POCKET

SCRABBLE
BRAND Crossword Game

DICTIONARY

POCKET

SCRABBLE®
BRAND Crossword Game

DICTIONARY

Collins

HarperCollins Publishers
Westerhill Road
Bishopbriggs
Glasgow
G64 2QT
Great Britain

Second Edition 2008

Reprint 10 9 8 7 6 5 4 3 2

© HarperCollins Publishers 2004, 2008

ISBN 978-0-00-726108-6

Collins® is a registered trademark of HarperCollins Publishers Limited

Scrabble® is a registered trademark of J. W. Spear & Sons Ltd, a subsidiary of Mattel, Inc.
© 2005 Mattel, Inc.

www.collinslanguage.com

A catalogue record for this book is available from the British Library

This book is set in Collins Fedra, a typeface specifically created for Collins dictionaries by Peter Bil'ak

Printed in Italy by
Rotolito Lombarda S.p.A.

Contributors

Editors
Sandra Anderson
Kay Cullen
Penny Hands
Helen Hucker
Andrew Holmes
Mike Munro

Project Manager
Justin Crozier

For the Publisher
Morven Dooner
Elaine Higgleton
Lucy Cooper

Computing Support
Thomas Callan

Collins Corpus Programmer
Nigel Rochford

Typesetting
Wordcraft

Contents

Introduction

Collins Pocket Scrabble Dictionary – Every Word Counts

The *Collins Pocket Scrabble Dictionary* is the ideal reference book for
people who play Scrabble for enjoyment, in a social or family
setting. This dictionary doesn't include every word eligible for
Scrabble, but does contain the most commonly used of the
260,000 words in *Collins Scrabble Words 2005*, the definitive
Scrabble wordlist. The concise definitions in the *Pocket Scrabble
Dictionary* allow players to check the meaning of words, as well
as using the book for settling arguments during games.

The *Collins Pocket Scrabble Dictionary* contains only words of up to
15 letters in length, as longer words cannot be used in
Scrabble. Because the dictionary is designed for family play, it
does not include offensive terms. Such words are,however,
included in *Collins Scrabble Words 2005*, the complete wordlist for
tournaments and club competitions.

Word order

In the *Collins Pocket Scrabble Dictionary*, all words are listed in
alphabetical order, rather than some being grouped at the
base form as in a conventional dictionary. Where words are
inflections of a base form, only the base form has a
definition, but the inflections are listed alphabetically as
individual entries for easy reference during a game. Base
forms and inflections are shown in black; inflections are
indented, with a cross-reference to the base form in blue.

Special Scrabble Words

To help family players learn and use some of the rarer and
higher-scoring words in the game, the Collins Pocket Scrabble
Dictionary includes a number of special panel entries. These

are unusual words which are particularly useful in Scrabble, either because they use the high-scoring 'power tiles' (J, Q, X, and Z), or because they have only two or three letters. There are also panel entries at the start of every letter section, which offer advice on useful words beginning with that letter.

The *Collins Pocket Scrabble Dictionary* is designed to be useful to new players and Scrabble veterans alike – we hope you enjoy using it!

Forming Words

The key to successful Scrabble is constant awareness of the opportunities for forming words on the board. The obvious way to play a new word is to place it so that it intersects a word already on the board through a common letter:

			D_2		
			O_1		
	L_1	U_1	C_3	K_5	
			T_1		
			O_1		
			R_1		

Other methods of forming words, however, create more than one new word in the process, giving a higher score. The two main ways of doing this are 'hooking' and 'tagging'.

Hooking

Hooking involves 'hanging' one word on another – the word already on the board acts as a 'hook' on which the other word can be hung – changing the first word in the process. When you form a word by hooking, you add a letter to the beginning or end of a word on the board, transforming it into a longer word as you do so:

C_3	O_1	M_3	E_1	T_1	

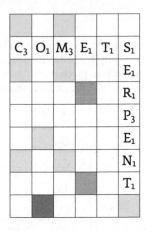

In this example, you get the points for COMETS as well as for SERPENTS. Plurals ending in S provide some of the most obvious – and useful – end-hooks. But there are plenty of other end-hooks as well. There are also lots of useful front-hooks. Consider the following example:

If you happened to have CEFIKL among the letters on your rack, you could play the following, taking full advantage of the valuable X played by your opponent:

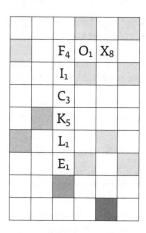

Here you get the 13 points for FOX as well as those for FICKLE. So you can see that hooking is generally a much more profitable method of word-formation than simply playing a word through one that is already on the board.

Obviously, only certain words can act as hooks. Some words cannot form other words by having a letter added to their front or back; these are known as 'blockers', as they prevent other players from adding words by hooking.

Tagging

Playing a word parallel to one already on the board, so that one or more tiles are in contact, is known as tagging. Tagging is more difficult than hooking because you need to form one additional word for each tile in contact with the word on the board. In most circumstances, these will be two-letter words, which is why short words are so vital to the game. The more two-letter words you know, the greater your opportunities for fitting words onto the board through tagging – and of running up some impressive scores!

For example, consider the following situation (your opponent has started the game with SHAM, and you have EEHISTX on your rack):

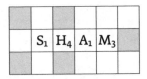

You could play HEXES so that it also forms SH, HE, AX and ME (all valid two-letter words), thus adding the scores for these three words to the points you make from HEXES:

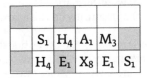

A particular advantage of tagging is that it allows you to benefit from valuable tiles twice in one go, as in the example above where X is used in both HEXES and AX.

Two-letter words are very important for tagging. The panel sections of this dictionary contain a number of unusual two-letter words: learning these is a good method of improving your game immediately!

ABBREVIATIONS USED IN THIS DICTIONARY

AD	anno Domini	Meteorol	Meteorology
adj	adjective	Mil	Military
adv	adverb	n	noun
Anat	Anatomy	N	North
Archit	Architecture	Naut	Nautical
Astrol	Astrology	NZ	New Zealand
Aust	Australia(n)	Obs	Obsolete
BC	before Christ	Offens	Offensive
Biol	Biology	orig.	originally
Brit	British	Photog	Photography
Chem	Chemistry	pl	plural
C of E	Church of England	prep	preposition
conj	conjunction	pron	pronoun
E	East	Psychol	Psychology
e.g.	for example	®	Trademark
esp.	especially	RC	Roman Catholic
etc.	et cetera	S	South
fem	feminine	S Afr	South Africa(n)
foll.	followed	Scot	Scottish
Geom	Geometry	sing	singular
Hist	History	US	United States
interj	interjection	usu.	usually
Lit	Literary	v	verb
masc	masculine	W	West
Med	Medicine	Zool	Zoology

Aa

A forms a two-letter word when followed by any one of A, B, D, E, G, H, I, M, N, R, S, T, W, X and Y – 15 letters out of 26 – so it's a really useful tile. There are also a number of short high-scoring words beginning with A. **Axe** (10 points) and **adze** (14 points) are good examples, but don't forget their US variants, **ax** (9 points) and **adz** (13 points). Also remember their plurals and the verb form **axed** (12 points). **Aye** (6) and **ay** (5) are handy for tight corners.

a *adj* indefinite article, used before a noun being mentioned for the first time

> **aa** aa n (**aas**). Aa is a type of volcanic rock. Aa scores 2 points, and is a good way of getting rid of annoying multiples of A.
>
> **aah** *interj*. Aah is a sound people make when they're pleased or amazed. Aah scores 6 points.
>
> **aal** *adj* Aal is a Scots word for **all**. Aal scores 3 points.

aardvark n (pl -s) S African anteater with long ears and snout

aardvarks n ▷ aardvark

ab n (pl -s) (*Informal*) (usually plural) abdominal muscle

> **aba** *noun* (**abas**). Cloth made from goat or camel hair. This is a useful word to remember for when you have more than one A on your rack. Aba scores 5 points.

aback *adv* startled or disconcerted

abacus (pl -es) n beads on a wire frame, used for doing calculations

abacuses n ▷ abacus

abalone (pl -s) [ab-a-**lone**-ee] n edible sea creature with a shell lined with mother of pearl

abalones n ▷ abalone

abandon v (-s, -ing, -ed) desert or leave (one's wife, children, etc.) ▸ n lack of inhibition > **abandonment** n (pl -s)

abandoned *adj* deserted ▸ v ▷ abandon

abandoning v ▷ abandon

abandonment n ▷ abandon

abandonments n ▷ abandon

abandons v ▷ abandon

abase v (-ses, -sing, -sed) humiliate or degrade (oneself) > **abasement** n (pl -s)

abased v ▷ abase

abasement n ▷ abase

abasements n ▷ abase

abases v ▷ abase

abashed *adj* embarrassed and ashamed

abasing v ▷ abase

abate v (-tes, -ting, -ted) make or become less strong > **abatement** n (pl -s)

abated v ▷ abate

abatement n ▷ abate

abatements n ▷ abate

abates v ▷ abate

abating v ▷ abate

abattoir [ab-a-twahr] n place where animals are killed for food (pl -s)

abattoirs n ▷ abattoir

> **abb** *noun* (**abbs**). Abb is yarn used in weaving. Remember this word for when you have two Bs on your rack, as there will probably already be an A on the board that you can use. Abb scores 7 points.

abbess n (pl -es) nun in charge of a convent

abbesses n ▷ abbess

abbey n (pl -s) dwelling place of, or a church belonging to, a community of monks or nuns

abbeys n ▷ abbey

abbot n (pl -s) head of an abbey of monks

abbots n ▷ abbot

abbreviate v (-tes, -ting, -ted) shorten (a word) by leaving out some letters

abbreviated v ▷ abbreviate

abbreviates v ▷ abbreviate

abbreviating v ▷ abbreviate

abbreviation n (pl -s) shortened form of a word or words

abbreviations n ▷ abbreviation

abdicate v (-tes, -ting, -ted) give up (the throne or a responsibility) > **abdication** n (pl -s)
abdicated v ▷ abdicate
abdicates v ▷ abdicate
abdicating v ▷ abdicate
abdication n ▷ abdicate
abdications n ▷ abdicate
abdomen n (pl -s) part of the body containing the stomach and intestines > **abdominal** adj
abdomens n ▷ abdomen
abdominal adj ▷ abdomen
abduct v (-s, -ing, -ed) carry off, kidnap > **abduction** n (pl -s) > **abductor** n (pl -s)
abducted v ▷ abduct
abducting v ▷ abduct
abduction n ▷ abduct
abductions n ▷ abduct
abductor n ▷ abduct
abductors n ▷ abduct
abducts v ▷ abduct
aberrant adj showing aberration
aberration n (pl -s) sudden change from what is normal, accurate, or correct
aberrations n ▷ aberration
abet v (-s, -ting, -ted) help or encourage in wrongdoing > **abettor** n (pl -s)
abets v ▷ abet
abetted v ▷ abet
abetting v ▷ abet
abettor n ▷ abet
abettors n ▷ abet
abeyance n (pl -s) not in use
abeyances n ▷ abeyance
abhor v (-s, -horring, -horred) detest utterly > **abhorrence** n (pl -s)
abhorred v ▷ abhor
abhorrence n ▷ abhor
abhorrences n ▷ abhor
abhorrent adj hateful, loathsome
abhorring v ▷ abhor
abhors v ▷ abhor
abide v (-des, -ding, -ded) endure, put up with
abided v ▷ abide
abides v ▷ abide
abiding adj lasting ► v ▷ abide
abilities n ▷ ability
ability n (pl -ties) competence, power
abject adj utterly miserable > **abjectly** adv
abjectly adv ▷ abject
abjure v (-res, -ring, -red) deny or renounce on oath
abjured v ▷ abjure
abjures v ▷ abjure
abjuring v ▷ abjure

ablative n (pl -s) case of nouns in Latin and other languages, indicating source, agent, or instrument of action
ablatives n ▷ ablative
ablaze adj burning fiercely
able adj (-r, -st) capable, competent > **ably** adv
abler adj ▷ able
ablest adj ▷ able
ablution n (pl -s) (usually plural) act of washing
ablutions n ▷ ablution
ably adv ▷ able
abnormal adj not normal or usual > **abnormally** adv > **abnormality** n (pl -ties)
abnormalities n ▷ abnormal
abnormality n ▷ abnormal
abnormally adv ▷ abnormal
aboard adv, prep on, in, onto, or into (a ship, train, or plane)
abode n (pl -s) home, dwelling
abodes n ▷ abode
abolish v (-shes, -shing, -shed) do away with > **abolition** n (pl -s)
abolished v ▷ abolish
abolishes v ▷ abolish
abolishing v ▷ abolish
abolition n ▷ abolish
abolitionist n (pl -s) person who wishes to do away with something, esp. slavery
abolitionists n ▷ abolitionist
abolitions n ▷ abolish
abominable adj detestable, very bad > **abominably** adv
abominably adv ▷ abominable
abomination n (pl -s) someone or something that is detestable
abominations n ▷ abomination
aboriginal n, adj ▷ aborigine
aboriginals n ▷ aborigine
aborigine, aboriginal [ab-or-**rij**-in-ee] n (pl -s) original inhabitant of a country or region, esp. (A-) Australia > **aboriginal** adj
aborigines n ▷ aborigine
abort v (-s, -ing, -ed) have an abortion or perform an abortion on
aborted v ▷ abort
aborting v ▷ abort
abortion n (pl -s) operation to end a pregnancy
abortionist n (pl -s) person who performs abortions, esp. illegally
abortionists n ▷ abortionist
abortions n ▷ abortion
abortive adj unsuccessful
aborts v ▷ abort
abound v (-s, -ing, -ed) be plentiful

> **abounding** adj
abounded v ▷ abound
abounding v, adj ▷ abound
abounds v ▷ abound
about prep concerning, on the subject of ▶ adv nearly, approximately
above adv, prep over or higher (than)
abracadabra n (pl -s) supposedly magic word
abracadabras n ▷ abracadabra
abrasion n (pl -s) scraped area on the skin
abrasions n ▷ abrasion
abrasive adj harsh and unpleasant in manner ▶ n (pl -s) substance for cleaning or polishing by rubbing
abrasives n ▷ abrasive
abreast adv, adj side by side
abridge v (-ges, -ging, -ged) shorten by using fewer words > **abridgment, abridgement** n (pl -s)
abridged v ▷ abridge
abridgement n ▷ abridge
abridgements n ▷ abridge
abridges v ▷ abridge
abridging v ▷ abridge
abridgment n ▷ abridge
abridgments n ▷ abridge
abroad adv to or in a foreign country
abrogate v (-tes, -ting, -ted) cancel (a law or agreement) formally > **abrogation** n (pl -s)
abrogated v ▷ abrogate
abrogates v ▷ abrogate
abrogating v ▷ abrogate
abrogation n ▷ abrogate
abrogations n ▷ abrogate
abrupt adj (-er, -est) sudden, unexpected > **abruptly** adv > **abruptness** n (pl -es)
abrupter adj ▷ abrupt
abruptest adj ▷ abrupt
abruptly adv ▷ abrupt
abruptness n ▷ abrupt
abruptnesses n ▷ abrupt
abs n ▷ ab
abscess n (pl abscesses) inflamed swelling containing pus
abscesses n ▷ abscess
abscond v (-s, -ing, -ed) leave secretly
absconded v ▷ abscond
absconding v ▷ abscond
absconds v ▷ abscond
abseil [ab-sale] v (-s, -ing, -ed) go down a steep drop by a rope fastened at the top and tied around one's body
abseiled v ▷ abseil
abseiling v ▷ abseil
abseils v ▷ abseil

absence n (pl -s) being away
absences n ▷ absence
absent adj not present ▶ v (-s, -ing, -ed) stay away > **absently** adv
absented v ▷ absent
absentee n (pl -s) person who should be present but is not
absenteeism n (pl -s) persistent absence from work or school
absenteeisms n ▷ absenteeism
absentees n ▷ absentee
absenting v ▷ absent
absently adv ▷ absent
absents v ▷ absent
absinthe n (pl -s) strong green aniseed-flavoured liqueur
absinthes n ▷ absinthe
absolute adj complete, perfect
absolutely adv completely ▶ interj certainly, yes
absolution n ▷ absolve
absolutions n ▷ absolve
absolutism n (pl -s) government by a ruler with unrestricted power
absolutisms n ▷ absolutism
absolve v (-ves, -ving, -ved) declare to be free from blame or sin > **absolution** n (pl -s)
absolved v ▷ absolve
absolves v ▷ absolve
absolving v ▷ absolve
absorb v (-s, -ing, -ed) soak up (a liquid) > **absorption** n (pl -s) > **absorbency** n (pl -s)
absorbed v ▷ absorb
absorbencies n ▷ absorb
absorbency n ▷ absorb
absorbent adj able to absorb liquid
absorbing v ▷ absorb
absorbs v ▷ absorb
absorption n ▷ absorb
absorptions n ▷ absorb
abstain v (-s, -ing, -ed) choose not to do something > **abstainer** n (pl -s)
abstained v ▷ abstain
abstainer n ▷ abstain
abstainers n ▷ abstain
abstaining v ▷ abstain
abstains v ▷ abstain
abstemious adj taking very little alcohol or food > **abstemiousness** n (pl -es)
abstemiousness n ▷ abstemious
abstemiousnesses n ▷ abstemious
abstention n (pl -s) abstaining, esp. from voting
abstentions n ▷ abstention
abstinence n (pl -s) abstaining, esp. from

drinking alcohol ▷ **abstinent** *adj*
abstinences *n* ▷ abstinence
abstinent *adj* ▷ abstinence
abstract *adj* existing as a quality
or idea rather than a material object ▶ *n* (*pl*
-s) summary ▶ *v* (-s, -ing, -ed) summarize
> **abstraction** *n* (*pl* -s)
abstracted *adj* lost in thought *v* ▷ abstract
abstracter *adj* ▷ abstract
abstractest *adj* ▷ abstract
abstracting *adj* ▷ abstract
abstraction *n* ▷ abstract
abstractions *n* ▷ abstract
abstracts *n*, *v* ▷ abstract
abstruse *adj* (-er, -est) not easy to understand
abstruser *adj* ▷ abstruse
abstrusest *adj* ▷ abstruse
absurd *adj* (-er, -est) incongruous or ridiculous
> **absurdly** *adv* > **absurdity** *n* (*pl* -ties)
absurder *adj* ▷ absurd
absurdest *adj* ▷ absurd
absurdities *n* ▷ absurd
absurdity *n* ▷ absurd
absurdly *adv* ▷ absurd
abundance *n* ▷ abundant
abundances *n* ▷ abundant
abundant *adj* plentiful > **abundantly** *adv*
> **abundance** *n* (*pl* -s)
abundantly *adv* ▷ abundant
abuse *v* (-ses, -sing, -sed) use wrongly ▶ *n* (*pl*
-s) prolonged ill-treatment > **abuser** *n* (*pl* -s)
> **abusive** *adj* > **abusively** *adv* > **abusiveness**
n (*pl* -es)
abused *v* ▷ abuse
abuser *n* ▷ abuse
abusers *n* ▷ abuse
abuses *v*, *n* ▷ abuse
abusing *v* ▷ abuse
abusive *adj* ▷ abuse
abusively *adv* ▷ abuse
abusiveness *n* ▷ abuse
abusivenesses *n* ▷ abuse
abut *v* (-s, abutting, abutted) be next to or
touching
abuts *v* ▷ abut
abutted *v* ▷ abut
abutting *v* ▷ abut

> **aby** *verb* (**abys abying abought**). Aby is
> an old word meaning to pay a penalty.
> If someone plays this word, remember
> that it can be expanded to **baby**,
> **abysmal** or **abyss**. Aby scores 8 points.

abysmal *adj* (*Informal*) extremely bad, awful
> **abysmally** *adv*
abysmally *adv* ▷ abysmal

abyss *n* (*pl* -es) very deep hole or chasm
abysses *n* ▷ abyss
acacia [a-kay-sha] *n* (*pl* -s) tree or shrub with
yellow or white flowers
acacias *n* ▷ acacia
academic *adj* of an academy or university ▶ *n*
(*pl* -s) lecturer or researcher at a university
> **academically** *adv*
academically *adv* ▷ academic
academician *n* (*pl* -s) member of an academy
academicians *n* ▷ academician
academics *n* ▷ academician
academies *n* ▷ academy
academy *n* (*pl* -mies) society to advance arts
or sciences
acanthus *n* (*pl* -es) prickly plant
acanthuses *n* ▷ acanthus
accede *v* (-des, -ding, -ded) consent or agree
(to)
acceded *v* ▷ accede
accedes *v* ▷ accede
acceding *v* ▷ accede
accelerate *v* (-tes, -ting, -ted) (cause to) move
faster > **acceleration** *n* (*pl* -s)
accelerated *v* ▷ accelerate
accelerates *v* ▷ accelerate
accelerating *v* ▷ accelerate
acceleration *n* ▷ accelerate
accelerations *n* ▷ accelerate
accelerator *n* (*pl* -s) pedal in a motor vehicle to
increase speed
accelerators *n* ▷ accelerator
accent *n* (*pl* -s) distinctive style of
pronunciation of a local, national, or social
group ▶ *v* (-s, -ing, -ed) place emphasis on
accented *v* ▷ accent
accenting *v* ▷ accent
accents *n*, *v* ▷ accent
accentuate *v* (-tes, -ting, -ted) stress,
emphasize > **accentuation** *n* (*pl* -s)
accentuated *v* ▷ accentuate
accentuates *v* ▷ accentuate
accentuating *v* ▷ accentuate
accentuation *n* ▷ accentuate
accentuations *n* ▷ accentuate
accept *v* (-s, -ing, -ed) receive willingly
> **acceptance** *n* (*pl* -s)
acceptabilities *n* ▷ acceptable
acceptability *n* ▷ acceptable
acceptable *adj* tolerable > **acceptably** *adv*
> **acceptability** *n* (*pl* -ties)
acceptably *adv* ▷ acceptable
acceptance *n* ▷ accept
acceptances *n* ▷ accept
accepted *v* ▷ accept

accepting v ▷ accept

accepts v ▷ accept

access n (pl -es) means of or right to approach or enter ▶ v (-es, -ing, -ed) obtain (data) from a computer

accessed v ▷ access

accesses n, v ▷ access

accessibilities n ▷ accessible

accessibility n ▷ accessible

accessible adj easy to reach > **accessibility** n (pl -ties)

accessing v ▷ access

accession n (pl -s) taking up of an office or position

accessions n ▷ accession

accessories n ▷ accessory

accessory n (pl -ries) supplementary part or object

accident n (pl -s) mishap, often causing injury

accidental adj happening by chance or unintentionally ▶ n (pl -s) (MUSIC) symbol indicating that a sharp, flat, or natural note is not a part of the key signature > **accidentally** adv

accidentally adv ▷ accidental

accidentals n ▷ accidental

accidents n ▷ accident

acclaim v (-s, -ing, -ed) applaud, praise ▶ n (pl -s) enthusiastic approval > **acclamation** n (pl -s)

acclaimed v ▷ acclaim

acclaiming v ▷ acclaim

acclaims v, n ▷ acclaim

acclamation n ▷ acclaim

acclamations n ▷ acclaim

acclimatization n ▷ acclimatize

acclimatizations n ▷ acclimatize

acclimatize v (-zes, -zing, -zed) adapt to a new climate or environment > **acclimatization** n (pl -s)

acclimatized v ▷ acclimatize

acclimatizes v ▷ acclimatize

acclimatizing v ▷ acclimatize

accolade n (pl -s) award, honour, or praise

accolades n ▷ accolade

accommodate v (-tes, -ting, -ted) provide with lodgings

accommodated v ▷ accommodate

accommodates v ▷ accommodate

accommodating adj obliging ▶ v ▷ accommodate

accommodation n (pl -s) house or room for living in

accommodations n ▷ accommodation

accompanied v ▷ accompany

accompanies v ▷ accompany

accompaniment n (pl -s) something that accompanies

accompaniments n ▷ accompaniment

accompanist n ▷ accompany

accompanists n ▷ accompany

accompany v (-nies, -nying, -nied) go along with > **accompanist** n (pl -s)

accompanying v ▷ accompany

accomplice n (pl -s) person who helps another to commit a crime

accomplices n ▷ accomplice

accomplish v (-es, -ing, -ed) manage to do

accomplished adj expert, proficient ▶ v ▷ accomplish

accomplishes v ▷ accomplish

accomplishing v ▷ accomplish

accomplishment n (pl -s) completion

accomplishments n ▷ accomplishment

accord n (pl -s) agreement, harmony ▶ v (-s, -ing, -ed) fit in with

accordance n (pl -s) conforming to or according to

accordances n ▷ accordance

accorded v ▷ accord

according adv as stated by ▶ v ▷ accord

accordingly adv in an appropriate manner

accordion n (pl -s) portable musical instrument played by moving the two sides apart and together, and pressing a keyboard or buttons to produce the notes > **accordionist** n

accordionist n (pl -s) ▷ accordion

accordionists n ▷ accordion

accordions n ▷ accordion

accords v ▷ accord

accost v (-s, -ing, -ed) approach and speak to, often aggressively

accosted v ▷ accost

accosting v ▷ accost

accosts v ▷ accost

account n (pl -s) report, description ▶ v (-s, -ing, -ed) judge to be

accountabilities n ▷ accountable

accountability n ▷ accountable

accountable adj responsible to someone or for something > **accountability** n (pl -ties)

accountancies n ▷ accountant

accountancy n ▷ accountant

accountant n (pl -s) person who maintains and audits business accounts > **accountancy** n (pl -cies)

accountants n ▷ accountant

accounted v ▷ account

accounting n (pl -s) skill or practice of

maintaining and auditing business accounts
▶ v ▷ account
accountings n ▷ accounting
accounts n, v ▷ account
accoutrement n (pl -s) an item of clothing and equipment for a particular activity
accoutrements n ▷ accoutrement
accredited adj authorized, officially recognized
accretion [ak-**kree**-shun] n (pl -s) gradual growth
accretions n ▷ accretion
accrual n ▷ accrue
accruals n ▷ accrue
accrue v (-crues, -cruing, -crued) increase gradually > **accrual** n (pl -s)
accrued v ▷ accrue
accrues v ▷ accrue
accruing v ▷ accrue
accumulate v (-tes, -ting, -ted) gather together in increasing quantity
> **accumulation** n (pl -s) > **accumulative** adj
accumulated v ▷ accumulate
accumulates v ▷ accumulate
accumulating v ▷ accumulate
accumulation n ▷ accumulate
accumulations v ▷ accumulate
accumulative adj ▷ accumulate
accumulator n (pl -s) (BRIT & AUST) rechargeable electric battery
accumulators n ▷ accumulator
accuracies n ▷ accurate
accuracy n ▷ accurate
accurate adj exact, correct > **accurately** adv
> **accuracy** n (pl -cies)
accurately adv ▷ accurate
accursed adj under a curse
accusation n ▷ accuse
accusations n ▷ accuse
accusative n (pl -s) grammatical case indicating the direct object
accusatives n ▷ accusative
accusatory adj ▷ accuse
accuse v (-ses, -sing, -sed) charge with wrongdoing > **accused** adj > **accuser** n (pl -s) > **accusing** adj > **accusation** n (pl -s)
> **accusatory** adj
accused v ▷ accuse
accused n ▷ accuse
accuser n ▷ accuse
accusers n ▷ accuser
accuses v ▷ accuse
accusing v, adj ▷ accuse
accusing adj ▷ accuse
accustom v (-s, -ing, -ed) make used to

accustomed adj usual v ▷ accustom
accustoming v ▷ accustom
accustoms v ▷ accustom
ace n (pl -s) playing card with one symbol on it
▶ adj (Informal) excellent
acerbic [ass-**sir**-bik] adj harsh or bitter
> **acerbity** n (pl -ties)
acerbities n ▷ acerbic
acerbity n ▷ acerbic
aces n ▷ ace
acetate [**ass**-it-tate] n (pl -s) (CHEM) salt or ester of acetic acid
acetates n ▷ acetate
acetic [ass-**see**-tik] adj of or involving vinegar
acetone [**ass**-it-tone] n (pl -s) colourless liquid used as a solvent
acetones n ▷ acetone
acetylene [ass-**set**-ill-een] n (pl -s) colourless flammable gas used in welding metals
acetylenes n ▷ acetylene
ache n (pl -s) dull continuous pain ▶ v (-ches, -ching, -ched) be in or cause continuous dull pain
ached n ▷ ache
aches v, n ▷ ache
achieve v (-ves, -ving, -ved) gain by hard work or ability
achieved v ▷ achieve
achievement n (pl -s) something accomplished
achievements n ▷ achievement
achieves v ▷ achieve
achieving v ▷ achieve
aching v ▷ ache
achromatic adj colourless
acid n (pl -s) (CHEM) one of a class of compounds, corrosive and sour when dissolved in water, that combine with a base to form a salt ▶ adj containing acid > **acidic** adj > **acidify** v > **acidity** n (pl -ties)
acidic adj ▷ acid
acidify v ▷ acid
acidities n ▷ acid
acidity n ▷ acid
acids n ▷ acid
acknowledge v (-ges, -ging, -ged) admit, recognize > **acknowledgment, acknowledgement** n (pl -s)
acknowledged v ▷ acknowledge
acknowledgement n ▷ acknowledge
acknowledgements n ▷ acknowledge
acknowledges v ▷ acknowledge
acknowledging v ▷ acknowledge
acknowledgment n ▷ acknowledge
acknowledgments n ▷ acknowledge

acme [ak-mee] *n* (*pl* -s) highest point of achievement or excellence
acmes *n* ▷ acme
acne [ak-nee] *n* (*pl* -s) pimply skin disease
acnes *n* ▷ acne
acolyte *n* (*pl* -s) follower or attendant
acolytes *n* ▷ acolyte
aconite *n* (*pl* -s) poisonous plant with hoodlike flowers
aconites *n* ▷ aconite
acorn *n* (*pl* -s) nut of the oak tree
acorns *n* ▷ acorn
acoustic *adj* of sound and hearing
 > **acoustically** *adv*
acoustically *adv* ▷ acoustic
acoustics *n* science of sounds
acquaint *v* (-s, -ing, -ed) make familiar, inform
 > **acquainted** *adj*
acquaintance *n* (*pl* -s) person known
acquaintances *n* ▷ acquaintance
acquainted *v, adj* ▷ acquaint
acquainting *v* ▷ acquaint
acquaints *v* ▷ acquaint
acquiesce [ak-wee-**ess**] *v* (-sces, -scing, -sced) agree to what someone wants
 > **acquiescence** *n* (*pl* -s) > **acquiescent** *adj*
acquiesced *v* ▷ acquiesce
acquiescence *n* ▷ acquiesce
acquiescences *n* ▷ acquiesce
acquiescent *adj* ▷ acquiesce
acquiesces *v* ▷ acquiesce
acquiescing *v* ▷ acquiesce
acquire *v* (-res, -ring, -red) gain, get
acquired *v* ▷ acquire
acquires *v* ▷ acquire
acquiring *v* ▷ acquire
acquisition *n* (*pl* -s) thing acquired
acquisitions *n* ▷ acquisition
acquisitive *adj* eager to gain material possessions > **acquisitiveness** *n* (*pl* -es)
acquisitiveness *n* ▷ acquisitive
acquisitivenesses *n* ▷ acquisitive
acquit *v* (-s, -quitting, -quitted) pronounce (someone) innocent > **acquittal** *n* (*pl* -s)
acquits *v* ▷ acquit
acquittal *n* ▷ acquit
acquittals *n* ▷ acquit
acquitted *v* ▷ acquit
acquitting *v* ▷ acquit
acre *n* (*pl* -s) measure of land, 4840 square yards (4046.86 square metres)
acreage [ake-er-rij] *n* (*pl* -s) land area in acres
acreages *n* ▷ acreage
acres *n* ▷ acre
acrid [ak-rid] *adj* (-er, -est) pungent, bitter

acrider *adj* ▷ acrid
acridest *adj* ▷ acrid
acrimonies *n* ▷ acrimonious
acrimonious *adj* bitter in speech or manner
 > **acrimony** *n* (*pl* -ies)
acrimony *n* ▷ acrimonious
acrobat *n* (*pl* -s) person skilled in gymnastic feats requiring agility and balance
 > **acrobatic** *adj*
acrobatic *adj* ▷ acrobatic
acrobatics *pl n* acrobatic feats
acrobats *n* ▷ acrobat
acronym *n* (*pl* -s) word formed from the initial letters of other words, such as NASA
acronyms *n* ▷ acronym
across *adv, prep* from side to side (of)
acrostic *n* (*pl* -s) lines of writing in which the first or last letters of each line spell a word or saying
acrostics *n* ▷ acrostic
acrylic *n* (*pl* -s) ▶ *adj* (synthetic fibre, paint, etc.) made from acrylic acid
acrylics *n* ▷ acrylic
act *n* (*pl* -s) thing done ▶ *v* (-s, -ing, -ed) do something
acted *v* ▷ act
acting *n* (*pl* -s) art of an actor ▶ *adj* temporarily performing the duties of ▶ *v* ▷ act
actings *n* ▷ acting
actinium *n* (*pl* -s) (CHEM) radioactive chemical element
actiniums *n* ▷ actinium
action *n* (*pl* -s) process of doing something
actionable *adj* giving grounds for a lawsuit
actions *n* ▷ action
activate *v* (-tes, -ting, -ted) make active
 > **activation** *n* (*pl* -s) > **activator** *n* (*pl* -s)
activated *v* ▷ activate
activates *v* ▷ activate
activating *v* ▷ activate
activation *n* ▷ activate
activations *n* ▷ activate
activator *n* ▷ activate
activators *n* ▷ activate
active *adj* moving, working > **actively** *adv*
actively *adv* ▷ active
activism *n* ▷ activist
activisms *n* ▷ activist
activist *n* (*pl* -s) person who works energetically to achieve political or social goals > **activism** *n* (*pl* -s)
activists *n* ▷ activist
activities *n* ▷ activity
activity *n* (*pl* -ties) state of being active
actor *n* (*pl* -s) person who acts in a play, film,

etc.

actors n ▷ actor

actress n (pl -es) woman who acts in a play, film, etc.

actresses n ▷ actress

acts n, v ▷ act

actual adj existing in reality > **actuality** n (pl -ties)

actualities n ▷ actual

actuality n ▷ actual

actually adv really, indeed

actuaries n ▷ actuary

actuary n (pl -ries) statistician who calculates insurance risks > **actuarial** adj

actuate v (-tes, -ting, -ted) start up (a device)

actuated v ▷ actuate

actuates v ▷ actuate

actuating v ▷ actuate

acuities n ▷ acuity

acuity [ak-kew-it-ee] n (pl -ties) keenness of vision or thought

acumen [ak-yew-men] n (pl -s) ability to make good judgments

acumens n ▷ acumen

acupuncture n (pl -s) medical treatment involving the insertion of needles at various points on the body > **acupuncturist** n (pl -s)

acupunctures n ▷ acupuncture

acupuncturist n ▷ acupuncture

acupuncturists n ▷ acupuncture

acute adj (-r, -st) severe ▶ n (pl -s) accent (´) over a letter to indicate the quality or length of its sound, as in café > **acutely** adv > **acuteness** n

acutely adv ▷ acute

acuteness n ▷ acute

acuter adj ▷ acute

acutes n ▷ acute

acutest adj ▷ acute

ad n (pl -s) (Informal) advertisement

adage n (pl -s) wise saying, proverb

adages n ▷ adage

adagio n (pl -gios) ▶ adv (MUSIC) (piece to be played) slowly and gracefully

adagios n ▷ adagio

adamant adj unshakable in determination or purpose > **adamantly** adv

adamantly adv ▷ adamant

adapt v (-s, -ing, -ed) alter for new use or new conditions > **adaptable** adj > **adaptability** n (pl -ties)

adaptabilities n ▷ adapt

adaptability n ▷ adapt

adaptable adj ▷ adapt

adaptation n (pl -s) thing produced by adapting something

adaptations n ▷ adaptation

adapted v ▷ adapt

adapter n ▷ adaptor

adapters n ▷ adaptor

adapting v ▷ adapt

adaptor, adapter n (pl -s) device for connecting several electrical appliances to a single socket

adaptors n ▷ adaptor

adapts v ▷ adapt

add v (-s, -ing, -ed) combine (numbers or quantities)

added v ▷ add

addenda n ▷ addendum

addendum n (pl -da) addition

adder n (pl -s) small poisonous snake

adders n ▷ adder

addict n (pl -s) person who is unable to stop taking drugs > **addicted** adj > **addiction** n (pl -s)

addicted adj ▷ addict

addiction n ▷ addict

addictions n ▷ addict

addictive adj causing addiction

addicts n ▷ addict

adding v ▷ add

addition n (pl -s) adding > **additional** adj > **additionally** adv

additional adj ▷ addition

additionally adv ▷ addition

additions n ▷ addition

additive n (pl -s) something added, esp. to a foodstuff, to improve it or prevent deterioration

additives n ▷ additive

addled adj confused or unable to think clearly

address n (pl -es) place where a person lives ▶ v (-es, -ing, -ed) mark the destination, as on an envelope

addressed v ▷ address

addressee n (pl -s) person addressed

addressees n ▷ addressee

addresses n, v ▷ address

addressing v ▷ address

adds v ▷ add

adduce v (-ces, -cing, -uced) mention something as evidence or proof

adduced v ▷ adduce

adduces v ▷ adduce

adducing v ▷ adduce

adenoid [ad-in-oid] n (pl -s) (usually plural) mass of tissue at the back of the throat

adenoidal adj having a nasal voice caused by

swollen adenoids
adenoids *n* ▷ adenoid
adept *adj* (-er, -est) ▶ *n* (*pl* -s) very skilful (person)
  adepter *adj* ▷ adept
  adeptest *adj* ▷ adept
  adepts *n* ▷ adept
adequacies *n* ▷ adequate
adequacy *n* ▷ adequate
adequate *adj* sufficient, enough **> adequately**
adv **> adequacy** *n* (*pl* -ies)
  adequately *adv* ▷ adequate
adherable *adj* ▷ adhere
adhere *v* (-res, -ring, -red) stick (to)
  > adherence *n* (*pl* -ces)
  adhered *v* ▷ adhere
  adherence *n* ▷ adhere
  adherences *n* ▷ adhere
adherent *n* (*pl* -s) devotee, follower
  adherents *n* ▷ adherent
  adheres *v* ▷ adhere
  adhering *v* ▷ adhere
adhesion *n* (*pl* -s) sticking (to)
  adhesions *n* ▷ adhesion
adhesive *n* (*pl* -s) substance used to stick
things together ▶ *adj* able to stick to things
  adhesives *n* ▷ adhesive
adieu [a-**dew**] *interj* (*Lit*) farewell, goodbye
adipose *adj* of or containing fat
adjacent *adj* near or next (to)
adjectival *adj* ▷ adjective
adjective *n* (*pl* -s) word that adds information
about a noun or pronoun **> adjectival** *adj*
  adjectives *n* ▷ adjective
adjoin *v* (-s, -ing, -ed) be next to **> adjoining** *adj*
  adjoined *v* ▷ adjoin
  adjoining *v*, *adj* ▷ adjoin
  adjoins *v* ▷ adjoin
adjourn *v* (-s, -ing, -ed) close (a court) at the
end of a session **> adjournment** *n* (*pl* -s)
  adjourned *v* ▷ adjourn
  adjourning *v* ▷ adjourn
  adjournment *n* ▷ adjourn
  adjournments *n* ▷ adjourn
  adjourns *v* ▷ adjourn
adjudge *v* (-ges, -ging, -ged) declare (to be)
  adjudged *v* ▷ adjudge
  adjudges *v* ▷ adjudge
  adjudging *v* ▷ adjudge
adjudicate *v* (-tes, -ting, -ted) give a formal
decision on (a dispute) **> adjudication** *n* (*pl* -s)
  > adjudicator *n* (*pl* -s)
  adjudicated *v* ▷ adjudicate
  adjudicates *v* ▷ adjudicate
  adjudicating *v* ▷ adjudicate
  adjudication *n* ▷ adjudicate

adjudications *n* ▷ adjudicate
  adjudicator *n* ▷ adjudicate
  adjudicators *n* ▷ adjudicate
adjunct *n* (*pl* -s) subordinate or additional
person or thing
  adjuncts *n* ▷ adjunct
adjure *v* (-res, -ring, -red) command (to do)
  adjured *v* ▷ adjure
  adjures *v* ▷ adjure
  adjuring *v* ▷ adjure
adjust *v* (-s, -ing, -ted) adapt to new
conditions **> adjustable** *adj* **> adjuster** *n* (*pl* -s)
  > adjustment *n* (*pl* -s)
  adjustable *adj* ▷ adjust
  adjusted *v* ▷ adjust
  adjuster *n* ▷ adjust
  adjusters *n* ▷ adjust
  adjustment *n* ▷ adjust
  adjustments *n* ▷ adjust
  adjusts *v* ▷ adjust
adjutant [**aj**-oo-tant] *n* (*pl* -s) army officer in
charge of routine administration
  adjutants *n* ▷ adjutant
admin *n* (*pl* -s) (*Informal*) administration
administer *v* (-s, -ing, -ed) manage (business
affairs)
  administered *v* ▷ administer
  administering *v* ▷ administer
  administers *v* ▷ administer
administrate *v* (-tes, -ting, -ated) manage (an
organization) **> administrator** *n* (*pl* -s)
  administrated *v* ▷ administrate
  administrates *v* ▷ administrate
  administrating *v* ▷ administrate
administration *n* (*pl* -s) management of an
organization
  administrations *n* ▷ administration
administrative *adj* of the management of an
organization
  administrator *n* ▷ administrate
  administrators *n* ▷ administrate
  admins *n* ▷ admin
  admirable *adj* ▷ admire
  admirably *adv* ▷ admire
admiral *n* (*pl* -s) highest naval rank
  admirals *n* ▷ admiral
  admiralties *n* ▷ admiralty
admiralty *n* (*pl* -ties) the office or jurisdiction
of an admiral
  admiration *n* ▷ admire
  admirations *n* ▷ admire
admire *v* (-res, -ring, -red) regard with esteem
and approval **> admirable** *adj* **> admirably**
adv **> admiration** *n* (*pl* -s) **> admirer** *n* (*pl* -s)
> admiring *adj* **> admiringly** *adv*

admired v ▷ admire
admirer n ▷ admire
admirers n ▷ admire
admires v ▷ admire
admiring v, adj ▷ admire
admiringly adv ▷ admire
admissibilities n ▷ admissible
admissibility n ▷ admissible
admissible adj allowed to be brought in as evidence in court **> admissibility** n (pl -ties)
admission n (pl -s) permission to enter
admissions n ▷ admission
admit v (-mits, -mitting, -mitted) confess, acknowledge
admits v ▷ admit
admittance n (pl -s) permission to enter
admittances n ▷ admittance
admitted v ▷ admit
admittedly adv it must be agreed
admitting v ▷ admit
admixture n (pl -s) mixture
admixtures n ▷ admixture
admonish v (-es, -ing, -ed) reprove sternly **> admonition** n (pl -s)
admonished v ▷ admonish
admonishes v ▷ admonish
admonishing v ▷ admonish
admonition n ▷ admonish
admonitions n ▷ admonish
ado n (pl -s) (Lit) fuss, trouble
adobe [ad-oh-bee] n (pl -s) sun-dried brick
adobes n ▷ adobe
adolescence n (pl -s) period between puberty and adulthood
adolescences n ▷ adolescence
adolescent n (pl -s), adj (person) between puberty and adulthood
adolescents n ▷ adolescent
adopt v (-s, -ing, -ed) take (someone else's child) as one's own **> adoption** n (pl -s)
adopted v ▷ adopt
adopting v ▷ adopt
adoption n ▷ adopt
adoptions n ▷ adopt
adoptive adj related by adoption
adopts v ▷ adopt
adorable adj ▷ adore
adoration n ▷ adore
adorations n ▷ adore
adore v (-res, -ring, -red) love intensely **> adorable** adj **> adoration** n (pl -s) **> adoring** adj **> adoringly** adv
adored v ▷ adore
adores v ▷ adore
adoring v, adj ▷ adore

adoringly adv ▷ adore
adorn v (-s, -ing, -ed) decorate, embellish **> adornment** n (pl -s)
adorned v ▷ adorn
adorning v ▷ adorn
adornment n ▷ adorn
adornments n ▷ adorn
adorns v ▷ adorn
ados n ▷ ado
adrenal [ad-reen-al] adj near the kidneys
adrenalin, adrenaline n (pl -s) hormone secreted by the adrenal glands in response to stress
adrenaline n ▷ adrenalin
adrenalines n ▷ adrenalin
adrenalins n ▷ adrenalin
adrenally adv ▷ adrenal
adrift adj, adv drifting
adroit adj quick and skilful **> adroitly** adv **> adroitness** n
adroitly adv ▷ adroit
adroitness n ▷ adroit
ads n ▷ ad
adsorb v (-s, -ing, -ed) (of a gas or vapour) condense and form a thin film on a surface **> adsorption** n (pl -s)
adsorbed v ▷ adsorb
adsorbing v ▷ adsorb
adsorbs v ▷ adsorb
adsorption n ▷ adsorb
adsorptions n ▷ adsorb
adulation n (pl -s) uncritical admiration
adulations n ▷ adulation
adult adj fully grown, mature ▶ n (pl -s) adult person or animal **> adulthood** n (pl -s)
adulterate v (-tes, -ting, -ted) spoil by adding inferior material **> adulteration** n (pl -s)
adulterated v ▷ adulterate
adulterates v ▷ adulterate
adulterating v ▷ adulterate
adulteration n ▷ adulterate
adulterations n ▷ adulterate
adulterer n ▷ adultery
adulterers n ▷ adultery
adulteress n ▷ adultery
adulteresses n ▷ adultery
adulteries n ▷ adultery
adulterous adj ▷ adultery
adultery n (pl -teries) sexual unfaithfulness of a husband or wife **> adulterer** n (pl -s) **> adulteress** n (pl -es) **> adulterous** adj
adulthood n ▷ adult
adulthoods n ▷ adult
adults n ▷ adult
advance v (-ces, -cing, -ced) go or bring

forward ► n (pl -s) forward movement ► adj done or happening before an event

advanced adj at a late stage in development ► v ▷ advance

advancement n (pl advancements) promotion

advancements n ▷ advancement

advances v, n ▷ advance

advancing v ▷ advance

advantage n (pl -s) more favourable position or state > **advantageous** adj > **advantageously** adv

advantageous adj ▷ advantage

advantageously adv ▷ advantage

advantages n ▷ advantage

advent n (pl -s) arrival

adventitious adj added or appearing accidentally

advents n ▷ advent

adventure n (pl -s) exciting and risky undertaking or exploit > **adventurous** adj

adventurer n (pl -s) person who unscrupulously seeks money or power

adventurers n ▷ adventurer

adventures n ▷ adventure

adventuress n (pl -es) woman who unscrupulously seeks money or power

adventuresses n ▷ adventuress

adventurous adj ▷ adventure

adverb n (pl -s) word that adds information about a verb, adjective, or other adverb > **adverbial** adj

adverbial adj ▷ adverb

adverbs n ▷ adverb

adversaries n ▷ adversary

adversary [ad-verse-er-ree] n (pl -ries) opponent or enemy

adverse adj unfavourable > **adversely** adv

adversely adv ▷ adverse

adversities n ▷ adversity

adversity n (pl -ties) very difficult or hard circumstances

advert n (pl -s) (Informal) advertisement

advertise v (-ses, -sing, -sed) present or praise (goods or services) to the public in order to encourage sales > **advertiser** n (pl -s) > **advertising** adj, n (pl -s)

advertised v ▷ advertise

advertisement n (pl -s) public announcement to sell goods or publicize an event

advertisements n ▷ advertisement

advertiser n ▷ advertise

advertises v ▷ advertise

advertising v, adj n ▷ advertise

advertisings n ▷ advertise

adverts n ▷ advert

advice n (pl -s) recommendation as to what to do

advices n ▷ advice

advisabilities n ▷ advisable

advisability n ▷ advisable

advisable adj prudent, sensible > **advisability** n (pl -ties)

advise v (-ses, -sing, -sed) offer advice to

advised adj considered, thought-out ► v ▷ advise

advisedly adv deliberately

adviser, advisor n (pl -s) person who offers advice, e.g. on careers to students

advisers n ▷ adviser

advises v ▷ advise

advising v ▷ advise

advisor n ▷ adviser

advisors n ▷ adviser

advisory adj giving advice

advocaat n (pl -s) liqueur with a raw egg base

advocaats n ▷ advocaat

advocacies n ▷ advocate

advocacy n ▷ advocate

advocate v (-tes, -ting, -ted) propose or recommend ► n (pl -s) person who publicly supports a cause > **advocacy** n (pl -cies)

advocated v ▷ advocate

advocates v, n ▷ advocate

advocating v ▷ advocate

adz n ▷ adze

adze, adz n (pl adzes) tool with an arched blade at right angles to the handle

adzed v ▷ adze

adzes n ▷ adze

■ **ae** adj. Ae is a Scots word that means **one**. This is a useful word to remember when you want to form words in two directions at once. Ae scores 2 points.

aegis [ee-jiss] n (pl -es) sponsorship, protection

aegises n ▷ aegis

aeon [ee-on] n (pl -s) immeasurably long period of time

aeons n ▷ aeon

aerate v (-tes, -ting, -ted) put gas into (a liquid), as when making a fizzy drink > **aeration** n (pl -s)

aerated v ▷ aerate

aerates v ▷ aerate

aerating v ▷ aerate

aeration n ▷ aerate

aerations n ▷ aerate

aerial adj in, from, or operating in the air ► n (pl -ls) metal pole, wire, etc., for receiving or transmitting radio or TV signals

aerials *n* ▷ aerial
aerobatic *adj* ▷ aerobatics
aerobatics *pl n* stunt flying > **aerobatic** *adj*
aerobic *adj* ▷ aerobics
aerobics *n* exercises designed to increase the amount of oxygen in the blood > **aerobic** *adj*
aerodrome *n* (*pl* -s) small airport
aerodromes *n* ▷ aerodrome
aerodynamic *adj* ▷ aerodynamics
aerodynamics *n* study of how air flows around moving solid objects > **aerodynamic** *adj*
aerofoil *n* (*pl* -s) part of an aircraft, such as the wing, designed to give lift
aerofoils *n* ▷ aerofoil
aerogram *n* (*pl* -s) airmail letter on a single sheet of paper that seals to form an envelope
aerograms *n* ▷ aerogram
aeronautical *adj* ▷ aeronautics
aeronautics *n* study or practice of aircraft flight > **aeronautical** *adj*
aeroplane *n* (*pl* -s) powered flying vehicle with fixed wings
aeroplanes *n* ▷ aeroplane
aerosol *n* (*pl* -s) pressurized can from which a substance can be dispensed as a fine spray
aerosols *n* ▷ aerosol
aerospace *n* (*pl* -s) earth's atmosphere and space beyond
aerospaces *n* ▷ aerospace
aesthete [eess-theet] *n* (*pl* -s) person who has or affects an extravagant love of art
> **aestheticism** *n* (*pl* -s)
aesthetes *n* ▷ aesthete
aesthetic [iss-thet-ik] *adj* relating to the appreciation of art and beauty
> **aesthetically** *adv*
aesthetically *adv* ▷ aesthetic
aestheticism *n* ▷ aesthete
aestheticisms *n* ▷ aesthete
aesthetics *n* study of art, beauty, and good taste
aether *n* (*pl* -s) ▷ ether
aethers *n* ▷ aether
aetiologies *n* ▷ aetiology
aetiology [ee-tee-ol-a-jee] *n* (*pl* -gies) ▷ etiology
afar *adv* from or at a great distance
affabilities *n* ▷ affable
affability *n* ▷ affable
affable *adj* friendly and easy to talk to > **affably** *adv* > **affability** *n* (*pl* -ties)
affably *adv* ▷ affable
affair *n* (*pl* -s) event or happening
affairs *n* ▷ affair
affect¹ *v* (-s, -ing, -ed) act on, influence

affect² *v* (-s, -ing, -ed) put on a show of
affectation *n* (*pl* -s) attitude or manner put on to impress
affectations *n* ▷ affectation
affected *adj* displaying affectation ▶ *v* ▷ affect¹, ²
affecting *v* ▷ affect¹, ²
affection *n* (*pl* -s) fondness or love
affectionate *adj* loving > **affectionately** *adv*
affectionately *adv* ▷ affectionate
affections *n* ▷ affection
affects *v* ▷ affect¹, ²
affianced [af-fie-anst] *adj* (*Old-fashioned*) engaged to be married
affidavit [af-fid-dave-it] *n* (*pl* -s) written statement made on oath
affidavits *n* ▷ affidavit
affiliate *v* (-tes, -ting, -ted) (of a group) link up with a larger group > **affiliation** *n* (*pl* -s)
affiliated *v* ▷ affiliate
affiliates *v* ▷ affiliate
affiliating *v* ▷ affiliate
affiliation *n* ▷ affiliate
affiliations *n* ▷ affiliate
affinities *n* ▷ affinity
affinity *n* (*pl* -ies) close connection or liking
affirm *v* (-s, -ing, -ed) declare to be true
> **affirmation** *n* (*pl* -s)
affirmation *n* ▷ affirm
affirmations *n* ▷ affirm
affirmative *n* (*pl* -s), *adj* (word or phrase) indicating agreement
affirmatives *n* ▷ affirmative
affirmed *v* ▷ affirm
affirming *v* ▷ affirm
affirms *v* ▷ affirm
affix *v* (-fixes, -fixing, -fixed) attach or fasten ▶ *n* (*pl* -fixes) word or syllable added to a word to change its meaning
affixed *v* ▷ affix
affixes *v, n* ▷ affix
affixing *v* ▷ affix
afflict *v* (-s, -ing, -ed) give pain or grief to
> **affliction** *n* (*pl* -s)
afflicted *v* ▷ afflict
afflicting *v* ▷ afflict
affliction *n* ▷ afflict
afflictions *n* ▷ afflict
afflicts *v* ▷ afflict
affluence *n* (*pl* -s) wealth
affluences *n* ▷ affluence
affluent *adj* having plenty of money
afford *v* (-s, -ing, -ed) have enough money to buy > **affordable** *adj*
affordable *adj* ▷ afford

afforded v ▷ afford

affording v ▷ afford

affords v ▷ afford

afforest v (-s, -ing, -ed) plant trees on > **afforestation** n (pl -s)

afforestation n ▷ afforest

afforestations n ▷ afforest

afforested v ▷ afforest

afforesting v ▷ afforest

afforests v ▷ afforest

affray n (pl -s) (BRIT, AUST & NZ) (LAW) noisy fight, brawl

affrays n ▷ affray

affront v (-s, -ing, -ed), n (pl -s) insult

affronted v ▷ affront

affronting v ▷ affront

affronts v, n ▷ affront

afghan adj of Afghanistan or its language

aficionado [af-fish-yo-**nah**-do] n (pl -dos) enthusiastic fan of something or someone

aficionados n ▷ aficionado

afield adv far away

aflame adj burning

afloat adv, adj floating

afoot adv, adj happening, in operation

aforementioned adj referred to previously

aforesaid adj referred to previously

aforethought adj premeditated

afraid adj frightened

afresh adv again, anew

aft adv at or towards the rear of a ship or aircraft

after prep following in time or place ▶ conj at a later time than ▶ adv at a later time

afterbirth n (pl -s) material expelled from the womb after childbirth

afterbirths n ▷ afterbirth

aftercare n (pl -s) support given to a person discharged from a hospital or prison

aftercares n ▷ aftercare

aftereffect n (pl -s) result occurring some time after its cause

aftereffects n ▷ aftereffect

afterglow n (pl -s) glow left after a source of light has gone

afterglows n ▷ afterglow

afterlife n (pl -lives) life after death

afterlives n ▷ afterlife

aftermath n (pl -s) results of an event considered together

aftermaths n ▷ aftermath

afternoon n (pl -s) time between noon and evening

afternoons n ▷ afternoon

afters pl n (BRIT) (Informal) dessert

aftershave n (pl -s) lotion applied to the face after shaving

aftershaves n ▷ aftershave

afterthought n (pl -s) idea occurring later

afterthoughts n ▷ afterthought

afterward adv ▷ afterwards

afterwards, afterward adv later

> **ag** adj. Ag means to do with **agriculture**. This is a good short word to remember, as it can come in handy when you need to form words in more than one direction. Ag scores 3 points.

again adv once more

against prep in opposition or contrast to

agape adj (of the mouth) wide open

agaric n (pl -s) fungus with gills on the underside of the cap, such as a mushroom

agarics n ▷ agaric

agate [**ag**-git] n (pl -s) semiprecious form of quartz with striped colouring

agates n ▷ agate

age n (pl -s) length of time a person or thing has existed ▶ v (-s, ageing or aging, -d) make or grow old > **ageing, aging** n, adj

aged adj [**ay**-jid] old ▷ age

ageing v, n, adj ▷ age

ageless adj apparently never growing old

agencies n ▷ agency

agency n (pl -cies) organization providing a service

agenda n (pl -s) list of things to be dealt with, esp. at a meeting

agendas n ▷ agenda

agent n (pl -s) person acting on behalf of another

agents n ▷ agent

ages n, v ▷ age

agglomeration n (pl -s) confused mass or cluster

agglomerations n ▷ agglomeration

aggrandize v (-zes, -zing, -zed) make greater in size, power, or rank > **aggrandizement** n (pl -s)

aggrandized v ▷ aggrandize

aggrandizement n ▷ aggrandize

aggrandizements n ▷ aggrandize

aggrandizes v ▷ aggrandize

aggrandizing v ▷ aggrandize

aggravate v (-tes, -ting, -ted) make worse > **aggravating** adj > **aggravation** n (pl -s)

aggravated v ▷ aggravate

aggravates v ▷ aggravate

aggravating v, adj ▷ aggravate

aggravation n ▷ aggravate

aggravations n ▷ aggravate

aggregate n (pl -s) total ► adj gathered into a mass ► v (-tes, -ting, -ted) combine into a whole > **aggregation** n (pl -s)
  aggregated v ▷ aggregate
  aggregates n, v ▷ aggregate
  aggregating v ▷ aggregate
  aggregation n ▷ aggregate
  aggregations n ▷ aggregate
aggression n (pl -s) hostile behaviour > **aggressor** n (pl -s)
  aggressions n ▷ aggression
aggressive adj showing aggression > **aggressively** adv > **aggressiveness** n
  aggressively adv ▷ aggressive
  aggressiveness n ▷ aggressive
  aggressor n ▷ aggression
  aggressors n ▷ aggression
aggrieved adj upset and angry
aggro n (pl -s) (BRIT, AUST & NZ) (Slang) aggressive behaviour
  aggros n ▷ aggro
aghast adj overcome with amazement or horror
agile adj (-r, -st) nimble, quick-moving > **agility** n (pl -ties)
  agileness n ▷ agile
  agiler adj ▷ agile
  agilest adj ▷ agile
  agilities n ▷ agile
  agility n ▷ agile
aging v, n, adj ▷ age
agitate v (-tes, -ting, -ted) disturb or excite > **agitation** n (pl -s) > **agitator** n (pl -s)
  agitated v ▷ agitate
  agitates v ▷ agitate
  agitating v ▷ agitate
  agitation n ▷ agitate
  agitations n ▷ agitate
  agitator n ▷ agitate
  agitators n ▷ agitate
aglow adj glowing
agnostic n (pl -s) person who believes that it is impossible to know whether God exists ► adj of agnostics > **agnosticism** n (pl -s)
  agnosticism n ▷ agnostic
  agnosticisms n ▷ agnostic
  agnostics n ▷ agnostic
ago adv in the past
agog adj eager or curious
  agonies n ▷ agony
agonize v (-zes, -zing, -zed) worry greatly > **agonizing** v
  agonized v ▷ agonize
  agonizes v ▷ agonize
  agonizing v, adj ▷ agonize

agony n (pl -nies) extreme physical or mental pain
agoraphobia n (pl -s) fear of open spaces > **agoraphobic** n (pl -s), adj
  agoraphobias n ▷ agoraphobia
  agoraphobic n, adj ▷ agoraphobia
  agoraphobics n ▷ agoraphobia
agrarian adj of land or agriculture
agree v (-s, -ing, -d) be of the same opinion
agreeable adj pleasant and enjoyable > **agreeably** adv
  agreeably adv ▷ agreeable
  agreed v ▷ agree
  agreeing v ▷ agree
agreement n (pl agreements) agreeing
  agreements n ▷ agreement
  agrees v ▷ agree
agricultural adj ▷ agriculture
agriculturalist n ▷ agriculture
agriculturalists n ▷ agriculture
agriculture n (pl -s) raising of crops and livestock > **agricultural** adj > **agriculturalist** n (pl -s)
  agricultures n ▷ agriculture
  agronomies n ▷ agronomy
  agronomist n ▷ agronomy
  agronomists n ▷ agronomy
agronomy [ag-ron-om-mee] n (pl -mies) science of soil management and crop production > **agronomist** n (pl -s)
aground adv onto the bottom of shallow water
ague [aig-yew] n (pl -s) (Old-fashioned) periodic fever with shivering
  agues n ▷ ague

> **ah** interj. Ah is a sound people make to show pleasure or pain. Ah scores 5 points, and is a good word to form as a result of playing a longer word.

ahead adv in front
ahoy interj shout used at sea to attract attention

> **ai** n (**ais**). An ai is a three-toed sloth. It's useful when trying to form several words at once. Ai scores 2 points.

aid v (-s, -ing, -ed) ► n (pl -s) (give) assistance or support
aide n (pl -s) assistant
  aided v ▷ aid
  aides n ▷ aide
  aiding v ▷ aid
  aids v, n ▷ aid
ail v (-s, -ing, -ed) trouble, afflict
  ailed v ▷ ail
aileron n (pl -s) movable flap on an aircraft

wing which controls rolling
ailerons n ▷ aileron
ailing adj sickly ▶ v ▷ ail
ailment n (pl -s) illness
ailments n ▷ ailment
ails v ▷ ail
aim v (-s, -ing, -ed) point (a weapon or missile) or direct (a blow or remark) at a target ▶ n (pl -s) aiming
aimed v ▷ aim
aiming v ▷ aim
aimless adj having no purpose > **aimlessly** adv
aimlessly adv ▷ aimless
aims v, n ▷ aim
air n (pl -s) mixture of gases forming the earth's atmosphere ▶ v (-s, -ing, -ed) make known publicly
airborne adj carried by air
airbrush n (pl -es) atomizer spraying paint by compressed air
airbrushes n ▷ airbrush
aircraft n any machine that flies, such as an aeroplane
aired v ▷ air
airfield n (pl -s) place where aircraft can land and take off
airfields n ▷ airfield
airier adj ▷ airy
airiest adj ▷ airy
airily adv ▷ airy
airing n (pl -s) exposure to air for drying or ventilation ▶ v ▷ air
airings n ▷ airing
airless adj stuffy
airlift n (pl -s) transport of troops or cargo by aircraft when other routes are blocked ▶ v (-s, -ing, -ed) transport by airlift
airlifted v ▷ airlift
airlifting v ▷ airlift
airlifts n, v ▷ airlift
airline n (pl -s) company providing scheduled flights for passengers and cargo
airliner n (pl -s) large passenger aircraft
airliners n ▷ airliner
airlines n ▷ airline
airlock n (pl -s) air bubble blocking the flow of liquid in a pipe
airlocks n ▷ airlock
airmail n system of sending mail by aircraft
airman n (pl -men) member of the air force
airmen n ▷ airman
airplay n (pl -s) broadcast performances of a record on radio
airplays n ▷ airplay
airport n (pl -s) airfield for civilian aircraft,

with facilities for aircraft maintenance and passengers
airports n ▷ airport
airs n, v ▷ air
airship n (pl -s) lighter-than-air self-propelled aircraft
airships n ▷ airship
airspace n (pl -s) atmosphere above a country, regarded as its territory
airspaces n ▷ airspace
airstrip n (pl -s) cleared area where aircraft can take off and land
airstrips n ▷ airstrip
airtight adj sealed so that air cannot enter
airworthiness n ▷ airworthy
airworthinesses n ▷ airworthy
airworthy adj (of aircraft) fit to fly
> **airworthiness** n (pl -es)
airy adj (-rier, -riest) well-ventilated > **airily** adv
aisle [rhymes with mile] n (pl -s) passageway separating seating areas in a church, theatre, etc., or row of shelves in a supermarket
aisles n ▷ aisle
ajar adj, adv (of a door) partly open
akimbo adv with hands on hips and elbows outwards
akin adj similar, related
al conj. Al is an old word for **if** or **although**. Al scores 2 points.
alabaster n (pl -s) soft white translucent stone
alabasters n ▷ alabaster
alacrities n ▷ alacrity
alacrity n (pl -ies) speed, eagerness
alarm n (pl -s) sudden fear caused by awareness of danger ▶ v (-s, -ing, -med) fill with fear > **alarming** adj
alarmed v ▷ alarm
alarming v, adj ▷ alarm
alarmist n (pl -s) person who alarms others needlessly
alarmists n ▷ alarmist
alarms n, v ▷ alarm
alas adv unfortunately, regrettably
albatross n (pl -es) large sea bird with very long wings
albatrosses n ▷ albatross
albeit conj even though
albino n (pl -nos) person or animal with white skin and hair and pink eyes
albinos n ▷ albino
album n (pl -s) book with blank pages for keeping photographs or stamps in
albumen n (pl -s) egg white
albumens n ▷ albumen
albumin n (pl -s) protein found in blood

plasma, egg white, milk, and muscle

albumins n ▷ albumin

albums n ▷ album

alchemies n ▷ alchemy

alchemist n ▷ alchemy

alchemists n ▷ alchemy

alchemy n (pl -ies) medieval form of chemistry concerned with trying to turn base metals into gold and to find the elixir of life > **alchemist** n (pl -s)

alcohol n (pl -s) colourless flammable liquid present in intoxicating drinks

alcoholic adj of alcohol ▶ n (pl -s) person addicted to alcohol

alcoholics n ▷ alcoholic

alcoholism n (pl -s) addiction to alcohol

alcoholisms n ▷ alcoholism

alcohols n ▷ alcohol

alcopop n (pl -s) (BRIT, AUST & S AFR) (Informal) alcoholic drink that tastes like a soft drink

alcopops n ▷ alcopop

alcove n (pl -s) recess in the wall of a room

alcoves n ▷ alcove

aldehyde n (pl -s) one of a group of chemical compounds derived from alcohol by oxidation

aldehydes n ▷ aldehyde

alder n (pl -s) tree related to the birch

alderman n (pl -men) formerly, senior member of a local council

aldermen n ▷ alderman

alders n ▷ alder

ale n (pl -s) kind of beer

alert adj (-er, -est) watchful, attentive ▶ n (pl -s) warning of danger ▶ v (-s, -ing, -ed) warn of danger > **alertness** n (pl -es)

alerted v ▷ alert

alerter adj ▷ alert

alertest adj ▷ alert

alerting v ▷ alert

alertness n ▷ alert

alertnesses n ▷ alert

alerts n, v ▷ alert

ales n ▷ ale

alfalfa n (pl -s) kind of plant used to feed livestock

alfalfas n ▷ alfalfa

alfresco adv, adj in the open air

alga n (pl -e) (usually plural) plant which lives in or near water and has no true stems, leaves, or roots

algae [al-jee] n ▷ alga

algebra n (pl -s) branch of mathematics using symbols to represent numbers > **algebraic** adj

algebraic adj ▷ algebra

algebras n ▷ algebra

algorithm n (pl -s) logical arithmetical or computational procedure for solving a problem

algorithms n ▷ algorithm

alias adv also known as ▶ n (pl -ses) false name

aliases n ▷ alias

alibi n (pl -s) plea of being somewhere else when a crime was committed

alibis n ▷ alibi

alien adj foreign ▶ n (pl -s) foreigner

alienate v (-tes, -ting, -ted) cause to become hostile > **alienation** n (pl -s)

alienated v ▷ alienate

alienates v ▷ alienate

alienating v ▷ alienate

alienation n ▷ alienate

alienations n ▷ alienate

aliens n ▷ alien

alight[1] v (-s, -ing, -ed) step out of (a vehicle)

alight[2] adj on fire

alighted v ▷ alight[1]

alighting v ▷ alight[1]

alights v ▷ alight[1]

align [a-line] v (-s, -ing, -ed) bring (a person or group) into agreement with the policy of another > **alignment** n (pl -s)

aligned v ▷ align

aligning v ▷ align

alignment n ▷ align

alignments n ▷ align

aligns v ▷ align

alike adj like, similar ▶ adv in the same way

alimentary adj of nutrition

alimonies n ▷ alimony

alimony n (pl -nies) allowance paid under a court order to a separated or divorced spouse

aliquot (MATHS) adj of or denoting an exact divisor of a number ▶ n (pl -s) exact divisor

aliquots n ▷ aliquot

alive adj living, in existence

alkali [alk-a-lie] n (pl -s) substance which combines with acid and neutralizes it to form a salt > **alkaline** adj > **alkalinity** n (pl -ties)

alkaline adj ▷ alkali

alkalinities n ▷ alkali

alkalinity n ▷ alkali

alkalis n ▷ alkali

alkaloid n (pl -s) any of a group of organic compounds containing nitrogen

alkaloids n ▷ alkaloid

all adj whole quantity or number (of) ▶ adv wholly, entirely

allay v (-s, -ing, -ed) reduce (fear or anger)

allayed v ▷ allay

allaying v ▷ allay
allays v ▷ allay
allegation n (pl -s) unproved accusation
allegations n ▷ allegation
allege v (-ges, -ging, -ged) state without proof
> **alleged** adj > **allegedly** adv
alleged v, adj ▷ allege
allegedly adv ▷ allege
alleges v ▷ allege
allegiance n (pl -s) loyalty to a person, country,
or cause
allegiances n ▷ allegiance
alleging v ▷ allege
allegorical adj ▷ allegory
allegories n ▷ allegory
allegory n (pl -ries) story with an underlying
meaning as well as the literal one
> **allegorical** adj
allegretto n (pl -s) ▶ adv (MUSIC) (piece to be
played) fairly quickly or briskly
allegrettos n ▷ allegretto
allegro n (pl -s) ▶ adv (MUSIC) (piece to be
played) in a brisk lively manner
allegros n ▷ allegro
alleluia interj ▷ hallelujah
allergen n (pl -s) substance capable of causing
an allergic reaction
allergens n ▷ allergen
allergic adj having or caused by an allergy
allergies n ▷ allergy
allergy n (pl -gies) extreme sensitivity to a
substance, which causes the body to react
to it
alleviate v (-tes, -ting, -ted) lessen (pain or
suffering) > **alleviation** n (pl -s)
alleviated v ▷ alleviate
alleviates v ▷ alleviate
alleviating v ▷ alleviate
alleviation n ▷ alleviate
alleviations n ▷ alleviate
alley n (pl -s) narrow street or path
alleys n ▷ alley
alliance n (pl -s) state of being allied
alliances n ▷ alliance
allied v, adj ▷ ally
allies n, v ▷ ally
alligator n (pl -s) reptile of the crocodile family,
found in the southern US and China
alligators n ▷ alligator
alliteration n (pl -s) use of the same sound at
the start of words occurring together, e.g.
moody music > **alliterative** adj
alliterations n ▷ alliteration
alliterative adj ▷ alliteration
allocate v (-tes, -ting, -ted) assign to someone

or for a particular purpose > **allocation** n
(pl -s)
allocated v ▷ allocate
allocates v ▷ allocate
allocating v ▷ allocate
allocation n ▷ allocate
allocations n ▷ allocate
allot v (-lots, -lotting, -lotted) assign as a share
or for a particular purpose
allotment n (pl -s) distribution
allotments n ▷ allotment
allotrope n (pl -s) any of two or more physical
forms in which an element can exist
allotropes n ▷ allotrope
allots v ▷ allot
allotted v ▷ allot
allotting v ▷ allot
allow v (-s, -ing, -ed) permit > **allowable** adj
allowable adj ▷ allow
allowance n (pl -s) amount of money given at
regular intervals
allowances n ▷ allowance
allowed v ▷ allow
allowing v ▷ allow
allows v ▷ allow
alloy n (pl -s) mixture of two or more metals ▶ v
(-s, -ing, -ed) mix (metals)
alloyed v ▷ alloy
alloying v ▷ alloy
alloys n, v ▷ alloy
allspice n (pl -s) spice made from the berries of
a tropical American tree
allspices n ▷ allspice
allude v (-des, -ding, -ded) (foll. by to) refer
indirectly to
alluded v ▷ allude
alludes v ▷ allude
alluding v ▷ allude
allure n (pl -s) attractiveness ▶ v (-s, -ing, -ed)
entice or attract > **alluring** adj
allured v ▷ allure
allures n, v ▷ allure
alluring v, adj ▷ allure
allusion n (pl -s) indirect reference > **allusive**
adj
allusions n ▷ allusion
allusive adj ▷ allusion
alluvial adj ▷ alluvium
alluvium n (pl -s) fertile soil deposited by
flowing water > **alluvial** adj
alluviums n ▷ alluvium
ally n (pl -lies) country, person, or group with
an agreement to support another ▶ v (-lies,
-lying, -lied) > **allied** adj
allying v ▷ ally

almanac n (pl -s) yearly calendar with detailed information on phases of the moon, etc.
almanacs n ▷ almanac
almighty adj having absolute power
almond n (pl -s) edible oval-shaped nut which grows on a small tree
almonds n ▷ almond
almondy adj ▷ almond
almoner n (pl -s) (BRIT) formerly, a hospital social worker
almoners n ▷ almoner
almost adv very nearly
alms [ahmz] pl n (Old-fashioned) gifts to the poor
aloe n (pl -s) plant with fleshy spiny leaves
aloes n ▷ aloe
aloft adv in the air
alone adj, adv without anyone or anything else
along prep over part or all the length of ▶ adv forward
alongside prep, adv beside (something)
aloof adj distant or haughty in manner
  > **aloofness** n (pl -es)
aloofness n ▷ aloof
aloofnesses n ▷ aloof
alopecia [al-loh-pee-sha] n (pl -s) loss of hair
alopecias n ▷ alopecia
aloud adv in an audible voice
alpaca n (pl -s) Peruvian llama
alpacas n ▷ alpaca
alpenstock n (pl -s) iron-tipped stick used by climbers
alpenstocks n ▷ alpenstock
alpha n (pl -s) first letter in the Greek alphabet
alphabet n (pl -s) set of letters used in writing a language
alphabetical adj in the conventional order of the letters of an alphabet > **alphabetically** adv
alphabetically adv ▷ alphabetical
alphabetize v (-zes, -zing, -zed) put in alphabetical order
alphabetized v ▷ alphabetize
alphabetizes v ▷ alphabetize
alphabetizing v ▷ alphabetize
alphabets n ▷ alphabet
alphas n ▷ alpha
alpine adj of high mountains ▶ n (pl -s) mountain plant
alpines n ▷ alpine
already adv before the present time
alright adj, interj all right
also adv in addition, too
altar n (pl -s) table used for Communion in Christian churches
altarpiece n (pl -s) work of art above and

behind the altar in some Christian churches
altarpieces n ▷ altarpiece
altars n ▷ altar
alter v (-s, -ing, -ed) make or become different
  > **alteration** n (pl -s)
alteration n ▷ alter
alterations n ▷ alter
altercation n (pl -s) heated argument
altercations n ▷ altercation
altered v ▷ alter
altering v ▷ alter
alternate v (-tes, -ting, -ted) (cause to) occur by turns ▶ adj occurring by turns
  > **alternately** adv > **alternation** n (pl -s)
alternated v ▷ alternate
alternately adv ▷ alternate
alternates v ▷ alternate
alternating v ▷ alternate
alternation n ▷ alternate
alternations n ▷ alternate
alternative n (pl -s) one of two choices ▶ adj able to be done or used instead of something else > **alternatively** adv
alternatively adv ▷ alternative
alternatives n ▷ alternative
alternator n (pl -s) electric generator for producing alternating current
alternators n ▷ alternator
alters v ▷ alter
although conj despite the fact that
altimeter [al-tim-it-er] n (pl -s) instrument that measures altitude
altimeters n ▷ altimeter
altitude n (pl -s) height above sea level
altitudes n ▷ altitude
alto n (pl -s) (MUSIC) (singer with) the highest adult male voice
altogether adv entirely
altos n ▷ alto
altruism n (pl -s) unselfish concern for the welfare of others > **altruist** n (pl -s) > **altruistic** adj > **altruistically** adv
altruisms n ▷ altruism
altruist n ▷ altruism
altruists n ▷ altruism
altruistic adj ▷ altruism
altruistically adv ▷ altruism
aluminium n (pl -s) (CHEM) light silvery-white metal that does not rust
aluminiums n ▷ aluminium
alumna n ▷ alumnus
alumnae n ▷ alumnus
alumni n ▷ alumnus
alumnus [al-lumm-nuss] n (pl -ni) [-nie] graduate of a college > **alumna** [al-lumm-na]

▶ *n fem* (*pl* **-nae**) [**-nee**]
always *adv* at all times
alyssum *n* (*pl* **-s**) garden plant with small yellow or white flowers
    alyssums *n* ▷ alyssum
am *v* ▷ be
amalgam *n* (*pl* **-s**) blend or combination
amalgamate *v* (**-tes, -ting, -ted**) combine or unite > **amalgamation** *n* (*pl* **-s**)
    amalgamated *v* ▷ amalgamate
    amalgamates *v* ▷ amalgamate
    amalgamating *v* ▷ amalgamate
    amalgamation *n* ▷ amalgamate
    amalgamations *n* ▷ amalgamate
    amalgams *n* ▷ amalgam
amandla [ah-**mand**-lah] *n* (s AFR) political slogan calling for power to the Black population
    amandlas *n* ▷ amandla
    amanuenses *n* ▷ amanuensis
amanuensis [am-man-yew-**en**-siss] *n* (*pl* **-ses**) [**-seez**] person who writes from dictation
amaranth *n* (*pl* **-s**) imaginary flower that never fades
    amaranths *n* ▷ amaranth
amaryllis *n* (*pl* **-ses**) lily-like plant with large red, pink, or white flowers
    amaryllises *n* ▷ amaryllis
amass *v* (**-ses, -sing, -sed**) collect or accumulate
    amassed *v* ▷ amass
    amasses *v* ▷ amass
    amassing *v* ▷ amass
amateur *n* (*pl* **-s**) person who engages in a sport or activity as a pastime rather than as a profession
amateurish *adj* lacking skill > **amateurishly** *adv*
    amateurishly *adv* ▷ amateurish
    amateurs *n* ▷ amateur
amatory *adj* relating to love
amaze *v* (**-zes, -zing, -zed**) surprise greatly, astound > **amazing** *adj* > **amazingly** *adv* > **amazement** *n* (*pl* **-s**)
    amazed *v* ▷ amaze
    amazement *n* ▷ amaze
    amazements *n* ▷ amaze
    amazes *v* ▷ amaze
    amazing *v, adj* ▷ amaze
    amazingly *adv* ▷ amaze
amazon *n* (*pl* **-s**) strong and powerful woman > **amazonian** *adj*
    amazonian *adj* ▷ amazon
    amazons *n* ▷ amazon
ambassador *n* (*pl* **-s**) senior diplomat who represents his or her country in another country > **ambassadorial** *adj*
    ambassadorial *adj* ▷ ambassador
    ambassadors *n* ▷ ambassador
amber *n* (*pl* **-s**) clear yellowish fossil resin ▶ *adj* brownish-yellow
ambergris [am-ber-**greece**] *n* (*pl* **-es**) waxy substance secreted by the sperm whale, used in making perfumes
    ambergrises *n* ▷ ambergris
    ambers *n* ▷ amber
ambidextrous *adj* able to use both hands with equal ease
ambience *n* (*pl* **-s**) atmosphere of a place
    ambiences *n* ▷ ambience
ambient *adj* surrounding
    ambiguities *n* ▷ ambiguous
    ambiguity *n* ▷ ambiguous
ambiguous *adj* having more than one possible meaning > **ambiguously** *adv* > **ambiguity** *n* (*pl* **-ties**)
    ambiguously *adv* ▷ ambiguous
ambit *n* (*pl* **-s**) limits or boundary
ambition *n* (*pl* **-s**) desire for success > **ambitious** *adj* > **ambitiously** *adv*
    ambitions *n* ▷ ambition
    ambitious *adj* ▷ ambition
    ambitiously *adv* ▷ ambition
    ambits *n* ▷ ambit
ambivalence *n* (*pl* **-s**) state of feeling two conflicting emotions at the same time > **ambivalent** *adj* > **ambivalently** *adv*
    ambivalences *n* ▷ ambivalence
    ambivalent *adj* ▷ ambivalence
    ambivalently *adv* ▷ ambivalence
amble *v* (**-les, -ling, -led**) walk at a leisurely pace ▶ *n* (*pl* **-s**) leisurely walk or pace
    ambled *v* ▷ amble
    ambles *v, n* ▷ amble
    ambling *v* ▷ amble
ambrosia *n* (*pl* **-s**) (MYTH) food of the gods > **ambrosial** *adj*
    ambrosial *adj* ▷ ambrosia
    ambrosias *n* ▷ ambrosia
ambulance *n* (*pl* **-s**) motor vehicle designed to carry sick or injured people
    ambulances *n* ▷ ambulance
ambush *n* (*pl* **-es**) act of waiting in a concealed position to make a surprise attack ▶ *v* (**-shes, -shing, -shed**) attack from a concealed position
    ambushed *v* ▷ ambush
    ambushes *n, v* ▷ ambush
    ambushing *v* ▷ ambush
ameliorate [am-**meal**-yor-rate] *v* (**-tes,**

-ting, -ted) make (something) better
> **amelioration** n (pl -s)
ameliorated v ▷ ameliorate
ameliorates v ▷ ameliorate
ameliorating v ▷ ameliorate
amelioration n ▷ ameliorate
ameliorations n ▷ ameliorate
amen interj so be it: used at the end of a prayer
amenable adj likely or willing to cooperate
amend v (-s, -ing, -ed) make small changes to correct or improve (something)
> **amendment** n (pl -s)
amended v ▷ amend
amending v ▷ amend
amendment n ▷ amend
amends pl n compensation for ▶ v ▷ amend
amenities n ▷ amenity
amenity n (pl -ties) useful or enjoyable feature
amethyst [am-myth-ist] n (pl -s) bluish-violet variety of quartz used as a gemstone
amethysts n ▷ amethyst
amiabilities n ▷ amiable
amiability n ▷ amiable
amiable adj friendly, pleasant-natured
> **amiably** adv > **amiability** n (pl -ties)
amiably adv ▷ amiable
amicable adj friendly > **amicably** adv
amicably adv ▷ amicable
amid, amidst prep in the middle of, among
amidships adv at or towards the middle of a ship
amidst prep ▷ amid
amiss adv wrongly, badly ▶ adj wrong, faulty
amities n ▷ amity
amity n (pl -ties) friendship
ammeter n (pl -s) instrument for measuring electric current
ammeters n ▷ ammeter
ammonia n (pl -s) strong-smelling alkaline gas containing hydrogen and nitrogen
ammonias n ▷ ammonia
ammonite n (pl -s) fossilized spiral shell of an extinct sea creature
ammonites n ▷ ammonite
ammunition n (pl -s) bullets, bombs, and shells that can be fired from or as a weapon
ammunitions n ▷ ammunition
amnesia n (pl -s) loss of memory > **amnesiac** adj, n (pl -s)
amnesiac adj, n ▷ amnesia
amnesiacs n ▷ amnesia
amnesias n ▷ amnesia
amnesties n ▷ amnesty
amnesty n (pl -ties) general pardon for offences against a government

amniocenteses n ▷ amniocentesis
amniocentesis n (pl -ses) removal of some amniotic fluid to test for possible abnormalities in a fetus
amoeba [am-mee-ba] n (pl -bae, -bas) microscopic single-celled animal able to change its shape
amoebae n ▷ amoeba
amoebas n ▷ amoeba
amok [a-muck, a-mock] adv in a violent frenzy
among, amongst prep in the midst of
amongst prep ▷ among
amoral [aim-mor-ral] adj without moral standards > **amorality** n (pl -ties)
amoralities n ▷ amoral
amorality n ▷ amoral
amorous adj feeling, showing, or relating to sexual love > **amorously** adv
amorously adv ▷ amorous
amorphous adj without distinct shape
amortize v (-zes, -zing, -zed) pay off (a debt) gradually by periodic transfers to a sinking fund
amortized v ▷ amortize
amortizes v ▷ amortize
amortizing v ▷ amortize
amount n (pl -s) extent or quantity ▶ v (-s, -ing, -ed) (foll. by **to**) be equal or add up to
amounted v ▷ amount
amounting v ▷ amount
amounts n, v ▷ amount
amour n (pl -s) (secret) love affair
amours n ▷ amour
amp n (pl -s) ampere
ampere [am-pair] n (pl -s) basic unit of electric current
amperes n ▷ ampere
ampersand n (pl -s) the character (&) meaning and
ampersands n ▷ ampersand
amphetamine [am-fet-am-mean] n (pl -s) drug used as a stimulant
amphetamines n ▷ amphetamine
amphibian n (pl -s) animal that lives on land but breeds in water
amphibians n ▷ amphibian
amphibious adj living or operating both on land and in water
amphitheatre n (pl -s) open oval or circular building with tiers of seats rising round an arena
amphitheatres n ▷ amphitheatre
amphora [am-for-ra] n (pl -phorae) two-handled ancient Greek or Roman jar
amphorae n ▷ amphora

ample *adj* (-r, -st) more than sufficient ▷ **amply** *adv*
  ampler *adj* ▷ ample
  amplest *adj* ▷ ample
  amplification *n* ▷ amplify
  amplifications *n* ▷ amplify
  amplified *v* ▷ amplify
amplifier *n* (*pl* -s) device used to amplify a current or sound signal
  amplifiers *n* ▷ amplifier
  amplifies *v* ▷ amplify
amplify *v* (-fies, -fying, -fied) increase the strength of (a current or sound signal) of ▷ **amplification** *n* (*pl* -s)
  amplifying *v* ▷ amplify
amplitude *n* (*pl* -s) greatness of extent
  amplitudes *n* ▷ amplitude
  amply *adv* ▷ ample
ampoule *n* (*pl* -s) small sealed glass vessel containing liquid for injection
  ampoules *n* ▷ ampoule
  amps *n* ▷ amp
amputate *v* (-tes, -ting, -ted) cut off (a limb or part of a limb) for medical reasons ▷ **amputation** *n* (*pl* -s)
  amputated *v* ▷ amputate
  amputates *v* ▷ amputate
  amputating *v* ▷ amputate
  amputation *n* ▷ amputate
  amputations *n* ▷ amputate
amuck *adv* ▷ amok
amulet *n* (*pl* -s) something carried or worn as a protection against evil
  amulets *n* ▷ amulet
amuse *v* (-ses, -sing, -sed) cause to laugh or smile ▷ **amusing** *adj*
  amused *v* ▷ amuse
amusement *n* (*pl* -s) state of being amused
  amusements *n* ▷ amusement
  amuses *v* ▷ amuse
  amusing *v, adj* ▷ amuse
an *adj* form of **a** used before vowels, and sometimes before h
anachronism [an-**nak**-kron-iz-zum] *n* (*pl* -s) person or thing placed in the wrong historical period or seeming to belong to another time ▷ **anachronistic** *adj*
  anachronisms *n* ▷ anachronism
  anachronistic *adj* ▷ anachronism
anaconda *n* (*pl* -s) large S American snake which kills by constriction
  anacondas *n* ▷ anaconda
anaemia [an-**neem**-ee-a] *n* (*pl* -s) deficiency in the number of red blood cells
  anaemias *n* ▷ anaemia

anaemic *adj* having anaemia
anaesthesia [an-niss-**theez**-ee-a] *n* (*pl* -s) loss of bodily feeling
  anaesthesias *n* ▷ anaesthesia
anaesthetic [an-niss-**thet**-ik] *n* (*pl* -s), *adj* (substance) causing loss of bodily feeling
  anaesthetics *n* ▷ anaesthetic
anaesthetist [an-**neess**-thet-ist] *n* (*pl* -s) doctor trained to administer anaesthetics ▷ **anaesthetize** *v* (-zes, -zing, -zed)
  anaesthetists *n* ▷ anaesthetist
  anaesthetize *v* ▷ anaesthetist
  anaesthetized *v* ▷ anaesthetist
  anaesthetizes *v* ▷ anaesthetist
  anaesthetizing *v* ▷ anaesthetist
anagram *n* (*pl* -s) word or phrase made by rearranging the letters of another word or phrase
  anagrams *n* ▷ anagram
anal [ain-al] *adj* of the anus
analgesia *n* (*pl* -s) absence of pain
  analgesias *n* ▷ analgesia
analgesic [an-nal-**jeez**-ik] *n* (*pl* -s) ▶ *adj* (drug) relieving pain
  analgesics *n* ▷ analgesic
  analogical *adj* ▷ analogy
  analogies *n* ▷ analogy
analogous *adj* similar in some respects
analogue *n* (*pl* -s) something that is similar in some respects to something else ▶ *adj* displaying information by means of a dial
  analogues *n* ▷ analogue
analogy *n* (*pl* -gies) similarity in some respects ▷ **analogical** *adj*
analyse *v* (-ses, -sing, -sed) make an analysis of (something)
  analysed *v* ▷ analyse
  analyses *v* ▷ analyse ▶ *n* ▷ analysis
  analysing *v* ▷ analyse
analysis *n* (*pl* -ses) separation of a whole into its parts for study and interpretation ▷ **analytical, analytic** *adj* ▷ **analytically** *adv*
analyst *n* (*pl* -s) person skilled in analysis
  analysts *n* ▷ analyst
  analytic *adj* ▷ analysis
  analytical *adj* ▷ analysis
  analytically *adv* ▷ analysis
  anarchic *adj* ▷ anarchy
  anarchies *n* ▷ anarchy
anarchism *n* (*pl* -s) doctrine advocating the abolition of government
  anarchisms *n* ▷ anarchism
anarchist *n* (*pl* -s) person who advocates the abolition of government ▷ **anarchistic** *adj*
  anarchistic *adj* ▷ anarchist

anarchists *n* ▷ anarchist

anarchy [an-ark-ee] *n* (*pl* -ies) lawlessness and disorder > **anarchic** *adj*

anathema [an-nath-im-a] *n* (*pl* -s) detested person or thing

anathemas *n* ▷ anathema

anatomical *adj* ▷ anatomy

anatomically *adv* ▷ anatomy

anatomies *n* ▷ anatomy

anatomist *n* (*pl* -s) expert in anatomy

anatomists *n* ▷ anatomist

anatomy *n* (*pl* -mies) science of the structure of the body > **anatomical** *adj* > **anatomically** *adv*

ancestor *n* (*pl* -s) person from whom one is descended > **ancestral** *adj*

ancestors *n* ▷ ancestor

ancestral *adj* ▷ ancestor

ancestries *n* ▷ ancestor

ancestry *n* (*pl* -ries) lineage or descent

anchor *n* (*pl* -s) heavy hooked device attached to a boat by a cable and dropped overboard to fasten the ship to the sea bottom ▶ *v* (-s, -ing, -ed) fasten with or as if with an anchor

anchorage *n* (*pl* -s) place where boats can be anchored

anchorages *n* ▷ anchorage

anchored *v* ▷ anchor

anchoring *v* ▷ anchor

anchorite *n* (*pl* -s) religious recluse

anchorites *n* ▷ anchorite

anchorman *n* (*pl* -men) broadcaster in a central studio who links up and presents items from outside camera units and other studios

anchormen *n* ▷ anchorman

anchors *n*, *v* ▷ anchor

anchorwoman *n* (*pl* -women) female broadcaster in a central studio who links up and presents items from outside camera units and other studios

anchorwomen *n* ▷ anchorwoman

anchovies *n* ▷ anchovy

anchovy [an-chov-ee] *n* (*pl* -vies) small strong-tasting fish

ancient *adj* dating from very long ago

ancients *pl n* people who lived very long ago

ancillary *adj* supporting the main work of an organization

and *conj* in addition to

andante [an-dan-tay] *n* (*pl* -s) ▶ *adv* (MUSIC) (piece to be played) moderately slowly

andantes *n* ▷ andante

andiron *n* (*pl* -s) iron stand for supporting logs in a fireplace

andirons *n* ▷ andiron

androgynous *adj* having both male and female characteristics

android *n* (*pl* -s) robot resembling a human

androids *n* ▷ android

anecdotal *adj* ▷ anecdote

anecdote *n* (*pl* -s) short amusing account of an incident > **anecdotal** *adj*

anecdotes *n* ▷ anecdote

anemometer *n* (*pl* -s) instrument for recording wind speed

anemometers *n* ▷ anemometer

anemone [an-nem-on-ee] *n* (*pl* -s) plant with white, purple, or red flowers

anemones *n* ▷ anemone

aneurism *n* ▷ aneurysm

aneurisms *n* ▷ aneurysm

aneurysm, aneurism [an-new-riz-zum] *n* (*pl* -s) permanent swelling of a blood vessel

aneurysms *n* ▷ aneurysm

anew *adv* once more

angel *n* (*pl* -s) spiritual being believed to be an attendant or messenger of God > **angelic** *adj* > **angelically** *adv*

angelic *adj* ▷ angel

angelica *n* (*pl* -s) aromatic plant

angelically *adv* ▷ angel

angelicas *n* ▷ angelica

angels *n* ▷ angel

angelus [an-jell-uss] *n* (*pl* -es) (in the Roman Catholic Church) prayers recited in the morning, at midday, and in the evening

angeluses *n* ▷ angelus

anger *n* (*pl* -s) fierce displeasure or extreme annoyance ▶ *v* (-s, -ing, -ed) make (someone) angry

angered *v* ▷ anger

angering *v* ▷ anger

angers *n*, *v* ▷ anger

angina [an-jine-a] *n* (*pl* -s) heart disorder causing sudden severe chest pains

anginas *n* ▷ angina

angle[1] *n* (*pl* -s) space between or shape formed by two lines or surfaces that meet ▶ *v* (-s, -ing, -ed) bend or place (something) at an angle

angle[2] *v* (-s, -ing, -ed) fish with a hook and line > **angling** *n* (*pl* -s)

angled *v* ▷ angle[1, 2]

angler *n* (*pl* -s) person who fishes with a hook and line

anglers *n* ▷ angler

angles *n* ▷ angle[1] ▶ *v* ▷ angle[1, 2]

anglicize *v* (-zes, -zing, -zed) make or become English in outlook, form, etc.

anglicized *v* ▷ anglicize

anglicizes v ▷ anglicize
anglicizing v ▷ anglicize
angling n ▷ angle² ▶ v ▷¹, ²
anglings n ▷ angle²

angophora n (pl -s) Australian tree related to the eucalyptus
angophoras n ▷ angophora

angora n (pl -s) variety of goat, cat, or rabbit with long silky hair
angoras n ▷ angora

angrier adj ▷ angry
angriest adj ▷ angry
angrily adv ▷ angry

angry adj (-grier, -griest) full of anger > **angrily** adv

angst n feeling of anxiety

angstrom n (pl angstroms) unit of length used to measure wavelengths
angstroms n ▷ angstrom

anguish n (pl -es) great mental pain > **anguished** adj
anguished adj ▷ anguish
anguishes n ▷ anguish

angular adj (of a person) lean and bony > **angularity** n (pl -ties)
angularities n ▷ angular
angularity n ▷ angular

anhydrous adj (CHEM) containing no water

aniline n (pl -s) colourless oily liquid used for making dyes, plastics, and explosives
anilines n ▷ aniline

animal n (pl -s) living creature with specialized sense organs and capable of voluntary motion, esp. one other than a human being ▶ adj of animals
animalian adj ▷ animal
animals n ▷ animal

animate v (-tes, -ting, -ted) give life to ▶ adj having life > **animated** adj > **animator** n (pl -s)
animated v, adj ▷ animate
animates v ▷ animate
animating v ▷ animate

animation n (pl -s) technique of making cartoon films
animations n ▷ animation
animator n ▷ animate
animators n ▷ animate

animism n (pl -s) belief that natural objects possess souls > **animist** n (pl -s) adj > **animistic** adj
animisms n ▷ animism
animist n, adj ▷ animism
animistic adj ▷ animism
animists n ▷ animism
animosities n ▷ animosity

animosity n (pl -ties) hostility, hatred
animus n (pl -es) hatred, animosity
animuses n ▷ animus

anion [an-eye-on] n (pl -s) ion with negative charge
anions n ▷ anion

anise [an-niss] n (pl -s) plant with liquorice-flavoured seeds

aniseed n (pl -s) liquorice-flavoured seeds of the anise plant
aniseeds n ▷ aniseed
anises n ▷ anise

ankle n (pl -s) joint between the foot and leg
ankles n ▷ ankle

anklet n (pl -s) ornamental chain worn round the ankle
anklets n ▷ anklet

annal n (usually plural) yearly record of events
annals n ▷ annal

anneal v (-s, -ing, -ed) toughen (metal or glass) by heating and slow cooling
annealed v ▷ anneal
annealing v ▷ anneal
anneals v ▷ anneal

annelid n (pl -s) worm with a segmented body, such as an earthworm
annelids n ▷ annelid

annex v (-es, -ing, -ed) seize (territory) > **annexation** n (pl -s)
annexation n ▷ annex
annexations n ▷ annex

annexe n (pl -s) extension to a building
annexed v ▷ annex
annexes v ▷ annex ▶ n ▷ annexe
annexing v ▷ annex

annihilate v (-tes, -ting, -ted) destroy utterly > **annihilation** n (pl -s)
annihilated v ▷ annihilate
annihilates v ▷ annihilate
annihilating v ▷ annihilate
annihilation n ▷ annihilate
annihilations n ▷ annihilate
anniversaries n ▷ anniversary

anniversary n (pl -ries) date on which something occurred in a previous year

annotate v (-tes, -ting, -ted) add notes to (a written work) > **annotation** n (pl -s)
annotated v ▷ annotate
annotates v ▷ annotate
annotating v ▷ annotate
annotation n ▷ annotate
annotations n ▷ annotate

announce v (-ces, -cing, -ced) make known publicly > **announcement** n (pl -s)
announced v ▷ announce

announcement n ▷ announce
announcements n ▷ announce
announcer n (pl -s) person who introduces radio or television programmes
announcers n ▷ announcer
announces v ▷ announce
announcing v ▷ announce
annoy v (-s, -ing, -ed) irritate or displease > **annoyance** n (pl -s)
annoyance n ▷ annoy
annoyances n ▷ annoy
annoyed v ▷ annoy
annoying v ▷ annoy
annoys v ▷ annoy
annual adj happening once a year ▶ n (pl -s) plant that completes its life cycle in a year > **annually** adv
annually adv ▷ annual
annuals n ▷ annual
annuities n ▷ annuity
annuity n (pl -ties) fixed sum paid every year
annul v (-ls, -lling, -lled) declare (something, esp. a marriage) invalid > **annulment** n (pl -s)
annular [an-new-lar] adj ring-shaped
annulled v ▷ annul
annulling v ▷ annul
annulment n ▷ annul
annulments n ▷ annul
annuls v ▷ annul
anode n (pl -s) (ELECTRICITY) positive electrode in a battery, valve, etc.
anodes n ▷ anode
anodize v (-zes, -zing, -zed) coat (metal) with a protective oxide film by electrolysis
anodized v ▷ anodize
anodizes v ▷ anodize
anodizing v ▷ anodize
anodyne n (pl -s) something that relieves pain or distress ▶ adj relieving pain or distress
anodynes n ▷ anodyne
anoint v (-s, -ing, -ed) smear with oil as a sign of consecration
anointed v ▷ anoint
anointing v ▷ anoint
anoints v ▷ anoint
anomalies n ▷ anomaly
anomalous adj ▷ anomaly
anomaly [an-nom-a-lee] n (pl -lies) something that deviates from the normal, irregularity > **anomalous** adj
anon adv (Obs) in a short time, soon
anonymity n ▷ anonymous
anonymous adj by someone whose name is unknown or withheld > **anonymously** adv > **anonymity** n

anonymously adv ▷ anonymous
anorak n (pl -s) light waterproof hooded jacket
anoraks n ▷ anorak
anorexia n (pl -s) psychological disorder characterized by fear of becoming fat and refusal to eat > **anorexic** adj, n
anorexias n ▷ anorexia
anorexic adj, n ▷ anorexia
another adj, pron one more
answer n (pl -s) reply to a question, request, letter, etc. ▶ v (-s, -ing, -ed) give an answer (to)
answerable adj (foll. by or or to) responsible for or accountable to
answered v ▷ answer
answering v ▷ answer
answers n, v ▷ answer
ant n (pl -s) small insect living in highly organized colonies
antacid n (pl -s) substance that counteracts acidity, esp. in the stomach
antacids n ▷ antacid
antagonism n (pl -s) open opposition or hostility
antagonisms n ▷ antagonism
antagonist n (pl -s) opponent or adversary > **antagonistic** adj
antagonistic adj ▷ antagonist
antagonists n ▷ antagonist
antagonize v (-zes, -zing, -zed) arouse hostility in, annoy
antagonized v ▷ antagonize
antagonizes v ▷ antagonize
antagonizing v ▷ antagonize
antarctic n area around the South Pole ▶ adj of this region
ante n (pl -s) player's stake in poker ▶ v (-tes, -teing, -ted or -teed) place (one's stake) in poker
anteater n (pl -s) mammal which feeds on ants by means of a long snout
anteaters n ▷ anteater
antecedent n (pl -s) event or circumstance happening or existing before another ▶ adj preceding, prior
antecedents n ▷ antecedent
anted v ▷ ante
antedate v (-tes, -ting, -ted) precede in time
antedated v ▷ antedate
antedates v ▷ antedate
antedating v ▷ antedate
antediluvian adj of the time before the biblical Flood
anteed v ▷ ante
anteing v ▷ ante
antelope n (pl -s) deerlike mammal with long

legs and horns
antelopes n ▷ antelope
antenatal adj during pregnancy, before birth
antenna n (pl -e) insect's feeler; (pl -s) aerial
antennae n ▷ antenna
antennas n ▷ antenna
anterior adj to the front
anteroom n (pl -s) small room leading into a larger one, often used as a waiting room
anterooms n ▷ anteroom
antes n, v ▷ ante
anthem n (pl -s) song of loyalty, esp. to a country
anthems n ▷ anthem
anther n (pl -s) part of a flower's stamen containing pollen
anthers n ▷ anther
anthologies n ▷ anthology
anthologist n ▷ anthology
anthologists n ▷ anthology
anthology n (pl -gies) collection of poems or other literary pieces by various authors
> **anthologist** n (pl -s)
anthraces n ▷ anthrax
anthracite n (pl -s) hard coal burning slowly with little smoke or flame but intense heat
anthracites n ▷ anthracite
anthrax n (pl -thraces) dangerous disease of cattle and sheep, communicable to humans
anthropoid adj like a human ▶ n (pl -s) ape, such as a chimpanzee, that resembles a human
anthropoids n ▷ anthropoid
anthropological adj ▷ anthropology
anthropologies n ▷ anthropology
anthropologist n ▷ anthropology
anthropologists n ▷ anthropology
anthropology n (pl -ies) study of human origins, institutions, and beliefs
> **anthropological** adj > **anthropologist** n (pl -s)
anthropomorphic adj attributing human form or personality to a god, animal, or object > **anthropomorphism** n (pl -s)
anthropomorphism n ▷ anthropomorphic
anthropomorphisms n ▷ anthropomorphic
antibiotic n (pl -s) chemical substance capable of destroying bacteria ▶ adj of antibiotics
antibiotics n ▷ antibiotic
antibodies n ▷ antibody
antibody n (pl -dies) protein produced in the blood, which destroys bacteria
anticipate v (-tes, -ting, -ted) foresee and act in advance of > **anticipation** n (pl -s)
> **anticipatory** adj

anticipated v ▷ anticipate
anticipates v ▷ anticipate
anticipating v ▷ anticipate
anticipation n ▷ anticipate
anticipations n ▷ anticipate
anticipatory adj ▷ anticipate
anticlimax n (pl -es) disappointing conclusion to a series of events
anticlimaxes n ▷ anticlimax
anticlockwise adv, adj in the opposite direction to the rotation of the hands of a clock
antics pl n absurd acts or postures
anticyclone n (pl -s) area of moving air of high pressure in which the winds rotate outwards
anticyclones n ▷ anticyclone
antidote n (pl -s) substance that counteracts a poison
antidotes n ▷ antidote
antifreeze n (pl -s) liquid added to water to lower its freezing point, used esp. in car radiators
antifreezes n ▷ antifreeze
antigen [an-tee-jen] n (pl -s) substance, usu. a toxin, causing the blood to produce antibodies
antigens n ▷ antigen
antihero n (pl -roes) central character in a book, film, etc., who lacks the traditional heroic virtues
antiheroes n ▷ antihero
antihistamine n (pl -s) drug used to treat allergies
antihistamines n ▷ antihistamine
antimacassar n (pl -s) cloth put over a chair-back to prevent soiling
antimacassars n ▷ antimacassar
antimonies n ▷ antimony
antimony n (pl -ies) (CHEM) brittle silvery-white metallic element
antipathetic adj ▷ antipathy
antipathies n ▷ antipathy
antipathy [an-tip-a-thee] n (pl -thies) dislike, hostility > **antipathetic** adj
antiperspirant n (pl -s) substance used to reduce or prevent sweating
antiperspirants n ▷ antiperspirant
antiphon n (pl -s) hymn sung in alternate parts by two groups of singers > **antiphonal** adj
antiphonal adj ▷ antiphon
antiphons n ▷ antiphon
antipodean adj ▷ antipodes
antipodes [an-tip-pod-deez] pl n any two places diametrically opposite one another on the earth's surface > **antipodean** adj

antipyretic adj reducing fever ▶ n (pl -s) drug that reduces fever
   antipyretics n ▷ antipyretic
antiquarian adj of or relating to antiquities or rare books ▶ n (pl -s) antiquary
   antiquarians n ▷ antiquarian
   antiquaries n ▷ antiquary
antiquary n (pl -ries) student or collector of antiques or ancient works of art
antiquated adj out-of-date
antique n (pl -s) object of an earlier period, valued for its beauty, workmanship, or age ▶ adj made in an earlier period
   antiques n ▷ antique
antiquities pl n objects dating from ancient times ▶ n ▷ antiquity
antiquity n (pl -ties) great age
antiracism n (pl -s) policy of challenging racism and promoting racial tolerance
   antiracisms n ▷ antiracism
antirrhinum n (pl -s) two-lipped flower of various colours
   antirrhinums n ▷ antirrhinum
antiseptic adj preventing infection by killing germs ▶ n (pl -s) antiseptic substance
   antiseptics n ▷ antiseptic
antisocial adj avoiding the company of other people
antistatic adj reducing the effects of static electricity
   antitheses n ▷ antithesis
antithesis [an-tith-iss-iss] n (pl -ses) [-seez] exact opposite > **antithetical** adj
   antithetical adj ▷ antithesis
antitoxin n (pl -s) (serum containing) an antibody that acts against a toxin
   antitoxins n ▷ antitoxin
antitrust adj (AUST & S AFR) (of laws) opposing business monopolies
antler n (pl -s) branched horn of male deer
   antlers n ▷ antler
antonym n (pl -s) word that means the opposite of another
   antonyms n ▷ antonym
   ants n ▷ ant
anus [ain-uss] n (pl -es) opening at the end of the alimentary canal, through which faeces are discharged
   anuses n ▷ anus
anvil n (pl -s) heavy iron block on which metals are hammered into particular shapes
   anvils n ▷ anvil
   anxieties n ▷ anxiety
anxiety n (pl -ties) state of being anxious
anxious adj worried and tense > **anxiously** adv

   anxiously adv ▷ anxious
any adj, pron one or some, no matter which ▶ adv at all ▷ **anything** pron
anybody pron anyone
anyhow adv anyway
anyone pron any person
   anything pron ▷ any
anyway adv at any rate, nevertheless
anywhere adv in, at, or to any place
aorta [eh-or-ta] n (pl -s) main artery of the body, carrying oxygen-rich blood from the heart
   aortas n ▷ aorta
apace adv (Lit) swiftly
   apalled v ▷ appal
apart adv to or in pieces
apartheid n (pl -s) former official government policy of racial segregation in S Africa
   apartheids n ▷ apartheid
apartment n (pl -s) room in a building
   apartments n ▷ apartment
apathetic adj ▷ apathy
apathy n (pl -thies) lack of interest or enthusiasm > **apathetic** adj
   apethies n ▷ apathy
ape n (pl -s) tailless monkey such as the chimpanzee ▶ v (apes, aping, aped) imitate
   aped v ▷ ape
aperient [ap-peer-ee-ent] adj having a mild laxative effect ▶ n (pl -s) mild laxative
   aperients n ▷ aperient
aperitif [ap-per-rit-teef] n (pl -s) alcoholic drink taken before a meal
   aperitifs n ▷ aperitif
   apertural adj ▷ aperture
aperture n (pl -s) opening or hole
   apertures n ▷ aperture
   apes n, v ▷ ape
apex n (pl -es) highest point
   apexes n ▷ apex
aphasia n disorder of the central nervous system that affects the ability to speak and understand words
aphid [eh-fid], **aphis** [eh-fiss] n (pl aphids) small insect which sucks the sap from plants
   aphids n ▷ aphid
   aphis n ▷ aphid
aphorism n (pl -s) short clever saying expressing a general truth
   aphorisms n ▷ aphorism
aphrodisiac [af-roh-diz-zee-ak] n (pl -s) substance that arouses sexual desire ▶ adj arousing sexual desire
   aphrodisiacs n ▷ aphrodisiac
   apiaries n ▷ apiary
apiary n (pl -ries) place where bees are kept

apiculture n (pl -s) breeding and care of bees
  apicultures n ▷ apiculture
apiece adv each
  aping v ▷ ape
aplomb n (pl -s) calm self-possession
  aplombs n ▷ aplomb
apocalypse n (pl -s) end of the world
  > **apocalyptic** adj
  apocalypses n ▷ apocalypse
  apocalyptic adj ▷ apocalypse
apocryphal [ap-**pok**-rif-al] adj (of a story) of
  questionable authenticity
apogee [ap-oh-jee] n (pl -s) point of the moon's
  or a satellite's orbit that is farthest from
  the earth
  apogees n ▷ apogee
apologetic adj showing or expressing regret
  > **apologetically** adv
  apologetically adv ▷ apologetic
apologetics n branch of theology concerned
  with the reasoned defence of Christianity
  apologies n ▷ apology
apologist n (pl -s) person who formally
  defends a cause
  apologists n ▷ apologist
apologize v (-zes, -zing, -zed) make an apology
  apologized v ▷ apologize
  apologizes v ▷ apologize
  apologizing v ▷ apologize
apology n (pl -gies) expression of regret for
  wrongdoing
apoplectic adj of apoplexy
  apoplexies n ▷ apoplexy
apoplexy n (pl -xies) (MED) stroke
  apostasies n ▷ apostasy
apostasy [ap-**poss**-stass-ee] n (pl -sies)
  abandonment of one's religious faith or other
  belief > **apostate** n (pl -s) adj
  apostate n, adj ▷ apostasy
  apostates n ▷ apostasy
apostle n (pl -s) ardent supporter of a cause or
  movement > **apostolic** adj
  apostles n ▷ apostle
  apostolic adj ▷ apostle
apostrophe [ap-**poss**-trof-fee] n (pl -s)
  punctuation mark (') showing the omission
  of a letter or letters in a word, e.g. don't, or
  forming the possessive, e.g. Jill's car
  apostrophes n ▷ apostrophe
  apothecaries n ▷ apothecary
apothecary n (pl -ries) (Obs) chemist
  apotheoses n ▷ apotheosis
apotheosis [ap-poth-ee-**oh**-siss] n (pl -ses)
  [-seez] perfect example
appal v (-s, -lling, -lled) dismay, terrify

appalled v ▷ appal
appalling adj dreadful, terrible ▶ v ▷ appal
appals v ▷ appal
apparatus n (pl -es) equipment for a particular
  purpose
  apparatuses n ▷ apparatus
apparel n (pl -s) (Old-fashioned) clothing
  apparels n ▷ apparel
apparent adj readily seen, obvious
  > **apparently** adv
  apparently adv ▷ apparent
apparition n (pl -s) ghost or ghostlike figure
  apparitions n ▷ apparition
appeal v (-s, -ing, -ed) make an earnest request
  ▶ n (pl -s) earnest request > **appealing** adj
  appealed v ▷ appeal
  appealing v, adj ▷ appeal
  appeals v, n ▷ appeal
appear v (-s, -ing, -ed) become visible or
  present
appearance n (pl -s) appearing
  appearances n ▷ appearance
  appeared v ▷ appear
  appearing v ▷ appear
  appears v ▷ appear
appease v (-s, -ing, -ed) pacify (a person)
  by yielding to his or her demands
  > **appeasement** n (pl -s)
  appeased v ▷ appease
  appeasement n ▷ appeal
  appeasements n ▷ appeal
  appeases v ▷ appease
  appeasing v ▷ appease
appellant n (pl -s) person who makes an
  appeal to a higher court
  appellants n ▷ appellant
appellation n (pl -s) (Formal) name, title
  appellations n ▷ appellation
append v (-s, -ing, -ed) join on, add
appendage n (pl -s) thing joined on or added
  appendages n ▷ appendage
  appended v ▷ append
  appendices n ▷ appendix
appendicitis n (pl -es) inflammation of the
  appendix
  appendicitises n ▷ appendicitis
  appending v ▷ append
appendix n (pl -dices, -dixes) separate
  additional material at the end of a book
  appendixes n ▷ appendix
  appends v ▷ append
appertain v (-s, -ing, -ed) (foll. by **to**) belong to
  appertained v ▷ appertain
  appertaining v ▷ appertain
  appertains v ▷ appertain

appetite n (pl -s) desire for food or drink
  appetites n ▷ appetite
appetizer n (pl -s) thing eaten or drunk to stimulate the appetite > **appetizing** adj stimulating the appetite
  appetizers n ▷ appetizer
  appetizing adj ▷ appetizer
applaud v (-s, -ing, -ed) show approval of by clapping one's hands
  applauded v ▷ applaud
  applauding v ▷ applaud
  applauds v ▷ applaud
applause n (pl -s) approval shown by clapping one's hands
  applauses n ▷ applause
apple n (pl -s) round firm fleshy fruit that grows on trees
  apples n ▷ apple
appliance n (pl -s) device with a specific function
  appliances n ▷ appliance
  applicabilities n ▷ applicable
  applicability n ▷ applicable
applicable adj relevant, appropriate > **applicability** n (pl -ties)
applicant n (pl -s) person who applies for something
  applicants n ▷ applicant
application n (pl -s) formal request
  applications n ▷ application
applied adj (of a skill, science, etc.) put to practical use ▶ v ▷ apply
  applies v ▷ apply
appliqué [ap-plee-kay] n (pl -s) kind of decoration in which one material is cut out and attached to another
  appliqués n ▷ appliqué
apply v (-plies, -plying, -plied) make a formal request
  applying v ▷ apply
appoint v (-s, -ing, -ed) assign to a job or position
  appointed v ▷ appoint
  appointing v ▷ appoint
appointment n (pl -s) arrangement to meet a person
  appointments n ▷ appointment
  appoints v ▷ appoint
apportion v (-s, -ing, -ed) divide out in shares
  apportioned v ▷ apportion
  apportioning v ▷ apportion
  apportions v ▷ apportion
apposite adj suitable, apt
apposition n (pl -s) grammatical construction in which two nouns or phrases referring to

the same thing are placed one after another without a conjunction
  appositions n ▷ apposition
appraisal n ▷ appraise
  appraisals n ▷ appraise
appraise v (-ses, -sing, -sed) estimate the value or quality of > **appraisal** n (pl -s)
  appraised v ▷ appraise
  appraises v ▷ appraise
  appraising v ▷ appraise
appreciable adj enough to be noticed > **appreciably** adv
  appreciably adv ▷ appreciable
appreciate v (-tes, -ting, -ted) value highly > **appreciation** n (pl -s)
  appreciated v ▷ appreciate
  appreciates v ▷ appreciate
  appreciating v ▷ appreciate
  appreciation n ▷ appreciate
  appreciations n ▷ appreciate
appreciative adj feeling or showing appreciation
apprehend v (-s, -ing, -ed) arrest and take into custody
  apprehended v ▷ apprehend
  apprehending v ▷ apprehend
  apprehends v ▷ apprehend
apprehension n (pl -s) dread, anxiety
  apprehensions n ▷ apprehension
apprehensive adj fearful or anxious
apprentice n (pl -s) someone working for a skilled person for a fixed period in order to learn his or her trade ▶ v (-ces, -cing, -ced) take or place (someone) as an apprentice > **apprenticeship** n (pl -s)
  apprenticed v ▷ apprentice
  apprentices n, v ▷ apprentice
  apprenticing v ▷ apprentice
apprise v (-ses, -sing, -sed) make aware (of)
  apprised v ▷ apprise
  apprises v ▷ apprise
  apprising v ▷ apprise
appro n (pl -s) (BRIT, AUST, NZ & S AFR) (Informal) on approval
approach v (-ches, -ching, -ched) come near or nearer (to) ▶ n (pl -es) approaching or means of approaching > **approachable** adj
  approachable adj ▷ approach
  approached v ▷ approach
  approaches v, n ▷ approach
  approaching v ▷ approach
approbation n (pl -s) approval
  approbations n ▷ approbation
appropriate adj suitable, fitting ▶ v (-tes, -ting, -ted) take for oneself > **appropriately**

adv > **appropriateness** *n* > **appropriation** *n* (*pl* -s)

appropriated *v* ▷ appropriate
appropriately *adv* ▷ appropriate
appropriateness *n* ▷ appropriate
appropriates *v* ▷ appropriate
appropriating *v* ▷ appropriate
appropriation *n* ▷ appropriate
appropriations *n* ▷ appropriate
appros *n* ▷ appro
approval *n* (*pl* -s) consent
approvals *n* ▷ approval
approve *v* (-ves, -ving, -ved) consider good or right
approved *v* ▷ approve
approves *v* ▷ approve
approving *v* ▷ approve
approximate *adj* almost but not quite exact
▶ *v* (-tes, -ting, -ted) (*foll. by* **to**) come close to > **approximately** *adv* > **approximation** *n* (*pl* -s)
approximated *v* ▷ approximate
approximately *adv* ▷ approximate
approximates *v* ▷ approximate
approximating *v* ▷ approximate
approximation *n* ▷ approximate
approximations *n* ▷ approximate
appurtenance *n* (*pl* -s) a minor or additional feature
appurtenances *n* ▷ appurtenance
apricot *n* (*pl* -s) yellowish-orange juicy fruit like a small peach ▶ *adj* yellowish-orange
apricots *n* ▷ apricot
apron *n* (*pl* -s) garment worn over the front of the body to protect the clothes
apronlike *adj* ▷ apron
aprons *n* ▷ apron
apropos [ap-prop-**poh**] *adj*, *adv* appropriate(ly)
apse *n* (*pl* -s) arched or domed recess
apses *n* ▷ apse
apt *adj* having a specified tendency > **aptly** *adv* > **aptness** *n* (*pl* -es)
aptitude *n* (*pl* -s) natural ability
aptitudes *n* ▷ aptitude
aptly *adv* ▷ apt
aptness *n* ▷ apt
aptnesses *n* ▷ apt
aqualung *n* (*pl* -s) mouthpiece attached to air cylinders, worn for underwater swimming
aqualungs *n* ▷ aqualung
aquamarine *n* (*pl* -s) greenish-blue gemstone ▶ *adj* greenish-blue
aquamarines *n* ▷ aquamarine
aquaplane *n* (*pl* -s) board on which a person stands to be towed by a motorboat ▶ *v* (-nes, -ning, -ned) ride on an aquaplane

aquaplaned *v* ▷ aquaplane
aquaplanes *n*, *v* ▷ aquaplane
aquaplaning *v* ▷ aquaplane
aquaria *n* ▷ aquarium
aquarium *n* (*pl* -s, -ria) tank in which fish and other underwater creatures are kept
aquariums *n* ▷ aquarium
aquatic *adj* living in or near water
aquatics *pl n* water sports
aquatint *n* (*pl* -s) print like a watercolour, produced by etching copper
aquatints *n* ▷ aquatint
aqueduct *n* (*pl* -s) structure carrying water across a valley or river
aqueducts *n* ▷ aqueduct
aqueous *adj* of, like, or containing water
aqueously *adv* ▷ aqueous
aquiline *adj* (of a nose) curved like an eagle's beak

> **ar** *n* (**ars**). Ar is the letter R. This is a good two-letter word to remember because it uses two very common tiles. Ar scores 2 points.

arabesque [ar-ab-**besk**] *n* (*pl* -s) ballet position in which one leg is raised behind and the arms are extended
arabesques *n* ▷ arabesque
arable *adj* suitable for growing crops on
arachnid [ar-**rak**-nid] *n* (*pl* -s) eight-legged invertebrate, such as a spider, scorpion, tick, or mite
arachnids *n* ▷ arachnid
arbiter *n* (*pl* -s) person empowered to judge in a dispute
arbiters *n* ▷ arbiter
arbitrarily *adv* ▷ arbitrary
arbitrary *adj* based on personal choice or chance, rather than reason > **arbitrarily** *adv*
arbitrate *v* ▷ arbitration
arbitrated *v* ▷ arbitration
arbitrates *v* ▷ arbitration
arbitrating *v* ▷ arbitration
arbitration *n* (*pl* -s) hearing and settling of a dispute by an impartial referee chosen by both sides > **arbitrate** *v* (-tes, -ting, -ted) > **arbitrator** *n* (*pl* -s)
arbitrations *n* ▷ arbitration
arbitrator *n* ▷ arbitration
arbitrators *n* ▷ arbitration
arboreal *adj* of or living in trees
arboreta *n* ▷ arboretum
arboretum [ahr-bore-**ee**-tum] *n* (*pl* -ta) place where rare trees or shrubs are cultivated
arboriculture *n* (*pl* -s) cultivation of trees or shrubs

arboricultures n ▷ arboriculture
arbour n (pl -s) glade sheltered by trees
   arbours n ▷ arbour
arc n (pl -s) part of a circle or other curve ▶ v (-s, -ing, -ed) form an arc
arcade n (pl -s) covered passageway lined with shops
   arcades n ▷ arcade
arcane adj mysterious and secret
   arced v ▷ arc
arch¹ n (pl -es) curved structure supporting a bridge or roof ▶ v (-es, -ing, -ed) (cause to) form an arch
arch² adj (-er, -est) superior, knowing ▷ **archly** adv ▷ **archness** n (pl -es)
   archaeological adj ▷ archaeology
   archaeologies n ▷ archaeology
   archaeologist n ▷ archaeology
   archaeologists n ▷ archaeology
archaeology n (pl -ies) study of ancient cultures from their physical remains ▷ **archaeological** adj ▷ **archaeologist** n (pl -s)
archaic [ark-kay-ik] adj ancient ▷ **archaism** [ark-kay-iz-zum] ▶ n (pl -s) archaic word or phrase
   archaism n ▷ archaic
   archaisms n ▷ archaic
archangel [ark-ain-jell] n (pl -s) chief angel
   archangels n ▷ archangel
archbishop n (pl -s) chief bishop
   archbishops n ▷ archbishop
archdeacon n (pl -s) priest ranking just below a bishop
   archdeacons n ▷ archdeacon
archdiocese n (pl -es) diocese of an archbishop
   archdioceses n ▷ archdiocese
   arched v ▷ arch¹
archer n (pl -s) person who shoots with a bow and arrow ▶ adj ▷ arch² ▷ **archery** n (pl -ries)
   archeries n ▷ archer
   archers n ▷ archer
   archery n ▷ archer
   arches n, v ▷ arch¹
   archest adj ▷ arch²
   archetypal adj ▷ archetype
archetype [ark-ee-type] n (pl -s) perfect specimen ▷ **archetypal** adj
   archetypes n ▷ archetype
   arching v ▷ arch¹
archipelago [ark-ee-pel-a-go] n (pl -gos) group of islands
   archipelagos n ▷ archipelago
architect n (pl -s) person qualified to design and supervise the construction of buildings
   architects n ▷ architect

   architectural adj ▷ architecture
architecture n (pl -s) style in which a building is designed and built ▷ **architectural** adj
   architectures n ▷ architecture
architrave n (pl -s) (ARCHIT) beam that rests on columns
   architraves n ▷ architrave
   archival adj ▷ archive
archive [ark-ive] n (pl -s) (often pl collection of records or documents ▷ **archival** adj
   archives n ▷ archive
archivist [ark-iv-ist] n (pl -s) person in charge of archives
   archivists n ▷ archivist
   archly adv ▷ arch²
   archness n ▷ arch²
   archnesses n ▷ arch²
archway n (pl -s) passageway under an arch
   archways n ▷ archway
   arcing v ▷ arc
   arcs n, v ▷ arc
arctic n (pl -s) area around the North Pole ▶ adj of this region
   arctics n ▷ arctic
ardent adj passionate ▷ **ardently** adv
   ardently adv ▷ ardent
ardour n (pl -s) passion
   ardours n ▷ ardour
arduous adj hard to accomplish, strenuous ▷ **arduously** adv
   arduously adv ▷ arduous
are¹ v ▷ be
are² n (pl -s) unit of measure, 100 square metres
area n (pl -s) part or region
   areas n ▷ area
arena n (pl -s) seated enclosure for sports events
   arenas n ▷ arena
areola n (pl -lae, -las) small circular area, such as the coloured ring around the human nipple
   areolae n ▷ areola
   areolas n ▷ areola
   ares n ▷ are²
argon n (pl -s) (CHEM) inert gas found in the air
   argons n ▷ argon
argot [ahr-go] n (pl -s) slang or jargon
   argots n ▷ argot
   arguable adj ▷ argue
   arguably adv ▷ argue
argue v (-gues, -guing, -gued) try to prove by giving reasons ▷ **arguable** adj ▷ **arguably** adv
   argued v ▷ argue
   argues v ▷ argue

arguing v ▷ argue

argument n (pl -s) quarrel

argumentation n (pl -s) process of reasoning methodically

argumentations n ▷ argumentation

argumentative adj given to arguing

arguments n ▷ argument

aria [ah-ree-a] n (pl -s) elaborate song for solo voice, esp. one from an opera

arias n ▷ aria

arid adj parched, dry > **aridity** n (pl -ties)

aridities n ▷ arid

aridity n ▷ arid

aright adv rightly

arise v (arises, arising, arose, arisen) come about

arisen v ▷ arise

arises v ▷ arise

arising v ▷ arise

aristocracies n ▷ aristocracy

aristocracy n (pl -cies) highest social class

aristocrat n (pl -s) member of the aristocracy > **aristocratic** adj

aristocratic adj ▷ aristocrat

aristocrats n ▷ aristocrat

arithmetic n (pl -s) calculation by or of numbers ▶ adj of arithmetic > **arithmetical** adj > **arithmetically** adv

arithmetical adj ▷ arithmetic

arithmetically adv ▷ arithmetic

arithmetics n ▷ arithmetic

ark n (pl -s) (OLD TESTAMENT) boat built by Noah, which survived the Flood

arks n ▷ ark

arm¹ n (pl -s) either of the upper limbs from the shoulder to the wrist

arm² v (-s, -ing, -ed) supply with weapons

armada n (pl -s) large number of warships

armadas n ▷ armada

armadillo n (pl -s) small S American mammal covered in strong bony plates

armadillos n ▷ armadillo

armament n (pl -s) military weapons

armaments n ▷ armament

armature n (pl -s) revolving structure in an electric motor or generator, wound with coils carrying the current

armatures n ▷ armature

armchair n (pl -s) upholstered chair with side supports for the arms

armchairs n ▷ armchair

armed v ▷ arm²

armful n (pl -s) as much as can be held in the arms

armfuls n ▷ armful

armhole n (pl -s) opening in a garment

through which the arm passes

armholes n ▷ armhole

armies n ▷ army

arming v ▷ arm²

armistice [arm-miss-stiss] n (pl -s) agreed suspension of fighting

armistices n ▷ armistice

armour n (pl -s) metal clothing formerly worn to protect the body in battle

armourer n (pl -s) maker, repairer, or keeper of arms or armour

armourers n ▷ armourer

armouries n ▷ armoury

armours n ▷ armour

armoury n (pl -ries) place where weapons are stored

armpit n (pl -s) hollow under the arm at the shoulder

armpits n ▷ armpit

arms pl n weapons ▶ n ▷ arm¹ ▶ v ▷ arm²

army n (pl -mies) military land forces of a nation

aroma n (pl -s) pleasant smell > **aromatic** adj

aromas n ▷ aroma

aromatherapies n ▷ aromatherapy

aromatherapy n (pl -pies) massage with fragrant oils to relieve tension

aromatic adj ▷ aroma

arose v ▷ arise

around prep, adv on all sides (of)

arouse v (-ses, -sing, -sed) stimulate, make active

aroused v ▷ arouse

arouses v ▷ arouse

arousing v ▷ arouse

arpeggio [arp-pej-ee-oh] n (pl -s) (MUSIC) notes of a chord played or sung in quick succession

arpeggios n ▷ arpeggio

arraign [ar-rain] v (-s, -ing, -ed) bring (a prisoner) before a court to answer a charge > **arraignment** n (pl -s)

arraigned v ▷ arraign

arraigning v ▷ arraign

arraignment n ▷ arraign

arraignments n ▷ arraign

arraigns v ▷ arraign

arrange v (-ges, -ging, -ged) plan > **arrangement** n (pl -s)

arranged v ▷ arrange

arrangement n ▷ arrange

arrangements n ▷ arrange

arranges v ▷ arrange

arranging v ▷ arrange

arrant adj utter, downright

arras n (pl -es) tapestry wall-hanging

arrases n ▷ arras

array n (pl -s) impressive display or collection

(*Poetic*) ▶ *v* (-s, -ing, -ed) arrange in order
arrayed *v* ▷ array
arraying *v* ▷ array
arrays *n*, *v* ▷ array
arrear *n* (*p* -s) (usually plural) money owed
arrears *n* ▷ arrear
arrest *v* (-s, -ing, -ed) take (a person) into custody ▶ *n* (*pl* -s) act of taking a person into custody
arrested *v* ▷ arrest
arresting *adj* attracting attention, striking ▶ *v* ▷ arrest
arrests *v*, *n* ▷ arrest
arrival *n* (*pl* -s) arriving
arrivals *n* ▷ arrival
arrive *v* (-ves, -ving, -ved) reach a place or destination
arrived *v* ▷ arrive
arrives *v* ▷ arrive
arriving *v* ▷ arrive
arrogance *n* ▷ arrogant
arrogances *n* ▷ arrogant
arrogant *adj* proud and overbearing > **arrogantly** *adv* > **arrogance** *n* (*pl* -s)
arrogantly *adv* ▷ arrogant
arrogate *v* (-tes, -ting, -ted) claim or seize without justification
arrogated *v* ▷ arrogate
arrogates *v* ▷ arrogate
arrogating *v* ▷ arrogate
arrow *n* (*pl* -s) pointed shaft shot from a bow
arrowhead *n* (*pl* -s) pointed tip of an arrow
arrowheads *n* ▷ arrowhead
arrowless *adj* ▷ arrow
arrowlike *adj* ▷ arrow
arrowroot *n* (*pl* -s) nutritious starch obtained from the root of a W Indian plant
arrowroots *n* ▷ arrowroot
arrows *n* ▷ arrow
arsenal *n* (*pl* -s) place where arms and ammunition are made or stored
arsenals *n* ▷ arsenal
arsenic *n* (*pl* -s) toxic grey element > **arsenical** *adj*
arsenical *adj* ▷ arsenic
arsenics *n* ▷ arsenic
arson *n* (*pl* -s) crime of intentionally setting property on fire > **arsonist** *n* (*pl* -s)
arsonist *n* ▷ arson
arsonists *n* ▷ arson
arsons *n* ▷ arson
art *n* (*pl* -s) creation of works of beauty, esp. paintings or sculpture
artefact *n* (*pl* -s) something man-made
artefacts *n* ▷ artefact

arterial *adj* of an artery
arteries *n* ▷ artery
artery *n* (*pl* -ries) one of the tubes carrying blood from the heart
artful *adj* cunning, wily > **artfully** *adv* > **artfulness** *n* (*pl* -es)
artfully *adv* ▷ artful
artfulness *n* ▷ artful
artfulnesses *n* ▷ artful
arthritic *adj*, *n* ▷ arthritis
arthritics *n* ▷ arthritis
arthritis *n* (*pl* -es) painful inflammation of a joint or joints > **arthritic** *adj*, *n* (*pl* -s)
arthritises *n* ▷ arthritis
arthropod *n* (*pl* -s) animal, such as an insect, with jointed limbs and a segmented body
arthropods *n* ▷ arthropod
artichoke *n* (*pl* -s) flower head of a thistle-like plant, cooked as a vegetable
artichokes *n* ▷ artichoke
article *n* (*pl* -s) written piece in a magazine or newspaper
articled *adj* bound (as an apprentice) by a written contract
articles *n* ▷ article
articulate *adj* able to express oneself clearly and coherently ▶ *v* (-tes, -ting, -ted) speak or say clearly and coherently > **articulately** *adv* > **articulation** *n* (*pl* -s)
articulated *adj* jointed ▶ *v* ▷ articulate
articulates *v* ▷ articulate
articulating *v* ▷ articulate
articulation *n* ▷ articulate
articulations *n* ▷ articulate
artier *adj* ▷ arty
artiest *adj* ▷ arty
artifice *n* (*pl* -s) clever trick
artificer [art-**tiff**-iss-er] *n* (*pl* -s) craftsman
artificers *n* ▷ artificer
artifices *n* ▷ artifice
artificial *adj* man-made, not occurring naturally > **artificially** *adv* > **artificiality** *n* (*pl* -ties)
artificialities *n* ▷ artificial
artificiality *n* ▷ artificial
artificially *adv* ▷ artificial
artilleries *n* ▷ artillery
artillery *n* (*pl* -ies) large-calibre guns
artisan *n* (*pl* -s) skilled worker, craftsman
artisans *n* ▷ artisan
artist *n* (*pl* -s) person who produces works of art, esp. paintings or sculpture > **artistic** *adj* > **artistically** *adv*
artiste *n* (*pl* -s) professional entertainer such as a singer or dancer

artistes n ▷ artiste
artistic adj ▷ artist
artistically adv ▷ artist
artistries n ▷ artistry
artistry n (pl -ries) artistic skill
artists n ▷ artist
artless adj free from deceit or cunning
> **artlessly** adv
artlessly adv ▷ artless
arts n ▷ art
arty adj (-tier, -tiest) (Informal) having an affected interest in art
arvie n (pl -s) (S AFR) (Informal) afternoon
arvies n ▷ arvie
as conj while, when ▶ adv, conj used to indicate amount or extent in comparisons ▶ prep in the role of, being
asafoetida n (pl -s) strong-smelling plant resin used as a spice in Eastern cookery
asafoetidas n ▷ asafoetida
asbestos n (pl -es) fibrous mineral which does not burn
asbestoses n ▷ asbestos, asbestosis
asbestosis n (pl -ses) lung disease caused by inhalation of asbestos fibre
ascend v (-s, -ing, -ed) go or move up
ascendancies n ▷ ascendancy
ascendancy n (pl -cies) condition of being dominant
ascendant adj dominant or influential
ascended v ▷ ascend
ascending v ▷ ascend
ascends v ▷ ascend
ascent n (pl -s) ascending
ascents n ▷ ascent
ascertain v (-s, -ing, -ed) find out definitely
> **ascertainable** adj ▷ **ascertainment** n (pl -s)
ascertainable adj ▷ ascertain
ascertained v ▷ ascertain
ascertaining v ▷ ascertain
ascertainment n ▷ ascertain
ascertainments n ▷ ascertain
ascertains v ▷ ascertain
ascetic [ass-**set**-tik] n (pl -s) ▶ adj (person) abstaining from worldly pleasures and comforts > **asceticism** n (pl -s)
asceticism n ▷ ascetic
asceticisms n ▷ ascetic
ascetics n ▷ ascetic
ascribe v (-bes, -bing, -bed) attribute, as to a particular origin > **ascription** n (pl -s)
ascribed v ▷ ascribe
ascribes v ▷ ascribe
ascribing v ▷ ascribe
ascription n ▷ ascribe

ascriptions n ▷ ascribe
aseptic [eh-**sep**-tik] adj free from harmful bacteria
asexual [eh-**sex**-yew-al] adj without sex
> **asexually** adv
asexually adv ▷ asexual
ash¹ n (pl -es) powdery substance left when something is burnt
ash² n (pl -es) tree with grey bark
ashamed adj feeling shame
ashen adj pale with shock
ashes n ▷ ash¹, ²
ashlar n (pl -s) square block of hewn stone used in building
ashlars n ▷ ashlar
ashore adv towards or on land
ashram n (pl -s) religious retreat where a Hindu holy man lives
ashrams n ▷ ashram
ashtray n (pl -s) receptacle for tobacco ash and cigarette butts
ashtrays n ▷ ashtray
aside adv to one side ▶ n (pl -s) remark not meant to be heard by everyone present
asides n ▷ aside
asinine adj stupid, idiotic
ask v (-s, -ing, -ed) say or write (something) in a form that requires an answer
askance [ass-**kanss**] adv with an oblique glance
asked v ▷ ask
askew adv, adj to one side, crooked
asking v ▷ ask
asks v ▷ ask
aslant adv, prep at a slant (to), slanting (across)
asleep adj sleeping
asp n (pl -s) small poisonous snake
asparagus n (pl -es) plant whose shoots are cooked as a vegetable
asparaguses n ▷ asparagus
aspect n (pl -s) feature or element
aspects n ▷ aspect
aspen n (pl -s) kind of poplar tree
aspens n ▷ aspen
asperities n ▷ asperity
asperity n (pl -ties) roughness of temper
aspersion n (pl -s) derogatory remark
aspersions n ▷ aspersion
asphalt n (pl -s) black hard tarlike substance used for road surfaces etc.
asphalts n ▷ asphalt
asphodel n (pl -s) plant with clusters of yellow or white flowers
asphodels n ▷ asphodel
asphyxia [ass-**fix**-ee-a] n (pl -s) suffocation
asphyxiate v (-tes, -ting, -ted) suffocate

> **asphyxiation** n (pl -s)
asphyxiated v ▷ asphyxiate
asphyxiates v ▷ asphyxiate
asphyxiating v ▷ asphyxiate
asphyxiation n ▷ asphyxiate
asphyxiations n ▷ asphyxiate
aspic n (pl -s) savoury jelly used to coat meat, eggs, fish, etc.
aspics n ▷ aspic
aspidistra n (pl -s) plant with long tapered leaves
aspidistras n ▷ aspidistra
aspirant n (pl -s) person who aspires
aspirants n ▷ aspirant
aspirate (PHONETICS) v (-tes, -ting, -ted) pronounce with an h sound ▶ n (pl -s) h sound
aspirated v ▷ aspirate
aspirates v, n ▷ aspirate
aspirating v ▷ aspirate
aspiration n (pl -s) strong desire or aim
aspirations n ▷ aspiration
aspire v (-res, -ring, -red) (foll. by to) yearn (for), hope (to do or be)
aspired v ▷ aspire
aspires v ▷ aspire
aspirin n (pl -s) drug used to relieve pain and fever
aspiring v ▷ aspire
aspirins n ▷ aspirin
asps n ▷ asp
ass n (pl -es) donkey
assail v (-s, -ing, -ed) attack violently
> **assailant** n (pl -s)
assailant n ▷ assail
assailants n ▷ assail
assailed v ▷ assail
assailing v ▷ assail
assails v ▷ assail
assassin n (pl -s) person who murders a prominent person
assassinate v (-tes, -ting, -ted) murder (a prominent person) > **assassination** n (pl -s)
assassinated v ▷ assassinate
assassinates v ▷ assassinate
assassinating v ▷ assassinate
assassination n ▷ assassinate
assassinations n ▷ assassinate
assassins n ▷ assassin
assault n (pl -ts) violent attack ▶ v (-s, -ing, -ed) attack violently
assaulted v ▷ assault
assaulting v ▷ assault
assaults n, v ▷ assault
assay n (pl -s) analysis of a substance, esp. a metal, to ascertain its purity ▶ v (-s, -ing, -ed)

assayed v ▷ assay
assaying v ▷ assay
assays n, v ▷ assay
assegai [ass-a-guy] n (pl -s) slender spear used in S Africa
assegais n ▷ assegai
assemblage n (pl -s) collection or group
assemblages n ▷ assemblage
assemble v (-bles, -bling, -bled) collect or congregate
assembled v ▷ assemble
assembles v ▷ assemble
assemblies n ▷ assembly
assembling v ▷ assemble
assembly n (pl -blies) assembled group
assent n (pl -s) agreement or consent ▶ v (-s, -ing, -ed) agree or consent
assented v ▷ assent
assenting v ▷ assent
assents n, v ▷ assent
assert v (-s, -ing, -ed) declare forcefully
> **assertion** n (pl -s) > **assertive** adj
> **assertively** adv
asserted v ▷ assert
asserting v ▷ assert
assertion n ▷ assert
assertions n ▷ assert
assertive adj ▷ assert
assertively adv ▷ assert
asserts v ▷ assert
asses n ▷ ass
assess v (-es, -ing, -ed) judge the worth or importance of > **assessment** n (pl -s)
> **assessor** n (pl -s)
assessed v ▷ assess
assesses v ▷ assess
assessing v ▷ assess
assessment n ▷ assess
assessments n ▷ assess
assessor n ▷ assess
assessors n ▷ assess
asset n (pl -s) valuable or useful person or thing
assets n ▷ asset
asseverate v (-tes, -ting, -ted) declare solemnly
asseverated v ▷ asseverate
asseverates v ▷ asseverate
asseverating v ▷ asseverate
assiduities n ▷ assiduous
assiduity n ▷ assiduous
assiduous adj hard-working > **assiduously** adv
> **assiduity** n (pl -ties)
assiduously adv ▷ assiduous
assign v (-s, -ing, -ed) appoint (someone) to a job or task

assignation n (pl -s) assigning
  assignations n ▷ assignation
  assigned v ▷ assign
  assigning v ▷ assign
assignment n (pl -s) task assigned
  assignments n ▷ assignment
  assigns v ▷ assign
  assimilable adj ▷ assimilate
assimilate v (-tes, -ting, -ted) learn and understand (information) > **assimilable** adj > **assimilation** n (pl -s)
  assimilated v ▷ assimilate
  assimilates v ▷ assimilate
  assimilating v ▷ assimilate
  assimilation n ▷ assimilate
  assimilations n ▷ assimilate
assist v (-s, -ing, -ed) give help or support > **assistance** n (pl -s)
  assistance n ▷ assist
  assistances n ▷ assist
assistant n (pl -s) helper ▶ adj junior or deputy
  assistants n ▷ assistant
  assisted v ▷ assist
  assisting v ▷ assist
  assists v ▷ assist
assizes pl n (BRIT) court sessions formerly held in each county of England and Wales
associate v (-tes, -ting, -ted) connect in the mind ▶ n (pl -s) partner in business ▶ adj having partial rights or subordinate status
  associated v ▷ associate
  associates v, n ▷ associate
  associating v ▷ associate
association n (pl -s) society or club
  associations n ▷ association
assonance n (pl -s) rhyming of vowel sounds but not consonants, as in *time* and *light*
  assonances n ▷ assonance
assorted adj consisting of various types mixed together
assortment n (pl -s) assorted mixture
  assortments n ▷ assortment
assuage [ass-**wage**] v (-ges, -ging, -ged) relieve (pain, grief, thirst, etc.)
  assuaged v ▷ assuage
  assuages v ▷ assuage
  assuaging v ▷ assuage
assume v (-mes, -ming, -med) take to be true without proof
  assumed v ▷ assume
  assumes v ▷ assume
  assuming v ▷ assume
assumption n (pl -s) thing assumed
  assumptions n ▷ assumption
assurance n (pl -s) assuring or being assured

assurances n ▷ assurance
assure v (-res, -ring, -red) promise or guarantee
assured adj confident ▶ v ▷ assure
assuredly adv definitely
  assures v ▷ assure
  assuring v ▷ assure
astatine n (pl -s) (CHEM) radioactive nonmetallic element
  astatines n ▷ astatine
aster n (pl -s) plant with daisy-like flowers
asterisk n (pl -s) star-shaped symbol (*) used in printing or writing to indicate a footnote etc. ▶ v (-s, -ing, -ed) mark with an asterisk
  asterisked v ▷ asterisk
  asterisking v ▷ asterisk
  asterisks n, v ▷ asterisk
astern adv at or towards the stern of a ship
asteroid n (pl -s) any of the small planets that orbit the sun between Mars and Jupiter
  asteroids n ▷ asteroid
  asters n ▷ aster
asthma [**ass**-ma] n (pl -s) illness causing difficulty in breathing > **asthmatic** adj, n (pl -s)
  asthmas n ▷ asthma
  asthmatic adj, n ▷ asthma
  asthmatics n ▷ asthma
astigmatism [eh-**stig**-mat-tiz-zum] n (pl -s) inability of a lens, esp. of the eye, to focus properly
  astigmatisms n ▷ astigmatism
astir adj (Old-fashioned) out of bed
astonish v (-es, -ing, -ed) surprise greatly > **astonishment** n (pl -s)
  astonished v ▷ astonish
  astonishes v ▷ astonish
  astonishing v ▷ astonish
  astonishment n ▷ astonish
  astonishments n ▷ astonish
astound v (-s, -ing, -ed) overwhelm with amazement > **astounding** adj
  astounded v ▷ astound
  astounding v, adj ▷ astound
  astounds v ▷ astound
astrakhan n (pl -s) dark curly fleece of lambs from Astrakhan in Russia
  astrakhans n ▷ astrakhan
astral adj of stars
astray adv off the right path
astride adv, prep with a leg on either side (of)
  astringencies n ▷ astringent
  astringency n ▷ astringent
astringent adj causing contraction of body tissue ▶ n (pl -s) astringent substance

> **astringency** n (pl -cies)
astringents n ▷ astringent
astrolabe n (pl -s) instrument formerly used to measure the altitude of stars and planets
astrolabes n ▷ astrolabe
astrologer n ▷ astrology
astrologers n ▷ astrology
astrological adj ▷ astrology
astrologies n ▷ astrology
astrology n (pl -gies) study of the alleged influence of the stars, planets, and moon on human affairs > **astrologer** n (pl -s) > **astrological** adj
astronaut n (pl -s) person trained for travelling in space
astronautical adj ▷ astronautics
astronautics n science and technology of space flight > **astronautical** adj
astronauts n ▷ astronaut
astronomer n ▷ astronomy
astronomers n ▷ astronomy
astronomical adj very large > **astronomically** adv
astronomically adv ▷ astronomical
astronomies n ▷ astronomy
astronomy n (pl -mies) scientific study of heavenly bodies > **astronomer** n (pl -s)
astrophysical adj ▷ astrophysics
astrophysicist n ▷ astrophysics
astrophysicists n ▷ astrophysics
astrophysics n science of the physical and chemical properties of stars, planets, etc. > **astrophysical** adj > **astrophysicist** n (pl -s)
astute adj perceptive or shrewd > **astutely** adv > **astuteness** n (pl -es)
astutely adv ▷ astute
astuteness n ▷ astute
astutenesses n ▷ astute
asunder adv (Obs or poetic) into parts or pieces
asylum n (pl -s) refuge or sanctuary
asylums n ▷ asylum
asymmetric adj ▷ asymmetry
asymmetrical adj ▷ asymmetry
asymmetries n ▷ asymmetry
asymmetry n (pl -tries) lack of symmetry > **asymmetrical, asymmetric** adj
asymptote [ass-im-tote] n (pl -s) straight line closely approached but never met by a curve
asymptotes n ▷ asymptote
at prep indicating position in space or time, movement towards an object, etc.
atavism [at-a-viz-zum] n (pl -s) recurrence of a trait present in distant ancestors > **atavistic** adj
atavisms n ▷ atavism
atavistic adj ▷ atavism

ate v ▷ eat
atheism [aith-ee-iz-zum] n (pl -s) belief that there is no God > **atheist** n (pl -s) > **atheistic** adj
atheisms n ▷ atheism
atheist n ▷ atheism
atheistic adj ▷ atheism
atheists n ▷ atheism
atherosclerosis n disease in which deposits of fat cause the walls of the arteries to thicken
athlete n (pl -s) person trained in or good at athletics
athletes n ▷ athlete
athletic adj physically fit or strong > **athletically** adv > **athleticism** n (pl -s)
athletically adv ▷ athletic
athleticism n ▷ athletic
athleticisms n ▷ athletic
athletics pl n track-and-field sports such as running, jumping, throwing, etc.
athwart prep across ► adv transversely
atlas n (pl -es) book of maps
atlases n ▷ atlas
atmosphere n (pl -s) mass of gases surrounding a heavenly body, esp. the earth > **atmospheric** adj
atmospheres n ▷ atmosphere
atmospheric adj ▷ atmosphere
atmospherics pl n radio interference due to electrical disturbance in the atmosphere
atoll n (pl -s) ring-shaped coral reef enclosing a lagoon
atolls n ▷ atoll
atom n (pl -s) smallest unit of matter which can take part in a chemical reaction
atomic adj of or using atomic bombs or atomic energy
atomize v (-zes, -zing, -zed) reduce to atoms or small particles
atomized v ▷ atomize
atomizer n (pl -s) device for discharging a liquid in a fine spray
atomizers n ▷ atomizer
atomizes v ▷ atomize
atomizing v ▷ atomize
atoms n ▷ atom
atonal [eh-tone-al] adj (of music) not written in an established key
atone v (-nes, -ning, -ned) make amends (for sin or wrongdoing) > **atonement** n (pl -s)
atoned v ▷ atone
atonement n ▷ atone
atonements n ▷ atone
atones v ▷ atone
atoning v ▷ atone

atop prep (Lit) on top of
atria n ▷ atrium
atrium n (pl atria) upper chamber of either half of the heart
atrocious adj extremely cruel or wicked > **atrociously** adv
atrociously adv ▷ atrocious
atrocities n ▷ atrocity
atrocity n (pl -ties) wickedness
atrophied v ▷ atrophy
atrophies n, v ▷ atrophy
atrophy [at-trof-fee] n (pl -phies) wasting away of an organ or part ▶ v (-phies, -phying, -phied) (cause to) waste away
atrophying v ▷ atrophy
attach v (-es, -ing, -ed) join, fasten, or connect > **attached** adj (foll. by **to**) fond of > **attachment** n (pl -s)
attaché [at-**tash**-shay] n (pl -s) specialist attached to a diplomatic mission
attached v, adj ▷ attach
attaches v ▷ attach
attachés n ▷ attaché
attaching v ▷ attach
attack v (-s, -ing, -ed) launch a physical assault (against) ▶ n (pl -s) act of attacking > **attacker** n (pl -s)
attacked v ▷ attack
attacker n ▷ attack
attackers n ▷ attack
attacking v ▷ attack
attacks v, n ▷ attack
attain v (-s, -ing, -ed) achieve or accomplish (a task or aim) > **attainable** adj
attainable adj ▷ attain
attained v ▷ attain
attaining v ▷ attain
attainment n (pl -s) accomplishment
attainments n ▷ attainment
attains v ▷ attain
attar n (pl -s) fragrant oil made from roses
attars n ▷ attar
attempt v (-s, -ing, -ed) try, make an effort ▶ n (pl -s) effort or endeavour
attempted v ▷ attempt
attempting v ▷ attempt
attempts v, n ▷ attempt
attend v (-s, -ing, -ed) be present at
attendance n (pl -s) attending
attendances n ▷ attendance
attendant n (pl -s) person who assists, guides, or provides a service ▶ adj accompanying
attendants n ▷ attendant
attended v ▷ attend
attending v ▷ attend

attends v ▷ attend
attention n (pl -s) concentrated direction of the mind
attentions n ▷ attention
attentive adj giving attention > **attentively** adv > **attentiveness** n (pl -es)
attentively adv ▷ attentive
attentiveness n ▷ attentive
attentivenesses n ▷ attentive
attenuated adj weakened > **attenuation** n (pl -s)
attenuation n ▷ attenuated
attenuations n ▷ attenuated
attest v (-s, -ing, -ed) affirm the truth of, be proof of > **attestation** n (pl -s)
attestation n ▷ attest
attestations n ▷ attest
attested v ▷ attest
attesting v ▷ attest
attests v ▷ attest
attic n (pl -s) space or room within the roof of a house
attics n ▷ attic
attire n (pl -s) (Formal) fine or formal clothes
attired adj dressed in a specified way
attires n ▷ attire
attitude n (pl -s) way of thinking and behaving
attitudes n ▷ attitude
attorney n (pl -s) person legally appointed to act for another (US & S AFR)
attorneys n ▷ attorney
attract v (-s, -ing, -ed) arouse the interest or admiration of
attracted v ▷ attract
attracting v ▷ attract
attraction n (pl -s) power to attract > **attractive** adj > **attractively** adv > **attractiveness** n
attractions n ▷ attraction
attractive adj ▷ attraction
attractively adv ▷ attraction
attractiveness n ▷ attraction
attracts v ▷ attract
attributable adj ▷ attribute
attribute v (-tes, -ting, -ted) (usu. foll. by **to**) regard as belonging to or produced by ▶ n (pl -s) quality or feature representative of a person or thing > **attributable** adj > **attribution** n (pl -s)
attributed v ▷ attribute
attributes v, n ▷ attribute
attributing v ▷ attribute
attributive adj (GRAMMAR) (of an adjective) preceding the noun modified
attrition n (pl -s) constant wearing down to weaken or destroy

attritions n ▷ attrition

attune v (-nes, -ning, -ned) adjust or accustom (a person or thing)

attuned v ▷ attune

attunes v ▷ attune

attuning v ▷ attune

atypical [eh-**tip**-ik-al] adj not typical

aubergine [oh-bur-zheen] n (pl -s) (BRIT) dark purple tropical fruit, cooked as a vegetable

aubergines n ▷ aubergine

aubrietia [aw-bree-sha] n (pl -s) trailing plant with purple flowers

aubrietias n ▷ aubrietia

auburn adj (of hair) reddish-brown

auction n (pl -s) public sale in which articles are sold to the highest bidder ▸ v (-s, -ing, -ed) sell by auction

auctioned v ▷ auction

auctioneer n (pl -s) person who conducts an auction

auctioneers n ▷ auctioneer

auctioning v ▷ auction

auctions n, v ▷ auction

audacious adj recklessly bold or daring > **audaciously** adv > **audacity** n (pl -ties)

audaciously adv ▷ audacious

audacities n ▷ audacious

audacity n ▷ audacious

audibilities n ▷ audible

audibility n ▷ audible

audible adj loud enough to be heard > **audibly** adv > **audibility** n (pl -ties)

audibly adv ▷ audible

audience n (pl -s) group of spectators or listeners

audiences n ▷ audience

audio adj of sound or hearing > **audiovisual** adj (esp. of teaching aids) involving both sight and hearing

audiovisual adj ▷ audio

audit n (pl -s) official examination of business accounts ▸ v (-s, -ing, -ted) examine (business accounts) officially > **auditor** n (pl -s)

audited v ▷ audit

auditing v ▷ audit

audition n (pl -s) test of a performer's ability for a particular role or job ▸ v (-s, -ing, -ed) test or be tested in an audition

auditioned v ▷ audition

auditioning v ▷ audition

auditions n, v ▷ audition

auditor n ▷ audit

auditoria n ▷ auditorium

auditorium n (pl -riums, -ria) area of a concert hall or theatre where the audience sits

auditoriums n ▷ auditorium

auditors n ▷ audit

auditory adj of or relating to hearing

audits n, v ▷ audit

> **auf** n (**aufs**). An auf is an elf-child left in place of a human baby. Auf scores 6 points.

auger n (pl -s) tool for boring holes

augers n ▷ auger

aught pron (Obs) anything whatever

augment v (-s, -ing, -ed) increase or enlarge > **augmentation** n (pl -s)

augmentation n ▷ augment

augmentations n ▷ augment

augmented v ▷ augment

augmenting v ▷ augment

augments v ▷ augment

augur v (-s, -ing, -ed) be a sign of (future events)

augured v ▷ augur

auguries n ▷ augury

auguring v ▷ augur

augurs v ▷ augur

augury n (pl -ries) foretelling of the future

august [aw-**gust**] adj dignified and imposing

auk n (pl -s) northern sea bird with short wings and black-and-white plumage

auks n ▷ auk

aunt n (pl -s) father's or mother's sister

auntie, aunty n (pl -ties) (Informal) aunt

aunties n ▷ auntie

aunts n ▷ aunt

aunty n ▷ auntie

aura n (pl -s) distinctive air or quality of a person or thing

aural adj of or using the ears or hearing

aurality n ▷ aura

auras n ▷ aura

aureola n ▷ aureole

aureolas n ▷ aureole

aureole, aureola n (pl -s) halo

aureoles n ▷ aureole

auricle n (pl -s) upper chamber of the heart > **auricular** adj

auricles n ▷ auricle

auricular adj ▷ auricle

aurochs n (pl aurochs) recently extinct European wild ox

aurora n (pl -ras, -rae) bands of light sometimes seen in the sky in polar regions

aurorae n ▷ aurora

auroras n ▷ aurora

auscultation n (pl -s) listening to the internal sounds of the body, usu. with a stethoscope, to help with diagnosis

auscultations n ▷ auscultation

auspice [aw-spiss] n (pl -s) (usually plural) patronage or guidance
  auspices n ▷ auspice
auspicious adj showing signs of future success, favourable > **auspiciously** adv
  auspiciously adv ▷ auspicious
austere adj (-r, -st) stern or severe > **austerely** adv > **austerity** n (pl -ties)
  austerely adv ▷ austere
  austerer adj ▷ austere
  austerest adj ▷ austere
  austerities n ▷ austere
  austerity n ▷ austere
  autarchies n ▷ autarchy
autarchy [aw-tar-kee] n (pl -chies) absolute power or autocracy
  autarkies n ▷ autarky
autarky [aw-tar-kee] n (pl -kies) policy of economic self-sufficiency
authentic adj known to be real, genuine
  > **authentically** adv > **authenticity** n (pl -ties)
  authentically adv ▷ authentic
authenticate v (-tes, -ting, -ted) establish as genuine > **authentication** n (pl -s)
  authenticated v ▷ authenticate
  authenticates v ▷ authenticate
  authenticating n ▷ authenticate
  authentication n ▷ authenticate
  authentications n ▷ authenticate
  authenticities n ▷ authentic
  authenticity n ▷ authentic
author n (pl -s) writer of a book etc.
  > **authorship** n (pl -s)
authoritarian n (pl -s) ▶ adj (person) insisting on strict obedience to authority
  authoritarians n ▷ authoritarian
authoritative adj recognized as being reliable
  > **authoritatively** adv
  authoritatively adv ▷ authoritative
  authorities n ▷ authority
authority n (pl -ties) power to command or control others
  authorization n ▷ authorize
  authorizations n ▷ authorize
authorize v (-zes, -zing, -zed) give authority to
  > **authorization** n (pl -s)
  authorized v ▷ authorize
  authorizes v ▷ authorize
  authorizing v ▷ authorize
  authors n ▷ author
  authorship n ▷ author
  authorships n ▷ author
autism n (pl -s) (PSYCHIATRY) disorder, usu. of children, characterized by lack of response to people and limited ability to communicate

> **autistic** adj
  autisms n ▷ autism
  autistic adj ▷ autism
  autobiographical adj ▷ autobiography
  autobiographically adv ▷ autobiography
  autobiographies n ▷ autobiography
autobiography n (pl -phies) account of a person's life written by that person
  > **autobiographical** adj > **autobiographically** adv
  autocracies n ▷ autocracy
autocracy n (pl -cies) government by an autocrat
autocrat n (pl -s) ruler with absolute authority
  > **autocratic** adj > **autocratically** adv
  autocratic adj ▷ autocrat
  autocratically adv ▷ autocrat
  autocrats n ▷ autocrat
autocross n (pl -es) motor-racing over a rough course
  autocrosses n ▷ autocross
autocue n (pl autocues)® electronic television prompting device displaying a speaker's script, unseen by the audience
  autocues n ▷ autocue
autogiro, autogyro n (pl -ros) self-propelled aircraft resembling a helicopter but with an unpowered rotor
  autogiros n ▷ autogiro
autograph n (pl -s) handwritten signature of a (famous) person ▶ v (-s, -ing, -ed) write one's signature on or in
  autographed v ▷ autograph
  autographing v ▷ autograph
  autographs n, v ▷ autograph
  autogyro n ▷ autogiro
  autogyros n ▷ autogiro
automat n (pl -s) (us) vending machine
automate v (-tes, -ting, -ted) make (a manufacturing process) automatic
  > **automation** n (pl -s)
  automated v ▷ automate
  automates v ▷ automate
automatic adj (of a device) operating mechanically by itself ▶ n (pl -s) self-loading firearm > **automatically** adv
  automatically adv ▷ automatic
  automatics n ▷ automatic
  automating v ▷ automate
  automation n ▷ automate
  automations n ▷ automate
automaton n (pl -s) robot
  automatons n ▷ automaton
  automats n ▷ automat
automobile n (pl -s) (us) motor car

automobiles n ▷ automobile
autonomies n ▷ autonomy
autonomous adj ▷ autonomy
autonomy n (pl -mies) self-government
   > **autonomous** adj
autopsies n ▷ autopsy
autopsist n ▷ autopsy
autopsy n (pl -sies) examination of a corpse to determine the cause of death
autosuggestion n (pl -s) process in which a person unconsciously influences his or her own behaviour or beliefs
autosuggestions n ▷ autosuggestion
autumn n (pl -s) season between summer and winter > **autumnal** adj
autumnal adj ▷ autumn
autumns n ▷ autumn
auxiliaries n ▷ auxiliary
auxiliary adj secondary or supplementary ▶ n (pl -ries) person or thing that supplements or supports
avail v (-s, -ing, -ed) be of use or advantage (to) ▶ n (pl -s) use or advantage
availabilities n ▷ available
availability n ▷ available
available adj obtainable or accessible
   > **availability** n (pl -ties)
availed v ▷ avail
availing v ▷ avail
avails v, n ▷ avail
avalanche n (pl -s) mass of snow or ice falling down a mountain
avalanches n ▷ avalanche
avarice [av-a-riss] n (pl -s) greed for wealth
   > **avaricious** adj
avarices n ▷ avarice
avaricious adj ▷ avarice
avast interj (NAUT) stop
avatar n (pl -s) (HINDUISM) appearance of a god in animal or human form
avatars n ▷ avatar
avenge v (-ges, -ging, -ged) take revenge in retaliation for (harm done) or on behalf of (a person harmed) > **avenger** n (pl -s)
avenged v ▷ avenge
avenger n ▷ avenge
avengers n ▷ avenge
avenges v ▷ avenge
avenging v ▷ avenge
avenue n (pl -s) wide street
avenues n ▷ avenue
aver [av-vur] v (avers, averring, averred) state to be true
average n (pl -s) typical or normal amount or quality ▶ adj usual or typical ▶ v (-ges, -ging,

-ged) calculate the average of
averaged v ▷ average
averages n, v ▷ average
averred v ▷ aver
averring v ▷ aver
avers v ▷ aver
averages n, v ▷ average
averse adj (usu. foll. by **to**) disinclined or unwilling
aversion n (pl -s) strong dislike
aversions n ▷ aversion
avert v (-s, -ing, -ed) turn away
averted v ▷ avert
averting v ▷ avert
averts v ▷ avert
aviaries n ▷ aviary
aviary n (pl -ries) large enclosure for birds
aviation n (pl -s) art of flying aircraft > **aviator** n (pl -s)
aviations n ▷ aviation
aviator n ▷ aviation
aviators n ▷ aviation
aviatrice n ▷ aviation
avid adj (-er, -est) keen or enthusiastic > **avidly** adv > **avidity** n (pl -ties)
avider adj ▷ avid
avidest adj ▷ avid
avidities n ▷ avid
avidity n ▷ avid
avidly adv ▷ avid
avocado n (pl -dos) pear-shaped tropical fruit with a leathery green skin
avocados n ▷ avocado
avocation n (pl -s) (Old-fashioned) occupation
avocations n ▷ avocation
avocet n (pl -s) long-legged wading bird with a long slender upward-curving bill
avocets n ▷ avocet
avoid v (-s, -ing, -ed) prevent from happening
   > **avoidable** adj > **avoidance** n (pl -s)
avoidable adj ▷ avoid
avoidance n ▷ avoid
avoidances n ▷ avoid
avoided v ▷ avoid
avoiding v ▷ avoid
avoids v ▷ avoid
avoirdupois [av-er-de-**poise**] n (pl -es) system of weights based on pounds and ounces
avoirdupoises n ▷ avoirdupois
avow v (-s, -ing, -ed) state or affirm > **avowal** n (pl -s) > **avowed** adj > **avowedly** adv
avowal n ▷ avow
avowals n ▷ avow
avowed v, adj ▷ avow
avowedly adv ▷ avow

avowing v ▷ avow
avows v ▷ avow
avuncular adj (of a man) friendly, helpful, and caring towards someone younger

aw interj. A sound people make when they're feeling sorry for someone. Aw scores 5 points.

await v (-s, -ing, -ed) wait for
awaited v ▷ await
awaiting v ▷ await
awaits v ▷ await
awake v (awakes, awaking, awoke, awoken) emerge or rouse from sleep ▶ adj not sleeping
awaken v (-s, -ing, -ed) awake
awakened v ▷ awaken
awakening v ▷ awaken
awakens v ▷ awaken
awakes v ▷ awake
awaking v ▷ awake
award v (-s, -ing, -ed) give (something, such as a prize) formally ▶ n (pl -s) something awarded, such as a prize
awarded v ▷ award
awarding v ▷ award
awards v, n ▷ award
aware adj having knowledge, informed
> awareness n (pl -es)
awareness n ▷ aware
awarenesses n ▷ aware
awash adv washed over by water
away adv from a place ▶ adj not present
awe n (pl -s) wonder and respect mixed with dread ▶ v (awes, awing, awed) fill with awe
awed v ▷ awe
awes n, v ▷ awe
awesome adj inspiring awe
awestruck adj filled with awe
awful adj (-ller, -llest) very bad or unpleasant
awfuller adj ▷ awful
awfullest adj ▷ awful
awfully adv in an unpleasant way
awhile adv for a brief time
awing v ▷ awe
awkward adj (-er, -est) clumsy or ungainly
> awkwardly adv > awkwardness n (pl -es)
awkwarder adj ▷ awkward
awkwardest adj ▷ awkward
awkwardly adv ▷ awkward
awkwardness n ▷ awkward
awkwardnesses n ▷ awkward
awl n (pl -s) pointed tool for piercing wood, leather, etc.
awls n ▷ awl
awning n (pl -s) canvas roof supported by a frame to give protection against the weather

awnings n ▷ awning
awoke v ▷ awake
awoken v ▷ awake
awry [a-rye] adv, adj with a twist to one side, askew
ax n ▷ axe
axe, ax n (pl axes) tool with a sharp blade for felling trees or chopping wood (Informal) ▶ v (axes, axing, axed) (Informal) dismiss (employees), restrict (expenditure), or terminate (a project)
axed v ▷ axe
axes n, v ▷ axe, axis
axial adj ▷ axis
axil n (pl -s) angle where the stalk of a leaf joins a stem
axils n ▷ axil
axing v ▷ axe
axiom n (pl -s) generally accepted principle
axiomatic adj self-evident
axioms n ▷ axiom
axis n (pl axes) (imaginary) line round which a body can rotate or about which an object or geometrical figure is symmetrical > axial adj
axle n (pl -s) shaft on which a wheel or pair of wheels turns
axles n ▷ axle
axolotl n (pl -s) aquatic salamander of central America
axolotls n ▷ axolotl
ay interj ▷ aye
ayatollah n (pl -s) Islamic religious leader in Iran
ayatollahs n ▷ ayatollah
aye, ay interj yes ▶ n (pl -s) affirmative vote or voter
ayes n ▷ aye
azalea [az-zale-ya] n (pl -s) garden shrub grown for its showy flowers
azaleas n ▷ azalea
azimuth n (pl -s) arc of the sky between the zenith and the horizon
azimuths n ▷ azimuth

azo adj. Azo describes a kind of chemical. Azo scores 12 points, and so is a very high-scoring word for only three letters.
azulejo n (azulejos). An azulejo is a painted and glazed tile. Azulejo scores 23 points, and if you are lucky enough to have all seven letters needed for it, you'll get the 50-point bonus for using all of your tiles.

azure adj, n (pl -s) (of) the colour of a clear blue sky
azures n ▷ azure

Bb

B forms a two-letter word with every vowel except U – and with Y as well. With a B in your rack, you can play lots of short everyday words that will give you relatively high scores. The best of these is **box** (12 points), but don't forget **bay** (8), **by** (7), **bow** (8), **boy** (8), **buy** (8) and **bye** (8).

ba n (**bas**). A ba is the human soul in Egyptian mythology, shown in paintings as a bird with a human head. Ba scores 4 points.

baa v (-s, -ing, -ed) make the characteristic bleating sound of a sheep ▶ n (pl -s) cry made by a sheep
  baaed v ▷ baa
  baaing v ▷ baa
  baas v, n ▷ baa

babble v (-les, -ling, -led) talk excitedly or foolishly ▶ n (pl -s) muddled or foolish speech
  babbled v ▷ babble
  babbles v, n ▷ babble
  babbling v ▷ babble

babe n (pl -s) baby

babel n (pl -s) confused mixture of noises or voices
  babels n ▷ babel
  babes n ▷ babe
  babies n ▷ baby

baboon n (pl -s) large monkey with a pointed face and a long tail
  baboons n ▷ baboon

baby n (pl -bies) very young child or animal ▶ adj comparatively small of its type
  > **babyish** adj
  babyish adj ▷ baby

babysitter n (pl -s) someone who looks after children when the parents are out
  babysitters n ▷ babysitter

baccarat [back-a-rah] n (pl -s) card game involving gambling
  baccarats n ▷ baccarat

bacchanalia [back-a-nail-ee-a] n (pl -s) wild drunken party or orgy
  bacchanalias n ▷ bacchanalia

bach [batch] (NZ) n (pl -es) small holiday cottage ▶ v (-es, -ing, -ed) look after oneself when one's spouse is away

bached v ▷ bach

bachelor n (pl -s) unmarried man
  bachelors n ▷ bachelor
  baches n, v ▷ bach
  baching v ▷ bach

bacilli n ▷ bacillus

bacillus [bass-ill-luss] n (pl -li) [-lie] rod-shaped bacterium

back n (pl -s) rear part of the human body, from the neck to the pelvis ▶ v (-s, -ing, -ed) (cause to) move backwards ▶ adv at, to, or towards the rear

backbencher n (pl -s) Member of Parliament who does not hold office in the government or opposition
  backbenchers n ▷ backbencher

backbiting n (pl -s) spiteful talk about an absent person
  backbitings n ▷ backbiting

backbone n (pl -s) spinal column
  backbones n ▷ backbone

backchat n (pl -s) (Informal) impudent replies
  backchats n ▷ backchat

backcloth n (pl -s) painted curtain at the back of a stage set
  backcloths n ▷ backcloth

backdate v (-tes, -ting, -ted) make (a document) effective from a date earlier than its completion
  backdated v ▷ backdate
  backdates v ▷ backdate
  backdating v ▷ backdate

backdrop n (pl -s) painted curtain at the back of a stage set
  backdrops n ▷ backdrop
  backed v ▷ back

backer n (pl -s) person who gives financial support
  backers n ▷ backer

backfire v (-res, -ring, -red) (of a plan) fail to

have the desired effect
backfired v ▷ backfire
backfires v ▷ backfire
backfiring v ▷ backfire
backgammon n (pl -s) game played with counters and dice
backgammons n ▷ backgammon
background n (pl -s) events or circumstances that help to explain something
backgrounds n ▷ background
backhand n (pl -s) (TENNIS ETC.) stroke played with the back of the hand facing the direction of the stroke
backhanded adj ambiguous or implying criticism
backhander n (pl -s) (Slang) bribe
backhanders n ▷ backhander
backhands n ▷ backhand
backing n (pl -s) support ▶ v ▷ back
backings n ▷ backing
backlash n (pl -es) sudden and adverse reaction
backlashes n ▷ backlash
backlog n (pl -s) accumulation of things to be dealt with
backlogs n ▷ backlog
backpack n (pl -s) large pack carried on the back
backpacks n ▷ backpack
backs n, v ▷ back
backside n (pl -s) (Informal) buttocks
backsides n ▷ backside
backslid v ▷ backslide
backslide v (-slides, -sliding, -slid) relapse into former bad habits > **backslider** n (pl -s)
backslider n ▷ backslide
backsliders n ▷ backslide
backslides v ▷ backslide
backsliding v ▷ backslide
backstage adv, adj behind the stage in a theatre
backstroke n (pl -s) swimming stroke performed on the back
backstrokes n ▷ backstroke
backtrack v (-s, -ing, -ed) return by the same route by which one has come
backtracked v ▷ backtrack
backtracking v ▷ backtrack
backtracks v ▷ backtrack
backup n (pl -s) support or reinforcement
backups n ▷ backup
backward adj directed towards the rear > **backwardness** n (pl -es)
backwardness n ▷ backward
backwardnesses n ▷ backwardness

backwards adv towards the rear
backwash n (pl -es) water washed backwards by the motion of a boat
backwashes n ▷ backwash
backwater n (pl -s) isolated or backward place or condition
backwaters n ▷ backwater
backwood n (pl -s) (usually plural) remote sparsely populated area
backwoods n ▷ backwood
bacon n (pl -s) salted or smoked pig meat
bacons n ▷ bacon
bacteria pl n (sing -rium) large group of microorganisms, many of which cause disease > **bacterial** adj
bacterial adj ▷ bacteria
bacteriologist n ▷ bacteriology
bacteriologists n ▷ bacteriology
bacteriology n study of bacteria > **bacteriologist** n (pl -s)
bacterium n ▷ bacteria
bad adj (worse, worst) of poor quality > **badly** adv > **badness** n (pl -es)
bade v ▷ bid
badge n (pl -s) emblem worn to show membership, rank, etc.
badger n (pl -s) nocturnal burrowing mammal of Europe, Asia, and N America with a black and white head ▶ v (-s, -ing, -ed) pester or harass
badgered v ▷ badger
badgering v ▷ badger
badgers n, v ▷ badger
badges n ▷ badge
badinage [bad-in-nahzh] n (pl -s) playful and witty conversation
badinages n ▷ badinage
badly adv ▷ bad
badminton n (pl -s) game played with rackets and a shuttlecock, which is hit back and forth over a high net
badmintons n ▷ badminton
badness n ▷ bad
badnesses n ▷ bad
baffle v (-les, -ling, -led) perplex or puzzle ▶ n (pl -s) device to limit or regulate the flow of fluid, light, or sound > **bafflement** n
baffled v ▷ baffle
bafflement n ▷ baffle
baffles v, n ▷ baffle
baffling v ▷ baffle
bag n (pl -s) flexible container with an opening at one end ▶ v (bags, bagging, bagged) put into a bag
bagatelle n (pl -s) something of little value

bagatelles n ▷ bagatelle
bagel n (pl -s) hard ring-shaped bread roll
  bagels n ▷ bagel
baggage n (pl -s) suitcases packed for a journey
  baggages n ▷ baggage
  bagged n ▷ bag
  baggier adj ▷ baggy
  baggiest adj ▷ baggy
  bagging n ▷ bag
baggy adj (-gier, -ggiest) (of clothes) hanging loosely
bagpipes pl n musical wind instrument with reed pipes and an inflatable bag
  bags n, v ▷ bag

> **bah** interj. Bah is something people say when they are annoyed or disgusted. Bah scores 8 points.

bail[1] n (pl -s) (LAW) money deposited with a court as security for a person's reappearance in court ▶ v (-s, -ing, -ed) pay bail for (a person)
bail[2], **bale** v (-s, -ing, -ed) (foll. by **out**) remove (water) from a boat) (Informal)
bail[3] n (pl -s) (CRICKET) either of two wooden bars across the tops of the stumps
  bailed v ▷ bail[1, 2]
bailey n (pl -s) outermost wall or court of a castle
  baileys n ▷ bailey
bailiff n (pl -s) sheriff's officer who serves writs and summonses
  bailiffs n ▷ bailiff
  bailing v ▷ bail[1,2]
  bails n ▷ bail[1,3] ▶ v ▷ bail[1, 2]
bairn n (pl -s) (SCOT) child
  bairns n ▷ bairn
bait n (pl -s) piece of food on a hook or in a trap to attract fish or animals ▶ v (-s, -ing, -ed) put a piece of food on or in (a hook or trap)
  baited v ▷ bait
  baiting v ▷ bait
  baits n, v ▷ bait
baize n (pl -s) woollen fabric used to cover billiard and card tables
  baizes n ▷ baize
bake v (-kes, -king, -ked) cook by dry heat as in an oven
  baked v ▷ bake
baker n (pl -s) person whose business is to make or sell bread, cakes, etc.
  bakeries n ▷ bakery
  bakers n ▷ baker
bakery n (pl -eries) place where bread, cakes, etc. are baked or sold

  bakes v ▷ bake
  baking v ▷ bake
bakkie n (pl -s) (S AFR) small truck
  bakkies n ▷ bakkie
balaclava n (pl -s) close-fitting woollen hood that covers the ears and neck
  balaclavas n ▷ balaclava
balalaika n (pl -s) guitar-like musical instrument with a triangular body
  balalaikas n ▷ balalaika
balance n (pl -s) state in which a weight or amount is evenly distributed ▶ v (-ces, -cing, -ced) weigh in a balance
  balanced v ▷ balance
  balances n, v ▷ balance
  balancing v ▷ balance
  balancings n ▷ balance
  balconies n ▷ balcony
balcony n (pl -nies) platform on the outside of a building with a rail along the outer edge
bald adj (-er, -est) having little or no hair on the scalp > **baldness** n (pl -es)
  balder adj ▷ bald
balderdash n (pl -es) stupid talk
  balderdashes n ▷ balderdash
  baldest adj ▷ bald
balding adj becoming bald
  baldness n ▷ bald
  baldnesses n ▷ bald
bale[1] n (pl -s) large bundle of hay or goods tightly bound together ▶ v (-les, -ling, -led) make or put into bales
  bale[2] v ▷ bail[2]
  baled v ▷ bale[1, 2]
baleful adj vindictive or menacing > **balefully** adv
  balefully adv ▷ baleful
  bales n, v ▷ bale[1, 2]
  baling v ▷ bale[1, 2]
balk, baulk v (-s, -ing, -ed) be reluctant to (do something)
  balked v ▷ balk
  balking v ▷ balk
  balks v ▷ balk
ball[1] n (pl -s) round or nearly round object, esp. one used in games ▶ v (-lls, -lling, -lled) form into a ball
ball[2] n (pl -s) formal social function for dancing > **ballroom** n (pl -s)
ballad n (pl -s) narrative poem or song
  ballads n ▷ ballad
ballast n (pl -s) substance used to stabilize a ship when it is not carrying cargo
  ballasts n ▷ ballast
  balled v ▷ ball[1]

ballerina *n* (*pl* -s) female ballet dancer
  ballerinas *n* ▷ ballerina
ballet *n* (*pl* -s) classical style of expressive dancing based on conventional steps
  ballets *n* ▷ ballet
  balling *v* ▷ ball¹
  ballistic *adj* ▷ ballistics
ballistics *n* study of the flight of projectiles, such as bullets > **ballistic** *adj*
balloon *n* (*pl* -s) inflatable rubber bag used as a plaything or decoration ▶ *v* (-s, -ing, -ed) fly in a balloon > **balloonist** *n* (*pl* -s)
  ballooned *v* ▷ balloon
  ballooning *v* ▷ balloon
  balloonist *n* ▷ balloon
  balloonists *n* ▷ balloonist
  balloons *n*, *v* ▷ balloon
ballot *n* (*pl* -s) method of voting ▶ *v* (-lots, -loting, -loted) vote or ask for a vote from
  balloted *v* ▷ ballot
  balloting *v* ▷ ballot
  ballots *n*, *v* ▷ ballot
ballpoint *n* (*pl* -s) pen with a tiny ball bearing as a writing point
  ballpoints *n* ▷ ballpoint
  ballroom *n* ▷ ball²
  ballrooms *n* ▷ ball²
  balls *n* ▷ ball¹, ² ▶ *v* ▷ ball¹
ballyhoo *n* (*pl* -s) exaggerated fuss
  ballyhoos *n* ▷ ballyhoo
balm *n* (*pl* -s) aromatic substance used for healing and soothing
  balmier *adj* ▷ balmy
  balmiest *adj* ▷ balmy
  balms *n* ▷ balm
balmy *adj* (-mier, -miest) (of weather) mild and pleasant
baloney, boloney *n* (*pl* -s) (*Informal*) nonsense
  baloneys *n* ▷ baloney
balsa [bawl-sa] *n* (*pl* -s) very light wood from a tropical American tree
balsam *n* (*pl* -s) soothing ointment
  balsams *n* ▷ balsam
  balsas *n* ▷ balsa
baluster *n* (*pl* -s) set of posts supporting a rail
  balusters *n* ▷ baluster
balustrade *n* (*pl* -s) ornamental rail supported by balusters
  balustrades *n* ▷ balustrade
bamboo *n* (*pl* -s) tall treelike tropical grass with hollow stems
  bamboos *n* ▷ bamboo
bamboozle *v* (-zles, -zling, -zled) (*Informal*) cheat or mislead
  bamboozled *v* ▷ bamboozle

  bamboozles *v* ▷ bamboozle
  bamboozling *v* ▷ bamboozle
ban *v* (-s, -nning, -nned) prohibit or forbid officially ▶ *n* (*pl* -s) official prohibition
banal [ban-nahl] *adj* (-er, -est) ordinary and unoriginal > **banality** *n* (*pl* -ties)
  banaler *adj* ▷ banal
  banalest *adj* ▷ banal
  banalities *n* ▷ banal
  banality *n* ▷ banal
banana *n* (*pl* -s) yellow crescent-shaped fruit
  bananas *n* ▷ banana
band¹ *n* (*pl* -s) group of musicians playing together > **bandsman** *n* (*pl* -men)
band² *n* (*pl* -s) strip of some material, used to hold objects
bandage *n* (*pl* -s) piece of material used to cover a wound or wrap an injured limb ▶ *v* (-ges, -ging, -ged) cover with a bandage
  bandaged *v* ▷ bandage
  bandages *n*, *v* ▷ bandage
  bandaging *v* ▷ bandage
  bandana *n* ▷ bandanna
  bandanas *n* ▷ bandanna
bandanna, bandana *n* (*pl* -s) large brightly coloured handkerchief or neckerchief
  bandannas *n* ▷ bandanna
bandicoot *n* (*pl* -s) ratlike Australian marsupial
  bandicoots *n* ▷ bandicoot
  bandied *v* ▷ bandy
  bandier *adj* ▷ bandy
  bandies *v* ▷ bandy
  bandiest *adj* ▷ bandy
bandit *n* (*pl* -s) robber, esp. a member of an armed gang > **banditry** *n*
  banditry *n* ▷ bandit
  bandits *n* ▷ bandit
bandolier *n* (*pl* -s) shoulder belt for holding cartridges
  bandoliers *n* ▷ bandolier
  bands *n* ▷ band¹, ²
  bandsman *n* ▷ band¹
  bandsmen *n* ▷ band¹
bandstand *n* (*pl* -s) roofed outdoor platform for a band
  bandstands *n* ▷ bandstand
bandwagon *n* (*pl* -s) a party or movement that seems assured of success
  bandwagons *n* ▷ bandwagon
bandy *adj* (-dier, -diest) ▶ *v* (-dies, -dying, -died) exchange (words) in a heated manner
  bandying *v* ▷ bandy
bane *n* (*pl* -s) person or thing that causes misery or distress > **baneful** *adj*

baneful *adj* ▷ bane
banes *n* ▷ bane
bang *n (pl -s)* short loud explosive noise ▶ *v* (-s, -ging, -ged) hit or knock, esp. with a loud noise ▶ *adv* precisely
banged *v* ▷ bang
banger *n (pl -s) (Informal)* (BRIT & AUST) old decrepit car
bangers *n* ▷ banger
banging *v* ▷ bang
bangle *n (pl -s)* bracelet worn round the arm or the ankle
bangles *n* ▷ bangle
bangs *n, v* ▷ bang
banish *v* (-es, -ing, -ed) send (someone) into exile > **banishment** *n (pl -s)*
banished *v* ▷ banish
banishes *v* ▷ banish
banishing *v* ▷ banish
banishment *n* ▷ banish
banishments *n* ▷ banish
banisters, bannisters *pl n* railing supported by posts on a staircase

> **banjax** *v* (**banjaxes, banjaxing, banjaxed**). If you banjax something, you wreck or ruin it. This is a great word to remember, with its high-scoring combination of J and X. Look out for chances to form it from either **ban** or **ax**. Banjax scores 22 points.

banjo *n (pl -jos, -joes)* guitar-like musical instrument with a circular body
banjoes *n* ▷ banjo
banjos *n* ▷ banjo
bank[1] *n (pl -s)* institution offering services such as the safekeeping and lending of money ▶ *v* (-s, -ing, -ed) deposit (cash or cheques) in a bank > **banking** *n*
bank[2] *n (pl -s)* raised mass, esp. of earth ▶ *v* (-s, -ing, -ed) form into a bank
bank[3] *n (pl -s)* arrangement of switches, keys, oars, etc. in a row or in tiers
banked *v* ▷ bank[1, 2]
banker *n (pl -s)* manager or owner of a bank
bankers *n* ▷ banker
banking *v* ▷ bank[1, 2] ▶ *n* ▷ bank[1]
banknote *n (pl -s)* piece of paper money
banknotes *n* ▷ banknote
bankrupt *n (pl -s)* person declared by a court to be unable to pay his or her debts ▶ *adj* financially ruined ▶ *v* (-s, -ing, -ed) make bankrupt > **bankruptcy** *n (pl -cies)*
bankruptcies *n* ▷ bankrupt
bankruptcy *n* ▷ bankrupt
bankrupted *v* ▷ bankrupt

bankrupting *v* ▷ bankrupt
bankrupts *n, v* ▷ bankrupt
banks *n* ▷ bank[1, 2, 3] ▶ *v* ▷ bank[1, 2]
banksia *n (pl -s)* Australian evergreen tree or shrub
banksias *n* ▷ banksia
banned *v* ▷ ban
banner *n (pl -s)* long strip of cloth displaying a slogan, advertisement, etc.
banners *n* ▷ banner
banning *v* ▷ ban
bannisters *pl n* ▷ banisters
banns *pl n* public declaration, esp. in a church, of an intended marriage
banquet *n (pl -s)* elaborate formal dinner
banquets *n* ▷ banquet
bans *v, n* ▷ ban
banshee *n (pl -s)* (in Irish folklore) female spirit whose wailing warns of a coming death
banshees *n* ▷ banshee
bantam *n (pl -s)* small breed of chicken
bantams *n* ▷ bantam
bantamweight *n (pl -s)* boxer weighing between 118lb (professional) or 54kg (amateur)
bantamweights *n* ▷ bantamweight
banter *v* (-s, -ing, -ed) tease jokingly ▶ *n (pl -s)* teasing or joking conversation
bantered *v* ▷ banter
bantering *v* ▷ banter
banters *v, n* ▷ banter
baobab [bay-oh-bab] *n (pl -s)* African tree with a thick trunk and angular branches
baobabs *n* ▷ baobab
baptism *n (pl -s)* Christian religious ceremony in which a person is immersed in or sprinkled with water as a sign of being cleansed from sin and accepted into the Church > **baptismal** *adj*
baptismal *adj* ▷ baptism
baptisms *n* ▷ baptism
baptist *n (pl -s)* member of a Protestant denomination that believes in adult baptism by immersion
baptists *n* ▷ baptist
baptize *v* (-zes, -zing, -zed) perform baptism on
baptized *v* ▷ baptize
baptizes *v* ▷ baptize
baptizing *v* ▷ baptize
bar[1] *n (pl -s)* rigid length of metal, wood, etc. ▶ *v* (bars, barring, barred) secure with a bar > **barman** *(pl -men)*, **barmaid** *(pl -s)* ▶ *n*
bar[2] *n (pl -s)* unit of atmospheric pressure
barb *n (pl -s)* cutting remark > **barbed** *adj*
barbarian *n (pl -s)* member of a primitive or

uncivilized people
barbarians n ▷ barbarian
barbaric adj cruel or brutal
barbarism n (pl -s) condition of being backward or ignorant
barbarisms n ▷ barbarism
barbarities n ▷ barbarity
barbarity n (pl -ties) state of being barbaric or barbarous
barbarous adj uncivilized
barbecue n (pl -s) grill on which food is cooked over hot charcoal, usu. outdoors ▶ v (-cues, -cuing, -cued) cook (food) on a barbecue
barbecued v ▷ barbecue
barbecues n, v ▷ barbecue
barbecuing v ▷ barbecue
barbed adj ▷ barb
barber n (pl -s) person who cuts men's hair and shaves beards
barbers n ▷ barber
barbiturate n (pl -s) drug used as a sedative
barbiturates n ▷ barbiturate
barbs n ▷ barb
bard n (pl -s) (Lit) poet
bards n ▷ bard
bare adj (-r, -st) unclothed, naked ▶ v (-res, -ring, -red) uncover > **bareness** n (pl -es)
bareback adj, adv (of horse-riding) without a saddle
bared v ▷ bare
barefaced adj shameless or obvious
barely adv only just
bareness n ▷ bare
barenesses n ▷ bare
barer adj ▷ bare
bares v ▷ bare
barest adj ▷ bare
bargain n (pl -s) agreement establishing what each party will give, receive, or perform in a transaction ▶ v (-s, -ing, -ed) negotiate the terms of an agreement
bargained v ▷ bargain
bargaining v ▷ bargain
bargains n, v ▷ bargain
barge n (pl -s) flat-bottomed boat used to transport freight ▶ v (-ges, -ging, -ged) (Informal) push violently
barged v ▷ barge
barges n, v ▷ barge
barging v ▷ barge
baring v ▷ bare
barista [bar-ee-sta] n (pl -s) person who makes and sells coffee in a coffee bar
baristas n ▷ barista
baritone n (pl -s) (singer with) the second

lowest adult male voice
baritones n ▷ baritone
barium n (pl -s) (CHEM) soft white metallic element
bariums n ▷ barium
bark[1] n (pl -s) loud harsh cry of a dog ▶ v (-s, -ing, -ed) (of a dog) make its typical cry
bark[2] n (pl -s) tough outer layer of a tree
barked v ▷ bark[1]
barking v ▷ bark[1]
barks n, v ▷ bark[1] ▶ n ▷ bark[2]
barley n (pl -s) tall grasslike plant cultivated for grain
barleys n ▷ barley
barmaid n ▷ bar[1]
barmaids n ▷ bar[1]
barman n ▷ bar[1]
barmen n ▷ bar[1]
barmier adj ▷ barmy
barmiest adj ▷ barmy
barmy adj (-mier, -miest) (Slang) insane
barn n (pl -s) large building on a farm used for storing grain
barnacle n (pl -s) shellfish that lives attached to rocks, ship bottoms, etc.
barnacles n ▷ barnacle
barney n (pl -s) (Informal) noisy fight or argument
barneys n ▷ barney
barns n ▷ barn
barometer n (pl -s) instrument for measuring atmospheric pressure > **barometric** adj
barometers n ▷ barometer
barometric adj ▷ barometer
baron n (pl -s) member of the lowest rank of nobility > **baroness** n (pl -es) > **baronial** adj
baroness n ▷ baron
baronesses n ▷ baron
baronet n (pl baronets) commoner who holds the lowest hereditary British title
baronets n ▷ baronet
baronial adj ▷ baron
barons n ▷ baron
baroque [bar-rock] n (pl -s) highly ornate style of art, architecture, or music from the late 16th to the early 18th century ▶ adj ornate in style
baroques n ▷ baroque
barque [bark] n (pl -s) sailing ship, esp. one with three masts
barques n ▷ barque
barra n (pl -s) (AUST) (Informal) ▷ barramundi
barrack v (-s, -ing, -ed) criticize loudly or shout against (a team or speaker)
barracked v ▷ barrack

barracking v ▷ barrack
barracks v ▷ barrack ▶ pl n building used to accommodate military personnel
barracouta n (pl -s) large Pacific fish with a protruding lower jaw and strong teeth
barracoutas n ▷ barracouta
barracuda n (pl barracuda) tropical sea fish
barrage [bar-rahzh] n (pl -s) continuous delivery of questions, complaints, etc.
barrages n ▷ barrage
barramundi n (pl -s) edible Australian fish
barramundis n ▷ barramundi
barras n ▷ barra
barred v ▷ bar¹
barrel n (pl -s) cylindrical container with rounded sides and flat ends
barrels n ▷ barrel
barren adj (-er, -est) (of a woman or female animal) incapable of producing offspring > **barrenness** n (pl -es)
barrener adj ▷ barren
barrenest adj ▷ barren
barrenness n ▷ barren
barrennesses n ▷ barren
barricade n (pl -s) barrier, esp. one erected hastily for defence ▶ v (-des, -ding, -ded) erect a barricade across (an entrance)
barricaded v ▷ barricade
barricades n, v ▷ barricade
barricading v ▷ barricade
barrier n (pl -s) anything that prevents access, progress, or union
barriers n ▷ barrier
barring v ▷ bar¹ ▶ prep except for
barrister n (pl -s) (BRIT, AUST & NZ) lawyer qualified to plead in a higher court
barristers n ▷ barrister
barrow¹ n (pl -s) wheelbarrow
barrow² n (pl -s) mound of earth over a prehistoric tomb
barrows n ▷ barrow¹, ²
bars n ▷ bar¹, ² ▶ v ▷ bar¹
barter v (-s, -ing, -ed) trade (goods) in exchange for other goods ▶ n (pl -s) trade by the exchange of goods
bartered v ▷ barter
bartering v ▷ barter
barters v, n ▷ barter
basalt [bass-awlt] n (pl -s) dark volcanic rock > **basaltic** adj
basaltic adj ▷ basalt
basalts n ▷ basalt
base¹ n (pl -s) bottom or supporting part of anything ▶ v (bases, basing, based) (foll. by on or upon) use as a basis (for) > **baseless** adj

base² adj (-r, -st) dishonourable or immoral > **baseness** n
baseball n (pl -s) team game in which runs are scored by hitting a ball with a bat then running round four bases
baseballs n ▷ baseball
based v ▷ base¹
baseless adj ▷ base¹
basement n (pl -s) partly or wholly underground storey of a building
basements n ▷ basement
baseness n ▷ base²
baser adj ▷ base²
bases n ▷ base¹, basis ▶ v ▷ base¹
basest adj ▷ base²
bash (Informal) v (-es, -ing, -ed) hit violently or forcefully ▶ n (pl bashes) heavy blow
bashed v ▷ bash
bashes v, n ▷ bash
bashful adj shy or modest > **bashfully** adv > **bashfulness** n
bashfully adv ▷ bash
bashfulness n ▷ bash
bashing v ▷ bash
basic adj of or forming a base or basis > **basically** adv
basically adv ▷ basic
basics pl n fundamental principles, facts, etc.
basil n (pl -s) aromatic herb used in cooking
basilica n (pl -s) rectangular church with a rounded end and two aisles
basilicas n ▷ basilica
basilisk n (pl -s) legendary serpent said to kill by its breath or glance
basilisks n ▷ basilisk
basils n ▷ basil
basin n (pl -s) round open container
basing v ▷ base¹
basins n ▷ basin
basis n (pl -ses) fundamental principles etc. from which something is started or developed
bask v (-s, -ing, -ed) lie in or be exposed to something, esp. pleasant warmth
basked v ▷ bask
basket n (pl -s) container made of interwoven strips of wood or cane ▶ **basketwork** n (pl -s)
basketball n (pl -s) team game in which points are scored by throwing the ball through a high horizontal hoop
basketballs n ▷ basketball
baskets n ▷ basket
basketwork n ▷ basket
basketworks n ▷ basket
basking v ▷ bask

basks v ▷ bask

bass¹ [base] n (pl -es) (singer with) the lowest adult male voice ▸ adj of the lowest range of musical notes

bass² n (pl bass) edible sea fish

basses n ▷ bass¹

bassoon n (pl -s) low-pitched woodwind instrument

bassoons n ▷ bassoon

bastard n (pl -s) (Offens) obnoxious or despicable person

bastards n ▷ bastard

baste¹ v (bastes, basting, basted) moisten (meat) during cooking with hot fat

baste² v (bastes, basting, basted) sew with loose temporary stitches

basted v ▷ baste¹,²

bastes v ▷ baste¹,²

basting v ▷ baste¹,²

bastion n (pl -s) projecting part of a fortification

bastions n ▷ bastion

bat¹ n (pl -s) any of various types of club used to hit the ball in certain sports ▸ v (bats, batting, batted) strike with or as if with a bat

bat² n (pl -s) nocturnal mouselike flying animal

batch n (pl -es) group of people or things dealt with at the same time

batches n ▷ batch

bath n (pl -s) large container in which to wash the body ▸ pl public swimming pool ▸ v (-s, -ing, -ed) wash in a bath

bathe v (-thes, -thing, -thed) swim in open water for pleasure ▸ **bather** n (pl -s)

bathed v ▷ bath ▷ bathe

bather n ▷ bathe

bathers n ▷ bathe

bathes v ▷ bath ▷ bathe

bathing v ▷ bath ▷ bathe

bathos [bay-thoss] n (pl -es) sudden ludicrous change in speech or writing from a serious subject to a trivial one

bathoses n ▷ bathos

bathroom n (pl -s) room with a bath, sink, and usu. a toilet

bathrooms n ▷ bathe

baths n, v ▷ bath

batik [bat-teek] n (pl -s) process of printing fabric using wax to cover areas not to be dyed

batiks n ▷ batik

batman n (pl -men) officer's servant in the armed forces

batmen n ▷ batman

baton n (pl -s) thin stick used by the conductor of an orchestra

batons n ▷ baton

bats n ▷ bat¹,² ▸ v ▷ bat¹

batsman n (pl -men) (CRICKET) person who bats or specializes in batting

batsmen n ▷ batsman

battalion n (pl -s) army unit consisting of three or more companies

battalions n ▷ battalion

batted v ▷ bat¹

batten n (pl -s) strip of wood fixed to something, esp. to hold it in place

battens n ▷ batten

batter¹ v (-s, -ing, -ed) hit repeatedly

batter² n (pl -s) mixture of flour, eggs, and milk, used in cooking

battered v ▷ batter¹

batteries n ▷ battery

battering v ▷ batter¹

batters v, n ▷ batter¹,²

battery n (pl -teries) device that produces electricity in a torch, radio, etc. ▸ adj kept in series of cages for intensive rearing

battier adj ▷ batty

battiest adj ▷ batty

batting adj ▷ bat¹

battle n (pl -s) fight between large armed forces ▸ v (battles, battling, battled) struggle

battled v ▷ battle

battlement n (pl -s) wall with gaps along the top for firing through

battlements n ▷ battlement

battles n, v ▷ battle

battleship n (pl -s) large heavily armoured warship

battleships n ▷ battleship

battling v ▷ battle

batty adj (-tier, -tiest) (Slang) eccentric or crazy

bauble n (pl -s) trinket of little value

baubles n ▷ bauble

bauera n (pl -s) small evergreen Australian shrub

baueras n ▷ bauera

baulk v (-s, -ing, -ed) ▷ balk

baulked v ▷ baulk

baulking v ▷ baulk

baulks v ▷ baulk

bauxite n (pl -s) claylike substance that is the chief source of aluminium

bauxites n ▷ bauxite

bawdier adj ▷ bawdy

bawdiest adj ▷ bawdy

bawdy adj (-ier, -iest) (of writing etc.) containing humorous references to sex

bawl v (-s, -ing, -ed) shout or weep noisily

bawled v ▷ bawl

bawling v ▷ bawl
bawls v ▷ bawl
bay[1] n (pl -s) stretch of coastline that curves inwards
bay[2] n (pl -s) recess in a wall
bay[3] v (-s, -ing, -ed) howl in deep prolonged tones
bay[4] n (pl -s) Mediterranean laurel tree
bay[5] adj, n (pl -s) reddish-brown (horse)
bayed v ▷ bay[3]
baying v ▷ bay[3]
bayonet n (pl -s) sharp blade that can be fixed to the end of a rifle ▶ v (-nets, -neting, -neted) stab with a bayonet
bayoneted v ▷ bayonet
bayoneting v ▷ bayonet
bayonets n, v ▷ bayonet
bays n ▷ bay[1, 2, 4, 5] ▶ v[3]
bazaar n (pl -s) sale in aid of charity
bazaars n ▷ bazaar
bazooka n (pl -s) portable rocket launcher that fires an armour-piercing projectile
bazookas n ▷ bazooka
be v (present sing (1st person am) (2nd person are) (3rd person is) (present pl are) (past sing (1st person was) (2nd person were) (3rd person was) (past pl were) (present participle being) (past participle been) exist or live
beach n (pl -es) area of sand or pebbles on a shore ▶ v (-es, -ing, -ed) run or haul (a boat) onto a beach
beached v ▷ beach
beaches n, v ▷ beach
beachhead n (pl -s) beach captured by an attacking army on which troops can be landed
beachheads v ▷ beachhead
beaching v ▷ beach
beacon n (pl -s) fire or light on a hill or tower, used as a warning
beacons n ▷ beacon
bead n (pl -s) small piece of plastic, wood, etc., pierced for threading on a string to form a necklace etc. > **beaded** adj
beaded v ▷ bead
beadier adj ▷ beady
beadiest adj ▷ beady
beadinesses n ▷ beady
beading n strip of moulding used for edging furniture
beads n ▷ bead
beady adj (-ier, -iest) small, round, and glittering
beagle n (pl -s) small hound with short legs and drooping ears

beagles n ▷ beagle
beak[1] n (pl -s) projecting horny jaws of a bird > **beaky** adj (-ier, -iest)
beak[2] n (pl -s) (BRIT, AUST & NZ) (Slang) judge, magistrate, or headmaster
beaker n (pl -s) large drinking cup
beakers n ▷ beaker
beakier adj ▷ beak[1]
beakiest adj ▷ beak[1]
beaks n ▷ beak[1, 2]
beaky adj ▷ beak[1]
beam n (pl -s) broad smile ▶ v (-s, -ing, -ed) smile broadly
beamed v ▷ beam
beaming v ▷ beam
beams n, v ▷ beam
bean n (pl -s) seed or pod of various plants, eaten or used to make coffee etc.
beanie n (pl -s) close-fitting woollen hat
beanies n ▷ beanie
beans n ▷ bean
bear[1] v (bears, bearing, bore, borne) support or hold up (passive born) > **bearable** adj
bear[2] n (pl -s) large heavy mammal with a shaggy coat
bearable adj ▷ bear[1]
beard n (pl -s) hair growing on the lower parts of a man's face > **bearded** adj
bearded adj ▷ beard
beards n ▷ beard
bearer n (pl -s) person who carries, presents, or upholds something
bearers n ▷ bearer
bearing n (pl -s) relevance (to) ▶ pl sense of one's own relative position ▶ v ▷ bear[1]
bearings n ▷ bearing
bears v ▷ bear[1] ▶ n ▷ bear[2]
bearskin n (pl -s) tall fur helmet worn by some British soldiers
bearskins n ▷ bearskin
beast n (pl -s) large wild animal
beastliness n ▷ beastly
beastly adj unpleasant or disagreeable > **beastliness** n
beasts n ▷ beast
beat v (beats, beating, beat, beaten or beat) hit hard and repeatedly ▶ n (pl beats) regular throb
beaten v ▷ beat
beatific adj displaying great happiness
beatification n ▷ beatify
beatifications n ▷ beatify
beatified v ▷ beatify
beatifies v ▷ beatify
beatify [bee-at-if-fie] v (-fies, -fying, -fied) (RC

CHURCH) declare (a dead person) to be among the blessed in heaven: the first step towards canonization > **beatification** n (pl -s)

beatifying v ▷ beatify

beating v ▷ beat

beatitude n (pl -s) (CHRISTIANITY) any of the blessings on the poor, meek, etc., in the Sermon on the Mount

beatitudes n ▷ beatitude

beats v, n ▷ beat

beau [boh] n (pl beaux, beaus) boyfriend or admirer

beaus n ▷ beau

beautician n (pl -s) person who gives beauty treatments professionally

beauticians n ▷ beautician

beauties n ▷ beauty

beautification n ▷ beautify

beautified v ▷ beautify

beautifies v ▷ beautify

beautiful adj very attractive to look at
> **beautifully** adv

beautifully adv ▷ beautiful

beautify v (-fies, -fying, -fied) make beautiful
> **beautification** n

beautifying v ▷ beautify

beauty n (pl -ties) combination of all the qualities of a person or thing that delight the senses and mind

beaux n ▷ beau

beaver n (pl -s) amphibious rodent with a big flat tail

beavers n ▷ beaver

becalmed adj (of a sailing ship) motionless through lack of wind

became v ▷ become

because conj on account of the fact that

beck n (pl -s) (N ENGLISH) stream

beckon v (-s, -ing, -ed) summon with a gesture

beckoned v ▷ beckon

beckoning v ▷ beckon

beckons v ▷ beckon

becks n ▷ beck

become v (-coming, -came, -come) come to be

becoming adj attractive or pleasing

bed n (pl -s) piece of furniture on which to sleep
> **bedroom** n (pl -s)

bedding n (pl -s) sheets and covers that are used on a bed

beddings n ▷ bedding

bedevil v (-s, -illing, -illed) harass, confuse, or torment

bedevilled v ▷ bedevil

bedevilling v ▷ bedevil

bedevils v ▷ bedevil

bedlam n (pl -s) noisy confused situation

bedlams n ▷ bedlam

bedpan n (pl -s) shallow bowl used as a toilet by bedridden people

bedpans n ▷ bedpan

bedraggled adj untidy, wet, or dirty

bedridden adj confined to bed because of illness or old age

bedrock n (pl -s) solid rock beneath the surface soil

bedrocks n ▷ bedrock

bedroom n ▷ bed

bedrooms n ▷ bed

beds n ▷ bed

bedsit, bedsitter n (pl -s) furnished sitting room with a bed

bedsits n ▷ bedsit

bedsitters n ▷ bedsit

bee n (pl -s) insect that makes wax and honey

beech n (pl -es) tree with a smooth greyish bark

beeches n ▷ beech

beef n (pl beeves) flesh of a cow, bull, or ox

beefburger n (pl -s) flat grilled or fried cake of minced beef

beefburgers n ▷ beefburger

beefeater n (pl -s) yeoman warder at the Tower of London

beefeaters n ▷ beefeater

beefier adj ▷ beefy

beefiest adj ▷ beefy

beefy adj (-fier, -fiest) like beef

beehive n (pl -s) structure in which bees live

beehives n ▷ beehive

been v ▷ be

beep n (pl -s) high-pitched sound, like that of a car horn ▶ v (-s, -ing, -ed) (cause to) make this noise

beeped v ▷ beep

beeping v ▷ beep

beeps n, v ▷ beep

beer n (pl -s) alcoholic drink brewed from malt and hops > **beery** (-ier, -iest) ▶ adj

beerier adj ▷ beer

beeriest adj ▷ beer

beers n ▷ beer

beery adj ▷ beer

bees n ▷ bee

beeswax n (pl -es) wax secreted by bees, used in polishes etc.

beeswaxes n ▷ beeswax

beet n (pl -s) plant with an edible root and leaves

beetle n (pl -s) insect with a hard wing cover on its back

beetles n ▷ beetle

beetroot n (pl -s) type of beet plant with a dark red root

beetroots n ▷ beetroot

beets n ▷ beet

beeves n ▷ beef

befall v (-falls, -falling, -fell, -fallen) (Old-fashioned) happen to (someone)

befallen v ▷ befall

befalling v ▷ befall

befalls v ▷ befall

befell v ▷ befall

befit v (-fits, -fitting, -fitted) be appropriate or suitable for ▷ **befitting** adj

befits v ▷ befit

befitted v ▷ befit

befitting v, adj ▷ befit

before conj, prep adv indicating something earlier in time, in front of, or preferred to

beforehand adv in advance

befriend v (-s, -ing, -ed) become friends with

befriended v ▷ befriend

befriending v ▷ befriend

befriends v ▷ befriend

beg v (begs, begging, begged) solicit (for money or food), esp. in the street

began v ▷ begin

begat v ▷ beget

beget v (-gets, -getting, -got or -gat; -gotten or -got) (Old-fashioned) cause or create

begets v ▷ beget

begetting v ▷ beget

beggar n (pl s) person who lives by begging ▷ **beggarly** adj ▷ **beggarliness** n

beggarliness n ▷ beggar

beggarly adj ▷ beggar

beggars n ▷ beggar

begged v ▷ beg

begging v ▷ beg

begin v (-gins, -ginning, -gan, -gun) start ▷ **beginning** n (pl -s)

beginner n (pl -s) person who has just started learning to do something

beginners n ▷ begin

beginning v, n ▷ begin

begins v ▷ begin

begonia n (pl -s) tropical plant with waxy flowers

begonias n ▷ begonia

begot v ▷ beget

begotten v ▷ beget

begrudge v (-grudges, -grudging, -grudged) envy (someone) the possession of something

begrudged v ▷ begrudge

begrudges v ▷ begrudge

begrudging v ▷ begrudge

begs v ▷ beg

beguile [big-gile] v (-guiles, -guiling, -guiled) cheat or mislead ▷ **beguiling** adj

beguiled v ▷ beguile

beguiles v ▷ beguile

beguiling v, adj ▷ beguile

begun v ▷ begin

behalf n in the interest of or for the benefit of

behave v (-haves, -having, -haved) act or function in a particular way

behaved v ▷ behave

behaves v ▷ behave

behaving v ▷ behave

behaviour n (pl -s) manner of behaving

behaviours n ▷ behaviour

behead v (-s, -ing, -ed) remove the head from

beheaded v ▷ behead

beheading v ▷ behead

beheads v ▷ behead

beheld v ▷ behold

behest n (pl -s) order or earnest request

behests n ▷ behest

behind prep, adv indicating position to the rear, lateness, responsibility, etc. ▶ n (pl -s) (Informal) buttocks

behinds n ▷ behind

behold v (-holds, -holding, -held) (Old-fashioned) look (at) ▷ **beholder** n (pl -s)

beholden adj indebted or obliged

beholder n ▷ behold

beholders n ▷ behold

beholding v ▷ behold

beholds v ▷ behold

behove v (-hoves, -hoving, -hoved) (Old-fashioned) be necessary or fitting for

behoved v ▷ behove

behoves v ▷ behove

behoving v ▷ behove

beige adj pale brown

being n (pl -s) state or fact of existing ▶ v ▷ be

beings n ▷ being

belabour v (-s, -ing, -ed) attack verbally or physically

belaboured v ▷ belabour

belabouring v ▷ belabour

belabours v ▷ belabour

belated adj late or too late ▷ **belatedly** adv

belatedly adv ▷ belated

belch v (-es, -ing, -ed) expel wind from the stomach noisily through the mouth ▶ n (pl belches) act of belching

belched v ▷ belch

belches v, n ▷ belch

belching v ▷ belch

beleaguered *adj* struggling against difficulties or criticism

belfries *n* ▷ belfry

belfry *n* (*pl* -fries) part of a tower where bells are hung

belie *v* (belies, belying, belied) show to be untrue

belied *v* ▷ belie

belief *n* (*pl* -s) faith or confidence

beliefs *n* ▷ belief

belies *v* ▷ belie

believable *adj* ▷ believe

believe *v* (-lieves, -lieving, -lieved) accept as true or real ▶ **believable** *adj* ▷ **believer** *n* (*pl* -s)

believed *v* ▷ believe

believer *n* ▷ believe

believers *n* ▷ believe

believes *v* ▷ believe

believing *v* ▷ believe

belittle *v* (-ttles, -ttling, -ttled) treat as having little value or importance

belittled *v* ▷ belittle

belittles *v* ▷ belittle

belittling *v* ▷ belittle

bell *n* (*pl* -s) hollow, usu. metal, cup-shaped instrument that emits a ringing sound when struck

belladonna *n* (*pl* -s) (drug obtained from) deadly nightshade

belladonnas *n* ▷ belladonna

bellbird *n* (*pl* -s) Australasian bird with bell-like call

bellbirds *n* ▷ bellbird

belle *n* (*pl* -s) beautiful woman, esp. the most attractive woman at a function

belles *n* ▷ belle

bellicose *adj* warlike and aggressive

bellied *v* ▷ belly

bellies *n*, *v* ▷ belly

belligerence *n* ▷ belligerent

belligerent *adj* hostile and aggressive ▶ *n* (*pl* -s) person or country engaged in war ▶ **belligerence** *n*

belligerents *n* ▷ belligerent

bellow *v* (-s, -ing, -ed) make a low deep cry like that of a bull ▶ *n* (*pl* -s) loud deep roar

bellowed *v* ▷ bellow

bellowing *v* ▷ bellow

bellows *v*, *n* ▷ bellow ▶ *pl n* instrument for pumping a stream of air into something

bells *n* ▷ bell

belly *n* (*pl* -lies) part of the body of a vertebrate which contains the intestines ▶ *v* (-lies, -lying, -lied) (cause to) swell out

bellyful *n* (*pl* -s) (*Slang*) more than one can tolerate

bellyfuls *n* ▷ bellyful

bellying *v* ▷ belly

belong *v* (-s, -ing, -ed) (foll. by **to**) be the property of

belonged *v* ▷ belong

belonging *v* ▷ belong

belongings *pl n* personal possessions

belongs *v* ▷ belong

beloved *adj* dearly loved ▶ *n* (*pl* -s) person dearly loved

beloveds *n* ▷ beloved

below *prep*, *adv* at or to a position lower than, under

belt *n* (*pl* -s) band of cloth, leather, etc., worn usu. around the waist ▶ *v* (-s, -ing, -ed) fasten with a belt

belted *v* ▷ belt

belting *v* ▷ belt

belts *n*, *v* ▷ belt

belying *v* ▷ belie

bemoan *v* (-s, -ing, -ed) express sorrow or dissatisfaction about

bemoaned *v* ▷ bemoan

bemoaning *v* ▷ bemoan

bemoans *v* ▷ bemoan

bemused *adj* puzzled or confused

bench *n* (*pl* -es) long seat

benches *n* ▷ bench

benchmark *n* (*pl* -s) criterion by which to measure something

benchmarks *n* ▷ benchmark

bend *v* (-s, -ing, bent) (cause to) form a curve ▶ *n* curved part ▷ **bendy** *adj* (-dier, -diest) ▷ **bendiness** *n* (*pl* -es)

bendier *adj* ▷ bend

bendiest *adj* ▷ bend

bendiness *n* ▷ bend

bendinesses *n* ▷ bend

bending *v* ▷ bend

bends *v* ▷ bend ▶ *pl n* (*Informal*) decompression sickness

bendy *adj* ▷ bend

beneath *adv*, *prep* below

benediction *n* (*pl* -s) prayer for divine blessing

benedictions *n* ▷ benediction

benefaction *n* ▷ benefactor

benefactions *n* ▷ benefactor

benefactor, benefactress (*pl* -s, -esses) someone who supports a person or institution by giving money ▷ **benefaction** *n* (*pl* -s)

benefactors *n* ▷ benefactor

benefactress *n* ▷ benefactor

benefactresses *n* ▷ benefactor

beneficence n ▷ beneficent
beneficent [bin-**eff**-iss-ent] adj charitable or generous > **beneficence** n
beneficial adj helpful or advantageous
beneficiaries n ▷ beneficiary
beneficiary n (pl -ciaries) person who gains or benefits
benefit n (pl -s) something that improves or promotes ▶ v (-s, -fiting, -fited) do or receive good
benefited v ▷ benefit
benefiting v ▷ benefit
benefits n, v ▷ benefit
benevolence n (pl -s) inclination to do good > **benevolent** adj > **benevolently** adv
benevolences n ▷ benevolence
benevolent adj ▷ benevolence
benevolently adv ▷ benevolence
benighted adj ignorant or uncultured
benign [bin-**nine**] adj showing kindliness > **benignly** adv
benignly adv ▷ benign
bent v ▷ bend ▶ adj curved ▶ n (pl -s) personal inclination or aptitude
bento n (pl -s) thin lightweight box divided into compartments, which contain small separate dishes comprising a Japanese meal
bentos n ▷ bento
bents n ▷ bent
benzene n (pl -s) flammable poisonous liquid used as a solvent, insecticide, etc.
benzenes n ▷ benzene
bequeath v (-s, -ing, -ed) dispose of (property) as in a will
bequeathed v ▷ bequeath
bequeathing v ▷ bequeath
bequeaths v ▷ bequeath
bequest n (pl -s) legal gift of money or property by someone who has died
bequests v ▷ bequest
berate v (-ates, -ating, -ated) scold harshly
berated v ▷ berate
berates v ▷ berate
berating v ▷ berate
bereaved adj having recently lost a close friend or relative through death > **bereavement** n (pl -s)
bereavements n ▷ bereavement
bereft adj (foll. by of) deprived
beret [ber-ray] n (pl -s) round flat close-fitting brimless cap
berets n ▷ beret
berg[1] n (pl -s) iceberg
berg[2] n (pl -s) (S AFR) mountain
bergamot n (pl -s) small Asian tree, the fruit of

which yields an oil used in perfumery
bergamots n ▷ bergamot
bergs n ▷ berg[1, 2]
beriberi n (pl -s) disease caused by vitamin B deficiency
beriberis n ▷ beriberi
berk n (pl -s) (BRIT, AUST & NZ) (Slang) stupid person
berks n ▷ berk
berm n (pl -s) (NZ) narrow grass strip between the road and the footpath in a residential area
berms n ▷ berm
berries n ▷ berry
berry n (pl -ries) small soft stoneless fruit
berserk adj violent or destructive
berth n (pl -s) bunk in a ship or train ▶ v (-s, -ing, -ed) dock (a ship)
berthed v ▷ berth
berthing v ▷ berth
berths n, v ▷ berth
beryl n (pl -s) hard transparent mineral
beryllium n (pl -s) (CHEM) toxic silvery-white metallic element
berylliums n ▷ beryllium
beryls n ▷ beryl
beseech v (-seeches, -seeching, -sought or -seeched) ask earnestly; beg
beseeched v ▷ beseech
beseeches v ▷ beseech
beseeching v ▷ beseech
beset v (-sets, -setting, -set) trouble or harass constantly
besets v ▷ beset
besetting v ▷ beset
beside prep at, by, or to the side of
besides adv, prep in addition
besiege v (-sieges, -sieging, -sieged) surround with military forces
besieged v ▷ besiege
besieges v ▷ besiege
besieging v ▷ besiege
besotted adj infatuated
besought v ▷ beseech
bespeak v (-speaks, -speaking, -spoke, -spoken) indicate or suggest
bespeaking v ▷ bespeak
bespeaks v ▷ bespeak
bespoke v ▷ bespeak ▶ adj (esp. of a suit) made to the customer's specifications
bespoken v ▷ bespeak
best adj most excellent of a particular group etc. ▶ adv in a manner surpassing all others ▶ n (pl -s) most outstanding or excellent person, thing, or group in a category

bestial adj brutal or savage ▷ **bestiality** n (pl
-ities)
  bestialities n ▷ bestial
  bestiality n ▷ bestial
bestir v (-stirs, -stirring, -stirred) cause
(oneself) to become active
  bestirred v ▷ bestir
  bestirring v ▷ bestir
  bestirs v ▷ bestir
bestow v (-s, -ing, -ed) present (a gift) or confer
(an honour) ▷ **bestowal** n (pl -s)
  bestowal n ▷ bestow
  bestowals n ▷ bestow
  bestowed v ▷ bestow
  bestowing v ▷ bestow
  bestows v ▷ bestow
  bestridden v ▷ bestride
bestride v (-strides, -striding, -strode,
-stridden) have or put a leg on either side of
  bestrides v ▷ bestride
  bestriding v ▷ bestride
  bestrode v ▷ bestride
  bests n ▷ best
bestseller n (pl -s) book or other product that
has sold in great numbers
  bestsellers n ▷ bestseller
bet n (pl -s) the act of staking a sum of money
or other stake on the outcome of an event ▶ v
(bets, betting, bet or **betted**) make or place
(a bet)
betel [bee-tl] n (pl -s) Asian climbing plant, the
leaves and nuts of which can be chewed
  betels n ▷ betels
betide v (-tides, -tiding, -tided) happen (to)
  betided v ▷ betide
  betides v ▷ betide
  betiding v ▷ betide
betoken v (-s, -ing, -ed) indicate or signify
  betokened v ▷ betoken
  betokening v ▷ betoken
  betokens v ▷ betoken
betray v (-s, -ing, -ed) hand over or expose
(one's nation, friend, etc.) treacherously to an
enemy ▷ **betrayal** n (pl -s) ▷ **betrayer** n (pl -s)
  betrayal n ▷ betray
  betrayals n ▷ betray
  betrayed v ▷ betray
  betrayer n ▷ betray
  betrayers n ▷ betray
  betraying v ▷ betray
  betrays v ▷ betray
betrothal n ▷ betrothed
  betrothals n ▷ betrothed
betrothed adj engaged to be married
▷ **betrothal** n (pl -s)

bets n, v ▷ bet
betted v ▷ bet
better adj more excellent than others ▶ adv in a
more excellent manner ▶ pl n one's superiors
▶ v (-s, -ing, -ed) improve upon
  bettered v ▷ better
  bettering v ▷ better
  betters n, v ▷ better
betting v ▷ bet
bettong n (pl -s) short-nosed rat kangaroo
  bettongs n ▷ bettong
between prep, adv indicating position in the
middle, alternatives, etc.
betwixt prep, adv (Old-fashioned) between
bevel n (pl -s) slanting edge ▶ v (-els, -elling,
-elled) cut a bevel on (a piece of timber etc.)
  bevelled v ▷ bevel
  bevelling v ▷ bevel
  bevels n, v ▷ bevel
beverage n (pl -s) drink
  beverages n ▷ beverage
  bevies n ▷ bevy
bevy n (pl bevies) flock or group
bewail v (-s, -ing, -ed) express great sorrow
over
  bewailed v ▷ bewail
  bewailing v ▷ bewail
  bewails v ▷ bewail
beware v (-wares, -waring, -wared) be on one's
guard (against)
  bewared v ▷ beware
  bewares v ▷ beware
  bewaring v ▷ beware
bewilder v (-s, -ing, -ed) confuse utterly
▷ **bewildering** adj ▷ **bewilderment** n (pl -s)
  bewildered v ▷ bewilder
  bewildering v, adj ▷ bewilder
  bewilderment n ▷ bewilder
  bewilderments n ▷ bewilder
  bewilders v ▷ bewilder
bewitch v (-es, -ing, -ed) attract and fascinate
▷ **bewitching** adj
  bewitched v ▷ bewitch
  bewitches v ▷ bewitch
  bewitching v, adj ▷ bewitch
    bey n (**beys**). A bey was an official in the
    Ottoman empire, and scores 8 points
beyond prep at or to a point on the other side
of ▶ adv at or to the far side of something
    bez n (**bezes**). A bez is the second spike
    of a deer's antler. This is a really handy
    word when you have Z on your rack.
    Bez scores 14 points.
    bezique n (**beziques**). Bezique is a card
    game; if you're lucky enough to be able

to play it, you'll score 27 points.

bi *adj, n (pl* -s) short for bisexual

biannual *adj* occurring twice a year
> **biannually** *adv*
  biannually *adv* ▷ biannual

bias *n (pl* -es) mental tendency, esp. prejudice
  ▶ *v* (-ases, -asing, -ased *or* -asses
  or -assed) cause to have a bias > **biased,
  biassed** *adj*
  biased *v* ▷ bias
  biases *n, v* ▷ bias
  biasing *v* ▷ bias
  biassed *v* ▷ bias
  biasses *n, v* ▷ bias
  biassing *v* ▷ bias

bib *n (pl* -s) piece of cloth or plastic worn to
  protect a young child's clothes when eating

bible *n (pl* -s) book regarded as authoritative
  > **biblical** *adj*
  bibles *n* ▷ bible
  biblical *n* ▷ bible
  bibliographer *n* ▷ bibliography
  bibliographers *n* ▷ bibliography
  bibliographies *n* ▷ bibliography

bibliography *n (pl* -phies) list of books on a
  subject > **bibliographer** *n (pl* -s)

bibliophile *n (pl* -s) person who collects or is
  fond of books
  bibliophiles *n* ▷ bibliophile
  bibs *n* ▷ bib

bibulous *adj* addicted to alcohol

bicarbonate *n (pl* -s) salt of carbonic acid
  bicarbonates *n* ▷ bicarbonate
  bicentenaries *n* ▷ bicentenary

bicentenary *n (pl* -naries) 200th anniversary

biceps *n (pl* -es) muscle with two origins, esp.
  the muscle that flexes the forearm

bicker *v* (-s, -ing, -ed) argue over petty matters
  bickered *v* ▷ bicker
  bickering *v* ▷ bicker
  bickers *v* ▷ bicker

bicycle *n (pl* -s) vehicle with two wheels, one
  behind the other, pedalled by the rider
  bicycles *n* ▷ bicycle

bid *v* (bids, bidding, bade, bidden) say (a
  greeting) (*past* bid) ▶ *n (pl* -s) offer of a
  specified amount > **bidder** *n (pl* -s)

biddable *adj* obedient
  bidden *v* ▷ bid
  bidder *n* ▷ bid
  bidders *n* ▷ bid

bidding *n (pl* -s) command ▶ *v* ▷ bid

bide *v* (bides, biding, bided) wait patiently for
  an opportunity
  bided *v* ▷ bide

bides *v* ▷ bide

bidet [bee-day] *n (pl* -s) low basin for washing
  the genital area
  bidets *n* ▷ bidet

biding *v* ▷ bide

bids *v, n* ▷ bid

biennial *adj* occurring every two years ▶ *n*
  (*pl* -s) plant that completes its life cycle in
  two years
  biennials *n* ▷ biennial

bier *n (pl* -s) stand on which a corpse or coffin
  rests before burial
  biers *n* ▷ bier

bifocals *pl n* spectacles with lenses permitting
  near and distant vision

big *adj* (bigger, biggest) of considerable size,
  height, number, or capacity ▶ *adv* on a grand
  scale
  bigamies *n* ▷ bigamy
  bigamist *n* ▷ bigamy
  bigamists *n* ▷ bigamy
  bigamous *adj* ▷ bigamy
  bigamously *adv* ▷ bigamy

bigamy *n (pl* -mies) crime of marrying a
  person while still legally married to someone
  else > **bigamist** *n (pl* -s) > **bigamous** *adj*
  > **bigamously** *adv*
  bigger *adj* ▷ big
  biggest *adj* ▷ big

bighead *n (pl* -s) (*Informal*) conceited person
  > **bigheaded** *adj*
  bigheaded *n* ▷ bighead
  bigheads *n* ▷ bighead

bigot *n (pl* -s) person who is intolerant, esp.
  regarding religion or race > **bigoted** *adj*
  > **bigotry** *n (pl* -tries)
  bigoted *adj* ▷ bigot
  bigotries *n* ▷ bigot
  bigotry *n* ▷ bigot
  bigots *n* ▷ bigot

bigwig *n (pl* -s) (*Informal*) important person
  bigwigs *n* ▷ bigwig

  bijou *n* (bijoux). A bijou is an intricate
  trinket. The plural form, bijoux, uses an
  X and allows you to score 22 points.

bike *n (pl* -s) (*Informal*) bicycle or motorcycle
  bikes *n* ▷ bike

bikini *n (pl* -s) woman's brief two-piece
  swimming costume
  bikinis *n* ▷ bikini

bilateral *adj* affecting or undertaken by two
  parties > **bilaterally** *adv*
  bilaterally *adv* ▷ bilateral
  bilberries *n* ▷ bilberry

bilberry *n (pl* -berries) bluish-black edible berry

bilbies n ▷ bilby

bilby n (pl -bies) Australian marsupial with long pointed ears and grey fur

bile n (pl -s) bitter yellow fluid secreted by the liver

biles n ▷ bile

bilge n (pl -s) (Informal) nonsense

bilges n ▷ bilge

bilingual adj involving or using two languages

bilious adj sick, nauseous > **biliousness** n

biliousness n ▷ bilious

bill¹ n (pl -s) statement of money owed for goods or services supplied ▶ v (-s, -ing, -ed) send or present a bill to

bill² n (pl -s) bird's beak

billabong n (pl -s) (AUST) stagnant pool in an intermittent stream

billabongs n ▷ billabong

billed v ▷ bill¹

billet v (-lets, -leting, -leted) assign a lodging to (a soldier) ▶ n (pl -s) accommodation for a soldier in civil lodgings

billeted v ▷ billet

billeting v ▷ billet

billets v, n ▷ billet

billhook n (pl -s) tool with a hooked blade, used for chopping etc.

billhooks n ▷ billhook

billiards n game played on a table with balls and a cue

billies n ▷ billy

billing v ▷ bill¹

billion n (pl -s) one thousand million > **billionth** adj

billions n ▷ billion

billionth adj ▷ billion

billow n (pl -s) large sea wave ▶ v (-s, -ing, -ed) rise up or swell out > **billowy, billowing** adj

billowed v ▷ billow

billowing v, adj ▷ billow

billows n, v ▷ billow

billowy adj ▷ billow

bills n ▷ bill¹, ² ▶ v ▷ bill¹

billy, billycan n (pl -lies, -s) metal can or pot for cooking on a camp fire

billycan n ▷ billy

billycans n ▷ billy

biltong n (pl -s) (S AFR) strips of dried meat

biltongs n ▷ biltong

bimbo n (pl -s) (Slang) attractive but empty-headed young person, esp. a woman

bimbos n ▷ bimbo

bin n (pl -s) container for rubbish or for storing grain, coal, etc.

binary adj composed of two parts (MATHS) (COMPUTERS)

bind v (binds, binding, bound) make secure with or as if with a rope ▶ n (pl -s) (Informal) annoying situation

binder n (pl -s) firm cover for holding loose sheets of paper together

binders n ▷ binder

binding n (pl -s) anything that binds or fastens ▶ n ▷ bind

bindings n ▷ binding

bindweed n (pl -s) plant that twines around a support

bindweeds n ▷ bindweed

binge n (pl -s) (Informal) bout of excessive indulgence, esp. in drink

binges n ▷ binge

bingo n (pl -s) gambling game in which numbers are called out and covered by the players on their individual cards

bingos n ▷ bingo

binoculars pl n optical instrument consisting of two small telescopes joined together

binomial n (pl -s), adj (mathematical expression) consisting of two terms

binomials n ▷ binomial

bins n ▷ bin

biochemistries n ▷ biochemistry

biochemistry n (pl -ries) study of the chemistry of living things > **biochemist** n (pl -s)

biochemists n ▷ biochemistry

biodegradable adj capable of being decomposed by natural means

biodiversities n ▷ biodiversity

biodiversity n (pl -ities) existence of a wide variety of species in their natural environment

biographer n (pl -s) person who writes an account of another person's life

biographers n ▷ biographer

biographical n ▷ biography

biographies n ▷ biography

biography n (pl -phies) account of a person's life by another person > **biographical** adj

biological adj of or relating to biology > **biologically** adv

biologically adv ▷ biological

biologies n ▷ biology

biologist n ▷ biology

biologists n ▷ biology

biology n (pl -ogies) study of living organisms > **biologist** n (pl -s)

biometric adj of any automated system using physiological or behavioural traits as a means of identification.

bionic *adj* having a part of the body that is operated electronically
  biopsies *n* ▷ biopsy

biopsy *n* (*pl* -sies) examination of tissue from a living body
  biotechnologies *n* ▷ biotechnology

biotechnology *n* (*pl* -ologies) use of microorganisms, such as cells or bacteria, in industry and technology

bioterrorism *n* (*pl* -s) use of viruses, bacteria, etc., by terrorists > **bioterrorist** *n* (*pl* -s)
  bioterrorisms *n* ▷ bioterrorism
  bioterrorists *n* ▷ bioterrorism

biped [bye-ped] *n* (*pl* -s) animal with two feet
  bipeds *n* ▷ biped

biplane *n* (*pl* -s) aeroplane with two sets of wings, one above the other
  biplanes *n* ▷ biplane

birch *n* (*pl* -es) tree with thin peeling bark
  birches *n* ▷ birch

bird *n* (*pl* -s) creature with feathers and wings, most types of which can fly

birdie *n* (*pl* -s) (GOLF) score of one stroke under par for a hole
  birdies *n* ▷ birdie
  birds *n* ▷ bird

biretta *n* (*pl* -s) stiff square cap worn by the Catholic clergy
  birettas *n* ▷ biretta

birth *n* (*pl* -s) process of bearing young; childbirth

birthday *n* (*pl* -s) anniversary of the day of one's birth
  birthdays *n* ▷ birthday

birthmark *n* (*pl* -s) blemish on the skin formed before birth
  birthmarks *n* ▷ birthmark

birthright *n* (*pl* -s) privileges or possessions that someone is entitled to as soon as he or she is born
  birthrights *n* ▷ birthright
  births *n* ▷ birth
  bis *n* ▷ bi

biscuit *n* (*pl* -s) small flat dry sweet or plain cake
  biscuits *n* ▷ biscuit

bisect *v* (-s, -ing, -ed) divide into two equal parts
  bisected *v* ▷ bisect
  bisecting *v* ▷ bisect
  bisects *v* ▷ bisect

bisexual *adj* sexually attracted to both men and women > **bisexuality** *n* (*pl* -ties)
  bisexualities *n* ▷ bisexual
  bisexuality *n* ▷ bisexual

bishop *n* (*pl* -s) clergyman who governs a diocese

bishopric *n* (*pl* -s) diocese or office of a bishop
  bishoprics *n* ▷ bishopric
  bishops *n* ▷ bishop

bismuth *n* (*pl* -s) (CHEM) pinkish-white metallic element
  bismuths *n* ▷ bismuth

bison *n* (*pl* -bison) large hairy animal of the cattle family, native to N America and Europe

bistro *n* (*pl* -s) small restaurant
  bistros *n* ▷ bistro

bit[1] *n* (*pl* -s) small piece, portion, or quantity

bit[2] *n* (*pl* -s) metal mouthpiece on a bridle
  bit3 *v* ▷ bite

bit[3] *n* (*pl* -s) (MATHS) (COMPUTERS) single digit of binary notation, either 0 or 1

bitch *n* (*pl* -es) female dog, fox, or wolf ▶ *v* (-es, -ing, -ed) (*Informal*) complain or grumble > **bitchy** *adj* (-ier, -iest) > **bitchiness** *n*
  bitched *v* ▷ bitch
  bitches *n, v* ▷ bitch
  bitchier *adj* ▷ bitch
  bitchiest *adj* ▷ bitch
  bitching *v* ▷ bitch
  bitchy *adj* ▷ bitch

bite *v* (bites, biting, bit, bitten) grip, tear, or puncture the skin, as with the teeth or jaws ▶ *n* (*pl* -s) act of biting > **biter** *n* (*pl* -s)
  biter *n* ▷ bite
  biters *n* ▷ bite
  bites *v, n* ▷ bite

biting *adj* piercing or keen ▶ *v* ▷ bite
  bits *n* ▷ bit[1, 2, 4]
  bitten *v* ▷ bite

bitter *adj* (-er, -est) having a sharp unpleasant taste ▶ *n* (*pl* -s) beer with a slightly bitter taste ▶ *pl* bitter-tasting alcoholic drink > **bitterly** *adv* > **bitterness** *n* (*pl* -es)
  bitterer *adj* ▷ bitter
  bitterest *adj* ▷ bitter
  bitterly *adv* ▷ bitter

bittern *n* (*pl* -s) wading marsh bird with a booming call
  bitterness *n* ▷ bitter
  bitternesses *n* ▷ bitter
  bitterns *n* ▷ bittern
  bitters *n* ▷ bitter

bitumen *n* (*pl* -s) black sticky substance obtained from tar or petrol
  bitumens *n* ▷ bitumen

bivalve *n* (*pl* -s) ▶ *adj* (marine mollusc) with two hinged segments to its shell
  bivalves *n* ▷ bivalve

bivouac *n* (*pl* -s) temporary camp in the

open air ▶ v (-acs, -acking, -acked) camp in a bivouac

bivouacked v ▷ bivouac

bivouacking v ▷ bivouac

bivouacs n, v ▷ bivouac

bizarre adj odd or unusual **> bizarrely** adv **> bizarreness** n

bizarrely adv ▷ bizarre

bizarreness n ▷ bizarre

blab v (blabs, blabbing, blabbed) reveal (secrets) indiscreetly

blabbed v ▷ blab

blabbing v ▷ blab

blabs v ▷ blab

black adj (-er, -est) of the darkest colour, like coal ▶ n (pl -s) darkest colour ▶ v (-s, -ing, -ed) make black **> blackness** n

blackball v (-balls, -balling, -balled) exclude from a group ▶ n (pl -balls) (NZ) hard boiled sweet with black-and-white stripes

blackballed v ▷ blackball

blackballing v ▷ blackball

blackballs v, n ▷ blackball

blackberries n ▷ blackberry

blackberry n (pl -rries) small blackish edible fruit

blackbird n (pl -s) common European thrush

blackbirds n ▷ blackbird

blackboard n (pl -s) hard black surface used for writing on with chalk

blackboards n ▷ blackboard

blackboy n (pl -s) Australian plant with grasslike leaves and a spike of small white flowers

blackboys n ▷ blackboy

blackbutt n (pl -s) Australian eucalyptus tree with hard wood used as timber

blackbutts n ▷ blackbutt

blackcurrant n (pl -s) very small blackish edible fruit that grows in bunches

blackcurrants n ▷ blackcurrant

blacked v ▷ black

blacken v (-s, -ing, -ed) make or become black

blackened v ▷ blacken

blackening v ▷ blacken

blackens v ▷ blacken

blacker adj ▷ black

blackest adj ▷ black

blackfish n (pl blackfish) small dark Australian estuary fish

blackguard [**blag**-gard] n (pl -s) unprincipled person

blackguards n ▷ blackguard

blackhead n (pl -s) black-tipped plug of fatty matter clogging a skin pore

blackheads n ▷ blackhead

blacking v ▷ black

blackleg n (pl -s) person who continues to work during a strike

blacklegs n ▷ blackleg

blacklist n (pl -s) list of people or organizations considered untrustworthy etc.

blacklists n ▷ blacklist

blackmail n (pl -s) act of attempting to extort money by threats ▶ v (-s, -ing, -ed) (attempt to) obtain money by blackmail

blackmailed v ▷ blackmail

blackmailing v ▷ blackmail

blackmails n, v ▷ blackmail

blackness n ▷ black

blackout n (pl -s) extinguishing of all light as a precaution against an air attack

blackouts n ▷ blackout

blacks n, v ▷ black

blacksmith n (pl -s) person who works iron with a furnace, anvil, etc.

blacksmiths n ▷ blacksmith

bladder n (pl -s) sac in the body where urine is held

bladders n ▷ bladder

blade n (pl -s) cutting edge of a weapon or tool

blades n ▷ blade

blame v (-mes, -ming, -med) consider (someone) responsible for ▶ n (pl -s) responsibility for something that is wrong **> blameless** adj

blamed v ▷ blame

blameless adj ▷ blame

blames v, n ▷ blame

blameworthy adj deserving blame

blaming v ▷ blame

blanch v (-es, -ing, -ed) become white or pale

blanched v ▷ blanch

blanches v ▷ blanch

blanching v ▷ blanch

blancmange [blam-**monzh**] n (pl -s) jelly-like dessert made with milk

blancmanges n ▷ blancmange

bland adj (-er, -est) dull and uninteresting **> blandly** adv

blander adj ▷ bland

blandest adj ▷ bland

blandishments pl n flattery intended to coax or persuade

blandly adj ▷ bland

blank adj not written on ▶ n (pl -s) empty space **> blankly** adv

blanket n (pl -s) large thick cloth used as covering for a bed ▶ v (-s, -ing, -ed) cover as with a blanket

blanketed v ▷ blanket
blanketing v ▷ blanket
blankets n, v ▷ blanket
blankly adv ▷ blank
blanks n ▷ blank
blare v (blares, blaring, blared) sound loudly and harshly ▶ n (pl -s) loud harsh noise
blared v ▷ blare
blares v, n ▷ blare
blaring v ▷ blare
blarney n (pl -s) flattering talk
blarneys n ▷ blarney
blasé [blah-zay] adj indifferent or bored through familiarity
blaspheme v (-phemes, -pheming, -phemed) speak disrespectfully of (God or sacred things) ▶ **blasphemy** n (pl -phemies) > **blasphemous** adj > **blasphemously** adv > **blasphemer** n (pl -s)
blasphemed v ▷ blaspheme
blasphemer n ▷ blaspheme
blasphemers n ▷ blaspheme
blasphemes v ▷ blaspheme
blasphemies n ▷ blaspheme
blaspheming v ▷ blaspheme
blasphemous v ▷ blaspheme
blasphemously v ▷ blaspheme
blast n (pl -s) explosion ▶ v (-s, -ing, -ed) blow up (a rock etc.) with explosives
blasted v ▷ blast
blasting v ▷ blast
blastoff n (pl -s) launching of a rocket
blastoffs n ▷ blastoff
blasts n, v ▷ blast
blatant adj glaringly obvious > **blatantly** adv
blatantly adv ▷ blatant
blaze¹ n (pl -s) strong fire or flame ▶ v (-s, -ing, -d) burn or shine brightly
blaze² n (pl -s) mark made on a tree to indicate a route
blazed v ▷ blaze¹
blazer n (pl -s) lightweight jacket, often in the colours of a school etc.
blazers n ▷ blazer
blazes n ▷ blaze¹,² ▶ v ▷ blaze¹
blazing v ▷ blaze¹
blazon v (-s, -ing, -ed) proclaim publicly
blazoned v ▷ blazon
blazoning v ▷ blazon
blazons v ▷ blazon
bleach v (-es, -ing, -ed) make or become white or colourless ▶ n (pl -es) bleaching agent
bleached v ▷ bleach
bleaches v, n ▷ bleach
bleaching v ▷ bleach

bleak adj (-er, -est) exposed and barren > **bleakly** adv > **bleakness** n (pl -es)
bleaker adj ▷ bleak
bleakest adj ▷ bleak
bleakly adv ▷ bleak
bleakness n ▷ bleak
bleaknesses n ▷ bleak
blearier adj ▷ bleary
bleariest adj ▷ bleary
blearily adv ▷ bleary
bleariness n ▷ bleary
blearinesses n ▷ bleary
bleary adj (-rier, -riest) with eyes dimmed, as by tears or tiredness > **blearily** adv > **bleariness** n (pl -es)
bleat v (-s, -ing, -ed) (of a sheep, goat, or calf) utter its plaintive cry ▶ n (pl -s) cry of sheep, goats, and calves
bleated v ▷ bleat
bleating v ▷ bleat
bleats v, n ▷ bleat
bled v ▷ bleed
bleed v (-s, -ing, bled) lose or emit blood
bleeding v ▷ bleed
bleeds v ▷ bleed
bleep n (pl -s) short high-pitched sound made by an electrical device ▶ v (-s, -ing, -ed) make a bleeping sound
bleeped v ▷ bleep
bleeper n (pl -s) small portable radio receiver that makes a bleeping signal
bleepers n ▷ bleeper
bleeping v ▷ bleep
bleeps n, v ▷ bleep
blemish n (pl -es) defect or stain ▶ v (-es, -ing, -ed) spoil or tarnish
blemished v ▷ blemish
blemishes n, v ▷ blemish
blemishing v ▷ blemish
blench v (-es, -ing, -ed) shy away, as in fear
blenched v ▷ blench
blenches v ▷ blench
blenching v ▷ blench
blend v (-s, -ing, -ed) mix or mingle (components or ingredients) ▶ n (pl -s) mixture
blended v ▷ blend
blender n (pl -s) electrical appliance for puréeing vegetables etc.
blenders n ▷ blender
blending v ▷ blend
blends v, n ▷ blend
bless v (-es, -ing, -ed) make holy by means of a religious rite
blessed adj holy ▶ v ▷ blessed > **blessedness** n

blessedness n ▷ blessed

blesses v ▷ bless

blessing n (pl -s) invoking of divine aid ▶ v ▷ bless

blessings n ▷ blessing

blether (Scot) v (-s, -ing, -ed) talk, esp. foolishly or at length ▶ n (pl -s) conversation

blethered v ▷ blether

blethering v ▷ blether

blethers v, n ▷ blether

blew v ▷ blow¹

blight n (pl -s) person or thing that spoils or prevents growth ▶ v (-s, -ing, -ed) frustrate or disappoint

blighted v ▷ blight

blighter n (pl -s) (Informal) irritating person

blighters n ▷ blighter

blighting v ▷ blight

blights n, v ▷ blight

blimp n (pl -s) small airship

blimps n ▷ blimp

blind adj (-er, -est) unable to see ▶ v (-s, -ing, -ed) deprive of sight ▶ n (pl -s) covering for a window > **blindly** adv > **blindness** n (pl -es)

blinded v ▷ blind

blinder adj ▷ blind

blindest adj ▷ blind

blindfold v (-s, -ing, -ed) prevent (a person) from seeing by covering the eyes ▶ n (pl -s) piece of cloth used to cover the eyes

blindfolded v ▷ blindfold

blindfolding v ▷ blindfold

blindfolds v, n ▷ blindfold

blinding adj, v ▷ blind

blindly adv ▷ blind

blindness n ▷ blind

blindnesses n ▷ blind

blinds v, n ▷ blind

blink v (-s, -ing, -ed) close and immediately reopen (the eyes) ▶ n (pl -s) act of blinking

blinked v ▷ blink

blinkers pl n leather flaps on a horse's bridle to prevent sideways vision

blinking v ▷ blink

blinks v, n ▷ blink

blip n (pl -s) spot of light on a radar screen indicating the position of an object

blips n ▷ blip

bliss n (pl -es) perfect happiness > **blissful** adj > **blissfully** adv

blisses n ▷ bliss

blissful adj ▷ bliss

blissfully adv ▷ bliss

blister n (pl -s) small bubble on the skin ▶ v (-s, -ing, -ed) (cause to) have blisters

blistered v ▷ blister

blistering adj (of weather) very hot ▶ v ▷ blister > **blisteringly** adv

blisteringly adv ▷ blistering

blisters n, v ▷ blister

blithe adj (-r, -st) casual and indifferent > **blithely** adv > **blitheness** n (pl -es)

blithely adv ▷ blithe

blitheness n ▷ blithe

blithenesses n ▷ blithe

blither adj ▷ blithe

blithest adj ▷ blithe

blitz n (pl -es) violent and sustained attack by aircraft ▶ v (-es, -ing, -ed) attack suddenly and intensively

blitzed v ▷ blitz

blitzes n, v ▷ blitz

blitzing v ▷ blitz

blizzard n (pl -s) blinding storm of wind and snow

blizzards n ▷ blizzard

bloat v (-s, -ing, -ed) cause to swell, as with liquid or air

bloated v ▷ bloat

bloater n (pl -s) (Brit) salted smoked herring

bloaters n ▷ bloater

bloating v ▷ bloat

bloats v ▷ bloat

blob n (pl -s) soft mass or drop

blobs n ▷ blob

bloc n (pl -s) people or countries combined by a common interest

block n (pl -s) large solid piece of wood, stone, etc. ▶ v (-s, -ing, -ed) obstruct or impede by introducing an obstacle > **blockage** n (pl -s)

blockade n (pl -s) sealing off of a place to prevent the passage of goods ▶ v (-ades, -ading, -aded) impose a blockade on

blockaded n ▷ blockade

blockades n, v ▷ blockade

blockading v ▷ blockade

blockage n ▷ block

blockages n ▷ block

blocked v ▷ block

blockhead n (pl -s) stupid person

blockheads n ▷ blockhead

blockie n (pl -s) (Aust) owner of a small property, esp. a farm

blockies n ▷ blockie

blocking v ▷ block

blocks n, v ▷ block

blocs n ▷ bloc

blog n (pl -s) ▷ weblog

blogs n ▷ blog

bloke n (pl -s) (Informal) man

blokes n ▷ bloke
blonde, *masc* **blond** *adj,* n (*pl* -es, -s) fair-haired (person)
blondes n ▷ blonde
blonds n ▷ blonde
blood n (*pl* -s) red fluid that flows around the body > **bloodless** *adj* > **bloodlessness** n
bloodhound n (*pl* -s) large dog formerly used for tracking
bloodhounds n ▷ bloodhound
bloodied v ▷ bloody
bloodies v ▷ bloody
bloodily *adv* ▷ bloody
bloodiness n ▷ bloody
bloodless *adj* ▷ bloody
bloodlessness n ▷ blood
bloods n ▷ blood
bloodshed n (*pl* -s) slaughter or killing
bloodsheds n ▷ bloodshed
bloodshot *adj* (of an eye) inflamed
bloodstream n (*pl* -s) flow of blood round the body
bloodstreams n ▷ bloodstream
bloodsucker n (*pl* -s) animal that sucks blood
bloodsuckers n ▷ bloodsucker
bloodthirstily *adv* ▷ bloodthirsty
bloodthirstiness n ▷ bloodthirsty
bloodthirsty *adj* taking pleasure in violence > **bloodthirstily** *adv* > **bloodthirstiness** n
bloody *adj* covered with blood ▶ *adj, adv* (Slang) extreme or extremely ▶ v (-dies, -dying, -died) stain with blood > **bloodily** *adv* > **bloodiness** n
bloodying v ▷ bloody
bloom n (*pl* -s) blossom on a flowering plant ▶ v (-s, -ing, -ed) bear flowers
bloomed v ▷ bloom
bloomer n (*pl* -s) (BRIT) (*Informal*) stupid mistake
bloomers n ▷ bloomer ▶ *pl* n woman's baggy knickers
blooming v ▷ bloom
blooms n, v ▷ bloom
blooper n (*pl* -s) (CHIEFLY US) (*Informal*) stupid mistake
bloopers n ▷ blooper
blossom n (*pl* -s) flowers of a plant ▶ v (-s, -ing, -ed) (of plants) flower
blossomed v ▷ blossom
blossoming v ▷ blossom
blossoms n, v ▷ blossom
blot n (*pl* -s) spot or stain ▶ v (-s, -tting, -tted) cause a blemish in or on > **blotter** n (*pl* -s)
blotch n (*pl* -es) discoloured area or stain > **blotchy** *adj*
blotches n ▷ blotch
blotchy *adj* ▷ blotch

blots n, v ▷ blot
blotted v ▷ blot
blotter n ▷ blot
blotters n ▷ blot
blotting v ▷ blot
blotto *adj* (BRIT, AUST & NZ) (*Slang*) extremely drunk
blouse n (*pl* -s) woman's shirtlike garment
blouses n ▷ blouse
blow¹ v (-s, -ing, blew, blown) (of air, the wind, etc.) move ▶ **blower** n (*pl* -s)
blow² n (*pl* -s) hard hit
blower n ▷ blow¹
blowers n ▷ blow¹
blowie n (*pl* blowies) (AUST) (*Informal*) bluebottle
blowier n ▷ blowy
blowies n ▷ blowie
blowiest n ▷ blowy
blowing v ▷ blow¹
blown v ▷ blow¹
blowout n (*pl* -s) sudden loss of air in a tyre
blowouts n ▷ blowout
blows v ▷ blow¹ ▶ n ▷ blow²
blowsier n ▷ blowsy
blowsiest n ▷ blowsy
blowsy *adj* (-sier, -siest) fat, untidy, and red-faced
blowy *adj* (-wier, -wiest) windy
blubber n (*pl* -s) fat of whales, seals, etc. ▶ v (-s, -ing, -ed) sob without restraint
blubbered v ▷ blubber
blubbering v ▷ blubber
blubbers n, v ▷ blubber
bludge (*Informal*) v (-s, -ging, -d) (AUST & NZ) evade work (AUST & NZ) ▶ n (*pl* -s) (AUST) easy task
bludged v ▷ bludge
bludgeon n (*pl* -s) short thick club ▶ v (-s, -ing, -ed) hit with a bludgeon
bludgeoned v ▷ bludgeon
bludgeoning v ▷ bludgeon
bludgeons n, v ▷ bludgeon
bludger n (*pl* -s) person who scrounges
bludgers n ▷ bludger
bludges v, n ▷ bludge
bludging v ▷ bludge
blue n (*pl* -s) colour of a clear unclouded sky ▶ *pl* feeling of depression ▶ *adj* (bluer, bluest) of the colour blue > **bluish** *adj*
bluebell n (*pl* -s) flower with blue bell-shaped flowers
bluebells n ▷ bluebell
bluebottle n (*pl* -s) large fly with a dark-blue body
bluebottles n ▷ bluebottle

blueprint *n* (*pl* -s) photographic print of a plan
blueprints *n* ▷ blueprint
bluer *adj* ▷ blue
blues *n* ▷ blue
bluest *adj* ▷ blue
bluetongue *n* (*pl* -s) Australian lizard with a blue tongue
bluetongues *n* ▷ bluetongue
bluff¹ *v* (-s, -ing, -ed) pretend to be confident in order to influence (someone) ▶ *n* (*pl* -s) act of bluffing
bluff² *n* (*pl* -s) steep cliff or bank ▶ *adj* good-naturedly frank and hearty
bluffed *v* ▷ bluff¹
bluffing *v* ▷ bluff¹
bluffs *v*, *n* ▷ bluff¹, ²
bluish *adj* ▷ blue
blunder *n* (*pl* -s) clumsy mistake ▶ *v* (-s, -ing, -ed) make a blunder
blunderbuss *n* (*pl* -es) obsolete gun with a wide flared muzzle
blunderbusses *n* ▷ blunderbuss
blundered *v* ▷ blunder
blundering *v* ▷ blunder
blunders *n*, *v* ▷ blunder
blunt *adj* (blunter, bluntest) not having a sharp edge or point ▶ *v* (-s, -ing, -ed) make less sharp > **bluntly** *adv* > **bluntness** *n*
blunted *v* ▷ blunt
blunter *adj* ▷ blunt
bluntest *adj* ▷ blunt
blunting *v* ▷ blunt
bluntly *adv* ▷ blunt
bluntness *n* ▷ blunt
blunts *v* ▷ blunt
blur *v* (-s, -rring, -rred) make or become vague or less distinct ▶ *n* (*pl* -s) something vague, hazy, or indistinct > **blurry** *adj* (-rier, -rriest)
blurb *n* (*pl* -s) promotional description, as on the jacket of a book
blurbs *n* ▷ blurb
blurred *v* ▷ blur
blurrier *adj* ▷ blur
blurriest *adj* ▷ blur
blurring *v* ▷ blur
blurry *adj* ▷ blur
blurs *v*, *n* ▷ blur
blurt *v* (-s, -ing, -ed) (*foll. by* out) utter suddenly and involuntarily
blurted *v* ▷ blurt
blurting *v* ▷ blurt
blurts *v* ▷ blurt
blush *v* (-es, -ing, -ed) become red in the face, esp. from embarrassment or shame ▶ *n* (*pl* -es) reddening of the face

blushed *v* ▷ blush
blushes *v*, *n* ▷ blush
blushing *v* ▷ blush
bluster *v* (-s, -ing, -ed) speak loudly or in a bullying way ▶ *n* (*pl* -s) empty threats or protests
blustered *v* ▷ bluster
blusteriness *n* ▷ blustery
blustering *v* ▷ bluster
blusters *v*, *n* ▷ bluster
blustery *adj* (of weather) rough and windy > **blusteriness** *n*

bo or **boh** interjection. Bo is an exclamation used to startle someone. Bo scores 4 points, while boh scores 8.

boa *n* (*pl* -s) large nonvenomous snake
boab [boh-ab] *n* (*pl* -s) (AUST) (*Informal*) ▷ baobab
boabs *n* ▷ boab
boar *n* (*pl* -s) uncastrated male pig
board *n* (*pl* -s) long flat piece of sawn timber ▶ *v* (-s, -ing, -ed) go aboard (a train, aeroplane, etc.)
boarded *v* ▷ board
boarder *n* (*pl* -s) person who pays rent in return for accommodation in someone else's home
boarders *n* ▷ boarder
boarding *v* ▷ board
boardroom *n* (*pl* -s) room where the board of a company meets
boardrooms *n* ▷ boardroom
boards *n*, *v* ▷ board
boars *n* ▷ boar
boas *n* ▷ boa
boast *v* (-s, -ing, -ed) speak too proudly about one's talents etc. ▶ *n* (*pl* -s) bragging statement > **boastful** *adj* > **boastfully** *adv* > **boastfulness** *n*
boasted *v* ▷ boast
boastful *adj* ▷ boast
boastfully *adv* ▷ boast
boastfulness *n* ▷ boast
boasting *v* ▷ boast
boasts *v*, *n* ▷ boast
boat *n* (*pl* -s) small vehicle for travelling across water > **boating** *n*
boater *n* (*pl* -s) flat straw hat
boaters *n* ▷ boater
boating *n* ▷ boat
boats *n* ▷ boat
boatswain *n* (*pl* -s) ▷ bosun
boatswains *n* ▷ boatswain
bob¹ *v* (bobs, bobbing, bobbed) move up and down repeatedly ▶ *n* (*pl* -s) short abrupt movement
bob² *n* (*pl* -s) hairstyle in which the hair is cut

short evenly all round the head ▸ v (bobs, bobbing, bobbed) cut (the hair) in a bob
bobbed v ▷ bob[1, 2]
bobbies n ▷ bobby
bobbin n (pl -s) reel on which thread is wound
bobbing v ▷ bob[1, 2]
bobbins n ▷ bobbin
bobble n (pl -s) small ball of material, usu. for decoration
bobbles n ▷ bobble
bobby n (pl -bies) (BRIT) (Informal) policeman
bobotie [ba-boot-ee] n (pl -s) (S AFR) dish of curried mince
boboties n ▷ bobotie
bobs v ▷ bob[1, 2] ▸ n[1, 2]
bobsleigh n (pl -s) sledge for racing down an icy track ▸ v (-s, -ing, -ed) ride on a bobsleigh
bobsleighed v ▷ bobsleigh
bobsleighing v ▷ bobsleigh
bobsleighs n, v ▷ bobsleigh
bode v (-s, -ding, -ed) be an omen of (good or ill)
boded v ▷ bode
bodes v ▷ bode
bodice n (pl -s) upper part of a dress
bodices n ▷ bodice
bodies n ▷ body
bodily adj relating to the body ▸ adv by taking hold of the body
boding v ▷ bode
bodkin n (pl -s) blunt large-eyed needle
bodkins n ▷ bodkin
body n (pl -dies) entire physical structure of an animal or human
bodyboard n (pl -s) small polystyrene surfboard
bodyboards n ▷ bodyboard
bodyguard n (pl -s) person or group of people employed to protect someone
bodyguards n ▷ bodyguard
bodywork n (pl -s) outer shell of a vehicle
bodyworks n ▷ bodywork
boerewors n (S AFR) spiced sausage
boffin n (pl -s) (BRIT, AUST, NZ & S AFR) (Informal) scientist or expert
boffins n ▷ boffin
bog n (pl -s) wet spongy ground > **boggy** adj (boggier, boggiest)
bogan n (pl -s) (AUST DATED & NZ) (Slang) youth who dresses and behaves rebelliously
bogans n ▷ bogan
bogey, bogy n (pl bogeys, bogies) something that worries or annoys
bogeys n ▷ bogey
boggier adj ▷ bog

boggiest adj ▷ bog
boggle v (boggles, boggling, boggled) be surprised, confused, or alarmed
boggled v ▷ boggle
boggles v ▷ boggle
boggling v ▷ boggle
boggy adj ▷ bog
bogies n ▷ bogey
bogong, bugong n (pl -s, -s) large nocturnal Australian moth
bogongs n ▷ bogong
bogs n ▷ bog
bogus adj not genuine
bogusnesses n ▷ bogus
bogy n (pl -gies) ▷ bogey
bohemian n (pl -s) ▸ adj (person) leading an unconventional life
bohemians n ▷ bohemian
boil[1] v (-s, -ing, -ed) (cause to) change from a liquid to a vapour so quickly that bubbles are formed ▸ n (pl -s) state or action of boiling
boil[2] n (pl -s) red pus-filled swelling on the skin
boiled v ▷ boil[1]
boiler n (pl -s) piece of equipment which provides hot water
boilers n ▷ boiler
boiling v ▷ boil[1]
boils v, n ▷ boil[1, 2]
boisterous adj noisy and lively > **boisterously** adv > **boisterousness** n
boisterously adv ▷ boisterous
boisterousness n ▷ boisterous

██ **bok** n (**boks**). A bok is a goat or antelope. Bok scores 9 points.

bold adj (-er, -est) confident and fearless > **boldly** adv > **boldness** n (pl -es)
bolder adj ▷ bold
boldest adj ▷ bold
boldly adv ▷ bold
boldness n ▷ bold
boldnesses n ▷ bold
bole n (pl -s) tree trunk
bolero n (pl -s) (music for) traditional Spanish dance
boleros n ▷ bolero
boles n ▷ bole
bollard n (pl -s) short thick post used to prevent the passage of motor vehicles
bollards n ▷ bollard
boloney n (pl -s) ▷ baloney
boloneys n ▷ boloney
bolshie, bolshy adj (Informal) difficult or rebellious
bolshy n ▷ bolshie
bolster v (-s, -ing, -ed) support or strengthen

▶ *n (pl* -s) long narrow pillow
bolstered *v* ▷ bolster
bolstering *v* ▷ bolster
bolsters *v, n* ▷ bolster
bolt *n (pl* -s) sliding metal bar for fastening a door etc. ▶ *v* (-s, -ing, -ed) run away suddenly
bolted *v* ▷ bolt
bolting *v* ▷ bolt
bolts *n, v* ▷ bolt
bomb *n (pl* -s) container fitted with explosive material ▶ *v* (-s, -ing, -ed) attack with bombs
bombard *v* (-s, -ing, -ed) attack with heavy gunfire or bombs > **bombardment** *n (pl* -s)
bombarded *v* ▷ bombard
bombarding *v* ▷ bombard
bombardment *n* ▷ bombard
bombardments *n* ▷ bombard
bombards *n* ▷ bombard
bombast *n (pl* -s) pompous language
> **bombastic** *adj*
bombastic *adj* ▷ bombast
bombasts *n* ▷ bombast
bombed *v* ▷ bomb
bomber *n (pl* -s) aircraft that drops bombs
bombers *n* ▷ bomber
bombing *v* ▷ bomb
bombs *n, v* ▷ bomb
bombshell *n (pl* -s) shocking or unwelcome surprise
bombshells *n* ▷ bombshell
bonanza *n (pl* -s) sudden good luck or wealth
bonanzas *n* ▷ bonanza
bond *n (pl* -s) something that binds, fastens or holds together ▶ *pl* something that restrains or imprisons ▶ *v* (-s, -ing, -ed) bind > **bonded** *adj*
bondage *n (pl* -s) slavery
bondages *n* ▷ bondage
bonded *v, adj* ▷ bond
bonding *v* ▷ bond
bonds *n, v* ▷ bond
bone *n (pl* -s) any of the hard parts in the body that form the skeleton ▶ *v* (-s, -ing, -d) remove the bones from (meat for cooking etc.)
> **boneless** *adj*
boned *v* ▷ bone
boneless *adj* ▷ bone
bones *n, v* ▷ bone
bonfire *n (pl* -s) large outdoor fire
bonfires *n* ▷ bonfire
bongo *n (pl* -gos, -goes) small drum played with the fingers
bongoes *n* ▷ bongo
bongos *n* ▷ bongo
bonhomie [bon-om-ee] *n (pl* -s) cheerful

friendliness
bonhomies *n* ▷ bonhomie
boning *v* ▷ bone
bonito [ba-nee-toh] *n (pl* -s) small tunny-like marine food fish
bonitos *n* ▷ bonito
bonnet *n (pl* -s) metal cover over a vehicle's engine
bonnets *n* ▷ bonnet
bonnier *adj* ▷ bonny
bonniest *adj* ▷ bonny
bonnily *adv* ▷ bonny
bonny *adj* (-nier, -niest) (Scot) beautiful
> **bonnily** *adv*
bonsai *n (pl* bonsai) ornamental miniature tree or shrub
bonus *n (pl* -es) something given, paid, or received above what is due or expected
bonuses *n* ▷ bonus
bony *adj* having many bones
boo *interj* shout of disapproval ▶ *v* (-s, -ing, -ed) shout 'boo' to show disapproval
boob (Slang) *n (pl* -s) foolish mistake
boobies *n* ▷ booby
boobook [boo-book] *n (pl* -s) small spotted Australian brown owl
boobooks *n* ▷ boobook
boobs *n* ▷ boob
booby *n (pl* -bies) foolish person
booed *v* ▷ boo
boogie *v* (-s, -ing, -ied) (Informal) dance to fast pop music
boogied *v* ▷ boogie
boogieing *v* ▷ boogie
boogies *v* ▷ boogie
booing *v* ▷ boo
book *n (pl* -s) number of pages bound together between covers ▶ *pl* record of transactions of a business or society ▶ *v* (-s, -ing, -ed) reserve (a place, passage, etc.) in advance
booked *n* ▷ book
booking *v* ▷ book
booklet *n (pl* -s) thin book with paper covers
booklets *v* ▷ booklet
bookmaker *n (pl* -s) person whose occupation is taking bets
bookmakers *n* ▷ bookmaker
bookmark *n (pl* -s) strip of material used to mark a place in a book ▶ *v* (-s, -ing, -ed) (COMPUTERS) identify and store (a website) so that one can return to it quickly and easily
bookmarked *v* ▷ bookmark
bookmarking *v* ▷ bookmark
bookmarks *n, v* ▷ bookmark
books *n, v* ▷ book

bookworm n (pl -s) person devoted to reading
bookworms n ▷ bookworm
boom[1] v (-s, -ing, -ed) make a loud deep echoing sound ▶ n (pl -s) loud deep echoing sound
boom[2] n (pl -s) pole to which the foot of a sail is attached
boomed v ▷ boom[1]
boomer n (pl -s) (AUST) large male kangaroo
boomerang n (pl -s) curved wooden missile which can be made to return to the thrower ▶ v (-s, -ing, -ed) (of a plan) recoil unexpectedly
boomeranged n ▷ boomerang
boomeranging v ▷ boomerang
boomerangs n, v ▷ boomerang
boomers n ▷ boomer
booming v ▷ boom[1]
booms v, n ▷ boom[1, 2]
boon n (pl -s) something helpful or beneficial
boongaries n ▷ boongary
boongary [boong-gar-ree] n (pl -garies) tree kangaroo of NE Queensland, Australia
boons n ▷ boon
boor n (pl -s) rude or insensitive person > **boorish** adj > **boorishly** adv > **boorishness** n
boorishly adv ▷ boor
boorishness n ▷ boor
boors n ▷ boor
boos v ▷ boo
boost n (pl -s) encouragement or help ▶ v (-s, -ing, -ed) improve
boosted v ▷ boost
booster n (pl -s) small additional injection of a vaccine
boosters n ▷ booster
boosting v ▷ boost
boosts n, v ▷ boost
boot n (pl -s) outer covering for the foot that extends above the ankle ▶ v (-s, -ing, -ed) (Informal) kick
booted v ▷ boot
bootee n (pl -s) baby's soft shoe
bootees n ▷ bootee
booth n (pl -s) small partly enclosed cubicle
booths n ▷ booth
booties n ▷ booty
booting v ▷ boot[1]
bootleg adj produced, distributed, or sold illicitly ▶ v (-legs, -legging, -legged) make, carry, or sell (illicit goods) > **bootlegger** n (pl -s)
bootlegged v ▷ bootleg
bootlegger n ▷ bootleg
bootleggers n ▷ bootleg

bootlegging v ▷ bootleg
bootlegs v ▷ bootleg
boots n ▶ v ▷ boot
booty n (pl -ties) valuable articles obtained as plunder
booze v (-zes, -zing, -zed) ▶ n (pl -s) (Informal) (consume) alcoholic drink > **boozy** adj (-zier, -ziest) > **boozily** adv
boozed v ▷ booze
boozer n (pl -s) (Informal) person who is fond of drinking
boozers n ▷ booze
boozes v, n ▷ booze
boozier adj ▷ booze
booziest adj ▷ booze
boozily adv ▷ booze
boozing v ▷ booze
boozy adj ▷ booze
bop v (-s, -pping, -pped) (Informal) dance to pop music
bopped v ▷ bop
bopping v ▷ bop
bops v ▷ bop
bora n (pl -s) (AUST) Aboriginal ceremony
boras n ▷ bora
borax n (pl -es) white mineral used in making glass
boraxes n ▷ borax
border n (pl -s) dividing line between political or geographical regions ▶ v (-s, -ing, -ed) provide with a border
bordered v ▷ border
bordering v ▷ border
borders n, v ▷ border
bore[1] v (-s, -ring, -d) make (a hole) with a drill etc. ▶ n (pl -s) (diameter of) the hollow of a gun barrel or other tube
bore[2] v (-s, -ring, -d) make weary by being dull or repetitious ▶ n dull or repetitious person or thing > **bored** adj > **boredom** n
bore[3] n (pl -s) high wave in a narrow estuary, caused by the tide
bore[4] v ▷ bear[1]
bored v, n ▷ bore[1, 2]
boree [baw-ree] n (pl -s) (AUST) ▷ **myall**
borees n ▷ boree
bores n ▷ bore[1, 2, 3] ▷ v ▷ bore[1, 2]
boring v ▷ bore[1, 2]
born v ▷ bear[1] ▶ adj possessing certain qualities from birth
borne v ▷ bear[1]
boron n (pl -s) (CHEM) element used in hardening steel
boronia n (pl -s) Australian aromatic flowering shrub

boronias n ▷ boronia
borons n ▷ boron
borough n (pl -s) (CHIEFLY BRIT) town or district with its own council
boroughs n ▷ borough
borrow v (-s, -ing, -ed) obtain (something) temporarily ▸ **borrower** n (pl -s)
borrowed v ▷ borrow
borrower n ▷ borrow
borrowers n ▷ borrow
borrowing v ▷ borrow
borrows v ▷ borrow
borstal n (pl -s) (formerly in Britain) prison for young criminals
borstals n ▷ borstal
borzoi n (pl -s) tall dog with a long silky coat
borzois n ▷ borzoi
bosh n (pl -es) (BRIT, AUST & NZ) (Informal) empty talk, nonsense
boshes n ▷ bosh
bosom n (pl -s) chest of a person, esp. the female breasts ▸ adj very dear
bosoms n ▷ bosom
boss[1] n (pl -es) person in charge of or employing others ▸ v (-es, -ing, -ed) be domineering towards > **bossy** adj > **bossiness** n
boss[2] n (pl -es) raised knob or stud
bossed v ▷ boss[1]
bosses n ▷ boss[1,2] ▸ v ▷ boss[1]
bossiness n ▷ boss[1]
bossing v ▷ boss[1]
bossy adj ▷ boss[1]
bosun n (pl -s) officer responsible for the maintenance of a ship
bosuns n ▷ bosun
botanic adj ▷ botany
botanical adj ▷ botany
botanies n ▷ botany
botanist n ▷ botany
botanists n ▷ botany
botany n (pl -ies) study of plants > **botanical**, **botanic** adj > **botanist** n (pl -s)
botch v (-es, -ing, -ed) spoil through clumsiness ▸ n (pl -es) (also **botch-up**) (pl -s) badly done piece of work or repair
botched v ▷ botch
botches v, n ▷ botch
botching v ▷ botch
both adj, pron two considered together
bother v (-s, -ing, -ed) take the time or trouble ▸ n (pl -s) trouble, fuss, or difficulty > **bothersome** adj
bothered v ▷ bother
bothering v ▷ bother

bothers v, n ▷ bother
bothersome adj ▷ bother
bottle n (pl -s) container for holding liquids ▸ v (-s, -ttling, -d) put in a bottle
bottled v ▷ bottle
bottleneck n (pl -s) narrow stretch of road where traffic is held up
bottlenecks n ▷ bottleneck
bottles n, v ▷ bottle
bottling v ▷ bottle
bottom n (pl -s) lowest, deepest, or farthest removed part of a thing ▸ adj lowest or last > **bottomless** adj
bottomless adj ▷ bottom
bottoms n ▷ bottom
botulism n (pl -s) severe food poisoning
botulisms n ▷ botulism
boudoir [boo-dwahr] n (pl -s) woman's bedroom or private sitting room
boudoirs n ▷ boudoir
bougainvillea n (pl -s) climbing plant with red or purple flowers
bougainvilleas n ▷ bougainvillea
bough n (pl -s) large branch of a tree
boughs n ▷ bough
bought v ▷ buy
boulder n (pl -s) large rounded rock
boulders n ▷ boulder
boulevard n (pl -s) wide, usu. tree-lined, street
boulevards n ▷ boulevard
bounce v (-s, -cing, -d) (of a ball etc.) rebound from an impact (Slang) ▸ n (pl -s) act of rebounding
bounced v ▷ bounce
bouncer n (pl -s) person employed at a disco etc. to remove unwanted people
bouncers n ▷ bouncer
bounces v, n ▷ bounce
bouncing v ▷ bounce ▸ adj vigorous and robust
bound[1] v (-s, -ing, -ed) ▷ bind ▸ adj destined or certain
bound[2] v (-s, -ing, -ed) move forwards by jumps ▸ n (pl -s) jump upwards or forwards
bound[3] v (-s, -ing, -ed) form a boundary of ▸ pl n limit
bound[4] adj going or intending to go towards
boundaries n ▷ boundary
boundary n (pl -aries) dividing line that indicates the farthest limit
bounded v ▷ bound[2,3]
bounding v ▷ bound[2,3]
bounds v, n ▷ bound[2,3]
bounteous adj ▷ bounty
bounties n ▷ bounty

bountiful *adj* ▷ bounty

bounty *n* (*pl* -ties) generosity > **bountiful**, **bounteous** *adj*

bouquet *n* (*pl* -s) bunch of flowers
bouquets *n* ▷ bouquet

bourbon [bur-bn] *n* (*pl* -s) whiskey made from maize
bourbons *n* ▷ bourbon

bourgeois [boor-zhwah] *adj*, *n* (*pl* bourgeois) middle-class (person)

bout *n* (*pl* -s) period of activity or illness

boutique *n* (*pl* -s) small clothes shop
boutiques *n* ▷ boutique

bouts *n* ▷ bout

bovine *adj* relating to cattle

bow[1] [rhymes with *now*] *v* (-s, -ing, -ed) lower (one's head) or bend (one's knee or body) as a sign of respect or shame ▶ *n* (*pl* -s) movement made when bowing

bow[2] [rhymes with *go*] *n* (*pl* -s) knot with two loops and loose ends

bow[3] [rhymes with *now*] *n* (*pl* -s) front end of a ship

bowdlerize *v* (-zes, -zing, -zed) remove words regarded as indecent from (a play, novel, etc.)
bowdlerized *v* ▷ bowdlerize
bowdlerizes *v* ▷ bowdlerize
bowdlerizing *v* ▷ bowdlerize
bowed *v* ▷ bow[1]

bowel *n* (*pl* -s) intestine, esp. the large intestine ▶ *pl* innermost part
bowels *n* ▷ bowel

bower *n* (*pl* -s) shady leafy shelter

bowerbird *n* (*pl* -s) songbird of Australia and New Guinea, the males of which build bower-like display grounds to attract females
bowerbirds *n* ▷ bowerbird
bowers *n* ▷ bower

bowing *v* ▷ bow[1]

bowl[1] *n* (*pl* -s) round container with an open top

bowl[2] *n* (*pl* -s) large heavy ball ▶ *pl* game played on smooth grass with wooden bowls ▶ *v* (-s, -ing, -ed) (CRICKET) send (a ball) towards the batsman
bowled *v* ▷ bowl[2]

bowlegged *adj* having legs that curve outwards at the knees

bowler[1] *n* (*pl* -s) (CRICKET) player who sends (a ball) towards the batsman

bowler[2] *n* (*pl* -s) stiff felt hat with a rounded crown
bowlers *n* ▷ bowler[1, 2]

bowling *n* game in which bowls are rolled at a group of pins ▶ *v* ▷ bowl[2]

bowls *n* ▷ bowl[1, 2] ▶ *v* ▷ bowl[2]

bows *v* ▷ bow[1] ▶ *n* ▷ bow[1, 2, 3]

box[1] *n* (*pl* -es) container with a firm flat base and sides ▶ *v* (-es, -ing, -ed) put into a box

box[2] *v* (-es, -ing, -ed) fight (an opponent) in a boxing match

box[3] *n* (*pl* -es) evergreen tree with shiny leaves bark

boxed *v* ▷ box[1, 2]

boxer *n* (*pl* -s) person who participates in the sport of boxing
boxers *n* ▷ boxer

boxes *v* ▷ box[1, 2] ▶ *n* ▷ box[1, 2, 3]

boxing *n* sport of fighting with the fists ▶ *v* ▷ box[1, 2]

boy *n* (*pl* -s) male child > **boyish** *adj* > **boyhood** *n* (*pl* -s)

boycott *v* (-cotts, -cotting, -cotted) refuse to deal with (an organization or country) ▶ *n* (*pl* -s) instance of boycotting
boycotted *v* ▷ boycott
boycotting *v* ▷ boycott
boycotts *v*, *n* ▷ boycott

boyfriend *n* (*pl* -s) male friend with whom a person is romantically or sexually involved
boyfriends *n* ▷ boyfriend
boyhood *n* ▷ boy
boyhoods *n* ▷ boy
boyish *n* ▷ boy
boys *n* ▷ boy

bra *n* (*pl* -s) woman's undergarment for supporting the breasts
braai *n* ▷ braaivlies
braaied *v* ▷ braaivlies
braaiing *v* ▷ braaivlies
braais *n*, *v* ▷ braaivlies

braaivlies [brye-flayss], **braai** (S AFR) *n* (*pl* braais) grill on which food is cooked over hot charcoal, usu. outdoors ▶ *v* (braais, braaiing, braaied) cook (food) on in this way

brace *n* (*pl* -s) object fastened to something to straighten or support it ▶ *pl* straps worn over the shoulders to hold up trousers ▶ *v* (-ces, -cing, -ced) steady or prepare (oneself) for something unpleasant
braced *n*, *v* ▷ brace

bracelet *n* (*pl* -s) ornamental chain or band for the wrist
bracelets *n* ▷ bracelet
braces *n*, *v* ▷ brace

bracing *adj* refreshing and invigorating ▶ *v* ▷ brace

bracken *n* (*pl* -s) large fern
brackens *n* ▷ bracken

bracket *n* (*pl* -s) either of a pair of characters

used to enclose a section of writing ▶ v (-ets, -eting, -eted) put in brackets
bracketed v ▷ bracket
bracketing v ▷ bracket
brackets n, v ▷ bracket
brackish adj (of water) slightly salty
> **brackishness** n
brackishness n ▷ bracket
bract n (pl -s) leaf at the base of a flower
bracts n ▷ bract
brag v (-s, -gging, -gged) speak arrogantly and boastfully ▶ **braggart** n (pl -s)
braggart n ▷ brag
braggarts n ▷ brag
bragged v ▷ brag
bragging v ▷ brag
brags v ▷ brag
braid v (-s, -ing, -ed) interweave (hair, thread, etc.) ▶ n (pl -s) length of hair etc. that has been braided
braided v ▷ braid
braiding v ▷ braid
braids v, n ▷ braid
braille n (pl -s) system of writing for the blind, consisting of raised dots interpreted by touch
brailles n ▷ braille
brain n (pl -s) soft mass of nervous tissue in the head ▶ v (-s, -ing, -ed) hit (someone) hard on the head
brainchild n (pl -children) idea produced by creative thought
brainchildren n ▷ brainchild
brained v ▷ brain
brainier adj ▷ brainy
brainiest adj ▷ brainy
braininess n ▷ brainy
braininesses n ▷ brainy
braining v ▷ brain
brainless adj stupid
brains n, v ▷ brain
brainwash v (-es, -ing, -ed) cause (a person) to alter his or her beliefs, esp. by methods based on isolation, sleeplessness, etc.
brainwashed v ▷ brainwash
brainwashes v ▷ brainwash
brainwashing v ▷ brainwash
brainwave n (pl -s) sudden idea
brainwaves v ▷ brainwave
brainy adj (-nier, -niest) (Informal) clever
> **braininess** n (pl -es)
braise v (-ses, -sing, -sed) cook slowly in a covered pan with a little liquid
braised v ▷ braise
braises v ▷ braise

braising v ▷ braise
brake n (pl -s) device for slowing or stopping a vehicle ▶ v (-kes, -king, -ked) slow down or stop by using a brake
braked v ▷ brake
brakes n, v ▷ brake
braking v ▷ brake
bramble n (pl -s) prickly shrub that produces blackberries
brambles n ▷ bramble
bran n (pl -s) husks of cereal grain
branch n (pl -es) secondary stem of a tree ▶ v (-es, -ing, -ed) (of stems, roots, etc.) divide, then develop in different directions
branched n ▷ branch
branches n, v ▷ branch
branching v ▷ branch
brand n (pl -s) particular product ▶ v (-s, -ing, -ed) mark with a brand
branded v ▷ brand
brandies n ▷ brandy
branding v ▷ brand
brandish v (-es, -ing, -ed) wave (a weapon etc.) in a threatening way
brandished v ▷ brandish
brandishes v ▷ brandish
brandishing v ▷ brandish
brands n, v ▷ brand
brandy n (pl -dies) alcoholic spirit distilled from wine
brans n ▷ bran
bras n ▷ bra
brash adj offensively loud, showy, or self-confident > **brashness** n
brashness n ▷ brash
brass n (pl -es) alloy of copper and zinc
brasses n ▷ brass
brassier adj ▷ brassy
brassiere n (pl -s) bra
brassieres n ▷ brassiere
brassiest adj ▷ brassy
brassiness adj ▷ brassy
brassinesses adj ▷ brassy
brassy adj (-ssier, -ssiest) brazen or flashy > **brassiness** n (pl -es)
brat n (pl -s) unruly child
brats n ▷ brat
bravado n (pl -oes) showy display of self-confidence
bravadoes n ▷ bravado
brave adj (-r, -st) having or showing courage, resolution, and daring ▶ n (pl -s) Native American warrior ▶ v (-ves, -ving, -ved) confront with resolution or courage > **bravery** n (pl -ies)

braved v ▷ brave
bravenesses n ▷ brave
braver adj ▷ brave
braveries n ▷ brave
bravery n ▷ brave
braves n, v ▷ brave
bravest adj ▷ brave
braving v ▷ brave
bravo interj well done!
brawl n (pl -s) noisy fight ▶ v (-s, -ing, -ed) fight noisily
brawled v ▷ brawl
brawling v ▷ brawl
brawls n, v ▷ brawl
brawn n (pl -s) physical strength > **brawny** (-nier, -niest) adj
brawnier adj ▷ brawn
brawniest adj ▷ brawn
brawns n ▷ brawn
brawny adj ▷ brawn
bray v (-s, -ing, -ed) (of a donkey) utter its loud harsh sound ▶ n (pl -s) donkey's loud harsh sound
brayed v ▷ bray
braying v ▷ bray
brays v, n ▷ bray
brazen adj shameless and bold ▶ v (-s, -ing, -ed) > **brazenly** adv > **brazenness** n
brazened v ▷ brazen
brazening v ▷ brazen
brazenly adv ▷ brazen
brazenness n ▷ brazen
brazens v ▷ brazen
brazier [bray-zee-er] n (pl -s) portable container for burning charcoal or coal
braziers n ▷ brazier
breach n (pl -es) breaking of a promise, obligation, etc. ▶ v (-es, -ing, -ed) break (a promise, law, etc.)
breached v ▷ breach
breaches n, v ▷ breach
breaching v ▷ breach
bread n (pl -s) food made by baking a mixture of flour and water or milk
breads n ▷ bread
breadth n (pl -s) extent of something from side to side
breadths n ▷ breadth
breadwinner n (pl -s) person whose earnings support a family
breadwinners n ▷ breadwinner
break v (breaks, breaking, broke, broken) separate or become separated into two or more pieces ▶ n (pl -s) act or result of breaking > **breakable** adj > **breakage** n (pl -s)

breakable adj ▷ break
breakage n ▷ break
breakages n ▷ break
breakdown n (pl -s) act or instance of breaking down
breakdowns n ▷ breakdown
breaker n (pl -s) large wave
breakers n ▷ breaker
breakfast v (-s, -ing, -ed) ▶ n (pl -s) (eat) the first meal of the day
breakfasted v ▷ breakfast
breakfasting v ▷ breakfast
breakfasts v, n ▷ breakfast
breaking v ▷ break
breakneck adj fast and dangerous
breaks v, n ▷ break
breakthrough n (pl -s) important development or discovery
breakthroughs n ▷ breakthrough
breakwater n (pl -s) wall that extends into the sea to protect a harbour or beach from the force of waves
breakwaters n ▷ breakwater
bream n (pl bream) silver freshwater fish
breast n (pl -s) either of the two soft fleshy milk-secreting glands on a woman's chest
breastbone n (pl -s) long flat bone in the front of the body, to which most of the ribs are attached
breastbones n ▷ breastbone
breasts n ▷ breast
breaststroke n (pl -s) swimming stroke in which the arms are extended in front of the head and swept back on either side
breaststrokes n ▷ breaststroke
breath n (pl -s) taking in and letting out of air during breathing > **breathless** adj > **breathlessly** adv > **breathlessness** n
breathalysed v ▷ breathalyser
breathalyser n (pl -s)® device for estimating the amount of alcohol in the breath > **breathalyse** v (-ses, -sing, -sed)
breathalysers n ▷ breathalyser
breathalyses v ▷ breathalyser
breathalysing v ▷ breathalyser
breathe v (-thes, -thing, -thed) take in oxygen and give out carbon dioxide > **breathing** n
breathed v ▷ breathe
breather n (pl -s) (Informal) short rest
breathers n ▷ breather
breathes v ▷ breathe
breathing v, n ▷ breathe
breathless adj ▷ breath
breathlessly adv ▷ breath
breathlessness n ▷ breath

breaths n ▷ breath

breathtaking adj causing awe or excitement

bred v ▷ breed

breech n (pl -es) buttocks

breeches pl n trousers extending to just below the knee ▶ n ▷ breech

breed v (-s, -ding, bred) produce new or improved strains of (domestic animals or plants) ▶ n (pl -s) group of animals etc. within a species that have certain clearly defined characteristics > **breeder** n (pl -s)

breeder n ▷ breed

breeders n ▷ breed

breeding n (pl -s) result of good upbringing or training ▶ v ▷ breed

breedings n ▷ breeding

breeds v, n ▷ breed

breeze n (pl -s) gentle wind ▶ v (-zes, -zing, -zed) move quickly or casually

breezed v ▷ breeze

breezes n, v ▷ breeze

breezier adj ▷ breezy

breeziest adj ▷ breezy

breezily adj ▷ breezy

breezing v ▷ breeze

breezy adj (-zier, -ziest) windy > **breezily** adv

brethren pl n (Old-fashioned) (used in religious contexts) brothers

brevities n ▷ brevity

brevity n (pl -ities) shortness

brew v (-s, -ing, -ed) make (beer etc.) by steeping, boiling, and fermentation ▶ n (pl -s) beverage produced by brewing

brewed v ▷ brew

brewer n (pl -s) person or company that brews beer

breweries n ▷ brewery

brewers n ▷ brewer

brewery n (pl -eries) place where beer etc. is brewed

brewing v ▷ brew

brews v, n ▷ brew

briar¹, brier n (pl -s) European shrub with a hard woody root

briar2 n (pl -s) ▷ brier¹

briars n ▷ briar¹, ²

bribe v (bribes, bribing, bribed) offer or give something to someone to gain favour, influence, etc. ▶ n (pl -s) something given or offered as a bribe > **bribery** n

bribed v ▷ bribe

bribes v, n ▷ bribe

bribing v ▷ bribe

brick n (pl -s) (rectangular block of) baked clay used in building ▶ v (-s, -ing, -ed) (foll. by **up** or

over) build, enclose, or fill with bricks

bricked v ▷ brick

bricking v ▷ brick

bricklayer n (pl -s) person who builds with bricks

bricklayers n ▷ bricklayer

bricks n, v ▷ brick

bridal adj ▷ bride

bride n (pl -s) woman who has just been or is about to be married > **bridal** adj

bridegroom n (pl -s) man who has just been or is about to be married

bridegrooms n ▷ bridegroom

brides n ▷ bride

bridesmaid n (pl -s) girl or woman who attends a bride at her wedding

bridesmaids n ▷ bridesmaid

bridge¹ n (pl -s) structure for crossing a river etc. ▶ v (-dges, -dging, -dged) build a bridge over (something)

bridge² n (pl -s) card game based on whist, played between two pairs

bridged v ▷ bridge¹

bridgehead n (pl -s) fortified position at the end of a bridge nearest the enemy

bridgeheads n ▷ bridgehead

bridges n ▷ bridge¹, ² ▶ v ▷ bridge¹

bridging v ▷ bridge¹

bridle n (pl -s) headgear for controlling a horse ▶ v (-dles, -dling, -dled) show anger or indignation

bridled v ▷ bridle

bridles n, v ▷ bridle

bridling v ▷ bridle

brief adj (-er, -est) short in duration ▶ n (pl -s) condensed statement or written synopsis (also **briefing**) (pl -s) ▶ pl men's or women's underpants ▶ v (-s, -ing, -ed) give information and instructions to (a person) > **briefly** adv

briefcase n (pl -s) small flat case for carrying papers, books, etc.

briefcases n ▷ briefcase

briefed v ▷ brief

briefer adj ▷ brief

briefest adj ▷ brief

briefing v, n ▷ brief

briefings n ▷ brief

briefly adv ▷ brief

briefs n, v ▷ brief

brier¹, briar n (pl -s) wild rose with long thorny stems

brier² n (pl -s) ▷ briar¹

briers n ▷ brier¹, ²

brig n (pl -s) two-masted square-rigged ship

brigade n (pl -s) army unit smaller than a

division
brigades n ▷ brigade
brigadier n (pl -s) high-ranking army officer
brigadiers n ▷ brigadier
brigalow n (pl -s) (AUST) type of acacia tree
brigalows n ▷ brigalow
brigand n (pl -s) (Lit) bandit
brigands n ▷ brigand
brigantine n (pl -s) two-masted sailing ship
brigantines n ▷ brigantine
bright adj (-er, -est) emitting or reflecting
much light ▷ **brightly** adv ▷ **brightness** n
▷ **brighten** v (-s, -ing, -ed)
brighten v ▷ bright
brightened v ▷ bright
brightening v ▷ bright
brightens v ▷ bright
brighter adj ▷ bright
brightest adj ▷ bright
brightly adj ▷ bright
brigs n ▷ brig
brilliance n ▷ brilliant
brilliancy n ▷ brilliant
brilliant adj shining with light ▷ **brilliance,
brilliancy** n ▷ **brilliantly** adv
brilliantly adv ▷ brilliant
brim n (pl -s) upper rim of a cup etc. ▶ v (brims,
brimming, brimmed) be full to the brim
brimmed v ▷ brim
brimming v ▷ brim
brims n, v ▷ brim
brimstone n (pl -s) (Obs) sulphur
brimstones n ▷ brimstone
brine n (pl -s) salt water
brines n ▷ brine
bring v (-s, -ing, brought) carry, convey, or take
to a designated place or person
bringing v ▷ bring
brings v ▷ bring
brinier adj ▷ briny
briniest adj ▷ briny
brinjal n (pl -s) (S AFR) aubergine
brinjals n ▷ brinjal
brink n (pl -s) edge of a steep place
brinks n ▷ brink
briny (brinier, briniest) adj very salty
brisk adj (-er, -est) lively and quick ▷ **briskly** adv
brisker adj ▷ brisk
briskest adj ▷ brisk
brisket n (pl -s) beef from the breast of a cow
briskets n ▷ brisket
briskly adv ▷ brisk
bristle n (pl -s) short stiff hair ▶ v (-les, -ling,
-led) (cause to) stand up like bristles ▷ **bristly**
adj (-lier, -liest)

bristled v ▷ bristle
bristles n, v ▷ bristle
bristlier adj ▷ bristle
bristliest adj ▷ bristle
bristling v ▷ bristle
bristly adj ▷ bristle
brit n (pl -s) (Informal) British person
brits n ▷ brit
brittle adj (-r, -st) hard but easily broken
▷ **brittleness** n (pl -es)
brittleness n ▷ brittle
brittlenesses n ▷ brittle
brittler adj ▷ brittle
brittlest adj ▷ brittle
broach v (-es, -ing, -ed) introduce (a topic) for
discussion
broached v ▷ broach
broaches v ▷ broach
broaching v ▷ broach
broad adj (-er, -est) having great breadth or
width ▷ **broadly** adv ▷ **broaden** v (-s, -ing, -ed)
broadband n (pl -s) telecommunication
transmission technique using a wide range
of frequencies
broadbands n ▷ broadband
broadcast n (pl -s) programme or
announcement on radio or television ▶ v
(-s, -ing, broadcast) transmit (a programme
or announcement) on radio or television
▷ **broadcaster** n (pl -s) ▷ **broadcasting** n
broadcaster n ▷ broadcast
broadcasters n ▷ broadcast
broadcasting v, n ▷ broadcast
broadcasts n, v ▷ broadcast
broaden v ▷ broad
broadened v ▷ broad
broadening v ▷ broad
broadens v ▷ broad
broader adj ▷ broad
broadest adj ▷ broad
broadly adv ▷ broad
broadminded adj tolerant
broadside n (pl -s) strong verbal or written
attack
broadsides n ▷ broadside
brocade n (pl -s) rich fabric woven with a
raised design
brocades n ▷ brocade
broccoli n (pl -s) type of cabbage with greenish
flower heads
broccolis n ▷ broccoli
brochure n (pl -s) booklet that contains
information about a product or service
brochures n ▷ brochure
broekies [brook-eez] pl n (S AFR) (Informal)

underpants

brogue[1] n (pl -s) sturdy walking shoe

brogue[2] n (pl -s) strong accent, esp. Irish
  brogues n ▷ brogue[1,2]

broil v (-s, -ing, -ed) (AUST, NZ, US & CANADIAN) cook by direct heat under a grill
  broiled v ▷ broil
  broiling v ▷ broil
  broils v ▷ broil

broke v ▷ break ▶ adj (Informal) having no money

broken v ▷ break ▶ adj fractured or smashed

brokenhearted adj overwhelmed by grief

broker n (pl -s) agent who buys or sells goods, securities, etc.
  brokers n ▷ broker

brolga n (pl -s) large grey Australian crane with a trumpeting call
  brolgas n ▷ brolga
  brollies n ▷ brolly

brolly n (pl -lies) (Informal) umbrella

bromide n (pl -s) chemical compound used in medicine and photography
  bromides n ▷ bromide

bromine n (pl -s) (CHEM) dark red liquid element that gives off a pungent vapour
  bromines n ▷ bromine

bronchi n ▷ bronchus

bronchial [bronk-ee-al] adj of the bronchi

bronchitis [bronk-eye-tiss] n inflammation of the bronchi

bronchus [bronk-uss] n (pl bronchi) [bronk-eye] either the two branches of the windpipe

bronco n (pl -s) (in the US) wild or partially tamed pony
  broncos n ▷ bronco

brontosaurus n (pl -es) very large plant-eating four-footed dinosaur
  brontosauruses n ▷ brontosaurus

bronze n (pl -s) alloy of copper and tin ▶ adj made of, or coloured like, bronze ▶ v (-zes, -zing, -zed) (esp. of the skin) make or become brown
  bronzed v ▷ bronze
  bronzes n, v ▷ bronze
  bronzing v ▷ bronze

brooch n (pl -es) ornament with a pin, worn fastened to clothes
  brooches n ▷ brooch

brood n (pl -s) number of birds produced at one hatching ▶ v (-s, -ing, -ed) think long and unhappily > **broody** adj moody and sullen (Informal)
  brooded v ▷ brood
  brooding v ▷ brood

broods n, v ▷ brood

broody adj ▷ brood

brook[1] n (pl -s) small stream

brook[2] v (-s, -ing, -ed) bear or tolerate
  brooked v ▷ brook[2]
  brooking v ▷ brook[2]
  brooks n ▷ brook[1] ▶ v ▷ brook[2]

broom n (pl -s) long-handled sweeping brush
  brooms n ▷ broom

broomstick n (pl -s) handle of a broom
  broomsticks n ▷ broomstick

broth n (pl -s) soup, usu. containing vegetables

brothel n (pl -s) house where men pay to have sex with prostitutes
  brothels n ▷ brothel

brother n (pl -s) boy or man with the same parents as another person > **brotherly** adj

brotherhood n (pl -s) fellowship
  brotherhoods n ▷ brotherhood
  brotherly adj ▷ brother
  brothers n ▷ brother
  broths n ▷ broth

brought v ▷ bring

brow n (pl -s) part of the face from the eyes to the hairline

browbeat v (-s, -ing, browbeat, -en) frighten (someone) with threats
  browbeaten v ▷ browbeat
  browbeating v ▷ browbeat
  browbeats v ▷ browbeat

brown n (pl -s) colour of earth or wood ▶ adj (-er, -est) of the colour brown ▶ v (-s, -ing, -ed) make or become brown > **brownish** adj
  browned v ▷ brown
  browner adj ▷ brown
  brownest adj ▷ brown
  browning v ▷ brown
  brownish adj ▷ brown
  browns n, v ▷ brown

brows n ▷ brow

browse v (-ses, -sing, -sed) look through (a book or articles for sale) in a casual manner ▶ n (pl -s) instance of browsing
  browsed v ▷ browse

browser n (pl -s) (COMPUTERS) software package that enables a user to read hypertext, esp. on the Internet
  browsers n ▷ browse
  browses v, n ▷ browse
  browsing v ▷ browse

bruise n (pl -s) discoloured area on the skin caused by an injury ▶ v (-ses, -sing, -sed) cause a bruise on
  bruised v ▷ bruise

bruiser n (pl -s) strong tough person

bruisers n ▷ bruiser

bruises n, v ▷ bruise

bruising v ▷ bruise

brumbies n ▷ brumby

brumby n (pl -bies) (AUST) wild horse

brunch n (pl -es) (Informal) breakfast and lunch combined

brunches n ▷ brunch

brunette n (pl -s) girl or woman with dark brown hair

brunettes n ▷ brunette

brunt n (pl -s) main force or shock of a blow, attack, etc.

brunts n ▷ brunt

brush¹ n (pl -es) device made of bristles, wires, etc. used for cleaning, painting, etc. ▶ v (-es, -ing, -ed) clean, scrub, or paint with a brush

brush² n (pl -es) thick growth of shrubs

brushed v ▷ brush¹

brushes v ▷ brush¹ ▶ n ▷ brush¹, ²

brushing v ▷ brush¹

brusque adj (-r, -st) blunt or curt in manner or speech ▷ **brusquely** adv ▷ **brusqueness** n (pl -es)

brusquely adv ▷ brusque

brusqueness n ▷ brusque

brusquenesses n ▷ brusque

brusquer adj ▷ brusque

brusquest adj ▷ brusque

brutal adj cruel and vicious ▷ **brutally** adv ▷ **brutality** n (pl -alities) ▷ **brutalize** v (-lizes, -lizing, -lized)

brutalities n ▷ brutal

brutality n ▷ brutal

brutalized v ▷ brutal

brutalizes v ▷ brutal

brutalizing v ▷ brutal

brutally adv ▷ brutal

brute n (pl -s) brutal person ▶ adj wholly instinctive or physical, like an animal

brutes n ▷ brute

brutish adj of or like an animal ▷ **brutishly** adv ▷ **brutishness** n

brutishly adv ▷ brutish

brutishness n ▷ brutish

bubble n (pl -s) ball of air in a liquid or solid ▶ v (-les, -ling, -led) form bubbles

bubbled v ▷ bubble

bubbles n, v ▷ bubble

bubblier adj ▷ bubbly

bubbliest adj ▷ bubbly

bubbling v ▷ bubble

bubbly adj (-lier, -liest) excited and lively

buccaneer n (pl -s) (HIST) pirate

buccaneers n ▷ buccaneer

buck¹ n (pl -s) male of the goat, hare, kangaroo, rabbit, and reindeer ▶ v (-s, -ing, -ed) (of a horse etc.) jump with legs stiff and back arched

buck² n (pl -s) (US, CANADIAN, AUST & NZ) (Slang) dollar

bucked v ▷ buck¹

bucket n (pl -s) open-topped round container with a handle ▶ v (-ets, -eting, -eted) rain heavily ▷ **bucketful** n (pl -s)

bucketed v ▷ bucket

bucketful n ▷ bucket

bucketfuls n ▷ bucket

bucketing v ▷ bucket

buckets n, v ▷ bucket

bucking v ▷ buck¹

buckle n (pl -s) clasp for fastening a belt or strap ▶ v (-les, -ling, -led) fasten or be fastened with a buckle

buckled v ▷ buckle

buckles n, v ▷ buckle

buckling v ▷ buckle

bucks v ▷ buck¹ ▶ n ▷ buck¹, ²

buckshee adj (Slang) free

buckteeth pl n projecting upper front teeth ▷ **buck-toothed** adj

buck-toothed adj ▷ buckteeth

buckwheat n (pl -s) small black grain used for making flour

buckwheats n ▷ buckwheat

bucolic [bew-koll-ik] adj of the countryside or country life

bud n (pl -s) swelling on a tree or plant that develops into a leaf or flower ▶ v (buds, budding, budded) produce buds

budded v ▷ bud

buddies n ▷ buddy

budding adj beginning to develop or grow ▶ v ▷ bud

buddleia n (pl -s) shrub with long spikes of purple flowers

buddleias n ▷ buddleia

buddy n (pl -dies) (Informal) friend

budge v (budges, budging, budged) move slightly

budged v ▷ budge

budgerigar n (pl -s) small cage bird bred in many different-coloured varieties

budgerigars n ▷ budgerigar

budges v ▷ budge

budget n (pl -s) financial plan for a period of time ▶ v (-ets, -eting, -eted) plan the expenditure of (money or time) ▶ adj cheap ▷ **budgetary** adj

budgeted v ▷ budget

budgeting v ▷ budget
budgets n, v ▷ budget
budgie n (pl -s) (Informal) ▷ budgerigar
budgies n ▷ budgie
budging v ▷ budge
buds n, v ▷ bud
buff¹ adj dull yellowish-brown ▶ v (-s, -ing, -ed) clean or polish with soft material
buff² n (pl -s) (Informal) expert on or devotee of a given subject
buffalo n (pl -oes) type of cattle (US)
buffaloes n ▷ buffalo
buffed v ▷ buff¹
buffer n (pl -s) something that lessens shock or protects from damaging impact, circumstances, etc.
buffers n ▷ buffer
buffet¹ [boof-ay, buff-ay] n (pl -s) counter where drinks and snacks are served
buffet² [buff-it] v (-s, -feting, -feted) knock against or about
buffeted v ▷ buffet²
buffeting v ▷ buffet²
buffets n ▷ buffet¹ ▶ v ▷ buffet²
buffing v ▷ buff¹
buffoon n (pl -s) clown or fool > **buffoonery** n (pl -ries)
buffooneries n ▷ buffoon
buffoonery n ▷ buffoon
buffoons n ▷ buffoon
buffs v ▷ buff¹ ▶ n ▷ buff²
bug n (pl -s) small insect ▶ v (bugs, bugging, bugged) (Informal) irritate (someone)
bugbear n (pl -s) thing that causes obsessive anxiety
bugbears n ▷ bugbear
bugged v ▷ bug
bugging v ▷ bug
bugle n (pl -s) instrument like a small trumpet > **bugler** n (pl -s)
bugler n ▷ bugle
buglers n ▷ bugle
bugles n ▷ bugle
bugong n ▷ bogong
bugongs n ▷ bogong
bugs n, v ▷ bug
build v (builds, building, built) make, construct, or form by joining parts or materials ▶ n (pl -s) shape of the body > **builder** n (pl -s)
builder n ▷ build
builders n ▷ build
building v ▷ build ▶ n (pl -s) structure with walls and a roof
buildings n ▷ building

builds v, n ▷ build
built v ▷ build
bulb n (pl -s) onion-shaped root which grows into a flower or plant
bulbous adj round and fat
bulbs n ▷ bulb
bulge n (pl -s) swelling on a normally flat surface ▶ v (bulges, bulging, bulged) swell outwards > **bulging** adj
bulged v ▷ bulge
bulges n, v ▷ bulge
bulging v, adj ▷ bulge
bulimia n (pl -s) disorder characterized by compulsive overeating followed by vomiting > **bulimic** adj, n (pl -s)
bulimias n ▷ bulimia
bulimic adj, n ▷ bulimia
bulimics n ▷ bulimia
bulk n (pl -s) size or volume, esp. when great > **bulky** adj (-ier, -iest)
bulkhead n (pl -s) partition in a ship or aeroplane
bulkheads n ▷ bulkhead
bulkier adj ▷ bulk
bulkiest adj ▷ bulk
bulks n ▷ bulk
bulky adj ▷ bulk
bull¹ n (pl -s) male of some animals, such as cattle, elephants, and whales
bull² n (pl -s) (Informal) complete nonsense
bull³ n (pl -s) papal decree
bulldog n (pl -s) thickset dog with a broad head and a muscular body
bulldogs n ▷ bulldog
bulldoze v ▷ bulldozer
bulldozed v ▷ bulldozer
bulldozer n (pl -s) powerful tractor for moving earth > **bulldoze** v (-zes, -zing, -zed)
bulldozers n ▷ bulldozer
bulldozes v ▷ bulldozer
bulldozing v ▷ bulldozer
bullet n (pl -s) small piece of metal fired from a gun
bulletin n (pl -s) short official report or announcement
bulletins n ▷ bulletin
bullets n ▷ bullet
bullfight n (pl -s) public show in which a matador kills a bull > **bullfighter** n (pl -s)
bullfighter n ▷ bullfight
bullfighters n ▷ bullfight
bullfights n ▷ bullfight
bullied v ▷ bully
bullies n, v ▷ bully

bullion n (pl -s) gold or silver in the form of bars
  bullions n ▷ bullion
bullock n (pl -s) castrated bull
  bullocks n ▷ bullock
  bulls n ▷ bull¹, ², ³
bullswool n (AUST DATED & NZ) (Slang) nonsense
bully n (pl -lies) person who hurts, persecutes, or intimidates a weaker person ▶ v (-lies, -lying, -lied) hurt, intimidate, or persecute (a weaker person)
  bullying v ▷ bully
bulrush n (pl -es) tall stiff reed
  bulrushes n ▷ bulrush
bulwark n (pl -s) wall used as a fortification
  bulwarks n ▷ bulwark
bum¹ n (pl -s) (Slang) buttocks or anus
bum² (Informal) n (pl -s) disreputable idler ▶ adj of poor quality
bumble v (-bles, -bling, -bled) speak, do, or move in a clumsy way ▶ **bumbling** adj, n
bumblebee n (pl -s) large hairy bee
  bumblebees n ▷ bumblebee
  bumbled v ▷ bumble
  bumbles v ▷ bumble
  bumbling v, adj n ▷ bumble
bumf, bumph n (pl -s) (Informal) official documents or forms
  bumfs n ▷ bumf
bump v (-s, -ing, -ed) knock or strike with a jolt ▶ n (pl -s) dull thud from an impact or collision > **bumpy** adj (-ier, -iest)
  bumped v ▷ bump
bumper¹ n (pl -s) bar on the front and back of a vehicle to protect against damage
bumper² adj unusually large or abundant
  bumpers n ▷ bumper¹
  bumph n ▷ bumf
  bumphs n ▷ bumf
  bumpier adj ▷ bump
  bumpiest adj ▷ bump
  bumping v ▷ bump
bumpkin n (pl -s) awkward simple country person
  bumpkins n ▷ bumpkin
  bumps v, n ▷ bump
bumptious adj offensively self-assertive > **bumptiously** adv > **bumptiousness** n
  bumptiously adj ▷ bumptious
  bumptiousness adj ▷ bumptious
  bumpy adj ▷ bump
  bums n ▷ bum¹, ²
bun n (pl -s) small sweet bread roll or cake
bunch n (pl -es) number of things growing, fastened, or grouped together ▶ v (-es, -ing, -ed) group or be grouped together in a bunch

  bunched v ▷ bunch
  bunches n, v ▷ bunch
  bunching v ▷ bunch
bundle n (pl -s) number of things gathered loosely together ▶ v (-dles, -dling, -dled) cause to go roughly or unceremoniously
  bundled v ▷ bundle
  bundles n, v ▷ bundle
  bundling v ▷ bundle
bung n (pl -s) stopper for a cask etc. ▶ v (-s, -ing, -ed) (foll. by **up**) (Informal) close with a bung
bungalow n (pl -s) one-storey house
  bungalows n ▷ bungalow
  bunged v ▷ bung
  bunging v ▷ bung
bungle v (-gles, -gling, -gled) spoil through incompetence > **bungler** n (pl -s) > **bungling** adj, n
  bungled v ▷ bungle
  bungler n ▷ bungle
  bunglers n ▷ bungle
  bungles v ▷ bungle
  bungling v, adj n ▷ bungle
  bungs n, v ▷ bung
bunion n (pl -s) inflamed swelling on the big toe
  bunions n ▷ bunion
bunk¹ n (pl -s) narrow shelflike bed
bunk² n (pl -s) ▷ bunkum
bunk³ (Slang) n (pl -s) (BRIT) make a hurried and secret departure ▶ v (-s, -ing, -ed) (BRIT, NZ & S AFR) be absent without permission
  bunked v ▷ bunk³
bunker n (pl -s) sand-filled hollow forming an obstacle on a golf course
  bunkers n ▷ bunker
  bunking v ▷ bunk³
  bunks n ▷ bunk¹, ², ³ ▶ v ▷ bunk³
bunkum n (pl -s) nonsense
  bunkums n ▷ bunkum
  bunnies n ▷ bunny
bunny n (pl -nies) child's word for a rabbit
  buns n ▷ bun
bunting n (pl -s) decorative flags
  buntings n ▷ bunting
bunya n (pl -s) tall dome-shaped Australian coniferous tree
  bunyas n ▷ bunya
bunyip n (pl -s) (AUST) legendary monster said to live in swamps and lakes
  bunyips n ▷ bunyip
buoy n (pl -s) floating marker anchored in the sea ▶ v (-s, -ing, -ed) prevent from sinking
  buoyancy n ▷ buoyant
buoyant adj able to float > **buoyancy** n

buoyed v ▷ buoy

buoying v ▷ buoy

buoys n, v ▷ buoy

bur n (pl -s) ▷ burr¹

burble v (-bles, -bling, -bled) make a bubbling sound

burbled v ▷ burble

burbles v ▷ burble

burbling v ▷ burble

burden¹ n (pl -s) heavy load ▶ v (-s, -ing, -ed) put a burden on **> burdensome** adj

burden² n (pl -s) theme of a speech etc.

burdened v ▷ burden¹

burdening v ▷ burden¹

burdens v ▷ burden¹ ▶ n ▷ burden¹, ²

burdensome adj ▷ burden¹

bureau n (pl -reaus, -reaux) office that provides a service

bureaucracies n ▷ bureaucracy

bureaucracy n (pl -cies) administrative system based on complex rules and procedures **> bureaucrat** n (pl -s) **> bureaucratic** adj

bureaucrat n ▷ bureaucracy

bureaucratic adj ▷ bureaucracy

bureaucrats n ▷ bureaucracy

bureaus n ▷ bureau

bureaux n ▷ bureau

burgeon v (-s, -ing, -ed) develop or grow rapidly

burgeoned v ▷ burgeon

burgeoning v ▷ burgeon

burgeons v ▷ burgeon

burgh n (pl -s) Scottish borough

burghs n ▷ burgh

burglar n (pl -s) person who enters a building to commit a crime, esp. theft **> burglary** n (pl -glaries) **> burgle** v (burgles, burgling, burgled)

burglaries n ▷ burglar

burglars n ▷ burglar

burglary n ▷ burglar

burgled v ▷ burglar

burgles v ▷ burglar

burgling v ▷ burglar

burgundy adj dark-purplish red

burial n (pl -s) burying of a dead body

burials n ▷ burial

buried v ▷ bury

buries v ▷ bury

burlesque n (pl -s) artistic work which satirizes a subject by caricature

burlesques n ▷ burlesque

burlier adj ▷ burly

burliest adj ▷ burly

burly adj (-lier, -liest) (of a person) broad and strong

burn¹ v (-s, -ing, -t or -ed) be or set on fire ▶ n (pl burns) injury or mark caused by fire or exposure to heat

burn² n (pl -s) (Scot) small stream

burned v ▷ burn¹

burning adj intense ▶ v ▷ burn¹

burnish v (-es, -ing, -ed) make smooth and shiny by rubbing

burnished v ▷ burnish

burnishes v ▷ burnish

burnishing v ▷ burnish

burns n ▷ burn¹, ² ▶ v ▷ burn¹

burnt v ▷ burn¹

burp v (-s, -ing, -ed) ▶ n (pl -s) (Informal) belch

burped v ▷ burp

burping v ▷ burp

burps v, n ▷ burp

burr¹, bur n (pl -s) head of a plant with prickles or hooks

burr² n (pl -s) soft trilling sound given to the letter r in some dialects

burrawang n (pl -s) Australian plant with fernlike leaves and an edible nut

burrawangs n ▷ burrawang

burrow n (pl -s) hole dug in the ground by a rabbit etc. ▶ v (-s, -ing, -ed) dig holes in the ground

burrowed v ▷ burrow

burrowing v ▷ burrow

burrows n, v ▷ burrow

burrs n ▷ burr¹, ²

burs n ▷ bur

bursar n (pl -s) treasurer of a school, college, or university

bursaries n ▷ bursary

bursars n ▷ bursar

bursary n (pl -ries) scholarship

burst v (-s, -ing, burst) (cause to) break open or apart noisily and suddenly ▶ n (pl -s) instance of breaking open suddenly

bursting v ▷ burst

bursts v, n ▷ burst

bury v (buries, burying, buried) place in a grave

burying v ▷ bury

bus n (pl buses) large motor vehicle for carrying passengers ▶ v (busses, bussing, bussed) travel or transport by bus

busbies n ▷ busby

busby n (pl -bies) tall fur hat worn by some soldiers

buses n ▷ bus

bush n (pl -es) dense woody plant, smaller than a tree

bushbabies n ▷ bushbaby

bushbaby n (pl -babies) small African tree-living mammal with large eyes

bushel n (pl -s) obsolete unit of measure equal to 8 gallons (36.4 litres)
  bushels n ▷ bushel

bushes n ▷ bush

bushier adj ▷ bushy

bushiest adj ▷ bushy

bushy adj (-shier, -shiest) (of hair) thick and shaggy
  busied v ▷ busy
  busier adj ▷ busy
  busies v ▷ busy
  busiest adj ▷ busy

business n (pl -es) purchase and sale of goods and services > **businessman** n (pl -men), **businesswoman** (pl -women)
  businesses n ▷ business

businesslike adj efficient and methodical
  businessman n ▷ business
  businessmen n ▷ business
  businesswoman n ▷ business
  businesswomen n ▷ business

busk v (-s, -ing, -ed) act as a busker
  busked v ▷ busk

busker n (pl -s) street entertainer
  buskers n ▷ busker
  busking v ▷ busk
  busks v ▷ busk
  bussed v ▷ bus
  busses v ▷ bus
  bussing v ▷ bus

bust¹ n (pl -s) woman's bosom

bust² (Informal) v (busts, busting, bust or busted) burst or break ▶ adj broken

bustard n (pl -s) bird with long strong legs, a heavy body, a long neck, and speckled plumage
  bustards n ▷ bustard
  busted v ▷ bust²
  busting v ▷ bust²

bustle¹ v (-les, -ling, -led) hurry with a show of activity or energy ▶ n (pl -s) energetic and noisy activity > **bustling** adj

bustle² n (pl -s) cushion or framework formerly worn under the back of a woman's skirt to hold it out
  bustled v ▷ bustle¹
  bustles v ▷ bustle¹ ▶ n ▷ bustle¹,²
  bustling v, adj ▷ bustle¹
  busts n ▷ bust¹ ▶ v ▷ bust²

busy adj (busier, busiest) actively employed ▶ v (busies, busying, busied) keep (someone, esp. oneself) busy > **busily** adv
  busybodies n ▷ busybody

busybody n (pl -bodies) meddlesome or nosy person
  busying v ▷ busy

but conj contrary to expectation ▶ prep except ▶ adv only

butane n (pl -s) gas used for fuel
  butanes n ▷ butane

butch adj (-er, -est) (Slang) markedly or aggressively masculine

butcher n (pl -s) person who slaughters animals or sells their meat ▶ v (-s, -ing, -ed) kill and prepare (animals) for meat > **butchery** n (pl -ries) adj ▷ butch

butcherbird n (pl -s) Australian magpie that impales its prey on thorns
  butcherbirds n ▷ butcherbird
  butchered v ▷ butcher
  butcheries n ▷ butcher
  butchering v ▷ butcher
  butchers n, v ▷ butcher
  butchery n ▷ butcher
  butchest adj ▷ butch

butler n (pl -s) chief male servant
  butlers n ▷ butler

butt¹ n (pl -s) thicker end of something

butt² n (pl -s) person or thing that is the target of ridicule

butt³ v (-s, -ing, -ed) strike with the head or horns

butt⁴ n (pl -s) large cask
  butted v ▷ butt³

butter n (pl -s) edible fatty solid made by churning cream ▶ v (-s, -ing, -ed) put butter on > **buttery** adj

buttercup n (pl -s) small yellow flower
  buttercups n ▷ buttercup
  buttered v ▷ butter

butterfingers n (pl -s) (Informal) person who drops things by mistake
  butterflies n ▷ butterfly

butterfly n (pl -flies) insect with brightly coloured wings
  buttering v ▷ butter

buttermilk n (pl -s) sourish milk that remains after the butter has been separated from milk
  buttermilks n ▷ buttermilk
  butters n, v ▷ butter

butterscotch n (pl -es) kind of hard brittle toffee
  butterscotches n ▷ butterscotch
  buttery adj ▷ butter
  butting v ▷ butt³

buttock n (pl -s) either of the two fleshy masses that form the human rump
  buttocks n ▷ buttock

button n (pl -s) small disc or knob sewn to clothing, which can be passed through a slit in another piece of fabric to fasten them ▶ v (-s, -ing, -ed) fasten with buttons
buttoned v ▷ button
buttonhole n (pl -s) slit in a garment through which a button is passed ▶ v (-holes, -holing, -holed) detain (someone) in conversation
buttonholed v ▷ buttonhole
buttonholes n, v ▷ buttonhole
buttonholing v ▷ buttonhole
buttoning v ▷ button
buttons n, v ▷ button
buttress n (pl -es) structure to support a wall ▶ v (-es, -ing, -ed) support with, or as if with, a buttress
buttressed v ▷ buttress
buttresses n, v ▷ buttress
buttressing v ▷ buttress
butts n ▷ butt[1, 2, 4] ▶ v ▷ butt[3]
buxom adj (-er, -est) (of a woman) healthily plump and full-bosomed
buxomer adj ▷ buxom
buxomest adj ▷ buxom
buy v (-s, -ing, bought) acquire by paying money for ▶ n (pl -s) thing acquired through payment
buyer n (pl -s) customer
buyers n ▷ buyer
buying v ▷ buy
buys v, n ▷ buy
buzz n (pl -es) rapidly vibrating humming sound (Informal) ▶ v (-es, -ing, -ed) make a humming sound > **buzzer** n (pl -s)
buzzard n (pl -s) bird of prey of the hawk family

buzzards n ▷ buzzard
buzzed v ▷ buzz
buzzer n ▷ buzz
buzzers n ▷ buzz
buzzes n, v ▷ buzz
buzzing v ▷ buzz
by prep indicating the doer of an action, nearness, movement past, time before or during which, etc. ▶ adv near
bye interj (Informal) goodbye
byelaw n ▷ bylaw
byelaws n ▷ bylaw
bygone adj past or former
bylaw, byelaw n (pl -s) rule made by a local authority
bylaws n ▷ bylaw
bypass n (pl -es) main road built to avoid a city ▶ v (-es, -ing, -ed) go round or avoid
bypassed v ▷ bypass
bypasses n, v ▷ bypass
bypassing v ▷ bypass
byre n (pl -s) (BRIT) shelter for cows
byres n ▷ byre
bystander n (pl -s) person present but not involved
bystanders n ▷ bystander
byte n (pl -s) (COMPUTERS) group of bits processed as one unit of data
bytes n ▷ byte
byway n (pl -s) minor road
byways n ▷ byway
byword n (pl -s) person or thing regarded as a perfect example of something
bywords n ▷ byword

Cc

C can be a tricky letter to use, especially as it only forms a single two-letter word **ch**. But if you remember this, you won't waste time racking your brains for two-letter words. There are, however, plenty of good three-letter words beginning with C. **Cox** scores 12 points, while **caw**, **cow** and **coy** are each worth 8. It's also a good idea to remember the short words starting with C that don't contain any vowels: **cly** and **cwm** as well as **ch**.

cab n (pl -s) taxi

cabal [kab-**bal**] n (pl -s) small group of political plotters
　　cabals n ▷ cabal

cabaret [kab-a-ray] n (pl -s) dancing and singing show in a nightclub
　　cabarets n ▷ cabaret

cabbage n (pl -s) vegetable with a large head of green leaves
　　cabbages n ▷ cabbage

cabbie, cabby n (pl -bies) (Informal) taxi driver
　　cabbies n ▷ cabbie
　　cabby n ▷ cabbie

caber n (pl -s) tree trunk tossed in competition at Highland games
　　cabers n ▷ caber

cabin n (pl -s) compartment in a ship or aircraft

cabinet n (pl -s) piece of furniture with drawers or shelves

cabinetmaker n (pl -s) person who makes fine furniture
　　cabinetmakers n ▷ cabinetmaker
　　cabinets n ▷ cabinet
　　cabins n ▷ cabin

cable n (pl -s) strong thick rope ▶ v (-les, -ling, -led) send (someone) a message by cable
　　cabled v ▷ cable
　　cables n, v ▷ cable
　　cabling v ▷ cable

caboodle n (Informal) the whole lot

cabriolet [kab-ree-oh-lay] n (pl -s) small horse-drawn carriage with a folding hood
　　cabriolets n ▷ cabriolet
　　cabs n ▷ cab

cacao [kak-**kah**-oh] n (pl -s) tropical tree with seed pods from which chocolate and cocoa are made
　　cacaos n ▷ cacao

cache [kash] n (pl -s) hidden store of weapons or treasure
　　caches n ▷ cache

cachet [kash-shay] n (pl -s) prestige, distinction
　　cachets n ▷ cachet

cackle v (-les, -ling, -led) laugh shrilly ▶ n (pl -s) cackling noise
　　cackled v ▷ cackle
　　cackles v, n ▷ cackle
　　cackling v ▷ cackle

cacophonies n ▷ cacophony
cacophonous adj ▷ cacophony

cacophony [kak-**koff**-on-ee] n (pl -phonies) harsh discordant sound > **cacophonous** adj
　　cacti n ▷ cactus

cactus n (pl -tuses, -ti) fleshy desert plant with spines but no leaves
　　cactuses n ▷ cactus

cad n (pl -s) (Old-fashioned) dishonourable man > **caddish** adj

cadaver [kad-**dav**-ver] n (pl -s) corpse
cadaverous adj pale, thin, and haggard
　　cadavers n ▷ cadaver

caddie, caddy n (pl -dies) person who carries a golfer's clubs ▶ v (-dies, -dying, -died) act as a caddie
　　caddies n ▷ caddie, caddy ▶ v ▷ caddie
　　caddish adj ▷ cad

caddy n (pl -dies) small container for tea
　　▷ caddie

cadence [kade-enss] n (pl -s) rise and fall in the pitch of the voice
　　cadences n ▷ cadence

cadenza n (pl -s) complex solo passage in a piece of music
　　cadenzas n ▷ cadenza

cadet n (pl -s) young person training for the armed forces or police

cadets n ▷ cadet

cadge v (cadges, cadging, cadged) (*Informal*) get (something) by taking advantage of someone's generosity > **cadger** n (pl -s)

cadged v ▷ cadge

cadger n ▷ cadge

cadgers n ▷ cadge

cadges v ▷ cadge

cadging v ▷ cadge

cadmium n (pl -s) (CHEM) bluish-white metallic element used in alloys

cadmiums n ▷ cadmium

cadre [kah-der] n (pl -s) small group of people selected and trained to form the core of a political organization or military unit

cadres n ▷ cadre

cads n ▷ cad

caeca n ▷ caecum

caecum [seek-um] n (pl -ca) [-ka] pouch at the beginning of the large intestine

caesium n (pl -s) (CHEM) silvery-white metallic element used in photocells

caesiums n ▷ caesium

café n (pl -s) small or inexpensive restaurant serving light refreshments

cafés n ▷ café

cafeteria n (pl -s) self-service restaurant

cafeterias n ▷ cafeteria

caffeine n (pl -s) stimulant found in tea and coffee

caffeines n ▷ caffeine

caftan n (pl -s) ▷ kaftan

caftans n ▷ caftan

cage n (pl -s) enclosure of bars or wires, for keeping animals or birds

caged adj kept in a cage

cages n ▷ cage

cagey adj (cagier, cagiest) (*Informal*) reluctant to go into details

cagier adj ▷ cagey

cagiest adj ▷ cagey

cagoule n (pl -s) (BRIT) lightweight hooded waterproof jacket

cagoules n ▷ cagoule

cahoots pl n (*Informal*) conspiring together

cairn n (pl -s) mound of stones erected as a memorial or marker

cairns n ▷ cairn

cajole v (-les, -ling, -led) persuade by flattery > **cajolery** n

cajoled v ▷ cajole

cajolery n ▷ cajole

cajoles v ▷ cajole

cajoling v ▷ cajole

cake n (pl -s) sweet food baked from a mixture of flour, eggs, etc. ▶ v (cakes, caking, caked) form into a hardened mass or crust

caked v ▷ cake

cakes n, v ▷ cake

caking v ▷ cake

calamine n (pl -s) pink powder consisting chiefly of zinc oxide, used in skin lotions and ointments

calamines n ▷ calamine

calamities n ▷ calamity

calamitous adj ▷ calamity

calamity n (pl -ties) disaster > **calamitous** adj

calcification v ▷ calcify

calcified v ▷ calcify

calcifies v ▷ calcify

calcify v (-fies, -fying, -fied) harden by the depositing of calcium salts > **calcification** n

calcifying v ▷ calcify

calcium n (pl -s) (CHEM) silvery-white metallic element found in bones, teeth, limestone, and chalk

calciums n ▷ calcium

calculable adj ▷ calculate

calculate v (-lates, -lating, -lated) solve or find out by a mathematical procedure or by reasoning > **calculable** adj > **calculation** n (pl -s)

calculated v ▷ calculate

calculates v ▷ calculate

calculating adj selfishly scheming ▶ v ▷ calculate

calculation n ▷ calculate

calculations n ▷ calculate

calculator n (pl -s) small electronic device for making calculations

calculators n ▷ calculator

calculus n (pl -es) branch of mathematics dealing with infinitesimal changes to a variable number or quantity

calculuses n ▷ calculus

calendar n (pl -s) chart showing a year divided up into months, weeks, and days

calendars n ▷ calendar

calendula n (pl -s) marigold

calendulas n ▷ calendula

calf¹ n (pl calves) young cow, bull, elephant, whale, or seal

calf² n (pl calves) back of the leg between the ankle and knee

calibrate v (-brates, -brating, -brated) mark the scale or check the accuracy of (a measuring instrument) > **calibration** n (pl -s)

calibrated v ▷ calibrate

calibrates v ▷ calibrate

calibrating v ▷ calibrate

calibration n ▷ calibrate

calibrations n ▷ calibrate

calibre n (pl -s) person's ability or worth

calibres n ▷ calibre

calico n (pl -coes) white cotton fabric

calicoes n ▷ calico

caliph n (pl -s) (HIST) Muslim ruler

caliphs n ▷ caliph

call v (-s, -ing, -ed) name ▶ n (pl -s) cry, shout > **caller** n (pl -s)

called v ▷ call

caller n ▷ call

callers n ▷ call

calligrapher n ▷ calligraphy

calligraphers n ▷ calligraphy

calligraphies n ▷ calligraphy

calligraphy n (pl -phies) (art of) beautiful handwriting > **calligrapher** n (pl -s)

calling n (pl -s) vocation, profession ▶ v ▷ call

callings n ▷ calling

calliper n (pl -s) metal splint for supporting the leg

callipers n ▷ calliper

callisthenics pl n light keep-fit exercises

callous adj showing no concern for other people's feelings > **callously** adv > **callousness** n

calloused adj (of skin) thickened and hardened

callously adv ▷ callous

callousness adv ▷ callous

callow adj (-er, -est) young and inexperienced > **callowness** n (pl -es)

callower adj ▷ callow

callowest adj ▷ callow

callowness adv ▷ callow

callownesses adv ▷ callow

calls v, n ▷ call

callus n (pl -es) area of thick hardened skin

calluses n ▷ callus

calm adj (-er, -est) not agitated or excited ▶ n (pl -s) peaceful state ▶ v (-s, -ing, -ed) (often foll. by **down**) make or become calm > **calmly** adv > **calmness** n (pl -es)

calmed v ▷ calm

calmer adj ▷ calm

calmest adj ▷ calm

calming v ▷ calm

calmly adv ▷ calm

calmness adv ▷ calm

calmnesses adv ▷ calm

calms n, v ▷ calm

calorie n (pl -s) unit of measurement for the energy value of food

calories n ▷ calorie

calorific adj of calories or heat

calumnies n ▷ calumny

calumny n (pl -nies) false or malicious statement

calve v (calves, calving, calved) give birth to a calf

calved v ▷ calve

calves v ▷ calve ▶ n ▷ calf[1, 2]

calving v ▷ calve

calyces n ▷ calyx

calypso n (pl -s) West Indian song with improvised topical lyrics

calypsos n ▷ calypso

calyx n (pl calyxes, calyces) outer leaves that protect a flower bud

calyxes n ▷ calyx

cam n (pl -s) device that converts a circular motion to a to-and-fro motion

camaraderie n (pl -s) comradeship

camaraderies n ▷ camaraderie

camber n (pl -s) slight upward curve to the centre of a surface

cambers n ▷ camber

cambric n (pl -s) fine white linen fabric

cambrics n ▷ cambric

camcorder n (pl -s) combined portable video camera and recorder

camcorders n ▷ camcorder

came v ▷ come

camel n (pl -s) humped mammal that can survive long periods without food or water in desert regions

camellia [kam-**meal**-ya] n (pl -s) evergreen ornamental shrub with white, pink, or red flowers

camellias n ▷ camellia

camels n ▷ camel

cameo n (pl -s) brooch or ring with a profile head carved in relief

cameos n ▷ cameo

camera n (pl -s) apparatus used for taking photographs or pictures for television or cinema

cameraman n (pl -men) man who operates a camera for television or cinema

cameramen n ▷ cameraman

cameras n ▷ camera

camiknickers pl n (BRIT) woman's undergarment consisting of knickers attached to a camisole

camisole n (pl -s) woman's bodice-like garment

camisoles n ▷ camisole

camomile n (pl -s) aromatic plant, used to make herbal tea

camomiles n ▷ camomile

camouflage [kam-moo-flahzh] *n* (*pl* -s) use of natural surroundings or artificial aids to conceal or disguise something ▶ *v* (-lages, -flaging, -flaged) conceal by camouflage
camouflaged *v* ▷ camouflage
camouflages *n, v* ▷ camouflage
camouflaging *v* ▷ camouflage

camp¹ *n* (*pl* -s) (place for) temporary lodgings consisting of tents, huts, or cabins ▶ *v* (-s, -ing, -ed) stay in a camp > **camper** *n* (*pl* -s)

camp² *adj* (-er, -est) (*Informal*) effeminate or homosexual

campaign *n* (*pl* -s) series of coordinated activities designed to achieve a goal ▶ *v* (-s, -ing, -ed) take part in a campaign
campaigned *v* ▷ campaign
campaigning *v* ▷ campaign
campaigns *n, v* ▷ campaign
campanologies *n* ▷ campanology
campanology *n* (*pl* -gies) art of ringing bells
campanula *n* (*pl* -s) plant with blue or white bell-shaped flowers
campanulas *n* ▷ campanula
camped *v* ▷ camp¹
camper *n* ▷ camp¹ ▶ *adj* ▷ camp²
campers *n* ▷ camp¹
campest *adj* ▷ camp²
camphor *n* (*pl* -s) aromatic crystalline substance used medicinally and in mothballs
camphors *n* ▷ camphor
camping *v* ▷ camp¹
campion *n* (*pl* -s) red, pink, or white wild flower
campions *n* ▷ campion
camps *n, v* ▷ camp¹
campus *n* (*pl* -es) grounds of a university or college
campuses *n* ▷ campus
cams *n* ▷ cam
camshaft *n* (*pl* -s) part of an engine consisting of a rod to which cams are fixed
camshafts *n* ▷ camshaft
can¹ *v* (*past* could) be able to
can² *n* (*pl* -s) metal container for food or liquids ▶ *v* (cans, canning, canned) put (something) into a can
canal *n* (*pl* -s) artificial waterway
canals *n* ▷ canal
canapé [kan-nap-pay] *n* (*pl* -s) small piece of bread or toast with a savoury topping
canapés *n* ▷ canapé
canaries *n* ▷ canary
canary *n* (*pl* -ries) small yellow songbird often kept as a pet
canasta *n* (*pl* -s) card game like rummy, played

with two packs
canastas *n* ▷ canasta
cancan *n* (*pl* -s) lively high-kicking dance performed by a female group
cancans *n* ▷ cancan
cancel *v* (-cels, -celling, -celled) stop (something that has been arranged) from taking place > **cancellation** *n* (*pl* -s)
cancellation *n* ▷ cancel
cancellations *n* ▷ cancel
cancelled *v* ▷ cancel
cancelling *v* ▷ cancel
cancels *v* ▷ cancel
cancer *n* (*pl* -s) serious disease resulting from a malignant growth or tumour > **cancerous** *adj*
cancerous *adj* ▷ cancer
cancers *n* ▷ cancer
candela [kan-dee-la] *n* (*pl* -s) unit of luminous intensity
candelabra *n* ▷ candelabrum
candelabrum *n* (*pl* -bra) large branched candle holder
candelas *n* ▷ candela
candid *adj* (-er, -est) honest and straightforward > **candidly** *adv* > **candidness** *n* (*pl* -es)
candidacies *n* ▷ candidate
candidacy *n* ▷ candidate
candidate *n* (*pl* -s) person seeking a job or position > **candidacy** (*pl* -acies), **candidature** *n* (*pl* -s)
candidates *n* ▷ candidate
candidature *n* ▷ candidate
candidatures *n* ▷ candidate
candider *adj* ▷ candid
candidest *adj* ▷ candid
candidly *adv* ▷ candid
candidness *n* ▷ candid
candidnesses *n* ▷ candid
candied *adj* coated with sugar
candies *n* ▷ candy
candle *n* (*pl* -s) stick of wax enclosing a wick, which is burned to produce light
candles *n* ▷ candle
candlestick *n* (*pl* -s) holder for a candle
candlesticks *n* ▷ candlestick
candlewick *n* (*pl* -s) cotton fabric with a tufted surface
candlewicks *n* ▷ candlewick
candour *n* (*pl* -s) honesty and straightforwardness
candours *n* ▷ candour
candy *n* (*pl* -dies) (us) sweet or sweets
candyfloss *n* (*pl* -es) light fluffy mass of spun sugar on a stick

candyflosses *n* ▷ candyfloss
cane *n* (*pl* -s) stem of the bamboo or similar plant ▶ *v* (canes, caning, caned) beat with a cane
caned *v* ▷ cane
canes *n*, *v* ▷ cane
canine *adj* of or like a dog ▶ *n* (*pl* -s) sharp pointed tooth between the incisors and the molars
canines *n* ▷ canine
caning *v* ▷ cane
canister *n* (*pl* -s) metal container
canisters *n* ▷ canister
canker *n* (*pl* -s) ulceration, ulcerous disease
cankers *n* ▷ canker
cannabis *n* (*pl* -es) Asian plant with tough fibres
cannabises *n* ▷ cannabis
canned *adj* preserved in a can ▶ *v* ▷ can²
cannelloni *pl n* tubular pieces of pasta filled with meat etc.
canneries *n* ▷ cannery
cannery *n* (*pl* -ries) factory where food is canned
cannibal *n* (*pl* -s) person who eats human flesh > **cannibalism** *n*
cannibalize *v* (-lizes, -lizing, -lized) use parts from (one machine) to repair another
cannibalized *v* ▷ cannibalize
cannibalizes *v* ▷ cannibalize
cannibalizing *v* ▷ cannibalize
cannibals *n* ▷ cannibal
cannier *adj* ▷ canny
canniest *adj* ▷ canny
cannily *adv* ▷ canny
canning *v* ▷ can²
cannon *n* (*pl* -s) large gun on wheels
cannonade *n* (*pl* -s) continuous heavy gunfire
cannonades *n* ▷ cannonade
cannonball *n* (*pl* -s) heavy metal ball fired from a cannon
cannonballs *n* ▷ cannonball
cannons *n* ▷ cannon
cannot *v* can not
canny *adj* (-nier, -niest) shrewd, cautious > **cannily** *adv*
canoe *n* (*pl* -s) light narrow open boat propelled by a paddle or paddles > **canoeist** *n* (*pl* -s)
canoeing *n* sport of rowing in a canoe
canoeist *n* ▷ canoe
canoeists *n* ▷ canoe
canoes *n* ▷ canoe
canon¹ *n* (*pl* -s) priest serving in a cathedral
canon² *n* (*pl* -s) Church decree regulating

morals or religious practices > **canonical** *adj*
canonical *adj* ▷ canon²
canonization *n* ▷ canonize
canonizations *n* ▷ canonize
canonize *v* (-izes, -izing, -ized) declare (a person) officially to be a saint > **canonization** *n* (*pl* -s)
canonized *v* ▷ canonize
canonizes *v* ▷ canonize
canonizing *v* ▷ canonize
canons *n* ▷ canon¹, ²
canoodle *v* (-les, -ling, -led) (*Slang*) kiss and cuddle
canoodled *v* ▷ canoodle
canoodles *v* ▷ canoodle
canoodling *v* ▷ canoodle
canopied *adj* covered with a canopy
canopies *n* ▷ canopy
canopy *n* (*pl* -pies) covering above a bed, door, etc
cans *n*, *v* ▷ can²
cant¹ *n* (*pl* -s) insincere talk
cant² *n* (*pl* -s) tilted position ▶ *v* (-s, -ing, -ed) tilt, overturn
cantaloupe, cantaloup *n* (*pl* -s) kind of melon with sweet orange flesh
cantaloupes *n* ▷ cantaloupe
cantaloups *n* ▷ cantaloupe
cantankerous *adj* quarrelsome, bad-tempered
cantata *n* (*pl* -s) musical work consisting of arias, duets, and choruses
cantatas *n* ▷ cantata
canted *v* ▷ cant²
canteen *n* (*pl* -s) restaurant attached to a workplace or school
canteens *n* ▷ canteen
canter *n* (*pl* -s) horse's gait between a trot and a gallop ▶ *v* (-s, -ing, -ed) move at a canter
cantered *v* ▷ canter
cantering *v* ▷ canter
canters *n*, *v* ▷ canter
canticle *n* (*pl* -s) short hymn with words from the Bible
canticles *n* ▷ canticle
cantilever *n* (*pl* -s) beam or girder fixed at one end only
cantilevers *n* ▷ cantilever
canting *v* ▷ cant²
canto *n* (*pl* -s) main division of a long poem
canton *n* (*pl* -s) political division of a country, esp. Switzerland
cantons *n* ▷ canton
cantor *n* (*pl* -s) man employed to lead services in a synagogue

cantors n ▷ cantor

cantos n ▷ canto

cants n ▷ cant[1, 2] ▶ v ▷ cant[2]

canvas n (pl -es) heavy coarse cloth used for sails and tents, and for oil painting

canvases n ▷ canvas

canvass v (-es, -ing, -ed) try to get votes or support (from) ▶ n (pl -es) canvassing

canvassed v ▷ canvass

canvasses v, n ▷ canvass

canvassing v ▷ canvass

canyon n (pl -s) deep narrow valley

canyons n ▷ canyon

cap n (pl -s) soft close-fitting covering for the head ▶ v (caps, capping, capped) cover or top with something

capabilities n ▷ capable

capability n ▷ capable

capable adj (foll. by of) having the ability (for) > **capably** adv > **capability** n (pl -ties)

capably adv ▷ capable

capacious adj roomy

capacitance n (pl -s) (measure of) the ability of a system to store electrical charge

capacitances n ▷ capacit

capacities n ▷ capacity

capacitor n (pl -s) device for storing electrical charge

capacitors n ▷ capacitor

capacity n (pl -ties) ability to contain, absorb, or hold

caparisoned adj magnificently decorated

cape[1] n (pl -s) short cloak

cape[2] n (pl -s) large piece of land that juts out into the sea

caper n (pl -s) high-spirited prank ▶ v (-s, -ing, -ed) skip about

capercaillie, capercailzie [kap-per-**kale**-yee] n (pl -s) large black European grouse

capercaillies n ▷ capercaillie

capercailzie n ▷ capercaillie

capercailzies n ▷ capercaillie

capered v ▷ caper

capering v ▷ caper

capers pl n pickled flower buds of a Mediterranean shrub used in sauces ▶ n ▷ caper ▶ v ▷ caper

capes n ▷ cape[1, 2]

capillaries n ▷ capillary

capillary n (pl -laries) very fine blood vessel

capital[1] n (pl -s) chief city of a country ▶ adj involving or punishable by death

capital[2] n (pl -s) top part of a pillar

capitalism n (pl -s) economic system based on the private ownership of industry

capitalisms n ▷ capitalism

capitalist adj of capitalists or capitalism ▶ n (pl -s) supporter of capitalism > **capitalistic** adj

capitalistic adj ▷ capitalist

capitalists n ▷ capitalist

capitalize v (-lizes, -lizing, -lized) write or print (words) in capitals

capitalized v ▷ capitalize

capitalizes v ▷ capitalize

capitalizing v ▷ capitalize

capitals n ▷ capital[1, 2]

capitation n (pl -s) tax of a fixed amount per person

capitations n ▷ capitation

capitulate v (-lates, -lating, -lated) surrender on agreed terms > **capitulation** n (pl -s)

capitulated v ▷ capitulate

capitulates v ▷ capitulate

capitulating v ▷ capitulate

capitulation n ▷ capitulate

capitulations n ▷ capitulate

capon n (pl -s) castrated cock fowl fattened for eating

capons n ▷ capon

capped v ▷ cap

capping v ▷ cap

cappuccino [kap-poo-**cheen**-oh] n (pl -s) coffee with steamed milk, sprinkled with powdered chocolate

cappuccinos n ▷ cappuccino

caprice [kap-**reess**] n (pl -s) sudden change of attitude

caprices n ▷ caprice

capricious adj tending to have sudden changes of attitude > **capriciously** adv

capriciously adv ▷ capricious

caps n, v ▷ cap

capsicum n (pl -s) kind of pepper used as a vegetable or as a spice

capsicums n ▷ capsicum

capsize v (-sizes, -sizing, -sized) (of a boat) overturn accidentally

capsized v ▷ capsize

capsizes v ▷ capsize

capsizing v ▷ capsize

capstan n (pl -s) rotating cylinder round which a ship's rope is wound

capstans n ▷ capstan

capsule n (pl -s) soluble gelatine case containing a dose of medicine

capsules n ▷ capsule

captain n (pl -s) commander of a ship or civil aircraft ▶ v (-s, -ing, -ed) be captain of > **captaincy** n (pl -cies)

captaincies n ▷ captain

captaincy n ▷ captain
captained v ▷ captain
captaining v ▷ captain
captains n, v ▷ captain
caption n (pl -s) title or explanation accompanying an illustration ▶ v (-s, -ing, -ed) provide with a caption
captioned v ▷ caption
captioning v ▷ caption
captions n, v ▷ caption
captious adj tending to make trivial criticisms > **captiously** adv > **captiousness** n
captiously adv ▷ captious
captiousness n ▷ captious
captivate v (-ates, -ating, -ated) attract and hold the attention of > **captivating** adj
captivated v ▷ captivate
captivates v ▷ captivate
captivating adj, v ▷ captivate
captive n (pl -s) person kept in confinement ▶ adj kept in confinement > **captivity** n
captives n ▷ captive
captivity n ▷ captive
captor n (pl -s) person who captures a person or animal
captors n ▷ captor
capture v (-tures, -turing, -tured) take by force ▶ n (pl -s) capturing
captured v ▷ capture
captures v, n ▷ capture
capturing v ▷ capture
car n (pl -s) motor vehicle designed to carry a small number of people
carafe [kar-**raff**] n (pl -s) glass bottle for serving water or wine
carafes n ▷ carafe
caramel n (pl -s) chewy sweet made from sugar and milk
caramelize v (-izes, -izing, -ized) turn into caramel
caramelized v ▷ caramelize
caramelizes v ▷ caramelize
caramelizing v ▷ caramelize
caramels n ▷ caramel
carapace n (pl -s) hard upper shell of tortoises and crustaceans
carapaces n ▷ carapace
carat n (pl -s) unit of weight of precious stones
carats n ▷ carat
caravan n (pl -s) large enclosed vehicle for living in, designed to be towed by a car or horse
caravans n ▷ caravan
caraway n (pl -s) plant whose seeds are used as a spice

caraways n ▷ caraway
carbide n (pl -s) compound of carbon with a metal
carbides n ▷ carbide
carbine n (pl -s) light automatic rifle
carbines n ▷ carbine
carbohydrate n (pl -s) any of a large group of energy-producing compounds in food, such as sugars and starches
carbohydrates n ▷ carbohydrate
carbon n (pl -s) nonmetallic element occurring as charcoal, graphite, and diamond, found in all organic matter
carbonate n (pl -s) salt or ester of carbonic acid
carbonated adj (of a drink) containing carbon dioxide
carbonates n ▷ carbonate
carbonize v (-izes, -izing, -ized) turn into carbon as a result of heating
carbonized v ▷ carbonize
carbonizes v ▷ carbonize
carbonizing v ▷ carbonize
carbons n ▷ carbon
carbuncle n (pl -s) inflamed boil
carbuncles n ▷ carbuncle
carburettor n (pl -s) device which mixes petrol and air in an internal-combustion engine
carburettors n ▷ carburettor
carcase n ▷ carcass
carcases n ▷ carcass
carcass, carcase n (pl -es, -es) dead body of an animal
carcasses n ▷ carcass
carcinogen n (pl -s) substance that produces cancer > **carcinogenic** adj
carcinogenic adj ▷ carcinogen
carcinogens n ▷ carcinogen
carcinoma n (pl -s) malignant tumour
carcinomas n ▷ carcinoma
card n (pl -s) piece of thick stiff paper or cardboard used for identification, reference, or sending greetings or messages ▶ pl any card game, or card games in general
cardboard n (pl -s) thin stiff board made from paper pulp
cardboards n ▷ cardboard
cardiac adj of the heart
cardigan n (pl -s) knitted jacket
cardigans n ▷ cardigan
cardinal n (pl -s) any of the high-ranking clergymen of the RC Church who elect the Pope and act as his counsellors ▶ adj fundamentally important
cardinals n ▷ cardinal
cardiogram n (pl -s) electrocardiogram

cardiograms n ▷ cardiogram
cardiograph n (pl -s) electrocardiograph
cardiographs n ▷ cardiograph
cardiologist n ▷ cardiology
cardiologists n ▷ cardiology
cardiology n study of the heart and its diseases ▷ **cardiologist** n (pl -s)
cardiovascular adj of the heart and the blood vessels
cards n ▷ card
cardsharp n (pl -s) professional card player who cheats
cardsharps n ▷ cardsharp
care v (cares, caring, cared) be concerned ▷ n (pl -s) careful attention, caution > **careful** adj (-ller, -llest) > **carefully** adv > **carefulness** n (pl -es) > **careless** adj > **carelessly** adv > **carelessness** n
cared v ▷ care
careen v (-s, -ing, -ed) tilt over to one side
careened v ▷ careen
careening v ▷ careen
careens v ▷ careen
career n (pl -s) series of jobs in a profession or occupation that a person has through their life ▷ v (-s, -ing, -ed) rush in an uncontrolled way
careered v ▷ career
careering v ▷ career
careerist n (pl -s) person who seeks advancement by any possible means
careerists n ▷ careerist
careers n, v ▷ career
carefree adj without worry or responsibility
careful adj ▷ care
carefuller adj ▷ care
carefullest adj ▷ care
carefully adv ▷ care
carefulness n ▷ care
carefulnesses n ▷ care
careless adj ▷ care
carelessly adv ▷ care
carelessness adv ▷ care
cares v, n ▷ care
caress n (pl -es) gentle affectionate touch or embrace ▷ v (-es, -ing, -ed) touch gently and affectionately
caressed v ▷ caress
caresses n, v ▷ caress
caressing v ▷ caress
caret [kar-rett] n (pl -s) symbol (⋀) indicating a place in written or printed matter where something is to be inserted
caretaker n (pl -s) person employed to look after a place

caretakers n ▷ caretaker
carets n ▷ caret
careworn adj showing signs of worry
cargo n (pl -es) goods carried by a ship, aircraft, etc.
cargoes n ▷ cargo
caribou n (pl -bou or -bous) large N American reindeer
caribous n ▷ caribou
caricature n (pl -s) drawing or description of a person that exaggerates features for comic effect ▷ v (-tures, -turing, -tured) make a caricature of
caricatured v ▷ caricature
caricatures n, v ▷ caricature
caricaturing v ▷ caricature
caries [care-reez] n (pl caries) tooth decay
carillon [kar-rill-yon] n (pl -s) set of bells played by keyboard or mechanically
carillons n ▷ carillon
caring v ▷ care
cark v (-s, -ing, -ed) (AUST & NZ) (Slang) die
carked v ▷ cark
carking v ▷ cark
carks v ▷ cark
carmine adj vivid red
carnage n (pl -s) extensive slaughter of people
carnages n ▷ carnage
carnal adj of a sexual or sensual nature > **carnally** adv
carnally adv ▷ carnal
carnation n (pl -s) cultivated plant with fragrant white, pink, or red flowers
carnations n ▷ carnation
carnival n (pl -s) festive period with processions, music, and dancing in the street
carnivals n ▷ carnival
carnivore n (pl -s) meat-eating animal > **carnivorous** adj
carnivores n ▷ carnivore
carnivorous adj ▷ carnivore
carob n (pl -s) pod of a Mediterranean tree, used as a chocolate substitute
carobs n ▷ carob
carol n (pl -s) joyful Christmas hymn ▷ v (-ls, -lling, -lled) sing carols
carolled v ▷ carol
carolling v ▷ carol
carols n, v ▷ carol
carotid adj, n (pl -s) (of) either of the two arteries supplying blood to the head
carotids n ▷ carotid
carouse v (-ouses, -ousing, -oused) have a merry drinking party
caroused v ▷ carouse

carousel [kar-roo-**sell**] *n* (*pl* -s) revolving conveyor belt for luggage or photographic slides

carousels *n* ▷ carousel

carouses *v* ▷ carouse

carousing *v* ▷ carouse

carp[1] *n* (*pl* carp) large freshwater fish

carp[2] *v* (-s, -ing, -ed) complain, find fault

carped *v* ▷ carp[2]

carpel *n* (*pl* -s) female reproductive organ of a flowering plant

carpels *n* ▷ carpel

carpenter *n* (*pl* -s) person who makes or repairs wooden structures > **carpentry** *n*

carpenters *n* ▷ carpenter

carpentry *n* ▷ carpenter

carpet *n* (*pl* -s) heavy fabric for covering floors ▶ *v* (-s, -ing, -ed) cover with a carpet

carpeted *v* ▷ carpet

carpeting *v* ▷ carpet

carpets *n*, *v* ▷ carpet

carpi *n* ▷ carpus

carping *v* ▷ carp[2]

carps *v* ▷ carp[2]

carpus *n* (*pl* -pi) set of eight bones of the wrist

carriage *n* (*pl* -s) one of the sections of a train for passengers

carriages *n* ▷ carriage

carriageway *n* (*pl* -s) (BRIT) part of a road along which traffic passes in one direction

carriageways *n* ▷ carriageway

carried *v* ▷ carry

carrier *n* (*pl* -s) person or thing that carries something

carriers *n* ▷ carrier

carries *v* ▷ carry

carrion *n* (*pl* -s) dead and rotting flesh

carrions *n* ▷ carrion

carrot *n* (*pl* -s) long tapering orange root vegetable

carrots *n* ▷ carrot

carroty *adj* (of hair) reddish-orange

carry *v* (-ries, -rying, -ried) take from one place to another

carrying *v* ▷ carry

cars *n* ▷ car

cart *n* (*pl* -s) open two-wheeled horse-drawn vehicle for carrying goods or passengers ▶ *v* (-s, -ing, -ed) carry, usu. with some effort

carted *v* ▷ cart

cartel *n* (*pl* -s) association of competing firms formed to fix prices

cartels *n* ▷ cartel

carthorse *n* (*pl* -s) large heavily built horse

carthorses *n* ▷ carthorse

cartilage *n* (*pl* -s) strong flexible tissue forming part of the skeleton > **cartilaginous** *adj*

cartilages *n* ▷ cartilage

cartilaginous *n* ▷ cartilage

carting *v* ▷ cart

cartographer *n* ▷ cartography

cartographers *n* ▷ cartography

cartographic *adj* ▷ cartography

cartographically *adj* ▷ cartography

cartographies *n* ▷ cartography

cartography *n* (*pl* -ies) map making > **cartographer** *n* (*pl* -s) > **cartographic** *adj* > **cartographically** *adv*

carton *n* (*pl* -s) container made of cardboard or waxed paper

cartons *n* ▷ carton

cartoon *n* (*pl* -s) humorous or satirical drawing > **cartoonist** *n* (*pl* -s)

cartoonist *n* ▷ cartoon

cartoonists *n* ▷ cartoon

cartoons *n* ▷ cartoon

cartridge *n* (*pl* -s) casing containing an explosive charge and bullet for a gun

cartridges *n* ▷ cartridge

carts *n*, *v* ▷ cart

cartwheel *n* (*pl* -s) sideways somersault supported by the hands with legs outstretched

cartwheels *n* ▷ cartwheel

carve *v* (carves, carving, carved) cut to form an object > **carving** *n* (*pl* -s)

carved *v* ▷ carve

carves *v* ▷ carve

carving *v*, *n* ▷ carve

carvings *n* ▷ carve

caryatid [kar-ree-**at**-id] *n* (*pl* -s) supporting column in the shape of a female figure

caryatids *n* ▷ caryatid

casbah *n* (*pl* -s) citadel of a N African city

casbahs *n* ▷ casbah

cascade *n* (*pl* -s) waterfall ▶ *v* (-cades, -cading, -caded) flow or fall in a cascade

cascaded *v* ▷ cascade

cascades *n*, *v* ▷ cascade

cascading *v* ▷ cascade

case[1] *n* (*pl* -s) instance, example

case[2] *n* (*pl* -s) container, protective covering ▶ *v* (cases, casing, cased) (*Slang*) inspect (a building) with the intention of burgling it

cased *v* ▷ case[2]

casement *n* (*pl* -s) window that is hinged on one side

casements *n* ▷ casement

cases *n* ▷ case[1, 2] ▶ *v* ▷ case[2]

cash n banknotes and coins ▶ v (-es, -ing, -ed) obtain cash for
  cashed v ▷ cash
  cashes v ▷ cash
cashew n (pl -s) edible kidney-shaped nut
  cashews n ▷ cashew
cashier¹ n (pl -s) person responsible for handling cash in a bank, shop, etc.
cashier² v (-s, -ing, -ed) dismiss with dishonour from the armed forces
  cashiered v ▷ cashier²
  cashiering v ▷ cashier²
  cashiers n ▷ cashier¹ ▶ v ▷ cashier²
  cashing v ▷ cash
cashmere n (pl -s) fine soft wool obtained from goats
  cashmeres n ▷ cashmere
casing n (pl -s) protective case, covering ▶ v ▷ case²
  casings n ▷ casing
casino n (pl -s) public building or room where gambling games are played
  casinos n ▷ casino
cask n (pl -s) barrel used to hold alcoholic drink
casket n (pl -s) small box for valuables
  caskets n ▷ casket
  casks n ▷ cask
cassava n (pl -s) starch obtained from the roots of a tropical American plant, used to make tapioca
  cassavas n ▷ cassava
casserole n (pl -s) covered dish in which food is cooked slowly, usu. in an oven ▶ v (-oles, -oling, -oled) cook in a casserole
  casseroled v ▷ casserole
  casseroles n, v ▷ casserole
  casseroling v ▷ casserole
cassette n (pl -s) plastic case containing a reel of film or magnetic tape
  cassettes n ▷ cassette
cassock n (pl -s) long tunic, usu. black, worn by priests
  cassocks n ▷ cassock
  cassowaries n ▷ cassowary
cassowary n (pl -waries) large flightless bird of Australia and New Guinea
cast n (pl -s) actors in a play or film collectively ▶ v (casts, casting, cast) select (an actor) to play a part in a play or film
castanets pl n musical instrument, used by Spanish dancers, consisting of curved pieces of hollow wood clicked together in the hand
castaway n (pl -s) shipwrecked person
  castaways n ▷ castaway
caste n (pl -s) any of the hereditary classes into which Hindu society is divided
castellated adj having battlements
  castes n ▷ caste
castigate v (-gates, -gating, -gated) reprimand severely > **castigation** n
  castigated v ▷ castigate
  castigates v ▷ castigate
  castigating v ▷ castigate
  castigation n ▷ castigate
  casting v ▷ cast
castle n (pl -s) large fortified building, often built as a ruler's residence
  castles n ▷ castle
castoff adj, n (pl -s) discarded (person or thing)
  castoffs n ▷ castoff
castor n (pl -s) small swivelling wheel fixed to the bottom of a piece of furniture for easy moving
  castors n ▷ castor
castrate v (-tes, -ting, -ted) remove the testicles of > **castration** n (pl -s)
  castrated v ▷ castrate
  castrates v ▷ castrate
  castrating v ▷ castrate
  castration n ▷ castrate
  castrations n ▷ castrate
  casts n, v ▷ cast
casual adj careless, nonchalant > **casually** adv
  casually adv ▷ casual
  casualties n ▷ casualty
casualty n (pl -ties) person killed or injured in an accident or war
casuarina [kass-yew-a-**reen**-a] n (pl -s) Australian tree with jointed green branches
  casuarinas n ▷ casuarina
  casuistries n ▷ casuistry
casuistry n (pl -ries) reasoning that is misleading or oversubtle
cat n (pl -s) small domesticated furry mammal
cataclysm [kat-a-**kliz**-zum] n (pl -s) violent upheaval > **cataclysmic** adj
  cataclysmic adj ▷ cataclysm
  cataclysms n ▷ cataclysm
catacombs [kat-a-koomz] pl n underground burial place consisting of tunnels with recesses for tombs
catafalque [kat-a-falk] n (pl -s) raised platform on which a body lies in state before or during a funeral
  catafalques n ▷ catafalque
  catalepsies n ▷ catalepsy
catalepsy n (pl -sies) trancelike state in which the body is rigid > **cataleptic** adj
  cataleptic adj ▷ catalepsy
catalogue n (pl -s) book containing details of

items for sale ▸ v (-logues, -loguing, -logued) make a systematic list of

catalogued v ▷ catalogue

catalogues n, v ▷ catalogue

cataloguing v ▷ catalogue

catalyse v (-lyses, -lysing, -lysed) speed up (a chemical reaction) by a catalyst

catalysed v ▷ catalyse

catalyses v ▷ catalyse

catalysing v ▷ catalyse

catalysis n ▷ catalyst

catalyst n (pl -s) substance that speeds up a chemical reaction without itself changing > **catalysis** n > **catalytic** adj > **catalytically** adv

catalysts n ▷ catalyst

catalytic adj ▷ catalyst

catalytically adv ▷ catalyst

catamaran n (pl -s) boat with twin parallel hulls

catamarans n ▷ catamaran

catapult n (pl -s) Y-shaped device with a loop of elastic, used by children for firing stones ▸ v (-s, -ing, -ed) shoot forwards or upwards violently

catapulted v ▷ catapult

catapulting v ▷ catapult

catapults n, v ▷ catapult

cataract n (pl -s) eye disease in which the lens becomes opaque

cataracts n ▷ cataract

catarrh [kat-**tar**] n (pl -s) excessive mucus in the nose and throat, during or following a cold > **catarrhal** adj

catarrhal adj ▷ catarrh

catarrhs n ▷ catarrh

catastrophe [kat-**ass**-trof-fee] n (pl -s) great and sudden disaster > **catastrophic** adj > **catastrophically** adv

catastrophes n ▷ catastrophe

catastrophic adj ▷ catastrophe

catastrophically adv ▷ catastrophe

catcall n (pl -s) derisive whistle or cry

catcalls n ▷ catcall

catch v (catches, catching, caught) seize, capture ▸ n (pl -es) device for fastening a door, window, etc.

catches v, n ▷ catch

catchier adj ▷ catchy

catchiest adj ▷ catchy

catchily adv ▷ catchy

catchiness n ▷ catchy

catchinesses n ▷ catchy

catching adj infectious ▸ v ▷ catch

catchword n (pl -s) well-known and frequently used phrase

catchwords n ▷ catchword

catchy adj (-chier, -chiest) (of a tune) pleasant and easily remembered > **catchily** adv > **catchiness** n (pl -es)

catechism [kat-ti-**kiz**-zum] n (pl -s) instruction on the doctrine of a Christian Church in a series of questions and answers

catechisms n ▷ catechism

categorical adj absolutely clear and certain > **categorically** adv

categorically adv ▷ categorical

categories n ▷ category

categorization n ▷ categorize

categorizations n ▷ categorize

categorize v (-izes, -izing, -ized) put in a category > **categorization** n (pl -s)

categorized v ▷ categorize

categorizes v ▷ categorize

categorizing v ▷ categorize

category n (pl -ries) class, group

cater v (-s, -ing, -ed) provide what is needed or wanted, esp. food or services > **caterer** n (pl -s)

catered v ▷ cater

caterer n ▷ cater

caterers n ▷ cater

catering v ▷ cater

caterpillar n (pl -s) wormlike larva of a moth or butterfly

caterpillars n ▷ caterpillar

caters v ▷ cater

caterwaul v (-s, -ing, -ed) wail, yowl

caterwauled v ▷ caterwaul

caterwauling v ▷ caterwaul

caterwauls v ▷ caterwaul

catfish n (pl catfish, catfishes) fish with whisker-like barbels round the mouth

catfishes n ▷ catfish

catgut n (pl -s) strong cord used to string musical instruments and sports rackets

catguts n ▷ catgut

catharses n ▷ catharsis

catharsis [kath-**thar**-siss] n (pl -ses) relief of strong suppressed emotions > **cathartic** adj

cathartic adj ▷ catharsis

cathedral n (pl -s) principal church of a diocese

cathedrals n ▷ cathedral

catheter [**kath**-it-er] n (pl -s) tube inserted into a body cavity to drain fluid

catheters n ▷ catheter

cathode n (pl -s) negative electrode, by which electrons leave a circuit

cathodes n ▷ cathode

catholic adj (of tastes or interests) covering a wide range > **catholicism** n (pl -s)

catholicism n ▷ catholic

catholicisms n ▷ catholic

cation [kat-eye-on] n (pl -s) positively charged ion

cations n ▷ cation

catkin n (pl -s) drooping flower spike of certain trees

catkins n ▷ catkin

catnap n (pl -s) ▶ v (-naps, -napping, -napped) doze

catnapped v ▷ catnap

catnapping v ▷ catnap

catnaps n, v ▷ catnap

cats n ▷ cat

cattier adj ▷ catty

cattiest adj ▷ catty

cattily adv ▷ catty

cattiness n ▷ catty

cattle pl n domesticated cows and bulls

catty adj (cattier, cattiest) (Informal) spiteful > **cattily** adv > **cattiness** n

catwalk n (pl -s) narrow pathway or platform

catwalks n ▷ catwalk

caucus n (pl -es) local committee or faction of a political party

caught v ▷ catch

cauldron n (pl -s) large pot used for boiling

cauldrons n ▷ cauldron

cauliflower n (pl -s) vegetable with a large head of white flower buds surrounded by green leaves

cauliflowers n ▷ cauliflower

caulk v (-s, -ing, -ed) fill in (cracks) with paste etc.

caulked v ▷ caulk

caulking v ▷ caulk

caulks v ▷ caulk

causal adj of or being a cause > **causally** adv

causality n ▷ causation

causally adv ▷ causal

causation, causality n relationship of cause and effect

cause n (pl -s) something that produces a particular effect ▶ v (causes, causing, caused) be the cause of

caused v ▷ cause

causes n, v ▷ cause

causeway n (pl -s) raised path or road across water or marshland

causeways n ▷ causeway

causing v ▷ cause

caustic adj capable of burning by chemical action > **caustically** adv

caustically adv ▷ caustic

cauterize v (-izes, -izing, -ized) burn (a wound) with heat or a caustic agent to prevent infection

cauterized v ▷ cauterize

cauterizes v ▷ cauterize

cauterizing v ▷ cauterize

caution n (pl -s) care, esp. in the face of danger ▶ v (-s, -ing, -ed) warn, advise

cautionary adj warning

cautioned v ▷ caution

cautioning v ▷ caution

cautions n, v ▷ caution

cautious adj showing caution > **cautiously** adv

cautiously adv ▷ cautious

cavalcade n (pl -s) procession of people on horseback or in cars

cavalcades n ▷ cavalcade

cavalier adj showing haughty disregard ▶ n (pl -s) (C-) supporter of Charles I in the English Civil War > **cavalierly** adv

cavalierly adv ▷ cavalier

cavaliers n ▷ cavalier

cavalries n ▷ cavalry

cavalry n (pl -ries) part of the army orig. on horseback, but now often using fast armoured vehicles

cave n (pl -s) hollow in the side of a hill or cliff

caveat [kav-vee-at] n (pl -s) warning

caveats n ▷ caveat

caveman n (pl -men) prehistoric cave dweller

cavemen n ▷ caveman

cavern n (pl -s) large cave > **cavernous** adj

cavernous adj ▷ cavern

caverns n ▷ cavern

caves n ▷ cave

caviar, caviare n (pl -s) salted sturgeon roe, regarded as a delicacy

caviar n ▷ caviar

caviares n ▷ caviar

caviars n ▷ caviar

cavil v (-ils, -illing, -illed) make petty objections ▶ n (pl -s) petty objection

cavilled v ▷ cavil

cavilling v ▷ cavil

cavils v, n ▷ cavil

caving n sport of exploring caves

cavities v ▷ cavity

cavity n (pl -ties) hollow space

cavort v (-s, -ing, -ed) skip about

cavorted v ▷ cavort

cavorting v ▷ cavort

cavorts v ▷ cavort

caw n (pl -s) cry of a crow, rook, or raven ▶ v (-s, -ing, -ed) make this cry

cawed v ▷ caw

cawing v ▷ caw

caws n, v ▷ caw

cay n (**cays**) A cay is a small low island. Cay scores 8 points.

cayman n (pl -s) S American reptile similar to an alligator

caymans n ▷ cayman

caz adj. Caz is a slang word for **casual**. It's a great word to have up your sleeve as it scores 14 points.

cazique n (**caziques**) A cazique is a chief among certain American Indian tribes. Cazique scores 27 points, and will earn you a 50-point bonus if you manage to use all of your tiles to score 14 points.

cease v (**ceases, ceasing, ceased**) bring or come to an end > **ceaseless** adj > **ceaselessly** adv

ceased v ▷ cease

ceasefire n (pl -s) temporary truce

ceasefires n ▷ ceasefire

ceaseless adj ▷ cease

ceaselessly adv ▷ cease

ceases v ▷ cease

ceasing v ▷ cease

cedar n (pl -s) evergreen coniferous tree

cedars n ▷ cedar

cede v (**cedes, ceding, ceded**) surrender (territory or legal rights)

ceded v ▷ cede

cedes v ▷ cede

cedilla n (pl -s) character (.) placed under a c in some languages, to show that it is pronounced s, not k

cedillas n ▷ cedilla

ceding v ▷ cede

ceilidh [kay-lee] n (pl -s) informal social gathering for singing and dancing, esp. in Scotland

ceilidhs n ▷ ceilidh

ceiling n (pl -s) inner upper surface of a room

ceilings n ▷ ceiling

celandine n (pl -s) wild plant with yellow flowers

celandines n ▷ celandine

celebrant n (pl -s) person who performs a religious ceremony

celebrants n ▷ celebrant

celebrate v (-rates, -rating, -rated) hold festivities to mark (a happy event, anniversary, etc.) > **celebration** n (pl -s)

celebrated adj well known ▶ v ▷ celebrate

celebrates v ▷ celebrate

celebrating v ▷ celebrate

celebration n ▷ celebrate

celebrations n ▷ celebrate

celebrities n ▷ celebrity

celebrity n (pl -rities) famous person

celeriac [sill-**ler**-ee-ak] n (pl -s) variety of celery with a large turnip-like root

celeriacs n ▷ celeriac

celeries n ▷ celery

celerities n ▷ celerity

celerity [sill-**ler**-rit-tee] n (pl -ties) swiftness

celery n (pl -ries) vegetable with long green crisp edible stalks

celestial adj heavenly, divine > **celestially** adv

celestially adv ▷ celestial

celibacy n ▷ celibate

celibate adj unmarried or abstaining from sex, esp. because of a religious vow of chastity ▶ n (pl -s) celibate person > **celibacy** n

celibates n ▷ celibate

cell n (pl -s) smallest unit of an organism that is able to function independently

cellar n (pl -s) underground room for storage

cellars n ▷ cellar

cellist n ▷ cello

cellists n ▷ cello

cello [**chell**-oh] n (pl -s) large low-pitched instrument of the violin family > **cellist** n (pl -s)

cellophane n (pl -s) ® thin transparent cellulose sheeting used as wrapping

cellophanes n ▷ cellophane

cellos n ▷ cello

cells n ▷ cell

cellular adj of or consisting of cells

celluloid n (pl -s) kind of plastic used to make toys and, formerly, photographic film

celluloids n ▷ celluloid

cellulose n (pl -s) main constituent of plant cell walls, used in making paper, plastics, etc.

celluloses n ▷ cellulose

cement n (pl -s) fine grey powder mixed with water and sand to make mortar or concrete ▶ v (-s, -ing, -ed) join, bind, or cover with cement

cemented v ▷ cement

cementing v ▷ cement

cements n, v ▷ cement

cemeteries n ▷ cemetery

cemetery n (pl -ries) place where dead people are buried

cenotaph n (pl -s) monument honouring soldiers who died in a war

cenotaphs n ▷ cenotaph

censer n (pl -s) container for burning incense

censers n ▷ censer

censor n (pl -s) person authorized to examine

films, books, etc., to ban or cut anything considered obscene or objectionable ▶ v (-s, -ing, -ed) ban or cut parts of (a film, book, etc.) > **censorship** n

censored v ▷ censor

censoring v ▷ censor

censorious adj harshly critical > **censoriously** adv

censoriously adv ▷ censorious

censors n, v ▷ censor

censorship n ▷ censor

censure n (pl -s) severe disapproval ▶ v (-sures, -suring, -sured) criticize severely

censured v ▷ censure

censures n, v ▷ censure

censuring v ▷ censure

census n (pl -es) official count of a population

censuses n ▷ census

cent n (pl -s) hundredth part of a monetary unit such as the dollar or euro

centaur n (pl -s) mythical creature with the head, arms, and torso of a man, and the lower body and legs of a horse

centaurs n ▷ centaur

centenarian n (pl -s) person at least 100 years old

centenarians n ▷ centenarian

centenaries n ▷ centenary

centenary [sen-**teen**-a-ree] n (CHIEFLY BRIT) (pl -naries) 100th anniversary or its celebration

centennial n (pl -s) 100th anniversary or its celebration

centennials n ▷ centennial

centigrade adj of, at, or forming the temperature in which water freezes at 0° and boils at 100°

centigram, centigramme n (pl -s) one hundredth of a gram

centigramme n ▷ centigram

centigrammes n ▷ centigram

centigrams n ▷ centigram

centilitre n (pl -s) one hundredth of a litre

centilitres n ▷ centilitre

centimetre n (pl -s) one hundredth of a metre

centimetres n ▷ centimetre

centipede n (pl -s) small wormlike creature with many legs

centipedes n ▷ centipede

central adj of, at, or forming the centre > **centrally** adv > **centrality** n

centralism n principle of central control of a country or organization > **centralist** n (pl -s)

centralist n ▷ centralism

centralists n ▷ centralism

centrality n ▷ central

centralization n ▷ centralize

centralizations n ▷ centralize

centralize v (-izes, -izing, -ized) bring under central control > **centralization** n (pl -s)

centralized v ▷ centralize

centralizes v ▷ centralize

centralizing v ▷ centralize

centrally adv ▷ central

centre n (pl -s) middle point or part (SPORT) ▶ v (centres, centring, centred) put in the centre of something

centred v ▷ centre

centres n, v ▷ centre

centrifugal adj moving away from a centre > **centrifugally** adv

centrifugally adv ▷ centrifugal

centrifuge n (pl -s) machine that separates substances by centrifugal force

centrifuges n ▷ centrifuge

centring v ▷ centre

centripetal adj moving towards a centre > **centripetally** adv

centripetally adv ▷ centripetal

centrist n (pl -s) person favouring political moderation

centrists n ▷ centrist

cents n ▷ cent

centuries n ▷ century

centurion n (pl -s) (in ancient Rome) officer commanding 100 men

centurions n ▷ centurion

century n (pl -ries) period of 100 years

cep n (ceps). A cep is an edible fungus. Cep scores 7 points.

cephalopod [seff-a-loh-pod] n (pl -s) sea mollusc with a head and tentacles, such as the octopus

cephalopods n ▷ cephalopod

ceramic n (pl -s) hard brittle material made by heating clay to a very high temperature ▶ pl art of producing ceramic objects ▶ adj made of ceramic

ceramics n ▷ ceramic

cereal n (pl -s) grass plant with edible grain, such as oat or wheat

cereals n ▷ cereal

cerebra n ▷ cerebrum

cerebral [ser-rib-ral, ser-reeb-ral] adj of the brain

cerebrum [serr-rib-rum] n (pl -brums, -bra) [-bra] main part of the brain

cerebrums n ▷ cerebrum

ceremonial adj ▷ ceremony

ceremonially adv ▷ ceremony

ceremonials n ▷ ceremony

ceremonies n ▷ ceremony

ceremonious adj excessively polite or formal

> **ceremoniously** adv
ceremoniously adv ▷ ceremonious
ceremony n (pl -nies) formal act or ritual
> **ceremonial** adj, n (pl -s) > **ceremonially** adv
cerise [ser-**reess**] adj cherry-red
certain adj (-er, -est) positive and confident
> **certainly** adv
certainer adj ▷ certain
certainest adj ▷ certain
certainly adv ▷ certain
certainties n ▷ certainty
certainty n (pl -ties) state of being sure
certifiable adj considered legally insane
> **certifiably** adv
certifiably adv ▷ certifiable
certificate n (pl -s) official document stating
the details of a birth, academic course, etc.
certificates n ▷ certificate
certification n ▷ certify
certifications n ▷ certify
certified v ▷ certify
certifies v ▷ certify
certify v (-fies, -fying, -fied) confirm, attest to
> **certification** n (pl -s)
certifying v ▷ certify
certitude n (pl -s) confidence, certainty
certitudes n ▷ certitude
cervical adj ▷ cervix
cervices n ▷ cervix
cervix n (pl cervixes, cervices) narrow
entrance of the womb > **cervical** adj
cervixes n ▷ cervix
cessation n (pl -s) ceasing
cessations n ▷ cessation
cesspit, cesspool n (pl -s) covered tank or pit
for sewage
cesspits n ▷ cesspit
cesspool n ▷ cesspit
cesspools n ▷ cesspit
cetacean [sit-**tay**-shun] n (pl -s) fish-shaped sea
mammal such as a whale or dolphin
cetaceans n ▷ cetacean

ch pron. This is an old dialect form of I.
It's the only two-letter word that can
be formed with the letter C, and it's
a good word to remember because
it doesn't use any vowels. Ch scores
7 points.
cha n (chas). Cha is a slang word for
tea. Cha scores 8 points.

chafe v (chafes, chafing, chafed) make sore or
worn by rubbing
chafed v ▷ chafe
chafes v ▷ chafe
chaff¹ n (pl -s) grain husks

chaff² v (-s, -ing, -ed) (Old-fashioned) tease
good-naturedly
chaffed v ▷ chaff²
chaffinch n (pl -es) small European songbird
chaffinches n ▷ chaffinch
chaffing v ▷ chaff²
chaffs n ▷ chaff¹ ▶ v ▷ chaff²
chafing v ▷ chafe
chagrin [shag-**grin**] n (pl -s) annoyance and
disappointment
chagrined adj annoyed and disappointed
chagrins n ▷ chagrin
chain n (pl -s) flexible length of connected
metal links ▶ v (-s, -ing, -ed) restrict or fasten
with or as if with a chain
chained v ▷ chain
chaining v ▷ chain
chains n, v ▷ chain
chair n (pl -s) seat with a back, for one person
▶ v (-s, -ing, -ed) preside over (a meeting)
chaired v ▷ chair
chairing v ▷ chair
chairlift (pl -s) series of chairs suspended from
a moving cable for carrying people up a slope
chairlifts n ▷ chairlift
chairman, chairwoman n (pl -men, -women)
person in charge of a company's board of
directors or a meeting (also **chairperson**)
(pl -s)
chairmen n ▷ chairman
chairperson n ▷ chairman
chairpersons n ▷ chairman
chairs n, v ▷ chair
chairwoman n ▷ chairman
chairwomen n ▷ chairman
chaise [shaze] n (pl -s) (HIST) light horse-drawn
carriage
chaises n ▷ chaise
chalcedonies n ▷ chalcedony
chalcedony [kal-**sed**-don-ee] n (pl -nies) variety
of quartz
chalet n (pl -s) kind of Swiss wooden house
with a steeply sloping roof
chalets n ▷ chalet
chalice n (pl -s) large goblet
chalices n ▷ chalice
chalk n (pl -s) soft white rock consisting of
calcium carbonate ▶ v (-s, -ing, -ed) draw or
mark with chalk > **chalky** adj (-kier, -kiest)
chalked v ▷ chalk
chalkier adj ▷ chalk
chalkiest adj ▷ chalk
chalking v ▷ chalk
chalks n, v ▷ chalk
chalky adj ▷ chalk

challenge n (pl -s) demanding or stimulating situation ▶ v (-ges, -ging, -ged) issue a challenge to > **challenger** n (pl -s)

challenged adj disabled as specified ▶ v ▷challenge

challenger n ▷challenge

challengers n ▷challenge

challenges n, v ▷challenge

challenging v ▷challenge

chamber n (pl -s) hall used for formal meetings (Old-fashioned) ▶ pl set of rooms used as offices by a barrister

chamberlain n (pl -s) (HIST) officer who managed the household of a king or nobleman

chamberlains n ▷chamberlain

chambermaid n (pl -s) woman employed to clean bedrooms in a hotel

chambermaids n ▷chambermaid

chambers n ▷chamber

chameleon [kam-**meal**-yon] n (pl -s) small lizard that changes colour to blend in with its surroundings

chameleons n ▷chameleon

chamfer [**cham**-fer] v (-s, -ing, -ed) bevel the edge of

chamfered v ▷chamfer

chamfering v ▷chamfer

chamfers v ▷chamfer

chamois [**sham**-wah] n (pl -ois) small mountain antelope

chamomile [**kam**-mo-mile] n (pl -s) ▷ camomile

chamomiles n ▷chamomile

champ[1] v (-s, -ing, -ed) chew noisily

champ[2] n (pl -s) ▷ champion

champagne n (pl -s) sparkling white French wine

champagnes n ▷champagne

champed v ▷champ[1]

champing v ▷champ[1]

champion n (pl -s) overall winner of a competition (foll. by **of**) ▶ v (-s, -ing, -ed) support ▶ adj (Dialect) excellent > **championship** n (pl -s)

championed v ▷champion

championing v ▷champion

champions n, v ▷champion

championship n ▷champion

championships n ▷champion

champs v ▷champ[1] ▶ n ▷champ[2]

chance n (pl -s) likelihood, probability ▶ v (chances, chancing, chanced) risk, hazard

chanced v ▷chance

chancel n (pl -s) part of a church containing the altar and choir

chancellor n (pl -s) head of government in some European countries > **chancellorship** n (pl -s)

chancellors n ▷chancellor

chancellorship n ▷chancellor

chancellorships n ▷chancellor

chancels n ▷chancel

chances n, v ▷chance

chancier adj ▷chancy

chanciest adj ▷chancy

chancing v ▷chance

chancy adj (-cier, -ciest) uncertain, risky

chandelier [shan-dill-**eer**] n (pl -s) ornamental light with branches and holders for several candles or bulbs

chandeliers n ▷chandelier

chandler n (pl -s) dealer, esp. in ships' supplies

chandlers n ▷chandler

change n (pl -s) becoming different ▶ v (changes, changing, changed) make or become different

changeable adj changing often

changed v ▷change

changeling n (pl -s) child believed to have been exchanged by fairies for another

changelings n ▷changeling

changes n, v ▷change

changing v ▷change

channel n (pl -s) band of broadcasting frequencies ▶ v (-nels, -nelling, -nelled) direct or convey through a channel

channelled v ▷channel

channelling v ▷channel

channels n, v ▷channel

chant v (-s, -ing, -ed) utter or sing (a slogan or psalm) ▶ n (pl -s) rhythmic or repetitious slogan

chanted v ▷chant

chanter n (pl -s) (on bagpipes) pipe on which the melody is played

chanters n ▷chanter

chanting v ▷chant

chants v, n ▷chant

chaos n complete disorder or confusion > **chaotic** adj > **chaotically** adv

chaotic adj ▷chaos

chaotically adv ▷chaos

chap n (pl -s) (Informal) man or boy

chapati, chapatti n (pl -s) (in Indian cookery) flat thin unleavened bread

chapatis n ▷chapati

chapatti n ▷chapati

chapattis n ▷chapati

chapel n (pl -s) place of worship with its own altar, within a church

chapels n ▷ chapel

chaperone [shap-per-rone] n (pl -s) older person who accompanies and supervises a young person or young people on a social occasion ▶ v (-ones, -oning, -oned) act as a chaperone to

chaperoned v ▷ chaperone

chaperones n, v ▷ chaperone

chaperoning v ▷ chaperone

chaplain n (pl -s) clergyman attached to a chapel, military body, or institution > **chaplaincy** n (pl -cies)

chaplaincies n ▷ chaplain

chaplaincy n ▷ chaplain

chaplains n ▷ chaplain

chaplet n (pl -s) garland for the head

chaplets n ▷ chaplet

chapped adj (of the skin) raw and cracked, through exposure to cold

chaps n ▷ chap

chapter n (pl -s) division of a book

chapters n ▷ chapter

char¹ v (chars, charring, charred) blacken by partial burning

char² (BRIT) (Informal) n (pl -s) charwoman ▶ v (chars, charring, charred) clean other people's houses as a job

char³ n (BRIT) (Old-fashioned slang) tea

charabanc [shar-rab-bang] n (pl -s) (Old-fashioned) coach for sightseeing

charabancs n ▷ charabanc

character n (pl -s) combination of qualities distinguishing a person, group, or place

characteristic n (pl -s) distinguishing feature or quality ▶ adj typical > **characteristically** adv

characteristically n ▷ characteristic

characteristics n ▷ characteristic

characterization n ▷ characterize

characterizations n ▷ characterize

characterize v (-rizes, -rizing, -rized) be a characteristic of (foll. by **as**) > **characterization** n (pl -s)

characterized v ▷ characterize

characterizes v ▷ characterize

characterizing v ▷ characterize

characters n ▷ character

charade [shar-rahd] n (pl -s) absurd pretence ▶ pl game in which one team acts out a word or phrase, which the other team has to guess

charades n ▷ charade

charcoal n (pl -s) black substance formed by partially burning wood

charcoals n ▷ charcoal

charge v (charges, charging, charged) ask as a

price ▶ n (pl -s) price charged > **chargeable** adj

chargeable adj ▷ charge

charged v ▷ charge

charger n (pl -s) device for charging an accumulator

chargers n ▷ charger

charges v, n ▷ charge

charging v ▷ charge

charier adj ▷ chary

chariest adj ▷ chary

chariot n (pl -s) two-wheeled horse-drawn vehicle used in ancient times in wars and races

charioteer n (pl -s) chariot driver

charioteers n ▷ charioteer

chariots n ▷ chariot

charisma [kar-rizz-ma] n (pl -s) person's power to attract or influence people > **charismatic** [kar-rizz-mat-ik] ▶ adj

charismas n ▷ charisma

charismatic adj ▷ charisma

charitable adj ▷ charity

charitably adv ▷ charity

charities n ▷ charity

charity n (pl -ties) organization that gives help, such as money or food, to those in need > **charitable** adj > **charitably** adv

charladies n ▷ charlady

charlady n (pl -ladies) (BRIT) (Informal) ▷ charwoman

charlatan [shar-lat-tan] n (pl -s) person who claims expertise that he or she does not have

charlatans n ▷ charlatan

charleston n (pl -s) lively dance of the 1920s

charlestons n ▷ charleston

charm n (pl -s) attractive quality ▶ v (-s, -ing, -ed) attract, delight > **charmer** n (pl -s)

charmed v ▷ charm

charmer n ▷ charm

charmers n ▷ charm

charming adj attractive ▶ v ▷ charm

charms n, v ▷ charm

charred v ▷ char¹, ²

charring v ▷ char¹, ²

chars v ▷ char¹, ² ▶ n ▷ char²

chart n (pl -s) graph, table, or diagram showing information ▶ v (-s, -ing, -ed) plot the course of

charted v ▷ chart

charter n (pl -s) document granting or demanding certain rights ▶ v (-s, -ing, -ed) hire by charter

chartered adj officially qualified to practise a profession ▶ v ▷ charter

chartering v ▷ charter

charters n, v ▷ charter
charting v ▷ chart
chartreuse [shar-**trerz**] n (pl -s) sweet-smelling green or yellow liqueur
chartreuses n ▷ chartreuse
charts n, v ▷ chart
charwoman n (pl **charwomen**) woman whose job is to clean other people's homes
charwomen n ▷ charwoman
chary [**chair**-ee] adj (-rier, -riest) wary, careful
chase¹ v (**chases**, **chasing**, **chased**) run after quickly in order to catch or drive away ▶ n (pl -s) chasing, pursuit
chase² v (**chases**, **chasing**, **chased**) engrave or emboss (metal)
chased v ▷ chase¹, ²
chaser n (pl -s) milder drink drunk after another stronger one
chasers n ▷ chaser
chases v ▷ chase¹, ² ▶ n ▷ chase¹
chasing v ▷ chase¹, ²
chasm [**kaz**-zum] n (pl -s) deep crack in the earth
chasms n ▷ chasm
chassis [**shass**-ee] n (pl -**sis**) frame, wheels, and mechanical parts of a vehicle
chaste adj (-r, -st) abstaining from sex outside marriage or altogether > **chastely** adv > **chasteness** n (pl -es) > **chastity** n (pl -ties)
chastely adv ▷ chaste
chasten [**chase**-en] v (-s, -ing, -ed) subdue by criticism
chastened v ▷ chasten
chasteness n ▷ chaste
chastenesses n ▷ chaste
chastening v ▷ chasten
chastens v ▷ chasten
chaster adj ▷ chaste
chastest adj ▷ chaste
chastise v (-ises, -ising, -ised) scold severely > **chastisement** n (pl -s)
chastised v ▷ chastise
chastisement n ▷ chastise
chastisements n ▷ chastise
chastises v ▷ chastise
chastising v ▷ chastise
chastities n ▷ chaste
chastity n ▷ chaste
chat n (pl -s) informal conversation ▶ v (**chats**, **chatting**, **chatted**) have an informal conversation > **chatty** adj (-tier, -tiest) > **chattily** adv > **chattiness** n (pl -es)
chateau [**shat**-toe] n (pl -**teaux**, -**teaus**) French castle
chateaus n ▷ chateau

chateaux n ▷ chateau
chatelaine [**shat**-tell-lane] n (pl -s) (formerly) mistress of a large house or castle
chatelaines n ▷ chatelaine
chatroom n (pl -s) site on the Internet where users have group discussions by e-mail
chatrooms n ▷ chatroom
chats n, v ▷ chat
chatted v ▷ chat
chattel n (pl -s) (usually plural) possessions
chattels n ▷ chattel
chatter v (-s, -ing, -ed) speak quickly and continuously about unimportant things ▶ n (pl -s) idle talk
chatterbox n (pl -es) person who chatters a lot
chatterboxes n ▷ chatterbox
chattered v ▷ chatter
chattering v ▷ chatter
chatters v, n ▷ chatter
chattier adj ▷ chat
chattiest adj ▷ chat
chattily adv ▷ chat
chattiness n ▷ chat
chattinesses n ▷ chat
chatting v ▷ chat
chatty adj ▷ chat
chauffeur n (pl -s) person employed to drive a car for someone
chauffeurs n ▷ chauffeur
chauvinism [**show**-vin-iz-zum] n (pl -s) irrational belief that one's own country, race, group, or sex is superior > **chauvinist** n (pl -s) adj > **chauvinistic** adj > **chauvinistically** adv
chauvinisms n ▷ chauvinism
chauvinist n ▷ chauvinism
chauvinistic adj ▷ chauvinism
chauvinistically adv ▷ chauvinism
chauvinists n ▷ chauvinism

    che pron. Like **ch**, che is an old dialect form of **I**. Che scores 8 points.

cheap adj (-er, -est) costing relatively little > **cheaply** adv
cheapen v (-s, -ing, -ed) lower the reputation of
cheapened v ▷ cheapen
cheapening v ▷ cheapen
cheapens v ▷ cheapen
cheaper adj ▷ cheap
cheapest adj ▷ cheap
cheaply adv ▷ cheap
cheapskate n (pl -s) (Informal) miserly person
cheapskates n ▷ cheapskate
cheat v (-s, -ing, -ed) act dishonestly to gain profit or advantage ▶ n (pl -s) person who cheats

cheated v ▷ cheat
cheating v ▷ cheat
cheats v, n ▷ cheat
check v (-s, -ing, -ed) examine, investigate ▶ n (pl -s) test to ensure accuracy or progress
checked v ▷ check
checking v ▷ check
checkmate n (pl -s) (CHESS) winning position in which an opponent's king is under attack and unable to escape ▶ v (-mates, -mating, -mated) (CHESS) place the king of (one's opponent) in checkmate
checkmated v ▷ checkmate
checkmates n, v ▷ checkmate
checkmating v ▷ checkmate
checkout n (pl -s) counter in a supermarket, where customers pay
checkouts n ▷ checkout
checks v, n ▷ check
checkup n (pl -s) thorough medical examination
checkups n ▷ checkup
cheddar n (pl -s) firm orange or yellowy-white cheese
cheddars n ▷ cheddar
cheek n (pl -s) either side of the face below the eye (Informal) ▶ v (-s, -ing, -ed) (BRIT, AUST & NZ) (Informal) speak impudently to
cheeked v ▷ cheek
cheekier adj ▷ cheeky
cheekiest adj ▷ cheeky
cheekily adv ▷ cheeky
cheekiness n ▷ cheeky
cheekinesses n ▷ cheeky
cheeking v ▷ cheek
cheeks n, v ▷ cheek
cheeky adj (-kier, -kiest) impudent, disrespectful > **cheekily** adv > **cheekiness** n (pl -es)
cheep n (pl -s) young bird's high-pitched cry ▶ v (-s, -ing, -ed) utter a cheep
cheeped v ▷ cheep
cheeping v ▷ cheep
cheeps n, v ▷ cheep
cheer v (-s, -ing, -ed) applaud or encourage with shouts ▶ n (pl -s) shout of applause or encouragement > **cheerful** adj (-ller, -llest) > **cheerfully** adv > **cheerfulness** n > **cheery** adj (-rier, -riest) > **cheerily** adv
cheered v ▷ cheer
cheerful adj ▷ cheer
cheerfuller adj ▷ cheer
cheerfullest adj ▷ cheer
cheerfully adv ▷ cheer
cheerfulness n ▷ cheer

cheerier adj ▷ cheer
cheeriest adj ▷ cheer
cheerily adv ▷ cheer
cheering v ▷ cheer
cheerio interj (Informal) goodbye ▶ n (pl -s) (AUST & NZ) small red cocktail sausage
cheerios n ▷ cheerio
cheerless adj dreary, gloomy > **cheerlessly** adv > **cheerlessness** n
cheerlessly adv ▷ cheerless
cheerlessness n ▷ cheerless
cheers v, n ▷ cheer
cheery adj ▷ cheer
cheese n (pl -s) food made from coagulated milk curd > **cheesy** adj (pl -sier, -siest) > **cheesily** adv > **cheesiness** n
cheeseburger n (pl -s) hamburger topped with melted cheese
cheeseburgers n ▷ cheeseburger
cheesecake n (pl -s) dessert with a biscuit-crumb base covered with a sweet cream-cheese mixture
cheesecakes n ▷ cheesecake
cheesecloth n (pl -s) light cotton cloth
cheesecloths n ▷ cheesecloth
cheeses n ▷ cheese
cheesier adj ▷ cheese
cheesiest adj ▷ cheese
cheesily adv ▷ cheese
cheesiness n ▷ cheese
cheesy adj ▷ cheese
cheetah n (pl -s) large fast-running spotted African wild cat
cheetahs n ▷ cheetah
chef n (pl -s) cook in a restaurant
chefs n ▷ chef
chemical n (pl -s) substance used in or resulting from a reaction involving changes to atoms or molecules ▶ adj of chemistry or chemicals > **chemically** adv
chemically adv ▷ chemical
chemicals n ▷ chemical
chemise [shem-meez] n (pl -s) (Old-fashioned) woman's loose-fitting slip
chemises n ▷ chemise
chemist n (pl -s) shop selling medicines and cosmetics
chemistries n ▷ chemistry
chemistry n (pl -ries) science of the composition, properties, and reactions of substances
chemists n ▷ chemist
chemotherapies n ▷ chemotherapy
chemotherapy n (pl -apies) treatment of disease, often cancer, using chemicals

chenille [shen-**neel**] n (pl -s) (fabric of) thick tufty yarn
chenilles n ▷ chenille
cheque n (pl -s) written order to one's bank to pay money from one's account
chequer n (pl chequers) piece used in Chinese chequers ▶ pl game of draughts
chequered adj marked by varied fortunes
chequers n ▷ chequer
cheques n ▷ cheque
cherish v (-es, -ing, -ed) cling to (an idea or feeling)
cherished v ▷ cherish
cherishes n ▷ cherish
cherishing v ▷ cherish
cheroot [sher-**root**] n (pl -s) cigar with both ends cut flat
cheroots n ▷ cheroot
cherries n ▷ cherry
cherry n (pl -ries) small red or black fruit with a stone ▶ adj deep red
cherub n (pl -s, -ubim) angel, often represented as a winged child > **cherubic** [cher-**rew**-bik] ▶ adj
cherubic adj ▷ cherub
cherubim n ▷ cherub
cherubs n ▷ cherub
chervil n (pl -s) aniseed-flavoured herb
chervils n ▷ chervil
chess n (pl -es) game for two players with 16 pieces each, played on a chequered board of 64 squares
chesses n ▷ chess
chessman n (pl -men) piece used in chess
chessmen n ▷ chessman
chest n (pl -s) front of the body, from neck to waist
chesterfield n (pl -s) couch with high padded sides and back
chesterfields n ▷ chesterfield
chestnut n (pl -s) reddish-brown edible nut (Informal) ▶ adj (of hair or a horse) reddish-brown
chestnuts n ▷ chestnut
chests n ▷ chest
chevron [**shev**-ron] n (pl -s) V-shaped pattern, esp. on the sleeve of a military uniform to indicate rank
chevrons n ▷ chevron
chew v (-s, -ing, -ed) grind (food) between the teeth
chewed v ▷ chew
chewier adj ▷ chewy
chewiest adj ▷ chewy
chewiness n ▷ chewy

chewinesses n ▷ chewy
chewing v ▷ chew
chews v ▷ chew
chewy adj (-ier, -iest) requiring a lot of chewing > **chewiness** n (pl -es)
chi n (chis). Chi is a letter of the Greek alphabet, and is worth 8 points.
chianti [kee-**ant**-ee] n (pl -s) dry red Italian wine
chiantis n ▷ chianti
chiaroscuro [kee-ah-roh-**skew**-roh] n (pl -s) distribution of light and shade in a picture
chiaroscuros n ▷ chiaroscuro
chic [**sheek**] adj (-er, -est) stylish, elegant ▶ n (pl -s) stylishness, elegance
chicane [shik-**kane**] n (pl -s) obstacle in a motor-racing circuit
chicaneries n ▷ chicanery
chicanery n (pl -eries) trickery, deception
chicanes n ▷ chicane
chicer adj ▷ chic
chicest adj ▷ chic
chick n (pl -s) baby bird
chicken n (pl -s) domestic fowl ▶ adj (Slang) cowardly
chickenpox n (pl -es) infectious disease with an itchy rash
chickenpoxes n ▷ chickenpox
chickens n ▷ chicken
chickpea n (pl -s) edible yellow pealike seed
chickpeas n ▷ chickpea
chicks n ▷ chick
chickweed n (pl -s) weed with small white flowers
chickweeds n ▷ chickweed
chicories n ▷ chicory
chicory n (pl -ries) plant whose leaves are used in salads
chics n ▷ chic
chid v ▷ chide
chidden v ▷ chide
chide v (chiding, chided or **chid**) (chid or **chidden**) rebuke, scold
chided v ▷ chide
chiding v ▷ chide
chief n (pl -s) head of a group of people ▶ adj most important
chiefly adv especially
chiefs n ▷ chief
chieftain n (pl -s) leader of a tribe
chieftains n ▷ chieftain
chiffon [**shif**-fon] n (pl -s) fine see-through fabric
chiffons n ▷ chiffon
chignon [**sheen**-yon] n (pl -s) knot of hair pinned up at the back of the head

chignons n ▷ chignon

chihuahua [chee-wah-wah] n (pl -s) tiny short-haired dog
  chihuahuas n ▷ chihuahua

chilblain n (pl -s) inflammation of the fingers or toes, caused by exposure to cold
  chilblains n ▷ chilblain

child n (pl children) young human being, boy or girl ▷ **childhood** n (pl -s) ▷ **childless** adj > **childlessness** n

childbirth n (pl -s) giving birth to a child
  childbirths n ▷ childbirth
  childhood n ▷ child
  childhoods n ▷ child

childish adj immature, silly > **childishly** adv > **childishness** n
  childishly adv ▷ childish
  childishness n ▷ childish
  childless adj ▷ child
  childlessness n ▷ child

childlike adj innocent, trustful
  children n ▷ child
  chili n ▷ chilli
  chilies n ▷ chilli

chill n (pl -s) feverish cold ▶ v (-s, -ing, -ed) make (something) cool or cold ▶ adj unpleasantly cold
  chilled v ▷ chill

chilli, chili n (pl -es) small red or green hot-tasting capsicum pod, used in cooking
  chillier adj ▷ chilly
  chillies n ▷ chilli
  chilliest adj ▷ chilly
  chilliness n ▷ chilly
  chillinesses n ▷ chilly
  chilling v ▷ chill
  chills n, v ▷ chill

chilly adj (-llier, -lliest) moderately cold > **chilliness** n (pl -es)

chime n (pl -s) musical ringing sound of a bell or clock ▶ v (-mes, -ming, -med) make a musical ringing sound
  chimed v ▷ chime

chimera [kime-meer-a] n (pl -s) unrealistic hope or idea
  chimeras n ▷ chimera
  chimes n, v ▷ chime
  chiming v ▷ chime

chimney n (pl -s) hollow vertical structure for carrying away smoke from a fire
  chimneys n ▷ chimney

chimp n (pl -s) (Informal) ▷ chimpanzee

chimpanzee n (pl -s) intelligent black African ape
  chimpanzees n ▷ chimpanzee

chimps n ▷ chimp

chin n (pl -s) part of the face below the mouth

china n (pl -s) fine earthenware or porcelain
  chinas n ▷ china

chinchilla n (pl -s) S American rodent bred for its soft grey fur
  chinchillas n ▷ chinchilla

chine n (pl -s) cut of meat including part of the backbone
  chines n ▷ chine

chink[1] n (pl -s) small narrow opening

chink[2] v (-s, -ing, -ed) ▶ n (pl -s) (make) a light ringing sound
  chinked v ▷ chink[2]
  chinking v ▷ chink[2]
  chinks n ▷ chink[1, 2] ▶ v ▷ chink[2]
  chins n ▷ chin

chintz n (pl -es) printed cotton fabric with a glazed finish
  chintzes n ▷ chintz

chinwag n (pl -s) (BRIT, AUST & NZ) (Informal) chat
  chinwags n ▷ chinwag

chip n (pl -s) strip of potato, fried in deep fat ▶ v (chips, chipping, chipped) break small pieces from

chipboard n (pl -s) thin board made of compressed wood particles
  chipboards n ▷ chipboard

chipmunk n (pl -s) small squirrel-like N American rodent with a striped back
  chipmunks n ▷ chipmunk
  chipped v ▷ chip

chippie n (pl -s) (BRIT, AUST & NZ) (Informal) carpenter
  chippies n ▷ chippie
  chipping v ▷ chip
  chips n, v ▷ chip

chiropodist [kir-rop-pod-ist] n (pl -s) person who treats minor foot complaints > **chiropody** n
  chiropodists n ▷ chiropodist
  chiropody n ▷ chiropodist

chiropractic [kire-oh-prak-tik] n (pl -s) system of treating bodily disorders by manipulation of the spine > **chiropractor** n (pl -s)
  chiropractics n ▷ chiropractic
  chiropractor n ▷ chiropractic
  chiropractors n ▷ chiropractic

chirp v (-s, -ing, -ed) (of a bird or insect) make a short high-pitched sound ▶ n (pl -s) chirping sound
  chirped v ▷ chirp
  chirpier adj ▷ chirpy
  chirpiest adj ▷ chirpy
  chirpily adv ▷ chirpy

chirpiness n ▷ chirpy
chirping v ▷ chirp
chirps v, n ▷ chirp
chirpy adj (-pier, -piest) (Informal) lively and cheerful > **chirpily** adv > **chirpiness** n
chisel n (pl -s) metal tool with a sharp end for shaping wood or stone ▶ v (-els, -elling, -elled) carve or form with a chisel
chiselled v ▷ chisel
chiselling v ▷ chisel
chisels n, v ▷ chisel
chit[1] n (pl -s) short official note, such as a receipt
chit[2] n (pl -s) (BRIT, AUST & NZ) (old-fashioned) pert or impudent girl
chitchat n (pl -s) chat, gossip
chitchats n ▷ chitchat
chits n ▷ chit[1, 2]
chitterlings pl n pig's intestines cooked as food
chivalries n ▷ chivalry
chivalrous adj ▷ chivalry
chivalrously adv ▷ chivalry
chivalry n (pl -ries) courteous behaviour, esp. by men towards women > **chivalrous** adj > **chivalrously** adv
chives pl n herb with a mild onion flavour
chivvied v ▷ chivvy
chivvies v ▷ chivvy
chivvy v (-vies, -vying, -vied) (Informal) harass, nag
chivvying v ▷ chivvy
chloride n (pl -s) compound of chlorine and another substance
chlorides n ▷ chloride
chlorinate v (-ates, -ating, -ated) disinfect (water) with chlorine > **chlorination** n
chlorinated v ▷ chlorinate
chlorinates v ▷ chlorinate
chlorinating v ▷ chlorinate
chlorination n ▷ chlorinate
chlorine n (pl -s) strong-smelling greenish-yellow gaseous element, used to disinfect water
chlorines n ▷ chlorine
chlorofluorocarbon n (pl -s) any of various gaseous compounds of carbon, hydrogen, chlorine, and fluorine, used in refrigerators and aerosol propellants, some of which break down the ozone in the atmosphere
chlorofluorocarbons n ▷ chlorofluorocarbon
chloroform n (pl -s) strong-smelling liquid formerly used as an anaesthetic
chloroforms n ▷ chloroform
chlorophyll n (pl -s) green colouring matter

of plants, which enables them to convert sunlight into energy
chlorophylls n ▷ chlorophyll
chock n (pl -s) block or wedge used to prevent a heavy object from moving
chockablock adj completely full
chocks n ▷ chock
chocolate n (pl -s) sweet food made from cacao seeds ▶ adj dark brown
chocolates n ▷ chocolate
choice n (pl -s) choosing ▶ adj (choicer, choicest) of high quality
choicer adj ▷ choice
choices n ▷ choice
choicest adj ▷ choice
choir n (pl -s) organized group of singers, esp. in church
choirs n ▷ choir
choke v (chokes, choking, choked) hinder or stop the breathing of (a person) by strangling or smothering ▶ n (pl -s) device controlling the amount of air that is mixed with the fuel in a petrol engine
choked v ▷ choke
choker n (pl -s) tight-fitting necklace
chokers n ▷ choker
chokes v, n ▷ choke
choking v ▷ choke
cholera [kol-ler-a] n (pl -s) serious infectious disease causing severe vomiting and diarrhoea
choleras n ▷ cholera
choleric [kol-ler-ik] adj bad-tempered
cholesterol [kol-lest-er-oll] n (pl -s) fatty substance found in animal tissue, an excess of which can cause heart disease
cholesterols n ▷ cholesterol
chomp v (-s, -ing, -ed) chew noisily
chomped v ▷ chomp
chomping v ▷ chomp
chomps v ▷ chomp
chook n (pl -s) (AUST & NZ) hen or chicken
chooks n ▷ chook
choose v (chooses, choosing, chose, chosen) select from a number of alternatives
chooses v ▷ choose
choosier adj ▷ choosy
choosiest adj ▷ choosy
choosing v ▷ choose
choosy adj (-sier, -siest) (Informal) fussy, hard to please
chop[1] v (chops, chopping, chopped) cut with a blow from an axe or knife (BOXING) (KARATE) ▶ n (pl -s) cutting or sharp blow
chop[2] v (chops, chopping, chopped) change

one's mind repeatedly
chopped v ▷ chop[1, 2]
chopper n (pl -s) (*Informal*) helicopter
choppers n ▷ chopper
choppier adj ▷ choppy
choppiest adj ▷ choppy
choppiness n ▷ choppy
choppinesses n ▷ choppy
chopping v ▷ choppy
choppy adj (-pier, -piest) (of the sea) fairly
rough > **choppiness** n (pl -es)
chops pl n (BRIT, AUST & NZ) (*Informal*) jaws,
cheeks ▶ v ▷ chop[1, 2] ▶ n ▷ chop[1]
chopsticks pl n pair of thin sticks used to eat
Chinese food
choral adj of a choir
chorale [kor-**rahl**] n (pl -s) slow stately hymn
tune
chorales n ▷ chorale
chord[1] n (pl -s) (MATHS) straight line joining two
points on a curve
chord[2] n (pl -s) simultaneous sounding of
three or more musical notes
chords n ▷ chord[1, 2]
chore n (pl -s) routine task
choreographer n ▷ choreography
choreographers n ▷ choreography
choreographic adj ▷ choreography
choreographies n ▷ choreography
choreography n (pl -phies) composition
of steps and movements for dancing
> **choreographer** n (pl -s) > **choreographic** adj
chores n ▷ chore
chorister n (pl -s) singer in a choir
choristers n ▷ chorister
chortle v (-tles, -tling, -tled) chuckle in
amusement ▶ n (pl -s) amused chuckle
chortled v ▷ chortle
chortles v, n ▷ chortle
chortling v ▷ chortle
chorus n (pl -es) large choir ▶ v (-es, -ing, -ed)
sing or say together
chorused v ▷ chorus
choruses n, v ▷ chorus
chorusing v ▷ chorus
chose v ▷ choose
chosen v ▷ choose
chow n (pl -s) thick-coated dog with a curled
tail, orig. from China
chowder n (pl -s) thick soup containing clams
or fish
chowders n ▷ chowder
chows n ▷ chow
christen v (-s, -ing, -ed) baptize > **christening**
n (pl -s)

christened v ▷ christen
christening v, n ▷ christen
christenings n ▷ christen
christens v ▷ christen
chromatic adj of colour or colours
> **chromatically** adv
chromatically adv ▷ chromatic
chromatographies n ▷ chromatic
chromatography n (pl -phies) separation and
analysis of the components of a substance
by slowly passing it through an adsorbing
material
chrome n ▷ chromium
chromes n ▷ chromium
chromium, chrome n (pl -s) (CHEM) grey
metallic element used in steel alloys and for
electroplating
chromiums n ▷ chromium
chromosome n (pl -s) microscopic gene-
carrying body in the nucleus of a cell
chromosomes n ▷ chromosome
chronic adj (of an illness) lasting a long time
> **chronically** adv
chronically adv ▷ chronic
chronicle n (pl -s) record of events in order of
occurrence ▶ v (-les, -ing, -led) record in or as
if in a chronicle > **chronicler** n (pl -s)
chronicled v ▷ chronicle
chronicler n ▷ chronicle
chroniclers n ▷ chronicle
chronicles n ▷ chronicle
chronicling v ▷ chronicle
chronological adj ▷ chronology
chronologically adv ▷ chronology
chronologies n ▷ chronology
chronology n (pl -gies) arrangement or list of
events in order of occurrence > **chronological**
adj > **chronologically** adv
chronometer n (pl -s) timepiece designed to
be accurate in all conditions
chronometers n ▷ chronometer
chrysalis [kriss-**a**-liss] n (pl -es) insect in the
stage between larva and adult, when it is in
a cocoon
chrysalises n ▷ chrysalis
chrysanthemum n (pl -s) garden flower with a
large head made up of thin petals
chrysanthemums n ▷ chrysanthemum
chub n (pl chub) European freshwater fish of
the carp family
chubbier adj ▷ chubby
chubbiest adj ▷ chubby
chubbiness n ▷ chubby
chubby adj (-bier, -biest) plump and round
> **chubbiness** n

chuck¹ v (-s, -ing, -ed) (Informal) throw

chuck² n (pl -s) cut of beef from the neck to the shoulder
chucked v ▷ chuck¹
chucking v ▷ chuck¹

chuckle v (-les, -ling, -led) laugh softly ▸ n (pl -s) soft laugh
chuckled v ▷ chuckle
chuckles v, n ▷ chuckle
chuckling v ▷ chuckle
chucks v ▷ chuck¹ ▸ n ▷ chuck²

chuffed adj (Informal) very pleased

chug n (pl -s) short dull sound like the noise of an engine ▸ v (chugs, chugging, chugged) operate or move with this sound
chugged v ▷ chug
chugging v ▷ chug
chugs n, v ▷ chug

chukka n (pl -s) period of play in polo
chukkas n ▷ chukka

chum (Informal) n (pl -s) close friend ▸ v (chums, chumming, chummed) form a close friendship with ▷ **chummy** adj (-mmier, -mmiest) ▷ **chumminess** n (pl -es)
chummed v ▷ chum
chummier adj ▷ chum
chummiest adj ▷ chum
chumminess n ▷ chum
chumminesses n ▷ chum
chumming v ▷ chum
chummy adj ▷ chum

chump n (pl -s) (Informal) stupid person
chumps n ▷ chump
chums n, v ▷ chum

chunk n (pl -s) thick solid piece
chunkier adj ▷ chunky
chunkiest adj ▷ chunky
chunkiness n ▷ chunky
chunkinesses n ▷ chunky
chunks n ▷ chunk

chunky adj (-kier, -kiest) (of a person) broad and heavy ▷ **chunkiness** n (pl -es)

church n (pl -s) building for public Christian worship
churches n ▷ church

churchgoer n (pl -s) person who attends church regularly
churchgoers n ▷ churchgoer

churchwarden n (pl -s) member of a congregation who assists the vicar
churchwardens n ▷ churchwarden

churchyard n (pl -s) grounds round a church, used as a graveyard
churchyards n ▷ churchyard

churlish adj surly and rude ▷ **churlishly** adv

> **churlishness** n
churlishly adv ▷ churlish
churlishness n ▷ churlish

churn n (pl -s) machine in which cream is shaken to make butter ▸ v (-s, -ing, -ed) stir (cream) vigorously to make butter
churned v ▷ churn
churning v ▷ churn
churns n, v ▷ churn

chute¹ [shoot] n (pl -s) steep slope down which things may be slid

chute² n (pl -s) (Informal) ▷ parachute
chutes n ▷ chute¹, ²

chutney n (pl -s) pickle made from fruit, vinegar, spices, and sugar
chutneys n ▷ chutney

cicada [sik-kah-da] n (pl -s) large insect that makes a high-pitched drone
cicadas n ▷ cicada
cicatrices n ▷ cicatrix

cicatrix [sik-a-trix] n (pl -trices) scar

cid n (cids). A cid is a hero or commander. Cid scores 6 points.

cider n (pl -s) alcoholic drink made from fermented apple juice
ciders n ▷ cider

cigar n (pl -s) roll of cured tobacco leaves for smoking

cigarette n (pl -s) thin roll of shredded tobacco in thin paper, for smoking
cigarettes n ▷ cigarette
cigars n ▷ cigar

cinch [sinch] n (pl -es) (Informal) easy task
cinches n ▷ cinch

cinder n (pl -s) piece of material that will not burn, left after burning coal
cinders n ▷ cinder

cinema n (pl -s) place for showing films
> **cinematic** adj
cinemas n ▷ cinema
cinematic adj ▷ cinema
cinematographer n ▷ cinematography
cinematographers n ▷ cinematography
cinematography n technique of making films
> **cinematographer** n (pl -s)

cineraria n (pl -s) garden plant with daisy-like flowers
cinerarias n ▷ cineraria

cinnamon n (pl -s) spice obtained from the bark of an Asian tree
cinnamons n ▷ cinnamon

cipher, cypher [sife-er] n (pl -s) system of secret writing
ciphers n ▷ cipher

circa [sir-ka] prep (LATIN) approximately, about

circle n (pl -s) perfectly round geometric figure, line, or shape ▶ v (**circles, circling, circled**) move in a circle (round)
circled v ▷ circle
circles n, v ▷ circle
circlet n (pl -s) circular ornament worn on the head
circlets n ▷ circlet
circling v ▷ circle
circuit n (pl -s) complete route or course, esp. a circular one
circuitous [sir-kew-it-uss] adj indirect and lengthy ▶ **circuitously** adv
circuitously adv ▷ circuitous
circuitry [sir-kit-tree] n electrical circuit(s)
circuits n ▷ circuit
circular adj in the shape of a circle ▶ n (pl -s) letter for general distribution ▶ **circularity** n
circularity n ▷ circular
circulars n ▷ circular
circulate v (-lates, -lating, -lated) send, go, or pass from place to place or person to person ▶ **circulatory** adj
circulated v ▷ circulate
circulates v ▷ circulate
circulating v ▷ circulate
circulation n flow of blood around the body
circulatory adj ▷ circulate
circumcise v (-cises, -cising, -cised) remove the foreskin of ▶ **circumcision** n (pl -s)
circumcised v ▷ circumcise
circumcises v ▷ circumcise
circumcising v ▷ circumcise
circumcision n ▷ circumcise
circumcisions n ▷ circumcise
circumference n (pl -s) boundary of a specified area or shape, esp. of a circle
circumferences n ▷ circumference
circumflex n (pl -es) mark (^) over a vowel to show that it is pronounced in a particular way
circumflexes n ▷ circumflex
circumlocution n (pl -s) indirect way of saying something
circumlocutions n ▷ circumlocution
circumnavigate v (-gates, -gating, -gated) sail right round ▶ **circumnavigation** n (pl -s)
circumnavigated v ▷ circumnavigate
circumnavigates v ▷ circumnavigate
circumnavigating v ▷ circumnavigate
circumnavigation n ▷ circumnavigate
circumnavigations n ▷ circumnavigate
circumscribe v (-scribes, -scribing, -scribed) limit, restrict ▶ **circumscription** n (pl -s)
circumscribed v ▷ circumscribe

circumscribes v ▷ circumscribe
circumscribing v ▷ circumscribe
circumscription n ▷ circumscribe
circumscriptions n ▷ circumscribe
circumspect adj cautious and careful not to take risks ▶ **circumspectly** adv ▶ **circumspection** n
circumspection n ▷ circumspect
circumspectly adv ▷ circumspect
circumstance n (pl -s) (usu. pl) occurrence or condition that accompanies or influences a person or event
circumstances n ▷ circumstance
circumstantial adj (of evidence) strongly suggesting something but not proving it
circumvent v (-s, -ing, -ed) avoid or get round (a rule etc.) ▶ **circumvention** n (pl -s)
circumvented v ▷ circumvent
circumventing v ▷ circumvent
circumvention n ▷ circumvent
circumventions n ▷ circumvent
circumvents v ▷ circumvent
circus n (pl -es) (performance given by) a travelling company of acrobats, clowns, performing animals, etc.
circuses n ▷ circus
cirrhosis [sir-roh-siss] n serious liver disease, often caused by drinking too much alcohol ▶ **cirrhotic** adj
cirrhotic adj ▷ cirrhosis
cirri n ▷ cirrus
cirrus n (pl -ri) high wispy cloud
cistern n (pl -s) water tank, esp. one that holds water for flushing a toilet
cisterns n ▷ cistern
citadel n (pl -s) fortress in a city
citadels n ▷ citadel
citation n ▷ cite
citations n ▷ cite
cite v (cites, citing, cited) quote, refer to ▶ **citation** n (pl -s)
cited v ▷ cite
cites v ▷ cite
cities n ▷ city
citing v ▷ cite
citizen n (pl -s) native or naturalized member of a state or nation ▶ **citizenship** n (pl -s)
citizens n ▷ citizen
citizenship n ▷ citizen
citizenships n ▷ citizen
city n (pl -ties) large or important town
civet [siv-vit] n (pl -s) spotted catlike African mammal
civets n ▷ civet
civic adj of a city or citizens

civics n study of the rights and responsibilities of citizenship

civil adj relating to the citizens of a state as opposed to the armed forces or the Church > **civilly** adv

civilian n (pl -s) ► adj (person) not belonging to the armed forces
civilians n ▷ civilian
civilities n ▷ civility

civility n (pl -ities) polite or courteous behaviour

civilization n (pl -s) high level of human cultural and social development
civilizations n ▷ civilization

civilize v (-izes, -izing, -ized) refine or educate (a person)
civilized v ▷ civilize
civilizes v ▷ civilize
civilizing v ▷ civilize
civilly adv ▷ civil

civvies pl n (BRIT, AUST & NZ) (Slang) ordinary clothes that are not part of a uniform

clack n (pl -s) sound made by two hard objects striking each other ► v (-s, -ing, -ed) make this sound
clacked v ▷ clack
clacking v ▷ clack
clacks n, v ▷ clack

clad v (clads, cladding, clad) ▷ clothe

cladding n (pl -s) material used to cover the outside of a building ► v ▷ clad
claddings n ▷ cladding
clads v ▷ clad

claim v (-s, -ing, -ed) assert as a fact ► n (pl -s) assertion that something is true > **claimant** n (pl -s)
claimant n ▷ claim
claimants n ▷ claim
claimed v ▷ claim
claiming v ▷ claim
claims v, n ▷ claim

clairvoyance n (pl -s) power of perceiving things beyond the natural range of the senses > **clairvoyant** n (pl -s) adj
clairvoyances n ▷ clairvoyance
clairvoyant n, adj ▷ clairvoyance
clairvoyants n ▷ clairvoyance

clam n (pl -s) edible shellfish with a hinged shell ► v (clams, clamming, clammed) (Informal) stop talking, esp. through nervousness

clamber v (-s, -ing, -ed) climb awkwardly
clambered v ▷ clamber
clambering v ▷ clamber
clambers v ▷ clamber

clammed v ▷ clam
clammier adj ▷ clammy
clammiest adj ▷ clammy
clamming v ▷ clam

clammy adj (-mier, -miest) unpleasantly moist and sticky

clamour n (pl -s) loud protest ► v (-s, -ing, -ed) make a loud noise or outcry > **clamorous** adj > **clamorously** adv > **clamorousness** n
clamoured v ▷ clamour
clamouring v ▷ clamour
clamourous adj ▷ clamour
clamourously adj ▷ clamour
clamourousness n ▷ clamour
clamours n, v ▷ clamour

clamp n (pl -s) tool with movable jaws for holding things together tightly ► v (-s, -ing, -ed) fasten with a clamp
clamped v ▷ clamp
clamping v ▷ clamp
clamps n, v ▷ clamp
clams v, n ▷ clam

clan n (pl -s) group of families with a common ancestor, esp. among Scottish Highlanders

clandestine adj secret and concealed > **clandestinely** adv
clandestinely adv ▷ clandestine

clang v (-s, -ing, -ed) make a loud ringing metallic sound ► n (pl -s) ringing metallic sound
clanged v ▷ clang

clanger n (pl -s) (Informal) obvious mistake
clangers n ▷ clanger
clanging v ▷ clang

clangour n (pl -s) loud continuous clanging sound
clangours n ▷ clangour
clangs v, n ▷ clang

clank n (pl -s) harsh metallic sound ► v (-s, -ing, -ed) make such a sound
clanked v ▷ clank
clanking v ▷ clank
clanks n, v ▷ clank

clannish adj (of a group) tending to exclude outsiders > **clannishness** n
clannishness n ▷ clannish
clans n ▷ clan

clap v (claps, clapping, clapped) applaud by hitting the palms of one's hands sharply together ► n (pl -s) act or sound of clapping
clapped v ▷ clap

clapper n (pl -s) piece of metal inside a bell, which causes it to sound when struck against the side

clapperboard n (pl -s) pair of hinged boards

clapped together during filming to help in synchronizing sound and picture
clapperboards *n* ▷ clapperboard
clappers *n* ▷ clapper
clapping *v* ▷ clap
claps *v*, *n* ▷ clap
claptrap *n* (*pl* -s) (*Informal*) foolish or pretentious talk
claptraps *n* ▷ claptrap
claret [klar-rit] *n* (*pl* -s) dry red wine from Bordeaux
clarets *n* ▷ claret
clarification *n* ▷ clarify
clarifications *n* ▷ clarify
clarified *v* ▷ clarify
clarifies *v* ▷ clarify
clarify *v* (-fies, -fying, -fied) make (a matter) clear and unambiguous > **clarification** *n* (*pl* -s)
clarifying *v* ▷ clarify
clarinet *n* (*pl* -s) keyed woodwind instrument with a single reed > **clarinettist** *n* (*pl* -s)
clarinets *n* ▷ clarinet
clarinettist *n* ▷ clarinet
clarinettists *n* ▷ clarinet
clarion *n* (*pl* -s) obsolete high-pitched trumpet
clarions *n* ▷ clarion
clarities *n* ▷ clarity
clarity *n* (*pl* -ities) clearness
clash *v* (-es, -ing, -ed) come into conflict ▶ *n* (*pl* -es) fight, argument
clashed *v* ▷ clash
clashes *v*, *n* ▷ clash
clashing *v* ▷ clash
clasp *n* (*pl* -s) device for fastening things ▶ *v* (-s, -ing, -ed) grasp or embrace firmly
clasped *v* ▷ clasp
clasping *v* ▷ clasp
clasps *n*, *v* ▷ clasp
class *n* (*pl* -es) group of people sharing a similar social position ▶ *v* (-es, -ing, -ed) place in a class
classed *v* ▷ class
classes *n*, *v* ▷ class
classic *adj* being a typical example of something ▶ *n* (*pl* -s) author, artist, or work of art of recognized excellence ▶ *pl* study of ancient Greek and Roman literature and culture
classical *adj* of or in a restrained conservative style > **classically** *adv* ▷ classical
classically *adv* ▷ classical
classicism *n* artistic style showing emotional restraint and regularity of form > **classicist** *n* (*pl* -s)

classicist *n* ▷ classicism
classicists *n* ▷ classicism
classics *n* ▷ classic
classier *adj* ▷ classy
classiest *adj* ▷ classy
classifiable *adj* ▷ classify
classification *n* ▷ classify
classifications *n* ▷ classify
classified *v* ▷ classify
classifies *v* ▷ classify
classify *v* (-fies, -fying, -fied) divide into groups with similar characteristics > **classifiable** *adj* > **classification** *n* (*pl* -s)
classifying *v* ▷ classify
classing *v* ▷ class
classy *adj* (classier, classiest) (*Informal*) stylish and elegant
clatter *v* (-s, -ing, -ed) ▶ *n* (*pl* -s) (make) a rattling noise
clattered *v* ▷ clatter
clattering *v* ▷ clatter
clatters *v*, *n* ▷ clatter
clause *n* (*pl* -s) section of a legal document
clauses *n* ▷ clause
claustrophobia *n* (*pl* -s) abnormal fear of confined spaces > **claustrophobic** *adj*
claustrophobia *n* ▷ claustrophobia
claustrophobias *n* ▷ claustrophobia
claustrophobic *adj* ▷ claustrophobia
clavichord *n* (*pl* -s) early keyboard instrument
clavichords *n* ▷ clavichord
clavicle *n* (*pl* -s) ▷ collarbone
clavicles *n* ▷ clavicle
claw *n* (*pl* -s) sharp hooked nail of a bird or beast ▶ *v* (-s, -ing, -ed) tear with claws or nails
clawed *v* ▷ claw
clawing *v* ▷ claw
claws *n*, *v* ▷ claw
clay *n* (*pl* -s) fine-grained earth, soft when moist and hardening when baked, used to make bricks and pottery > **clayey** *adj*
clayey *adj* ▷ clay
claymore *n* (*pl* -s) large two-edged sword formerly used by Scottish Highlanders
claymores *n* ▷ claymore
clays *n* ▷ clay
clean *adj* (-er, -est) free from dirt or impurities ▶ *v* (-s, -ing, -ed) make (something) free from dirt ▶ *adv* (*Not standard*) completely > **cleaner** *n* (*pl* -s) > **cleanly** *adv* > **cleanliness** *n* (*pl* -es)
cleaned *v* ▷ clean
cleaner *n*, *adj* ▷ clean
cleaners *n* ▷ clean
cleanest *adj* ▷ clean
cleaning *v* ▷ clean

cleanliness n ▷ clean
cleanlinesses n ▷ clean
cleanly adv ▷ clean
cleans v ▷ clean
cleanse v (-ses, -sing, -sed) make clean
> **cleanser** n (pl -s)
cleansed v ▷ cleanse
cleanser n ▷ cleanse
cleansers n ▷ cleanse
cleanses v ▷ cleanse
cleansing v ▷ cleanse
clear adj (-er, -est) free from doubt or confusion
▶ adv out of the way ▶ v (-s, -ing, -ed) make or
become clear > **clearly** adv
clearance n (pl -s) clearing
clearances n ▷ clear
cleared v ▷ clear
clearer adj ▷ clear
clearest adj ▷ clear
clearing n (pl -s) treeless area in a wood ▶ v
▷ clear
clearings n ▷ clearing
clearly adv ▷ clear
clears v ▷ clear
clearway n (pl -s) stretch of road on which
motorists may stop in an emergency
clearways n ▷ clearway
cleat n (pl -s) wedge
cleats n ▷ cleat
cleavage n (pl -s) space between a woman's
breasts, as revealed by a low-cut dress
cleavages n ▷ cleavage
cleave¹ v (-ves, -ving, cleft, -ved or clove) (cleft,
cleaved or cloven) split apart
cleave² v (-ves, -ving, cleft, cleft) cling or stick
cleaved v ▷ cleave¹
cleaver n (pl -s) butcher's heavy knife with a
square blade
cleavers n ▷ cleaver
cleaves v ▷ cleave¹, ²
cleaving v ▷ cleave¹, ²
clef n (pl -s) (MUSIC) symbol at the beginning of
a stave to show the pitch
clefs n ▷ clef
cleft n (pl -s) narrow opening or crack ▶ v
▷ cleave¹, ²
clefted v ▷ cleft
clefting v ▷ cleft
clefts n, v ▷ cleft
clematis n climbing plant with large colourful
flowers
clemencies n ▷ clemency
clemency n (pl -cies) kind or lenient treatment
clement adj (of weather) mild
clementine n (pl -s) small orange citrus fruit

clementines n ▷ clementine
clench v (-es, -ing, -ed) close or squeeze (one's
teeth or fist) tightly
clenched v ▷ clench
clenches v ▷ clench
clenching v ▷ clench
clerestories n ▷ clerestory
clerestory [clear-store-ee] n (pl -ries) row
of windows at the top of a wall above an
adjoining roof
clergies n ▷ clergy
clergy n (pl clergies) priests and ministers as a
group > **clergyman** n (pl -men)
clergyman n ▷ clergy
clergymen n ▷ clergy
cleric n (pl -s) member of the clergy
clerical adj of clerks or office work
clerics n ▷ cleric
clerk n (pl -s) employee in an office, bank, or
court who keeps records, files, and accounts
clerks n ▷ clerk
clever adj (-er, -est) intelligent, quick at
learning > **cleverly** adv > **cleverness** n (pl -es)
cleverer adj ▷ clever
cleverest adj ▷ clever
cleverly adv ▷ clever
cleverness n ▷ clever
clevernesses n ▷ clever
clianthus [klee-**anth**-us] n (pl -es) Australian or
NZ plant with slender scarlet flowers
clianthuses n ▷ clianthus
cliché [klee-shay] n (pl -s) expression or idea
that is no longer effective because of overuse
> **clichéd** adj
clichéd n ▷ cliché
clichés n ▷ cliché
click n (pl -s) short sharp sound ▶ v (-s, -ing, -ed)
make this sound
clicked v ▷ click
clicking v ▷ click
clicks n, v ▷ click
client n (pl -s) person who uses the services of a
professional person or company
clientele [klee-on-**tell**] n (pl -s) clients
collectively
clienteles n ▷ clientele
clients n ▷ client
cliff n (pl -s) steep rock face, esp. along the
sea shore
cliffhanger n (pl -s) film, game, etc., that is
tense and exciting because its outcome is
uncertain
cliffhangers n ▷ cliffhanger
cliffs n ▷ cliff
climactic adj ▷ climax

climate n (pl -s) typical weather conditions of an area > **climatic** adj
climates n ▷ climate
climatic adj ▷ climate
climax n (pl -es) most intense point of an experience, series of events, or story > **climactic** adj
climaxes n ▷ climax
climb v (-s, -ing, -ed) go up, ascend ▶ n (pl -s) climbing > **climber** n (pl -s)
climbed v ▷ climb
climber n ▷ climb
climbers n ▷ climb
climbing v ▷ climb
climbs v, n ▷ climb
clime n (pl -s) (Poetic) place or its climate
climes n ▷ clime
clinch v (-es, -ing, -ed) settle (an argument or agreement) decisively
clinched v ▷ clinch
clincher n (pl -s) (Informal) something decisive
clinchers n ▷ clincher
clinches v ▷ clinch
clinching v ▷ clinch
cling v (clings, clinging, clung) hold tightly or stick closely
clingfilm n (pl -s) thin polythene material for wrapping food
clingfilms n ▷ clingfilm
clinging v ▷ cling
clings v ▷ cling
clinic n (pl -s) building where outpatients receive medical treatment or advice
clinical adj of a clinic > **clinically** adv
clinically adv ▷ clinic
clinics n ▷ clinic
clink¹ v (-s, -ing, -ed) ▶ n (pl -s) (make) a light sharp metallic sound
clink² n (pl -s) (BRIT, AUST & NZ) (Slang) prison
clinked v ▷ clink¹
clinker n (pl -s) fused coal left over in a fire or furnace
clinkers n ▷ clinker
clinking v ▷ clink¹
clinks n ▷ clink¹, ² ▶ v ▷ clink¹
clip¹ v (clips, clipping, clipped) cut with shears or scissors ▶ n (-s) short extract of a film
clip² n device for attaching or holding things together ▶ v (clips, clipping, clipped) attach or hold together with a clip
clipped v ▷ clip¹, ²
clipper n (pl -s) fast commercial sailing ship
clippers pl n tool for clipping ▶ n ▷ clipper
clipping n (-s) something cut out, esp. an article from a newspaper ▶ v ▷ clip¹, ²

clippings n ▷ clipping
clips n, v ▷ clip¹, ²
clique [kleek] n (pl -s) small exclusive group
cliques n ▷ clique
clitoral adj ▷ clitoris
clitoris [klit-or-iss] n (pl -es) small sexually sensitive organ at the front of the vulva > **clitoral** adj
clitorises n ▷ clitoris
cloak n (pl -s) loose sleeveless outer garment ▶ v (-s, -ing, -ed) cover or conceal
cloaked v ▷ cloak
cloaking v ▷ cloak
cloakroom n (pl -s) room where coats may be left temporarily
cloakrooms n ▷ cloakroom
cloaks n, v ▷ cloak
clobber¹ v (-s, -ing, -ed) (Informal) hit
clobber² n (pl -s) (BRIT, AUST & NZ) (Informal) belongings, esp. clothes
clobbered v ▷ clobber¹
clobbering v ▷ clobber¹
clobbers v ▷ clobber¹ ▶ n ▷ clobber²
cloche [klosh] n (pl -s) cover to protect young plants
cloches n ▷ cloche
clock n (pl -s) instrument for showing the time
clocks n ▷ clock
clockwise adv, adj in the direction in which the hands of a clock rotate
clockwork n mechanism similar to the kind in a clock, used in wind-up toys
clod n (pl -s) lump of earth
clods n ▷ clod
clog v (clogs, clogging, clogged) obstruct ▶ n (pl -s) wooden or wooden-soled shoe
clogged v ▷ clog
clogging v ▷ clog
clogs v, n ▷ clog
cloister n (pl -s) covered pillared arcade, usu. in a monastery
cloistered adj sheltered
cloisters n ▷ cloister
clone n (pl -s) animal or plant produced artificially from the cells of another animal or plant, and identical to the original (Informal) ▶ v (clones, cloning, cloned) produce as a clone
cloned v ▷ clone
clones n, v ▷ clone
cloning v ▷ clone
close¹ v (-ses, -sing, -sed) [rhymes with nose] shut ▶ n (pl -s) end, conclusion
close² adj (-r, -st) [rhymes with dose] near ▶ adv closely, tightly > **closely** adv > **closeness** n

(pl -es)

closed v ▷ close¹

closely adv ▷ close²

closeness n ▷ close²

closenesses n ▷ close²

closer adj ▷ close²

closes v, n ▷ close¹

closest adj ▷ close²

closet n (pl -s) (us) cupboard ▶ adj private, secret ▶ v (-s, -ing, -ed) shut (oneself) away in private

closeted v ▷ closet

closeting v ▷ closet

closets n, v ▷ closet

closing v ▷ close¹

closure n (pl -s) closing

closures n ▷ closure

clot n (pl -s) soft thick lump formed from liquid ▶ v (-s, -tting, -tted) form soft thick lumps

cloth n (pl -s) (piece of) woven fabric

clothe v (clothes, clothing, clothed or clad) put clothes on

clothed v ▷ clothe

clothes pl n articles of dress ▶ v ▷ clothe

clothing n clothes collectively ▶ v ▷ clothe

cloths n ▷ cloth

clots n, v ▷ clot

clotted v ▷ clot

clotting v ▷ clot

cloud n (pl -s) mass of condensed water vapour floating in the sky ▶ v (-s, -ing, -ed) (foll. by over) become cloudy > cloudless adj

cloudburst n (pl -s) heavy fall of rain

cloudbursts n ▷ cloudburst

clouded v ▷ cloud

cloudier adj ▷ cloud

cloudiest adj ▷ cloud

cloudiness n ▷ cloudy

clouding v ▷ cloud

cloudless adj ▷ cloud

clouds n, v ▷ cloud

cloudy adj (-dier, -diest) having a lot of clouds > cloudiness n

clout (Informal) n (pl -s) hard blow ▶ v (-s, -ed, -ing) hit hard

clouted v ▷ clout

clouting v ▷ clout

clouts n, v ▷ clout

clove¹ n (pl -s) dried flower bud of a tropical tree, used as a spice

clove² n (pl -s) segment of a bulb of garlic

clove³ v ▷ cleave¹

cloven v ▷ cleave¹

clover n (pl -s) plant with three-lobed leaves

clovers n ▷ clover

cloves n ▷ clove¹, ²

clown n (pl -s) comic entertainer in a circus ▶ v (-s, -ing, -ed) behave foolishly ▶ clownish adj > clownishly adv > clownishness n

clowned v ▷ clown

clowning v ▷ clown

clownish adj ▷ clown

clownishly adv ▷ clown

clownishness n ▷ clown

clowns n, v ▷ clown

club n (pl -s) association of people with common interests ▶ v (clubs, clubbing, clubbed) hit with a club

clubbed v ▷ club

clubbing v ▷ club

clubs n, v ▷ club

cluck n (pl -s) low clicking noise made by a hen ▶ v (-s, -ing, -ed) make this noise

clucked v ▷ cluck

clucking v ▷ cluck

clucks n, v ▷ cluck

clue n (pl -s) something that helps to solve a mystery or puzzle

clueless adj stupid > cluelessly adv > cluelessness n

cluelessly adv ▷ clueless

cluelessness n ▷ clueless

clues n ▷ clue

clump n (pl -s) small group of things or people ▶ v (-s, -ing, -ed) walk heavily

clumped v ▷ clump

clumping v ▷ clump

clumps n, v ▷ clump

clumsier adj ▷ clumsy

clumsiest adj ▷ clumsy

clumsily adv ▷ clumsy

clumsiness n ▷ clumsy

clumsy adj (-sier, -siest) lacking skill or physical coordination > clumsily adv > clumsiness n

clung v ▷ cling

clunk n (pl -s) dull metallic sound ▶ v (-s, -ing, -ed) make such a sound

clunked v ▷ clunk

clunking v ▷ clunk

clunks n, v ▷ clunk

cluster n (pl -s) small close group ▶ v (-s, -ing, -ed) gather in clusters

clustered v ▷ cluster

clustering v ▷ cluster

clusters n, v ▷ cluster

clutch¹ v (-es, -ing, -ed) grasp tightly (foll. by at) ▶ n (pl -es) device enabling two revolving shafts to be connected and disconnected, esp. in a motor vehicle

clutch² n (pl -es) set of eggs laid at the same time
clutched v ▷ clutch¹
clutches v ▷ clutch¹ ▸ n ▷ clutch¹, ²
clutching v ▷ clutch¹
clutter v (-s, -ing, -ed) scatter objects about (a place) untidily ▸ n (pl -s) untidy mess
cluttered v ▷ clutter
cluttering v ▷ clutter
clutters v, n ▷ clutter

> **cly** verb (**clys, clying, clyed**). Cly is an old word meaning steal. The various forms of this word can be useful when you are short of vowels. Cly scores 8 points.

coach n (pl -es) long-distance bus ▸ v (-es, -ing, -ed) train, teach
coached v ▷ coach
coaches n, v ▷ coach
coaching v ▷ coach
coagulant n (pl -s) substance causing coagulation
coagulants n ▷ coagulant
coagulate [koh-**ag**-yew-late] v (-lates, -lating, -lated) change from a liquid to a semisolid mass > **coagulation** n (pl -s)
coagulated v ▷ coagulate
coagulates v ▷ coagulate
coagulating v ▷ coagulate
coagulation n ▷ coagulate
coagulations n ▷ coagulate
coal n (pl -s) black rock consisting mainly of carbon, used as fuel
coalesce [koh-a-**less**] v (-lesces, -lescing, -lesced) come together, merge > **coalescence** n (pl -s)
coalesced v ▷ coalesce
coalescence n ▷ coalesce
coalescences n ▷ coalesce
coalesces v ▷ coalesce
coalescing v ▷ coalesce
coalfield n (pl -s) area with coal under the ground
coalfields n ▷ coalfield
coalition [koh-a-**lish**-un] n (pl -s) temporary alliance, esp. between political parties
coalitions n ▷ coalition
coals n ▷ coal
coarse adj (-r, -st) rough in texture > **coarsely** adv > **coarseness** n (pl -es) > **coarsen** v (-s, -ing, -ed)
coarsely adv ▷ coarse
coarsen v ▷ coarse
coarsened v ▷ coarse
coarseness n ▷ coarse
coarsenesses n ▷ coarse

coarsening v ▷ coarse
coarsens v ▷ coarse
coarser adj ▷ coarse
coarsest adj ▷ coarse
coast n (pl -s) place where the land meets the sea ▸ v (-s, -ing, -ed) move by momentum, without the use of power > **coastal** adj
coastal adj ▷ coast
coasted v ▷ coast
coaster n (pl -s) small mat placed under a glass
coasters n ▷ coaster
coastguard n (pl -s) organization that aids ships and swimmers in trouble and prevents smuggling
coastguards n ▷ coastguard
coasting v ▷ coast
coastline n (pl -s) outline of a coast
coastlines n ▷ coastline
coasts n, v ▷ coast
coat n (pl -s) outer garment with long sleeves ▸ v (-s, -ing, -ed) cover with a layer
coated v ▷ coat
coating n (pl -s) covering layer ▸ v ▷ coat
coatings n ▷ coating
coats n, v ▷ coat
coax v (-es, -ing, -ed) persuade gently
coaxed v ▷ coax
coaxes v ▷ coax
coaxial [koh-**ax**-ee-al] adj (of a cable) transmitting by means of two concentric conductors separated by an insulator
coaxing v ▷ coax
cob n (pl -s) stalk of an ear of maize
cobalt n (pl -s) (CHEM) brittle silvery-white metallic element
cobalts n ▷ cobalt
cobber n (pl -s) (AUST & OLD-FASHIONED NZ) (Informal) friend
cobbers n ▷ cobber
cobble n (pl -s) cobblestone
cobbler n (pl -s) shoe mender
cobblers n ▷ cobbler
cobbles n ▷ cobble
cobblestone n (pl -s) rounded stone used for paving
cobblestones n ▷ cobblestone
cobia [koh-bee-a] n (pl -s) large dark-striped game fish of tropical and subtropical seas
cobias n ▷ cobia
cobra n (pl -s) venomous hooded snake of Asia and Africa
cobras n ▷ cobra
cobs n ▷ cob
cobweb n (pl -s) spider's web
cobwebs n ▷ cobweb

cocaine n (pl -s) addictive drug used as a narcotic and as an anaesthetic
cocaines n ▷ cocaine
coccyges n ▷ coccyx
coccyx [kok-six] n (pl coccyges) [kok-**sije**-eez] bone at the base of the spinal column
cochineal n (pl -s) red dye obtained from a Mexican insect, used for food colouring
cochineals n ▷ cochineal
cock n (pl -s) male bird, esp. of domestic fowl ▶ v (-s, -ing, -ed) draw back (the hammer of a gun) to firing position
cockade n (pl -s) feather or rosette worn on a hat as a badge
cockades n ▷ cockade
cockatiel n ▷ cockatiel
cockatiels n ▷ cockatiel
cockatiel, cockateel n (pl -s) crested Australian parrot with a greyish-brown and yellow plumage
cockatiels n ▷ cockatiel
cockatoo n (pl -s) crested parrot of Australia or the East Indies
cockatoos n ▷ cockatoo
cocked v ▷ cock
cockerel n (pl -s) young domestic cock
cockerels n ▷ cockerel
cockeyed adj (Informal) crooked, askew
cockie, cocky n (pl -kies) (AUST & NZ) (Informal) farmer
cockier adj ▷ cocky
cockies n ▷ cockie
cockiest adj ▷ cocky
cockily adv ▷ cocky
cockiness n ▷ cocky
cocking v ▷ cock
cockle n (pl -s) edible shellfish
cockles n ▷ cockle
cockney n (pl -s) native of the East End of London
cockneys n ▷ cockney
cockpit n (pl -s) pilot's compartment in an aircraft
cockpits n ▷ cockpit
cockroach n (pl -es) beetle-like insect which is a household pest
cockroaches n ▷ cockroach
cocks n, v ▷ cock
cocksure adj overconfident, arrogant
cocktail n (pl -s) mixed alcoholic drink
cocktails n ▷ cocktail
cocky adj (cockier, cockiest) conceited and overconfident ▶ n ▷ cockie > **cockily** adv > **cockiness** n
cocoa n (pl -s) powder made from the seed of

the cacao tree
cocoas n ▷ cocoa
coconut n (pl -s) large hard fruit of a type of palm tree
coconuts n ▷ coconut
cocoon n (pl -s) silky protective covering of a silkworm ▶ v (-s, -ing, -ed) wrap up tightly for protection
cocooned v ▷ cocoon
cocooning v ▷ cocoon
cocoons n, v ▷ cocoon
cod n (pl cod) large food fish of the North Atlantic
coda n (pl -s) final part of a musical composition
codas n ▷ coda
coddle v (coddles, coddling, coddled) pamper, overprotect
coddled v ▷ coddle
coddles v ▷ coddle
coddling v ▷ coddle
code n (pl -s) system of letters, symbols, or prearranged signals by which messages can be communicated secretly or briefly ▶ v (codes, coding, coded) put into code
coded v ▷ code
codeine [kode-een] n (pl -s) drug used as a painkiller
codeines v ▷ codeine
codes n, v ▷ code
codex n (pl codices) volume of manuscripts of an ancient text
codger n (pl -s) (BRIT, AUST & NZ) (Informal) old man
codgers n ▷ codger
codices n ▷ codex
codicil [kode-iss-ill] n (pl -s) addition to a will
codicils n ▷ codicil
codification n ▷ codify
codifications n ▷ codify
codified v ▷ codify
codifies v ▷ codify
codify v (-fies, -fying, -fied) organize (rules or procedures) systematically > **codification** n (pl -s)
codifying v ▷ codify
coding v ▷ code
coeducation n education of boys and girls together > **coeducational** adj
coeducational adj ▷ coeducation
coefficient n (pl -s) (MATHS) number or constant placed before and multiplying a quantity
coefficients n ▷ coefficient
coelacanth [seel-a-kanth] n (pl -s) primitive marine fish

coelacanths n ▷ coelacanth

coerce [koh-**urss**] v (-ces, -cing, -ced) compel, force > **coercion** n > **coercive** adj

coerced v ▷ coerce

coerces v ▷ coerce

coercing v ▷ coerce

coercion n ▷ coerce

coercive adj ▷ coerce

coeval [koh-**eev**-al] adj, n (pl -s) contemporary

coevals n ▷ coeval

coexist v (-s, -ing, -ed) exist together, esp. peacefully despite differences > **coexistence** n

coexisted v ▷ coexist

coexistence n ▷ coexist

coexisting v ▷ coexist

coexists v ▷ coexist

coffee n (pl -s) drink made from the roasted and ground seeds of a tropical shrub ▶ adj medium-brown

coffees n ▷ coffee

coffer n (pl -s) chest for valuables ▶ pl store of money

coffers n ▷ coffer

coffin n (pl -s) box in which a corpse is buried or cremated

coffins n ▷ coffin

cog n (pl -s) one of the teeth on the rim of a gearwheel

cogency n ▷ cogent

cogent [koh-**jent**] adj forcefully convincing > **cogency** n > **cogently** adv

cogently n ▷ cogent

cogitate [koj-it-tate] v (-tates, -tating, -tated) think deeply about > **cogitation** n (pl -s)

cogitated v ▷ cogitate

cogitates v ▷ cogitate

cogitating v ▷ cogitate

cogitation n ▷ cogitate

cogitations n ▷ cogitate

cognac [kon-yak] n (pl -s) French brandy

cognacs n ▷ cognac

cognate adj derived from a common original form

cognition n (pl -s) act or experience of knowing or acquiring knowledge > **cognitive** adj

cognitions n ▷ cognition

cognitive adj ▷ cognition

cognizance n (pl -s) knowledge, understanding > **cognizant** adj

cognizances n ▷ cognizance

cognizant adj ▷ cognizance

cognoscenti [kon-yo-**shen**-tee] pl n connoisseurs

cogs n ▷ cog

cohabit v (-s, -ing, -ed) live together as husband and wife without being married > **cohabitation** n (pl -s)

cohabitation n ▷ cohabit

cohabitations n ▷ cohabit

cohabited v ▷ cohabit

cohabiting v ▷ cohabit

cohabits v ▷ cohabit

cohere v (-heres, -hering, -hered) hold or stick together

cohered v ▷ cohere

coherence n ▷ coherent

coherent adj logical and consistent > **coherence** n > **coherently** adv

coherently n ▷ coherent

coheres v ▷ cohere

cohering v ▷ cohere

cohesion n sticking together

cohesive adj sticking together to form a whole

cohort n (pl -s) band of associates

cohorts n ▷ cohort

coiffeur n ▷ coiffure

coiffeurs n ▷ coiffure

coiffeuse n ▷ coiffure

coiffeuses n ▷ coiffure

coiffure n (pl -s) hairstyle > **coiffeur, coiffeuse** n (pl -s) hairdresser

coiffures n ▷ coiffure

coil v (-s, -ing, -ed) wind in loops ▶ n (pl -s) something coiled

coiled v ▷ coil

coiling v ▷ coil

coils v, n ▷ coil

coin n (pl -s) piece of metal money ▶ v (-s, -ing, -ed) invent (a word or phrase)

coinage n (pl -s) coins collectively

coinages n ▷ coinage

coincide v (-cides, -ciding, -cided) happen at the same time

coincided v ▷ coincide

coincidence n (pl -s) occurrence of simultaneous or apparently connected events

coincidences n ▷ coincidence

coincident adj in agreement

coincidental adj resulting from coincidence > **coincidentally** adv

coincidentally adv ▷ coincidental

coincides v ▷ coincide

coinciding v ▷ coincide

coined v ▷ coin

coining v ▷ coin

coins n, v ▷ coin

coir n (pl -s) coconut fibre, used for matting

coirs *n* ▷ coir

coital *adj* ▷ coitus

coition *n* ▷ coitus

coitions *n* ▷ coitus

coitus [koh-it-uss], **coition** [koh-ish-un] *n* (*pl* -s) sexual intercourse > **coital** *adj*

coke¹ *n* (*pl* -s) solid fuel left after gas has been distilled from coal

coke² *n* (*pl* -s) (*Slang*) cocaine

cokes *n* ▷ coke¹, ²

col *n* (*pl* -s) high mountain pass

cola *n* (*pl* -s) dark brown fizzy soft drink

colander *n* (*pl* -s) perforated bowl for straining or rinsing foods

colanders *n* ▷ colander

colas *n* ▷ cola

cold *adj* (-er, -est) lacking heat ▶ *n* (*pl* -s) lack of heat > **coldly** *adv* > **coldness** *n* (*pl* -es)

colder *adj* ▷ cold

coldest *adj* ▷ cold

coldly *adv* ▷ cold

coldness *n* ▷ cold

coldnesses *n* ▷ cold

colds *n* ▷ cold

coleslaw *n* (*pl* -s) salad dish of shredded raw cabbage in a dressing

coleslaws *n* ▷ coleslaw

coley *n* (*pl* -s) codlike food fish of the N Atlantic

coleys *n* ▷ coley

colic *n* (*pl* -s) severe pains in the stomach and bowels > **colicky** *adj* (-ckier, -ckiest)

colickier *adj* ▷ colic

colickiest *adj* ▷ colic

colicky *adj* ▷ colic

colics *n* ▷ colic

colitis [koh-lie-tiss] *n* inflammation of the colon

collaborate *v* (-ates, -ating, -ated) work with another on a project > **collaboration** *n* (*pl* -s) > **collaborative** *adj* > **collaboratively** *adv* > **collaborator** *n* (*pl* -s)

collaborated *v* ▷ collaborate

collaborates *v* ▷ collaborate

collaborating *v* ▷ collaborate

collaboration *n* ▷ collaborate

collaborations *n* ▷ collaborate

collaborative *adj* ▷ collaborate

collaboratively *adv* ▷ collaborate

collaborator *n* ▷ collaborate

collaborators *n* ▷ collaborate

collage [kol-lahzh] *n* (*pl* -s) art form in which various materials or objects are glued onto a surface

collages *n* ▷ collage

collapse *v* (-lapses, -lapsing, -lapsed) fall down suddenly ▶ *n* (*pl* -s) collapsing > **collapsible** *adj*

collapsed *v* ▷ collapse

collapses *v, n* ▷ collapse

collapsible *adj* ▷ collapse

collapsing *v* ▷ collapse

collar *n* (*pl* -s) part of a garment round the neck ▶ *v* (-s, -ing, -ed) (BRIT, AUST & NZ) (*Informal*) seize, arrest

collarbone *n* (*pl* -s) bone joining the shoulder blade to the breastbone

collarbones *n* ▷ collarbone

collared *v* ▷ collar

collaring *v* ▷ collar

collars *n, v* ▷ collar

collate *v* (-lates, -lating, -lated) gather together, examine, and put in order

collated *v* ▷ collate

collateral *n* (*pl* -s) security pledged for the repayment of a loan

collaterals *n* ▷ collateral

collates *v* ▷ collate

collating *v* ▷ collate

collation *n* (*pl* -s) collating

collations *n* ▷ collation

colleague *n* (*pl* -s) fellow worker, esp. in a profession

colleagues *n* ▷ colleague

collect¹ *v* (-s, -ing, -ed) gather together > **collector** *n* (*pl* -s)

collect² *n* (*pl* -s) short prayer

collected *adj* calm and controlled ▶ *v* ▷ collect¹ > **collectedly** *adv* > **collectedness** *n*

collectedly *adv* ▷ collected

collectedness *n* ▷ collected

collecting *v* ▷ collect¹

collection *n* (*pl* -s) things collected

collections *n* ▷ collection

collective *adj* of or done by a group ▶ *n* (*pl* -s) group of people working together on an enterprise and sharing the benefits from it > **collectively** *adv*

collectively *adv* ▷ collective

collectives *n* ▷ collective

collects *v* ▷ collect¹ ▶ *n* ▷ collect²

colleen *n* (*pl* -s) (IRISH) girl

colleens *n* ▷ colleen

college *n* (*pl* -s) place of higher education > **collegiate** *adj*

colleges *n* ▷ college

collegiate *adj* ▷ college

collide *v* (-lides, -liding, -lided) crash together violently > **collision** *n* (*pl* -s)

collided *v* ▷ collide

collides *v* ▷ collide

colliding *v* ▷ collide

collie n (pl -s) silky-haired sheepdog
collier n (pl -s) coal miner
  collieries n ▷ colliery
  colliers n ▷ collier
colliery n (pl -lieries) coal mine
  collies n ▷ collie
  collision n ▷ collide
  collisions n ▷ collide
collocate v (-cates, -cating, -cated) (of words) occur together regularly > **collocation** n (pl -s)
  collocated v ▷ collocate
  collocates v ▷ collocate
  collocating v ▷ collocate
  collocation n ▷ collocate
  collocations n ▷ collocate
colloid n (pl -s) suspension of particles in a solution
  colloids n ▷ colloid
colloquial adj suitable for informal speech or writing > **colloquially** adv
colloquialism n (pl -s) colloquial word or phrase
  colloquialisms n ▷ colloquialism
  colloquially adv ▷ colloquial
collude v (-ludes, -luding, -luded) act in collusion
  colluded v ▷ collude
  colludes v ▷ collude
  colluding v ▷ collude
collusion n (pl -s) secret or illegal cooperation
  collusions n ▷ collusion
collywobbles pl n (Slang) nervousness
cologne n (pl -s) mild perfume
  colognes n ▷ cologne
colon[1] n (pl -s) punctuation mark (:)
colon[2] n (pl -s) part of the large intestine connected to the rectum
colonel n (pl -s) senior commissioned army or air-force officer
  colonels n ▷ colonel
colonial adj, n (pl -s) (inhabitant) of a colony
colonialism n policy of acquiring and maintaining colonies
  colonials n ▷ colonial
  colonies n ▷ colony
colonist n (pl -s) settler in a colony
  colonists n ▷ colonist
colonization n ▷ colonize
  colonizations n ▷ colonize
colonize v (-izes, -izing, -ized) make into a colony > **colonization** n (pl -s)
  colonized v ▷ colonize
  colonizes v ▷ colonize
  colonizing v ▷ colonize
colonnade n (pl -s) row of columns

colonnades n ▷ colonnade
colons n ▷ colon[1, 2]
colony n (pl -nies) group of people who settle in a new country but remain under the rule of their homeland
coloration n (pl -s) arrangement of colours
  colorations n ▷ coloration
  colosally adv ▷ colossal
colossal adj very large > **colossally** adv
  colossi n ▷ colossus
colossus n (pl -si, -suses) huge statue
  colossuses n ▷ colossus
  colostomies n ▷ colostomy
colostomy n (pl -mies) operation to form an opening from the colon onto the surface of the body, for emptying the bowel
colour n (pl -s) appearance of things as a result of reflecting light ▶ pl flag of a country or regiment (SPORT) ▶ v (-s, -ing, -ed) apply colour to > **colourless** adj > **colourlessly** adv
coloured adj having colour ▶ v ▷ colour
colourful adj with bright or varied colours > **colourfully** adv
  colourfully adv ▷ colourful
  colouring v ▷ colour
  colourless adj ▷ colour
  colourlessly adv ▷ colour
  colours n, v ▷ colour
  cols n ▷ col
colt n (pl -s) young male horse
  colts n ▷ colt
columbine n (pl -s) garden flower with five petals
  columbines n ▷ columbine
column n (pl -s) pillar
columnist n (pl -s) journalist who writes a regular feature in a newspaper
  columnists n ▷ columnist
  columns n ▷ column
coma n (pl -s) state of deep unconsciousness
  comas n ▷ coma
comatose adj in a coma
comb n (pl -s) toothed implement for arranging the hair ▶ v (-s, -ing, -ed) use a comb on
combat n (pl -s) ▶ v (-s, -ing, -ed) fight, struggle > **combatant** n (pl -s) > **combative** adj > **combativeness** n
  combatant n ▷ combat
  combatants n ▷ combat
  combated v ▷ combat
  combating v ▷ combat
  combats n, v ▷ combat
  combed v ▷ comb
combination n (pl -s) combining ▶ pl (BRIT) old-

fashioned undergarment with long sleeves and long legs

combinations n ▷ combination

combine v (-bines, -bining, -bined) join together ▶ n (pl -s) association of people or firms for a common purpose

combined v ▷ combine

combines v, n ▷ combine

combing v ▷ comb

combining v ▷ combine

combs n, v ▷ comb

combustible adj burning easily

combustion n (pl -s) process of burning

combustions n ▷ combustion

come v (comes, coming, came, come) move towards a place, arrive

comeback n (pl -s) (Informal) return to a former position

comebacks n ▷ comeback

comedian, comedienne n (pl -s) entertainer who tells jokes

comedians n ▷ comedian

comedienne n ▷ comedian

comediennes n ▷ comedian

comedies n ▷ comedy

comedown n (pl -s) decline in status

comedowns n ▷ comedown

comedy n (pl -dies) humorous play, film, or programme

comelier adj ▷ comely

comeliest adj ▷ comely

comeliness n ▷ comely

comely adj (-lier, -liest) (Old-fashioned) nice-looking > **comeliness** n

comes v ▷ come

comestibles pl n (Formal) food

comet n (pl -s) heavenly body with a long luminous tail

comets n ▷ comet

comeuppance n (Informal) deserved punishment

comfier adj ▷ comfy

comfiest adj ▷ comfy

comfit n (pl -s) (Old-fashioned) sugar-coated sweet

comfits n ▷ comfit

comfort n (pl -s) physical ease or wellbeing ▶ v (-s, -ing, -ed) soothe, console > **comforter** n (pl -s)

comfortable adj giving comfort > **comfortably** adv

comfortably adv ▷ comfortable

comforted v ▷ comfort

comforter n ▷ comfort

comforters n ▷ comfort

comforting v ▷ comfort

comforts n, v ▷ comfort

comfrey n (pl -s) tall plant with bell-shaped flowers

comfreys n ▷ comfrey

comfy adj (-fier, -fiest) (Informal) comfortable

comic adj humorous, funny ▶ n (pl -s) comedian

comical adj amusing > **comically** adv

comically adv ▷ comical

comics n ▷ comic

coming v ▷ come

comma n (pl -s) punctuation mark (,)

command v (-s, -ing, -ed) order ▶ n (pl -s) authoritative instruction that something must be done

commandant n (pl -s) officer commanding a military group

commandants n ▷ commandant

commanded v ▷ command

commandeer v (-s, -ing, -ed) seize for military use

commandeered v ▷ commandeer

commandeering v ▷ commandeer

commandeers v ▷ commandeer

commander n (pl -s) military officer in command of a group or operation

commanders n ▷ commander

commanding v ▷ command

commandment n (pl -s) command from God

commandments n ▷ commandment

commando n (pl -dos, -does) (member of) a military unit trained for swift raids in enemy territory

commandoes n ▷ commando

commandos n ▷ commando

commands v, n ▷ command

commas n ▷ comma

commemorate v (-rates, -rating, -rated) honour the memory of > **commemoration** n (pl -s) > **commemorative** adj

commemorated v ▷ commemorate

commemorates v ▷ commemorate

commemorating v ▷ commemorate

commemoration n ▷ commemorate

commemorations n ▷ commemorate

commemorative adj ▷ commemorate

commence v (-mences, -mencing, -menced) begin > **commencement** n (pl -s)

commenced v ▷ commence

commencement n ▷ commence

commencements n ▷ commence

commences v ▷ commence

commencing v ▷ commence

commend v (-s, -ing, -ed) praise

> **commendable** adj > **commendably** adv
> **commendation** n (pl -s)
commendable adj ▷ commend
commendably adv ▷ commend
commendation n ▷ commend
commendations n ▷ commend
commended v ▷ commend
commending v ▷ commend
commends v ▷ commend
commensurable adj measurable by the same standards
commensurate adj corresponding in degree, size, or value
comment n (pl -s) remark ▶ v (-s, -ing, -ed) make a comment
commentaries n ▷ commentary
commentary n (pl -taries) spoken accompaniment to a broadcast or film
commentate v (-tates, -tating, -tated) provide a commentary > **commentator** n (pl -s)
commentated v ▷ commentate
commentates v ▷ commentate
commentating v ▷ commentate
commentator n ▷ commentate
commentators n ▷ commentate
commented v ▷ comment
commenting v ▷ comment
comments n, v ▷ comment
commerce n (pl -s) buying and selling, trade
commerces n ▷ commerce
commercial adj of commerce ▶ n (pl -s) television or radio advertisement
commercialization n ▷ commercialize
commercialize v (-izes, -izing, -ized) make commercial > **commercialization** n
commercialized v ▷ commercialize
commercializes v ▷ commercialize
commercializing v ▷ commercialize
commercials n ▷ commercial
commiserate v (-rates, -rating, -rated) (foll. by with) express sympathy (for) > **commiseration** n (pl -s)
commiserated v ▷ commiserate
commiserates v ▷ commiserate
commiserating v ▷ commiserate
commiseration n ▷ commiserate
commiserations n ▷ commiserate
commissar n (pl -s) (formerly) official responsible for political education in Communist countries
commissariat n (pl -s) (BRIT, AUST & NZ) military department in charge of food supplies
commissariats n ▷ commissariat
commissars n ▷ commissar

commission n (pl -s) piece of work that an artist is asked to do (MIL) ▶ v (-s, -ing, -ed) place an order for
commissionaire n (pl -s) uniformed doorman at a hotel, theatre, etc.
commissionaires n ▷ commissionaire
commissioned v ▷ commission
commissioner n (pl -s) appointed official in a government department
commissioners n ▷ commissioner
commissioning v ▷ commission
commissions n, v ▷ commission
commit v (-mits, -mitting, -mitted) perform (a crime or error)
commitment n (pl -s) dedication to a cause
commitments n ▷ commitment
commits v ▷ commit
committal n (pl -s) sending someone to prison or hospital
committals n ▷ committal
committed v ▷ commit
committee n (pl -s) group of people appointed to perform a specified service or function
committees n ▷ committee
committing v ▷ commit
commode n (pl -s) seat with a hinged flap concealing a chamber pot
commodes n ▷ commode
commodious adj roomy
commodities n ▷ commodity
commodity n (pl -ities) something that can be bought or sold
commodore n (pl -s) senior commissioned officer in the navy
commodores n ▷ commodore
common adj (-er, -est) occurring often ▶ n (pl -s) area of grassy land belonging to a community > **commonly** adv
commoner n (pl -s) person who does not belong to the nobility ▶ adj ▷ common
commoners n ▷ commoner
commonest adj ▷ common
commonly adv ▷ common
commonplace adj ordinary, everyday ▶ n (pl -s) trite remark
commonplaces n ▷ commonplace
commons n ▷ common
commonwealth n (pl -s) state or nation viewed politically
commonwealths n ▷ commonwealth
commotion n (pl -s) noisy disturbance
commotions n ▷ commotion
communal adj shared > **communally** adv
communally n ▷ communal
commune[1] n (pl -s) group of people who live

together and share everything

commune² v (-munes, -muning, -muned) (foll. by **with**) feel very close (to)
  communed v ▷ commune²
  communes n ▷ commune¹ ▶ v ▷ commune²

communicable adj (of a disease) able to be passed on

communicant n (pl -s) person who receives Communion
  communicants n ▷ communicant

communicate v (-cates, -cating, -cated) make known or share (information, thoughts, or feelings)
  communicated v ▷ communicate
  communicates v ▷ communicate

communicating adj (of a door) joining two rooms ▶ v ▷ communicate

communication n communicating ▶ pl (-s) means of travelling or sending messages
  communications n ▷ communication

communicative adj talking freely

  communing v ▷ commune²

communion n (pl -s) sharing of thoughts or feelings
  communions n ▷ communion

communiqué [kom-mune-ik-kay] n (pl -s) official announcement
  communiqués n ▷ communiqué

communism n belief that all property and means of production should be shared by the community > **communist** n (pl -s) adj
  communists n ▷ communism
  communities n ▷ community

community n (pl -ties) all the people living in one district

commutator n (pl -s) device used to change alternating electric current into direct current
  commutators n ▷ commutator

commute v (-mutes, -muting, -muted) travel daily to and from work
  commuted v ▷ commute

commuter n (pl -s) person who commutes to and from work
  commuters n ▷ commuter
  commutes v ▷ commute
  commuting v ▷ commute

compact¹ adj (-er, -est) closely packed ▶ n (pl -s) small flat case containing a mirror and face powder ▶ v (-s, -ing, -ed) pack closely together > **compactly** adv > **compactness** n

compact² n (pl -s) contract, agreement
  compacted v ▷ compact¹
  compacter adj ▷ compact¹
  compactest adj ▷ compact¹

  compacting v ▷ compact¹
  compactly adv ▷ compact¹
  compactness n ▷ compact¹
  compacts n ▷ compact¹, ² ▶ v ▷ compact¹

companies n ▷ company

companion n (pl -s) person who associates with or accompanies someone > **companionship** n (pl -s)

companionable adj friendly > **companionably** adv
  companionably adv ▷ companionable
  companions n ▷ companion
  companionship n ▷ companion
  companionships n ▷ companion

companionway n (pl -s) ladder linking the decks of a ship
  companionways n ▷ companionway

company n (pl -nies) business organization

comparability n ▷ compare

comparable adj ▷ compare

comparative adj relative ▶ n (pl -s) (GRAMMAR) comparative form of a word > **comparatively** adv
  comparatively adv ▷ comparative
  comparatives n ▷ comparative

compare v (-pares, -paring, -pared) examine (things) and point out the resemblances or differences (foll. by **to**) (foll. by **with**) > **comparable** adj > **comparability** n
  compared v ▷ compare
  compares v ▷ compare
  comparing v ▷ compare

comparison n (pl -s) comparing
  comparisons n ▷ comparison

compartment n (pl -s) section of a railway carriage
  compartments n ▷ compartment

compass n (pl -es) instrument for showing direction, with a needle that points north ▶ pl hinged instrument for drawing circles
  compasses n ▷ compass

compassion n pity, sympathy > **compassionate** adj > **compassionately** adv
  compassionate adj ▷ compassion
  compassionately adj ▷ compassion
  compatibility n ▷ compatible

compatible adj able to exist, work, or be used together > **compatibility** n

compatriot n (pl -s) fellow countryman or countrywoman
  compatriots n ▷ compatriot

compel v (-pels, -pelling, -pelled) force (to be or do)
  compelled v ▷ compel
  compelling v ▷ compel

compels v ▷ compel
compendia n ▷ compendium
compendious adj brief but comprehensive
compendium n (pl -diums, -dia) selection of board games in one box
compendiums n ▷ compendium
compensate v (-sates, -sating, -sated) make amends to (someone), esp. for injury or loss (foll. by **for**) ▷ **compensatory** adj
compensated v ▷ compensate
compensates v ▷ compensate
compensating v ▷ compensate
compensation n (pl -s) payment to make up for loss or injury
compensations n ▷ compensation
compensatory adj ▷ compensate
compere n (pl -s) person who presents a stage, radio, or television show ▶ v (-peres, -pering, -pered) be the compere of
compered v ▷ compere
comperes n, v ▷ compere
compering v ▷ compere
compete v (-petes, -peting, -peted) try to win or achieve (a prize, profit, etc.) ▷ **competitive** adj ▷ **competitively** adv ▷ **competitiveness** n ▷ **competitor** n (pl -s)
competed v ▷ compete
competence n ▷ competent
competent adj having the skill or knowledge to do something well ▷ **competently** adv ▷ **competence** n
competently adv ▷ competent
competes v ▷ compete
competing v ▷ compete
competition n (pl -s) competing
competitions n ▷ competition
competitive adj ▷ compete
competitively adv ▷ compete
competitiveness n ▷ compete
competitor n ▷ compete
competitors n ▷ compete
compilation n ▷ compile
compilations n ▷ compile
compile v (-piles, -piling, -piled) collect and arrange (information), esp. to make a book ▷ **compilation** n (pl -s) ▷ **compiler** n (pl -s)
compiled v ▷ compile
compiler n ▷ compile
compilers n ▷ compile
compiles v ▷ compile
compiling v ▷ compile
complacencies n ▷ complacent
complacency n ▷ complacent
complacent adj self-satisfied ▷ **complacently** (pl -cies) adv ▷ **complacency** n

complacently adv ▷ complacent
complain v (-s, -ing, -ed) express resentment or displeasure
complainant n (pl -s) (LAW) plaintiff
complainants n ▷ complainant
complained v ▷ complain
complaining v ▷ complain
complains v ▷ complain
complaint n (pl -s) complaining
complaints n ▷ complaint
complaisance n ▷ complaisant
complaisant [kom-**play**-zant] adj willing to please ▷ **complaisance** n
complement n (pl -s) thing that completes something (GRAMMAR) ▶ v (-s, -ing, -ed) make complete ▷ **complementary** adj
complementary adj ▷ complement
complemented v ▷ complement
complementing v ▷ complement
complements n, v ▷ complement
complete adj thorough, absolute ▶ v (-pletes, -pleting, -pleted) finish ▷ **completely** adv ▷ **completeness** n
completed v ▷ complete
completely adv ▷ complete
completeness n ▷ complete
completes v ▷ complete
completing v ▷ complete
completion n finishing
complex adj (-er, -est) made up of parts ▶ n (pl -es) whole made up of parts ▷ **complexity** n (pl -ities)
complexer adj ▷ complex
complexes n ▷ complex
complexest adj ▷ complex
complexion n (pl -s) skin of the face
complexions n ▷ complexion
complexities n ▷ complex
complexity n ▷ complex
compliance n (pl -s) complying ▷ **compliant** adj
compliances n ▷ compliance
compliant adj ▷ compliance
complicate v (-cates, -cating, -cated) make or become complex or difficult to deal with ▷ **complication** n (pl -s)
complicated v ▷ complicate
complicates v ▷ complicate
complicating v ▷ complicate
complication n ▷ complicate
complications n ▷ complicate
complicities n ▷ complicity
complicity n (pl -ities) fact of being an accomplice in a crime
complied v ▷ comply

complies v ▷ comply
compliment n (pl -s) expression of praise ▶ pl formal greetings ▶ v (-s, -ing, -ed) praise
complimentary adj expressing praise
complimented v ▷ compliment
complimenting v ▷ compliment
compliments n, v ▷ compliment
compline n (pl -s) last service of the day in the Roman Catholic Church
complines n ▷ compline
comply v (-plies, -plying, -plied) (foll. by with) act in accordance (with)
complying v ▷ comply
component n (pl -s) ▶ adj (being) part of a whole
components n ▷ component
comport v (-s, -ing, -ed) (Formal) behave (oneself) in a specified way
comported v ▷ comport
comporting v ▷ comport
comports v ▷ comport
compose v (-poses, -posing, -posed) put together
composed v ▷ compose
composer n (pl -s) person who writes music
composers n ▷ composer
composes v ▷ compose
composing v ▷ compose
composite n (pl -s) ▶ adj (something) made up of separate parts
composites n ▷ composite
composition n (pl -s) way that something is put together or arranged
compositions n ▷ composition
compositor n (pl -s) person who arranges type for printing
compositors n ▷ compositor
compost n (pl -s) decayed plants used as a fertilizer
composts n ▷ compost
composure n calmness
compote n (pl -s) fruit stewed with sugar
compotes n ▷ compote
compound[1] n (pl -s) ▶ adj (thing, esp. chemical) made up of two or more combined parts or elements ▶ v (-s, -ing, -ed) combine or make by combining
compound[2] n (pl -s) fenced enclosure containing buildings
compounded v ▷ compound[1]
compounding v ▷ compound[1]
compounds v ▷ compound[1] ▶ n ▷ compound[1, 2]
comprehend v (-s, -ing, -ed) understand
 > **comprehensible** adj > **comprehensibly** adv
 > **comprehension** n (pl -s)

comprehended v ▷ comprehend
comprehending v ▷ comprehend
comprehends v ▷ comprehend
comprehensible adj ▷ comprehend
comprehensibly adv ▷ comprehend
comprehension n ▷ comprehend
comprehensions n ▷ comprehend
comprehensive adj of broad scope, fully inclusive ▶ n (pl -s) (BRIT) comprehensive school > **comprehensively** adv
 > **comprehensiveness** n
comprehensively adv ▷ comprehensive
comprehensiveness n ▷ comprehensive
comprehensives n ▷ comprehensive
compress v (-es, -ing, -ed) [kum-**press**] squeeze together ▶ n (pl -es) [kom-press] pad applied to stop bleeding or cool inflammation
 > **compression** n (pl -s)
compressed v ▷ compress
compresses v, n ▷ compress
compressing v ▷ compress
compression n ▷ compress
compressions n ▷ compress
compressor n (pl -s) machine that compresses gas or air
compressors n ▷ compressor
comprise v (-ises, -ising, -ised) be made up of or make up
comprised v ▷ comprise
comprises v ▷ comprise
comprising v ▷ comprise
compromise [kom-**prom**-mize] n (pl -s) settlement reached by concessions on each side ▶ v (-ises, -ising, -ised) settle a dispute by making concessions
compromised v ▷ compromise
compromises n, v ▷ compromise
compromising v ▷ compromise
comptroller n (pl -s) (in titles) financial controller
comptrollers n ▷ comptroller
compulsion n (pl -s) irresistible urge
 > **compulsive** adj > **compulsively** adv
compulsions n ▷ compulsion
compulsive adj ▷ compulsion
compulsively adv ▷ compulsion
compulsorily adv ▷ compulsory
compulsoriness n ▷ compulsory
compulsory adj required by rules or laws
 > **compulsorily** adv > **compulsoriness** n
compunction n (pl -s) feeling of guilt or shame
compunctions n ▷ compunction
computation n ▷ compute
computations n ▷ compute
compute v (-putes, -puting, -puted) calculate,

esp. using a computer > **computation** n (pl -s)
computed v ▷ compute
computer n (pl -s) electronic machine that stores and processes data > **computerize** v (-izes, -izing, -ized) adapt (a system) to be handled by computer > **computerization** n (pl -s)
computerization n ▷ computerize
computerizations n ▷ computerize
computerized v ▷ computerize
computerizes v ▷ computerize
computerizing v ▷ computerize
computers n ▷ computer
computes v ▷ compute
computing v ▷ compute
comrade n (pl -s) fellow member of a union or socialist political party > **comradeship** n
comrades n ▷ comrade
comradeship n ▷ comrade
con[1] (Informal) n (pl -s) ▷ confidence trick ▶ v (cons, conning, conned) deceive, swindle
con[2] n (pl -s) ▷ **pro**[1]
concatenation n (pl -s) series of linked events
concatenations n ▷ concatenation
concave adj curving inwards
conceal v (-s, -ing, -ed) cover and hide > **concealment** n
concealed v ▷ conceal
concealing v ▷ conceal
concealment n ▷ conceal
conceals v ▷ conceal
concede v (-cedes, -ceding, -ceded) admit to be true
conceded v ▷ concede
concedes v ▷ concede
conceding v ▷ concede
conceit n (pl -s) too high an opinion of oneself > **conceited** adj > **conceitedly** adv > **conceitedness** n
conceited adj ▷ conceit
conceitedly adv ▷ conceit
conceitedness adv ▷ conceit
conceits n ▷ conceit
conceivable adj imaginable, possible > **conceivably** adv
conceivably adv ▷ conceivable
conceive v (-ceives, -ceiving, -ceived) imagine, think
conceived v ▷ conceive
conceives v ▷ conceive
conceiving v ▷ conceive
concentrate v (-rates, -rating, -rated) fix one's attention or efforts on something ▶ n (pl -s) concentrated liquid
concentrated v ▷ concentrate

concentrates v, n ▷ concentrate
concentrating v ▷ concentrate
concentration n (pl -s) concentrating
concentrations n ▷ concentration
concentric adj having the same centre
concept n (pl -s) abstract or general idea
conception n (pl -s) general idea
conceptions n ▷ conception
concepts n ▷ concept
conceptual adj of or based on concepts > **conceptually** adv
conceptualize v (-izes, -izing, -ized) form a concept of
conceptualized v ▷ conceptualize
conceptualizes v ▷ conceptualize
conceptualizing v ▷ conceptualize
conceptually adv ▷ conceptual
concern n (pl -s) anxiety, worry ▶ v (-s, -ing, -ed) worry (someone)
concerned adj interested, involved ▶ v ▷ concern
concerning prep about, regarding ▶ v ▷ concern
concerns n, v ▷ concern
concert n (pl -s) musical entertainment
concerted adj done together
concerti n ▷ concerto
concertina n (pl -s) small musical instrument similar to an accordion ▶ v (-nas, -naing, -naed) collapse or fold up like a concertina
concertinaed v ▷ concertina
concertinaing v ▷ concertina
concertinas n, v ▷ concertina
concerto [kon-**chair**-toe] n (pl -tos, -ti) large-scale composition for a solo instrument and orchestra
concertos n ▷ concerto
concerts n ▷ concert
concession n (pl -s) grant of rights, land, or property > **concessionary** adj
concessionary adj ▷ concession
concessions n ▷ concession
conch n (pl -s) shellfish with a large spiral shell
conchs n ▷ conch
concierge [kon-see-**airzh**] n (pl -s) (in France) caretaker in a block of flats
concierges n ▷ concierge
conciliate v (-ates, -ating, -ated) try to end a disagreement (with) > **conciliation** n > **conciliator** n (pl -s)
conciliated v ▷ conciliate
conciliates v ▷ conciliate
conciliating v ▷ conciliate
conciliation n ▷ conciliate
conciliator n ▷ conciliate

conciliators n ▷ conciliate

conciliatory adj intended to end a disagreement

concise adj (-r, -st) brief and to the point > **concisely** adv > **concision, conciseness** n (pl -s, -es)

concisely adv ▷ concise

conciseness n ▷ concise

concisenesses n ▷ concise

conciser adj ▷ concise

concisest adj ▷ concise

concision n ▷ concise

concisions n ▷ concise

conclave n (pl -s) secret meeting

conclaves n ▷ conclave

conclude v (-cludes, -cluding, -cluded) decide by reasoning

concluded v ▷ conclude

concludes v ▷ conclude

concluding v ▷ conclude

conclusion n (pl -s) decision based on reasoning

conclusions n ▷ conclusion

conclusive adj ending doubt, convincing > **conclusively** adv

conclusively adv ▷ conclusive

concoct v (-s, -ing, -ed) make up (a story or plan) > **concoction** n (pl -s)

concocted v ▷ concoct

concocting v ▷ concoct

concoction n ▷ concoct

concoctions n ▷ concoct

concocts v ▷ concoct

concomitant adj existing along with something else

concord n (pl -s) state of peaceful agreement, harmony

concordance n (pl -s) similarity or consistency

concordances n ▷ concordance

concordant adj agreeing > **concordantly** adv

concordantly adv ▷ concordant

concords n ▷ concord

concourse n (pl -s) large open public place where people can gather

concourses n ▷ concourse

concrete n (pl -s) mixture of cement, sand, stone, and water, used in building ▶ adj made of concrete

concretes n ▷ concrete

concubine [kon-kew-bine] n (pl -s) (HIST) woman living in a man's house but not married to him and kept for his sexual pleasure

concubines n ▷ concubine

concupiscence [kon-**kew**-piss-enss] n (Formal) lust

concur v (-curs, -curring, -curred) agree > **concurrence** n (pl -s)

concurred v ▷ concur

concurrence n ▷ concur

concurrent adj happening at the same time or place

concurrently adv at the same time

concurring v ▷ concur

concurs v ▷ concur

concussed adj having concussion

concussion n (pl -s) period of unconsciousness caused by a blow to the head

concussions n ▷ concussion

condemn v (-s, -ing, -ed) express disapproval of > **condemnation** n (pl -s) > **condemnatory** adj

condemnation n ▷ condemn

condemnations n ▷ condemn

condemnatory adj ▷ condemn

condemned v ▷ condemn

condemning v ▷ condemn

condemns v ▷ condemn

condensation n ▷ condense

condense v (-denses, -densing, -densed) make shorter > **condensation** n

condensed v ▷ condense

condenser n (pl -s) (ELECTRICITY) capacitor

condensers n ▷ condenser

condenses v ▷ condense

condensing v ▷ condense

condescend v (-s, -ing, -ed) behave patronizingly towards someone > **condescension** n

condescended v ▷ condescend

condescending v ▷ condescend

condescends v ▷ condescend

condescension n ▷ condescend

condiment n (pl -s) seasoning for food, such as salt or pepper

condiments n ▷ condiment

condition n (pl -s) particular state of being ▶ pl circumstances ▶ v (-s, -ed, -ing) train or influence to behave in a particular way

conditional adj depending on circumstances > **conditionally** adv

conditionally adv ▷ conditional

conditioned v ▷ condition

conditioner n (pl -s) thick liquid used when washing to make hair or clothes feel softer

conditioning v ▷ condition

conditioners n ▷ condition

conditions n, v ▷ condition

condolence n (pl -s) sympathy ▶ pl expression of sympathy

condolences n ▷ condolence
condom n (pl -s) rubber sheath worn on the penis or in the vagina during sexual intercourse to prevent conception or infection
condominium n (pl -s) (AUST, US & CANADIAN) block of flats in which each flat is owned by the occupant
condominiums n ▷ condominium
condoms n ▷ condom
condone v (-dones, -doning, -doned) overlook or forgive (wrongdoing)
condoned v ▷ condone
condones v ▷ condone
condoning v ▷ condone
condor n (pl -s) large vulture of S America
condors n ▷ condor
conducive adj (foll. by **to**) likely to lead (to)
conduct n (pl -s) management of an activity
▶ v (-s, -ing, -ed) carry out (a task)
conducted v ▷ conduct
conducting v ▷ conduct
conduction n transmission of heat or electricity
conductive adj ▷ conductivity
conductivities n ▷ conductivity
conductivity n (pl -vities) ability to transmit heat or electricity > **conductive** adj
conductor n (pl -s) person who conducts musicians, fem **conductress** ▶ n (pl -es)
conductors n ▷ conductor
conductress n ▷ conductor
conductresses n ▷ conductor
conductresses n ▷ conductor
conducts n, v ▷ conduct
conduit [kon-dew-it] n (pl -s) channel or tube for fluid or cables
conduits n ▷ conduit
cone n (pl -s) object with a circular base, tapering to a point
cones n ▷ cone
coney n (pl -s) ▷ cony
coneys n ▷ coney
confab n (pl -s) (Informal) conversation (also **confabulation**)
confabs n ▷ confab
confabulation n ▷ confab
confabulations n ▷ confab
confection n (pl -s) any sweet food (Old-fashioned)
confectioner n (pl -s) maker or seller of confectionery
confectioneries n ▷ confectionery
confectioners n ▷ confectioner
confectionery n (pl -eries) sweets
confections n ▷ confection

confederacies n ▷ confederacy
confederacy n (pl -cies) union of states or people for a common purpose
confederate n (pl -s) member of a confederacy ▶ adj united, allied ▶ v (-rates, -rating, -rated) unite in a confederacy
confederated v ▷ confederate
confederates n, v ▷ confederate
confederating v ▷ confederate
confederation n (pl -s) alliance of political units
confederations n ▷ confederation
confer v (-fers, -ferring, -ferred) discuss together
conference n (pl -s) meeting for discussion
conferences n ▷ conference
conferment n (pl -s) granting, giving
conferments n ▷ conferment
conferred v ▷ confer
conferring v ▷ confer
confers v ▷ confer
confess v (-es, -ing, -ed) admit (a fault or crime)
confessed v ▷ confess
confesses v ▷ confess
confessing v ▷ confess
confession n (pl -s) something confessed
confessional n (pl -s) small stall in which a priest hears confessions
confessionals n ▷ confessional
confessions n ▷ confession
confessor n (pl -s) priest who hears confessions
confessors n ▷ confessor
confetti n (pl -s) small pieces of coloured paper thrown at weddings
confettis n ▷ confetti
confidant n (pl -s) person confided in > **confidante** n fem (pl -s)
confidante n ▷ confidant
confidantes n ▷ confidant
confidants n ▷ confidant
confide v (-fides, -fiding, -fided) tell someone (a secret)
confided v ▷ confide
confidence n (pl -s) trust
confidences n ▷ confidence
confident adj sure, esp. of oneself > **confidently** adv
confidential adj private, secret > **confidentially** adv > **confidentiality** n
confidentiality n ▷ confidential
confidentially adv ▷ confidential
confidently adv ▷ confident
confides v ▷ confide

confiding v ▷ confide
configuration n (pl -s) arrangement of parts
  configurations n ▷ configuration
confine v (-fines, -fining, -fined) keep within bounds
  confined v ▷ confine
confinement n (pl -s) being confined
confines pl n boundaries, limits ▶ v ▷ confine
  confining v ▷ confine
confirm v (-s, -ing, -ed) prove to be true
confirmation n (pl -s) confirming
  confirmations n ▷ confirmation
confirmed adj firmly established in a habit or condition ▶ v ▷ confirm
  confirming v ▷ confirm
  confirms v ▷ confirm
confiscate v (-cates, -cating, -cated) seize (property) by authority > **confiscation** n (pl -s)
  confiscated v ▷ confiscate
  confiscates v ▷ confiscate
  confiscating v ▷ confiscate
  confiscation n ▷ confiscate
  confiscations n ▷ confiscate
conflagration n (pl -s) large destructive fire
  conflagrations n ▷ conflagration
conflate v (-ates, -ating, -ated) combine or blend into a whole > **conflation** n (pl -s)
  conflated v ▷ conflate
  conflates v ▷ conflate
  conflating v ▷ conflate
  conflation n ▷ conflate
  conflations n ▷ conflate
conflict n (pl -s) disagreement ▶ v (-s, -ing, -ed) be incompatible
  conflicted v ▷ conflict
  conflicting v ▷ conflict
  conflicts n, v ▷ conflict
confluence n (pl -s) place where two rivers join
  confluences n ▷ confluence
conform v (-s, -ing, -ed) comply with accepted standards or customs
  conformed v ▷ conform
  conforming v ▷ conform
conformist n (pl -s) ▶ adj (person) complying with accepted standards or customs
  conformists n ▷ conformist
  conformities n ▷ conformity
conformity n (pl -ities) compliance with accepted standards or customs
  conforms v ▷ conform
confound v (-s, -ing, -ed) astound, bewilder
confounded adj (Old-fashioned) damned ▶ v ▷ confound > **confoundedly** adv
  confoundedly adv ▷ confounded
  confounding v ▷ confound

confounds v ▷ confound
confront v (-s, -ing, -ed) come face to face with
confrontation n (pl -s) serious argument > **confrontational** adj
  confrontational adj ▷ confrontation
  confrontations n ▷ confrontation
  confronted v ▷ confront
  confronting v ▷ confront
  confronts v ▷ confront
confuse v (-fuses, -fusing, -fused) mix up > **confusion** n (pl -s)
  confused v ▷ confuse
  confuses v ▷ confuse
  confusing v ▷ confuse
  confusion n ▷ confuse
  confusions n ▷ confuse
confute v (-futes, -futing, -futed) prove wrong
  confuted v ▷ confute
  confutes v ▷ confute
  confuting v ▷ confute
conga n (pl -s) dance performed by a number of people in single file
  congas n ▷ conga
congeal v (-s, -ing, -ed) (of a liquid) become thick and sticky
  congealed v ▷ congeal
  congealing v ▷ congeal
  congeals v ▷ congeal
congenial adj pleasant, agreeable > **congeniality** n > **congenially** adv
  congeniality n ▷ congenial
  congenially adv ▷ congenial
congenital adj (of a condition) existing from birth > **congenitally** adv
  congenitally adv ▷ congenital
conger n (pl -s) large sea eel
  congers n ▷ conger
congested adj crowded to excess > **congestion** n
  congestion n ▷ congested
conglomerate n (pl -s) large corporation made up of many companies ▶ v (-rates, -rating, -rated) form into a mass ▶ adj made up of several different elements > **conglomeration** n (pl -s)
  conglomerated v ▷ conglomerate
  conglomerates n, v ▷ conglomerate
  conglomerating v ▷ conglomerate
  conglomeration n ▷ conglomerate
  conglomerations n ▷ conglomerate
congratulate v (-lates, -lating, -lated) express one's pleasure to (someone) at his or her good fortune or success > **congratulations** pl n, interj > **congratulatory** adj
  congratulated v ▷ congratulate

congratulates v ▷ congratulate
congratulating v ▷ congratulate
congratulations n ▷ congratulate
congratulatory adj ▷ congratulate
congregate v (-gates, -gating, -gated) gather together in a crowd
congregated v ▷ congregate
congregates v ▷ congregate
congregating v ▷ congregate
congregation n (pl -s) people who attend a church > **congregational** adj
congregational adj ▷ congregation
congregations n ▷ congregation
congress n (pl congresses) formal meeting for discussion > **congressional** adj
congresses n ▷ congress
congressional n ▷ congress
congressman, congresswoman n (pl -men, -women) member of Congress
congressmen n ▷ congressman
congresswoman n ▷ congressman
congresswomen n ▷ congressman
congruence n ▷ congruent
congruent adj similar, corresponding > **congruence** n
conical adj cone-shaped
conies n ▷ cony
conifer n (pl -s) cone-bearing tree, such as the fir or pine > **coniferous** adj
coniferous adj ▷ conifer
conifers n ▷ conifer
conjectural adj ▷ conjecture
conjecture n (pl -s) ▶ v (-tures, -turing, -tured) guess > **conjectural** adj
conjectured v ▷ conjecture
conjectures n, v ▷ conjecture
conjecturing v ▷ conjecture
conjugal adj of marriage > **conjugally** adv
conjugally adv ▷ conjugal
conjugate v (-gates, -gating, -gated) give the inflections of (a verb)
conjugated v ▷ conjugate
conjugates v ▷ conjugate
conjugating v ▷ conjugate
conjugation n (pl -s) complete set of inflections of a verb
conjugations n ▷ conjugation
conjunction n (pl -s) combination
conjunctions n ▷ conjunction
conjunctiva n (pl -s) the membrane covering the eyeball and inner eyelid
conjunctivas n ▷ conjunctiva
conjunctivitis n inflammation of the conjunctiva
conjure v (-jures, -juring, -jured) perform

tricks that appear to be magic > **conjuror** n (pl -s)
conjured v ▷ conjure
conjures v ▷ conjure
conjuring v ▷ conjure
conjuror n ▷ conjure
conjurors n ▷ conjure
conk n (pl -s) (BRIT, AUST & NZ) (Slang) nose
conker n (pl -s) (Informal) nut of the horse chestnut
conkers n ▷ conker
conks n ▷ conk
connect v (-s, -ing, -ed) join together > **connection, connexion** n (pl -s) relationship, association > **connective** adj
connected v ▷ connect
connecting v ▷ connect
connection n ▷ connect
connections n ▷ connect
connective n ▷ connect
connects v ▷ connect
conned v ▷ con[1]
connexion n ▷ connect
connexions n ▷ connect
conning v ▷ con[1]
connivance n ▷ connive
connivances n ▷ connive
connive v (-nives, -niving, -nived) (foll. by at) allow (wrongdoing) by ignoring it > **connivance** n (pl -s)
connived v ▷ connive
connives v ▷ connive
conniving v ▷ connive
connoisseur [kon-noss-**sir**] n (pl -s) person with special knowledge of the arts, food, or drink
connoisseurs n ▷ connoisseur
connotation n (pl -s) associated idea conveyed by a word > **connote** v (-notes, -noting, -noted)
connotations n ▷ connotation
connoted v ▷ connotation
connotes v ▷ connotation
connoting v ▷ connotation
connubial adj (Formal) of marriage
conquer v (-s, -ing, -ed) defeat > **conqueror** n (pl -s)
conquered v ▷ conquer
conquering v ▷ conquer
conqueror n ▷ conquer
conquerors n ▷ conquer
conquers v ▷ conquer
conquest n (pl -s) conquering
conquests n ▷ conquest
cons n ▷ con[1, 2]
conscience n (pl -s) sense of right or wrong as

regards thoughts and actions
consciences *n* ▷ conscience
conscientious *adj* painstaking
> **conscientiously** *adv*
conscientiously *adv* ▷ conscientious
conscious *adj* alert and awake > **consciously**
adv > **consciousness** *n*
consciously *adv* ▷ conscious
consciousness *n* ▷ conscious
conscript *n* (*pl* -s) person enrolled for
compulsory military service ▶ *v* (-s, -ing, -ed)
enrol (someone) for compulsory military
service > **conscription** *n* (*pl* -s)
conscripted *v* ▷ conscript
conscripting *v* ▷ conscript
conscription *n* ▷ conscript
conscriptions *n* ▷ conscript
conscripts *n*, *v* ▷ conscript
consecrate *v* (-rates, -rating, -rated) make
sacred > **consecration** *n* (*pl* -s)
consecrated *v* ▷ consecrate
consecrates *v* ▷ consecrate
consecrating *v* ▷ consecrate
consecration *n* ▷ consecrate
consecrations *n* ▷ consecrate
consecutive *adj* in unbroken succession
> **consecutively** *adv*
consecutively *adv* ▷ consecutive
consensus *n* general agreement
consent *n* (*pl* -s) agreement, permission ▶ *v* (-s,
-ing, -ed) (*foll. by* **to**) permit, agree to
consented *v* ▷ consent
consenting *v* ▷ consent
consents *v*, *n* ▷ consent
consequence *n* (*pl* -s) result, effect
consequences *n* ▷ consequence
consequent *adj* resulting
consequential *adj* important
consequently *adv* as a result, therefore
conservancies *n* ▷ conservancy
conservancy *n* (*pl* -cies) environmental
conservation
conservation *n* (*pl* -s) protection of
natural resources and the environment
> **conservationist** *n* (*pl* -s)
conservationist *n* ▷ conservation
conservationists *n* ▷ conservation
conservations *n* ▷ conservation
conservatism *adv* ▷ conservative
conservative *adj* opposing change ▶ *n* (*pl* -s)
conservative person > **conservatively** *adv*
> **conservatism** *n*
conservatively *adv* ▷ conservative
conservatives *n* ▷ conservative
conservatoire [kon-**serv**-a-twahr] *n* (*pl* -s)

school of music
conservatoires *n* ▷ conservatoire
conservatories *n* ▷ conservatory
conservatory *n* (*pl* -ries) room with glass walls
and a glass roof, attached to a house
conserve *v* (-serves, -serving, -served) protect
from harm, decay, or loss ▶ *n* (*pl* -s) jam
containing large pieces of fruit
conserved *v* ▷ conserve
conserves *v*, *n* ▷ conserve
conserving *v* ▷ conserve
consider *v* (-s, -ing, -ed) regard as
considerable *adj* large in amount or degree
> **considerably** *adv*
considerably *adv* ▷ considerable
considerate *adj* thoughtful towards others
> **considerately** *adv*
considerately *adv* ▷ considerate
consideration *n* (*pl* -s) careful thought
considerations *n* ▷ consideration
considered *v* ▷ consider
considering *prep* taking (a specified fact) into
account ▶ *v* ▷ consider
considers *v* ▷ consider
consign *v* (-s, -ing, -ed) put somewhere
consigned *v* ▷ consign
consigning *v* ▷ consign
consignment *n* (*pl* -s) shipment of goods
consignments *n* ▷ consignment
consigns *v* ▷ consign
consist *v* (-s, -ing, -ed) be made up of
consisted *v* ▷ consist
consistencies *n* ▷ consistency
consistency *n* (*pl* -cies) being consistent
consistent *adj* unchanging, constant (*foll. by*
with) > **consistently** *adv*
consistently *adv* ▷ consistent
consisting *v* ▷ consist
consists *v* ▷ consist
consolation *n* (*pl* -s) consoling
consolations *n* ▷ consolation
console¹ *v* (-soles, -soling, -soled) comfort in
distress
console² *n* (*pl* -s) panel of controls for
electronic equipment
consoled *v* ▷ console¹
consoles *v* ▷ console¹ ▶ *n* ▷ console²
consolidate *v* (-dates, -dating, -dated)
make or become stronger or more stable
> **consolidation** *n* (*pl* -s)
consolidated *v* ▷ consolidate
consolidates *v* ▷ consolidate
consolidating *v* ▷ consolidate
consolidation *n* ▷ consolidate
consolidations *n* ▷ consolidate

consoling v ▷ console¹

consommé [kon-**som**-may] n (pl -s) thin clear meat soup

consommés n ▷ consommé

consonance n agreement, harmony

consonant n (pl -s) speech sound made by partially or completely blocking the breath stream, such as b or f ▶ adj (foll. by **with**) agreeing (with) > **consonantly** adv

consonantly adv ▷ consonant

consonants n ▷ consonant

consort v (-s, -ing, -ed) (foll. by **with**) keep company (with) ▶ n (pl -s) husband or wife of a monarch

consorted v ▷ consort

consortia n ▷ consortium

consorting v ▷ consort

consortium n (pl -tia) association of business firms

consorts v, n ▷ consort

conspectus n (pl -es) (Formal) survey or summary

conspectuses n ▷ conspectus

conspicuous adj clearly visible > **conspicuously** adv > **conspicuousness** n

conspicuously adv ▷ conspicuous

conspicuousness n ▷ conspicuous

conspiracies n ▷ conspiracy

conspiracy n (pl -cies) conspiring > **conspirator** n (pl -s) > **conspiratorial** adj

conspirator n ▷ conspiracy

conspiratorial adj ▷ conspiracy

conspirators n ▷ conspiracy

conspire v (-spires, -spiring, -spired) plan a crime together in secret

conspired v ▷ conspire

conspires v ▷ conspire

conspiring v ▷ conspire

constable n (pl -s) police officer of the lowest rank

constables n ▷ constable

constabularies n ▷ constabulary

constabulary n (pl -laries) police force of an area

constancy n ▷ constant

constant adj continuous ▶ n (pl -s) unvarying quantity > **constantly** adv > **constancy** n

constantly adv ▷ constant

constants n ▷ constant

constellation n (pl -s) group of stars

constellations n ▷ constellation

consternation n anxiety or dismay

constipated adj having constipation

constipation n difficulty in defecating

constituencies n ▷ constituency

constituency n (pl -cies) area represented by a Member of Parliament

constituent n (pl -s) member of a constituency ▶ adj forming part of a whole

constituents n ▷ constituent

constitute v (-tutes, -tuting, -tuted) form, make up

constituted v ▷ constitute

constitutes v ▷ constitute

constituting v ▷ constitute

constitution n (pl -s) principles on which a state is governed

constitutional adj of a constitution ▶ n (pl -s) walk taken for exercise > **constitutionally** adv

constitutionally adv ▷ constitutional

constitutionals n ▷ constitutional

constitutions n ▷ constitution

constrain v (-s, -ing, -ed) compel, force > **constraint** n (pl -s)

constrained v ▷ constrain

constraining v ▷ constrain

constrains v ▷ constrain

constraint n ▷ constrain

constraints n ▷ constrain

constrict v (-s, -ing, -ed) make narrower by squeezing > **constriction** n (pl -s) > **constrictive** adj

constricted v ▷ constrict

constricting v ▷ constrict

constriction n ▷ constrict

constrictions n ▷ constrict

constrictive adj ▷ constrict

constrictor n (pl -s) large snake that squeezes its prey to death

constrictors n ▷ constrictor

constricts v ▷ constrict

construct v (-s, -ing, -ed) build or put together

constructed v ▷ construct

constructing v ▷ construct

construction n (pl -s) constructing

constructions n ▷ construction

constructive adj (of advice, criticism, etc.) useful and helpful > **constructively** adv

constructively adv ▷ constructive

constructs v ▷ construct

construe v (-strues, -struing, -strued) interpret

construed v ▷ construe

construes v ▷ construe

construing v ▷ construe

consul n (pl -s) official representing a state in a foreign country > **consular** adj > **consulship** n (pl -s)

consular adj ▷ consul

consulate n (pl -s) workplace or position of

a consul
consulates n ▷ consulate
consuls n ▷ consul
consulship n ▷ consul
consulships n ▷ consul
consult v (-s, -ing, -ed) go to for advice or information
consultancies n ▷ consultancy
consultancy n (pl -cies) work or position of a consultant
consultant n (pl -s) specialist doctor with a senior position in a hospital
consultants n ▷ consultant
consultation n (pl -s) (meeting for) consulting
consultations n ▷ consultation
consultative adj giving advice
consulted v ▷ consult
consulting v ▷ consult
consults v ▷ consult
consume v (-sumes, -suming, -sumed) eat or drink
consumed v ▷ consume
consumer n (pl -s) person who buys goods or uses services
consumers n ▷ consumer
consumes v ▷ consume
consuming v ▷ consume
consummate [kon-sum-mate] v (-mates, -mating, -mated) make (a marriage) legal by sexual intercourse ▶ adj [kon-**sum**-mit] supremely skilled ▷ **consummately** adv ▷ **consummation** n (pl -s)
consummated v ▷ consummate
consummately adv ▷ consummate
consummates v ▷ consummate
consummating v ▷ consummate
consummation n ▷ consummate
consummations n ▷ consummate
consumption n (pl -s) amount consumed
consumptions n ▷ consumption
consumptive n (pl -s) ▶ adj (Old-fashioned) (person) having tuberculosis
consumptives n ▷ consumptive
contact n (pl -s) communicating ▶ v (-s, -ing, -ed) get in touch with
contacted v ▷ contact
contacting v ▷ contact
contacts n, v ▷ contact
contagion n (pl -s) passing on of disease by contact
contagions n ▷ contagion
contagious adj spreading by contact, catching
contain v (-s, -ing, -ed) hold or be capable of holding

contained v ▷ contain
container n (pl -s) object used to hold or store things in
containers n ▷ container
containing v ▷ contain
containment n prevention of the spread of something harmful
contains v ▷ contain
contaminant n (pl -s) contaminating substance
contaminants n ▷ contaminant
contaminate v (-nates, -nating, -nated) make impure, pollute ▷ **contamination** n (pl -s)
contaminated v ▷ contaminate
contaminates v ▷ contaminate
contaminating v ▷ contaminate
contamination n ▷ contaminate
contaminations n ▷ contaminate
contemplate v (-lates, -lating, -lated) think deeply ▷ **contemplation** n (pl -s) ▷ **contemplative** adj
contemplated v ▷ contemplate
contemplates v ▷ contemplate
contemplating v ▷ contemplate
contemplation n ▷ contemplate
contemplations n ▷ contemplate
contemplative adj ▷ contemplate
contemporaneous adj happening at the same time
contemporaries n ▷ contemporary
contemporary adj present-day, modern ▶ n (pl -raries) person or thing living or occurring at the same time as another
contempt n (pl -s) dislike and disregard
contemptible adj deserving contempt ▷ **contemptibly** adv
contemptibly adv ▷ contemptible
contempts n ▷ contempt
contemptuous adj showing contempt ▷ **contemptuously** adv
contemptuously adv ▷ contemptuous
contend v (-s, -ing, -ed) (foll. by with) deal with
contended v ▷ contend
contender n (pl -s) competitor, esp. a strong one
contenders n ▷ contender
contending v ▷ contend
contends v ▷ contend
content[1] n (pl -s) meaning or substance of a piece of writing ▶ pl what something contains
content[2] adj satisfied with things as they are ▶ v (-s, -ing, -ed) make (someone) content ▶ n happiness and satisfaction ▷ **contented** adj ▷ **contentedly** adv ▷ **contentment** n

contented v, adj ▷ content²
contentedly adv ▷ content²
contenting v ▷ content²
contention n (pl -s) disagreement or dispute
contentions n ▷ contention
contentious adj causing disagreement
> **contentiously** adv > **contentiousness** n
contentiously adv ▷ contentious
contentiousness n ▷ contentious
contentment n ▷ content²
contents n ▷ content¹ ▶ v ▷ content²
contest n (pl -s) competition or struggle ▶ v
(-s, -ing, -ed) dispute, object to > **contestant**
n (pl -s)
contestant n ▷ contest
contestants n ▷ contest
contested v ▷ contest
contesting v ▷ contest
contests n, v ▷ contest
context n (pl -s) circumstances of an event or
fact > **contextual** adj
contexts n ▷ context
contextual adj ▷ context
contiguous adj very near or touching
> **contiguously** adv
contiguously adv ▷ contiguous
continence n ▷ continent²
continent¹ n (pl -s) one of the earth's
large masses of land > **continental** adj
> **continentally** adv
continent² adj able to control one's bladder
and bowels > **continence** n
continental adj ▷ continent¹
continentally adv ▷ continent¹
continents n ▷ continent¹
contingencies n ▷ contingency
contingency n (pl -cies) something that may
happen
contingent n (pl -s) group of people that
represents or is part of a larger group ▶ adj
(foll. by **on**) dependent on (something
uncertain)
contingents n ▷ contingent
continua n ▷ continuum
continual adj constant > **continually** adv
continually adv ▷ continual
continuance n continuing
continuation n (pl -s) continuing
continuations n ▷ continuation
continue v (-tinues, -tinuing, -tinued) (cause
to) remain in a condition or place
continued v ▷ continue
continues v ▷ continue
continuing v ▷ continue
continuities n ▷ continuity

continuity n (pl -ities) smooth development
or sequence
continuo n (pl -s) (MUSIC) continuous bass part,
usu. played on a keyboard instrument
continuos n ▷ continuo
continuous adj continuing uninterrupted
> **continuously** adv
continuously adv ▷ continuous
continuum n (pl -tinua, -tinuums) continuous
series
continuums n ▷ continuum
contort v (-s, -ing, -ed) twist out of shape
> **contortion** n (pl -s)
contorted v ▷ contort
contorting v ▷ contort
contortion n ▷ contort
contortionist n (pl -s) performer who contorts
his or her body to entertain
contortionists n ▷ contortionist
contortions n ▷ contort
contorts v ▷ contort
contour n (pl -s) outline
contours n ▷ contour
contraband n, adj smuggled (goods)
contraception n (pl -s) prevention of
pregnancy by artificial means
contraceptions n ▷ contraception
contraceptive n (pl -s) device used or pill
taken to prevent pregnancy ▶ adj preventing
pregnancy
contraceptives n ▷ contraceptive
contract n (pl -s) (document setting out) a
formal agreement ▶ v (-s, -ing, -ed) make
a formal agreement (to do something)
> **contraction** n (pl -s) > **contractual** adj
> **contractually** adv
contracted v ▷ contract
contracting v ▷ contract
contraction n ▷ contract
contractions n ▷ contract
contractor n (pl -s) firm that supplies
materials or labour
contractors n ▷ contractor
contracts n, v ▷ contract
contractual adj ▷ contract
contractually adv ▷ contract
contradict v (-s, -ing, -ed) declare the opposite
of (a statement) to be true > **contradiction** n
(pl -s) > **contradictory** adj
contradicted v ▷ contradict
contradicting v ▷ contradict
contradiction n ▷ contradict
contradictions n ▷ contradict
contradictory adj ▷ contradict
contradicts v ▷ contradict

contraflow *n* (*pl* -s) flow of traffic going alongside but in an opposite direction to the usual flow
contraflows *n* ▷ contraflow
contralto *n* (*pl* -s) (singer with) the lowest female voice
contraltos *n* ▷ contralto
contraption *n* (*pl* -s) strange-looking device
contraptions *n* ▷ contraption
contrapuntal *adj* (MUSIC) of or in counterpoint > **contrapuntally** *adv*
contrapuntally *adv* ▷ contrapuntal
contraries *n* ▷ contrary
contrarily *adv* ▷ contrary
contrariness *n* ▷ contrary
contrariwise *adv* ▷ contrary
contrary *n* (*pl* -aries) complete opposite ▶ *adj* opposed, completely different ▶ *adv* in opposition > **contrarily** *adv* > **contrariness** *n* > **contrariwise** *adv*
contrast *n* (*pl* -s) obvious difference ▶ *v* (-s, -ing, -ed) compare in order to show differences (foll. by **with**)
contrasted *v* ▷ contrast
contrasting *v* ▷ contrast
contrasts *n*, *v* ▷ contrast
contravene *v* (-venes, -vening, -vened) break (a rule or law) > **contravention** *n* (*pl* -s)
contravened *v* ▷ contravene
contravenes *v* ▷ contravene
contravening *v* ▷ contravene
contravention *n* ▷ contravene
contraventions *n* ▷ contravene
contretemps [kon-tra-tahn] *n* (*pl* -temps) embarrassing minor disagreement
contribute *v* (-butes, -buting, -buted) give for a common purpose or fund (foll. by **to**) > **contribution** *n* (*pl* -s) > **contributor** *n* (*pl* -s) > **contributory** *adj*
contributed *v* ▷ contribute
contributes *v* ▷ contribute
contributing *v* ▷ contribute
contribution *n* ▷ contribute
contributions *n* ▷ contribute
contributor *n* ▷ contribute
contributors *n* ▷ contribute
contributory *adj* ▷ contribute
contrite *adj* sorry and apologetic > **contritely** *adv* > **contrition** *n*
contritely *adv* ▷ contrite
contrition *n* ▷ contrite
contrivance *n* (*pl* -s) device
contrivances *n* ▷ contrivance
contrive *v* (-trives, -triving, -trived) make happen

contrived *adj* planned or artificial ▶ *v* ▷ contrive
contrives *v* ▷ contrive
contriving *v* ▷ contrive
control *n* (*pl* -s) power to direct something ▶ *pl* instruments used to operate a machine ▶ *v* (-trols, -trolling, -trolled) have power over > **controllable** *adj* > **controller** *n* (*pl* -s)
controllable *adj* ▷ control
controlled *v* ▷ control
controller *n* ▷ control
controllers *n* ▷ control
controlling *v* ▷ control
controls *n*, *v* ▷ control
controversial *adj* causing controversy > **controversially** *adv*
controversially *adv* ▷ controversial
controversies *adv* ▷ controversy
controversy *n* (*pl* -sies) fierce argument or debate
contumelies *n* ▷ contumely
contumely [kon-tume-mill-ee] *n* (*pl* -melies) (Lit) scornful or insulting treatment
contusion *n* (*pl* -s) (Formal) bruise
contusions *n* ▷ contusion
conundrum *n* (*pl* -s) riddle
conundrums *n* ▷ conundrum
conurbation *n* (*pl* -s) large urban area formed by the growth and merging of towns
conurbations *n* ▷ conurbation
convalesce *v* (-lesces, -lescing, -lesced) recover after an illness or operation > **convalescence** *n* (*pl* -s) > **convalescent** *n* (*pl* -s) *adj*
convalesced *v* ▷ convalesce
convalescence *n* ▷ convalesce
convalescences *n* ▷ convalesce
convalescent *n* ▷ convalesce
convalescents *n* ▷ convalesce
convalesces *v* ▷ convalesce
convalescing *v* ▷ convalesce
convection *n* (*pl* -s) transmission of heat in liquids or gases by the circulation of currents
convections *n* ▷ convection
convector *n* (*pl* -s) heater that gives out hot air
convectors *n* ▷ convector
convene *v* (-venes, -vening, -vened) gather or summon for a formal meeting
convened *v* ▷ convene
convener, convenor *n* (*pl* -s) person who calls a meeting
conveners *n* ▷ convener
convenes *v* ▷ convene
convenience *n* (*pl* -s) quality of being convenient

conveniences n ▷ convenience
convenient adj suitable or opportune
  > **conveniently** adv
conveniently adv ▷ convenient
convening v ▷ convene
convenor n ▷ convener
convenors n ▷ convener
convent n (pl -s) building where nuns live
convention n (pl -s) widely accepted view of
  proper behaviour
conventional adj (unthinkingly) following
  the accepted customs > **conventionally** adv
  > **conventionality** n
conventionality n ▷ conventional
conventionally adv ▷ conventional
conventions n ▷ convention
convents n ▷ convent
converge v (-verges, -verging, -verged) meet
  or join > **convergence** n
converged v ▷ converge
converges v ▷ converge
converging v ▷ converge
conversant adj having knowledge or
  experience of
conversation n (pl -s) informal talk
  > **conversational** adj
conversational adj ▷ conversation
conversationalist n (pl -s) person with a
  specified ability at conversation
  conversationalists n ▷ conversationalist
  conversations n ▷ conversation
converse[1] v (-verses, -versing, versed) have a
  conversation
converse[2] adj, n (pl -s) opposite or contrary
  > **conversely** adv
  conversed v ▷ converse[1]
  conversely adv ▷ converse[2]
  converses v ▷ converse[1] ▷ n ▷ converse[2]
  conversing v ▷ converse[1]
conversion n (pl -s) (thing resulting from)
  converting
  conversions n ▷ conversion
convert v (-s, -ing, ed) change in form,
  character, or function ▶ n (pl -s) person who
  has converted to a different belief or religion
  converted v ▷ convert
convertible adj capable of being converted ▶ n
  (pl -s) car with a folding or removable roof
  convertibles n ▷ convertible
  converting v ▷ convert
  converts v, n ▷ convert
convex adj curving outwards
convey v (-s, -ing, -ed) communicate
  (information)
conveyance n (pl -s) (Old-fashioned) vehicle

conveyances n ▷ conveyance
conveyancing n branch of law dealing with
  the transfer of ownership of property
conveyed v ▷ convey
conveying v ▷ convey
conveys v ▷ convey
convict v (-s, -ing, -ed) declare guilty ▶ n (pl -s)
  person serving a prison sentence
  convicted v ▷ convict
  convicting v ▷ convict
conviction n (pl -s) firm belief
  convictions n ▷ conviction
  convicts v, n ▷ convict
convince v (-vinces, -vincing, -vinced)
  persuade by argument or evidence
  > **convincing** adj > **convincingly** adv
  convinced v ▷ convince
  convinces v ▷ convince
  convincing v, adj ▷ convince
  convincingly adv ▷ convince
convivial adj sociable, lively > **conviviality** n
  > **convivially** adv
  conviviality n ▷ convivial
  convivially adv ▷ convivial
convocation n (pl -s) calling together
  convocations n ▷ convocation
convoke v (-vokes, -voking, -voked) call
  together
  convoked v ▷ convoke
  convokes v ▷ convoke
  convoking v ▷ convoke
convoluted adj coiled, twisted > **convolution**
  n (pl -s)
  convolution n ▷ convoluted
  convolutions n ▷ convoluted
convolvulus n (pl -es) twining plant with
  funnel-shaped flowers
  convolvuluses n ▷ convolvulus
convoy n (pl -s) group of vehicles or ships
  travelling together
  convoys n ▷ convoy
convulse v (-vulses, -vulsing, -vulsed) (of
  part of the body) undergo violent spasms
  (Informal) > **convulsive** adj > **convulsively** adv
  convulsed v ▷ convulse
  convulses v ▷ convulse
  convulsing v ▷ convulse
convulsion n (pl -s) violent muscular spasm
  ▶ pl uncontrollable laughter
  convulsions n ▷ convulsion
  convulsive adj ▷ convulse
  convulsively adv ▷ convulse
cony, coney n (pl conies, -s) (BRIT) rabbit
coo v (coos, cooing, cooed) (of a dove or
  pigeon) make a soft murmuring sound

cooed v ▷ coo

cooee interj (BRIT, AUST & NZ) call to attract attention

cooing v ▷ coo

cook v (-s, -ing, -ed) prepare (food) by heating ▶ n (pl -s) person who cooks food

cooked v ▷ cook

cooker n (pl -s) (CHIEFLY BRIT) apparatus for cooking heated by gas or electricity

cookers n ▷ cooker

cookery n art of cooking

cookie n (pl -s) (US) biscuit

cookies n ▷ cookie

cooking v ▷ cook

cooks v, n ▷ cook

cool adj (-er, -est) moderately cold (Informal) ▶ v (-s, -ing, -ed) make or become cool ▶ n (pl -s) coolness > **coolly** adv > **coolness** n (pl -es)

coolant n (pl -s) fluid used to cool machinery while it is working

coolants n ▷ coolant

cooled v ▷ cool

cooler n (pl -s) container for making or keeping things cool ▶ adj ▷ cool

coolers n ▷ cooler

coolest adj ▷ cool

coolibah n (pl -s) Australian eucalypt that grows beside rivers

coolibahs n ▷ coolibah

cooling v ▷ cool

coolly adv ▷ cool

coolness n ▷ cool

coolnesses n ▷ cool

cools v, n ▷ cool

coomb, coombe n (pl -s) (S ENGLISH) short valley or deep hollow

coombe n ▷ coomb

coombes n ▷ coomb

coombs n ▷ coomb

coop¹ n (pl -s) cage or pen for poultry

coop² [koh-op] n (pl -s) (BRIT, US & AUST) (shop run by) a cooperative society

cooper n (pl -s) person who makes or repairs barrels

cooperate v (-rates, -rating, -rated) work or act together > **cooperation** n

cooperated v ▷ cooperate

cooperates v ▷ cooperate

cooperating v ▷ cooperate

cooperation n ▷ cooperate

cooperative adj willing to cooperate ▶ n (pl -s) cooperative organization

cooperatives n ▷ cooperative

coopers n ▷ cooper

coops n ▷ coop¹, ²

coopt [koh-opt] v (-s, -ing, -ed) add (someone) to a group by the agreement of the existing members

coopted v ▷ coopt

coopting v ▷ coopt

coopts v ▷ coopt

coordinate v (-nates, -nating, -nated) bring together and cause to work together efficiently ▶ n (pl -s) (MATHS) any of a set of numbers defining the location of a point ▶ pl clothes designed to be worn together > **coordination** n > **coordinator** n (pl -s)

coordinated v ▷ coordinate

coordinates v, n ▷ coordinate

coordinating v ▷ coordinate

coordination n ▷ coordinate

coordinator n ▷ coordinate

coordinators n ▷ coordinate

coos v ▷ coo

coot n (pl -s) small black water bird

coots n ▷ coot

cop (Slang) n (pl -s) policeman ▶ v (cops, copping, copped) take or seize

cope¹ v (copes, coping, coped) (often foll. by **with**) deal successfully (with)

cope² n (pl -s) large ceremonial cloak worn by some Christian priests

coped v ▷ cope¹

copes v ▷ cope¹ ▶ n ▷ cope²

copied v ▷ copy

copies n, v ▷ copy

coping v ▷ cope¹ ▶ n (pl -s) sloping top row of a wall

copings n ▷ coping

copious [kope-ee-uss] adj abundant, plentiful > **copiously** adv

copiously adv ▷ copious

copped v ▷ cop

copper¹ n (pl -s) soft reddish-brown metal

copper² n (pl -s) (BRIT) (Slang) policeman

copperplate n (pl -s) fine handwriting style

copperplates n ▷ copperplate

coppers n ▷ copper¹, ²

coppice, copse n (pl -s) small group of trees growing close together

coppices n ▷ coppice

copping v ▷ cop

copra n (pl -s) dried oil-yielding kernel of the coconut

copras n ▷ copra

cops n, v ▷ cop

copse n ▷ coppice

copses n ▷ coppice

copulate v (-lates, -lating, -lated) have sexual intercourse > **copulation** n (pl -s)

copulated v ▷ copulate
copulates v ▷ copulate
copulating v ▷ copulate
copulation n ▷ copulate
copulations n ▷ copulate
copy n (pl copies) thing made to look exactly like another ▶ v (copies, copying, copied) make a copy of
copying v ▷ copy
copyright n (pl -s) exclusive legal right to reproduce and control a book, work of art, etc. ▶ v (-s, -ing, -ed) take out a copyright on ▶ adj protected by copyright
copyrighted v ▷ copyright
copyrighting v ▷ copyright
copyrights n, v ▷ copyright
copywriter n (pl -s) person who writes advertising copy
copywriters n ▷ copywriter
coquette n (pl -s) woman who flirts
> **coquettish** adj
coquettes n ▷ coquette
coquettish adj ▷ coquette
coracle n (pl -s) small round boat of wicker covered with skins
coracles n ▷ coracle
coral n (pl -s) hard substance formed from the skeletons of very small sea animals ▶ adj orange-pink
corals n ▷ coral
cord n (pl -s) thin rope or thick string ▶ pl corduroy trousers
cordial adj warm and friendly ▶ n (pl -s) drink with a fruit base > **cordially** adv > **cordiality** n
cordiality n ▷ cordial
cordially adv ▷ cordial
cordials n ▷ cordial
cordite n (pl -s) explosive used in guns and bombs
cordites n ▷ cordite
cordon n (pl -s) chain of police, soldiers, etc., guarding an area
cordons n ▷ cordon
cords n ▷ cord
corduroy n (pl -s) cotton fabric with a velvety ribbed surface
corduroys n ▷ corduroy
core n (pl -s) central part of certain fruits, containing the seeds ▶ v (cores, coring, cored) remove the core from
cored v ▷ core
corella n (pl -s) white Australian cockatoo
corellas n ▷ corella
cores n, v ▷ core
corgi n (pl -s) short-legged sturdy dog

corgis n ▷ corgi
coriander n (pl -s) plant grown for its aromatic seeds and leaves
corianders n ▷ coriander
coring v ▷ core
cork n (pl -s) thick light bark of a Mediterranean oak ▶ v (-s, -ing, -ed) seal with a cork
corkage n (pl -s) restaurant's charge for serving wine bought elsewhere
corkages n ▷ corkage
corked v ▷ cork
corking v ▷ cork
corks n, v ▷ cork
corkscrew n (pl -s) spiral metal tool for pulling corks from bottles
corkscrews n ▷ corkscrew
corm n (pl -s) bulblike underground stem of certain plants
cormorant n (pl -s) large dark-coloured long-necked sea bird
cormorants n ▷ cormorant
corms n ▷ corm
corn[1] n (pl -s) cereal plant such as wheat or oats
corn[2] n (pl -s) painful hard skin on the toe
cornea [korn-ee-a] n (pl -neas, -neae) transparent membrane covering the eyeball
> **corneal** adj
corneae n ▷ cornea
corneal adj ▷ cornea
corneas n ▷ cornea
corner n (pl -s) area or angle where two converging lines or surfaces meet (SPORT) ▶ v (-s, -ing, -ed) force into a difficult or inescapable position
cornered v ▷ corner
cornering v ▷ corner
corners n, v ▷ corner
cornerstone n (pl -s) indispensable part or basis
cornerstones n ▷ cornerstone
cornet n (pl -s) brass instrument similar to the trumpet
cornets n ▷ cornet
cornflakes pl n breakfast cereal made from toasted maize
cornflour n (pl -s) (CHIEFLY BRIT) fine maize flour
cornflours n ▷ cornflour
cornflower n (pl -s) plant with blue flowers
cornflowers n ▷ cornflower
cornice n (pl -s) decorative moulding round the top of a wall
cornices n ▷ cornice
cornier adj ▷ corny
corniest adj ▷ corny

corns *n* ▷ corn¹, ²

cornucopia [korn-yew-**kope**-ee-a] *n* (*pl* -s) great abundance

cornucopias *n* ▷ cornucopia

corny (-nier, -niest) *adj* (*Slang*) unoriginal or oversentimental

corolla *n* (*pl* -s) petals of a flower collectively

corollaries *n* ▷ corollary

corollary *n* (*pl* -laries) idea, fact, or proposition which is the natural result of something else

corollas *n* ▷ corolla

corona *n* (*pl* -nas, -nae) ring of light round the moon or sun

coronae *n* ▷ corona

coronaries *n* ▷ coronary

coronary [kor-ron-a-ree] *adj* of the arteries surrounding the heart ▶ *n* (*pl* -naries)

coronas *n* ▷ corona

coronation *n* (*pl* -s) ceremony of crowning a monarch

coronations *n* ▷ coronation

coroner *n* (*pl* -s) (BRIT, AUST & NZ) official responsible for the investigation of violent, sudden, or suspicious deaths

coroners *n* ▷ coroner

coronet *n* (*pl* -s) small crown

coronets *n* ▷ coronet

corpora *n* ▷ corpus

corporal¹ *n* (*pl* -s) noncommissioned officer in an army

corporal² *adj* of the body ▷ **corporally** *adv*

corporally *adv* ▷ corporal²

corporals *n* ▷ corporal¹

corporate *adj* of business corporations

corporation *n* (*pl* -s) large business or company

corporations *n* ▷ corporation

corporeal [kore-**pore**-ee-al] *adj* physical or tangible

corps [kore] *n* (*pl* corps) military unit with a specific function

corpse *n* (*pl* -s) dead body

corpses *n* ▷ corpse

corpulence *n* ▷ corpulent

corpulent *adj* fat or plump ▷ **corpulence** *n*

corpus *n* (*pl* corpora) collection of writings, esp. by a single author

corpuscle *n* (*pl* -s) red or white blood cell

corpuscles *n* ▷ corpuscle

corral (US) *n* (*pl* -s) enclosure for cattle or horses ▶ *v* (-rals, -ralling, -ralled) put in a corral

corralled *v* ▷ corral

corralling *v* ▷ corral

corrals *n*, *v* ▷ corral

correct *adj* free from error, true ▶ *v* (-s, -ing, -ed)

put right ▷ **correctly** *adv* ▷ **correctness** *n*

corrected *v* ▷ correct

correcting *v* ▷ correct

correction *n* (*pl* -s) correcting

corrections *n* ▷ correction

corrective *adj* intended to put right something wrong

correctly *adv* ▷ correct

correctness *n* ▷ correct

corrects *v* ▷ correct

correlate *v* (-lates, -lating, -lated) place or be placed in a mutual relationship ▷ **correlation** *n* (*pl* -s)

correlated *v* ▷ correlate

correlates *v* ▷ correlate

correlating *v* ▷ correlate

correlation *n* ▷ correlate

correlations *n* ▷ correlate

correspond *v* (-s, -ing, -ed) be consistent or compatible (with) ▷ **corresponding** *adj* ▷ **correspondingly** *adv*

corresponded *v* ▷ correspond

correspondence *n* communication by letters

correspondent *n* (*pl* -s) person employed by a newspaper etc. to report on a special subject or from a foreign country

correspondents *n* ▷ correspondent

corresponding *v*, *adj* ▷ correspond

correspondingly *adv* ▷ correspond

corresponds *v* ▷ correspond

corridor *n* (*pl* -s) passage in a building or train

corridors *n* ▷ corridor

corrigenda *n* ▷ corrigendum

corrigendum [kor-rij-**end**-um] *n* (*pl* -da) error to be corrected

corroborate *v* (-rates, -rating, -rated) support (a fact or opinion) by giving proof ▷ **corroboration** *n* (*pl* -s) ▷ **corroborative** *adj*

corroborated *v* ▷ corroborate

corroborates *v* ▷ corroborate

corroborating *v* ▷ corroborate

corroboration *n* ▷ corroborate

corroborations *n* ▷ corroborate

corroborative *adj* ▷ corroborate

corroboree *n* (*pl* -s) (AUST) Aboriginal gathering or dance

corroborees *n* ▷ corroboree

corrode *v* (-rodes, -roding, -roded) eat or be eaten away by chemical action or rust ▷ **corrosion** *n* ▷ **corrosive** *adj* ▷ **corrosively** *adv* ▷ **corrosiveness** *n*

corroded *v* ▷ corrode

corrodes *v* ▷ corrode

corroding *v* ▷ corrode

corrosion *n* ▷ corrode

corrosive v ▷ corrode

corrosively adv ▷ corrode

corrosiveness n ▷ corrode

corrugated adj folded into alternate grooves and ridges

corrupt adj (-er, -est) open to or involving bribery ▶ v (-s, -ing, -ed) make corrupt > **corruptly** adv > **corruption** n > **corruptible** adj

corrupted v ▷ corrupt

corrupter adj ▷ corrupt

corruptest adj ▷ corrupt

corruptible adj ▷ corrupt

corrupting v ▷ corrupt

corruption n ▷ corrupt

corruptly adv ▷ corrupt

corrupts v ▷ corrupt

corsage [kor-**sahzh**] n (pl -s) small bouquet worn on the bodice of a dress

corsages n ▷ corsage

corsair n (pl -s) pirate

corsairs n ▷ corsair

corset n (pl -s) women's close-fitting undergarment worn to shape the torso

corsets n ▷ corset

cortege [kor-**tayzh**] n (pl -s) funeral procession

corteges n ▷ cortege

cortex n (pl -tices) (ANAT) outer layer of the brain or other internal organ > **cortical** adj

cortical adj ▷ cortex

cortices n ▷ cortex

cortisone n (pl -s) steroid hormone used to treat various diseases

cortisones n ▷ cortisone

corundum n (pl -s) hard mineral used as an abrasive

corundums n ▷ corundum

coruscate v (-cates, -cating, -cated) (Formal) sparkle

coruscated v ▷ coruscate

coruscates v ▷ coruscate

coruscating v ▷ coruscate

corvette n (pl -s) lightly armed escort warship

corvettes n ▷ corvette

cosh n (pl -es) (BRIT) heavy blunt weapon ▶ v (-es, -ing, -ed) hit with a cosh

coshed v, n ▷ cosh

coshes v ▷ cosh

coshing v ▷ cosh

cosier adj ▷ cosy

cosies adj ▷ cosy

cosiest adj ▷ cosy

cosily adv ▷ cosy

cosine [koh-sine] n (pl -s) (in trigonometry) ratio of the length of the adjacent side to that of the hypotenuse in a right-angled triangle

cosines n ▷ cosine

cosiness n ▷ cosy

cosmetic n (pl -s) preparation used to improve the appearance of a person's skin ▶ adj improving the appearance only

cosmetics n ▷ cosmetic

cosmic adj of the whole universe > **cosmically** adv

cosmically adv ▷ cosmic

cosmological adj ▷ cosmology

cosmologist n ▷ cosmology

cosmologists n ▷ cosmology

cosmology n study of the origin and nature of the universe > **cosmological** adj > **cosmologist** n (pl -s)

cosmonaut n (pl -s) Russian name for an astronaut

cosmonauts n ▷ cosmonaut

cosmopolitan adj composed of people or elements from many countries ▶ n (pl -s) cosmopolitan person > **cosmopolitanism** n

cosmopolitanism n ▷ cosmopolitan

cosmopolitans n ▷ cosmopolitan

cosmos n (pl cosmos) the universe

cossack n (pl -s) member of a S Russian people famous as horsemen and dancers

cossacks n ▷ cossack

cosset v (-s, -ing, -ed) pamper

cosseted v ▷ cosset

cosseting v ▷ cosset

cossets v ▷ cosset

cost n (pl -s) amount of money, time, labour, etc., required for something ▶ pl expenses of a lawsuit ▶ v (costs, costing, cost) have as its cost

costermonger n (pl -s) (BRIT) person who sells fruit and vegetables from a street barrow

costermongers n ▷ costermonger

costing v ▷ cost

costlier adj ▷ costly

costliest adj ▷ costly

costliness n ▷ costly

costlinesses n ▷ costly

costly adj (-lier, -liest) expensive > **costliness** n (pl -es)

costs n, v ▷ cost

costume n (pl -s) style of dress of a particular place or time, or for a particular activity

costumes n ▷ costume

costumier n (pl -s) maker or seller of costumes

costumiers n ▷ costumier

cosy adj (-sier, -siest) warm and snug ▶ n (pl -sies) cover for keeping things warm > **cosily** adv > **cosiness** n

cot n (pl -s) baby's bed with high sides

cote n (pl -s) shelter for birds or animals

coterie [kote-er-ee] n (pl -s) exclusive group, clique

  coteries n ▷ coterie

  cotes n ▷ cote

cotoneaster [kot-tone-ee-ass-ter] n (pl -s) garden shrub with red berries

  cotoneasters n ▷ cotoneaster

  cots n ▷ cot

cottage n (pl -s) small house in the country

  cottages n ▷ cottage

cotter n (pl -s) pin or wedge used to secure machine parts

  cotters n ▷ cotter

cotton n (pl -s) white downy fibre covering the seeds of a tropical plant > **cottony** adj

  cottons n ▷ cotton

  cottony adj ▷ cotton

cotyledon [kot-ill-ee-don] n (pl -s) first leaf of a plant embryo

  cotyledons n ▷ cotyledon

couch n (pl couches) piece of upholstered furniture for seating more than one person ▶ v (-es, -ing, -ed) express in a particular way

  couched v ▷ couch

  couches n, v ▷ couch

couchette [koo-shett] n (pl -s) bed converted from seats on a train or ship

  couchettes n ▷ couchette

  couching v ▷ couch

cougan n (pl -s) (AUST) (Slang) drunk and rowdy person

  cougans n ▷ cougan

cougar n (pl -s) puma

  cougars n ▷ cougar

cough v (-s, -ing, -ed) expel air from the lungs abruptly and noisily ▶ n (pl -s) act or sound of coughing

  coughed v ▷ cough

  coughing v ▷ cough

  coughs v, n ▷ cough

  could v ▷ can¹

coulomb [koo-lom] n (pl -s) SI unit of electric charge

  coulombs n ▷ coulomb

coulter n (pl -s) blade at the front of a ploughshare

  coulters n ▷ coulter

council n (pl -s) group meeting for discussion or consultation ▶ adj of or by a council

councillor n (pl -s) member of a council

  councillors n ▷ councillor

  councils n ▷ council

counsel n (pl -s) advice or guidance ▶ v

(-sels, -selling, -selled) give guidance to > **counsellor** n (pl -s)

  counselled v ▷ counsel

  counselling v ▷ counsel

  counsellor n ▷ counsel

  counsellors n ▷ counsel

  counsels n, v ▷ counsel

count¹ v (-s, -ing, -ed) say numbers in order ▶ n (pl -s) counting

count² n (pl -s) European nobleman

countdown n (pl -s) counting backwards to zero of the seconds before an event

  countdowns n ▷ countdown

  counted v ▷ count¹

countenance n (pl -s) (expression of) the face ▶ v (-nances, -nancing, -nanced) allow or tolerate

  countenanced v ▷ countenance

  countenances n, v ▷ countenance

  countenancing v ▷ countenance

counter¹ n (pl -s) long flat surface in a bank or shop, on which business is transacted

counter² v (-s, -ing, -ed) oppose, retaliate against ▶ adv in the opposite direction ▶ n (pl -s) opposing or retaliatory action

counteract v (-s, -ing, -ed) act against or neutralize > **counteraction** n

  counteracted v ▷ counteract

  counteracting v ▷ counteract

  counteraction n ▷ counteract

  counteracts v ▷ counteract

counterattack n (pl -s) ▶ v (-s, -ing, -ed) attack in response to an attack

  counterattacked v ▷ counterattack

  counterattacking v ▷ counterattack

  counterattacks n, v ▷ counterattack

counterbalance n (pl -s) weight or force balancing or neutralizing another ▶ v (-ces, -cing, -ced) act as a counterbalance to

  counterbalanced v ▷ counterbalance

  counterbalances n, v ▷ counterbalance

  counterbalancing v ▷ counterbalance

counterblast n (pl -s) aggressive response to a verbal attack

  counterblasts n ▷ counterblast

  countered v ▷ counter

counterfeit adj fake, forged ▶ n (pl -s) fake, forgery ▶ v (-s, -ing, -ed) fake, forge

  counterfeited v ▷ counterfeit

  counterfeiting v ▷ counterfeit

  counterfeits n, v ▷ counterfeit

counterfoil n (pl -s) part of a cheque or receipt kept as a record

  counterfoils n ▷ counterfoil

  countering v ▷ counter

countermand v (-s, -ing, -ed) cancel (a previous order)
countermanded v ▷ countermand
countermanding v ▷ countermand
countermands v ▷ countermand
counterpane n (pl -s) bed covering
counterpanes n ▷ counterpane
counterpart n (pl -s) person or thing complementary to or corresponding to another
counterparts n ▷ counterpart
counterpoint n (pl -s) (MUSIC) technique of combining melodies
counterpoints n ▷ counterpoint
counterpoise n (pl -s) ▶ v (-ses, -sing, -sed) counterbalance
counterpoised v ▷ counterpoise
counterpoises n, v ▷ counterpoise
counterpoising v ▷ counterpoise
counterproductive adj having an effect opposite to the one intended
counters n ▷ counter¹, ² ▶ v ▷ counter²
countersank v ▷ countersink
countersign v (-s, -ing, -ed) sign (a document already signed by someone) as confirmation
countersigned v ▷ countersign
countersigning v ▷ countersign
countersigns v ▷ countersign
countersink v (-sinks, -sinking, -sank, -sunk) drive (a screw) into a shaped hole so that its head is below the surface
countersinking v ▷ countersink
countersinks v ▷ countersink
countersunk v ▷ countersink
countertenor n (pl -s) male alto
countertenors n ▷ countertenor
counterterrorism n measures to prevent terrorist attacks or eradicate terrorist groups
countess n (pl -es) woman holding the rank of count or earl
countesses n ▷ countess
counties n ▷ county
counting v ▷ count¹
countless adj too many to count
countries n ▷ country
countrified adj rustic in manner or appearance
country n (pl -tries) nation
countryman, countrywoman n (pl -men, -women) person from one's native land
countrymen n ▷ countryman
countryside n land away from cities
countrywoman n ▷ countryman
countrywomen n ▷ countryman
counts v ▷ count¹ ▶ n ▷ count¹, ²

county n (pl -ties) (in some countries) division of a country
coup [koo] n (pl -s) successful action
coupé [koo-pay] n (pl -s) sports car with two doors and a sloping fixed roof
coupés n ▷ coupé
couple n (pl -s) two people who are married or romantically involved ▶ v (-ples, -pling, -pled) connect, associate
coupled v ▷ couple
couples n, v ▷ couple
couplet n (pl -s) two consecutive lines of verse, usu. rhyming and of the same metre
couplets n ▷ couplet
coupling n (pl -s) device for connecting things, such as railway carriages ▶ v ▷ couple
couplings n ▷ coupling
coupon n (pl -s) piece of paper entitling the holder to a discount or gift
coupons n ▷ coupon
coups n ▷ coup
courage n ability to face danger or pain without fear > **courageous** adj > **courageously** adv
courageous adj ▷ courage
courageously adv ▷ courage
courgette n (pl -s) type of small vegetable marrow
courgettes n ▷ courgette
courier n (pl -s) person employed to look after holiday-makers
couriers n ▷ courier
course n (pl -s) series of lessons or medical treatment ▶ v (-ses, -sing, -sed) (of liquid) run swiftly
coursed v ▷ course
courses n, v ▷ course
coursing v ▷ course
court n (pl -s) body which decides legal cases ▶ v (-s, -ing, -ed) (Old-fashioned) try to gain the love of
courted v ▷ court
courteous adj polite > **courteously** adv
courteously adv ▷ courteous
courtesan [kor-tiz-zan] n (pl -s) (HIST) mistress or high-class prostitute
courtesans n ▷ courtesan
courtesies n ▷ courtesy
courtesy n (pl -sies) politeness, good manners
courtier n (pl -s) attendant at a royal court
courtiers n ▷ courtier
courting v ▷ court
courtlier adj ▷ courtly
courtliest adj ▷ courtly
courtliness n ▷ courtly

courtlinesses n ▷ courtly

courtly adj (-lier, -liest) ceremoniously polite
> **courtliness** n (pl -es)

courts n, v ▷ court

courtship n (pl -s) courting of an intended spouse or mate
courtships n ▷ courtship

courtyard n (pl -s) paved space enclosed by buildings or walls
courtyards n ▷ courtyard

cousin n (pl -s) child of one's uncle or aunt
cousins n ▷ cousin

couture [koo-toor] n (pl -s) high-fashion designing and dressmaking
coutures n ▷ couture

couturier n (pl -s) person who designs women's fashion clothes
couturiers n ▷ couturier

cove n (pl -s) small bay or inlet

coven [kuv-ven] n (pl -s) meeting of witches
covens n ▷ coven

covenant [kuv-ven-ant] n (pl -s) contract ▶ v (-s, -ing, -ed) agree by a covenant
covenanted v ▷ covenant
covenanting v ▷ covenant
covenants n, v ▷ covenant

cover v (-s, -ing, -ed) place something over, to protect or conceal ▶ n (pl -s) anything that covers

coverage n amount or extent covered
covered v ▷ cover
covering v ▷ cover

coverlet n (pl -s) bed cover
coverlets v ▷ coverlet
covers v, n ▷ cover

covert adj concealed, secret ▶ n (pl -s) thicket giving shelter to game birds or animals
> **covertly** adv
covertly adv ▷ covert
coverts n ▷ covert
coves n ▷ cove

covet v (-s, -ing, -ed) long to possess (what belongs to someone else) > **covetous** adj
> **covetousness** n
coveted v ▷ covet
coveting v ▷ covet
covetous adj ▷ covet
covetousness n ▷ covet
covets v ▷ covet

covey [kuv-vee] n (pl -s) small flock of grouse or partridge
coveys n ▷ covey

cow¹ n (pl -s) mature female of cattle and of certain other mammals, such as the elephant or seal

cow² v (-s, -ing, -ed) intimidate, subdue

coward n (pl -s) person who lacks courage
> **cowardly** adj > **cowardliness** n

cowardice n lack of courage
cowardliness n ▷ coward
cowardly adj ▷ coward
cowards n ▷ coward

cowboy n (pl -s) (in the US) ranch worker who herds and tends cattle, usu. on horseback
cowboys n ▷ cowboy
cowed v ▷ cow²

cower v (-s, -ing, -ed) cringe in fear
cowered v ▷ cower
cowering v ▷ cower
cowers v ▷ cower
cowing v ▷ cow²

cowl n (pl -s) loose hood

cowling n (pl -s) cover on an engine
cowlings n ▷ cowling
cowls n ▷ cowl

cowrie n (pl -s) brightly-marked sea shell
cowries n ▷ cowrie
cows n ▷ cow¹ ▶ v ▷ cow²

cowslip n (pl -s) small yellow wild European flower
cowslips n ▷ cowslip

cox n (pl -es) coxswain ▶ v (-es, -ing, -ed) act as cox of (a boat)
coxed v ▷ cox
coxes n, v ▷ cox
coxing v ▷ cox

coxswain [kok-sn] n (pl -s) person who steers a rowing boat
coxswains n ▷ coxswain

coy adj (-er, -est) affectedly shy or modest
> **coyly** adv > **coyness** n (pl -es)
coyer adj ▷ coy
coyest adj ▷ coy
coyly adv ▷ coy
coyness n ▷ coy
coynesses n ▷ coy

coyote [koy-ote-ee] n (pl -s) prairie wolf of N America
coyotes n ▷ coyote

coypu n (pl -s) beaver-like aquatic rodent native to S America, bred for its fur
coypus n ▷ coypu

> **coz** n (cozes). Coz is an old word for **cousin**, and a good one to know as it scores 14 points.

cozen v (-s, -ing, -ed) (Lit) cheat, trick
cozened v ▷ cozen
cozening v ▷ cozen
cozens v ▷ cozen

crab n (pl -s) edible shellfish with ten legs, the

first pair modified into pincers

crabbed adj (of handwriting) hard to read (also **crabby**) (crabbier, crabbiest)

crabbier adj ▷ crabbed

crabbiest adj ▷ crabbed

crabby adj ▷ crabbed

crabs n ▷ crab

crack v (-s, -ing, -ed) break or split partially ▶ n (pl -s) sudden sharp noise ▶ adj (Informal) first-rate, excellent

crackdown n (pl -s) severe disciplinary measures

crackdowns n ▷ crackdown

cracked v ▷ crack

cracker n (pl -s) thin dry biscuit

crackers n ▷ cracker ▶ adj (Slang) insane

cracking adj very good ▶ v ▷ crack

crackle v (-ckles, -ckling, -ckled) make small sharp popping noises ▶ n (pl -ckles) crackling sound

crackled v ▷ crackle

crackles v, n ▷ crackle

crackling n crackle ▶ v ▷ crackle

crackpot n (pl -s) ▶ adj (Informal) eccentric (person)

crackpots n ▷ crackpot

cracks v, n ▷ crack

cradle n (pl -s) baby's bed on rockers ▶ v (-dles, -dling, -dled) hold gently as if in a cradle

cradled v ▷ cradle

cradles n, v ▷ cradle

cradling v ▷ cradle

craft n (pl -s) occupation requiring skill with the hands

craftier adj ▷ crafty

craftiest adj ▷ crafty

craftily adv ▷ crafty

craftiness n ▷ crafty

craftinesses n ▷ crafty

crafts n ▷ craft

craftsman, craftswoman n (pl -men, -women) skilled worker > **craftsmanship** n (pl -s)

craftsmanship n ▷ craftsman

craftsmanships n ▷ craftsman

craftsmen n ▷ craftsman

craftswoman n ▷ craftsman

craftswomen n ▷ craftsman

crafty adj (-tier, -tiest) skilled in deception > **craftily** adv > **craftiness** n (pl -es)

crag n (pl -s) steep rugged rock > **craggy** adj (-ggier, -ggiest)

craggier adj ▷ crag

craggiest adj ▷ crag

craggy adj ▷ crag

crags n ▷ crag

cram v (-s, -mming, -mmed) force into too small a space

crammed v ▷ cram

cramming v ▷ cram

cramp[1] n (pl -s) painful muscular contraction

cramp[2] v (-s, -ing, -ed) confine, restrict

cramped v ▷ cramp[2]

cramping v ▷ cramp[2]

crampon n (pl -s) spiked plate strapped to a boot for climbing on ice

crampons n ▷ crampon

cramps n ▷ cramp[1] ▶ v ▷ cramp[2]

crams v ▷ cram

cranberries n ▷ cranberry

cranberry n (pl -berries) sour edible red berry

crane n (pl -s) machine for lifting and moving heavy weights ▶ v (cranes, craning, craned) stretch (one's neck) to see something

craned v ▷ crane

cranes n, v ▷ crane

crania n ▷ cranium

cranial adj ▷ cranium

craning v ▷ crane

cranium n (pl -niums, -nia) (ANAT) skull > **cranial** adj

craniums n ▷ cranium

crank n (pl -s) arm projecting at right angles from a shaft, for transmitting or converting motion (Informal) ▶ v (-s, -ing, -ed) start (an engine) with a crank

cranked v ▷ crank

crankier adj ▷ cranky

crankiest adj ▷ cranky

cranking v ▷ crank

cranks n, v ▷ crank

crankshaft n (pl -s) shaft driven by a crank

crankshafts n ▷ crankshaft

cranky adj (-kier, -kiest) (Informal) eccentric

crannies n ▷ cranny

cranny n (pl -nies) narrow opening

crape n (pl -s) ▷ crepe

crapes n ▷ crape

craps n gambling game played with two dice

crash n (pl -es) collision involving a vehicle or vehicles ▶ v (-es, -ing, -ed) (cause to) collide violently with a vehicle, a stationary object, or the ground

crashed v ▷ crash

crashes n, v ▷ crash

crashing v ▷ crash

crass adj (-er, -est) stupid and insensitive > **crassly** adv > **crassness** n (pl -es)

crasser adj ▷ crass

crassest adj ▷ crass

crassly adv ▷ crass
crassness n ▷ crass
crassnesses n ▷ crass
crate n (pl -s) large wooden container for packing goods
crater n (pl -s) very large hole in the ground or in the surface of the moon
craters n ▷ crater
crates n ▷ crate
cravat n (pl -s) man's scarf worn like a tie
cravats n ▷ cravat
crave v (craves, craving, craved) desire intensely > **craving** n (pl -s)
craved v ▷ crave
craven adj cowardly
craves v ▷ crave
craving n, v ▷ crave
cravings n ▷ crave
crawfish n (pl crawfish) ▷ crayfish
crawl v (-s, -ing, -ed) move on one's hands and knees ▸ n (pl -s) crawling motion or pace > **crawler** n (pl -s)
crawled v ▷ crawl
crawler n ▷ crawl
crawlers n ▷ crawl
crawling v ▷ crawl
crawls v, n ▷ crawl
crayfish n (pl crayfish) edible shellfish like a lobster
crayon v (-s, -ing, -ed), n (pl -s) (draw or colour with) a stick or pencil of coloured wax or clay
crayoned v ▷ crayon
crayoning v ▷ crayon
crayons v, n ▷ crayon
craze n (pl -s) short-lived fashion or enthusiasm
crazed adj wild and uncontrolled
crazes n ▷ craze
crazier adj ▷ crazy
craziest adj ▷ crazy
crazily adv ▷ crazy
craziness n ▷ crazy
crazinesses n ▷ crazy
crazy adj (-zier, -ziest) ridiculous > **crazily** adv > **craziness** n (pl -es)
creak v, n (pl -s) (make) a harsh squeaking sound > **creaky** adj (-kier, -kiest)
creakier adj ▷ creak
creakiest adj ▷ creak
creaks n ▷ creak
creaky adj ▷ creak
cream n (pl -s) fatty part of milk ▸ adj yellowish-white ▸ v (-s, -ing, -ed) beat to a creamy consistency > **creamy** adj > **creaminess** n

creamed v ▷ cream
creaminess n ▷ cream
creaming v ▷ cream
creams n, v ▷ cream
creamy adj ▷ cream
crease n (pl -s) line made by folding or pressing ▸ v (creases, creasing, creased) crush or line
creased v ▷ crease
creases n, v ▷ crease
creasing v ▷ crease
create v (creates, creating, created) make, cause to exist > **creation** n (pl -s) > **creator** n (pl -s)
created v ▷ create
creates v ▷ create
creating v ▷ create
creation n ▷ create
creations n ▷ create
creative adj imaginative or inventive > **creatively** adv > **creativity** n
creatively adv ▷ creative
creativity n ▷ creative
creator n ▷ create
creators n ▷ create
creature n (pl -s) animal, person, or other being
creatures n ▷ creature
crèche n (pl -s) place where small children are looked after while their parents are working, shopping, etc.
crèches n ▷ crèche
credence n (pl -s) belief in the truth or accuracy of a statement
credences n ▷ credence
credentials pl n document giving evidence of a person's identity or qualifications
credibility n ▷ credible
credible adj believable > **credibly** adv > **credibility** n
credibly adv ▷ credible
credit n (pl -s) system of allowing customers to receive goods and pay later ▸ v (-s, -ing, -ed) enter as a credit in an account
creditable adj praiseworthy > **creditably** adv
creditably adv ▷ creditable
credited v ▷ credit
crediting v ▷ credit
creditor n (pl -s) person to whom money is owed
creditors n ▷ creditor
credits n, v ▷ credit
credulity n ▷ credulous
credulous adj too willing to believe > **credulity** n > **credulously** adv
credulously adv ▷ credulous

creed n (pl -s) statement or system of (Christian) beliefs or principles
creeds n ▷ creed

creek n (pl -s) narrow inlet or bay (AUST, NZ, US & CANADIAN)
creeks n ▷ creek

creel n (pl -s) wicker basket used by anglers
creels n ▷ creel

creep v (creeps, creeping, crept) move quietly and cautiously ▶ n (pl -s) (Slang) obnoxious or servile person

creeper n (pl -s) creeping plant
creepers n ▷ creeper
creepier adj ▷ creepy
creepiest adj ▷ creepy
creepily adv ▷ creepy
creepiness n ▷ creepy
creepinesses n ▷ creepy
creeping v ▷ creep
creeps v, n ▷ creep

creepy adj (-pier, -piest) (Informal) causing a feeling of fear or disgust > **creepily** adv > **creepiness** n (pl -es)

cremate v (-mates, -mating, -mated) burn (a corpse) to ash > **cremation** n (pl -s)
cremated v ▷ cremate
cremates v ▷ cremate
cremating v ▷ cremate
cremation n ▷ cremate
cremations n ▷ cremate
crematoria n ▷ crematorium

crematorium n (pl -iums, -ia) building where corpses are cremated
crematoriums n ▷ crematorium

crenellated adj having battlements

creole n (pl -s) language developed from a mixture of languages
creoles n ▷ creole

creosote n (pl -s) dark oily liquid made from coal tar and used for preserving wood ▶ v (-sotes, -soting, -soted) treat with creosote
creosoted v ▷ creosote
creosotes n, v ▷ creosote
creosoting v ▷ creosote

crepe, crape [krayp] n (pl -s) fabric or rubber with a crinkled texture
crepes n ▷ crepe
crept v ▷ creep

crepuscular adj (Lit) of or like twilight

crescendo [krish-end-oh] n (pl -s) gradual increase in loudness, esp. in music
crescendos n ▷ creep

crescent n (pl -s) (curved shape of) the moon as seen in its first or last quarter
crescents n ▷ crescent

cress n (pl -es) plant with strong-tasting leaves, used in salads
cresses n ▷ cress

crest n (pl -s) top of a mountain, hill, or wave > **crested** adj
crested adj ▷ crest
crestfallen adj disheartened
crests n ▷ crest

cretin n (pl -s) (Informal) stupid person > **cretinous** adj
cretinous adj ▷ cretin
cretins n ▷ cretin

crevasse n (pl -s) deep open crack in a glacier
crevasses n ▷ crevasse

crevice n (pl -s) narrow crack or gap in rock
crevices n ▷ crevice

crew n (pl -s) people who work on a ship or aircraft (Informal) ▶ v (-s, -ing, -ed) serve as a crew member (on)
crewed v ▷ crew

crewel n (pl -s) fine worsted yarn used in embroidery
crewels n ▷ crewel
crewing v ▷ crew
crews n, v ▷ crew

crib n (pl -s) piece of writing stolen from elsewhere ▶ v (cribs, cribbing, cribbed) copy (someone's work) dishonestly

cribbage n card game for two to four players
cribbed v ▷ crib
cribbing v ▷ crib
cribs n, v ▷ crib

crick n (pl -s) muscle spasm or cramp in the back or neck ▶ v (-s, -ing, -ed) cause a crick in
cricked v ▷ crick

cricket¹ n (pl -s) outdoor game played with bats, a ball, and wickets by two teams of eleven > **cricketer** n (pl -s)

cricket² n (pl -s) chirping insect like a grasshopper
cricketer n ▷ cricket¹
cricketers n ▷ cricket¹
crickets n ▷ cricket¹, ²
cricking v ▷ crick
cricks n, v ▷ crick
cried v ▷ cry
cries v ▷ cry

crime n (pl -s) unlawful act
crimes n ▷ crime

criminal n (pl -s) person guilty of a crime ▶ adj of crime > **criminally** adv > **criminality** n
criminality n ▷ criminal
criminally adv ▷ criminal
criminals n ▷ criminal
criminologist n ▷ criminology

criminologists n ▷ criminology
criminology n study of crime ▷ **criminologist** n (pl -s)
crimp v (-s, -ing, -ed) fold or press into ridges
  crimped v ▷ crimp
  crimping v ▷ crimp
  crimps v ▷ crimp
crimson adj deep purplish-red
cringe v (cringes, cringing, cringed) flinch in fear
  cringed v ▷ cringe
  cringes v ▷ cringe
  cringing v ▷ cringe
crinkle v (-kles, -kling, -kled) ▶ n (pl -s) wrinkle, crease, or fold
  crinkled v ▷ crinkle
  crinkles v, n ▷ crinkle
  crinkling v ▷ crinkle
crinoline n (pl -s) hooped petticoat
  crinolines n ▷ crinoline
cripple n (pl -s) person who is lame or disabled ▶ v (-pples, -ppling, -ppled) make lame or disabled
  crippled v ▷ cripple
  cripples n, v ▷ cripple
  crippling v ▷ cripple
  crises n ▷ crisis
crisis n (pl -ses) crucial stage, turning point
crisp adj (-er, -est) fresh and firm ▶ n (pl -s) (BRIT) very thin slice of potato fried till crunchy ▷ **crisply** adv ▷ **crispness** n (pl -es)
crispbread n (pl -s) thin dry biscuit
  crispbreads n ▷ crispbread
  crisper adj ▷ crisp
  crispest adj ▷ crisp
  crispier adj ▷ crisp
  crispiest adj ▷ crisp
  crisply adv ▷ crisp
  crispness adv ▷ crisp
  crispnesses adv ▷ crisp
  crisps n ▷ crisp
crispy adj (-pier, -piest) hard and crunchy
crisscross v (-s, -ing, -ed) move in or mark with a crosswise pattern ▶ adj (of lines) crossing in different directions
  crisscrossed v ▷ crisscross
  crisscrosses v ▷ crisscross
  crisscrossing v ▷ crisscross
  criteria n ▷ criterion
criterion n (pl -ria) standard of judgment
critic n (pl -s) professional judge of any of the arts
critical adj very important or dangerous ▷ **critically** adv
  critically adv ▷ critical

criticism n (pl -s) fault-finding
  criticisms n ▷ criticism
criticize v (-cizes, -cizing, -cized) find fault with
  criticized v ▷ criticize
  criticizes v ▷ criticize
  criticizing v ▷ criticize
  critics n ▷ critic
critique n (pl -s) critical essay
  critiques n ▷ critique
croak v (-s, -ing, -ed) (of a frog or crow) give a low hoarse cry ▶ n (pl -s) low hoarse sound
  croaked v ▷ croak
  croakiness n ▷ croaky
  croaking v ▷ croak
  croaks v, n ▷ croak
croaky adj hoarse ▷ **croakiness** n
crochet [kroh-shay] v (-chets, -cheting, -cheted) make by looping and intertwining yarn with a hooked needle ▶ n (pl -s) work made in this way
  crocheted v ▷ crochet
  crocheting v ▷ crochet
  crochets v, n ▷ crochet
crock[1] n (pl -s) earthenware pot or jar
crock[2] n (pl -s) (BRIT, AUST & NZ) (Informal) old or decrepit person or thing
crockery n dishes
  crocks n ▷ crock[1, 2]
crocodile n (pl -s) large amphibious tropical reptile
  crocodiles n ▷ crocodile
crocus n (pl -cuses) small plant with yellow, white, or purple flowers in spring
  crocuses n ▷ crocus
croft n (pl -s) small farm worked by one family in Scotland ▷ **crofter** n (pl -s)
  crofter n ▷ croft
  crofters n ▷ croft
  crofts n ▷ croft
croissant [krwah-son] n (pl -s) rich flaky crescent-shaped roll
  croissants n ▷ croissant
cromlech n (pl -s) (BRIT) circle of prehistoric standing stones
  cromlechs n ▷ cromlech
crone n (pl -s) witchlike old woman
  crones n ▷ crone
  cronies n ▷ crony
crony n (pl -nies) close friend
crook n (pl -s) (Informal) criminal ▶ adj (AUST & NZ) (Slang) unwell, injured
crooked adj bent or twisted ▷ **crookedly** adv ▷ **crookedness** n
  crookedly adv ▷ crooked

crookedness n ▷ crooked

crooks n ▷ crook

croon v (-s, -ing, -ed) sing, hum, or speak in a soft low tone

crooned v ▷ croon

crooner n (pl -s) male singer of sentimental ballads

crooners n ▷ crooner

crooning v ▷ croon

croons v ▷ croon

crop n (pl -s) cultivated plant ▶ v (crops, cropping, cropped) cut very short > **cropper** n (pl -s)

cropped v ▷ crop

cropper n ▷ crop

croppers n ▷ crop

cropping v ▷ crop

crops n, v ▷ crop

croquet [kroh-kay] n (pl -s) game played on a lawn in which balls are hit through hoops

croquets n ▷ croquet

croquette [kroh-kett] n (pl -s) fried cake of potato, meat, or fish

croquettes n ▷ croquette

crosier n (pl -s) ▷ crozier

crosiers n ▷ crosier

cross v (-es, -ing, -ed) move or go across (something) ▶ n (pl -es) structure, symbol, or mark of two intersecting lines ▶ adj (-er, -est) angry, annoyed > **crossly** adv > **crossness** n (pl -es)

crossbar n (pl -s) horizontal bar across goalposts or on a bicycle

crossbars n ▷ crossbar

crossbow n (pl -s) weapon consisting of a bow fixed across a wooden stock

crossbows n ▷ crossbow

crossbred adj bred from two different types of animal or plant

crossbreed n (pl -s) crossbred animal or plant

crossbreeds n ▷ crossbreed

crossed v ▷ cross

crosser adj ▷ cross

crosses v, n ▷ cross

crossest adj ▷ cross

crossfire n (pl -s) gunfire crossing another line of fire

crossfires n ▷ crossfire

crossing n (pl -s) place where a street may be crossed safely ▶ v ▷ cross

crossings n ▷ crossing

crossly adv ▷ cross

crossness n ▷ cross

crossnesses n ▷ cross

crossroads n place where two roads intersect

crosswise adj, adv across

crossword n (pl -s) puzzle in which words suggested by clues are written into a grid of squares

crosswords n ▷ crossword

crotch n (pl -es) part of the body between the tops of the legs

crotches n ▷ crotch

crotchet n (pl -s) musical note half the length of a minim

crotchetier adj ▷ crotchety

crotchetiest adj ▷ crotchety

crotchets n ▷ crotchet

crotchety adj (-tier, -tiest) (Informal) bad-tempered

crouch v (-es, -ing, -ed) bend low with the legs and body close ▶ n (pl -es) this position

crouched v ▷ crouch

crouches v, n ▷ crouch

crouching v ▷ crouch

croup[1] [kroop] n (pl -s) throat disease of children, with a cough

croup[2] [kroop] n (pl -s) hind quarters of a horse

croupier [kroop-ee-ay] n (pl -s) person who collects bets and pays out winnings at a gambling table in a casino

croupiers n ▷ croupier

croups n ▷ croup[1, 2]

crouton n (pl -s) small piece of fried or toasted bread served in soup

croutons n ▷ crouton

crow[1] n (pl -s) large black bird with a harsh call

crow[2] v (-s, -ing, -ed) (of a cock) make a shrill squawking sound

crowbar n (pl -s) iron bar used as a lever

crowbars n ▷ crowbar

crowd n (pl -s) large group of people or things ▶ v (-s, -ing, -ed) gather together in large numbers

crowded v ▷ crowd

crowding v ▷ crowd

crowds n, v ▷ crowd

crowed v ▷ crow[2]

crowing v ▷ crow[2]

crown n (pl -s) monarch's headdress of gold and jewels ▶ v (-s, -ing, -ed) put a crown on the head of (someone) to proclaim him or her monarch

crowned v ▷ crown

crowning v ▷ crown

crowns n, v ▷ crown

crows n ▷ crow[1] ▶ v ▷ crow[2]

crozier, crosier n (pl -s) bishop's hooked staff

croziers n ▷ crozier

crucial adj very important > **crucially** adv

crucially adv ▷ crucial

crucible n (pl -s) pot in which metals are melted

crucibles n ▷ crucible

crucified v ▷ crucify

crucifies v ▷ crucify

crucifix n (pl -es) model of Christ on the Cross

crucifixes n ▷ crucify

crucifixion n (pl -s) crucifying

crucifixions n ▷ crucifixion

cruciform adj cross-shaped

crucify v (-fies, -fying, -fied) put to death by fastening to a cross

crucifying v ▷ crucify

crude adj (-r, -st) rough and simple > **crudely** adv > **crudeness** n (pl -es) > **crudity** n (pl -ties)

crudely adv ▷ crude

crudeness n ▷ crude

crudenesses n ▷ crude

cruder adj ▷ crude

crudest adj ▷ crude

crudities n ▷ crude

crudity n ▷ crude

cruel adj (-ler, -llest) delighting in others' pain > **cruelly** adv > **cruelty** n (pl -ties)

crueller adj ▷ cruel

cruellest adj ▷ cruel

cruelly adv ▷ cruel

cruelties n ▷ cruel

cruelty n ▷ cruel

cruet n (pl -s) small container for salt, pepper, etc., at table

cruets n ▷ cruet

cruise n (pl -s) sail for pleasure ▶ v (cruises, cruising, cruised) sail from place to place for pleasure

cruised n ▷ cruise

cruiser n (pl -s) fast warship

cruisers n ▷ cruiser

cruises n, v ▷ cruise

cruising v ▷ cruise

crumb n (pl -s) small fragment of bread or other dry food

crumble v (-bles, -bling, -bled) break into fragments ▶ n (pl -s) pudding of stewed fruit with a crumbly topping > **crumbly** adj (-blier, -bliest)

crumbled v ▷ crumble

crumbles v, n ▷ crumble

crumblier adj ▷ crumble

crumbliest adj ▷ crumble

crumbling v ▷ crumble

crumbly adj ▷ crumble

crumbs n ▷ crumb

crummier adj ▷ crummy

crummiest adj ▷ crummy

crummy adj (-mier, -miest) (Slang) of poor quality

crumpet n (pl -s) round soft yeast cake, eaten buttered

crumpets n ▷ crumpet

crumple v (-ples, -pling, -pled) crush, crease > **crumpled** adj

crumpled v, adj ▷ crumple

crumples v ▷ crumple

crumpling v ▷ crumple

crunch v (-es, -ing, -ed) bite or chew with a noisy crushing sound ▶ n (pl -es) crunching sound (Informal) > **crunchy** adj (-chier, -chiest)

crunched v ▷ crunch

crunches v, n ▷ crunch

crunchier adj ▷ crunch

crunchiest adj ▷ crunch

crunching v ▷ crunch

crunchy adj ▷ crunch

crupper n (pl -s) strap that passes from the back of a saddle under a horse's tail

cruppers n ▷ crupper

crusade n (pl -s) medieval Christian war to recover the Holy Land from the Muslims ▶ v (-sades, -sading, -saded) take part in a crusade

crusaded v ▷ crusade

crusader n (pl -s) person who took part in the medieval Christian war to recover the Holy Land from the Muslims

crusaders n ▷ crusader

crusades n, v ▷ crusade

crusading v ▷ crusade

crush v (-es, -ing, -ed) compress so as to injure, break, or crumple ▶ n (pl -es) dense crowd

crushed v ▷ crush

crushes v, n ▷ crush

crushing v ▷ crush

crust n (pl -s) hard outer part of something, esp. bread ▶ v (-s, -ing, -ed) cover with or form a crust

crustacean n (pl -s) hard-shelled, usu. aquatic animal with several pairs of legs, such as the crab or lobster

crustaceans n ▷ crustacean

crusted v ▷ crust

crustier adj ▷ crusty

crustiest adj ▷ crusty

crusting v ▷ crust

crusts n, v ▷ crust

crusty adj (-tier, -tiest) having a crust

crutch n (pl -es) long sticklike support with a rest for the armpit, used by a lame person

crutches n ▷ crutch

crux n (pl -es) crucial or decisive point
  cruxes n ▷ crux
cry v (cries, crying, cried) shed tears ▶ n (pl cries) fit of weeping
  crybabies n ▷ crybaby
crybaby n (pl -babies) person, esp. a child, who cries too readily
  crying v ▷ cry
  cryogenic adj ▷ cryogenics
cryogenics n branch of physics concerned with very low temperatures > **cryogenic** adj
crypt n (pl -s) vault under a church, esp. one used as a burial place
cryptic adj obscure in meaning, secret > **cryptically** adv
  cryptographer n ▷ cryptography
  cryptographers n ▷ cryptography
cryptography n art of writing in and deciphering codes > **cryptographer** n (pl -s)
  crypts n ▷ crypt
crystal n (pl -s) (single grain of) a symmetrically shaped solid formed naturally by some substances ▶ adj bright and clear
crystalline adj of or like crystal or crystals
  crystallization n ▷ crystallize
  crystallizations n ▷ crystallize
crystallize v (-lizes, -lizing, -lized) make or become definite > **crystallization** n (pl -s)
  crystallized v ▷ crystallize
  crystallizes v ▷ crystallize
  crystallizing v ▷ crystallize
  crystals n ▷ crystal
cub n (pl -s) young wild animal such as a bear or fox ▶ v (cubs, cubbing, cubbed) give birth to cubs
  cubbed v ▷ cub
  cubbing v ▷ cub
cubbyhole n (pl -s) small enclosed space or room
  cubbyholes n ▷ cubbyhole
cube n (pl -s) object with six equal square sides ▶ v (cubes, cubing, cubed) cut into cubes
  cubed v ▷ cube
  cubes n, v ▷ cube
cubic adj having three dimensions
cubicle n (pl -s) enclosed part of a large room, screened for privacy
  cubicles n ▷ cubicle
  cubing v ▷ cube
cubism n style of art in which objects are represented by geometrical shapes > **cubist** adj, n (pl -s)
  cubists n ▷ cubist
  cubs n, v ▷ cub
cuckold n (pl -s) man whose wife has been unfaithful ▶ v (-s, -ing, -ed) be unfaithful to (one's husband)
  cuckolded v ▷ cuckold
  cuckolding v ▷ cuckold
  cuckolds n, v ▷ cuckold
cuckoo n (pl -s) migratory bird with a characteristic two-note call, which lays its eggs in the nests of other birds ▶ adj (Informal) insane or foolish
  cuckoos n ▷ cuckoo
cucumber n (pl -s) long green-skinned fleshy fruit used in salads
  cucumbers n ▷ cucumber
cud n (pl -s) partially digested food which a ruminant brings back into its mouth to chew again
cuddle v (cuddles, cuddling, cuddled) ▶ n (pl -s) hug > **cuddly** adj (-lier, -liest)
  cuddled v ▷ cuddle
  cuddles v, n ▷ cuddle
  cuddlier adj ▷ cuddle
  cuddliest adj ▷ cuddle
  cuddling v ▷ cuddle
  cuddly adj ▷ cuddle
cudgel n (pl -s) short thick stick used as a weapon
  cudgels n ▷ cudgel
  cuds n ▷ cud
cue¹ n (pl -s) signal to an actor or musician to begin speaking or playing ▶ v (cues, cueing, cued) give a cue to
cue² n long tapering stick used in billiards, snooker, or pool ▶ v (cues, cueing, cued) hit (a ball) with a cue
  cued v ▷ cue¹, ²
  cueing v ▷ cue¹, ²
  cues n, v ▷ cue¹, ²
cuff¹ n (pl -s) end of a sleeve
cuff² (BRIT, AUST & NZ) v (-s, -ing, -ed) hit with an open hand ▶ n (pl -s) blow with an open hand
  cuffed v ▷ cuff²
  cuffing v ▷ cuff²
  cuffs n ▷ cuff¹, ² v ▷ cuff²
cuisine [quiz-zeen] n (pl -s) style of cooking
  cuisines n ▷ cuisine
culinary adj of kitchens or cookery
cull v (-s, -ing, -ed) choose, gather ▶ n (pl -s) culling
  culled v ▷ cull
  culling v ▷ cull
  culls v, n ▷ cull
culminate v (-nates, -nating, -nated) reach the highest point or climax > **culmination** n (pl -s)
  culminated v ▷ culminate

culminates v ▷ culminate

culminating v ▷ culminate

culmination n ▷ culminate

culminations n ▷ culminate

culottes pl n women's knee-length trousers cut to look like a skirt

culpabilities n ▷ culpable

culpability n ▷ culpable

culpable adj deserving blame > **culpability** n (pl -ties)> **culpably** adv

culpably adv ▷ culpable

culprit n (pl -s) person guilty of an offence or misdeed

culprits n ▷ culprit

cult n (pl -s) specific system of worship

cultivate v (-vates, -vating, -vated) prepare (land) to grow crops > **cultivation** n

cultivated adj well-educated ▶ v ▷ cultivate

cultivates v ▷ cultivate

cultivating v ▷ cultivate

cultivation n ▷ cultivate

cults n ▷ cult

cultural adj ▷ culture

culturally adv ▷ culture

culture n (pl -s) ideas, customs, and art of a particular society > **cultural** adj > **culturally** adv

cultured adj showing good taste or manners

cultures n ▷ culture

culvert n (pl -s) drain under a road or railway

culverts n ▷ culvert

cumbersome adj awkward because of size or shape

cumin, cummin n (pl -s) sweet-smelling seeds of a Mediterranean plant, used in cooking

cumins n ▷ cumin

cummerbund n (pl -s) wide sash worn round the waist

cummerbunds n ▷ cummerbund

cummin n ▷ cumin

cummins n ▷ cumin

cumulative adj increasing steadily > **cumulatively** adv

cumulatively adv ▷ cumulative

cumuli n ▷ cumulus

cumulus [kew-myew-luss] n (pl -li) thick white or dark grey cloud

cuneiform [kew-nif-form] n, adj (written in) an ancient system of writing using wedge-shaped characters

cunjevoi n (pl -s) (AUST) plant of tropical Asia and Australia with small flowers, cultivated for its edible rhizome

cunjevois n ▷ cunjevoi

cunning adj clever at deceiving ▶ n cleverness at deceiving > **cunningly** adv

cunningly adv ▷ cunning

cup n (pl -s) small bowl-shaped drinking container with a handle ▶ v (cups, cupping, cupped) form (one's hands) into the shape of a cup > **cupful** n (pl -s)

cupboard n (pl -s) piece of furniture or alcove with a door, for storage

cupboards n ▷ cupboard

cupful n ▷ cup

cupfuls n ▷ cup

cupidity [kew-pid-it-ee] n greed for money or possessions

cupola [kew-pol-la] n (pl -s) domed roof or ceiling

cupolas n ▷ cupola

cupped v ▷ cup

cupping v ▷ cup

cups n, v ▷ cup

cur n (pl -s) (Lit) mongrel dog

curable adj ▷ cure

curaçao [kew-rah-so] n orange-flavoured liqueur

curacies n ▷ curacy

curacy [kew-rah-see] n (pl -cies) work or position of a curate

curare [kew-rah-ree] n (pl -s) poisonous resin of a S American tree, used as a muscle relaxant in medicine

curares n ▷ curare

curate n (pl -s) clergyman who assists a parish priest

curates n ▷ curate

curative adj, n (pl -s) (something) able to cure

curatives n ▷ curative

curator n (pl -s) person in charge of a museum or art gallery > **curatorship** n (pl -s)

curators n ▷ curator

curatorship n ▷ curator

curatorships n ▷ curator

curb n (pl -s) something that restrains ▶ v (-s, -ing, -ed) control, restrain

curbed v ▷ curb

curbing v ▷ curb

curbs n, v ▷ curb

curd n (pl -s) coagulated milk, used to make cheese

curdle v (-dles, -dling, -dled) turn into curd, coagulate

curdled v ▷ curdle

curdles v ▷ curdle

curdling v ▷ curdle

curds n ▷ curd

cure v (cures, curing, cured) get rid of (an illness or problem) ▶ n (pl -s) (treatment

causing) curing of an illness or person
> **curable** adj
cured v ▷ cure
cures v, n ▷ cure
curettage n ▷ curette
curettages n ▷ curette
curette n (pl -s) surgical instrument for
scraping tissue from body cavities ▶ v
(curettes, curetting, curetted) scrape with a
curette > **curettage** n (pl -s)
curetted v ▷ curette
curettes n, v ▷ curette
curetting v ▷ curette
curfew n (pl -s) law ordering people to stay
inside their homes after a specific time at
night
curfews n ▷ curfew
curie n (pl -s) standard unit of radioactivity
curies n ▷ curie
curing v ▷ cure
curio n (pl -s) rare or unusual object valued as a
collector's item
curios n ▷ curio
curiosities n ▷ curiosity
curiosity n eagerness to know or find out
(pl -ties)
curiously adv ▷ curious
curious adj eager to learn or know > **curiously**
adv
curl n (pl -s) curved piece of hair ▶ v (-s, -ing,
-ed) make (hair) into curls or (of hair) grow in
curls > **curler** n (pl -s) > **curly** adj (-lier, -liest)
curled v ▷ curl
curler n ▷ curl
curlers n ▷ curl
curlew n (pl -s) long-billed wading bird
curlews n ▷ curlew
curlier adj ▷ curl
curliest adj ▷ curl
curling n game like bowls, played with heavy
stones on ice ▶ v ▷ curl
curls n, v ▷ curl
curly adj ▷ curl
curmudgeon n (pl -s) bad-tempered person
> **curmudgeonly** adj
curmudgeonly adj ▷ curmudgeon
curmudgeons n ▷ curmudgeon
currajong n (pl -s) ▷ kurrajong
currajongs n ▷ currajong
currant n (pl -s) small dried grape
currants n ▷ currant
currawong n (pl -s) Australian songbird
currawongs n ▷ currawong
currencies n ▷ currency
currency n (pl -cies) money in use in a

particular country
current adj of the immediate present ▶ n
(pl -s) flow of water or air in one direction
> **currently** adv
currently adv ▷ current
currents n ▷ current
curricula n ▷ curriculum
curriculum n (pl -la, -lums) all the courses of
study offered by a school or college
curriculums n ▷ curriculum
curried v ▷ curry¹,²
curries n ▷ curry¹ ▶ v ▷ curry¹,²
curry¹ n (pl -ries) Indian dish of meat or
vegetables in a hot spicy sauce ▶ v (-ries,
-rying, -ried) prepare (food) with curry
powder
curry² v (-ries, -rying, -ried) groom (a horse)
currying v ▷ curry¹,²
curs n ▷ cur
curse v (curses, cursing, cursed) swear (at) ▶ n
(pl -s) swearword > **cursed** adj
cursed adj, v ▷ curse
curses v, n ▷ curse
cursing v ▷ curse
cursive adj, n (pl -s) (handwriting) done with
joined letters > **cursively** adv
cursively adv ▷ cursive
cursives n ▷ cursive
cursor n (pl -s) movable point of light that
shows a specific position on a visual display
unit
cursorily adv ▷ cursory
cursoriness n ▷ cursory
cursors n ▷ cursor
cursory adj quick and superficial > **cursorily**
adv > **cursoriness** n
curt adj (-er, -est) brief and rather rude > **curtly**
adv > **curtness** n (pl -es)
curtail v (-s, -ing, -ed) cut short > **curtailment**
n (pl -s)
curtailed v ▷ curtail
curtailing v ▷ curtail
curtailment n ▷ curtail
curtailments n ▷ curtail
curtails v ▷ curtail
curtain n (pl -s) piece of cloth hung at a
window or opening as a screen ▶ v (-s, -ing,
-ed) provide with curtains
curtained v ▷ curtain
curtaining v ▷ curtain
curtains n, v ▷ curtain
curter adj ▷ curt
curtest adj ▷ curt
curtly adv ▷ curt
curtness n ▷ curt

curtnesses n ▷ curt
curtsey n ▷ curtsy
curtseyed v ▷ curtsy
curtseying v ▷ curtsy
curtseys n, v ▷ curtsy
curtsied v ▷ curtsy
curtsies n, v ▷ curtsy
curtsy, curtsey n (pl -sies, -seys) woman's gesture of respect made by bending the knees and bowing the head ▶ v (-sies, -seys, -sying, -sied or -seying) (-seyed) make a curtsy
curtsying v ▷ curtsy
curvaceous adj (Informal) (of a woman) having a shapely body
curvature n (pl -s) curved shape
curvatures n ▷ curvature
curve n (pl -s) continuously bending line with no straight parts ▶ v (curves, curving, curved) form or move in a curve > **curvy** adj (-vier, -viest)
curved v ▷ curve
curves n, v ▷ curve
curvier adj ▷ curve
curviest adj ▷ curve
curvilinear adj consisting of or bounded by a curve
curving v ▷ curve
curvy adj ▷ curve
cuscus n (pl -ses) large Australian nocturnal possum
cuscuses n ▷ cuscus
cushier adj ▷ cushy
cushiest adj ▷ cushy
cushion n (pl -s) bag filled with soft material, to make a seat more comfortable ▶ v (-s, -ing, -ed) lessen the effects of
cushioned v ▷ cushion
cushioning v ▷ cushion
cushions n, v ▷ cushion
cushy adj (cushier, cushiest) (Informal) easy
cusp n (pl -s) pointed end, esp. on a tooth
cusps n ▷ cusp
cuss (Informal) n (pl -es) curse, oath ▶ v (-es, -ing, -ed) swear (at)
cussed [kuss-id] adj (Informal) obstinate ▶ v ▷ cuss > **cussedly** adv > **cussedness** n
cussedly adv ▷ cussed
cussedness n ▷ cussed
cusses n, v ▷ cuss
cussing v ▷ cuss
custard n (pl -s) sweet yellow sauce made from milk and eggs
custards n ▷ custard
custodial adj ▷ custody

custodian n (pl -s) person in charge of a public building
custodians n ▷ custodian
custodies n ▷ custody
custody n (pl -dies) protective care > **custodial** adj
custom n (pl -s) long-established activity or action ▶ pl duty charged on imports or exports
customarily adv ▷ customary
customary adj usual > **customarily** adv
customer n (pl s) person who buys goods or services
customers n ▷ customer
customs n ▷ custom
cut v (cuts, cutting, cut) open up, penetrate, wound, or divide with a sharp instrument ▶ n (pl -s) stroke or incision made by cutting
cutaneous [kew-tane-ee-uss] adj of the skin
cute adj (cuter, cutest) appealing or attractive > **cutely** adv > **cuteness** n
cutely adv ▷ cute
cuteness n ▷ cute
cuter adj ▷ cute
cutest adj ▷ cute
cuticle n (pl -s) skin at the base of a fingernail or toenail
cuticles n ▷ cuticle
cutlass n (pl -es) curved one-edged sword formerly used by sailors
cutlasses n ▷ cutlass
cutler n (pl -s) maker of cutlery
cutlers n ▷ cutler
cutlery n knives, forks, and spoons
cutlet n (pl -s) small piece of meat like a chop
cutlets n ▷ cutlet
cuts v, n ▷ cut
cutter n (pl -s) person or tool that cuts
cutters n ▷ cutter
cutting n (pl -s) article cut from a newspaper or magazine ▶ adj (of a remark) hurtful ▶ v ▷ cut > **cuttingly** adv
cuttingly adv ▷ cutting
cuttings n ▷ cutting
cuttlefish n (pl cuttlefish) squidlike sea mollusc

> **cuz** n (cuzzes) Like **coz**, cuz is an old word for **cousin**. You need a blank tile for the second Z if you're going to play the plural. Cuz scores 14 points.
> **cwm** n (cwms) Cwm is a Welsh word for a valley. It's a useful one to remember because it doesn't contain any vowels. Cwm scores 10 points.

cyanide n (pl -s) extremely poisonous chemical

compound

cyanides n ▷ cyanide

cybernetics n branch of science in which electronic and mechanical systems are studied and compared to biological systems

cyberspace n place said to contain all the data stored in computers

cyclamen [**sik**-la-men] n (pl -s) plant with red, pink, or white flowers

cyclamens n ▷ cyclamen

cycle v (**cycles, cycling, cycled**) ride a bicycle ▶ n (pl -s) (BRIT, AUST & NZ) bicycle

cycled v ▷ cycle

cycles v, n ▷ cycle

cyclic adj ▷ cyclical

cyclical, cyclic adj occurring in cycles > **cyclically** adv

cyclically adv ▷ cyclical

cycling v ▷ cycle

cyclist n (pl -s) person who rides a bicycle

cyclists n ▷ cyclist

cyclone n (pl -s) violent wind moving round a central area

cyclones n ▷ cyclone

cyclotron n (pl -s) apparatus that accelerates charged particles by means of a strong vertical magnetic field

cyclotrons n ▷ cyclotron

cygnet n (pl -s) young swan

cygnets n ▷ cygnet

cylinder n (pl -s) solid or hollow body with straight sides and circular ends > **cylindrical** adj

cylinders n ▷ cylinder

cylindrical adj ▷ cylinder

cymbal n (pl -s) percussion instrument consisting of a brass plate which is struck against another or hit with a stick

cymbals n ▷ cymbal

cynic [**sin**-ik] n (pl -s) person who believes that people always act selfishly > **cynical** adj > **cynically** adv > **cynicism** n

cynical adj ▷ cynic

cynically adv ▷ cynic

cynicism n ▷ cynic

cynics n ▷ cynic

cynosure [**sin**-oh-**zyure**] n (pl -s) centre of attention

cynosures n ▷ cynosure

cypher n (pl -s) ▷ cipher

cyphers n ▷ cypher

cypress n (pl -es) evergreen tree with dark green leaves

cypresses n ▷ cypress

cyst [**sist**] n (pl -s) (abnormal) sac in the body containing fluid or soft matter > **cystic** adj

cystic adj ▷ cyst

cystitis [siss-**tite**-iss] n inflammation of the bladder

cysts n ▷ cyst

cytological adj ▷ cytology

cytologically adv ▷ cytology

cytologies n ▷ cytology

cytologist n ▷ cytology

cytologists n ▷ cytology

cytology [site-**ol**-a-jee] n (pl -logies) study of plant and animal cells > **cytological** adj > **cytologically** adv > **cytologist** n (pl -s)

czar [**zahr**] n (pl -s) ▷ tsar > **czarism** n > **czarist** adj, n (pl -s)

czarism n ▷ czar

czarist n ▷ czar

czarists n ▷ czar

czars n ▷ czar

Dd

D only starts a handful of two-letter words, but it does form a two-letter word before every vowel except U. There are plenty of good three-letter words beginning with D, particularly those with a Y or W: **day**, **dye** and **dew** are worth 7 points each, for example.

da n (**das**). A da is a Burmese knife. Da scores 3 points.

dab¹ v (-s, -bbing, -bbed) pat lightly ▸ n (pl -s) small amount of something soft or moist

dab² n (pl -s) small European flatfish with rough scales

　dabbed v ▷ dab¹

　dabbing v ▷ dab¹

dabble v (-les, -ling, -led) be involved in something superficially > **dabbler** n (pl -s)

　dabbled v ▷ dabble

　dabbler n ▷ dabble

　dabblers n ▷ dabble

　dabbles v ▷ dabble

　dabbling v ▷ dabble

　dabs n ▷ dab¹, ² ▸ v ▷ dab¹

dace n (pl dace) small European freshwater fish

dachshund n (pl -s) dog with a long body and short legs

　dachshunds n ▷ dachshund

dad n (pl -s) (Informal) father

　daddies n ▷ daddy

daddy n (pl -dies) (Informal) father

dado [day-doe] n (pl -does, -dos) lower part of an interior wall, below a rail, decorated differently from the upper part

　dadoes n ▷ dado

　dados n ▷ dado

　dads n ▷ dad

daffodil n (pl -s) yellow trumpet-shaped flower that blooms in spring

　daffodils n ▷ daffodil

daft adj (-er, -est) (Informal) foolish or crazy > **daftness** n (pl -es)

　dafter adj ▷ daft

　daftest adj ▷ daft

　daftness n ▷ daft

　daftnesses n ▷ daft

dag (NZ) n (pl -s) dried dung on a sheep's rear (Informal) ▸ v (-s, -gging, -gged) remove the dags from a sheep

dagga n (pl -s) (S AFR) (Informal) cannabis

　daggas n ▷ dagga

　dagged v ▷ dag

dagger n (pl -s) short knifelike weapon with a pointed blade

　daggers n ▷ dagger

　daggier adj ▷ daggy

　daggiest adj ▷ daggy

　dagging v ▷ dag

daggy adj (-ggier, -ggiest) (NZ) (Informal) amusing

　dags n, v ▷ dag

daguerreotype [dag-**gair**-oh-type] n (pl -s) type of early photograph produced on chemically treated silver

　daguerreotypes n ▷ daguerreotype

dahlia [day-lya] n (pl -s) brightly coloured garden flower

　dahlias n ▷ dahlia

　dailies n ▷ daily

daily adj occurring every day or every weekday ▸ adv every day ▸ n (pl -lies) daily newspaper

　daintier adj ▷ dainty

　daintiest adj ▷ dainty

　daintily adv ▷ dainty

dainty adj (-tier, -tiest) delicate or elegant > **daintily** adv

daiquiri [dak-**eer**-ee] n (pl -s) iced drink containing rum, lime juice, and sugar

　daiquiris n ▷ daiquiri

　dairies n ▷ dairy

dairy n (pl -ies) place for the processing or sale of milk and its products ▸ adj of milk or its products

dais [day-iss, **dayss**] n (pl -es) raised platform in a hall, used by a speaker

　daises n ▷ dais

　daisies n ▷ daisy

daisy n (pl -sies) small wild flower with a

yellow centre and white petals

dak n (daks) A dak is an old Indian mail or transport system. This is a good word to know if you have a K on your rack but can't think of a longer word in which to use it. Dak scores 8 points.

dale n (pl -s) (esp. in N England) valley
  dales n ▷ dale

dalliance n (pl -s) flirtation
  dalliances n ▷ dalliance
  dallied v ▷ dally
  dallies v ▷ dally

dally v (-lies, -lying, -lied) waste time
  dallying v ▷ dally

dalmatian n (pl -s) large dog with a white coat and black spots
  dalmatians n ▷ dalmatian

dam¹ n (pl -s) barrier built across a river to create a lake ▶ v (dams, damming, dammed) build a dam across (a river)

dam² n (pl -s) mother of an animal such as a sheep or horse

damage v (-ages, -aging, -aged) harm, spoil ▶ n (pl -s) harm to a person or thing ▶ pl money awarded as compensation for injury or loss
  damaged v ▷ damage
  damages v, n ▷ damage
  damaging v ▷ damage

damask n (pl -s) fabric with a pattern woven into it, used for tablecloths etc.
  damasks n ▷ damask

dame n (pl -s) (CHIEFLY US & CANADIAN) (Slang) woman
  dames n ▷ dame
  dammed v ▷ dam¹
  damming v ▷ dam¹

damn interj (Slang) exclamation of annoyance ▶ adv, adj (also **damned**) (Slang) extreme(ly) ▶ v (-s, -ing, -ed) condemn as bad or worthless > **damnation** interj, n (pl -s)

damnable adj annoying > **damnably** adv
  damnably adv ▷ damnable
  damnation interj, n ▷ damn
  damnations n ▷ damn
  damned v ▷ damn

damning adj proving or suggesting guilt ▶ v ▷ damn
  damns v ▷ damn

damp adj (-er, -est) slightly wet ▶ n (pl -s) slight wetness, moisture ▶ v (-s, -ing, -ed) (also **dampen**) (-s, -ing, -ed) make damp (foll. by **down**) > **damply** adv > **dampness** n
  damped v ▷ damp
  dampen v ▷ dampen
  dampened v ▷ dampen

dampening v ▷ dampen
dampens v ▷ dampen
damper n (pl -s) movable plate to regulate the draught in a fire ▶ adj ▷ damp
dampers n ▷ damper
dampest adj ▷ damp
damping v ▷ damp
damply adv ▷ damp
dampness n ▷ damp
damps v, n ▷ damp
dams n ▷ dam¹, ² ▶ v ▷ dam¹
damsel n (pl -s) (Old-fashioned) young woman
damsels n ▷ damsel
damson n (pl -s) small blue-black plumlike fruit
damsons n ▷ damson
dance v (dances, dancing, danced) move the feet and body rhythmically in time to music ▶ n (pl -s) series of steps and movements in time to music > **dancer** n (pl -s)
danced v ▷ dance
dancer n ▷ dance
dancers n ▷ dance
dances v, n ▷ dance
dancing v ▷ dance
dandelion n (pl -s) yellow-flowered wild plant
dandelions n ▷ dandelion
dander n (pl -s) (Slang) anger
danders n ▷ dander
dandier adj ▷ dandy
dandies n ▷ dandy
dandiest adj ▷ dandy
dandified adj ▷ dandy
dandle v (-dles, -dling, -dled) move (a child) up and down on one's knee
dandled v ▷ dandle
dandles v ▷ dandle
dandling v ▷ dandle
dandruff n (pl -s) loose scales of dry dead skin shed from the scalp
dandruffs n ▷ dandruff
dandy n (pl -dies) man who is overconcerned with the elegance of his appearance ▶ adj (-dier, -diest) (Informal) very good > **dandified** adj
danger n (pl -s) possibility of being injured or killed > **dangerous** adj > **dangerously** adv
dangerous adj ▷ danger
dangerously adv ▷ danger
dangers n ▷ danger
dangle v (-gles, -gling, -gled) hang loosely
dangled v ▷ dangle
dangles v ▷ dangle
dangling v ▷ dangle
dank adj (-er, -est) unpleasantly damp and

chilly ▷ **dankly** adv ▷ **dankness** n (pl -es)

danker adj ▷ dank

dankest adj ▷ dank

dankly adv ▷ dank

dankness n ▷ dank

danknesses n ▷ dank

dapper adj (-er, -est) (of a man) neat in appearance > **dapperly** adv > **dapperness** n (pl -es)

dapperer adj ▷ dapper

dapperest adj ▷ dapper

dapperly adv ▷ dapper

dapperness n ▷ dapper

dappernesses n ▷ dapper

dappled adj marked with spots of a different colour

dare v (dares, daring, dared) be courageous enough to try (to do something) ▶ n (pl -s) challenge to do something risky

dared v ▷ dare

daredevil adj, n (pl -s) recklessly bold (person)

daredevils n ▷ daredevil

dares v, n ▷ dare

daring adj willing to take risks ▶ n courage to do dangerous things ▶ v ▷ dare > **daringly** adv

daringly adv ▷ daring

dark adj (-er, -est) having little or no light ▶ n (pl -s) absence of light > **darkly** adv > **darkness** n (pl -es) ▶ **darken** v (-s, -ing, -ed)

darken v ▷ dark

darkened v ▷ dark

darkening v ▷ dark

darkens v ▷ dark

darker adj ▷ dark

darkest adj ▷ dark

darkly adv ▷ dark

darkness n ▷ dark

darknesses n ▷ dark

darkroom n (pl -s) darkened room for processing photographic film

darkrooms n ▷ darkroom

darks n ▷ dark

darling n (pl -s) much-loved person ▶ adj much-loved

darlings n ▷ darling

darn¹ v (-s, -ing, -ed) mend (a garment) with a series of interwoven stitches ▶ n (pl -s) patch of darned work

darn² interj, adv, adj, v (-s, -ing, -ed) (Euphemistic) damn

darned v ▷ darn¹, ²

darning v ▷ darn¹, ²

darns v, ² ▶ n ▷ darn¹

dart n (pl -s) small narrow pointed missile that is thrown or shot, esp. in the game of

darts ▶ pl game in which darts are thrown at a circular numbered board ▶ v (-s, -ing, -ed) move or direct quickly and suddenly

darted v ▷ dart

darting v ▷ dart

darts n, v ▷ dart

dash v (-es, -ing, -ed) move quickly ▶ n (pl -es) sudden quick movement

dashboard n (pl -s) instrument panel in a vehicle

dashboards n ▷ dashboard

dashed v ▷ dash

dashes v, n ▷ dash

dashing adj stylish and attractive ▶ v ▷ dash > **dashingly** adv

dashingly adv ▷ dashing

dassie n (pl -s) type of hoofed rodent-like animal (also hyrax)

dassies n ▷ dassie

dastardliness n ▷ dastardly

dastardly adj wicked and cowardly > **dastardliness** n

dasyure [dass-ee-your] n (pl -s) small marsupial of Australia, New Guinea, and adjacent islands

dasyures n ▷ dasyure

data n information consisting of observations, measurements, or facts

date¹ n (pl -s) specified day of the month ▶ v (dates, dating, dated) mark with the date

date² n (pl -s) dark-brown sweet-tasting fruit of the date palm

dated adj old-fashioned ▶ v ▷ date¹

dates n ▷ date¹, ² ▶ v ▷ date¹

dating v ▷ date¹

dative n (pl -s) (in certain languages) the form of the noun that expresses the indirect object

datives n ▷ dative

datum n (pl data) single piece of information in the form of a fact or statistic

daub v (-s, -ing, -ed) smear or spread quickly or clumsily

daubed v ▷ daub

daubing v ▷ daub

daubs v ▷ daub

daughter n (pl -s) female child > **daughterly** adj

daughterly adj ▷ daughter

daughters n ▷ daughter

daunting adj intimidating or worrying > **dauntingly** adv

dauntingly adv ▷ daunting

dauntless adj fearless > **dauntlessly** adv > **dauntlessness** n

dauntlessly adv ▷ dauntless

dauntlessness n ▷ dauntless

dauphin [doe-fan] n (pl -s) (formerly) eldest son of the king of France

dauphins n ▷ dauphin

davenport n (pl -s) (CHIEFLY BRIT) small writing table with drawers

davenports n ▷ davenport

davit [dav-vit] n (pl -s) crane, usu. one of a pair, at a ship's side, for lowering and hoisting a lifeboat

davits n ▷ davit

daw n (daws). A daw is another name for a **jackdaw**. Daw scores 7 points.

dawdle v (-dles, -dling, -dled) walk slowly, lag behind

dawdled v ▷ dawdle

dawdles v ▷ dawdle

dawdling v ▷ dawdle

dawn n (pl -s) daybreak ▶ v (-s, -ing, -ed) begin to grow light

dawned v ▷ dawn

dawning v ▷ dawn

dawns n, v ▷ dawn

day n (pl -s) period of 24 hours

daybreak n time in the morning when light first appears

daydream n (pl -s) pleasant fantasy indulged in while awake ▶ v (-s, -ing, -ed) indulge in idle fantasy ▷ **daydreamer** n (pl -s)

daydreamed v ▷ daydream

daydreamer n ▷ daydream

daydreamers n ▷ daydream

daydreaming v ▷ daydream

daydreams n, v ▷ daydream

daylight n light from the sun

days n ▷ day

daze v (dazes, dazing, dazed) stun, by a blow or shock ▶ n (pl -s) state of confusion or shock

dazed v ▷ daze

dazes v, n ▷ daze

dazing v ▷ daze

dazzle v (-zles, -zling, -zled) impress greatly ▶ n (pl -s) bright light that dazzles ▷ **dazzling** adj ▷ **dazzlingly** adv

dazzled v ▷ dazzle

dazzles v, n ▷ dazzle

dazzling v, adj ▷ dazzle

dazzlingly adv ▷ dazzle

de prep. De means of or from. This is a useful little word to fit in when trying to form several words at once. De scores 3 points.

deacon n (pl -s) (CHRISTIANITY) ordained minister ranking immediately below a priest

deacons n ▷ deacon

dead adj (-er, -est) no longer alive ▶ n (pl -s)

period during which coldness or darkness is most intense ▶ adv extremely

deadbeat n (pl -s) (Informal) lazy useless person

deadbeats n ▷ deadbeat

deaden v (-s, -ing, -ed) make less intense

deadened v ▷ deaden

deadening v ▷ deaden

deadens v ▷ deaden

deader adj ▷ dead

deadest adj ▷ dead

deadlier adj ▷ deadly

deadliest adj ▷ deadly

deadline n (pl -s) time limit

deadlines n ▷ deadline

deadliness n ▷ deadly

deadlock n (pl -s) point in a dispute at which no agreement can be reached ▷ **deadlocked** adj

deadlocked adj ▷ deadlock

deadlocks n ▷ deadlock

deadly adj (-lier, -liest) likely to cause death ▶ adv extremely ▷ **deadliness** n

deadpan adj, adv showing no emotion or expression

deads n ▷ dead

deaf adj (-er, -est) unable to hear ▷ **deafness** n (pl -es)

deafen v (-s, -ing, -ed) make deaf, esp. temporarily

deafened v ▷ deafen

deafening v ▷ deafen

deafens v ▷ deafen

deafer adj ▷ deaf

deafest adj ▷ deaf

deafness n ▷ deaf

deafnesses n ▷ deaf

deal¹ n (pl -s) agreement or transaction ▶ v (deals, dealing, dealt) inflict (a blow) on ▷ **dealer** n (pl -s)

deal² n (pl -s) plank of fir or pine wood

dealer n ▷ deal¹

dealers n ▷ deal¹

dealing v ▷ deal¹

dealings pl n transactions or business relations

deals v ▷ deal¹ ▶ n ▷ deal¹, ²

dealt v ▷ deal¹

dean n (pl -s) chief administrative official of a college or university faculty

deaneries n ▷ deanery

deanery n (pl -eries) office or residence of a dean

deans n ▷ dean

dear n (pl -s) someone regarded with affection ▶ adj (-er, -est) much-loved ▷ **dearly** adv

> **dearness** n (pl -es)

dearer adj ▷ dear

dearest adj ▷ dear

dearly adv ▷ dear

dearness n ▷ dear

dearnesses n ▷ dear

dears n ▷ dear

dearth [dirth] n (pl -s) inadequate amount, scarcity

dearths n ▷ dearth

death n (pl -s) permanent end of life in a person or animal

deathly adj, adv like death

deaths n ▷ death

deb n (pl -s) (Informal) debutante

debacle [day-bah-kl] n (pl -s) disastrous failure

debacles n ▷ debacle

debar v (-bars, -barring, -barred) prevent, bar

debarred v ▷ debar

debarring v ▷ debar

debars v ▷ debar

debase v (-bases, -basing, -based) lower in value, quality, or character > **debasement** n (pl -s)

debased v ▷ debase

debasement n ▷ debase

debasements n ▷ debase

debases v ▷ debase

debasing v ▷ debase

debatable adj not absolutely certain > **debatably** adv

debate n (pl -s) discussion ▶ v (-bates, -bating, -bated) discuss formally

debated v ▷ debate

debates n, v ▷ debate

debating v ▷ debate

debauch [dib-bawch] v (-es, -ing, -ed) make (someone) bad or corrupt, esp. sexually > **debauchery** n (pl -eries)

debauched adj immoral, sexually corrupt ▶ v ▷ debauch

debaucheries n ▷ debauch

debauchery n ▷ debauch

debauches v ▷ debauch

debauching v ▷ debauch

debenture n (pl -s) long-term bond bearing fixed interest, issued by a company or a government agency

debentures n ▷ debenture

debilitate v (-tates, -tating, -tated) weaken, make feeble > **debilitation** n

debilitated v ▷ debilitate

debilitates v ▷ debilitate

debilitating v ▷ debilitate

debilitation n ▷ debilitate

debilities n ▷ debility

debility n (pl -ities) weakness, infirmity

debit n (pl -s) acknowledgment of a sum owing by entry on the left side of an account ▶ v (-s, -ing, -ed) charge (an account) with a debt

debited v ▷ debit

debiting v ▷ debit

debits n, v ▷ debit

debonair adj (of a man) charming and refined

debouch v (-es, -ing, -ed) move out from a narrow place to a wider one

debouched v ▷ debouch

debouches v ▷ debouch

debouching v ▷ debouch

debrief v (-s, -ing, -ed) receive a report from (a soldier, diplomat, etc.) after an event

> **debriefing** n (pl -s)

debriefed v ▷ debrief

debriefing v, n ▷ debrief

debriefings n ▷ debrief

debriefs v ▷ debrief

debris [deb-ree] n fragments of something destroyed

debs n ▷ deb

debt n (pl -s) something owed, esp. money

> **debtor** n (pl -s)

debtor n ▷ debt

debtors n ▷ debt

debts n ▷ debt

debunk v (-s, -ing, -ed) (Informal) expose the falseness of

debunked v ▷ debunk

debunking v ▷ debunk

debunks v ▷ debunk

debut [day-byoo] n (pl -s) first public appearance of a performer

debutante [day-byoo-tont] n (pl -s) young upper-class woman being formally presented to society

debutantes n ▷ debutante

debuts n ▷ debut

decade n (pl -s) period of ten years

decadence n (pl -s) deterioration in morality or culture > **decadent** adj > **decadently** adv

decadences n ▷ decadence

decadent adj ▷ decadence

decadently adv ▷ decadence

decades n ▷ decade

decaffeinated [dee-kaf-fin-ate-id] adj (of coffee, tea, or cola) with caffeine removed

decagon n (pl -s) geometric figure with ten faces > **decagonal** adj

decagonal adj ▷ decagon

decagons n ▷ decagon

decahedral adj ▷ decahedron

decahedron [deck-a-heed-ron] n (pl -s) solid figure with ten sides > **decahedral** adj
  decahedrons n ▷ decahedron

decamp v (-s, -ing, -ed) depart secretly or suddenly
  decamped v ▷ decamp
  decamping v ▷ decamp
  decamps v ▷ decamp

decant v (-s, -ing, -ed) pour (a liquid) from one container to another
  decanted v ▷ decant

decanter n (pl -s) stoppered bottle for wine or spirits
  decanters n ▷ decanter
  decanting v ▷ decant
  decants v ▷ decant

decapitate v (-tates, -tating, -tated) behead > **decapitation** n (pl -s)
  decapitated v ▷ decapitate
  decapitates v ▷ decapitate
  decapitating v ▷ decapitate
  decapitation n ▷ decapitate
  decapitations n ▷ decapitate
  decathlete n ▷ decathlon
  decathletes n ▷ decathlon

decathlon n (pl -s) athletic contest with ten events > **decathlete** n (pl -s)
  decathlons n ▷ decathlon

decay v (-s, -ing, -ed) become weaker or more corrupt ▶ n (pl -s) process of decaying
  decayed v ▷ decay
  decaying v ▷ decay
  decays v, n ▷ decay

decease n (pl -s) (Formal) death
  deceases n ▷ decease

deceased adj (Formal) dead

deceit n (pl -s) behaviour intended to deceive > **deceitful** adj > **deceitfully** adv
  deceitful adj ▷ deceit
  deceitfully adv ▷ deceit
  deceits n ▷ deceit

deceive v (-ceives, -ceiving, -ceived) mislead by lying > **deceiver** n (pl -s)
  deceived v ▷ deceive
  deceiver n ▷ deceive
  deceivers n ▷ deceive
  deceives v ▷ deceive
  deceiving v ▷ deceive

decelerate v (-rates, -rating, -rated) slow down > **deceleration** n (pl -s)
  decelerated v ▷ decelerate
  decelerates v ▷ decelerate
  decelerating v ▷ decelerate
  deceleration n ▷ decelerate
  decelerations n ▷ decelerate

  decencies n ▷ decent
  decency n ▷ decent

decent adj (-er, -est) (of a person) polite and morally acceptable > **decently** adv > **decency** n (pl -cies)
  decenter adj ▷ decent
  decentest adj ▷ decent
  decently adv ▷ decent

decentralization n ▷ decentralize

decentralize v (-lizes, -lizing, -lized) reorganize into smaller local units > **decentralization** n
  decentralized v ▷ decentralize
  decentralizes v ▷ decentralize
  decentralizing v ▷ decentralize

deception n (pl -s) deceiving
  deceptions n ▷ deception

deceptive adj likely or designed to deceive > **deceptively** adv > **deceptiveness** n
  deceptively adv ▷ deceptive
  deceptiveness n ▷ deceptive

decibel n (pl -s) unit for measuring the intensity of sound
  decibels n ▷ decibel

decide v (-cides, -ciding, -cided) (cause to) reach a decision

decided adj unmistakable ▶ v ▷ decide > **decidedly** adv
  decidedly adv ▷ decided
  decides v ▷ decide
  deciding v ▷ decide

deciduous adj (of a tree) shedding its leaves annually

decimal n (pl -s) fraction written in the form of a dot followed by one or more numbers ▶ adj relating to or using powers of ten > **decimalization** n > **decimally** adv
  decimalization n ▷ decimal
  decimally adv ▷ decimal
  decimals n ▷ decimal

decimate v (-mates, -mating, -mated) destroy or kill a large proportion of > **decimation** n (pl -s)
  decimated v ▷ decimate
  decimates v ▷ decimate
  decimating v ▷ decimate
  decimation n ▷ decimate
  decimations n ▷ decimate

decipher v (-s, -ing, -ed) work out the meaning of (something illegible or in code) > **decipherable** adj
  decipherable adj ▷ decipher
  deciphered v ▷ decipher
  deciphering v ▷ decipher
  deciphers v ▷ decipher

decision n (pl -s) judgment, conclusion, or resolution

decisions n ▷ decision

decisive adj having a definite influence > **decisively** adv > **decisiveness** n

decisively adv ▷ decisive

decisiveness n ▷ decisive

deck n (pl -s) area of a ship that forms a floor

decking n wooden platform in a garden

decks n ▷ deck

declaim v (-s, -ing, -ed) speak loudly and dramatically > **declamation** n (pl -s) > **declamatory** adj

declaimed v ▷ declaim

declaiming v ▷ declaim

declaims v ▷ declaim

declamation n ▷ declaim

declamations n ▷ declaim

declamatory adj ▷ declaim

declaration n ▷ declare

declarations n ▷ declare

declaratory adj ▷ declare

declare v (-clares, -claring, -clared) state firmly and forcefully > **declaration** n (pl -s) > **declaratory** adj

declared v ▷ declare

declares v ▷ declare

declaring v ▷ declare

declension n (pl -s) (GRAMMAR) changes in the form of nouns, pronouns, or adjectives to show case, number, and gender

declensions n ▷ declension

decline v (-clines, -clining, -clined) become smaller, weaker, or less important ▶ n (pl -s) gradual weakening or loss

declined v ▷ decline

declines v, n ▷ decline

declining v ▷ decline

declivities n ▷ declivity

declivity n (pl -ties) downward slope

declutch v (-es, -ing, -ed) disengage the clutch of a motor vehicle

declutched v ▷ declutch

declutches v ▷ declutch

declutching v ▷ declutch

decoct v (-s, -ing, -ed) extract the essence from (a substance) by boiling > **decoction** n (pl -s)

decocted v ▷ decoct

decocting v ▷ decoct

decoction n ▷ decoct

decoctions n ▷ decoct

decocts v ▷ decoct

decode v (-codes, -coding, -coded) convert from code into ordinary language > **decoder** n (pl -s)

decoded v ▷ decode

decoder n ▷ decode

decoders n ▷ decode

decodes v ▷ decode

decoding v ▷ decode

décolleté [day-kol-tay] adj (of a woman's garment) low-cut

decommission v (-s, -ing, -ed) dismantle (a nuclear reactor, weapon, etc.) which is no longer needed

decommissioned v ▷ decommission

decommissioning v ▷ decommission

decommissions v ▷ decommission

decompose v (-poses, -posing, -posed) be broken down through chemical or bacterial action > **decomposition** n (pl -s)

decomposed v ▷ decompose

decomposes v ▷ decompose

decomposing v ▷ decompose

decomposition n ▷ decompose

decompositions n ▷ decompose

decompress v (-presses, -pressing, -pressed) free from pressure > **decompression** n (pl -s)

decompressed v ▷ decompress

decompresses v ▷ decompress

decompressing v ▷ decompress

decompression n ▷ decompress

decompressions n ▷ decompress

decongestant n (pl -s) medicine that relieves nasal congestion

decongestants n ▷ decongestant

decontaminate v (-nates, -nating, -nated) make safe by removing poisons, radioactivity, etc. > **decontamination** n (pl -s)

decontaminated v ▷ decontaminate

decontaminates v ▷ decontaminate

decontaminating v ▷ decontaminate

decontamination n ▷ decontaminate

decontaminations n ▷ decontaminate

decor [day-core] n (pl -s) style in which a room or house is decorated

decorate v (-rates, -rating, -rated) make more attractive by adding something ornamental > **decoration** n (pl -s) > **decorative** adj > **decorator** n (pl -s)

decorated v ▷ decorate

decorates v ▷ decorate

decorating v ▷ decorate

decoration n ▷ decorate

decorations n ▷ decorate

decorator n ▷ decorate

decorators n ▷ decorate

decorous [dek-a-russ] adj polite, calm, and sensible in behaviour > **decorously** adv > **decorousness** n

decorously adv ▷ decorous

decorousness n ▷ decorous

decors n ▷ decor

decorum [dik-**core**-um] n (pl -s) polite and socially correct behaviour

decorums n ▷ decorum

decoy n (pl -s) person or thing used to lure someone into danger ▶ v (-s, -ing, -ed) lure away by means of a trick

decoyed v ▷ decoy

decoying v ▷ decoy

decoys n, v ▷ decoy

decrease v (-creases, -creasing, -creased) make or become less ▶ n (pl -s) lessening, reduction

decreased v ▷ decrease

decreases v, n ▷ decrease

decreasing v ▷ decrease

decree n (pl -s) law made by someone in authority ▶ v (-crees, -creeing, -creed) order by decree

decreed v ▷ decree

decreeing v ▷ decree

decrees n, v ▷ decree

decrepit adj weakened or worn out by age or long use ▷ **decrepitude** n (pl -s)

decrepitude n ▷ decrepit

decrepitudes n ▷ decrepit

decried v ▷ decry

decries v ▷ decry

decry v (-cries, -crying, -cried) express disapproval of

decrying v ▷ decry

dedicate v (-cates, -cating, -cated) commit (oneself or one's time) wholly to a special purpose or cause ▷ **dedication** n (pl -s)

dedicated adj devoted to a particular purpose or cause ▶ v ▷ dedicate

dedicates v ▷ dedicate

dedicating v ▷ dedicate

dedication n ▷ dedicate

dedications n ▷ dedicate

deduce v (-duces, -ducing, -duced) reach (a conclusion) by reasoning from evidence ▷ **deducible** adj

deduced v ▷ deduce

deduces v ▷ deduce

deducible adj ▷ deduce

deducing v ▷ deduce

deduct v (-s, -ing, -ed) subtract

deducted v ▷ deduct

deducting v ▷ deduct

deduction n (pl -s) deducting ▷ **deductive** adj

deductions n ▷ deduction

deductive adj ▷ deduction

deducts v ▷ deduct

deed n (pl -s) something that is done

deeds n ▷ deed

deem v (-s, -ing, -ed) consider, judge

deemed v ▷ deem

deeming v ▷ deem

deems v ▷ deem

deep adj (-er, -est) extending or situated far down, inwards, backwards, or sideways ▷ **deepen** v (-s, -ing, -ed)

deepen v ▷ deep

deepened v ▷ deep

deepening v ▷ deep

deepens v ▷ deep

deeper adj ▷ deep

deepest adj ▷ deep

deepfreeze n (pl -s) ▷ freezer

deepfreezes n ▷ deepfreeze

deeply adv profoundly or intensely

deer n (pl deer) large wild animal, the male of which has antlers

deerstalker n (pl -s) cloth hat with peaks at the back and front and earflaps

deerstalkers n ▷ deerstalker

deface v (-faces, -facing, -faced) deliberately spoil the appearance of ▷ **defacement** n (pl -s)

defaced v ▷ deface

defacement n ▷ deface

defacements n ▷ deface

defaces v ▷ deface

defacing v ▷ deface

defamation n ▷ defame

defamations n ▷ defame

defamatory adj ▷ defame

defame v (-fames, -faming, -famed) attack the good reputation of ▷ **defamation** n (pl -s) ▷ **defamatory** [dif-**fam**-a-tree] adj

defamed v ▷ defame

defames v ▷ defame

defaming v ▷ defame

default n (pl -s) failure to do something ▶ v (-s, -ing, -ed) fail to fulfil an obligation ▷ **defaulter** n (pl -s)

defaulted v ▷ default

defaulter n ▷ default

defaulters n ▷ default

defaulting v ▷ default

defaults n, v ▷ default

defeat v (-s, -ing, -ed) win a victory over ▶ n (pl -s) defeating

defeated v ▷ defeat

defeating v ▷ defeat

defeatism n ready acceptance or expectation of defeat ▷ **defeatist** adj, n (pl -s)

defeatist n, adj ▷ defeatism

defeatists n ▷ defeatism
defeats v, n ▷ defeat
defecate v (-cates, -cating, -cated) discharge waste from the body through the anus > **defecation** n (pl -s)
defecated v ▷ defecate
defecates v ▷ defecate
defecating v ▷ defecate
defecation n ▷ defecate
defecations n ▷ defecate
defect n (pl -s) imperfection, blemish ▶ v (-s, -ing, -ed) desert one's cause or country to join the opposing forces > **defection** n (pl -s) > **defector** n (pl -s)
defected v ▷ defect
defecting v ▷ defect
defection n ▷ defect
defections n ▷ defect
defective adj imperfect, faulty > **defectiveness** n
defectiveness n ▷ defective
defector n ▷ defect
defectors n ▷ defect
defects n, v ▷ defect
defence n (pl -s) resistance against attack > **defenceless** adj
defenceless adj ▷ defence
defences n ▷ defence
defend v (-s, -ing, -ed) protect from harm or danger
defendant n (pl -s) person accused of a crime
defendants n ▷ defendant
defended v ▷ defend
defender n (pl -s) person who supports someone or something in the face of criticism
defenders n ▷ defender
defending v ▷ defend
defends v ▷ defend
defensibilities n ▷ defensible
defensibility n ▷ defensible
defensible adj capable of being defended because believed to be right > **defensibility** n (pl -ities)
defensive adj intended for defence > **defensively** adv
defensively adv ▷ defensive
defer[1] v (-fers, -ferring, -ferred) delay (something) until a future time > **deferment**, **deferral** n (pl -s)
defer[2] v (-fers, -ferring, -ferred) (foll. by to) comply with the wishes (of)
deference n polite and respectful behaviour > **deferential** adj > **deferentially** adv
deferential adj ▷ deference

deferentially adv ▷ deference
deferment n ▷ defer[1]
deferments n ▷ defer[1]
deferral n ▷ defer[1]
deferrals n ▷ defer[1]
deferred v ▷ defer[1, 2]
deferring v ▷ defer[1, 2]
defers v ▷ defer[1, 2]
defiance n ▷ defy
defiances n ▷ defy
defiant adj ▷ defy
defiantly adv ▷ defy
deficiencies n ▷ deficiency
deficiency n (pl -cies) state of being deficient
deficient adj lacking some essential thing or quality > **deficiently** adv
deficiently adv ▷ deficient
deficit n (pl -s) amount by which a sum of money is too small
deficits n ▷ deficit
defied v ▷ defy
defies v ▷ defy
defile[1] v (-files, -filing, -filed) treat (something sacred or important) without respect > **defilement** n (pl -s)
defile[2] n (pl -s) narrow valley or pass
defiled v ▷ defile[1]
defilement n ▷ defile[1]
defilements n ▷ defile[1]
defiles v ▷ defile[1] ▶ n ▷ defile[1, 2]
defiling v ▷ defile[1]
definable adj ▷ define
define v (-fines, -fining, -fined) state precisely the meaning of > **definable** adj
defined v ▷ define
defines v ▷ define
defining v ▷ define
definite adj firm, clear, and precise > **definitely** adv
definitely adv ▷ definite
definition n (pl -s) statement of the meaning of a word or phrase
definitions n ▷ definition
definitive adj providing an unquestionable conclusion > **definitively** adv
definitively adv ▷ definitive
deflate v (-flates, -flating, -flated) (cause to) collapse through the release of air
deflated v ▷ deflate
deflates v ▷ deflate
deflating v ▷ deflate
deflation n (pl -s) (ECONOMICS) reduction in economic activity resulting in lower output and investment > **deflationary** adj
deflationary adj ▷ deflation

deflations n ▷ deflation
deflect v (-flects, -flecting, -flected) (cause to) turn aside from a course > **deflection** n (pl -s) > **deflector** n (pl -s)
  deflected v ▷ deflect
  deflecting v ▷ deflect
  deflection n ▷ deflect
  deflections n ▷ deflect
  deflector n ▷ deflect
  deflectors n ▷ deflect
  deflects v ▷ deflect
deflower v (-flowers, -flowering, -flowered) (Lit) deprive (a woman) of her virginity
  deflowered v ▷ deflower
  deflowering v ▷ deflower
  deflowers v ▷ deflower
  defoliant n ▷ defoliate
  defoliants n ▷ defoliate
defoliate v (-ates, -ating, -ated) deprive (a plant) of its leaves > **defoliant** n (pl -s) > **defoliation** n (pl -s)
  defoliated v ▷ defoliate
  defoliates v ▷ defoliate
  defoliating v ▷ defoliate
  defoliation n ▷ defoliate
  defoliations n ▷ defoliate
deforestation n (pl -s) destruction of all the trees in an area
  deforestations n ▷ deforestation
deform v (-s, -ing, -ed) put out of shape or spoil the appearance of > **deformation** n (pl -s) > **deformity** n (pl -ties)
  deformation n ▷ deform
  deformations n ▷ deform
  deformed v ▷ deform
  deforming v ▷ deform
  deformities n ▷ deform
  deformity n ▷ deform
  deforms v ▷ deform
defraud v (-s, -ing, -ed) cheat out of money, property, etc.
  defrauded v ▷ defraud
  defrauding v ▷ defraud
  defrauds v ▷ defraud
defray v (-s, -ing, -ed) provide money for (costs or expenses)
  defrayed v ▷ defray
  defraying v ▷ defray
  defrays v ▷ defray
defrock v (-s, -ing, -ed) deprive (a priest) of priestly status
  defrocked v ▷ defrock
  defrocking v ▷ defrock
  defrocks v ▷ defrock
defrost v (-s, -ing, -ed) make or become free of ice
  defrosted v ▷ defrost
  defrosting v ▷ defrost
  defrosts v ▷ defrost
deft adj quick and skilful in movement > **deftly** adv > **deftness** n (pl -es)
  deftly adv ▷ deft
  deftness n ▷ deft
  deftnesses n ▷ deft
defunct adj no longer existing or operative
defuse v (-fuses, -fusing, -fused) remove the fuse of (an explosive device)
  defused v ▷ defuse
  defuses v ▷ defuse
  defusing v ▷ defuse
defy v (-fies, -fying, -fied) resist openly and boldly > **defiance** n (pl -s) > **defiant** adj > **defiantly** adv
  defying v ▷ defy
  degeneracies n ▷ degeneracy
degeneracy n (pl -acies) degenerate behaviour
degenerate adj having deteriorated to a lower mental, moral, or physical level ▶ n (pl -s) degenerate person ▶ v (-ates, -ating, -ated) become degenerate > **degeneration** n (pl -s)
  degenerated v ▷ degenerate
  degenerates n, v ▷ degenerate
  degenerating v ▷ degenerate
  degeneration n ▷ degenerate
  degenerations n ▷ degenerate
  degradation n ▷ degrade
  degradations n ▷ degrade
degrade v (-grades, -grading, -graded) reduce to dishonour or disgrace (CHEM) > **degradation** n (pl -s)
  degraded v ▷ degrade
  degrades v ▷ degrade
  degrading v ▷ degrade
degree n (pl -s) stage in a scale of relative amount or intensity
  degrees n ▷ degree
  dehumanization n ▷ dehumanize
  dehumanizations n ▷ dehumanize
dehumanize v (-izes, -izing, -ized) deprive of human qualities > **dehumanization** n (pl -s)
  dehumanized v ▷ dehumanize
  dehumanizes v ▷ dehumanize
  dehumanizing v ▷ dehumanize
dehydrate v (-ates, -ating, -ated) remove water from (food) to preserve it > **dehydration** n (pl -s)
  dehydrated v ▷ dehydrate
  dehydrates v ▷ dehydrate
  dehydrating v ▷ dehydrate
  dehydration n ▷ dehydrate

dehydrations n ▷ dehydrate
deification n ▷ deify
deifications n ▷ deify
deified v ▷ deify
deifies v ▷ deify
deify [day-if-fie] v (-fies, -fying, -fied) treat or worship as a god > **deification** n (pl -s)
deifying v ▷ deify
deign [dane] v (-s, -ing, -ed) agree (to do something), but as if doing someone a favour
deigned v ▷ deign
deigning v ▷ deign
deigns v ▷ deign
deities n ▷ deity
deity [dee-it-ee, day-it-ee] n (pl -ties) god or goddess
dejected adj unhappy > **dejectedly** adv > **dejection** n (pl -s)
dejectedly adv ▷ dejected
dejection n ▷ dejected
dejections n ▷ dejected
dekko n (pl -s) (BRIT, AUST & NZ) (Slang) look
dekkos n ▷ dekko
delay v (-s, -ing, -ed) put off to a later time ▶ n (pl -s) act of delaying
delayed v ▷ delay
delaying v ▷ delay
delays v, n ▷ delay
delectable adj delightful, very attractive
delectation n (pl -s) (Formal) great pleasure
delectations n ▷ delectation
delegate n (pl -s) person chosen to represent others, esp. at a meeting ▶ v (-gates, -gating, -gated) entrust (duties or powers) to someone
delegated v ▷ delegate
delegates n, v ▷ delegate
delegating v ▷ delegate
delegation n (pl -s) group chosen to represent others
delegations n ▷ delegation
delete v (-letes, -leting, -leted) remove (something written or printed) > **deletion** n (pl -s)
deleted v ▷ delete
deleterious [del-lit-eer-ee-uss] adj harmful, injurious
deletes v ▷ delete
deleting v ▷ delete
deletion n ▷ delete
deletions n ▷ delete
deliberate adj planned in advance, intentional ▶ v (-ates, -ating, -ated) think something over > **deliberately** adv > **deliberation** n (pl -s) > **deliberative** adj

deliberated v ▷ deliberate
deliberately adv ▷ deliberate
deliberates v ▷ deliberate
deliberating v ▷ deliberate
deliberation n ▷ deliberate
deliberations n ▷ deliberate
deliberative adj ▷ deliberate
delicacies n ▷ delicacy
delicacy n (pl -cies) being delicate
delicate adj fine or subtle in quality or workmanship > **delicately** adv
delicately adv ▷ delicate
delicatessen n (pl -s) shop selling imported or unusual foods, often already cooked or prepared
delicatessens n ▷ delicatessen
delicious adj very appealing to taste or smell > **deliciously** adv > **deliciousness** n
deliciously adv ▷ delicious
deliciousness n ▷ delicious
delight n (pl -s) (source of) great pleasure ▶ v (-s, -ing, -ed) please greatly > **delightful** adj > **delightfully** adv
delighted v ▷ delight
delightful adj ▷ delight
delightfully adv ▷ delight
delighting v ▷ delight
delights n, v ▷ delight
delimit v (-s, -ing, -ed) mark or lay down the limits of > **delimitation** n (pl -s)
delimitation n ▷ delimit
delimitations n ▷ delimit
delimited v ▷ delimit
delimiting v ▷ delimit
delimits v ▷ delimit
delineate [dill-lin-ee-ate] v (-ates, -ating, -ated) show by drawing > **delineation** n (pl -s)
delineated v ▷ delineate
delineates v ▷ delineate
delineating v ▷ delineate
delineation n ▷ delineate
delineations n ▷ delineate
delinquencies n ▷ delinquent
delinquency n ▷ delinquent
delinquent n (pl -s) someone, esp. a young person, who repeatedly breaks the law ▶ adj repeatedly breaking the law > **delinquency** n (pl -cies)
delinquents n ▷ delinquent
delirious adj ▷ delirium
deliriously adv ▷ delirium
delirium n (pl -s) state of excitement and mental confusion, often with hallucinations > **delirious** adj > **deliriously** adv
deliriums n ▷ delirium

deliver v (-s, -ing, -ed) carry (goods etc.) to a destination

deliverance n (pl -s) rescue from captivity or evil

deliverances n ▷ deliverance

delivered v ▷ deliver

deliveries n ▷ delivery

delivering v ▷ deliver

delivers v ▷ deliver

delivery n (pl -eries) delivering

dell n (pl -s) (CHIEFLY BRIT) small wooded hollow

dells n ▷ dell

delphinium n (pl -s) large garden plant with blue flowers

delphiniums n ▷ delphinium

delta n (pl -s) fourth letter in the Greek alphabet

deltas n ▷ delta

delude v (-ludes, -luding, -luded) deceive

deluded v ▷ delude

deludes v ▷ delude

deluding v ▷ delude

deluge [del-lyooj] n (pl -s) great flood ▶ v (-luges, -luging, -luged) flood

deluged v ▷ deluge

deluges n, v ▷ deluge

deluging v ▷ deluge

delusion n (pl -s) mistaken idea or belief > **delusive** adj

delusions n ▷ delusion

delusive adj ▷ delusion

delve v (delves, delving, delved) research deeply (for information)

delved v ▷ delve

delves v ▷ delve

delving v ▷ delve

demagogic adj ▷ demagogue

demagogies v ▷ demagogue

demagogue n (pl -s) political agitator who appeals to the prejudice and passions of the mob > **demagogic** adj > **demagogy** n (pl -gies)

demagogues n ▷ demagogue

demagogy n ▷ demagogue

demand v (-s, -ing, -ed) request forcefully ▶ n (pl -s) forceful request

demanded v ▷ demand

demanding adj requiring a lot of time or effort ▶ v ▷ demand

demands v, n ▷ demand

demarcation n (pl -s) (Formal) establishing limits or boundaries, esp. between the work performed by different trade unions

demarcations n ▷ demarcation

demean v (-s, -ing, -ed) do something unworthy of one's status or character

demeaned v ▷ demean

demeaning v ▷ demean

demeanour n (pl -s) way a person behaves

demeanours n ▷ demeanour

demeans v ▷ demean

demented adj mad > **dementedly** adv

dementedly adv ▷ demented

dementia [dim-men-sha] n (pl -s) state of serious mental deterioration

dementias n ▷ dementia

demerit n (pl -s) fault, disadvantage

demerits n ▷ demerit

demesne [dim-mane] n (pl -s) land surrounding a house

demesnes n ▷ demesne

demijohn n (pl -s) large bottle with a short neck, often encased in wicker

demijohns n ▷ demijohn

demilitarization n ▷ demilitarize

demilitarizations n ▷ demilitarize

demilitarize v (-izes, -izing, -ized) remove the military forces from > **demilitarization** n (pl -s)

demilitarized v ▷ demilitarize

demilitarizes v ▷ demilitarize

demilitarizing v ▷ demilitarize

demimonde n (pl -s) (esp. in the 19th century) class of women considered to be outside respectable society because of promiscuity

demimondes n ▷ demimonde

demise n (pl -s) eventual failure (of something successful)

demises n ▷ demise

demo n (pl -s) (Informal) demonstration, organized expression of public opinion

demob v (-mobs, -mobbing, -mobbed) (BRIT, AUST & NZ) (Informal) demobilize

demobbed v ▷ demob

demobbing v ▷ demob

demobilization n ▷ demobilize

demobilizations n ▷ demobilize

demobilize v (-lizes, -lizing, -lized) release from the armed forces > **demobilization** n (pl -s)

demobilized v ▷ demobilize

demobilizes v ▷ demobilize

demobilizing v ▷ demobilize

demobs v ▷ demob

democracies n ▷ democracy

democracy n (pl -cies) government by the people or their elected representatives

democrat n (pl -s) advocate of democracy

democratic adj of democracy > **democratically** adv

democratically adv ▷ democratic

democrats n ▷ democrat
demographer n ▷ demography
demographers n ▷ demography
demographic adj ▷ demography
demographies n ▷ demography
demography n (pl -phies) study of population statistics, such as births and deaths > **demographer** n (pl -s) > **demographic** adj
demolish v (-es, -ing, -ed) knock down or destroy (a building) > **demolition** n (pl -s)
demolished v ▷ demolish
demolishes v ▷ demolish
demolishing v ▷ demolish
demolition n ▷ demolish
demolitions n ▷ demolish
demon n (pl -s) evil spirit
demoniac adj ▷ demonic
demoniacal adj ▷ demonic
demoniacally adv ▷ demonic
demonic adj evil > **demoniac, demoniacal** adj appearing to be possessed by a devil > **demoniacally** adv
demonologies n ▷ demonology
demonologist n ▷ demonology
demonologists n ▷ demonology
demonology n (pl -logies) study of demons > **demonologist** n (pl -s)
demons n ▷ demon
demonstrable adj able to be proved > **demonstrably** adv
demonstrably adv ▷ demonstrable
demonstrate v (-rates, -rating, -rated) show or prove by reasoning or evidence
demonstrated v ▷ demonstrate
demonstrates v ▷ demonstrate
demonstrating v ▷ demonstrate
demonstration n (pl -s) organized expression of public opinion
demonstrations n ▷ demonstration
demonstrative adj tending to show one's feelings unreservedly > **demonstratively** adv
demonstratively adv ▷ demonstrative
demonstrator n (pl -s) person who demonstrates how a device or machine works
demonstrators n ▷ demonstrator
demoralization n ▷ demoralize
demoralizations n ▷ demoralize
demoralize v (-lizes, -lizing, -lized) undermine the morale of > **demoralization** n (pl -s)
demoralized v ▷ demoralize
demoralizes v ▷ demoralize
demoralizing v ▷ demoralize
demos n ▷ demo
demote v (-motes, -moting, -moted) reduce in

status or rank > **demotion** n (pl -s)
demoted v ▷ demote
demotes v ▷ demote
demoting v ▷ demote
demotion n ▷ demote
demotions n ▷ demote
demur v (-murs, -murring, -murred) show reluctance
demure adj (-r, -st) quiet, reserved, and rather shy > **demurely** adv
demurely adv ▷ demure
demurer adj ▷ demure
demurest adj ▷ demure
demurred v ▷ demur
demurring v ▷ demur
demurs v ▷ demur
den n (pl -s) home of a wild animal
denationalization n ▷ denationalize
denationalizations n ▷ denationalize
denationalize v (-lizes, -lizing, -lized) transfer (an industry) from public to private ownership > **denationalization** n (pl -s)
denationalized v ▷ denationalize
denationalizes v ▷ denationalize
denationalizing v ▷ denationalize
denature v (-tures, -turing, -tured) change the nature of
denatured v ▷ denature
denatures v ▷ denature
denaturing v ▷ denature
deniable adj ▷ deny
deniably adv ▷ deny
denial n (pl -s) statement that something is not true
denials n ▷ denial
denied v ▷ deny
denier [den-yer] n (pl -s) unit of weight used to measure the fineness of nylon or silk
deniers n ▷ denier
denies v ▷ deny
denigrate v (-grates, -grating, -grated) criticize unfairly > **denigration** n (pl -s)
denigrated v ▷ denigrate
denigrates v ▷ denigrate
denigrating v ▷ denigrate
denigration n ▷ denigrate
denigrations n ▷ denigrate
denim n (pl -s) hard-wearing cotton fabric, usu. blue ▶ pl jeans made of denim
denims n ▷ denim
denizen n (pl -s) inhabitant
denizens n ▷ denizen
denominate v (-nates, -nating, -nated) give a specific name to
denominated v ▷ denominate

denominates v ▷ denominate

denominating v ▷ denominate

denomination n (pl -s) group having a distinctive interpretation of a religious faith > **denominational** adj

denominational adj ▷ denomination

denominations n ▷ denomination

denominator n (pl -s) number below the line in a fraction

denominators n ▷ denominator

denotation n ▷ denote

denotations n ▷ denote

denote v (-notes, -noting, -noted) be a sign of > **denotation** n (pl -s)

denoted v ▷ denote

denotes v ▷ denote

denoting v ▷ denote

denouement [day-noo-mon] n (pl -s) final outcome or solution in a play or book

denouements n ▷ denouement

denounce v (-ces, -cing, -ced) speak vehemently against

denounced v ▷ denounce

denounces v ▷ denounce

denouncing v ▷ denounce

dens n ▷ den

dense adj (-r, -st) closely packed > **densely** adv

densely adv ▷ dense

denser adj ▷ dense

densest adj ▷ dense

densities n ▷ density

density n (pl -ties) degree to which something is filled or occupied

dent n (pl -s) hollow in the surface of something, made by hitting it ▶ v (-s, -ing, -ed) make a dent in

dental adj of teeth or dentistry

dented v ▷ dent

dentine [den-teen] n (pl -s) hard dense tissue forming the bulk of a tooth

dentines n ▷ dentine

denting v ▷ dent

dentist n (pl -s) person qualified to practise dentistry

dentistries n ▷ dentistry

dentistry n (pl -ries) branch of medicine concerned with the teeth and gums

dentists n ▷ dentist

dents n, v ▷ dent

denture n (pl -s) false tooth

dentures n ▷ denture

denude v (-nudes, -nuding, -nuded) remove the covering or protection from

denuded v ▷ denude

denudes v ▷ denude

denuding v ▷ denude

denunciation n (pl -s) open condemnation

denunciations n ▷ denunciation

deny v (-nies, -nying, -nied) declare to be untrue > **deniable** adj > **deniably** adv

denying v ▷ deny

deodorant n (pl -s) substance applied to the body to mask the smell of perspiration

deodorants n ▷ deodorant

deodorize v (-izes, -izing, -ized) remove or disguise the smell of

deodorized v ▷ deodorize

deodorizes v ▷ deodorize

deodorizing v ▷ deodorize

depart v (-s, -ing, -ed) leave > **departed** > **departure** n (pl -s)

departed adj (Euphemistic) dead ▶ v ▷ depart

departing v ▷ depart

department n (pl -s) specialized division of a large organization > **departmental** adj

departmental adj ▷ department

departments n ▷ department

departs v ▷ depart

departure n ▷ depart

departures n ▷ depart

depend v (-s, -ing, -ed) (foll. by on) put trust (in) > **dependable** adj > **dependably** adv > **dependability** n (pl -ities)

dependabilities n ▷ depend

dependability n ▷ depend

dependable adj ▷ depend

dependably adv ▷ depend

dependant n (pl -s) person who depends on another for financial support

dependants n ▷ dependant

depended v ▷ depend

dependence n (pl -s) state of being dependent

dependences n ▷ dependence

dependencies n ▷ dependency

dependency n (pl -cies) country controlled by another country

dependent adj depending on someone or something > **dependently** adv

dependently adv ▷ dependent

depending v ▷ depend

depends v ▷ depend

depict v (-s, -ing, -ed) produce a picture of > **depiction** n (pl -s)

depicted v ▷ depict

depicting v ▷ depict

depiction n ▷ depict

depictions n ▷ depict

depicts v ▷ depict

depilatories n ▷ depilatory

depilatory [dip-pill-a-tree] n (pl -tories) ▶ adj

(substance) designed to remove unwanted hair

deplete v (-letes, -leting, -leted) use up
> **depletion** n (pl -s)
depleted v ▷ deplete
depletes v ▷ deplete
depleting v ▷ deplete
depletion n ▷ deplete
depletions n ▷ deplete

deplorable adj very bad or unpleasant
> **deplorably** adv
deplorably adv ▷ deplorable

deplore v (-lores, -loring, -lored) condemn strongly
deplored v ▷ deplore
deplores v ▷ deplore
deploring v ▷ deplore

deploy v (-s, -ing, -ed) organize (troops or resources) into a position ready for immediate action > **deployment** n (pl -s)
deployed v ▷ deploy
deploying v ▷ deploy
deployment n ▷ deploy
deployments n ▷ deploy
deploys v ▷ deploy

depopulate v (-lates, -lating, -lated) reduce the population of > **depopulation** n (pl -s)
depopulated v ▷ depopulate
depopulates v ▷ depopulate
depopulating v ▷ depopulate
depopulation n ▷ depopulate
depopulations n ▷ depopulate

deport v (-s, -ing, -ed) remove forcibly from a country > **deportation** n (pl -s) > **deportee** n (pl -s)
deportation n ▷ deport
deportations n ▷ deport
deported v ▷ deport
deportee n ▷ deport
deportees n ▷ deport
deporting v ▷ deport

deportment n (pl -s) way in which a person moves or stands
deportments n ▷ deportment
deports v ▷ deport

depose v (-poses, -posing, -posed) remove from an office or position of power
deposed v ▷ depose
deposes v ▷ depose
deposing v ▷ depose

deposit v (-s, -ing, -ed) put down ▶ n (pl -s) sum of money paid into a bank account
> **depositor** n (pl -s)
depositaries n ▷ depositary

depositary n (pl -aries) person to whom

something is entrusted for safety
deposited v ▷ deposit
depositing v ▷ deposit

deposition n (pl -s) (LAW) sworn statement of a witness used in court in his or her absence
depositions n ▷ deposition
depositor n ▷ deposit
depositories n ▷ deposit
depositors n ▷ deposit

depository n (pl -ories) store for furniture etc.
deposits v, n ▷ deposit

depot [dep-oh] n (pl -s) building where goods or vehicles are kept when not in use
depots n ▷ depot

depraved adj morally bad > **depravity** n (pl -ities)
depravities n ▷ depraved
depravity n ▷ depraved

deprecate v (-cates, -cating, -cated) express disapproval of > **deprecation** n (pl -s)
> **deprecatory** adj
deprecated v ▷ deprecate
deprecates v ▷ deprecate
deprecating v ▷ deprecate
deprecation n ▷ deprecate
deprecations n ▷ deprecate
deprecatory adj ▷ deprecate

depreciate v (-ates, -ating, -ated) decline in value or price > **depreciation** n (pl -s)
depreciated v ▷ depreciate
depreciates v ▷ depreciate
depreciating v ▷ depreciate
depreciation n ▷ depreciate
depreciations n ▷ depreciate

depredation n (pl -s) plundering
depredations n ▷ depredation

depress v (-es, -ing, -ed) make sad
> **depressing** adj > **depressingly** adv

depressant n (pl -s) ▶ adj (drug) able to reduce nervous activity
depressants n ▷ depressant
depressed v ▷ depress
depresses v ▷ depress
depressing v, adj ▷ depress
depressingly adv ▷ depress

depression n (pl -s) mental state in which a person has feelings of gloom and inadequacy
depressions n ▷ depression

depressive adj tending to cause depression
▶ n (pl -s) person who suffers from depression
> **depressively** adv
depressively adv ▷ depressive
depressives n ▷ depressive
deprivation n ▷ deprive
deprivations n ▷ deprive

deprive v (-rives, -riving, -rived) (foll. by of) prevent from (having or enjoying) > **deprivation** n (pl -s)

deprived adj lacking adequate living conditions, education, etc. ▶ v ▷ deprive

deprives v ▷ deprive

depriving v ▷ deprive

depth n (pl -s) distance downwards, backwards, or inwards

depths n ▷ depth

deputation n (pl -s) body of people appointed to represent others

deputations n ▷ deputation

depute v (-putes, -puting, -puted) appoint (someone) to act on one's behalf

deputed v ▷ depute

deputes v ▷ depute

deputies n ▷ deputy

deputing v ▷ depute

deputize v (-izes, -izing, -ized) act as deputy

deputized v ▷ deputize

deputizes v ▷ deputize

deputizing v ▷ deputize

deputy n (pl -ties) person appointed to act on behalf of another

derail v (-s, -ing, -ed) cause (a train) to go off the rails > **derailment** n (pl -s)

derailed v ▷ derail

derailing v ▷ derail

derailment n ▷ derail

derailments n ▷ derail

derails v ▷ derail

deranged adj insane or uncontrolled > **derangement** n (pl -s)

derangement n ▷ derange

derangements n ▷ derange

derbies n ▷ derby

derby [dah-bee] n (pl -bies) sporting event between teams from the same area ▶ n any of various horse races

deregulate v (-ates, -ating, -ated) remove regulations or controls from > **deregulation** n (pl -s)

deregulated v ▷ deregulate

deregulates v ▷ deregulate

deregulating v ▷ deregulate

deregulation n ▷ deregulate

deregulations n ▷ deregulate

derelict adj unused and falling into ruins ▶ n (pl -s) social outcast, vagrant

dereliction n (pl -s) state of being abandoned

derelictions n ▷ dereliction

derelicts n ▷ derelict

deride v (-rides, -riding, -rided) treat with contempt or ridicule > **derision** n (pl -s)

derided v ▷ deride

derides v ▷ deride

deriding v ▷ deride

derision n ▷ deride

derisions n ▷ deride

derisive adj mocking, scornful > **derisively** adv > **derisiveness** n

derisively adv ▷ derisive

derisiveness n ▷ derisive

derisory adj too small or inadequate to be considered seriously

derivation n ▷ derive

derivations n ▷ derive

derivative adj word, idea, etc., derived from another > **derivatively** adv

derivatively adv ▷ derivative

derive v (-rives, -riving, -rived) (foll. by from) take or develop (from) > **derivation** n (pl -s)

derived v ▷ derive

derives v ▷ derive

deriving v ▷ derive

dermatitis n inflammation of the skin

dermatologies n ▷ dermatology

dermatologist n ▷ dermatology

dermatologists n ▷ dermatology

dermatology n (pl -ogies) branch of medicine concerned with the skin > **dermatologist** n (pl -s)

derogatorily adv ▷ derogatory

derogatory [dir-rog-a-tree] adj intentionally offensive > **derogatorily** adv

derrick n (pl -s) simple crane

derricks n ▷ derrick

derv n (pl -s) (BRIT) diesel oil, when used for road transport

dervish n (pl -es) member of a Muslim religious order noted for a frenzied whirling dance

dervishes n ▷ dervish

dervs n ▷ derv

descant n (pl -s) (MUSIC) tune played or sung above a basic melody

descants n ▷ descant

descend v (-s, -ing, -ed) move down (a slope etc.)

descendant n (pl -s) person or animal descended from an individual, race, or species

descendants n ▷ descendant

descended v ▷ descend

descendent adj descending

descending v ▷ descend

descends v ▷ descend

descent n (pl -s) descending

descents v ▷ descent

describe v (-ribes, -ribing, -ribed) give an account of (something or someone) in words
described v ▷ describe
describes v ▷ describe
describing v ▷ describe
descried v ▷ descry
descries v ▷ descry
description n (pl -s) statement that describes something or someone > **descriptive** adj > **descriptively** adv > **descriptiveness** n
descriptions n ▷ description
descriptive adj ▷ description
descriptively adv ▷ description
descriptiveness n ▷ description
descry v (-scries, -scrying, -scried) catch sight of
descrying v ▷ descry
desecrate v (-rates, -rating, -rated) damage or insult (something sacred) > **desecration** n (pl -s)
desecrated v ▷ desecrate
desecrates v ▷ desecrate
desecrating v ▷ desecrate
desecration n ▷ desecrate
desecrations n ▷ desecrate
desegregate v (-gates, -gating, -gated) end racial segregation in > **desegregation** n (pl -s)
desegregated v ▷ desegregate
desegregates v ▷ desegregate
desegregating v ▷ desegregate
desegregation n ▷ desegregate
desegregations n ▷ desegregate
deselect v (-s, -ing, -ed) (BRIT) (POLITICS) refuse to select (an MP) for re-election > **deselection** n (pl -s)
deselected v ▷ deselect
deselecting v ▷ deselect
deselection n ▷ deselect
deselections n ▷ deselect
deselects v ▷ deselect
desert[1] n (pl -s) region with little or no vegetation because of low rainfall
desert[2] v (-s, -ing, -ed) abandon (a person or place) without intending to return > **deserter** n (pl -s) > **desertion** n (pl -s)
deserted v ▷ desert[2]
deserter n ▷ desert[2]
deserters n ▷ desert[2]
deserting v ▷ desert[2]
desertion n ▷ desert[2]
desertions n ▷ desert[2]
deserts n ▷ desert[1] ▶ pl n the punishment one deserves ▶ v ▷ desert[2]
deserve v (-serves, -serving, -served) be entitled to or worthy of

deserved adj rightfully earned ▶ v ▷ deserve > **deservedly** adv
deservedly adv ▷ deserved
deserves v ▷ deserve
deserving adj worthy of help, praise, or reward ▶ v ▷ deserve
deshabille [day-zab-**beel**] n (pl -s) state of being partly dressed
deshabilles n ▷ deshabille
desiccate v (-siccates, -siccating, -siccated) remove most of the water from > **desiccation** n (pl -s)
desiccated v ▷ desiccate
desiccates v ▷ desiccate
desiccating v ▷ desiccate
desiccation n ▷ desiccate
desiccations n ▷ desiccate
design v (-s, -ing, -ed) work out the structure or form of (something), by making a sketch or plans ▶ n (pl -s) preliminary drawing
designate [**dez**-zig-nate] v (-nates, -nating, -nated) give a name to ▶ adj appointed but not yet in office
designated v ▷ designate
designates v ▷ designate
designating v ▷ designate
designation n (pl -s) name
designations n ▷ designation
designed v ▷ design
designedly [dee-zine-id-lee] adv intentionally
designer n (pl -s) person who draws up original sketches or plans from which things are made ▶ adj designed by a well-known designer
designers n ▷ designer
designing adj cunning and scheming ▶ v ▷ design
designs v, n ▷ design
desirabilities n ▷ desirable
desirability n ▷ desirable
desirable adj worth having > **desirability** n (pl -ities) > **desirably** adv
desirably adv ▷ desirable
desire v (-sires, -siring, -sired) want very much ▶ n (pl -s) wish, longing
desired v ▷ desire
desires v, n ▷ desire
desiring v ▷ desire
desist v (-s, -ing, -ed) (foll. by **from**) stop (doing something)
desisted v ▷ desist
desisting v ▷ desist
desists v ▷ desist
desk n (pl -s) piece of furniture with a writing surface and drawers

desks *n* ▷ desk

desktop *adj* (of a computer) small enough to use at a desk

desolate *adj* uninhabited and bleak ▶ *v* (-lates, -lating, -lated) deprive of inhabitants > **desolately** *adv* > **desolateness** *n* > **desolation** *n* (*pl* -s)

desolated *v* ▷ desolate

desolately *adv* ▷ desolate

desolateness *n* ▷ desolate

desolates *v* ▷ desolate

desolating *v* ▷ desolate

desolation *n* ▷ desolate

desolations *n* ▷ desolate

despair *n* (*pl* -s) total loss of hope ▶ *v* (-s, -ing, -ed) lose hope > **despairingly** *adv*

despaired *v* ▷ despair

despairing *v* ▷ despair

despairingly *adv* ▷ despair

despairs *n*, *v* ▷ despair

despatch *v* (-es, -ing, -ed) ▶ *n* (*pl* -es) ▷ dispatch

despatched *v* ▷ despatch

despatches *v*, *n* ▷ despatch

despatching *v* ▷ despatch

desperado *n* (*pl* -does, -dos) reckless person ready to commit any violent illegal act

desperadoes *v* ▷ desperado

desperados *v* ▷ desperado

desperate *adj* in despair and reckless > **desperately** *adv* > **desperateness** *n* > **desperation** *n* (*pl* -s)

desperately *adv* ▷ desperate

desperateness *n* ▷ desperate

desperation *n* ▷ desperate

desperations *n* ▷ desperate

despicable *adj* deserving contempt > **despicably** *adv*

despicably *adv* ▷ despicable

despise *v* (-pises, -pising, -pised) regard with contempt

despised *v* ▷ despise

despises *v* ▷ despise

despising *v* ▷ despise

despite *prep* in spite of

despoil *v* (-s, -ing, -ed) (*Formal*) plunder > **despoliation** *n* (*pl* -s)

despoiled *v* ▷ despoil

despoiling *v* ▷ despoil

despoils *v* ▷ despoil

despoliation *n* ▷ despoil

despoliations *n* ▷ despoil

despondencies *n* ▷ despondent

despondency *n* ▷ despondent

despondent *adj* unhappy > **despondently** *adv* > **despondency** *n* (*pl* -cies)

despondently *adv* ▷ despondent

despot *n* (*pl* -s) person in power who acts unfairly or cruelly > **despotic** *adj* > **despotically** *adv*

despotic *adj* ▷ despot

despotically *adv* ▷ despot

despotism *n* (*pl* -s) unfair or cruel government or behaviour

despotisms *n* ▷ despotism

despots *n* ▷ despot

dessert *n* (*pl* -s) sweet course served at the end of a meal

desserts *n* ▷ dessert

dessertspoon *n* (*pl* -s) spoon between a tablespoon and a teaspoon in size

dessertspoons *n* ▷ dessertspoon

destination *n* (*pl* -s) place to which someone or something is going

destinations *n* ▷ destination

destined *adj* certain to be or to do something

destinies *n* ▷ destiny

destiny *n* (*pl* -nies) future marked out for a person or thing

destitute *adj* having no money or possessions > **destitution** *n*

destitution *n* ▷ destitute

destroy *v* (-s, -ing, -ed) ruin, demolish

destroyed *v* ▷ destroy

destroyer *n* (*pl* -s) small heavily armed warship

destroyers *n* ▷ destroyer

destroying *v* ▷ destroy

destroys *v* ▷ destroy

destruction *n* (*pl* -s) destroying

destructions *n* ▷ destruction

destructive *adj* (capable of) causing destruction > **destructively** *adv* > **destructiveness** *n*

destructively *adv* ▷ destructive

destructiveness *n* ▷ destructive

desuetude [diss-syoo-it-tude] *n* (*pl* -s) condition of not being in use

desuetudes *n* ▷ desuetude

desultorily *adv* ▷ desultory

desultoriness *n* ▷ desultory

desultory [dez-zl-tree] *adj* jumping from one thing to another, disconnected > **desultorily** *adv* > **desultoriness** *n*

detach *v* (-es, -ing, -ed) disengage and separate > **detachable** *adj*

detachable *adj* ▷ detach

detached *adj* (BRIT, AUST & S AFR) (of a house) not joined to another house ▶ *v* ▷ detach

detaches *v* ▷ detach

detaching *v* ▷ detach

detachment *n* (*pl* -s) lack of emotional

involvement

detachments n ▷ detachment

detail n (pl -s) individual piece of information ▶ v (-s, -ing, -ed) list fully

detailed v ▷ detail

detailing v ▷ detail

details n, v ▷ detail

detain v (-s, -ing, -ed) delay (someone) > **detainee** n (pl -s)

detained v ▷ detain

detainee n ▷ detain

detainees n ▷ detain

detaining v ▷ detain

detains v ▷ detain

detect v (-s, -ing, -ed) notice > **detectable** adj > **detection** n (pl -s)

detectable adj ▷ detect

detected v ▷ detect

detecting v ▷ detect

detection n ▷ detect

detections n ▷ detect

detective n (pl -s) policeman or private agent who investigates crime

detectives n ▷ detective

detector n (pl -s) instrument used to find something

detectors n ▷ detector

detects v ▷ detect

detente [day-tont] n (pl -s) easing of tension between nations

detentes n ▷ detente

detention n (pl -s) imprisonment

detentions n ▷ detention

deter v (-ters, -terring, -terred) discourage (someone) from doing something by instilling fear or doubt

detergent n (pl -s) chemical substance for washing clothes or dishes

detergents n ▷ detergent

deteriorate v (-rates, -rating, -rated) become worse > **deterioration** n (pl -s)

deteriorated v ▷ deteriorate

deteriorates v ▷ deteriorate

deteriorating v ▷ deteriorate

deterioration n ▷ deteriorate

deteriorations n ▷ deteriorate

determinant n (pl -s) factor that determines

determinants n ▷ determinant

determinate adj definitely limited or fixed > **determinateness** n

determinateness n ▷ determinate

determination n (pl -s) being determined or resolute

determinations n ▷ determination

determine v (-mines, -mining, -mined) settle (an argument or a question) conclusively

determined adj firmly decided, unable to be dissuaded ▶ v ▷ determine > **determinedly** adv

determiner n (pl -s) (GRAMMAR) word that determines the object to which a noun phrase refers

determiners n ▷ determiner

determines v ▷ determine

determining v ▷ determine

determinism n theory that human choice is not free, but decided by past events > **determinist** n (pl -s) adj

determinist n ▷ determinism

determinists n ▷ determinism

deterred v ▷ deter

deterrent n (pl -s) something that deters ▶ adj tending to deter

deterrents n ▷ deterrent

deterring v ▷ deter

deters v ▷ deter

detest v (-s, -ing, -ed) dislike intensely > **detestable** adj > **detestably** adv > **detestation** n (pl -s)

detestable adj ▷ detest

detestably adv ▷ detest

detestation n ▷ detest

detestations n ▷ detest

detested v ▷ detest

detesting v ▷ detest

detests v ▷ detest

dethrone v (-rones, -roning, -roned) remove from a throne or position of power

dethroned v ▷ dethrone

dethrones v ▷ dethrone

dethroning v ▷ dethrone

detonate v (-nates, -nating, -nated) explode > **detonation** n (pl -s)

detonated v ▷ detonate

detonates v ▷ detonate

detonating v ▷ detonate

detonation n ▷ detonate

detonations n ▷ detonate

detonator n (pl -s) small amount of explosive, or a device, used to set off an explosion

detonators n ▷ detonator

detour n (pl -s) route that is not the most direct one

detours n ▷ detour

detract v (-s, -ing, -ed) (foll. by from) make (something) seem less good > **detractor** n (pl -s)

detracted v ▷ detract

detracting v ▷ detract

detractor n ▷ detract

detractors n ▷ detract
detracts v ▷ detract
detriment n (pl -s) disadvantage or damage
> **detrimental** adj > **detrimentally** adv
detrimental adj ▷ detract
detrimentally adv ▷ detract
detriments n ▷ detract
detritus [dit-**trite**-uss] n loose mass of stones
and silt worn away from rocks
deuce [**dyewss**] n (pl -s) (TENNIS) score of forty all
deuces n ▷ deuce

> **deus** n (**di**). Deus is a Latin word for a
> god. Its plural, di, is a very handy word
> to know when trying to form several
> words at once. Di scores 3 points.

deuterium n (pl -s) isotope of hydrogen twice
as heavy as the normal atom
deuteriums n ▷ deuterium

> **dev** n (**devs**). A dev is a Hindu god. Dev
> scores 7 points.

devaluation n ▷ devalue
devaluations n ▷ devalue
devalue v (-lues, -luing, -lued) reduce the
exchange value of (a currency) > **devaluation**
n (pl -s)
devalued v ▷ devalue
devalues v ▷ devalue
devaluing v ▷ devalue
devastate v (-tates, -tating, -tated) destroy
> **devastation** n (pl -s)
devastated adj shocked and extremely upset
▶ v ▷ devastate
devastates v ▷ devastate
devastating v ▷ devastate
devastation n ▷ devastate
devastations n ▷ devastate
develop v (-s, -ing, -ed) grow or bring to a later,
more elaborate, or more advanced stage
> **development** n (pl -s)
developed v ▷ develop
developer n (pl -s) person who develops
property
developers n ▷ developer
developing v ▷ develop
development n ▷ develop
developments n ▷ develop
develops v ▷ develop
deviance n ▷ deviant
deviances n ▷ deviant
deviant n (pl -s) ▶ adj (person) deviating from
what is considered acceptable behaviour
> **deviance** n (pl -s)
deviants n ▷ deviant
deviate v (-ates, -ating, -ated) differ from
others in belief or thought > **deviation** n (pl -s)

deviated v ▷ deviate
deviates v ▷ deviate
deviating v ▷ deviate
deviation n ▷ deviate
deviations n ▷ deviate
device n (pl -s) machine or tool used for a
specific task
devices n ▷ device
devil n (pl -s) evil spirit (Informal) ▶ v (-ils, -illing,
-illed) prepare (food) with a highly flavoured
spiced mixture
devilish adj cruel or unpleasant ▶ adv (also
devilishly) (Informal) extremely
devilishly adv ▷ devilish
devilled v ▷ devil
devilling v ▷ devil
devil-may-care adj carefree and cheerful
devilment n (pl -s) mischievous conduct
devilments n ▷ devilment
devilries n ▷ devilry
devilry n (pl -ries) mischievousness
devils n, v ▷ devil
devious adj insincere and dishonest
> **deviously** adv > **deviousness** n
deviously adv ▷ devious
deviousness n ▷ devious
devise v (-vises, -vising, -vised) work out
(something) in one's mind
devised v ▷ devise
devises v ▷ devise
devising v ▷ devise
devoid adj (foll. by **of**) completely lacking (in)
devolution n (pl -s) transfer of authority from a
central government to regional governments
devolutions n ▷ devolution
devolve v (-volves, -volving, -volved) (foll.
by **on** or **to**) pass (power or duties) or (of
power or duties) be passed to a successor or
substitute
devolved v ▷ devolve
devolves v ▷ devolve
devolving v ▷ devolve
devote v (-votes, -voting, -voted) apply or
dedicate to a particular purpose
devoted adj showing loyalty or devotion ▶ v
▷ devote > **devotedly** adv
devotedly adv ▷ devoted
devotee n (pl -s) person who is very
enthusiastic about something
devotees n ▷ devotee
devotes v ▷ devote
devoting v ▷ devote
devotion n (pl -s) strong affection for or
loyalty to someone or something ▶ pl prayers
> **devotional** adj

devotional adj ▷ devotion
devotions adj ▷ devotion
devour v (-s, -ing, -ed) eat greedily
devoured v ▷ devour
devouring v ▷ devour
devours v ▷ devour
devout adj deeply religious > **devoutly** adv
> **devoutness** n
devoutly adv ▷ devout
devoutness n ▷ devout
dew n (pl -s) drops of water that form on the
ground at night from vapour in the air > **dewy**
adj (-wier, -wiest)
dewier adj ▷ dew
dewiest adj ▷ dew
dewlap n (pl -s) loose fold of skin hanging
under the throat in dogs, cattle, etc.
dewlaps n ▷ dewlap
dews n ▷ dew
dewy adj ▷ dew

dex n (**dexes**). Dex is a slang word for a
kind of amphetamine. This is an easy
way to pick up a some points after
another player has used an X. Dex
scores 11 points.

dexterities n ▷ dexterity
dexterity n (pl -ities) skill in using one's hands
> **dexterous** adj > **dexterously** adv
dexterous adj ▷ dexterity
dexterously adv ▷ dexterity
dextrose n (pl -s) glucose occurring in fruit,
honey, and the blood of animals
dextroses n ▷ dextrose

dey n (**deys**). A dey is an Ottoman
governor. Dey scores 7 points.

diabetes [die-a-beet-eez] n disorder in which
an abnormal amount of urine containing
an excess of sugar is excreted > **diabetic** n
(pl -s) adj
diabetic n ▷ diabetes
diabetics n ▷ diabetes
diabolic adj of the Devil
diabolical adj (Informal) extremely bad
> **diabolically** adv > **diabolicalness** n
diabolically adv ▷ diabolical
diabolicalness n ▷ diabolical
diabolism n witchcraft, devil worship
> **diabolist** n (pl -s)
diabolist n ▷ diabolism
diabolists n ▷ diabolism
diaconate n (pl -s) position or period of office
of a deacon
diaconates n ▷ diaconate
diacritic n (pl -s) sign above or below a
character to indicate phonetic value or stress

diacritics n ▷ diacritic
diadem n (pl -s) (Old-fashioned) crown
diadems n ▷ diadem
diaereses n ▷ diaeresis
diaeresis n (pl -ses) mark (¨) placed over
a vowel to show that it is pronounced
separately from the preceding one, for
example in Noël
diagnosed v ▷ diagnosis
diagnoses n, v ▷ diagnosis
diagnosing v ▷ diagnosis
diagnosis [die-ag-no-siss] n (pl -ses) [-seez]
discovery and identification of diseases from
the examination of symptoms > **diagnose** v
(-noses, -nosing, -nosed) > **diagnostic** adj
diagnostic adj ▷ diagnosis
diagonal adj from corner to corner ▶ n (pl -s)
diagonal line > **diagonally** adv
diagonally adv ▷ diagonal
diagonals n ▷ diagonal
diagram n (pl -s) sketch showing the form or
workings of something > **diagrammatic** adj
diagrammatic adj ▷ diagram
diagrams n ▷ diagram
dial n (pl -s) face of a clock or watch ▶ v (dials,
dialling, dialled) operate the dial or buttons
on a telephone in order to contact (a number)
dialect n (pl -s) form of a language spoken in
a particular area > **dialectal** adj > **dialectally** adv
dialectal adj ▷ dialect
dialectally adv ▷ dialect
dialectic n (pl -s) logical debate by question
and answer to resolve differences between
two views > **dialectical** adj > **dialectically** adv
dialectical adj ▷ dialectic
dialectically adv ▷ dialectic
dialectics n ▷ dialectic
dialects n ▷ dialect
dialled v ▷ dial
dialling v ▷ dial
dialogue n (pl -s) conversation between two
people, esp. in a book, film, or play
dialogues n ▷ dialogue
dials n, v ▷ dial
dialyses ▷ dialysis
dialysis [die-al-iss-iss] n (pl -ses) (MED) filtering
of blood through a membrane to remove
waste products
diamanté [die-a-man-tee] adj decorated with
artificial jewels or sequins
diameter n (pl -s) (length of) a straight line
through the centre of a circle or sphere
diameters n ▷ diameter
diametric, diametrical adj of a diameter

> **diametrically** adv
diametrical adj ▷ diametric
diametrically adv ▷ diametric
diamond n (pl -s) exceptionally hard, usu. colourless, precious stone
　diamonds n ▷ diamond
diaper n (pl -s) (us) nappy
　diapers n ▷ diaper
diaphanous [die-**af**-fan-ous] adj fine and almost transparent > **diaphanously** adv
　diaphanously adv ▷ diaphanous
diaphragm [die-**a**-fram] n (pl -s) muscular partition that separates the abdominal cavity and chest cavity
　diaphragms n ▷ diaphragm
　diaries n ▷ diary
　diarist n ▷ diary
　diarists n ▷ diary
diarrhoea [die-a-**ree**-a] n (pl -s) frequent discharge of abnormally liquid faeces
　diarrhoeas n ▷ diarrhoea
diary n (pl -ries) (book for) a record of daily events, appointments, or observations
> **diarist** n (pl -s)
diatribe n (pl -s) bitter critical attack
　diatribes n ▷ diatribe
dibble n (pl -s) small hand tool used to make holes in the ground for seeds or plants
　dibbles n ▷ dibble
dice n (pl dice) small cube each of whose sides has a different number of spots (1 to 6), used in games of chance ▶ v (dices, dicing, diced) cut (food) into small cubes
　diced v ▷ dice
　dices v ▷ dice
dicey adj (dicier, diciest) (Informal) dangerous or risky
　dichotomies n ▷ dichotomy
dichotomy [die-**kot**-a-mee] n (pl -mies) division into two opposed groups or parts
　dicier adj ▷ dice
　diciest adj ▷ dice
　dicing v ▷ dice
　dickier adj ▷ dicky²
　dickies n ▷ dicky¹
　dickiest adj ▷ dicky²
dicky¹ n (pl dickies) false shirt front
dicky² adj (dickier, dickiest) (Informal) shaky or weak
dickybird n (pl -s) child's word for a bird
　dickybirds n ▷ dickybird
　dicta n ▷ dictum
dictate v (-tes, -ting, -ted) say aloud for someone else to write down (foll. by to) ▶ n (pl -s) authoritative command > **dictation**

n (pl -s)
　dictated v ▷ dictate
　dictates v, n ▷ dictate
　dictating v ▷ dictate
　dictation n ▷ dictate
　dictations n ▷ dictate
dictator n (pl -s) ruler who has complete power
> **dictatorship** n (pl -s)
dictatorial adj like a dictator > **dictatorially** adv
　dictatorially adv ▷ dictatorial
　dictators n ▷ dictator
　dictatorship n ▷ dictator
　dictatorships n ▷ dictator
diction n (pl -s) manner of pronouncing words and sounds
　dictionaries n ▷ dictionary
dictionary n (pl -aries) book consisting of an alphabetical list of words with their meanings
　dictions n ▷ diction
dictum n (pl -tums, -ta) formal statement
　dictums n ▷ dictum
　did v ▷ do
didactic adj intended to instruct > **didactically** adv
　didactically adv ▷ didactic
diddle v (-dles, -dling, -dled) (Informal) swindle
　diddled v ▷ diddle
　diddles v ▷ diddle
　diddling v ▷ diddle
didgeridoo n (pl -s) Australian musical instrument made from a long hollow piece of wood
　didgeridoos n ▷ didgeridoo
　didn't did not
die¹ v (dies, dying, died) (of a person, animal, or plant) cease all biological activity permanently
die² n (pl -s) shaped block used to cut or form metal
　died v ▷ die¹
diehard n (pl -s) person who resists change
　diehards n ▷ diehard
　diereses n ▷ dieresis
dieresis [die-**air**-iss-iss] n (pl -ses) [-seez] ▷ diaeresis
　dies v ▷ die¹ ▶ n ▷ die²
diesel n (pl -s) diesel engine
　diesels n ▷ diesel
diet¹ n (pl -s) food that a person or animal regularly eats ▶ v (-s, -ing, -ed) follow a special diet so as to lose weight ▶ adj (of food) suitable for a weight-reduction diet > **dietary** adj > **dieter** n (pl -s)

diet² n (pl -s) parliament of some countries
  dietary adj ▷ diet
  dieted v ▷ diet
  dieter n ▷ diet
  dieters n ▷ diet
dietetic adj prepared for special dietary requirements
dietetics n study of diet and nutrition
dietician n (pl -s) person who specializes in dietetics
  dieticians n ▷ dietician
  dieting v ▷ diet
  diets v ▷ diet¹ ▶ n ▷ diet¹, ²
differ v (-s, -ing, -ed) be unlike
  differed v ▷ differ
difference n (pl -s) state of being unlike
  differences n ▷ difference
different adj unlike > **differently** adv
differential adj of or using a difference ▶ n (pl -s) factor that differentiates between two comparable things > **differentially** adv
  differentially adv ▷ differential
  differentials n ▷ differential
differentiate v, v (-te, -ting, -ted) perceive or show the difference (between)
  > **differentiation** n (pl -s)
  differentiated v ▷ differentiate
  differentiates v ▷ differentiate
  differentiating v ▷ differentiate
  differentiation n ▷ differentiate
  differentiations n ▷ differentiate
  differently n ▷ different
  differing v ▷ differ
  differs v ▷ differ
difficult adj requiring effort or skill to do or understand > **difficultly** adv > **difficulty** n (pl -ties)
  difficulties n ▷ difficult
  difficultly adv ▷ difficult
  difficulty n ▷ difficult
  diffidence n ▷ diffident
  diffidences n ▷ diffident
diffident adj lacking self-confidence
  > **diffidence** n (pl -s) > **diffidently** adv
  diffidently adv ▷ diffident
diffraction n (pl -s) (PHYSICS) deviation in the direction of a wave at the edge of an obstacle in its path
  diffractions n ▷ diffraction
diffuse v (-fuses, -fusing, -fused) spread over a wide area ▶ adj widely spread > **diffusely** adv
  > **diffuseness** n > **diffusion** n (pl -s)
  diffused v ▷ diffuse
  diffusely adv ▷ diffuse
  diffuseness n ▷ diffuse

  diffuses v ▷ diffuse
  diffusing v ▷ diffuse
  diffusion n ▷ diffuse
  diffusions n ▷ diffuse
dig v (digs, digging, dug) cut into, break up, and turn over or remove (earth), esp. with a spade ▶ n (pl -s) digging ▶ pl (pl -s) (BRIT, AUST & S AFR) (informal) lodgings
digest v (-s, -ing, -ed) subject to a process of digestion ▶ n (pl -s) shortened version of a book, report, or article > **digestible** adj
  > **digestibility** n > **digestive** adj > **digestively** adv
  digested v ▷ digest
  digestibility n ▷ digest
  digestible adj ▷ digest
  digesting v ▷ digest
digestion n (pl -s) (body's system for) breaking down food into easily absorbed substances
  digestions n ▷ digestion
  digestive adj ▷ digest
  digestively adv ▷ digest
  digests v, n ▷ digest
digger n (pl -s) machine used for digging
  diggers n ▷ digger
  digging v ▷ dig
  diggings n ▷ dig
digit [dij-it] n (pl -s) finger or toe
digital adj displaying information as numbers rather than with hands and a dial > **digitally** adv
digitalis n drug made from foxglove leaves, used as a heart stimulant
  digitally adv ▷ digital
  digits n ▷ digit
  dignified n ▷ dignify
  dignifies n ▷ dignify
dignify v (-s, -ing, -ed) add distinction to
  dignifying v ▷ dignify
  dignitaries n ▷ dignitary
dignitary n (pl -aries) person of high official position
  dignities n ▷ dignity
dignity n (pl -ties) serious, calm, and controlled behaviour or manner
digress v (-es, -ing, -ed) depart from the main subject in speech or writing > **digression** n (pl -s)
  digressed v ▷ digress
  digresses v ▷ digress
  digressing v ▷ digress
  digression n ▷ digress
  digressions n ▷ digress
  digs v, n ▷ dig
dike n (pl -s) ▷ dyke

dikes n ▷ dike

dilapidated adj (of a building) having fallen into ruin > **dilapidation** n (pl -s)

dilapidation n ▷ dilapidated

dilapidations n ▷ dilapidated

dilatation n ▷ dilate

dilatations n ▷ dilate

dilate v (-lates, -lating, -lated) make or become wider or larger > **dilation, dilatation** n (pl -s)

dilated v ▷ dilate

dilates v ▷ dilate

dilating v ▷ dilate

dilation n ▷ dilate

dilations n ▷ dilate

dilatorily adv ▷ dilatory

dilatoriness n ▷ dilatory

dilatory [dill-a-tree] adj tending or intended to waste time > **dilatorily** adv > **dilatoriness** n

dilemma n (pl -s) situation offering a choice between two equally undesirable alternatives

dilemmas n ▷ dilemma

dilettante [dill-it-tan-tee] n (pl -tantes, -tanti) person whose interest in a subject is superficial rather than serious > **dilettantism** n

dilettantes n ▷ dilettante

dilettanti n ▷ dilettante

dilettantism n ▷ dilettante

diligence n ▷ diligent

diligent adj careful and persevering in carrying out duties > **diligently** adv > **diligence** n

diligently adv ▷ diligent

dill n (pl -s) sweet-smelling herb

dills n ▷ dill

dilute v (-lutes, -luting, -luted) make (a liquid) less concentrated, esp. by adding water > **dilution** n (pl -s)

diluted v ▷ dilute

dilutes v ▷ dilute

diluting v ▷ dilute

dilution n ▷ dilute

dilutions n ▷ dilute

diluvial, diluvian adj of a flood, esp. the great Flood described in the Old Testament

diluvian adj ▷ diluvial

dim adj (dimmer, dimmest) badly lit ▶ v (dims, dimming, dimmed) make or become dim > **dimly** adv > **dimness** n

dime n (pl -s) coin of the US and Canada, worth ten cents

dimension n (pl -s) measurement of the size of something in a particular direction

dimensions n ▷ dimension

dimes n ▷ dime

diminish v (-es, -ing, -ed) make or become smaller, fewer, or less > **diminution** n (pl -s)

diminished v ▷ diminish

diminishes v ▷ diminish

diminishing v ▷ diminish

diminuendo n (pl -s) (MUSIC) gradual decrease in loudness

diminuendos n ▷ diminuendo

diminution n ▷ diminish

diminutions n ▷ diminish

diminutive adj very small ▶ n (pl -s) word or affix which implies smallness or unimportance > **diminutively** adv > **diminutiveness** n

diminutively adv ▷ diminutive

diminutiveness n ▷ diminutive

diminutives n ▷ diminutive

dimly adv ▷ dim

dimmed v ▷ dim

dimmer n (pl -s) device for dimming an electric light ▶ adj ▷ dim

dimmers n ▷ dimmer

dimmest adj ▷ dim

dimming v ▷ dim

dimness n ▷ dim

dimple n (pl -s) small natural dent, esp. in the cheeks or chin ▶ v (-ples, -pling, -pled) produce dimples by smiling

dimpled v ▷ dimple

dimples n, v ▷ dimple

dimpling v ▷ dimple

dims v ▷ dim

din n (pl -s) loud unpleasant confused noise ▶ v (dins, dinning, dinned) (foll. by into) instil (something) into someone by constant repetition

dinar [dee-nahr] n (pl -s) monetary unit of various Balkan, Middle Eastern, and North African countries

dinars n ▷ dinar

dine v (dines, dining, dined) eat dinner

dined v ▷ dine

diner n (pl -s) person eating a meal

diners n ▷ diner

dines v ▷ dine

ding n (pl -s) (AUST DATED & NZ) (Informal) small dent in a vehicle

dinghies n ▷ dinghy

dinghy [ding-ee] n (pl -ghies) small boat, powered by sails, oars, or a motor

dingier adj ▷ dingy

dingiest adj ▷ dingy

dinginess n ▷ dingy

dingo n (pl -goes) Australian wild dog

dingoes n ▷ dingo

dings n ▷ ding

dingy [din-jee] adj (-gier, -giest) (BRIT, AUST & NZ) dull and drab > **dinginess** n

dining v ▷ dine

dinkier adj ▷ dinky

dinkiest adj ▷ dinky

dinkum adj (AUST & NZ) (Informal) genuine or right

dinky adj (-kier, -kiest) (BRIT, AUST & NZ) (Informal) small and neat

dinned v ▷ din

dinner n (pl -s) main meal of the day, eaten either in the evening or at midday

dinners n ▷ dinner

dinning v ▷ din

dinosaur n (pl -s) type of extinct prehistoric reptile, many of which were of gigantic size

dinosaurs n ▷ dinosaur

dins n, v ▷ din

dint n (pl -s) means

dints n ▷ dint

diocesan adj ▷ diocese

diocese [die-a-siss] n (pl -s) district over which a bishop has control > **diocesan** adj

dioceses n ▷ diocese

diode n (pl -s) semiconductor device for converting alternating current to direct current

diodes n ▷ diode

dioptre [die-op-ter] n (pl -s) unit for measuring the refractive power of a lens

dioptres n ▷ dioptre

dioxide n (pl -s) oxide containing two oxygen atoms per molecule

dioxides n ▷ dioxide

dip v (dips, dipping, dipped) plunge quickly or briefly into a liquid ▶ n (pl -s) dipping

diphtheria [dif-theer-ya] n (pl -s) contagious disease producing fever and difficulty in breathing and swallowing

diphtherias n ▷ diphtheria

diphthong n (pl -s) union of two vowel sounds in a single compound sound

diphthongs n ▷ diphthong

diploma n (pl -s) qualification awarded by a college on successful completion of a course

diplomacies n ▷ diplomacy

diplomacy n (pl -macies) conduct of the relations between nations by peaceful means

diplomas n ▷ diploma

diplomat n (pl -s) official engaged in diplomacy

diplomatic adj of diplomacy > **diplomatically** adv

diplomatically adv ▷ diplomatic

diplomats n ▷ diplomat

dipped v ▷ dip

dipper n (pl -s) ladle used for dipping

dippers n ▷ dipper

dipping v ▷ dip

diprotodont [die-pro-toe-dont] n (pl -s) marsupial with fewer than three upper incisor teeth on each side of the jaw

diprotodonts n ▷ diprotodont

dips v, n ▷ dip

dipsomania n (pl -s) compulsive craving for alcohol > **dipsomaniac** n (pl -s) adj

dipsomaniac n, adj ▷ dipsomania

dipsomaniacs n ▷ dipsomania

dipsomanias n ▷ dipsomania

diptych [dip-tik] n (pl -s) painting on two hinged panels

diptychs n ▷ diptych

dire adj (-er, -est) disastrous, urgent, or terrible > **direly** adv > **direness** n (pl -es)

direct adj (of a route) shortest, straight ▶ adv in a direct manner ▶ v (-s, -ing, -ed) lead and organize > **directness** n

directed v ▷ direct

directing v ▷ direct

direction n (pl -s) course or line along which a person or thing moves, points, or lies ▶ pl instructions for doing something or for reaching a place > **directional** adj

directional adj ▷ direction

directions n ▷ direction

directive n (pl -s) instruction, order

directives n ▷ directive

directly adv in a direct manner ▶ conj as soon as

directness n ▷ direct

director n (pl -s) person or thing that directs or controls > **directorial** adj > **directorship** n (pl -s)

directorate n (pl -s) board of directors

directorates n ▷ directorate

directorial adj ▷ director

directories n ▷ directory

directors n ▷ director

directorship n ▷ director

directorships n ▷ director

directory n (pl -ries) book listing names, addresses, and telephone numbers

directs v ▷ direct

direly adv ▷ dire

direness n ▷ dire

direnesses n ▷ dire

direr adj ▷ dire

direst adj ▷ dire

dirge n (pl -s) slow sad song of mourning
  dirges n ▷ dirge

dirigible [dir-rij-jib-bl] adj able to be steered ▶ n
  (pl -s) airship
  dirigibles n ▷ dirigible

dirk n (pl -s) dagger, formerly worn by Scottish
  Highlanders
  dirks n ▷ dirk

dirndl n (pl -s) full gathered skirt originating
  from Tyrolean peasant wear
  dirndls n ▷ dirndl

dirt n (pl -s) unclean substance, filth
  dirtied v ▷ dirty
  dirtier adj ▷ dirty
  dirties v ▷ dirty
  dirtiest adj ▷ dirty
  dirtily adv ▷ dirty
  dirtiness n ▷ dirty
  dirts n ▷ dirt

dirty adj (dirtier, dirtiest) covered or marked
  with dirt ▶ v (dirties, dirtying, dirtied) make
  dirty > **dirtily** adv > **dirtiness** n
  dirtying v ▷ dirty
  disabilities n ▷ disability

disability n (pl -ties) condition of being
  disabled

disable v (-bles, -bling, -bled) make ineffective,
  unfit, or incapable > **disablement** n

disabled adj lacking a physical power, such as
  the ability to walk ▶ v ▷ disable
  disablement n ▷ disable
  disables v ▷ disable
  disabling v ▷ disable

disabuse v (-buses, -busing, -bused) (foll. by of)
  rid (someone) of a mistaken idea
  disabused v ▷ disabuse
  disabuses v ▷ disabuse
  disabusing v ▷ disabuse

disadvantage n (pl -s) unfavourable or
  harmful circumstance > **disadvantageous**
  adj > **disadvantageously** adv
  > **disadvantageousness** n

disadvantaged adj socially or economically
  deprived
  disadvantageous adj ▷ disadvantage
  disadvantageously adv ▷ disadvantage
  disadvantageousness n ▷ disadvantage
  disadvantages n ▷ disadvantage

disaffected adj having lost loyalty to or
  affection for someone or something
  > **disaffectedly** adv > **disaffection** n (pl -s)
  disaffectedly adv ▷ disaffected
  disaffection n ▷ disaffected
  disaffections n ▷ disaffected

disagree v (-grees, -greeing, -greed) argue

or have different opinions > **disagreement**
n (pl -s)

disagreeable adj unpleasant
  > **disagreeableness** n > **disagreeably** adv
  disagreeableness n ▷ disagreeable
  disagreeably adv ▷ disagreeable
  disagreed v ▷ disagree
  disagreeing v ▷ disagree
  disagreement n ▷ disagree
  disagreements n ▷ disagree
  disagrees v ▷ disagree

disallow v (-s, -ing, -ed) reject as untrue or
  invalid
  disallowed v ▷ disallow
  disallowing v ▷ disallow
  disallows v ▷ disallow

disappear v (-s, -ing, -ed) cease to be visible
  > **disappearance** n (pl -s)
  disappearance n ▷ disappear
  disappearances n ▷ disappear
  disappeared v ▷ disappear
  disappearing v ▷ disappear
  disappears v ▷ disappear

disappoint v (-s, -ing, -ed) fail to meet the
  expectations or hopes of > **disappointingly**
  adv
  disappointed v ▷ disappoint
  disappointing v ▷ disappoint
  disappointingly adv ▷ disappoint

disappointment n (pl -s) feeling of being
  disappointed
  disappointments n ▷ disappointment
  disappoints v ▷ disappoint

disapprobation n (pl -s) disapproval
  disapprobations n ▷ disapprobation
  disapproval n ▷ disapprove
  disapprovals n ▷ disapprove

disapprove v (-proves, -proving, -proved) (foll.
  by of) consider wrong or bad > **disapproval**
  n (pl -s)
  disapproved v ▷ disapprove
  disapproves v ▷ disapprove
  disapproving v ▷ disapprove

disarm v (-s, -ing, -ed) deprive of weapons
  > **disarmament** n (pl -s)
  disarmament n ▷ disarm
  disarmaments n ▷ disarm
  disarmed v ▷ disarm

disarming adj removing hostility or suspicion
  ▶ v ▷ disarm > **disarmingly** adv
  disarmingly adv ▷ disarming
  disarms v ▷ disarm

disarrange v (-ranges, -ranging, -ranged)
  throw into disorder
  disarranged v ▷ disarrange

disarranges v ▷ disarrange
disarranging v ▷ disarrange
disarray n (pl -s) confusion and lack of discipline
disarrays n ▷ disarray
disaster n (pl -s) occurrence that causes great distress or destruction > **disastrous** adj > **disastrously** adv
disasters n ▷ disaster
disastrous adj ▷ disaster
disastrously adv ▷ disaster
disavow v (-s, -ing, -ed) deny connection with or responsibility for > **disavowal** n (pl -s)
disavowal n ▷ disavow
disavowals n ▷ disavow
disavowed v ▷ disavow
disavowing v ▷ disavow
disavows v ▷ disavow
disband v (-s, -ing, -ed) (cause to) cease to function as a group
disbanded v ▷ disband
disbanding v ▷ disband
disbands v ▷ disband
disbelief n ▷ disbelieve
disbelieve v (-lieves, -lieving, -lieved) reject as false (foll. by in) > **disbelief** n
disbelieved v ▷ disbelieve
disbelieves v ▷ disbelieve
disbelieving v ▷ disbelieve
disburse v (-burses, -bursing, -bursed) pay out > **disbursement** n (pl -s)
disbursed v ▷ disburse
disbursement n ▷ disburse
disbursements n ▷ disburse
disburses v ▷ disburse
disbursing v ▷ disburse
disc n (pl -s) flat circular object ▷ disk
discard v (-s, -ing, -ed) get rid of (something or someone) as useless or undesirable
discarded v ▷ discard
discarding v ▷ discard
discards v ▷ discard
discern v (-s, -ing, -ed) see or be aware of (something) clearly > **discernible** adj > **discernibly** adv > **discernment** n (pl -s)
discerned v ▷ discern
discernible adj ▷ discern
discernibly adv ▷ discern
discerning adj having good judgment ▶ v ▷ discern
discernment n ▷ discern
discernments n ▷ discern
discerns v ▷ discern
discharge v (-charges, -charging, -charged) release, allow to go ▶ n (pl -s) substance that comes out from a place
discharged v ▷ discharge
discharges v, n ▷ discharge
discharging v ▷ discharge
disciple [diss-**sipe**-pl] n (pl -s) follower of the doctrines of a teacher, esp. Jesus Christ
disciples n ▷ disciple
disciplinarian n (pl -s) person who practises strict discipline
disciplinarians n ▷ disciplinarian
disciplinary adj ▷ discipline
discipline n (pl -s) practice of imposing strict rules of behaviour ▶ v (-plines, -plining, -plined) attempt to improve the behaviour of (oneself or another) by training or rules > **disciplinary** adj
disciplined adj able to behave and work in a controlled way ▶ v ▷ discipline
disciplines n, v ▷ discipline
disciplining v ▷ discipline
disclaimed v ▷ disclaimer
disclaimer n (pl -s) statement denying responsibility > **disclaim** v (-s, -ing, -ed)
disclaimers n ▷ disclaimer
disclaiming v ▷ disclaimer
disclaims v ▷ disclaimer
disclose v (-closes, -closing, -closed) make known > **disclosure** n (pl -s)
disclosed v ▷ disclose
discloses v ▷ disclose
disclosing v ▷ disclose
disclosure n ▷ disclose
disclosures n ▷ disclose
disco n (pl -s) nightclub where people dance to amplified pop records
discoloration n ▷ discolour
discolorations n ▷ discolour
discolour v (-s, -ing, -ed) change in colour, fade > **discoloration** n (pl -s)
discoloured v ▷ discolour
discolouring v ▷ discolour
discolours v ▷ discolour
discomfit v (-s, -ing, -ed) make uneasy or confused > **discomfiture** n (pl -s)
discomfited v ▷ discomfit
discomfiting v ▷ discomfit
discomfits v ▷ discomfit
discomfiture n ▷ discomfit
discomfitures n ▷ discomfit
discomfort n (pl -s) inconvenience, distress, or mild pain
discomforts n ▷ discomfort
discommode v (-modes, -moding, -moded) cause inconvenience to
discommoded v ▷ discommode

discommodes v ▷ discommode
discommoding v ▷ discommode
disconcert v (-s, -ing, -ed) embarrass or upset
disconcerted v ▷ disconcert
disconcerting v ▷ disconcert
disconcerts v ▷ disconcert
disconnect v (-s, -ing, -ed) undo or break the connection between (two things) > **disconnection** n (pl -s)
disconnected adj (of speech or ideas) not logically connected ▶ v ▷ disconnect
disconnecting v ▷ disconnect
disconnection n ▷ disconnect
disconnections n ▷ disconnect
disconnects v ▷ disconnect
disconsolate adj sad beyond comfort > **disconsolately** adv
disconsolately adv ▷ disconsolate
discontent n (pl -s) lack of contentment > **discontented** adj > **discontentedly** adv
discontented adj ▷ discontent
discontentedly adv ▷ discontent
discontents n ▷ discontent
discontinue v (-nues, -nuing, -nued) come or bring to an end
discontinued v ▷ discontinue
discontinues v ▷ discontinue
discontinuing v ▷ discontinue
discontinuities n ▷ discontinuous
discontinuity n ▷ discontinuous
discontinuous adj characterized by interruptions > **discontinuity** n (pl -nuities)
discord n (pl -s) lack of agreement or harmony between people > **discordant** adj > **discordantly** adv > **discordance** n (pl -s)
discordance n ▷ discord
discordances n ▷ discord
discordant adj ▷ discord
discordantly adv ▷ discord
discords n ▷ discord
discos n ▷ disco
discotheque n (pl -s) ▷ disco
discotheques n ▷ discotheque
discount v (-s, -ing, -ed) take no account of (something) because it is considered to be unreliable, prejudiced, or irrelevant ▶ n (pl -s) deduction from the full price of something
discounted v ▷ discount
discounting v ▷ discount
discounts v, n ▷ discount
discourage v (-rages, -raging, -raged) deprive of the will to persist in something > **discouragement** n (pl -s)
discouraged v ▷ discourage
discouragement n ▷ discourage

discouragements n ▷ discourage
discourages v ▷ discourage
discouraging v ▷ discourage
discourse n (pl -s) conversation ▶ v (-ses, -sing, -sed) (foll. by on) speak or write (about) at length
discoursed v ▷ discourse
discourses n, v ▷ discourse
discoursing v ▷ discourse
discourteous adj showing bad manners > **discourteously** adv > **discourtesy** n (pl -esies)
discourteously adv ▷ discourteous
discourtesies n ▷ discourteous
discourtesy n ▷ discourteous
discover v (-s, -ing, -ed) be the first to find or to find out about > **discoverer** n (pl -s)
discovered v ▷ discover
discoverer n ▷ discover
discoverers n ▷ discover
discoveries n ▷ discovery
discovering v ▷ discover
discovers v ▷ discover
discovery n (pl -eries) discovering
discredit v (-s, -ing, -ed) damage the reputation of ▶ n (pl -s) damage to someone's reputation
discreditable adj bringing shame
discredited v ▷ discredit
discrediting v ▷ discredit
discredits v, n ▷ discredit
discreet adj (-er, -est) careful to avoid embarrassment, esp. by keeping confidences secret > **discreetly** adv > **discreetness** n (pl -es)
discreeter adj ▷ discreet
discreetest adj ▷ discreet
discreetly adv ▷ discreet
discreetness n ▷ discreet
discreetnesses n ▷ discreet
discrepancies n ▷ discrepancy
discrepancy n (pl -cies) conflict or variation between facts, figures, or claims
discrete adj (-r, -st) separate, distinct > **discretely** adv > **discreteness** n (pl -es)
discretely adv ▷ discrete
discreteness n ▷ discrete
discretenesses n ▷ discrete
discreter adj ▷ discrete
discretest adj ▷ discrete
discretion n (pl -s) quality of behaving in a discreet way > **discretionary** adj
discretionary adj ▷ discretion
discretions n ▷ discretion
discriminate v (-nates, -nating, -nated) (foll. by **against** or **in favour of**) single

out (a particular person or group) for
worse or better treatment than others
> discrimination n (pl -s)
discriminated v ▷ discriminate
discriminates v ▷ discriminate
discriminating adj showing good taste and
judgment ▶ v ▷ discriminate
discrimination n ▷ discriminate
discriminations n ▷ discriminate
discriminatory adj based on prejudice
discs n ▷ disc
discursive adj passing from one topic to
another **> discursively** adv **> discursiveness** n
discursively adv ▷ discursive
discursiveness n ▷ discursive
discus n (pl -es) heavy disc-shaped object
thrown in sports competitions
discuses n ▷ discus
discuss v (-es, -ing, -ed) consider (something)
by talking it over **> discussion** n (pl -s)
discussed v ▷ discuss
discusses v ▷ discuss
discussing v ▷ discuss
discussion n ▷ discuss
discussions n ▷ discuss
disdain n feeling of superiority and dislike ▶ v
(-s, -ing, -ed) refuse with disdain **> disdainful**
adj **disdainfully** adv
disdained v ▷ disdain
disdainful adj ▷ disdain
disdainfully adv ▷ disdain
disdaining v ▷ disdain
disdains v ▷ disdain
disease n (pl -s) illness, sickness **> diseased** adj
diseased n ▷ disease
diseases n ▷ disease
disembark v (-s, -ing, -ed) get off a ship,
aircraft, or bus **> disembarkation** n (pl -s)
disembarkation n ▷ disembark
disembarkations n ▷ disembark
disembarked v ▷ disembark
disembarking v ▷ disembark
disembarks v ▷ disembark
disembodied adj lacking a body
disembowel v (-els, -elling, -elled) remove the
entrails of
disembowelled v ▷ disembowel
disembowelling v ▷ disembowel
disembowels v ▷ disembowel
disenchanted adj disappointed and
disillusioned **> disenchantment** n (pl -s)
disenchantment n ▷ disenchant
disenchantments n ▷ disenchant
disenfranchise, disfranchise v (-ises,
-ising, -ised) deprive (someone) of the right

to vote or of other rights of citizenship
> disenfranchisement n (pl -s)
disenfranchised v ▷ disenfranchise
disenfranchisement n ▷ disenfranchise
disenfranchisements n ▷ disenfranchise
disenfranchises v ▷ disenfranchise
disenfranchising v ▷ disenfranchise
disengage v (-gages, -gaging, -gaged) release
from a connection **> disengagement** n (pl -s)
disengaged v ▷ disengage
disengagement n ▷ disengage
disengagements n ▷ disengage
disengages v ▷ disengage
disengaging v ▷ disengage
disentangle v (-tangles, -tangling, -tangled)
release from entanglement or confusion
disentangled v ▷ disentangle
disentangles v ▷ disentangle
disentangling v ▷ disentangle
disfavour n (pl -s) disapproval or dislike
disfavours n ▷ disfavour
disfigure v (-gures, -guring, -gured) spoil the
appearance of **> disfigurement** n (pl -s)
disfigured v ▷ disfigure
disfigurement n ▷ disfigure
disfigurements n ▷ disfigure
disfigures v ▷ disfigure
disfiguring v ▷ disfigure
disfranchise v (-ises, -ising, -ised)
▷ disenfranchise
disfranchised v ▷ disfranchise
disfranchises v ▷ disfranchise
disfranchising v ▷ disfranchise
disgorge v (-gorges, -gorging, -gorged) empty
out, discharge
disgorged v ▷ disgorge
disgorges v ▷ disgorge
disgorging v ▷ disgorge
disgrace n (pl -s) condition of shame, loss of
reputation, or dishonour ▶ v (-graces,
-gracing, -graced) bring shame upon (oneself
or others) **> disgraceful** adj **> disgracefully**
adv
disgraced v ▷ disgrace
disgraceful adj ▷ disgrace
disgracefully adv ▷ disgrace
disgraces n, v ▷ disgrace
disgracing v ▷ disgrace
disgruntled adj sulky or discontented
> disgruntlement n
disgruntlement n ▷ disgruntled
disguise v (-guises, -guising, -guised) change
the appearance or manner in order to conceal
the identity of (someone or something)
▶ n (pl -s) mask, costume, or manner that

disguises
disguised v ▷ disguise
disguises v, n ▷ disguise
disguising v ▷ disguise
disgust n (pl -s) great loathing or distaste ▶ v (-s, -ing, -ed) sicken, fill with loathing
disgusted v ▷ disgust
disgusting v ▷ disgust
disgusts v ▷ disgust
dish n (pl -es) shallow container used for holding or serving food
dishabille [diss-a-beel] n (pl -s) ▷ deshabille
dishabilles n ▷ dishabille
dishcloth n (pl -s) cloth for washing dishes
dishcloths n ▷ dishcloth
dishearten v (-s, -ing, -ed) weaken or destroy the hope, courage, or enthusiasm of
disheartened v ▷ dishearten
disheartening v ▷ dishearten
disheartens v ▷ dishearten
dishes n ▷ dish
dishevelled adj (of a person's hair, clothes, or general appearance) disordered and untidy
dishonest adj not honest or fair > **dishonestly** adv > **dishonesty** n (pl -ties)
dishonesties n ▷ dishonesty
dishonestly adv ▷ dishonest
dishonesty n ▷ dishonest
dishonour v (-s, -ing, -ed) treat with disrespect ▶ n (pl -s) lack of respect > **dishonourable** adj > **dishonourably** adv
dishonourable adj ▷ dishonour
dishonourably adv ▷ dishonour
dishonoured v ▷ dishonour
dishonouring v ▷ dishonour
dishonours v, n ▷ dishonour
disillusion v (-s, -ing, -ed) destroy the illusions or false ideas of (also **disillusionment**) ▶ n (pl -s) state of being disillusioned
disillusioned v ▷ disillusion
disillusioning v ▷ disillusion
disillusionment n ▷ disillusion
disillusionments n ▷ disillusion
disillusions v, n ▷ disillusion
disincentive n (pl -s) something that acts as a deterrent
disincentives n ▷ disincentive
disinclination n ▷ disinclined
disinclinations n ▷ disinclined
disinclined adj unwilling, reluctant > **disinclination** n (pl -s)
disinfect v (-s, -ing, -ed) rid of harmful germs, chemically > **disinfection** n (pl -s)
disinfectant n (pl -s) substance that destroys harmful germs

disinfectants n ▷ disinfectant
disinfected v ▷ disinfect
disinfecting v ▷ disinfect
disinfection n ▷ disinfect
disinfections n ▷ disinfect
disinfects v ▷ disinfect
disinformation n false information intended to mislead
disingenuous adj not sincere > **disingenuously** adv > **disingenuousness** n
disingenuously adv ▷ disingenuous
disingenuousness n ▷ disingenuous
disinherit v (-s, -ing, -ed) (LAW) deprive (an heir) of inheritance > **disinheritance** n (pl -s)
disinheritance n ▷ disinherit
disinheritances n ▷ disinherit
disinherited v ▷ disinherit
disinheriting v ▷ disinherit
disinherits v ▷ disinherit
disintegrate v (-rates, -rating, -rated) break up > **disintegration** n (pl -s)
disintegrated v ▷ disintegrate
disintegrates v ▷ disintegrate
disintegrating v ▷ disintegrate
disintegration n ▷ disintegrate
disintegrations n ▷ disintegrate
disinter v (-ters, -terring, -terred) dig up
disinterest n ▷ disinterested
disinterested adj free from bias or involvement > **disinterest** n ▷ **disinterestedly** adv > **disinterestedness** n
disinterestedly adv ▷ disinterested
disinterestedness n ▷ disinterested
disinterred v ▷ disinter
disinterring v ▷ disinter
disinters v ▷ disinter
disjointed adj having no coherence, disconnected > **disjointedly** adv
disjointedly adv ▷ disjointed
disk n (pl -s) (COMPUTERS) storage device, consisting of a stack of plates coated with a magnetic layer, which rotates rapidly as a single unit
disks n ▷ disk
dislike v (-likes, -liking, -liked) consider unpleasant or disagreeable ▶ n (pl -s) feeling of not liking something or someone
disliked v ▷ dislike
dislikes v, n ▷ dislike
disliking v ▷ dislike
dislocate v (-cates, -cating, -cated) displace (a bone or joint) from its normal position > **dislocation** n (pl -s)
dislocated v ▷ dislocate
dislocates v ▷ dislocate

dislocating v ▷ dislocate
dislocation n ▷ dislocate
dislocations n ▷ dislocate
dislodge v (-lodges, -lodging, -lodged) remove (something) from a previously fixed position
dislodged v ▷ dislodge
dislodges v ▷ dislodge
dislodging v ▷ dislodge
disloyal adj not loyal, deserting one's allegiance ▷ **disloyalty** n (pl -ties)
disloyalties n ▷ disloyalty
dismal adj gloomy and depressing ▷ **dismally** adv ▷ **dismalness** n
dismally adv ▷ dismal
dismalness n ▷ dismal
dismantle v (-mantles, -mantling, -mantled) take apart piece by piece
dismantled v ▷ dismantle
dismantles v ▷ dismantle
dismantling v ▷ dismantle
dismay v (-s, -ing, -ed) fill with alarm or depression ▶ n (pl -s) alarm mixed with sadness
dismayed v ▷ dismay
dismaying v ▷ dismay
dismays v, n ▷ dismay
dismember v (-s, -ing, -ed) remove the limbs of ▷ **dismemberment** n (pl -s)
dismembered v ▷ dismember
dismembering v ▷ dismember
dismemberment n ▷ dismember
dismemberments n ▷ dismember
dismembers v ▷ dismember
dismiss v (-es, -ing, -ed) remove (an employee) from a job ▷ **dismissal** n (pl -s)
dismissal n ▷ dismiss
dismissals n ▷ dismiss
dismissed v ▷ dismiss
dismisses v ▷ dismiss
dismissing v ▷ dismiss
dismissive adj scornful, contemptuous
dismount v (-s, -ing, -ed) get off a horse or bicycle
dismounted v ▷ dismount
dismounting v ▷ dismount
dismounts v ▷ dismount
disobedience n ▷ disobey
disobedient adj ▷ disobey
disobediently adv ▷ disobey
disobey v (-s, -ing, -ed) neglect or refuse to obey ▷ **disobedient** adj ▷ **disobediently** adv ▷ **disobedience** n
disobeyed v ▷ disobey
disobeying v ▷ disobey
disobeys v ▷ disobey

disobliging adj unwilling to help
disorder n (pl -s) state of untidiness and disorganization
disordered adj untidy
disorderliness n ▷ disorderly
disorderly adj untidy and disorganized ▷ **disorderliness** n
disorders n ▷ disorder
disorganization n ▷ disorganize
disorganizations n ▷ disorganize
disorganize v (-nizes, -nizing, -nized) disrupt the arrangement or system of ▷ **disorganization** n (pl -s)
disorganized v ▷ disorganize
disorganizes v ▷ disorganize
disorganizing v ▷ disorganize
disorientate, disorient v (-tates, -tating, -tated, -s, -ing, -ed) cause (someone) to lose his or her bearings ▷ **disorientation** n (pl -s)
disorientated v ▷ disorientate
disorientates v ▷ disorientate
disorientating v ▷ disorientate
disorientation n ▷ disorientate
disorientations n ▷ disorientate
disoriented v ▷ disorientate
disorienting v ▷ disorientate
disorients v ▷ disorientate
disown v (-s, -ing, -ed) deny any connection with (someone)
disowned v ▷ disown
disowning v ▷ disown
disowns v ▷ disown
disparage v (-rages, -raging, -raged) speak contemptuously of ▷ **disparagement** n (pl -s)
disparaged v ▷ disparage
disparagement n ▷ disparage
disparagements n ▷ disparage
disparages v ▷ disparage
disparaging v ▷ disparage
disparate adj completely different ▷ **disparately** adv ▷ **disparateness** n ▷ **disparity** n (pl -ities)
disparately adv ▷ disparate
disparateness n ▷ disparate
disparities n ▷ disparate
disparity n ▷ disparate
dispassionate adj not influenced by emotion ▷ **dispassionately** adv
dispassionately adv ▷ dispassionate
dispatch v (-es, -ing, -ed) send off to a destination or to perform a task ▶ n (pl -es) official communication or report, sent in haste
dispatched v ▷ dispatch
dispatches v, n ▷ dispatch

dispatching v ▷ dispatch
dispel v (-pels, -pelling, -pelled) destroy or remove
dispelled v ▷ dispel
dispelling v ▷ dispel
dispels v ▷ dispel
dispensability n ▷ dispensable
dispensable adj not essential > **dispensability** n
dispensaries n ▷ dispensary
dispensary n (pl -saries) place where medicine is dispensed
dispensation n (pl -s) dispensing
dispensations n ▷ dispensation
dispense v (-penses, -pensing, -pensed) distribute in portions > **dispenser** n (pl -s)
dispensed v ▷ dispense
dispenser n ▷ dispense
dispensers n ▷ dispense
dispenses v ▷ dispense
dispensing v ▷ dispense
dispersal n ▷ disperse
dispersals n ▷ disperse
disperse v (-perses, -persing, -persed) scatter over a wide area > **dispersal, dispersion** n (pl -s)
dispersed v ▷ disperse
disperses v ▷ disperse
dispersing v ▷ disperse
dispersion n ▷ disperse
dispersions n ▷ disperse
dispirit v (-s, -ing, -ed) make downhearted
dispirited v ▷ dispirit
dispiriting v ▷ dispirit
dispirits v ▷ dispirit
displace v (-places, -placing, -placed) move from the usual location > **displacement** n (pl -s)
displaced v ▷ displace
displacement n ▷ displace
displacements n ▷ displace
displaces v ▷ displace
displacing v ▷ displace
display v (-s, -ing, -ed) make visible or noticeable ▶ n (pl -s) displaying
displayed v ▷ display
displaying v ▷ display
displays v, n ▷ display
displease v (-ses, -sing, -sed) annoy or upset > **displeasure** n (pl -s)
displeased v ▷ displease
displeases v ▷ displease
displeasing v ▷ displease
displeasure n ▷ displease
displeasures n ▷ displease

disport v (-s, -ing, -ed) indulge oneself in pleasure
disported v ▷ disport
disporting v ▷ disport
disports v ▷ disport
disposability n ▷ disposable
disposable adj designed to be thrown away after use > **disposability** n
disposal n (pl -s) getting rid of something
disposals n ▷ disposal
dispose v (-poses, -posing, -posed) place in a certain order
disposed adj willing or eager ▶ v ▷ dispose
disposes v ▷ dispose
disposing v ▷ dispose
disposition n (pl -s) person's usual temperament
dispositions n ▷ disposition
dispossess v (-es, -ing, -ed) (foll. by **of**) deprive (someone) of (a possession) > **dispossession** n (pl -s)
dispossessed v ▷ dispossess
dispossesses v ▷ dispossess
dispossessing v ▷ dispossess
dispossession n ▷ dispossess
dispossessions n ▷ dispossess
disproportion n (pl -s) lack of proportion or equality
disproportionate adj out of proportion > **disproportionately** adv
disproportionately adv ▷ disproportionate
disproportions n ▷ disproportion
disprove v (-proves, -proving, -proved) show (an assertion or claim) to be incorrect
disproved v ▷ disprove
disproves v ▷ disprove
disproving v ▷ disprove
dispute n (pl -s) disagreement, argument ▶ v (-putes, -puting, -puted) argue about (something)
disputed v ▷ dispute
disputes n, v ▷ dispute
disputing v ▷ dispute
disqualification n ▷ disqualify
disqualifications n ▷ disqualify
disqualified v ▷ disqualify
disqualifies v ▷ disqualify
disqualify v (-fies, -fying, -fied) stop (someone) officially from taking part in something for wrongdoing > **disqualification** n (pl -s)
disqualifying v ▷ disqualify
disquiet n (pl -s) feeling of anxiety ▶ v (-s, -ing, -ed) make (someone) anxious > **disquietude** n (pl -s)

disquieted v ▷ disquiet
disquieting v ▷ disquiet
disquiets v, n ▷ disquiet
disquietude n ▷ disquiet
disquietudes n ▷ disquiet
disregard v (-s, -ing, -ed) give little or no attention to ▶ n (pl -s) lack of attention or respect
disregarded v ▷ disregard
disregarding v ▷ disregard
disregards v, n ▷ disregard
disrepair n (pl -s) condition of being worn out or in poor working order
disrepairs n ▷ disrepair
disreputable adj having or causing a bad reputation > **disreputably** adv
disreputably adv ▷ disreputable
disrepute n (pl -s) loss or lack of good reputation
disreputes n ▷ disrepute
disrespect n (pl -s) lack of respect > **disrespectful** adj > **disrespectfully** adv
disrespectful adj ▷ disrespect
disrespectfully adv ▷ disrespect
disrespects n ▷ disrespect
disrobe v (-robes, -robing, -robed) undress
disrobed v ▷ disrobe
disrobes v ▷ disrobe
disrobing v ▷ disrobe
disrupt v (-s, -ing, -ed) interrupt the progress of > **disruption** n (pl -s) > **disruptive** adj
disrupted v ▷ disrupt
disrupting v ▷ disrupt
disruption n ▷ disrupt
disruptions n ▷ disrupt
disruptive adj ▷ disrupt
disrupts v ▷ disrupt
dissatisfaction n ▷ dissatisfied
dissatisfactions n ▷ dissatisfied
dissatisfied adj not pleased or contented > **dissatisfaction** n (pl -s)
dissect v (-s, -ing, -ed) cut open (a corpse) to examine it > **dissection** n (pl -s)
dissected v ▷ dissect
dissecting v ▷ dissect
dissection n ▷ dissect
dissections n ▷ dissect
dissects v ▷ dissect
dissemble v (-bles, -bling, -bled) conceal one's real motives or emotions by pretence
dissembled v ▷ dissemble
dissembles v ▷ dissemble
dissembling v ▷ dissemble
disseminate v (-nates, -nating, -nated) spread (information) > **dissemination** n (pl -s)

disseminated v ▷ disseminate
disseminates v ▷ disseminate
disseminating v ▷ disseminate
dissemination n ▷ disseminate
disseminations n ▷ disseminate
dissension n ▷ dissent
dissensions n ▷ dissent
dissent v (-s, -ing, -ed) disagree ▶ n (pl -s) disagreement > **dissension** n (pl -s) > **dissenter** n (pl -s)
dissented v ▷ dissent
dissenter n ▷ dissent
dissenters n ▷ dissent
dissenting v ▷ dissent
dissents v ▷ dissent
dissertation n (pl -s) written thesis, usu. required for a higher university degree
dissertations n ▷ dissertation
disservice n (pl -s) harmful action
disservices n ▷ disservice
dissidence n ▷ dissident
dissidences n ▷ dissident
dissident n (pl -s) person who disagrees with and criticizes the government ▶ adj disagreeing with the government > **dissidence** n (pl -s)
dissidents n ▷ dissident
dissimilar adj not alike, different > **dissimilarity** n (pl -ities)
dissimilarities n ▷ dissimilar
dissimilarity n ▷ dissimilar
dissimulate v (-lates, -lating, -lated) conceal one's real feelings by pretence > **dissimulation** n (pl -s)
dissimulated v ▷ dissimulate
dissimulates v ▷ dissimulate
dissimulating v ▷ dissimulate
dissimulation n ▷ dissimulate
dissimulations n ▷ dissimulate
dissipate v (-pates, -pating, -pated) waste or squander > **dissipation** n (pl -s)
dissipated adj showing signs of overindulgence in alcohol and other physical pleasures ▶ v ▷ dissipate
dissipates v ▷ dissipate
dissipating v ▷ dissipate
dissipation n ▷ dissipate
dissipations n ▷ dissipate
dissociate v (-ciates, -ciating, -ciated) regard or treat as separate > **dissociation** n (pl -s)
dissociated v ▷ dissociate
dissociates v ▷ dissociate
dissociating v ▷ dissociate
dissociation n ▷ dissociate
dissociations n ▷ dissociate

dissolute *adj* leading an immoral life
> **dissolutely** *adv* > **dissoluteness** *n*
  dissolutely *adv* > dissolute
  dissoluteness *n* > dissolute
dissolution *n* (*pl* -s) official breaking up of
  an organization or institution, such as
  Parliament
  dissolutions *n* > dissolution
dissolve *v* (-solves, -solving, -solved) (cause to)
  become liquid
  dissolved *v* > dissolve
  dissolves *v* > dissolve
  dissolving *v* > dissolve
dissonance *n* (*pl* -s) lack of agreement or
  harmony > **dissonant** *adj*
  dissonances *n* > dissonance
  dissonant *adj* > dissonance
dissuade *v* (-suades, -suading, -suaded)
  deter (someone) by persuasion from doing
  something > **dissuasion** *n* (*pl* -s)
  dissuaded *v* > dissuade
  dissuades *v* > dissuade
  dissuading *v* > dissuade
  dissuasion *n* > dissuade
  dissuasions *n* > dissuade
distaff *n* (*pl* -s) rod on which wool etc. is
  wound for spinning
  distaffs *n* > distaff
distance *n* (*pl* -s) space between two points
  distances *n* > distance
distant *adj* far apart > **distantly** *adv*
  distantly *adv* > distant
distaste *n* (*pl* -s) dislike, disgust
distasteful *adj* unpleasant, offensive
  > **distastefulness** *n*
  distastefulness *n* > distasteful
  distastes *n* > distaste
distemper¹ *n* (*pl* -s) highly contagious viral
  disease of dogs
distemper² *n* (*pl* -s) paint mixed with water,
  glue, etc., used for painting walls
  distempers *n* > distemper¹, ²
distend *v* (-s, -ing, -ed) (of part of the body)
  swell > **distension** *n* (*pl* -s)
  distended *v* > distend
  distending *v* > distend
  distends *v* > distend
  distension *n* > distend
  distensions *n* > distend
distil *v* (-tils, -tilling, -tilled) subject to or
  obtain by distillation
  distillate *n* > distillation
  distillates *n* > distillation
distillation *n* (*pl* -s) process of evaporating
  a liquid and condensing its vapour (*also*

distillate) (*pl* -s)
  distillations *n* > distillation
  distilled *v* > distil
distiller *n* (*pl* -s) person or company that
  makes strong alcoholic drink, esp. whisky
  distilleries *n* > distillery
  distillers *n* > distiller
distillery *n* (*pl* -leries) place where a strong
  alcoholic drink, esp. whisky, is made
  distilling *v* > distil
  distils *v* > distil
distinct *adj* (-er, -est) not the same > **distinctly**
  adv > **distinctness** *n* (*pl* -es)
  distincter *adj* > distinct
  distinctest *adj* > distinct
distinction *n* (*pl* -s) act of distinguishing
  distinctions *n* > distinction
distinctive *adj* easily recognizable
  > **distinctively** *adv* > **distinctiveness** *n*
  distinctively *adv* > distinctive
  distinctiveness *n* > distinctive
  distinctly *adv* > distinct
  distinctness *n* > distinct
  distinctnesses *n* > distinct
distinguish *v* (-es, -ing, -ed) (*usu. foll. by*
  between) make, show, or recognize a
  difference (between) > **distinguishable** *adj*
  distinguishable *adj* > distinguish
distinguished *adj* dignified in appearance ▶ *v*
  > distinguish
  distinguishes *v* > distinguish
  distinguishing *v* > distinguish
distort *v* (-s, -ing, -ed) misrepresent (the truth
  or facts) > **distortion** *n* (*pl* -s)
  distorted *v* > distort
  distorting *v* > distort
  distortion *n* > distort
  distortions *n* > distort
  distorts *v* > distort
distract *v* (-s, -ing, -ed) draw the attention
  of (a person) away from something
  > **distraction** *n* (*pl* -s)
distracted *adj* unable to concentrate,
  preoccupied ▶ *v* > distract > **distractedly** *adv*
  distractedly *adv* > distracted
  distracting *v* > distract
  distraction *n* > distract
  distractions *n* > distract
  distracts *v* > distract
distrait [diss-tray] *adj* absent-minded or
  preoccupied
distraught [diss-trawt] *adj* extremely anxious
  or agitated
distress *n* (*pl* -es) extreme unhappiness ▶ *v*
  (-es, -ing, -ed) upset badly > **distressing** *adj*

> **distressingly** adv

distressed adj extremely upset ► v ▷ distress

distresses n, v ▷ distress

distressing v, adj ▷ distress

distressingly adv ▷ distress

distribute v (-butes, -buting, -buted) hand out or deliver > **distributive** adj > **distributively** adv

distributed v ▷ distribute

distributes v ▷ distribute

distributing v ▷ distribute

distribution n (pl -s) distributing

distributions n ▷ distribution

distributive adj ▷ distribute

distributively adv ▷ distribute

distributor n (pl -s) wholesaler who distributes goods to retailers in a specific area

distributors n ▷ distributor

district n (pl -s) area of land regarded as an administrative or geographical unit

districts n ▷ district

distrust v (-s, -ing, -ed) regard as untrustworthy ► n (pl -s) feeling of suspicion or doubt > **distrustful** adj

distrusted v ▷ distrust

distrustful adj ▷ distrust

distrusting v ▷ distrust

distrusts v, n ▷ distrust

disturb v (-s, -ing, -ed) intrude on > **disturbance** n (pl -s) > **disturbing** adj > **disturbingly** adv

disturbance n ▷ disturb

disturbances n ▷ disturb

disturbed adj (PSYCHIATRY) emotionally upset or maladjusted ► v ▷ disturb

disturbing v, adj ▷ disturb

disturbingly adv ▷ disturb

disturbs v ▷ disturb

disunite v (-nites, -niting, -nited) cause disagreement among > **disunity** n (pl -ities)

disunited v ▷ disunite

disunites v ▷ disunite

disunities n ▷ disunite

disuniting v ▷ disunite

disunity n ▷ disunite

disuse n (pl -s) state of being no longer used > **disused** adj

disused adj ▷ disuse

disuses n ▷ disuse

ditch n (pl -es) narrow channel dug in the earth for drainage or irrigation ► v (-es, -ing, -ed) (Slang) abandon

ditched v ▷ ditch

ditches n, v ▷ ditch

ditching v ▷ ditch

dither v (-s, -ing, -ed) be uncertain or indecisive ► n (pl -s) state of indecision or agitation > **ditherer** n (pl -s) > **dithery** adj > **ditheriness** n

dithered v ▷ dither

ditheriness n ▷ dither

dithering v ▷ dither

dithers v, n ▷ dither

dithery adj ▷ dither

ditties n ▷ ditty

ditto n (pl -tos) the same ► adv in the same way

dittos n ▷ ditto

ditty n (pl -ties) short simple poem or song

diuretic [die-yoor-et-ik] n (pl -s) drug that increases the flow of urine

diuretics n ▷ diuretic

diurnal [die-urn-al] adj happening during the day or daily > **diurnally** adv

diurnally adv ▷ diurnal

diva n (pl -s) distinguished female singer

divan n (pl -s) low backless bed

divans n ▷ divan

divas n ▷ diva

dive v (dives, diving, dived) plunge headfirst into water (foll. by in or into) ► n (pl -s) diving

dived v ▷ dive

diver n (pl -s) person who works or explores underwater

diverge v (-verges, -verging, -verged) separate and go in different directions > **divergence** n (pl -s) > **divergent** adj

diverged v ▷ diverge

divergence n ▷ diverge

divergences n ▷ diverge

divergent adj ▷ diverge

diverges v ▷ diverge

diverging v ▷ diverge

divers adj (Old-fashioned) various ► n ▷ diver

diverse adj having variety, assorted > **diversely** adv > **diversify** v (-fies, -fying, -fied) > **diversification** n (pl -s)

diversely adv ▷ diverse

diversification n ▷ diverse

diversifications n ▷ diverse

diversified v ▷ diverse

diversifies v ▷ diverse

diversify v ▷ diverse

diversifying v ▷ diverse

diversion n (pl -s) official detour used by traffic when a main route is closed > **diversionary** adj

diversionary adj ▷ diversion

diversions n ▷ diversion

diversities n ▷ diversity

diversity n (pl -ties) quality of being different or varied

divert v (-s, -ing, -ed) change the direction of
diverted v ▷ divert
diverting v ▷ divert
diverts v ▷ divert
dives v, n ▷ dive

divest v (-s, -ing, -ed) strip (of clothes)
divested v ▷ divest
divesting v ▷ divest
divests v ▷ divest

divide v (-vides, -viding, -vided) separate into parts ▶ n (pl -s) division, split
divided v ▷ divide

dividend n (pl -s) sum of money representing part of the profit made, paid by a company to its shareholders
dividends n ▷ dividend

divider n (pl -s) screen used to divide a room into separate areas ▶ pl compasses with two pointed arms, used for measuring or dividing lines
dividers n ▷ divider
divides v, n ▷ divide
dividing v ▷ divide

divination n (pl -s) art of discovering future events, as though by supernatural powers
divinations n ▷ divination

divine adj (-r, -st) of God or a god ▶ v (-nes, -ning, -ned) discover (something) by intuition or guessing > **divinely** adv
divined v ▷ divine
divinely adv ▷ divine
diviner adj ▷ divine
divines v ▷ divine
divinest adj ▷ divine
diving v ▷ dive
divining v ▷ divine
divinities n ▷ divinity

divinity n study of religion (pl -ties)
divisibility n ▷ divisible
divisible adj > **divisibility** n

division n (pl -s) dividing, sharing out
divisional adj of a division in an organization > **divisionally** adv
divisionally adv ▷ divisional
divisions n ▷ division

divisive adj tending to cause disagreement > **divisively** adv > **divisiveness** n
divisively adv ▷ divisive
divisiveness n ▷ divisive

divisor n (pl -s) number to be divided into another number
divisors n ▷ divisor

divorce n (pl -s) legal ending of a marriage ▶ v

(-ces, -cing, -ced) legally end one's marriage (to)
divorcé n ▷ divorcée
divorced v ▷ divorce

divorcée, masc **divorcé** n (pl -s) person who is divorced
divorcées n ▷ divorcée
divorces n, v ▷ divorce
divorcés n ▷ divorcée
divorcing v ▷ divorce

divulge v (-ges, -ging, -ged) make known, disclose > **divulgence** n (pl -s)
divulged v ▷ divulge
divulgence n ▷ divulge
divulgences n ▷ divulge
divulges v ▷ divulge
divulging v ▷ divulge

dizzied v ▷ dizzy
dizzier adj ▷ dizzy
dizzies v ▷ dizzy
dizziest adj ▷ dizzy
dizzily adv ▷ dizzy
dizziness n ▷ dizzy

dizzy adj (-zier, -ziest) having or causing a whirling sensation ▶ v (-zies, -zying, -zied) make dizzy > **dizzily** adv > **dizziness** n
dizzying v ▷ dizzy

do v (does, doing, did, done) perform or complete (a deed or action) ▶ n (pl dos, do's) (Informal) party, celebration

docile adj (-r, -st) (of a person or animal) easily controlled > **docilely** adv > **docility** n (pl -ties)
docilely adv ▷ docile
dociler adj ▷ docile
docilest adj ▷ docile
docilities n ▷ docile
docility n ▷ docile

dock[1] n (pl -s) enclosed area of water where ships are loaded, unloaded, or repaired ▶ v (-s, -ing, -ed) bring or be brought into dock
dock[2] v (docks, docking, docked) deduct money from (a person's wages)
dock[3] n (pl -s) enclosed space in a court of law where the accused person sits or stands
dock[4] n (pl -s) weed with broad leaves
docked v ▷ dock

docker n (pl -s) (BRIT) person employed to load and unload ships
dockers n ▷ docker

docket n (pl dockets) label on a package or other delivery, stating contents, delivery instructions, etc.
dockets n ▷ docket
docking v ▷ dock
docks n ▷ dock[1, 3, 4] ▶ v ▷ dock[1, 2]

dockyard n (pl -s) place where ships are built or repaired
  dockyards n ▷ dockyard
doctor n (pl -s) person licensed to practise medicine ▶ v (-s, -ing, -ed) alter in order to deceive > **doctoral** adj
  doctoral adj ▷ doctor
doctorate n (pl -s) highest academic degree in any field of knowledge
  doctorates n ▷ doctorate
  doctored v ▷ doctor
  doctoring v ▷ doctor
  doctors n, v ▷ doctor
doctrinaire adj stubbornly insistent on the application of a theory without regard to practicality
doctrinal adj of doctrines > **doctrinally** adv
  doctrinally adv ▷ doctrinal
doctrine n (pl -s) body of teachings of a religious, political, or philosophical group
  doctrines n ▷ doctrine
document n (pl -s) piece of paper providing an official record of something ▶ v (-s, -ing, -ed) record or report (something) in detail > **documentation** n (pl -s)
  documentaries n ▷ documentary
documentary n (pl -ries) film or television programme presenting the facts about a particular subject ▶ adj (of evidence) based on documents
  documentation n ▷ document
  documentations n ▷ document
  documented v ▷ document
  documenting v ▷ document
  documents n, v ▷ document
dodder v (-s, -ing, -ed) move unsteadily > **doddery** adj (-rier, -riest)
  doddered v ▷ dodder
  dodderier adj ▷ dodder
  dodderiest adj ▷ dodder
  doddering v ▷ dodder
  dodders v ▷ dodder
  doddery adj ▷ dodder
dodecagon [doe-**deck**-a-gon] n (pl -s) geometric figure with twelve sides
  dodecagons n ▷ dodecagon
dodge v (dodges, dodging, dodged) avoid (a blow, being seen, etc.) by moving suddenly ▶ n (pl -s) cunning or deceitful trick
  dodged v ▷ dodge
dodger n (pl -s) person who evades a responsibility or duty
  dodgers n ▷ dodger
  dodges v, n ▷ dodge
  dodgier adj ▷ dodgy

  dodgiest adj ▷ dodgy
  dodging v ▷ dodge
dodgy adj (-gier, -giest) (Informal) dangerous, risky
dodo n (pl -s, -es) large flightless extinct bird
  dodoes n ▷ dodo
  dodos n ▷ dodo
doe n (pl -s) female deer, hare, or rabbit
  does n ▷ doe ▶ v ▷ do
doesn't does not
doff v (-s, -ing, -ed) take off or lift (one's hat) in polite greeting
  doffed v ▷ doff
  doffing v ▷ doff
  doffs v ▷ doff
dog n (pl -s) domesticated four-legged mammal of many different breeds ▶ v (dogs, dogging, dogged) follow (someone) closely
dogcart n (pl -s) light horse-drawn two-wheeled cart
  dogcarts n ▷ dogcart
doge [doje] n (pl -s) (formerly) chief magistrate of Venice or Genoa
dogeared adj (of a book) having pages folded down at the corner
  doges n ▷ doge
dogfight n (pl -s) close-quarters combat between fighter aircraft
  dogfights n ▷ dogfight
dogfish n (pl -es) small shark
  dogfishes n ▷ dogfish
dogged [dog-gid] adj obstinately determined ▶ v ▷ dog > **doggedly** adv > **doggedness** n (pl -es)
  doggedly adv ▷ dogged
  doggedness n ▷ dogged
  doggednesses n ▷ dogged
doggerel n (pl -s) poorly written poetry, usu. comic
  doggerels n ▷ doggerel
  doggie n ▷ doggy
  doggies n ▷ doggy
  dogging v ▷ dog
doggo adv (Informal) in hiding and keeping quiet
doggy, doggie n (pl -gies) child's word for a dog
doghouse n (pl -s) (US) kennel
  doghouses n ▷ doghouse
dogleg n (pl -s) sharp bend
  doglegs n ▷ dogleg
dogma n (pl -s) doctrine or system of doctrines proclaimed by authority as true > **dogmatic** adj habitually stating one's opinions forcefully or arrogantly > **dogmatically** adv

> **dogmatism** n
dogmas n ▷ dogma
dogs n, v ▷ dog
dogsbodies n ▷ dogsbody
dogsbody n (pl -**bodies**) (*Informal*) person who carries out boring tasks for others

doh interj. Doh is a sound people make when things go wrong. Doh scores 7 points.

doilies n ▷ doily
doily n (pl -**lies**) decorative lacy paper mat, laid on a plate
doing v ▷ do
doldrums pl n depressed state of mind
dole n (pl -s) (BRIT, AUST & NZ) (*Informal*) money received from the state while unemployed ▶ v (**doles, doling, doled**) (foll. by **out**) distribute in small quantities
doled v ▷ dole
doleful adj dreary, unhappy > **dolefully** adv
> **dolefulness** n
dolefully adv ▷ doleful
dolefulness n ▷ doleful
doles v, n ▷ dole
doling v ▷ dole
doll n (pl -s) small model of a human being, used as a toy
dollar n (pl -s) standard monetary unit of many countries
dollars n ▷ dollar
dollies n ▷ dolly
dollop n (pl -s) (*Informal*) lump (of food)
dollops n ▷ dollop
dolls n ▷ doll
dolly n (pl -**lies**) child's word for a doll
dolmen n (pl -s) prehistoric monument consisting of a horizontal stone supported by vertical stones
dolmens n ▷ dolmen
dolomite n (pl -s) mineral consisting of calcium magnesium carbonate
dolomites n ▷ dolomite
dolorous adj sad, mournful > **dolorously** adv
dolorously adv ▷ dolorous
dolphin n (pl -s) sea mammal of the whale family, with a beaklike snout
dolphinaria n ▷ dolphinarium
dolphinarium n (pl -**ariums, -aria**) aquarium for dolphins
dolphinariums n ▷ dolphinarium
dolphins n ▷ dolphin
dolt n (pl -s) stupid person > **doltish** adj
> **doltishness** n
doltish adj ▷ dolt
doltishness n ▷ dolt

dolts n ▷ dolt
domain n (pl -s) field of knowledge or activity
domains n ▷ domain
dome n (pl -s) rounded roof built on a circular base > **domed** adj
domes n ▷ dome
domestic adj of one's own country or a specific country ▶ n (pl -s) person whose job is to do housework in someone else's house
> **domestically** adv > **domesticity** n
domestically adv ▷ domestic
domesticate v (-**cates, -cating, -cated**) bring or keep (a wild animal or plant) under control or cultivation > **domestication** n (pl -s)
domesticated v ▷ domesticate
domesticates v ▷ domesticate
domesticating v ▷ domesticate
domestication n ▷ domesticate
domestications n ▷ domesticate
domesticity n ▷ domestic
domestics n ▷ domestic
domicile [dom-miss-ile] n (pl -s) place where one lives
domiciles n ▷ domicile
dominance n ▷ dominant
dominances n ▷ dominant
dominant adj having authority or influence
> **dominance** n (pl -s)
dominate v (-**nates, -nating, -nated**) control or govern > **domination** n (pl -s)
dominated v ▷ dominate
dominates v ▷ dominate
dominating v ▷ dominate
domination n ▷ dominate
dominations n ▷ dominate
domineering adj forceful and arrogant
dominion n (pl -s) control or authority
dominions n ▷ dominion
domino n (pl -**noes**) small rectangular block marked with dots, used in dominoes ▶ pl game in which dominoes with matching halves are laid together
dominoes n ▷ domino
don[1] v (**dons, donning, donned**) put on (clothing)
don[2] n (pl -s) (BRIT) member of the teaching staff at a university or college
donate v (-**nates, -nating, -nated**) give, esp. to a charity or organization
donated v ▷ donate
donates v ▷ donate
donating v ▷ donate
donation n (pl -s) donating
donations n ▷ donation
done v ▷ do

donga [dong-ga] n (pl -s) (S AFR, AUST & NZ) steep-sided gully created by soil erosion
dongas n ▷ donga
donkey n (pl -s) long-eared member of the horse family
donkeys n ▷ donkey
donkeywork n (pl -s) tedious hard work
donkeyworks n ▷ donkeywork
donned v ▷ don¹
donning v ▷ don¹
donnish adj serious and academic
> **donnishness** n (pl -es)
donnishness n ▷ donnish
donnishnesses n ▷ donnish
donor n (pl -s) (MED) person who gives blood or organs for use in the treatment of another person
donors n ▷ donor
dons v ▷ don¹ ▶ n ▷ don²
doodle v (-dles, -dling, -dled) scribble or draw aimlessly ▶ n (pl -s) shape or picture drawn aimlessly
doodled v ▷ doodle
doodles v, n ▷ doodle
doodling v ▷ doodle
doom n (pl -s) death or a terrible fate ▶ v (-s, -ing, -ed) destine or condemn to death or a terrible fate
doomed v ▷ doom
dooming v ▷ doom
dooms n, v ▷ doom
doomsday n (pl -s) (CHRISTIANITY) day on which the Last Judgment will occur
doomsdays n ▷ doomsday
door n (pl -s) hinged or sliding panel for closing the entrance to a building, room, etc.
doormat n (pl -s) mat for wiping dirt from shoes before going indoors
doormats n ▷ doormat
doors n ▷ door
doorway n (pl -s) opening into a building or room
doorways n ▷ doorway
dope n (pl -s) (Slang) illegal drug, usu. cannabis ▶ v (dopes, doping, doped) give a drug to, esp. in order to improve performance in a race
doped v ▷ dope
dopes n, v ▷ dope
dopey, dopy (dopier, dopiest) adj half-asleep, drowsy
dopier adj ▷ dopey
dopiest adj ▷ dopey
doping v ▷ dope
dopy adj ▷ dopey
dorb n ▷ dorba

dorba n (pl -s) (AUST) (Slang) stupid, inept, or clumsy person (also **dorb**) (pl -s)
dorbas n ▷ dorba
dorbs n ▷ dorba
dories n ▷ dory
dork n (pl -s) (Slang) stupid person
dorks n ▷ dork
dormancy n ▷ dormant
dormant adj temporarily quiet, inactive, or not being used > **dormancy** n
dormer n (pl -s) window that sticks out from a sloping roof
dormers n ▷ dormer
dormice n ▷ dormouse
dormitories n ▷ dormitory
dormitory n (pl -ries) large room, esp. at a school, containing several beds
dormouse n (pl -mice) small mouselike rodent with a furry tail
dorp n (pl -s) (S AFR) small town
dorps n ▷ dorp
dorsal adj of or on the back
dory n (pl -ries) spiny-finned edible sea fish
dos n ▷ do
do's n ▷ do
dosage n (pl -s) size of a dose
dosages n ▷ dosage
dose n (pl -s) specific quantity of a medicine taken at one time ▶ v (doses, dosing, dosed) give a dose to
dosed v ▷ dose
doses n, v ▷ dose
dosing v ▷ dose
doss v (-es, -ing, -ed) (Slang) sleep in an uncomfortable place
dossed v ▷ doss
dosses v ▷ doss
dosshouse n (pl -s) (BRIT & S AFR) (Slang) cheap lodging house for homeless people
dosshouses n ▷ dosshouse
dossier [doss-ee-ay] n (pl -s) collection of documents about a subject or person
dossiers n ▷ dossier
dossing v ▷ doss
dot n (pl -s) small round mark ▶ v (dots, dotting, dotted) mark with a dot
dotage n (pl -s) weakness as a result of old age
dotages n ▷ dotage
dotcom n (pl -s) company that does most of its business on the Internet
dotcoms n ▷ dotcom
dote v (dotes, doting, doted) love to an excessive degree
doted v ▷ dote
dotes v ▷ dote

doting v ▷ dote
dots n, v ▷ dot
dotted v ▷ dot
dottier adj ▷ dotty
dottiest adj ▷ dotty
dottily adv ▷ dotty
dottiness n ▷ dotty
dottinesses n ▷ dotty
dotting v ▷ dot
dotty adj (-tier, -ttiest) (Slang) rather eccentric > **dottily** adv > **dottiness** n (pl -es)
double adj as much again in number, amount, size, etc. ▶ adv twice over ▶ n (pl -s) twice the number, amount, size, etc. ▶ pl game between two pairs of players ▶ v (-bles, -bling, -bled) make or become twice as much or as many > **doubly** adv
doubled v ▷ double
doubles n, v ▷ double
doublet [dub-lit] n (pl -s) (HIST) man's close-fitting jacket, with or without sleeves
doublets n ▷ doublet
doubling v ▷ double
doubloon n (pl -s) former Spanish gold coin
doubloons n ▷ doubloon
doubly adv ▷ double
doubt n (pl -s) uncertainty about the truth, facts, or existence of something ▶ v (-s, -ing, -ed) question the truth of > **doubter** n (pl -s)
doubted v ▷ doubt
doubter n ▷ doubt
doubters n ▷ doubt
doubtful adj unlikely > **doubtfully** adv
doubtfully adv ▷ doubtful
doubting v ▷ doubt
doubtless adv probably or certainly > **doubtlessly** adv
doubtlessly adv ▷ doubtless
doubts n, v ▷ doubt
douche [doosh] n (pl -s) (instrument for applying) a stream of water directed onto or into the body for cleansing or medical purposes ▶ v (-es, -ing, -ed) cleanse or treat by means of a douche
douched v ▷ douche
douches n, v ▷ douche
douching v ▷ douche
dough n (pl -s) thick mixture of flour and water or milk, used for making bread etc.
doughnut n (pl -s) small cake of sweetened dough fried in deep fat
doughnuts n ▷ doughnut
doughs n ▷ dough
doughtier adj ▷ doughty
doughtiest adj ▷ doughty

doughtily adv ▷ doughty
doughtiness n ▷ doughty
doughtinesses n ▷ doughty
doughty [dowt-ee] adj (-tier, -tiest) (Old-fashioned) brave and determined > **doughtily** adv > **doughtiness** n (pl -es)
dour [doo-er] adj (-er, -est) sullen and unfriendly > **dourly** adv > **dourness** n (pl -es)
dourer adj ▷ dour
dourest adj ▷ dour
dourly adv ▷ dour
dourness n ▷ dour
dournesses n ▷ dour
douse [rhymes with **mouse**] v (-ses, -sing, -sed) drench with water or other liquid
doused v ▷ douse
douses v ▷ douse
dousing v ▷ douse
dove n (pl -s) bird with a heavy body, small head, and short legs
dovecot n ▷ dovecote
dovecote, dovecot n (pl -s) structure for housing pigeons
dovecotes n ▷ dovecote
dovecots n ▷ dovecote
doves n ▷ dove
dovetail n (pl -s) joint containing wedge-shaped tenons ▶ v (-s, -ing, -ed) fit together neatly
dovetailed v ▷ dovetail
dovetailing v ▷ dovetail
dovetails v ▷ dovetail

> **dow** n (**dows**). A dow is an Arab ship. Dow scores 7 points.

dowager n (pl -s) widow possessing property or a title obtained from her husband
dowagers n ▷ dowager
dowdier adj ▷ dowdy
dowdiest adj ▷ dowdy
dowdily adv ▷ dowdy
dowdiness n ▷ dowdy
dowdy adj (-dier, -diest) dull and old-fashioned > **dowdily** adv > **dowdiness** n
dowel n (pl -s) wooden or metal peg that fits into two corresponding holes to join two adjacent parts
dowels n ▷ dowel
dower n (pl -s) life interest in a part of her husband's estate allotted to a widow by law
dowers n ▷ dower
down¹ prep, adv indicating movement to or position in a lower place ▶ adv indicating completion of an action, lessening of intensity, etc. ▶ adj depressed, unhappy ▶ v (-s, -ing, -ed) (Informal) drink quickly

down² n (pl -s) soft fine feathers > **downiness** n
> **downy** adj (-nier, -niest)

downbeat adj (Informal) gloomy

downcast adj sad, dejected
downed v ▷ down¹

downfall n (pl -s) (cause of) a sudden loss of
position or reputation
downfalls n ▷ downfall

downgrade v (-grades, -grading, -graded)
reduce in importance or value
downgraded v ▷ downgrade
downgrades v ▷ downgrade
downgrading v ▷ downgrade

downhearted adj sad and discouraged
> **downheartedly** adv
downheartedly adv ▷ downhearted

downhill adj going or sloping down ▶ adv
towards the bottom of a hill
downier adj ▷ down²
downiest adj ▷ down²
downiness n ▷ down²
downing v ▷ down¹

download v (-s, -ing, -ed) transfer (data) from
the memory of one computer to that of
another, especially over the Internet ▶ n (pl -s)
file transferred in such a way
downloaded v ▷ download
downloading v ▷ download
downloads v, n ▷ download

downpour n (pl -s) heavy fall of rain
downpours n ▷ downpour

downright adj, adv extreme(ly)

downs pl n low grassy hills, esp. in S England
▶ v ▷ down¹ ▶ n ▷ down²

downstairs adv to or on a lower floor ▶ n lower
or ground floor

downtrodden adj oppressed and lacking the
will to resist

downward adj, adv (descending) from a higher
to a lower level, condition, or position

downwards adv from a higher to a lower level,
condition, or position

downy adj ▷ down²

dowries n ▷ dowry

dowry n (pl -ries) property brought by a
woman to her husband at marriage

dowse [rhymes with **cows**] v (-ses, -sing, -sed)
search for underground water or minerals
using a divining rod
dowsed v ▷ dowse
dowses v ▷ dowse
dowsing v ▷ dowse

doxologies n ▷ doxology

doxology n (pl -gies) short hymn of praise
to God

doy n (**doys**). Doy is a dialect word for a
beloved person. Doy scores 7 points.

doyen [doy-en] n (pl -s) senior member of a
group, profession, or society > **doyenne**
[doy-en] ▶ n fem
doyenne n ▷ doyen
doyennes n ▷ doyen
doyens n ▷ doyen

doze v (dozes, dozing, dozed) sleep lightly or
briefly ▶ n (pl -s) short sleep
dozed v ▷ doze

dozen adj, n (pl -s) twelve > **dozenth** adj
dozens n ▷ dozen
dozenth adj ▷ dozen
dozes v, n ▷ doze
dozier adj ▷ dozy
doziest adj ▷ dozy
dozily adv ▷ dozy
doziness n ▷ dozy
dozing v ▷ doze

dozy adj (dozier, doziest) feeling sleepy
> **dozily** adv > **doziness** adv

drab adj (drabber, drabbest) dull and dreary
> **drably** adv > **drabness** n (pl -es)
drabber adj ▷ drab
drabbest adj ▷ drab
drably adv ▷ drab
drabness n ▷ drab
drabnesses n ▷ drab

drachm [dram] n (pl -s) (BRIT) one eighth of a
fluid ounce

drachma n (pl -mas, -mae) former monetary
unit of Greece
drachmae n ▷ drachma
drachmas n ▷ drachma
drachms n ▷ drachm

draconian adj severe, harsh

draft n (pl -s) plan, sketch, or drawing of
something (US & AUST) ▶ v (-s, -ing, -ed) draw
up an outline or plan of
drafted v ▷ draft
drafting v ▷ draft
drafts n, v ▷ draft

drag v (-s, -gging, -gged) pull with force, esp.
along the ground (foll. by **on** or **out**) ▶ n (pl -s)
person or thing that slows up progress
dragged v ▷ drag
dragging v ▷ drag

dragnet n (pl -s) net used to scour the bottom
of a pond or river to search for something
dragnets n ▷ dragnet

dragon n (pl -s) mythical fire-breathing
monster like a huge lizard
dragonflies n ▷ dragonfly

dragonfly n (pl -flies) brightly coloured insect

with a long slender body and two pairs of wings

dragons n ▷ dragon

dragoon n (pl -s) heavily armed cavalryman ▶ v (-s, -ing, -ed) coerce, force

dragooned v ▷ dragoon

dragooning v ▷ dragoon

dragoons n, v ▷ dragoon

drags v, n ▷ drag

drain n (pl -s) pipe or channel that carries off water or sewage ▶ v (-s, -ing, -ed) draw off or remove liquid from

drainage n (pl -s) system of drains

drainages n ▷ drainage

drained v ▷ drain

draining v ▷ drain

drains n, v ▷ drain

drake n (pl -s) male duck

drakes n ▷ drake

dram n (pl -s) small amount of a strong alcoholic drink, esp. whisky

drama n (pl -s) serious play for theatre, television, or radio

dramas n ▷ drama

dramatic adj of or like drama > **dramatically** adv

dramatically adv ▷ dramatic

dramatist n (pl -s) person who writes plays

dramatists n ▷ dramatist

dramatization n ▷ dramatize

dramatizations n ▷ dramatize

dramatize v (-tizes, -tizing, -tized) rewrite (a book) in the form of a play > **dramatization** n (pl -s)

dramatized v ▷ dramatize

dramatizes v ▷ dramatize

dramatizing v ▷ dramatize

drams n ▷ dram

drank v ▷ drink

drape v (drapes, draping, draped) cover with material, usu. in folds ▶ n (pl -s) (AUST, US & CANADIAN) piece of cloth hung at a window or opening as a screen

draped v ▷ drape

draper n (pl -s) (BRIT) person who sells fabrics and sewing materials

draperies n ▷ drapery

drapers n ▷ draper

drapery n (pl -peries) fabric or clothing arranged and draped

drapes v, n ▷ drape

draping v ▷ drape

drastic adj strong and severe > **drastically** adv

drastically adv ▷ drastic

draught n (pl -s) current of cold air, esp. in an enclosed space ▶ pl game for two players using a chessboard and twelve draughts each ▶ adj (of an animal) used for pulling heavy loads

draughtier adj ▷ draughty

draughtiest adj ▷ draughty

draughtiness n ▷ draughty

draughts n ▷ draught

draughtsman n (pl -men) person employed to prepare detailed scale drawings of machinery, buildings, etc. > **draughtsmanship** n

draughtsmanship n ▷ draughtsman

draughtsmen n ▷ draughtsman

draughty adj (-tier, -tiest) exposed to draughts of air > **draughtiness** n

draw v (draws, drawing, drew, drawn) sketch (a figure, picture, etc.) with a pencil or pen ▶ n (pl -s) raffle or lottery

drawback n (pl -s) disadvantage

drawbacks n ▷ drawback

drawbridge n (pl -s) bridge that may be raised to prevent access or to enable vessels to pass

drawbridges n ▷ drawbridge

drawer n (pl -s) sliding box-shaped part of a piece of furniture, used for storage ▶ pl (Old-fashioned) undergarment worn on the lower part of the body

drawers n ▷ drawer

drawing n (pl -s) picture or plan made by means of lines on a surface ▶ v ▷ draw

drawl v (-s, -ing, -ed) speak slowly, with long vowel sounds ▶ n (pl drawls) drawling manner of speech

drawled v ▷ drawl

drawling v ▷ drawl

drawls v ▷ drawl

drawls n ▷ drawl

drawn v ▷ draw ▶ adj haggard, tired, or tense in appearance

draws n, v ▷ draw

drawstring n (pl -s) cord run through a hem around an opening, so that when it is pulled tighter, the opening closes

drawstrings n ▷ drawstring

dray n (pl -s) low cart used for carrying heavy loads

drays n ▷ dray

dread v (-s, -ing, -ed) anticipate with apprehension or fear ▶ n (pl -s) great fear

dreaded v ▷ dread

dreadful adj very disagreeable or shocking > **dreadfully** adv

dreadfully adv ▷ dreadful

dreading v ▷ dread

dreadlocks pl n hair worn in the Rastafarian style of tightly twisted strands

dreads v, n ▷ dread

dream n (pl -s) imagined series of events experienced in the mind while asleep (Informal) ▶ v (-s, -ing, -ed or -t) see imaginary pictures in the mind while asleep (often foll. by of or about) (foll. by of) ▶ adj ideal > **dreamer** n (pl -s)

dreamed v ▷ dream

dreamer n ▷ dream

dreamers n ▷ dream

dreamier adj ▷ dreamy

dreamiest adj ▷ dreamy

dreamily adv ▷ dreamy

dreaminess n ▷ dreamy

dreaminesses n ▷ dreamy

dreaming v ▷ dream

dreams n, v ▷ dream

dreamt v ▷ dream

dreamy adj (-mier, -miest) vague or impractical > **dreamily** adv > **dreaminess** n (pl -es)

drearier adj ▷ dreary

dreariest adj ▷ dreary

drearily adv ▷ dreary

dreariness n ▷ dreary

dreary adj (drearier, dreariest) dull, boring > **drearily** adv > **dreariness** n

dredge¹ v (dredges, dredging, dredged) clear or search (a river bed or harbour) by removing silt or mud

dredge² v (dredges, dredging, dredged) sprinkle (food) with flour etc.

dredged v ▷ dredge¹, ²

dredger n (pl -s) boat fitted with machinery for dredging

dredgers n ▷ dredger

dredges v ▷ dredge¹, ²

dredging v ▷ dredge¹, ²

dregs pl n solid particles that settle at the bottom of some liquids

drench v (-es, -ing, -ed) make completely wet

drenched v ▷ drench

drenches v ▷ drench

drenching v ▷ drench

dress n (pl -es) one-piece garment for a woman or girl, consisting of a skirt and bodice and sometimes sleeves ▶ v (-es, -ing, -ed) put clothes on

dressage [dress-ahzh] n (pl -s) training of a horse to perform manoeuvres in response to the rider's body signals

dressages n ▷ dressage

dressed v ▷ dress

dresser¹ n (pl -s) piece of furniture with shelves and with cupboards, for storing or displaying dishes

dresser² n (pl -s) (THEATRE) person employed to assist actors with their costumes

dressers n ▷ dresser¹, ²

dresses n, v ▷ dress

dressier adj ▷ dressy

dressiest adj ▷ dressy

dressiness n ▷ dressy

dressinesses n ▷ dressy

dressing n (pl -s) sauce for salad ▶ v ▷ dress

dressings n ▷ dressing

dressmaker n (pl -s) person who makes women's clothes > **dressmaking** n

dressmakers n ▷ dressmaker

dressmaking n ▷ dressmaker

dressy adj (-ssier, -ssiest) (of clothes) elegant > **dressiness** n (pl -es)

drew v ▷ draw

drey n (pl -s) squirrel's nest

dreys n ▷ drey

dribble v (-les, -ling, -led) (allow to) flow in drops ▶ n (pl -s) small quantity of liquid falling in drops > **dribbler** n (pl -s)

dribbled v ▷ dribble

dribbler n ▷ dribble

dribblers n ▷ dribble

dribbles v, n ▷ dribble

dribbling v ▷ dribble

dried v ▷ dry

drier¹ adj ▷ dry

drier² n (pl -s) ▷ dryer

driers n ▷ drier²

dries v ▷ dry

driest adj ▷ dry

drift v (-s, -ing, -ed) be carried along by currents of air or water ▶ n (pl -s) something piled up by the wind or current, such as a snowdrift

drifted v ▷ drift

drifter n (pl -s) person who moves aimlessly from place to place or job to job

drifters n ▷ drifter

drifting v ▷ drift

drifts v, n ▷ drift

driftwood n (pl -s) wood floating on or washed ashore by the sea

driftwoods n ▷ driftwood

drill¹ n (pl -s) tool or machine for boring holes ▶ v (-s, -ing, -ed) bore a hole in (something) with or as if with a drill

drill² n (pl -s) machine for sowing seed in rows

drill³ n (pl -s) hard-wearing cotton cloth

drilled v ▷ drill¹

drilling v ▷ drill¹
drills n ▷ drill¹, ², ³ ▶ v ▷ drill¹
drily adv ▷ dry
drink v (drinks, drinking, drank, drunk) swallow (a liquid) ▶ n (pl -s) (portion of) a liquid suitable for drinking > **drinkable** adj > **drinker** n (pl -s)
drinkable adj ▷ drink
drinker n ▷ drink
drinkers n ▷ drink
drinking v ▷ drink
drinks v, n ▷ drink
drip v (drips, dripping, dripped) (let) fall in drops ▶ n (pl -s) falling of drops of liquid
dripped v ▷ drip
dripping n (pl -s) fat that comes from meat while it is being roasted or fried ▶ v ▷ drip
drippings n ▷ dripping
drips v, n ▷ drip
drive v (drives, driving, drove, driven) guide the movement of (a vehicle) ▶ n (pl -s) journey by car, van, etc.; path for vehicles (also **driveway**) (pl -s)
drivel n (pl -s) foolish talk ▶ v (-els, -elling, -elled) speak foolishly
drivelled v ▷ drivel
drivelling v ▷ drivel
drivels v, n ▷ drivel
driven v ▷ drive
driver n (pl -s) person who drives a vehicle
drivers n ▷ driver
drives v, n ▷ drive
driveway n ▷ drive
driveways n ▷ drive
driving v ▷ drive
drizzle n (pl -s) very light rain ▶ v (-zles, -zling, -zled) rain lightly > **drizzly** adj
drizzled v ▷ drizzle
drizzles n, v ▷ drizzle
drizzling v ▷ drizzle
drizzly adj ▷ drizzle
droll adj (-er, -est) quaintly amusing > **drolly** adv > **drollery** n (pl -ries) > **drollness** n (pl -es)
droller adj ▷ droll
drolleries n ▷ droll
drollery n ▷ droll
drollest adj ▷ droll
drollness n ▷ droll
drollnesses n ▷ droll
drolly adv ▷ droll
dromedaries n ▷ dromedary
dromedary [drom-mid-er-ee] n (pl -daries) camel with a single hump
drone¹ n (pl -s) male bee
drone² v (drones, droned, droning) ▶ n (pl -s) (make) a monotonous low dull sound
droned v ▷ drone²
drones n ▷ drone¹, ² ▶ v ▷ drone²
drongo n (pl -gos) tropical songbird with a glossy black plumage, a forked tail, and a stout bill
drongos n ▷ drongo
droning v ▷ drone²
drool v (-s, -ing, -ed) (foll. by **over**) show excessive enthusiasm (for)
drooled v ▷ drool
drooling v ▷ drool
drools v ▷ drool
droop v (-s, -ing, -ed) hang downwards loosely > **droopy** adj (-pier, -piest)
drooped v ▷ droop
droopier adj ▷ droop
droopiest adj ▷ droop
drooping v ▷ droop
droops v ▷ droop
droopy adj ▷ droop
drop v (-s, -pping, -pped) (allow to) fall vertically ▶ n (pl -s) small quantity of liquid forming a round shape ▶ pl liquid medication applied in small drops > **droplet** n (pl -s)
droplet n ▷ drop
droplets n ▷ drop
dropout n (pl -s) person who rejects conventional society
dropouts n ▷ dropout
dropped v ▷ drop
dropping v ▷ drop
droppings pl n faeces of certain animals, such as rabbits or birds
drops v, n ▷ drop
dropsical adj ▷ dropsy
dropsies n ▷ dropsy
dropsy n (pl -sies) illness in which watery fluid collects in the body > **dropsical** adj
dross n (pl -es) scum formed on the surfaces of molten metals
drosses n ▷ dross
drought n (pl -s) prolonged shortage of rainfall
droughts n ▷ drought
drove¹ v ▷ drive
drove² n (pl -s) very large group, esp. of people
drover n (pl -s) person who drives sheep or cattle
drovers n ▷ drover
droves n ▷ drove²
drown v (-s, -ing, -ed) die or kill by immersion in liquid
drowned v ▷ drown
drowning v ▷ drown
drowns v ▷ drown

drowse v (-ses, -sing, -sed) be sleepy, dull, or sluggish > **drowsy** adj (-sier, -siest) > **drowsily** adv > **drowsiness** n (pl -es)

drowsed v ▷ drowse

drowses v ▷ drowse

drowsier adj ▷ drowse

drowsiest adj ▷ drowse

drowsily adv ▷ drowse

drowsiness n ▷ drowse

drowsinesses n ▷ drowse

drowsing v ▷ drowse

drowsy adj ▷ drowse

drubbing n (pl -s) utter defeat in a contest etc.

drubbings n ▷ drubbing

drudge n (pl -s) person who works hard at uninteresting tasks > **drudgery** n (pl -eries)

drudgeries n ▷ drudge

drudgery n ▷ drudge

drudges n ▷ drudge

drug n (pl -s) substance used in the treatment or prevention of disease ▶ v (drugs, drugging, drugged) give a drug to (a person or animal) to cause sleepiness or unconsciousness

drugged v ▷ drug

drugging v ▷ drug

drugs v, n ▷ drug

drugstore n (pl -s) (US) pharmacy where a wide range of goods are available

drugstores n ▷ drugstore

druid n (pl -s) member of an ancient order of Celtic priests > **druidic, druidical** adj

druidic adj ▷ druid

druidical adj ▷ druid

druids adj ▷ druid

drum n (pl -s) percussion instrument sounded by striking a membrane stretched across the opening of a hollow cylinder ▶ v (drums, drumming, drummed) play (music) on a drum

drummed v ▷ drum

drummer n (pl -s) person who plays a drum or drums

drummers n ▷ drummer

drumming v ▷ drum

drums n, v ▷ drum

drumstick n (pl -s) stick used for playing a drum

drumsticks n ▷ drumstick

drunk v ▷ drink ▶ adj (-er, -est) intoxicated with alcohol to the extent of losing control over normal functions ▶ n (pl -s) person who is drunk or who frequently gets drunk

drunkard n (pl -s) person who frequently gets drunk

drunkards n ▷ drunkard

drunken adj drunk or frequently drunk > **drunkenly** adv > **drunkenness** n (pl -es)

drunkenly adv ▷ drunken

drunkenness n ▷ drunken

drunkennesses n ▷ drunken

drunker adj ▷ drunk

drunkest adj ▷ drunk

drunks n ▷ drunk

dry adj (drier, driest or dryer, dryest) lacking moisture ▶ v (dries, drying, dried) make or become dry > **drily, dryly** adv > **dryness** n (pl -es)

dryad n (pl -s) wood nymph

dryads n ▷ dryad

dryer, drier n (pl -s) apparatus for removing moisture

dryer adj ▷ dry

dryers n ▷ dryer

dryest adj ▷ dry

drying v ▷ dry

dryly adv ▷ dry

dryness n ▷ dry

drynesses n ▷ dry

> **dso** n (**dsos**). Dso is one of several spelling for a Tibetan animal bred from yaks and cattle. The other forms are **dzo, zho** and **zo**, and it's worth remembering all of them. Dso scores 4 points.

dual adj having two parts, functions, or aspects > **duality** n (pl -ities) > **dually** adv

dualities n ▷ dual

duality n ▷ dual

dually adv ▷ dual

dub[1] v (dubs, dubbing, dubbed) give (a person or place) a name or nickname

dub[2] v (dubs, dubbing, dubbed) provide (a film) with a new soundtrack, esp. in a different language

dubbed v ▷ dub[1, 2]

dubbin n (pl -s) (BRIT) thick grease applied to leather to soften and waterproof it

dubbing v ▷ dub[1, 2]

dubbins n ▷ dubbin

dubieties n ▷ dubious

dubiety n ▷ dubious

dubious [dew-bee-uss] adj feeling or causing doubt > **dubiously** adv > **dubiousness** n > **dubiety** [dew-by-it-ee] n (pl -ities)

dubiously adv ▷ dubious

dubiousness n ▷ dubious

dubs v ▷ dub[1, 2]

ducal [duke-al] adj of a duke

ducat [duck-it] n (pl -s) former European gold or silver coin

ducats n ▷ ducat

duchess n (pl -es) woman who holds the rank of duke

duchesse n (pl -s) (NZ) dressing table with a mirror

duchesses n ▷ duchess, duchesse

duchies n ▷ duchy

duchy n (pl duchies) territory of a duke or duchess

duck¹ n (pl -s) water bird with short legs, webbed feet, and a broad blunt bill

duck² v (-s, -ing, -ed) move (the head or body) quickly downwards, to avoid being seen or to dodge a blow

ducked v ▷ duck²

ducking v ▷ duck²

duckling n (pl -s) baby duck

ducklings n ▷ duckling

ducks n ▷ duck¹ ▶ v ▷ duck²

duct n (pl -s) tube, pipe, or channel through which liquid or gas is conveyed

ductile adj (of a metal) able to be shaped into sheets or wires

ducts n ▷ duct

dud (Informal) n (pl -s) ineffectual person or thing ▶ adj bad or useless

dude n (pl -s) (US) (Informal) man

dudes n ▷ dude

dudgeon n (pl -s) anger, resentment

dudgeons n ▷ dudgeon

duds n ▷ dud

due adj expected or scheduled to be present or arrive ▶ n (pl -s) something that is owed or required ▶ pl charges for membership of a club or organization ▶ adv directly or exactly

duel n (pl -s) formal fight with deadly weapons between two people, to settle a quarrel ▶ v (-s, -lling, -lled) fight in a duel > **duellist** n (pl -s)

duelled v ▷ duel

duelling v ▷ duel

duellist n ▷ duel

duellists n ▷ duel

duels n, v ▷ duel

dues n ▷ due

duet n (pl -s) piece of music for two performers

duets n ▷ duet

duff adj (-er, -est) (CHIEFLY BRIT) broken or useless

duffel, duffle n (pl -s) heavy woollen cloth

duffels n ▷ duffel

duffer n (pl -s) (Informal) dull or incompetent person ▶ adj ▷ duff

duffers n ▷ duffer

duffest adj ▷ duff

duffle n ▷ duffel

duffles n ▷ duffel

dug¹ v ▷ dig

dug² n (pl -s) teat or udder

dugite [doo-gyte] n (pl -s) medium-sized Australian venomous snake

dugites n ▷ dugite

dugong n (pl -s) whalelike mammal of tropical waters

dugongs n ▷ dugong

dugout n (pl -s) (BRIT) (at a sports ground) covered bench where managers and substitutes sit

dugouts n ▷ dugout

dugs n ▷ dug²

duke n (pl -s) nobleman of the highest rank > **dukedom** n (pl -s)

dukedom n ▷ duke

dukedoms n ▷ duke

dukes n ▷ duke

dulcet [dull-sit] adj (of a sound) soothing or pleasant

dulcimer n (pl -s) tuned percussion instrument consisting of a set of strings stretched over a sounding board and struck with hammers

dulcimers n ▷ dulcimer

dull adj (-er, -est) not interesting ▶ v (-s, -ing, -ed) make or become dull > **dullness** n (pl -es) > **dully** adv

dullard n (pl -s) dull or stupid person

dullards n ▷ dullard

dulled v ▷ dull

duller adj ▷ dull

dullest adj ▷ dull

dulling v ▷ dull

dullness n ▷ dull

dullnesses n ▷ dull

dulls v ▷ dull

dully adv ▷ dull

duly adv in a proper manner

dumb adj (dumber, dumbest) lacking the power to speak > **dumbly** adv > **dumbness** n

dumbbell n (pl -s) short bar with a heavy ball or disc at each end, used for physical exercise

dumbbells n ▷ dumbbell

dumber adj ▷ dumb

dumbest adj ▷ dumb

dumbfounded adj speechless with astonishment

dumbly adv ▷ dumb

dumbness n ▷ dumb

dumdum n (pl -s) soft-nosed bullet that expands on impact and causes serious wounds

dumdums n ▷ dumdum

dummies n ▷ dummy

dummy n (pl -mies) figure representing the human form, used for displaying clothes etc. ▶ adj imitation, substitute

dump v (-s, -ing, -ed) drop or let fall in a careless manner ▶ n (pl -s) place where waste materials are left

dumped v ▷ dump

dumpier adj ▷ dumpy

dumpiest adj ▷ dumpy

dumpily adv ▷ dumpy

dumpiness n ▷ dumpy

dumping v ▷ dump

dumpling n (pl -s) small ball of dough cooked and served with stew

dumplings n ▷ dumpling

dumps v, n ▷ dump

dumpy adj (dumpier, dumpiest) short and plump > **dumpily** adv > **dumpiness** n

dun (dunner, dunnest) adj brownish-grey

dunce n (pl -s) person who is stupid or slow to learn

dunces n ▷ dunce

dunderhead n (pl -s) slow-witted person

dunderheads n ▷ dunderhead

dune n (pl -s) mound or ridge of drifted sand

dunes n ▷ dune

dung n (pl -s) faeces from animals such as cattle

dungarees pl n trousers with a bib attached

dungeon n (pl -s) underground prison cell

dungeons n ▷ dungeon

dungs n ▷ dung

dunk v (-s, -ing, -ed) dip (a biscuit or bread) in a drink or soup before eating it

dunked v ▷ dunk

dunking v ▷ dunk

dunks v ▷ dunk

dunner adj ▷ dun

dunnest adj ▷ dun

dunnies n ▷ dunny

dunny n (pl -nies) (AUST & OLD-FASHIONED NZ) (Informal) toilet

duo n (pl -s) pair of performers

duodena n ▷ duodenum

duodenal adj ▷ duodenum

duodenum [dew-oh-deen-um] n (pl -na, -nums) first part of the small intestine, just below the stomach > **duodenal** adj

duodenums n ▷ duodenum

duos n ▷ duo

dupe v (dupes, duping, duped) deceive or cheat ▶ n (pl -s) person who is easily deceived

duped v ▷ dupe

dupes v, n ▷ dupe

duping v ▷ dupe

duple adj (MUSIC) having two beats in a bar

duplex n (pl -es) (CHIEFLY US) apartment on two floors

duplexes n ▷ duplex

duplicate adj copied exactly from an original ▶ n (pl -s) exact copy ▶ v (-cates, -cating, -cated) make an exact copy of > **duplication** n (pl -s) > **duplicator** n (pl -s)

duplicated v ▷ duplicate

duplicates n, v ▷ duplicate

duplicating v ▷ duplicate

duplication n ▷ duplicate

duplications n ▷ duplicate

duplicator n ▷ duplicate

duplicators n ▷ duplicate

duplicities n ▷ duplicity

duplicity n (pl -ities) deceitful behaviour

durability n ▷ durable

durable adj long-lasting > **durability** n > **durably** adv

durables pl n goods that require infrequent replacement

durably adv ▷ durable

duration n (pl -s) length of time that something lasts

durations n ▷ duration

duress n compulsion by use of force or threats

during prep throughout or within the limit of (a period of time)

dusk n (pl -s) time just before nightfall, when it is almost dark

duskier adj ▷ dusky

duskiest adj ▷ dusky

duskily adv ▷ dusky

duskiness n ▷ dusky

dusks n ▷ dusk

dusky adj (duskier, duskiest) dark in colour > **duskily** adv > **duskiness** n

dust n (pl -s) small dry particles of earth, sand, or dirt ▶ v (-s, -ing, -ed) remove dust from (furniture) by wiping

dustbin n (pl -s) large container for household rubbish

dustbins n ▷ dustbin

dusted v ▷ dust

duster n (pl -s) cloth used for dusting

dusters n ▷ duster

dustier adj ▷ dusty

dustiest adj ▷ dusty

dusting v ▷ dust

dustman n (pl -men) (BRIT) man whose job is to collect household rubbish

dustmen n ▷ dustman

dustpan n (pl -s) short-handled shovel into which dust is swept from floors

dustpans n ▷ dustpan

dusts n, v ▷ dust

dusty adj (dustier, dustiest) covered with dust

dutiability n ▷ dutiable

dutiable adj (of goods) requiring payment of duty > **dutiability** n

duties n ▷ duty

dutiful adj doing what is expected > **dutifully** adv

dutifully adv ▷ dutiful

duty n (pl -ties) work or a task performed as part of one's job

duvet [doo-vay] n (pl -s) kind of quilt used in bed instead of a top sheet and blankets

duvets n ▷ duvet

> **dux** n (**duces**). A dux is the top pupil in a school. This is a handy word to have ready if someone else has played a word containing X. Dux scores 11 points.

dwang n (pl -s) (NZ & S AFR) short piece of wood inserted in a timber-framed wall

dwangs n ▷ dwang

dwarf n (pl dwarfs, dwarves) person who is smaller than average ▶ adj (of an animal or plant) much smaller than the usual size for the species ▶ v (dwarfs, dwarfing or dwarfed) cause (someone or something) to seem small by being much larger

dwarfed v ▷ dwarf

dwarfing v ▷ dwarf

dwarfs n, v ▷ dwarf

dwarves n ▷ dwarf

dwell v (dwells, dwelling, dwelt or dwelled) live, reside

dwelled v ▷ dwell

dweller n (pl -s) person who lives in a specified place

dwellers n ▷ dweller

dwelling n (pl -s) place of residence ▶ v ▷ dwell

dwellings n ▷ dwelling

dwells v ▷ dwell

dwelt v ▷ dwell

dwindle v (-dles, -dling, -dled) grow less in size, strength, or number

dwindled v ▷ dwindle

dwindles v ▷ dwindle

dwindling v ▷ dwindle

dye n (pl -s) colouring substance ▶ v (dyes, dyeing, dyed) colour (hair or fabric) by applying a dye > **dyer** n (pl -s)

dyed v ▷ dye

dyeing v ▷ dye

dyer n ▷ dye

dyers n ▷ dye

dyes n, v ▷ dye

dying v ▷ die¹

dyke n (pl -s) wall built to prevent flooding

dykes n ▷ dyke

dynamic adj full of energy, ambition, and new ideas > **dynamically** adv

dynamically adv ▷ dynamic

dynamics n branch of mechanics concerned with the forces that change or produce the motions of bodies ▶ pl forces that produce change in a system

dynamism n great energy and enthusiasm

dynamite n (pl -s) explosive made of nitroglycerine ▶ v (-mites, -miting, -mited) blow (something) up with dynamite

dynamited v ▷ dynamite

dynamites n, v ▷ dynamite

dynamiting v ▷ dynamite

dynamo n (pl -s) device for converting mechanical energy into electrical energy

dynamos n ▷ dynamo

dynastic adj ▷ dynasty

dynasties n ▷ dynasty

dynasty n (pl -ties) sequence of hereditary rulers > **dynastic** adj

dysenteries n ▷ dysentery

dysentery n (pl -teries) infection of the intestine causing severe diarrhoea

dysfunction n (pl -s) (MED) disturbance or abnormality in the function of an organ or part > **dysfunctional** adj > **dysfunctionally** adv

dysfunctional adj ▷ dysfunction

dysfunctionally adv ▷ dysfunction

dysfunctions n ▷ dysfunction

dyslexia n (pl -s) disorder causing impaired ability to read > **dyslexic** adj

dyslexias n ▷ dyslexia

dyslexic adj ▷ dyslexia

dysmenorrhoea n (pl -s) painful menstruation

dysmenorrhoeas n ▷ dysmenorrhoea

dyspepsia n (pl -s) indigestion > **dyspeptic** adj

dyspepsias n ▷ dyspepsia

dyspeptic adj ▷ dyspepsia

dystrophic adj ▷ dystrophy

dystrophies n ▷ dystrophy

dystrophy [diss-trof-fee] n (pl -phies) wasting disorder > **dystrophic** adj

dzho *n* (**dzhos**). A dzho is one of several ways of spelling the name of a Tibetan animal bred from yaks and cattle. This spelling is less useful than the others (**dso, dzo, zho** and **zo**) because it has four letters rather than two or three. It is, however, a very useful word to know when someone else has played zho, as you can use D to hook another word onto zho, or just to take advantage of the Z already on the board. Dzho scores 17 points.

dzo *n* (**dzos**). Dzo is one of several spelling for a Tibetan animal bred from yaks and cattle. The other forms are **dso, dzho, zho** and **zo,** and it's worth remembering all of them. Dzo scores 13 points.

Ee

E is the most common tile in the game and, while it is only worth one point, as the most frequent letter in English it is extremely useful. Many words contain two or more Es, so, unlike many tiles, it's good to have several Es on your rack. Keep in mind three-letter words formed by two Es either side of a consonant, like **eye, ewe** and **eve** (6 points each), and **eke** (7). E can also be handy for getting rid of double consonants: think of words like **egg** or **ebb** (each 5 points). E also combines well with K: as well as **eke**, we have **elk** and **eek** (both 7), and **ewk** (10). If you have an X on your rack, E offers you all kinds of options: just think of all the words that begin with ex-, like **exhaust** (17), which will give you a 50-point bonus if you use all of your tiles to form it. And don't forget **ex** itself, a nice little word that earns you 9 points.

ea n (**eas**). Ea is a dialect word for a river. This word won't earn you many points, but it does provide many opportunities to play longer words that form ea in the process. Ea scores 2 points.

each adj, pron every (one) taken separately

eager adj (-er, -est) showing or feeling great desire, keen > **eagerly** adv > **eagerness** n (pl -es)
  eagerer adj ▷ eager
  eagerest adj ▷ eager
  eagerly adv ▷ eager
  eagerness n ▷ eager
  eagernesses n ▷ eager

eagle n (pl -s) large bird of prey with keen eyesight
  eagles n ▷ eagle

eaglet n (pl -s) young eagle
  eaglets n ▷ eaglet

ear¹ n (pl -s) organ of hearing, esp. the external part of it

ear² n (pl -s) head of corn

earache n (pl -s) pain in the ear
  earaches n ▷ earache

earbash v (-es, -ing, -ed) (AUST & NZ) (Informal) talk incessantly > **earbashing** n (pl -s)
  earbashed n ▷ earbash
  earbashes n ▷ earbash
  earbashing v, n ▷ earbash
  earbashings n ▷ earbash

eardrum n (pl -s) thin piece of skin inside the ear which enables one to hear sounds
  eardrums n ▷ eardrum

earl n (pl -s) British nobleman ranking next below a marquess > **earldom** n (pl -s)
  earldom n ▷ earl
  earldoms n ▷ earl

earlier adj, adv ▷ early

earliest adj, adv ▷ early

earls n ▷ earl

early adj, adv (-ier, -iest) before the expected or usual time

earmark v (-s, -ing, -ed) set (something) aside for a specific purpose
  earmarked v ▷ earmark
  earmarking v ▷ earmark
  earmarks v ▷ earmark

earn v (-s, -ing, -ed) obtain by work or merit
  earned v ▷ earn

earnest¹ adj serious and sincere > **earnestly** adv

earnest² n (pl -s) part payment given in advance, esp. to confirm a contract
  earnests n ▷ earnest²
  earning v ▷ earn

earnings pl n money earned
  earns v ▷ earn

earphone n (pl -s) receiver for a radio etc., held to or put in the ear
  earphones n ▷ earphone

earring n (pl -s) ornament for the lobe of the ear
  earrings n ▷ earring
  ears n ▷ ear¹, ²

earshot n (pl -s) hearing range
  earshots n ▷ earshot

earth n (pl -s) land, the ground ▶ v (-s, -ing, -ed)

connect (a circuit) to earth
earthed v ▷ earth
earthen adj made of baked clay or earth
earthenware n (pl -s) pottery made of baked
clay
earthenwares n ▷ earthenwares
earthier adj ▷ earthy
earthiest adj ▷ earthy
earthing v ▷ earth
earthly adj conceivable or possible
earthquake n (pl -s) violent vibration of the
earth's surface
earthquakes n ▷ earthquake
earths n, v ▷ earth
earthwork n (pl -s) fortification made of earth
earthworks n ▷ earthwork
earthworm n (pl -s) worm which burrows in
the soil
earthworms n ▷ earthworm
earthy adj (-thier, -thiest) coarse or crude
earwig n (pl -s) small insect with a pincer-like
tail
earwigs n ▷ earwig
ease n (pl -ses) freedom from difficulty,
discomfort, or worry ▶ v (-ses, -sing, -sed)
give bodily or mental ease to
eased v ▷ ease
easel n (pl -s) frame to support an artist's
canvas or a blackboard
easels n ▷ easel
eases n, v ▷ ease
easier adj ▷ easy
easily adv ▷ easy
easiest adj ▷ easy
easiness n ▷ easy
easinesses n ▷ easy
easing v ▷ ease
east n (pl -s) (direction towards) the part of
the horizon where the sun rises ▶ adj to or
in the east ▶ adv in, to, or towards the east
> **easterly** adj > **eastern** adj > **eastward** adj,
adv > **eastwards** adv
easterly adj ▷ east
eastern adj ▷ east
easts n ▷ east
eastward adj, adv ▷ east
eastwards adv ▷ east
easy adj (-ier, -iest) not needing much work or
effort > **easily** adv > **easiness** n (pl -s)
eat v (eats, eating, ate, eaten) take (food) into
the mouth and swallow it
eatable adj fit or suitable for eating
eaten v ▷ eat
eating v ▷ eat
eats v ▷ eat

eaves pl n overhanging edges of a roof
eavesdrop v (-s, -pping, -pped) listen secretly
to a private conversation > **eavesdropper** n
(pl -s) > **eavesdropping** n (pl -s)
eavesdropped v ▷ eavesdrop
eavesdropper n ▷ eavesdrop
eavesdroppers n ▷ eavesdrop
eavesdropping v, n ▷ eavesdrop
eavesdroppings n ▷ eavesdrop
eavesdrops v ▷ eavesdrop
ebb v (-s, -ing, -ed) (of tide water) flow back ▶ n
(pl -s) flowing back of the tide
ebbed v ▷ ebb
ebbing v ▷ ebb
ebbs v, n ▷ ebb
ebonies n ▷ ebony
ebony n (pl -ies) hard black wood ▶ adj deep
black
ebullience n ▷ ebullient
ebulliences n ▷ ebullient
ebullient adj full of enthusiasm or excitement
> **ebullience** n (pl -s)
eccentric adj odd or unconventional ▶ n (pl
-s) eccentric person > **eccentrically** adv
> **eccentricity** n (pl -ies)
eccentrically adv ▷ eccentric
eccentricities n ▷ eccentric
eccentricity n ▷ eccentric
eccentrics n ▷ eccentric
ecclesiastic n (pl -s) member of the clergy ▶ adj
(also **ecclesiastical**) of the Christian Church
or clergy
ecclesiastical adj ▷ ecclesiastic
ecclesiastics n ▷ ecclesiastic

> **ech** v (**echs**, **eching**, **eched**). Ech is
> an old word that Shakespeare uses,
> and means **eke**. It's a good one to
> have ready if you have C and H but no
> obvious place to play them. Ech scores
> 8 points.

echelon [esh-a-lon] n (pl -s) level of power or
responsibility
echelons n ▷ echelon
echidna [ik-kid-na] n (pl -nas, -nae) [-nee]
Australian spiny egg-laying mammal
echidnae n ▷ echidna
echidnas n ▷ echidna
echo n (pl -es) repetition of sounds by
reflection of sound waves off a surface ▶ v
(-es, -ing, -ed) repeat or be repeated as an
echo
echoed v ▷ echo
echoes v, n ▷ echo
echoing v ▷ echo
éclair n (pl -s) finger-shaped pastry filled with

cream and covered with chocolate
éclairs n ▷ éclair
éclat [ake-lah] n brilliant success
eclectic adj selecting from various styles,
ideas, or sources > **eclecticism** n (pl -s)
eclecticism n ▷ eclectic
eclecticisms n ▷ eclectic
eclipse n (pl -es) temporary obscuring of one
star or planet by another ▶ v (-ses, -sing, -sed)
surpass or outclass
eclipsed v ▷ eclipse
eclipses v ▷ eclipse
eclipsing v ▷ eclipse
ecliptic n (pl -s) apparent path of the sun
ecliptics n ▷ ecliptic
ecological adj of ecology > **ecologically** adv
ecologically adv ▷ ecological
ecologist n ▷ ecology
ecologists n ▷ ecology
ecology n study of the relationships between
living things and their environment
> **ecologist** n (pl -s)
economic adj of economics
economical adj not wasteful, thrifty
> **economically** adv
economically adv ▷ economical
economics n social science concerned with
the production and consumption of goods
and services
economies n ▷ economy
economist n (pl -s) specialist in economics
economists n ▷ economist
economize v (-izes, -izing, -ized) reduce
expense or waste
economized v ▷ economize
economizes v ▷ economize
economizing v ▷ economize
economy n (pl -ies) system of interrelationship
of money, industry, and employment in a
country
ecosystem n (pl -s) system involving
interactions between a community and its
environment
ecosystems n ▷ ecosystem
ecru adj pale creamy-brown
ecstasies n ▷ ecstasy
ecstasy n (pl -ies) state of intense delight
> **ecstatic** adj > **ecstatically** adv
ecstatic adj ▷ ecstasy
ecstatically adv ▷ ecstasy
ectoplasm n (pl -s) (SPIRITUALISM) substance
that supposedly is emitted from the body of a
medium during a trance
ectoplasms n ▷ ectoplasm
ecumenical adj of the Christian Church

throughout the world
eczema [ek-sim-a] n (pl s) skin disease causing
intense itching
eczemas n ▷ eczema
eddied v ▷ eddy
eddies n, v ▷ eddy
eddy n (pl eddies) circular movement of air,
water, etc. ▶ v (eddies, eddying, eddied) move
with a circular motion
eddying v ▷ eddy
edelweiss [ade-el-vice] n (pl -es) alpine plant
with white flowers
edelweisses n ▷ edelweiss
edge n (pl -s) border or line where something
ends or begins ▶ v (edges, edging, edged)
provide an edge or border for
edged v ▷ edge
edges n, v ▷ edge
edgeways adv with the edge forwards or
uppermost
edgier adj ▷ edgy
edgiest adj ▷ edgy
edging v ▷ edge ▶ n (pl -s) anything placed
along an edge to finish it
edgings n ▷ edging
edgy adj (edgier, edgiest) nervous or irritable
edibilities n ▷ edible
edibility n ▷ edible
edible adj fit to be eaten > **edibility** n (pl -ties)
edict [ee-dikt] n (pl -s) order issued by an
authority
edicts n ▷ edict
edification n ▷ edify
edifications n ▷ edify
edifice [ed-if-iss] n (pl -s) large building
edifices n ▷ edifice
edified v ▷ edify
edifies v ▷ edify
edify [ed-if-fie] v (-fies, -fying, -fied) improve
morally by instruction > **edification** n (pl -s)
edifying v ▷ edify
edit v (-s, -ing, -ed) prepare (a book, film, etc.)
for publication or broadcast
edited v ▷ edit
editing v ▷ edit
editings n ▷ edit
edition n (pl -s) number of copies of a new
publication printed at one time
editions n ▷ edition
editor n (pl -s) person who edits
editorial n (pl -s) newspaper article stating
the opinion of the editor ▶ adj of editing or
editors
editorials n ▷ editorial
editors n ▷ editor

edits v ▷ edit

educate v (-tes, -ting, -ted) teach > **education** n (pl -s) > **educational** adj > **educationally** adv

educated v ▷ educate

educates v ▷ educate

educating v ▷ educate

educational adj ▷ educate

educationalist n (pl -s) expert in the theory of education

educationalists n ▷ educationalist

educationally adv ▷ educate

educations n ▷ educate

educative adj educating

> **ee** n (**een**). Ee is a Scots word for eye. While this word won't earn you a big score on its own, it can be very useful when you're trying to form several words at once. Ee scores 2 points.
> **eek** interj. Eek is a noise that people make when they are startled or frightened. Eek scores 7 points.

eel n (pl -s) snakelike fish

eels n ▷ eel

eerie adj (-ier, -iest) uncannily frightening or disturbing > **eerily** adv

eerier adj ▷ eerie

eeriest adj ▷ eerie

eerily adv ▷ eerie

> **ef** n (**efs**). Ef is the letter F, and is a handy word to know when you want to play a longer word parallel to one that's already on the board. Ef scores 5 points.

efface v (-ces, -cing, -ced) remove by rubbing > **effacement** n (pl -s)

effaced v ▷ efface

effacement n ▷ efface

effacements n ▷ efface

effaces v ▷ efface

effacing v ▷ efface

effect n (pl -s) change or result caused by someone or something ▶ pl personal belongings ▶ v (-s, -ing, -ed) cause to happen, accomplish

effected v ▷ effect

effecting v ▷ effect

effective adj producing a desired result > **effectively** adv

effectively adv ▷ effective

effects n, v ▷ effect

effectual adj producing the intended result > **effectually** adv

effectually adv ▷ effectual

effeminacies n ▷ effeminate

effeminacy n ▷ effeminate

effeminate adj (of a man) displaying characteristics thought to be typical of a woman > **effeminacy** n (pl -ies)

effervescence n ▷ effervescent

effervescences n ▷ effervescent

effervescent adj (of a liquid) giving off bubbles of gas > **effervescence** n (pl -s)

effete [if-**feet**] adj powerless, feeble

efficacies n ▷ efficacious

efficacious adj producing the intended result > **efficacy** n (pl -ies)

efficacy n ▷ efficacious

efficiencies n ▷ efficient

efficiency n ▷ efficient

efficient adj functioning effectively with little waste of effort > **efficiently** adv > **efficiency** n (pl -ies)

efficiently adv ▷ efficient

effigies n ▷ effigy

effigy [**ef**-fij-ee] n (pl -ies) image or likeness of a person

efflorescence n (pl -s) flowering

efflorescences n ▷ efflorescence

effluent n (pl -s) liquid discharged as waste

effluents n ▷ effluent

effluvia n ▷ effluvium

effluvium n (pl -via) unpleasant smell, as of decaying matter or gaseous waste

effort n (pl -s) physical or mental exertion > **effortless** adj

effortless adj ▷ effort

efforts n ▷ effort

effronteries n ▷ effrontery

effrontery n (pl -ies) brazen impudence

effusion n (pl -s) unrestrained outburst

effusions n ▷ effusion

effusive adj openly emotional, demonstrative > **effusively** adv

effusively adv ▷ effusive

egalitarian adj upholding the equality of all people ▶ n (pl -s) person who holds egalitarian beliefs > **egalitarianism** n (pl -s)

egalitarianism n ▷ egalitarian

egalitarianisms n ▷ egalitarian

egalitarians n ▷ egalitarian

egg[1] n (pl -s) oval or round object laid by the females of birds and other creatures, containing a developing embryo

egg[2] v (-s, -ing, -ed) encourage or incite, esp. to do wrong

egged v ▷ egg[2]

egghead n (pl -s) (Informal) intellectual person

eggheads n ▷ egghead

egging v ▷ egg[2]

eggplant n (pl -s) (US, CANADIAN, AUST & NZ) aubergine

eggplants n ▷ eggplant
eggs n, v ▷ egg¹,²
ego n (pl -s) the conscious mind of an individual
egocentric adj self-centred
egoism, egotism n excessive concern for one's own interests > **egoist, egotist** n (pl -s) > **egoistic, egotistic** adj
egoist n ▷ egoism
egoistic adj ▷ egoism
egoists n ▷ egoism
egos n ▷ ego
egotist n ▷ egoism
egotistic adj ▷ egoism
egotists n ▷ egoism
egregious [ig-**greej**-uss] adj outstandingly bad
egress [ee-gress] n (pl -es) departure
egresses n ▷ egress
egret [ee-grit] n (pl -s) lesser white heron
egrets n ▷ egret
eider n (pl -s) Arctic duck
eiderdown n (pl -s) quilt (orig. stuffed with eider feathers)
eiderdowns n ▷ eiderdown
eiders n ▷ eider
eight adj, n (pl -s) one more than seven
eighteen adj, n (pl -s) eight and ten > **eighteenth** adj, n (pl -s)
eighteens n ▷ eighteen
eighteenth adj, n ▷ eighteen
eighteenths n ▷ eighteen
eighth adj, n (pl -s) (of) number eight in a series
eighths n ▷ eighth
eighties n ▷ eighty
eightieth n ▷ eighty
eightieths n ▷ eighty
eights n ▷ eight
eighty adj, n (pl -ies) eight times ten > **eightieth** adj, n (pl -s)
eisteddfod [ice-**sted**-fod] n (pl -s) Welsh festival with competitions in music and other performing arts
eisteddfods n ▷ eisteddfod
either adj, pron one or the other (of two) ▶ conj used preceding two or more possibilities joined by or ▶ adv likewise
ejaculate v (-tes, -ting, -ted) eject (semen) > **ejaculation** n (pl -s)
ejaculated v ▷ ejaculate
ejaculates v ▷ ejaculate
ejaculating v ▷ ejaculate
ejaculation n ▷ ejaculate
ejaculations n ▷ ejaculate
eject v (-s, -ing, -ed) force out, expel > **ejection** n (pl -s) > **ejector** n (pl -s)

ejected v ▷ eject
ejecting v ▷ eject
ejection n ▷ eject
ejections n ▷ eject
ejector n ▷ eject
ejectors n ▷ eject
ejects v ▷ eject
eke v (ekes, eking, eked) (usu. foll. by **out**) make (a living) with difficulty
eked v ▷ eke
ekes v ▷ eke
eking v ▷ eke
elaborate adj with a lot of fine detail ▶ v (-tes, -ting, -ted) expand upon > **elaboration** n (pl -s)
elaborated v ▷ elaborate
elaborates v ▷ elaborate
elaborating v ▷ elaborate
elaboration n ▷ elaborate
elaborations n ▷ elaborate
élan [ale-an] n (pl -s) style and vigour
eland [eel-and] n (pl -s) large antelope of southern Africa
elands n ▷ eland
élans n ▷ élan
elapse v (-ses, -sing, -sed) (of time) pass by
elapsed v ▷ elapse
elapses v ▷ elapse
elapsing v ▷ elapse
elastic adj resuming normal shape after distortion ▶ n (pl -s) tape or fabric containing interwoven strands of flexible rubber > **elasticity** n (pl -ies)
elasticities n ▷ elastic
elasticity n ▷ elastic
elastics n ▷ elastic
elate v (-tes, -ting, -ted) make extremely happy and excited > **elation** n (pl -s)
elated v ▷ elate
elates v ▷ elate
elating v ▷ elate
elation n ▷ elate
elations n ▷ elate
elbow n (pl -s) joint between the upper arm and the forearm ▶ v (-s, -ing, -ed) shove or strike with the elbow
elbowed v ▷ elbow
elbowing v ▷ elbow
elbows n, v ▷ elbow
elder¹ adj older ▶ n (pl -s) older person
elder² n (pl -s) small tree with white flowers and black berries
elderly adj (fairly) old
elders n ▷ elder¹,²
eldest adj oldest

eldritch adj (SCOT) weird, uncanny

elect v (-s, -ing, -ed) choose by voting ▶ adj appointed but not yet in office
　elected v ▷ elect
　electing v ▷ elect

election n (pl -s) choosing of representatives by voting

electioneering n (pl -s) active participation in a political campaign
　electioneerings n ▷ electioneering
　elections n ▷ election

elective adj chosen by election

elector n (pl -s) someone who has the right to vote in an election > **electoral** adj
　electoral adj ▷ elector

electorate n (pl -s) people who have the right to vote
　electorates n ▷ electorate
　electors n ▷ elector

electric adj produced by, transmitting, or powered by electricity

electrical adj using or concerning electricity

electrician n (pl -s) person trained to install and repair electrical equipment
　electricians n ▷ electrician
　electricities n ▷ electricity

electricity n (pl -ies) form of energy associated with stationary or moving electrons or other charged particles

electrics pl n (BRIT) electric appliances
　electrification n ▷ electrify
　electrifications n ▷ electrify
　electrified v ▷ electrify
　electrifies v ▷ electrify

electrify v (-fies, -fying, -fied) adapt for operation by electric power > **electrification** n
　electrifying v ▷ electrify

electrocute v (-tes, -ting, -ted) kill or injure by electricity > **electrocution** n (pl -s)
　electrocuted v ▷ electrocute
　electrocutes v ▷ electrocute
　electrocuting v ▷ electrocute
　electrocution n ▷ electrocute
　electrocutions n ▷ electrocute

electrode n (pl -s) conductor through which an electric current enters or leaves a battery, vacuum tube, etc
　electrodes n ▷ electrode

electrodynamics n branch of physics concerned with the interactions between electrical and mechanical forces
　electrolyses n ▷ electrolysis

electrolysis [ill-lek-**troll**-iss-iss] n (pl -ses) conduction of electricity by an electrolyte, esp. to induce chemical change

electrolyte n (pl -s) solution or molten substance that conducts electricity
> **electrolytic** adj
　electrolytes n ▷ electrolyte
　electrolytic adj ▷ electrolyte

electromagnet n (pl -s) magnet containing a coil of wire through which an electric current is passed

electromagnetic adj of or operated by an electomagnet
　electromagnets n ▷ electromagnet

electron n (pl -s) elementary particle in all atoms that has a negative electrical charge

electronic adj (of a device) dependent on the action of electrons

electronics n technology concerned with the development of electronic devices and circuits
　electrons n ▷ electron

electronvolt n (pl -s) unit of energy used in nuclear physics
　electronvolts n ▷ electronvolt

electroplate v (-tes, -ting, -ted) coat with silver etc. by electrolysis
　electroplated v ▷ electroplate
　electroplates v ▷ electroplate
　electroplating v ▷ electroplate
　elects v ▷ elect
　elegance n ▷ elegant
　elegances n ▷ elegant

elegant adj pleasing or graceful in dress, style, or design > **elegance** n (pl -s)

elegiac adj mournful or plaintive
　elegies n ▷ elegy

elegy [el-lij-ee] n (pl -ies) mournful poem, esp. a lament for the dead

element n (pl -s) component part ▶ pl basic principles of something

elemental adj of primitive natural forces or passions

elementary adj simple and straightforward
　elements n ▷ element

elephant n (pl -s) huge four-footed thick-skinned animal with ivory tusks and a long trunk

elephantiasis [el-lee-fan-**tie**-a-siss] n disease with hardening of the skin and enlargement of the legs etc.

elephantine adj unwieldy, clumsy
　elephants n ▷ elephant

elevate v (-ates, -ating, -ated) raise in rank or status
　elevated v ▷ elevate
　elevates v ▷ elevate

elevating v ▷ elevate
elevation n (pl -s) raising
elevator n (pl -s) (AUST, US & CANADIAN) lift for carrying people
 elevators n ▷ elevator
eleven adj, n (pl -s) one more than ten
 elevens n ▷ eleven
elevenses n (BRIT & S AFR) (Informal) mid-morning snack
eleventh adj, n (pl -s) (of) number eleven in a series
 elevenths n ▷ eleventh
elf n (pl elves) (in folklore) small mischievous fairy
elfin adj small and delicate
elicit v (-s, -ing, -ed) bring about (a response or reaction)
 elicited v ▷ elicit
 eliciting v ▷ elicit
 elicits v ▷ elicit
elide v (-des, -ding, -ded) omit (a vowel or syllable) from a spoken word ▷ **elision** n (pl -s)
 elided v ▷ elide
 elides v ▷ elide
 eliding v ▷ elide
 eligibilities n ▷ eligible
 eligibility n ▷ eligible
eligible adj meeting the requirements or qualifications needed ▷ **eligibility** n (pl -ties)
eliminate v (-tes, -ting, -ted) get rid of ▷ **elimination** n (pl -s)
 eliminated v ▷ eliminate
 eliminates v ▷ eliminate
 eliminating v ▷ eliminate
 elimination n ▷ eliminate
 eliminations n ▷ eliminate
 elision n ▷ elide
 elisions n ▷ elide
elite [ill-eet] n (pl -s) most powerful, rich, or gifted members of a group
 elites n ▷ elite
elitism n (pl -s) belief that society should be governed by a small group of superior people ▷ **elitist** n, adj (pl -s)
 elitisms n ▷ elitism
 elitists n ▷ elitist
elixir [ill-ix-er] n (pl -s) imaginary liquid that can prolong life or turn base metals into gold
 elixirs n ▷ elixir
elk n (pl -s) large deer of N Europe and Asia
 elks n ▷ elk
ellipse n (pl -ses) oval shape
 ellipses n ▷ ellipse, ellipsis
ellipsis n (pl -ses) omission of letters or words in a sentence

elliptical adj oval-shaped
elm n (pl -s) tree with serrated leaves
 elms n ▷ elm
elocution n (pl -s) art of speaking clearly in public
 elocutions n ▷ elocution
elongate [eel-long-gate] v (-tes, -ting, -ted) make or become longer ▷ **elongation** n (pl -s)
 elongated v ▷ elongate
 elongates v ▷ elongate
 elongating v ▷ elongate
 elongation n ▷ elongate
 elongations n ▷ elongate
elope v (-s, -ing, -ed) (of two people) run away secretly to get married ▷ **elopement** n (pl -s)
 eloped v ▷ elope
 elopement n ▷ elope
 elopements n ▷ elope
 elopes v ▷ elope
 eloping v ▷ elope
eloquence n (pl -s) fluent powerful use of language ▷ **eloquent** adj ▷ **eloquently** adv
 eloquencies n ▷ eloquence
 eloquent adj ▷ eloquence
 eloquently adv ▷ eloquence
else adv in addition or more
elsewhere adv in or to another place
elucidate v (-tes, -ting, -ted) make (something difficult) clear ▷ **elucidation** n (pl -s)
 elucidated v ▷ elucidate
 elucidates v ▷ elucidate
 elucidating v ▷ elucidate
 elucidation n ▷ elucidate
 elucidations n ▷ elucidate
elude v (-s, -ing, -ed) escape from by cleverness or quickness
 eluded v ▷ elude
 eludes v ▷ elude
 eluding v ▷ elude
elusive adj difficult to catch or remember
elver n (pl -s) young eel
 elvers n ▷ elver
 elves n ▷ elf
emaciated [im-mace-ee-ate-id] adj abnormally thin ▷ **emaciation** n (pl -s)
 emaciation n ▷ emaciated
 emaciations n ▷ emaciated
emanate [em-a-nate] v (-tes, -ting, -ted) issue, proceed from a source ▷ **emanation** n (pl -s)
 emanated v ▷ emanate
 emanates v ▷ emanate
 emanating v ▷ emanate
 emanation n ▷ emanate
 emanations n ▷ emanate
emancipate v (-tes, -ting, -ted) free

from social, political, or legal restraints
> emancipation n (pl -s)
emancipated v ▷ emancipate
emancipates v ▷ emancipate
emancipating v ▷ emancipate
emancipation n ▷ emancipate
emancipations n ▷ emancipate
emasculate v (-tes, -ting, -ted) deprive of power **> emasculation** n (pl -s)
emasculated v ▷ emasculate
emasculates v ▷ emasculate
emasculating v ▷ emasculate
emasculation n ▷ emasculate
emasculations n ▷ emasculate
embalm v (-s, -ing, -ed) preserve (a corpse) from decay by the use of chemicals etc.
embalmed v ▷ embalm
embalming v ▷ embalm
embalms v ▷ embalm
embankment n (pl -s) man-made ridge that carries a road or railway or holds back water
embankments n ▷ embankment
embargo n (pl -oes) order by a government prohibiting trade with a country ▶ v (-oes, -oing, -oed) put an embargo on
embargoed v ▷ embargo
embargoes n, v ▷ embargo
embargoing v ▷ embargo
embark v (-s, -ing, -ed) board a ship or aircraft (foll. by on) **> embarkation** n (-s)
embarkation n ▷ embark
embarkations n ▷ embark
embarked v ▷ embark
embarking v ▷ embark
embarks v ▷ embark
embarrass v (-es, -ing, -ed) cause to feel self-conscious or ashamed **> embarrassed** adj **> embarrassing** adj **> embarrassment** n (pl -s)
embarrassed v, adj ▷ embarrass
embarrasses v ▷ embarrass
embarrassing v, adj ▷ embarrass
embarrassment n ▷ embarrass
embarrassments n ▷ embarrass
embassies n ▷ embassy
embassy n (pl -ies) offices or official residence of an ambassador
embattled adj having a lot of difficulties
embed v (-s, -dding, -dded) fix firmly in something solid
embedded adj (of a journalist) assigned to accompany an active military unit ▶ v ▷ embed
embedding v ▷ embed
embeds v ▷ embed
embellish v (-es, -ing, -ed) decorate

> embellishment n (pl -s)
embellished v ▷ embellish
embellishes v ▷ embellish
embellishing v ▷ embellish
embellishment n ▷ embellish
embellishments n ▷ embellish
ember n (pl -s) glowing piece of wood or coal in a dying fire
embers n ▷ ember
embezzle v (-s, -ing, -ed) steal money that has been entrusted to one **> embezzlement** n (pl -s) **> embezzler** n (pl -s)
embezzled v ▷ embezzle
embezzlement n ▷ embezzle
embezzlements n ▷ embezzle
embezzler n ▷ embezzle
embezzlers n ▷ embezzle
embezzles v ▷ embezzle
embezzling v ▷ embezzle
embittered adj feeling anger as a result of misfortune
emblazon v (-s, -ing, -ed) decorate with bright colours
emblazoned v ▷ emblazon
emblazoning v ▷ emblazon
emblazons v ▷ emblazon
emblem n (pl -s) object or design that symbolizes a quality, type, or group **> emblematic** adj
emblematic adj ▷ emblem
emblems n ▷ emblem
embodied v ▷ embody
embodies v ▷ embody
embodiment n ▷ embody
embodiments n ▷ embody
embody v (-dies, -dying, -died) be an example or expression of **> embodiment** n (pl -s)
embodying v ▷ embody
embolden v (-s, -ing, -ed) encourage (someone)
emboldened v ▷ embolden
emboldening v ▷ embolden
emboldens v ▷ embolden
embolism n (pl -s) blocking of a blood vessel by a blood clot or air bubble
embolisms n ▷ embolism
embossed adj (of a design or pattern) standing out from a surface
embrace v (-ces, -cing, -ced) clasp in the arms, hug ▶ n (pl -s) act of embracing
embraced v ▷ embrace
embraces v, n ▷ embrace
embracing v ▷ embrace
embrasure n (pl -s) door or window having splayed sides so that the opening is larger

on the inside

embrasures n ▷ embrasure

embrocation n (pl -s) lotion for rubbing into the skin to relieve pain

embrocations n ▷ embrocation

embroider v (-s, -ing, -ed) decorate with needlework > **embroidery** n (pl -ies)

embroidered v ▷ embroider

embroideries n ▷ embroider

embroidering v ▷ embroider

embroiders v ▷ embroider

embroidery n ▷ embroider

embroil v (-s, -ing, -ed) involve (a person) in problems

embroiled v ▷ embroil

embroiling v ▷ embroil

embroils v ▷ embroil

embryo [em-bree-oh] n (pl -s) unborn creature in the early stages of development > **embryology** n (pl -ies)

embryologies n ▷ embryo

embryology n ▷ embryo

embryonic adj at an early stage

embryos n ▷ embryo

emend v (-s, -ing, -ed) remove errors from > **emendation** n (pl emendations)

emendation n ▷ emend

emendations n ▷ emend

emended v ▷ emend

emending v ▷ emend

emends v ▷ emend

emerald n (pl -s) bright green precious stone ▶ adj bright green

emeralds n ▷ emerald

emerge v (-ges, -ging, -ged) come into view > **emergence** n (pl -s) > **emergent** adj

emerged v ▷ emerge

emergence n ▷ emerge

emergences n ▷ emerge

emergencies n ▷ emergency

emergency n (pl -ies) sudden unforeseen occurrence needing immediate action

emergent adj ▷ emerge

emerges v ▷ emerge

emerging v ▷ emerge

emeries n ▷ emery

emeritus [im-mer-it-uss] adj retired, but retaining an honorary title

emery n (pl -ies) hard mineral used for smoothing and polishing

emetic [im-met-ik] n (pl -s) substance that causes vomiting ▶ adj causing vomiting

emetics n ▷ emetic

emigrant n ▷ emigrate

emigrants n ▷ emigrate

emigrate v (-tes, -ting, -ted) go and settle in another country > **emigrant** n (pl -s) > **emigration** n (pl -s)

emigrated v ▷ emigrate

emigrates v ▷ emigrate

emigrating v ▷ emigrate

emigration n ▷ emigrate

emigrations n ▷ emigrate

émigré [em-mig-gray] n (pl -s) someone who has left his native country for political reasons

émigrés n ▷ émigré

eminence n (pl -s) position of superiority or fame

eminences n ▷ eminence

eminent adj distinguished, well-known > **eminently** adv

eminently adv ▷ eminent

emir [em-meer] n (pl -s) Muslim ruler

emirate n (pl -s) country ruled by an emir

emirates n ▷ emirate

emirs n ▷ emir

emissaries n ▷ emissary

emissary n (pl -ies) agent sent on a mission by a government

emission n ▷ emit

emissions ▷ emit

emit v (-s, -tting, -tted) give out (heat, light, or a smell) > **emission** n (pl -s)

emits v ▷ emit

emitted v ▷ emit

emitting v ▷ emit

emollient adj softening, soothing ▶ n (pl -s) substance which softens or soothes the skin

emollients n ▷ emollient

emolument n (pl -s) (formal) fees or wages from employment

emoluments n ▷ emolument

emoticon [i-mote-i-kon] n (pl -s) (COMPUTERS) ▷ smiley

emoticons n ▷ emoticon

emotion n (pl -s) strong feeling

emotional adj readily affected by or appealing to the emotions > **emotionally** adv

emotionally adv ▷ emotional

emotions n ▷ emotion

emotive adj tending to arouse emotion

empathies n ▷ empathy

empathy n (pl -ies) ability to understand someone else's feelings as if they were one's own

emperor n (pl -s) ruler of an empire > **empress** n fem (pl -es)

emperors n ▷ emperor

emphases n ▷ emphasis

emphasis n (pl -ses) special importance or significance > **emphasize** v (-s, -ing, -ed)
emphasize v ▷ emphasis
emphasized v ▷ emphasis
emphasizes v ▷ emphasis
emphasizing v ▷ emphasis
emphatic adj showing emphasis
  > **emphatically** adv
emphatically adv ▷ emphatic
emphysema [em-fiss-see-ma] n (pl -s) condition in which the air sacs of the lungs are grossly enlarged, causing breathlessness
emphysemas n ▷ emphysema
empire n (pl -s) group of territories under the rule of one state or person
empires n ▷ empire
empirical adj relying on experiment or experience, not on theory > **empirically** adv
empirically adv ▷ empirical
empiricism n (pl -s) doctrine that all knowledge derives from experience
  > **empiricist** n (pl -s)
empiricisms n ▷ empiricism
empiricist n ▷ empiricism
empiricists n ▷ empiricism
emplacement n (pl -s) prepared position for a gun
emplacements n ▷ emplacement
employ v (-s, -ing, -ed) hire (a person) ▶ n (pl -s) state of being employed > **employee** n (pl -s)
employed v ▷ employ
employee n ▷ employ
employees n ▷ employ
employer n (pl -s) person or organization that employs someone
employers n ▷ employer
employing v ▷ employ
employment n (pl -s) state of being employed
employments n ▷ employment
employs v, n ▷ employ
emporia n ▷ emporium
emporium n (pl -riums, -ria) (Old-fashioned) large general shop
emporiums n ▷ emporia
empower v (-s, -ing, -ed) enable, authorize
empowered v ▷ empower
empowering v ▷ empower
empowers v ▷ empower
empress n ▷ emperor
empresses n ▷ emperor
emptied v ▷ empty
emptier adj ▷ empty
empties pl n empty boxes, bottles, etc. ▶ v ▷ empty
emptiest adj ▷ empty

emptiness n ▷ empty
emptinesses n ▷ empty
empty adj (-ier, -iest) containing nothing ▶ v (-ies, -ying, -ied) make or become empty
  > **emptiness** n (pl -es)
emptying v ▷ empty
emu n (pl -s) large Australian flightless bird with long legs
emulate v (-tes, -ting, -ted) attempt to equal or surpass by imitating > **emulation** n (pl -s)
emulated v ▷ emulate
emulates v ▷ emulate
emulating v ▷ emulate
emulation n ▷ emulate
emulations n ▷ emulate
emulsified v ▷ emulsify
emulsifier n ▷ emulsify
emulsifiers n ▷ emulsify
emulsifies v ▷ emulsify
emulsify v (-fies, -fying, -fied) (of two liquids) join together or join (two liquids) together
  > **emulsifier** n (pl -s)
emulsifying v ▷ emulsify
emulsion n (pl -s) light-sensitive coating on photographic film ▶ v (-s, -ing, -ed) paint with emulsion paint
emulsioned v ▷ emulsion
emulsioning v ▷ emulsion
emulsions n, v ▷ emulsion
emus n ▷ emu
enable v (-les, -ling, -led) provide (a person) with the means, opportunity, or authority (to do something)
enabled v ▷ enable
enables v ▷ enable
enabling v ▷ enable
enact v (-s, -ing, -ed) establish by law
  > **enactment** n (pl -s)
enacted v ▷ enact
enacting v ▷ enact
enactment n ▷ enact
enactments n ▷ enact
enacts v ▷ enact
enamel n (pl -s) glasslike coating applied to metal etc. to preserve the surface ▶ v (-s, -lling, -lled) cover with enamel
enamelled v ▷ enamel
enamelling v ▷ enamel
enamels n, v ▷ enamel
enamoured adj inspired with love
encamp v (-s, -ing, -ed) set up in a camp
  > **encampment** n (pl -s)
encamped v ▷ encamp
encamping v ▷ encamp
encampment n ▷ encamp

encampments n ▷ encamp
encamps v ▷ encamp
encapsulate v (-tes, -ting, -ted) summarize
   encapsulated v ▷ encapsulate
   encapsulates v ▷ encapsulate
   encapsulating v ▷ encapsulate
encephalitis [en-sef-a-**lite**-iss] n (pl -es)
   inflammation of the brain
   encephalitises n ▷ encephalitis
enchant v (-s, -ing, -ed) delight and fascinate
   > enchantment n (pl -s) > enchanter n (pl -s)
   > enchantress n fem (pl -es)
   enchanted v ▷ enchant
   enchanter n ▷ enchant
   enchanters n ▷ enchant
   enchanting v ▷ enchant
   enchantment n ▷ enchant
   enchantments n ▷ enchant
   enchantress n ▷ enchant
   enchantresses n ▷ enchant
   enchants v ▷ enchant
encircle v (-s, -ling, -led) form a circle around
   > encirclement n (pl -s)
   encircled v ▷ encircle
   encirclement n ▷ encircle
   encirclements n ▷ encircle
   encircles v ▷ encircle
   encircling v ▷ encircle
enclave n (pl -s) part of a country entirely
   surrounded by foreign territory
   enclaves n ▷ enclave
enclose v (-s, -sing, -sed) surround completely
   > enclosure n (pl -s)
   enclosed v ▷ enclose
   encloses v ▷ enclose
   enclosing v ▷ enclose
   enclosure n ▷ enclose
   enclosures n ▷ enclose
encomia n ▷ encomium
encomium n (pl -miums, -mia) formal
   expression of praise
   encomiums n ▷ encomiums
encompass v (-es, -ing, -ed) surround
   encompassed v ▷ encompass
   encompasses v ▷ encompass
   encompassing v ▷ encompass
encore interj again, once more ▶ n (pl -s) extra
   performance due to enthusiastic demand
   encores n ▷ encore
encounter v (-s, -ing, -ed) meet unexpectedly
   ▶ n (pl -s) unexpected meeting
   encountered v ▷ encounter
   encountering v ▷ encounter
   encounters v, n ▷ encounter
encourage v (-ges, -ging, -ged) inspire with

confidence > encouragement n (pl -s)
   encouraged v ▷ encourage
   encouragement n ▷ encourage
   encouragements n ▷ encourage
   encourages v ▷ encourage
   encouraging v ▷ encourage
encroach v (-s, -ing, -ed) intrude gradually
   on a person's rights or land > encroachment
   n (pl -s)
   encroached v ▷ encroach
   encroaches v ▷ encroach
   encroaching v ▷ encroach
   encroachment n ▷ encroach
   encroachments n ▷ encroach
encrust v (-s, -ing, -ed) cover with a layer of
   something
   encrusted v ▷ encrust
   encrusting v ▷ encrust
   encrusts v ▷ encrust
encumber v (-s, -ing, -ed) hinder or impede
   encumbered v ▷ encumber
   encumbering v ▷ encumber
   encumbers v ▷ encumber
encumbrance n (pl -s) something that
   impedes or is burdensome
   encumbrances n ▷ encumbrance
encyclical [en-**sik**-lik-kl] n (pl -s) letter sent by
   the Pope to all bishops
   encyclicals n ▷ encyclical
   encyclopaedia n ▷ encyclopedia
   encyclopaedias n ▷ encyclopedia
   encyclopaedic adj ▷ encyclopedia
encyclopedia, encyclopaedia n (pl -s) book
   or set of books containing facts about
   many subjects, usu. in alphabetical order
   > encyclopedic, encyclopaedic adj
   encyclopedias n ▷ encyclopedia
   encyclopedic adj ▷ encyclopedia
end n (pl -s) furthest point or part ▶ v (-s, -ing,
   -ed) bring or come to a finish > ending n (pl -s)
   > endless adj
endanger v (-s, -ing, -ed) put in danger
   endangered v ▷ endanger
   endangering v ▷ endanger
   endangers v ▷ endanger
endear v (-s, -ing, -ed) cause to be liked
   > endearing adj
   endeared v ▷ endear
   endearing v, adj ▷ endear
endearment n (pl -s) affectionate word or
   phrase
   endearments n ▷ endearment
   endears v ▷ endear
endeavour v (-s, -ing, -ed) try ▶ n (pl -s) effort
   endeavoured v ▷ endeavour

endeavouring v ▷ endeavour
endeavours v, n ▷ endeavour
ended v ▷ end
endemic adj present within a localized area or peculiar to a particular group of people
ending v, n ▷ end
endings n ▷ end
endive n (pl -s) curly-leaved plant used in salads
endives n ▷ endive
endless adj ▷ end
endocrine adj relating to the glands which secrete hormones directly into the bloodstream
endogenous [en-**dodge**-in-uss] adj originating from within
endorse v (-ses, -sing, -sed) give approval to > **endorsement** n (pl -s)
endorsed v ▷ endorse
endorsement n ▷ endorse
endorsements n ▷ endorse
endorses v ▷ endorse
endorsing v ▷ endorse
endow v (-s, -ing, -ed) provide permanent income for > **endowment** n (pl -s)
endowed v ▷ endow
endowing v ▷ endow
endowment n ▷ endow
endowments n ▷ endow
endows v ▷ endow
ends n, v ▷ end
endurable adj ▷ endure
endurance n (pl -s) act or power of enduring
endurances n ▷ endurance
endure v (-res, -ring, -red) bear (hardship) patiently > **endurable** adj
endured v ▷ endure
endures v ▷ endure
enduring v ▷ endure
endways adv having the end forwards or upwards
enema [en-**im**-a] n (pl -s) medicine injected into the rectum to empty the bowels
enemas n ▷ enema
enemies n ▷ enemy
enemy n (pl -ies) hostile person or nation, opponent
energetic adj ▷ energy
energetically adv ▷ energy
energies n ▷ energy
energize v (-izes, -izing, -ized) give vigour to
energized v ▷ energize
energizes v ▷ energize
energizing v ▷ energize
energy n (pl -ies) capacity for intense activity

> **energetic** adj > **energetically** adv
enervate v (-tes, -ting, -ted) deprive of strength or vitality > **enervation** n (pl -s)
enervated v ▷ enervate
enervates v ▷ enervate
enervating v ▷ enervate
enervation n ▷ enervate
enervations n ▷ enervate
enfeeble v (-les, -ling, -led) weaken
enfeebled v ▷ enfeeble
enfeebles v ▷ enfeeble
enfeebling v ▷ enfeeble
enfold v (-s, -ing, -ed) cover by wrapping something around
enfolded v ▷ enfold
enfolding v ▷ enfold
enfolds v ▷ enfold
enforce v (-ces, -cing, -ced) impose obedience (to a law etc.) > **enforceable** adj
> **enforcement** n (pl -s)
enforced v ▷ enforce
enforcement n ▷ enforce
enforcements n ▷ enforce
enforces v ▷ enforce
enforcing v ▷ enforce
enfranchise v (-ses, -sing, -sed) grant (a person) the right to vote > **enfranchisement** n (pl -s)
enfranchised v ▷ enfranchise
enfranchisement n ▷ enfranchise
enfranchisements n ▷ enfranchise
enfranchises v ▷ enfranchise
enfranchising v ▷ enfranchise
engage v (-ges, -ging, -ged) take part, participate > **engagement** n (pl -s)
engaged adj pledged to be married ▶ v ▷ engage
engagement n ▷ engage
engagements n ▷ engage
engages v ▷ engage
engaging adj charming ▶ v ▷ engage
engender v (-s, -ing, -ed) produce, cause to occur
engendered v ▷ engender
engendering v ▷ engender
engenders v ▷ engender
engine n (pl -s) any machine which converts energy into mechanical work
engineer n (pl -s) person trained in any branch of engineering ▶ v (-s, -ing, -ed) plan in a clever manner
engineered v ▷ engineer
engineering v ▷ engineer ▶ n (pl -s) profession of applying scientific principles to the design and construction of engines, cars, buildings,

or machines
engineerings n ▷ engineering
engineers n, v ▷ engineer
engines n ▷ engine
English n (pl -es) official language of Britain, Ireland, Australia, New Zealand, South Africa, Canada, the US, and several other countries ▶ adj relating to England
Englishes n ▷ English
engrave v (-ves, -ving, -ved) carve (a design) onto a hard surface > **engraver** n (pl -s)
engraved v ▷ engrave
engraver n ▷ engrave
engravers n ▷ engrave
engraves v ▷ engrave
engraving v ▷ engrave ▶ n (pl -s) print made from an engraved plate
engravings n ▷ engraving
engross [en-**groce**] v (-es, -ing, -ed) occupy the attention of (a person) completely
engrossed v ▷ engross
engrosses v ▷ engross
engrossing v ▷ engross
engulf v (-s, -ing, -ed) cover or surround completely
engulfed v ▷ engulf
engulfing v ▷ engulf
engulfs v ▷ engulf
enhance v (-s, -ing, -ed) increase in quality, value, or attractiveness > **enhancement** n (pl -s)
enhanced v ▷ enhance
enhancement n ▷ enhance
enhancements n ▷ enhance
enhances v ▷ enhance
enhancing v ▷ enhance
enigma n (pl -s) puzzling thing or person > **enigmatic** adj > **enigmatically** adv
enigmas n ▷ enigma
enigmatic adj ▷ enigma
enigmatically adv ▷ enigma
enjoin v (-s, -ing, -ed) order (someone) to do something
enjoined v ▷ enjoin
enjoining v ▷ enjoin
enjoins v ▷ enjoin
enjoy v (-s, -ing, -ed) take joy in > **enjoyable** adj > **enjoyment** n (pl -s)
enjoyable adj ▷ enjoy
enjoyed v ▷ enjoy
enjoying v ▷ enjoy
enjoyment n ▷ enjoy
enjoyments n ▷ enjoy
enjoys v ▷ enjoy
enlarge v (-ges, -ging, -ged) make or grow

larger (foll. by **on**) > **enlargement** n (pl -s)
enlarged v ▷ enlarge
enlargement n ▷ enlarge
enlargements n ▷ enlarge
enlarges v ▷ enlarge
enlarging v ▷ enlarge
enlighten v (-s, -ing, -ed) give information to > **enlightenment** n (pl -s)
enlightened v ▷ enlighten
enlightening v ▷ enlighten
enlightenment n ▷ enlighten
enlightenments n ▷ enlighten
enlightens v ▷ enlighten
enlist v (-s, -ing, -ed) enter the armed forces > **enlistment** n (pl -s)
enlisted v ▷ enlist
enlisting v ▷ enlist
enlistment n ▷ enlist
enlistments n ▷ enlist
enlists v ▷ enlist
enliven v (-s, -ing, -ed) make lively or cheerful
enlivened v ▷ enliven
enlivening v ▷ enliven
enlivens v ▷ enliven
enmeshed adj deeply involved
enmities n ▷ enmity
enmity n (pl -ies) ill will, hatred
ennoble v (-s, -ing, -ed) make noble, elevate
ennobled v ▷ ennoble
ennobles v ▷ ennoble
ennobling v ▷ ennoble
ennui [on-**nwee**] n (pl -s) boredom, dissatisfaction
ennuis n ▷ ennui
enormities n ▷ enormity
enormity n (pl -ies) great wickedness
enormous adj very big, vast
enough adj as much or as many as necessary ▶ pron sufficient quantity ▶ adv sufficiently
enquire v (-res, -ring, -red) ▷ inquire > **enquiry** n (pl -ies)
enquired v ▷ enquire
enquires v ▷ enquire
enquiries n ▷ enquire
enquiring v ▷ enquire
enquiry n ▷ enquire
enraptured adj filled with delight and fascination
enrich v (-es, -ing, -ed) improve in quality
enriched v ▷ enrich
enriches v ▷ enrich
enriching v ▷ enrich
enrol v (-s, -lling, -lled) (cause to) become a member > **enrolment** n (pl -s)

enrolled v ▷ enrol
enrolling v ▷ enrol
enrolment n ▷ enrol
enrolments n ▷ enrol
enrols v ▷ enrol
ensconce v (-ces, -cing, -ced) settle firmly or comfortably
ensconced v ▷ ensconce
ensconces v ▷ ensconce
ensconcing v ▷ ensconce
ensemble [on-**som**-bl] n (pl -s) all the parts of something taken together
ensembles n ▷ ensemble
enshrine v (-nes, -ning, -ned) cherish or treasure
enshrined v ▷ enshrine
enshrines v ▷ enshrine
enshrining v ▷ enshrine
ensign n (pl -s) naval flag
ensigns n ▷ ensign
enslave v (-ves, -ving, -ved) make a slave of (someone) > **enslavement** n (pl -s)
enslaved v ▷ enslave
enslavement n ▷ enslave
enslavements n ▷ enslave
enslaves v ▷ enslave
enslaving v ▷ enslave
ensnare v (-res, -ring, -red) catch in or as if in a snare
ensnared v ▷ ensnare
ensnares v ▷ ensnare
ensnaring v ▷ ensnare
ensue v (-sues, -suing, -sued) come next, result
ensued v ▷ ensue
ensues v ▷ ensue
ensuing v ▷ ensue
ensure v (-re, -ring, -red) make certain or sure
ensured v ▷ ensure
ensures v ▷ ensure
ensuring v ▷ ensure
entail v (-s, -ing, -ed) bring about or impose inevitably
entailed v ▷ entail
entailing v ▷ entail
entails v ▷ entail
entangle v (-les, -ling, -led) catch or involve in or as if in a tangle > **entanglement** n (pl -s)
entangled v ▷ entangle
entanglement n ▷ entangle
entanglements n ▷ entangle
entangles v ▷ entangle
entangling v ▷ entangle
entente [on-**tont**] n (pl -s) friendly understanding between nations
ententes n ▷ entente

enter v (-s, -ing, -ed) come or go in
entered v ▷ enter
enteric [en-**ter**-ik] adj intestinal
entering v ▷ enter
enteritis [en-ter-**rite**-iss] n (pl -es) inflammation of the intestine, causing diarrhoea
enteritises n ▷ enteritis
enterprise n (pl -s) company or firm
enterprises n ▷ enterprise
enterprising adj full of boldness and initiative
enters v ▷ enter
entertain v (-s, -ing, -ed) amuse > **entertainer** n (pl -s) > **entertainment** n (pl -s)
entertained v ▷ entertain
entertainer n ▷ entertain
entertainers n ▷ entertain
entertaining v ▷ entertain
entertainment n ▷ entertain
entertainments n ▷ entertain
entertains v ▷ entertain
enthral [en-**thrawl**] v (-s, -lling, -lled) hold the attention of > **enthralling** adj
enthralled v ▷ enthral
enthralling v, adj ▷ enthral
enthrals v ▷ enthral
enthuse v (-s, -ing, -ed) (cause to) show enthusiasm
enthused v ▷ enthuse
enthuses v ▷ enthuse
enthusiasm n (pl -s) ardent interest, eagerness
enthusiasms n ▷ enthusiasm
enthusiast n (pl -s) ardent supporter of something > **enthusiastic** adj > **enthusiastically** adv
enthusiastic adj ▷ enthusiast
enthusiastically adv ▷ enthusiast
enthusiasts n ▷ enthusiast
enthusing v ▷ enthuse
entice v (-ces, -cing, -ced) attract by exciting hope or desire, tempt > **enticement** n (pl -s)
enticed v ▷ entice
enticement n ▷ entice
enticements n ▷ entice
entices v ▷ entice
enticing v ▷ entice
entire adj including every detail, part, or aspect of something > **entirely** adv > **entirety** n (pl -ties)
entirely adv ▷ entire
entireties n ▷ entire
entirety n ▷ entire
entities n ▷ entity
entitle v (-les, -ling, -led) give a right to > **entitlement** n (pl -s)

entitled v ▷ entitle

entitlement n ▷ entitle

entitlements n ▷ entitle

entitles v ▷ entitle

entitling v ▷ entitle

entity n (pl -ties) separate distinct thing

entomological adj ▷ entomology

entomologies n ▷ entomology

entomologist n ▷ entomology

entomologists n ▷ entomology

entomology n (pl -ies) study of insects
> **entomological** adj > **entomologist** n (pl -s)

entourage [on-toor-ahzh] n (pl -s) group of
people who assist an important person

entourages n ▷ entourage

entrails pl n intestines

entrance¹ n (pl -s) way into a place

entrance² v (-s, -ing, -ed) delight

entranced v ▷ entrance²

entrances n ▷ entrance¹ ▶ v ▷ entrance²

entrancing v ▷ entrance²

entrant n (pl -s) person who enters a
university, contest, etc.

entrants n ▷ entrant

entreat v (-s, -ing, -ed) ask earnestly

entreated v ▷ entreat

entreaties n ▷ entreaty

entreating v ▷ entreat

entreats v ▷ entreat

entreaty n (pl -ties) earnest request

entrée [on-tray] n (pl -s) dish served before a
main course

entrées n ▷ entrée

entrench v (-es, -ing, -ed) establish firmly
> **entrenchment** n (pl -s)

entrenched v ▷ entrench

entrenches v ▷ entrench

entrenching v ▷ entrench

entrenchment n ▷ entrench

entrenchments n ▷ entrench

entrepreneur n (pl -s) business person
who attempts to make a profit by risk and
initiative

entrepreneurs n ▷ entrepreneur

entries n ▷ entry

entropies n ▷ entropy

entropy [en-trop-ee] n (pl -ies) lack of
organization

entrust v (-s, -ing, -ed) put into the care or
protection of

entrusted v ▷ entrust

entrusting v ▷ entrust

entrusts v ▷ entrust

entry n (pl -ies) entrance

entwine v (-s, -ing, -ed) twist together or
around

entwined v ▷ entwine

entwines v ▷ entwine

entwining v ▷ entwine

enumerate v (-tes, -ting, -ted) name one by
one > **enumeration** n (pl -s)

enumerated v ▷ enumerate

enumerates v ▷ enumerate

enumerating v ▷ enumerate

enumeration n ▷ enumerate

enumerations n ▷ enumerate

enuncation n ▷ enunciate

enunciate v (-tes, -ting, -ted) pronounce
clearly > **enunciation** n (pl -s)

enunciated v ▷ enunciate

enunciates v ▷ enunciate

enunciating v ▷ enunciate

enunciation n ▷ enunciate

enunciations n ▷ enunciate

envelop v (-s, -ing, -ed) wrap up, enclose
> **envelopment** n (pl -s)

envelope n (pl -s) folded gummed paper cover
for a letter

enveloped v ▷ envelop

envelopes n ▷ envelope

enveloping v ▷ envelop

envelopment n ▷ envelop

envelopments n ▷ envelop

envelops v ▷ envelop

enviable adj arousing envy, fortunate

envied v ▷ envy

envies n, v ▷ envy

envious adj full of envy

environment [en-vire-on-ment] n (pl -s)
external conditions and surroundings
in which people, animals, or plants live
> **environmental** adj

environmental adj ▷ environment

environmentalist n (pl -s) person concerned
with the protection of the natural
environment

environmentalists n ▷ environmentalist

environments n ▷ environment

environs pl n surrounding area, esp. of a town

envisage v (-ges, -ging, -ged) conceive of as a
possibility

envisaged v ▷ envisage

envisages v ▷ envisage

envisaging v ▷ envisage

envoy n (pl -s) messenger

envoys n ▷ envoy

envy n (pl -ies) feeling of discontent aroused by
another's good fortune ▶ v (-ies, -ying, -ied)
grudge (another's good fortune, success, or
qualities)

envying v ▷ envy

enzyme n (pl -s) any of a group of complex proteins that act as catalysts in specific biochemical reactions

enzymes n ▷ enzyme

eolithic adj of the early part of the Stone Age

epaulette n (pl -s) shoulder ornament on a uniform

epaulettes n ▷ epaulette

ephemeral adj short-lived

epic n (pl -s) long poem, book, or film about heroic events or actions ▶ adj very impressive or ambitious

epicentre n (pl -s) point on the earth's surface immediately above the origin of an earthquake

epicentres n ▷ epicentre

epics n ▷ epic

epicure n (pl -s) person who enjoys good food and drink

epicurean adj devoted to sensual pleasures, esp. food and drink ▶ n (pl -s) epicure

epicureans n ▷ epicurean

epicures n ▷ epicure

epidemic n (pl -s) widespread occurrence of a disease

epidemics n ▷ epidemic

epidermis n (pl -ses) outer layer of the skin

epidermises n ▷ epidermis

epidural [ep-pid-**dure**-al] adj, n (pl -s) (of) spinal anaesthetic injected to relieve pain during childbirth

epidurals n ▷ epidural

epiglottis n (pl -ses) thin flap that covers the opening of the larynx during swallowing

epiglottises n ▷ epiglottis

epigram n (pl -s) short witty remark or poem > **epigrammatic** adj

epigrammatic adj ▷ epigram

epigrams n ▷ epigram

epigraph n (pl -s) quotation at the start of a book

epigraphs n ▷ epigraph

epilepsies n ▷ epilepsy

epilepsy n (pl -ies) disorder of the nervous system causing loss of consciousness and sometimes convulsions

epileptic adj of or having epilepsy ▶ n (pl -s) person who has epilepsy

epileptics n ▷ epileptic

epilogue n (pl -s) short speech or poem at the end of a literary work, esp. a play

epilogues n ▷ epilogue

epiphanies n ▷ epiphany

epiphany n (pl -ies) a moment of great or sudden realization

episcopal [ip-**piss**-kop-al] adj of or governed by bishops

episcopalian adj advocating Church government by bishops ▶ n (pl -s) advocate of such Church government

episcopalians n ▷ episcopalian

episode n (pl -s) incident in a series of incidents

episodes n ▷ episode

episodic adj occurring at irregular intervals

epistemological adj ▷ epistemology

epistemologies n ▷ epistemology

epistemology [ip-iss-stem-**ol**-a-jee] n (pl -ies) study of the source, nature, and limitations of knowledge > **epistemological** adj

epistle n (pl -s) letter, esp. of an apostle > **epistolary** adj

epistles n ▷ epistle

epistolary adj ▷ epistle

epitaph n (pl -s) commemorative inscription on a tomb

epitaphs n ▷ epitaph

epithet n (pl -s) descriptive word or name

epithets n ▷ epithet

epitome [ip-**pit**-a-mee] n (pl -s) typical example

epitomes n ▷ epitome

epitomize v (-izes, -izing, -ized) be the epitome of

epitomized v ▷ epitomize

epitomizes v ▷ epitomize

epitomizing v ▷ epitomize

epoch [**ee**-pok] n (pl -s) period of notable events

epochs n ▷ epoch

eponymous [ip-**pon**-im-uss] adj after whom a book, play, etc. is named

equable [**ek**-wab-bl] adj even-tempered > **equably** adv

equably adv ▷ equable

equal adj identical in size, quantity, degree, etc. ▶ n (pl -s) person or thing equal to another ▶ v (-s, -lling, -lled) be equal to > **equally** adv

equalities n ▷ equality

equality n (pl -ies) state of being equal

equalization n ▷ equalize

equalizations n ▷ equalize

equalize v (-izes, -izing, -ized) make or become equal > **equalization** n (pl -s)

equalized v ▷ equalize

equalizes v ▷ equalize

equalizing v ▷ equalize

equalled v ▷ equal

equalling v ▷ equal

equally adv ▷ equal

equals n, v ▷ equal

equanimities *n* ▷ equanimity

equanimity *n* (*pl* -ies) calmness of mind

equate *v* (-tes, -ting, -ted) make or regard as equivalent

equated *v* ▷ equate

equates *v* ▷ equate

equating *v* ▷ equate

equation *n* (*pl* -s) mathematical statement that two expressions are equal

equations *n* ▷ equation

equator *n* (*pl* -s) imaginary circle round the earth, equidistant from the poles > **equatorial** *adj*

equatorial *adj* ▷ equator

equators *n* ▷ equator

equerries *n* ▷ equerry

equerry [ek-kwer-ee] *n* (*pl* -ies) (BRIT) officer who acts as an attendant to a member of a royal family

equestrian *adj* of horses and riding

equidistant *adj* equally distant

equilateral *adj* having equal sides

equilibria *n* ▷ equilibriums

equilibrium *n* (*pl* -ria) steadiness or stability

equine *adj* of or like a horse

equinoctial *adj* ▷ equinox

equinox *n* (*pl* -es) time of year when day and night are of equal length > **equinoctial** *adj*

equinoxes *n* ▷ equinox

equip *v* (-s, -pping, -pped) provide with supplies, components, etc.

equipment *n* (*pl* -s) set of tools or devices used for a particular purpose

equipments *n* ▷ equipment

equipoise *n* (*pl* -s) perfect balance

equipoises *n* ▷ equipoise

equipped *v* ▷ equip

equipping *v* ▷ equip

equips *v* ▷ equips

equitable *adj* fair and reasonable > **equitably** *adv*

equitably *adv* ▷ equitable

equities *n* ▷ equity

equity *n* (*pl* -ties) fairness ▸ *pl* interest of ordinary shareholders in a company

equivalence *n* ▷ equivalent

equivalences *n* ▷ equivalent

equivalent *adj* equal in value ▸ *n* (*pl* -s) something that is equivalent > **equivalence** *n* (*pl* -s)

equivalents *n* ▷ equivalent

equivocal *adj* ambiguous > **equivocally** *adv*

equivocally *adv* ▷ equivocal

equivocate *v* (-tes, -ting, -ted) use vague or ambiguous language to mislead people

> **equivocation** *n* (*pl* -s)

equivocated *v* ▷ equivocate

equivocates *v* ▷ equivocate

equivocating *v* ▷ equivocate

equivocation *n* ▷ equivocate

equivocations *n* ▷ equivocate

era *n* (*pl* -s) period of time considered as distinctive

eradicate *v* (-tes, -ting, -ted) destroy completely > **eradication** *n* (*pl* -s)

eradicated *v* ▷ eradicate

eradicates *v* ▷ eradicate

eradicating *v* ▷ eradicate

eradication *n* ▷ eradicate

eradications *n* ▷ eradicate

eras *n* ▷ era

erase *v* (-ses, -sing, -sed) rub out

erased *v* ▷ erase

eraser *n* (*pl* -s) object for erasing something written

erasers *n* ▷ eraser

erases *v* ▷ erase

erasing *v* ▷ erase

erasure *n* (*pl* -s) erasing

erasures *n* ▷ erasure

ere *prep, conj* (Poetic) before

erect *v* (-s, -ing, -ed) build ▸ *adj* upright

> **erection** *n* (*pl* -s)

erected *v* ▷ erect

erectile *adj* capable of becoming erect from sexual excitement

erecting *v* ▷ erect

erection *n* ▷ erect

erections *n* ▷ erect

erects *v* ▷ erect

erg *n* (*pl* -s) unit of work or energy

ergonomic *adj* ▷ ergonomics

ergonomics *n* (*pl* study of the relationship between workers and their environment

> **ergonomic** *adj*

ergot *n* (*pl* -s) fungal disease of cereal

ergots *n* ▷ ergot

ergs *n* ▷ erg

ermine *n* (*pl* -s) stoat in northern regions

ermines *n* ▷ ermine

erode *v* (-s, -ing, -ed) wear away > **erosion** *n* (*pl* -s)

eroded *v* ▷ erode

erodes *v* ▷ erode

eroding *v* ▷ erode

erogenous [ir-roj-in-uss] *adj* sensitive to sexual stimulation

erosion *n* ▷ erode

erosions *n* ▷ erode

erotic *adj* relating to sexual pleasure or desire

> **eroticism** n (pl -s)
erotica n sexual literature or art
  eroticism n ▷ erotic
  eroticisms n ▷ erotic
err v (-s, -ing, -ed) make a mistake
errand n (pl -s) short trip to do something for someone
  errands n ▷ errand
errant adj behaving in a manner considered to be unacceptable
  errata n ▷ erratum
erratic adj irregular or unpredictable
> **erratically** adv
  erratically adv ▷ erratic
erratum n (pl -ta) error in writing or printing
  erred v ▷ err
  erring v ▷ err
erroneous adj incorrect, mistaken
error n (pl -s) mistake, inaccuracy, or misjudgment
  errors n ▷ error
  errs v ▷ err
ersatz [air-zats] adj made in imitation
erstwhile adj former
erudite adj having great academic knowledge
> **erudition** n (pl -s)
  erudition v ▷ erudite
  eruditions n ▷ erudite
erupt v (-s, -ing, -ed) eject (steam, water, or volcanic material) violently > **eruption** n (pl -s)
  erupted v ▷ erupt
  erupting v ▷ erupt
  eruption n ▷ erupt
  eruptions n ▷ erupt
  erupts v ▷ erupt
erysipelas [err-riss-**sip**-pel-ass] n (pl -es) acute skin infection causing purplish patches
  erysipelases n ▷ erysipelas

> **es** n (**eses**). Es is the letter S. This is a useful word when you want to play a high-scoring word that will touch words already on the board. Es scores 2 points.

escalate v (-tes, -ting, -ted) increase in extent or intensity > **escalation** n (pl -s)
  escalated v ▷ escalate
  escalates v ▷ escalate
  escalating v ▷ escalate
  escalation n ▷ escalate
  escalations n ▷ escalate
escalator n (pl -s) moving staircase
  escalators n ▷ escalator
escalope [ess-kal-lop] n (pl -s) thin slice of meat, esp. veal

  escalopes n ▷ escalope
escapade n (pl -s) mischievous adventure
  escapades n ▷ escapade
escape v (-pes, -ping, -ped) get free (of) ▶ n (pl -s) act of escaping
  escaped v ▷ escape
escapee n (pl -s) person who has escaped
  escapees n ▷ escapee
  escapes v, n ▷ escape
  escaping v ▷ escape
escapism n (pl -s) taking refuge in fantasy to avoid unpleasant reality
  escapisms n ▷ escapism
  escapologies n ▷ escapologist
escapologist n (pl -s) entertainer who specializes in freeing himself from confinement > **escapology** n (pl -ies)
  escapologists n ▷ escapologist
  escapology n ▷ escapologist
escarpment n (pl -s) steep face of a ridge or mountain
  escarpments n ▷ escarpment
eschew [iss-**chew**] v (-s, -ing, -ed) abstain from, avoid
  eschewed v ▷ eschew
  eschewing v ▷ eschew
  eschews v ▷ eschew
escort n (pl -s) people or vehicles accompanying another person for protection or as an honour ▶ v (-s, -ing, -ed) act as an escort to
  escorted v ▷ escort
  escorting v ▷ escort
  escorts n, v ▷ escort
escudo [ess-**kyoo**-doe] n (pl -dos) former monetary unit of Portugal
  escudos n ▷ escudo
escutcheon n (pl -s) shield with a coat of arms
  escutcheons n ▷ escutcheon
esoteric [ee-so-**ter**-rik] adj understood by only a small number of people with special knowledge
espadrille [ess-pad-drill] n (pl -s) light canvas shoe with a braided cord sole
  espadrilles n ▷ espadrille
espalier [ess-**pal**-yer] n (pl -s) shrub or fruit tree trained to grow flat
  espaliers n ▷ espalier
esparto n (pl -s) grass of S Europe and N Africa used for making rope etc.
  espartos n ▷ esparto
especial adj (Formal) special
especially adv particularly
  espied v ▷ espy
  espies v ▷ espy

espionage [ess-pyon-ahzh] *n* (*pl* -s) spying
  espionages *n* ▷ espionage
esplanade *n* (*pl* -s) wide open road used as a public promenade
  esplanades *n* ▷ esplanade
  espousal *n* ▷ espouse
  espousals *n* ▷ espouse
espouse *v* (-ses, -sing, -sed) adopt or give support to (a cause etc.) ▷ **espousal** *n* (*pl* -s)
  espoused *v* ▷ espouse
  espouses *v* ▷ espouse
  espousing *v* ▷ espouse
espresso *n* (*pl* -s) strong coffee made by forcing steam or boiling water through ground coffee beans
  espressos *n* ▷ espresso
esprit [ess-pree] *n* (*pl* -s) spirit, liveliness, or wit
  esprits *n* ▷ esprit
espy *v* (-ies, -ying, -ied) catch sight of
  espying *v* ▷ espy
esquire *n* (*pl* -s) courtesy title placed after a man's name
  esquires *n* ▷ esquire
essay *n* (*pl* -s) short literary composition ▶ *v* (-s, -ing, -ed) attempt ▷ **essayist** *n* (*pl* -s)
  essayed *v* ▷ essay
  essaying *v* ▷ essay
  essayist *n* ▷ essay
  essayists *n* ▷ essay
  essays *n*, *v* ▷ essay
essence *n* (*pl* -s) most important feature of a thing which determines its identity
  essences *n* ▷ essence
essential *adj* vitally important ▶ *n* (*pl* -s) something fundamental or indispensable ▷ **essentially** *adv*
  essentially *adv* ▷ essential
  essentials *n* ▷ essential
establish *v* (-es, -ing, -ed) set up on a permanent basis
  established *v* ▷ establish
  establishes *v* ▷ establish
  establishing *v* ▷ establish
establishment *n* (*pl* -s) act of establishing
  establishments *n* ▷ establishment
estate *n* (*pl* -s) landed property
  estates *n* ▷ estate
esteem *n* (*pl* -s) high regard ▶ *v* (-s, -ing, -ed) think highly of
  esteemed *v* ▷ esteem
  esteeming *v* ▷ esteem
  esteems *n*, *v* ▷ esteem
ester *n* (*pl* -s) (CHEM) compound produced by the reaction between an acid and an alcohol
  esters *n* ▷ ester

estimable *adj* worthy of respect
estimate *v* (-tes, -ting, -ted) calculate roughly ▶ *n* (*pl* -s) approximate calculation
  estimated *v* ▷ estimate
  estimates *v*, *n* ▷ estimate
  estimating *v* ▷ estimate
estimation *n* (*pl* -s) considered opinion
  estimations *n* ▷ estimation
estranged *adj* no longer living with one's spouse ▷ **estrangement** *n* (*pl* -s)
  estrangement *n* ▷ estranged
  estrangements *n* ▷ estranged
  estuaries *n* ▷ estuary
estuary *n* (*pl* --ies) mouth of a river
etch *v* (-es, -ing, -ed) wear away or cut the surface of (metal, glass, etc.) with acid ▷ **etching** *n* (*pl* -s)
  etched *v* ▷ etch
  etches *v* ▷ etch
  etching *v*, *n* ▷ etch
eternal *adj* without beginning or end ▷ **eternally** *adv*
  eternally *adv* ▷ eternal
  eternities *n* ▷ eternity
eternity *n* (*pl* -ies) infinite time
ether *n* (*pl* -s) colourless sweet-smelling liquid used as an anaesthetic
ethereal [eth-eer-ee-al] *adj* extremely delicate
  ethers *n* ▷ ether
ethic *n* (*pl* -s) moral principle ▷ **ethical** *adj* ▷ **ethically** *adv*
  ethical *adj* ▷ ethic
  ethically *adv* ▷ ethic
  ethics *n* ▷ ethic
ethnic *adj* relating to a people or group that shares a culture, religion, or language
  ethnological *adj* ▷ ethnology
  ethnologies *n* ▷ ethnology
  ethnologist *n* ▷ ethnology
  ethnologists *n* ▷ ethnology
ethnology *n* (*pl* -ies) study of human races ▷ **ethnological** *adj* ▷ **ethnologist** *n* (*pl* -s)
ethos [eeth-oss] *n* (*pl* -es) distinctive spirit and attitudes of a people, culture, etc.
  ethoses *n* ▷ ethos
ethyl [eeth-ile] *adj* of, consisting of, or containing the hydrocarbon group C_2H_5
ethylene *n* (*pl* -s) poisonous gas used as an anaesthetic and as fuel
  ethylenes *n* ▷ ethylene
etiolate [ee-tee-oh-late] *v* (-tes, -ting, -ted) become pale and weak (BOTANY)
  etiolated *v* ▷ etiolate
  etiolates *v* ▷ etiolate
  etiolating *v* ▷ etiolate

etiologies n ▷ etiology

etiology n (pl -ies) study of the causes of diseases

etiquette n (pl -s) conventional code of conduct

etiquettes n ▷ etiquette

étude [ay-tewd] n (pl -s) short musical composition for a solo instrument, esp. intended as a technical exercise

études n ▷ étude

etymological adj ▷ etymology

etymologies n ▷ etymology

etymology n (pl -gies) study of the sources and development of words > **etymological** adj

eucalypt n ▷ eucalyptus

eucalypts n ▷ eucalyptus

eucalyptus, eucalypt n (pl -ses, -s) tree, mainly grown in Australia, that provides timber, gum, and medicinal oil from the leaves

eucalyptuses n ▷ eucalyptus

eugenics [yew-jen-iks] n (pl study of methods of improving the human race

eulogies n ▷ eulogy

eulogistic adj ▷ euology

eulogize v (-s, -ing, -ed) praise (a person or thing) highly in speech or writing

eulogized v ▷ eulogize

eulogizes v ▷ eulogize

eulogizing v ▷ eulogize

eulogy n (pl -ies) speech or writing in praise of a person > **eulogistic** adj

eunuch n (pl -s) castrated man, esp. (formerly) a guard in a harem

eunuchs n ▷ eunuch

euphemism n (pl -s) inoffensive word or phrase substituted for one considered offensive or upsetting > **euphemistic** adj > **euphemistically** adv

euphemisms n ▷ euphemism

euphemistic ▷ euphemism

euphemistically ▷ euphemism

euphonies n ▷ euphony

euphonious adj pleasing to the ear

euphonium n (pl -s) brass musical instrument, tenor tuba

euphoniums n ▷ euphonium

euphony n (pl -nies) pleasing sound

euphoria n (pl -s) sense of elation > **euphoric** adj

euphorias n ▷ euphoria

euphoric adj ▷ euphoria

eureka [yew-reek-a] interj exclamation of triumph at finding something

euro n (pl -s) unit of the single currency of the European Union

euros n ▷ euro

euthanasia n (pl -s) act of killing someone painlessly, esp. to relieve his or her suffering

euthanasias n ▷ euthanasia

evacuate v (-tes, -ting, -ted) send (someone) away from a place of danger > **evacuation** n (pl -s) > **evacuee** n (pl -s)

evacuated v ▷ evacuate

evacuates v ▷ evacuate

evacuating v ▷ evacuate

evacuation n ▷ evacuate

evacuations n ▷ evacuate

evacuee n ▷ evacuate

evacuees n ▷ evacuate

evade v (-des, -ding, -ded) get away from or avoid > **evasion** n (pl -s)

evaded v ▷ evade

evades v ▷ evade

evading v ▷ evade

evaluate v (-tes, -ting, -ted) find or judge the value of > **evaluation** n (pl -s)

evaluated v ▷ evaluate

evaluates v ▷ evaluate

evaluating v ▷ evaluate

evaluation n ▷ evaluate

evaluations n ▷ evaluate

evanescence n ▷ evanescent

evanescences n ▷ evanescent

evanescent adj quickly fading away > **evanescence** n (pl -s)

evangelical adj of or according to gospel teaching ▶ n (pl -s) member of an evangelical sect > **evangelicalism** n (pl -s)

evangelicalism n ▷ evangelical

evangelicalisms n ▷ evangelical

evangelicals n ▷ evangelical

evangelism n (pl -s) teaching and spreading of the Christian gospel

evangelisms n ▷ evangelism

evangelist n (pl -s) writer of one of the four gospels

evangelists n ▷ evangelist

evangelization n ▷ evangelize

evangelizations n ▷ evangelize

evangelize v (-zes, -zing, -zed) preach the gospel > **evangelization** n (pl -s)

evangelized v ▷ evangelize

evangelizes v ▷ evangelize

evangelizing v ▷ evangelize

evaporate v (-tes, -ing, -ted) change from a liquid or solid to a vapour > **evaporation** n (pl -s)

evaporated v ▷ evaporate

evaporates v ▷ evaporate

evaporating v ▷ evaporate

evaporation n ▷ evaporate

evaporations n ▷ evaporate

evasion n ▷ evade

evasions n ▷ evade

evasive adj not straightforward > **evasively** adv

evasively adv ▷ evasive

evasiveness n ▷ evasive

eve n (pl -s) evening or day before some special event

even (-er, -est) adj flat or smooth (foll. by with) ▶ adv equally ▶ v (-s, -ing, -ed) make even

evened v ▷ even

evener adj ▷ even

evenest adj ▷ even

evening n (pl -s) end of the day or early part of the night ▶ adj of or in the evening ▶ v ▷ even

evenings n ▷ evening

evens v ▷ even

evensong n (pl -s) evening prayer

evensongs n ▷ evensong

event n (pl -s) anything that takes place

eventful adj full of exciting incidents

eventing n (pl -s) (BRIT, AUST & NZ) riding competitions, usu. involving cross-country, jumping, and dressage

eventings n ▷ eventing

events n ▷ event

eventual adj ultimate

eventualities n ▷ eventuality

eventuality n (pl -ies) possible event

eventually adv at the end of a situation or process

ever adv at any time > **everlasting** adj

evergreen adj, n (pl -s) (tree or shrub) having leaves throughout the year

evergreens n ▷ evergreen

everlasting adj ▷ ever

evermore adv for all time to come

every adj each without exception

everybody pron every person

everyday adj usual or ordinary

everyone pron every person

everything pron all things

everywhere adv in all places

eves n ▷ eve

evict v (-s, -ing, -ed) legally expel (someone) from his or her home > **eviction** n (pl -s)

evicted v ▷ evict

evicting v ▷ evict

eviction n ▷ evict

evictions n ▷ evict

evicts v ▷ evict

evidence n (pl -s) ground for belief ▶ v (-ces,

-cing, -ced) demonstrate, prove

evidenced v ▷ evidence

evidences n, v ▷ evidence

evidencing v ▷ evidence

evident adj easily seen or understood > **evidently** adv

evidential adj of, serving as, or based on evidence

evidently adv ▷ evident

evil n (pl -s) wickedness ▶ adj (-ller, -llest) harmful > **evilly** adv

evildoer n (pl -s) wicked person

evildoers n ▷ evildoer

eviller adj ▷ evil

evillest adj ▷ evil

evilly adv ▷ evil

evils n ▷ evil

evince v (-s, -ing, -ed) make evident

evinced v ▷ evince

evinces v ▷ evince

evincing v ▷ evince

eviscerate v (-tes, -ting, -ted) disembowel > **evisceration** n (pl -s)

eviscerated v ▷ eviscerate

eviscerates v ▷ eviscerate

eviscerating v ▷ eviscerate

evisceration n ▷ eviscerate

eviscerations n ▷ eviscerate

evocation n ▷ evoke

evocations n ▷ evoke

evocative adj ▷ evoke

evoke v (-s, -ing, -ed) call or summon up (a memory, feeling, etc.) > **evocation** n (pl -s) > **evocative** adj

evoked v ▷ evoke

evokes v ▷ evoke

evoking v ▷ evoke

evolution n (pl -s) gradual change in the characteristics of living things over successive generations, esp. to a more complex form > **evolutionary** adj

evolutionary n ▷ evolution

evolutions n ▷ evolution

evolve v (-kes, -king, -ked) develop gradually

evolved v ▷ evolve

evolves v ▷ evolve

evolving v ▷ evolve

ewe n (pl -s) female sheep

ewer n (pl -s) large jug with a wide mouth

ewers n ▷ ewer

ewes n ▷ ewe

> **ewk** n (ewks). Ewk is a dialect word for **itch**. It's a handy little word and a good one to remember in case you end up with both K and W, as you're very likely

to be able to play it from an E already
on the board. Ewk scores 10 points.

ex *n (pl -es) (Informal)* former wife or husband

exacerbate [ig-**zass**-er-bate] *v (-tes, -ting, -ted)*
make (pain, emotion, or a situation) worse
> **exacerbation** *n (pl -s)*

  exacerbated *v* ▷ exacerbate

  exacerbates *v* ▷ exacerbate

  exacerbating *v* ▷ exacerbate

  exacerbation *n* ▷ exacerbate

  exacerbations *n* ▷ exacerbate

exact *adj (-er, -est)* correct and complete
in every detail ▶ *v (-s, -ing, -ed)* demand
(payment or obedience) > **exactness** *n (pl -es)*
> **exactitude** *n (pl -s)*

  exacted *v* ▷ exact

  exacter *adj* ▷ exact

  exactest *adj* ▷ exact

exacting *adj* making rigorous or excessive
demands ▶ *v* ▷ exact

  exactitude *n* ▷ exact

  exactitudes *n* ▷ exact

exactly *adv* precisely, in every respect

  exactness *n* ▷ exact

  exactnesses *n* ▷ exact

  exacts *v* ▷ exact

exaggerate *v (-tes, -ting, -ted)* regard
or represent as greater than is true
> **exaggeratedly** *adv* > **exaggeration** *n (pl -s)*

  exaggerated *v* ▷ exaggerate

  exaggeratedly *adv* ▷ exaggerate

  exaggerates *v* ▷ exaggerate

  exaggerating *v* ▷ exaggerate

  exaggeration *n* ▷ exaggerate

  exaggerations *n* ▷ exaggerate

exalt *v (-s, -ing, -ed)* praise highly > **exalted** *adj*
> **exaltation** *n (pl -s)*

  exaltation *n* ▷ exalt

  exaltations *n* ▷ exalt

  exalted *v, adj* ▷ exalt

  exalting *v* ▷ exalt

  exalts *v* ▷ exalt

exam *n (pl -s)* ▷ examination

examination *n (pl -s)* examining

  examinations *n* ▷ examination

examine *v (-nes, -ning, -ned)* look at closely
> **examinee** *n (pl -s)* > **examiner** *n (pl -s)*

  examined *v* ▷ examine

  examinee *n* ▷ examine

  examinees *n* ▷ examine

  examiner *n* ▷ examine

  examiners *n* ▷ examine

  examines *v* ▷ examine

  examining *v* ▷ examine

example *n (pl -s)* specimen typical of its group

  examples *n* ▷ example

  exams *n* ▷ exam

exasperate *v (-tes, -ting, -ted)* cause great
irritation to > **exasperation** *n (pl -s)*

  exasperated *v* ▷ exasperate

  exasperates *v* ▷ exasperate

  exasperating *v* ▷ exasperate

  exasperation *n* ▷ exasperate

  exasperations *n* ▷ exasperate

excavate *v (-tes, -ting, -ted)* unearth buried
objects from (a piece of land) methodically to
learn about the past > **excavation** *n (pl -s)*

  excavated *v* ▷ excavate

  excavates *v* ▷ excavate

  excavating *v* ▷ excavate

  excavation *n* ▷ excavate

  excavations *n* ▷ excavate

excavator *n (pl -s)* large machine used for
digging

  excavators *n* ▷ excavator

exceed *v (-s, -ing, -ed)* be greater than

  exceeded *v* ▷ exceed

  exceeding *v* ▷ exceed

exceedingly *adv* very

  exceeds *v* ▷ exceed

excel *v (-s, -lling, -lled)* be superior to

  excelled *v* ▷ excel

  excellence *n* ▷ excellent

  excellences *n* ▷ excellent

excellent *adj* exceptionally good > **excellence**
n (pl -s)

  excelling *v* ▷ excel

  excels *v* ▷ excel

except *prep (sometimes foll. by* **for***)* other than,
not including ▶ *v (-s, -ing, -ed)* not include

  excepted *v* ▷ except

  excepting *prep* except ▶ *v* ▷ except

exception *n (pl -s)* excepting

exceptional *adj* not ordinary

  exceptions *n* ▷ exception

  excepts *v* ▷ except

excerpt *n (pl -s)* passage taken from a book,
speech, etc.

  excerpts *n* ▷ excerpt

excess *n (pl -es)* state or act of exceeding
the permitted limits > **excessive** *adj*
> **excessively** *adv*

  excesses *n* ▷ excess

  excessive *adj* ▷ excess

  excessively *adv* ▷ excess

exchange *v (-ges, -ging, -ged)* give or receive
(something) in return for something else ▶ *n
(pl -s)* act of exchanging > **exchangeable** *adj*

  exchangeable *adj* ▷ exchange

  exchanged *v* ▷ exchange

exchanges v, n ▷ exchange
exchanging v ▷ exchange
exchequer n (pl -s) (BRIT) government department in charge of state money
exchequers n ▷ exchequer
excise v (-ses, -sing, -sed) cut out or away
> **excision** n (pl -s)
excised v ▷ excise
excises v ▷ excise
excising v ▷ excise
excision n ▷ excise
excisions n ▷ excise
excitabilities n ▷ excitable
excitability n ▷ excitable
excitable adj easily excited > **excitability** n (pl -s)
excite v (-s, -ing, -ed) arouse to strong emotion
> **excitement** n (pl -s)
excited v ▷ excite
excitement n ▷ excite
excitements n ▷ excite
excites v ▷ excite
exciting v ▷ excite
exclaim v (-s, -ing, -ed) speak suddenly, cry out
> **exclamation** n > **exclamatory** adj
exclaimed v ▷ exclaim
exclaiming v ▷ exclaim
exclaims v ▷ exclaim
exclamation n ▷ exclaim
exclamations n ▷ exclaim
exclamatory adj ▷ exclaim
exclude v (-s, -ing, -ed) keep out, leave out
> **exclusion** n (pl -s)
excluded v ▷ exclude
excludes v ▷ exclude
excluding v ▷ exclude
exclusion n ▷ exclude
exclusions n ▷ exclude
exclusive adj excluding everything else ► n (pl -s) story reported in only one newspaper
> **exclusively** adv > **exclusivity** n (pl -ies)
> **exclusiveness** n (pl -es)
exclusively adv ▷ exclusive
exclusiveness n ▷ exclusive
exclusivenesses n ▷ exclusive
exclusives n ▷ exclusive
exclusivities n ▷ exclusive
exclusivity n ▷ exclusive
excommunicate v (-tes, -ting, -ted) exclude from membership and the sacraments of the Church > **excommunication** n (pl -s)
excommunicated v ▷ excommunicate
excommunicates v ▷ excommunicate
excommunicating v ▷ excommunicate
excommunication n ▷ excommunicate

excommunications n ▷ excommunicate
excoriate v (-tes, -ting, -ted) censure severely
> **excoriation** n (pl -s)
excoriated v ▷ excoriate
excoriates v ▷ excoriate
excoriating v ▷ excoriate
excoriation n ▷ excoriate
excoriations n ▷ excoriate
excrement n (pl -s) waste matter discharged from the body
excrements n ▷ excrement
excrescence n (pl -s) lump or growth on the surface of an animal or plant
excrescences n ▷ excrescence
excreta [ik-**skree**-ta] n excrement
excrete v (-tes, -ting, -ted) discharge (waste matter) from the body > **excretion** n (pl -s)
> **excretory** adj
excreted v ▷ excrete
excretes v ▷ excrete
excreting v ▷ excrete
excretion n ▷ excrete
excretions n ▷ excrete
excretory adj ▷ excrete
excruciating adj agonizing > **excruciatingly** adv
excruciatingly adv ▷ excruciating
exculpate v (-tes, -ting, -ted) free from blame or guilt
exculpated v ▷ exculpate
exculpates v ▷ exculpate
exculpating v ▷ exculpate
excursion n (pl -s) short journey, esp. for pleasure
excursions n ▷ excursion
excusable adj ▷ excuse
excuse n (pl -s) explanation offered to justify (a fault etc.) ► v (-ses, -sing, -sed) put forward a reason or justification for (a fault etc.)
> **excusable** adj
excused v ▷ excuse
excuses n, v ▷ excuse
excusing v ▷ excuse
execrable [**eks**-sik-rab-bl] adj of very poor quality
execute v (-tes, -ting, -ted) put (a condemned person) to death > **execution** n (pl -s)
> **executioner** n (pl -s)
executed v ▷ execute
executes v ▷ execute
executing v ▷ execute
execution n ▷ execute
executioner n ▷ execute
executioners n ▷ execute
executions n ▷ execute

executive n (pl -s) person or group in an administrative position ▸ adj having the function of carrying out plans, orders, laws, etc.
executives n ▷ executive

executor n (pl -s) person appointed to perform the instructions of a will
executors n ▷ executor
executrices n ▷ executrix

executrix n (pl -ixes, -ices) woman appointed to perform the instructions of a will
executrixes n ▷ executrix
exegeses n ▷ exegesis

exegesis [eks-sij-**jee**-siss] n (pl -ses) [-seez] explanation of a text, esp. of the Bible

exemplar n (pl -s) person or thing to be copied, model
exemplars n ▷ exemplar

exemplary adj being a good example
exemplifications n ▷ exemplify
exemplified v ▷ exemplify
exemplifies v ▷ exemplify

exemplify v (-ies, -fying, -ied) show an example of > **exemplification** n (pl -s)
exemplifying v ▷ exemplify

exempt adj not subject to an obligation etc. ▸ v (-s, -ing, -ed) release from an obligation etc. > **exemption** n (pl -s)
exempted v ▷ exempt
exempting v ▷ exempt
exemption n ▷ exempt
exemptions n ▷ exempt
exempts v ▷ exempt

exequy n (**exequies**). An exequy is a funeral rite. This is a great word if you have the tiles for it, combining X and Q. Even better, if you have all the letters for the plural, exequies, and can play it, you'll score an extra 50 points for using all your tiles. Exequy scores 25 points.

exercise n (pl -s) activity to train the body or mind ▸ v (-ses, -sing, -sed) make use of
exercised v ▷ exercise
exercises n, v ▷ exercise
exercising v ▷ exercise

exert v (-s, -ing, -ed) use (influence, authority, etc.) forcefully or effectively > **exertion** n (pl -s)
exerted v ▷ exert
exerting v ▷ exert
exertion n ▷ exert
exertions n ▷ exert
exerts v ▷ exert
exes n ▷ ex

exeunt [eks-see-unt] (LATIN) they go out: used as a stage direction
exhalation n ▷ exhale
exhalations n ▷ exhale

exhale v (-les, -ling, -led) breathe out > **exhalation** n (pl -s)
exhaled v ▷ exhale
exhales v ▷ exhale
exhaling v ▷ exhale

exhaust v (-s, -ing, -ed) tire out ▸ n (pl -s) gases ejected from an engine as waste products
exhausted v ▷ exhaust
exhausting v ▷ exhaust

exhaustion n (pl -s) extreme tiredness
exhaustions n ▷ exhaustion

exhaustive adj comprehensive > **exhaustively** adv
exhaustively adv ▷ exhaustive
exhausts v, n ▷ exhaust

exhibit v (-s, -ing, -ed) display to the public ▸ n (pl -s) object exhibited to the public (LAW) > **exhibitor** n (pl -s)
exhibited v ▷ exhibit
exhibiting v ▷ exhibit

exhibition n (pl -s) public display of art, skills, etc.

exhibitionism n (pl -s) compulsive desire to draw attention to oneself > **exhibitionist** n (pl -s)
exhibitionisms n ▷ exhibitionism
exhibitionist n ▷ exhibitionism
exhibitionists n ▷ exhibitionism
exhibitions n ▷ exhibition
exhibitor n ▷ exhibit
exhibitors n ▷ exhibit
exhibits v, n ▷ exhibit

exhilarate v (-tes, -ting, -ted) make lively and cheerful > **exhilaration** n (pl -s)
exhilarated v ▷ exhilarate
exhilarates v ▷ exhilarate
exhilarating v ▷ exhilarate
exhilaration n ▷ exhilarate
exhilarations n ▷ exhilarate

exhort v (-s, -ing, -ed) urge earnestly > **exhortation** n (pl -s)
exhortation n ▷ exhort
exhortations n ▷ exhort
exhorted v ▷ exhort
exhorting v ▷ exhort
exhorts v ▷ exhort
exhumation n ▷ exhume
exhumations n ▷ exhume

exhume [ig-**zyume**] v (-mes, -ming, -med) dig up (something buried, esp. a corpse) > **exhumation** n (pl -s)

exhumed v ▷ exhume
exhumes v ▷ exhume
exhuming v ▷ exhume
exigencies n ▷ exigency
exigency n (pl -cies) urgent demand or need
  > **exigent** adj
exigent adj ▷ exigency
exiguous adj scanty or meagre
exile n (pl -s) prolonged, usu. enforced, absence
  from one's country ▶ v (-les, -ling, -led) expel
  from one's country
exiled v ▷ exile
exiles n ▷ exile
exiles n, v ▷ exile
exiling v ▷ exile
exist v (-s, -ing, -ed) have being or reality
  > **existence** n (pl -s) > **existent** adj
existed v ▷ exist
existence n ▷ exist
existences n ▷ exist
existent adj ▷ exist
existential adj of or relating to existence, esp.
  human existence
existentialism n (pl -s) philosophical
  movement stressing the personal experience
  and responsibility of the individual, who
  is seen as a free agent > **existentialist** adj,
  n (pl -s)
existentialisms n ▷ existentialism
existentialist adj, n ▷ existentialism
existentialists n ▷ existentialism
existing v ▷ exist
exists v ▷ exist
exit n (pl -s) way out ▶ v (-s, -ing, -ed) go out
exited v ▷ exit
exiting v ▷ exit
exits n, v ▷ exit

> **exo** adj. Exo is an informal Australian
> way of saying excellent. This is a great
> little word as it allows you to combine
> X with two of the most common tiles
> in the game, E and O. Exo scores 10
> points.

exocrine adj relating to a gland, such as the
  sweat gland, that secretes externally through
  a duct
exodus [eks-so-duss] n (pl -es) departure of a
  large number of people
exoduses n ▷ exodus
exonerate v (-tes, -ting, -ted) free from blame
  or a criminal charge > **exoneration** n (pl -s)
exonerates v ▷ exonerate
exonerated v ▷ exonerate
exonerating v ▷ exonerate
exoneration v ▷ exonerate

exonerations v ▷ exonerate
exorbitant adj (of prices, demands, etc.)
  excessive, immoderate > **exorbitantly** adv
exorbitantly adv ▷ exorbitant
exorcism n ▷ exorcize
exorcisms n ▷ exorcize
exorcist n ▷ exorcize
exorcists n ▷ exorcize
exorcize v (-zes, -zing, -zed) expel (evil spirits)
  by prayers and religious rites > **exorcism** n (pl
  -s) > **exorcist** n (pl -s)
exorcized v ▷ exorcize
exorcizes v ▷ exorcize
exorcizing v ▷ exorcize
exotic adj having a strange allure or beauty ▶ n
  (pl -s) non-native plant > **exotically** adv
exotica pl n (collection of) exotic objects
exotically adv ▷ exotic
exotics n ▷ exotic
expand v (-s, -ing, -ed) make or become larger
  (foll. by on) > **expansion** n (pl -s)
expanded v ▷ expand
expanding v ▷ expand
expands v ▷ expand
expanse n (pl -s) uninterrupted wide area
expanses n ▷ expanse
expansion n ▷ expand
expansions n ▷ expand
expansive adj wide or extensive
expat adj, n (pl -s) short for expatriate
expatiate [iks-pay-shee-ate] v (-tes, -ting, -ted)
  (foll. by on) speak or write at great length (on)
expatiated v ▷ expatiate
expatiates v ▷ expatiate
expatiating v ▷ expatiate
expatriate [eks-pat-ree-it] adj living outside
  one's native country ▶ n (pl -s) person
  living outside his or her native country
  > **expatriation** n (pl -s)
expatriates n ▷ expatriate
expatriation n ▷ expatriate
expatriations n ▷ expatriate
expats n ▷ expat
expect v (-s, -ing, -ed) regard as probable
expectancies n ▷ expectancy
expectancy n (pl -ies) something expected on
  the basis of an average
expectant adj expecting or hopeful
  > **expectantly** adv
expectantly adv ▷ expectant
expectation n (pl -s) act or state of expecting
expectations n ▷ expectation
expected v ▷ expect
expecting v ▷ expect
expectorant n (pl -s) medicine that helps

to bring up phlegm from the respiratory passages

expectorants *n* ▷ expectorant

expectorate *v* (-tes, -ting, -ted) spit out (phlegm etc.) > **expectoration** *n* (*pl* -s)

expectorated *v* ▷ expectorate

expectorates *v* ▷ expectorate

expectorating *v* ▷ expectorate

expectoration *n* ▷ expectorate

expectorations *n* ▷ expectorate

expects *v* ▷ expect

expediencies *n* ▷ expedient

expediency *n* ▷ expedient

expedient *n* (*pl* -s) something that achieves a particular purpose ▶ *adj* suitable to the circumstances, appropriate > **expediency** *n* (*pl* -ies)

expedients *n* ▷ expedient

expedite *v* (-s, -ing, -ed) hasten the progress of

expedited *v* ▷ expedite

expedites *v* ▷ expedite

expediting *v* ▷ expedite

expedition *n* (*pl* -s) organized journey, esp. for exploration

expeditionary *adj* relating to an expedition, esp. a military one

expeditions *n* ▷ expedition

expeditious *adj* done quickly and efficiently

expel *v* (-s, -lling, -lled) drive out with force > **expulsion** *n* (*pl* -s)

expelled *v* ▷ expel

expelling *v* ▷ expel

expels *v* ▷ expel

expend *v* (-s, -ing, -ed) spend, use up

expendable *adj* able to be sacrificed to achieve an objective

expended *v* ▷ expend

expending *v* ▷ expend

expenditure *n* (*pl* -s) something expended, esp. money

expenditures *n* ▷ expenditure

expends *v* ▷ expend

expense *n* (*pl* -s) cost ▶ *pl* charges, outlay incurred

expenses *n* ▷ expense

expensive *adj* high-priced

experience *n* (*pl* -s) direct personal participation ▶ *v* (-ces, -cing, -ced) participate in

experienced *v* ▷ experience ▶ *adj* skilful from extensive participation

experiences *n, v* ▷ experience

experiencing *v* ▷ experience

experiment *n* (*pl* experiments) test to provide evidence to prove or disprove a theory

▶ *v* (-s, -ing, -ed) carry out an experiment
> **experimental** *adj* > **experimentally** *adv*
> **experimentation** *n* (*pl* -s)

experimental *adj* ▷ experiment

experimentally *adv* ▷ experiment

experimentation *n* ▷ experiment

experimentations *n* ▷ experiment

experimented *v* ▷ experiment

experimenting *v* ▷ experiment

experiments *n, v* ▷ experiment

expert *n* (*pl* -s) person with extensive skill or knowledge in a particular field ▶ *adj* skilful or knowledgeable

expertise [eks-per-**teez**] *n* (*pl* -s) special skill or knowledge

expertises *n* ▷ expertise

experts *n* ▷ expert

expiate *v* (-tes, -ting, -ted) make amends for > **expiation** *n* (*pl* -s)

expiated *v* ▷ expiate

expiates *v* ▷ expiate

expiating *v* ▷ expiate

expiation *n* ▷ expiate

expiations *n* ▷ expiate

expiration *n* ▷ expire

expirations *n* ▷ expire

expire *v* (-res, -ring, -red) finish or run out (*Lit*) > **expiration** *n* (*pl* -s)

expired *v* ▷ expire

expires *v* ▷ expire

expiries *n* ▷ expiry

expiring *v* ▷ expire

expiry *n* (*pl* -ies) end, esp. of a contract period

explain *v* (-s, -ing, -ed) make clear and intelligible > **explanation** *n* (*pl* -s) > **explanatory** *adj*

explained *v* ▷ explain

explaining *v* ▷ explain

explains *v* ▷ explain

explanation *n* ▷ explain

explanations *n* ▷ explain

explanatory *adj* ▷ explain

expletive *n* (*pl* -s) swearword

expletives *n* ▷ expletive

explicable *adj* able to be explained

explicate *v* (-tes, -ting, -ted) (*Formal*) explain > **explication** *n* (*pl* -s)

explicated *v* ▷ explicate

explicates *v* ▷ explicate

explicating *v* ▷ explicate

explication *n* ▷ explicate

explications *n* ▷ explicate

explicit *adj* precisely and clearly expressed > **explicitly** *adv*

explicitly *adv* ▷ explicit

explode v (-des, -ding, -ded) burst with great violence, blow up ▸ **explosion** n (pl -s)
  exploded v ▷ explode
  explodes v ▷ explode
  exploding v ▷ explode
exploit v (pl -s) take advantage of for one's own purposes ▸ n (pl -s) notable feat or deed ▸ **exploitation** n (pl -s) ▸ **exploiter** n (pl -s)
  exploitation n ▷ exploit
  exploitations n ▷ exploit
  exploited v ▷ exploit
  exploiter n ▷ exploit
  exploiters n ▷ exploit
  exploiting v ▷ exploit
  exploits v, n ▷ exploit
  exploration n ▷ explore
  explorations n ▷ explore
  exploratory adj ▷ explore
explore v (-res, -ring, -red) investigate ▸ **exploration** n (pl -s) ▸ **explorer** n (pl -s)
  explored v ▷ explore
  explorer n ▷ explore
  explorers n ▷ explore
  explores v ▷ explore
  exploring v ▷ explore
  explosion n ▷ explode
  explosions n ▷ explode
explosive adj tending to explode ▸ n (pl -s) substance that causes explosions
  explosives n ▷ explosive
expo n (pl -s) (Informal) exposition, large public exhibition
exponent n (pl -s) person who advocates an idea, cause, etc.
exponential adj (Informal) very rapid ▸ **exponentially** adv
  exponentially adv ▷ exponential
  exponents n ▷ exponent
export n (pl -s) selling or shipping of goods to a foreign country ▸ v (-s, -ing, -ed) sell or ship (goods) to a foreign country ▸ **exporter** n (pl -s)
  exported v ▷ export
  exporter n ▷ export
  exporters n ▷ export
  exporting v ▷ export
  exports n, v ▷ export
  expos n ▷ expo
expose v (-ses, -sing, -sed) uncover or reveal ▸ **exposure** n (pl -s) exposing
exposé [iks-pose-ay] n (pl -s) bringing of a crime, scandal, etc. to public notice
  exposed v ▷ expose
  exposes v ▷ expose

  exposés n ▷ exposé
  exposing v ▷ expose
  exposition n ▷ expound
  expositions n ▷ expound
expostulate v (-tes, -ting, -ted) (foll. by **with**) reason (with), esp. to dissuade
  expostulated v ▷ expostulate
  expostulates v ▷ expostulate
  expostulating v ▷ expostulate
  exposure n ▷ expose
  exposures n ▷ expose
expound v (-s, -ing, -ed) explain in detail ▸ **exposition** n (pl -s) explanation
  expounded v ▷ expound
  expounding v ▷ expound
  expounds v ▷ expound
express v (-es, -ing, -ed) put into words ▸ adj explicitly stated ▸ n (pl -es) fast train or bus stopping at only a few stations ▸ adv by express delivery
  expressed v ▷ express
  expresses v, n ▷ express
  expressing v ▷ express
expression n (pl -s) expressing ▸ **expressionless** adj ▸ **expressive** adj
expressionism n (pl -s) early 20th-century artistic movement which sought to express emotions rather than represent the physical world ▸ **expressionist** adj, n (pl -s)
  expressionisms n ▷ expressionism
  expressionist adj, n ▷ expressionism
  expressionists n ▷ expressionism
  expressionless adj ▷ expression
  expressions n ▷ expression
  expressive adj ▷ expression
expropriate v (-tes, -ting, -ted) deprive an owner of (property) ▸ **expropriation** n (pl -s)
  expropriated v ▷ expropriate
  expropriates v ▷ expropriate
  expropriating v ▷ expropriate
  expropriation n ▷ expropriate
  expropriations n ▷ expropriate
  expulsion n ▷ expel
  expulsions n ▷ expel
expunge v (-ges, -ging, -ged) delete, erase, blot out
  expunged v ▷ expunge
  expunges v ▷ expunge
  expunging v ▷ expunge
expurgate v (-tes, -ting, -ted) remove objectionable parts from (a book etc.)
  expurgated v ▷ expurgate
  expurgates v ▷ expurgate
  expurgating v ▷ expurgate
exquisite adj of extreme beauty or delicacy

> **exquisitely** *adv*
exquisitely *adv* ▷ exquisite
extant *adj* still existing
extemporize *v* (-zes, -zing, -zed) speak, perform, or compose without preparation
extemporized *v* ▷ extemporize
extemporizes *v* ▷ extemporize
extemporizing *v* ▷ extemporize
extend *v* (-s, -ing, -ed) draw out or be drawn out, stretch (foll. by **to**) > **extendable** *adj*
extendable *adj* ▷ extend
extended *v* ▷ extend
extending *v* ▷ extend
extends *v* ▷ extend
extension *n* (*pl* -s) room or rooms added to an existing building
extensions *n* ▷ extension
extensive *adj* having a large extent, widespread
extensor *n* (*pl* -s) muscle that extends a part of the body
extensors *n* ▷ extensor
extent *n* (*pl* -s) range over which something extends, area
extents *n* ▷ extent
extenuate *v* (-tes, -ting, -ted) make (an offence or fault) less blameworthy
> **extenuation** *n* (*pl* -s)
extenuated *v* ▷ extenuate
extenuates *v* ▷ extenuate
extenuating *v* ▷ extenuate
extenuation *n* ▷ extenuate
extenuations *n* ▷ extenuate
exterior *n* (*pl* -s) part or surface on the outside ▶ *adj* of, on, or coming from the outside
exteriors *n* ▷ exterior
exterminate *v* (-tes, -ting, -ted) destroy (animals or people) completely
> **extermination** *n* (*pl* -s) > **exterminator** *n* (*pl* -s)
exterminated *v* ▷ exterminate
exterminates *v* ▷ exterminate
exterminating *v* ▷ exterminate
extermination *n* ▷ exterminate
exterminations *n* ▷ exterminate
exterminator *n* ▷ exterminate
exterminators *n* ▷ exterminate
external *adj* of, situated on, or coming from the outside > **externally** *adv*
externally *adv* ▷ external
extinct *adj* having died out > **extinction** *n* (*pl* -s)
extinction *n* ▷ extinct
extinctions *n* ▷ extinct
extinguish *v* (-es, -ing, -ed) put out (a fire or light)

extinguished *v* ▷ extinguish
extinguisher *n* (*pl* -s) device for extinguishing a fire or light
extinguishers *n* ▷ extinguisher
extinguishes *v* ▷ extinguish
extinguishing *v* ▷ extinguish
extirpate *v* (-tes, -ting, -ted) destroy utterly
extirpated *v* ▷ extirpate
extirpates *v* ▷ extirpate
extirpating *v* ▷ extirpate
extol *v* (-s, -lling, -lled) praise highly
extolled *v* ▷ extol
extolling *v* ▷ extol
extols *v* ▷ extol
extort *v* (-s, -ing, -ed) get (something) by force or threats > **extortion** *n* (*pl* -s)
extorted *v* ▷ extort
extorting *v* ▷ extort
extortion *n* ▷ extort
extortionate *adj* (of prices) excessive
extortions *n* ▷ extort
extorts *v* ▷ extort
extra *adj* more than is usual, expected or needed ▶ *n* (*pl* -s) additional person or thing ▶ *adv* unusually or exceptionally
extract *v* (-s, -ing, -ed) pull out by force ▶ *n* (*pl* -s) something extracted, such as a passage from a book etc. > **extraction** *n* (*pl* -s) > **extractor** (*pl* -s) *n*
extracted *v* ▷ extract
extracting *v* ▷ extract
extraction *n* ▷ extract
extractions *n* ▷ extract
extractor *n* ▷ extract
extractors *n* ▷ extract
extracts *n, v* ▷ extract
extradite *v* (-tes, -ting, -ted) send (an accused person) back to his or her own country for trial > **extradition** *n* (*pl* -s)
extradited *v* ▷ extradite
extradites *v* ▷ extradite
extraditing *v* ▷ extradite
extradition *n* ▷ extradite
extraditions *n* ▷ extradite
extramural *adj* connected with but outside the normal courses of a university or college
extraneous [iks-**train**-ee-uss] *adj* irrelevant
extraordinarily *adv* ▷ extraordinary
extraordinary *adj* very unusual > **extraordinarily** *adv*
extrapolate *v* (-tes, -ting, -ted) infer (something not known) from the known facts (MATHS) > **extrapolation** *n* (*pl* -s)
extrapolated *v* ▷ extrapolate

extrapolates v ▷ extrapolate
extrapolating v ▷ extrapolate
extrapolation n ▷ extrapolate
extrapolations n ▷ extrapolate
extras n ▷ extra
extrasensory adj beyond the normal range of the senses
extravagance n ▷ extravagant
extravagances n ▷ extravagant
extravagant adj spending money excessively > **extravagance** n (pl -s)
extravaganza n (pl -s) elaborate and lavish entertainment, display, etc.
extravaganzas n ▷ extravaganza
extreme adj of a high or the highest degree or intensity ▶ n (pl -s) either of the two limits of a scale or range > **extremely** adv
extremely adv ▷ extreme
extremes n ▷ extreme
extremist n (pl -s) person who favours immoderate methods ▶ adj holding extreme opinions
extremists n ▷ extremist
extremities n ▷ extremity
extremity n (pl -ies) farthest point
extricate v (-tes, -ting, -ted) free from complication or difficulty > **extrication** n (pl -s)
extricated v ▷ extricate
extricates v ▷ extricate
extricating v ▷ extricate
extrication n ▷ extricate
extrications n ▷ extricate
extrovert adj lively and outgoing ▶ n (pl -s) extrovert person
extroverts n ▷ extrovert
extrude v (-des, -ding, -ded) squeeze or force out > **extrusion** n (pl -s)
extruded v ▷ extrude
extrudes v ▷ extrude
extruding v ▷ extrude
extrusion n ▷ extrude
extrusions n ▷ extrude
exuberance n ▷ exuberant
exuberances n ▷ exuberant
exuberant adj high-spirited > **exuberance** n (pl -s)
exude v (-s, -ing, -ed) (of a liquid or smell) seep or flow out slowly and steadily

exuded v ▷ exude
exudes v ▷ exude
exuding v ▷ exude
exult v (-s, -ing, -ed) be joyful or jubilant > **exultation** n (pl -s) > **exultant** adj
exultant adj ▷ exult
exultation n ▷ exult
exultations n ▷ exult
exulted v ▷ exult
exulting v ▷ exult
exults v ▷ exult
eye n (pl -s) organ of sight ▶ v (-s, eyeing or **eyeing**, eyed) look at carefully or warily > **eyeless** adj
eyeball n (pl -s) ball-shaped part of the eye
eyeballs n ▷ eyeball
eyebrow n (pl -s) line of hair on the bony ridge above the eye
eyebrows n ▷ eyebrow
eyed v ▷ eye
eyeglass n (pl -es) lens for aiding defective vision
eyeglasses n ▷ eyeglass
eyeing v ▷ eye
eyelash n (pl -es) short hair that grows out from the eyelid
eyelashes n ▷ eyelash
eyeless adj ▷ eye
eyelet n (pl -s) small hole for a lace or cord to be passed through
eyelets n ▷ eyelet
eyelid n (pl -s) fold of skin that covers the eye when it is closed
eyelids n ▷ eyelid
eyeliner n (pl -s) cosmetic used to outline the eyes
eyeliners n ▷ eyeliner
eyes n, v ▷ eye
eyesight n (pl -s) ability to see
eyesights n ▷ eyesight
eyesore n (pl -s) ugly object
eyesores n ▷ eyesore
eyewitness n (pl -es) person who was present at an event and can describe what happened
eyewitnesses n ▷ eyewitness
eying v ▷ eye
eyrie n (pl -s) nest of an eagle
eyries n ▷ eyrie

Ff

F can be an awkward letter in Scrabble: there are only two two-letter words beginning with F, for example (**fa** and **fy**). But if you're aware of this, you won't waste time trying to think of other two-letter words. There are also quite a few words that combine F with X or Z, allowing high scores particularly if you can hit a bonus square with them. **Fax**, **fix** and **fox** are good examples (13 points each), and don't forgets **fez** (15). If you have a blank tile, you can use it for the second Z in **fuzz** (15) or **fuzzy** (19). **Fey**, **fly** and **fry** can also be useful (9 each).

fa n (**fas**). Fa is the musical note F. This word isn't going to win you a game on its own, but it's useful when you're trying to form several words at once. Fa scores 5 points.

fab adj Fab is a short form of **fabulous**. Fab scores 8 points.

fable n (pl -s) story with a moral

fabled adj made famous in legend

fables n ▷ fable

fabric n (pl -s) knitted or woven cloth

fabricate v (-tes, -ting, -ted) make up (a story or lie) > **fabrication** n (pl -s)

fabricated v ▷ fabricate

fabricates v ▷ fabricate

fabricating v ▷ fabricate

fabrication n ▷ fabricate

fabrications n ▷ fabricate

fabrics n ▷ fabric

fabulous adj (Informal) excellent > **fabulously** adv

fabulously adv ▷ fabulous

facade [fas-sahd] n (pl -s) front of a building

facades n ▷ facade

face n (pl -s) front of the head ▶ v (-ces, -cing, -ced) look or turn towards

faced v ▷ face

faceless adj impersonal, anonymous

faces n, v ▷ face

facet n (pl -s) aspect

facetious [fas-see-shuss] adj funny or trying to be funny, esp. at inappropriate times

facets n ▷ facet

facia n (pl -ciae) ▷ fascia

faciae n ▷ fascia

facial adj of the face ▶ n (pl -s) beauty treatment for the face

facials n ▷ facial

facile [fas-sile] adj (of a remark, argument, etc.) superficial and showing lack of real thought

facilitate v (-tes, -ting, -ted) make easy > **facilitation** n (pl -s)

facilitated v ▷ facilitate

facilitates v ▷ facilitate

facilitating v ▷ facilitate

facilitation n ▷ facilitate

facilitations n ▷ facilitate

facilities n ▷ facility

facility n (pl -ties) skill ▶ pl means or equipment for an activity

facing v ▷ face

facing n (pl -s) lining or covering for decoration or reinforcement ▶ pl contrasting collar and cuffs on a jacket

facings n ▷ facing

facsimile [fak-sim-ill-ee] n (pl -s) exact copy

facsimiles n ▷ facsimile

fact n (pl -s) event or thing known to have happened or existed > **factual** adj

faction n (pl -s) (dissenting) minority group within a larger body

factions n ▷ faction

factious adj of or producing factions

factitious adj artificial

factor n (pl -s) element contributing to a result

factorial n (pl -s) product of all the integers from one to a given number

factorials n ▷ factorial

factories n ▷ factory

factorize v (-zes, -zing, -zed) calculate the factors of (a number)

factorized v ▷ factorize

factorizes v ▷ factorize

factorizing v ▷ factorize

factors n ▷ factor
factory n (pl -ies) building where goods are manufactured
factotum n (pl -s) person employed to do all sorts of work
factotums n ▷ factotum
facts n ▷ fact
factual adj ▷ fact
faculties n ▷ faculty
faculty n (pl -ties) physical or mental ability
fad n (pl -s) short-lived fashion > **faddy** (-ddier, -ddiest), **faddish** adj
faddier adj ▷ fad
faddiest adj ▷ fad
faddish adj ▷ fad
faddy adj ▷ fad
fade v (-des, -ding, -ded) (cause to) lose brightness, colour, or strength
faded v ▷ fade
fades v ▷ fade
fading v ▷ fade
fads n ▷ fad
faecal adj ▷ faeces
faeces [fee-seez] pl n waste matter discharged from the anus > **faecal** [fee-kl] ▶ adj
fag¹ n (pl -s) (Informal) boring task (BRIT) ▶ v (-gs, -gging, -gged) (BRIT) do menial chores in a public school
fag² n (BRIT) (Slang) cigarette
fagged v ▷ fag¹
fagging v ▷ fag¹
faggot n (pl -s) (BRIT, AUST & NZ) ball of chopped liver, herbs, and bread
faggots n ▷ faggot
fags n, v ▷ fag¹, ²
faïence [fie-ence] n (pl -s) tin-glazed earthenware
faïences n ▷ faïence
fail v (-s, -ing, -ed) be unsuccessful ▶ n (pl -s) instance of not passing an exam or test
failed v ▷ fail
failing n (pl -s) weak point ▶ prep in the absence of ▶ v ▷ fail
failings n ▷ failing
fails v, n ▷ fail
failure n (pl -s) act or instance of failing
failures n ▷ failure
fain adv (Obs) gladly
faint adj lacking clarity, brightness, or volume ▶ v (-s, -ing, -ed) lose consciousness temporarily ▶ n (pl -s) temporary loss of consciousness
fainted v ▷ faint
fainting v ▷ faint
faints v, n ▷ faint

fair¹ adj (-er, -est) unbiased and reasonable ▶ adv fairly > **fairness** n (pl -s)
fair² n (pl -s) travelling entertainment with sideshows, rides, and amusements
fairer adj ▷ fair¹
fairest adj ▷ fair¹
fairground n (pl -s) open space used for a fair
fairgrounds n ▷ fairground
fairies n ▷ fairy
fairly adv moderately
fairness n ▷ fair¹
fairnesses n ▷ fair¹
fairs n ▷ fair¹, ²
fairway n (pl -s) (GOLF) smooth area between the tee and the green
fairways n ▷ fairway
fairy n (pl -ries) imaginary small creature with magic powers > **fairyland** n (pl -s)
fairyland n ▷ fairy
fairylands n ▷ fairy
faith n (pl -s) strong belief, esp. without proof
faithful adj loyal > **faithfully** adv
faithfully adv ▷ faithful
faithless adj disloyal or dishonest
faiths n ▷ faith
fake v (-kes, -king, -ked) cause something not genuine to appear real or more valuable by fraud ▶ n (pl -s) person, thing, or act that is not genuine ▶ adj not genuine
faked v ▷ fake
fakes v, n ▷ fake
faking v ▷ fake
fakir [fay-keer] n (pl -s) Muslim who spurns worldly possessions
fakirs n ▷ fakir
falcon n (pl -s) small bird of prey
falconer n ▷ falconry
falconers n ▷ falconry
falconries n ▷ falconry
falconry n (pl -ries) art of training falcons > **falconer** n (pl -s)
falcons n ▷ falcon
fall v (-s, -ing, fell, fallen) drop from a higher to a lower place through the force of gravity ▶ n (pl -s) falling
fallacies n ▷ fallacy
fallacious adj ▷ fallacy
fallacy n (pl -cies) false belief > **fallacious** adj
fallen v ▷ fall
fallibilities n ▷ fallible
fallibility n ▷ fallible
fallible adj (of a person) liable to make mistakes > **fallibility** n (pl -ties)
falling v ▷ fall
fallout n (pl -s) radioactive particles spread as

a result of a nuclear explosion
fallouts n ▷ fallout
fallow adj (of land) ploughed but left unseeded to regain fertility
falls v, n ▷ fall
false adj (-r, -st) not true or correct > **falsely** adv > **falseness** n (pl -es) > **falsity** n (pl -ties)
falsehood n (pl -s) quality of being untrue
falsehoods n ▷ falsehood
falsely adv ▷ false
falseness n ▷ false
falsenesses n ▷ false
falser adj ▷ false
falsest adj ▷ false
falsetto n (pl -tos) voice pitched higher than one's natural range
falsettos n ▷ falsetto
falsification n ▷ falsify
falsifications n ▷ falsify
falsified v ▷ falsify
falsifies v ▷ falsify
falsify v (-fies, -fying, -fied) alter fraudulently > **falsification** n (pl -s)
falsifying v ▷ falsify
falsities n ▷ false
falsity n ▷ false
falter v (-s, -ing, -ed) be hesitant, weak, or unsure
faltered v ▷ falter
faltering v ▷ falter
falters v ▷ falter
fame n (pl -s) state of being widely known or recognized
famed adj famous
famed adj ▷ fame
fames n ▷ fame
familial adj ▷ family
familiar adj well-known ▶ n (pl -s) demon supposed to attend a witch > **familiarly** adv > **familiarity** n (pl -ties)
familiarities n ▷ familiarity
familiarity n ▷ familiarity
familiarize (-zes, -zing, -zed) v acquaint fully with a particular subject > **familiarization** n (pl -s)
familiarization n ▷ familiarize
familiarizations n ▷ familiarize
familiarized v ▷ familiarize
familiarizes v ▷ familiarize
familiarizing v ▷ familiarize
familiarly adv ▷ familiar
familiars n ▷ familiar
families n ▷ family
family n (pl -lies) group of parents and their children ▶ adj suitable for parents and

children together > **familial** adj
famine n (pl -s) severe shortage of food
famines n ▷ famine
famished adj very hungry
famous adj very well-known
famously adv (Informal) excellently
fan¹ n (pl -s) hand-held or mechanical object used to create a current of air for ventilation or cooling ▶ v (-s, -nning, -nned) blow or cool with a fan
fan² n (pl -s) (Informal) devotee of a pop star, sport, or hobby
fanatic n (pl -s) person who is excessively enthusiastic about something > **fanatical** adj > **fanatically** adv > **fanaticism** n (pl -s)
fanatical adj ▷ fanatic
fanatically adv ▷ fanatic
fanaticism n ▷ fanatic
fanaticisms n ▷ fanatic
fanatics n ▷ fanatic
fanbase n (pl -s) body of admirers of a particular pop singer, sports team, etc
fanbases n ▷ fanbase
fancied v ▷ fancy
fancier adj ▷ fancy
fancies n, v ▷ fancy
fanciest adj ▷ fancy
fanciful adj not based on fact > **fancifully** adv
fancifully adv ▷ fanciful
fancy adj (-cier, -ciest) elaborate, not plain ▶ n (pl -cies) sudden irrational liking or desire ▶ v (-cies, -cying, -cied) (Informal) be sexually attracted to
fancy-free adj not in love
fancying v ▷ fancy
fandango n (pl -os) lively Spanish dance
fandangos n ▷ fandango
fanfare n (pl -s) short loud tune played on brass instruments
fanfares n ▷ fanfare
fang n (pl -s) snake's tooth which injects poison
fangs n ▷ fang
fanned n ▷ fan
fanning n ▷ fan
fans n, v ▷ fan
fantail n (pl -s) small New Zealand bird with a tail like a fan
fantails n ▷ fantail
fantasia n (pl -s) musical composition of an improvised nature
fantasias n ▷ fantasia
fantasies n ▷ fantasy
fantasize v (-zes, -zing, -zed) indulge in daydreams

fantasized v ▷ fantasize
fantasizes v ▷ fantasize
fantasizing v ▷ fantasize
fantastic adj (Informal) very good
  > **fantastically** adv
  fantastically adv ▷ fantastic
fantasy n (pl -sies) far-fetched notion
far adv (farther or further, farthest or furthest)
  at, to, or from a great distance ▶ adj remote in
  space or time
farad n (pl -s) unit of electrical capacitance
  farads n ▷ farad
farce n (pl -s) boisterous comedy
  farces n ▷ farce
farcical adj ludicrous > **farcically** adv
  farcically adv ▷ farcical
fare n (pl -s) charge for a passenger's journey
  ▶ v (-res, -ring, -red) get on (as specified)
  fared v ▷ fare
  fares n, v ▷ fare
farewell interj goodbye ▶ n (pl -s) act of saying
  goodbye and leaving ▶ v (-s, -ing, -ed) (NZ) say
  goodbye
  farewelled v ▷ farewell
  farewelling v ▷ farewell
  farewells n, v ▷ farewell
farinaceous adj containing starch or having a
  starchy texture
  faring v ▷ fare
farm n (pl -s) area of land for growing crops or
  rearing livestock ▶ v (-s, -ing, -ed) cultivate
  (land) > **farmyard** n (pl -s) > **farmyard** n (pl -s)
  farmed v ▷ farm
farmer n (pl -s) person who owns or runs a
  farm
  farmers n ▷ farmer
  farmhouse n ▷ farm
  farmhouses n ▷ farm
  farming v ▷ farm
  farms n, v ▷ farm
farmstead n (pl -s) farm and its buildings
  farmsteads n ▷ farmstead
  farmyard n ▷ farm
  farmyards n ▷ farm
farrago [far-**rah**-go] n (pl -gos, -goes) jumbled
  mixture of things
  farragoes n ▷ farrago
  farragos n ▷ farrago
farrier n (pl -s) person who shoes horses
  farriers n ▷ farrier
farrow n (pl -s) litter of piglets ▶ v (-s, -ing, -ed)
  (of a sow) give birth
  farrowed v ▷ farrow
  farrowing v ▷ farrow
  farrows n, v ▷ farrow

farther, farthest adv, adj ▷ far
farthing n (pl -s) former British coin
  equivalent to a quarter of a penny
  farthings n ▷ farthing
fascia [**fay**-shya] n (pl -ciae, -cias) outer surface
  of a dashboard
  fasciae n ▷ fascia
  fascias n ▷ fascia
fascinate v (-tes, -ting, -ted) attract
  and interest strongly > **fascinating** adj
  > **fascination** n (pl -s)
  fascinated v ▷ fascinate
  fascinates v ▷ fascinate
  fascinating v, adj ▷ fascinate
  fascination n ▷ fascinate
  fascinations n ▷ fascinate
fascism [**fash**-iz-zum] n (pl -s) right-wing
  totalitarian political system characterized
  by state control and extreme nationalism
  > **fascist** adj, n (pl -s)
  fascisms n ▷ fascism
  fascist n ▷ fascism
  fascists n ▷ fascism
fashion n (pl -s) style in clothes, hairstyle, etc.,
  popular at a particular time ▶ v (-s, -ing, -ed)
  form or make into a particular shape
fashionable adj currently popular
  > **fashionably** adv
  fashionably adv ▷ fashionable
  fashioned v ▷ fashion
  fashioning v ▷ fashion
  fashions n, v ▷ fashion
fast¹ adj (-er, -est) (capable of) acting or
  moving quickly ▶ adv quickly
fast² v (-s, -ing, -ed) go without food, esp. for
  religious reasons ▶ n (pl -s) period of fasting
  fasted v ▷ fast²
fasten v (-s, -ing, -ed) make or become firmly
  fixed or joined
  fastened v ▷ fasten
fastener n (pl -s) device that fastens
  fasteners n ▷ fastener
  fastening v ▷ fasten ▶ n (pl -s) device that
  fastens
  fastenings n ▷ fastening
  fastens v ▷ fasten
  faster adj ▷ fast¹
  fastest adj ▷ fast¹
fastidious adj very fussy about details
  > **fastidiously** adv > **fastidiousness** n
  fastidiously adv ▷ fastidious
  fastidiousness n ▷ fastidious
  fastidiousnesses n ▷ fastidious
  fasting v ▷ fast²
fastness n (pl -es) fortress, safe place

fastnesses n ▷ fastness

fasts v, n ▷ fast²

fat adj (-er, -est) having excess flesh on the body ▶ n (pl -s) extra flesh on the body >**fatness** n (pl -es)

fatal adj causing death or ruin >**fatally** adv

fatalism n (pl -s) belief that all events are predetermined and people are powerless to change their destinies >**fatalist** n (pl -s) >**fatalistic** adj

fatalisms n ▷ fatalism

fatalist n ▷ fatalism

fatalistic adj ▷ fatalism

fatalists n ▷ fatalism

fatalities n ▷ fatality

fatality n (pl -ties) death caused by an accident or disaster

fatally adv ▷ fatal

fate n (pl -s) power supposed to predetermine events

fated adj destined

fateful adj having important, usu. disastrous, consequences

fates n ▷ fate

fathead n (pl -s) (Informal) stupid person >**fat-headed** adj

fatheaded adj ▷ fathead

fatheads n ▷ fathead

father n (pl -s) male parent ▶ v (-s, -ing, -ed) be the father of (offspring) >**fatherhood** n (pl -s) >**fatherless** adj >**fatherly** adj

fathered v ▷ father

fatherhood n ▷ father

fatherhoods n ▷ fatherhood

fathering v ▷ father

fatherland n one's native country

fatherlands n ▷ fatherland

fatherless adj ▷ father

fatherly adj ▷ father

fathers n, v ▷ father

fathom n (pl -s) unit of length, used in navigation, equal to six feet (1.83 metres) ▶ v (-s, -ing, -ed) understand >**fathomable** adj

fathomable adj ▷ fathom

fathomed v ▷ fathom

fathoming v ▷ fathom

fathomless adj too deep or difficult to fathom

fathoms n, v ▷ fathom

fatigue [fat-**eeg**] n (pl -s) extreme physical or mental tiredness ▶ v (-gues, -guing, -gued) tire out

fatigued v ▷ fatigue

fatigues v, n ▷ fatigue

fatiguing v ▷ fatigue

fatness n ▷ fat

fatnesses n ▷ fat

fats n ▷ fat

fatten v (-s, -ing, -ed) (cause to) become fat

fattened v ▷ fatten

fattening v ▷ fatten

fattens v ▷ fatten

fattier adj ▷ fatty

fattiest adj ▷ fatty

fatty adj (-ier, -iest) containing fat

fatuities n ▷ fatuous

fatuity n ▷ fatuous

fatuous adj foolish >**fatuously** adv >**fatuity** n (pl -s)

fatuously adv ▷ fatuous

faucet [faw-set] n (pl -s) (US) tap

faucets n ▷ faucet

fault n (pl -s) responsibility for something wrong ▶ v (-s, -ing, -ed) criticize or blame >**faulty** adj (-tier, -tiest) >**faultless** adj >**faultlessly** adv

faulted v ▷ fault

faultier adj ▷ fault

faultiest adj ▷ fault

faulting v ▷ fault

faultless adj ▷ fault

faultlessly adv ▷ fault

faults v ▷ fault

faulty adj ▷ fault

faun n (pl -s) (in Roman legend) creature with a human face and torso and a goat's horns and legs

fauna n (pl -as, -ae) animals of a given place or time

faunae n ▷ fauna

faunas n ▷ fauna

fauns n ▷ faun

favour n (pl -s) approving attitude ▶ v (-s, -ing, -ed) prefer

favourable adj encouraging or advantageous >**favourably** adv

favourably adv ▷ favourable

favoured v ▷ favour

favouring v ▷ favour

favourite adj most liked ▶ n (pl -s) preferred person or thing

favourites n ▷ favourite

favouritism n (pl -s) practice of giving special treatment to a person or group

favouritisms n ▷ favouritism

favours n, v ▷ favour

faw n (faws). A faw is a gypsy. This is a good word for taking advantage of a nearby bonus square. Faw scores 9 points.

fawn¹ n (pl -s) young deer ▶ adj light yellowish-brown

fawn² v (-s, -ing, -ed) (foll. by **on**) seek attention from (someone) by insincere flattery

fawned v ▷ fawn²

fawning v ▷ fawn²

fawns n, v ▷ fawn¹, ²

fax n (pl -es) electronic system for sending facsimiles of documents by telephone ▶ v (-xes, -xing, -xed) send (a document) by this system

faxed n ▷ fax

faxes n, v ▷ fax

faxing v ▷ fax

> **fay** n (**fays**). A fay is a fairy. This is a fairly high-scoring short word. Fay scores 9 points.

fealties n ▷ fealty

fealty n (pl -ies) (in feudal society) subordinate's loyalty to his ruler or lord

fear n (pl -s) distress or alarm caused by impending danger or pain ▶ v (-s, -ing, -ed) be afraid of (something or someone) > **fearless** adj > **fearlessly** adv

feared v ▷ fear

fearful adj feeling fear (Informal) > **fearfully** adv

fearfully adv ▷ fearful

fearing v ▷ fear

fearless n ▷ fear

fearlessly adv ▷ fear

fears n, v ▷ fear

fearsome adj terrifying

feasibilities n ▷ feasible

feasibility n ▷ feasible

feasible adj able to be done, possible > **feasibly** adv > **feasibility** n (pl -ies)

feasibly adv ▷ feasible

feast n (pl -s) lavish meal ▶ v (-s, -ing, -ed) eat a feast

feasted v ▷ feast

feasting v ▷ feast

feasts n, v ▷ feast

feat n (pl -s) remarkable, skilful, or daring action

feather n (pl -s) one of the barbed shafts forming the plumage of birds ▶ v (-s, -ing, -ed) fit or cover with feathers > **feathered** adj > **feathery** adj (-rier, -riest)

feathered v, adj ▷ feather

featherier adj ▷ feather

featheriest adj ▷ feather

feathering v ▷ feather

feathers n, v ▷ feather

featherweight n (pl -s) boxer weighing up to 126lb (professional) or 57kg (amateur)

featherweights n ▷ featherweight

feathery adj ▷ feather

featliness n ▷ feat

feats n ▷ feat

feature n (pl -s) part of the face, such as the eyes ▶ v (-res, -ring, -red) have as a feature or be a feature in > **featureless** adj

featured v ▷ feature

featureless adj ▷ feature

features n, v ▷ feature

featuring v ▷ feature

febrile [fee-brile] adj feverish

feckless adj ineffectual or irresponsible

fecund adj fertile > **fecundity** n (pl -ties)

fecundities n ▷ fecund

fecundity n ▷ fecund

fed v ▷ feed

federal adj of a system in which power is divided between one central government and several regional governments > **federalism** n (pl -s) > **federalist** n (pl -s)

federalism n ▷ federal

federalisms n ▷ federal

federalist n ▷ federal

federalists n ▷ federal

federate v (-tes, -ting, -ted) unite in a federation

federated v ▷ federate

federates v ▷ federate

federating v ▷ federate

federation n (pl -s) union of several states, provinces, etc.

federations n ▷ federation

fedora [fid-or-a] n (pl -s) man's soft hat with a brim

fedoras n ▷ fedora

fee n (pl -s) charge paid to be allowed to do something

feeble adj (-r, -st) lacking physical or mental power > **feebleness** n (pl -es) > **feebly** adv

feebleminded adj unable to think or understand effectively

feebleness n ▷ feeble

feeblenesses n ▷ feeble

feebler adj ▷ feeble

feeblest adj ▷ feeble

feebly adv ▷ feeble

feed v (-s, -ing, fed) give food to ▶ n (pl -s) act of feeding

feedback n (pl -s) information received in response to something done

feedbacks n ▷ feedback

feeder n (pl -s) road or railway line linking outlying areas to the main traffic network

feeders n ▷ feeder

feeding v ▷ feed

feeds v, n ▷ feed

feel (-s, -ing, felt) have a physical or emotional sensation of ▶ n (pl -s) act of feeling

feeler n (pl -s) organ of touch in some animals

feelers n ▷ feeler

feeling n (pl -s) emotional reaction

feelings n ▷ feeling ▶ v ▷ feel

feels v, n ▷ feel

fees n ▷ fee

feet n ▷ foot

feign [fane] v (-s, -ing, -ed) pretend

feigned v ▷ feign

feigning v ▷ feign

feigns v ▷ feign

feint¹ [faint] n (pl -s) sham attack or blow meant to distract an opponent ▶ v (-s, -ing, -ed) make a feint

feint² [faint] n (pl -s) narrow lines on ruled paper

feinted v ▷ feint¹

feinting v ▷ feint¹

feints n, v ▷ feint¹, ²

feldspar n (pl -s) hard mineral that is the main constituent of igneous rocks

feldspars n ▷ feldspar

felicitations pl n congratulations

felicities n ▷ felicity

felicitous adj ▷ felicity

felicity n (pl -ties) happiness > **felicitous** adj

feline adj of cats ▶ n (pl -s) member of the cat family

felines n ▷ feline

fell¹ v ▷ fall

fell² v (-s, -ing, -ed) cut down (a tree)

fell³ adj (-er, -est) deadly

fell⁴ n (pl -s) (SCOT & N ENGLISH) mountain, hill, or moor

felled v ▷ fell²

feller adj ▷ fell³

fellest adj ▷ fell³

felling v ▷ fell²

felloe n (pl -oes) (segment of) the rim of a wheel

felloes n ▷ felloe

fellow n (pl -s) man or boy ▶ adj in the same group or condition

fellows n ▷ fellow

fellowship n (pl -s) sharing of aims or interests

fellowships n ▷ fellowship

fells v, n ▷ fell², ⁴

felon n (pl -s) (CRIMINAL LAW) (formerly) person guilty of a felony

felonies n ▷ felony

felonious adj ▷ felony

felons n ▷ felon

felony n (pl -nies) serious crime > **felonious** adj

felspar n (pl -s) ▷ feldspar

felspars n ▷ felspar

felt¹ v ▷ feel

felt² n (pl -s) matted fabric made by bonding fibres by pressure

felts n ▷ felt²

female adj of the sex which bears offspring ▶ n (pl -s) female person or animal

females n ▷ female

feminine adj having qualities traditionally regarded as suitable for, or typical of, women > **femininity** n (pl -ties)

femininities n ▷ feminine

femininity n ▷ feminine

feminism n (pl -s) advocacy of equal rights for women > **feminist** adj, n (pl -s)

feminisms n ▷ feminism

feminist n ▷ feminism

feminists n ▷ feminism

femoral adj of the thigh

femur [fee-mer] n (pl -s) thighbone

femurs n ▷ femur

fen n (pl -s) (BRIT) low-lying flat marshy land

fence n (pl -s) barrier of posts linked by wire or wood, enclosing an area ▶ v (-ces, -cing, -ced) enclose with or as if with a fence

fenced v ▷ fence

fencer n ▷ fencing

fencers n ▷ fencing

fences n, v ▷ fence

fencing n (pl -s) sport of fighting with swords ▶ v ▷ fence > **fencer** n (pl -s)

fencings n ▷ fencing

fend v (-s, -ing, -ed) provide (for oneself)

fended v ▷ fend

fender n (pl -s) low metal frame in front of a fireplace

fenders n ▷ fender

fending v ▷ fend

fends v ▷ fend

fennel n (pl -s) fragrant plant whose seeds, leaves, and root are used in cookery

fennels n ▷ fennel

fens n ▷ fen

fenugreek n (pl -s) Mediterranean plant grown for its heavily scented seeds

fenugreeks n ▷ fenugreek

feral adj wild

ferment n (pl -s) commotion, unrest ▶ v (-s, -ing, -ed) undergo or cause to undergo fermentation

fermentation n (pl -s) reaction in which

an organic molecule splits into simpler substances, esp. the conversion of sugar to alcohol

fermentations *n* ▷ fermentation
fermented *n* ▷ ferment
fermenting *v* ▷ ferment
ferments *n, v* ▷ ferment
fern *n* (*pl* -s) flowerless plant with fine fronds
ferns *n* ▷ fern
ferocious *adj* savagely fierce or cruel > **ferocity** *n* (*pl* -ties)
ferocities *n* ▷ ferocious
ferocity *n* ▷ ferocious
ferret *n* (*pl* -s) tamed polecat used to catch rabbits or rats ▶ *v* (-s, -ing, -ed) hunt with ferrets
ferreted *v* ▷ ferret
ferreting *v* ▷ ferret
ferrets *n, v* ▷ ferret
ferric, ferrous *adj* of or containing iron
ferried *v* ▷ ferry
ferries *n, v* ▷ ferry
ferrous *adj* ▷ ferric
ferry *n* (*pl* -rries) boat for transporting people and vehicles ▶ *v* (-rries, -rrying, -rried) carry by ferry > **ferryman** *n* (*pl* -men)
ferrying *v* ▷ ferry
ferryman *n* ▷ ferry
ferrymen *n* ▷ ferry
fertile *adj* capable of producing young, crops, or vegetation > **fertility** *n* (*pl* -ties)
fertilities *n* ▷ fertile
fertility *n* ▷ fertile
fertilization *n* ▷ fertilize
fertilizations *n* ▷ fertilize
fertilize *v* (-zes, -zing, -zed) provide (an animal or plant) with sperm or pollen to bring about fertilization > **fertilization** *n* (*pl* -s)
fertilized *v* ▷ fertilize
fertilizer *n* (*pl* -s) substance added to the soil to increase its productivity
fertilizers *n* ▷ fertilizer
fertilizes *v* ▷ fertilize
fertilizing *v* ▷ fertilize
fervent, fervid *adj* intensely passionate and sincere > **fervently** *adv*
fervently *adv* ▷ fervent
fervid *adj* ▷ fervent
fervour *n* (*pl* -s) intensity of feeling
fervours *n* ▷ fervour
fescue *n* (*pl* -s) pasture and lawn grass with stiff narrow leaves
fescues *n* ▷ fescue
fester *v* (-s, -ing, -ed) grow worse and increasingly hostile

festered *v* ▷ fester
festering *v* ▷ fester
festers *v* ▷ fester
festival *n* (*pl* -s) organized series of special events or performances
festivals *n* ▷ festival
festive *adj* of or like a celebration
festivities *n* ▷ festivity
festivity *n* (*pl* -ties) happy celebration ▶ *pl* celebrations
festoon *v* (-s, -ing, -ed) hang decorations in loops
festooned *v* ▷ festoon
festooning *v* ▷ festoon
festoons *v* ▷ festoon
feta *n* (*pl* -as) white salty Greek cheese
fetal *adj* ▷ fetus
fetas *n* ▷ feta
fetch *v* (-es, -ing, -ed) go after and bring back (*Informal*)
fetched *v* ▷ fetch
fetches *v* ▷ fetch
fetching *v* ▷ fetch ▶ *adj* attractive
fete [fate] *n* (*pl* -s) gala, bazaar, etc., usu. held outdoors ▶ *v* (-tes, -ting, -ted) honour or entertain regally
feted *v* ▷ fete
fetes *n, v* ▷ fete
fetid *adj* (-er, -est) stinking
fetider *adj* ▷ fetid
fetidest *adj* ▷ fetid
feting *v* ▷ fete
fetish *n* (*pl* -es) form of behaviour in which sexual pleasure is derived from looking at or handling an inanimate object > **fetishism** *n* (*pl* -s) > **fetishist** (*pl* -s) *n*
fetishes *n* ▷ fetish
fetishism *n* ▷ fetish
fetishisms *n* ▷ fetish
fetishist *n* ▷ fetish
fetishists *n* ▷ fetish
fetlock *n* (*pl* -s) projection behind and above a horse's hoof
fetlocks *n* ▷ fetlock
fetter *n* (*pl* -s) chain or shackle for the foot ▶ *pl* restrictions ▶ *v* (-s, -ing, -ed) restrict
fettered *v* ▷ fetter
fettering *v* ▷ fetter
fetters *n, v* ▷ fetter
fettle *n* (*pl* -s) state of health or spirits
fettles *n* ▷ fettle
fetus [fee-tuss] *n* (*pl* -tuses) embryo of a mammal in the later stages of development > **fetal** *adj*
fetuses *n* ▷ fetus

feu n (pl -s) (in Scotland) right of use of land in return for a fixed annual payment

feud n (pl -s) long bitter hostility between two people or groups ▷ v (-s, -ing, -ed) carry on a feud

feudal adj of or like feudalism

feudalism n (pl -s) medieval system in which people held land from a lord, and in return worked and fought for him
  feudalisms n ▷ feudalism
  feuded v ▷ feud
  feuding v ▷ feud
  feuds n, v ▷ feud
  feus n ▷ feu

fever n (pl -s) (illness causing) high body temperature > **fevered** adj
  fevered adj ▷ fever

feverish adj suffering from fever > **feverishly** adv
  feverishly adv ▷ feverish
  fevers n ▷ fever

few adj (-er, -est) not many
  fewer adj ▷ few
  fewest adj ▷ few

fey adj (-er, -est) whimsically strange
  feyer adj ▷ fey
  feyest adj ▷ fey

fez n (pl fezzes) brimless tasselled cap, orig. from Turkey
  fezzes n ▷ fez

fiancé [fee-on-say] n (pl -cés) man engaged to be married > **fiancée** fem (pl -cées)
  fiancée n ▷ fiancé
  fiancées n ▷ fiancé
  fiancés n ▷ fiancé

fiasco n (pl -cos, -coes) ridiculous or humiliating failure
  fiascoes n ▷ fiasco
  fiascos n ▷ fiasco

fiat [fee-at] n (pl -s) arbitrary order
  fiats n ▷ fiat

fib n (pl -s) trivial lie ▷ v (-s, -bbing, -bbed) tell a lie > **fibber** n (pl -s)
  fibbed v ▷ fib
  fibber n ▷ fib
  fibbers n ▷ fib
  fibbing v ▷ fib

fibre n (pl -s) thread that can be spun into yarn > **fibrous** adj

fibreglass n (pl -es) material made of fine glass fibres
  fibreglasses n ▷ fibreglass
  fibres n ▷ fibre

fibro n (pl -ros) (AUST) mixture of cement and asbestos fibre, used in sheets for building

(also **fibrocement**)

fibroid [**fibe**-royd] n (pl -s) benign tumour composed of fibrous connective tissue
  fibroids n ▷ fibroid
  fibros n ▷ fibro
  fibrosites n ▷ fibrositis

fibrositis [fibe-roh-**site**-iss] n (pl -es) inflammation of the tissues of muscle sheaths
  fibrous adj ▷ fibre
  fibs n, v ▷ fib

fibula n (pl -lae, -las) slender outer bone of the lower leg
  fibulae n ▷ fibula
  fibulas n ▷ fibula

fiche [feesh] n (pl -s) sheet of film for storing publications in miniaturized form
  fiches n ▷ fiche

fickle adj changeable, inconstant > **fickleness** n (pl -ess)
  fickleness n ▷ fickle
  ficklenesses n ▷ fickle

fiction n (pl -s) literary works of the imagination, such as novels > **fictional** adj
  fictional adj ▷ fiction

fictionalize v (-zes, -zing, -zed) turn into fiction
  fictionalized v ▷ fictionalize
  fictionalizes v ▷ fictionalize
  fictionalizing v ▷ fictionalize
  fictions n ▷ fiction

fictitious adj not genuine

fiddle n (pl -s) violin (Informal) ▷ v (-les, -ling, -led) play the violin
  fiddled v ▷ fiddle
  fiddles n, v ▷ fiddle

fiddlesticks interj expression of annoyance or disagreement
  fiddlier adj ▷ fiddly
  fiddliest adj ▷ fiddly
  fiddling v ▷ fiddle ▶ adj trivial

fiddly adj (-lier, -liest) awkward to do or use
  fidelities n ▷ fidelity

fidelity n (pl -ies) faithfulness

fidget v (-s, -ing, -ed) move about restlessly ▶ n (pl -s) person who fidgets ▶ pl restlessness > **fidgety** adj (-tier, -tiest)
  fidgeted v ▷ fidget
  fidgetier adj ▷ fidget
  fidgetiest adj ▷ fidget
  fidgeting v ▷ fidget
  fidgets v, n ▷ fidget
  fidgety adj ▷ fidget
  fiduciaries n ▷ fiduciary

fiduciary [fid-**yew**-she-er-ee] (LAW) n (pl -ies)

person bound to act for someone else's
benefit, as a trustee ▸ adj of a trust or trustee
fief [feef] n (pl -s) (HIST) land granted by a lord in
return for war service
fiefs n ▷ fief
field n (pl -s) enclosed piece of agricultural
land ▸ v (-s, -ing, -ed) (SPORT) catch and return
(a ball)
fielded v ▷ field
fielder n (pl -s) (SPORT) player whose task is to
field the ball
fielders n ▷ fielder
fieldfare n (pl -s) type of large Old World thrush
fieldfares n ▷ fieldfare
fielding v ▷ field
fields n, v ▷ field
fieldwork n (pl -s) investigation made in the
field as opposed to the classroom or the
laboratory
fieldworks n ▷ fieldwork
fiend [feend] n (pl -s) evil spirit (Informal)
> **fiendish** adj > **fiendishly** adv
fiendish adj ▷ fiend
fiendishly adv ▷ fiend
fiends n ▷ fiend
fierce adj (-r, -st) wild or aggressive > **fiercely**
adv > **fierceness** n (pl -es)
fiercely adv ▷ fierce
fierceness n ▷ fierce
fiercenesses n ▷ fierce
fiercer adj ▷ fierce
fiercest adj ▷ fierce
fierier adj ▷ fiery
fieriest adj ▷ fiery
fiery adj (-rier, -riest) consisting of or like fire
fiesta n (pl -s) religious festival, carnival
fiestas n ▷ fiesta
fife n (pl -s) small high-pitched flute
fifes n ▷ fife
fifteen adj, n (pl -s) five and ten > **fifteenth**
adj, n (pl -s)
fifteens n ▷ fifteen
fifteenth adj, n ▷ fifteen
fifteenths n ▷ fifteenth
fifth adj, n (pl -s) (of) number five in a series
fifths n ▷ fifth
fifties n ▷ fifty
fiftieth adj, n ▷ fifty
fiftieths n ▷ fifty
fifty adj, n (pl -ties) five times ten > **fiftieth**
adj, n (pl -s)
fig n (pl -s) soft pear-shaped fruit
fight v (-s, -ing, fought) struggle (against) in
battle or physical combat ▸ n (pl -s) aggressive
conflict between two (groups of) people

fighter n (pl -s) boxer
fighters n ▷ fighter
fighting v ▷ fight
fights n, v ▷ fight
figment n (pl -s) something imagined
figments n ▷ figment
figs n ▷ fig
figurative adj (of language) abstract,
imaginative, or symbolic > **figuratively** adv
figuratively adv ▷ figurative
figure n (pl -s) numerical symbol (MATHS) ▸ v
(-res, -ring, -red) consider, conclude
figured v ▷ figure
figurehead n (pl -s) nominal leader
figureheads n ▷ figurehead
figures n, v ▷ figure
figurine n (pl -s) statuette
figurines n ▷ figurine
figuring v ▷ figure
filament n (pl -s) fine wire in a light bulb that
gives out light
filaments n ▷ filament
filbert n (pl -s) hazelnut
filberts n ▷ filbert
filch v (-es, -ing, -ed) steal (small amounts)
filched v ▷ filch
filches v ▷ filch
filching v ▷ filch
file[1] n (pl -s) box or folder used to keep
documents in order ▸ v (-les, -ling, -led) place
(a document) in a file
file[2] n (pl -s) tool with a roughened blade for
smoothing or shaping ▸ v (-les, -ling, -led)
shape or smooth with a file
filed v ▷ file[1, 2]
files n, v ▷ file[1, 2]
filial adj of or befitting a son or daughter
filibuster n (pl -s) obstruction of legislation
by making long speeches ▸ v (-s, -ing, -ed)
obstruct (legislation) with such delaying
tactics
filibustered v ▷ filibuster
filibustering v ▷ filibuster
filibusters n, v ▷ filibuster
filigree n (pl -s) delicate ornamental work of
gold or silver wire ▸ adj made of filigree
filigrees n ▷ filigree
filing v ▷ file[1, 2]
filings pl n shavings removed by a file
fill v (-s, -ing, -ed) make or become full
filled v ▷ fill
filler n (pl -s) substance that fills a gap or
increases bulk
fillers n ▷ filler
fillet n (pl -s) boneless piece of meat or fish ▸ v

(-s, -ing, -ed) remove the bones from
filleted v ▷ fillet
filleting v ▷ fillet
fillets n, v ▷ fillet
fillies n ▷ filly
filling n (pl -s) substance that fills a gap
or cavity, esp. in a tooth ▶ adj (of food)
substantial and satisfying ▶ v ▷ fill
fillings n ▷ filling
fillip n (pl -s) something that adds stimulation
or enjoyment
fillips n ▷ fillip
fills v ▷ fill
filly n (pl -lies) young female horse
film n (pl -s) sequence of images projected on
a screen, creating the illusion of movement
▶ v (-s, -ing, -ed) photograph with a movie or
video camera ▶ adj connected with films or
the cinema
filmed v ▷ film
filmier adj ▷ filmy
filmiest adj ▷ filmy
filming v ▷ film
films n, v ▷ film
filmy adj (-mier, -miest) very thin, delicate
filter n (pl -s) material or device permitting
fluid to pass but retaining solid particles
▶ v (-s, -ing, -ed) remove impurities from (a
substance) with a filter
filtered v ▷ filter
filtering v ▷ filter
filters n, v ▷ filter
filth n (pl -s) disgusting dirt > **filthy** adj (-thier,
-thiest) > **filthiness** n (pl -es)
filthier adj ▷ filth
filthiest adj ▷ filth
filthiness n ▷ filth
filthinesses n ▷ filth
filths n ▷ filth
filthy adj ▷ filth
filtrate n (pl -s) filtered gas or liquid ▶ v (-tes,
-ting, -ted) remove impurities with a filter
> **filtration** n (pl -s)
filtrated v ▷ filtrate
filtrates n, v ▷ filtrate
filtrating v ▷ filtrate
filtration n ▷ filtrate
filtrations n ▷ filtrate
fin n (pl -s) projection from a fish's body
enabling it to balance and swim
finagle [fin-nay-gl] v (-les, -ling, -led) get or
achieve by craftiness or trickery
finagled v ▷ finagle
finagles v ▷ finagle
finagling v ▷ finagle

final adj at the end ▶ n (pl -s) deciding contest
between winners of previous rounds
in a competition ▶ pl (BRIT & S AFR) last
examinations in an educational course
> **finally** adv > **finality** n (pl -ties)
finale [fin-nah-lee] (pl -s) n concluding part of a
dramatic performance or musical work
finales n ▷ finale
finalist n (pl -s) competitor in a final
finalists n ▷ finalist
finalities n ▷ final
finality n ▷ final
finalize v (-zes, -zing, -zed) put into final form
finalized v ▷ finalize
finalizes v ▷ finalize
finalizing v ▷ finalize
finally adv ▷ final
finals n ▷ final
finance v (-ces, -cing, -ced) provide or obtain
funds for ▶ n (pl -s) management of money,
loans, or credits ▶ pl money resources
> **financial** adj > **financially** adv
financed v ▷ finance
finances v, n ▷ finance
financial adj ▷ finance
financially adv ▷ finance
financier n (pl -s) person involved in large-
scale financial business
financiers n ▷ financier
financing v ▷ finance
finch n (pl -es) small songbird with a short
strong beak
finches n ▷ finch
find v (-s, -ing, found) discover by chance ▶ n (pl
-s) person or thing found, esp. when valuable
> **finder** n (pl -s)
finder n ▷ find
finders n ▷ find
finding n (pl -s) conclusion from an
investigation ▶ v ▷ find
findings n ▷ finding
finds v, n ▷ find
fine[1] adj (-r, -st) very good > **finely** adv
> **fineness** n (pl -es)
fine[2] n (pl -s) payment imposed as a penalty ▶ v
(-nes, -ning, -ned) impose a fine on
fined v ▷ fine[2]
finely adv ▷ fine[1]
fineness n ▷ fine[1]
finenesses n ▷ fine[1]
finer adj ▷ fine[1]
fineries n ▷ finery
finery n (pl -ries) showy clothing
fines n, v ▷ fine[1, 2]
finesse [fin-ness] n (pl -s) delicate skill

finesses *n* ▷ finesse
finest *adj* ▷ fine¹
finger *n* (*pl* -s) one of the four long jointed parts of the hand ▶ *v* (-s, -ing, -ed) touch or handle with the fingers
fingerboard *n* part of a stringed instrument against which the strings are pressed
fingerboards *n* ▷ fingerboard
fingered *v* ▷ finger
fingering *n* technique of using the fingers in playing a musical instrument ▶ *v* ▷ finger
fingerprint *n* (*pl* -s) impression of the ridges on the tip of the finger ▶ *v* take the fingerprints of (someone)
fingerprints *n* ▷ fingerprint
fingers *n, v* ▷ finger
finickier *adj* ▷ finicky
finickiest *adj* ▷ finicky
finicky *adj* (-ckier, -ckiest) excessively particular, fussy
fining *v* ▷ fine
finish *v* (-es, -ing, -ed) bring to an end, stop ▶ *n* (*pl* -es) end, last part
finished *v* ▷ finish
finishes *v, n* ▷ finish
finishing *v* ▷ finish
finite *adj* having limits in space, time, or size
fins *n* ▷ fin
fiord *n* (*pl* -s) ▷ fjord
fiords *n* ▷ fiord
fir *n* (*pl* -s) pyramid-shaped tree with needle-like leaves and erect cones
fire *n* (*pl* -s) state of combustion producing heat, flames, and smoke ▶ *v* (-res, -ring, -red) operate (a weapon) so that a bullet or missile is released
firearm *n* (*pl* -s) rifle, pistol, or shotgun
firearms *n* ▷ firearm
firebrand *n* (*pl* -s) person who causes unrest
firebrands *n* ▷ firebrand
firebreak *n* strip of cleared land to stop the advance of a fire
firebreaks *n* ▷ firebreak
fired *v* ▷ fire
firedamp *n* (*pl* -s) explosive gas, composed mainly of methane, formed in mines
firedamps *n* ▷ firedamp
firefighter *n* (*pl* -s) member of a fire brigade
firefighters *n* ▷ firefighter
fireflies *n* ▷ firefly
firefly *n* (*pl* -flies) beetle that glows in the dark
fireguard *n* (*pl* -s) protective grating in front of a fire
fireguards *n* ▷ fireguard
fireplace *n* (*pl* -s) recess in a room for a fire

fireplaces *n* ▷ fireplace
fires *n, v* ▷ fire
firewall *n* (*pl* -s) (COMPUTERS) computer that prevents unauthorized access to a computer network from the Internet
firewalls *n* ▷ firewall
firework *n* (*pl* -s) device containing chemicals that is ignited to produce spectacular explosions and coloured sparks ▶ *pl* show of fireworks
fireworks *n* ▷ firework
firing *v* ▷ fire
firm¹ *adj* (-er, -est) not soft or yielding ▶ *adv* in an unyielding manner ▶ *v* (-s, -ing, -ed) make or become firm > **firmly** *adv* > **firmness** *n* (*pl* -es)
firm² *n* (*pl* -s) business company
firmament *n* (*pl* -s) (Lit) sky or the heavens
firmaments *n* ▷ firmament
firmed *v* ▷ firm¹
firmer *adj* ▷ firm¹
firmest *adj* ▷ firm¹
firming *v* ▷ firm¹
firmly *adv* ▷ firm¹
firmness *n* ▷ firm¹
firmnesses *n* ▷ firm¹
firms *v, n* ▷ firm¹, ²
firs *n* ▷ fir
first *adj* earliest in time or order ▶ *n* (*pl* -s) person or thing coming before all others ▶ *adv* before anything else > **firstly** *adv*
firsthand *adj, adv* (obtained) directly from the original source
firstly *adv* ▷ first
firsts *n* ▷ first
firth *n* (*pl* -s) narrow inlet of the sea, esp. in Scotland
firths *n* ▷ firth
fiscal *adj* of government finances, esp. taxes
fish *n* (*pl* fish, fishes) cold-blooded vertebrate with gills, that lives in water ▶ *v* (-es, -ing, -ed) try to catch fish
fished *v* ▷ fish
fisheries *n* ▷ fishery
fisherman *n* (*pl* -men) person who catches fish for a living or for pleasure
fishermen *n* ▷ fisherman
fishery *n* (*pl* -ries) area of the sea used for fishing
fishes *n, v* ▷ fish
fishfinger *n* (*pl* -s) oblong piece of fish covered in breadcrumbs
fishfingers *n* ▷ fishfinger
fishier *adj* ▷ fishy
fishiest *adj* ▷ fishy

fishing v ▷ fish
fishmeal n (pl -s) dried ground fish used as animal feed or fertilizer
  fishmeals n ▷ fishmeal
fishmonger n (pl -s) seller of fish
  fishmongers n ▷ fishmonger
fishnet n (pl -s) open mesh fabric
  fishnets n ▷ fishnet
fishplate n (pl -s) metal plate holding rails together
  fishplates n ▷ fishplate
fishwife n (pl -wives) coarse scolding woman
  fishwives n ▷ fishwife
fishy adj (-shier, -shiest) of or like fish
fissile adj capable of undergoing nuclear fission
fission n (pl -s) splitting > **fissionable** adj
  fissionable adj ▷ fission
  fissions n ▷ fission
fissure [fish-er] n (pl -s) long narrow cleft or crack
  fissures n ▷ fissure
fist n (pl -s) clenched hand
fisticuffs pl n fighting with the fists
  fists n ▷ fist
fit[1] v (-s, -tting, -tted) be appropriate or suitable for ▶ adj appropriate ▶ n (-tter, -ttest) (pl -s) way in which something fits > **fitness** n (pl -es)
fit[2] n (pl -s) sudden attack or convulsion, such as an epileptic seizure
fitful adj occurring in irregular spells > **fitfully** adv
  fitfully adv ▷ fitful
fitment n (pl -s) detachable part of the furnishings of a room
  fitments n ▷ fitment
  fitness n ▷ fit[1]
  fitnesses n ▷ fit[1]
  fits v, n ▷ fit[1, 2]
  fitted v ▷ fit[1]
fitter n (pl -s) person skilled in the installation and adjustment of machinery ▶ adj ▷ fit[1]
  fitters n ▷ fitter
  fittest adj ▷ fit[1]
fitting adj appropriate, suitable ▶ n (pl -s) accessory or part ▶ pl furnishings and accessories in a building ▶ v ▷ fit
  fittings n ▷ fitting
five adj, n (pl -s) one more than four
fiver n (pl -s) (Informal) five-pound note
  fivers n ▷ fiver
fives n ball game resembling squash but played with bats or the hands ▶ n ▷ five
fix v (-xes, -xing, -xed) make or become firm,

stable, or secure ▶ n (pl -es) (Informal) difficult situation > **fixed** adj > **fixedly** adv steadily
fixated adj obsessed
fixation n (pl -s) obsessive interest in something
  fixations n ▷ fixation
fixative n (pl -s) liquid used to preserve or hold things in place
  fixatives n ▷ fixative
  fixed v, adj ▷ fix
  fixedly adv ▷ fix
fixer n (pl -s) solution used to make a photographic image permanent
  fixers n ▷ fixer
  fixes v, n ▷ fix
  fixing v ▷ fix
fixture n (pl -s) permanently fitted piece of household equipment
  fixtures n ▷ fixture
fizz v (-es, -ing, -ed) make a hissing or bubbling noise ▶ n (pl -es) hissing or bubbling noise > **fizzy** adj (-zzier, -zziest)
  fizzed v ▷ fizz
  fizzes v ▷ fizz
  fizzier adj ▷ fizz
  fizziest adj ▷ fizz
  fizzinesses n ▷ fizz
  fizzing v ▷ fizz
fizzle v (-les, -ling, -led) make a weak hissing or bubbling sound
  fizzled v ▷ fizzle
  fizzles v ▷ fizzle
  fizzling v ▷ fizzle
  fizzy adj ▷ fizz
fjord [fee-ord] n (pl -s) long narrow inlet of the sea between cliffs, esp. in Norway
  fjords n ▷ fjord
flab n (pl -s) (Informal) unsightly body fat
flabbergasted adj completely astonished
  flabbier adj ▷ flabby
  flabbiest adj ▷ flabby
flabby adj (-bbier, -bbiest) having flabby flesh
  flabs n ▷ flab
flaccid [flas-sid] adj (-er, -est) soft and limp > **flaccidity** n (pl -ties)
  flaccider adj ▷ flaccid
  flaccidest adj ▷ flaccid
  flaccidities n ▷ flaccid
  flaccidity n ▷ flaccid
flag[1] n (pl -s) piece of cloth attached to a pole as an emblem or signal ▶ v (-s, -gging, -gged) mark with a flag or sticker
flag[2] v (-s, -gging, -gged) lose enthusiasm or vigour
flag[3], **flagstone** (pl -s) n flat paving-stone

flagellant n (pl -s) person who whips himself or herself
  flagellants n ▷ flagellant
flagellate [flaj-a-late] v (-tes, -ting, -ted) whip, esp. in religious penance or for sexual pleasure > **flagellation** n (pl -s)
  flagellated v ▷ flagellate
  flagellates v ▷ flagellate
  flagellating v ▷ flagellate
  flagellation n ▷ flagellate
  flagellations n ▷ flagellate
flageolet [flaj-a-let] n (pl -s) small instrument like a recorder
  flageolets n ▷ flageolet
flagged adj paved with flagstones ▶ v ▷ flag[1, 2]
  flagged v ▷ flag[1, 2]
  flagging v ▷ flag[1, 2]
flagon n (pl -s) wide bottle for wine or cider
  flagons n ▷ flagon
flagpole, flagstaff (pl -s) n pole for a flag
  flagpoles n ▷ flagpole
flagrant [flayg-rant] adj openly outrageous > **flagrantly** adv
  flagrantly adv ▷ flagrant
  flagrantnesses n ▷ flagrant
  flags v, n ▷ flag[1, 2, 3]
flagship n (pl -s) admiral's ship
  flagships n ▷ flagship
  flagstaff n ▷ flagpole
  flagstaffs n ▷ flagpole
  flagstone n ▷ flag[3]
  flagstones n ▷ flag[3]
flail v (-s, -ing, -ed) wave about wildly ▶ n (pl -s) tool formerly used for threshing grain
  flailed v ▷ flail
  flailing v ▷ flail
  flails n, v ▷ flail
flair n (pl -s) natural ability
  flairs n ▷ flair
flak n (pl -s) anti-aircraft fire
flake[1] n (pl -s) small thin piece, esp. chipped off something ▶ v (-kes, -king, -ked) peel off in flakes > **flaky** adj (-kier, -kiest)
flake[2] n (pl -s) (in Australia) the commercial name for the meat of the gummy shark
  flaked v ▷ flake
  flakes v, n ▷ flake[1, 2]
  flakier adj ▷ flaky
  flakiest adj ▷ flaky
  flaking v ▷ flake
  flaks n ▷ flak
  flaky adj ▷ flake[1]
flambé [flahm-bay] v (-bés, -béing, -béed) cook or serve (food) in flaming brandy
  flambéed v ▷ flambé

  flambéing v ▷ flambé
  flambés v ▷ flambé
  flamboyances n ▷ flamboyant
flamboyant adj behaving in a very noticeable, extravagant way > **flamboyance** n (pl -s)
  flamboyance n ▷ flamboyant
flame n (pl -s) luminous burning gas coming from burning material ▶ v (-mes, -ming, -med) burn brightly
  flamed v ▷ flame
flamenco n (pl -cos) rhythmical Spanish dance accompanied by a guitar and vocalist
  flamencos n ▷ flamenco
  flames n, v ▷ flame
  flaming v ▷ flame
flamingo n (pl -gos, -goes) large pink wading bird with a long neck and legs
  flamingoes n ▷ flamingo
  flamingos n ▷ flamingo
  flammabilities n ▷ flammable
  flammability n ▷ flammable
flammable adj easily set on fire > **flammability** n (pl -ties)
flan n (pl -s) open sweet or savoury tart
flange n (pl -s) projecting rim or collar
  flanges n ▷ flange
flank n (pl -s) part of the side between the hips and ribs ▶ v (-s, -ing, -ed) be at or move along the side of
  flanked v ▷ flank
  flanking v ▷ flank
  flanks n, v ▷ flank
flannel n (pl -s) (BRIT) small piece of cloth for washing the face ▶ pl trousers made of flannel ▶ v (-s, -nelling, -nelled) (Informal) talk evasively
flannelette n (pl -s) cotton imitation of flannel
  flannelettes n ▷ flannelette
  flannelled v ▷ flannel
  flannelling v ▷ flannel
  flannels n, v ▷ flannel
  flans n ▷ flan
flap v (-s, -pping, -pped) move back and forwards or up and down ▶ n (pl -s) action or sound of flapping
flapjack n (pl -s) chewy biscuit made with oats
  flapjacks n ▷ flapjack
  flapped v ▷ flap
  flapping v ▷ flap
  flaps v, n ▷ flap
flare v (-res, -ring, -red) blaze with a sudden unsteady flame ▶ n (pl -s) sudden unsteady flame ▶ pl flared trousers
flared adj (of a skirt or trousers) becoming wider towards the hem ▶ v ▷ flare

flares v, n ▷ flare

flaring v ▷ flare

flash n (pl -es) sudden burst of light or flame ▶ v (-es, -ing, -ed) (cause to) burst into flame

flashback n (pl -s) scene in a book, play, or film, that shows earlier events

flashbacks n ▷ flashback

flashed v ▷ flash

flasher n (pl -s) (Slang) man who exposes himself indecently

flashers n ▷ flasher

flashes n, v ▷ flash

flashier adj ▷ flashy

flashiest adj ▷ flashy

flashing n (pl -s) watertight material used to cover joins in a roof ▶ v ▷ flash

flashings n ▷ flashing

flashlight n (pl -s) (US) torch

flashlights n ▷ flashlight

flashy adj (-shier, -shiest) vulgarly showy

flask n (pl -s) ▷ **vacuum flask** flat bottle for carrying alcoholic drink in the pocket

flasks n ▷ flask

flat¹ adj (-ter, -ttest) level and horizontal ▶ adv in or into a flat position ▶ n (pl -s) (MUSIC) symbol lowering the pitch of a note by a semitone > **flatly** adv > **flatness** n (pl -es) > **flatten** v (-s, -ing, -ed)

flat² n (pl -s) set of rooms for living in which are part of a larger building ▶ v (-s, -tting, -tted) (AUST & NZ) live in a flat

flatfish n (pl -fish, -fishes) sea fish, such as the sole, which has a flat body

flatfishes n ▷ flatfish

flatlet n (pl -s) (BRIT, AUST & S AFR) small flat

flatlets n ▷ flatlet

flatly adv ▷ flat¹

flatmate n (pl -s) person with whom one shares a flat

flatmates n ▷ flatmate

flatness n ▷ flat¹

flatnesses n ▷ flat¹

flat-pack adj (of furniture, etc.) supplied in pieces in a flat box for assembly by the buyer

flats n, v ▷ flat¹, ²

flatted v ▷ flat²

flatten v ▷ flat¹

flattened v ▷ flat¹

flattening v ▷ flat¹

flatter¹ v (-s, -ing, -ed) praise insincerely > **flatterer** n (pl -s) > **flattery** n (pl -ries)

flatter² adj ▷ flat¹

flattered v ▷ flatter¹

flatterer n ▷ flatter

flatterers n ▷ flatter

flatteries n ▷ flatter

flattering v ▷ flatter¹

flatters v ▷ flatter¹

flattery n ▷ flatter

flattest adj ▷ flat¹

flattie n (pl -s) (NZ & S AFR) (Informal) flat tyre

flatties n ▷ flattie

flatting v ▷ flat²

flatulence n ▷ flatulent

flatulences n ▷ flatulent

flatulent adj suffering from or caused by too much gas in the intestines > **flatulence** n (pl -s)

flaunt v (-s, -ing, -ed) display (oneself or one's possessions) arrogantly

flaunted v ▷ flaunt

flaunting v ▷ flaunt

flaunts v ▷ flaunt

flautist n (pl -s) flute player

flautists n ▷ flautist

flavour n (pl -s) distinctive taste ▶ v (-s, -ing, -ed) give flavour to > **flavourless** adj

flavoured v ▷ flavour

flavouring n (pl -s) substance used to flavour food ▶ v ▷ flavour

flavourings n ▷ flavouring

flavourless adj ▷ flavour

flavours n, v ▷ flavour

flaw n (pl -s) imperfection or blemish > **flawed** adj > **flawless** adj

flawed adj ▷ flaw

flawless adj ▷ flaw

flaws n ▷ flaw

flax n (pl -es) plant grown for its stem fibres and seeds

flaxen adj (of hair) pale yellow

flaxes n ▷ flax

flay v (-s, -ing, -ed) strip the skin off

flayed v ▷ flay

flaying v ▷ flay

flays v ▷ flay

flea n (pl -s) small wingless jumping bloodsucking insect

fleapit n (pl -s) (Informal) shabby cinema or theatre

fleapits n ▷ fleapit

fleas n ▷ flea

fleck n (pl -s) small mark, streak, or speck ▶ v (-s, -ing, -ed) speckle

flecked n ▷ fleck

flecking v ▷ fleck

flecks n, v ▷ fleck

fled v ▷ flee

fledged adj (of young birds) able to fly

fledgelings n ▷ fledgling

fledgling, fledgeling (*pl* -s) *n* young bird ▶ *adj* new or inexperienced
  fledglings *n* ▷ fledgling

flee *v* (-lees, -leeing, fled) run away (from)

fleece *n* (*pl* -s) sheep's coat of wool ▶ *v* (-ces, -cing, -ced) defraud or overcharge
  fleeced *v* ▷ fleece
  fleeces *n*, *v* ▷ fleece
  fleecier *adj* ▷ fleecy
  fleeciest *adj* ▷ fleecy
  fleecing *v* ▷ fleece

fleecy *adj* (-cier, -ciest) made of or like fleece
  fleeing *v* ▷ flee
  flees *v* ▷ flee

fleet[1] *n* (*pl* -s) number of warships organized as a unit

fleet[2] *adj* swift in movement

fleeting *adj* rapid and soon passing
  > **fleetingly** *adv*
  fleetingly *adv* ▷ fleeting
  fleets *n* ▷ fleet

flesh *n* (*pl* -es) soft part of a human or animal body (*Informal*)
  fleshes *n* ▷ flesh
  fleshier *adj* ▷ fleshy
  fleshiest *adj* ▷ fleshy

fleshly *adj* carnal

fleshy *adj* (-shier, -shiest) plump

flew *v* ▷ fly[1]

flex *n* (*pl* -xes) flexible insulated electric cable ▶ *v* (-xes, -xing, -xed) bend
  flexed *v* ▷ flex
  flexes *n*, *v* ▷ flex
  flexibility *n* ▷ flexible

flexible *adj* easily bent > **flexibly** *adv*
  > **flexibility** *n* (*pl* -ties)
  flexibilities *n* ▷ flexible
  flexibly *adv* ▷ flexible
  flexing *v* ▷ flex

fleximtime, flextime *n* (*pl* -s) system permitting variation in starting and finishing times of work
  flexitimes *n* ▷ flexitime
  flextimes *n* ▷ flexitime

flick *v* (-s, -ing, -ed) touch or move with the finger or hand in a quick movement ▶ *n* (*pl* -s) tap or quick stroke ▶ *pl* (*Slang*) the cinema
  flicked *v* ▷ flick

flicker *v* (-s, -ing, -ed) shine unsteadily or intermittently ▶ *n* (*pl* -s) unsteady brief light
  flickered *v* ▷ flicker
  flickering *v* ▷ flicker
  flickers *v*, *n* ▷ flicker
  flicking *v* ▷ flick
  flicks *v*, *n* ▷ flick

flier[1] *adj* ▷ fly[3]

flier[2] *n* ▷ flyer

fliers *n* ▷ flyer

flies *v*, *n* ▷ fly[1, 2]

fliest *adj* ▷ fly[3]

flight[1] *n* (*pl* -s) journey by air

flight[2] *n* (*pl* -s) act of running away
  flightier *adj* ▷ flighty
  flightiest *adj* ▷ flighty

flightless *adj* (of certain birds or insects) unable to fly
  flights *n* ▷ flight[1, 2]

flighty *adj* (-tier, -tiest) frivolous and fickle
  flimsier *adj* ▷ flimsy
  flimsiest *adj* ▷ flimsy
  flimsily *adv* ▷ flimsy
  flimsiness *n* ▷ flimsy
  flimsinesses *n* ▷ flimsy

flimsy *adj* (-sier, -siest) not strong or substantial > **flimsily** *adv* > **flimsiness** *n* (*pl* -es)

flinch *v* (-es, -ing, -ed) draw back or wince, as from pain
  flinched *v* ▷ flinch
  flinches *v* ▷ flinch
  flinching *v* ▷ flinch

fling *v* (-s, -ing, flung) throw, send, or move forcefully or hurriedly ▶ *n* (*pl* -s) spell of self-indulgent enjoyment
  flinging *v* ▷ fling
  flings *v*, *n* ▷ fling

flint *n* (*pl* -s) hard grey stone
  flintier *adj* ▷ flinty
  flintiest *adj* ▷ flinty
  flints *n* ▷ flint

flinty (-tier, -tiest) *adj* cruel

flip *v* (-s, -pping, -pped) throw (something small or light) carelessly ▶ *adj* (*Informal*) flippant
  flippancies *n* ▷ flippant
  flippancy *n* ▷ flippant

flippant *adj* treating serious things lightly
  > **flippancy** *n* (*pl* -cies)
  flipped *v* ▷ flip

flipper (*pl* -s) *n* limb of a sea animal adapted for swimming
  flippers *n* ▷ flipper
  flipping *v* ▷ flip
  flips *v* ▷ flip

flirt *v* (-s, -ing, -ed) behave as if sexually attracted to someone ▶ *n* (*pl* -s) person who flirts > **flirtation** *n* (*pl* -s) > **flirtatious** *adj*
  flirtation *n* ▷ flirt
  flirtations *n* ▷ flirt
  flirtatious *adj* ▷ flirt

flirted v ▷ flirt
flirting v ▷ flirt
flirts v, n ▷ flirt
flit v (-s, -tting, -tted) move lightly and rapidly ▶ n (pl -s) act of flitting
flits v, n ▷ flit
flitted v ▷ flit
flitting v ▷ flit
float v (-s, -ing, -ed) rest on the surface of a liquid ▶ n (pl -s) light object used to help someone or something float
floated v ▷ float
floating adj moving about, changing ▶ v ▷ float
floats v, n ▷ float
flock¹ n (pl -s) number of animals of one kind together ▶ v (-s, -ing, -ed) gather in a crowd
flock² n (pl -s) wool or cotton waste used as stuffing ▶ adj (of wallpaper) with a velvety raised pattern
flocked v ▷ flock¹
flocking v ▷ flock¹·²
flocks n, v ▷ flock¹·²
floe n (pl -s) sheet of floating ice
floes n ▷ floe
flog v (-s, -gging, -gged) beat with a whip or stick ▷ **flogging** n (pl -s)
flogged v ▷ flog
flogging v, n ▷ flog
floggings n ▷ flog
flogs v ▷ flog
flood n (pl -s) overflow of water onto a normally dry area ▶ v (-s, -ing, -ed) cover or become covered with water
flooded v ▷ flood
floodgate n (pl -s) gate used to control the flow of water
floodgates n ▷ floodgate
flooding v ▷ flood
floodlight n (pl -s) lamp that casts a broad intense beam of light ▶ v (-lights, -lighting, -lit) illuminate by floodlight
floodlighting v ▷ floodlight
floodlights n, v ▷ floodlight
floodlit v ▷ floodlight
floods n, v ▷ flood
floor n (pl -s) lower surface of a room ▶ v (-s, -ing, -ed) knock down
floored adj covered with a floor ▶ v ▷ floor
flooring n (pl -s) material for floors ▶ v ▷ floor
floorings n ▷ flooring
floors n, v ▷ floor
floozies n ▷ floozy
floozy n (pl -zies) (Old-fashioned slang) disreputable woman

flop v (-s, -pping, -pped) bend, fall, or collapse loosely or carelessly ▶ n (pl -s) failure
flopped v ▷ flop
floppier adj ▷ floppy
floppies n ▷ floppy
floppiest adj ▷ floppy
flopping v ▷ flop
floppy adj (-ppier, -ppiest) hanging downwards, loose ▶ n (pl -ppies) (COMPUTERS) a flexible magnetic disk that stores information
flops v, n ▷ flop
flora n (pl -s) plants of a given place or time
floral adj consisting of or decorated with flowers
floras n ▷ flora
floret n (pl -s) small flower forming part of a composite flower head
florets n ▷ floret
floribunda n (pl -s) type of rose whose flowers grow in large clusters
floribundas n ▷ floribunda
florid adj (-er, -est) with a red or flushed complexion
florider adj ▷ florid
floridest adj ▷ florid
florin n (pl -s) former British and Australian coin
florins n ▷ florin
florist n (pl -s) seller of flowers
florists n ▷ florist
floss n (pl -es) fine silky fibres
flosses n ▷ floss
flotation n (pl -s) launching or financing of a business enterprise
flotations n ▷ flotation
flotilla n (pl -s) small fleet or fleet of small ships
flotillas n ▷ flotilla
flotsam n (pl -s) floating wreckage
flotsams n ▷ flotsam
flounce¹ v (-ces, -cing, -ced) go with emphatic movements ▶ n (pl -s) flouncing movement
flounce² n (pl -s) ornamental frill on a garment
flounced v ▷ flounce
flounces v, n ▷ flounce¹·²
flouncing v ▷ flounce
flounder¹ v (-s, -ing, -ed) move with difficulty, as in mud
flounder² n (pl -s) edible flatfish
floundered v ▷ flounder
floundering v ▷ flounder
flounders v, n ▷ flounder¹·²
flour n (pl -s) powder made by grinding grain, esp. wheat ▶ v (-s, -ing, -ed) sprinkle with flour ▷ **floury** adj (-rier, -riest)

floured v ▷ flour
flourier adj ▷ flour
flouriest adj ▷ flour
flouring v ▷ flour
flourish v (-es, -ing, -ed) be active, successful, or widespread ▶ n (pl -es) dramatic waving motion > **flourishing** adj
flourished v ▷ flourish
flourishes v, n ▷ flourish
flourishing n, adj ▷ flourish
flours n, v ▷ flour
floury adj ▷ flour
flout v (-s, -ing, -ed) deliberately disobey (a rule, law, etc.)
flouted v ▷ flout
flouting v ▷ flout
flouts v ▷ flout
flow v (-s, -ing, -ed) (of liquid) move in a stream ▶ n (pl -s) act, rate, or manner of flowing
flowed v ▷ flow
flower n (pl -s) part of a plant that produces seeds ▶ v (-s, -ing, -ed) produce flowers, bloom
flowerbed n (pl -s) piece of ground for growing flowers
flowerbeds n ▷ flowerbed
flowered adj decorated with a floral design ▶ v ▷ flower
flowerier adj ▷ flowery
floweriest adj ▷ flowery
flowering v ▷ flower
flowers n, v ▷ flower
flowery adj (-rier, -riest) decorated with a floral design
flowing v ▷ flow
flown v ▷ fly¹
flows v, n ▷ flow
flu n (pl flus) ▷ influenza
fluctuate v (-tes, -ting, -ted) change frequently and erratically > **fluctuation** n (pl -s)
fluctuated v ▷ fluctuate
fluctuates v ▷ fluctuate
fluctuating v ▷ fluctuate
fluctuation n ▷ fluctuate
fluctuations n ▷ fluctuate
flue n (pl -s) passage or pipe for smoke or hot air
fluencies n ▷ fluent
fluency n ▷ fluent
fluent adj able to speak or write with ease > **fluently** adv > **fluency** n (pl -cies)
fluently adv ▷ fluent
flues n ▷ flue
fluff n (pl -s) soft fibres ▶ v (-s, -ing, -ed) make

or become soft and puffy > **fluffy** adj (-ffier, -ffiest)
fluffed v ▷ fluff
fluffier adj ▷ fluff
fluffiest adj ▷ fluff
fluffing v ▷ fluff
fluffs n, v ▷ fluff
fluffy adj ▷ fluff
fluid n (pl -s) substance able to flow and change its shape; a liquid or a gas ▶ adj able to flow or change shape easily > **fluidity** n (pl -ies)
fluidities n ▷ fluid
fluidity n ▷ fluid
fluids n ▷ fluid
fluke¹ n (pl -s) accidental stroke of luck
fluke² (pl -s) n flat triangular point of an anchor
fluke³ (pl -s) n parasitic worm
flukes n ▷ fluke¹,²,³
flume n (pl -s) narrow sloping channel for water
flumes n ▷ flume
flummox v (-xes, -xing, -xed) puzzle or confuse
flummoxed v ▷ flummox
flummoxes v ▷ flummox
flummoxing v ▷ flummox
flung v ▷ fling
flunk v (flunks, flunking, flunked) (US, AUST, NZ & S AFR) (Informal) fail
flunked v ▷ flunk
flunkey n ▷ flunky
flunkeys n ▷ flunky
flunkies n ▷ flunky
flunking v ▷ flunk
flunks v ▷ flunk
flunky, flunkey n (pl -kies, -keys) servile person
fluoresce v (-ces, -cing, -ced) exhibit fluorescence
fluoresced v ▷ fluoresce
fluorescence n (pl -s) emission of light from a substance bombarded by particles, such as electrons, or by radiation
fluorescences n ▷ fluorescence
fluorescent adj of or resembling fluorescence
fluoresces v ▷ fluoresce
fluorescing v ▷ fluoresce
fluoridate v (-tes, -ting, -ted) add fluoride to (water) as protection against tooth decay > **fluoridation** n (pl -s)
fluoridated v ▷ fluoridate
fluoridates v ▷ fluoridate
fluoridating v ▷ fluoridate
fluoridation n ▷ fluoridate
fluoridations n ▷ fluoridate

fluoride n (pl -s) compound containing fluorine
fluorides n ▷ fluoride
fluorine n (pl -s) (CHEM) toxic yellow gas, most reactive of all the elements
fluorines n ▷ fluorine
flurried v ▷ flurry
flurries n, v ▷ flurry
flurry n (pl -rries) sudden commotion ▶ v (-rries, -rrying, -rried) confuse
flus n ▷ flu
flush v (-es, -ing, -ed) blush or cause to blush ▶ n (pl -es) blush
flush² adj level with the surrounding surface
flush³ v (-es, -ing, -ed) drive out of a hiding place
flush⁴ n (pl -es) (in card games) hand all of one suit
flushed v ▷ flush¹,³
flushes v, n ▷ flush¹,³,⁴
flushing v ▷ flush¹,³
fluster v (-s, -ing, -ed) make nervous or upset ▶ n (pl -s) nervous or upset state
flustered v ▷ fluster
flustering v ▷ fluster
flusters v, n ▷ fluster
flute n (pl -s) wind instrument consisting of a tube with sound holes and a mouth hole in the side
fluted adj having decorative grooves
flutes n ▷ flute
flutter v (-s, -ing, -ed) wave rapidly ▶ n (pl -s) flapping movement
fluttered v ▷ flutter
fluttering v ▷ flutter
flutters v, n ▷ flutter
fluvial adj of rivers
flux n (pl -es) constant change or instability
fluxes n ▷ flux
fly¹ v (flying, flew, flown) move through the air on wings or in an aircraft ▶ n (pl flies) (often pl (BRIT)) fastening at the front of trousers ▶ pl space above a stage, used for storage
fly² n (pl flies) two-winged insect
fly³ adj (flier, fliest) (Slang) sharp and cunning
flycatcher n (pl -s) small insect-eating songbird
flycatchers n ▷ flycatcher
flyer, flier (pl -s) n small advertising leaflet
flyers n ▷ flyer
flying adj hurried and brief ▶ v ▷ fly
flyleaf n (pl -leaves) blank leaf at the beginning or end of a book
flyleaves n ▷ flyleaf
flyover n (pl -s) road passing over another by a bridge
flyovers n ▷ flyover
flypaper n (pl -s) paper with a sticky poisonous coating, used to kill flies
flypapers n ▷ flypaper
flyweight n (pl -s) boxer weighing up to 112lb (professional) or 51kg (amateur)
flyweights n ▷ flyweight
flywheel n (pl -s) heavy wheel regulating the speed of a machine
flywheels n ▷ flywheel
foal n (pl -s) young of a horse or related animal ▶ v (-s, -ing, -ed) give birth to a foal
foaled v ▷ foal
foaling v ▷ foal
foals n, v ▷ foal
foam n (pl -s) mass of small bubbles on a liquid ▶ v (-s, -ing, -ed) produce foam > **foamy** adj (-ier, -iest)
foamed v ▷ foam
foamier adj ▷ foam
foamiest adj ▷ foam
foaming v ▷ foam
foams n, v ▷ foam
foamy adj ▷ foam
fob n (pl -s) short watch chain
fobs n ▷ fob
focal adj of or at a focus
foci n ▷ focus
fo'c's'le n (pl fo'c's'les) ▷ forecastle
fo'c's'les n ▷ fo'c's'le
focus n (pl -cuses, -ci) [-sye] point at which light or sound waves converge ▶ v (-cuses, -cusing, -cused or -cusses, -cussing, -cussed) bring or come into focus
focused v ▷ focus
focuses n, v ▷ focus
focusing v ▷ focus
focussed v ▷ focus
focussing v ▷ focus
fodder n (pl -s) feed for livestock
fodders n ▷ fodder
foe n (pl foes) enemy, opponent
foes n ▷ foe
foetid adj (-er, -est) ▷ fetid
foetider adj ▷ foetid
foetidest adj ▷ foetid
foetus n (pl -tuses) ▷ fetus
foetuses n ▷ foetus
fog n (pl -s) mass of condensed water vapour in the lower air, often greatly reducing visibility ▶ v (-s, fogging, fogged) cover with steam > **foggy** adj (-ggier, -ggiest)
fogey, fogy n (pl -geys, -gies) old-fashioned person

fogeys *n* ▷ fogey
fogged *v* ▷ fog
foggier *adj* ▷ fog
foggiest *adj* ▷ fog
fogging *v* ▷ fog
foggy *adj* ▷ fog
foghorn *n* (*pl* -s) large horn sounded to warn ships in fog
foghorns *n* ▷ foghorn
fogies *n* ▷ fogey
fogs *n* ▷ fog
fogy *n* ▷ fogey
foible *n* (*pl* -s) minor weakness or slight peculiarity
foibles *n* ▷ foible
foil¹ *v* (-s, -ing, -ed) ruin (someone's plan)
foil² *n* (*pl* -s) metal in a thin sheet, esp. for wrapping food
foil³ *n* (*pl* -s) light slender flexible sword tipped with a button
foiled *v* ▷ foil
foiling *v* ▷ foil
foils *v, n* ▷ foil¹, ², ³
foist *v* (-s, -ing, -ed) (*foll. by* **on** *or* **upon**) force or impose on
foisted *v* ▷ foist
foisting *v* ▷ foist
foists *v* ▷ foist
fold¹ *v* (-s, -ing, -ed) bend so that one part covers another ▶ *n* (*pl* -s) folded piece or part
fold² *n* (*pl* -s) (BRIT, AUST & S AFR) enclosure for sheep
folded *v* ▷ fold
folder *n* (*pl* -s) piece of folded cardboard for holding loose papers
folders *n* ▷ folder
folding *v* ▷ fold
folds *v, n* ▷ fold¹, ²
foliage *n* (*pl* -s) leaves
foliages *n* ▷ foliage
foliation *n* (*pl* -s) process of producing leaves
foliations *n* ▷ foliation
folio *n* (*pl* -lios) sheet of paper folded in half to make two leaves of a book
folios *n* ▷ folio
folk *n* (*pl* -s) people in general ▶ *pl* relatives
folklore *n* (*pl* -s) traditional beliefs and stories of a people
folklores *n* ▷ folklore
folks *n* ▷ folk
folksier *adj* ▷ folksy
folksiest *adj* ▷ folksy
folksy *adj* (-sier, -siest) simple and unpretentious
follicle *n* (*pl* -s) small cavity in the body, esp.
one from which a hair grows
follicles *n* ▷ follicle
follies *n* ▷ folly
follow *v* (-s, -ing, -ed) go or come after
followed *v* ▷ follow
follower *n* (*pl* -s) disciple or supporter
followers *n* ▷ follower
following *adj* about to be mentioned ▶ *n* (*pl* -s) group of supporters ▶ *prep* as a result of ▶ *v* ▷ follow
followings *n* ▷ following
follows *v* ▷ follow
folly *n* (*pl* -llies) foolishness
foment [foam-ent] *v* (-s, -ing, -ed) encourage or stir up (trouble)
fomented *v* ▷ foment
fomenting *v* ▷ foment
foments *v* ▷ foment
fond *adj* (-er, -est) tender, loving > **fondly** *adv* > **fondness** *n* (*pl* -es)
fondant *n* (*pl* -s) (sweet made from) flavoured paste of sugar and water
fondants *n* ▷ fondant
fonder *adj* ▷ fond
fondest *adj* ▷ fond
fondle *v* (-les, -ling, -led) caress
fondled *v* ▷ fondle
fondles *v* ▷ fondle
fondling *v* ▷ fondle
fondly *adv* ▷ fond
fondness *n* ▷ fond
fondnesses *n* ▷ fond
fondue *n* (*pl* -dues) Swiss dish of a hot melted cheese sauce into which pieces of bread are dipped
fondues *n* ▷ fondue
font¹ *n* (*pl* -s) bowl in a church for baptismal water
font² (*pl* -s) *n* set of printing type of one style and size
fontanelle *n* (*pl* -s) soft membranous gap between the bones of a baby's skull
fontanelles *n* ▷ fontanelle
fonts *n* ▷ font¹, ²
food *n* (*pl* -dies) what one eats, solid nourishment
foodie *n* (*pl* -s) (*Informal*) gourmet
foodies *n* ▷ foodie
foods *n* ▷ food
foodstuff *n* (*pl* -s) substance used as food
foodstuffs *n* ▷ foodstuff
fool¹ *n* (*pl* -s) person lacking sense or judgment (HIST) ▶ *v* (-s, -ing, -ed) deceive (someone)
fool² (*pl* -s) *n* dessert of puréed fruit mixed with cream

fooled v ▷ fool

fooleries n ▷ foolery

foolery n (pl -ries) foolish behaviour

foolhardiness n ▷ foolhardy

foolhardinesses n ▷ foolhardy

foolhardy adj recklessly adventurous
>foolhardiness n (pl -es)

fooling v ▷ fool

foolish adj (-er, -est) unwise, silly, or absurd
>foolishly adv >foolishness n (pl -es)

foolisher adj ▷ foolish

foolishest adj ▷ foolish

foolishly adv ▷ foolish

foolishness n ▷ foolish

foolishnesses n ▷ foolish

foolproof adj unable to fail

fools n, v ▷ fool¹, ²

foolscap n (pl -s) size of paper, 34.3 × 43.2
centimetres

foolscaps n ▷ foolscap

foot n (pl feet) part of the leg below the ankle

footage n (pl -s) amount of film used

footages n ▷ footage

football n (pl -s) game played by two teams of
eleven players kicking a ball in an attempt to
score goals >footballer n (pl -s)

footballer n ▷ football

footballers n ▷ footballs

footballs n ▷ football

footbridge n (pl -s) bridge for pedestrians

footbridges n ▷ footbridge

footfall n (pl -s) sound of a footstep

footfalls n ▷ footfall

foothills pl n hills at the foot of a mountain

foothold n (pl -s) secure position from which
progress may be made

footholds n ▷ foothold

footing n (pl -s) basis or foundation

footings n ▷ footing

footlight n light at the front of a stage

footlights pl n ▷ footlight

footling adj (CHIEFLY BRIT) (Informal) trivial

footloose adj free from ties

footman n (pl -men) male servant in uniform

footmen n ▷ footman

footnote n note printed at the foot of a page

footnotes n ▷ footnote

footpath n (pl -s) narrow path for walkers only

footpaths n ▷ footpath

footplate n (pl -s) platform in the cab of a
locomotive for the driver

footplates n ▷ footplate

footprint n (pl -s) mark left by a foot

footprints n ▷ footprint

footsie n (pl -s) (Informal) flirtation involving
the touching together of feet

footsies n ▷ footsie

footstep n step in walking

footsteps n ▷ footstep

footstool n (pl -s) low stool used to rest the
feet on while sitting

footstools n ▷ footstool

footwear n (pl -s) anything worn to cover
the feet

footwears n ▷ footwear

footwork n (pl -s) skilful use of the feet, as in
sport or dancing

footworks n ▷ footwork

fop n (pl -s) man excessively concerned
with fashion >foppery n (pl -ies) >foppish
adj

fopperies n ▷ fop

foppery n ▷ fop

foppish n ▷ fop

fops n ▷ fop

for prep indicating a person intended to
benefit from or receive something, span of
time or distance, person or thing represented
by someone, etc. ▷ conj because

forage v (-ges, -ging, -ged) search about (for)
▶ n (pl -s) food for cattle or horses

foraged v ▷ forage

forages v, n ▷ forage

foraging v ▷ forage

foray n (pl -s) brief raid or attack

forays n ▷ foray

forbade v ▷ forbid

forbear v (-s, -ing, forbore, forborne) cease or
refrain (from doing something)

forbearance n (pl -s) tolerance, patience

forbearances n ▷ forbearance

forbearing v ▷ forbear

forbears v ▷ forbear

forbid v (-s, -dding, forbade, forbidden)
prohibit, refuse to allow >forbidden adj

forbidden v, adj ▷ forbid

forbidding adj severe, threatening ▶ v ▷ forbid

forbids v ▷ forbid

forbore v ▷ forbear

forborne v ▷ forbear

force n (pl -s) strength or power ▶ v (-ces, -cing,
-ced) compel, make (someone) do something

forced adj compulsory ▶ v ▷ force

forceful adj emphatic and confident
>forcefully adv

forceps pl n surgical pincers

forces n, v ▷ force

forcible adj involving physical force or violence
>forcibly adv

forcibly adv ▷ forcible

forcing v ▷ force
ford n (pl -s) shallow place where a river may be crossed ▶ v (-s, -ing, -ed) cross (a river) at a ford
  forded v ▷ ford
  fording v ▷ ford
  fords n, v ▷ ford
fore adj in, at, or towards the front ▶ n (pl -s) front part
forearm[1] n (pl -s) arm from the wrist to the elbow
forearm[2] v (-s, -ing, -ed) prepare beforehand
  forearmed v ▷ forearm[2]
  forearming v ▷ forearm[2]
  forearms n, v ▷ forearm[1, 2]
forebear n (pl -s) ancestor
  forebears n ▷ forebear
foreboding n (pl -s) feeling that something bad is about to happen
  forebodings n ▷ foreboding
forecast v (-casts, -casting, -cast or -casted) predict (weather, events, etc.) ▶ n (pl -s) prediction
  forecasted v ▷ forecast
  forecasting v ▷ forecast
forecastle [foke-sl] n (pl -s) raised front part of a ship
  forecastles n ▷ forecastle
  forecasts v, n ▷ forecast
foreclose v (-ses, -sing, -sed) take possession of (property bought with borrowed money which has not been repaid) > **foreclosure** n (pl -s)
  foreclosed v ▷ foreclose
  forecloses v ▷ foreclose
  foreclosing v ▷ foreclose
  foreclosure n ▷ foreclose
  foreclosures n ▷ foreclose
forecourt n (pl -s) courtyard or open space in front of a building
  forecourts n ▷ forecourt
forefather n (pl -s) ancestor
  forefathers n ▷ forefather
forefinger n (pl -s) finger next to the thumb
  forefingers n ▷ forefinger
forefront n (pl -s) most active or prominent position
  forefronts n ▷ forefront
foregather v (-s, -ing, -ed) meet together or assemble
  foregathered v ▷ foregather
  foregathering v ▷ foregather
  foregathers v ▷ foregather
forego v (-goes, -going, -went, -gone) ▷ forgo
  foregoes v ▷ forgo

foregoing adj going before, preceding ▶ v ▷ forego
  foregone v ▷ forego
foreground n (pl -s) part of a view, esp. in a picture, nearest the observer
  foregrounds n ▷ foreground
forehand n (pl -s) (TENNIS ETC.) stroke played with the palm of the hand facing forward
  forehands n ▷ forehand
forehead n (pl -s) part of the face above the eyebrows
  foreheads n ▷ forehead
foreign adj not of, or in, one's own country > **foreigner** n (pl -s)
  foreigner n ▷ foreign
  foreigners n ▷ foreign
foreleg n (pl -s) either of the front legs of an animal
  forelegs n ▷ foreleg
forelock n (pl -s) lock of hair over the forehead
  forelocks n ▷ forelock
foreman n (pl -men) person in charge of a group of workers
foremast n (pl -s) mast nearest the bow of a ship
  foremasts n ▷ foremast
  foremen n ▷ foreman
foremost adj, adv first in time, place, or importance
forename n (pl -s) first name
  forenames n ▷ forename
forenoon n (pl -s) (CHIEFLY US & CANADIAN) morning
  forenoons n ▷ forenoon
forensic adj used in or connected with courts of law
foreplay n (pl -s) sexual stimulation before intercourse
  foreplays n ▷ foreplay
forerunner n (pl -s) person or thing that goes before, precursor
  forerunners n ▷ forerunner
  fores n ▷ fore
foresail n (pl -s) main sail on the foremast of a ship
  foresails n ▷ foresail
  foresaw v ▷ foresee
foresee v (-sees, -seeing, -saw, -seen) see or know beforehand > **foreseeable** adj
  foreseeable adj ▷ foresee
  foreseeing v ▷ foresee
  foreseen v ▷ foresee
  foresees v ▷ foresee
foreshadow v (-s, -ing, -ed) show or indicate beforehand

foreshadowed v ▷ foreshadow
foreshadowing v ▷ foreshadow
foreshadows v ▷ foreshadow
foreshore n (pl -s) part of the shore between high- and low-tide marks
foreshores n ▷ foreshore
foreshorten v (-s, -ing, -ed) represent (an object) in a picture as shorter than it really is, in accordance with perspective
foreshortened v ▷ foreshorten
foreshortening v ▷ foreshorten
foreshortens v ▷ foreshorten
foresight n (pl -s) ability to anticipate and provide for future needs
foresights n ▷ foresight
foreskin n (pl -s) fold of skin covering the tip of the penis
foreskins n ▷ foreskin
forest n (pl -s) large area with a thick growth of trees > **forested** adj
forestall v (-s, -ing, -ed) prevent or guard against in advance
forestalled v ▷ forestall
forestalling v ▷ forestall
forestalls v ▷ forestall
forested adj ▷ forest
forester n (pl -s) person skilled in forestry
foresters n ▷ foresters
forestries n ▷ forestry
forestry n (pl -ries) science of planting and caring for trees
forests n ▷ forest
foretaste n (pl -s) early limited experience of something to come
foretastes n ▷ foretaste
foretell v (-s, f -ing, -told) tell or indicate beforehand
foretelling v ▷ foretell
foretells v ▷ foretell
forethought n (pl -s) thoughtful planning for future events
forethoughts n ▷ forethought
foretold v ▷ foretell
forever adv without end
forewarn v (-s, -ing, -ed) warn beforehand
forewarned v ▷ forewarn
forewarning v ▷ forewarn
forewarns v ▷ forewarn
forewent v ▷ forego
foreword n (pl -s) introduction to a book
forewords n ▷ foreword
forfeit [for-fit] n (pl -s) thing lost or given up as a penalty for a fault or mistake ▶ v (-s, -ing, -ed) lose as a forfeit ▶ adj lost as a forfeit > **forfeiture** n (pl -s)

forfeited v ▷ forfeit
forfeiting v ▷ forfeit
forfeits n, v ▷ forfeit
forfeiture n ▷ forfeit
forfeitures n ▷ forfeit
forgave v ▷ forgive
forge¹ n (pl -s) place where metal is worked, smithy ▶ v (-ges, -ging, -ged) make a fraudulent imitation of (something)
forge² v (-ges, -ging, -ged) advance steadily
forged v ▷ forge¹'²
forger n (pl -s) person who makes an illegal copy of something
forgeries n ▷ forgery
forgers n ▷ forger
forgery n (pl -ries) illegal copy of something
forges v, n ▷ forge¹'²
forget v (-s, -getting, -got, -gotten) fail to remember
forgetful adj tending to forget > **forgetfulness** n (pl -es)
forgetfulness n ▷ forgetful
forgetfulnesses n ▷ forgetful
forgets v ▷ forget
forgetting v ▷ forget
forging v ▷ forge¹'²
forgive v (-giving, -gave, -given) cease to blame or hold resentment against, pardon > **forgiveness** n (pl -es)
forgiven v ▷ forgive
forgiveness n ▷ forgive
forgivenesses n ▷ forgive
forgiving v ▷ forgive
forgo v (-goes, -going, -went, -gone) do without or give up
forgoes v ▷ forgo
forgoing v ▷ forgo
forgone v ▷ forgo
forgot v ▷ forget
forgotten v ▷ forget
fork n (pl -s) tool for eating food, with prongs and a handle ▶ v (-s, -ing, -ed) pick up, dig, etc. with a fork > **forked** adj
forked v, adj ▷ fork
forking v ▷ fork
forks n, v ▷ fork
forlorn adj lonely and unhappy > **forlornly** adv
forlornly adv ▷ forlorn
form n (pl -s) shape or appearance ▶ v (-s, -ing, -ed) give a (particular) shape to or take a (particular) shape > **formless** adj
formal adj of or characterized by established conventions of ceremony and behaviour > **formally** adv
formaldehyde [for-mal-de-hide] n (pl -s)

colourless pungent gas
formaldehydes *n* ▷ formaldehyde
formalin *n* (*pl* -s) solution of formaldehyde in water, used as a disinfectant or a preservative for biological specimens
formalins *n* ▷ formalin
formalities *n* ▷ formality
formality *n* (*pl* -ties) requirement of custom or etiquette
formalize *v* (-zes, -zing, -zed) make official or formal
formalized *v* ▷ formalize
formalizes *v* ▷ formalize
formalizing *v* ▷ formalize
formally *adv* ▷ formal
format *n* (*pl* -s) style in which something is arranged ▶ *v* (-s, -matting, -matted) arrange in a format
formation *n* (*pl* -s) forming
formations *n* ▷ formation
formative *adj* of or relating to development
formativenesses *n* ▷ formative
formats *n*, *v* ▷ format
formatting *v* ▷ format
formed *v* ▷ form
former *adj* of an earlier time, previous ▷ **formerly** *adv*
formerly *adv* ▷ former
formidable *adj* frightening because difficult to overcome or manage ▷ **formidably** *adv*
formidably *adv* ▷ formidable
forming *v* ▷ form
formless *adj* ▷ form
forms *n*, *v* ▷ form
formula *n* (*pl* -las, -lae) group of numbers, letters, or symbols expressing a scientific or mathematical rule ▷ **formulaic** *adj*
formulae *n* ▷ formula
formulaic *adj* ▷ formula
formulas *n* ▷ formula
formulate *v* (-tes, -ting, -ted) plan or describe precisely and clearly ▷ **formulation** *n* (*pl* -s)
formulated *v* ▷ formulate
formulates *v* ▷ formulate
formulating *v* ▷ formulates
formulation *n* ▷ formulate
formulations *n* ▷ formulate
fornicate *v* (-tes, -ting, -ted) have sexual intercourse without being married ▷ **fornication** *n* (*pl* -s) ▷ **fornicator** *n* (*pl* -s)
fornicated *v* ▷ fornicate
fornicates *v* ▷ fornicate
fornicating *v* ▷ fornicate
fornication ▶ *n* ▷ fornicate

fornications *n* ▷ fornicate
fornicator *n* ▷ fornicate
fornicators *n* ▷ fornicate
forsake *v* (-sakes, -saking, -sook, -saken) withdraw support or friendship from
forsaken *v* ▷ forsake
forsakes *v* ▷ forsake
forsaking *v* ▷ forsake
forsook *v* ▷ forsake
forsooth *adv* (*Obs*) indeed
forswear *v* (-s, -swearing, -swore, -sworn) renounce or reject
forswearing *v* ▷ forswear
forswears *v* ▷ forswear
forswore *v* ▷ forswear
forsworn *v* ▷ forswear
forsythia [for-**syth**-ee-a] *n* (*pl* -as) shrub with yellow flowers in spring
forsythias *n* ▷ forsythia
fort *n* (*pl* -s) fortified building or place
forte¹ [for-tay] *n* (*pl* -s) thing at which a person excels
forte² [for-tay] *adv* (MUSIC) loudly
fortes *n* ▷ forte
forth *adv* forwards, out, or away
forthcoming *adj* about to appear or happen
forthright *adj* direct and outspoken
forthwith *adv* at once
forties *n* ▷ forty
fortieth *adj*, *n* ▷ forty
fortieths *n* ▷ forty
fortifications *n* ▷ fortify
fortified *v* ▷ fortify
fortifies *v* ▷ fortify
fortify *v* (-fies, -fying, -fied) make (a place) defensible, as by building walls ▷ **fortification** *n* (*pl* -s)
fortification *n* ▷ fortify
fortifying *v* ▷ fortify
fortissimo *adv* (MUSIC) very loudly
fortitude *n* (*pl* -s) courage in adversity or pain
fortitudes *n* ▷ fortitude
fortnight *n* (*pl* -s) two weeks ▷ **fortnightly** *adv*, *adj*
fortnightly *adv*, *adj* ▷ fortnight
fortnights *n* ▷ fortnight
fortress *n* (*pl* -es) large fort or fortified town
fortresses *n* ▷ fortress
forts *n* ▷ fort
fortuitous [for-**tyew**-it-uss] *adj* happening by (lucky) chance ▷ **fortuitously** *adv*
fortuitously *adv* ▷ fortuitous
fortunate *adj* having good luck ▷ **fortunately** *adv*
fortunately *adv* ▷ fortunate

fortune n (pl -s) luck, esp. when favourable ▶ pl person's destiny
fortunes n ▷ fortune
forty adj, n (pl -ties) four times ten > **fortieth** adj, n (pl -s)
forum n (pl -ums) meeting or medium for open discussion or debate
forums n ▷ forum
forward adj directed or moving ahead ▶ n (pl -s) attacking player in various team games, such as soccer or hockey ▶ adv forwards ▶ v (-s, -ing, -ed) send (a letter etc.) on to an ultimate destination
forwarded v ▷ forward
forwarding v ▷ forward
forwards adv towards or at a place further ahead in space or time ▶ n ▷ forward
fossick v (-s, -ing, -ed) (AUST & NZ) search, esp. for gold or precious stones
fossicked v ▷ fossick
fossicking v ▷ fossick
fossicks v ▷ fossick
fossil n (pl -s) hardened remains of a prehistoric animal or plant preserved in rock
fossilize v (-zes, -zing, -zed) turn into a fossil
fossilized v ▷ fossilize
fossilizes v ▷ fossilize
fossilizing v ▷ fossilize
fossils n ▷ fossil
foster v (-s, -ing, -ed) promote the growth or development of ▶ adj of or involved in fostering a child
fostered v ▷ foster
fostering v ▷ foster
fosters v ▷ foster
fought v ▷ fight
foul adj (-er, -est) loathsome or offensive ▶ n (pl -s) (SPORT) violation of the rules ▶ v (-s, -ing, -ed) make dirty or polluted
fouled v ▷ foul
fouler adj ▷ foul
foulest adj ▷ foul
fouling v ▷ foul
foulmouthed adj habitually using foul language
fouls n, v ▷ foul
found¹ v ▷ find
found² v (-s, -ing, -ed) establish or bring into being (foll. by on or upon) > **founder** n (pl -s)
found³ v (-s, -ing, -ed) cast (metal or glass) by melting and setting in a mould
foundation n (pl -s) basis or base
foundations n ▷ foundation
founded v ▷ found²,³
founder¹ n ▷ found²

founder² v (-s, -ing, -ed) break down or fail
foundered v ▷ founder
foundering v ▷ founder
founders¹ n ▷ found²
founders² v ▷ founder
founding v ▷ found²,³
foundling n (pl -s) (CHIEFLY BRIT) abandoned baby
foundlings n ▷ foundling
foundries n ▷ foundry
foundry n (pl -dries) place where metal is melted and cast
founds v ▷ found²,³
fount¹ n (pl -s) (Lit) fountain
fount² (pl -s) n set of printing type of one style and size
fountain n (pl -s) jet of water
fountainhead n (pl -s) original source
fountainheads n ▷ fountainhead
fountains n ▷ fountain
founts n ▷ fount¹,²
four adj, n (pl -s) one more than three
fours n ▷ four
foursome n group of four people
foursomes n (pl -s) ▷ foursome
fourteen adj, n (pl -s) four and ten > **fourteenth** adj, n (pl -s)
fourteens n ▷ fourteen
fourteenth adj, n ▷ fourteen
fourteenths n ▷ fourteen
fourth adj, n (pl -s) (of) number four in a series ▶ n quarter
fourths n ▷ fourth
fowl n (pl -s) domestic cock or hen
fowls n ▷ fowl
fox n (pl -es) reddish-brown bushy-tailed animal of the dog family ▶ v (-s, -ing, -ed) (Informal) perplex or deceive
foxed v ▷ fox
foxes n, v ▷ fox
foxglove n (pl -s) tall plant with purple or white flowers
foxgloves n ▷ foxglove
foxhole n (pl -s) (MIL) small pit dug for protection
foxholes n ▷ foxhole
foxhound n (pl -s) dog bred for hunting foxes
foxhounds n ▷ foxhound
foxier adj ▷ foxy
foxiest adj ▷ foxy
foxing v ▷ fox
foxtrot n (pl -s) ballroom dance with slow and quick steps
foxtrots n ▷ foxtrot
foxy adj (-xier, -xiest) of or like a fox, esp. in

craftiness

> **foy** n (**foys**). Foy is an old dialect word meaning a farewell meal or gift. This unusual word can be useful when there is little space to form longer words. Foy scores 9 points.

foyer [**foy**-ay] n (pl-s) entrance hall in a theatre, cinema, or hotel
  foyers n ▷ foyer
fracas [**frak**-ah] n (pl-es) noisy quarrel
  fracases n ▷ fracas
fraction n (pl-s) numerical quantity that is not a whole number > **fractional** adj
  > **fractionally** adv
  fractional adj ▷ fraction
  fractionally adv ▷ fraction
  fractions n ▷ fraction
fractious adj easily upset and angered
fracture n (pl-s) breaking, esp. of a bone ▶ v (-res, -ring, -red) break
  fractured v ▷ fracture
  fractures n, v ▷ fracture
  fracturing v ▷ fracture
fragile adj easily broken or damaged > **fragility** n (pl-lities)
  fragilities n ▷ fragile
  fragility n ▷ fragile
fragment n (pl-s) piece broken off ▶ v (-s, -ing, -ed) break into pieces > **fragmentary** adj
  > **fragmentation** n (pl-s)
  fragmentary adj ▷ fragment
  fragmentation n ▷ fragment
  fragmentations n ▷ fragment
  fragmented v ▷ fragment
  fragmenting v ▷ fragment
  fragments n, v ▷ fragment
fragrance n (pl-s) pleasant smell
  fragrances n ▷ fragrance
fragrant adj sweet-smelling
frail adj (-er, -est) physically weak
  frailer adj ▷ frail
  frailest adj ▷ frail
  frailities n ▷ fraility
frailty n (pl-ties) physical or moral weakness
frame n (pl-s) structure giving shape or support ▶ v (-mes, -ming, -med) put together, construct
  framed v ▷ frame
  frames n, v ▷ frame
framework n (pl-s) supporting structure
  frameworks n ▷ framework
  framing v ▷ frame
franc n (pl-s) monetary unit of Switzerland, various African countries, and formerly of France and Belgium

franchise n (pl-s) right to vote
  franchises n ▷ franchise
francium n (pl-s) (CHEM) radioactive metallic element
  franciums n ▷ francium
  francs n ▷ franc
frangipani [fran-jee-**pah**-nee] n (pl-nis) Australian evergreen tree with large yellow fragrant flowers
  frangipanis n ▷ frangipani
frank adj (-er, -est) honest and straightforward in speech or attitude ▶ n (pl-s) official mark on a letter permitting delivery ▶ v (-s, -ing, -ed) put such a mark on (a letter) > **frankly** adv
  > **frankness** n (pl-es)
  franked v ▷ frank
  franker adj ▷ frank
  frankest adj ▷ frank
frankfurter n (pl-s) smoked sausage
  frankfurters n ▷ frankfurter
frankincense n (pl-es) aromatic gum resin burned as incense
  frankincenses n ▷ frankincense
  franking v ▷ frank
  frankly adv ▷ frank
  frankness n ▷ frank
  franknesses n ▷ frank
  franks n, v ▷ frank
frantic adj distracted with rage, grief, joy, etc.
  > **frantically** adv
  frantically adv ▷ frantic
fraternal adj of a brother, brotherly
  > **fraternally** adv
fraternity n (pl-ties) group of people with shared interests, aims, etc. (US)
fraternize v associate on friendly terms
  > **fraternization** n
fratricide n (pl-s) crime of killing one's brother
  fratricides n ▷ fratricide
frau [rhymes with **how**] n (pl fraus, frauen) married German woman
fraud n (pl-s) (criminal) deception, swindle
  > **fraudulent** adj > **fraudulence** n (pl-s)
  frauds n ▷ fraud
  fraudulence n ▷ fraud
  fraudulences n ▷ fraud
  fraudulent adj ▷ fraud
  frauen n ▷ frau
fraught [**frawt**] adj (-er, -est) tense or anxious
  fraughter adj ▷ fraught
  fraughtest adj ▷ fraught
fräulein [**froy**-line] n (pl-leins, -lein) unmarried German woman
  fräuleins n ▷ fräulein
  fraus n ▷ frau

fray¹ n (pl -s) (BRIT, AUST & NZ) noisy quarrel

fray² v (-s, -ing, -ed) make or become ragged at the edge
  frayed v ▷ fray²
  fraying v ▷ fray²
  frays n, v ▷ fray¹, ²

frazzle n (pl -s) (Informal) exhausted state
  frazzles n ▷ frazzle

freak n (pl -s) abnormal person or thing ▶ adj abnormal > **freakish** adj
  freakish adj ▷ freak
  freaks n ▷ freak

freckle n (pl -s) small brown spot on the skin
freckled adj marked with freckles
  freckles n ▷ freckle

free adj (freer, freest) able to act at will, not compelled or restrained ▶ v (frees, freeing, freed) release, liberate > **freely** adv
  freed v ▷ free

freedom n (pl -s) being free
  freedoms n ▷ freedom

freehand adj drawn without guiding instruments

freehold n (pl -s) tenure of land for life without restrictions > **freeholder** n (pl -s)
  freeholder n ▷ freehold
  freeholders n ▷ freehold
  freeholds n ▷ freehold
  freeing v ▷ free

freelance adj, n (pl -s) (of) a self-employed person doing specific pieces of work for various employers
  freelances n ▷ freelance

freeloader n (pl -s) (Slang) habitual scrounger
  freeloaders n ▷ freeloader
  freely adv ▷ free

freemason n (pl -s) member of a secret fraternity pledged to help each other
  freemasons n ▷ freemason
  freer adj ▷ free
  frees v ▷ free

freesia n (pl -s) plant with fragrant tubular flowers
  freesias n ▷ freesia
  freest adj ▷ free

freeway n (pl -s) (US & AUST) motorway
  freeways n ▷ freeway

freewheel v (-s, -ing, -ed) travel downhill on a bicycle without pedalling
  freewheeled v ▷ freewheel
  freewheeling v ▷ freewheel
  freewheels v ▷ freewheel

freeze v (-zes, -zing, froze, frozen) change from a liquid to a solid by the reduction of temperature, as water to ice ▶ n period of very cold weather

freezer n (pl -s) insulated cabinet for cold-storage of perishable foods
  freezers n ▷ freezer
  freezes v ▷ freeze

freezing adj (Informal) very cold ▶ v ▷ freeze

freight [frate] n (pl -s) commercial transport of goods ▶ v (-s, -ing, -ed) send by freight
  freighted v ▷ freight

freighter n (pl -s) ship or aircraft for transporting goods
  freighters n ▷ freighter
  freighting v ▷ freight
  freights n, v ▷ freight

frenetic [frin-net-ik] adj uncontrolled, excited > **frenetically** adv
  frenetically adv ▷ frenetic
  freneticnesses n ▷ frenetic
  frenzied adj ▷ frenzy
  frenziedly adv ▷ frenzy
  frenzies n ▷ frenzy

frenzy n (pl -zies) violent mental derangement > **frenzied** adj > **frenziedly** adv
  frequencies n ▷ frequency

frequency n (pl -cies) rate of occurrence

frequent adj happening often ▶ v (-s, -ing, -ed) visit habitually > **frequently** adv
  frequented v ▷ frequent
  frequenting v ▷ frequent
  frequently adv ▷ frequent
  frequents v ▷ frequent

fresco n (pl -coes, -cos) watercolour painting done on wet plaster on a wall
  frescoes n ▷ fresco
  frescos n ▷ fresco

fresh adj (-er, -est) newly made, acquired, etc. > **freshly** adv > **freshness** n (pl -es)

freshen v (-s, -ing, -ed) make or become fresh or fresher
  freshened v ▷ freshen
  freshening v ▷ freshen
  freshens v ▷ freshen

fresher n (pl -s) first-year student ▶ adj ▷ fresh
  freshers n ▷ fresher
  freshest adj ▷ fresh
  freshly adv ▷ fresh

freshman n (pl -men) (BRIT & US) first-year student
  freshmen n ▷ freshman
  freshness n ▷ fresh
  freshnesses n ▷ fresh

fret¹ v (-s, -tting, -tted) be worried

fret² n (pl -s) small bar on the fingerboard of a guitar etc.

fretful adj irritable

frets n ▷ fret[1,2]

fretsaw n (pl -s) fine saw with a narrow blade, used for fretwork

fretsaws n ▷ fretsaw

fretted v ▷ fret[1]

fretting v ▷ fret[1]

fretwork n (pl -s) decorative carving in wood

fretworks n ▷ fretwork

friable adj easily crumbled

friar n (pl -s) member of a male Roman Catholic religious order

friaries n ▷ friary

friars n ▷ friar

friary n (pl -ries) house of friars

fricassee n (pl -s) stewed meat served in a thick white sauce

fricassees n ▷ fricassee

friction n (pl -s) resistance met with by a body moving over another > **frictional** adj

frictional adj ▷ friction

frictions n ▷ friction

fridge n (pl -s) apparatus in which food and drinks are kept cool

fridges n ▷ fridge

fried v ▷ fry[1]

friend n (pl -s) person whom one knows well and likes > **friendless** adj > **friendship** n (pl -s)

friendless adj ▷ friend

friendlier adj ▷ friendly

friendlies n ▷ friendly

friendliest adj ▷ friendly

friendliness n ▷ friendly

friendlinesses n ▷ friendly

friendly adj (-lier, -liest) showing or expressing liking ▶ n (pl -lies) (SPORT) match played for its own sake and not as part of a competition > **friendliness** n (pl -es)

friends n ▷ friend

friendship n ▷ friend

friendships n ▷ friend

fries v, n ▷ fry[1]

Friesian [free-zhan] n (pl -s) breed of black-and-white dairy cattle

Friesians n ▷ Friesian

frieze [freeze] n (pl -s) ornamental band on a wall

friezes n ▷ frieze

frigate [frig-it] n (pl -s) medium-sized fast warship

frigates n ▷ frigate

fright n (pl -s) sudden fear or alarm

frighten v (-s, -ing, -ed) scare or terrify > **frightening** adj

frightened v ▷ frighten

frightened v ▷ frighten

frightening v, adj ▷ frighten

frightful adj horrifying (Informal) > **frightfully** adv

frightfully adv ▷ frightful

frights n ▷ fright

frigid [frij-id] adj (of a woman) sexually unresponsive > **frigidity** n (pl -ties)

frigidities n ▷ frigid

frigidity n ▷ frigid

frill n (pl -s) gathered strip of fabric attached at one edge ▶ pl superfluous decorations or details > **frilled** adj > **frilly** adj (-ier, -iest)

frilled adj ▷ frill

frillier adj ▷ frill

frilliest adj ▷ frill

frills n ▷ frill

frilly adj ▷ frill

fringe n (pl -es) hair cut short and hanging over the forehead ▶ v (-ges, -ging, -ged) decorate with a fringe ▶ adj (of theatre) unofficial or unconventional > **fringed** adj

fringed v, adj ▷ fringe

fringes n, v ▷ fringe

fringing v ▷ fringe

fripperies n ▷ frippery

frippery n (pl -ries) useless ornamentation

frisk v (-s, -ing, -ed) move or leap playfully

frisked v ▷ frisk

friskier adj ▷ frisky

friskiest adj ▷ frisky

frisking v ▷ frisk

frisks v ▷ frisk

frisky adj (-kier, -kiest) lively or high-spirited

frisson [frees-sonn] n (pl -s) shiver of fear or excitement

frissons n ▷ frisson

fritter n (pl -s) piece of food fried in batter

fritters n ▷ fritter

frivolities n ▷ frivolous

frivolity n ▷ frivolous

frivolous adj not serious or sensible > **frivolity** n (pl -ties)

frizz v (-es, -ing, -ed) form (hair) into stiff wiry curls > **frizzy** adj (-zzier, -zziest)

frizzed v ▷ frizz

frizzes v ▷ frizz

frizzier adj ▷ frizz

frizziest adj ▷ frizz

frizzing v ▷ frizz

frizzle v (-les, -ling, -led) cook or heat until crisp and shrivelled

frizzled v ▷ frizzle

frizzles v ▷ frizzle

frizzling v ▷ frizzle

frizzy adj ▷ frizz

frock n (pl -s) dress
  frocks n ▷ frock

frog n (pl -s) smooth-skinned tailless
amphibian with long back legs used for
jumping

frogman n (pl -men) swimmer with a rubber
suit and breathing equipment for working
underwater
  frogmen n ▷ frogman
  frogs n ▷ frog

frogspawn n (pl -s) jelly-like substance
containing frog's eggs
  frogspawns n ▷ frogspawn

frolic v (-lics, -licking, -licked) run and play
in a lively way ▸ n (pl -s) lively and merry
behaviour
  frolicked v ▷ frolic
  frolicking v ▷ frolic
  frolics v, n ▷ frolic

frolicsome adj playful

from prep indicating the point of departure,
source, distance, cause, change of state, etc.

frond n (pl -s) long leaf or leaflike part of a fern,
palm, or seaweed
  fronds n ▷ frond

front n (pl -s) fore part ▸ adj of or at the front ▸ v
(-s, -ing, -ed) face (onto) > **frontal** adj

frontage n (pl -s) facade of a building
  frontages n ▷ frontage
  frontal adj ▷ front
  fronted v ▷ front

frontier n (pl -s) area of a country bordering
on another
  frontiers n ▷ frontier
  fronting v ▷ front

frontispiece n (pl -s) illustration facing the
title page of a book
  frontispieces n ▷ frontispiece

frontrunner (pl -s) n (Informal) person regarded
as most likely to win a race, election, etc.
  frontrunners n ▷ frontrunner
  fronts n, v ▷ front

frost n (pl -s) white frozen dew or mist ▸ v (-s,
-ing, -ed) become covered with frost

frostbite n destruction of tissue, esp. of the
fingers or ears, by cold (pl -s) > **frostbitten** adj
  frostbites n ▷ frostbite
  frostbitten adj ▷ frostbite

frosted v ▷ frost ▸ adj (of glass) having a rough
surface to make it opaque
  frostier adj ▷ frosty
  frostiest adj ▷ frosty
  frostily adv ▷ frosty
  frostiness n ▷ frosty
  frostinesses n ▷ frosty

frosting v ▷ frost ▸ n (pl -s) (CHIEFLY US) sugar
icing
  frostings n ▷ frosting
  frosts n, v ▷ frost

frosty adj (-tier, -tiest) characterized or
covered by frost > **frostily** adv > **frostiness**
n (-es)

froth n (pl -s) mass of small bubbles ▸ v (-s, -ing,
-ed) foam > **frothy** adj (-thier, -thiest)
  frothed v ▷ froth
  frothier adj ▷ froth
  frothiest adj ▷ froth
  frothing v ▷ froth
  froths n, v ▷ froth
  frothy adj ▷ froth
  frowiest adj ▷ frowzy

frown v (-s, -ing, -ed) wrinkle one's brows in
worry, anger, or thought ▸ n (pl -s) frowning
expression
  frowned v ▷ frown
  frowning v ▷ frown
  frowns v, n ▷ frown
  frowsier adj ▷ frowzy
  frowsiest adj ▷ frowzy
  frowstier adj ▷ frowsty
  frowstiest adj ▷ frowsty

frowsty adj (-ier, -iest) (BRIT) stale or musty
  frowzier adj ▷ frowzy

frowzy, frowsy adj (-zier, -ziest) dirty or
unkempt
  froze v ▷ freeze
  frozen v ▷ freeze

frugal adj thrifty, sparing > **frugally** adv
> **frugality** n (pl -ties)
  frugalities n ▷ frugal
  frugality n ▷ frugal
  frugally adv ▷ frugal

fruit n (pl -s) part of a plant containing seeds,
esp. if edible ▸ v (-s, -ing, -ed) bear fruit
  fruited v ▷ fruit

fruiterer n (pl -s) person who sells fruit
  fruiterers n ▷ fruiterer

fruitful adj useful or productive > **fruitfully** adv
  fruitfully adv ▷ fruitful
  fruitier adj ▷ fruity
  fruitiest adj ▷ fruity
  fruiting v ▷ fruit

fruition [froo-ish-on] n (pl -s) fulfilment of
something worked for or desired
  fruitions n ▷ fruition

fruitless adj useless or unproductive
> **fruitlessly** adv
  fruitlessly adv ▷ fruitless
  fruits n, v ▷ fruit

fruity adj (-tier, -tiest) of or like fruit

frump n (pl -s) dowdy woman > **frumpy** adj (-pier, -piest)
frumpier adj ▷ frump
frumpiest adj ▷ frump
frumps n ▷ frump
frumpy adj ▷ frump
frustrate v (-tes, -ting, -ted) upset or anger > **frustrated** adj > **frustrating** adj > **frustration** n (pl -s)
frustrated v, adj ▷ frustrate
frustrates v ▷ frustrate
frustrating v, adj ▷ frustrate
frustration n ▷ frustrate
frustrations n ▷ frustrate
fry¹ v (-ries, -rying, -ried) cook or be cooked in fat or oil ▶ n (pl fries) potato chip
fry² pl n young fishes
frying v ▷ fry
fuchsia [fyew-sha] n (pl -s) ornamental shrub with hanging flowers
fuchsias n ▷ fuchsia
fuddle v (-les, -ling, -led) cause to be intoxicated or confused > **fuddled** adj
fuddled v, adj ▷ fuddle
fuddles v ▷ fuddle
fuddling v ▷ fuddle
fudge¹ n (pl -s) soft caramel-like sweet
fudge² v (-ges, -ging, -ged) avoid making a firm statement or decision
fudged v ▷ fudge²
fudges n, v ▷ fudge¹, ²
fudging v ▷ fudge²
fuel n (pl -s) substance burned or treated to produce heat or power ▶ v (-s, -lling, -lled) provide with fuel
fuelled v ▷ fuel
fuelling v ▷ fuel
fuels n, v ▷ fuel
fug n (pl -s) hot stale atmosphere > **fuggy** adj (-ggier, -ggiest)
fuggier adj ▷ fug
fuggiest adj ▷ fug
fuggy adj ▷ fug
fugitive [fyew-jit-iv] n (pl -s) person who flees, esp. from arrest or pursuit ▶ adj fleeing
fugitives n ▷ fugitive
fugs n ▷ fug
fugue [fyewg] n (pl -s) musical composition in which a theme is repeated in different parts
fugues n ▷ fugue
fulcra n ▷ fulcrum
fulcrum n (pl -crums, -cra) pivot about which a lever turns
fulcrums n ▷ fulcrum
fulfil v (-s, -lling, -lled) bring about the

achievement of (a desire or promise) > **fulfilment** n (pl -s)
fulfilled n ▷ fulfil
fulfilling v ▷ fulfil
fulfilment n ▷ fulfil
fulfilments n ▷ fulfil
fulfils v ▷ fulfil
full adj (-er, -est) containing as much or as many as possible ▶ adv completely > **fully** adv > **fullness** n (pl -es)
fuller adj ▷ full
fullest adj ▷ full
fullness n ▷ full
fullnesses n ▷ full
fully adv ▷ full
fulmar n (pl -s) Arctic sea bird
fulmars n ▷ fulmar
fulminate v (-tes, -ting, -ted) (foll. by **against**) criticize or denounce angrily
fulminated v ▷ fulminate
fulminates v ▷ fulminate
fulminating v ▷ fulminate
fulsome adj distastefully excessive or insincere
fumble v (-les, -ling, -led) handle awkwardly ▶ n (pl -s) act of fumbling
fumbled v ▷ fumble
fumbles n, v ▷ fumble
fumbling v ▷ fumble
fume v (-s, -ing, -ed) be very angry ▶ pl n pungent smoke or vapour
fumed v ▷ fume
fumes v, n ▷ fume
fumigate [fyew-mig-gate] v (-tes, -ting, -ted) disinfect with fumes > **fumigation** n (pl -s)
fumigated v ▷ fumigate
fumigates v ▷ fumigate
fumigating v ▷ fumigate
fumigation n ▷ fumigate
fumigations n ▷ fuminate
fuming v ▷ fume
fun n (pl -s) enjoyment or amusement
function n (pl -s) purpose something exists for ▶ v (-s, -ing, -ed) operate or work (foll. by **as**)
functional adj of or as a function > **functionally** adv
functionally adv ▷ functional
functionaries n ▷ functionary
functionary n (pl -ries) official
functioned v ▷ function
functioning v ▷ function
functions n, v ▷ function
fund n (pl -s) stock of money for a special purpose ▶ pl money resources ▶ v (-s, -ing, -ed) provide money to > **funding** n (pl -s)

fundamental *adj* essential or primary ▸ *n* (*pl* -s) basic rule or fact > **fundamentally** *adv*
fundamentalism *n* (*pl* -s) literal or strict interpretation of a religion > **fundamentalist** *adj*, *n* (*pl* -s)
　fundamentalisms *n* ▷ fundamentalism
fundamentalist *adj*, *n* ▷ fundamentalism
　fundamentalists *n* ▷ fundamentalism
　fundamentally *adv* ▷ fundamental
　fundamentals *n* ▷ fundamental
　funded *v* ▷ fund
fundi *n* (*pl* -dis) (S AFR) expert or boffin
　funding *v*, *n* ▷ fund
　fundings *n* ▷ fund
　fundis *n* ▷ fundi
　funds *n*, *v* ▷ fund
funeral *n* (*pl* -s) ceremony of burying or cremating a dead person
　funerals *n* ▷ funeral
funerary *adj* of or for a funeral
funereal [fyew-**neer**-ee-al] *adj* gloomy or sombre
funfair *n* (*pl* -s) entertainment with machines to ride on and stalls
　funfairs *n* ▷ funfair
fungal *adj* ▷ fungus
　fungi *n* ▷ fungus
fungicide *n* (*pl* -s) substance that destroys fungi
　fungicides *n* ▷ fungicides
　fungous *adj* ▷ fungus
fungus *n* (*pl* -gi, -guses) plant without leaves, flowers, or roots, such as a mushroom or mould > **fungal, fungous** *adj*
　funguses *n* ▷ fungus
funicular *n* (*pl* -s) cable railway on a mountainside or cliff
　funiculars *n* ▷ funicular
funk[1] *n* (*pl* -s) style of dance music with a strong beat
funk[2] (*Informal*) *n* nervous or fearful state ▸ *v* (-s, -ing, -ed) avoid (doing something) through fear
　funked *v* ▷ funk
　funkier *adj* ▷ funky
　funkiest *adj* ▷ funky
　funking *v* ▷ funk
　funks *n*, *v* ▷ funk[1, 2]
funky *adj* (-kier, -kiest) (of music) having a strong beat
funnel *n* (*pl* -s) cone-shaped tube for pouring liquids into a narrow opening ▸ *v* (-s, -lling, -lled) (cause to) move through or as if through a funnel
　funnelled *v* ▷ funnel

　funnelling *v* ▷ funnel
　funnels *n*, *v* ▷ funnel
　funnier *adj* ▷ funny
　funniest *adj* ▷ funny
　funnily *adv* ▷ funny
funny *adj* (-nnier, -nniest) comical, humorous > **funnily** *adv*
　funs *n* ▷ fun
fur *n* (*pl* -s) soft hair of a mammal ▸ *v* (-s, -rring, -rred) cover or become covered with fur > **furry** (-rrier, -rriest) ▸ *adj*
furbish *v* (-es, -ing, -ed) smarten up
　furbished *v* ▷ furbish
　furbishes *v* ▷ furbish
　furbishing *v* ▷ furbish
　furies *n* ▷ fury
furious *adj* very angry > **furiously** *adv*
　furiously *adv* ▷ furious
furl *v* (-s, -ing, -ed) roll up and fasten (a sail, umbrella, or flag)
　furled *v* ▷ furl
　furling *v* ▷ furl
furlong *n* (*pl* -s) unit of length equal to 220 yards (201.168 metres)
　furlongs *n* ▷ furlongs
furlough [**fur**-loh] *n* (*pl* -s) leave of absence
　furloughs *n* ▷ furlough
　furls *v* ▷ furl
furnace *n* (*pl* -s) enclosed chamber containing a very hot fire
　furnaces *n* ▷ furnace
furnish *v* (-es, -ing, -ed) provide (a house or room) with furniture
　furnished *v* ▷ furnish
　furnishes *v* ▷ furnish
　furnishing *v* ▷ furnish
furnishings *pl n* furniture, carpets, and fittings
furniture *n* (*pl* -s) large movable articles such as chairs and wardrobes
　furnitures *n* ▷ furniture
furore [fyew-**ror**-ee] *n* (*pl* -s) very excited or angry reaction
　furores *n* ▷ furore
　furred *v* ▷ fur
furrier *n* (*pl* -s) dealer in furs ▸ *adj* ▷ fur
　furriers *n* ▷ furrier
　furriest *adj* ▷ fur
　furring *v* ▷ fur
furrow *n* (*pl* -s) trench made by a plough ▸ *v* (-s, -ing, -ed) make or become wrinkled
　furrowed *v* ▷ furrow
　furrowing *v* ▷ furrow
　furrows *n*, *v* ▷ furrow
　furry *adj* ▷ fur

furrying v ▷ flurry
furs n, v ▷ fur
further adv in addition ▸ adj additional ▸ v (-s, -ing, -ed) assist the progress of > **furtherance** n (pl -s)
furtherance n ▷ further
furtherances n ▷ further
furthered v ▷ further
furthering v ▷ further
furthermore adv besides
furthermost adj most distant
furthers v ▷ further
furthest adv to the greatest distance or extent ▸ adj most distant
furtive adj sly and secretive > **furtively** adv
furtively adv ▷ furtive
fury n (pl -ries) wild anger
furze n (pl -s) gorse
furzes n ▷ furze
fuse¹ n (pl -s) cord containing an explosive for detonating a bomb
fuse² n (pl -s) safety device for electric circuits, containing a wire that melts and breaks the connection when the circuit is overloaded ▸ v (-ses, -sing, -sed) (cause to) fail as a result of a blown fuse
fused v ▷ fuse
fuselage [fyew-zill-lahzh] n (pl -s) body of an aircraft
fuselages n ▷ fuselage
fuses v, n ▷ fuse
fusilier [fyew-zill-**leer**] n (pl -s) soldier of certain regiments
fusiliers n ▷ fusilier
fusillade [fyew-zill-**lade**] n (pl -s) continuous discharge of firearms
fusillades n ▷ fusillade
fusing v ▷ fuse
fusion n (pl -s) melting ▸ adj of a style of cooking that combines traditional Western techniques and ingredients with those used in Eastern cuisine
fusions n ▷ fusion
fuss n (pl -es) needless activity or worry ▸ v (-es, -ing, -ed) make a fuss

fussed v ▷ fuss
fusses n, v ▷ fuss
fussier adj ▷ fussy
fussiest adj ▷ fussy
fussily adv ▷ fussy
fussiness n ▷ fussy
fussinesses n ▷ fussy
fussing v ▷ fuss
fussy adj (-ssier, -ssiest) inclined to fuss > **fussily** adv > **fussiness** n (pl -es)
fustier adj ▷ fusty
fustiest adj ▷ fusty
fustiness n ▷ fusty
fustinesses n ▷ fusty
fusty adj (-tier, -tiest) stale-smelling > **fustiness** n (pl -es)
futile adj unsuccessful or useless > **futility** n (pl -ties)
futilities n ▷ futile
futility n ▷ futile
futon [foo-tonn] n (pl -s) Japanese-style bed
futons n ▷ futon
future n (pl -s) time to come ▸ adj yet to come or be
futures n ▷ future
futuristic adj of a design appearing to belong to some future time
fuzz¹ n (pl -es) mass of fine or curly hairs or fibres
fuzz² n (Slang) police
fuzzes n ▷ fuzz¹
fuzzier adj ▷ fuzzy
fuzziest adj ▷ fuzzy
fuzzily adv ▷ fuzzy
fuzziness n ▷ fuzzy
fuzzinesses n ▷ fuzzy
fuzzy adj (-zzier, -zziest) of, like, or covered with fuzz > **fuzzily** adv > **fuzziness** n (pl -es)

> **fy** interj. Fy is an old word that people said when they were disgusted or dismayed. This very unusual word can be really useful when you're trying to form words in more than one direction. Fy scores 8 points.

Gg

Only three two-letter words begin with G (**gi**, **go** and **gu**). Knowing these will save you worrying about other possibilities. There are quite a few short words beginning with G that use Y, which can prove very useful. These include **gay**, **gey**, **goy** and **guy** (7 points each), as well as **gym** and **gyp** (9 points each).

gab n (pl -s) ▶ v (-s, -ing, -ed) (Informal) talk or chatter
  gababouts n ▷ gadabout
gabardine, gaberdine n (pl -s) strong twill cloth used esp. for raincoats
  gabardines n ▷ gabardine
  gabbed v ▷ gab
  gabbier adj ▷ gabby
  gabbiest adj ▷ gabby
  gabbing v ▷ gab
gabble v (-s, -ing, -ed) speak rapidly and indistinctly ▶ n (pl -s) rapid indistinct speech
  gabbled v ▷ gabble
  gabbles v, n ▷ gabble
  gabbling v ▷ gabble
gabby adj (-bier, -bbiest) (Informal) talkative
gable n (pl -s) triangular upper part of a wall between sloping roofs > **gabled** adj
  gabled adj ▷ gable
  gables n ▷ gable
  gabs n, v ▷ gab
gad v (-s, -dding, -dded) go around in search of pleasure
  gadabout n (pl -s) pleasure-seeker
  gadded v ▷ gad
  gadding v ▷ gad
  gadflies n ▷ gadfly
gadfly n (pl -flies) fly that bites cattle
gadget n (pl -s) small mechanical device or appliance
  gadgetries n ▷ gadgetry
gadgetry n (pl -ries) gadgets
  gadgets n ▷ gadget
  gads v ▷ gad
gaff n (pl -s) stick with an iron hook for landing large fish
gaffe n (pl -s) social blunder
gaffer n (pl -s) (BRIT) (Informal) foreman or boss

  gaffers n ▷ gaffer
  gaffes n ▷ gaffe
  gaffs n ▷ gaff
gag[1] v (-s, -gging, -gged) choke or retch ▶ n (pl -s) cloth etc. put into or tied across the mouth
gag[2] n (pl -s) (Informal) joke
gaga [gah-gah] adj (Slang) senile
  gagged v ▷ gag[1]
  gagging v ▷ gag[1]
gaggle n (pl -s) (Informal) disorderly crowd
  gaggles n ▷ gaggle
  gags v, n ▷ gag[1, 2]
  gaieties n ▷ gaiety
gaiety n (pl -ties) cheerfulness
gaily adv merrily
gain v (-s, -ing, -ed) acquire or obtain ▶ n (pl -s) profit or advantage
  gained v ▷ gain
gainful adj useful or profitable > **gainfully** adv
  gainfully adv ▷ gainful
  gaining v ▷ gain
  gains v, n ▷ gain
  gainsaid v ▷ gainsay
gainsay v (-s, -ing, -said) deny or contradict
  gainsaying v ▷ gainsay
  gainsays v ▷ gainsay
gait n (pl -s) manner of walking
gaiter n (pl -s) cloth or leather covering for the lower leg
  gaiters n ▷ gaiter
  gaits n ▷ gait
gala [gah-la] n (pl -s) festival
galactic adj ▷ galaxy
  galas n ▷ gala
  galaxies n ▷ galaxy
galaxy n (pl -xies) system of stars > **galactic** adj
gale n (pl -s) strong wind
  gales n ▷ gale

gall¹ [gawl] *n* (*pl* -s) (*Informal*) impudence

gall² [gawl] *v* (-s, -ing, -ed) annoy

gall³ [gawl] *n* (*pl* -s) abnormal outgrowth on a tree or plant

gallant *adj* (-er, -est) brave and noble
> **gallantly** *adv*

  gallanter *adj* ▷ gallant

  gallantest *adj* ▷ gallant

  gallantly *adv* ▷ gallant

  gallantries *n* ▷ gallantry

gallantry *n* (*pl* -tries) showy, attentive treatment of women

  galled *v* ▷ gall²

galleon *n* (*pl* -s) large three-masted sailing ship of the 15th-17th centuries

  galleons *n* ▷ galleon

  galleries *n* ▷ gallery

gallery *n* (*pl* -ries) room or building for displaying works of art

galley *n* (*pl* -s) kitchen of a ship or aircraft

  galleys *n* ▷ galley

  galling *v* ▷ gall²

gallium *n* (*pl* -iums) (CHEM) soft grey metallic element used in semiconductors

  galliums *n* ▷ gallium

gallivant *v* (-s, -ing, -ed) go about in search of pleasure

  gallivanted *v* ▷ gallivant

  gallivanting *v* ▷ gallivant

  gallivants *v* ▷ gallivant

gallon *n* (*pl* -s) liquid measure of eight pints, equal to 4.55 litres

  gallons *n* ▷ gallon

gallop *n* (*pl* -s) horse's fastest pace ▶ *v* (-s, -ing, -ed) go or ride at a gallop

  galloped *v* ▷ gallop

  galloping *v* ▷ gallop

  gallops *n, v* ▷ gallop

gallows *n* (*pl* -ses) wooden structure used for hanging criminals

  gallowses *n* ▷ gallows

  galls *v, n* ▷ gall¹, ², ³

gallstone *n* (*pl* -s) hard mass formed in the gall bladder or its ducts

  gallstones *n* ▷ gallstone

galore *adv* in abundance

galoshes *pl n* (BRIT, AUST & NZ) waterproof overshoes

galumph *v* (-s, -ing, -ed) (BRIT, AUST & NZ) (*Informal*) leap or move about clumsily

  galumphed *v* ▷ galumph

  galumphing *v* ▷ galumph

  galumphs *v* ▷ galumph

galvanic *adj* of or producing an electric current generated by chemical means

galvanize *v* (-zes, -zing, -zed) stimulate into action

  galvanized *v* ▷ galvanize

  galvanizes *v* ▷ galvanize

  galvanizing *v* ▷ galvanize

gambit *n* (*pl* -s) opening line or move intended to secure an advantage (CHESS)

  gambits *n* ▷ gambit

gamble *v* (-les, -ling, -led) play games of chance to win money ▶ *n* (*pl* -s) risky undertaking > **gambler** *n* (*pl* -s) > **gambling** *n* (*pl* -s)

  gambled *v* ▷ gamble

  gambler *n* ▷ gamble

  gamblers *n* ▷ gamble

  gambles *v, n* ▷ gamble

  gambling *v, n* ▷ gamble

  gamblings *n* ▷ gamble

gamboge [gam-**boje**] *n* (*pl* -s) gum resin used as a yellow pigment and purgative

  gamboges *n* ▷ gamboge

gambol *v* (-s, -bolling, -bolled) jump about playfully, frolic ▶ *n* (*pl* -s) frolic

  gambolled *v* ▷ gambol

  gambolling *v* ▷ gambol

  gambols *v, n* ▷ gambol

game¹ *n* (*pl* -s) amusement or pastime ▶ *v* (-mes, -ming, -med) gamble ▶ *adj* (-er, -est) brave > **gamely** *adv*

game² *adj* (-er, -est) (BRIT, AUST & NZ) lame, crippled

  gamed *v* ▷ game¹

gamekeeper *n* (*pl* -s) (BRIT, AUST & S AFR) person employed to breed game and prevent poaching

  gamekeepers *n* ▷ gamekeeper

  gamely *adv* ▷ game¹

gamer *n* person who plays computer games ▶ *adj* ▷ game¹, ²

  gamers *n* ▷ gamer

  games *n, v* ▷ game¹

gamesmanship *n* (-s) art of winning by cunning practices without actually cheating

  gamesmanships *n* ▷ gamesmanship

  gamest *adj* ▷ game¹, ²

gamete *n* (*pl* -s) (BIOL) reproductive cell

  gametes *n* ▷ gamete

gamine [gam-**een**] *n* (*pl* -s) slim boyish young woman

  gamines *n* ▷ gamine

gaming *n* gambling ▶ *v* ▷ game¹

gamma *n* (*pl* -s) third letter of the Greek alphabet

  gammas *n* ▷ gamma

  gammier *adj* ▷ gammy

gammiest adj ▷ gammy
gammon n (pl -s) cured or smoked ham
gammons n ▷ gammon
gammy adj (-mier, -miest) ▷ game²
gamut n (pl -s) whole range or scale (of music, emotions, etc.)
gamuts n ▷ gamut
gander n (pl -s) male goose
ganders n ▷ gander
gang n (pl -s) (criminal) group
gangland n (pl -s) criminal underworld
ganglands n ▷ gangland
gangling adj lanky and awkward
ganglion n (pl -s) group of nerve cells
ganglions n ▷ ganglion
gangplank n (pl -s) portable bridge for boarding or leaving a ship
gangplanks n ▷ gangplank
gangrene n (pl -s) decay of body tissue as a result of disease or injury > **gangrenous** adj
gangrenes n ▷ gangrene
gangs n ▷ gang
gangster n (pl -s) member of a criminal gang
gangsters n ▷ gangster
gangway n (pl -s) passage between rows of seats
gangways n ▷ gangway
gannet n (pl -s) large sea bird
gannets n ▷ gannet
gantries n ▷ gantry
gantry n (pl -ries) structure supporting something such as a crane or rocket
gaol [jayl] n (pl -s) ▷ jail
gaols n ▷ gaol
gap n (pl -s) break or opening > **gappy** adj (-pier, -ppiest)
gape v (-pes, -ping, -ped) stare in wonder > **gaping** adj
gaped v ▷ gape
gapes v ▷ gape
gaping v, adj ▷ gape
gappier adj ▷ gap
gappiest adj ▷ gap
gappy adj ▷ gap
gaps n ▷ gap
garage n (pl -s) building used to house cars ▶ v (-ges, -ging, -ged) put or keep a car in a garage
garaged v ▷ garage
garages n, v ▷ garage
garaging v ▷ garage
garb n (pl -s) clothes ▶ v (-s, -ing, -ed) clothe
garbage n (pl -s) rubbish
garbages n ▷ garbage
garbed v ▷ garb
garbing v ▷ garb

garbled adj (of a story etc.) jumbled and confused
garbs n, v ▷ garb
garden n (pl -s) piece of land for growing flowers, fruit, or vegetables ▶ pl ornamental park ▶ v (-s, -ing, -ed) cultivate a garden > **gardener** n (pl -s) > **gardening** n (pl -s)
gardened v ▷ garden
gardenia [gar-**deen**-ya] n (pl -s) large fragrant white waxy flower
gardenias n ▷ gardenia
gardening v ▷ garden
gardens n, v ▷ garden
garfish n (pl -fishes) freshwater fish with a long body and very long toothed jaws
garfishes n ▷ garfish
gargantuan adj huge
gargle v (-les, -ling, -led) wash the throat with (a liquid) by breathing out slowly through the liquid ▶ n (pl -s) liquid used for gargling
gargled v ▷ gargle
gargles v, n ▷ gargle
gargling v ▷ gargle
gargoyle n (pl -s) waterspout carved in the form of a grotesque face, esp. on a church
gargoyles n ▷ gargoyle
garish adj crudely bright or colourful > **garishly** adv > **garishness** n (pl -es)
garishly adv ▷ garish
garishness n ▷ garish
garishnesses n ▷ garish
garland n (pl -s) wreath of flowers worn or hung as a decoration ▶ v (-s, -ing, -ed) decorate with garlands
garlanded v ▷ garland
garlanding v ▷ garland
garlands n, v ▷ garland
garlic n (pl -s) pungent bulb of a plant of the onion family, used in cooking
garlics n ▷ garlic
garment n (pl -s) article of clothing ▶ pl clothes
garments n ▷ garment
garner v (-s, -ing, -ed) collect or store
garnered v ▷ garner
garnering v ▷ garner
garners v ▷ garner
garnet n (pl -s) red semiprecious stone
garnets n ▷ garnet
garnish v (-es, -ing, -ed) decorate (food) ▶ n (pl -es) decoration for food
garnished v ▷ garnish
garnishes v, n ▷ garnish
garnishing v ▷ garnish
garotte n ▷ garrotte
garotted v ▷ garrotte

garottes n, v ▷ garrotte
garotting v ▷ garrotte
garret n (pl -s) attic in a house
   garrets n ▷ garret
garrison n (pl -s) troops stationed in a town or fort ▶ v (-s, -ing, -ed) station troops in
   garrisoned v ▷ garrison
   garrisoning v ▷ garrison
   garrisons n, v ▷ garrison
garrotte, garotte n (pl -s) Spanish method of execution by strangling ▶ v (-tes, -ting, -ted) kill by this method
   garrotted v ▷ garrotte
   garrottes n, v ▷ garrotte
   garrotting v ▷ garrotte
garrulous adj talkative
garter n (pl -s) band worn round the leg to hold up a sock or stocking
   garters n ▷ garter
gas n (pl gases, gasses) airlike substance that is not liquid or solid ▶ v (gases, gasses, gassing, gassed) poison or render unconscious with gas
gasbag n (pl -s) (Informal) person who talks too much
   gasbags n ▷ gasbag
gaseous adj of or like gas
   gases n, v ▷ gas
gash v (-es, -ing, -ed) make a long deep cut in ▶ n (pl -es) long deep cut
   gashed v ▷ gash
   gashes v, n ▷ gash
   gashing v ▷ gash
gasholder, gasometer [gas-**som**-it-er] (pl -s) n large tank for storing gas
   gasholders n ▷ gasholder
gasket n (pl -s) piece of rubber etc. placed between the faces of a metal joint to act as a seal
   gaskets n ▷ gasket
gasoline n (pl -s) (US) petrol
   gasolines n ▷ gasoline
   gasometers n ▷ gasholder
gasp v (-s, -ing, -ed) draw in breath sharply or with difficulty ▶ n (pl -s) convulsive intake of breath
   gasped v ▷ gasp
   gasping v ▷ gasp
   gasps v, n ▷ gasp
   gassed v ▷ gas
   gasses n, v ▷ gas
   gassier adj ▷ gassy
   gassiest adj ▷ gassy
   gassing v ▷ gas
gassy adj (-ssier, -ssiest) filled with gas

gastric adj of the stomach
gastritis n (pl -tes) inflammation of the stomach lining
   gastritises n ▷ gastritis
gastroenteritis n inflammation of the stomach and intestines
   gastronomies n ▷ gastronomy
gastronomy n (pl -mies) art of good eating > **gastronomic** adj
gastropod n (pl -s) mollusc, such as a snail, with a single flattened muscular foot
   gastropodans n ▷ gastropod
   gastropods n ▷ gastropod
gate n (pl -s) movable barrier, usu. hinged, in a wall or fence
gâteau [gat-toe] n (pl -teaux) [-toes] rich elaborate cake
   gâteaux n ▷ gâteau
gatecrash v (-es, -ing, -ed) enter (a party) uninvited
   gatecrashed v ▷ gatecrash
   gatecrashes v ▷ gatecrash
   gatecrashing v ▷ gatecrash
gatehouse n (pl -s) building at a gateway
   gatehouses n ▷ gatehouse
   gates n ▷ gate
gateway n (pl -s) entrance with a gate
   gateways n ▷ gateway
gather v (-s, -ing, -ed) assemble
   gathered v ▷ gather
gathering n (pl -s) assembly ▶ v ▷ gather
   gatherings n ▷ gathering
gathers pl n gathered folds in material ▶ v ▷ gather
gauche [gohsh] adj (-r, -st) socially awkward > **gaucheness** n (pl -es)
   gaucheness n ▷ gauche
   gauchenesses n ▷ gauche
   gaucher adj ▷ gauche
   gauchest adj ▷ gauche
gaucho [gow-choh] n (pl -hos) S American cowboy
   gauchos n ▷ gaucho
   gaudier adj ▷ gaudy
   gaudiest adj ▷ gaudy
   gaudily adv ▷ gaudy
   gaudiness n ▷ gaudy
   gaudinesses n ▷ gaudy
gaudy adj (-dier, -diest) vulgarly bright or colourful > **gaudily** adv > **gaudiness** n (pl -es)
gauge [gayj] v (-ges, -ging, -ged) estimate or judge ▶ n (pl -s) measuring instrument
   gauged v ▷ gauge
   gauges v, n ▷ gauge
   gauging v ▷ gauge

gaunt *adj* (-er, -est) lean and haggard
> **gauntness** *n* (*pl* -es)
  gaunter *adj* ▷ gaunt
  gauntest *adj* ▷ gaunt
gauntlet *n* (*pl* -s) heavy glove with a long cuff
  gauntlets *n* ▷ gauntlet
  gauntness *n* ▷ gaunt
  gauntnesses *n* ▷ gaunt
gauze *n* (*pl* -s) transparent loosely-woven
  fabric, often used for surgical dressings
  > **gauzy** *adj* (-zier, -ziest)
  gauzes *n* ▷ gauze
  gauzier *adj* ▷ gauze
  gauziest *adj* ▷ gauze
  gauzy *adj* ▷ gauze
gave *v* ▷ give
gavel [gav-el] *n* (*pl* -s) small hammer used by a
  judge, auctioneer, etc, to call for attention
  gavels *n* ▷ gavel
gavotte *n* (*pl* -s) old formal dance
  gavottes *n* ▷ gavotte
gawk *v* (-s, -ing, -ed) stare stupidly
  gawked *v* ▷ gawk
  gawkier *adj* ▷ gawky
  gawkiest *adj* ▷ gawky
  gawkiness *n* ▷ gawky
  gawkinesses *n* ▷ gawky
  gawking *v* ▷ gawk
  gawks *v* ▷ gawk
gawky *adj* (-kier, -kiest) clumsy or awkward
  > **gawkiness** *n* (*pl* -es)
gawp *v* (-s, -ing, -ed) (*Slang*) stare stupidly
  gawped *v* ▷ gawp
  gawping *v* ▷ gawp
  gawps *v* ▷ gawp
gay *adj* (-er, -est) homosexual ▶ *n* (*pl* -s)
  homosexual
  gayer *adj* ▷ gay
  gayest *adj* ▷ gay
gayness *n* (*pl* -es) homosexuality
  gaynesses *n* ▷ gayness
  gays *n* ▷ gay
gaze *v* (-zes, -zing, -zed) look fixedly ▶ *n* (*pl* -s)
  fixed look
gazebo [gaz-zee-boh] *n* (*pl* -bos, -boes)
  summerhouse with a good view
  gazeboes *n* ▷ gazebo
  gazebos *n* ▷ gazebo
  gazed *v* ▷ gaze
gazelle *n* (*pl* -s) small graceful antelope
  gazelles *n* ▷ gazelle
  gazes *v, n* ▷ gaze
gazette *n* (*pl* -s) official publication containing
  announcements
gazetteer *n* (part of) a book that lists and

describes places
  gazetteers *n* ▷ gazetteer
  gazettes *n* ▷ gazette
gazillion *n* (*pl* -s) (*Informal*) extremely large,
  unspecified amount
gazillionaire *n* (*Informal*) enormously rich
  person
  gazillionaires *n* ▷ gazillionaire
  gazillions *n* ▷ gazillion
  gazing *v* ▷ gaze
  gazings *n* ▷ gaze
gazump *v* (-s, -ing, -ed) (BRIT & AUST) raise the
  price of a property after verbally agreeing it
  with (a prospective buyer)
  gazumped *v* ▷ gazump
  gazumping *v* ▷ gazump
  gazumps *v* ▷ gazump
gear *n* (*pl* -s) set of toothed wheels connecting
  with another or with a rack to change the
  direction or speed of transmitted motion
  ▶ *v* (-s, -ing, -ed) prepare or organize for
  something
gearbox *n* (*pl* -es) case enclosing a set of gears
  in a motor vehicle
  gearboxes *n* ▷ gearbox
  geared *v* ▷ gear
  gearing *v* ▷ gear
  gears *n, v* ▷ gear
gecko *n* (*pl* -kos, -koes) small tropical lizard
  geckoes *n* ▷ gecko
  geckos *n* ▷ gecko
geebung [gee-bung] *n* (*pl* -s) Australian tree or
  shrub with an edible but tasteless fruit
  geebungs *n* ▷ geebung
geek *n* (*pl* -s) (*Informal*) boring, unattractive
  person > **geeky** *adj* (-kier, -kiest)
  geekier *adj* ▷ geek
  geekiest *adj* ▷ geek
  geeks *n* ▷ geek
  geeky *adj* ▷ geek
geelbek *n* (*pl* -s) (S AFR) edible marine fish
  geelbeks *n* ▷ geelbek
  geese *n* ▷ goose
geezer *n* (*pl* -s) (BRIT, AUST & NZ) (*Informal*) man
  geezers *n* ▷ geezer
geisha [gay-sha] *n* (*pl* -sha, -shas) (in Japan)
  professional female companion for men
  geishas *n* ▷ geisha
gel [jell] *n* (*pl* -s) jelly-like substance, esp. one
  used to secure a hairstyle ▶ *v* (-s, gelling,
  gelled) form a gel
gelatine [jel-at-teen], **gelatin** *n* (*pl* -s)
  substance made by boiling animal bones
  gelatines *n* ▷ gelatine
gelatinous [jel-at-in-uss] *adj* of or like jelly

geld v (gelds, gelding, gelded) castrate
gelded v ▷ geld
gelding n (pl -s) castrated horse ▶ v ▷ geld
geldings n ▷ gelding
gelds v ▷ geld
gelignite n (pl -s) type of dynamite used for blasting
gelignites v ▷ gelignite
gelled v ▷ gell
gelling v ▷ gell
gels n, v ▷ gel
gem n (pl -s) precious stone or jewel
gemfish (pl -fishes) n Australian food fish
gemfishes n ▷ gemfish
gems n ▷ gem
gen n (pl -s) (Informal) information
gendarme [zhohn-darm] n (pl -s) member of the French police force
gendarmes n ▷ gendarme
gender n (pl -s) state of being male or female
genders n ▷ gender
gene [jean] n (pl -s) part of a cell which determines inherited characteristics
genealogical adj ▷ genealogy
genealogies n ▷ genealogy
genealogist n ▷ genealogy
genealogists n ▷ genealogy
genealogy [jean-ee-al-a-gee] n (pl -gies) (study of) the history and descent of a family or families > **genealogical** adj > **genealogist** n (pl -s)
genera [jen-er-a] ▷ genus
general adj common or widespread ▶ n (pl -s) very senior army officer > **generally** adv
generalities n ▷ generality
generality n (pl -ties) general principle
generalization n ▷ generalize
generalizations n ▷ generalize
generalize v (-zes, -zing, -zed) draw general conclusions > **generalization** n (pl -s)
generalized v ▷ generalize
generalizes v ▷ generalize
generalizing v ▷ generalize
generalnesses n ▷ general
generally adv ▷ general
generals n ▷ general
generate v (-tes, -ting, -ted) produce or bring into being
generated v ▷ generate
generates v ▷ generate
generating v ▷ generate
generation n (pl -s) all the people born about the same time
generations n ▷ generation
generative adj capable of producing

generator n (pl -s) machine for converting mechanical energy into electrical energy
generators n ▷ generator
generic [jin-ner-ik] adj of a class, group, or genus > **generically** adv
generically adv ▷ generic
generosities n ▷ generous
generosity n ▷ generous
generous adj free in giving > **generously** adv > **generosity** n (pl -ties)
generously adv ▷ generous
genes n ▷ gene
geneses n ▷ genesis
genesis [jen-iss-iss] n (pl -ses) [-iss-eez] beginning or origin
genetic [jin-net-tik] adj of genes or genetics
geneticist n ▷ genetics
geneticists n ▷ genetics
genetics n study of heredity and variation in organisms > **geneticist** n (pl -s)
genial [jean-ee-al] adj cheerful and friendly > **genially** adv > **geniality** n (pl -ties)
genialities n ▷ genial
geniality n ▷ genial
genially adv ▷ genial
genie [jean-ee] n (pl -s) (in fairy tales) servant who appears by magic and grants wishes
genies n ▷ genie
genital adj of the sexual organs or reproduction
genitalia n ▷ genitals
genitals, genitalia [jen-it-ail-ya] pl n external sexual organs
genitive n (pl -s) grammatical case indicating possession or association
genitives n ▷ genitive
genius [jean-yuss] n (pl -es) (person with) exceptional ability in a particular field
geniuses n ▷ genius
genocide [jen-no-side] n (pl -s) murder of a race of people
genocides n ▷ genocide
genre [zhohn-ra] n (pl -s) style of literary, musical, or artistic work
genres n ▷ genre
gens n ▷ gen
gent n (pl -s) (BRIT, AUST & NZ) (Informal) gentleman
genteel adj (-er, -est) affectedly proper and polite > **genteelly** adv
genteeler adj ▷ genteel
genteelest adj ▷ genteel
genteelly adv ▷ genteel
gentian [jen-shun] n (pl -s) mountain plant with deep blue flowers

gentians n ▷ gentian
gentile adj, n (pl -s) non-Jewish (person)
gentiles n ▷ gentile
gentle adj (-r, -st) mild or kindly ▷ **gentleness** n (pl -es) ▷ **gently** adv
gentleman n (pl -men) polite well-bred man ▷ **gentlemanly** adj ▷ **gentlewoman** n fem (pl -women)
gentlemanly adj ▷ gentleman
gentlemen n ▷ gentleman
gentleness n ▷ gentle
gentlenesses n ▷ gentle
gentler adj ▷ gentle
gentlest adj ▷ gentle
gentlewoman n ▷ gentleman
gentlewomen n ▷ gentleman
gently adv ▷ gentle
gentries n ▷ gentry
gentries n ▷ gentry
gentrification n (pl -s) taking-over of a traditionally working-class area by middle-class incomers ▷ **gentrify** v (-fies, -fying, -fied)
gentrifications n ▷ gentrification
gentrified v ▷ gentrification
gentrifies v ▷ gentrification
gentrifying v ▷ gentrification
gentry n (pl -ies) people just below the nobility in social rank
gents n men's public toilet ▶ n ▷ gent
genuflect v (-s, -ing, -ed) bend the knee as a sign of reverence or deference ▷ **genuflection, genuflexion** n (pl -s)
genuflected v ▷ genuflect
genuflecting v ▷ genuflect
genuflection n ▷ genuflect
genuflections n ▷ genuflect
genuflects v ▷ genuflect
genuflexion n ▷ genuflect
genuflexions n ▷ genuflect
genuine adj not fake, authentic ▷ **genuinely** adv ▷ **genuineness** n (-es)
genuinely adv ▷ genuine
genuineness n ▷ genuine
genuinenesses n ▷ genuine
genus [jean-uss] n (pl genera) group into which a family of animals or plants is divided
geocentric adj having the earth as a centre
geographer n ▷ geography
geographers n ▷ geography
geographic adj ▷ geography
geographical adj ▷ geography
geographically adv ▷ geography
geographies n ▷ geography
geography n (pl -phies) study of the earth's

physical features, climate, population, etc. ▷ **geographer** n (pl -s) ▷ **geographical, geographic** adj ▷ **geographically** adv
geological adj ▷ geology
geologically adv ▷ geology
geologies n ▷ geology
geologist n ▷ geology
geologists n ▷ geology
geology n (pl -gies) study of the earth's origin, structure, and composition ▷ **geological** adj ▷ **geologically** adv ▷ **geologist** n (pl -s)
geometric adj ▷ geometry
geometrical adj ▷ geometry
geometrically adv ▷ geometry
geometries n ▷ geometry
geometry n (pl -tries) branch of mathematics dealing with points, lines, curves, and surfaces ▷ **geometric, geometrical** adj ▷ **geometrically** adv
geostationary adj (of a satellite) orbiting so as to remain over the same point of the earth's surface
geothermal adj of or using the heat in the earth's interior
geranium n (pl -s) cultivated plant with red, pink, or white flowers
geraniums n ▷ geranium
gerbil [jer-bill] n (pl -s) burrowing desert rodent of Asia and Africa
gerbils n ▷ gerbil
geriatric adj, n (pl -s) old (person)
geriatrics n (pl branch of medicine dealing with old age and its diseases ▶ n ▷ **geriatric**
germ n (pl -s) microbe, esp. one causing disease
germane adj relevant to
germanium n (pl -s) (CHEM) brittle grey element that is a semiconductor
germaniums n ▷ germanium
germinal adj of or in the earliest stage of development
germinate v (-tes, -ting, -ted) (cause to) sprout or begin to grow ▷ **germination** n (pl -s)
germinated v ▷ germinate
germinates v ▷ germinate
germinating v ▷ germinate
germination n ▷ germinate
germinations n ▷ germinate
germs n ▷ germ
gerrymandering n (pl -s) alteration of voting constituencies in order to give an unfair advantage to one party

gerrymanderings *n* ▷ gerrymandering

gerund [jer-rund] *n* (*pl* -s) noun formed from a verb

gerunds *n* ▷ gerund

gestation *n* (*pl* -s) (period of) carrying of young in the womb between conception and birth

gestations *n* ▷ gestation

gesticulate *v* (-tes, -ting, -ted) make expressive movements with the hands and arms > **gesticulation** *n* (*pl* -s)

gesticulated *v* ▷ gesticulate

gesticulates *v* ▷ gesticulate

gesticulating *v* ▷ gesticulate

gesticulation *n* ▷ gesticulate

gesticulations *n* ▷ gesticulate

gesture *n* (*pl* -s) movement to convey meaning ▶ *v* (-res, -ring, -red) gesticulate

gestured *v* ▷ gesture

gestures *n*, *v* ▷ gesture

gesturing *v* ▷ gesture

get *v* (-s, -tting, got) obtain or receive

getaway *adj*, *n* (*pl* -s) (used in) escape

getaways *n* ▷ getaway

gets *v* ▷ get

getting *v* ▷ get

> **gey** *adv*. Gey is a Scots word meaning **very**. If you have a G and a Y, it's highly likley that there will be an E you can use somewhere on the board. Gey scores 7 points.

geyser [geez-er] *n* (*pl* -s) spring that discharges steam and hot water (BRIT & S AFR)

geysers *n* ▷ geyser

ghastlier *adj* ▷ ghastly

ghastliest *adj* ▷ ghastly

ghastliness *n* ▷ ghastly

ghastlinesses *n* ▷ ghastly

ghastly *adj* (-lier, -liest) (*Informal*) unpleasant > **ghastliness** *n* (*pl* -es)

ghat *n* (*pl* -s) (in India) steps leading down to a river

ghats *n* ▷ ghat

ghee [gee] *n* (*pl* -s) (in Indian cookery) clarified butter

ghees *n* ▷ ghee

gherkin *n* (*pl* -s) small pickled cucumber

gherkins *n* ▷ gherkin

ghetto *n* (*pl* -ttos, -ttoes) slum area inhabited by a deprived minority

ghettoblaster *n* (*Informal*) large portable cassette recorder or CD player

ghettoblasters *n* ▷ ghettoblaster

ghettoes *n* ▷ ghetto

ghettos *n* ▷ ghetto

ghillie *n* (*pl* -s) ▷ gillie

ghillies *n* ▷ ghillie

ghost *n* (*pl* -s) disembodied spirit of a dead person ▶ *v* (-s, -ing, -ed) ghostwrite > **ghostly** *adj* (-ier, -iest)

ghosted *v* ▷ ghost

ghosting *v* ▷ ghost

ghostlier *adj* ▷ ghost

ghostliest *adj* ▷ ghost

ghostly *adj* ▷ ghost

ghosts *n*, *v* ▷ ghost

ghostwriter *n* (*pl* -s) writer of a book or article on behalf of another person who is credited as the author

ghostwriters *n* ▷ ghostwriter

ghoul [gool] *n* (*pl* -s) person with morbid interests > **ghoulish** *adj*

ghoulish *adj* ▷ ghoul

ghouls *n* ▷ ghoul

> **gi** *n*. A gi is a suit worn by judo or karate practitioners. Gi is one of only three two-letter words beginning with G, and so is worth knowing. Gi scores 3 points.

giant *n* (*pl* -s) mythical being of superhuman size ▶ *adj* huge

giants *n* ▷ giant

gibber[1] [jib-ber] *v* (-s, -ing, -ed) speak or utter rapidly and unintelligibly

gibber[2] [gib-ber] *n* (*pl* -s) (AUST) boulder

gibbered *v* ▷ gibber[1]

gibbering *v* ▷ gibber[1]

gibberish *n* rapid unintelligible talk

gibbers *n*, *v* ▷ gibber[1, 2]

gibbet [jib-bit] *n* (*pl* -s) gallows for displaying executed criminals

gibbets *n* ▷ gibbet

gibbon [gib-bon] *n* (*pl* -s) agile tree-dwelling ape of S Asia

gibbons *n* ▷ gibbon

gibbous *adj* (of the moon) more than half but less than fully illuminated

gibe [jibe] *v*, *n* (*pl* -s) ▷ jibe[1]

gibes *n* ▷ gibe

giblets [jib-lets] *pl n* gizzard, liver, heart, and neck of a fowl

gidday, g'day *interj* (AUST & NZ) expression of greeting

giddier *adj* ▷ giddy

giddiest *adj* ▷ giddy

giddily *adv* ▷ giddy

giddiness *n* ▷ giddy

giddinesses *n* ▷ giddy

giddy *adj* (-dier, -ddiest) having or causing a feeling of dizziness > **giddily** *adv* > **giddiness**

n (*pl* -es)

gift *n* (*pl* -s) present ▶ *v* (-s, -ing, -ed) make a present of

gifted *adj* talented ▶ *v* ▷ gift

  gifting *v* ▷ gift

  gifts *n*, *v* ▷ gift

gig¹ *n* (*pl* -s) single performance by pop or jazz musicians ▶ *v* (-s, -gging, -gged) play a gig or gigs

gig² (*pl* -s) *n* light two-wheeled horse-drawn carriage

gigantic *adj* enormous

  giganticnesses *n* ▷ gigantic

  gigged *v* ▷ gig¹

  gigging *v* ▷ gig¹

giggle *v* (-les, -ling, -led) laugh nervously or foolishly ▶ *n* (*pl* -s) such a laugh ▷ **giggly** *adj* (-lier, -liest)

  giggled *v* ▷ giggle

  giggles *v*, *n* ▷ giggle

  gigglier *adj* ▷ giggle

  giggliest *adj* ▷ giggle

  giggling *v* ▷ giggle

  giggly *adj* ▷ giggle

gigolo [jig-a-lo] *n* (*pl* -los) man paid by an older woman to be her escort or lover

  gigolos *n* ▷ gigolo

gigot *n* (*pl* -s) (CHIEFLY BRIT) leg of lamb or mutton

  gigots *n* ▷ gigot

  gigs *n*, *v* ▷ gig¹, ²

gild *v* (-s, -ing, -ed or -gilt) put a thin layer of gold on

  gilded *v* ▷ gild

  gilding *v* ▷ gild

  gilds *v* ▷ gild

gill [jill] *n* (*pl* -s) liquid measure of quarter of a pint, equal to 0.142 litres

gillie *n* (*pl* -s) (in Scotland) attendant for hunting or fishing

  gillies *n* ▷ gillie

gills [gillz] *pl n* breathing organs in fish and other water creatures ▶ *n* ▷ gill

gilt *adj* covered with a thin layer of gold ▶ *n* (*pl* -s) thin layer of gold used as decoration ▶ *v* ▷ gild

  gilts *n* ▷ gilt

gimbals *pl n* set of pivoted rings which allow nautical instruments to remain horizontal

gimcrack [jim-krak] *adj* showy but cheap

gimlet [gim-let] *n* (*pl* -s) small tool with a screwlike tip for boring holes in wood

  gimlets *n* ▷ gimlet

gimmick *n* (*pl* -s) something designed to attract attention or publicity ▷ **gimmickry** *n*

(*pl* -ries) ▷ **gimmicky** *adj* (-ier, -iest)

  gimmickier *adj* ▷ gimmick

  gimmickiest *adj* ▷ gimmick

  gimmickries *n* ▷ gimmick

  gimmickry *n* ▷ gimmick

  gimmicks *n* ▷ gimmick

  gimmicky *adj* ▷ gimmick

gin¹ *n* (*pl* -s) spirit flavoured with juniper berries

gin² *n* (*pl* -s) wire noose used to trap small animals

gin³ *n* (*pl* -s) (AUST) (Offens) Aboriginal woman

ginger *n* (*pl* -s) root of a tropical plant, used as a spice ▷ **gingery** *adj*

gingerbread *n* (*pl* -s) moist cake flavoured with ginger

  gingerbreads *n* ▷ gingerbread

gingerly *adv* cautiously

  gingers *n* ▷ ginger

  gingery *adj* ▷ ginger

gingham *n* (*pl* -s) cotton cloth, usu. checked or striped

  ginghams *n* ▷ gingham

gingivitis [jin-jiv-vite-iss] *n* (*pl* -tes) inflammation of the gums

  gingivitises *n* ▷ gingivitis

ginkgo [gink-go] *n* (*pl* -goes) ornamental Chinese tree

  ginkgoes *n* ▷ ginkgo

  gins *n* ▷ gin¹, ², ³

ginseng [jin-seng] *n* (*pl* -s) (root of) a plant believed to have tonic and energy-giving properties

  ginsengs *n* ▷ ginseng

  gipsies *n* ▷ gipsy

gipsy *n* (*pl* -sies) ▷ gypsy

giraffe *n* (*pl* -s) African ruminant mammal with a spotted yellow skin and long neck and legs

  giraffes *n* ▷ giraffe

gird *v* (-s, girding, girded or -girt) put a belt round

  girded *v* ▷ gird

girder *n* (*pl* -s) large metal beam

  girders *n* ▷ girder

  girding *v* ▷ gird

girdle¹ *n* (*pl* -s) woman's elastic corset ▶ *v* (-les, -ling, -led) surround or encircle

girdle² *n* (*pl* -s) (SCOT) griddle

  girdled *v* ▷ girdle¹

  girdles *v*, *n* ▷ girdle¹, ²

  girdling *v* ▷ girdle¹

  girds *v* ▷ gird

girl *n* (*pl* -s) female child (Informal) ▷ **girlhood** *n* ▷ **girlish** *adj*

girlfriend n (pl -s) girl or woman with whom a person is romantically or sexually involved
  girlfriends n ▷ girlfriend
girlhood n ▷ girl
  girlhoods n ▷ girl
girlie, girly adj (Informal) featuring photographs of naked or scantily clad women
  girlish adj ▷ girl
  girls n ▷ girl
  girly n ▷ girlie
giro [jire-oh] n (pl -os) (in some countries) system of transferring money within a post office or bank directly from one account to another
  giros n ▷ giro
  girt v ▷ gird
girth n (pl -s) measurement round something
  girths n ▷ girth
gist [jist] n (pl -s) substance or main point of a matter
  gists n ▷ gist
give v (-s, giving, gave, given) present (something) to another person ▶ n (pl -s) resilience or elasticity
giveaway n (pl -s) something that reveals hidden feelings or intentions ▶ adj very cheap or free
  giveaways n ▷ giveaway
  given v ▷ give
  gives v, n ▷ give
  giving v ▷ give
gizzard n (pl -s) part of a bird's stomach
  gizzards n ▷ gizzard

> **gju** n (**gjus**). A gju (also spelt **gu**) is a kind of violin from Shetland. This unusual term is a great little word, especially when there's not much space on the board. Gju scores 11 points.

glacé [glass-say] adj preserved in a thick sugary syrup
glacial adj of ice or glaciers
glaciated adj covered with or affected by glaciers > **glaciation** n (pl -s)
  glaciation n ▷ glaciated
  glaciations n ▷ glaciated
glacier n (pl -s) slow-moving mass of ice formed by accumulated snow
  glaciers n ▷ glacier
glad adj (-dder, -ddest) pleased and happy > **gladly** adv > **gladness** n (pl -es)
gladden v (-s, -ing, -ed) make glad
  gladdened v ▷ gladden
  gladdening v ▷ gladden

gladdens v ▷ gladden
gladder adj ▷ glad
gladdest adj ▷ glad
glade n (pl -s) open space in a forest
  glades n ▷ glade
gladiator n (pl -s) (in ancient Rome) man trained to fight in arenas to provide entertainment
  gladiators n ▷ gladiator
  gladioli n ▷ gladiolus
gladiolus n (pl -lus, -li, -luses) garden plant with sword-shaped leaves
  gladioluses n ▷ gladiolus
  gladly adv ▷ glad
  gladness n ▷ glad
  gladnesses n ▷ glad
gladwrap ® (AUST, NZ & S AFR) n (pl -wraps) thin polythene material for wrapping food ▶ v (-wraps, -wrapping, -wrapped) wrap in gladwrap
  gladwrapped v ▷ gladwrap
  gladwrapping v ▷ gladwrap
  gladwraps n, v ▷ gladwrap
  glamorize v ▷ glamorous
  glamorized v ▷ glamorous
  glamorizes v ▷ glamorous
  glamorizing v ▷ glamorous
glamorous adj alluring > **glamorize** v (-zes, -zing, -zed)
glamour n (pl -s) alluring charm or fascination
  glamours n ▷ glamour
glance v (-ces, -cing, -ced) look rapidly or briefly ▶ n (pl -s) brief look
  glanced v ▷ glance
  glances v, n ▷ glance
glancing adj hitting at an oblique angle ▶ v ▷ glance
gland n (pl -s) organ that produces and secretes substances in the body > **glandular** adj
  glands n ▷ gland
  glandular adj ▷ gland
glare v (-res, -ring, -red) stare angrily ▶ n (pl -s) angry stare
  glared v ▷ glare
  glares v, n ▷ glare
glaring adj conspicuous ▶ v ▷ glare > **glaringly** adv
  glaringly adv ▷ glaring
glass n (pl -es) hard brittle, usu. transparent substance consisting of metal silicates or similar compounds ▶ pl spectacles
  glasses n ▷ glass
glasshouse n greenhouse
  glasshouses n ▷ glasshouse

glassier *adj* ▷ glassy

glassiest *adj* ▷ glassy

glassy *adj* (-sier, -siest) like glass

glaucoma *n* (*pl* -s) eye disease

  glaucomas *n* ▷ glaucoma

glaze *v* (-zes, -zing, -zed) fit or cover with glass ▶ *n* (*pl* -s) transparent coating

  glazed *v* ▷ glaze

  glazes *v*, *n* ▷ glaze

glazier (*pl* -s) *n* person who fits windows with glass

  glaziers *n* ▷ glazier

  glazing *v* ▷ glaze

gleam *n* (*pl* -s) small beam or glow of light ▶ *v* (-s, -ing, -ed) emit a gleam > **gleaming** *adj*

  gleamed *v* ▷ gleam

  gleaming *v*, *adj* ▷ gleam

  gleams *n*, *v* ▷ gleam

glean *v* (-s, -ing, -ed) gather (facts etc.) bit by bit > **gleaner** *n* (*pl* -s)

  gleaned *v* ▷ glean

  gleaner *n* ▷ glean

  gleaners *n* ▷ glean

  gleaning *v* ▷ glean

  gleans *v* ▷ glean

glee *n* (*pl* -s) triumph and delight > **gleeful** *adj* > **gleefully** *adv*

  gleeful *adj* ▷ glee

  gleefully *adv* ▷ glee

  glees *n* ▷ glee

glen *n* (*pl* -s) deep narrow valley, esp. in Scotland

  glens *n* ▷ glen

glib *adj* (-bber, -bbest) fluent but insincere or superficial > **glibly** *adv* > **glibness** *n* (*pl* -es)

  glibber *adj* ▷ glib

  glibbest *adj* ▷ glib

  glibly *adv* ▷ glib

  glibness *n* ▷ glib

  glibnesses *n* ▷ glib

glide *v* (-des, -ding, -ded) move easily and smoothly ▶ *n* (*pl* -s) smooth easy movement

  glided *v* ▷ glide

glider *n* (AUST) flying phalanger

  gliders *n* ▷ glider

  glides *v* ▷ glide

gliding *n* sport of flying gliders ▶ *v* ▷ glide

glimmer *v* (-s, -ing, -ed) shine faintly, flicker ▶ *n* (*pl* -s) faint gleam

  glimmered *v* ▷ glimmer

  glimmering *v* ▷ glimmer

  glimmers *v*, *n* ▷ glimmer

glimpse *n* (*pl* -s) brief or incomplete view ▶ *v* (-ses, -sing, -sed) catch a glimpse of

  glimpsed *v* ▷ glimpse

  glimpses *n*, *v* ▷ glimpse

  glimpsing *v* ▷ glimpse

glint *v* (-s, -ing, -ed) gleam brightly ▶ *n* (*pl* -s) bright gleam

  glinted *v* ▷ glint

  glinting *v* ▷ glint

  glints *v*, *n* ▷ glint

glissando *n* (*pl* -dos) (MUSIC) slide between two notes in which all intermediate notes are played

  glissandos *n* ▷ glissando

glisten *v* (-s, -ing, -ed) gleam by reflecting light

  glistened *v* ▷ glisten

  glistening *v* ▷ glisten

  glistens *v* ▷ glisten

glitch *n* (*pl* -es) small problem that stops something from working properly

  glitches *n* ▷ glitch

glitter *v* (-s, -ing, -ed) shine with bright flashes ▶ *n* (*pl* -s) sparkle or brilliance

  glittered *v* ▷ glitter

  glittering *v* ▷ glitter

  glitters *v*, *n* ▷ glitter

gloaming *n* (*pl* -s) (SCOT) (*poetic*) twilight

  gloamings *n* ▷ gloaming

gloat *v* (-s, -ing, -ed) regard one's own good fortune or the misfortune of others with smug or malicious pleasure

  gloated *v* ▷ gloat

  gloating *v* ▷ gloat

  gloats *v* ▷ gloat

glob *n* (*pl* -s) rounded mass of thick fluid

global *adj* worldwide > **globally** *adv*

globalization *n* (*pl* -s) process by which a company, etc., expands to operate internationally

  globalizations *n* ▷ globalization

  globally *adv* ▷ global

globe *n* (*pl* globes) sphere with a map of the earth on it

  globes *n* ▷ globe

globetrotter *n* habitual worldwide traveller > **globetrotting** *adj*, *n* (*pl* -s)

  globetrotters *n* ▷ globetrotter

  globetrotting *n* ▷ globetrotter

  globetrottings *n* ▷ globetrotter

  globs *n* ▷ glob

globular *adj* ▷ globule

globule *n* (*pl* -s) small round drop > **globular** *adj*

  globules *n* ▷ globule

glockenspiel *n* (*pl* -s) percussion instrument consisting of small metal bars played with hammers

  glockenspiels *n* ▷ glockenspiel

gloom *n* (*pl* glooms) melancholy or depression

> gloomy adj (-mier, -miest) **> gloomily** adv
gloomier adj ▷ gloom
gloomiest adj ▷ gloom
gloomily adv ▷ gloom
glooms n ▷ gloom
gloomy adj ▷ gloom
gloried v ▷ glory
glories n, v ▷ glory
glorification n ▷ glorify
glorifications n ▷ glorify
glorified v ▷ glorify
glorifies v ▷ glorify
glorify v (-fies, -fying, -fied) make (something) seem more worthy than it is **> glorification** n (pl -s)
glorifying v ▷ glorify
glorious adj brilliantly beautiful **> gloriously** adv
gloriously adv ▷ glorious
glory n (pl -ries) praise or honour ▶ v (-ries, -rying, -ried) (foll. by **in**) triumph or exalt
glorying v ▷ glory
gloss¹ n (pl -es) surface shine or lustre
gloss² n (pl -es) explanatory comment added to the text of a book ▶ v (-es, -ing, -ed) add glosses to
glossaries n ▷ glossary
glossary n (pl -ries) list of special or technical words with definitions
glossed v ▷ gloss²
glosses n, v ▷ gloss¹, ²
glossier adj ▷ glossy
glossiest adj ▷ glossy
glossily adv ▷ glossy
glossiness n ▷ glossy
glossinesses n ▷ glossy
glossing v ▷ gloss²
glossy adj (-ssier, -ssiest) smooth and shiny **> glossily** adv **> glossiness** n (pl -es)
glottal adj of the glottis
glottides n ▷ glottis
glottis n (pl -tises, -tides) vocal cords and the space between them
glottises n ▷ glottis
glove n (pl -s) covering for the hand with individual sheaths for each finger and the thumb
gloved adj covered by a glove or gloves
gloves n ▷ glove
glow v (-s, -ing, -ed) emit light and heat without flames ▶ n (pl -s) glowing light
glowed v ▷ glow
glower [rhymes with **power**] v (-s, -ing, -ed) ▶ n (pl -s) scowl
glowered v ▷ glower

glowering v ▷ glower
glowers v, n ▷ glower
glowing v ▷ glow
glows v, n ▷ glow
glowworm n (pl -s) insect giving out a green light
glowworms n ▷ glowworm
gloxinia n (pl -s) tropical plant with large bell-shaped flowers
gloxinias n ▷ gloxinia
glucose n (pl -s) kind of sugar found in fruit
glucoses n ▷ glucose
glue n (pl glues) natural or synthetic sticky substance used as an adhesive ▶ v (glues, gluing or glueing, glued) fasten with glue **> gluey** adj
glued v ▷ glue
glueing v ▷ glue
glues n, v ▷ glue
gluey adj ▷ glue
gluier adj ▷ glue
gluiest adj ▷ glue
gluing v ▷ glue
glum adj (-mmer, -mmest) sullen or gloomy **> glumly** adv
glumly adv ▷ glum
glummer adj ▷ glum
glummest adj ▷ glum
glut n (pl -s) excessive supply ▶ v (-s, -tting, -tted) oversupply
gluten [gloo-ten] n (pl -s) protein found in cereal grain
glutens n ▷ gluten
glutinous [gloo-tin-uss] adj sticky or gluey
gluts n, v ▷ glut
glutted v ▷ glut
glutting v ▷ glut
glutton n (pl -s) greedy person **> gluttonous** adj **> gluttony** n (pl -nies)
gluttonies n ▷ glutton
gluttonous adj ▷ glutton
gluttons n ▷ glutton
gluttony n ▷ glutton
glycerine, glycerin n (pl -s) colourless sweet liquid used widely in chemistry and industry
glycerines n ▷ glycerine
glycerins n ▷ glycerine
glycerol [gliss-ser-ol] n (pl -s) ▷ glycerine
glycerols n ▷ glycerol
gnarled adj rough, twisted, and knobbly
gnash v (-es, -ing, -ed) grind (the teeth) together in anger or pain
gnashed v ▷ gnash
gnashes v ▷ gnash
gnashing v ▷ gnash

gnat n (pl -s) small biting two-winged fly
　gnats n ▷ gnat
gnaw v (-s, -ing, -ed or gnawn) bite or chew steadily
　gnawed v ▷ gnaw
　gnaws v ▷ gnaw
gneiss n (pl -es) coarse-grained metamorphic rock
　gneisses n ▷ gneiss
gnome n (pl -s) imaginary creature like a little old man
　gnomes n ▷ gnome
gnomic [no-mik] adj of pithy sayings
gnu [noo] n (pl -s) oxlike S African antelope
　gnus n ▷ gnu
go v (going, went, gone) move to or from a place (pl gos) ▶ n attempt
goad v (-s, -ing, -ed) provoke (someone) to take some kind of action, usu. in anger ▶ n (pl -s) spur or provocation
　goaded v ▷ goad
　goading v ▷ goad
　goads v, n ▷ goad
goal n (pl -s) (SPORT) posts through which the ball or puck has to be propelled to score
goalie n (pl -s) (Informal) goalkeeper
　goalies n ▷ goalie
goalkeeper n (pl -s) player whose task is to stop shots entering the goal
　goalkeepers n ▷ goalkeeper
goalpost (pl -s) one of the two posts marking the limit of a goal
　goalposts n ▷ goalpost
　goals n ▷ goal
goanna n (pl -s) large Australian lizard
　goannas n ▷ goanna
goat n (pl -s) sure-footed ruminant animal with horns
goatee n (pl -s) pointed tuftlike beard
　goatees n ▷ goatee
　goats n ▷ goat
gob n (pl -s) lump of a soft substance (BRIT, AUST & NZ)
gobbet n (pl -s) lump, esp. of food
　gobbets n ▷ gobbet
gobble[1] v (-les, -ling, -led) eat hastily and greedily
gobble[2] n (pl -s) rapid gurgling cry of the male turkey ▶ v (-les, -ling, -led) make this noise
　gobbled v ▷ gobble[1, 2]
　gobbledegooks n ▷ gobbledegook
　gobbledygooks n ▷ gobbledegook
　gobbles v, n ▷ gobble[1, 2]

gobbledegook, gobbledygook n (pl -s) unintelligible (official) language or jargon
gobbling v ▷ gobble[1, 2]
　gobies n ▷ goby
goblet n (pl -s) drinking cup without handles
　goblets n ▷ goblet
goblin n (pl -s) (in folklore) small malevolent creature
　goblins n ▷ goblin
　gobs n ▷ gob
goby n (pl -by, -bies) small spiny-finned fish
god n (pl -s) spirit or being worshipped as having supernatural power
　> godlike adj
godchild n (pl -s) child for whom a person stands as godparent
　> goddaughter n (pl -s)
　> godson n (pl -s)
　goddaughter n ▷ godchild
　goddaughters n ▷ godchild
goddess n fem (pl -es) female god
　goddesses n ▷ goddess
godetia n (pl -s) plant with showy flowers
　godetias n ▷ godetia
godfather n (pl -s) male godparent
　> godmother n (pl -s)
　godfathers n ▷ godfather
godforsaken adj desolate or dismal
　godlier adj ▷ godly
　godliest adj ▷ godly
　godlike adj ▷ god
　godliness n ▷ godly
　godlinesses n ▷ godly
godly adj (-lier, -liest) devout or pious
　> godliness n (pl -es)
　godmother n ▷ godfather
　godmothers n ▷ godfather
godparent n (pl -s) person who promises at a child's baptism to bring the child up as a Christian
　godparents n ▷ godparent
　gods n ▷ god
godsend n (pl -s) something unexpected but welcome
　godsends n ▷ godsend
　godson n ▷ godchild
　godsons n ▷ godchild
gogga n (pl -s) (S AFR) (Informal) any small insect
　goggas n ▷ gogga
goggle v (-les, -ling, -led) (of the eyes) bulge
　goggled v ▷ goggle
goggles pl n protective spectacles ▶ v ▷ goggle
　goggling v ▷ goggle
going n (pl -s) condition of the ground for

walking or riding over ▸ *adj* thriving ▸ *v* ▷ go
goings *n* ▷ going
goitre [goy-ter] *n* (*pl* -s) swelling of the thyroid gland in the neck
goitres *n* ▷ goitre
gold *n* (*pl* -s) yellow precious metal ▸ *adj* made of gold
goldcrest *n* (*pl* -s) small bird with a yellow crown
goldcrests *n* ▷ goldcrest
golden *adj* made of gold
goldfinch *n* (*pl* -es) kind of finch, the male of which has yellow-and-black wings
goldfinches *n* ▷ goldfinch
goldfish *n* (*pl* -es) orange fish kept in ponds or aquariums
goldfishes *n* ▷ goldfish
golds *n* ▷ gold
golf *n* (*pl* -s) outdoor game in which a ball is struck with clubs into a series of holes ▸ *v* (-s, -ing, -ed) play golf ▸ **golfer** *n* (*pl* -s)
golfed *v* ▷ golf
golfer *n* ▷ golf
golfers *n* ▷ golf
golfing *v* ▷ golf
golfs *n*, *v* ▷ golf
golliwog *n* (*pl* -s) soft black-faced doll
golliwogs *n* ▷ golliwog
gonad *n* (*pl* -s) organ producing reproductive cells, such as a testicle or ovary
gonads *n* ▷ gonad
gondola *n* (*pl* -s) long narrow boat used in Venice
gondolas *n* ▷ gondola
gondolier *n* (*pl* -s) person who propels a gondola
gondoliers *n* ▷ gondoliers
gone *v* ▷ go
goner *n* (*pl* -s) (*Informal*) person or thing beyond help or recovery
goners *n* ▷ goner
gong *n* (*pl* -s) rimmed metal disc that produces a note when struck
gongs *n* ▷ gong
gonorrhoea [gon-or-ree-a] *n* (*pl* -s) venereal disease with a discharge from the genitals
gonorrhoeas *n* ▷ gonorrhoea
good *adj* (better, best) giving pleasure ▸ *n* benefit ▸ *adj* merchandise > **goodness** *n* (*pl* -es)
goodbye *interj*, *n* (*pl* -s) expression used on parting
goodbyes *n* ▷ goodbye
goodies *n* ▷ goody
goodly *adj* considerable
goodness *n* ▷ good

goodnesses *n* ▷ good
goodwill *n* (*pl* -s) kindly feeling
goodwills *n* ▷ goodwill
goody *n* (*pl* -dies) (*Informal*) hero in a book or film
gooey *adj* (gooier, gooiest) (*Informal*) sticky and soft
goof (*Informal*) *n* (*pl* -s) mistake ▸ *v* (-s, -ing, -ed) make a mistake
goofed *v* ▷ goof
goofing *v* ▷ goof
goofs *n*, *v* ▷ goof
googlies *n* ▷ googly
googly *n* (*pl* -lies) (CRICKET) ball that spins unexpectedly from off to leg on the bounce
gooier *adj* ▷ gooey
gooiest *adj* ▷ gooey
goon *n* (*pl* -s) (*Informal*) stupid person
goons *n* ▷ goon
goose *n* (*pl* geese) web-footed bird like a large duck
gooseberries *n* ▷ gooseberry
gooseberry *n* (*pl* -ries) edible yellowy-green berry
gopher [go-fer] *n* (*pl* -s) American burrowing rodent
gophers *n* ▷ gopher
gore[1] *n* (*pl* -s) blood from a wound
gore[2] *v* (-res, -ring, -red) pierce with horns
gored *v* ▷ gore[2]
gores *n*, *v* ▷ gore[1, 2]
gorge *n* (*pl* -s) deep narrow valley ▸ *v* (-ges, -ging, -ged) eat greedily
gorged *v* ▷ gorge
gorgeous *adj* strikingly beautiful or attractive (*Informal*) > **gorgeously** *adv*
gorgeously *adv* ▷ gorgeous
gorges *n*, *v* ▷ gorge
gorging *v* ▷ gorge
gorgon *n* (*pl* -s) terrifying or repulsive woman
gorgons *n* ▷ gorgon
gorier *adj* ▷ gory
goriest *adj* ▷ gory
gorilla *n* (*pl* -s) largest of the apes, found in Africa
gorillas *n* ▷ gorilla
goring *v* ▷ gore[2]
gormless *adj* (*Informal*) stupid
gorse *n* (*pl* -s) prickly yellow-flowered shrub
gorses *n* ▷ gorse
gory *adj* (-rier, -riest) horrific or bloodthirsty
gos *n* ▷ go
goshawk *n* (*pl* -s) large hawk
goshawks *n* ▷ goshawk
gosling *n* (*pl* -s) young goose

goslings n ▷ gosling
gospel n (pl -s) any of the first four books of the New Testament
gospels n ▷ gospel
gossamer n (pl -s) very fine fabric
gossamers n ▷ gossamer
gossip n (pl -s) idle talk, esp. about other people ▶ v (-s, -ing, -ed) engage in gossip
> **gossipy** adj (-ier, -iest)
gossiped v ▷ gossip
gossipier adj ▷ gossip
gossipiest adj ▷ gossip
gossiping v ▷ gossip
gossips n, v ▷ gossip
gossipy adj ▷ gossip
got v ▷ get
gouache n (pl -s) (painting using) watercolours mixed with glue
gouaches n ▷ gouache
gouge [gowj] v (-ges, -ging, -ged) scoop or force out ▶ n (pl -s) hole or groove
gouged v ▷ gouge
gouges v, n ▷ gouge
gouging v ▷ gouge
goulash [goo-lash] n (pl -es) rich stew seasoned with paprika
goulashes n ▷ goulash
gourd [goord] n (pl -s) fleshy fruit of a climbing plant
gourds n ▷ gourd
gourmand [goor-mand] n (pl -s) person who is very keen on food and drink
gourmands n ▷ gourmand
gourmet [goor-may] n (pl -s) connoisseur of food and drink
gourmets n ▷ gourmet
gout [gowt] n (pl -s) disease causing inflammation of the joints
gouts n ▷ gout
govern v (-s, -ing, -ed) rule, direct, or control
> **governable** adj
governable adj ▷ govern
governance n (pl -s) governing
governances n ▷ governance
governed v ▷ govern
governess n (pl -es) woman teacher in a private household
governesses n ▷ governess
governing v ▷ govern
government n (pl -s) executive policy-making body of a state
> **governmental** adj
governmental adj ▷ government
governments n ▷ government
governor n (pl -s) official governing a province

or state
governors n ▷ governor
governs v ▷ govern
gown n (pl -s) woman's long formal dress
gowns n ▷ gown
goy n (pl -yim, -ys) (Slang) Jewish word for a non-Jew
goyim n ▷ goy
goys n ▷ goy

> **gox** n (**goxes**). Gox is a short word meaning gaseous oxygen. This unusual word can come in very useful, especially if you can use it to hit a bonus square. Gox scores 11 points.
> **goy** n (**goyim**) or (**goys**). Goy is a Yiddish word for someone who isn't Jewish. For a short word, this earns you a reasonable number of points, and the two plural forms can come in useful too. Goy scores 7 points.

grab v (-s, -bbing, -bbed) grasp suddenly, snatch ▶ n sudden snatch
grabbed v ▷ grab
grabbing v ▷ grab
grabs v ▷ grab
grace n (pl -s) beauty and elegance ▶ v (-ces, -cing, -ced) add grace to > **graceful** adj
> **gracefully** adv
> **graceless** adj
graced v ▷ grace
graceful adj ▷ grace
gracefully adv ▷ grace
graceless adj ▷ grace
graces n, v ▷ grace
gracing v ▷ grace
gracious adj kind and courteous > **graciously** adv
graciously adv ▷ gracious
gradation n (pl -s) (stage in) a series of degrees or steps
gradations n ▷ gradation
grade n (pl -s) place on a scale of quality, rank, or size ▶ v (-des, -ding, -ded) arrange in grades
graded v ▷ grade
grades n, v ▷ grade
gradient n (pl -s) (degree of) slope
gradients n ▷ gradient
grading v ▷ grade
gradual adj occurring, developing, or moving in small stages
> **gradually** adv
gradually adv ▷ gradual
graduate v (-tes, -ting, -ted) receive a degree or diploma ▶ n (pl -s) holder of a degree
> **graduation** n (pl -s)

graduated v ▷ graduate

graduates v, n ▷ graduate

graduating v ▷ graduate

graduation n ▷ graduate

graduations n ▷ graduate

graffiti [graf-**fee**-tee] pl n words or drawings scribbled or sprayed on walls etc.

graft¹ n (pl -s) surgical transplant of skin or tissue ▶ v (-s, -ing, -ed) transplant (living tissue) surgically

graft² (BRIT) (*Informal*) n hard work ▶ v work hard > **grafter** n (pl -s)

grafted v ▷ graft¹, ²

grafter n ▷ graft

grafters n ▷ graft

grafting v ▷ graft¹, ²

grafts n, v ▷ graft¹, ²

grain n (pl -s) seedlike fruit of a cereal plant > **grainy** adj (-ier, -iest)

grainier adj ▷ grain

grainiest adj ▷ grain

grains n ▷ grain

grainy adj ▷ grain

gram, gramme n (pl -s) metric unit of mass equal to one thousandth of a kilogram

grammar n (pl -s) branch of linguistics dealing with the form, function, and order of words > **grammarian** n (pl -s)

grammarian n ▷ grammar

grammarians n ▷ grammar

grammars n ▷ grammar

grammatical adj according to the rules of grammar > **grammatically** adv

grammatically adv ▷ grammatical

gramophone n (pl -s) old-fashioned type of record player

gramophones n ▷ gramophone

grampus n (pl -es) dolphin-like mammal

grampuses n ▷ grampus

grams n ▷ gram

gran n (pl -s) (BRIT, AUST & NZ) (*Informal*) grandmother

granaries n ▷ granary

granary n (pl -ries) storehouse for grain

grand adj large or impressive, imposing ▶ n (pl -s) (*Slang*) thousand pounds or dollars

grandchild n (pl -children) child of one's child

grandchildren n ▷ grandchild

granddaughter n (pl -s) female grandchild

granddaughters n ▷ granddaughter

grandee n (pl -s) person of high station

grandees n ▷ grandee

grandeur n (pl -s) magnificence

grandeurs n ▷ grandeur

grandfather n (pl -s) male grandparent

grandfathers n ▷ grandfather

grandiloquences n ▷ grandiloquent

grandiloquent adj using pompous language > **grandiloquence** n (pl -s)

grandiloquence n ▷ grandiloquent

grandiose adj imposing > **grandiosity** n (pl -ties)

grandiosities n ▷ grandiose

grandiosity n ▷ grandiose

grandmother n (pl -s) female grandparent

grandmothers n ▷ grandmother

grandparent n (pl -s) parent of one's parent

grandparents n ▷ grandparent

grands n ▷ grand

grandson n (pl -s) male grandchild

grandsons n ▷ grandson

grandstand n (pl -s) terraced block of seats giving the best view at a sports ground

grandstands n ▷ grandstand

grange n (pl -s) (BRIT) country house with farm buildings

granges n ▷ grange

granite [**gran**-nit] n (pl -s) very hard igneous rock often used in building

granites n ▷ granite

grannies n ▷ granny

granny, grannie n (pl -nies) (*Informal*) grandmother

grans n ▷ gran

grant v (-s, -ing, -ed) consent to fulfil (a request) ▶ n (pl -s) sum of money provided by a government for a specific purpose, such as education

granted v ▷ grant

granting v ▷ grant

grants v, n ▷ grant

granular adj of or like grains

granulated adj (of sugar) in the form of coarse grains

granule n (pl -s) small grain

granules n ▷ granule

grape n (pl -s) small juicy green or purple berry, eaten raw or used to produce wine, raisins, currants, or sultanas

grapefruit n (pl -s) large round yellow citrus fruit

grapefruits n ▷ grapefruit

grapes n ▷ grape

grapevine n (pl -s) grape-bearing vine

grapevines n ▷ grapevine

graph n (pl -s) drawing showing the relation of different numbers or quantities plotted against a set of axes

graphic adj vividly descriptive > **graphically** adv

graphically *adv* ▷ graphic

graphics *pl n* diagrams, graphs, etc., as used in a television programme or computer screen

graphite *n* (*pl* -s) soft black form of carbon, used in pencil leads

graphites *n* ▷ graphite

graphologies *n* ▷ graphology

graphologist *n* ▷ graphology

graphologists *n* ▷ graphology

graphology *n* (*pl* -gies) study of handwriting > **graphologist** *n* (*pl* -s)

graphs *n* ▷ graph

grapnel *n* (*pl* -s) device with several hooks, used to grasp or secure things

grapnels *n* ▷ grapnel

grapple *v* (-les, -ling, -led) try to cope with (something difficult)

grappled *v* ▷ grapple

grapples *v* ▷ grapple

grappling *v* ▷ grapple

grasp *v* (-s, -ing, -ed) grip something firmly ▶ *n* (*pl* -s) grip or clasp

grasped *v* ▷ grasp

grasping *adj* greedy or avaricious ▶ *v* ▷ grasp

grasps *v*, *n* ▷ grasp

grass *n* (*pl* -es) common type of plant with jointed stems and long narrow leaves, including cereals and bamboo ▶ *v* (-es, -ing, -ed) cover with grass > **grassy** *adj* (-ssier, -ssiest)

grassed *v* ▷ grass

grasses *n*, *v* ▷ grass

grasshopper *n* (*pl* -s) jumping insect with long hind legs

grasshoppers *n* ▷ grasshopper

grassier *adj* ▷ grass

grassiest *adj* ▷ grass

grassing *v* ▷ grass

grassroots *adj* of the ordinary members of a group, rather than its leaders

grassy *adj* ▷ grass

grate[1] *v* (-tes, -ting, -ted) rub into small bits on a rough surface > **grater** *n* (*pl* -s)

grate[2] *n* (*pl* -s) framework of metal bars for holding fuel in a fireplace

grated *v* ▷ grate[1]

grateful *adj* feeling or showing gratitude > **gratefully** *adv*

gratefully *adv* ▷ grateful

grater *n* ▷ grate[1]

graters *n* ▷ grate[1]

grates *v*, *n* ▷ grate[1, 2]

gratification *n* ▷ gratify

gratifications *n* ▷ gratify

gratified *v* ▷ gratify

gratifies *v* ▷ gratify

gratify *v* (-fies, -fying, -fied) satisfy or please > **gratification** *n* (*pl* -s)

gratifying *v* ▷ gratify

grating *n* (*pl* -s) framework of metal bars covering an opening ▶ *adj* harsh or rasping ▶ *v* ▷ grate[1]

gratings *n* ▷ grating

gratis *adv*, *adj* free, for nothing

gratitude *n* (*pl* -s) feeling of being thankful for a favour or gift

gratitudes *n* ▷ gratitude

gratuities *n* ▷ gratuity

gratuitous *adj* unjustified > **gratuitously** *adv*

gratuitously *adv* ▷ gratuitous

gratuity *n* (*pl* -ies) money given for services rendered, tip

grave[1] *n* (*pl* -s) hole for burying a corpse

grave[2] *adj* causing concern > **gravely** *adv*

grave[3] [rhymes with **halve**] *n* (*pl* -s) accent (`) over a vowel to indicate a special pronunciation

gravel *n* (*pl* -s) mixture of small stones and coarse sand

gravelled *adj* covered with gravel

gravellier *adj* ▷ gravelly

gravelliest *adj* ▷ gravelly

gravelly *adj* (-llier, -lliest) covered with gravel

gravels *n* ▷ gravel

gravely *adv* ▷ grave[2]

graven *adj* carved or engraved

graves *n* ▷ grave[1, 3]

gravestone *n* (*pl* -s) stone marking a grave

gravestones *n* ▷ gravestone

graveyard *n* (*pl* -s) cemetery

graveyards *n* ▷ graveyard

gravid [grav-id] *adj* (MED) pregnant

gravies *n* ▷ gravy

gravitate *v* (-tes, -ting, -ted) be influenced or drawn towards > **gravitation** *n* (*pl* -s) > **gravitational** *adj*

gravitated *v* ▷ gravitate

gravitates *v* ▷ gravitate

gravitating *v* ▷ gravitate

gravitation *n* ▷ gravitate

gravitational *adj* ▷ gravitate

gravitations *n* ▷ gravitate

gravities *n* ▷ gravity

gravity *n* (*pl* -ties) force of attraction of one object for another, esp. of objects to the earth

gravy *n* (*pl* -vies) juices from meat in cooking

grawing *v* ▷ gnaw

grawn *v* ▷ gnaw

gray *adj* (-er, -est) (CHIEFLY US) grey

grayer adj ▷ gray
grayest adj ▷ gray
grayling n (pl -s) fish of the salmon family
graylings n ▷ grayling
graze¹ v (-zes, -zing, -zed) feed on grass
graze² v (-zes, -zing, -zed) scratch or scrape the skin ▶ n (pl -s) slight scratch or scrape
grazed v ▷ graze¹, ²
grazes v, n ▷ graze¹, ²
grazing v ▷ graze¹, ²
grease n (pl -s) soft melted animal fat ▶ v (-ses, -sing, -sed) apply grease to
greased v ▷ grease
greasepaint n (pl -s) theatrical make-up
greasepaints n ▷ greasepaint
greases n, v ▷ grease
greasier adj ▷ greasy
greasiest adj ▷ greasy
greasiness n ▷ greasy
greasinesses n ▷ greasy
greasing v ▷ grease
greasy adj (-sier, -siest) covered with or containing grease ▷ **greasiness** n (pl -s)
great adj (-er, -est) large in size or number (Informal) ▷ **greatly** adv ▷ **greatness** n (pl -es)
greatcoat n (pl -s) heavy overcoat
greatcoats n ▷ greatcoat
greater adj ▷ great
greatest adj ▷ great
greatly adv ▷ great
greatness n ▷ great
greatnesses n ▷ great
greave n (pl -s) piece of armour for the shin
greaves n ▷ greave
grebe n (pl -s) diving water bird
grebes n ▷ grebe
greed n (pl -s) excessive desire for food, wealth, etc. ▷ **greedy** adj (-dier, -diest) ▷ **greedily** adv ▷ **greediness** n (pl -es)
greedier adj ▷ greed
greediest adj ▷ greed
greedily adv ▷ greed
greediness n ▷ greed
greedinesses n ▷ greed
greeds n ▷ greed
greedy adj ▷ greed
green adj (-er, -est) of a colour between blue and yellow ▶ n (pl -s) colour between blue and yellow ▶ pl green vegetables ▶ v (-s, -ing, -ed) make or become green ▷ **greenness** n (pl -es) ▷ **greenish, greeny** adj
greened v ▷ green
greener adj ▷ green
greeneries n ▷ greenery
greenery n (pl -ries) vegetation

greenest adj ▷ green
greenfinch n (pl -es) European finch with dull green plumage in the male
greenfinches n ▷ greenfinch
greenflies n ▷ greenfly
greenfly n (pl -flies) green aphid, a common garden pest
greengage n (pl -s) sweet green plum
greengages n ▷ greengage
greengrocer n (pl -s) (BRIT) shopkeeper selling vegetables and fruit
greengrocers n ▷ greengrocers
greenhorn n (pl -s) (CHIEFLY US) novice
greenhorns n ▷ greenhorn
greenhouse n (pl -s) glass building for rearing plants
greenhouses n ▷ greenhouse
greening v ▷ green
greenish adj ▷ green
greenness n ▷ green
greennesses n ▷ green
greens n, v ▷ green
greenshank (pl -s) n large European sandpiper
greenshanks n ▷ greenshanks
greenstone n (pl -s) (NZ) type of green jade used for Maori ornaments
greenstones n ▷ greenstone
greeny adj ▷ green
greet v (-s, -ing, -ed) meet with expressions of welcome ▷ **greeting** n (pl -s)
greeted v ▷ greet
greeting v, n ▷ greet
greetings n ▷ greet
greets v ▷ greet
gregarious adj fond of company
gremlin n (pl -s) imaginary being blamed for mechanical malfunctions
gremlins n ▷ gremlin
grenade n (pl -s) small bomb thrown by hand or fired from a rifle
grenades n ▷ grenade
grenadier n (pl -s) soldier of a regiment formerly trained to throw grenades
grenadiers n ▷ grenadier
grenadine [gren-a-**deen**] n (pl -s) syrup made from pomegranates
grenadines n ▷ grenadine
grevillea n (pl -s) any of various Australian evergreen trees and shrubs
grevilleas n ▷ grevillea
grew v ▷ grow
grey adj (-er, -est) of a colour between black and white ▶ n (pl -s) grey colour
greyer adj ▷ grey
greyest adj ▷ grey

greyhound *n* (*pl* -s) swift slender dog used in racing
  greyhounds *n* ▷ greyhound
greying *adj* (of hair) turning grey > **greyish** *adj*
  > **greyness** *n* (*pl* -es)
  greyish *adj* ▷ grey
  greyness *n* ▷ grey
  greynesses *n* ▷ grey
  greys *n* ▷ grey
grid *n* (*pl* -s) network of horizontal and vertical lines, bars, etc.
griddle *n* (*pl* -s) flat iron plate for cooking
  griddles *n* ▷ griddle
gridiron *n* (*pl* -s) frame of metal bars for grilling food
  gridirons *n* ▷ gridiron
gridlock *n* (*pl* -s) situation where traffic is not moving
  gridlocked *adj* ▷ gridlock
  gridlocks *n* ▷ gridlock
  grids *n* ▷ grid
grief *n* (*pl* -s) deep sadness
  griefs *n* ▷ grief
grievance (*pl* -s) *n* real or imaginary cause for complaint
  grievances *n* ▷ grievance
grieve *v* (-ves, -ving, -ved) (cause to) feel grief
  grieved *v* ▷ grieve
  grieves *v* ▷ grieve
  grieving *adj* ▷ grieve
grievous *adj* very severe or painful
griffin *n* (*pl* -s) mythical monster with an eagle's head and wings and a lion's body
  griffins *n* ▷ griffin
grill *n* (*pl* -s) device on a cooker that radiates heat downwards ▶ *v* (-s, -ing, -ed) cook under a grill
grille, grill *n* (*pl* -s) grating over an opening
  grilled *v* ▷ grill
  grilles *n* ▷ grille
grilling *n* (*pl* -s) relentless questioning ▶ *v* ▷ grill
  grillings *n* ▷ grilling
  grills¹ *n*, *v* ▷ grill
  grills² *n* ▷ grille
grilse [grilss] *n* (*pl* -s) salmon on its first return from the sea to fresh water
  grilses *n* ▷ grilse
grim *adj* (-mmer, -mmest) stern > **grimly** *adv*
  > **grimness** *n* (*pl* -es)
grimace *n* (*pl* -s) ugly or distorted facial expression of pain, disgust, etc. ▶ *v* (-ces, -cing, -ced) make a grimace
  grimaced *v* ▷ grimace
  grimaces *n*, *v* ▷ grimace

grimacing *v* ▷ grimace
grime *n* (*pl* -s) ingrained dirt ▶ *v* (-mes, -ming, -med) make very dirty > **grimy** *adj* (-mier, -miest)
  grimed *v* ▷ grime
  grimes *n*, *v* ▷ grime
  grimier *adj* ▷ grime
  grimiest *adj* ▷ grime
  griming *v* ▷ grime
  grimly *adv* ▷ grim
  grimmer *adj* ▷ grim
  grimmest *adj* ▷ grim
  grimness *n* ▷ grim
  grimnesses *n* ▷ grim
  grimy *adj* ▷ grime
grin *v* (-s, -nning, -nned) smile broadly, showing the teeth ▶ *n* (-s) broad smile
grind *v* (-s, -ing, ground) crush or rub to a powder ▶ *n* (*pl* -s) (*Informal*) hard work
  grinding *v* ▷ grind
  grinds *v*, *n* ▷ grind
grindstone *n* (*pl* -s) stone used for grinding
  grindstones *n* ▷ grindstone
  grinned *v* ▷ grin
  grinning *v* ▷ grin
  grins *v*, *n* ▷ grin
grip *n* (*pl* -s) firm hold or grasp (us) ▶ *v* (-s, -pping, -pped) grasp or hold tightly
  > **gripping** *adj*
gripe *v* (-pes, -ping, -ped) (*Informal*) complain persistently ▶ *n* (*pl* -s) (*Informal*) complaint
  griped *v* ▷ gripe
  gripes *v*, *n* ▷ gripe
  griping *v* ▷ gripe
  gripped *v* ▷ grip
  gripping *v*, *adj* ▷ grip
  grips *n*, *v* ▷ grip
  grislier *adj* ▷ grisly
  grisliest *adj* ▷ grisly
grisly *adj* (-lier, -liest) horrifying or ghastly
grist *n* (*pl* -s) grain for grinding
gristle *n* (*pl* -s) tough stringy animal tissue found in meat > **gristly** *adj* (-lier, -liest)
  gristles *n* ▷ gristle
  gristlier *adj* ▷ gristle
  gristliest *adj* ▷ gristle
  gristly *adj* ▷ gristle
  grists *n* ▷ grist
grit *n* (*pl* -s) rough particles of sand ▶ *pl* coarsely ground grain ▶ *v* (-s, -tting, -tted) spread grit on (an icy road etc.) > **gritty** *adj* (-ttier, -ttiest) > **grittiness** *n* (*pl* -es)
  grits *v* ▷ grit
  gritted *v* ▷ grit
  grittier *adj* ▷ grit

grittiest adj ▷ grit
grittiness n ▷ grit
grittinesses n ▷ grit
gritting v ▷ grit
gritty adj ▷ grit
grizzle v (-les, -ling, -led) (BRIT, AUST & NZ) (Informal) whine or complain
grizzled adj grey-haired ▶ v ▷ grizzle
 grizzles v ▷ grizzle
 grizzlies n ▷ grizzly
 grizzling v ▷ grizzle
grizzly n (pl -lies) large American bear
groan n (pl -s) deep sound of grief or pain ▶ v (-s, -ing, -ed) utter a groan
 groaned v ▷ groan
 groaning v ▷ groan
 groans n, v ▷ groan
groat n (pl -s) (HIST) fourpenny piece
 groats n ▷ groat
grocer n (pl -s) shopkeeper selling foodstuffs
 groceries n ▷ grocery
 grocers n ▷ grocer
grocery n (pl -ceries) business or premises of a grocer ▶ pl goods sold by a grocer
grog n (pl -s) (BRIT, AUST & NZ) spirit, usu. rum, and water
 groggier adj ▷ groggy
 groggiest adj ▷ groggy
groggy adj (-gier, -giest) (Informal) faint, shaky, or dizzy
 grogs n ▷ grog
groin n (pl -s) place where the legs join the abdomen
 groins n ▷ groin
grommet n (pl -s) ring or eyelet
 grommets n ▷ grommet
groom n (pl -s) person who looks after horses ▶ v (-s, -ing, -ed) make or keep one's clothes and appearance neat and tidy
 groomed v ▷ groom
 grooming v ▷ groom
 grooms n, v ▷ groom
groove n (pl -s) long narrow channel in a surface
 grooves n ▷ groove
grope v (-pes, -ping, -ped) feel about or search uncertainly > **groping** n (pl -s)
 groped v ▷ grope
 gropes v ▷ grope
 groping v, n ▷ grope
 gropings n ▷ grope
gross adj flagrant ▶ n (pl -es) twelve dozen ▶ v (-es, -ing, -ed) make as total revenue before deductions > **grossly** adv > **grossness** n (pl -es)
 grossed v ▷ gross

 grosses n, v ▷ gross
 grossing v ▷ gross
 grossly adv ▷ gross
 grossness n ▷ gross
 grossnesses n ▷ gross
grotesque [grow-**tesk**] adj (-quer, -quest) strangely distorted ▶ n (pl -s) grotesque person or thing > **grotesquely** adv
 grotesquely adv ▷ grotesque
 grotesquer adj ▷ grotesque
 grotesques n ▷ grotesque
 grotesquest adj ▷ grotesque
 grottier adj ▷ grotty
 grottiest adj ▷ grotty
grotto n (pl -ttoes, -ttos) small picturesque cave
 grottoes n ▷ grotto
 grottos n ▷ grotto
grotty adj (-ttier, -ttiest) (Informal) nasty or in bad condition
grouch (Informal) v (-es, -ing, -ed) grumble or complain ▶ n (pl -es) person who is always complaining > **grouchy** adj (-chier, -chiest)
 grouched v ▷ grouch
 grouches v, n ▷ grouch
 grouchier adj ▷ grouch
 grouchiest adj ▷ grouch
 grouching v ▷ grouch
 grouchy adj ▷ grouch
ground¹ n (pl -s) surface of the earth ▶ pl enclosed land round a house ▶ v (-s, -ing, -ed) base or establish
ground² v ▷ grind
groundbreaking adj innovative
 grounded v ▷ ground¹
grounding n (pl -s) basic knowledge of a subject ▶ v ▷ ground¹
 groundings n ▷ grounding
groundless adj without reason
groundnut n (pl -s) peanut
 groundnuts n ▷ groundnut
 grounds n, v ▷ ground¹
groundsheet n (pl -s) waterproof sheet put on the ground under a tent
 groundsheets n ▷ groundsheet
groundsman n (pl -men) person employed to maintain a sports ground or park
 groundsmen n ▷ groundsman
groundswell n (pl -s) rapidly developing general feeling or opinion
 groundswells n ▷ groundswell
groundwork n (pl -s) preliminary work
 groundworks n ▷ groundwork
group n (pl -s) number of people or things regarded as a unit ▶ v (-s, -ing, -ed) place or

form into a group
grouped v ▷ group
grouping v ▷ group
groups n, v ▷ group
grouse[1] n (pl -s) stocky game bird
grouse[2] v (-ses, -sing, -sed) grumble or complain ▶ n (pl -s) complaint
groused v ▷ grouse[2]
grouses n, v ▷ grouse[1, 2]
grousing v ▷ grouse[2]
grout n (pl -s) thin mortar ▶ v (-s, -ing, -ed) fill up with grout
grouted v ▷ grout
grouting v ▷ grout
grouts n, v ▷ grout
grove n (pl -s) small group of trees
grovel [grov-el] v (-s, -elling, -elled) behave humbly in order to win a superior's favour
grovelled v ▷ grovel
grovelling v ▷ grovel
grovels v ▷ grovel
groves n ▷ grove
grow v (-s, growing, grew, grown) develop physically
growing v ▷ grow
growl v (-s, -ing, -ed) make a low rumbling sound ▶ n (pl -s) growling sound
growled v ▷ growl
growling v ▷ growl
growls v, n ▷ growl
grown v ▷ grow
grownup adj, n (pl -s) adult
grownups n ▷ grownup
grows v ▷ grow
growth n (pl -s) growing
growths n ▷ growth
groyne n (pl -s) wall built out from the shore to control erosion
groynes n ▷ groyne
grub n (pl -s) legless insect larva ▶ v (-s, -bbing, -bbed) search carefully for something by digging or by moving things about
grubbed v ▷ grub
grubbier adj ▷ grubby
grubbiest adj ▷ grubby
grubbiness n ▷ grubby
grubbinesses n ▷ grubby
grubbing v ▷ grub
grubby adj (-bbier, -bbiest) dirty > **grubbiness** n (pl -es)
grubs n, v ▷ grub
grudge v (-ges, -ging, -ged) be unwilling to give or allow ▶ n (pl -s) resentment
grudged v ▷ grudge
grudges v, n ▷ grudge

grudging v ▷ grudge
gruel n (pl -s) thin porridge
gruelling adj exhausting or severe
gruels n ▷ gruel
gruesome adj (-er, -est) causing horror and disgust
gruesomer adj ▷ gruesome
gruesomest adj ▷ gruesome
gruff adj (-er, -est) rough or surly in manner or voice > **gruffly** adv > **gruffness** n (pl -es)
gruffer adj ▷ gruff
gruffest adj ▷ gruff
gruffly adv ▷ gruff
gruffness n ▷ gruff
gruffnesses n ▷ gruff
grumble v (-les, -ling, -led) complain ▶ n (pl -s) complaint > **grumbler** n (pl -s) > **grumbling** adj, n (pl -s)
grumbled v ▷ grumble
grumbler n ▷ grumble
grumblers n ▷ grumble
grumbles v, n ▷ grumble
grumbling v, n ▷ grumble
grumblings n ▷ grumble
grumpier adj ▷ grumpy
grumpiest adj ▷ grumpy
grumpily adv ▷ grumpy
grumpiness n ▷ grumpy
grumpinesses n ▷ grumpy
grumpy adj (-pier, -piest) bad-tempered > **grumpily** adv > **grumpiness** n (pl -es)
grunge n (pl -s) style of rock music with a fuzzy guitar sound
grunges n ▷ grunge
grunt v (-s, -ing, -ed) make a low short gruff sound, like a pig ▶ n (pl -s) pig's sound
grunted v ▷ grunt
grunting v ▷ grunt
grunts v, n ▷ grunt
gryphon n (pl -s) ▷ griffin
gryphons n ▷ gryphon

> **gu** n (**gus**). A gu (also spelt **gju**) is a kind of violin from Shetland. This is one of only three two-letter words beginning with G, and so is a good one to remember. Gu scores 3 points.

guano [gwah-no] n (pl -nos) dried sea-bird manure, used as fertilizer
guanos n ▷ guano
guarantee n (pl -s) formal assurance, esp. in writing, that a product will meet certain standards ▶ v (-s, -teeing, -teed) give a guarantee
guaranteed v ▷ guarantee
guaranteeing v ▷ guarantee

guarantees n, v ▷ guarantee
guarantor n (pl -s) person who gives or is bound by a guarantee
guarantors n ▷ guarantor
guard v (-s, -ing, -ed) watch over to protect or to prevent escape ▶ n (pl -s) person or group that guards ▶ (**G-**) pl regiment with ceremonial duties
guarded adj cautious or noncommittal ▶ v ▷ guard > **guardedly** adv
guardedly adv ▷ guarded
guardian n (pl -s) keeper or protector > **guardianship** n (pl -s)
guardians n ▷ guardian
guardianship n ▷ guardian
guardianships n ▷ guardian
guarding v ▷ guard
guards v, n ▷ guard
guardsman n (pl -s) member of the Guards
guardsmen n ▷ guardsman
guava [gwah-va] n (pl -s) yellow-skinned tropical American fruit
guavas n ▷ guava
gudgeon n (pl -s) small freshwater fish
gudgeons n ▷ gudgeon
guerillas n ▷ guerrilla
guerrilla, guerilla n (pl -s) member of an unofficial armed force fighting regular forces
guerrillas n ▷ guerrilla
guess v (-es, -ing, -ed) estimate or draw a conclusion without proper knowledge ▶ n (pl -es) estimate or conclusion reached by guessing
guessed v ▷ guess
guesses v, n ▷ guess
guessing v ▷ guess
guesswork n (pl -s) process or results of guessing
guessworks n ▷ guesswork
guest n (pl -s) person entertained at another's house or at another's expense ▶ v (-s, -ing, -ed) appear as a visiting player or performer
guested v ▷ guest
guesthouse n (pl -s) boarding house
guesthouses n ▷ guesthouse
guesting v ▷ guest
guests n, v ▷ guest
guff n (pl -s) (BRIT, AUST & NZ) (Slang) nonsense
guffaw n (pl -s) crude noisy laugh ▶ v (-s, -ing, -ed) laugh in this way
guffawed v ▷ guffaw
guffawing v ▷ guffaw
guffaws n, v ▷ guffaw
guffs n ▷ guff
guidance n (pl -s) leadership, instruction, or advice

guidances n ▷ guidance
guide n (pl -s) person who conducts tour expeditions ▶ v (-s, -ing, -ed) act as a guide for
guided v ▷ guide
guideline n set principle for doing something
guidelines n ▷ guideline
guides n, v ▷ guide
guiding v ▷ guide
guild n (pl -s) organization or club
guilder n (pl -s) former monetary unit of the Netherlands
guilders n ▷ guilder
guilds n ▷ guild
guile [gile] n (pl -s) cunning or deceit > **guileful** adj > **guileless** adj
guileful adj ▷ guile
guileless adj ▷ guile
guiles n ▷ guile
guillemot [gil-lee-mot] n (pl -s) black-and-white diving sea bird of N hemisphere
guillemots n ▷ guillemot
guillotine n (pl -s) machine for beheading people ▶ v (-s, -ing, -ed) behead by guillotine
guillotined v ▷ guillotine
guillotines n, v ▷ guillotine
guillotining v ▷ guillotine
guilt n (pl -s) fact or state of having done wrong
guiltier adj ▷ guilty
guiltiest adj ▷ guilty
guiltily adv ▷ guilty
guiltless adj innocent
guilts n ▷ guilt
guilty adj (-tier, -tiest) responsible for an offence or misdeed > **guiltily** adv
guinea n (pl -s) former British monetary unit worth 21 shillings (1.05 pounds)
guineas n ▷ guinea
guise [rhymes with size] n (pl -s) false appearance
guises n ▷ guise
guitar n (pl -s) stringed instrument with a flat back and a long neck, played by plucking or strumming > **guitarist** n
guitarist n ▷ guitar
guitarists n ▷ guitar
guitars n ▷ guitar
gulch n (pl -es) (US) deep narrow valley
gulches n ▷ gulch
gulf n (pl -s) large deep bay
gulfs n ▷ gulf
gull n (pl -s) long-winged sea bird
gullet n (pl -s) muscular tube through which food passes from the mouth to the stomach
gullets n ▷ gullet

gullibilities n ▷ gullible
gullibility n ▷ gullible
gullible adj easily tricked > **gullibility** n (pl -ties)
gullies n ▷ gully
gulls n ▷ gull
gully n (pl -llies) channel cut by running water
gulp v (-s, -ing, -ed) swallow hastily ▶ n (pl -s) gulping
gulped v ▷ gulp
gulping v ▷ gulp
gulps v, n ▷ gulp
gum¹ n (pl -s) firm flesh in which the teeth are set
gum² n (pl -s) sticky substance obtained from certain trees ▶ v (-s, -mming, -mmed) stick with gum
gumboot n (pl -s) (CHIEFLY BRIT) Wellington boot
gumboots n ▷ gumboot
gumdrop n (pl -s) hard jelly-like sweet
gumdrops n ▷ gumdrop
gummed v ▷ gum²
gummier adj ▷ gummy¹, ²
gummiest adj ▷ gummy¹, ²
gumming v ▷ gum²
gummy¹ adj (-mmier, -mmiest) toothless
gummy² adj (-mmier, -mmiest) sticky
gumption n (pl -s) (Informal) resourcefulness
gumptions n ▷ gumption
gums n ▷ gum¹, ²
gun n (pl -s) weapon with a metal tube from which missiles are fired by explosion ▶ v (-s, -nning, -nned) cause (an engine) to run at high speed
gunboat n (pl -s) small warship
gunboats n ▷ gunboat
gunge n (pl -s) (Informal) sticky unpleasant substance > **gungy** adj (-gier, -giest)
gunges n ▷ gunge
gungier adj ▷ gung
gungiest adj ▷ gung
gungy adj ▷ gung
gunman n (pl -men) armed criminal
gunmen n ▷ gunman
gunmetal n (pl -s) alloy of copper, tin, and zinc ▶ adj dark grey
gunmetals n ▷ gunmetal
gunned v ▷ gun
gunnel n ▷ gunwale
gunnels n ▷ gunwale
gunner n (pl -s) artillery soldier
gunneries n ▷ gunnery
gunners n ▷ gunner
gunnery n (pl -ries) use or science of large guns
gunnies n ▷ gunny

gunning v ▷ gun
gunny n (pl -ies) strong coarse fabric used for sacks
gunpowder n (pl -s) explosive mixture of potassium nitrate, sulphur, and charcoal
gunpowders n ▷ gunpowder
gunrunner n ▷ gunrunning
gunrunners n ▷ gunrunning
gunrunning n (pl -s) smuggling of guns and ammunition > **gunrunner** n (pl -s)
gunrunnings n ▷ gunrunning
guns n, v ▷ gun
gunshot n (pl -s) shot or range of a gun
gunshots n ▷ gunshot
gunwale, gunnel [gun-nel] n (pl -s) top of a ship's side
gunwales n ▷ gunwale
gunyah n (pl -s) (AUST) hut or shelter in the bush
gunyahs n ▷ gunyah
guppies n ▷ guppy
guppy n (pl -ppies) small colourful aquarium fish
gurgle v (-les, -ling, -led) ▶ n (pl -s) (make) a bubbling noise
gurgled v ▷ gurgle
gurgles v, n ▷ gurgle
gurgling v ▷ gurgle
guru n (pl -s) Hindu or Sikh religious teacher or leader
gurus n ▷ guru
gush v (-es, -ing, -ed) flow out suddenly and profusely ▶ n (pl -es) sudden copious flow
gushed v ▷ gush
gusher n (pl -s) spurting oil well
gushers n ▷ gusher
gushes v, n ▷ gush
gushing v ▷ gush
gusset n (pl -s) piece of material sewn into a garment to strengthen it
gussets n ▷ gusset
gust n (pl -s) sudden blast of wind ▶ v (-s, -ing, -ed) blow in gusts > **gusty** adj (-tier, -tiest)
gusted v ▷ gust
gustier adj ▷ gust
gustiest adj ▷ gust
gusting v ▷ gust
gusto n (pl -tos) enjoyment or zest
gustos n ▷ gusto
gusts n, v ▷ gust
gusty adj ▷ gust
gut n (pl -s) intestine (Informal) ▷ catgut ▶ pl internal organs ▶ v (-s, -tting, -tted) remove the guts from ▶ adj basic or instinctive
guts n ▷ gut
gutsier adj ▷ gutsy

gutsiest adj ▷ gutsy

gutsy adj (-sier, -siest) (Informal) courageous

gutted adj (BRIT, AUST & NZ) (Informal) disappointed and upset ▶ v ▷ gut

gutter n (pl -s) shallow channel for carrying away water from a roof or roadside ▶ v (-s, -ing, -ed) (of a candle) burn unsteadily, with wax running down the sides

guttered v ▷ gutter

guttering n material for gutters ▶ v ▷ gutter

gutters n, v ▷ gutter

guttersnipe n (pl -s) (BRIT) neglected slum child

guttersnipes n ▷ guttersnipe

gutting v ▷ gut

guttural adj (of a sound) produced at the back of the throat

gutturalnesses n ▷ guttural

guy¹ n (pl -s) (Informal) man or boy

guy² n (pl -s) rope or chain to steady or secure something

guys n ▷ guy¹, ²

guzzle v (-les, -ling, -led) eat or drink greedily

guzzled v ▷ guzzle

guzzles v ▷ guzzle

guzzling v ▷ guzzle

gybe [jibe] v (-bes, -bing, -bed) (of a fore-and-aft sail) swing suddenly from one side to the other

gybed v ▷ gybe

gybes v ▷ gybe

gybing v ▷ gybe

gym n (pl -s) gymnasium

gymkhana [jim-kah-na] n (pl -s) horse-riding competition

gymkhanas n ▷ gymkhana

gymnasium n (pl -s) large room with equipment for physical training

gymnasiums n ▷ gymnasium

gymnast n (pl -s) expert in gymnastics

gymnastic n ▷ gymnastics

gymnastics pl n exercises to develop strength and agility > **gymnastic** adj

gymnasts n ▷ gymnast

gyms n ▷ gym

gynaecological adj ▷ gynaecology

gynaecologies n ▷ gynaecology

gynaecologist n ▷ gynaecology

gynaecologists n ▷ gynaecology

gynaecology [guy-nee-**kol**-la-jee] n (pl -ies) branch of medicine dealing with diseases and conditions specific to women > **gynaecological** adj > **gynaecologist** n (pl -s)

> **gyp** n (gyps, gypping, gyped). Gyp is a slang word meaning to cheat or swindle. This word and its inflections can be very useful when there is a word ending in Y on the board. Gyp scores 9 points.

gypsies n ▷ gypsy

gypsophila n (pl -s) garden plant with small white flowers

gypsophilas n ▷ gypsophila

gypsum n (pl -s) chalklike mineral used to make plaster of Paris

gypsums n ▷ gypsy

gypsy n (pl -sies) member of a travelling people found throughout Europe

gypsyhood n ▷ gypsy

gyrate [jire-**rate**] v (-tes, -ting, -ted) rotate or spiral about a point or axis > **gyration** n (pl -s)

gyrated v ▷ gyrate

gyrates v ▷ gyrate

gyrating v ▷ gyrate

gyration n ▷ gyrate

gyrations n ▷ gyrate

gyratory adj gyrating

gyrocompass n (pl -es) compass using a gyroscope

gyrocompasses n ▷ gyrocompass

gyroscope [jire-oh-skohp] n (pl -s) disc rotating on an axis that can turn in any direction, so the disc maintains the same position regardless of the movement of the surrounding structure > **gyroscopic** adj

gyroscopes n ▷ gyroscope

gyroscopic adj ▷ gyroscope

Hh

H forms a two-letter word in front of every vowel except U (and you can make **uh** with U), making it a versatile tile when you want to form words in more than one direction. As H is worth 4 points on its own, you can earn some very high scores by doing this: even **ha**, **he**, **hi** and **ho** will give 5 points each. There are lots of good short words beginning with H, like **haw**, **hew**, **how**, **hay**, **hey** and **hoy** (9 each).

ha *interj*. Ha is a sound people make to express triumph or surprise. This gives a reasonable score for a two-letter word, and is a good one to form when making a longer word in another direction at the same time. Ha scores 5 points.

haberdasher *n (pl -s)* (BRIT, AUST & NZ) dealer in small articles used for sewing > **haberdashery** *n (pl -ries)*
haberdasheries *n* ▷ haberdasher
haberdashers *n* ▷ haberdasher
haberdashery *n (pl -s)*
habit *n (pl -s)* established way of behaving
habitable *adj* fit to be lived in
habitat *n (pl -s)* natural home of an animal or plant
habitation *n (pl -s)* (occupation of) a dwelling place
habitations *n* ▷ habitation
habitats *n* ▷ habitat
habits *n* ▷ habit
habitual *adj* done regularly and repeatedly > **habitually** *adv*
habitually *adv* ▷ habitual
habituate *v (-tes, -ting, -ted)* accustom > **habituation** *n (pl -s)*
habituated *v* ▷ habituate
habituates *v* ▷ habituate
habituating *v* ▷ habituate
habituation *n* ▷ habituate
habituations *n* ▷ habituate
habitué *n (pl -s)* frequent visitor to a place
habitués *n* ▷ habitué
hacienda *n (pl -s)* ranch or large estate in Latin America
haciendas *n* ▷ hacienda
hack¹ *v (-s, -ing, -ed)* cut or chop violently (BRIT

& NZ) (*Informal*)
hack² *n (pl -s)* (inferior) writer or journalist
hacked *v* ▷ hack¹
hacker *n (pl -s)* (*Slang*) computer enthusiast, esp. one who breaks into the computer system of a company or government
hackers *n* ▷ hacker
hacking *v* ▷ hack¹
hackles *pl n* hairs on the neck and back of an animal
hackney *n (pl -s)* (BRIT) taxi
hackneyed *adj* (of a word or phrase) unoriginal and overused
hackneys *n* ▷ hackney
hacks *v* ▷ hack¹ ▶ *n* ▷ hack²
hacksaw *n (pl -s)* small saw for cutting metal
hacksaws *n* ▷ hacksaw
had *v* ▷ have
haddock *n (pl -s)* edible sea fish of N Atlantic
haddocks *n* ▷ haddock
hadj *n (pl -es)* ▷ hajj
hadjes *n* ▷ hadj
haematologies *n* ▷ haematology
haematology *n (pl -gies)* study of blood and its diseases
haemoglobin [hee-moh-**globe**-in] *n (pl -s)* protein found in red blood cells which carries oxygen
haemoglobins *n* ▷ haemoglobin
haemophilia [hee-moh-**fill**-lee-a] *n (pl -s)* hereditary illness in which the blood does not clot > **haemophiliac** *n (pl -s)*
haemophiliac *n* ▷ haemophilia
haemophiliacs *n* ▷ haemophilia
haemophilias *n* ▷ haemophilia
haemorrhage [**hem**-or-ij] *n (pl -ges)* heavy bleeding ▶ *v (-ges, -ging, -ged)* bleed heavily
haemorrhaged *v* ▷ haemorrhage
haemorrhages *n, v* ▷ haemorrhage

haemorrhaging v ▷ haemorrhage

haemorrhoids [hem-or-oydz] pl n swollen veins in the anus (also **piles**)

hafnium n (pl -s) (CHEM) metallic element found in zirconium ores

hafniums n ▷ hafnium

haft n (pl -s) handle of an axe, knife, or dagger

hafts n ▷ haft

hag n (pl -s) ugly old woman

haggard adj looking tired and ill

haggis n (pl -es) Scottish dish made from sheep's offal, oatmeal, suet, and seasonings, boiled in a bag made from the sheep's stomach

haggises n ▷ haggis

haggle v (-les, -ling, -led) bargain or wrangle over a price

haggled v ▷ haggle

haggles v ▷ haggle

haggling v ▷ haggle

hagiographies n ▷ hagiography

hagiography n (pl -phies) writing about the lives of the saints

hags n ▷ hag

hail¹ n (pl -s) (shower of) small pellets of ice ▶ v (-s, -ing, -ed) fall as or like hail > **hailstone** n (pl -s)

hail² v (-s, -ing, -ed) call out to, greet

hailed v ▷ hail¹, ²

hailing v ▷ hail¹, ²

hails v ▷ hail¹, ² ▶ n ▷ hail¹

hailstone n ▷ hail¹

hailstones n ▷ hail¹

hair n (pl hairs) threadlike growth on the skin

hairclip n (pl -s) small bent metal hairpin

hairclips n ▷ hairclip

hairdo n (pl -s) (Informal) hairstyle

hairdos n ▷ hairdo

hairdresser n (pl -s) person who cuts and styles hair

hairdressers n ▷ hairdresser

hairgrip n (BRIT) (pl -s) ▷ hairclip

hairgrips n ▷ hairgrip

hairier adj ▷ hairy

hairiest adj ▷ hairy

hairiness n ▷ hairy

hairinesses n ▷ hairy

hairline n (pl -s) edge of hair at the top of the forehead ▶ adj very fine or narrow

hairlines n ▷ hairline

hairpin n (pl -s) U-shaped wire used to hold the hair in place

hairpins n ▷ hairpin

hairs n ▷ hair

hairsplitting n (pl -s) ▶ adj making petty distinctions

hairsplittings n ▷ hairsplitting

hairstyle n (pl -s) cut and arrangement of a person's hair

hairstyles n ▷ hairstyle

hairy adj (-rier, -riest) covered with hair > **hairiness** n (pl -es)

> **haj** n. Haj is the same as **hajj**. This is a very useful word, especially when there isn't much space on the board. Remember that this spelling doesn't have a plural form. Haj scores 13 points.

hajj n (pl -es) pilgrimage a Muslim makes to Mecca

hajjes n ▷ hajj

haka n (pl -s) (NZ) ceremonial Maori dance with chanting

hakas n ▷ haka

hake n (pl hakes) edible sea fish of N hemisphere (AUST) ▷ barracouta

hakea [hah-kee-a] n (pl -s) Australian tree or shrub with hard woody fruit

hakeas n ▷ hakea

hakes n ▷ hake

halal n (pl -s) meat from animals slaughtered according to Muslim law

halals n ▷ halal

halberd n (pl -s) (HIST) spear with an axe blade

halberds n ▷ halberd

halcyon [hal-see-on] adj peaceful and happy

hale adj (-ler, -lest) healthy, robust

haler adj ▷ hale

halest adj ▷ hale

half n (pl -lves) either of two equal parts ▶ adj denoting one of two equal parts ▶ adv to the extent of half

halfhearted adj unenthusiastic

halflife n (pl -ves) time taken for half the atoms in radioactive material to decay

halflives n ▷ halflife

halfpennies n ▷ halfpenny

halfpenny [hayp-nee] n (pl -nnies) former British coin worth half an old penny

halftime n (pl -s) (SPORT) short rest period between two halves of a game

halftimes n ▷ halftime

halftone n (pl -s) illustration showing lights and shadows by means of very small dots

halftones n ▷ halftone

halfway adv, adj at or to half the distance

halfwit n (pl -s) foolish or stupid person

halfwits n ▷ halfwit

halibut n (pl halibuts) large edible flatfish of N Atlantic

halibuts n ▷ halibut

halitosis n (pl -ises) unpleasant-smelling breath
 halitosises n ▷ halitosis
hall n (pl -s) (also **hallway**) entrance passage
hallelujah [hal-ee-loo-ya] interj exclamation of praise to God
hallmark n (pl -s) typical feature ▶ v (-s, -ing, -ed) stamp with a hallmark
 hallmarked v ▷ hallmark
 hallmarking v ▷ hallmark
 hallmarks n, v ▷ hallmark
 hallo interj ▷ hello
hallowed adj regarded as holy
Halloween, Hallowe'en n (pl -s) October 31, celebrated by children by dressing up as ghosts, witches, etc.
 Halloweens n ▷ Halloween
 halls n ▷ hall
hallucinate v (-tes, -ting, -ted) seem to see something that is not really there
 > **hallucination** n (pl -s) > **hallucinatory** adj
 hallucinated v ▷ hallucinate
 hallucinates v ▷ hallucinate
 hallucinating v ▷ hallucinate
 hallucination n ▷ hallucinate
 hallucinations n ▷ hallucinate
 hallucinatory adj ▷ hallucinate
hallucinogen n (pl -s) drug that causes hallucinations > **hallucinogenic** adj
 hallucinogenic adj ▷ hallucinogen
 hallucinogens n ▷ hallucinogen
halo [hay-loh] n (pl -loes, -los) ring of light round the head of a sacred figure
 haloes n ▷ halo
halogen [hal-oh-jen] n (pl -s) (CHEM) any of a group of nonmetallic elements including chlorine and iodine
 halogens n ▷ halogen
 halos n ▷ halo
halt v (-s, -ing, -ed) come or bring to a stop ▶ n (pl -s) temporary stop
 halted v ▷ halt
halter n (pl -s) strap round a horse's head with a rope to lead it with
halterneck n (pl -s) woman's top or dress with a strap fastened at the back of the neck
 halternecks n ▷ halterneck
 halters n ▷ halter
halting adj hesitant, uncertain ▶ v ▷ halt
 halts v, n ▷ halt
halve v (-ves, -ving, -ved) divide in half
 halved v ▷ halve
 halves v ▷ halve ▶ n ▷ half
 halving v ▷ halve
halyard n (pl -s) rope for raising a ship's sail

or flag
 halyards n ▷ halyard
ham¹ n (pl -s) smoked or salted meat from a pig's thigh
ham² (Informal) n (pl -s) amateur radio operator ▶ v (-s, -mming, -mmed) overact
hamburger n (pl -s) minced beef shaped into a flat disc, cooked and usu. served in a bread roll
 hamburgers n ▷ hamburger
hamlet n (pl -s) small village
 hamlets n ▷ hamlet
 hammed v ▷ ham²
hammer n (pl -s) tool with a heavy metal head and a wooden handle, used to drive in nails etc. ▶ v (-s, -ing, -ed) hit (as if) with a hammer
 hammered v ▷ hammer
hammerhead n (pl -s) shark with a wide flattened head
 hammerheads n ▷ hammerhead
 hammering v ▷ hammer
 hammers n, v ▷ hammer
 hamming v ▷ ham²
hammock n (pl -s) hanging bed made of canvas or net
 hammocks n ▷ hammock
hamper¹ v (-s, -ing, -ed) make it difficult for (someone or something) to move or progress
hamper² n (pl -s) large basket with a lid
 hampered v ▷ hamper¹
 hampering v ▷ hamper¹
 hampers v, n ▷ hamper¹, ²
 hams n, v ▷ ham¹, ²
hamster n (pl -s) small rodent with a short tail and cheek pouches
 hamsters n ▷ hamster
hamstring n (pl -s) tendon at the back of the knee ▶ v (-s, -ing, -rung) make it difficult for (someone) to take any action
 hamstringing v ▷ hamstring
 hamstrings n, v ▷ hamstring
 hamstrung v ▷ hamstring
hand n (pl -s) part of the body at the end of the arm, consisting of a palm, four fingers, and a thumb ▶ v (-s, -ing, -ed) pass, give
handbag n (pl -s) woman's small bag for carrying personal articles in
 handbags n ▷ handbag
handbill n (pl -s) small printed notice
 handbills n ▷ handbill
handbook n (pl -s) small reference or instruction book
 handbooks n ▷ handbook
handcuff n (pl -s) one of a linked pair of metal rings designed to be locked round a

prisoner's wrists by the police ▶ v (-s, -ing, -ed) put handcuffs on

handcuffed v ▷ handcuff

handcuffing v ▷ handcuff

handcuffs n, v ▷ handcuff

handed v ▷ hand

handful n (pl -s) amount that can be held in the hand

handfuls n ▷ handful

handheld adj (of a film camera) held rather than mounted, as in close-up action shots ▶ n (pl -s) computer that can be held in the hand

handhelds n ▷ handheld

handicap n (pl -s) physical or mental disability ▶ v (-s, -pping, -pped) make it difficult for (someone) to do something

handicapped v ▷ handicap

handicapping v ▷ handicap

handicaps n, v ▷ handicap

handicraft n (pl -s) objects made by hand

handicrafts n ▷ handicraft

handier adj ▷ handy

handiest adj ▷ handy

handily adv ▷ handy

handing v ▷ hand

handiwork n (pl -s) result of someone's work or activity

handiworks n ▷ handiwork

handkerchief n (pl -s) small square of fabric used to wipe the nose

handkerchiefs n ▷ handkerchief

handle n (pl -s) part of an object that is held so that it can be used ▶ v (-les, -ling, -led) hold, feel, or move with the hands

handlebars pl n curved metal bar used to steer a cycle

handled v ▷ handle

handler n (pl -s) person who controls an animal

handlers n ▷ handler

handles n, v ▷ handle

handling v ▷ handle

handout n (pl -s) clothing, food, or money given to a needy person

handouts n ▷ handout

hands n, v ▷ hand

handsome adj (esp. of a man) good-looking

handstand n (pl -s) act of supporting the body on the hands in an upside-down position

handstands n ▷ handstand

handwriting n (pl -s) (style of) writing by hand

handwritings n ▷ handwriting

handy adj (-dier, -diest) convenient, useful > **handily** adv

handyman n (pl -men) man who is good at

making or repairing things

handymen n ▷ handyman

hang v (-s, -ing, hung or hanged) attach or be attached at the top with the lower part free

hangar n (pl -s) large shed for storing aircraft

hangars n ▷ hangar

hangdog adj guilty, ashamed

hanged v ▷ hang

hanger n (pl -s) curved piece of wood, wire, or plastic, with a hook, for hanging up clothes (also **coat hanger**)

hangers n ▷ hanger

hangi n (pl -gi, -gis) (NZ) Maori oven consisting of a hole in the ground filled with hot stones

hanging v ▷ hang

hangis n ▷ hangi

hangman n (pl -men) man who executes people by hanging

hangmen n ▷ hangman

hangover n (pl -s) headache and nausea as a result of drinking too much alcohol

hangovers n ▷ hangover

hangs v ▷ hang

hangup n (pl -s) (Informal) emotional or psychological problem

hangups n ▷ hangup

hank n (pl -s) coil, esp. of yarn

hanker v (-s, -ing, -ed) (foll. by **after** or **for**) desire intensely

hankered v ▷ hanker

hankering v ▷ hanker

hankers v ▷ hanker

hankie n ▷ hanky

hankies n ▷ hanky

hanks n ▷ hank

hanky, hankie n (pl hankies) (Informal) handkerchief

haphazard adj not organized or planned > **haphazardly** adv

haphazardly adv ▷ haphazard

hapless adj unlucky

happen v (-s, -ing, -ed) take place, occur

happened v ▷ happen

happening n (pl -s) event, occurrence ▶ v ▷ happen

happenings n ▷ happening

happens v ▷ happen

happier adj ▷ happy

happiest adj ▷ happy

happily adv ▷ happy

happiness n ▷ happy

happinesses n ▷ happiness

happy adj (-ppier, -ppiest) feeling or causing joy > **happily** adv > **happiness** n (pl -es)

harangue v (-gues, -guing, -gued) address

angrily or forcefully ▶ n (pl -gues) angry or forceful speech

harangued v ▷ harangue

harangues v, n ▷ harangue

haranguing v ▷ harangue

harass v (-es, -ing, -ssed) annoy or trouble constantly > **harassed** adj > **harassment** n (pl -s)

harassed v, adj ▷ harass

harasses v ▷ harass

harassing v ▷ harass

harassment n ▷ harrass

harassments n ▷ harassment

harbinger [har-binj-a] n (pl -s) someone or something that announces the approach of something

harbingers n ▷ harbinger

harbour n (pl -s) sheltered port ▶ v (-s, -ing, -ed) maintain secretly in the mind

harboured v ▷ harbour

harbouring v ▷ harbour

harbours n, v ▷ harbour

hard adj firm, solid, or rigid ▶ adv with great energy or effort > **harden** v (-s, -ing, -ed) > **hardness** n (pl -es)

hardboard n (pl -s) thin stiff board made of compressed sawdust and wood chips

hardboards n ▷ hardboard

harden v ▷ hard

hardened v ▷ hard

hardening v ▷ hard

hardens v ▷ hard

hardfill n (pl -s) (NZ & S AFR) stone waste material used for landscaping

hardfills n ▷ hardfill

hardheaded adj shrewd, practical

hardhearted adj unsympathetic, uncaring

hardier adj ▷ hardy

hardiest adj ▷ hardy

hardiness n ▷ hardy

hardinesses n ▷ hardy

hardly adv scarcely or not at all

hardness n ▷ hard

hardnesses n ▷ hard

hardship n (pl -s) suffering

hardships n ▷ hardship

hardware n (pl -s) metal tools or implements

hardwares n ▷ hardware

hardwood n (pl -s) wood of a broadleaved tree such as oak or ash

hardwoods n ▷ hardwood

hardy adj (-dier, -diest) able to stand difficult conditions > **hardiness** n (pl -es)

hare n (pl -s) animal like a large rabbit, with longer ears and legs ▶ v (-res, -ring, -red) (usu.

foll. by **off**) run (away) quickly

harebell n (pl -s) blue bell-shaped flower

harebells n ▷ harebell

harebrained adj foolish or impractical

hared v ▷ hare

harelip n (pl -s) slight split in the upper lip

harelips n ▷ harelip

harem n (pl -s) (apartments of) a Muslim man's wives and concubines

harems n ▷ harem

hares v, n ▷ hare

haring v ▷ hare

hark v (-s, -ing, -ed) (Old-fashioned) listen

harked v ▷ hark

harking v ▷ hark

harks v ▷ hark

harlequin n (pl -s) stock comic character with a diamond-patterned costume and mask ▶ adj in many colours

harlequins n ▷ harlequin

harlot n (pl -s) (Lit) prostitute

harlots n ▷ harlot

harm v (-s, -ing, -ed) injure physically, mentally, or morally ▶ n (pl -s) physical, mental, or moral injury > **harmful** adj > **harmless** adj

harmed v ▷ harm

harmful adj ▷ harm

harming v ▷ harm

harmless adj ▷ harm

harmonic adj of harmony

harmonica n (pl -s) small wind instrument played by sucking and blowing

harmonicas n ▷ harmonica

harmonics n science of musical sounds

harmonies n ▷ harmony

harmonious adj ▷ harmony

harmoniously adv ▷ harmony

harmonium n (pl -s) keyboard instrument like a small organ

harmoniums n ▷ harmonium

harmonization v ▷ harmonize

harmonizations v ▷ harmonize

harmonize v (-zes, -zing, -zed) blend well together > **harmonization** n (pl -s)

harmonized v ▷ harmonize

harmonizes v ▷ harmonize

harmonizing v ▷ harmonize

harmony n (pl -nies) peaceful agreement and cooperation > **harmonious** adj > **harmoniously** adv

harms v, n ▷ harm

harness n (pl -es) arrangement of straps for attaching a horse to a cart or plough ▶ v (-es, -ing, -ed) put a harness on

harnessed v ▷ harness
harnesses n, v ▷ harness
harnessing v ▷ harness
harp n (pl -s) large triangular stringed instrument played with the fingers > **harpist** n (pl -s)
harpies n ▷ harpy
harpist n ▷ harp
harpists n ▷ harp
harpoon n (pl -s) barbed spear attached to a rope used for hunting whales ▶ v (-s, -ing, -ed) spear with a harpoon
harpooned v ▷ harpoon
harpooning v ▷ harpoon
harpoons n, v ▷ harpoon
harps n ▷ harp
harpsichord n (pl -s) stringed keyboard instrument
harpsichords n ▷ harpsichord
harpy n (pl -pies) nasty or bad-tempered woman
harridan n (pl -s) nagging or vicious woman
harridans n ▷ harridan
harried v ▷ harry
harrier n (pl -s) cross-country runner
harriers n ▷ harrier
harries v ▷ harry
harrow n (pl -s) implement used to break up lumps of soil ▶ v (-s, -ing, -ed) draw a harrow over
harrowed v ▷ harrow
harrowing adj very distressing ▶ v ▷ harrow
harrows n, v ▷ harrow
harry v (-rries, -rrying, -rried) keep asking (someone) to do something, pester
harrying v ▷ harry
harsh adj severe and difficult to cope with > **harshly** adv > **harshness** n (pl -es)
harshly adv ▷ harsh
harshness n ▷ harsh
harshnesses n ▷ harsh
hart n (pl -s) adult male deer
harts n ▷ hart
harvest n (pl -s) (season for) the gathering of crops ▶ v (-s, -ing, -ed) gather (a ripened crop) > **harvester** n (pl -s)
harvested v ▷ harvest
harvester n ▷ harvest
harvesters n ▷ harvest
harvesting v ▷ harvest
harvests n, v ▷ harvest
has v ▷ have
hash¹ n (pl -es) dish of diced cooked meat and vegetables reheated
hash² n (pl -es) (Informal) hashish

hashes n ▷ hash¹, ²
hashish [hash-eesh] n (pl -es) drug made from the cannabis plant, smoked for its intoxicating effects
hashishes n ▷ hashish
hasp n (pl -s) clasp that fits over a staple and is secured by a bolt or padlock, used as a fastening
hasps n ▷ hasp
hassle (Informal) n (pl -s) trouble, bother ▶ v (-les, -ling, -led) bother or annoy
hassled v ▷ hassle
hassles n, v ▷ hassle
hassling v ▷ hassle
hassock n (pl -s) cushion for kneeling on in church
hassocks n ▷ hassock
haste n (pl -s) (excessive) quickness
hasten v (-s, -ing, -ed) (cause to) hurry
hastened v ▷ hasten
hastening n ▷ hasten
hastens n ▷ hasten
hastes n ▷ haste
hastier adj ▷ hasty
hastiest adj ▷ hasty
hastily adv ▷ hasty
hasty adj (-tier, -tiest) (too) quick > **hastily** adv
hat n (pl -s) covering for the head, often with a brim, usu. worn to give protection from the weather
hatch¹ v (-es, -ing, -ed) (cause to) emerge from an egg
hatch² n (pl -es) hinged door covering an opening in a floor or wall
hatchback n (pl -s) car with a lifting door at the back
hatchbacks n ▷ hatchback
hatched v ▷ hatch¹
hatches v ▷ hatch¹ ▶ n ▷ hatch²
hatchet n (pl -s) small axe
hatchets n ▷ hatchet
hatching v ▷ hatch¹
hatchway n (pl -s) opening in the deck of a ship
hatchways n ▷ hatchway
hate v (-tes, -ting, -ted) dislike intensely ▶ n (pl -s) intense dislike > **hater** n (pl -s)
hated v ▷ hate
hateful adj causing or deserving hate
hater n ▷ hate
haters n ▷ hate
hates v, n ▷ hate
hating v ▷ hate
hatred n (pl -s) intense dislike
hatreds n ▷ hatred

hats n ▷ hat
haughtier adj ▷ haughty
haughtiest adj ▷ haughty
haughtily adv ▷ haughty
haughtiness n ▷ haughty
haughtinesses n ▷ haughty
haughty adj (-tier, -tiest) proud, arrogant
  > **haughtily** adv > **haughtiness** n (pl -es)
haul v (-s, -ing, -ed) pull or drag with effort ▶ n
  (pl -s) amount gained by effort or theft
haulage n (pl -s) (charge for) transporting
  goods
haulages n ▷ haulage
hauled v ▷ haul
haulier n (pl -s) firm or person that transports
  goods by road
hauliers n ▷ haulier
hauling v ▷ haul
hauls v, n ▷ haul
haunch n (pl -es) human hip or fleshy
  hindquarter of an animal
haunches n ▷ haunch
haunt v (-s, -ing, -ed) visit in the form of a
  ghost ▶ n (pl -s) place visited frequently
haunted adj frequented by ghosts ▶ v ▷ haunt
haunting adj memorably beautiful or sad ▶ v
  ▷ haunt
haunts v, n ▷ haunt
hauteur [oat-ur] n (pl -s) haughtiness
hauteurs n ▷ hauteur
have v (has, having, had) possess, hold
haven n (pl -s) place of safety
havens n ▷ haven
haversack n (pl -s) canvas bag carried on the
  back or shoulder
haversacks n ▷ haversack
having v ▷ have
havoc n (pl -s) disorder and confusion
havocs n ▷ havoc
haw n (pl -s) hawthorn berry
hawk¹ n (pl -s) bird of prey with a short hooked
  bill and very good eyesight > **hawkish,
  hawklike** adj
hawk² v (-s, -ing, -ed) offer (goods) for sale in
  the street or door-to-door > **hawker** n (pl -s)
hawk³ v (-s, -ing, -ed) cough noisily
hawked v ▷ hawk²,³
hawker n ▷ hawk²
hawkers n ▷ hawk²
hawk-eyed adj having very good eyesight
hawking v ▷ hawk²,³
hawkish adj ▷ hawk¹
hawks n ▷ hawk¹ v ▷ hawk²,³
hawlike adj ▷ hawk¹
haws n ▷ haw

hawser n (pl -s) large rope used on a ship
hawsers n ▷ hawser
hawthorn n (pl -s) thorny shrub or tree
hawthorns n ▷ hawthorn
hay n (pl hays) grass cut and dried as fodder
hays n ▷ hay
haystack n (pl -s) large pile of stored hay
haystacks n ▷ haystack
haywire adj (Informal) not functioning properly
hazard n (pl -s) something that could be
  dangerous ▶ v (-s, -ing, -ed) put in danger
  > **hazardous** adj
hazarded v ▷ hazard
hazarding v ▷ hazard
hazardous adj ▷ hazard
hazards n, v ▷ hazard
haze n (pl -s) mist, often caused by heat
hazel n (pl -s) small tree producing edible nuts
  ▶ adj (of eyes) greenish-brown > **hazelnut**
  n (pl -s)
hazelnut n ▷ hazel
hazelnuts n ▷ hazel
hazels n ▷ hazel
hazes n ▷ haze
hazier adj ▷ hazy
haziest adj ▷ hazy
hazy adj (-zier, -ziest) not clear, misty
he pron refers to: male person or animal ▶ n (pl
  -s) male person or animal
head n (pl -s) upper or front part of the body,
  containing the sense organs and the brain
  ▶ adj chief, principal ▶ v (-s, -ing, -ed) be at the
  top or front of
headache n (pl -s) continuous pain in the head
headaches n ▷ headache
headboard n (pl -s) vertical board at the top
  end of a bed
headboards n ▷ headboard
headdress n (pl -s) decorative head covering
headdresses n ▷ headdress
headed v ▷ head
header n (pl -s) striking a ball with the head
headers n ▷ header
headhunt v (-s, -ing, -ed) (of a company)
  approach and offer a job to (a person working
  for a rival company) > **headhunter** n (pl -s)
headhunted v ▷ headhunt
headhunter n ▷ headhunt
headhunters n ▷ headhunt
headhunting v ▷ headhunt
headhunts v ▷ headhunt
headier adj ▷ heady
headiest adj ▷ heady
heading n (pl -s) title written or printed at the
  top of a page ▶ v ▷ head

headings n ▷ heading
headland n (pl -s) area of land jutting out into the sea
  headlands n ▷ headland
headlight n (pl -s) powerful light on the front of a vehicle
  headlights n ▷ headlight
headline n (pl -s) title at the top of a newspaper article, esp. on the front page
  headlines n ▷ headline ▶ pl n main points of a news broadcast
headlong adv, adj with the head first
headphones pl n two small loudspeakers held against the ears
headquarters pl n centre from which operations are directed
heads adv (Informal) with the side of a coin which has a portrait of a head on it uppermost ▶ n, v ▷ head
headstone n (pl -s) memorial stone on a grave
  headstones n ▷ headstone
headstrong adj self-willed, obstinate
headway n (pl -s) progress
  headways n ▷ headway
headwind n (pl -s) wind blowing against the course of an aircraft or ship
  headwinds n ▷ headwind
heady adj (-dier, -diest) intoxicating or exciting
heal v (-s, -ing, -ed) make or become well
  > **healer** n (pl -s)
  healed v ▷ heal
  healer n ▷ heal
  healers n ▷ heal
  healing v ▷ heal
  heals v ▷ heal
health n (pl -s) normal (good) condition of someone's body
  healthier adj ▷ healthy
  healthiest adj ▷ healthy
  healthily adv ▷ healthy
  healths n ▷ health
healthy adj (-thier, -thiest) having good health
  > **healthily** adv
heap n (pl -s) pile of things one on top of another ▶ v (-s, -ing, -ed) gather into a pile
  heaped v ▷ heap
  heaping v ▷ heap
  heaps n, v ▷ heap
hear v (-s, -ing, heard) perceive (a sound) by ear
  > **hearer** n (pl -s)
  heard v ▷ hear
  hearer n ▷ hear
  hearers n ▷ hear
hearing n (pl -s) ability to hear ▶ v ▷ hear

hearings n ▷ hearing
hears v ▷ hear
hearsay n (pl -s) gossip, rumour
  hearsays n ▷ hearsay
hearse n (pl -s) funeral car used to carry a coffin
  hearses n ▷ hearse
heart n (pl -s) organ that pumps blood round the body
heartache n (pl -s) intense anguish
  heartaches n ▷ heartache
heartbeat n (pl -s) one complete pulsation of the heart
  heartbeats n ▷ heartbeat
heartbreak n (pl -s) intense grief
  heartbreaks n ▷ heartbreak
heartburn n (pl -s) burning sensation in the chest caused by indigestion
  heartburns n ▷ heartburn
hearten v (-s, -ing, -ed) encourage, make cheerful
  heartened v ▷ hearten
  heartening v ▷ hearten
  heartens v ▷ hearten
heartfelt adj felt sincerely or strongly
hearth n (pl -s) floor of a fireplace
  hearths n ▷ hearth
  heartier adj ▷ hearty
  heartiest adj ▷ hearty
  heartily adv ▷ hearty
heartless adj cruel, unkind
heartrending adj causing great sorrow
  hearts n ▷ heart
heartthrob n (pl -s) (Slang) very attractive man, esp. a film or pop star
  heartthrobs n ▷ heartthrob
hearty adj (-tier, -tiest) substantial, nourishing > **heartily** adv
heat v (-s, -ing, -ed) make or become hot ▶ n (pl -s) state of being hot > **heater** n (pl -s)
  heated v ▷ heat ▶ adj angry and excited > **heatedly** adv
  heatedly adv ▷ heated
  heater n ▷ heat
  heaters n ▷ heat
heath n (pl -s) (BRIT) area of open uncultivated land
heathen adj, n (pl -s) (of) a person who does not believe in an established religion
  heathens n ▷ heathen
heather n (pl -s) low-growing plant with small purple, pinkish, or white flowers, growing on heaths and mountains
  heathers n ▷ heather
  heaths n ▷ heath
  heating v ▷ heat

heats v, n ▷ heat

heave v (-ves, -ving, -ved) lift with effort ▶ n (pl -s) heaving

heaved v ▷ heave

heaven n (pl -s) place believed to be the home of God, where good people go when they die

heavenly adj of or like heaven

heavens n ▷ heaven

heaves v, n ▷ heave

heavier adj ▷ heavy

heaviest adj ▷ heavy

heavily adv ▷ heavy

heaviness n ▷ heavy

heavinesses n ▷ heavy

heaving v ▷ heave

heavy adj (-vier, -viest) of great weight > **heavily** adv > **heaviness** n (pl -es)

heavyweight n (pl -s) boxer weighing over 175lb (professional) or 81kg (amateur)

heavyweights n ▷ heavyweight

heckle v (-les, -ling, -led) interrupt (a public speaker) with comments, questions, or taunts > **heckler** n (pl -s)

heckled v ▷ heckle

heckler n ▷ heckle

hecklers n ▷ heckle

heckles v ▷ heckle

heckling v ▷ heckle

hectare n (pl -s) one hundred ares or 10 000 square metres (2.471 acres)

hectares n ▷ hectare

hectic adj rushed or busy

hector v (-s, -ing, -ed) bully

hectored v ▷ hector

hectoring v ▷ hector

hectors v ▷ hector

hedge n (pl -s) row of bushes forming a barrier or boundary ▶ v (-ges, -ging, -ged) be evasive or noncommittal

hedged v ▷ hedge

hedgehog n (pl -s) small mammal with a protective covering of spines

hedgehogs n ▷ hedgehog

hedgerow n (pl -s) bushes forming a hedge

hedgerows n ▷ hedgerow

hedges n, v ▷ hedge

hedging v ▷ hedge

hedonism n (pl -s) doctrine that pleasure is the most important thing in life > **hedonist** n (pl -s) > **hedonistic** adj

hedonisms n ▷ hedonism

hedonist n ▷ hedonism

hedonistic n ▷ hedonism

hedonists n ▷ hedonism

heed n (pl -s) careful attention ▶ v (-s, -ing, -ed) pay careful attention to

heeded v ▷ heed

heeding v ▷ heed

heedless adj taking no notice of

heeds v, n ▷ heed

heel¹ n (pl -s) back part of the foot ▶ v (-s, -ing, -ed) repair the heel of (a shoe)

heel² v (-s, -ing, -ed) (foll. by over) lean to one side

heeled v ▷ heel¹, ²

heeler n (pl -s) (AUST & NZ) dog that herds cattle by biting at their heels

heelers n ▷ heeler

heeling v ▷ heel¹, ²

heels n ▷ heel¹ ▶ v ▷ heel¹, ²

heftier adj ▷ hefty

heftiest adj ▷ hefty

hefty adj (-tier, -tiest) large, heavy, or strong

hegemonies n ▷ hegemony

hegemony [hig-**em**-on-ee] n (pl -nies) political domination

hegira n (pl -s) Mohammed's flight from Mecca to Medina in 622 AD

hegiras n ▷ hegira

heifer [**hef**-fer] n (pl -s) young cow

heifers n ▷ heifer

height n (pl -s) distance from base to top

heighten v (-s, -ing, -ed) make or become higher or more intense

heightened v ▷ heighten

heightening v ▷ heighten

heightens v ▷ heighten

heights n ▷ height

heinous adj evil and shocking

heir n (pl -s) person entitled to inherit property or rank > **heiress** n fem (pl -es)

heiresses n ▷ heir

heirloom n (pl -s) object that has belonged to a family for generations

heirlooms n ▷ heirloom

heirs n ▷ heir

held v ▷ hold¹

helical adj spiral

helices n ▷ helix

helicopter n (pl -s) aircraft lifted and propelled by rotating overhead blades

helicopters n ▷ helicopter

heliotrope n (pl -s) plant with purple flowers ▶ adj light purple

heliotropes n ▷ heliotrope

heliport n (pl -s) airport for helicopters

heliports n ▷ heliport

helium [**heel**-ee-um] n (pl -s) (CHEM) very light colourless odourless gas

heliums n ▷ helium

helix [heel-iks] n (pl **-ices, -ixes**) spiral
  helixes n ▷ helix
hell n (pl -s) place believed to be where wicked people go when they die > **hellish** adj
hellbent adj (foll. by **on**) intent
  hellish adj ▷ hell
hello interj expression of greeting or surprise
  hells n ▷ hell
helm n (pl -s) tiller or wheel for steering a ship
helmet n (pl -s) hard hat worn for protection
  helmets n ▷ helmet
  helms n ▷ helm
help v (-s, -ing, -ed) make something easier, better, or quicker for (someone) ▶ n (pl -s) assistance or support > **helper** n (pl -s) > **helpful** adj
  helped v ▷ help
  helper n ▷ help
  helpers n ▷ help
  helpful adj ▷ help
helping n (pl -s) single portion of food ▶ v ▷ help
  helpings n ▷ helping
helpless adj weak or incapable > **helplessly** adv
  helplessly adv ▷ helpless
helpline n (pl -s) telephone line set aside for callers to contact an organization for help with a problem
  helplines n ▷ helpline
helpmate n (pl -s) companion and helper, esp. a husband or wife
  helpmates n ▷ helpmate
  helps v, n ▷ help
hem n (pl -s) bottom edge of a garment, folded under and stitched down ▶ v (-s, -mming, -mmed) provide with a hem
hemisphere n (pl -s) half of a sphere, esp. the earth > **hemispherical** adj
  hemispheres n ▷ hemisphere
hemline n (pl -s) level to which the hem of a skirt hangs
  hemlines n ▷ hemline
hemlock n (pl -s) poison made from a plant with spotted stems and small white flowers
  hemlocks n ▷ hemlock
  hemmed v ▷ hem
  hemming v ▷ hem
hemp n (pl -s) (also **cannabis**) Asian plant with tough fibres
  hemps n ▷ hemp
  hems n, v ▷ hem
hen n (pl -s) female domestic fowl
hence conj for this reason ▶ adv from this time
henceforth adv from now on
henchman n (pl -men) person employed by

someone powerful to carry out orders
  henchmen n ▷ henchman
henna n (pl -s) reddish dye made from a shrub or tree ▶ v (-s, -ing, -ed) dye (the hair) with henna
  hennaed v ▷ henna
  hennaing v ▷ henna
  hennas n, v ▷ henna
henpecked adj (of a man) dominated by his wife
  henries n ▷ henry
henry n (pl **-ries, -rys**) unit of electrical inductance
  henrys n ▷ henry
  hens n ▷ hen
hepatitis n (pl **-es**) inflammation of the liver
  hepatitises n ▷ hepatitis
heptagon n (pl -s) geometric figure with seven sides
  heptagons n ▷ heptagon
heptathlon n (pl -s) athletic contest for women, involving seven events
  heptathlons n ▷ heptathlon
her pron refers to a female person or animal or anything personified as feminine when the object of a sentence or clause ▶ adj belonging to her
herald n (pl -s) person who announces important news ▶ v (-s, -ing, -ed) signal the approach of
  heralded v ▷ herald
  heraldic adj ▷ heraldry
  heralding v ▷ herald
  heraldries n ▷ heraldry
heraldry n (pl **-ries**) study of coats of arms and family trees > **heraldic** adj
  heralds n, v ▷ herald
herb n (pl -s) plant used for flavouring in cookery, and in medicine > **herbal** adj
herbaceous adj (of a plant) soft-stemmed
  herbal adj ▷ herb
herbalist n (pl -s) person who grows or specializes in the use of medicinal herbs
  herbalists n ▷ herbalist
herbicide n (pl -s) chemical used to destroy plants, esp. weeds
  herbicides n ▷ herbicide
herbivore n (pl -s) animal that eats only plants > **herbivorous** [her-biv-or-uss] ▶ adj
  herbivores n ▷ herbivore
  herbivorous adj ▷ herbivore
  herbs n ▷ herb
herculean [her-kew-lee-an] adj requiring great strength or effort
herd n (pl -s) group of animals feeding and

living together ▸ v (-s, -ing, -ed) collect into a herd

herded v ▷ herd

herding v ▷ herd

herds n, v ▷ herd

herdsman n (pl -men) man who looks after a herd of animals

herdsmen n ▷ herd

here adv in, at, or to this place or point

hereabouts adv near here

hereafter adv after this point or time

hereby adv by means of or as a result of this

hereditary adj passed on genetically from one generation to another

heredities n ▷ heredity

heredity [hir-red-it-ee] n (pl -ties) passing on of characteristics from one generation to another

herein adv in this place, matter, or document

heresies n ▷ heresy

heresy [herr-iss-ee] n (pl -sies) opinion contrary to accepted opinion or belief

heretic [herr-it-ik] n (pl -s) person who holds unorthodox opinions > **heretical** [hir-ret-ik-al] ▸ adj

heretical n ▷ heretic

heretics n ▷ heretic

herewith adv with this

heritage n (pl -s) something inherited

heritages n ▷ heritage

hermaphrodite [her-maf-roe-dite] n (pl -s) animal, plant, or person with both male and female reproductive organs

hermaphrodites n ▷ hermaphrodite

hermetic adj sealed so as to be airtight > **hermetically** adv

hermetically adv ▷ hermetic

hermit n (pl -s) person living in solitude, esp. for religious reasons

hermitage n (pl -s) home of a hermit

hermitages n ▷ hermitage

hermits n ▷ hermit

hernia n (pl -s) protrusion of an organ or part through the lining of the surrounding body cavity

hernias n ▷ hernia

hero n (pl -es) principal character in a film, book, etc. > **heroine** n fem (pl -s) > **heroism** [herr-oh-izz-um] n (pl -s)

heroes n ▷ hero

heroic adj courageous > **heroically** adv

heroically adv ▷ heroic

heroics pl n extravagant behaviour

heroin n (pl -s) highly addictive drug derived from morphine

heroine n ▷ hero

heroines n ▷ hero

heroins n ▷ heroin

heroism n ▷ hero

heroisms n ▷ hero

heron n (pl -s) long-legged wading bird

herons n ▷ heron

herpes [her-peez] n (pl -es) any of several inflammatory skin diseases, including shingles and cold sores

herpeses n ▷ herpes

herring n (pl -s) important food fish of northern seas

herringbone n (pl -s) pattern of zigzag lines

herringbones n ▷ herringbone

herrings n ▷ herring

hertz n (pl -es) (PHYSICS) unit of frequency

hertzes n ▷ hertz

hes n ▷ he

hesitancies n ▷ hesitant

hesitancy n ▷ hesitant

hesitant adj undecided or wavering > **hesitantly** adv > **hesitancy** n (pl -cies)

hesitantly adv ▷ hesitant

hesitate v (-tes, -ting, -ted) be slow or uncertain in doing something > **hesitation** n (pl -s)

hesitated v ▷ hesitate

hesitates v ▷ hesitate

hesitating v ▷ hesitate

hesitation n ▷ hesitate

hesitations n ▷ hesitate

hessian n (pl -s) coarse jute fabric

hessians n ▷ hessian

heterodox adj differing from accepted doctrines or beliefs > **heterodoxy** n (pl -xies)

heterodoxies n ▷ heterodox

heterodoxy n ▷ heterodox

heterogeneities n ▷ heterogeneous

heterogeneity n ▷ heterogeneous

heterogeneous [het-er-oh-jean-ee-uss] adj composed of diverse elements > **heterogeneity** n (pl -ties)

heterosexual n (pl -s) person sexually attracted to members of the opposite sex ▸ adj > **heterosexuality** n (pl -ties)

heterosexualities n ▷ heterosexual

heterosexuality n ▷ heterosexual

heterosexuals n ▷ heterosexual

heuristic [hew-rist-ik] adj involving learning by investigation

hew v (-s, -ing, -ed or hewn) cut with an axe

hewed v ▷ hew

hewing v ▷ hew

hewn v ▷ hew

hews *v* ▷ hew

hex *n* hexes. A hex is a curse or spell. This is a really useful word to remember when you have an X, as there is likely to be an E or H on the board already.

hexagon *n* (*pl* -s) geometrical figure with six sides > **hexagonal** *adj*

hexagonal *adj* ▷ hexagon

hexagons *n* ▷ hexagon

hey *interj* expression of surprise or for catching attention

heyday *n* (*pl* -s) time of greatest success, prime

heydays *n* ▷ heyday

hi *interj*. Hi is an informal word for hello. This everyday word is worth keeping in mind when you want to form a word adjacent to a parallel word above or below. Hi scores 5 points.

hiatus [hie-**ay**-tuss] *n* (*pl* -tuses, -tus) pause or interruption in continuity

hiatuses *n* ▷ hiatus

hibernate *v* (-tes, -ting, -ted) (of an animal) pass the winter as if in a deep sleep > **hibernation** *n* (*pl* -s)

hibernated *v* ▷ hibernate

hibernates *v* ▷ hibernate

hibernating *v* ▷ hibernate

hibernation *n* ▷ hibernate

hibernations *n* ▷ hibernate

hibiscus *n* (*pl* -cuses) tropical plant with large brightly coloured flowers

hibiscuses *n* ▷ hibiscus

hiccough *n, v* ▷ hiccup

hiccoughed *v* ▷ hiccup

hiccoughing *v* ▷ hiccup

hiccoughs *n, v* ▷ hiccup

hiccup, hiccough *n* (*pl* -s) spasm of the breathing organs with a sharp coughlike sound (*Informal*) ▷ *v* (-s, -pping, -pped) make a hiccup

hiccupped *v* ▷ hiccup

hiccupping *v* ▷ hiccup

hiccups *n, v* ▷ hiccup

hick *n* (*pl* -s) (US, AUST & NZ) (*Informal*) unsophisticated country person

hickories *n* ▷ hickory

hickory *n* (*pl* -ries) N American nut-bearing tree

hicks *n* ▷ hick

hid *v* ▷ hide¹

hidden *v* ▷ hide¹

hide¹ *v* (-des, -ding, hid, hidden) put (oneself or an object) somewhere difficult to see or find ▷ *n* (*pl* -s) place of concealment, esp. for a bird-watcher

hide² *n* (*pl* -s) skin of an animal

hidebound *adj* unwilling to accept new ideas

hideous [**hid**-ee-uss] *adj* ugly, revolting > **hideously** *adv*

hideously *adv* ▷ hideous

hideout *n* (*pl* -s) place to hide in

hideouts *n* ▷ hideout

hides *v* ▷ hide¹ ▷ *n* ▷ hide¹, ²

hiding *n* (*pl* -s) (*Slang*) severe beating ▷ *v* ▷ hide¹

hidings *n* ▷ hiding

hierarchical *adj* ▷ hierarchy

hierarchies *n* ▷ hierarchy

hierarchy [**hire**-ark-ee] *n* (*pl* -chies) system of people or things arranged in a graded order > **hierarchical** *adj*

hieroglyphic [hire-oh-**gliff**-ik] *adj* of a form of writing using picture symbols, as used in ancient Egypt ▷ *n* (*pl* -s) symbol that is difficult to decipher (also **hieroglyph**)

hieroglyphics *n* ▷ hieroglyphic

high *adj* (-er, -est) of a great height ▷ *adv* at or to a high level > **highly** *adv*

highbrow *adj, n* (*pl* -s) intellectual and serious (person)

highbrows *n* ▷ highbrow

higher *adj* ▷ high

highest *adj* ▷ high

highlands *pl n* area of high ground

highlight *n* (*pl* -s) outstanding part or feature ▷ *v* (-s, -ing, -ed) give emphasis to

highlighted *v* ▷ highlight

highlighting *v* ▷ highlight

highlights *n, v* ▷ highlight

highly *adv* ▷ high

highway *n* (*pl* -s) (US, AUST & NZ) main road

highwayman *n* (*pl* -men) (formerly) robber, usu. on horseback, who robbed travellers at gunpoint

highwaymen *n* ▷ highwayman

highways *n* ▷ highway

hijack *v* (-s, -ing, -ed) seize control of (an aircraft or other vehicle) while travelling > **hijacker** *n* (*pl* -s)

hijacked *v* ▷ hijack

hijacker *n* ▷ hijack

hijackers *n* ▷ hijack

hijacking *v* ▷ hijack

hijacks *v* ▷ hijack

hike *n* (*pl* -s) long walk in the country, esp. for pleasure ▷ *v* (-kes, -king, -ked) go for a long walk > **hiker** *n* (*pl* -s)

hiked *v* ▷ hike

hiker *n* ▷ hike

hikers *n* ▷ hike

hikes n, v ▷ hike
hiking v ▷ hike
hilarious adj very funny > **hilariously** adv
> **hilarity** n (pl -ties)
hilariously adv ▷ hilarious
hilarities n ▷ hilarious
hilarity n ▷ hilarious
hill n (pl -s) raised part of the earth's surface,
less high than a mountain > **hilly** adj (-llier,
-lliest)
hillbillies n ▷ hillbilly
hillbilly n (pl -llies) (us) unsophisticated
country person
hillier adj ▷ hill
hilliest adj ▷ hill
hillock n (pl -s) small hill
hillocks n ▷ hillock
hills n ▷ hill
hilly adj ▷ hill
hilt n (pl -s) handle of a sword or knife
hilts n ▷ hilt
him pron refers to a male person or animal
when the object of a sentence or clause
hind[1] adj (-er, -most) situated at the back
hind[2] n (pl -s) female deer
hinder adj ▷ hind[1] ▶ v (-s, -ing, -ed) get in the
way of > **hindrance** n (pl -s)
hindered v ▷ hinder
hindering v ▷ hinder
hinders v ▷ hinder
hindmost adj ▷ hind[1]
hindrance n ▷ hinder
hindrances n ▷ hinder
hinds n ▷ hind[2]
hinge n (pl -s) device for holding together two
parts so that one can swing freely ▶ v (-ges,
-ging, -ged) (foll. by **on**) depend (on)
hinged v ▷ hinge
hinges n, v ▷ hinge
hinging v ▷ hinge
hint n (pl -s) indirect suggestion ▶ v (-s, -ing,
-ed) suggest indirectly
hinted v ▷ hint
hinterland n (pl -s) land lying behind a coast or
near a city, esp. a port
hinterlands n ▷ hinterland
hinting v ▷ hint
hints n, v ▷ hint
hip[1] n (pl -s) either side of the body between
the pelvis and the thigh
hip[2] n (pl -s) rosehip
hippie adj, n (pl -s) ▷ hippy
hippies n ▷ hippie
hippo n (pl -ppos) (Informal) hippopotamus
hippodrome n (pl -s) music hall, variety

theatre, or circus
hippodromes n ▷ hippodrome
hippopotami n ▷ hippopotamus
hippopotamus n (pl -muses, -mi) large African
mammal with thick wrinkled skin, living
near rivers
hippopotamuses n ▷ hippopotamus
hippos n ▷ hippo
hippy adj, n (pl -ppies) (esp. in the 1960s) (of)
a person whose behaviour and dress imply a
rejection of conventional values
hips n ▷ hip[1, 2]
hire v (-res, -ring, -red) pay to have temporary
use of ▶ n (pl -s) hiring
hired v ▷ hire
hireling n (pl -s) person who works only for
wages
hirelings n ▷ hireling
hires v, n ▷ hire
hiring v ▷ hire
hirsute [her-suit] adj hairy
his pron, adj (something) belonging to him
hiss n (pl -es) sound like that of a long s (as an
expression of contempt) ▶ v (-es, -ing, -ed)
utter a hiss
hissed v ▷ hiss
hisses n, v ▷ hiss
hissing v ▷ hiss
histamine [hiss-ta-meen] n (pl -s) substance
released by the body tissues in allergic
reactions
histamines n ▷ histamine
histogram n (pl -s) statistical graph in which
the frequency of values is represented by
vertical bars of varying heights and widths
histograms n ▷ histogram
histologies n ▷ histology
histology n (pl -gies) study of the tissues of an
animal or plant
historian n (pl -s) writer of history
historians n ▷ historian
historic adj famous or significant in history
historical adj occurring in the past
> **historically** adv
historically adv ▷ historical
histories n ▷ history
history n (pl -ries) (record or account of) past
events and developments
histrionic adj excessively dramatic
histrionics pl n excessively dramatic
behaviour
hit v (-s, -tting, hit) strike, touch forcefully ▶ n
(pl -s) hitting ▶ adj sometimes successful and
sometimes not
hitch n (pl -es) minor problem ▶ v (-es, -ing, -ed)

(*Informal*) obtain (a lift) by hitchhiking
hitched *v* ▷ hitch
hitches *n*, *v* ▷ hitch
hitchhike *v* (-kes, -king, -ked) travel by obtaining free lifts ▶ **hitchhiker** *n* (*pl* -s)
hitchhiked *n* ▷ hitchhike
hitchhiker *n* ▷ hitchhike
hitchhikers *n* ▷ hitchhike
hitchhikes *n* ▷ hitchhike
hitchhiking *n* ▷ hitchhike
hitching *v* ▷ hitch
hither *adv* (*Old-fashioned*) to or towards this place
hitherto *adv* until this time
hits *n*, *v* ▷ hit
hitting *v* ▷ hit
hive *n* (*pl* -s) ▷ beehive
hives *v* ▷ hive

hm or **hmm** *interj*. This is a noise that people make when they are thinking or considering something. Both forms of this word are useful because neither contains a vowel, which is great if you have no vowels on your rack. Hm scores 5 points, while hmm scores 8.
ho *interj*. Ho is a noise people make when they laugh. This little word is useful when you want to go in two directions at once. It's also worth remembering that ho is oh backwards: if you can't use one, you might be able to use the other. Ho scores 5 points.

hoard *n* (*pl* -s) store hidden away for future use ▶ *v* (-s, -ing, -ed) save or store ▶ **hoarder** *n* (*pl* -s)
hoarded *v* ▷ hoard
hoarder *n* ▷ hoard
hoarders *n* ▷ hoard
hoarding *n* (*pl* -s) large board for displaying advertisements ▶ *v* ▷ hoard
hoardings *n* ▷ hoarding
hoards *n*, *v* ▷ hoard
hoarfrost *n* (*pl* -s) white ground frost
hoarfrosts *n* ▷ hoarfrost
hoarier *adj* ▷ hoary
hoariest *adj* ▷ hoary
hoarse *adj* (-ser, -sest) (of a voice) rough and unclear ▶ **hoarsely** *adv* ▶ **hoarseness** *n* (*pl* -es)
hoarsely *adv* ▷ hoarse
hoarseness *n* ▷ hoarse
hoarsenesses *n* ▷ hoarse
hoarsest *adj* ▷ hoarse
hoarsest *adj* ▷ hoarse
hoary *adj* (-rier, -riest) grey or white(-haired)
hoax *n* (*pl* -es) deception or trick ▶ *v* (-es, -ing,

-ed) deceive or play a trick upon ▶ **hoaxer** *n*
hoaxed *v* ▷ hoax
hoaxer *n* ▷ hoax
hoaxers *n* ▷ hoax
hoaxes *n*, *v* ▷ hoax
hoaxing *v* ▷ hoax
hob *n* (*pl* -s) (BRIT) flat top part of a cooker, or a separate flat surface, containing gas or electric rings for cooking on
hobbies *n* ▷ hobby
hobble *v* (-les, -ling, -led) walk lamely
hobbled *v* ▷ hobble
hobbles *v* ▷ hobble
hobbling *v* ▷ hobble
hobby *n* (*pl* -bbies) activity pursued in one's spare time
hobbyhorse *n* (*pl* -s) favourite topic
hobbyhorses *n* ▷ hobbyhorse
hobgoblin *n* (*pl* -s) mischievous goblin
hobgoblins *n* ▷ hobgoblin
hobnob *v* (-s, -nobbing, -nobbed) (*foll. by* with) be on friendly terms (with)
hobnobbed *v* ▷ hobnob
hobnobbing *v* ▷ hobnob
hobnobs *v* ▷ hobnob
hobo *n* (*pl* -s) (US, AUST & NZ) tramp or vagrant
hobos *n* ▷ hobo
hobs *n* ▷ hob
hock[1] *n* (*pl* -s) joint in the back leg of an animal such as a horse that corresponds to the human ankle
hock[2] *n* (*pl* -s) white German wine
hock[3] *v* (-s, -ing, -ed) (*Informal*) pawn
hocked *v* ▷ hock
hockey *n* (*pl* -s) team game played on a field with a ball and curved sticks
hockeys *n* ▷ hockey
hocking *v* ▷ hock
hocks *n* ▷ hock[1, 2] *v* ▷ hock[3]
hod *n* (*pl* -s) open wooden box attached to a pole, for carrying bricks or mortar
hods *n* ▷ hod
hoe *n* (*pl* -s) long-handled tool used for loosening soil or weeding ▶ *v* (-oes, -oeing, -oed) scrape or weed with a hoe
hoed *v* ▷ hoe
hoeing *v* ▷ hoe
hoes *n*, *v* ▷ hoe
hog *n* (*pl* -s) castrated male pig (*Informal*) ▶ *v* (-s, -gging, -gged) (*Informal*) take more than one's share of
hogged *v* ▷ hog
hogging *v* ▷ hog
hogmanay *n* (*pl* -s) (in Scotland) New Year's Eve

hogmanays n ▷ hogmanay
hogs n, v ▷ hog
hogshead n (pl -s) large cask
hogsheads n ▷ hogshead
hogwash n (pl -es) (Informal) nonsense
hogwashes n ▷ hogwash
hoick v (-s, -ing, -ed) raise abruptly and sharply
  hoicked v ▷ hoick
  hoicking v ▷ hoick
  hoicks v ▷ hoick
hoist v (-s, -ing, -ed) raise or lift up ▶ n (pl -s) device for lifting things
  hoisted v ▷ hoist
  hoisting v ▷ hoist
  hoists v, n ▷ hoist
hold¹ v (-s, -ing, held) keep or support in or with the hands or arms ▶ n (pl -s) act or way of holding ▷ **holder** n (pl -s)
hold² n (pl -s) cargo compartment in a ship or aircraft
holdall n (pl -s) large strong travelling bag
  holdalls n ▷ holdall
  holder n ▷ hold¹
  holders n ▷ hold¹
holding n (pl -s) property, such as land or stocks and shares ▶ v ▷ hold¹
  holds n ▷ hold¹, ² v ▷ hold¹
holdup n (pl -s) armed robbery
  holdups n ▷ holdup
hole n (pl -s) area hollowed out in a solid ▶ v (-les, -ling, -led) make holes in
  holed v ▷ hole
  holes n, v ▷ hole
holiday n (pl -s) time spent away from home for rest or recreation
  holidays n ▷ holiday
  holier adj ▷ holy
  holiest adj ▷ holy
holiness n (pl -es) state of being holy
  holinesses n ▷ holiness
  holing v ▷ hole
  holisms n ▷ holism
holistic adj considering the complete person, physically and mentally, in the treatment of an illness ▷ **holism** n (pl -s)
  hollies n ▷ holly
  holloganism n ▷ hooligan
hollow adj having a hole or space inside ▶ n (pl -s) cavity or space ▶ v (-s, -ing, -ed) form a hollow in
  hollowed v ▷ hollow
  hollowing v ▷ hollow
  hollows n, v ▷ hollow
holly n (pl -llies) evergreen tree with prickly leaves and red berries

hollyhock n (pl -s) tall garden plant with spikes of colourful flowers
  hollyhocks n ▷ hollyhock
holocaust n (pl -s) destruction or loss of life on a massive scale
  holocausts n ▷ holocaust
hologram n (pl -s) three-dimensional photographic image
  holograms n ▷ hologram
holograph n (pl -s) document handwritten by the author
  holographs n ▷ holograph
holster n (pl -s) leather case for a pistol, hung from a belt
  holsters n ▷ holster
holy adj (-lier, -liest) of God or a god
homage n (pl -s) show of respect or honour towards someone or something
  homages n ▷ homage
home n (pl -s) place where one lives ▶ adj of one's home, birthplace, or native country (SPORT) ▶ adv to or at home ▶ v (-mes, -ming, -med) (foll. by **in** or **in on**) direct towards (a point or target) > **homeward** adj, adv
  > **homewards** adv
  homed v ▷ home
homeland n (pl -s) country from which a person's ancestors came
  homelands n ▷ homeland
homeless adj having nowhere to live
  ▶ pl n people who have nowhere to live
  > **homelessness** n (pl -es)
  homelessness n ▷ homeless
  homelessnesses n ▷ homeless
  homelier adj ▷ homely
  homeliest adj ▷ homely
homely adj (-lier, -liest) simple, ordinary, and comfortable
homemade adj made at home or on the premises
homeopath n (pl -s) person who practises homeopathy > **homeopathic** adj
  homeopathic adj ▷ homeopath
  homeopathies n ▷ homeopathy
  homeopaths n ▷ homeopath
homeopathy [home-ee-op-ath-ee] n (pl -thies) treatment of disease by small doses of a drug that produces symptoms of the disease in healthy people
  homes n, v ▷ home
homesick adj sad because missing one's home and family > **homesickness** n (pl -es)
  homesickness n ▷ homesick
  homesicknesses n ▷ homesick
homeward adj, adv ▷ home

homewards adv ▷ home
homework n (pl -s) school work done at home
homeworks n ▷ homework
homicidal adj ▷ homicide
homicide n (pl -s) killing of a human being
> **homicidal** adj
homicides n ▷ homicide
homilies n ▷ homily
homily n (pl -lies) speech telling people how they should behave
homing v ▷ home
hominid n (pl -s) man or any extinct forerunner of man
hominids n ▷ hominid
homogeneities n ▷ homogeneous
homogeneity n ▷ homogeneous
homogeneous [home-oh-**jean**-ee-uss] adj formed of similar parts > **homogeneity** n (pl -ties)
homogenize v (-zes, -zing, -zed) break up fat globules in (milk or cream) to distribute them evenly
homogenized v ▷ homogenize
homogenizes v ▷ homogenize
homogenizing v ▷ homogenize
homograph n (pl -s) word spelt the same as another, but with a different meaning
homographs n ▷ homograph
homologous [hom-ol-log-uss] adj having a related or similar position or structure
homonym n (pl -s) word spelt or pronounced the same as another, but with a different meaning
homonyms n ▷ homonym
homophobia n (pl -s) hatred or fear of homosexuals > **homophobic** adj
homophobias n ▷ homophobia
homophobic adj ▷ homophobia
homophone n (pl -s) word pronounced the same as another, but with a different meaning or spelling
homophones n ▷ homophone
homosexual n (pl -s) ▸ adj (person) sexually attracted to members of the same sex
> **homosexuality** n (pl -ties)
homosexualities n ▷ homosexual
homosexuality n ▷ homosexual
homosexuals n ▷ homosexual
hone v (-nes, -ning, -ned) sharpen
honed v ▷ hone
hones v ▷ hone
honest adj (-er, -est) truthful and moral
> **honestly** adv
honester adj ▷ honest
honestest adj ▷ honest

honesties n ▷ honesty
honestly adv ▷ honest
honesty n (pl -ties) quality of being honest
honey n (pl -s) sweet edible sticky substance made by bees from nectar
honeycomb n (pl -s) waxy structure of six-sided cells in which honey is stored by bees in a beehive
honeycombs n ▷ honeycomb
honeymoon n (pl -s) holiday taken by a newly married couple
honeymoons n ▷ honeymoon
honeys n ▷ honey
honeysuckle n (pl -s) climbing shrub with sweet-smelling flowers
honeysuckles n ▷ honeysuckle
hongi [hong-jee] n (pl -s) (NZ) Maori greeting in which people touch noses
hongis n ▷ hongi
honing v ▷ hone
honk n (pl -s) sound made by a car horn ▸ v (-s, -ing, -ed) (cause to) make this sound
honked v ▷ honk
honking v ▷ honk
honks n, v ▷ honk
honorary adj held or given only as an honour
honorific adj showing respect
honour n (pl -s) sense of honesty and fairness ▸ v (-s, -ing, -ed) give praise and attention to
honourable adj worthy of respect or esteem
> **honourably** adv
honourably adv ▷ honourable
honoured v ▷ honour
honouring v ▷ honour
honours n, v ▷ honour ▸ pl n university degree of a higher standard than an ordinary degree
hood¹ n (pl -s) head covering, often attached to a coat or jacket
hood² n (pl -s) (CHIEFLY US) (Slang) hoodlum
hooded adj (of a garment) having a hood
hoodlum n (pl -s) (Slang) violent criminal, gangster
hoodlums n ▷ hoodlum
hoodoo n (pl -s) (cause of) bad luck
hoodoos n ▷ hoodoo
hoods n ▷ hood¹,²
hoodwink v (-s, -ing, -ed) trick, deceive
hoodwinked v ▷ hoodwink
hoodwinking v ▷ hoodwink
hoodwinks v ▷ hoodwink
hoof n (pl hooves, hoofs) horny covering of the foot of a horse, deer, etc.
hoofs n ▷ hoof
hook n (pl -s) curved piece of metal, plastic, etc., used to hang, hold, or pull something

▶ v (-s, -ing, -ed) fasten or catch (as if) with a hook
hookah n (pl -s) oriental pipe in which smoke is drawn through water and a long tube
　hookahs n ▷ hookah
hooked adj bent like a hook ▶ v ▷ hook
hooker n (pl -s) (CHIEFLY US) (Slang) prostitute
　hookers n ▷ hooher
　hooking v ▷ hook
　hooks n, v ▷ hook
hookup n (pl -s) linking of radio or television stations
　hookups n ▷ hookup
hookworm n (pl -s) blood-sucking worm with hooked mouthparts
　hookworms n ▷ hookworm
hooligan n (pl -s) rowdy young person
　> **hooliganism** n (pl -s)
　hooliganisms n ▷ hooligan
　hooligans n ▷ hooligan
hoon n (pl -s) (AUST & NZ) (Slang) loutish youth who drives irresponsibly
　hoons n ▷ hoon
hoop n (pl -s) rigid circular band, used esp. as a child's toy or for animals to jump through in the circus
hoopla n (pl -s) fairground game in which hoops are thrown over objects in an attempt to win them
　hooplas n ▷ hoopla
　hoops n ▷ hoop
　hooray interj ▷ hurrah
hoot n (pl -s) sound of a car horn ▶ v (-s, -ing, -ed) sound (a car horn)
　hooted v ▷ hoot
hooter n (pl -s) device that hoots
　hooters n ▷ hooter
　hooting v ▷ hoot
　hoots n, v ▷ hoot
hoover n ® (pl -s) vacuum cleaner ▶ v (-s, -ing, -ed) clean with a vacuum cleaner
　hoovered v ▷ hoover
　hoovering v ▷ hoover
　hoovers n, v ▷ hoover
　hooves n ▷ hoof
hop¹ v (-s, -pping, -pped) jump on one foot ▶ n (pl -s) instance of hopping
hop² n (often pl) climbing plant, the dried flowers of which are used to make beer
hope v (-pes, -ping, -ped) want (something) to happen or be true ▶ n (pl -s) expectation of something desired > **hopeless** adj
　hoped v ▷ hope
hopeful adj having, expressing, or inspiring hope ▶ n (pl -s) person considered to be on the

brink of success
　hopefully adv in a hopeful manner
　hopefuller adj ▷ hopeful
　hopefuls n ▷ hopeful
　hopeless adj ▷ hope
　hopes v, n ▷ hope
　hoping v ▷ hope
　hopped v ▷ hop¹
hopper n (pl -s) container for storing substances such as grain or sand
　hoppers n ▷ hopper
　hopping v ▷ hop¹
　hops n ▷ hop¹,² ▶ v ▷ hop¹
hopscotch n (pl -es) children's game of hopping in a pattern drawn on the ground
　hopscotches n ▷ hopscotch
horde n (pl -s) large crowd
　hordes n ▷ horde
horizon n (pl -s) apparent line that divides the earth and the sky
　horizons n ▷ horizon ▶ pl n limits of scope, interest, or knowledge
horizontal adj parallel to the horizon, level, flat > **horizontally** adv
　horizontally adv ▷ horizontal
　hormonal adj ▷ hormone
hormone n (pl -s) substance secreted by certain glands which stimulates certain organs of the body > **hormonal** adj
　hormones n ▷ hormone
horn n (pl -s) one of a pair of bony growths sticking out of the heads of cattle, sheep, etc. > **horned** adj
hornbeam n (pl -s) tree with smooth grey bark
　hornbeams n ▷ hornbeam
hornbill n (pl -s) bird with a bony growth on its large beak
　hornbills n ▷ hornbill
hornblende n (pl -s) mineral containing aluminium, calcium, sodium, magnesium, and iron
　hornblendes n ▷ hornblende
　horned adj ▷ horn
hornet n (pl -s) large wasp with a severe sting
　hornets n ▷ hornet
hornpipe n (pl -s) (music for) a solo dance, traditionally performed by sailors
　hornpipes n ▷ hornpipe
　horns n ▷ horn
horny adj (-nier, -niest) of or like horn
horoscope n (pl -s) prediction of a person's future based on the positions of the planets, sun, and moon at his or her birth
　horoscopes n ▷ horoscope
horrendous adj very unpleasant and shocking

horrible adj disagreeable, unpleasant
  ▷ **horribly** adv
  horribly adv ▷ horrible
horrid adj disagreeable, unpleasant
horrific adj causing horror
  horrified v ▷ horrify
  horrifies v ▷ horrify
horrify v (-fies, -fying, -fied) cause to feel
  horror or shock
  horrifying v ▷ horrify
horror n (pl -s) (thing or person causing) terror
  or hatred
  horrors n ▷ horror
horse n (pl -s) large animal with hooves, a
  mane, and a tail, used for riding and pulling
  carts etc.
  horseflies n ▷ horsefly
horsefly n (pl -flies) large bloodsucking fly
horsehair n (pl -s) hair from the tail or mane
  of a horse
  horsehairs n ▷ horsehair
horseman n (pl -men) person riding a horse
  horsemen n ▷ horseman
horseplay n (pl -s) rough or rowdy play
  horseplays n ▷ horseplay
horsepower n (pl -s) unit of power (equivalent
  to 745.7 watts), used to measure the power
  of an engine
  horsepowers n ▷ horsepower
horseradish n (pl -es) strong-tasting root of a
  plant, usu. made into a sauce
  horseradishes n ▷ horseradish
  horses n ▷ horse
horseshoe n (pl -s) protective U-shaped piece
  of iron nailed to a horse's hoof, regarded as a
  symbol of good luck
  horseshoes n ▷ horseshoe
horsewoman n (pl -men) woman riding a
  horse
  horsewomen n ▷ horsewoman
horsey, horsy adj (-sier, -siest) very keen on
  horses
  horsier adj ▷ horsey
  horsiest adj ▷ horsey
  horsy adj ▷ horsey
  horticultural adj ▷ horticulture
  horticulturalist n ▷ horticulture
  horticulturalists n ▷ horticulture
horticulture n (pl -s) art or science of
  cultivating gardens ▷ **horticultural** adj
  ▷ **horticulturalist, horticulturist** n (pl -s)
  horticultures n ▷ horticulture
  horticulturist n ▷ horticulture
  horticulturists n ▷ horticulture
hosanna interj exclamation of praise to God

hose[1] n (pl -s) flexible pipe for conveying liquid
  ▶ v (-ses, -sing, -sed) water with a hose
hose[2] n (pl -s) stockings, socks, and tights
  hosed v ▷ hose[1]
  hoses n, v ▷ hose[1, 2] ▶ v ▷ hose[1]
  hosieries n ▷ hosiery
hosiery n (pl -ries) stockings, socks, and tights
  collectively
  hosing v ▷ hose[1]
hospice [hoss-piss] n (pl -s) nursing home for
  the terminally ill
  hospices n ▷ hospice
hospitable adj welcoming to strangers or
  guests
hospital n (pl -s) place where people who are ill
  are looked after and treated
  hospitalities n ▷ hospitality
  hospitalities n ▷ hospitality
hospitality n (pl -ties) kindness in welcoming
  strangers or guests
  hospitalization n ▷ hospitalize
  hospitalizations n ▷ hospitalize
hospitalize v (-izes, -izing, -ized) send or
  admit to hospital ▷ **hospitalization** n (pl -s)
  hospitalized v ▷ hospitalize
  hospitalizes v ▷ hospitalize
  hospitalizing v ▷ hospitalize
  hospitals n ▷ hospital
host[1] n (pl -s) man who entertains guests,
  esp. in his own home ▶ v (-s, -ing, -ed) be the
  host of
host[2] n (pl -s) large number
hostage n (pl -s) person who is illegally held
  prisoner until certain demands are met by
  other people
  hostages n ▷ hostage
  hosted v ▷ host[1]
hostel n (pl -s) building providing
  accommodation at a low cost for a specific
  group of people such as students, travellers,
  homeless people, etc.
  hostelries n ▷ hostelry
hostelry n (pl -ries) (Old-fashioned or facetious)
  inn, pub
  hostels n ▷ hostel
hostess n (pl -es) woman who entertains
  guests, esp. in her own home
  hostesses n ▷ hostess
hostile adj unfriendly
  hostilities n ▷ hostility ▶ pl n acts of warfare
hostility n (pl -ties) unfriendly and aggressive
  feelings or behaviour
  hosting v ▷ host[1]
  hosts n ▷ host[1, 2] ▶ v ▷ host[1]
hot adj (-tter, -ttest) having a high

temperature in trouble > **hotly** adv

hotbed n (pl -s) any place encouraging a particular activity
  hotbeds n ▷ hotbed
hotchpotch n (pl -es) jumbled mixture
  hotchpotches n ▷ hotchpotch
hotel n (pl -s) commercial establishment providing lodging and meals
hotelier n (pl -s) owner or manager of a hotel
  hoteliers n ▷ hotelier
  hotels n ▷ hotel
hotfoot adv (Informal) quickly and eagerly
hotheaded adj rash, having a hot temper
hothouse n (pl -s) greenhouse
  hothouses n ▷ hothouse
hotline n (pl -s) direct telephone link for emergency use
  hotlines n ▷ hotline
  hotly adv ▷ hot
hotplate n (pl -s) heated metal surface on an electric cooker
  hotplates n ▷ hotplate
  hotter adj ▷ hot
  hottest adj ▷ hot
hound n (pl -s) hunting dog ▶ v (-s, -ing, -ed) pursue relentlessly
  hounded v ▷ hound
  hounding v ▷ hound
  hounds n, v ▷ hound
hour n (pl -s) twenty-fourth part of a day, sixty minutes
hourglass n (pl -es) device with two glass compartments, containing a quantity of sand that takes an hour to trickle from the top section to the bottom one
  hourglasses n ▷ hourglass
houri n (pl -s) (ISLAM) any of the nymphs of paradise
  houris n ▷ houri
hourly adj, adv (happening) every hour
hours pl n period regularly appointed for work or business ▶ n ▷ hour
house n (pl -s) building used as a home ▶ v (-ses, -sing, -sed) give accommodation to
houseboat n (pl -s) stationary boat used as a home
  houseboats n ▷ houseboat
housebreaker n (pl -s) burglar
  housebreakers n ▷ housebreaker
housecoat n (pl -s) woman's long loose coat-shaped garment for wearing at home
  housecoats n ▷ housecoat
  housed v ▷ house
household n (pl -s) all the people living in a house

householder n (pl -s) person who owns or rents a house
  householders n ▷ householder
  households n ▷ household
housekeeper n (pl -s) person employed to run someone else's household
  housekeepers n ▷ housekeeper
housekeeping n (pl -s) (money for) running a household
  housekeepings n ▷ housekeeping
housemaid n (pl -s) female servant employed to do housework
  housemaids n ▷ housemaid
  houses n, v ▷ house
housewarming n (pl -s) party to celebrate moving into a new home
  housewarmings n ▷ housewarming
housewife n (pl -wives) woman who runs her own household and does not have a job
  housewives n ▷ housewife
housework n (pl -s) work of running a home, such as cleaning, cooking, and shopping
  houseworks n ▷ housework
housing n (pl -s) (providing of) houses ▶ v ▷ house
  housings n ▷ housing
hovea n (pl -s) Australian plant with purple flowers
  hoveas n ▷ hovea
hovel n (pl -s) small dirty house or hut
  hovels n ▷ hovel
hover v (-s, -ing, -red) (of a bird etc.) remain suspended in one place in the air
hovercraft n (pl -s) vehicle which can travel over both land and sea on a cushion of air
  hovercrafts n ▷ hovercraft
  hovered v ▷ hover
  hovering v ▷ hover
  hovers v ▷ hover
how adv in what way, by what means
howdah n (pl -s) canopied seat on an elephant's back
  howdahs n ▷ howdah
however adv nevertheless
howitzer n (pl -s) large gun firing shells at a steep angle
  howitzers n ▷ howitzer
howl n (pl -s) loud wailing cry ▶ v (-s, -ing, -ed) utter a howl
  howled v ▷ howl
howler n (pl -s) (Informal) stupid mistake
  howlers n ▷ howler
  howling v ▷ howl
  howls n, v ▷ howl
hoyden n (pl -s) (Old-fashioned) wild or

boisterous girl

hoydens n ▷ hoyden

hox v (hoxes, hoxing, hoxed). This is a word found in Shakespeare's plays, and means to cut a horse's hamstring. This unusual word is a handy one to remember if you draw an X. Hox scores 12 points.

hub n (pl -s) centre of a wheel, through which the axle passes

hubbies n ▷ hubby

hubbub n (pl -s) confused noise of many voices

hubbubs n ▷ hubbub

hubby n (pl -s) (Informal) husband

hubris [hew-briss] n (pl -es) (Formal) pride, arrogance

hubrises ▷ hubris

hubs n ▷ hub

huckster n (pl -s) person using aggressive methods of selling

hucksters n ▷ huckster

huddle v (-les, -ling, -led) hunch (oneself) through cold or fear ▶ n (pl -s) small group

huddled v ▷ huddle

huddles n, v ▷ huddle

huddling v ▷ huddle

hue n (pl -s) colour, shade

hues n ▷ hue

huff n (pl -s) passing mood of anger or resentment ▶ v (-s, -ing, -ed) blow or puff heavily ▷ **huffy** adj (-ffier, -ffiest) ▷ **huffily** adv

huffed v ▷ huff

huffier adj ▷ huff

huffiest adj ▷ huff

huffily adv ▷ huff

huffing v ▷ huff

huffs n, v ▷ huff

huffy adj ▷ huff

hug v (-s, -gging, -gged) clasp tightly in the arms, usu. with affection ▶ n (pl -s) tight or fond embrace

huge adj (-r, -st) very big ▷ **hugely** adv

huger adj ▷ huge

hugest adj ▷ huge

hugged v ▷ hug

hugging v ▷ hug

hugs n, v ▷ hug

huh interj exclamation of derision, bewilderment, or inquiry

hui [hoo-ee] n (pl huies) (NZ) meeting of Maori people

huies n ▷ hui

hula n (pl -s) swaying Hawaiian dance

hulas n ▷ hula

hulk n (pl -s) body of an abandoned ship

hulking adj bulky, unwieldy

hulks n ▷ hulk

hull n (pl -s) main body of a boat ▶ v (-s, -ing, -ed) remove the hulls from

hullabaloo n (pl -loos) loud confused noise or clamour

hullabaloos n ▷ hullabaloo

hulled v ▷ hull

hulling v ▷ hull

hulls n, v ▷ hull

hum v (-s, -mming, -mmed) make a low continuous vibrating sound ▶ n (pl -s) humming sound

human adj of or typical of people ▶ n (pl -s) human being

humane adj (-r, -st) kind or merciful ▷ **humanely** adv

humanely adv ▷ humane

humaner adj ▷ humane

humanest adj ▷ humane

humanism n (pl -s) belief in human effort rather than religion ▷ **humanist** n (pl -s)

humanisms n ▷ humanism

humanist n ▷ humanism

humanists n ▷ humanism

humanitarian adj, n (pl -s) (person) having the interests of humankind at heart

humanitarians n ▷ humanitarian

humanities n ▷ humanity ▶ pl n study of literature, philosophy, and the arts

humanity n (pl -ties) human race

humanize v (-zes, -zing, -zed) make human or humane

humanized v ▷ humanize

humanizes v ▷ humanize

humanizing v ▷ humanize

humankind n (pl -s) human race

humankinds n ▷ humankind

humanly adv by human powers or means

humans n ▷ human

humble adj (-r, -st) conscious of one's failings ▶ v (-les, -ling, -led) cause to feel humble, humiliate ▷ **humbly** adv

humbled v ▷ humble

humbler adj ▷ humble

humbles v ▷ humble

humblest adj ▷ humble

humbling v ▷ humble

humbly adv ▷ humble

humbug n (pl -s) (BRIT) hard striped peppermint sweet

humbugs n ▷ humbug

humdinger n (pl -s) (Slang) excellent person or thing

humdingers n ▷ humdinger

humdrum *adj* ordinary, dull
humeri *n* ▷ humerus
humerus [hew-mer-uss] *n* (*pl* -meri) [-mer-rye] bone from the shoulder to the elbow
humid *adj* (-er, -est) damp and hot **> humidity** *n* (*pl* -ties) **> humidify** *v* (-fies, -fying, -fied)
  humider *adj* ▷ humid
  humidest *adj* ▷ humid
  humidified *v* ▷ humid
humidifier *n* (*pl* -s) device for increasing the amount of water vapour in the air in a room
  humidifiers *n* ▷ humidifier
  humidifies *v* ▷ humid
  humidifying *v* ▷ humidify
  humidities *n* ▷ humid
  humidity *n* ▷ humid
humiliate *v* (-tes, -ting, -ted) lower the dignity or hurt the pride of **> humiliating** *adj* **> humiliation** *n* (*pl* -s)
  humiliated *v* ▷ humiliate
  humiliates *v* ▷ humiliate
humiliating *v, adj* ▷ humiliate
  humiliation *n* ▷ humiliate
  humiliations *n* ▷ humiliate
  humilities *n* ▷ humility
humility *n* (*pl* humilities) quality of being humble
  hummed *v* ▷ hum
  humming *v* ▷ hum
hummingbird *n* (*pl* -s) very small American bird whose powerful wings make a humming noise as they vibrate
  hummingbirds *n* ▷ hummingbird
hummock *n* (*pl* -s) very small hill
  hummocks *n* ▷ hummock
humorist *n* (*pl* -s) writer or entertainer who uses humour in his or her work
  humorists *n* ▷ humorist
  humorous *adj* ▷ humour
  humorously *adj* ▷ humour
humour *n* (*pl* -s) ability to say or perceive things that are amusing ▶ *v* (-s, -ing, -ed) be kind and indulgent to **> humorous** *adj* **> humorously** *adv*
  humoured *v* ▷ humour
  humouring *v* ▷ humour
  humours *n, v* ▷ humour
hump *n* (*pl* -s) raised piece of ground ▶ *v* (-s, -ing, -ed) (*Slang*) carry or heave
  humped *v* ▷ hump
  humping *v* ▷ hump
  humps *n, v* ▷ hump
  hums *v, n* ▷ hum
humus [hew-muss] *n* (*pl* -es) decomposing vegetable and animal mould in the soil

humuses *n* ▷ humus
hunch *n* (*pl* -es) feeling or suspicion not based on facts ▶ *v* (-es, -ing, -ed) draw (one's shoulders) up or together
hunchback *n* (*pl* -s) (*Offens*) person with an abnormal curvature of the spine
  hunchbacks *n* ▷ hunchback
  hunched *v* ▷ hunch
  hunches *n, v* ▷ hunch
  hunching *v* ▷ hunch
hundred *adj* ten times ten ▶ *n* (*pl* -s) (*often pl*) large but unspecified number **> hundredth** *adj, n* (*pl* -s)
  hundreds *n* ▷ hundred
  hundredth *n* ▷ hundred
  hundredths *n* ▷ hundred
hundredweight *n* (*pl* -s) (*BRIT*) unit of weight of 112 pounds (50.8 kilograms)
  hundredweights *n* ▷ hundredweight
hung *v* ▶ hang ▶ *adj* (of a parliament or jury) with no side having a clear majority
hunger *n* (*pl* -s) discomfort or weakness from lack of food ▶ *v* (-s, -ing, -ed) (*foll. by* for) want very much
  hungered *v* ▷ hunger
  hungering *v* ▷ hunger
  hungers *n, v* ▷ hunger
  hungrier *adj* ▷ hungry
  hungriest *adj* ▷ hungry
  hungrily *adv* ▷ hungry
hungry *adj* (-rier, -riest) desiring food (*foll. by* for) **> hungrily** *adv*
hunk *n* (*pl* -s) large piece
  hunks *n* ▷ hunk
hunt *v* (-s, -ing, -ed) seek out and kill (wild animals) for food or sport ▶ *n* (*pl* -s) hunting
huntaway *n* (*pl* -s) (*NZ*) sheepdog trained to drive sheep by barking
  huntaways *n* ▷ huntaway
  hunted *v* ▷ hunt
hunter *n* (*pl* -s) person or animal that hunts wild animals for food or sport
  hunters *n* ▷ hunter
  hunting *v* ▷ hunt
  hunts *v, n* ▷ hunt
huntsman *n* (*pl* -men) man who hunts wild animals, esp. foxes
  huntsmen *n* ▷ huntsman
hurdle *n* (*pl* -s) (*SPORT*) light barrier for jumping over in some races ▶ *v* (-les, -ling, -led) jump over (something) **> hurdler** *n* (*pl* -s)
  hurdled *v* ▷ hurdle
  hurdler *n* ▷ hurdle
  hurdlers *n* ▷ hurdle
hurdles *n, v* ▷ hurdle ▶ *pl n* race involving

hurdles
hurdling v ▷ hurdle
hurl v (-s, -ing, -ed) throw or utter forcefully
  hurled v ▷ hurl
  hurley n ▷ hurling
  hurleys n ▷ hurling
hurling, hurley n (pl -s) Irish game like hockey
  ▶ v ▷ hurl
  hurlings n ▷ hurling
  hurls v ▷ hurl
hurrah, hurray interj exclamation of joy or
  applause
hurricane n (pl -s) very strong, often
  destructive, wind or storm
  hurricanes n ▷ hurricane
  hurried v ▷ hurry
  hurriedly adv ▷ hurry
  hurries v, n ▷ hurry
hurry v (-ries, -rying, -ried) (cause to) move or
  act very quickly ▶ n (pl -ries) doing something
  quickly or the need to do something quickly
  > **hurriedly** adv
  hurrying v ▷ hurry
hurt v (-s, -ing, hurt) cause physical or
  mental pain to ▶ n (pl -s) physical or mental
  pain
hurtful adj unkind
  hurting v ▷ hurt
hurtle v (-les, -ling, -led) move quickly or
  violently
  hurtled v ▷ hurtle
  hurtles v ▷ hurtle
  hurtling v ▷ hurtle
  hurts v, n ▷ hurt
husband n (pl -s) woman's partner in marriage
  ▶ v (-s, -ing, -ed) use economically
  husbanded v ▷ husband
  husbanding v ▷ husband
  husbandries n ▷ husbandry
husbandry n (pl -ries) farming
  husbands n, v ▷ husband
hush v (-es, -ing, -ed) make or be silent ▶ n (pl
  -es) stillness or silence
  hushed v ▷ hush
  hushes v, n ▷ hush
  hushing v ▷ hush
husk n (pl -s) outer covering of certain seeds
  and fruits ▶ v (-s, -ing, -ed) remove the husk
  from
  husked v ▷ husk
  huskier adj ▷ husky¹
  huskies n ▷ husky²
  huskiest adj ▷ husky¹
  huskily adv ▷ husky¹
  husking v ▷ husk

husks n, v ▷ husk
husky¹ adj (-kier, -kiest) slightly hoarse
  > **huskily** adv
husky² n (pl -kies) Arctic sledge dog with thick
  hair and a curled tail
hussar [hoo-zar] n (pl -s) (HIST) lightly armed
  cavalry soldier
  hussars n ▷ hussar
  hussies n ▷ hussy
hussy n (pl -sies) immodest or promiscuous
  woman
hustings pl n political campaigns and
  speeches before an election
hustle v (-les, -ling, -led) push about, jostle ▶ n
  (pl -les) lively activity or bustle
  hustled v ▷ hustle
  hustles v, n ▷ hustle
  hustling v ▷ hustle
hut n (pl -s) small house, shelter, or shed
hutch n (pl -es) cage for pet rabbits etc.
  hutches n ▷ hutch
  huts n ▷ hut
hyacinth n (pl -s) sweet-smelling spring flower
  that grows from a bulb
  hyacinths n ▷ hyacinth
hyaena n (pl -s) ▷ hyena
  hyaenas n ▷ hyena
hybrid n (pl -s) offspring of two plants or
  animals of different species ▶ adj of mixed
  origin
  hybrids n ▷ hybrid
hydra n (pl -s) mythical many-headed water
  serpent
hydrangea n (pl -s) ornamental shrub with
  clusters of pink, blue, or white flowers
  hydrangeas n ▷ hydrangea
hydrant n (pl -s) outlet from a water main with
  a nozzle for a hose
  hydrants n ▷ hydrant
  hydras n ▷ hydra
hydrate n (pl -tes) chemical compound of
  water with another substance
  hydrates n ▷ hydrate
hydraulic adj operated by pressure forced
  through a pipe by a liquid such as water or oil
  hydraulically adv ▷ hydraulics
hydraulics n study of the mechanical
  properties of fluids as they apply to practical
  engineering > **hydraulically** adv
hydro¹ n (pl -s) hotel offering facilities for
  hydropathy
hydro² adj ▷ hydroelectric
hydrocarbon n (pl -s) compound of hydrogen
  and carbon
  hydrocarbons n ▷ hydrocarbon

hydroelectric *adj* of the generation of electricity by water pressure

hydrofoil *n* (*pl* -s) fast light boat with its hull raised out of the water on one or more pairs of fins
　hydrofoils *n* ▷ hydrofoil

hydrogen *n* (*pl* -s) (CHEM) light flammable colourless gas that combines with oxygen to form water
　hydrogens *n* ▷ hydrogen
　hydrolyses *n* ▷ hydrolysis

hydrolysis [hie-**drol**-iss-iss] *n* (*pl* -yses) decomposition of a chemical compound reacting with water

hydrometer [hie-**drom**-it-er] *n* (*pl* -s) instrument for measuring the density of a liquid
　hydrometers *n* ▷ hydrometer
　hydropathies *n* ▷ hydropathy

hydropathy *n* (*pl* -thies) method of treating disease by the use of large quantities of water both internally and externally

hydrophobia *n* (*pl* -s) rabies
　hydrophobias *n* ▷ hydrophobia

hydroplane *n* (*pl* -s) light motorboat that skims the water
　hydroplanes *n* ▷ hydroplane

hydroponics *n* method of growing plants in water rather than soil
　hydros *n* ▷ hydro¹
　hydrotherapies *n* ▷ hydrotherapy

hydrotherapy *n* (*pl* -pies) (MED) treatment of certain diseases by exercise in water

hyena *n* (*pl* -s) scavenging doglike mammal of Africa and S Asia
　hyenas *n* ▷ hyena

hygiene *n* (*pl* -s) principles and practice of health and cleanliness > **hygienic** *adj* > **hygienically** *adv*
　hygienic *adj* ▷ hygiene
　hygienically *adj* ▷ hygiene

hymen *n* (*pl* -s) membrane partly covering the opening of a girl's vagina, which breaks before puberty or at the first occurrence of sexual intercourse
　hymens *n* ▷ hymen

hymn *n* (*pl* -s) Christian song of praise sung to God or a saint

hymnal *n* (*pl* -s) book of hymns (*also* **hymn book**)
　hymnals *n* ▷ hymnal
　hymns *n* ▷ hymn

hype *n* (*pl* -s) intensive or exaggerated publicity or sales promotion ▶ *v* (-pes, -ping, -ped) promote (a product) using intensive or exaggerated publicity

hyped *v* ▷ hype

hyper *adj* (*Informal*) overactive or overexcited

hyperbola [hie-**per**-bol-a] *n* (*pl* -s) (GEOM) curve produced when a cone is cut by a plane at a steeper angle to its base than its side
　hyperbolas *n* ▷ hyperbola

hyperbole [hie-**per**-bol-ee] *n* (*pl* -s) deliberate exaggeration for effect
　> **hyperbolic** *adj*
　hyperboles *n* ▷ hyperbole
　hyperbolic *adj* ▷ hyperbole

hyperlink (COMPUTERS) *n* (*pl* -s) link from a hypertext file that gives users instant access to related material in another file ▶ *v* (-s, -ing, -ed) link (files) in this way
　hyperlinked *v* ▷ hyperlink
　hyperlinking *v* ▷ hyperlink
　hyperlinks *v*, *n* ▷ hyperlink

hypermarket *n* (*pl* -s) huge self-service store
　hypermarkets *n* ▷ hypermarket

hypersensitive *adj* extremely sensitive to certain drugs, extremes of temperature, etc.

hypersonic *adj* having a speed of at least five times the speed of sound

hypertension *n* (*pl* -s) very high blood pressure
　hypertensions *n* ▷ hypertension
　hypertensions *n* ▷ hypertension

hypertext *n* (*pl* -s) computer software and hardware that allows users to store and view text and move between related items easily
　hypertexts *n* ▷ hypertext
　hypes *n*, *v* ▷ hype

hyphen *n* (*pl* -s) punctuation mark (-) indicating that two words or syllables are connected

hyphenated *adj* (of two words or syllables) having a hyphen between them
　> **hyphenation** *n* (*pl* -s)
　hyphenation *n* ▷ hyphenated
　hyphenations *n* ▷ hyphenated
　hyphens *n* ▷ hyphen
　hyping *v* ▷ hype
　hypnoses *n* ▷ hypnosis

hypnosis *n* (*pl* -noses) artificially induced state of relaxation in which the mind is more than usually receptive to suggestion

hypnotic *adj* of or (as if) producing hypnosis

hypnotism *n* (*pl* -s) inducing hypnosis in someone > **hypnotist** *n* (*pl* -s) > **hypnotize** *v* (-tizes, -tizing, -tized)
　hypnotisms *n* ▷ hypnotism
　hypnotist *n* ▷ hypnotism
　hypnotists *n* ▷ hypnotism
　hypnotize *v* ▷ hypnotism

hypnotized v ▷ hypnotism
hypnotizes v ▷ hypnotism
hypnotizing v ▷ hypnotism
hypoallergenic adj (of cosmetics) not likely to cause an allergic reaction
hypochondria n (pl -s) undue preoccupation with one's health > **hypochondriac** n (pl -s)
　hypochondriac n ▷ hypochondria
　hypochondriacs n ▷ hypochondria
　hypochondrias n ▷ hypochondria
　hypocrisies n ▷ hypocrisy
hypocrisy [hip-**ok**-rass-ee] n (pl -sies) (instance of) pretence of having standards or beliefs that are contrary to one's real character or actual behaviour
hypocrite [hip-oh-krit] n (pl -s) person who pretends to be what he or she is not > **hypocritical** adj > **hypocritically** adv
　hypocrites n ▷ hypocrite
　hypocritical adj ▷ hypocrite
　hypocritically adv ▷ hypocrite
hypodermic adj, n (pl -s) (denoting) a syringe or needle used to inject a drug beneath the skin
　hypodermics n ▷ hypodermic
hypotension n (pl -s) very low blood pressure
hypotenuse [hie-**pot**-a-news] n (pl -s) side of a right-angled triangle opposite the right angle
　hypotenuses n ▷ hypotenuse
hypothermia n (pl -s) condition in which a person's body temperature is dangerously low as a result of prolonged exposure to severe cold
　hypothermias n ▷ hypothermia
　hypotheses n ▷ hypothesis
hypothesis [hie-**poth**-iss-iss] n (pl -ses) [-seez] suggested but unproved explanation of something
hypothetical adj based on assumption rather than fact or reality > **hypothetically** adv
　hypothetically adj ▷ hypothetical
　hyraces n ▷ hyrax
hyrax n (pl -raxes or -races) type of hoofed rodent-like animal of Africa and Asia
　hyraxes n ▷ hyrax
　hysterectomies n ▷ hysterectomy
hysterectomy n (pl -mies) surgical removal of the womb
hysteria n (pl -s) state of uncontrolled excitement, anger, or panic > **hysterical** adj > **hysterically** adv
　hysterias n ▷ hysteria
　hysterical adj ▷ hysteria
　hysterically adj ▷ hysteria
hysterics pl n attack of hysteria

I i

The letter I can prove a difficult tile to use effectively in Scrabble. It's one of the most common tiles in the game, so you often end up with two or more on your rack, but it can be hard to get rid of. Where I does come in very useful, though, is in the number of everyday short words that can be formed from it, which are very helpful when you need to form short words in addition to the main word that you want to play. These words include **in**, **is**, **it** (2 points each), **id** (3) and **if** (5). Other handy words are **icy** (8), **ivy** (9) and **imp** (7). Don't forget the three-letter words that use K: **ilk**, **ink** and **irk** (7 each).

ibex [ibe-eks] *n* (*pl* -es) wild goat of N with large backward-curving horns
   ibexes *n* ▷ ibex
ibis [ibe-iss] *n* (*pl* -es) large wading bird with long legs
   ibises *n* ▷ ibis
ice *n* (*pl* -s) frozen water ▶ *v* (-ces, -cing, -ced) (*foll. by* up *or* over) become covered with ice
iceberg *n* (*pl* -s) large floating mass of ice
   icebergs *n* ▷ iceberg
icebox *n* (*pl* -es) (us) refrigerator
   iceboxes *n* ▷ icebox
icecap *n* (*pl* -s) mass of ice permanently covering an area
   icecaps *n* ▷ icecap
iced *adj* covered with icing ▶ *v* ▷ ice
   ices *v*, *n* ▷ ice

    ich *pron.* Ich is an old dialect form of I. This is a useful little word that is worth remembering because of its unusual combination of letters and relatively high score. Ich scores 8 points.

   ichthyologies *n* ▷ ichthyology
ichthyology [ik-thi-ol-a-jee] *n* (*pl* -gies) scientific study of fish
icicle *n* (*pl* -s) tapering spike of ice hanging where water has dripped
   icicles *n* ▷ icicle
   icier *adj* ▷ icy
   iciest *adj* ▷ icy
   icily *adv* ▷ icy
   iciness *n* ▷ icy
   icinesses *n* ▷ icy
icing *v* ▷ ice ▶ *n* (*pl* -s) mixture of sugar and water etc., used to cover and decorate cakes
   icings *n* ▷ icing

    ick *interj.* Ick is something that people

say when they encounter something unpleasant or disgusting. Ick is a good word to remember because, in addition to being useful when there's little space, it's one of the highest-scoring three-letter word beginning with I. Ick scores 9 points.

icon *n* (*pl* -s) picture of Christ or another religious figure, regarded as holy in the Orthodox Church
iconoclast *n* (*pl* -s) person who attacks established ideas or principles > **iconoclastic** *adj*
   iconoclastic *adj* ▷ iconoclastic
   iconoclasts *n* ▷ iconoclast
   icons *n* ▷ icon
icy *adj* (-cier, -ciest) very cold > **icily** *adv* > **iciness** *n* (*pl* -es)
id *n* (*pl* -s) (PSYCHOANALYSIS) the mind's instinctive unconscious energies

    ide (*ides*). An ide is a kind of fish. This combination of letters is a good one to keep in mind because it is both a suffix that can be added to words already on the board and a word in its own right. Ide scores 4 points.

idea *n* (*pl* -s) plan or thought formed in the mind
ideal *adj* most suitable ▶ *n* (*pl* -s) conception of something that is perfect > **idealist** *n* (*pl* -s) > **idealistic** *adj* > **ideally** *adv*
idealism *n* (*pl* -s) tendency to seek perfection in everything
   idealisms *n* ▷ idealism
   idealist *n* ▷ ideal
   idealistic *adj* ▷ ideal
   idealists *n* ▷ ideal

idealization n ▷ idealize
idealizations n ▷ idealize
idealize v (-izes, -izing, -ized) regard or portray as perfect or nearly perfect > **idealization** n (pl -s)
idealized n ▷ idealize
idealizes n ▷ idealize
idealizing n ▷ idealize
ideally adv ▷ ideal
ideals n ▷ ideal
ideas n ▷ idea
idem pron, adj (LATIN) the same: used to refer to an article, chapter, or book already quoted
identical adj exactly the same > **identically** adv
identically adv ▷ identical
identifiable adj ▷ identify
identification n ▷ identify
identifications n ▷ identify
identified v ▷ identify
identifies v ▷ identify
identify v (-fies, -fying, -fied) prove or recognize as being a certain person or thing > **identifiable** adj > **identification** n (pl -s)
identifying v ▷ identify
identities n ▷ identity
identity n (pl -ties) state of being a specified person or thing
ideological adj ▷ ideology
ideologies n ▷ ideology
ideologist n ▷ ideology
ideologists n ▷ ideology
ideology n (pl -gies) body of ideas and beliefs of a group, nation, etc. > **ideological** adj > **ideologist** n (pl -s)
idiocies n ▷ idiocy
idiocy n (pl -cies) utter stupidity
idiom n (pl -s) group of words which when used together have a different meaning from the words individually > **idiomatic** adj > **idiomatically** adv
idiomatic adj ▷ idiom
idiomatically adv ▷ idiom
idioms n ▷ idiom
idiosyncrasies n ▷ idiosyncrasy
idiosyncrasy n (pl -sies) personal peculiarity of mind, habit, or behaviour
idiot n (pl -s) foolish or stupid person > **idiotic** adj > **idiotically** adv
idiotic adj ▷ idiot
idiotically adv ▷ idiot
idiots n ▷ idiot
idle adj not doing anything ▶ v (-les, -ling, -led) (usu. foll. by away) spend (time) doing very little > **idleness** n (pl -s) > **idler** n (pl -s) > **idly** adv

idled v ▷ idle
idleness n ▷ idle
idlenesses n ▷ idle
idler n ▷ idle
idlers n ▷ idle
idles v ▷ idle
idling v ▷ idle
idly adj ▷ idle
idol n (pl -s) object of excessive devotion
idolatries n ▷ idolatry
idolatrous adj ▷ idolatry
idolatry n (pl -ries) worship of idols > **idolatrous** adj
idolize v (-izes, -izing, -ized) love or admire excessively
idolized v ▷ idolize
idolizes v ▷ idolize
idolizing v ▷ idolize
idols n ▷ idol
ids n ▷ id
idyll [id-ill] n (pl -s) scene or time of great peace and happiness > **idyllic** adj > **idyllically** adv
idyllic adj ▷ idyll
idyllically adj ▷ idyll
idylls n ▷ idyll
if conj on the condition or supposition that ▶ n (pl -s) uncertainty or doubt

iff conj. Iff is a word used in logic to mean if and only if. This word is worth remembering: not only can it come in handy when there isn't much space on the board, but it's also one of the highest-scoring three-letter word beginning with I. Iff scores 9 points.

iffy adj (Informal) doubtful, uncertain
ifs n ▷ if
igloo n (pl -loos) dome-shaped Inuit house made of snow and ice
igloos n ▷ igloo
igneous [ig-nee-uss] adj (of rock) formed as molten rock cools and hardens
ignite v (-tes, -ting, -ted) catch fire or set fire to
ignited v ▷ ignite
ignites v ▷ ignite
igniting v ▷ ignite
ignition n (pl -s) system that ignites the fuel-and-air mixture to start an engine
ignitions n ▷ ignition
ignoble adj dishonourable
ignominies n ▷ ignominy
ignominious adj ▷ ignominy
ignominiously adj ▷ ignominy
ignominy [ig-nom-in-ee] n (pl -nies) humiliating disgrace > **ignominious** adj > **ignominiously** adv

ignoramus n (pl -muses) ignorant person
  ignoramuses n ▷ ignoramus
  ignorance n ▷ ignorant
  ignorances n ▷ ignorance
ignorant adj lacking knowledge > **ignorance** n (pl -s)
ignore v (-res, -ring, -red) refuse to notice, disregard deliberately
  ignored v ▷ ignore
  ignores v ▷ ignore
  ignoring v ▷ ignore
iguana n (pl -s) large tropical American lizard
  iguanas n ▷ iguana
ileum n (pl -s) lowest part of the small intestine
  ileums n ▷ ileum
ilk n (pl -s) type
  ilks n ▷ ilk
ill adj not in good health ▶ n (pl -s) evil, harm ▶ adv badly > **illness** n (pl -s)
illegal adj against the law > **illegally** adv > **illegality** n (pl -ties)
  illegalities n ▷ illegal
  illegality n ▷ illegal
  illegally adv ▷ illegal
illegible adj unable to be read or deciphered
  illegitimacies n ▷ illegitimate
  illegitimacy n ▷ illegitimate
illegitimate adj born of parents not married to each other > **illegitimacy** n (pl -s)
illicit adj illegal
  illiteracies n ▷ illiterate
  illiteracy n ▷ illiterate
illiterate n (pl -s) ▶ adj (person) unable to read or write > **illiteracy** n (pl -s)
  illiterates n ▷ illiterate
  illness n ▷ ill
  illnesses n ▷ ill
illogical adj unreasonable > **illogicality** n (pl -lities)
  illogicalities adj ▷ illogical
  illogicality adj ▷ illogical
  ills n ▷ ill
illuminate v (-tes, -ting, -ted) light up > **illumination** n (pl -s) > **illuminating** adj
  illuminated v ▷ illuminate
  illuminates v ▷ illuminate
  illuminating adj, v ▷ illuminate
  illumination n ▷ illuminate
  illuminations n ▷ illuminate
illusion n (pl -s) deceptive appearance or belief
illusionist n (pl -s) conjuror
  illusionists n ▷ illusionist
  illusions n ▷ illusion
illusory adj seeming to be true, but actually false
illustrate v (-tes, -ting, -ted) explain by use of examples > **illustrative** adj > **illustrator** n (pl -s)
  illustrated v ▷ illustrate
  illustrates v ▷ illustrate
  illustrating v ▷ illustrate
illustration n (pl -s) picture or diagram
  illustrations n ▷ illustrate
  illustrative adj ▷ illustrate
  illustrator n ▷ illustrate
  illustrators n ▷ illustrate
illustrious adj famous and distinguished
image n (pl -s) mental picture of someone or something
  imageries n ▷ imagery
imagery n (pl -ries) images collectively, esp. in the arts
  images n ▷ image
  imaginable adj ▷ imagine
imaginary adj existing only in the imagination
imagination n (pl -s) ability to make mental images of things that may not exist in real life
  imaginations n ▷ imagination
imaginative adj having or showing a lot of creative mental ability > **imaginatively** adv
  imaginatively adv ▷ imaginative
imagine v (-nes, -ning, -ned) form a mental image of > **imaginable** adj
  imagined v ▷ imagine
  imagines v ▷ imagine ▶ n ▷ imago
  imagining v ▷ imagine
imago [im-**may**-go] n (pl -goes, -gines) [im-**maj**-in-ees] sexually mature adult insect
  imagoes n ▷ imago
imam n (pl -s) leader of prayers in a mosque
  imams n ▷ imam
imbalance n (pl -s) lack of balance or proportion
  imbalances n ▷ imbalance
imbecile [imb-ess-eel] n (pl -s) stupid person ▶ adj (also **imbecilic**) stupid or senseless > **imbecility** n (pl -ties)
  imbeciles n ▷ imbecile
  imbecilic adj ▷ imbecile
  imbecilities n ▷ imbecile
  imbecility n ▷ imbecile
imbibe v (-bes, -bing, -bed) drink (alcoholic drinks)
  imbibed v ▷ imbibe
  imbibes v ▷ imbibe
  imbibing v ▷ imbibe
imbroglio [imb-**role**-ee-oh] n (pl -ios) confusing and complicated situation

imbroglios *n* ▷ imbroglio
imbue *v* (-ues, -uing, -ued) (*usu. foll. by* with) fill or inspire with (ideals or principles)
  imbued *v* ▷ imbue
  imbues *v* ▷ imbue
  imbuing *v* ▷ imbue
imitate *v* (-tes, -ting, -ted) take as a model > imitative *adj* > imitator *n* (*pl* -s)
  imitated *v* ▷ imitate
  imitates *v* ▷ imitate
  imitating *v* ▷ imitate
imitation *n* (*pl* -s) copy of an original
  imitations *n* ▷ imitation
  imitative *adj* ▷ imitate
  imitator *n* ▷ imitate
  imitators *n* ▷ imitate
immaculate *adj* completely clean or tidy > immaculately *adv*
  immaculately *adv* ▷ immaculate
  immanence *n* ▷ immanent
  immanences *n* ▷ immanent
immanent *adj* present within and throughout something > immanence *n* (*pl* -s)
immaterial *adj* not important, not relevant
immature *adj* not fully developed > immaturity *n* (*pl* -ties)
  immaturities *n* ▷ immature
  immaturity *n* ▷ immature
  immediacies *n* ▷ immediate
  immediacy *n* ▷ immediate
immediate *adj* occurring at once > immediately *adv* > immediacy *n* (*pl* -cies)
  immediately *adv* ▷ immediate
immemorial *adj* longer than anyone can remember
immense *adj* extremely large > immensity *n* (*pl* -ties)
immensely *adv* to a very great degree
  immensities *n* ▷ immense
  immensity *n* ▷ immense
immerse *v* (-ses, -sing, -sed) involve deeply, engross > immersion *n* (*pl* -s)
  immersed *v* ▷ immerse
  immerses *v* ▷ immerse
  immersing *v* ▷ immerse
  immersion *n* ▷ immerse
  immersions *n* ▷ immerse
  immigrant *n* ▷ immigration
  immigrants *n* ▷ immigration
immigration *n* (*pl* -s) coming to a foreign country in order to settle there > immigrant *n* (*pl* -s)
  immigrations *n* ▷ immigration
  imminence *n* ▷ imminent
  imminences *n* ▷ imminent

imminent *adj* about to happen > imminently *adv* > imminence *n* (*pl* -s)
  imminently *adv* ▷ imminent
immobile *adj* not moving > immobility *n* (*pl* -ties)
  immobilities *adj* ▷ immobile
  immobility *adj* ▷ immobile
immobilize *v* (-izes, -izing, -ized) make unable to move or work
  immobilized *v* ▷ immobilize
  immobilizes *v* ▷ immobilize
  immobilizing *v* ▷ immobilize
immoderate *adj* excessive or unreasonable
immolate *v* (-tes, -ting, -ted) kill as a sacrifice > immolation *n* (*pl* -s)
  immolated *v* ▷ immolate
  immolates *v* ▷ immolate
  immolating *v* ▷ immolate
  immolation *n* ▷ immolate
  immolations *n* ▷ immolate
immoral *adj* morally wrong, corrupt > immorality *n* (*pl* -ties)
  immoralities *n* ▷ immoral
  immorality *n* ▷ immoral
immortal *adj* living forever ▶ *n* (*pl* -s) person whose fame will last for all time > immortality *n* (*pl* -s) > immortalize *v* (-lizes, -lizing, -lized)
  immortalities *n* ▷ immortal
  immortality *n* ▷ immortal
  immortalized *v* ▷ immortal
  immortalizes *v* ▷ immortal
  immortalizing *v* ▷ immortal
  immortals *n* ▷ immortal
immune *adj* protected against a specific disease
  immunities *n* ▷ immunity
immunity *n* (*pl* -ties) ability to resist disease
  immunization *n* ▷ immunize
  immunizations *n* ▷ immunize
immunize *v* (-izes, -izing, -ized) make immune to a disease > immunization *n* (*pl* -s)
  immunized *v* ▷ immunize
  immunizes *v* ▷ immunize
  immunizing *v* ▷ immunize
  immunodeficiencies *n* ▷ immunodeficiency
immunodeficiency *n* (*pl* -cies) deficiency in or breakdown of a person's ability to fight diseases
  immunological *adj* ▷ immunology
  immunologies *n* ▷ immunology
  immunologist *n* ▷ immunology
  immunologists *n* ▷ immunology
immunology *n* (*pl* -gies) branch of medicine concerned with the study of immunity

> **immunological** adj > **immunologist** n (pl -s)
immutabilities n > immutable
immutability n > immutable
immutable [im-**mute**-a-bl] adj unchangeable
> **immutability** n (pl -ties)
imp n (pl -s) (in folklore) mischievous small creature with magical powers
impact n (pl -s) strong effect ▶ v (-s, -ing, -ed) press firmly into something
impacted v > impact
impacting v > impact
impacts n, v > impact
impair v (-s, -ing, -ed) weaken or damage
> **impairment** n (pl -s)
impaired v > impair
impairing v > impair
impairment n > impair
impairments n > impair
impairs v > impair
impala [im-**ah**-la] n (pl -s) southern African antelope
impalas n > impala
impale v (-les, -ling, -led) pierce with a sharp object
impaled v > impale
impales v > impale
impaling v > impale
impalpable adj difficult to define or understand
impart v (-s, -ing, -ed) communicate (information)
imparted v > impart
impartial adj not favouring one side or the other > **impartially** adv > **impartiality** n (pl -ties)
impartialities n > impartial
impartiality n > impartial
impartially adv > impartial
imparting v > impart
imparts v > impart
impassable adj (of a road etc.) impossible to travel through or over
impasse [am-**pass**] n (pl -s) situation in which progress is impossible
impasses n > impasse
impassioned adj full of emotion
impassive adj showing no emotion, calm
impatience n > impatient
impatiences n > impatient
impatient adj irritable at any delay or difficulty > **impatiently** adv > **impatience** n (pl -s)
impatiently adv > impatient
impeach v (-es, -ing, -ed) charge with a serious crime against the state > **impeachment** n

(pl -s)
impeached v > impeach
impeaches v > impeach
impeaching v > impeach
impeachment n > impeach
impeachments n > impeach
impeccable adj without fault, excellent
> **impeccably** adv
impeccably adv > impeccable
impecunious adj penniless, poor
impedance [imp-**eed**-anss] n (pl -s) (ELECTRICITY) measure of the opposition to the flow of an alternating current
impedances n > impedance
impede v (-des, -ding, -ded) hinder in action or progress
impeded v > impede
impedes v > impede
impediment n (pl -s) something that makes action, speech, or progress difficult
impedimenta pl n objects impeding progress, esp. baggage or equipment
impediments n > impediment
impeding v > impede
impel v (-s, -lling, -lled) push or force (someone) to do something
impelled v > impel
impelling v > impel
impels v > impel
impending adj (esp. of something bad) about to happen
impenetrable adj impossible to get through
imperative adj extremely urgent, vital ▶ n (pl -s) (GRAMMAR) imperative mood
imperatives n > imperative
imperceptible adj too slight or gradual to be noticed > **imperceptibly** adv
imperceptibly adv > imperceptible
imperfect adj having faults or mistakes ▶ n (pl -s) (GRAMMAR) imperfect tense > **imperfection** n (pl -s)
imperfection n > imperfect
imperfections n > imperfect
imperfects n > imperfect
imperial adj of or like an empire or emperor
imperialism n (pl -s) rule by one country over many others > **imperialist** adj, n (pl -s)
imperialisms n > imperialism
imperialist adj, n > imperial
imperialists n > imperialist
imperil v (-s, -lling, -lled) put in danger
imperilled v > imperil
imperilling v > imperil
imperils v > imperil
imperious adj proud and domineering

impersonal adj not relating to any particular person, objective > **impersonality** n (pl -ties)
  impersonalities n ▷ impersonal
  impersonality n ▷ impersonal
impersonate v (-tes, -ting, -ted) pretend to be (another person) > **impersonation** n (pl -s) > **impersonator** n (pl -s)
  impersonated v ▷ impersonate
  impersonates v ▷ impersonate
  impersonating v ▷ impersonate
  impersonation n ▷ impersonate
  impersonations n ▷ impersonate
  impersonator n ▷ impersonate
  impersonators n ▷ impersonate
  impertinence n ▷ impertinent
  impertinences n ▷ impertinent
impertinent adj disrespectful or rude > **impertinently** adv > **impertinence** n (pl -s)
  impertinently adv ▷ impertinent
imperturbable adj calm, not excitable
impervious adj (foll. by **to**) not letting (water etc.) through
impetigo [imp-it-**tie**-go] n (pl -s) contagious skin disease
  impetigos n ▷ impetigo
  impetuosities n ▷ impetuous
  impetuosity n ▷ impetuous
impetuous adj done or acting without thought, rash > **impetuously** adv > **impetuosity** n (pl -ties)
  impetuously adv ▷ impetuous
impetus [imp-it-uss] n (pl -es) incentive, impulse
  impetuses n ▷ impetus
impinge v (-ges, -ging, -ged) (foll. by **on**) affect or restrict
  impinged v ▷ impinge
  impinges v ▷ impinge
  impinging v ▷ impinge
impious [imp-ee-uss] adj showing a lack of respect or reverence
impish adj mischievous
  implacabilities n ▷ implacable
  implacability n ▷ implacable
implacable adj not prepared to be appeased, unyielding > **implacably** adv > **implacability** n (pl -ties)
  implacably adv ▷ implacable
implant n (pl -s) (MED) something put into someone's body, usu. by surgical operation ▶ v (-s, -ing, -ed) put (something) into someone's body, usu. by surgical operation > **implantation** n (pl -s)
  implantation n ▷ implant
  implantations n ▷ implant

implanted v ▷ implant
implanting v ▷ implant
implants n, v ▷ implant
implement v (-s, -ing, -ed) carry out (instructions etc.) ▶ n (pl -s) tool, instrument > **implementation** n (pl -s)
  implementation n ▷ implement
  implementations n ▷ implement
  implemented v ▷ implement
  implementing v ▷ implement
implements v, n ▷ implement
implicate v (-tes, -ting, -ted) show to be involved, esp. in a crime
  implicated v ▷ implicate
  implicates v ▷ implicate
  implicating v ▷ implicate
implication n (pl -s) something implied
  implications n ▷ implication
implicit adj expressed indirectly > **implicitly** adv
  implicitly adv ▷ implicit
  implied v ▷ imply
  implies v ▷ imply
implore v (-res, -ring, -red) beg earnestly
  implored v ▷ implore
  implores v ▷ implore
  imploring v ▷ implore
imply v (-lies, -lying, -lied) indicate by hinting, suggest
  implying v ▷ imply
impolitic adj unwise or inadvisable
imponderable n (pl -s) ▶ adj (something) impossible to assess
  imponderables n ▷ imponderable
import v (-s, -ing, -ed) bring in (goods) from another country ▶ n (pl -s) something imported > **importation** n (pl -s) > **importer** n (pl -s)
  importance n ▷ important
  importances n ▷ important
important adj of great significance or value > **importance** n (pl -s)
  importation n ▷ import
  importations n ▷ import
  imported v ▷ import
  importer n ▷ import
  importers n ▷ import
  importing v ▷ import
  imports v, n ▷ import
importunate adj persistent or demanding
importune v (-nes, -ning, -ned) harass with persistent requests > **importunity** n (pl -ties)
  importuned v ▷ importune
  importunes v ▷ importune
  importuning v ▷ importune

importunities *n* ▷ importune
importunity *n* ▷ importune
impose *v* (-ses, -sing, -sed) force the acceptance of
  imposed *v* ▷ impose
  imposes *v* ▷ impose
imposing *adj* grand, impressive ▶ *v* ▷ impose
imposition *n* (*pl* -s) unreasonable demand
  impositions *n* ▷ imposition
  impossibilities *n* ▷ impossible
  impossibility *n* ▷ impossible
impossible *adj* not able to be done or to happen > **impossibly** *adv* > **impossibility** *n* (*pl* -ties)
  impossibly *adv* ▷ impossible
imposter, impostor *n* (*pl* -s) person who cheats or swindles by pretending to be someone else
  imposters *n* ▷ imposter
  impostor *n* ▷ imposter
  impostors *n* ▷ imposter
  impotence *n* ▷ impotent
  impotences *n* ▷ impotent
impotent [imp-a-tent] *adj* powerless > **impotence** *n* (*pl* -s) > **impotently** *adv*
  impotently *adv* ▷ impotent
impound *v* (-s, -ing, -ed) take legal possession of, confiscate
  impounded *v* ▷ impound
  impounding *v* ▷ impound
  impounds *v* ▷ impound
impoverish *v* (-es, -ing, -ed) make poor or weak > **impoverishment** *n* (*pl* -s)
  impoverished *v* ▷ impoverish
  impoverishes *v* ▷ impoverish
  impoverishing *v* ▷ impoverish
  impoverishment *n* ▷ impoverish
  impoverishments *n* ▷ impoverish
impracticable *adj* incapable of being put into practice
impractical *adj* not sensible
imprecation *n* (*pl* -s) curse
  imprecations *n* ▷ imprecation
  impregnabilities *n* ▷ impregnable
  impregnability *n* ▷ impregnable
impregnable *adj* impossible to break into > **impregnability** *n* (*pl* -ties)
impregnate *v* (-tes, -ting, -ted) saturate, spread all through > **impregnation** *n* (*pl* -s)
  impregnated *v* ▷ impregnate
  impregnates *v* ▷ impregnate
  impregnating *v* ▷ impregnate
  impregnation *n* ▷ impregnate
  impregnations *n* ▷ impregnate
impresario *n* (*pl* -s) person who runs theatre performances, concerts, etc.
  impresarios *n* ▷ impresario
impress *v* (-es, -ing, -ed) affect strongly, usu. favourably
  impressed *v* ▷ impress
  impresses *v* ▷ impress
  impressing *v* ▷ impress
impression *n* (*pl* -s) effect, esp. a strong or favourable one
impressionable *adj* easily impressed or influenced
impressionism *n* (*pl* -s) art style that gives a general effect or mood rather than form or structure > **impressionist** *n* (*pl* -s) > **impressionistic** *adj*
  impressionisms *n* ▷ impressionism
  impressionist *n* ▷ impressionism
  impressionistic *adj* ▷ impressionism
  impressionists *n* ▷ impressionism
  impressions *n* ▷ impression
impressive *adj* making a strong impression, esp. through size, importance, or quality
imprimatur [imp-rim-**ah**-ter] *n* (*pl* -s) official approval to print a book
  imprimaturs *n* ▷ imprimatur
imprint *n* (*pl* -s) mark made by printing or stamping ▶ *v* (-s, -ing, -ed) produce (a mark) by printing or stamping
  imprinted *v* ▷ imprint
  imprinting *v* ▷ imprint
  imprints *n*, *v* ▷ imprint
imprison *v* (-s, -ing, -ed) put in prison > **imprisonment** *n* (*pl* -s)
  imprisoned *v* ▷ imprison
  imprisoning *v* ▷ imprison
  imprisonment *n* ▷ imprison
  imprisonments *n* ▷ imprisonment
  imprisons *v* ▷ imprison
  improbabilities *n* ▷ improbable
  improbability *n* ▷ improbable
improbable *adj* not likely to be true or to happen > **improbability** *n* (*pl* -ties)
impromptu *adj* without planning or preparation
improper *adj* indecent
  improprieties *n* ▷ impropriety
impropriety [imp-roe-**pry**-a-tee] *n* (*pl* -ties) unsuitable or slightly improper behaviour
improve *v* (-ves, -ving, -ved) make or become better > **improvement** *n* (*pl* -s)
  improved *v* ▷ improve
  improvement *n* ▷ improvement
  improvements *n* ▷ improvement
  improves *v* ▷ improve
  improvidence *n* ▷ improvident

improvidences n ▷ improvident
improvident adj not planning for future needs
> **improvidence** n (pl -s)
improving v ▷ improve
improvisation n ▷ improvise
improvisations n ▷ improvise
improvise v (-ises, -sing, -sed) make use
of whatever materials are available
> **improvisation** n (pl -s)
improvised v ▷ improvise
improvises v ▷ improvise
improvising v ▷ improvise
imps n ▷ imp
impudence n ▷ impudent
impudences n ▷ impudent
impudent adj cheeky, disrespectful
> **impudence** n ▷ **impudence** n (pl -s)
> **impudently** adv ▷ impudently
impudently adv ▷ impudently
impugn [imp-yoon] v (-s, -ing, -ed) challenge
the truth or validity of
impugned v ▷ impugn
impugning v ▷ impugn
impugns n ▷ impugn
impulse n (pl -s) sudden urge to do something
> **impulsive** adj acting or done without
careful consideration > **impulsively** adv
impulses n ▷ impulse
impulsive adj ▷ impulse
impulsively adv ▷ impulse
impunities n ▷ impunity
impunity [imp-yoon-it-ee] n (pl -ties) without
punishment
impure adj having dirty or unwanted
substances mixed in > **impurity** n (pl -ties)
impurities n ▷ impure
impurity n ▷ impure
imputation n ▷ impute
imputations n ▷ impute
impute v (-tes, -ting, -ted) attribute
responsibility to > **imputation** n (pl -s)
imputed v ▷ impute
imputes v ▷ impute
imputing v ▷ impute
in prep indicating position inside, state or
situation, etc. ▶ adv indicating position
inside, entry into, etc. ▶ adj fashionable
inabilities n ▷ inability
inability n (pl -ties) lack of means or skill to do
something
inaccuracies n ▷ inaccurate
inaccuracy n ▷ inaccurate
inaccurate adj not correct > **inaccuracy** n
(pl -cies)
inadequacies n ▷ inadequate
inadequacy n ▷ inadequate

inadequate adj not enough > **inadequacy** n
(pl -cies)
inadvertent adj unintentional
> **inadvertently** adv
inadvertently adv ▷ inadvertent
inalienable adj not able to be taken away
inane adj senseless, silly > **inanity** n (pl -ties)
inanimate adj not living
inanities n ▷ inane
inanity n ▷ inane
inappropriate adj not suitable
inarticulate adj unable to express oneself
clearly or well
inaugural adj ▷ inaugurate
inaugurate v (-tes, -ting, -ted) open or begin
the use of, esp. with ceremony > **inaugural**
adj > **inauguration** n (pl -s)
inaugurated v ▷ inaugurate
inaugurates v ▷ inaugurate
inaugurating v ▷ inaugurate
inauguration n ▷ inaugurate
inaugurations n ▷ inaugurate
inauspicious adj unlucky, likely to have an
unfavourable outcome
inboard adj (of a boat's engine) inside the hull
inborn adj existing from birth, natural
inbred adj produced as a result of inbreeding
inbreeding n (pl -s) breeding of animals or
people that are closely related
inbreedings n ▷ inbreeding
inbuilt adj present from the start
incalculable adj too great to be estimated
incandescence n ▷ incandescent
incandescences n ▷ incandescent
incandescent adj glowing with heat
> **incandescence** n (pl -s)
incantation n (pl -s) ritual chanting of magic
words or sounds
incantations n ▷ incantation
incapable adj (foll. by of) unable (to do
something)
incapacitate v (-tates, -tating, -tated) deprive
of strength or ability > **incapacity** n (pl -ties)
incapacitated v ▷ incapacitate
incapacitates v ▷ incapacitate
incapacitating v ▷ incapacitate
incapacities n ▷ incapacitate
incapacity n ▷ incapacitate
incarcerate v (-tes, -ting, -ted) imprison
> **incarceration** n (pl -s)
incarcerated v ▷ incarcerate
incarcerates v ▷ incarcerate
incarcerating v ▷ incarcerate
incarceration n ▷ incarcerate
incarcerations n ▷ incarcerate

incarnate *adj* in human form > **incarnation** *n* (*pl* -s)
  incarnation *n* ▷ incarnate
  incarnations *n* ▷ incarnate
  incendiaries *n* ▷ incendiary
incendiary [in-**send**-ya-ree] *adj* (of a bomb, attack, etc.) designed to cause fires ▶ *n* (*pl* -ries) bomb designed to cause fires
incense¹ *v* (-ses, -sing, -sed) make very angry
incense² *n* (*pl* incenses) substance that gives off a sweet perfume when burned
  incensed *v* ▷ incense¹
  incenses *v* ▷ incense¹ ▶ *n* ▷ incense²
  incensing *v* ▷ incense¹
incentive *n* (*pl* -s) something that encourages effort or action
  incentives *n* ▷ incentive
inception *n* (*pl* -s) beginning
  inceptions *n* ▷ inception
incessant *adj* never stopping > **incessantly** *adv*
  incessantly *adv* ▷ incessant
incest *n* (*pl* -s) sexual intercourse between two people too closely related to marry > **incestuous** *adj*
  incests *n* ▷ incest
  incestuous *adj* ▷ incest
inch *n* (*pl* -es) unit of length equal to one twelfth of a foot or 2.54 centimetres ▶ *v* (-ches, -ching, -ched) move slowly and gradually
  inched *v* ▷ inch
  inches *v, n* ▷ inch
  inching *v* ▷ inch
inchoate [in-**koe**-ate] *adj* just begun and not yet properly developed
incidence *n* (*pl* -s) extent or frequency of occurrence
  incidences *n* ▷ incidence
incident *n* (*pl* -s) something that happens
incidental *adj* occurring in connection with or resulting from something more important > **incidentally** *adv*
  incidentally *adv* ▷ incidental
  incidents *n* ▷ incident
incinerate *v* (-tes, -ting, -ted) burn to ashes > **incineration** *n* (*pl* -s)
  incinerated *v* ▷ incinerate
  incinerates *v* ▷ incinerate
  incinerating *v* ▷ incinerate
  incineration *n* ▷ incinerate
  incinerations *n* ▷ incinerate
incinerator *n* (*pl* -s) furnace for burning rubbish
  incinerators *n* ▷ incinerator
incipient *adj* just starting to appear or happen

incise *v* (-ses, -sing, -sed) cut into with a sharp tool > **incision** *n* (*pl* -s)
  incised *v* ▷ incise
  incises *v* ▷ incise
  incising *v* ▷ incise
  incision *n* ▷ incise
  incisions *n* ▷ incise
incisive *adj* direct and forceful
incisor *n* (*pl* -s) front tooth, used for biting into food
  incisors *n* ▷ incisor
incite *v* (-tes, -ting, -ted) stir up, provoke > **incitement** *n* (*pl* -s)
  incited *v* ▷ incite
  incitement *n* ▷ incite
  incitements *n* ▷ incite
  incites *v* ▷ incite
  inciting *v* ▷ incite
  incivilities *n* ▷ incivility
incivility *n* (*pl* -ties) rudeness or a rude remark
inclement *adj* (of weather) stormy or severe
inclination *n* (*pl* -s) liking, tendency, or preference
  inclinations *n* ▷ inclination
incline *v* (-nes, -ning, -ned) lean, slope ▶ *n* (*pl* -s) slope
  inclined *v* ▷ incline
  inclines *v, n* ▷ incline
  inclining *v* ▷ incline
include *v* (-des, -ding, -ded) have as part of the whole > **inclusion** *n* (*pl* -s)
  included *v* ▷ include
  includes *v* ▷ include
  including *v* ▷ include
  inclusion *n* ▷ include
  inclusions *n* ▷ include
inclusive *adj* including everything (specified) > **inclusively** *adv*
  inclusively *adv* ▷ inclusive
incognito [in-kog-**nee**-toe] *adj, adv* having adopted a false identity ▶ *n* (*pl* -tos) false identity
  incognitos *n* ▷ incognito
  incoherence *n* ▷ incoherent
  incoherences *n* ▷ incoherent
incoherent *adj* unclear and impossible to understand > **incoherence** *n* (*pl* -s) > **incoherently** *adv*
  incoherently *adv* ▷ incoherent
income *n* (*pl* -s) amount of money earned from work, investments, etc.
  incomes *n* ▷ income
incoming *adj* coming in
incommode *v* (-des, -ding, -ded) cause inconvenience to

incommoded v ▷ incommode
incommodes v ▷ incommode
incommoding v ▷ incommode
incommunicado adj, adv deprived of communication with other people
incomparable adj beyond comparison, unequalled > **incomparably** adv
incomparably adv ▷ incomparable
incompatibilities n ▷ incompatible
incompatibility n ▷ incompatible
incompatible adj inconsistent or conflicting > **incompatibility** n (pl -ties)
incompetence n ▷ incompetent
incompetences n ▷ incompetent
incompetent adj not having the necessary ability or skill to do something > **incompetence** n (pl -s)
inconceivable adj extremely unlikely, unimaginable
inconclusive adj not giving a final decision or result
incongruities n ▷ incongruous
incongruity n ▷ incongruous
incongruous adj inappropriate or out of place > **incongruously** adv > **incongruity** n (pl -ties)
incongruously adv ▷ incongruous
inconsequential adj unimportant, insignificant
inconsiderable adj fairly large
inconstant adj liable to change one's loyalties or opinions
incontinence n ▷ incontinent
incontinences n ▷ incontinent
incontinent adj unable to control one's bladder or bowels > **incontinence** n (pl -s)
incontrovertible adj impossible to deny or disprove
inconvenience n (pl -s) trouble or difficulty ▶ v (-ces, -ncing, -nced) cause trouble or difficulty to > **inconvenient** adj
inconvenienced v ▷ inconvenience
inconveniences n, v ▷ inconvenience
inconveniencing v ▷ inconvenience
inconvenient adj ▷ inconvenience
incorporate v (-tes, -ting, -ted) include or be included as part of a larger unit
incorporated v ▷ incorporate
incorporates v ▷ incorporate
incorporating v ▷ incorporate
incorporeal adj without material form
incorrigible adj beyond correction or reform
incorruptible adj too honest to be bribed or corrupted
increase v (-ses, -sing, -sed) make or become greater in size, number, etc. ▶ n (pl -s) rise in

number, size, etc. > **increasingly** adv
increased v ▷ increase
increases v, n ▷ increase
increasing v ▷ increase
increasingly adv ▷ increase
incredible adj hard to believe or imagine > **incredibly** adv
incredibly adv ▷ incredible
incredulities n ▷ incredulous
incredulity n ▷ incredulous
incredulous adj not willing to believe something > **incredulity** n (pl -ties)
increment n (pl -s) increase in money or value, esp. a regular salary increase > **incremental** adj
incremental adj ▷ increment
increments n ▷ increment
incriminate v (-tes, -ting, -ted) make (someone) seem guilty of a crime > **incriminating** adj
incriminated v ▷ incriminate
incriminates v ▷ incriminate
incriminating v, adj ▷ incriminate
incubate [in-cube-ate] v (-tes, -ting, -ted) (of a bird) hatch (eggs) by sitting on them > **incubation** n (pl -s)
incubated v ▷ incubate
incubates v ▷ incubate
incubating v ▷ incubate
incubation n ▷ incubate
incubations n ▷ incubate
incubator n (pl -s) heated enclosed apparatus for rearing premature babies
incubators n ▷ incubator
incubi n ▷ incubus
incubus [in-cube-uss] n (pl -bi, -buses) (in folklore) demon believed to have sex with sleeping women
incubuses n ▷ incubus
inculcate v (-tes, -ting, -ted) fix in someone's mind by constant repetition > **inculcation** n (pl -s)
inculcated v ▷ inculcate
inculcates v ▷ inculcate
inculcating v ▷ inculcate
inculcation n ▷ inculcate
inculcations n ▷ inculcate
incumbencies n ▷ incumbent
incumbency n ▷ incumbent
incumbent n (pl -s) person holding a particular office or position ▶ adj it is the duty of > **incumbency** n (pl -cies)
incumbents n ▷ incumbent
incur v (-s, -rring, -rred) cause (something unpleasant) to happen

incurable *adj* not able to be cured > **incurably** *adv*

incurably *adv* ▷ incurable

incurious *adj* showing no curiosity or interest

incurred *v* ▷ incur

incurring *v* ▷ incur

incurs *v* ▷ incur

incursion *n* (*pl* -s) sudden brief invasion

incursions *n* ▷ incursion

indebted *adj* owing gratitude for help or favours > **indebtedness** *n* (*pl* -es)

indebtedness *n* ▷ indebted

indebtednesses *n* ▷ indebted

indecencies *n* ▷ indecent

indecency *n* ▷ indecent

indecent *adj* morally or sexually offensive > **indecently** *adv* **indecency** *n* (*pl* -cies)

indecently *adv* ▷ indecent

indecipherable *adj* impossible to read

indeed *adv* really, certainly ▶ *interj* expression of indignation or surprise

indefatigable *adj* never getting tired > **indefatigably** *adv*

indefatigably *adv* ▷ indefatigable

indefensible *adj* unable to be justified

indefinite *adj* without exact limits > **indefinitely** *adv*

indefinitely *adv* ▷ indefinite

indelible *adj* impossible to erase or remove > **indelibly** *adv*

indelibly *adv* ▷ indelible

indelicate *adj* offensive or embarrassing

indemnified *v* ▷ indemnify

indemnifies *v* ▷ indemnify

indemnify *v* (-fies, -fying, -fied) secure against loss, damage, or liability

indemnifying *v* ▷ indemnify

indemnities *v* ▷ indemnify

indemnity *n* (*pl* -ties) insurance against loss or damage

indent *v* (-s, -ing, -ed) start (a line of writing) further from the margin than the other lines

indentation *n* (*pl* -s) dent in a surface or edge

indentations *n* ▷ indentation

indented *v* ▷ indent

indenting *v* ▷ indent

indents *v* ▷ indent

indenture *n* (*pl* -s) contract, esp. one binding an apprentice to his or her employer

indentures *n* ▷ indenture

independence *n* ▷ independent

independences *n* ▷ independent

independent *adj* free from the control or influence of others ▶ *n* (*pl* -s) politician who does not represent any political party

> **independently** *adv* > **independence** *n* (*pl* -s)

independently *adsv* ▷ independent

independents *n* ▷ independent

indescribable *adj* too intense or extreme for words > **indescribably** *adv*

indescribably *adv* ▷ indescribable

indeterminacies *n* ▷ indeterminate

indeterminacy *n* ▷ indeterminate

indeterminate *adj* uncertain in extent, amount, or nature > **indeterminacy** *n* (*pl* -cies)

index *n* (*pl* -dices) [in-diss-eez] alphabetical list of names or subjects dealt with in a book ▶ *v* (-dexes, -dexing, -dexed) provide (a book) with an index

indexed *v* ▷ index

indexes *v* ▷ index

indexing *v* ▷ index

indicate *v* (-tes, -ting, -ted) be a sign or symptom of > **indication** *n* (*pl* -s)

indicated *v* ▷ indicate

indicates *v* ▷ indicate

indicating *v* ▷ indicate

indication *n* ▷ indicate

indications *n* ▷ indicate

indicative *adj* (foll. by *of*) suggesting ▶ *n* (*pl* -s) (GRAMMAR) indicative mood

indicatives *n* ▷ indicative

indicator *n* (*pl* -s) something acting as a sign or indication

indicators *n* ▷ indicator

indices *n* ▷ index

indict [in-**dite**] *v* (-s, -ing, -ed) formally charge with a crime > **indictable** *adj* > **indictment** *n* (*pl* -s)

indictable *adj* ▷ indict

indicted *v* ▷ indict

indicting *v* ▷ indict

indictment *n* ▷ indict

indictments *n* ▷ indict

indicts *v* ▷ indict

indie *adj* (*Informal*) (of rock music) released by an independent record company

indifference *n* ▷ indifferent

indifferences *n* ▷ indifferent

indifferent *adj* showing no interest or concern > **indifference** *n* (*pl* -s) > **indifferently** *adv*

indifferently *adv* ▷ indifferent

indigence *n* ▷ indigent

indigences *n* ▷ indigent

indigenous [in-**dij**-in-uss] *adj* born in or natural to a country

indigent *adj* extremely poor > **indigence** *n* (*pl* -s)

indigestible *adj* ▷ indigestion

indigestion *n* (*pl* -s) (discomfort or pain

caused by) difficulty in digesting food
> **indigestible** adj

indigestions n ▷ indigestion

indignant adj feeling or showing indignation
> **indignantly** adv

indignantly adv ▷ indignant

indignation n (pl -s) anger at something
unfair or wrong

indignations n ▷ indignation

indignities n ▷ indignity

indignity n (pl -ties) embarrassing or
humiliating treatment

indigo adj deep violet-blue ▶ n (pl -s) dye of
this colour

indigos n ▷ indigo

indirect adj done or caused by someone or
something else

indiscreet adj incautious or tactless
in revealing secrets > **indiscreetly** adv
> **indiscretion** n (pl -s)

indiscreetly adv ▷ indiscreet

indiscretion n ▷ indiscreet

indiscretions n ▷ indiscreet

indiscriminate adj showing lack of careful
thought

indispensable adj absolutely essential

indisposed adj unwell, ill > **indisposition** n
(pl -s)

indisposition n ▷ indisposed

indispositions n ▷ indisposed

indisputable adj beyond doubt > **indisputably**
adv

indisputably adv ▷ indisputable

indissoluble adj permanent

indium n (pl -s) (CHEM) soft silvery-white
metallic element

indiums n ▷ indium

individual adj characteristic of or meant for a
single person or thing ▶ n (pl -s) single person
or thing > **individually** adv > **individuality**
n (pl -ties)

individualism n (pl -s) principle of living one's
life in one's own way > **individualist** n (pl -s)
> **individualistic** adj

individualisms n ▷ individualism

individualist n ▷ individualism

individualistic adj ▷ individualism

individualists n ▷ individualism

individualities n ▷ individual

individuality n ▷ individual

individually adv ▷ individual

individuals n ▷ individual

indoctrinate v (-tes, -ting, -ted) teach
(someone) to accept a doctrine or belief
uncritically > **indoctrination** n (pl -s)

indoctrinated v ▷ indoctrinate

indoctrinates v ▷ indoctrinate

indoctrinating v ▷ indoctrinate

indoctrination n ▷ indoctrinate

indoctrinations n ▷ indoctrinate

indolence n ▷ indolent

indolences n ▷ indolent

indolent adj lazy > **indolence** n (pl -s)

indomitable adj too strong to be defeated or
discouraged > **indomitably** adv

indomitably adv ▷ indomitable

indoor adj inside a building > **indoors** adv

indoors adv ▷ indoor

indubitable adj beyond doubt, certain
> **indubitably** adv

indubitably adv ▷ indubitable

induce v (-ces, -cing, -ced) persuade or
influence

induced v ▷ induce

inducement n (pl -s) something used to
persuade someone to do something

inducements n ▷ inducement

induces v ▷ induce

inducing v ▷ induce

induct v (-s, -ing, -ed) formally install
(someone, esp. a clergyman) in office

inductance n (pl -s) property of an electric
circuit creating voltage by a change of
current

inductances n ▷ inductance

inducted v ▷ induct

inducting v ▷ induct

induction n (pl -s) reasoning process by
which general conclusions are drawn from
particular instances > **inductive** adj

inductions n ▷ induction

inductive adj ▷ induction

inducts v ▷ induct

indulge v (-ges, -ging, -ged) allow oneself
pleasure > **indulgent** adj > **indulgently** adv

indulged v ▷ indulge

indulgence n (pl -s) something allowed
because it gives pleasure

indulgences n ▷ indulgence

indulgent adj ▷ indulge

indulgently adv ▷ indulge

indulges v ▷ indulge

indulging v ▷ indulge

industrial adj of, used in, or employed in
industry

industrialization n ▷ industrialize

industrializations n ▷ industrialize

industrialize v (-izes, -izing, -ized) develop
large-scale industry in (a country or region)
> **industrialization** n (pl -s)

industrialized v ▷ industrialize
industrializes v ▷ industrialize
industrializing v ▷ industrialize
industries n ▷ industry
industrious adj ▷ industry
industry n (pl -tries) manufacture of goods > **industrious** adj hard-working
inebriate n (pl -s) ▸ adj (person who is) habitually drunk
inebriated adj drunk > **inebriation** n (pl -s)
inebriates n ▷ inebriate
inebriation n ▷ inebriated
inebriations n ▷ inebriated
inedible adj not fit to be eaten
ineffable adj too great for words > **ineffably** adv
ineffably adv ▷ ineffable
ineffectual adj having very little effect
ineligible adj not qualified for or entitled to something
ineluctable adj impossible to avoid
inept adj clumsy, lacking skill > **ineptitude** n (pl -s)
ineptitude n ▷ inept
ineptitudes n ▷ inept
inequitable adj unfair
ineradicable adj impossible to remove
inert adj without the power of motion or resistance > **inertness** n (pl -es)
inertia n (pl -s) feeling of unwillingness to do anything
inertias n ▷ inertia
inertness n ▷ inert
inertnesses n ▷ inert
inescapable adj unavoidable
inestimable adj too great to be estimated > **inestimably** adv
inestimably adv ▷ inestimable
inevitabilities n ▷ inevitable
inevitability n ▷ inevitable
inevitable adj unavoidable, sure to happen > **inevitably** adv > **inevitability** n (pl -ties)
inevitably adv ▷ inevitable
inexorable adj unable to be prevented from continuing or progressing > **inexorably** adv
inexorably adv ▷ inexorable
inexpert adj lacking skill
inexplicable adj impossible to explain > **inexplicably** adv
inexplicably adv ▷ inexplicable
inextricable adj impossible to escape from
infallibilities adv ▷ infallible
infallibility adv ▷ infallible
infallible adj never wrong > **infallibly** adv > **infallibility** n (pl -ties)

infallibly adv ▷ infallible
infamies n ▷ infamous
infamous [in-fam-uss] adj well-known for something bad > **infamously** adv > **infamy** n (pl -mies)
infamously adv ▷ infamous
infamy n ▷ infamous
infancies n ▷ infancy
infancy n (pl -cies) early childhood
infant n (pl -s) very young child
infanticide n (pl -s) murder of an infant
infanticides n ▷ infanticide
infantile adj childish
infantries n ▷ infantry
infantry n (pl -ries) soldiers who fight on foot
infants n ▷ infant
infatuated adj feeling intense unreasoning passion
infatuation n (pl -s) intense unreasoning passion
infatuations n ▷ infatuation
infect v (-s, -ing, -ed) affect with a disease > **infection** n (pl -s)
infected v ▷ infect
infecting v ▷ infect
infection n ▷ infect
infections n ▷ infect
infectious adj (of a disease) spreading without actual contact
infects v ▷ infect
infer v (-s, -rring, -rred) work out from evidence > **inference** n (pl -s)
inference n ▷ infer
inferences n ▷ infer
inferior adj lower in quality, position, or status ▸ n (pl -s) person of lower position or status > **inferiority** n (pl -ties)
inferiorities n ▷ inferior
inferiority n ▷ inferior
inferiors n ▷ inferior
infernal adj of hell (Informal) > **infernally** adv
infernally adv ▷ infernal
inferno n (pl -s) intense raging fire
infernos n ▷ inferno
inferred v ▷ infer
inferring v ▷ infer
infers v ▷ infer
infertile adj unable to produce offspring > **infertility** n (pl -ties)
infertilities n ▷ infertile
infertility n ▷ infertile
infest v (-s, -ing, -ed) inhabit or overrun in unpleasantly large numbers > **infestation** n (pl -s)
infestation n ▷ infest

infestations n ▷ infest
infested v ▷ infest
infesting v ▷ infest
infests v ▷ infest
infidel n (pl -s) person with no religion
infidelities n ▷ infidelity
infidelity n (pl -ties) (act of) sexual unfaithfulness to one's husband, wife, or lover
infidels n ▷ infidel
infighting n (pl -s) quarrelling within a group
infightings n ▷ infighting
infiltrate v (-tes, -ting, -ted) enter gradually and secretly > **infiltration** n (pl -s) > **infiltrator** n (pl -s)
infiltrated v ▷ infiltrate
infiltrates v ▷ infiltrate
infiltrating v ▷ infiltrate
infiltration n ▷ infiltrate
infiltrations n ▷ infiltrate
infiltrator n ▷ infiltrate
infiltrators n ▷ infiltrate
infinite [in-fin-it] adj without any limit or end > **infinitely** adv
infinitely adv ▷ infinite
infinitesimal adj extremely small
infinities n ▷ infinity
infinitive n (pl -s) (GRAMMAR) form of a verb not showing tense, person, or number
infinitives n ▷ infinitive
infinity n (pl -ties) endless space, time, or number
infirm adj physically or mentally weak > **infirmity** n (pl -ties)
infirmaries n ▷ infirmary
infirmary n (pl -ries) hospital
infirmities n ▷ infirm
infirmity n ▷ infirm
inflame v (-mes, -ming, -med) make angry or excited
inflamed adj (of part of the body) red, swollen, and painful because of infection ▶ v ▷ inflame > **inflammation** n (pl -s)
inflames v ▷ inflame
inflaming v ▷ inflame
inflammable adj easily set on fire
inflammation n ▷ inflamed
inflammations n ▷ inflamed
inflammatory adj likely to provoke anger
inflatable adj able to be inflated ▶ n (pl -s) plastic or rubber object which can be inflated
inflatables n ▷ inflatable
inflate v (-tes, -ting, -ted) expand by filling with air or gas
inflated v ▷ inflate
inflates v ▷ inflate

inflating v ▷ inflate
inflation n (pl -s) inflating > **inflationary** adj
inflationary adj ▷ inflationary
inflations n ▷ inflation
inflection, inflexion n (pl -s) change in the pitch of the voice
inflections n ▷ inflection
inflexibilities n ▷ inflexible
inflexibility n ▷ inflexible
inflexible adj unwilling to be persuaded, obstinate > **inflexibly** adv > **inflexibility** n (pl -ties)
inflexibly n ▷ inflexibly
inflexion n ▷ inflection
inflexions n ▷ inflection
inflict v (-s, -ing, -ed) impose (something unpleasant) on > **infliction** n (pl -s)
inflicted v ▷ inflict
inflicting v ▷ inflict
infliction n ▷ inflict
inflictions n ▷ inflict
inflicts v ▷ inflict
inflorescence n (pl -s) (BOTANY) arrangement of flowers on a stem
inflorescences n ▷ inflorescence
influence n (pl -s) effect of one person or thing on another ▶ v (-ces, -cing, -ced) have an effect on > **influential** adj
influenced v ▷ influence
influences n, v ▷ influence
influencing v ▷ influence
influential adj ▷ influence
influenza n (pl -s) contagious viral disease causing headaches, muscle pains, and fever
influenzas n ▷ influenza
influx n (pl -es) arrival or entry of many people or things
influxes n ▷ influx
info n (pl -s) (Informal) information
inform v (-s, -ing, -ed) tell
informal adj relaxed and friendly > **informally** adv > **informality** n (pl -s)
informalities n ▷ informal
informality n ▷ informal
informally adv ▷ informal
informant n (pl -s) person who gives information
informants n ▷ informant
information n (pl -s) knowledge or facts
informations n ▷ information
informative adj giving useful information
informed v ▷ inform
informer n (pl -s) person who informs to the police
informers n ▷ informer

informing v ▷ inform
informs v ▷ inform
infos n ▷ info
infrared adj of or using rays below the red end of the visible spectrum
infrastructure n (pl -s) basic facilities, services, and equipment needed for a country or organization to function properly
infrastructures n ▷ infrastructure
infringe v (-ges, -ging, -ged) break (a law or agreement) > **infringement** n (pl -s)
infringed v ▷ infringe
infringement n ▷ infringe
infringements n ▷ infringe
infringes v ▷ infringe
infringing v ▷ infringe
infuriate v (-tes, -ting, -ted) make very angry
infuriated v ▷ infuriate
infuriates v ▷ infuriate
infuriating v ▷ infuriate
infuse v (-ses, -sing, -sed) fill (with an emotion or quality) > **infusion** n (pl -s) infusing
infused v ▷ infuse
infuses v ▷ infuse
infusing v ▷ infuse
infusion n ▷ infuse
infusions n ▷ infuse
ingenious [in-**jean**-ee-uss] adj showing cleverness and originality > **ingeniously** adv > **ingenuity** [in-jen-**new**-it-ee] n (pl -ties)
ingeniously adv ▷ ingenious
ingénue [an-jay-new] n (pl -s) naive young woman, esp. as a role played by an actress
ingénues n ▷ ingénue
ingenuities n ▷ ingenious
ingenuity n ▷ ingenious
ingenuous [in-**jen**-new-uss] adj unsophisticated and trusting > **ingenuously** adv
ingenuously adv ▷ ingenuous
ingest v (-s, -ing, -ed) take (food or liquid) into the body > **ingestion** n (pl -s)
ingested v ▷ ingest
ingesting v ▷ ingest
ingestion n ▷ ingest
ingestions n ▷ ingest
ingests v ▷ ingest
inglorious adj dishonourable, shameful
ingot n (pl -s) oblong block of cast metal
ingots n ▷ ingot
ingrained adj firmly fixed
ingratiate v (-iates, -iating, -iated) try to make (oneself) popular with someone > **ingratiating** adj > **ingratiatingly** adv
ingratiated v ▷ ingratiate
ingratiates v ▷ ingratiate

ingratiating v, adj ▷ ingratiate
ingratiatingly adv ▷ ingratiate
ingredient n (pl -s) component of a mixture or compound
ingredients n ▷ ingredient
ingress n (pl -es) act or right of entering
ingresses n ▷ ingress
ingrowing adj (of a toenail) growing abnormally into the flesh
inhabit v (-s, -ing, -ed) live in > **inhabitable** adj > **inhabitant** n (pl -s)
inhabitable adj ▷ inhabitable
inhabitant n ▷ inhabit
inhabitants n ▷ inhabit
inhabited v ▷ inhabit
inhabiting v ▷ inhabit
inhabits v ▷ inhabit
inhalant n (pl -s) medical preparation inhaled to help breathing problems
inhalants n ▷ inhalant
inhalations n ▷ inhalation
inhale v (-les, -ling, -led) breathe in (air, smoke, etc.) > **inhalation** n (pl -s)
inhaled v ▷ inhale
inhaler n (pl -s) container for an inhalant
inhalers n ▷ inhaler
inhales v ▷ inhale
inhaling v ▷ inhale
inherent adj existing as an inseparable part > **inherently** adv
inherently adv ▷ inherent
inherit v (-s, -ing, -ed) receive (money etc.) from someone who has died > **inheritance** n (pl -s) > **inheritor** n (pl -s)
inheritance n ▷ inherit
inheritances n ▷ inherit
inherited v ▷ inherit
inheriting v ▷ inherit
inheritor n ▷ inherit
inheritors n ▷ inherit
inherits v ▷ inherit
inhibit v (-s, -ing, -ed) restrain (an impulse or desire) > **inhibited** adj
inhibited v, adj ▷ inhibit
inhibiting v ▷ inhibit
inhibition n (pl -s) feeling of fear or embarrassment that stops one from behaving naturally
inhibitions n ▷ inhibition
inhibits v ▷ inhibit
inhospitable adj not welcoming, unfriendly
inhuman adj cruel or brutal
inhumane adj cruel or brutal > **inhumanity** n (pl -ties)
inhumanities n ▷ inhumane

inhumanity n ▷ inhumane

inimical adj unfavourable or hostile

inimitable adj impossible to imitate, unique

iniquities n ▷ iniquity

iniquitous adj ▷ iniquity

iniquity n (pl -ties) injustice or wickedness > **iniquitous** adj

initial adj first, at the beginning ▶ n (pl -s) first letter, esp. of a person's name ▶ v (-s, -lling, -lled) sign with one's initials > **initially** adv

initialled v ▷ initial

initialling v ▷ initial

initially adv ▷ initial

initials n, v ▷ initial

initiate v (-tes, -ting, -ted) begin or set going ▶ n (pl -s) recently initiated person > **initiation** n (pl -s) > **initiator** n (pl -s)

initiated v ▷ initiate

initiates v, n ▷ initiate

initiating v ▷ initiate

initiation n ▷ initiate

initiations n ▷ initiate

initiative n (pl -ves) first step, commencing move

initiatives n ▷ initiative

initiator n ▷ initiation

initiators n ▷ initiation

inject v (-s, -ing, -ed) put (a fluid) into the body with a syringe > **injection** n (pl -s)

injected v ▷ inject

injecting v ▷ inject

injection n ▷ inject

injections n ▷ inject

injects v ▷ inject

injudicious adj showing poor judgment, unwise

injunction n (pl -s) court order not to do something

injunctions n ▷ injunction

injure v (-res, -ring, -red) hurt physically or mentally ▶ **injury** n (pl -ries) > **injurious** adj

injured v ▷ injure

injures v ▷ injure

injuries n ▷ injure

injuring v ▷ injure

injurious adj ▷ injure

injury n ▷ injure

injustice n (pl -s) unfairness

injustices n ▷ injustice

ink n (pl -s) coloured liquid used for writing or printing ▶ v (-s, -ing, -ed) (foll. by **in**) mark in ink (something already marked in pencil)

inked v ▷ ink

inking v ▷ ink

inkling n (pl -s) slight idea or suspicion

inklings n ▷ inkling

inks v, n ▷ ink

inky adj dark or black

inlaid adj set in another material so that the surface is smooth

inland adj, adv in or towards the interior of a country, away from the sea

inlay n (pl -s) inlaid substance or pattern

inlays n ▷ inlay

inlet n (pl -s) narrow strip of water extending from the sea into the land

inlets n ▷ inlet

inmate n (pl -s) person living in an institution such as a prison

inmates n ▷ inmate

inmost adj innermost

inn n (pl -s) pub or small hotel, esp. in the country > **innkeeper** n (pl -s)

innards pl n (Informal) internal organs

innate adj being part of someone's nature, inborn

inner adj happening or located inside

innermost adj furthest inside

innings n (SPORT) player's or side's turn of batting

innkeeper n ▷ inn

innkeepers n ▷ inn

innocence n ▷ innocent

innocences n ▷ innocent

innocent adj not guilty of a crime ▶ n (pl -s) innocent person, esp. a child > **innocently** adv > **innocence** n (pl -s)

innocently adv ▷ innocent

innocents n ▷ innocent

innocuous adj not harmful > **innocuously** adv

innocuously adv ▷ innocuous

innovated v ▷ innovation

innovates v ▷ innovation

innovating v ▷ innovation

innovation n (pl -s) new idea or method > **innovate** v (-tes, -ting, -ted) > **innovative** adj > **innovator** n (pl -s)

innovations n ▷ innovation

innovative adj ▷ innovation

innovator n ▷ innovation

innovators n ▷ innovation

inns n ▷ inn

innuendo n (pl -does) (remark making) an indirect reference to something rude or unpleasant

innuendoes n ▷ innuendo

innumerable adj too many to be counted

innumeracies n ▷ innumerate

innumeracy n ▷ innumerate

innumerate adj having no understanding

of mathematics or science ▷ **innumeracy** *n*
(*pl* -cies)

inoculate *v* (-tes, -ting, -ted) protect
against disease by injecting with a vaccine
▷ **inoculation** *n* (*pl* -s)
 inoculated *v* ▷ inoculate
 inoculates *v* ▷ inoculate
 inoculating *v* ▷ inoculate
 inoculation *n* ▷ inoculate
 inoculations *n* ▷ inoculate
inoperable *adj* (of a tumour or cancer) unable
to be surgically removed
inopportune *adj* badly timed, unsuitable
inordinate *adj* excessive
inorganic *adj* not having the characteristics of
living organisms
inpatient *n* (*pl* -s) patient who stays in a
hospital for treatment
 inpatients *n* ▷ inpatient
input *n* (*pl* -s) resources put into a project etc.
▶ *v* (-s, -tting, -put) enter (data) in a computer
 inputs *v*, *n* ▷ input
 inputting *v*, *n* ▷ input
inquest *n* (*pl* -s) official inquiry into a sudden
death
 inquests *n* ▷ inquest
inquire *v* (-res, -ring, -red) seek information or
ask (about) ▷ **inquirer** *n* (*pl* -s)
 inquired *v* ▷ inquire
 inquirer *n* ▷ inquire
 inquirers *n* ▷ inquire
 inquires *v* ▷ inquire
 inquiries *n* ▷ inquiry
 inquiring *v* ▷ inquire
inquiry *n* (*pl* -ries) question
inquisition *n* (*pl* -s) thorough investigation
▷ **inquisitor** *n* (*pl* -s) ▷ **inquisitorial** *adj*
 inquisitions *n* ▷ inquisition
inquisitive *adj* excessively curious about
other people's affairs ▷ **inquisitively** *adv*
 inquisitively *adv* ▷ inquisitive
 inquisitor *n* ▷ inquisition
 inquisitorial *adj* ▷ inquisition
 inquisitors *n* ▷ inquisition
inquorate *adj* without enough people present
to make a quorum
inroads *pl n* start affecting or reducing
insalubrious *adj* unpleasant, unhealthy, or
sordid
insane *adj* mentally ill ▷ **insanely** *adv*
▷ **insanity** *n* (*pl* -ties)
 insanely *adv* ▷ insane
insanitary *adj* dirty or unhealthy
 insanities *n* ▷ insane
 insanity *n* ▷ insane

insatiable [in-**saysh**-a-bl] *adj* unable to be
satisfied
inscribe *v* (-bes, -bing, -bed) write or carve
words on
 inscribed *v* ▷ inscribe
 inscribes *v* ▷ inscribe
 inscribing *v* ▷ inscribe
inscription *n* (*pl* -s) words inscribed
 inscriptions *n* ▷ inscription
inscrutable *adj* mysterious, enigmatic
▷ **inscrutably** *adv*
 inscrutably *adv* ▷ inscrutable
insect *n* (*pl* -s) small animal with six legs and
usu. wings, such as an ant or fly
insecticide *n* (*pl* -s) substance for killing
insects
 insecticides *n* ▷ insecticide
insectivorous *adj* insect-eating
 insects *n* ▷ insect
insecure *adj* anxious, not confident
 inseminated *v* ▷ insemination
 inseminates *v* ▷ insemination
 inseminating *v* ▷ insemination
insemination *n* (*pl* -s) putting semen into a
woman's or female animal's body to try to
make her pregnant ▷ **inseminate** *v* (-tes,
-ting, -ted)
 inseminations *n* ▷ insemination
insensate *adj* without sensation, unconscious
insensible *adj* unconscious, without feeling
insensitive *adj* unaware of or ignoring other
people's feelings ▷ **insensitivity** *n* (*pl* -ties)
 insensitivities *n* ▷ insensitive
 insensitivity *n* ▷ insensitive
inseparable *adj* (of two people) spending
most of the time together
insert *v* (-s, -ing, -ed) put inside or include ▶ *n*
(*pl* -s) something inserted ▷ **insertion** *n* (*pl* -s)
 inserted *v* ▷ insert
 inserting *v* ▷ insert
 insertion *n* ▷ insert
 insertions *n* ▷ insert
 inserts *v*, *n* ▷ insert
inset *n* (*pl* -s) small picture inserted within a
larger one
 insets *n* ▷ inset
inshore *adj* close to the shore ▶ *adj*, *adv*
towards the shore
inside *prep* in or to the interior of ▶ *adj* on or
of the inside ▶ *adv* on, in, or to the inside,
indoors ▶ *n* (*pl* -s) inner side, surface, or part
insider *n* (*pl* -s) member of a group who has
privileged knowledge about it
 insiders *n* ▷ insider
 insides *n* ▷ inside ▶ *pl n* (*Informal*) stomach

and bowels

insidious adj subtle or unseen but dangerous > **insidiously** adv

insidiously adv ▷ insidious

insight n (pl -s) deep understanding

insights n ▷ insight

insignia n (pl -s) badge or emblem of honour or office

insignias n ▷ insignia

insignificance n ▷ insignificant

insignificances n ▷ insignificant

insignificant adj not important > **insignificance** n (pl -s)

insincere adj showing false feelings, not genuine > **insincerely** adv > **insincerity** n (pl -ties)

insincerely adv ▷ insincerely

insincerities n ▷ insincere

insincerity n ▷ insincere

insinuate v (-tes, -ting, -ted) suggest indirectly > **insinuation** n (pl -s)

insinuated v ▷ insinuate

insinuates v ▷ insinuate

insinuating v ▷ insinuate

insinuation n ▷ insinuate

insinuations n ▷ insinuate

insipid adj lacking interest, spirit, or flavour

insist v (-s, -ing, -ed) demand or state firmly > **insistent** adj making persistent demands > **insistently** adv > **insistence** n (pl -s)

insisted v ▷ insist

insistence n ▷ insist

insistences n ▷ insist

insistent adj ▷ insist

insistently adv ▷ insist

insisting v ▷ insist

insists v ▷ insist

insole n (pl -s) inner sole of a shoe or boot

insolence n ▷ insolent

insolences n ▷ insolent

insolent adj rude and disrespectful > **insolence** n (pl -s) > **insolently** adv

insolently adv ▷ insolent

insoles n ▷ insole

insoluble adj incapable of being solved

insolvencies n ▷ insolvent

insolvency n ▷ insolvent

insolvent adj unable to pay one's debts > **insolvency** n (pl -cies)

insomnia n (pl -s) inability to sleep > **insomniac** n (pl -s)

insomniac n ▷ insomnia

insomniacs n ▷ insomnia

insomnias n ▷ insomnia

insouciance n ▷ insouciant

insouciances n ▷ insouciant

insouciant adj carefree and unconcerned > **insouciance** n (pl -s)

inspect v (-s, -ing, -ed) check closely or officially > **inspection** n (pl -s)

inspected v ▷ inspect

inspecting v ▷ inspect

inspection n ▷ inspect

inspections n ▷ inspect

inspector n (pl -s) person who inspects

inspectors n ▷ inspector

inspects v ▷ inspect

inspiration n (pl -s) creative influence or stimulus > **inspirational** adj

inspirational adj ▷ inspiration

inspirations n ▷ inspiration

inspire v (-res, -ring, -red) fill with enthusiasm, stimulate

inspired v ▷ inspire

inspires v ▷ inspire

inspiring v ▷ inspire

instabilities n ▷ instability

instability n (pl -ties) lack of steadiness or reliability

install v (-lls, -lling, -lled) put in and prepare (equipment) for use

installation n (pl -s) installing

installations n ▷ installation

installed v ▷ install

installing v ▷ install

installs v ▷ install

instalment n (pl -s) any of the portions of a thing presented or a debt paid in successive parts

instalments n ▷ instalment

instance n (pl -s) particular example ▶ v (-ces, -cing, -ced) mention as an example

instanced v ▷ instance

instances n, v ▷ instance

instancing v ▷ instance

instant n (pl -s) very brief time ▶ adj happening at once > **instantly** adv

instantaneous adj happening at once > **instantaneously** adv

instantaneously adv ▷ instantaneous

instantly adv ▷ instant

instants n ▷ instant

instead adv as a replacement or substitute

instep n (pl -s) part of the foot forming the arch between the ankle and toes

insteps n ▷ instep

instigate v (-tes, -ting, -ted) cause to happen > **instigation** n (pl -s) > **instigator** n (pl -s)

instigated v ▷ instigate

instigates v ▷ instigate

instigating v ▷ instigate
instigation n ▷ instigate
instigations n ▷ instigate
instigator n ▷ instigate
instigators n ▷ instigate
instil v (-s, -lling, -lled) introduce (an idea etc.) gradually into someone's mind
instilled v ▷ instil
instilling v ▷ instil
instils v ▷ instil
instinct n (pl -s) inborn tendency to behave in a certain way > **instinctive** adj > **instinctively** adv
instinctive adj ▷ instinct
instinctively adv ▷ instinct
instincts n ▷ instinct
institute n (pl -s) organization set up for a specific purpose, esp. research or teaching ▶ v (-tutes, -tuting, -tuted) start or establish
instituted v ▷ institute
institutes n, v ▷ institute
instituting v ▷ institute
institution n (pl -s) large important organization such as a university or bank > **institutional** adj > **institutionalize** v (-izes, -izing, -ized)
institutional adj ▷ institution
institutionalize v ▷ institution
institutionalized v ▷ institution
institutionalizes v ▷ institution
institutionalizing n ▷ institution
institutions n ▷ institution
instruct v (-s, -ing, -ed) order to do something > **instructor** n (pl -s)
instructed v ▷ instruct
instructing v ▷ instruct
instruction n (pl -s) order to do something **instructions** n ▷ instruction ▶ pl n information on how to do or use something
instructive adj informative or helpful
instructor n ▷ instruct
instructors n ▷ instruct
instructs v ▷ instruct
instrument n (pl -s) tool used for particular work
instrumental adj (foll. by **in**) having an important function in
instrumentalist n (pl -s) player of a musical instrument
instrumentalists n ▷ instrumentalist
instrumentation n (pl -s) set of instruments in a car etc.
instrumentations n ▷ instrumentation
instruments n ▷ instrument
insubordinate adj not submissive to

authority > **insubordination** n (pl -s)
insubordination n ▷ insubordinate
insubordinations n ▷ insubordinate
insufferable adj unbearable
insular adj not open to new ideas, narrow-minded > **insularity** n (pl -ties)
insularities n ▷ insular
insularity n ▷ insular
insulate v (-tes, -ting, -ted) prevent or reduce the transfer of electricity, heat, or sound by surrounding or lining with a nonconducting material > **insulation** n (pl -s) > **insulator** n (pl -s)
insulated v ▷ insulate
insulates v ▷ insulate
insulating v ▷ insulate
insulation n ▷ insulate
insulations n ▷ insulate
insulator n ▷ insulate
insulators n ▷ insulate
insulin n (pl -s) hormone produced in the pancreas that controls the amount of sugar in the blood
insulins n ▷ insulin
insult v (-s, -ing, -ed) behave rudely to, offend ▶ n (pl -s) insulting remark or action > **insulting** adj
insulted v ▷ insult
insulting v, adj ▷ insult
insults v, n ▷ insult
insuperable adj impossible to overcome
insupportable adj impossible to tolerate
insurance n (pl -ces) agreement by which one makes regular payments to a company who pay an agreed sum if damage, loss, or death occurs
insurances n ▷ insurance
insure v (-res, -ring, -red) protect by insurance
insured v ▷ insure
insures v ▷ insure
insurgent n (pl -s) ▶ adj (person) in revolt against an established authority
insurgents n ▷ insurgent
insuring v ▷ insure
insurrection n (pl -s) rebellion
insurrections n ▷ insurrection
intact adj not changed or damaged in any way
intaglio [in-tah-lee-oh] n (pl -s) (gem carved with) an engraved design
intaglios n ▷ intaglio
intake n (pl -kes) amount or number taken in
intakes n ▷ intake
integer n (pl -s) positive or negative whole number or zero
integers n ▷ integer

integral adj being an essential part of a whole ▶ n (pl -s) (MATHS) sum of a large number of very small quantities

integrals n ▷ integral

integrate v (-tes, -ting, -ted) combine into a whole > **integration** n (pl -s)

integrated v ▷ integrate

integrates v ▷ integrate

integrating v ▷ integrate

integration n ▷ integrate

integrations n ▷ integrate

integrities n ▷ integrity

integrity n (pl -ties) quality of having high moral principles

intellect n (pl -s) power of thinking and reasoning

intellects n ▷ intellect

intellectual adj of or appealing to the intellect ▶ n (pl -s) intellectual person > **intellectually** adv

intellectually adv ▷ intellectual

intellectuals n ▷ intellectual

intelligence n (pl -s) quality of being intelligent

intelligences n ▷ intelligence

intelligent adj able to understand, learn, and think things out quickly > **intelligently** adv

intelligently adv ▷ intelligent

intelligentsia n (pl -s) intellectual or cultured people in a society

intelligentsias n ▷ intelligentsia

intelligibilities n ▷ intelligibile

intelligibility n ▷ intelligibile

intelligible adj able to be understood > **intelligibility** n (pl -ties)

intemperance n ▷ intemperate

intemperances n ▷ intemperate

intemperate adj unrestrained, uncontrolled > **intemperance** n (pl -s)

intend v (-s, -ing, -ed) propose or plan (to do something)

intended v ▷ intend

intending v ▷ intend

intends v ▷ intend

intense adj of great strength or degree > **intensity** n (pl -ties)

intensification n ▷ intensify

intensifications n ▷ intensify

intensified v ▷ intensify

intensifies v ▷ intensify

intensify v (-fies, -fying, -fied) make or become more intense > **intensification** n (pl -s)

intensifying v ▷ intensify

intensities n ▷ intense

intensity n ▷ intense

intensive adj using or needing concentrated effort or resources > **intensively** adv

intensively adv ▷ intensive

intent n (pl -s) intention ▶ adj paying close attention > **intently** adv > **intentness** n (pl -s)

intention n (pl -s) something intended

intentional adj planned in advance, deliberate > **intentionally** adv

intentionally adv ▷ intentional

intentions n ▷ intention

intently adv ▷ intent

intentness n ▷ intent

intentnesses n ▷ intent

intents n ▷ intent

inter [in-ter] v (-s, -rring, -rred) bury (a corpse) > **interment** n (pl -s)

interact v (-s, -ing, -ed) act on or in close relation with each other > **interaction** n (pl -s) > **interactive** adj

interacted v ▷ interact

interacting v ▷ interact

interaction n ▷ interact

interactions n ▷ interact

interactive adj ▷ interact

interacts v ▷ interact

interbred v ▷ interbreed

interbreed v (-s, -ing, -bred) breed within a related group

interbreeding v ▷ interbreed

interbreeds v ▷ interbreed

intercede v (-des, -ding, -ded) try to end a dispute between two people or groups > **intercession** n (pl -s)

interceded v ▷ intercede

intercedes v ▷ intercede

interceding v ▷ intercede

intercept v (-s, -ing, -ed) seize or stop in transit > **interception** n (pl -s)

intercepted v ▷ intercept

intercepting v ▷ intercept

interception n ▷ intercept

interceptions n ▷ intercept

intercepts v ▷ intercept

intercession n ▷ intercede

intercessions n ▷ intercede

interchange v (-ges, -ging, -ged) (cause to) exchange places ▶ n (pl -ges) motorway junction > **interchangeable** adj

interchangeable adj ▷ interchange

interchanged v ▷ interchange

interchanges v, n ▷ interchange

interchanging v ▷ interchange

intercom n (pl -s) internal communication system with loudspeakers

intercoms n ▷ intercom

intercontinental adj travelling between or linking continents

intercourse n (pl -s) sexual intercourse

intercourses n ▷ intercourse

interdict n ▷ interdiction

interdiction, interdict n (pl -s) formal order forbidding something

interdictions n ▷ interdiction

interdicts n, v ▷ interdiction

interdisciplinary adj involving more than one branch of learning

interest n (pl -s) desire to know or hear more about something ▶ v (-s, -ing, -ed) arouse the interest of > **interesting** adj > **interestingly** adv

interested adj feeling or showing interest ▶ v ▷ interest

interesting v, adj ▷ interest

interestingly adv ▷ interest

interests n, v ▷ interest

interface n (pl -s) area where two things interact or link

interfaces n ▷ interface

interfere v (-res, -ring, -red) try to influence other people's affairs where one is not involved or wanted > **interfering** adj > **interference** n (pl -s) interfering

interfered v ▷ interfere

interference n ▷ interfere

interferes v ▷ interfere

interfering v, adj ▷ interfere

interferon n (pl -s) protein that stops the development of an invading virus

interferons n ▷ interferon

interim adj temporary or provisional

interior n (pl -s) inside ▶ adj inside, inner

interiors n ▷ interior

interject v (-s, -ing, -ed) make (a remark) suddenly or as an interruption > **interjection** n (pl -s)

interjected v ▷ interject

interjecting v ▷ interject

interjection n ▷ interject

interjections n ▷ interject

interjects v ▷ interject

interlace v (-ces, -cing, -ced) join together as if by weaving

interlaced v ▷ interlace

interlaces v ▷ interlace

interlacing v ▷ interlace

interlink v (-s, -ing, -ed) connect together

interlinked v ▷ interlink

interlinking v ▷ interlink

interlinks v ▷ interlink

interlock v (-s, -ing, -ed) join firmly together

interlocked v ▷ interlock

interlocking v ▷ interlock

interlocks v ▷ interlock

interlocutor [in-ter-**lok**-yew-ter] n (pl -s) person who takes part in a conversation

interlocutors n ▷ interlocutor

interloper [in-ter-lope-er] n (pl -s) person in a place or situation where he or she has no right to be

interlopers n ▷ interloper

interlude n (pl -s) short rest or break in an activity or event

interludes n ▷ interlude

intermarriage n ▷ intermarry

intermarriages n ▷ intermarry

intermarried v ▷ intermarry

intermarries v ▷ intermarry

intermarry v (-rries, -rrying, -rried) (of families, races, or religions) become linked by marriage > **intermarriage** n (pl -s)

intermarrying v ▷ intermarry

intermediaries n ▷ intermediary

intermediary n (pl -ries) person trying to create agreement between others

intermediate adj coming between two points or extremes

interment n ▷ inter

interments n ▷ inter

intermezzo [in-ter-**met**-so] n (pl -s) short piece of music, esp. one performed between the acts of an opera

intermezzos n ▷ intermezzo

interminable adj seemingly endless because boring > **interminably** adv

interminably adv ▷ interminable

intermingle v (-les, -ling, -led) mix together

intermingled v ▷ intermingle

intermingles v ▷ intermingle

intermingling v ▷ intermingle

intermission n (pl -s) interval between parts of a play, film, etc.

intermissions n ▷ intermission

intermittent adj occurring at intervals > **intermittently** adv

intermittently adv ▷ intermittent

intern v (-s, -ing, -ed) imprison, esp. during a war ▶ n (pl -s) trainee doctor in a hospital > **internment** n (pl -s)

internal adj of or on the inside > **internally** adv

internally adv ▷ internal

international adj of or involving two or more countries ▶ n (pl -s) game or match between teams of different countries > **internationally** adv

internationally adv ▷ international
internationals n ▷ international
internecine adj mutually destructive
interned v ▷ intern
internee n (pl -s) person who is interned
internees n ▷ internee
interning v ▷ intern
internment n ▷ intern
internments n ▷ intern
interns v, n ▷ intern
interplanetary adj of of linking planets
interplay n (pl -s) action and reaction of two things upon each other
interplays n ▷ interplay
interpolate [in-ter-pole-ate] v (-tes, -ting, -ted) insert (a comment or passage) into (a conversation or text) ▷ **interpolation** n (pl -s)
interpolated v ▷ interpolate
interpolates v ▷ interpolate
interpolating v ▷ interpolate
interpolation n ▷ interpolate
interpolations n ▷ interpolate
interpose v (-ses, -sing, -sed) insert between or among things
interposed v ▷ interpose
interposes v ▷ interpose
interposing v ▷ interpose
interpret v (-s, -ing, -ed) explain the meaning of ▷ **interpretation** n (pl -s)
interpretation n ▷ interpret
interpretations n ▷ interpret
interpreted v ▷ interpret
interpreter n (pl -s) person who translates orally from one language into another
interpreters n ▷ interpreter
interpreting v ▷ interpret
interprets v ▷ interpret
interred v ▷ inter
interregna n ▷ interregnum
interregnum n (pl -nums, -na) interval between reigns
interregnums n ▷ interregnum
interring v ▷ inter
interrogate v (-tes, -ting, -ted) question closely ▷ **interrogation** n (pl -s)
interrogated v ▷ interrogate
interrogates v ▷ interrogate
interrogating v ▷ interrogate
interrogation n ▷ interrogate
interrogations n ▷ interrogate
interrogative adj questioning ▶ n (pl -s) word used in asking a question, such as how or why ▷ **interrogator** n (pl -s)
interrogatives n ▷ interrogative
interrogator n ▷ interrogative

interrogators n ▷ interrogative
interrupt v (-s, -ing, -ed) break into (a conversation etc.) ▷ **interruption** n (pl -s)
interrupted v ▷ interrupt
interrupting v ▷ interrupt
interruption n ▷ interrupt
interruptions n ▷ interrupt
interrupts v ▷ interrupt
inters v ▷ inter
intersect v (-s, -ing, -ed) (of roads) meet and cross ▷ **intersection** n (pl -s)
intersected v ▷ intersect
intersecting v ▷ intersect
intersection n ▷ intersect
intersections n ▷ intersect
intersects v ▷ intersect
interspersed adj scattered (among, between, or on)
interstellar adj between or among stars
interstice [in-ter-stiss] n (pl -ces) small crack or gap between things
interstices n ▷ interstice
intertwine v (-nes, -ning, -ned) twist together
intertwined v ▷ intertwine
intertwines v ▷ intertwine
intertwining v ▷ intertwine
interval n (pl -s) time between two particular moments or events
intervals n ▷ interval
intervene v (-nes, -ning, -ned) involve oneself in a situation, esp. to prevent conflict ▷ **intervention** n (pl -s)
intervened v ▷ intervene
intervenes v ▷ intervene
intervening v ▷ intervene
intervention n ▷ intervene
interventions n ▷ intervene
interview n (pl -s) formal discussion, esp. between a job-seeker and an employer ▶ v (-s, -ing, -ed) conduct an interview with ▷ **interviewee** n (pl -s) ▷ **interviewer** n (pl -s)
interviewed v ▷ interview
interviewee n ▷ interview
interviewees n ▷ interview
interviewer n ▷ interview
interviewers n ▷ interview
interviewing v ▷ interview
interviews n, v ▷ interview
interweave v (-ves, -ving, -wove, -woven) weave together
interweaves v ▷ interweave
interweaving v ▷ interweave
interwove v ▷ interweave
interwoven v ▷ interweave
intestacies n ▷ intestate

intestacy *n* ▷ intestate
intestate *adj* not having made a will
  > **intestacy** *n* (*pl* -cies)
intestinal *adj* ▷ intestine
intestinally *adv* ▷ intestine
intestine *n* (*pl* -s) (*often pl* lower part of the alimentary canal between the stomach and the anus > **intestinal** *adj* > **intestinally** *adv*
intestines *n* ▷ intestine
intimacies *n* ▷ intimate¹
intimacy *n* ▷ intimate¹
intimate¹ *adj* having a close personal relationship ▶ *n* (*pl* -s) close friend
  > **intimately** *adv* > **intimacy** *n* (*pl* -cies)
intimate² *v* (-tes, -ting, -ted) hint at or suggest
  > **intimation** *n* (*pl* -s)
intimated *v* ▷ intimate²
intimately *adv* ▷ intimate¹
intimates *n* ▷ intimate¹ ▶ *v* ▷ intimate²
intimating *v* ▷ intimate²
intimation *n* ▷ intimate²
intimations *n* ▷ intimate²
intimidate *v* (-tes, -ting, -ted) subdue or influence by fear > **intimidating** *adj*
  > **intimidation** *n* (*pl* -s)
intimidated *v* ▷ intimidate
intimidates *v* ▷ intimidate
intimidating *v, adj* ▷ intimidate
intimidation *n* ▷ intimidate
intimidations *n* ▷ intimidate
into *prep* indicating motion towards the centre, result of a change, division, etc.
intolerable *adj* more than can be endured
  > **intolerably** *adv*
intolerably *adv* ▷ intolerable
intolerance *n* ▷ intolerant
intolerances *n* ▷ intolerant
intolerant *adj* refusing to accept practices and beliefs different from one's own
  > **intolerance** *n* (*pl* -s)
intonation *n* (*pl* -s) sound pattern produced by variations in the voice
intonations *n* ▷ intonation
intone *v* (-nes, -ning, -ned) speak or recite in an unvarying tone of voice
intoned *v* ▷ intone
intones *v* ▷ intone
intoning *v* ▷ intone
intoxicant *n* (*pl* -s) intoxicating drink
intoxicants *n* ▷ intoxicant
intoxicate *v* (-tes, -ting, -ted) make drunk
intoxicated *v* ▷ intoxicate
intoxicates *v* ▷ intoxicate
intoxicating *v* ▷ intoxicate
intoxication *n* (*pl* -s) state of being drunk

intoxications *n* ▷ intoxication
intractable *adj* (of a person) difficult to control
intranet *n* (*pl* -s) (COMPUTERS) internal network that makes use of Internet technology
intranets *n* ▷ intranet
intransigence *n* ▷ intransigent
intransigences *n* ▷ intransigent
intransigent *adj* refusing to change one's attitude > **intransigence** *n* (*pl* -s)
intransitive *adj* (of a verb) not taking a direct object
intrauterine *adj* within the womb
intravenous [in-tra-vee-nuss] *adj* into a vein
  > **intravenously** *adv*
intravenously *adv* ▷ intravenous
intrepid *adj* fearless, bold > **intrepidity** *n* (*pl* -ties)
intrepidities *n* ▷ intrepid
intrepidity *n* ▷ intrepid
intricacies *n* ▷ intricate
intricacy *n* ▷ intricate
intricate *adj* involved or complicated
  > **intricately** *adv* > **intricacy** *n* (*pl* -cies)
intricately *adv* ▷ intricate
intrigue *v* (-gues, -guing, -gued) make interested or curious ▶ *n* (*pl* -gues) secret plotting > **intriguing** *adj*
intrigued *v* ▷ intrigue
intrigues *v, n* ▷ intrigue
intriguing *v, adj* ▷ intrigue
intrinsic *adj* essential to the basic nature of something > **intrinsically** *adv*
intrinsically *adv* ▷ intrinsic
introduce *v* (-ces, -cing, -ced) present (someone) by name (to another person)
introduced *v* ▷ introduce
introduces *v* ▷ introduce
introducing *v* ▷ introduce
introduction *n* (*pl* -s) presentation of one person to another > **introductory** *adj*
introductions *n* ▷ introduction
introductory *adj* ▷ introduction
introspection *n* (*pl* -s) examination of one's own thoughts and feelings > **introspective** *adj*
introspections *n* ▷ introspection
introspective *adj* ▷ introspection
introversion *n* ▷ introvert
introversions *n* ▷ introvert
introvert *n* (*pl* -s) person concerned more with his or her thoughts and feelings than with the outside world > **introverted** *adj*
  > **introversion** *n* (*pl* -s)
introverted *adj* ▷ introvert
introverts *n* ▷ introvert
intrude *v* (-des, -ding, -ded) come in or join

in without being invited ▷ **intrusion** n (pl -s)
▷ **intrusive** adj
intruded v ▷ intrude
intruder n (pl -s) person who enters a place
without permission
intruders n ▷ intruder
intrudes v ▷ intrude
intruding v ▷ intrude
intrusion n ▷ intrude
intrusions n ▷ intrude
intrusive adj ▷ intrude
intuition n (pl -s) instinctive knowledge
or insight without conscious reasoning
▷ **intuitive** adj ▷ **intuitively** adv
intuitions n ▷ intuition
intuitive adj ▷ intuition
intuitively adv ▷ intuition
inundate v (-tes, -ting, -ted) flood
▷ **inundation** n (pl -s)
inundated v ▷ inundate
inundates v ▷ inundate
inundating v ▷ inundate
inundation n ▷ inundate
inundations n ▷ inundate
inured adj accustomed, esp. to hardship or
danger
invade v (-des, -ding, -ded) enter (a country) by
military force ▷ **invader** n (pl -s)
invaded v ▷ invade
invader n ▷ invade
invaders n ▷ invade
invades v ▷ invade
invading v ▷ invade
invalid[1] adj, n (pl -s) disabled or chronically ill
(person) ▶ v (-s, -ing, -ed) (often foll. by out)
dismiss from active service because of illness
or injury ▷ **invalidity** n (pl -ties)
invalid[2] adj having no legal force
invalidate v (-tes, -ting, -ted) make or show
to be invalid
invalidated v ▷ invalidate
invalidates v ▷ invalidate
invalidating v ▷ invalidate
invalided v ▷ invalid[1]
invaliding v ▷ invalid[1]
invalidities n ▷ invalid[1]
invalidity n ▷ invalid[1]
invalids n, v ▷ invalid[1]
invaluable adj of very great value or worth
invasion n (pl -s) invading
invasions n ▷ invasion
invective n (pl -s) abusive speech or writing
invectives n ▷ invective
inveigh [in-vay] v (-s, -ing, -ed) (foll. by **against**)
criticize strongly

inveighed v ▷ inveigh
inveighing v ▷ inveigh
inveighs v ▷ inveigh
inveigle v (-les, -ling, -led) coax by cunning
or trickery
inveigled v ▷ inveigle
inveigles v ▷ inveigle
inveigling v ▷ inveigle
invent v (-s, -ing, -ed) think up or create
(something new)
invented v ▷ invent
inventing v ▷ invent
invention n (pl -s) something invented
inventive adj creative and resourceful
▷ **inventiveness** n (pl -s) ▷ **inventor** n (pl -s)
inventiveness n ▷ inventive
inventivenesses n ▷ inventive
inventor n ▷ inventive
inventories v ▷ inventory
inventors n ▷ inventive
inventory n (pl -ries) detailed list of goods or
furnishings
invents v ▷ invent
inverse adj reversed in effect, sequence,
direction, etc. ▷ **inversely** adv
inversely adv ▷ inverse
inversion n ▷ invert
inversions n ▷ invert
invert v (-s, -ing, -ed) turn upside down or
inside out ▷ **inversion** n (pl -s)
invertebrate n (pl -s) animal with no
backbone
invertebrates n ▷ invertebrate
inverted v ▷ invert
inverting v ▷ invert
inverts v ▷ invert
invest v (-s, -ing, -ed) spend (money, time, etc.)
on something with the expectation of profit
invested v ▷ invest
investigate v (-tes, -ting, -ted) inquire
into, examine ▷ **investigation** n (pl -s)
▷ **investigative** adj ▷ **investigator** n (pl -s)
investigated v ▷ investigate
investigates v ▷ investigate
investigating v ▷ investigate
investigation n ▷ investigate
investigations n ▷ investigate
investigative adj ▷ investigate
investigator n ▷ investigate
investigators n ▷ investigate
investing v ▷ invest
investiture n (pl -s) formal installation of a
person in an office or rank
investitures n ▷ investiture
investment n (pl -s) money invested

> **investor** n (pl -s)
investments n ▷ investment
investor n ▷ investment
investors n ▷ investment
invests v ▷ invest
inveterate adj firmly established in a habit or condition
invidious adj likely to cause resentment
invigilate v (-tes, -ting, -ted) supervise people sitting an examination > **invigilator** n (pl -s)
invigilated v ▷ invigilate
invigilates v ▷ invigilate
invigilating v ▷ invigilate
invigilation n ▷ invigilate
invigilations n ▷ invigilate
invigilator n ▷ invigilate
invigilators n ▷ invigilate
invigorate v (-tes, -ting, -ted) give energy to, refresh
invigorated v ▷ invigorate
invigorates v ▷ invigorate
invigorating v ▷ invigorate
invincibilities n ▷ invincible
invincibility n ▷ invincible
invincible adj impossible to defeat > **invincibility** n (pl -ties)
inviolable adj unable to be broken or violated
inviolate adj unharmed, unaffected
invisibilities n ▷ invisible
invisibility adv ▷ invisible
invisible adj not able to be seen > **invisibly** adv > **invisibility** n (pl -ties)
invisibly adv ▷ invisible
invitation n ▷ invite
invitations n ▷ invite
invite v (-tes, -ting, -ted) request the company of ▶ n (pl -s) (Informal) invitation > **invitation** n (pl -s)
invited v ▷ invite
invites v, n ▷ invite
inviting adj tempting, attractive ▶ v ▷ invite
invocation n ▷ invoke
invocations n ▷ invoke
invoice v (-ces, -cing, -ced) ▶ n (pl -s) (present with) a bill for goods or services supplied
invoiced v ▷ invoice
invoices n, v ▷ invoice
invoicing v ▷ invoice
invoke v (-kes, -king, -ked) put (a law or penalty) into operation > **invocation** n (pl -s)
invoked v ▷ invoke
invokes v ▷ invoke
invoking v ▷ invoke
involuntarily adv ▷ involuntary
involuntary adj not done consciously,

unintentional > **involuntarily** adv
involve v (-lves, -lving, -lved) include as a necessary part > **involved** adj complicated > **involvement** n (pl -s)
involved v, adj ▷ involve
involvement n ▷ involve
involvements n ▷ involve
involves v ▷ involve
involving v ▷ involve
invulnerable adj not able to be wounded or harmed
inward adj directed towards the middle ▶ adv (also **inwards**) towards the inside or middle > **inwardly** adv
inwardly adv ▷ inward
inwards adv ▷ inward

> **io** n (**ios**). An io is a cry of joy or grief. While io doesn't earn many points, it's useful when you want to form words in more than one direction: I and O are two of the most common tiles in the game, so there's a good chance that you'll be able to use io when forming a word in another direction. Io scores 2 points.

iodine n (pl -s) (CHEM) bluish-black element used in medicine and photography
iodines n ▷ iodine
iodize v (-izes, -izing, -ized) treat with iodine
iodized n ▷ iodize
iodizes n ▷ iodize
iodizing n ▷ iodize
ion n (pl -s) electrically charged atom > **ionic** adj
ionic adj ▷ ion
ionization n ▷ ionize
ionizations n ▷ ionize
ionize v (-izes, -izing, -ized) change into ions > **ionization** n (pl -s)
ionized v ▷ ionize
ionizes v ▷ ionize
ionizing v ▷ ionize
ionosphere n (pl -s) region of ionized air in the upper atmosphere that reflects radio waves
ionospheres n ▷ ionosphere
ions n ▷ ion
iota n (pl -s) very small amount
iotas n ▷ iota
irascibilities n ▷ irascible
irascibility n ▷ irascible
irascible adj easily angered > **irascibility** n (pl -ties)
irate adj very angry
ire n (pl -s) (Lit) anger
ires n ▷ ire
iridescence n ▷ iridescent

iridescences n ▷ iridescent
iridescent adj having shimmering changing colours like a rainbow > **iridescence** n (pl -s)
iridium n (pl -s) (CHEM) very hard corrosion-resistant metal
iridiums n ▷ iridium
iris n (pl -ses) coloured circular membrane of the eye containing the pupil
irises n ▷ iris
irk v (-s, -ing, -ed) irritate, annoy
irked v ▷ irk
irking v ▷ irk
irks v ▷ irk
irksome adj irritating, annoying
iron n (pl -s) strong silvery-white metallic element, widely used for structural and engineering purposes ▶ adj made of iron ▶ (-s, -ing, -ed) smooth (clothes or fabric) with an iron
ironbark n (pl -s) Australian eucalyptus with hard rough bark
ironbarks n ▷ ironbark
ironed v ▷ iron
ironic, ironical adj using irony > **ironically** adv
ironical adj ▷ ironic
ironically adv ▷ ironic
ironies n ▷ irony
ironing n (pl -s) clothes to be ironed ▶ v ▷ iron
ironings n ▷ ironing
ironmonger n (pl -s) shopkeeper or shop dealing in hardware > **ironmongery** n (pl -ries)
ironmongeries n ▷ ironmonger
ironmongers n ▷ ironmonger
ironmongery n ▷ ironmonger
irons n, v ▷ iron ▶ pl n chains, restraints
ironstone n (pl -s) rock consisting mainly of iron ore
ironstones n ▷ ironstone
irony n (pl -nies) mildly sarcastic use of words to imply the opposite of what is said
irradiate v (-tes, -ting, -ted) subject to or treat with radiation > **irradiation** n (pl -s)
irradiated v ▷ irradiate
irradiates v ▷ irradiate
irradiating v ▷ irradiate
irradiation n ▷ irradiate
irradiations n ▷ irradiate
irrational adj not based on or not using logical reasoning
irredeemable adj not able to be reformed or corrected
irreducible adj impossible to put in a simpler form
irrefutable adj impossible to deny or disprove

irregular adj not regular or even > **irregularly** adv > **irregularity** n (pl -ties)
irregularities n ▷ irregular
irregularity n ▷ irregular
irregularly adv ▷ irregular
irrelevance n ▷ irrelevant
irrelevances n ▷ irrelevant
irrelevant adj not connected with the matter in hand > **irrelevantly** adv > **irrelevance** n (pl -s)
irrelevantly adv ▷ irrelevant
irreparable adj not able to be repaired or put right > **irreparably** adv
irreparably adv ▷ irreparable
irreplaceable adj impossible to replace
irreproachable adj blameless, faultless
irresistible adj too attractive or strong to resist > **irresistibly** adv
irresistibly adv ▷ irresistible
irresponsibilities n ▷ irresponsible
irresponsibility n ▷ irresponsible
irresponsible adj not showing or not done with due care for the consequences of one's actions or attitudes > **irresponsibility** n (pl -ties)
irreverence n ▷ irreverent
irreverences n ▷ irreverent
irreverent adj not showing due respect > **irreverence** n (pl -s)
irreversible adj not able to be reversed or put right again > **irreversibly** adv
irreversibly adv ▷ irreversible
irrevocable adj not possible to change or undo > **irrevocably** adv
irrevocably adv ▷ irrevocable
irrigate v (-tes, -ting, -ted) supply (land) with water by artificial channels or pipes > **irrigation** n (pl -s)
irrigated v ▷ irrigate
irrigates v ▷ irrigate
irrigating v ▷ irrigate
irrigation n ▷ irrigate
irrigations n ▷ irrigate
irritable adj easily annoyed > **irritably** adv
irritably adv ▷ irritable
irritant n (pl -s) ▶ adj (person or thing) causing irritation
irritants n ▷ irritant
irritate v (-tes, -ting, -ted) annoy, anger > **irritation** n (pl -s)
irritated v ▷ irritate
irritates v ▷ irritate
irritating v ▷ irritate
irritation n ▷ irritate
irritations n ▷ irritate

is v ▷ be

> **ish** n (**ishes**). An ish is a word for an issue in Scots law. If you have I, S and H on your rack, remember that as well as adding **ish** to the end of many words, you can also play those letters as a word in its own right. Ish scores 6 points.

isinglass [**ize**-ing-glass] n (pl -**es**) kind of gelatine obtained from some freshwater fish
isinglasses n ▷ isinglass
island n (pl -**s**) piece of land surrounded by water
islander n (pl -**s**) person who lives on an island
islanders n ▷ islander
islands n ▷ island
isle n (pl -**s**) (*Poetic*) island
isles n ▷ isle
islet n small island
islets n ▷ islet

> **ism** n (**isms**). An ism is an informal word for a belief or doctrine. While **ism** can be added to the ends of many words as a suffix, it's worth remembering it as a word in its own right. Ism scores 5 points.

isobar [**ice**-oh-bar] n (pl -**s**) line on a map connecting places of equal atmospheric pressure
isobars n ▷ isobar
isolate v (-**tes**, -**ting**, -**ted**) place apart or alone
> **isolation** n (pl -**s**)
isolated v ▷ isolate
isolates v ▷ isolate
isolating v ▷ isolate
isolation n ▷ isolate
isolationism n (pl -**s**) policy of not participating in international affairs
> **isolationist** n (pl -**s**) adj
isolationisms n ▷ isolationism
isolationist n, adj ▷ isolationism
isolationists n ▷ isolationsim
isolations n ▷ isolate
isomer [**ice**-oh-mer] n (pl -**s**) substance whose molecules contain the same atoms as another but in a different arrangement
isomers n ▷ isomer
isometric adj relating to muscular contraction without shortening of the muscle
isometrics pl n isometric exercises
isotherm [**ice**-oh-therm] n (pl -**s**) line on a map connecting points of equal temperature
isotherms n ▷ isotherm
isotope [**ice**-oh-tope] n (pl -**s**) one of two or more atoms with the same number of protons in the nucleus but a different number of neutrons
isotopes n ▷ isotope
issue n (pl -**s**) topic of interest or discussion ▶ v (-**ssues**, -**ssuing**, -**ssued**) make (a statement etc.) publicly
issued v ▷ issue
issues n, v ▷ issue
issuing v ▷ issue
isthmus [**iss**-muss] n (pl -**muses**) narrow strip of land connecting two areas of land
isthmuses n ▷ isthmus
it pron refers to a nonhuman, animal, plant, or inanimate object ▷ **its** adj, pron belonging to it
italic adj (of printing type) sloping to the right
italicize v (-**izes**, -**izing**, -**ized**) put in italics
italicized v ▷ italicize
italicizes v ▷ italicize
italicizing v ▷ italicize
italics pl n this type, used for emphasis
itch n (pl -**es**) skin irritation causing a desire to scratch ▶ v (-**es**, -**ing**, -**ed**) have an itch
> **itchy** adj
itched v ▷ itch
itches n, v ▷ itch
itching v ▷ itch
itchy adj ▷ itch
item n (pl -**s**) single thing in a list or collection
> **itemize** v (-**izes**, -**izing**, -**ized**) make a list of
itemized n ▷ item
itemizes n ▷ item
itemizing n ▷ item
items n ▷ item
iterate v (-**tes**, -**ting**, -**ted**) repeat > **iteration** n (pl -**s**)
iterated v ▷ iterate
iterates v ▷ iterate
iterating v ▷ iterate
iteration n ▷ iterate
iterations n ▷ iterate
itinerant adj travelling from place to place
itineraries n ▷ itinerary
itinerary n (pl -**aries**) detailed plan of a journey
itself pron ▷ it
ivies n ▷ ivy
ivories n ▷ ivory
ivory n (pl -**ries**) hard white bony substance forming the tusks of elephants ▶ adj yellowish-white
ivy n (pl -**vies**) evergreen climbing plant
iwi n (pl -**s**) (NZ) Maori tribe
iwis n ▷ iwi

J

J is one of the best tiles to have in Scrabble, as it is worth 8 points on its own. J also forms a number of words with X and Z, allowing you to earn some huge scores if you get the right tiles to go with it. Even better, some of these words are seven letters in length, so the right combination of tiles will give you a 50-point bonus if you are lucky enough to have it on your rack. On the other hand, J isn't the easiest tile to use when forming words in different directions. There's only one two-letter word that begins with J, **jo**. If you remember this, you won't waste time trying to think of others. As J has such a high value, look out for double- and triple-letter squares when playing it. There are plenty of good three-letter words starting with J: **jab** (12 points), **jam** (12), **jar** (10), **jaw** (13), **jay** (13), **jet** (10), **jib** (12), **jig** (11), **job** (12), **jog** (11), **jot** (10), **joy** (13), **jug** (11) and **jut** (10). In addition to these, there are other fantastic words beginning with J. **Jazz** (19) is very useful – you'll need a blank tile for the second Z, but if you can form it, you may also be able to play **jazzes** (21) or **jazzy** (23). **Jinx** (18) is also handy, and don't forget **jukebox** (27), which can be formed from **box** or **ox** if someone has played those.

jab v (-s, -bbing, -bbed) poke sharply ▶ n (pl -s)
  jabbed v ▷ jab
jabber v (-s, -ing, -ed) talk rapidly or incoherently
  jabbered v ▷ jabber
  jabbering v ▷ jabber
  jabbers v ▷ jabber
  jabbing v ▷ jab
jabiru n (pl -s) large white-and-black Australian stork
  jabirus n ▷ jabiru
  jabs v, n ▷ jab
jacaranda n (pl -s) tropical tree with sweet-smelling wood
  jacarandas n ▷ jacaranda
jack n (pl -s) device for raising a motor vehicle or other heavy object
  jacks n ▷ jack
jackal n (pl -s) doglike wild animal of Africa and Asia
  jackals n ▷ jackal
jackaroo, jackeroo n (pl -roos) (AUST) trainee on a sheep station
  jackaroos n ▷ jackaroo
jackass n (pl -es) fool
  jackasses n ▷ jackass
jackboot n (pl -s) high military boot
  jackboots n ▷ jackboot

jackdaw n (pl -s) black-and-grey Eurasian bird of the crow family
  jackdaws n ▷ jackdaw
  jackeroo n ▷ jackaroo
  jackeroos n ▷ jackaroo
jacket n (pl -s) short coat
  jackets n ▷ jacket
  jackings n ▷ jack
jackknife v (-s, -fing, -fed) (of an articulated truck) go out of control so that the trailer swings round at a sharp angle to the cab ▶ n (pl -knives) large clasp knife
  jackknifed v ▷ jackknife
  jackknifes v ▷ jackknife
  jackknifing v ▷ jackknife
  jackknives n ▷ jackknife
jackpot n (pl -s) largest prize that may be won in a game
  jackpots n ▷ jackpot
jacuzzi [jak-oo-zee] n ® (pl -s) circular bath with a device that swirls the water
  jacuzzis n ▷ jacuzzi
jade n (pl -s) ornamental semiprecious stone, usu. dark green ▶ adj bluish-green
jaded adj tired and unenthusiastic
  jades n ▷ jade
jagged [jag-gid] adj having an uneven edge

with sharp points

jaguar n (pl -s) large S American spotted cat
  jaguars n ▷ jaguar

jail n (pl -s) prison ▶ v (-s, -ing, -ed) send to prison > **jailer** n (pl -s)

jailbird n (pl -s) (Informal) person who has often been in prison
  jailbirds n ▷ jailbird
  jailed v ▷ jail
  jailer n ▷ jail
  jailers n ▷ jail
  jailing v ▷ jail
  jails n, v ▷ jail
  jalopies n ▷ jalopy

jalopy [jal-**lop**-ee] n (pl -pies) (Informal) old car

jam¹ v (-s, -mming, -mmed) pack tightly into a place ▶ n (pl -s) hold-up of traffic

jam² n (pl -s) food made from fruit boiled with sugar

jamb n (pl -s) side post of a door or window frame

jamboree n (pl -s) large gathering or celebration
  jamborees n ▷ jamboree
  jambs n ▷ jamb
  jammed v ▷ jam¹
  jamming v ▷ jam¹
  jams v ▷ jam¹ ▶ n ▷ jam¹, ²

jandal n (pl -s) (NZ) sandal with a strap between the toes
  jandals n ▷ jandal

jangle v (-les, -ling, -led) (cause to) make a harsh ringing noise
  jangled v ▷ jangle
  jangles v ▷ jangle
  jangling v ▷ jangle

janitor n (pl -s) caretaker of a school or other building
  janitors n ▷ janitor

> **janizar** or **janizary** n (janizars, janizaries). A janizar was an elite soldier in the armies of the Ottoman Empire. This is a very useful word, and will earn you a 50-point bonus if you are able to use all your letters in playing it. Also, if janizar is already on the board, you have an opportunity to earn a good score by adding an S, Y or IES. Janizar scores 23 points.

japan n (pl -s) very hard varnish, usu. black ▶ v (-s, -nning, -nned) cover with this varnish
  japanned v ▷ japan
  japanning v ▷ japan
  japans n, v ▷ japan

jape n (pl -s) (Old-fashioned) joke or prank

japes n ▷ jape

japonica n (pl -s) shrub with red flowers
  japonicas n ▷ japonica

jar¹ n (pl -s) wide-mouthed container, usu. round and made of glass

jar² v (-s, -rring, -rred) have a disturbing or unpleasant effect ▶ n (pl -s) jolt or shock

jargon n (pl -s) specialized technical language of a particular subject
  jargons n ▷ jargon

jarrah n (pl -s) Australian eucalypt yielding valuable timber
  jarrahs n ▷ jarrah
  jarred v ▷ jar²
  jarring v ▷ jar²
  jars v ▷ jar² ▶ n ▷ jar¹, ²

jasmine n (pl -s) shrub with sweet-smelling yellow or white flowers
  jasmines n ▷ jasmine

jasper n (pl -s) red, yellow, dark green, or brown variety of quartz
  jaspers n ▷ jasper

jaundice n (pl -s) disease marked by yellowness of the skin

jaundiced adj (of an attitude or opinion) bitter or cynical
  jaundices n ▷ jaundice

jaunt n (pl -s) short journey for pleasure
  jauntier adj ▷ jaunty
  jauntiest adj ▷ jaunty
  jauntily adv ▷ jaunty
  jaunts n ▷ jaunt

jaunty adj (-tier, -tiest) sprightly and cheerful > **jauntily** adv

javelin n (pl -s) light spear thrown in sports competitions
  javelins n ▷ javelin

jaw n (pl -s) one of the bones in which the teeth are set ▶ v (-s, -ing, -ed) (Slang) talk lengthily

> **jawbox** n (jawboxes). Jawbox is a Scots word for a sink. Watch out for opportunities to form this if someone else has played either jaw or box, and if jawbox itself is on the board, you can earn 27 points just by making it plural with es. Jawbox scores 25 points.

  jawed v ▷ jaw
  jawing v ▷ jaw
  jaws n, v ▷ jaw ▶ pl n mouth

jay n (pl -s) bird with a pinkish body and blue-and-black wings
  jays n ▷ jay

jaywalker n (pl -s) person who crosses the road in a careless or dangerous manner > **jaywalking** n (pl -s)

jaywalkers n ▷ jaywalker
jaywalking n ▷ jaywalker
jaywalkings n ▷ jaywalker

> **jazy** n (**jazies**). Jazy is an old word for a wig. This is a marvellous word, combining J and Z. If you get this combination and have either an A or a Y, look for the missing letter on the board, as it's highly likely to be there. Jazy scores 23 points.

jazz n (pl -es) kind of music with an exciting rhythm, usu. involving improvisation
jazzes n ▷ jazz
jazzier adj ▷ jazzy
jazziest adj ▷ jazzy
jazzy adj (-zier, -ziest) flashy or showy
jealous adj fearful of losing a partner or possession to a rival > **jealously** adv > **jealousy** n (pl -sies)
jealousies n ▷ jealous
jealously adv ▷ jealous
jealousy n ▷ jealous
jeans pl n casual denim trousers
jeer v (-s, -ing, -ed) scoff or deride ▶ n (pl -s) cry of derision
jeered v ▷ jeer
jeering v ▷ jeer
jeers v, n ▷ jeer
jejune adj simple or naive
jell v (-s, -ing, -ed) form into a jelly-like substance
jelled v ▷ jell
jellied adj prepared in a jelly
jelling v ▷ jell
jells v ▷ jell
jellies n ▷ jelly
jelly n (pl -llies) soft food made of liquid set with gelatine
jellyfish n (pl jellyfish) small jelly-like sea animal
jemmies n ▷ jemmy
jemmy n (pl -mmies) short steel crowbar used by burglars
jennies n ▷ jenny
jenny n (pl -nnies) female ass or wren
jeopardies n ▷ jeopardy
jeopardize v (-izes, -izing, -ized) place in danger
jeopardized n ▷ jeopardy
jeopardizes n ▷ jeopardy
jeopardizing n ▷ jeopardy
jeopardy n (pl -dies) danger
jerboa n (pl -s) small mouselike rodent with long hind legs
jerboas n ▷ jerboa

jerk v (-s, -ing, -ed) move or throw abruptly ▶ n (pl -s) sharp or abruptly stopped movement
jerked v ▷ jerk
jerkily adv ▷ jerky
jerkin n (pl -s) sleeveless jacket
jerkiness n ▷ jerky
jerkinesses n ▷ jerky
jerking v ▷ jerk
jerkins n ▷ jerkin
jerks v, n ▷ jerk
jerky adj sudden or abrupt > **jerkily** adv > **jerkiness** n (pl -s)

> **jerque** v (**jerques, jerquing, jerqued**), n (**jerquer, jerquers, jerquing, jerquings**). Jerque means to search a ship for smuggled goods. If you have all the tiles for jerques, jerquer or jerqued, you'll get a 50-point bonus for using all your letters, which will give you a fantastic score. Jerque scores 22 points.

jersey n (pl -s) knitted jumper
jerseys n ▷ jersey
jest n (pl -s) ▶ v (-s, -ing, -ed) joke
jested v ▷ jest
jester n (pl -s) (HIST) professional clown at court
jesters n ▷ jester
jesting v ▷ jest
jests n, v ▷ jest
jet[1] n (pl -s) aircraft driven by jet propulsion ▶ v (-s, jetting, jetted) fly by jet aircraft
jet[2] n (pl -s) hard black mineral
jetboat n (pl -s) motorboat propelled by a jet of water
jetboats n ▷ jetboat
jets n ▷ jet[1, 2] ▶ v ▷ jet[1]
jetsam n (pl -s) goods thrown overboard to lighten a ship
jetsams n ▷ jetsam
jetted v ▷ jet[1]
jetties n ▷ jetty
jetting v ▷ jet[1]
jettison v (-s, -ing, -ed) abandon
jettisoned v ▷ jettison
jettisoning v ▷ jettison
jettisons v ▷ jettison
jetty n (pl -ties) small pier

> **jeu** n (**jeux**). Jeu is the French word for **game** or **play**. The plural form, jeux, is a great little word, using both J and X particularly if you can play it on a double- or triple-word square. Jeux scores 18 points.

jewel n (pl -s) precious stone
jeweller n (pl -s) dealer in jewels
jewelleries n ▷ jewellery

jewellers n ▷ jeweller
jewellery n (pl -s) objects decorated with precious stones
jewels n ▷ jewel
jewfish n (pl jewfish) (AUST) freshwater catfish

jezail n (jezails). A jezail is a kind of heavy Afghan musket. This word is potentially a very high scorer, as its plural uses seven tiles. If you can play all of these at once, you'll earn the 50-point bonus for a total of 73 points! Jezail scores 22 points.

jib¹ n (pl -s) triangular sail set in front of a mast
jib² v (-s, -bbing, -bbed) (of a horse, person, etc.) stop and refuse to go on
jib³ n (pl -s) projecting arm of a crane or derrick
jibbed v ▷ jib²
jibbing v ▷ jib²
jibe¹ n (pl -s) ▷ v (-jibes, -jibing, -jibed) taunt or jeer
jibed v ▷ jibe¹
jibes n, v ▷ jibe¹
jibing v ▷ jibe¹
jibs n ▷ jib¹,³ ▷ v ▷ jib²
jiffies n ▷ jiffy
jiffy n (pl -ffies) (Informal) very short period of time
jig n (pl -s) type of lively dance ▷ v (-s, -gging, -gged) make jerky up-and-down movements
jigged v ▷ jig
jigging v ▷ jig
jiggle v (-ggles, -ggling, -ggled) move up and down with short jerky movements
jiggled v ▷ jiggle
jiggles v ▷ jiggle
jiggling v ▷ jiggle
jigs n, v ▷ jig
jigsaw n (pl -s) (also **jigsaw puzzle**) picture cut into interlocking pieces, which the user tries to fit together again
jigsaws n ▷ jigsaw
jihad n (pl -s) Islamic holy war against unbelievers
jihads n ▷ jihad
jilt v (-s, -ing, -ed) leave or reject (one's lover)
jilted v ▷ jilt
jilting v ▷ jilt
jilts v ▷ jilt
jingle n (pl -s) catchy verse or song used in a radio or television advert ▷ v (-les, -ling, -led) (cause to) make a gentle ringing sound
jingled v ▷ jingle
jingles n, v ▷ jingle
jingling v ▷ jingle
jingoism n (pl -s) aggressive nationalism

> **jingoistic** adj
jingoisms n ▷ jingoism
jingoistic adj ▷ jingoism
jinks pl n boisterous merrymaking
jinn n ▷ jinni
jinni n (pl jinn) spirit in Muslim mythology
jinx n (pl -es) person or thing bringing bad luck
  ▶ v (-xes, -xing, -xed) be or put a jinx on
jinxed v ▷ jinx
jinxes n, v ▷ jinx
jinxing v ▷ jinx
jitters pl n worried nervousness
jittery adj nervous
jive n (pl -s) lively dance of the 1940s and '50s
  ▶ v (-ves, -ving, -ved) dance the jive
jived v ▷ jive
jives n, v ▷ jive
jiving v ▷ jive

jiz n (jizes). Jiz is an old word for a wig. This is a very useful word for when you find yourself with J and Z but nothing else that looks promising: there will almost certainly be an I on the board around which you can form jiz. Jiz scores 19 points.

jizz n (jizzes). A jizz is the combination of characteristics used to identify a bird or plant species. A blank tile is required to form jizz because it contains two Zs. If **jiz** is already on the board, a blank or a blank and ES will earn you 19 or 21 points. Jizz scores 19 points.

jo n (joes). Jo is a Scots word for a sweetheart. This is the only two-letter word that starts with J, and is worth remembering for that reason. It's also a good word to form when playing in more than one direction at once. Jo scores 9 points.

job n (pl -s) occupation or paid employment
jobbing adj doing individual jobs for payment
jobless adj, pl n unemployed (people)
jobs n ▷ job
jockey n (pl -s) (professional) rider of racehorses ▶ v (-ys, -ying, -yed) manoeuvre to obtain an advantage
jockeyed v ▷ jockey
jockeying v ▷ jockey
jockeys n, v ▷ jockey
jockstrap n (pl -s) belt with a pouch to support the genitals, worn by male athletes
jockstraps n ▷ jockstrap
jocose [joke-kohss] adj playful or humorous
jocular adj fond of joking > **jocularity** n (pl

-ties) > **jocularly** adv
jocularities n ▷ jocular
jocularity n ▷ jocular
jocularly adv ▷ jocular
jocund [jok-kund] adj (Lit) merry or cheerful
jodhpurs pl n riding trousers, loose-fitting above the knee but tight below
joey n (pl -ys) (AUST) young kangaroo
joeys n ▷ joey
jog v (-s, -gging, -gged) run at a gentle pace, esp. for exercise ▶ n (pl -s) slow run > **jogger** n (pl -s) > **jogging** n (pl -s)
jogged v ▷ jog
jogger n ▷ jog
joggers n ▷ jog
jogging n, v ▷ jog
joggings n ▷ jog
joggle v (-les, -ling, -led) shake or move jerkily
joggled v ▷ joggle
joggles v ▷ joggle
joggling v ▷ joggle
jogs n, v ▷ jog
join v (-s, -ing, -ed) become a member (of) ▶ n (pl -s) place where two things are joined
joined v ▷ join
joiner n (pl -s) maker of finished woodwork
joineries n ▷ joinery
joiners n ▷ joiner
joinery n (pl -ries) joiner's work
joining v ▷ join
joins n, v ▷ join
joint adj shared by two or more ▶ n (pl -s) place where bones meet but can move ▶ v (-s, -ing, -ed) divide meat into joints > **jointed** adj > **jointly** adv
jointed v, adj ▷ joint
jointing v ▷ joint
jointly adv ▷ joint
joints n, v ▷ joint
joist n (pl -s) horizontal beam that helps support a floor or ceiling
joists n ▷ joist
jojoba [hoe-hoe-ba] n (pl -s) shrub of SW North America whose seeds yield oil used in cosmetics
jojobas n ▷ jojoba
joke n (pl -s) thing said or done to cause laughter ▶ v (-kes, -king, -ked) make jokes > **jokey** adj > **jokingly** adv
joked v ▷ joke
joker n (pl -s) person who jokes
jokers n ▷ joker
jokes n, v ▷ joke
jokey adj ▷ joke
joking v ▷ joke

jokingly adv ▷ joke
jollied v ▷ jolly
jollier adj ▷ jolly
jollies v ▷ jolly
jolliest adj ▷ jolly
jollities n ▷ jolly
jollity n ▷ jolly
jolly adj (-llier, -lliest) (of a person) happy and cheerful ▶ v (-lies, -lying, -lied) try to keep (someone) cheerful by flattery or coaxing > **jollity** n (pl -ties)
jollification n (pl -s) merrymaking
jollifications n ▷ jolly
jollying v ▷ jolly
jolt n (pl -s) unpleasant surprise or shock ▶ v (-s, -ing, -ed) surprise or shock
jolted v ▷ jolt
jolting v ▷ jolt
jolts n, v ▷ jolt
jonquil n (pl -s) fragrant narcissus
jonquils n ▷ jonquil
josh v (-es, -ing, -ed) (CHIEFLY US) (Slang) tease
joshed v ▷ josh
joshes v ▷ josh
joshing v ▷ josh
jostle v (-les, -ling, -led) knock or push against
jostled v ▷ jostle
jostles v ▷ jostle
jostling v ▷ jostle
jot v (-s, -tting, -tted) write briefly ▶ n (pl -s) very small amount
jotted v ▷ jot
jotting v ▷ jot
jotter n (pl -s) notebook
jotters n ▷ jotter
jottings pl n notes jotted down
jots v, n ▷ jot
joule [jool] n (pl -s) (PHYSICS) unit of work or energy
joules n ▷ joule
journal n (pl -s) daily newspaper or magazine
journalese n (pl -s) superficial style of writing, found in some newspapers
journaleses n ▷ journalese
journalism n (pl -s) writing in or editing of newspapers and magazines > **journalist** n (pl -s) > **journalistic** adj
journalisms n ▷ journalism
journalist n ▷ journalism
journalistic adj ▷ journalism
journalists n ▷ journalism
journals n ▷ journal
journey n (pl -s) act or process of travelling from one place to another ▶ v (-s, -ing, -ed) travel

journeyed v ▷ journey

journeying v ▷ journey

journeyman n (pl -men) qualified craftsman employed by another

journeymen n ▷ journeyman

journeys n, v ▷ journey

joust (HIST) n (pl -s) combat with lances between two mounted knights ▶ v (-s, -ing, -ed) fight on horseback using lances

jousted v ▷ joust

jousting v ▷ joust

jousts n, v ▷ joust

jovial adj happy and cheerful > **jovially** adv > **joviality** n (pl -ties)

jovialities n ▷ jovial

joviality n ▷ jovial

jovially adv ▷ jovial

jowl¹ n (pl -s) lower jaw

jowl² n (pl -s) fatty flesh hanging from the lower jaw

jowls n ▷ jowl¹,² ▶ pl n cheeks

joy n (pl -s) feeling of great delight or pleasure > **joyful** adj > **joyless** adj

joyful adj ▷ joy

joyless adj ▷ joy

joyous adj extremely happy and enthusiastic

joyride n ▷ joyriding

joyrider n ▷ joyriding

joyriders n ▷ joyriding

joyrides n ▷ joyriding

joyriding n (pl -s) driving for pleasure, esp. in a stolen car > **joyride** n (pl -s) > **joyrider** n (pl -s)

joyridings n ▷ joyriding

joystick n (pl -s) control device for an aircraft or computer

joysticks n ▷ joystick

joys n ▷ joy

jubilant adj feeling or expressing great joy > **jubilantly** adv > **jubilation** n (pl -s)

jubilantly adv ▷ jubilant

jubilation n ▷ jubilant

jubilations n ▷ jubilant

jubilee n (pl -s) special anniversary, esp. 25th (**silver jubilee**) or 50th (**golden jubilee**)

jubilees n ▷ jubilee

judder v (-s, -ing, -ed) vibrate violently ▶ n (pl -s) violent vibration

juddered v ▷ judder

juddering v ▷ judder

judders v, n ▷ judder

judge n (pl -s) public official who tries cases and passes sentence in a court of law ▶ v (-dges, -dging, -dged) act as a judge

judged v ▷ judge

judgement n ▷ judgment

judgements n ▷ judgment

judgemental adj ▷ judgment

judges n, v ▷ judge

judging v ▷ judge

judgment, judgement n (pl -s) opinion reached after careful thought > **judgmental, judgemental** adj

judgmental adj ▷ judgment

judgments n ▷ judgment

judicial adj of or by a court or judge > **judicially** adv

judicially adv ▷ judicial

judiciary n (pl -ries) system of courts and judges

judiciaries n ▷ judiciary

judicious adj well-judged and sensible > **judiciously** adv

judiciously adv ▷ judicious

judo n sport in which two opponents try to throw each other to the ground

jug n (pl -s) container for liquids, with a handle and small spout

juggernaut n (pl -s) (BRIT) large heavy truck

juggernauts n ▷ juggernaut

juggle v (-les, -ling, -led) throw and catch (several objects) so that most are in the air at the same time > **juggler** n (pl -s)

juggled v ▷ juggle

juggler n ▷ juggle

jugglers n ▷ juggle

juggles v ▷ juggle

juggling v ▷ juggle

jugs n ▷ jug

jugular n (pl -s) one of three large veins of the neck that return blood from the head to the heart

jugulars n ▷ jugular

juice n (pl -s) liquid part of vegetables, fruit, or meat

juices n ▷ juice

juicier adj ▷ juicy

juiciest adj ▷ juicy

juicy adj (-cier, -ciest) full of juice

jujitsu n (pl -s) Japanese art of wrestling and self-defence

jujitsus n ▷ jujitsu

juju n (pl -s) W African magic charm or fetish

jujus n ▷ juju

jukebox n (pl -es) coin-operated machine on which records, CDs, or videos can be played

jukeboxes n ▷ jukebox

julep n (pl -s) sweet alcoholic drink

juleps n ▷ julep

jumble n (pl -s) confused heap or state ▶ v (-les, -ling, -led) mix in a disordered way

jumbled v ▷ jumble

jumbles n, v ▷ jumble

jumbling v ▷ jumble

jumbo adj (Informal) very large ▶ n (pl -s) (also **jumbo jet**) large jet airliner

jumbos n ▷ jumbo

jumbuck n (pl -s) (AUST) (Old-fashioned slang) sheep

jumbucks n ▷ jumbuck

jump v (-s, -ing, -ed) leap or spring into the air using the leg muscles ▶ n (pl -s) act of jumping

jumped v ▷ jump

jumper n (pl -s) sweater or pullover

jumpers n ▷ jumper

jumpier adj ▷ jumpy

jumpiest adj ▷ jumpy

jumping v ▷ jump

jumpings n ▷ jump

jumps v, n ▷ jump

jumpy adj (-pier, -piest) nervous

junction n (pl -s) place where routes, railway lines, or roads meet

junctions n ▷ junction

juncture n (pl -s) point in time, esp. a critical one

junctures n ▷ juncture

jungle n (pl -s) tropical forest of dense tangled vegetation

jungles n ▷ jungle

junior adj of lower standing ▶ n (pl -s) junior person

juniors n ▷ junior

juniper n (pl -s) evergreen shrub with purple berries

junipers n ▷ juniper

junk[1] n (pl -s) discarded or useless objects

junk[2] n (pl -s) flat-bottomed Chinese sailing boat

junket n (pl -s) excursion by public officials paid for from public funds

junkets n ▷ junket

junkie, junky n (pl -kies) (Slang) drug addict

junkies n ▷ junkie

junks n ▷ junk[1, 2]

junky n ▷ junkie

junta n (pl -s) group of military officers holding power in a country, esp. after a coup

juntas n ▷ junta

juridical adj of law or the administration of justice

juries n ▷ jury

jurisdiction n (pl -s) right or power to administer justice and apply laws

jurisdictions n ▷ jurisdiction

jurisprudence n (pl -s) science or philosophy of law

jurisprudences n ▷ jurisprudence

jurist n (pl -s) expert in law

jurists n ▷ jurist

juror n (pl -s) member of a jury

jurors n ▷ juror

jury n (pl -ries) group of people sworn to deliver a verdict in a court of law

just adv very recently ▶ adj fair or impartial in action or judgment > **justly** adv > **justness** n (pl -s)

justice n (pl -s) quality of being just

justices n ▷ justice

justifiable adj ▷ justify

justifiably adv ▷ justify

justification n ▷ justify

justifications n ▷ justify

justified v ▷ justify

justifies v ▷ justify

justify v (-fies, -fying, -fied) prove right or reasonable > **justifiable** adj > **justifiably** adv > **justification** n (pl -s)

justifying v ▷ justify

justly adv ▷ just

justness n ▷ just

justnesses n ▷ just

jut v (-s, -tting, -tted) project or stick out

jute n (pl -s) plant fibre, used for rope, canvas, etc.

jutes n ▷ jute

juts v ▷ jut

jutted v ▷ jut

jutting v ▷ jut

juvenilia pl n works produced in an author's youth

juvenile adj young ▶ n (pl -s) young person or child

juveniles n ▷ juvenile

juxtapose v (-ses, -sing, -sed) put side by side > **juxtaposition** n (pl -s)

juxtaposed v ▷ juxtapose

juxtaposes v ▷ juxtapose

juxtaposing v ▷ juxtapose

juxtaposition n ▷ juxtapose

juxtapositions n ▷ juxtapose

jynx n (**jynxes**). A jynx is a kind of woodpecker. This unusual word is unique in combining J, Y and Z without using any vowels. Jynx scores 21 points.

Kk

Worth 5 points, K is a valuable tile to have in your rack. However, it's not the most useful tile for the short words that you need when forming words in different directions at the same time. There are only three two-letter words beginning with K: **ka**, **ko** and **ky**. Remembering these will stop you wasting time trying to think of others. There aren't very many three-letter words either, but remember **kak** (11 points), **keg** (8), **ken** (7), **key** (10), **kid** (8), **kin** (7), **kip** (9) and **kit** (7).

ka n (**kas**). A ka is a supernatural being in ancient Egyptian mythology. Along with **ko** and **ky**, it's one of only three two-letter words starting with K. Ka scores 6 points.

kaftan n (pl -s) long loose Eastern garment
  kaftans n ▷ kaftan
kaiser [kize-er] n (pl -s) (HIST) German or Austro-Hungarian emperor
  kaisers n ▷ kaiser
kak n (pl -s) (S AFR) (Slang) faeces
  kaks n (offensive) ▷ kak
kalashnikov n (pl -s) Russian-made automatic rifle
  kalashnikovs n ▷ kalashnikov
kale n (pl -s) cabbage with crinkled leaves
  kales n ▷ kale
kaleidoscope n (pl -s) tube-shaped toy containing loose coloured pieces reflected by mirrors so that intricate patterns form when the tube is twisted ▷ **kaleidoscopic** adj
  kaleidoscopes n ▷ kaleidoscope
  kaleidoscopic adj ▷ kaleidoscope
kamikaze [kam-mee-kah-zee] n (pl -s) (in World War II) Japanese pilot who performed a suicide mission ▶ adj (of an action) undertaken in the knowledge that it will kill or injure the person performing it
  kamikazes n ▷ kamikaze
kangaroo n (pl -s) Australian marsupial which moves by jumping with its powerful hind legs
  kangaroos n ▷ kangaroo
kaolin n (pl -s) fine white clay used to make porcelain and in some medicines
  kaolins n ▷ kaolin
kapok n (pl -s) fluffy fibre from a tropical tree, used to stuff cushions etc.

kapoks n ▷ kapok
kaput [kap-**poot**] adj (Informal) ruined or broken
karaoke n (pl -s) form of entertainment in which people sing over a prerecorded backing tape
  karaokes n ▷ karaoke
karate n (pl -s) Japanese system of unarmed combat using blows with the feet, hands, elbows, and legs
  karates n ▷ karate
karma n (pl -s) (BUDDHISM, HINDUISM) person's actions affecting his or her fate in the next reincarnation
  karmas n ▷ karma
karri n (pl -s) Australian eucalypt
  karris n ▷ karri
katipo n (pl -s) small poisonous New Zealand spider
  katipos n ▷ katipo
kayak n (pl -s) Inuit canoe made of sealskins stretched over a frame
  kayaks n ▷ kayak
kebab n (pl -s) dish of small pieces of meat grilled on skewers
  kebabs n ▷ kebab
kedgeree n (pl -s) dish of fish with rice and eggs
  kedgerees n ▷ kedgeree
keel n (pl -s) main lengthways timber or steel support along the base of a ship
  keels n ▷ keel
keen¹ adj (-er, -est) eager or enthusiastic ▷ **keenly** adv ▷ **keenness** n
keen² v (-s, -ing, -ed) wail over the dead
  keened v ▷ keen²
  keener adj ▷ keen¹
  keenest adj ▷ keen¹
  keening v ▷ keen²

keenly adv ▷ keen[1]
keenness n ▷ keen[1]
keens v ▷ keen[2]
keep v (-s, -ing, kept) have or retain possession of ▶ n (-s) cost of food and everyday expenses
keeper n (-s) person who looks after animals in a zoo ▶ n ▷ keeper
keeping v ▷ keep ▶ n (-s) care or charge ▶ n ▷ keeping ▶ v ▷ keep ▶ n ▷ keep > **keepsake** n (-s) gift treasured for the sake of the giver
keepsakes n ▷ keepsake
keg n (pl -s) small metal beer barrel
kegs n ▷ keg
kelp n (pl -s) large brown seaweed
kelpie n (pl -s) Australian sheepdog with a smooth coat and upright ears
kelpies n ▷ kelpie
kelps n ▷ kelp
kelvin n (pl -s) SI unit of temperature
kelvins n ▷ kelvin
ken v (-s, -nning, -nned or kent) (SCOT) know
kenning v ▷ ken
kenned v ▷ ken
kendo n (pl -s) Japanese sport of fencing using wooden staves
kendos n ▷ kendo
kennel n (pl -s) hutlike shelter for a dog
kennels n ▷ kennel
kens v ▷ ken
kent v ▷ ken
kept v ▷ keep
keratin n (pl -s) fibrous protein found in the hair and nails
keratins n ▷ keratin
kerb n (pl -s) edging to a footpath
kerbs n ▷ kerb
kerchief n (pl -s) piece of cloth worn over the head or round the neck
kerchiefs n ▷ kerchief
kerfuffle n (pl -s) (Informal) commotion or disorder
kerfuffles n ▷ kerfuffle
kernel n (pl -s) seed of a nut, cereal, or fruit stone
kernels n ▷ kernel
kerosene n (pl -s) (US, CANADIAN, AUST & NZ) liquid mixture distilled from petroleum and used as a fuel or solvent
kerosenes n ▷ kerosene
kestrel n (pl -s) type of small falcon
kestrels n ▷ kestrel
ketch n (pl -es) two-masted sailing ship
ketches n ▷ ketch
ketchup n (pl -s) thick cold sauce, usu. made of tomatoes

ketchups n ▷ ketchup
kettle n (pl -s) container with a spout and handle used for boiling water
kettledrum n (pl -s) large bowl-shaped metal drum
kettledrums n ▷ kettledrum
kettles n ▷ kettle
key n (pl -s) device for operating a lock by moving a bolt ▶ adj of great importance ▶ v (-s, -ing, -ed) enter (text) using a keyboard
keyboard n (pl -s) set of keys on a piano, computer, etc. ▶ v (-s, -ing, -ed) enter (text) using a keyboard
keyboarded v ▷ keyboard
keyboarding v ▷ keyboard
keyboards n, v ▷ keyboard
keyed v ▷ key
keyhole n (pl -s) opening for inserting a key into a lock
keyholes n ▷ keyhole
keying v ▷ key
keyings n ▷ key
keynote n (pl -s) dominant idea of a speech etc.
keynotes n ▷ keynote
keys n, v ▷ key
keystone n (pl -s) most important part of a process, organization, etc.
keystones n ▷ keystone

> **kex** n (**kexes**). A kex is a hollow-stemmed plant. This is a great three-letter word, combining K with X. If you have these letters on your rack, you can be confident that there will be, or will soon be, an E on the board, around which you can form kex. Kex scores 14 points.

khaki adj dull yellowish-brown ▶ n (pl -s) hard-wearing fabric of this colour
khakis n ▷ khaki

> **khi** n (**khis**). Khi is a letter of the Greek alphabet, also spelt **chi**. This is one of the higher-scoring three-letter words starting with K, and so is worth remembering. Khi scores 10 points.

kibbutz n (pl -im) communal farm or factory in Israel
kibbutzim n ▷ kibbutz
kick v (-s, -ing, -ed) drive, push, or strike with the foot ▶ n (pl kicks) thrust or blow with the foot
kickback (Informal) n (pl -s) money paid illegally for favours done
kickbacks n ▷ kickback
kicked v ▷ kick

kicking *n, v* ▷ kick
kicks *n, v* ▷ kick
kid[1] *n (pl -s)* (*Informal*) child
kid[2] *v (-s, -dding, -dded)* (*Informal*) tease or deceive (someone)
  kidded *v* ▷ kid[2]
  kidding *v* ▷ kid[2]
  kiddishnesses *n* ▷ kid[1,2]
kidnap *v (-s, -pping, -pped)* seize and hold (a person) to ransom ▷ **kidnapper** *n (pl -s)*
  kidnapped *n* ▷ kidnap
  kidnapper *n* ▷ kidnap
  kidnappers *n* ▷ kidnap
  kidnapping *n* ▷ kidnap
  kidnaps *n* ▷ kidnap
kidney *n (pl kidneys)* either of the pair of organs that filter waste products from the blood to produce urine
  kidneys *n* ▷ kidney
  kids *n* ▷ kid[1] ▶ *v* ▷ kid[2]
kill *v (-s, -ing, -ed)* cause the death of (*Informal*) ▶ *n (pl -s)* act of killing ▷ **killer** *n (pl killers)*
  killed *v* ▷ kill
  killer *n* ▷ kill
  killers *n* ▷ kill
killing (*Informal*) *adj* very tiring ▶ *n (pl -s)* sudden financial success ▶ *v* ▷ kill
  killings *n* ▷ killing
killjoy *n (pl -s)* person who spoils others' pleasure
  killjoys *n* ▷ killjoy
  kills *v, n* ▷ kill
kiln *n (pl -s)* oven for baking, drying, or processing pottery, bricks, etc.
  kilns *n* ▷ kiln
kilobyte *n (pl -s)* (COMPUTERS) 1024 units of information
  kilobytes *n* ▷ kilobyte
kilogram, kilogramme *n (pl -s)* one thousand grams
  kilogrammes *n* ▷ kilogram
  kilograms *n* ▷ kilogram
kilohertz *n (pl -es)* one thousand hertz
  kilohertzes *n* ▷ kilohertz
kilometre *n (pl -s)* one thousand metres
  kilometres *n* ▷ kilometre
kilowatt *n (pl -s)* (ELECTRICITY) one thousand watts
  kilowatts *n* ▷ kilowatt
kilt *n (pl -s)* knee-length pleated tartan skirt worn orig. by Scottish Highlanders ▷ **kilted** *adj*
  kilted *n* ▷ kilt
  kilts *n* ▷ kilt
kimono *n (pl -s)* loose wide-sleeved Japanese robe, fastened with a sash
  kimonos *n* ▷ kimono
kin, kinsfolk *n* person's relatives collectively ▷ **kinship** *(pl -s)* ▶ *n*
kind[1] *adj (-er, -est)* considerate, friendly, and helpful ▷ **kindness** *n (pl -es)* ▷ **kindliness** *n (pl -es)* ▷ **kind-hearted** *adj*
kind[2] *n (pl -s)* class or group with common characteristics
  kinder *adj* ▷ kind[1]
kindergarten *n (pl -s)* class or school for children under six years old
  kindergartens *n* ▷ kindergarten
  kindest *adj* ▷ kind[1]
  kindhearted *adj* ▷ kind[1]
  kindies *n* ▷ kindy
kindliness *n (pl -es)* ▷ kind[1]
  kindlinesses *n* ▷ kind[1]
kindle *v (-les, -ling, -led)* set (a fire) alight
  kindled *v* ▷ kindle
  kindles *v* ▷ kindle
kindling *n (pl -s)* dry wood or straw for starting fires ▶ *v* ▷ kindle
kindly *adj* having a warm-hearted nature ▶ *adv* in a considerate way
kindness *n (pl -es)* ▷ kind[1]
  kindnesses *n* ▷ kind[1]
  kinds *n* ▷ kind[2]
kindred *adj* having similar qualities ▶ *n (pl -s)* ▷ kin
kindy, kindie *n (pl -dies)* (AUST & NZ) (*Informal*) kindergarten
kinetic [kin-**net**-ik] *adj* relating to or caused by motion
king *n (pl kings)* male ruler of a monarchy ▷ **kingship** *n (pl -s)*
kingdom *n (pl -s)* state ruled by a king or queen
  kingdoms *n* ▷ kingdom
  kings *n* ▷ king
kingship *n (pl -s)* ▷ king
  kingships *n* ▷ king
kingfisher *n (pl -s)* small bird, often with a bright-coloured plumage, that dives for fish
  kingfishers *n* ▷ kingfisher
kingpin *n (pl -s)* most important person in an organization
  kingpins *n* ▷ kingpin
kink *n (pl -s)* twist or bend in rope, wire, etc.
  kinks *n* ▷ kink
kinky *adj* (*Slang*) given to unusual sexual practices
  kinships *n* ▷ kinship
kiosk *n (pl -s)* small booth selling drinks, cigarettes, newspapers, etc.
  kiosks *n* ▷ kiosk

kip (*Informal*) *n* (*pl* -s) sleep ▶ *v* (-s, -pping, -pped) sleep
  kipped *v* ▷ kip
kipper *n* (*pl* -s) cleaned, salted, and smoked herring
  kippers *n* ▷ kipper
  kipping *v* ▷ kip
  kips *v* ▷ kip
kirk *n* (*pl* -s) (SCOT) church
  kirks *n* ▷ kirk
kismet *n* (*pl* -s) fate or destiny
  kismets *n* ▷ kismet
kiss *v* (-es, -ing, -ed) touch with the lips in affection or greeting ▶ *n* (*pl* -es) touch with the lips
kissagram *n* (*pl* -s) greetings service in which a messenger kisses the person celebrating
  kissagrams *n* ▷ kissagram
  kissed *v* ▷ kiss
kisser *n* (*pl* -s) (*Slang*) mouth or face
  kissers *n* ▷ kisser
  kisses *v*, *n* ▷ kiss
  kissing *v* ▷ kiss
kist *n* (*pl* -s) (S AFR) large wooden chest
  kists *n* ▷ kist
kit *n* (*pl* -s) outfit or equipment for a specific purpose
kitbag *n* (*pl* -s) bag for a soldier's or traveller's belongings
  kitbags *n* ▷ kitbag
  kits *n* ▷ kit
kitset *n* (*pl* -s) (NZ) unassembled pieces for constructing a piece of furniture
kitchen *n* (*pl* -s) room used for cooking
kitchenette *n* (*pl* -s) small kitchen
  kitchenettes *n* ▷ kitchenette
  kitchens *n* ▷ kitchen
  kitches *n* ▷ kitch
kite *n* (*pl* -s) light frame covered with a thin material flown on a string in the wind
  kites *n* ▷ kite
kith *n* (*pl* -s) friends and relatives
  kiths *n* ▷ kith
kitsch *n* (*pl* -es) art or literature with popular sentimental appeal
kitten *n* (*pl* -s) young cat
kittenish *adj* lively and flirtatious
  kittens *n* ▷ kitten
  kitties *n* ▷ kitty
kittiwake *n* (*pl* -s) type of seagull
  kittiwakes *n* ▷ kittiwake
kitty *n* (*pl* -ties) communal fund
kiwi *n* (*pl* -s) New Zealand flightless bird with a long beak and no tail
  kiwis *n* ▷ kiwi

klaxon *n* (*pl* -s) loud horn used on emergency vehicles as a warning signal
  klaxons *n* ▷ klaxon
kleptomania *n* (*pl* -s) compulsive tendency to steal > **kleptomaniac** *n* (*pl* -s)
kleptomaniac *n* (*pl* -s) ▷ kleptomania
  kleptomaniacs *n* ▷ kleptomania
kloof *n* (*pl* kloofs) (S AFR) mountain pass or gorge
  kloofs *n* ▷ kloof
knack *n* (*pl* knacks) skilful way of doing something
  knacks *n* ▷ knack
knacker *n* (*pl* -s) (BRIT) buyer of old horses for killing
knackered *adj* (*Slang*) extremely tired
  knackers *n* ▷ knacker
knapsack *n* (*pl* -s) soldier's or traveller's bag worn strapped on the back
  knapsacks *n* ▷ knapsack
knave *n* (*pl* -s) jack at cards (*Obs*)
  knaves *n* ▷ knave
knead *v* (-s, -ing, -ed) work (dough) into a smooth mixture with the hands
  kneaded *v* ▷ knead
  kneading *v* ▷ knead
  kneads *v* ▷ knead
knee *n* (*pl* knees) joint between thigh and lower leg ▶ *v* (-s, -ing, -d) strike or push with the knee
kneecap *n* (*pl* kneecaps) bone in front of the knee ▶ *v* (-pping, -pped) shoot in the kneecap
  kneed *v* ▷ knee
  kneeing *v* ▷ knee
kneejerk *adj* (of a reply or reaction) automatic and predictable
kneel *v* (-s, -ing, -ed or knelt) fall or rest on one's knees
  kneeled, knelt *v* ▷ kneel
  kneeling *v* ▷ kneel
  kneels *v* ▷ kneel
  knees *n*, *v* ▷ knee
knell *n* (*pl* -s) sound of a bell, esp. at a funeral or death
  knells *n* ▷ knell
  knelt *v* ▷ kneel
  knew *v* ▷ know
knickerbockers *pl n* loose-fitting short trousers gathered in at the knee
knickers *pl n* woman's or girl's undergarment covering the lower trunk and having legs or legholes
knife *n* (*pl* knives) cutting tool or weapon consisting of a sharp-edged blade with a handle ▶ *v* (-s, -ing, -ed) cut or stab with a

knife
knifed v ▷ knife
knifes v ▷ knife
knifing v ▷ knife
knight n (pl -s) man who has been given
a knighthood ▶ v (-s, -ing, -ed) award a
knighthood to > knightly adj > knighthood
n (pl -s) honorary title given to a man by the
British sovereign
knighted v ▷ knight
knighthoods n ▷ knighthood
knighting v ▷ knight
knights n, v ▷ knight
knit v (-s, -tting, -tted or knit) make (a
garment) by interlocking a series of loops in
wool or other yarn > knitting n (pl -s)
knits v ▷ knit
knitted v ▷ knit
knitting v ▷ knit
knittings n ▷ knit
knitwear n (pl -s) knitted clothes, such as
sweaters
knitwears n ▷ knitwear
knives n ▷ knife
knob n (pl -s) rounded projection, such as a
switch on a radio
knobblier adj ▷ knobbly
knobbliest adj ▷ knobbly
knobbly adj (-lier, -liest) covered with small
bumps
knobkerrie n (pl -s) (S AFR) club with a rounded
end
knobkerries n ▷ knobkerrie
knobs n ▷ knob
knock v (-s, -ing, -ed) give a blow or push to ▶ n
(pl -s) blow or rap
knockabout adj (of comedy) boisterous
knockdown adj (of a price) very low
knocked v ▷ knock
knocker n (pl -s) metal fitting for knocking
on a door
knockers n ▷ knocker
knocking v ▷ knock
knockout n (pl -s) blow that renders an
opponent unconscious
knockouts n ▷ knockout
knocks v, n ▷ knock
knoll n (pl -s) small rounded hill
knolls n ▷ knoll
knot n (pl -s) fastening made by looping and
pulling tight strands of string, cord, or
rope ▶ v (-s, -tting, -tted) tie with or into a
knot
knots n ▷ knot
knotted n ▷ knot

knotting n ▷ knot
knotty adj full of knots
know v (-s, -ing, knew, known) be or feel
certain of the truth of (information etc.)
> knowable adj
knowing v ▷ know ▶ adj suggesting secret
knowledge
knowingly adv deliberately
knowhow n (pl -s) (Informal) ingenuity,
aptitude, or skill
knowhows n ▷ know-how
knowledgable n ▷ knowledgeable
knowledge n (pl -s) facts or experiences
known by a person
knowledgeable, knowledgable adj
intelligent or well-informed
knowledges n ▷ knowledge
known v ▷ know
knows v ▷ know
knuckle n (pl -s) bone at the finger
joint
knuckles n ▷ knuckle

> ko n (kos). A ko is a Maori digging-
> stick. This is worth remembering as,
> along with ka and ky, it's one of only
> three two-letter words starting with K.
> Ko scores 6 points.

koala n (pl -s) tree-dwelling Australian
marsupial with dense grey fur
koalas n ▷ koala
kohl n (pl -s) cosmetic powder used to darken
the edges of the eyelids
kohls n ▷ kohls
kookaburra n (pl -s) large Australian
kingfisher with a cackling cry
kookaburras n ▷ kookaburra
koori n (pl -s) Australian Aborigine
kooris n ▷ koori
kopje, koppie n (pl -s) (S AFR) small hill
kopjes n ▷ kopje
kosher [koh-sher] adj conforming to Jewish
religious law, esp. (of food) to Jewish dietary
law ▶ n (pl -s) kosher food
koshers n ▷ kosher
kowhai n (pl -s) New Zealand tree with clusters
of yellow flowers
kowhais n ▷ kowhai

> kow n (kows). A kow is a Scots word
> for a bunch of twigs. Kow is relatively
> high-scoring for a three-letter word,
> and so can be a good one to form when
> playing in more than one direction.
> Kow scores 10 points.

kowtow v (-s, -ing, -ed) be servile (towards)
kowtowed v ▷ kowtow

kowtowing v ▷ kowtow
kowtows v ▷ kowtow
kraal n (pl -s) S African village surrounded by a strong fence
  kraals n ▷ kraal
krill n small shrimplike sea creature(s)
krypton n (pl -s) (CHEM) colourless gas present in the atmosphere and used in fluorescent lights
  kryptons n ▷ krypton
kudos n (pl -es) fame or credit
  kudoses n ▷ kudoses
kugel [koog-el] n (pl -s) (S AFR) rich, fashion-conscious, materialistic young woman
  kugels n ▷ kugel
kumara n (pl -s) (NZ) tropical root vegetable with yellow flesh
  kumaras n ▷ kumara

kumquat [kumm-kwott] n (pl -s) citrus fruit resembling a tiny orange
  kumquats n ▷ kumquat
kurrajong n (pl -s) Australian tree or shrub with tough fibrous bark
  kurrajongs n ▷ kurrajong

> **ky** or **kye** n. Ky is a Scots word for **cows.** If you are playing a longer word beginning with K, you may be able to use ky to tag onto a word on the board that ends in Y. Ky scores 9 points.
>
> **kyu** n (**kyus**). A kyu is a beginner's grade in judo. The unusual combination of letters makes this a useful word to have when you have an unpromising set of letters on your rack. Kyu scores 10 points.

Ll

L can be a difficult letter to use well, especially when you need to play short words. Just three two-letter words begin with L: **la**, **li** and **lo**. Knowing this will save you valuable time in a game, especially when you are trying to fit words into a crowded board. There aren't a great number of three-letter words either, but don't forget common words like **lab** (5 points), **law** (6), **lay** (6), **low** (6) and **lye** (6). Try to remember the three-letter words that combine L with X: **lax**, **lex**, **lox** and **lux** (10 points each). These are particularly useful towards the end of a game if you have an X but little opportunity to play it.

la n (**las**). In music, la is the sixth note of a major scale. La is also spelt **lah**. La scores 2 points.

label n (pl **-s**) piece of card or other material fixed to an object to show its ownership, destination, etc. ▶ v (**-s, -lling, -lled**) give a label to
  labels n ▷ label

labia pl n (sing **-bium**) four liplike folds of skin forming part of the female genitals

labial [lay-bee-al] adj of the lips
  labium n ▷ labia

labor n (pl **-s**) (US & AUST) ▷ labour

laboratories n ▷ laboratory

laboratory n (pl **-ies**) building or room designed for scientific research or for the teaching of practical science

laborious adj involving great prolonged effort > **laboriously** adv
  laboriously adv ▷ laborious
  labors n ▷ labor

labour, (US & AUST) **labor** n (pl **-s**) physical work or exertion ▶ v (**-s, -ing, -ed**) work hard

laboured adj uttered or done with difficulty
  ▶ v ▷ labour
  labourednesses n ▷ laboured

labourer n (pl **-s**) person who labours, esp. someone doing manual work for wages
  labourers n ▷ labourer
  labouring v ▷ labour
  labours n, v ▷ labour

labrador n (pl **-s**) large retriever dog with a usu. gold or black coat
  labradors n ▷ labrador

laburnum n (pl **-s**) ornamental tree with yellow hanging flowers
  laburnums n ▷ laburnum

labyrinth [lab-er-inth] n (pl **-s**) complicated network of passages > **labyrinthine** adj
  labyrinthine adj ▷ labyrinth
  labyrinths n ▷ labyrinth

lace n (pl **-s**) delicate decorative fabric made from threads woven into an open weblike pattern ▶ v (**-ces, -cing, -ced**) fasten with laces
  laced v ▷ lace
  laces n, v ▷ lace
  lacing v ▷ lace

lacerate [lass-er-rate] v (**-tes, -ting, -ted**) tear (flesh) > **laceration** n (pl **-s**)
  lacerated v ▷ lacerate
  lacerates v ▷ lacerate
  lacerating v ▷ lacerate
  lacerations v ▷ lacerate

lachrymose adj tearful

lack n (pl **-s**) shortage or absence of something needed or wanted ▶ v (**-s, -ing, -ed**) need or be short of (something)
  lacked v ▷ lack

lackadaisical adj lazy and careless in a dreamy way
  lacked v ▷ lack

lackey n (pl **-s**) servile follower
  lackeys n ▷ lackey
  lacking v ▷ lack

lacklustre adj lacking brilliance or vitality

laconic adj using only a few words, terse > **laconically** adv
  laconically adv ▷ laconic

lacquer n (pl **-s**) hard varnish for wood or metal
  lacquers n ▷ lacquer

lacrimal adj of tears or the glands which produce them

lacrosse n (pl **-s**) sport in which teams catch

and throw a ball using long sticks with a pouched net at the end
lacks n, v ▷ lack

lactation n (pl -s) secretion of milk by female mammals to feed young
lactations n ▷ lactation

lactic adj of or derived from milk

lactose n (pl -s) white crystalline sugar found in milk
lactoses n ▷ lactose

lacuna [lak-kew-na] n (pl -e) gap or missing part, esp. in a document or series
lacunosities n ▷ lacuna

lacy adj fine, like lace

lad n (pl -s) boy or young man
lads n ▷ lad

ladder n (pl -s) frame of two poles connected by horizontal steps used for climbing ▶ v (-s, -ing, -ed) have or cause to have such a line of undone stitches
laddered v ▷ ladder
laddering v ▷ ladder
ladders n, v ▷ ladder

laden adj loaded

ladle n (pl -s) spoon with a long handle and a large bowl, used for serving soup etc. ▶ v (-les, -ling, -led) serve out
ladled v ▷ ladle
ladles n, v ▷ ladle
ladling v ▷ ladle

lady n (pl -dies) woman regarded as having characteristics of good breeding or high rank

ladybird n (pl -s) small red beetle with black spots
ladybirds n ▷ ladybird

ladykiller n (pl -s) (Informal) man who is or thinks he is irresistible to women
ladykillers n ▷ ladykiller

ladylike adj polite and dignified

lag¹ v (-s, -gging, -gged) go too slowly, fall behind ▶ n (pl -s) delay between events

lag² v (-s, -gging, -gged) wrap (a boiler, pipes, etc.) with insulating material

lag³ n (pl -s) (BRIT, AUST & NZ) (Slang) convict

laggard n (pl -s) person who lags behind
laggards n ▷ laggard

lagging n (pl -s) insulating material ▶ v ▷ lag¹,²
laggings n ▷ lagging

lager n (pl -s) light-bodied beer
lagers n ▷ lager

lagoon n (pl -s) body of water cut off from the open sea by coral reefs or sand bars
lagoons n ▷ lagoon
lags n ▷ lag¹,³
laid v ▷ lay¹

lain v ▷ lie²

lair n (pl -s) resting place of an animal
lairs n ▷ lair

laird n (pl -s) Scottish landowner
lairds n ▷ laird

laity [lay-it-ee] n (pl -ties) people who are not members of the clergy
laities n ▷ laity

lake¹ n (pl -s) expanse of water entirely surrounded by land > **lakeside** n (pl -s)

lake² n (pl -s) red pigment
lakes n ▷ lake¹,²
lakesides n ▷ lake¹

lama n (pl -s) Buddhist priest in Tibet or Mongolia
lamas n ▷ lama

lamb n (pl -s) young sheep ▶ v (-s, -ing, -ed) (of sheep) give birth to a lamb or lambs > **lambskin** n (pl -s) > **lambswool** n (pl -s)

lambast, lambaste v (-s, -ing, -ed) beat or thrash
lambasted v ▷ lambast
lambasting v ▷ lambast
lambasts v ▷ lambast
lambed v ▷ lamb

lambent adj (Lit) (of a flame) flickering softly
lambing v ▷ lamb
lambs n, v ▷ lamb
lambskin v ▷ lamb
lambswool v ▷ lamb

lame adj (-er, -est) having an injured or disabled leg or foot ▶ v (-mes, -ming, -med) make lame > **lamely** adv > **lameness** n (pl -s)

lamé [lah-may] n (pl -s) ▶ adj (fabric) interwoven with gold or silver thread
lamed v ▷ lame
lamely adv ▷ lame
lamenesses n ▷ lame

lament v (-s, -ing, -ed) feel or express sorrow (for) ▶ n (pl -s) passionate expression of grief > **lamentation** n (pl -s)

lamentable adj very disappointing
lamentations v ▷ lament

lamented adj grieved for ▶ v ▷ lament
lamenting v ▷ lament
laments v, n ▷ lament
lamer adj ▷ lame
lames v ▷ lame
lamés v ▷ lamé
lamest adj ▷ lame

laminate v (-tes, -ting, -ted) make (a sheet of material) by sticking together thin sheets ▶ n (pl -s) laminated sheet > **laminated** adj
laminated v, adj ▷ laminate
laminates v, n ▷ laminate

laminating v ▷ laminate

laming v ▷ lame

lamington n (pl -s) (AUST & NZ) sponge cake coated with a sweet coating

lamingtons n ▷ lamington

lamp n (pl -s) device which produces light from electricity, oil, or gas > **lampshade** (pl -s) ▶ n

lamppost n (pl -s) post supporting a lamp in the street

lampposts n ▷ lamppost

lamps n ▷ lamp

lampoon n (pl -s) humorous satire ridiculing someone ▶ v (-s, -ing, -ed) satirize or ridicule

lampooned v ▷ lampoon

lampooning v ▷ lampoon

lampoons n, v ▷ lampoon

lamprey n (pl -s) eel-like fish with a round sucking mouth

lampreys n ▷ lamprey

lampshades n ▷ lampshade

lance n (pl -s) long spear used by a mounted soldier ▶ v (-ces, -cing, -ced) pierce (a boil or abscess) with a lancet

lanced v ▷ lance

lancer n (pl -s) formerly, cavalry soldier armed with a lance

lancers n ▷ lancer

lances n, v ▷ lance

lancing v ▷ lance

lancet n (pl -s) pointed two-edged surgical knife

lancets n ▷ lancet

land n (pl -s) solid part of the earth's surface ▶ v (-s, -ing, -ed) come or bring to earth after a flight, jump, or fall ▶ **landless** adj

landau [lan-daw] n (pl -s) four-wheeled carriage with two folding hoods

landaus n ▷ landau

landed adj possessing or consisting of lands ▶ v ▷ land

landfall n (pl -s) ship's first landing after a voyage

landfalls n ▷ landfall

landing n (pl -s) floor area at the top of a flight of stairs ▶ v ▷ land

landings n ▷ landing

landlocked adj completely surrounded by land

lands n, v ▷ land

landlady n (pl -dies) woman who rents out land, houses, etc.

landladies n ▷ landlady

landless v ▷ land

landlord n (pl -s) man who rents out land, houses, etc.

landlords n ▷ landlord

landlubber n (pl -s) person who is not experienced at sea

landlubbers n ▷ landlubber

landmark n (pl -s) prominent object in or feature of a landscape

landmarks n ▷ landmark

landscape n (pl -s) extensive piece of inland scenery seen from one place ▶ v (-pes, -ping, -ped) improve natural features of (a piece of land)

landscaped v ▷ landscape

landscapes n, v ▷ landscape

landscaping v ▷ landscape

landslide (also **landslip**) n (pl -s) falling of soil, rock, etc. down the side of a mountain

landslides n ▷ landslide

landslip n ▷ landslide

landslips n ▷ landslide ▶ adj nearest to or facing the land ▶ adv (also **landwards**) towards land

landwards adv ▷ landward

lane n (pl -s) narrow road

lanes n ▷ lane

language n (pl -s) system of sounds, symbols, etc. for communicating thought

languages n ▷ language

languid adj lacking energy or enthusiasm > **languidly** adv

languidly adv ▷ languid

languish v (-es, -ing, -ed) suffer neglect or hardship

languished v ▷ languish

languishes v ▷ languish

languishing v ▷ languish

languor [lang-ger] n (pl -s) state of dreamy relaxation > **languorous** adj

languorous n ▷ languor

languors n ▷ languor

lank adj (-er, -est) (of hair) straight and limp

lanker adj ▷ lank

lankest adj ▷ lank

lankier adj ▷ lanky

lankiest adj ▷ lanky

lanky adj (-kier, -kiest) ungracefully tall and thin

lanolin n (pl -s) grease from sheep's wool used in ointments etc.

lanolins n ▷ lanolin

lantana [lan-tay-na] n (pl -s) shrub with orange or yellow flowers, considered a weed in Australia

lantanas n ▷ lantana

lantern n (pl -s) light in a transparent protective case

lanterns n ▷ lantern

lanthanum n (pl -s) (CHEM) silvery-white metallic element
  lanthanums n ▷ lanthanum
lanyard n (pl -s) cord worn round the neck to hold a knife or whistle
  lanyards n ▷ lanyard
lap¹ n (pl -s) part between the waist and knees of a person when sitting
lap² n (pl -s) single circuit of a racecourse or track ▸ v (-s, -pping, -pped) overtake an opponent so as to be one or more circuits ahead
lap³ v (-s, -pping, -pped) (of waves) beat softly against (a shore etc.)
lapel [lap-**pel**] n (pl -s) part of the front of a coat or jacket folded back towards the shoulders
  lapels n ▷ lapel
lapidary adj of or relating to stones
  lapped v ▷ lap²,3
  lapping v ▷ lap²,3
  laps n ▷ lap¹,² ▸ v ▷ lap²,3
lapse n (pl -s) temporary drop in a standard, esp. through forgetfulness or carelessness ▸ v (-ses, -sing, -sed) drop in standard ▷ **lapsed** adj
  lapsed v ▷ lapse
  lapses n, v ▷ lapse
  lapsing v ▷ lapse
laptop adj (of a computer) small enough to fit on a user's lap ▸ n (pl -s) computer small enough to fit on a user's lap
  laptops n ▷ laptop
lapwing n (pl -s) plover with a tuft of feathers on the head
  lapwings n ▷ lapwing
larboard adj, n (pl -s) (Old-fashioned) port (side of a ship)
  larboards n ▷ larboard
  larcenies n ▷ larceny
larceny n (pl -nies) (LAW) theft
larch n (pl -es) deciduous coniferous tree
  larches n ▷ larch
lard n (pl -s) soft white fat obtained from a pig ▸ v (-s, -ing, -ed) insert strips of bacon in (meat) before cooking
  larded v ▷ lard
larder n (pl -s) storeroom for food
  larders n ▷ larder
  larding v ▷ lard
  lards n, v ▷ lard
large adj (-r, -st) great in size, number, or extent ▷ **largely** adv ▷ **largish** adj
  largely adv ▷ large
  larger adj ▷ large
  largess n (pl -es) ▷ largesse
largesse, largess [lar-**jess**] n (pl -(es)) generous

giving, esp. of money
  largesses n ▷ largesse
  largest adj ▷ large
  largish adj ▷ large
largo n (pl -s) ▸ adv (MUSIC) (piece to be played) in a slow and dignified manner
  largos n ▷ largo
lariat n (pl -s) lasso
  lariats n ▷ lariat
lark¹ n (pl -s) small brown songbird, skylark
lark² n (pl -s) (Informal) harmless piece of mischief or fun
  larkishnesses n ▷ lark²
  larks n ▷ lark¹,²
larkspur n (pl -s) plant with spikes of blue, pink, or white flowers with spurs
  larkspurs n ▷ larkspur
larrikin n (pl -s) (AUST & NZ) (Old-fashioned slang) mischievous or unruly person
  larrikins n ▷ larrikin
larva n (pl -e) insect in an immature stage, often resembling a worm ▷ **larval** adj
  larval adj ▷ larva
  larynges n ▷ larynx
  laryngeal adj ▷ larynx
laryngitis n (pl -ses) inflammation of the larynx
  laryngitises n ▷ laryngitis
larynx n (pl -nges) part of the throat containing the vocal cords ▷ **laryngeal** adj
lasagne, lasagna [laz-**zan**-ya] n (pl -s) pasta in wide flat sheets
  lasagnas n ▷ lasagne
  lasagnes n ▷ lasagne
lascivious [lass-**iv**-ee-uss] adj showing or producing sexual desire ▷ **lasciviously** adv
  lasciviously adv ▷ lascivious
laser [**lay**-zer] n (pl -s) device that produces a very narrow intense beam of light, used for cutting hard materials and in surgery etc.
  lasers n ▷ laser
lash¹ n (pl -es) eyelash ▸ v (-es, -ing, -ed) hit with a whip
lash² v (-es, -ing, -ed) fasten or bind tightly with cord etc.
  lashed v ▷ lash¹,²
  lashes n ▷ lash¹ ▸ v ▷ lash¹,²
  lashing v ▷ lash¹,²
lashings pl n (Old-fashioned) large amounts
lass, lassie n (pl -es, -s) (SCOT & N ENGLISH) girl
  lasses n ▷ lass
  lassies n ▷ lass
lassitude n (pl -s) physical or mental weariness
  lassitudes n ▷ lassitude
lasso [lass-**oo**] n (pl -s, -es) rope with a noose for

catching cattle and horses ▶ v (-s, -ing, -ed) catch with a lasso
lassoed v ▷ lasso
lassoes v ▷ lasso
lassoing v ▷ lasso
lassos n, v ▷ lasso
last¹ adj, adv coming at the end or after all others ▶ adj only remaining ▶ n (pl -s) last person or thing ▶ **lastly** adv
last² v (-s, -ing, -ed) continue > **lasting** adj
last³ n (pl -s) model of a foot on which shoes and boots are made or repaired
lasted v ▷ last²
lasting v, adj ▷ last²
lastly adv ▷ last¹
lasts n ▷ last¹,³ ▶ v ▷ last²
latch n (pl -es) fastening for a door with a bar and lever ▶ v (-es, -ing, -ed) fasten with a latch
latched v ▷ latch
latches n, v ▷ latch
latching v ▷ latch
late adj (-r, -st) after the normal or expected time ▶ adv after the normal or expected time > **lateness** n (pl -es)
lately adv in recent times
latencies n ▷ latent
lateness n ▷ late
latenesses n ▷ late
latent adj hidden and not yet developed
> **latency** n (pl -cies)
later adj ▷ late
lateral [lat-ter-al] adj of or relating to the side or sides > **laterally** adv
latest adj ▷ late
latex n (pl -es) milky fluid found in some plants, esp. the rubber tree, used in making rubber
latexes n ▷ latex
lath n (pl -s) thin strip of wood used to support plaster, tiles, etc.
laths n ▷ lath
lathe n (pl -s) machine for turning wood or metal while it is being shaped
lathes n ▷ lathe
lather n (pl -s) froth of soap and water ▶ v (-s, -ing, -ed) make frothy
lathered v ▷ lather
lathering v ▷ lather
lathers n, v ▷ lather
lathery adj (-rier, -riest) frothy
latherier adj ▷ lathery
latheriest adj ▷ lathery
latitude n (pl -s) angular distance measured in degrees N or S of the equator
latitudes n ▷ latitude
latrine n (pl -s) toilet in a barracks or camp

latrines n ▷ latrine
latter adj second of two > **latterly** adv
latter-day adj modern
latterly adv ▷ latter
lattice [lat-iss] n (pl -s) framework of intersecting strips of wood, metal, etc.
> **latticed** adj
latticed adj ▷ lattice
lattices n ▷ lattice
laud v (-s, -ing, -ed) praise or glorify > **laudably** adv
laudable adj praiseworthy
laudably adv ▷ laudable
laudanum [lawd-a-num] n (pl -s) opium-based sedative
laudanums n ▷ laudanum
laudatory adj praising or glorifying
lauded v ▷ laud
lauding v ▷ laud
lauds v ▷ laud
laugh v (-s, -ing, -ed) make inarticulate sounds with the voice expressing amusement, merriment, or scorn ▶ n (pl -s) act or instance of laughing
laughable adj ▷ laugh
laughed v ▷ laugh
laughing v ▷ laugh
laughs v, n ▷ laugh
laughter n (pl -s) sound or action of laughing
laughters n ▷ laughter
launch¹ v (-es, -ing, -ed) put (a ship or boat) into the water, esp. for the first time ▶ n (pl -es) launching > **launcher** n (pl -s)
launch² n (pl -s) open motorboat
launched v ▷ launch¹
launchers n ▷ launch¹
launches v ▷ launch¹ ▶ n ▷ launch¹,²
launches n ▷ launch¹
launching v ▷ launch¹
launder v (-s, -ing, -ed) wash and iron (clothes and linen)
launderette n ® (pl -s) shop with coin-operated washing and drying machines
laundered v ▷ launder
launderettes n ▷ launderette
laundering v ▷ launder
launders v ▷ launder
laundry n (pl -ries) clothes etc. for washing or which have recently been washed
laundries n ▷ laundry
laureate [lor-ee-at] adj (of a poet) appointed to the court of Britain
laurel n (pl -s) glossy-leaved shrub, bay tree ▶ pl wreath of laurel, an emblem of victory or merit

laurels n ▷ laurel
lava n (pl -e) molten rock thrown out by volcanoes, which hardens as it cools
lavae n ▷ lava
lavatory n (pl -ries) toilet
lavatories n ▷ lavatory
lavender n (pl -s) shrub with fragrant flowers ▶ adj bluish-purple
lavenders n ▷ lavender
lavish adj great in quantity or richness ▶ v (-es, -ing, -ed) give or spend generously
> **lavishly** adv
lavished v ▷ lavish
lavishes v ▷ lavish
lavishing v ▷ lavish
lavishly adv ▷ lavish
law n (pl -s) rule binding on a community
> **lawfully** adv > **lawlessness** n (pl -es) > **law-breaker** n (pl -s)
lawful adj allowed by law
lawfully adv ▷ law
lawless adj breaking the law, esp. violently
lawlessness n ▷ law
lawlessnesses n ▷ law
lawn¹ n (pl -s) area of tended and mown grass
lawn² n (pl -s) fine linen or cotton fabric
lawns n ▷ lawn¹,²
laws n ▷ law
lawsuit n (pl -s) court case brought by one person or group against another
lawsuits n ▷ lawsuit
lawyer n (pl -s) professionally qualified legal expert
lawyers n ▷ lawyer
lax adj not strict > **laxity** n (pl -ties)
laxative n (pl -s) ▶ adj (medicine) inducing the emptying of the bowels
laxatives n ▷ laxative
laxities n ▷ lax
laxity n ▷ lax
lay¹ v (-s, -ing, laid) cause to lie
lay² v ▷ lie²
lay³ adj of or involving people who are not clergymen
lay⁴ n (pl -s) short narrative poem designed to be sung
layabout n (pl -s) lazy person
layabouts n ▷ layabout
layer n (pl -s) single thickness of some substance, as a cover or coating on a surface ▶ v (-s, -ing, -ed) form a layer > **layered** adj
layered v, adj ▷ layer
layering v ▷ layer
layers n, v ▷ layer
layette n (pl -s) clothes for a newborn baby

layettes n ▷ layette
laying v ▷ lay¹
layman n (pl -men) person who is not a member of the clergy
laymen n ▷ layman
layout n (pl -s) arrangement, esp. of matter for printing or of a building
layouts n ▷ layout
lays v ▷ lay¹ ▶ n ▷ lay⁴
laze v (-s, -ing, -ed) be idle or lazy ▶ n (pl -s) time spent lazing
lazed v ▷ laze
lazes v, n ▷ laze
lazily adv ▷ lazy
laziness adv ▷ lazy
lazinesses adv ▷ lazy
lazing v ▷ laze
lazy adj (-zier, -ziest) not inclined to work or exert oneself > **lazily** adv > **laziness** n (pl -s)
lea n (pl -s) (Poetic) meadow
leas n ▷ lea
leach v (-es, -ing, -ed) remove or be removed from a substance by a liquid passing through it
leached v ▷ leach
leaches v ▷ leach
leaching v ▷ leach
lead¹ v (-s, -ing, led) guide or conduct ▶ n (pl -s) first or most prominent place ▶ adj acting as a leader or lead
lead² n (pl -s) soft heavy grey metal
leaded adj (of windows) made from many small panes of glass held together by lead strips
leaden adj heavy or sluggish
leader n (pl -s) person who leads > **leadership** n (pl -s)
leaders n ▷ leader
leaderships n ▷ leader
leading adj principal
leads n ▷ lead¹,² ▶ v ▷ lead¹
leaf n (pl leaves) flat usu. green blade attached to the stem of a plant > **leafy** (-fier, -fiest) ▶ adj > **leafless** adj
leafier adj ▷ leaf
leafiest adj ▷ leaf
leafless adj ▷ leaf
leaflessnesses n ▷ leaf
leaflet n (pl -s) sheet of printed matter for distribution
leaflets n ▷ leaflet
leafy adj ▷ leaf
league¹ n (pl -s) association promoting the interests of its members
league² n (Obs) measure of distance, about

three miles

leagues n ▷ league[1,2]

leak n (pl -s) hole or defect that allows the escape or entrance of liquid, gas, radiation, etc. ▶ v (-s, -ing, -ed) let liquid etc. in or out > **leaky** (-kier, -kiest) ▶ adj

leakage n (pl -s) act or instance of leaking

leakages n ▷ leakage

leaked v ▷ leak

leakier adj ▷ leak

leakiest adj ▷ leak

leaking v ▷ leak

leaks n, v ▷ leak

leaky adj (-kier, -kiest) ▷ leak

lean[1] v (-ing, -ed or leant) rest against

lean[2] adj (-er, -est) thin but healthy-looking ▶ n (pl -s) lean part of meat > **leanness** n (pl -es)

leaner adj ▷ lean

leanest adj ▷ lean

leaning n (pl -s) tendency ▶ v ▷ lean[1]

leanings n ▷ leaning

leanness n ▷ lean[2]

leannesses n ▷ lean[2]

leans v, n ▷ lean[1]

leant n ▷ lean[1]

leap v (-s, -ing, leapt or -ed) make a sudden powerful jump ▶ n (pl -s) sudden powerful jump

leaped v ▷ leap

leapfrog n (pl -s) game in which a player vaults over another bending down

leapfrogs n ▷ leapfrog

leaping v ▷ leap

leaps v, n ▷ leap

leapt v ▷ leap

learn v (-s, -ing, -ed or learnt) gain skill or knowledge by study, practice, or teaching > **learner** n (pl -s)

learned adj erudite, deeply read

learner n ▷ learn

learners n ▷ learn

learning n (pl -s) knowledge got by study ▶ v ▷ learn

learnings n ▷ learning

lease n (pl -s) contract by which land or property is rented for a stated time by the owner to a tenant ▶ v (-ses, -sing, -sed) let or rent by lease > **leaseholder** n (pl -s)

leasehold n, adj (land or property) held on lease

leaseholder n ▷ lease

leaseholders n ▷ lease

leaseholds n ▷ leasehold

leased v ▷ lease

leases n, v ▷ lease

leash n (pl -es) lead for a dog

leashes n ▷ leash

leasing v ▷ lease

least adj ▷ little smallest ▶ n smallest one ▶ adv in the smallest degree

leather n (pl -s) material made from specially treated animal skins ▶ adj made of leather ▶ v (-s, -ing, -ed) beat or thrash

leathered v ▷ leather

leatherier adj ▷ leathery

leatheriest adj ▷ leathery

leathering v ▷ leather

leathers n, v ▷ leather

leathery adj (-rier, -riest) like leather, tough

leave[1] v (-s, -ing, left) go away from

leave[2] n (pl -s) permission to be absent from work or duty

leaven [lev-ven] n substance that causes dough to rise ▶ v (-s, -ing, -ed) raise with leaven

leavens v ▷ leaven

leavening v ▷ leaven

leavened v ▷ leaven

leaves v ▷ leave

leaving v ▷ leave

lecher n (pl -s) man who has or shows excessive sexual desire > **lechery** n (pl -ries)

lecheries n ▷ lechery

lecherous [letch-er-uss] adj (of a man) having or showing excessive sexual desire

lechers n ▷ lecher

lectern n (pl -s) sloping reading desk, esp. in a church

lecterns n ▷ lectern

lecture n (pl -s) informative talk to an audience on a subject ▶ v (-s, -ing, -ed) give a talk

lectured v ▷ lecture

lecturer n (pl -s) person who lectures, esp. in a university or college

lecturers n ▷ lecturer

lectures n, v ▷ lecture

lectureship n (pl -s) appointment as a lecturer

lectureships n ▷ lectureship

lecturing v ▷ lecture

ledge n (pl -s) narrow shelf sticking out from a wall

ledger n (pl -s) book of debit and credit accounts of a firm

ledgers n ▷ ledger

ledges n ▷ ledge

lee n (pl -s) sheltered part or side ▶ adv towards this side

leech n (pl -es) species of bloodsucking worm

leeches n ▷ leech

leek n (pl -s) vegetable of the onion family with

a long bulb and thick stem
leeks n ▷ leek
leer v (-s, -ing, -ed) look or grin at in a sneering or suggestive manner ▶ n (pl -s) sneering or suggestive look or grin
leered v ▷ leer
leerier adj ▷ leery
leeriest adj ▷ leery
leering v ▷ leer
leers v, n ▷ leer
leery adj (Informal) (-rier, -riest) suspicious or wary (of)
lees pl n sediment of wine ▶ n ▷ lee
leeward adj, n (pl -s) (on) the lee side
leewards n ▷ leeward
leeway n (pl -s) room for free movement within limits
leeways n ▷ leeway
left[1] adj of the side that faces west when the front faces north ▶ adv on or towards the left ▶ n (pl -s) left hand or part
left[2] v ▷ leave[1]
leftist n (pl -s) ▶ adj (person) of the political left
leftists n ▷ leftist
leftover n (pl -s) unused portion of food or material
leftovers n ▷ leftover
lefts n ▷ left[1]
leg n (pl -s) one of the limbs on which a person or animal walks, runs, or stands
legacies n ▷ legacy
legacy n (pl -cies) thing left in a will
legal adj established or permitted by law > **legally** adv > **legality** n (pl -ties) > **legalization** n (pl -s)
legalities n ▷ legal
legality n ▷ legal
legalization n ▷ legal
legalizations n ▷ legal
legalize v (-zes, -zing, -zed) make legal
legalized adv ▷ legalize
legalizes adv ▷ legalize
legalizing adv ▷ legalize
legally adv ▷ legal
legate n (pl -s) messenger or representative, esp. from the Pope
legatee n (pl -s) recipient of a legacy
legatees n ▷ legatee
legates n ▷ legate
legation n (pl -s) diplomatic minister and his staff
legations n ▷ legation
legato [leg-**ah**-toe] n (pl -s), adv (MUSIC) (piece to be played) smoothly
legatos n ▷ legato

legend n (pl -s) traditional story or myth
legendary adj famous
legends n ▷ legend
legerdemain [lej-er-de-**main**] n (pl -s) sleight of hand
legerdemains n ▷ legerdemain
leggier adj ▷ leggy
leggiest adj ▷ leggy
leggings pl n covering of leather or other material for the legs
leggy adj (-gier, -giest) having long legs
legibilities n ▷ legible
legibility n ▷ legible
legible adj easily read > **legibility** n (pl -ties) > **legibly** adv
legibly adv ▷ legible
legion n (pl -s) large military force > **legionary** adj, n (pl -ries)
legionaries n ▷ legion
legionary adj, n ▷ legion
legionnaire n (pl -s) member of a legion
legionnaires n ▷ legionnaire
legions n ▷ legion
legislate v (-tes, -ting, -ted) make laws > **legislative** adj
legislated v ▷ legislate
legislates v ▷ legislate
legislating v ▷ legislate
legislation n (pl -s) legislating
legislations n ▷ legislation
legislative v ▷ legislate
legislator n (pl -s) maker of laws
legislators n ▷ legislator
legislature n (pl -s) body of people that makes, amends, or repeals laws
legislatures n ▷ legislature
legitimacies n ▷ legitimate
legitimacy n ▷ legitimate
legitimate adj authorized by or in accordance with law ▶ v (-tes, -ting, -ted) make legitimate > **legitimacy** n (pl -cies) > **legitimately** adv
legitimated v ▷ legitimate
legitimately adv ▷ legitimate
legitimates v ▷ legitimate
legitimating v ▷ legitimate
legitimize v (-zes, -zing, -zed) make legitimate, legalize > **legitimization** n (pl -s)
legitimization n ▷ legitimize
legitimizations n ▷ legitimize
legitimized v ▷ legitimize
legitimizes v ▷ legitimize
legitimizing v ▷ legitimize
legless adj without legs
legs n ▷ leg

leguaan [leg-oo-ahn] n (pl -s) large S African lizard
  leguaans n ▷leguaan
legume n (pl -s) pod of a plant of the pea or bean family ▸ pl peas or beans
  legumes n ▷legume
leguminous adj (of plants) pod-bearing
lei n (pl -s) (in Hawaii) garland of flowers
  leis n ▷lei
leisure n (pl -s) time for relaxation or hobbies
leisured adj with plenty of spare time
leisurely adj deliberate, unhurried ▸ adv slowly
  leisures n ▷leisure
leitmotif [lite-mote-eef] n (pl -s) (MUSIC) recurring theme associated with a person, situation, or thought
  leitmotifs n ▷leitmotif
lekker adj (S AFR) (Slang) attractive or nice
lemming n (pl -s) rodent of arctic regions, reputed to run into the sea and drown during mass migrations
  lemmings n ▷lemming
lemon n (pl -s) yellow oval fruit that grows on trees ▸ adj pale-yellow
lemonade n (pl -s) lemon-flavoured soft drink, often fizzy
  lemonades n ▷lemonade
  lemons n ▷lemon
lemur n (pl -s) nocturnal animal like a small monkey, found in Madagascar
  lemurs n ▷lemur
lend v (-s, -ing, lent) give the temporary use of > **lender** n (pl -s)
  lending v ▷lend
  lender n ▷lend
  lenders n ▷lend
  lends v ▷lend
length n (pl -s) extent or measurement from end to end > **lengthily** adv > **lengthways, lengthwise** adj, adv
lengthen v (-s, -ing, -ed) make or become longer
  lengthened v ▷lengthen
  lengthening v ▷lengthen
  lengthens v ▷lengthen
  lengthier adj ▷length
  lengthiest adj ▷length
  lengthily adv ▷length
  lengths n ▷length
  lengthways adj, adv ▷length
  lengthwise adj, adv ▷lengthen
lengthy adj (-thier, -thiest) very long or tiresome
  leniencies n ▷lenient
  leniency n ▷lenient

lenient [lee-nee-ent] adj tolerant, not strict or severe > **leniency** n (pl -cies) > **leniently** adv
  leniently adv ▷lenient
lens n (pl -es) piece of glass or similar material with one or both sides curved, used to bring together or spread light rays in cameras, spectacles, telescopes, etc.
  lenses n ▷lens
  lent v ▷lend
lentil n (pl -s) edible seed of a leguminous Asian plant
  lentils n ▷lentil
lento n (pl -tos), adv (MUSIC) (piece to be played) slowly
  lentos n ▷lento
  Lents n ▷Lent
leonine adj like a lion
leopard n (pl -s) large spotted carnivorous animal of the cat family
  leopards n ▷leopard
leotard n (pl -s) tight-fitting garment covering the upper body, worn for dancing or exercise
  leotards n ▷leotard
leper n (pl -s) person suffering from leprosy
  lepers n ▷leper
lepidoptera pl n order of insects with four wings covered with fine gossamer scales, as moths and butterflies
lepidopterist n (pl -s) person who studies or collects butterflies or moths
  lepidopterists n ▷lepidopterist
leprechaun n (pl -s) mischievous elf of Irish folklore
  leprechauns n ▷leprechaun
leprosy n (pl -sies) disease attacking the nerves and skin, resulting in loss of feeling in the affected parts > **leprous** adj
  leprosies n ▷leprosy
  leprous adj ▷leprosy
lesbian n (pl -s) homosexual woman ▸ adj of homosexual women > **lesbianism** n (pl -s)
  lesbians n ▷lesbian
  lesbianisms n ▷lesbian
lesion n (pl -s) structural change in an organ of the body caused by illness or injury
  lesions n ▷lesion
less adj smaller in extent, degree, or duration ▷little ▸ pron smaller part or quantity ▸ adv to a smaller extent or degree ▸ prep after deducting, minus
lessee n (pl -s) person to whom a lease is granted
  lessees n ▷lessee
lessen v (-s, -ing, -ed) make or become smaller or not as much

lessened v ▷ lessen
lessening v ▷ lessen
lessens v ▷ lessen
lesser adj not as great in quantity, size, or worth
lesson n (pl -s) single period of instruction in a subject
lessons n ▷ lesson
lest conj so as to prevent any possibility that
let¹ v (-s, -tting, let) allow, enable, or cause
let² n (pl -s) (TENNIS) minor infringement or obstruction of the ball requiring a replay of the point
letdown n (pl -s) disappointment
letdowns n ▷ letdown
lets v ▷ let¹ ▶ n ▷ let²
lethal adj deadly
lethargic adj ▷ lethargy
lethargically adv ▷ lethargy
lethargies n ▷ lethargy
lethargy n (pl -gies) sluggishness or dullness > **lethargic** adj > **lethargically** adv
letter n (pl -s) written message, usu. sent by post ▶ pl literary knowledge or ability > **lettering** n (pl -s)
lettered adj learned
letterhead n (pl -s) printed heading on stationery giving the sender's name and address
letterheads n ▷ letterhead
lettering n ▷ letter
letterings n ▷ letter
letters n ▷ letter
letting v ▷ let¹
lettuce n (pl -s) plant with large green leaves used in salads
lettuces n ▷ lettuce
leucocyte [loo-koh-site] n (pl -s) white blood cell
leucocytes n ▷ leucocyte
leukaemia [loo-kee-mee-a] n (pl -s) disease caused by uncontrolled overproduction of white blood cells
leukaemias n ▷ leukaemia
levee n (pl -s) (US) natural or artificial river embankment
levees n ▷ levee
level adj (-llest, -ller) horizontal ▶ v (-s, -lling, -lled, -ller) make even or horizontal ▶ n (pl -s) horizontal line or surface
levelled v ▷ level
leveller v ▷ level
levellest adj ▷ level
levelling v ▷ level
levels v, n ▷ level
lever n (pl -s) handle used to operate

machinery ▶ v (-s, -ing, -ed) prise or move with a lever
leverage n (pl -s) action or power of a lever
leverages n ▷ leverage
levered v ▷ lever
levering v ▷ lever
levers n, v ▷ lever
leveret [lev-ver-it] n (pl -s) young hare
leverets n ▷ leveret
leviathan [lev-vie-ath-an] n (pl -s) sea monster
leviathans n ▷ leviathan
levitate v (-tes, -ting, -ted) rise or cause to rise into the air
levitated v ▷ levitate
levitates v ▷ levitate
levitating v ▷ levitate
levitation n (pl -s) raising of a solid body into the air supernaturally
levitations n ▷ levitation
levities n ▷ levity
levity n (pl -ties) inclination to make a joke of serious matters
levy [lev-vee] v (-vies, -ing, -vied) impose and collect (a tax) ▶ n (pl -vies) imposition or collection of taxes
levied v ▷ levy
levies v, n ▷ levy
levying v ▷ levy
lewd adj (-er, -est) lustful or indecent > **lewdly** adv > **lewdness** n (pl -es)
lewder adj ▷ lewd
lewdest adj ▷ lewd
lewdly adv ▷ lewd
lewdness n ▷ lewd
lewdnesses n ▷ lewd

> **lex** n (**leges**). A lex is a system or body of laws. This is a really handy word when you have L and X, as there is likely to be an E available on the board. Lex scores 10 points.

lexical adj relating to the vocabulary of a language
lexicographer n (pl -s) writer of dictionaries
lexicographers n ▷ lexicographer
lexicography n ▷ lexicon
lexicographies n ▷ lexicon
lexicon n (pl -s) dictionary > **lexicography** n (pl -phies)
lexicons n ▷ lexicon

> **li** n (**lis**). The li is a Chinese unit of length. This low-scoring word is worth knowing for when you want to form words in more than one direction at the same time. Li scores 2 points.

liability n (pl -ties) hindrance or disadvantage

liable *adj* legally obliged or responsible
liaise *v* (-ses, -sing, -sed) establish and maintain communication (with)
  liaised *v* ▷ liaise
  liaises *v* ▷ liaise
  liaising *v* ▷ liaise
liaison *n* (*pl* -s) communication and contact between groups
  liaisons *n* ▷ liaison
liana *n* (*pl* -s) climbing plant in tropical forests
  lianas *n* ▷ liana
liar *n* (*pl* -s) person who tells lies
  liars *n* ▷ liar
libation [lie-**bay**-shun] *n* (*pl* -s) drink poured as an offering to the gods
  libations *n* ▷ libation
libel *n* (*pl* -s) published statement falsely damaging a person's reputation ▶ *v* (-s, -lling, -lled) falsely damage the reputation of (someone) > **libellous** *adj*
  libelled *v* ▷ libel
  libelling *v* ▷ libel
  libellous *adj* ▷ libel
  libels *n, v* ▷ libel
liberal *adj* having social and political views that favour progress and reform ▶ *n* (*pl* -s) person who has liberal ideas or opinions > **liberally** *adv* > **liberalization** *n* (*pl* -s)
liberalism *n* (*pl* -s) belief in democratic reforms and individual freedom
  liberalisms *n* ▷ liberalism
  liberalities *n* ▷ liberality
liberality *n* (*pl* -ties) generosity
  liberalization *n* ▷ liberal
  liberalizations *n* ▷ liberal
liberalize *v* (-zes, -zing, -zed) make (laws, a country, etc.) less restrictive
  liberalized *v* ▷ liberalize
  liberalizes *v* ▷ liberalize
  liberalizing *v* ▷ liberalize
  liberally *adv* ▷ liberal
  liberals *n* ▷ liberal
liberate *v* (-tes, -ting, -ted) set free > **liberation** *n* (*pl* -s) > **liberator** *n* (*pl* -s)
  liberated *v* ▷ liberate
  liberates *v* ▷ liberate
  liberating *v* ▷ liberate
  liberation *n* ▷ liberate
  liberations *n* ▷ liberate
  liberator *n* ▷ liberate
  liberators *n* ▷ liberate
libertarian *n* (*pl* -s) believer in freedom of thought and action ▶ *adj* having such a belief
  libertarians *n* ▷ libertarian
libertine [lib-er-teen] *n* (*pl* -s) morally dissolute person
  libertines *n* ▷ libertine
  liberties *n* ▷ liberty
liberty *n* (*pl* -ties) freedom
libidinous *adj* lustful
libido [lib-ee-doe] *n* (*pl* -s) psychic energy
  libidos *n* ▷ libido
librarian *n* (*pl* -s) keeper of or worker in a library > **librarianship** *n* (*pl* -s)
  librarians *n* ▷ librarian
  librarianship *n* ▷ librarian
  librarianships *n* ▷ librarian
  libraries *n* ▷ library
library *n* (*pl* -ries) room or building where books are kept
  libretti *n* ▷ libretto
  librettist *n* ▷ libretto
  librettists *n* ▷ libretto
libretto *n* (*pl* -ttos, -tti) words of an opera > **librettist** *n* (*pl* -s)
  librettos *n* ▷ libretto
  lice *n* ▷ louse
licence *n* (*pl* -s) document giving official permission to do something
  licences *n* ▷ licence
license *v* (-ses, -sing, -sed) grant a licence to > **licensed** *adj*
  licensed *v, adj* ▷ license
licensee *n* (*pl* -s) holder of a licence
  licensees *n* ▷ licensee
  licenses *v* ▷ license
  licensing *v* ▷ license
licentiate *n* (*pl* -s) person licensed as competent to practise a profession
  licentiates *n* ▷ licentiate
licentious *adj* sexually unrestrained or promiscuous
lichen *n* (*pl* -s) small flowerless plant forming a crust on rocks, trees, etc.
  lichens *n* ▷ lichen
licit *adj* lawful, permitted
  licitnesses *n* ▷ licit
lick *v* (-s, -ing, -ed) pass the tongue over ▶ *n* (*pl* -s) licking
  licked *v* ▷ lick
  licking *v* ▷ lick
  licks *v, n* ▷ lick
  licorice *n* (*pl* -s) ▷ liquorice
  licorices *n* ▷ licorice
lid *n* (*pl* -s) movable cover
  lids *n* ▷ lid
lido [lee-doe] *n* (*pl* -s) open-air centre for swimming and water sports
  lidos *n* ▷ lido
lie¹ *v* (-s, lying, lied) make a deliberately false

statement ▶ n (pl -s) deliberate falsehood

lie² v (-s, lying, lay, lain) place oneself or be in a horizontal position ▶ n (pl -s) way something lies

lied¹ v ▷ lie¹

lied² [leed] n (pl lieder) (MUSIC) setting for voice and piano of a romantic poem

liege [leej] adj bound to give or receive feudal service ▶ n (pl -s) lord

lieges n ▷ liege

lien n (pl -s) (LAW) right to hold another's property until a debt is paid

liens n ▷ lien

lies v, n ▷ lie¹,²

lieutenant [lef-ten-ant] n (pl -s) junior officer in the army or navy

lieutenants n ▷ lieutenant

life n (pl lives) state of living beings, characterized by growth, reproduction, and response to stimuli > **lifelike** adj

lifeboat n (pl -s) boat used for rescuing people at sea

lifeboats adj ▷ lifeboat

lifeless adj dead

lifelike adj ▷ life

lifeline n (pl -s) means of contact or support

lifelines n ▷ lifeline

lifelong adj lasting all of a person's life

lifestyle n (pl -s) particular attitudes, habits, etc.

lifestyles n ▷ lifestyle

lifetime n (pl -s) length of time a person is alive

lifetimes n ▷ lifetime

lift v (lifts, lifting, lifted) move upwards in position, status, volume, etc. ▶ n (pl lifts) cage raised and lowered in a vertical shaft to transport people or goods

liftoff n moment a rocket leaves the ground

lifts v ▷ lift

lifting v ▷ lift

lifted v ▷ lift

lifts n ▷ lift

ligament n (pl -s) band of tissue joining bones

ligaments n ▷ ligament

ligature n (pl -s) link, bond, or tie

ligatures n ▷ ligature

light¹ n (pl -s) electromagnetic radiation by which things are visible ▶ pl traffic lights ▶ adj bright ▶ v (-s, -ing, lit) ignite

light² adj (-er, -est) not heavy, weighing relatively little ▶ adv with little equipment or luggage ▶ v (-s, -ing, -ed, lit) (esp. of birds) settle after flight > **lightly** adv > **lightness** n (pl -s)

lighted v ▷ light²

lighten¹ v (-s, -ing, -ed) make less dark

lighten² v (-s, -ing, -ed) make less heavy or burdensome

lightened v ▷ lighten¹,²

lightening v ▷ lighten¹,²

lightens v ▷ lighten¹,²

lighter adj ▷ light²

lightest adj ▷ light²

lighthouse n (pl -s) tower with a light to guide ships

lighthouses n ▷ lighthouse

lighting n (pl -s) apparatus for and use of artificial light in theatres, films, etc. ▶ v ▷ light¹,²

lightings n ▷ lighting

lighter¹ n (pl -s) device for lighting cigarettes etc.

lighter² n (pl -s) flat-bottomed boat for unloading ships

lighters n ▷ lighter¹,²

lightly adv ▷ light²

lightness n ▷ light²

lightnesses n ▷ light²

lightning n (pl -s) visible discharge of electricity in the atmosphere ▶ adj fast and sudden

lightnings n ▷ lightning

lights pl n lungs of animals as animal food ▶ n ▷ light¹ ▶ v ▷ light¹,²

lightweight n (pl -s) ▶ adj (person) of little importance

lightweights n ▷ lightweight

ligneous adj of or like wood

lignite [lig-nite] n (pl -s) woody textured rock used as fuel

lignites n ▷ lignite

like¹ prep, conj adj, pron indicating similarity, comparison, etc.

like² v (-s, -ing, -ed) find enjoyable > **likeable, likable** adj > **liking** n fondness

liked v ▷ like

liken v (-s, -ing, -ed) compare

likelier adj ▷ likely

likeliest adj ▷ likely

likelihood n (pl -s) probability

likelihoods n ▷ likelihood

likely adj (-lier, -liest) tending or inclined ▶ adv probably

likened v ▷ liken

likeness n resemblance

likening v ▷ liken

likens v ▷ liken

likes v ▷ like

likewise adv similarly

liking v ▷ like

lilac n (pl -s) shrub with pale mauve or white flowers ▶ adj light-purple
lilacs n ▷ lilac
lilt n (pl -s) pleasing musical quality in speaking > **lilting** adj
lilting adj ▷ lilt
lilts n ▷ lilt
lily n (pl -lies) plant which grows from a bulb and has large, often white, flowers
limb n (pl -s) arm, leg, or wing
limbs n ▷ limb
limber adj pliant or supple
limbo n (pl -s) West Indian dance in which dancers lean backwards to pass under a bar
limbos n ▷ limbo
lime¹ n (pl -s) calcium compound used as a fertilizer or in making cement
lime² n (pl -s) small green citrus fruit
lime³ n (pl -s) deciduous tree with heart-shaped leaves and fragrant flowers
limelight n (pl -s) glare of publicity
limelights n ▷ lime
limerick [lim-mer-ik] n (pl -s) humorous verse of five lines
limericks n ▷ limerick
limes n ▷ lime¹,²,³
limestone n (pl -s) sedimentary rock used in building
limestones n ▷ limestone
limey n (pl -s) (US) (Slang) British person
limeys n ▷ limey
limit n (pl -s) ultimate extent, degree, or amount of something ▶ v (-s, -ing, -ed) restrict or confine > **limitation** n (pl -s) > **limitless** adj
limitation n ▷ limit
limitations n ▷ limit
limited v ▷ limit
limiting v ▷ limit
limitless v ▷ limit
limits n, v ▷ limit
limousine n (pl -s) large luxurious car
limousines n ▷ limousine
limp¹ v (-s, -ing, -ed) walk with an uneven step ▶ n (pl -s) limping walk
limp² (-er, -est) adj without firmness or stiffness ▶ **limply** adv
limped v ▷ limp¹
limper adj ▷ limp²
limpest adj ▷ limp²
limping v ▷ limp¹
limply adv ▷ limp²
limps v, n ▷ limp¹
limpet n (pl -s) shellfish which sticks tightly to rocks

limpets n ▷ limpet
limpid adj clear or transparent > **limpidity** n (pl -ties)
limpidities n ▷ limpid
limpidity n ▷ limpid
linchpin, lynchpin n (pl -s) pin to hold a wheel on its axle
linchpins n ▷ linchpin
linctus n (pl -es) syrupy cough medicine
linctuses n ▷ linctus
linden n (pl -s) ▷ lime³
lindens n ▷ linden
line¹ n (pl -s) long narrow mark ▶ pl words of a theatrical part ▶ v (-s, -ing, -ed) mark with lines
line² v (-s, -ning, -ned) give a lining to
lined v ▷ line¹,²
lines n, v ▷ line¹,²
lining v ▷ line¹,²
lineage [lin-ee-ij] n (pl -s) descent from an ancestor
lineages n ▷ lineage
lineament n (pl -s) facial feature
lineaments n ▷ lineament
linear [lin-ee-er] adj of or in lines
linen n (pl -s) cloth or thread made from flax
linens n ▷ linen
liner¹ n (pl -s) large passenger ship or aircraft
liner² n something used as a lining
liners n ▷ liner¹,²
linesman n (pl -men) (in some sports) an official who helps the referee or umpire
linesmen n ▷ linesman
ling¹ n slender food fish
ling² n (pl lings) heather
linger v (-s, -ing, -ed) delay or prolong departure
lingered v ▷ linger
lingerie [lan-zher-ee] n (pl -s) women's underwear or nightwear
lingeries n ▷ lingerie
lingering v ▷ linger
lingers v ▷ linger
lingo n (pl -s) (Informal) foreign or unfamiliar language or jargon
lingos n ▷ lingo
lings n ▷ ling²
lingual adj of the tongue
linguist n (pl -s) person skilled in foreign languages
linguistic adj of languages
linguistics n (pl -s) scientific study of language
linguists n ▷ linguist
liniment n (pl -s) medicated liquid rubbed on the skin to relieve pain or stiffness

liniments *n* ▷ liniment

lining *n* (*pl* -s) layer of cloth attached to the inside of a garment etc.
linings *n* ▷ lining

link *n* (*pl* -s) any of the rings forming a chain ▶ *v* (-s, -ing, -ed) connect with or as if with links > **linkage** *n* (*pl* -s)
linkage *n* ▷ link
linkages *n* ▷ link
linked *v* ▷ link
linking *v* ▷ link

links *pl n* golf course, esp. one by the sea
links *n*, *v* ▷ link

linnet *n* (*pl* -s) songbird of the finch family
linnets *n* ▷ linnet

linoleum *n* (*pl* -s) floor covering of hessian or jute with a smooth decorative coating of powdered cork
linoleums *n* ▷ linoleum

linseed *n* (*pl* -s) seed of the flax plant
linseeds *n* ▷ linseeds

lint *n* (*pl* -s) soft material for dressing a wound

lintel *n* (*pl* -s) horizontal beam at the top of a door or window
lintels *n* ▷ lintel
lints *n* ▷ lint

lion *n* (*pl* -s) large animal of the cat family, the male of which has a shaggy mane > **lioness** *n fem*
lioness *n* ▷ lion
lions *n* ▷ lion

lip *n* (*pl* -s) either of the fleshy edges of the mouth
lips *n* ▷ lip

lipstick *n* (*pl* -s) cosmetic in stick form, for colouring the lips

liquefy *v* (-fies, -fying, -fied) make or become liquid > **liquefaction** *n* (*pl* -s)
liquefaction *n* ▷ liquefy
liquefactions *n* ▷ liquefy
liquefied *v* ▷ liquefy
liquefies *v* ▷ liquefy
liquefying *v* ▷ liquefy

liqueur [lik-**cure**] *n* (*pl* -s) flavoured and sweetened alcoholic spirit
liqueurs *n* ▷ liqueur

liquid *n* (*pl* -s) substance in a physical state which can change shape but not size ▶ *adj* of or being a liquid

liquidate *v* (-tes, -ting, -ted) pay (a debt) > **liquidation** *n* (*pl* -s)
liquidated *v* ▷ liquidate
liquidates *v* ▷ liquidate
liquidating *v* ▷ liquidate
liquidation *n* ▷ liquidate

liquidations *n* ▷ liquidate
liquidities *n* ▷ liquidity
liquidator *n* (*pl* -s) official appointed to liquidate a business
liquidators *n* ▷ liquidator

liquidity *n* (*pl* -ties) state of being able to meet financial obligations ▶ *v* (-zes, -zing, -zed) make or become liquid
liquidized *v* ▷ liquidize
liquidizer *n* (*pl* -s) kitchen appliance that liquidizes food
liquidizers *v* ▷ liquidizer
liquidizes *v* ▷ liquidize
liquidizing *v* ▷ liquidize
liquids *n* ▷ liquid

liquor *n* (*pl* -s) alcoholic drink, esp. spirits
liquors *n* ▷ liquor

liquorice [lik-ker-iss] *n* (*pl* -s) black substance used in medicine and as a sweet
liquorices *n* ▷ liquorice

lira *n* (*pl* -re, -ras) monetary unit of Turkey and formerly of Italy
liras *n* ▷ lira
lire *n* ▷ lira

lisle [rhymes with **mile**] *n* (*pl* -s) strong fine cotton thread or fabric
lisles *n* ▷ lisle

lisp *n* (*pl* -s) speech defect in which *s* and *z* are pronounced *th* ▶ *v* (-s, -ing, -ed) speak or utter with a lisp
lisped *v* ▷ lisp
lisping *v* ▷ lisp
lisps *n*, *v* ▷ lisp

lissom, lissome *adj* supple, agile
lissome *adj* ▷ lissom

list¹ *n* (*pl* -s) item-by-item record of names or things, usu. written one below another ▶ *v* (-s, -ing, -ed) make a list of

list² *v* (-s, -ing, -ed) (of a ship) lean to one side ▶ *n* (*pl* -s) leaning to one side
listed *v* ▷ list¹,²
listing *v* ▷ list¹,²
lists *n*, *v* ▷ list¹,²

listen *v* (-s, -ing, -ed) concentrate on hearing something > **listener** *n* (*pl* -s)
listened *v* ▷ listen
listener *n* ▷ listen
listeners *n* ▷ listen
listening *v* ▷ listen
listens *v* ▷ listen

listeriosis *n* (*pl* -ses) dangerous form of food poisoning
listerioses *n* ▷ listeriosis

listless *adj* lacking interest or energy > **listlessly** *adv*

listlessly adv ▷ listless
lit v ▷ light¹,²
litanies n ▷ litany
litany n (pl -nies) prayer with responses from
the congregation
literacies n ▷ literacy
literacy n (pl -cies) ability to read and write
literal adj according to the explicit meaning of
a word or text, not figurative > literally adv
literally adv ▷ literal
literary adj of or knowledgeable about
literature
literate adj able to read and write
literati pl n literary people
literature n (pl -s) written works such as
novels, plays, and poetry
literatures n ▷ literature
lithe adj (-ther, -thest) flexible or supple, pliant
lither adj ▷ lithe
lithest adj ▷ lithe
lithium n (pl -s) (CHEM) chemical element, the
lightest known metal
lithograph n (pl -s) print made by lithography
lithographer n ▷ lithography
lithographers n ▷ lithography
lithographic adj ▷ lithography
lithographied v ▷ lithography
lithographies n, v ▷ lithography
lithographs n ▷ lithography
lithography [lith-og-ra-fee] n (pl -phies)
method of printing from a metal or stone
surface in which the printing areas are made
receptive to ink ▶ v (-phies, -ying, -phied)
reproduce by lithography > lithographer n (pl
-s) > lithographic adj
lithographying v ▷ lithography
litigant n (pl -s) person involved in a lawsuit
litigants n ▷ litigant
litigate v (-tes, -ting, -ted) bring or contest
a lawsuit
litigated v ▷ litigate
litigates v ▷ litigate
litigating v ▷ litigate
litigation n (pl -s) legal action
litigations n ▷ litigation
litigious [lit-ij-uss] adj frequently going to law
litmus n (pl -es) blue dye turned red by acids
and restored to blue by alkalis
litmuses n ▷ litmus
litotes [lie-toe-teez] n ironical understatement
used for effect
litre n (pl -s) unit of liquid measure equal to
1000 cubic centimetres or 1.76 pints
litres n ▷ litre
litter n (pl -s) untidy rubbish dropped in public

places ▶ v (-s, -ing, -ed) strew with litter
littered v ▷ litter
littering v ▷ litter
litters n, v ▷ litter
little adj small or smaller than average
▶ adv not a lot ▶ n small amount, extent, or
duration
littoral adj of or by the seashore ▶ n (pl -s)
coastal district
littorals n ▷ littoral
liturgical n ▷ liturgy
liturgies n ▷ liturgy
liturgy n (pl -gies) prescribed form of public
worship > liturgical adj
live¹ v (-s, -ing, -ed) be alive
live² adj living, alive ▶ adv in the form of a live
performance > liveliness n (pl -es)
lived v ▷ live¹
liveliness n ▷ live²
livelinesses n ▷ live²
lively adj full of life or vigour
livelihood n (pl livelihoods) occupation or
employment
livelihoods n ▷ livelihood
lively adj full of life or vigour
liver¹ n (pl -s) organ secreting bile
liver² n (pl -s) person who lives in a specified
way
liveried adj ▷ livery
liverish adj having a disorder of the liver
livers n ▷ liver¹,²
livery n (pl -ries) distinctive dress, esp. of a
servant or servants > liveried adj
lives v ▷ live¹ ▶ n ▷ life
livestock n (pl -s) farm animals
livestocks n ▷ livestock
livid adj (Informal) (-er, -est) angry or furious
livider adj ▷ livid
lividest adj ▷ livid
living adj possessing life, not dead or
inanimate ▶ n (pl -s) condition of being alive
▶ v ▷ live
livings n ▷ living
lizard n (pl -s) four-footed reptile with a long
body and tail
lizards n ▷ lizard
llama n (pl -s) woolly animal of the camel
family used as a beast of burden in S America
llamas n ▷ llama

lo interj. Lo is a command that means
look! Along with la and li, lo is one of
just three two-letter words that begin
with L. Lo scores 2 points.

loach n (pl -es) carplike freshwater fish
loaches n ▷ loach

load n (pl -s) burden or weight ▶ pl (Informal) lots ▶ v (-s, -ing, -ed) put a load on or into
loaded adj (of a question) containing a hidden trap or implication
loaded v, adj ▷ load
loads n, v ▷ load
loading v ▷ load
loaf¹ n (pl loaves) shaped mass of baked bread
loaf² v (-s, -ing, -ed) idle, loiter ▶ **loafer** n (pl -s)
loafed v ▷ loaf²
loafer n ▷ loaf²
loafers n ▷ loaf²
loafing v ▷ loaf²
loafs v ▷ loaf²
loam n (pl -s) fertile soil
loams n ▷ loam
loan n (pl -s) money lent at interest ▶ v (-s, -ing, -ed) lend
loaned v ▷ loan
loaning v ▷ loan
loans n, v ▷ loan
loath, loth [rhymes with both] adj unwilling or reluctant (to)
loathe v (-s, -thing, -thed) hate, be disgusted by ▷ **loathing** n (pl -s) ▷ **loathsome** adj
loathed v ▷ loathe
loathes v ▷ loathe
loathing v, n ▷ loathe
loathings n ▷ loathe
loathsome adj ▷ loathe
loaves n ▷ loaf¹
lob (SPORT) n (pl -s) ball struck or thrown in a high arc ▶ v (-s, -bbing, -bbed) strike or throw (a ball) in a high arc
lobbed v ▷ lob
lobbied v ▷ lobby
lobbies n, v ▷ lobby
lobbing v ▷ lob
lobby n (pl -bies) corridor into which rooms open ▶ v (-bies, -bying, -bied) try to influence (legislators) in the formulation of policy ▷ **lobbyist** n
lobbying v ▷ lobby
lobe n (pl -s) rounded projection ▷ **lobed** adj
lobed n ▷ lobe
lobelia n (pl -s) garden plant with blue, red, or white flowers
lobelias n ▷ lobelia
lobes n ▷ lobe
lobola [law-bawl-a] n (pl -s) (S AFR) (in African custom) price paid by a bridegroom's family to his bride's family
lobolas n ▷ lobola
lobotomy n (pl -mies) surgical incision into a lobe of the brain to treat mental disorders

lobotomies n ▷ lobotomy
lobs n, v ▷ lob
lobster n (pl -s) shellfish with a long tail and claws, which turns red when boiled
lobsters n ▷ lobster
local adj of or existing in a particular place ▶ n (pl -s) person belonging to a particular district > **locally** adv
locale [loh-kahl] n (pl -s) scene of an event
localities n ▷ locality
locality n (pl -ties) neighbourhood or area
localize v (-zes, -zing, -zed) restrict to a particular place
localized v ▷ localize
localizes v ▷ localize
localizing v ▷ localize
locally adv ▷ local
locals n ▷ local
locate v (-s, -ing, -ed) discover the whereabouts of
located v ▷ locate
locates v ▷ locate
locating v ▷ locate
location n (pl -s) site or position
locations n ▷ location
loch n (pl -s) (SCOT) lake
lochs n ▷ loch
loci n ▷ locus
lock¹ n (pl -s) appliance for fastening a door, case, etc. ▶ v (-s, -ing, -ed) fasten or become fastened securely
lock² n (pl -s) strand of hair
locked v ▷ lock¹
locker n (pl -s) small cupboard with a lock
lockers n ▷ locker
locket n (pl -s) small hinged pendant for a portrait etc.
lockets n ▷ locket
locking v ▷ lock¹
lockjaw n (pl -s) tetanus
lockjaws n ▷ lockjaw
locomotion n (pl -s) action or power of moving
locomotions n ▷ locomotion
locomotive n (pl -s) self-propelled engine for pulling trains ▶ adj of locomotion
locomotives n ▷ locomotive
lockout n (pl -s) closing of a workplace by an employer to force workers to accept terms
lockouts n ▷ lockout
locks n ▷ lock¹,² ▶ v ▷ lock¹
locksmith n (pl -s) person who makes and mends locks
locksmiths n ▷ locksmith
lockup n (pl -s) prison
lockups n ▷ lockup

locum n (pl -s) temporary stand-in for a doctor or clergyman
locums n ▷ locum
locus [loh-kuss] n (pl -ci) [loh-sigh] area or place where something happens
locust n (pl -s) destructive African insect that flies in swarms and eats crops
locusts n ▷ locust
lode n (pl -s) vein of ore
lodes n ▷ lode
lodestar n (pl -s) star used in navigation or astronomy as a point of reference
lodestars n ▷ lodestar
lodestone n (pl -s) magnetic iron ore
lodestones n ▷ lodestone
lodge n (pl -s) (CHIEFLY BRIT) gatekeeper's house ▶ v (-dges, -dging, -dged) live in another's house at a fixed charge ▶ **lodger** n (pl -s)
lodged v ▷ lodge
lodger n ▷ lodge
lodgers n ▷ lodge
lodges n, v ▷ lodge
lodging n (pl -s) temporary residence ▶ pl rented room or rooms in another person's house ▶ v ▷ lodge
lodgings n ▷ lodging
loft n (pl -s) space between the top storey and roof of a building ▶ v (-s, -ing, -ed) (SPORT) strike, throw, or kick (a ball) high into the air
lofted v ▷ loft
loftier adj ▷ lofty
loftiest adj ▷ lofty
loftily adv haughtily
lofting v ▷ loft
lofts n, v ▷ loft
lofty adj (-tier, -tiest) of great height
log¹ n (pl -s) portion of a felled tree stripped of branches ▶ v (-s, -gging, -gged) saw logs from a tree
log² n ▷ logarithm
loganberry n (pl -rries) purplish-red fruit, similar to a raspberry
loganberries n ▷ loganberry
logarithm n (pl -s) one of a series of arithmetical functions used to make certain calculations easier
logarithms n ▷ logarithm
logbook n (pl -s) book recording the details about a car or a ship's journeys
logbooks n ▷ logbook
logged v ▷ log¹
loggerheads pl n quarrelling, disputing
loggia [loj-ya] n (pl -s) covered gallery at the side of a building
loggias n ▷ loggia

logging n (pl -s) work of cutting and transporting logs ▶ v ▷ log¹
loggings n ▷ logging
logic n (pl -s) philosophy of reasoning > **logically** adv > **logician** n (pl -s)
logical adj of logic
logically adv ▷ logic
logician n ▷ logic
logicians n ▷ logic
logics n ▷ logic
logistical adj ▷ logistics
logistics n detailed planning and organization of a large, esp. military, operation > **logistical, logistic** adj
logo [loh-go] n (pl -s) emblem used by a company or other organization
logos n ▷ logo
logs n ▷ log¹
loin n (pl -s) part of the body between the ribs and the hips
loincloth n (pl -s) piece of cloth covering the loins only
loincloths n ▷ loincloth
loins n ▷ loin
loiter v (-s, -ing, -ed) stand or wait aimlessly or idly
loitered v ▷ loiter
loitering v ▷ loiter
loiters v ▷ loiter
loll v (-s, -ing, -ed) lounge lazily
lolled v ▷ loll
lollies n ▷ lolly
lolling v ▷ loll
lollipop n (pl -s) boiled sweet on a small wooden stick
lollipops n ▷ lollipop
lolls v ▷ loll
lolly n (pl -llies) (Informal) lollipop or ice lolly
lone adj solitary > **lonesome** adj lonely
loneliness n ▷ lonely
lonelinesses n ▷ lonely
lonely adj sad because alone > **loneliness** n (pl -s)
loner n (pl -s) (Informal) person who prefers to be alone
loners n ▷ -s
lonesome adj ▷ lone
long¹ adj (-er, -est) having length, esp. great length, in space or time ▶ adv for an extensive period
long² v (-s, -ing, -ed) have a strong desire (for)
longed v ▷ long²
longer adj ▷ long¹
longest adj ▷ long¹
longevities n ▷ longevity

longevity [lon-**jev**-it-ee] *n* (*pl* -**ties**) long life
longhand *n* (*pl* -**s**) ordinary writing, not shorthand or typing
  longhands *n* ▷ longhand
longing *n* (*pl* -**s**) yearning ▶ *v* ▷ long²
  > **longingly** *adv*
  longingly *adv* ▷ longing
  longings *n* ▷ longing
longitude *n* (*pl* -**s**) distance east or west from a standard meridian
  longitudes *n* ▷ longitude
longitudinal *adj* of length or longitude
  longs *v* ▷ long²
longshoreman *n* (*pl* -**men**) (US) docker
  longshoremen *n* ▷ longshoreman
loo *n* (*pl* -**s**) (*Informal*) toilet
  loos *n* ▷ loo
loofah *n* (*pl* -**s**) sponge made from the dried pod of a gourd
  loofahs *n* ▷ loofah
look *v* (-**s**, -**ing**, -**ed**) direct the eyes or attention (towards) ▶ *n* (*pl* -**s**) instance of looking
lookalike *n* (*pl* -**s**) person who is the double of another
  lookalikes *n* ▷ lookalike
  looked *v* ▷ look
  looking *v* ▷ look
lookout *n* (*pl* -**s**) guard
  lookouts *n* ▷ lookout
  looks *v*, *n* ▷ look
loom¹ *n* (*pl* -**s**) machine for weaving cloth
loom² *v* (-**s**, -**ing**, -**ed**) appear dimly
  loomed *v* ▷ loom²
  looming *v* ▷ loom²
  looms *n* ▷ loom¹ ▶ *v* loom²
  loonies *n* ▷ loony
loony (*Slang*) *adj* (-**nier**, -**niest**) foolish or insane ▶ *n* (*pl* -**nies**) foolish or insane person
loop *n* (*pl* -**s**) rounded shape made by a curved line or rope crossing itself ▶ *v* (-**s**, -**ing**, -**ed**) form or fasten with a loop
  looped *v* ▷ loop
loophole *n* (*pl* -**s**) means of evading a rule without breaking it
  loopholes *n* ▷ loophole
  looping *v* ▷ loop
  loops *n*, *v* ▷ loop
loose *adj* (-**r**, -**est**) not tight, fastened, fixed, or tense ▶ *adv* in a loose manner ▶ *v* (-**s**, -**sing**, -**sed**) free > **loosely** *adv* > **looseness** *n* (*pl* -**s**)
  loosed *v* ▷ loose
  loosely *adv* ▷ loose
loosen *v* (-**s**, -**ing**, -**ed**) make loose
  loosened *v* ▷ loosen
  looseness *n* ▷ loose

loosenesses *n* ▷ loose
loosening *v* ▷ loosen
loosens *v* ▷ loosen
looser *adj* ▷ loose
looses *v* ▷ loose
loosest *adj* ▷ loose
loosing *v* ▷ loose
loot *n*, *v* (-**s**, -**ing**, -**ed**) plunder ▶ *n* (*pl* -**s**) (*Informal*) money > **looter** *n* (*pl* -**s**) > **looting** *n* (*pl* -**s**)
  looted *v* ▷ loot
  looter *n* ▷ loot
  looters *n* ▷ loot
  looting *v*, *n* ▷ loot
  lootings *n* ▷ loot
  loots *v*, *n* ▷ loot
lop *v* (-**s**, -**pping**, -**pped**) cut away twigs and branches
lope *v* (-**s**, -**ing**, -**ed**) run with long easy strides
  loped *v* ▷ lope
  lopes *v* ▷ lope
  loping *v* ▷ lope
lopsided *adj* greater in height, weight, or size on one side
loquacious *adj* talkative > **loquacity** *n* (*pl* -**ties**)
  loquacities *n* ▷ loquacity
lord *n* (*pl* -**s**) person with power over others, such as a monarch or master
  lordlier *adj* ▷ lordly
  lordliest *adj* ▷ lordly
lordly *adj* (-**lier**, -**liest**) imperious, proud
  lords *n* ▷ lord
lore *n* (*pl* -**s**) body of traditions on a subject
  lores *n* ▷ lore
lorgnette [lor-**nyet**] *n* (*pl* -**s**) pair of spectacles mounted on a long handle
  lorgnettes *n* ▷ lorgnette
  lorries *n* ▷ lorry
lorikeet *n* (*pl* -**s**) small brightly coloured Australian parrot
  lorikeets *n* ▷ lorikeet
lorry *n* (*pl* -**rries**) (BRIT & S AFR) large vehicle for transporting loads by road
lose *v* (-**s**, -**sing**, **lost**) come to be without, esp. by accident or carelessness
loser *n* (*pl* -**s**) person or thing that loses
  losers *n* ▷ loser
  loses *v* ▷ lose
  losing *v* ▷ lose
loss *n* (*pl* -**es**) losing
  losses *n* ▷ loss
  lost *v* ▷ lose ▶ *adj* unable to find one's way
lot *pron* great number ▶ *n* (*pl* -**s**) collection of people or things
  lots *n* ▷ lot

loth adj ▷ loath

lotion n (pl -s) medical or cosmetic liquid for use on the skin
  lotions n ▷ lotion

lottery n (pl -ries) method of raising money by selling tickets that win prizes by chance

lotto n (pl -s) game of chance like bingo
  lottos n ▷ lotto

lotus n (pl -es) legendary plant whose fruit induces forgetfulness
  lotuses n ▷ lotus

loud adj (-er, -est) relatively great in volume
  > **loudly** adv > **loudness** n (pl -es)
  louder adj ▷ loud
  loudest adj ▷ loud
  loudly adv ▷ loud
  loudness n ▷ loud
  loudnesses n ▷ loud

loudspeaker n (pl -s) instrument for converting electrical signals into sound
  loudspeakers n ▷ loudspeaker

lough n (pl -s) (IRISH) loch
  loughs n ▷ lough

lounge n (pl -s) living room in a private house
  ▶ v (-s, -ging, -ged) sit, lie, or stand in a relaxed manner
  lounged v ▷ lounge
  lounges n, v ▷ lounge
  lounging v ▷ lounge

lour v (-s, -ing, -ed) ▷ lower[2]
  loured v ▷ lour
  louring v ▷ lour
  lours v ▷ lour

louse n (pl lice, louses) wingless parasitic insect
  louses n ▷ louse
  lousier adj ▷ lousy
  lousiest adj ▷ lousy

lousy adj (-sier, -siest) (Slang) mean or unpleasant

lout n (pl -s) crude, oafish, or aggressive person
  > **loutish** adj
  loutish adj ▷ lout
  louts n ▷ lout

louvre [loo-ver] n (pl -s) one of a set of parallel slats slanted to admit air but not rain
  > **louvred** adj
  louvred adj ▷ louvre
  louvres n ▷ louvre

love v (-s, -ving, -ved) have a great affection for
  ▶ n (pl -s) great affection > **lovable, loveable** adj > **loveless** adj > **lovemaking** n (pl -s)
  lovable adj ▷ love
  loveable adj ▷ love

lovebird n (pl -s) small parrot

lovebirds n ▷ lovebird

loved v ▷ love

loveless adj ▷ love

lovelier adj ▷ lovely

loveliest adj ▷ lovely

lovelorn adj miserable because of unhappiness in love

lovely adj (-lier, -liest) very attractive

lovemaking n ▷ love

lovemakings n ▷ love

lover n (pl -s) person having a sexual relationship outside marriage
  lovers n ▷ lover

loves v, n ▷ love

loving adj affectionate, tender ▶ v ▷ love
  > **lovingly** adv

lovingly adv ▷ loving

low[1] adj not tall, high, or elevated ▶ adv in or to a low position, level, or degree ▶ n (pl -s) low position, level, or degree > **lowland** n (pl -s)

low[2] n (pl -s) cry of cattle, moo ▶ v (-s, -ing, -ed) moo

lowbrow n (pl -s) ▶ adj (person) with nonintellectual tastes and interests
  lowbrows n ▷ lowbrow

lowdown n (pl -s) (Informal) inside information
  lowdowns n ▷ lowdown

lowed v ▷ low[2]

lower[1] adj (-est) below one or more other things ▶ v (-s, -ing, -ed) cause or allow to move down

lower[2], **lour** v (of the sky or weather) look gloomy or threatening
  lowered v ▷ lower[1,2]
  lowering v ▷ lower[1,2]
  lowers v ▷ lower[1,2]
  lowest adj ▷ lower
  lowing v ▷ low[2]

lowland n (pl -s) low-lying country
  lowlands n ▷ lowland
  lowlier adj ▷ lowly
  lowliest adj ▷ lowly
  lowliness n ▷ lowly
  lowlinesses n ▷ lowly

lowly adj (-lier, -liest) modest, humble
  > **lowliness** n (pl -es)
  lows n ▷ low[1,2] ▶ v ▷ low[2]

> **lox** n (**loxes**). Lox is a kind of smoked salmon. This is a good word if you get have an X and L in the late stages of the game: there's likely to be a usable O on the board already. Lox scores 10 points.

loyal adj (-er, -est) faithful to one's friends, country, or government > **loyally** adv > **loyalty** n (pl -ties) > **loyalist** n (pl -s)

loyalist *n* ▷ loyal
loyalists *n* ▷ loyal
loyaller *adj* ▷ loyal
loyallest *adj* ▷ loyal
loyally *adv* ▷ loyal
loyalties *n* ▷ loyal
loyalty *n* ▷ loyal
lozenge *n* (*pl* -s) medicated tablet held in the mouth until it dissolves
lozenges *n* ▷ lozenge
lubricate [loo-brik-ate] *v* (-tes, -ting, -ted) oil or grease to lessen friction ▷ **lubrication** *n* (*pl* -s)
lubricant *n* (*pl* -s) lubricating substance, such as oil
lubricants *n* ▷ lubricant
lubricated *v* ▷ lubricate
lubricates *v* ▷ lubricate
lubricating *v* ▷ lubricate
lubrication *n* ▷ lubricate
lubrications *n* ▷ lubricate
lubricious *adj* (Lit) lewd
lucerne *n* (*pl* -s) fodder plant like clover, alfalfa
lucernes *n* ▷ lucerne
lucid *adj* clear and easily understood ▷ **lucidly** *adv* ▷ **lucidity** *n* (*pl* -ties)
lucidities *n* ▷ lucid
lucidity *n* ▷ lucid
lucidly *adv* ▷ lucid
luck *n* (*pl* -s) fortune, good or bad
luckily *adv* fortunately
luckless *adj* having bad luck
lucrative *adj* very profitable
lucre [loo-ker] *n* (*pl* -s) (Facetious) money
lucks *n* having bad luck
lucky *adj* having or bringing good luck
luderick *n* (*pl* -s) Australian fish, usu. black or dark brown in colour
ludericks *n* ▷ luderick
ludicrous *adj* absurd or ridiculous ▷ **ludicrously** *adv*
ludicrously *adv* ▷ ludicrous
ludo *n* (*pl* -s) game played with dice and counters on a board
lug¹ *v* (-s, -gging, -gged) carry or drag with great effort
lug² *n* (*pl* -s) projection serving as a handle
luggage *n* (*pl* -s) traveller's cases, bags, etc.
luggages *n* projection serving as a handle ▷ luggage
lugs *v* ▷ lug¹ ▶ *n* ▷ lug²
lugubrious *adj* mournful, gloomy ▷ **lugubriously** *adv*
lugubriously *adv* ▷ lugubrious
lugworm *n* (*pl* -s) large worm used as bait
lugworms *n* ▷ lugworm

lukewarm *adj* moderately warm, tepid
lull *v* (-s, -ing, -ed) soothe (someone) by soft sounds or motions ▶ *n* (*pl* -s) brief time of quiet in a storm etc.
lullabies *n* ▷ lullaby
lullaby *n* (*pl* -bies) quiet song to send a child to sleep
lulled *v* ▷ lull
lulling *v* ▷ lull
lulls *v*, *n* ▷ lull
lumbago [lum-**bay**-go] *n* (*pl* -s) pain in the lower back
lumbagos *n* ▷ lumbago
lumbar *adj* relating to the lower back
lumber¹ *n* (*pl* -s) (BRIT) unwanted disused household articles ▶ *v* (-s, -ing, -ed) (Informal) burden with something unpleasant
lumber² *v* move heavily and awkwardly ▷ **lumbering** *adj*
lumbered *v* ▷ lumber¹,²
lumbering *v* ▷ lumber¹,² ▶ *adj* ▷ lumber²
lumberjack *n* (*pl* -s) (US) man who fells trees and prepares logs for transport
lumberjacks *n* ▷ lumberjack
lumbers *n*¹ ▶ *v* ▷ lumber¹,²
luminary *n* (*pl* -s) famous person
luminescence *n* (*pl* -s) emission of light at low temperatures by any process other than burning
luminescences *n* ▷ luminescence
luminescent *adj* ▷ luminous
luminosities *n* ▷ luminous
luminosity *n* ▷ luminous
luminous *adj* reflecting or giving off light ▷ **luminosity** *n* (*pl* -s) ▷ **luminescent** *adj*
lump¹ *n* (*pl* -s) shapeless piece or mass ▶ *v* (-s, -ing, -ed) consider as a single group ▷ **lumpy** *adj* (-pier, -piest)
lump² *v* (Informal) tolerate or put up with it
lumped *v* ▷ lump¹,²
lumpier *adj* ▷ lump¹
lumpiest *adj* ▷ lump¹
lumping *v* ▷ lump¹,²
lumps *n*, *v* ▷ lump¹,²
lumpy *adj* ▷ lump¹
lunar *adj* relating to the moon
lunacies *n* ▷ lunacy
lunatic *adj* foolish and irresponsible ▶ *n* (*pl* -s) foolish or annoying person ▷ **lunacy** *n* (*pl* -cies)
lunatics *n* ▷ lunatic
lunch *n* (*pl* lunches) meal taken in the middle of the day ▶ *v* (-es, -ing, -ed) eat lunch
lunched *v* ▷ lunch
luncheon *n* (*pl* -s) formal lunch

luncheons n ▷ luncheon
lunches n, v ▷ lunch
lunching v ▷ lunch
lung n (pl -s) organ that allows an animal or bird to breathe air: humans have two lungs in the chest
lungfish n freshwater bony fish with an air-breathing lung of South America and Australia
lungs n ▷ lung
lunge n (pl -s) sudden forward motion ▶ v (-s, -ging, -ged) move with or make a lunge
lunged v ▷ lunge
lunges n, v ▷ lunge
lunging v ▷ lunge
lupin n (pl -s) garden plant with tall spikes of flowers
lupins n ▷ lupin
lupine adj like a wolf
lurch v (-es, -ing, -ed) tilt or lean suddenly to one side ▶ n (pl -es) lurching movement
lurched v ▷ lurch
lurcher n (pl -s) crossbred dog trained to hunt silently
lurchers n ▷ lurcher
lurches v, n ▷ lurch
lurching v ▷ lurch
lure v (-s, -red, -ring) tempt or attract by the promise of reward ▶ n (pl -s) person or thing that lures
lured v ▷ lure
lures v, n ▷ lure
luring v ▷ lure
lurid adj (-er, -est) vivid in shocking detail, sensational > **luridly** adv
lurider adj ▷ lurid
luridest adj ▷ lurid
luridly adv ▷ lurid
luring v ▷ lure
lurk v (-s, -ing, -ed) lie hidden or move stealthily, esp. for sinister purposes
lurked v ▷ lurk
lurking v ▷ lurk
lurks v ▷ lurk
luscious [lush-uss] adj extremely pleasurable to taste or smell
lush[1] adj (-er, -est) (of grass etc.) growing thickly and healthily
lush[2] n (pl -es) (Slang) alcoholic
lusher adj ▷ lush[1]
lushes n ▷ lush[2]
lushest adj ▷ lush[1]
lust n (pl -s) strong sexual desire ▶ v (-s, -ing, -ed) have passionate desire (for) > **lustful** adj > **lusty** adj vigorous, healthy > **lustily** adv

lusted v ▷ lust
lustful adj ▷ lust
lustier adj ▷ lusty
lustiest adj ▷ lusty
lustily adv ▷ lusty
lusting v ▷ lust
lustre n (pl -s) gloss, sheen
lustres n ▷ lustre
lustrous adj shining, luminous
lusts n, v ▷ lust
lusty adj (-tier, -tiest) vigorous, healthy
lute n (pl -s) ancient guitar-like musical instrument with a body shaped like a half pear
lutes n ▷ lute

> **lux** n (**lux**). A lux is a unit of illumination. This is a great word to know when you have an X but little opportunity to play it. Lux scores 10 points.

luxuriant adj rich and abundant > **luxuriance** n (pl -ces) > **luxuriantly** adv
luxuriance n ▷ luxuriant
luxuriances n ▷ luxuriant
luxuriantly adv ▷ luxuriant
luxuriate v (-tes, -ting, -ted) take self-indulgent pleasure (in)
luxuriated v ▷ luxuriate
luxuriates v ▷ luxuriate
luxuriating v ▷ luxuriate
luxurious adj full of luxury, sumptuous > **luxuriously** adv
luxuriously adv ▷ luxurious
luxury n (pl -ries) enjoyment of rich, very comfortable living ▶ adj of or providing luxury

> **luz** n (**luzzes**). In traditional Jewish writings, the luz was a bone that was supposed to be indestructible. This very unusual word is very useful, especially if you have a Z at the end of a game when there is little opportunity to use it in a longer word. Luz scores 12 points.

lychee [lie-chee] n (pl -s) Chinese fruit with a whitish juicy pulp
lychees n ▷ lychee
lye n (pl -s) caustic solution obtained by leaching wood ash
lyes n ▷ lye
lying v ▷ lie[1,2]
lymph n (pl -s) colourless bodily fluid consisting mainly of white blood cells > **lymphatic** adj
lymphatic adj ▷ lymph
lymphocyte n (pl -s) type of white blood cell
lymphocytes n ▷ lymphocyte

lymphs *n* ▷ lymph
lynch *v* (-es, -ing, -ed) put to death without a trial
  lynched *v* ▷ lynch
  lynches *v* ▷ lynch
  lynching *v* ▷ lynch
  lynchpin *n* ▷ lynchpin
  lynchpins *n* ▷ lynchpin
lynx *n* (*pl* -es) animal of the cat family with tufted ears and a short tail
  lynxes *n* ▷ lynx

lyre *n* (*pl* -s) ancient musical instrument like a U-shaped harp
  lyres *n* ▷ lyre
lyric *adj* (of poetry) expressing personal emotion in songlike style ▶ *n* (*pl* -s) short poem in a songlike style > **lyrical** *adj* lyric
  lyrical *n* ▷ lyric
lyricist *n* (*pl* -s) person who writes the words of songs or musicals
  lyricists *n* ▷ lyricist
  lyrics *n* ▷ lyric

M m

M is a very useful letter when you need to form short words as it starts a two-letter word with every vowel, as well as with Y and with another M. Remembering this allows you to use M effectively when you're forming a word parallel to, and in contact with, a word that is already on the board. M also combines well with X and Z, so there is a lot of potential for high-scoring words. Keep **max**, **mix** and **mux** (12 points each) in mind, as well as **miz** and **muz** (14 each). It's also worth remembering the three-letter words ending in W: **maw**, **mew** and **mow** (8 points each).

ma n (pl -s) (Informal) mother
   mas n ▷ ma
mac n (pl -s) (BRIT) (Informal) mackintosh
   macs n ▷ mac
macabre [mak-**kahb**-ra] adj strange and horrible, gruesome
macadam n (pl -s) road surface of pressed layers of small broken stones
   macadams n ▷ macadam
macadamia n (pl -s) Australian tree with edible nuts
   macadamias n ▷ macadamia
macaroni n (pl -s) pasta in short tube shapes
   macaronis n ▷ macaroni
macaroon n (pl -s) small biscuit or cake made with ground almonds
   macaroons n ▷ macaroon
macaw n (pl -s) large tropical American parrot
   macaws n ▷ macaw
mace¹ n (pl -s) ceremonial staff of office
mace² n (pl -s) spice made from the dried husk of the nutmeg
   maces n ▷ mace¹,²
macerate [**mass**-er-ate] v (-tes, -ting, -ted) soften by soaking ▷ **maceration** n (pl -s)
   macerated v ▷ macerate
   macerates v ▷ macerate
   macerating v ▷ macerate
   maceration n ▷ macerate
   macerations n ▷ macerate
machete [mash-**ett**-ee] n (pl -s) broad heavy knife used for cutting or as a weapon
   machetes n ▷ machete
machinations [mak-in-**nay**-shunz] pl n cunning plots and ploys
machine n (pl -s) apparatus, usu. powered by electricity, designed to perform a particular task ▶ v (-nes, -ning, -ned) make or produce by machine
   machined v ▷ machine
machinegun v (-s, -nning, -nned) fire at with such a gun
   machinegunned v ▷ machinegun
   machinegunning v ▷ machinegun
   machineguns v ▷ machinegun
   machineries n ▷ machinery
machinery n (pl -ries) machines or machine parts collectively
   machines n, v ▷ machine
   machining v ▷ machine
machinist n (pl -s) person who operates a machine
   machinists n ▷ machinist
machismo [mak-**izz**-moh] n (pl -s) exaggerated or strong masculinity
   machismos n ▷ machismo
macho [**match**-oh] adj strongly or exaggeratedly masculine
mackerel n edible sea fish
mackintosh n (pl -es) waterproof raincoat of rubberized cloth
   mackintoshes n ▷ mackintosh
macramé [mak-**rah**-mee] n (pl -s) ornamental work of knotted cord
   macramés n ▷ macramé
macrobiotics n dietary system advocating whole grains and vegetables grown without chemical additives > **macrobiotic** adj
   macrobiotic adj ▷ macrobiotics
macrocosm n (pl -s) the universe
   macrocosms n ▷ macrocosm
mad adj (madder, maddest) mentally deranged, insane > **madly** adv > **madness** n (pl -es) > **madman** n (pl -men) > **madwoman**

n (pl -women)

madam *n (pl* madams) polite form of address to a woman
  madams *n* ▷ madam

madame [mad-**dam**] *n (pl* mesdames) [may-dam] French title equivalent to *Mrs*

madcap *adj* foolish or reckless

madden *v (*-s, -ed, -ing) infuriate or irritate
  > **maddening** *adj*
  maddened *v* ▷ madden
  maddening *v* ▷ madden ▶ *adj* ▷ madden
  maddens *v* ▷ madden

madder *n (pl*-s) climbing plant ▶ *adj* ▷ mad
  maddest *adj* ▷ mad
  made *v* ▷ make

madeira [mad-**deer**-a] *n (pl* -s) fortified white wine
  madeiras *n* ▷ madeira

mademoiselle [mad-mwah-**zel**, maid-mwah-zel] *n (pl* -s) French title equivalent to *Miss*
  mademoiselles *n* ▷ mademoiselle

madonna *n (pl* -s) the Virgin Mary

madly *adv* ▷ mad
  madman *n* ▷ mad
  madmen *n* ▷ mad
  madness *n* ▷ mad
  madnesses *n* ▷ madness
  madonnas *n* ▷ madonna

madrigal *n (pl* -s) 16th–17th-century part song for unaccompanied voices
  madrigals *n* ▷ madrigal
  madwoman *n* ▷ mad
  madwomen *n* ▷ mad

maelstrom [**male**-strom] *n (pl* -s) great whirlpool
  maelstroms *n* ▷ maelstrom
  maestri *n* ▷ maestro

maestro [**my**-stroh] *n (pl* -tri, -tros) outstanding musician or conductor
  maestros *n* ▷ maestro

mafia *n (pl* -s) international secret criminal organization
  mafias *n* ▷ mafia
  mafiosi *n* ▷ mafioso

mafioso *n (pl* -sos, -si) member of the Mafia
  mafiosos *n* ▷ mafioso

magazine *n (pl* -s) periodical publication with articles by different writers
  magazines *n* ▷ magazine

magenta [maj-**jen**-ta] *adj* deep purplish-red

maggot *n (pl* -s) larva of an insect > **maggoty** *adj*
  maggots *n* ▷ maggot
  maggoty *adj* ▷ maggot

magi [**maje**-eye] *pl n* wise men from the East who came to worship the infant Jesus

magic *n (pl* -s) supposed art of invoking supernatural powers to influence events
  ▶ *adj (also* **magical**) of, using, or like magic
  > **magically** *adv*
  magical *adj* ▷ magic
  magically *adv* ▷ magic

magician *n (pl* -s) conjuror
  magicians *n* ▷ magician
  magics *n* ▷ magic

magisterial *adj* commanding or authoritative

magistrate *n (pl* -s) public officer administering the law
  magistrates *n* ▷ magistrate

magma *n (pl* -s) molten rock inside the earth's crust
  magmas *n* ▷ magma

magnanimous *adj* noble and generous
  > **magnanimously** *adv* > **magnanimity** *n (pl* -ties)
  magnanimities *n* ▷ magnanimous
  magnanimity *n* ▷ magnanimous
  magnanimously *n* ▷ magnanimous

magnate *n (pl* -s) influential or wealthy person, esp. in industry
  magnates *n* ▷ magnate

magnesia *n (pl* -s) white tasteless substance used as an antacid and a laxative; magnesium oxide
  magnesias *n* ▷ magnesia

magnesium *n (pl* -s) (CHEM) silvery-white metallic element
  magnesiums *n* ▷ magnesium

magnet *n (pl* -s) piece of iron or steel capable of attracting iron and pointing north when suspended

magnetic *adj* having the properties of a magnet > **magnetically** *adv*
  magnetically *adv* ▷ magnetic

magnetism *n (pl* -s) magnetic property
  magnetisms *n* ▷ magnetism

magnetize *v (*-zes, -zed, -zing) make into a magnet
  magnetized *v* ▷ magnetize
  magnetizes *v* ▷ magnetize
  magnetizing *v* ▷ magnetize
  magnets *n* ▷ magnet

magneto [mag-**nee**-toe] *n (pl* -s) apparatus for ignition in an internal-combustion engine

magnificent *adj* splendid or impressive
  > **magnificently** *adv* > **magnificence** *n (pl* -s)
  magnificence *n* ▷ magnificent
  magnificences *n* ▷ magnificent
  magnificently *adv* ▷ magnificent

magnify *v (*-fies, -ing, -fied) increase in

apparent size > **magnification** n (pl -s)

magnification n ▷ magnify

magnifications n ▷ magnify

magnified v ▷ magnify

magnifies v ▷ magnify

magnifying v ▷ magnify

magnitude n (pl -s) relative importance or size

magnitudes n ▷ magnitude

magnolia n (pl -s) shrub or tree with showy white or pink flowers

magnolias n ▷ magnolia

magnum n (pl s) large wine bottle holding about 1.5 litres

magnums n ▷ magnum

magpie n (pl -s) black-and-white bird

magpies n ▷ magpie

maharajah n (pl -s) former title of some Indian princes > **maharani** n fem (pl -s)

maharajahs n ▷ maharajah

maharani n ▷ maharajah

maharanis n ▷ maharajah

mahogany n (pl -nies) hard reddish-brown wood of several tropical trees

mahoganies n ▷ mahogany

mahout [ma-**howt**] n (pl s) (in India and the East Indies) elephant driver or keeper

mahouts n ▷ mahout

maid (also **maidservant**) n (pl -s) female servant

maiden n (pl -s) (Lit) young unmarried woman ▶ adj unmarried

maidenhair n (pl -s) fern with delicate fronds

maidenhairs n ▷ maidenhair

maidenhead n (pl -s) virginity

maidenheads n ▷ maidenhead

maidenly adj modest

maidens n ▷ maiden

maidishnesses n ▷ maid

maids n ▷ maid

maidservant n ▷ maid

maidservants n ▷ maid

mail¹ n (pl -s) letters and packages transported and delivered by the post office ▶ v (-s, -ing, -ed) send by mail

mail² n (pl -s) flexible armour of interlaced rings or links

mailbox n (pl -es) (US, CANADIAN & AUST) box into which letters and parcels are delivered

mailboxes n ▷ mailbox

mailed v ▷ mail¹

mailing v ▷ mail¹

mails n ▷ mail¹,² ▶ v ▷ mail²

mailshot n (pl -s) (BRIT) posting of advertising material to many selected people at once

mailshots n ▷ mailshot

maim v (-s, -ing, -ed) cripple or mutilate

maimed v ▷ maim

maiming v ▷ maim

maims v ▷ maim

main adj chief or principal ▶ n (pl -s) principal pipe or line carrying water, gas, or electricity

mainframe n (pl -s) ▶ adj (COMPUTERS) (denoting) a high-speed general-purpose computer

mainframes n ▷ mainframe

mainland n (pl -s) stretch of land which forms the main part of a country

mainlands n ▷ mainland

mainly adv for the most part, chiefly

mainmast n (pl -s) chief mast of a ship

mainmasts n ▷ mainmast

mains n ▷ main

mainsail n (pl -s) largest sail on a mainmast

mainsails n ▷ mainsail

mainspring n (pl -s) chief cause or motive

mainsprings n ▷ mainspring

mainstay n (pl -s) chief support

mainstays n ▷ mainstay

mainstream adj (of) a prevailing cultural trend

maintain v (-s, -ing, -ed) continue or keep in existence

maintained v ▷ maintain

maintaining v ▷ maintain

maintains v ▷ maintain

maintenance n (pl -s) maintaining

maintenances n ▷ maintenance

maisonette n (pl -s) (BRIT) flat with more than one floor

maisonettes n ▷ maisonette

maize n (pl -s) type of corn with spikes of yellow grains

maizes n ▷ maize

majesty n (pl -ties) stateliness or grandeur > **majestic** adj > **majestically** adv

majestic adj ▷ majesty

majestically adv ▷ majesty

majesties n ▷ majesty

major adj greater in number, quality, or extent ▶ n (pl -s) middle-ranking army officer ▶ v (-s, -ing, -ed) (foll. by **in**) (US, CANADIAN, S AFR, AUST & NZ) do one's principal study in (a particular subject)

majordomo n (pl -s) chief steward of a great household

majordomos n ▷ majordomo

majored v ▷ major

majoring v ▷ major

majorities n ▷ majority

majority n (pl -ties) greater number

majors n, v ▷ major
make v (-kes, -king, made) create, construct, or establish ▶ n (pl -s) brand, type, or style
maker n (pl -s) ▷ **makeweight** n (pl -s) something unimportant added to make up a lack
maker n ▷ make
makers n ▷ make
makes n, v ▷ make
makeshift adj serving as a temporary substitute
makeup n (pl -s) cosmetics
makeups n ▷ makeup
making v ▷ make ▶ n (pl -s) creation or production
makings n ▷ making
malachite [mal-a-kite] n (pl -s) green mineral
malachites n ▷ malachite
maladjusted adj (PSYCHOL) unable to meet the demands of society ▷ **maladjustment** n (pl -s)
maladjustment n ▷ maladjusted
maladjustments n ▷ maladjusted
maladministration n (pl -s) inefficient or dishonest administration
maladministrations n ▷ maladministration
maladroit adj clumsy or awkward
malady n (pl -dies) disease or illness
maladies n ▷ malady
malaise [mal-laze] n (pl -s) vague feeling of unease, illness, or depression
malaises n ▷ malaise
malapropism n (pl -s) comical misuse of a word by confusion with one which sounds similar, e.g. I am not under the affluence of alcohol
malapropisms n ▷ malapropism
malaria n (pl -s) infectious disease caused by the bite of some mosquitoes ▷ **malarial** adj
malarias n ▷ malaria
malarial adj ▷ malaria
malcontent n (pl -s) discontented person
malcontents n ▷ malcontent
male adj of the sex which can fertilize female reproductive cells ▶ n (pl males) male person or animal
males n ▷ male
malediction [mal-lid-dik-shun] n (pl -s) curse
maledictions n ▷ malediction
malefactor [mal-if-act-or] n (pl -s) criminal or wrongdoer
malefactors n ▷ malefactor
malevolent [mal-lev-a-lent] adj wishing evil to others ▷ **malevolently** adv ▷ **malevolence** n (pl -s)
malevolence n ▷ malevolent

malevolences n ▷ malevolent
malevolently adv ▷ malevolent
malfeasance [mal-fee-zanss] n (pl -s) misconduct, esp. by a public official
malfeasances n ▷ malfeasance
malformed adj misshapen or deformed > **malformation** n (pl -s)
malformation n ▷ malformed
malformations n ▷ malformed
malfunction v (-s, -ing, -ed) function imperfectly or fail to function ▶ n (pl -s) defective functioning or failure to function
malfunctioned v ▷ malfunction
malfunctioning v ▷ malfunction
malfunctions v, n ▷ malfunction
malice [mal-iss] n (pl -s) desire to cause harm to others > **malicious** adj > **maliciously** adv
malices n ▷ malice
malicious adj ▷ malice
maliciously adj ▷ malice
malign [mal-line] v (-s, -ing, -ed) slander or defame ▶ adj evil in influence or effect > **malignity** n (pl -nities) evil disposition
malignancies n ▷ malignant
malignancy n ▷ malignant
malignant [mal-lig-nant] adj seeking to harm others > **malignancy** n (pl -cies)
maligned v ▷ malign
maligning v ▷ malign
malignities n ▷ malign
malignity n ▷ malign
maligns v ▷ malign
malinger v (-s, -ing, -ed) feign illness to avoid work > **malingerer** n (pl -s)
malingered v ▷ malinger
malingerer n ▷ malinger
malingering v ▷ malinger
malingerers n ▷ malinger
malingers v ▷ malinger
mall [mawl] n (pl -s) street or shopping area closed to vehicles
mallard n wild duck
malleable [mal-lee-a-bl] adj capable of being hammered or pressed into shape > **malleability** n (pl -ties)
malleability n ▷ malleable
malleabilities n ▷ malleable
mallee n (pl -s) (AUST) low-growing eucalypt in dry regions
mallees n ▷ mallee
mallet n (pl -s) (wooden) hammer
mallets n ▷ mallet
mallow n (pl -s) plant with pink or purple flowers
mallows n ▷ mallow

malls *n* ▷ mall
malnutrition *n* (*pl* -s) inadequate nutrition
malnutritions *n* ▷ malnutrition
malodorous [mal-**lode**-or-uss] *adj* bad-smelling
malpractice *n* (*pl* -s) immoral, illegal, or unethical professional conduct
malpractices *n* ▷ malpractice
malt *n* (*pl* -s) grain, such as barley, prepared for use in making beer or whisky
malts *n* ▷ malt
maltreat *v* (-s, -ing, -ed) treat badly
▷ **maltreatment** *n* (*pl* -s)
maltreated *v* ▷ maltreat
maltreating *v* ▷ maltreat
maltreatment *n* ▷ maltreat
maltreatments *n* ▷ maltreat
maltreats *v* ▷ maltreat
mama *n* (*pl* -s) (*Old-fashioned*) mother
mamas *n* ▷ mama
mamba *n* (*pl* -s) deadly S African snake
mambas *n* ▷ mamba
mamma *n* (*pl* -s) ▷ mama
mammas *n* ▷ mamma
mammal *n* (*pl* -s) animal of the type that suckles its young ▷ **mammalian** *adj*
mammalian *adj* ▷ mammal
mammals *n* ▷ mammal
mammary *adj* of the breasts or milk-producing glands
mammon *n* (*pl* -s) wealth regarded as a source of evil
mammons *n* ▷ mammon
mammoth *n* (*pl* -s) extinct elephant-like mammal ▶ *adj* colossal
mammoths *n* ▷ mammoth
man *n* (*pl* men) adult male ▶ *v* (-s, -nning, -nned) supply with sufficient people for operation or defence ▷ **manhood** *n* (*pl* -s)
mana *n* (*pl* -s) (NZ) authority, influence
manacle [man-a-kl] *n* (*pl* -s) handcuff or fetter
▶ *v* (-les, -ling, -led) handcuff or fetter
manacled *v* ▷ manacle
manacling *v* ▷ manacle
manacles *n*, *v* ▷ manacle
manage *v* (-ges, -ging, -ged) succeed in doing
▷ **manageable** *adj* ▷ **management** *n* (*pl* -s) managers collectively
manageable *adj* ▷ manage
managed *v* ▷ manage
managing *v* ▷ manage
management *n* ▷ manage
managements *n* ▷ manage
manages *v* ▷ manage
manager *n* (*pl* -s) person in charge of a business, institution, actor, sports team, etc.

▷ **managerial** *adj*
manageress *n* (*pl* -es) woman in charge of a business, institution, actor, sports team, etc.
manageresses *n* ▷ manager
managerial *adj* ▷ manager
managers *n* ▷ manager
manas *n* ▷ mana
manatee *n* (*pl* -s) large tropical plant-eating aquatic mammal
manatees *n* ▷ manatee
mandarin *n* (*pl* -s) high-ranking government official
mandarins *n* ▷ mandarin
mandate *n* (*pl* -s) official or authoritative command ▶ *v* (-tes, -ting, -ted) give authority to
mandated *v* ▷ mandate
mandates *n*, *v* ▷ mandate
mandating *v* ▷ mandate
mandatory *adj* compulsory
mandible *n* (*pl* -s) lower jawbone or jawlike part
mandibles *n* ▷ mandible
mandolin *n* (*pl* s) musical instrument with four pairs of strings
mandolins *n* ▷ mandolin
mandrake *n* (*pl* -s) plant with a forked root, formerly used as a narcotic
mandrakes *n* ▷ mandrake
mandrel *n* (*pl* -s) shaft on which work is held in a lathe
mandrels *n* ▷ mandrel
mandrill *n* (*pl* -s) large blue-faced baboon
mandrills *n* ▷ mandrill
mane *n* (*pl* -s) long hair on the neck of a horse, lion, etc.
manes *n* ▷ mane
manful *adj* determined and brave ▷ **manfully** *adv*
manfully *adv* ▷ manful
manganese *n* (*pl* -s) (CHEM) brittle greyish-white metallic element
manganeses *n* ▷ manganese
mange *n* (*pl* -s) skin disease of domestic animals
manges *n* ▷ mange
mangelwurzel *n* (*pl* -s) variety of beet used as cattle food
mangelwurzels *n* ▷ mangelwurzel
manger *n* (*pl* -s) eating trough in a stable or barn
mangers *n* ▷ manger
mangetout [mawnzh-too] *n* (*pl* -s) variety of pea with an edible pod
mangetouts *n* ▷ mangetout

mangier *adj* ▷ mangy
mangiest *adj* ▷ mangy
mangle[1] *v* (-les, -ling, -led) destroy by crushing and twisting
mangle[2] *n* (*pl* -s) machine with rollers for squeezing water from washed clothes ▶ *v* (-les, -ling, -led) put through a mangle
mangled *v* ▷ mangle[1,2]
mangling *v* ▷ mangle[1,2]
mangles *v* ▷ mangle[1,2] ▶ *n* ▷ mangle[2]
mango *n* (*pl* -goes, -gos) tropical fruit with sweet juicy yellow flesh
mangoes *n* ▷ mango
mangos *n* ▷ mango
mangrove *n* (*pl* -s) tropical tree with exposed roots, which grows beside water
mangroves *n* ▷ mangrove
mangy *adj* (-gier, -giest) having mange
manhandle *v* (-les, -ling, -led) treat roughly
manhandled *v* ▷ manhandle
manhandling *v* ▷ manhandle
manhandles *v* ▷ manhandle
manhole *n* (*pl* -s) hole with a cover, through which a person can enter a drain or sewer
manholes *n* ▷ manhole
manhood *n* ▷ man
manhoods *n* ▷ man
mania *n* (*pl* -s) extreme enthusiasm
> **maniacal** [man-**eye**-a-kl] ▶ *adj*
maniac *n* (*pl* -s) mad person
maniacal *adj* ▷ mania
maniacs *n* ▷ mania
manias *n* ▷ mania
manic *adj* affected by mania
manicure *n* (*pl* -s) cosmetic care of the fingernails and hands ▶ *v* (-res, -ring, -red) care for (the fingernails and hands) in this way > **manicurist** *n* (*pl* -s)
manicured *v* ▷ manicure
manicures *n*, *v* ▷ manicure
manicuring *v* ▷ manicure
manicurist *n* ▷ manicure
manicurists *n* ▷ manicure
manifest *adj* easily noticed, obvious ▶ *v* (-s, -ing, -ed) show plainly ▶ *n* (*pl* -s) list of cargo or passengers for customs > **manifestation** *n* (*pl* -s)
manifestation *n* ▷ manifest
manifestations *n* ▷ manifest
manifested *v* ▷ manifest
manifesting *v*, *n* ▷ manifest
manifesto *n* (*pl* -tos, -toes) declaration of policy as issued by a political party
manifestos *n* ▷ manifesto
manifestoes *n* ▷ manifesto

manifests *v* ▷ manifest
manifold *adj* numerous and varied ▶ *n* (*pl* -s) pipe with several outlets, esp. in an internal-combustion engine
manifolds *n* ▷ manifold
manikin *n* (*pl* -s) little man or dwarf
manikins *n* ▷ manikin
manila, manilla *n* (*pl* -s) strong brown paper used for envelopes
manilas *n* ▷ manila
manillas *n* ▷ manila
manipulate *v* (-tes, -ting, -ted) handle skilfully > **manipulation** *n* (*pl* -s) > **manipulative** *adj* > **manipulator** *n* (*pl* -s)
manipulated *v* ▷ manipulate
manipulates *v* ▷ manipulate
manipulating *v* ▷ manipulate
manipulation *n* ▷ manipulate
manipulations *n* ▷ manipulate
manipulative *adj* ▷ manipulate
manipulator *n* ▷ manipulate
manipulators *n* ▷ manipulate
mankind *n* (*pl* -s) human beings collectively
mankinds *n* ▷ mankind
manlier *adj* ▷ manly
manliest *adj* ▷ manly
manliness *n* ▷ manly
manlinesses *n* ▷ manly
manly *adj* (-lier, -liest) (possessing qualities) appropriate to a man > **manliness** *n* (*pl* -s)
manna *n* (BIBLE) miraculous food which sustained the Israelites in the wilderness
mannas *n* ▷ manna
manned *v* ▷ man
mannequin *n* (*pl* -s) woman who models clothes at a fashion show
mannequins *n* ▷ mannequin
manner *n* (*pl* -s) way a thing happens or is done > **mannered** *adj* affected
mannered *adj* ▷ manner
mannerism *n* (*pl* -s) person's distinctive habit or trait
mannerisms *n* ▷ manner
manners *n* ▷ manner
mannikin *n* (*pl* -s) ▷ manikin
mannikins *n* ▷ mannikin
manning *v* ▷ man
mannish *adj* (of a woman) like a man
manoeuvre [man-**noo**-ver] *n* (*pl* -s) skilful movement military or naval exercises ▶ *v* (-res, -ring, -red) manipulate or contrive skilfully or cunningly > **manoeuvrable** *adj*
manoeuvred *v* ▷ manoeuvre
manoeuvres *n*, *v* ▷ manoeuvre
manoeuvring *v* ▷ manoeuvre

manor *n* (*pl* -s) (BRIT) large country house and its lands ▷ **manorial** *adj*
manorial *adj* ▷ manor
manors *n* ▷ manor
manpower *n* (*pl* -s) available number of workers
manpowers *n* ▷ manpower
manqué [mong-kay] *adj* would-be
mans *v* ▷ man
manse *n* (*pl* -s) house provided for a minister in some religious denominations
manses *n* ▷ manse
manservant *n* (*pl* menservants) male servant, esp. a valet
mansion *n* (*pl* -s) large house
mansions *n* ▷ mansion
manslaughter *n* (*pl* -s) unlawful but unintentional killing of a person
manslaughters *n* ▷ manslaughter
mantel *n* (*pl* -s) structure round a fireplace
mantelpiece *n* (*pl* -es) shelf above a fireplace
mantelpieces *n* ▷ mantelpiece
mantels *n* ▷ mantel
mantilla *n* (*pl* -s) (in Spain) a lace scarf covering a woman's head and shoulders
mantillas *n* ▷ mantilla
mantis *n* (*pl* -ses, -tes) carnivorous insect like a grasshopper
mantes *n* ▷ mantis
mantises *n* ▷ mantis
mantle *n* (*pl* -s) loose cloak
mantles *n* ▷ mantle
mantra *n* (*pl* -s) (HINDUISM, BUDDHISM) any sacred word or syllable used as an object of concentration
mantras *n* ▷ mantra
manual *adj* of or done with the hands ▶ *n* (*pl* -s) handbook ▷ **manually** *adv*
manually *adv* ▷ manual
manuals *n* ▷ manual
manufacture *v* (-res, -ring, -red) process or make (goods) on a large scale using machinery ▶ *n* (*pl* -s) process of manufacturing goods
manufactured *v* ▷ manufacture
manufacturer *n* (*pl* -s) company that manufactures goods
manufacturers *n* ▷ manufacturer
manufactures *v*, *n* ▷ manufacture
manufacturing *v* ▷ manufacture
manure *n* (*pl* -s) animal excrement used as a fertilizer
manures *n* ▷ manure
manuscript *n* (*pl* -s) book or document, orig. one written by hand

manuscripts *n* ▷ manuscript
many *adj* (more, most) numerous ▶ *n* large number
map *n* (*pl* -s) representation of the earth's surface or some part of it, showing geographical features ▶ *v* (-s, -pping, -pped) make a map of
maple *n* (*pl* -s) tree with broad leaves, a variety of which (**sugar maple**) yields sugar
maples *n* ▷ maple
mapped *v* ▷ map
mapping *v* ▷ map
maps *n*, *v* ▷ map
mar *v* (-s, -rring, -rred) spoil or impair
marabou *n* (*pl* -s) large black-and-white African stork
marabous *n* ▷ marabou
maraca [mar-rak-a] *n* (*pl* -s) shaken percussion instrument made from a gourd containing dried seeds etc.
maracas *n* ▷ maraca
marae *n* (*pl* -s) (NZ) enclosed space in front of a Maori meeting house
maraes *n* ▷ marae
marathon *n* (*pl* -s) long-distance race of 26 miles 385 yards (42.195 kilometres)
marathons *n* ▷ marathon
marauder *n* ▷ marauding
marauders *n* ▷ marauder
marauding *adj* wandering or raiding in search of plunder ▷ **marauder** *n* (*pl* -s)
marble *n* (*pl* -s) kind of limestone with a mottled appearance, which can be highly polished ▷ **marbled** *adj* having a mottled appearance like marble
marbled *n* ▷ marble
marbles *n* ▷ marble
march¹ *v* (-es, -ing, -ed) walk with a military step ▶ *n* (*pl* -es) action of marching ▷ **marcher** *n* (*pl* -s)
march² *n* (*pl* -s) border or frontier
marched *v* ▷ march¹
marches *v* ▷ march¹ ▶ *n* ▷ march¹,²
marching *v* ▷ march¹
marchioness [marsh-on-**ness**] *n* (*pl* -es) woman holding the rank of marquis
marchionesses *n* ▷ marchioness
mare *n* (*pl* -s) female horse or zebra
mares *n* ▷ mare
margarine *n* (*pl* -s) butter substitute made from animal or vegetable fats
margarines *n* ▷ margarine
marge *n* (*pl* -s) (*Informal*) margarine
marges *n* ▷ marge
margin *n* (*pl* -s) edge or border ▷ **marginal** *adj*

insignificant, unimportant ▷ **marginally** adv
marginal adj ▷ margin
marginalize v (-zes, -zing, -zed) make or treat as insignificant
  marginalized v ▷ marginalize
  marginalizes v ▷ marginalize
  marginalizing v ▷ marginalize
  margins n ▷ margin
marguerite n (pl -s) large daisy
  marguerites n ▷ marguerite
marigold n (pl -s) plant with yellow or orange flowers
  marigolds n ▷ marigold
marijuana [mar-ree-**wah**-na] n (pl -s) dried flowers and leaves of the cannabis plant, used as a drug, esp. in cigarettes
  marijuanas n ▷ marijuana
marina n (pl -s) harbour for yachts and other pleasure boats
  marinas n ▷ marina
marinade n (pl -s) seasoned liquid in which fish or meat is soaked before cooking ▶ v (-des, -ding, -ded) ▷ marinate
  marinaded v ▷ marinade
  marinades n, v ▷ marinade
  marinading v ▷ marinade
marinate v (-tes, -ting, -ted) soak in marinade
  marinated v ▷ marinate
  marinates v ▷ marinate
  marinating v ▷ marinate
marine adj of the sea or shipping ▶ n (pl -s) (esp. in Britain and the US) soldier trained for land and sea combat
mariner n (pl -s) sailor
  mariners n ▷ mariner
  marines n ▷ marine
marionette n (pl -s) puppet worked with strings
  marionettes n ▷ marionette
marital adj relating to marriage
maritime adj relating to shipping
marjoram n (pl -s) aromatic herb used for seasoning food and in salads
  marjorams n ▷ marjoram
mark¹ n (pl -s) line, dot, scar, etc. visible on a surface ▶ v (-s, -ing, -ed) make a mark on ▷ **marked** adj noticeable ▷ **markedly** adv ▷ **marker** n (pl -s)
mark² n ▷ Deutschmark
marked v, adj ▷ mark¹
  markedly adv ▷ mark¹
  marker n ▷ mark¹
  markers n ▷ mark
  marking v ▷ mark¹
  marks n ▷ mark¹,² ▶ v ▷ mark¹

market n (pl -s) assembly or place for buying and selling ▶ v (-s, -ing, -ed) offer or produce for sale ▷ **marketable** adj
  marketable adj ▷ market
marketing n (pl -s) part of a business that controls the way that goods or services are sold
  marketings n ▷ marketing
marketplace n (pl -s) market
  marketplaces n ▷ marketplace
  markets n, v ▷ market
marksman n (pl -men) person skilled at shooting ▷ **marksmanship** n (pl -s)
  marksmanship n ▷ marksman
  marksmanships n ▷ marksman
  marksmen n ▷ marksman
marl n (pl -s) soil formed of clay and lime, used as fertilizer
  marls n ▷ marl
marlin n large food and game fish of warm and tropical seas, with a very long upper jaw
marlinespike, marlinspike n (pl -s) pointed hook used to separate strands of rope
  marlinespikes n ▷ marlinespike
  marlinspikes n ▷ marlinspike
marmalade n (pl -s) jam made from citrus fruits
  marmalades n ▷ marmalade
marmoreal adj of or like marble
marmoset n (pl -s) small bushy-tailed monkey
  marmosets n ▷ marmoset
marmot n (pl -s) burrowing rodent
  marmots n ▷ marmot
maroon¹ adj reddish-purple
maroon² v (-s, -ing, -ed) abandon ashore, esp. on an island
  marooned v ▷ maroon
  marooning v ▷ maroon
  maroons v ▷ maroon
marquee n (pl -s) large tent used for a party or exhibition
  marquees n ▷ marquee
marquess [mar-kwiss] n (pl -es) (BRIT) nobleman of the rank below a duke
  marquesses n ▷ marquess
marquetry n (pl -ries) ornamental inlaid work of wood
  marquetries n ▷ marquetry
marquis n (pl -es) (in some European countries) nobleman of the rank above a count
  marquises n ▷ marquis
  marred v ▷ mar
marriage n (pl -s) state of being married ▷ **marriageable** adj

marriageable adj ▷ marriage
marriages n ▷ marriage
married v ▷ marry
marries v ▷ marry
marring v ▷ mar
marrow n (pl -s) fatty substance inside bones
marrows n ▷ marrow
marry v (-ries, -ing, -ried) take as a husband or wife
marrying v ▷ marry
mars v ▷ mar
marsala [mar-**sah**-la] n (pl -s) dark sweet wine
marsh n (pl -es) low-lying wet land ► **marshy** adj (-shier, -shiest)
marshal n (pl -s) officer of the highest rank ► v (-s, -shalling, -shalled) arrange in order
marshalled v ▷ marshal
marshalling v ▷ marshal
marshals n, v ▷ marshal
marshes n ▷ marsh
marshier adj ▷ marsh
marshiest adj ▷ marsh
marshmallow n (pl -s) spongy pink or white sweet
marshmallows n ▷ marshmallow
marshy n ▷ marsh
marsupial [mar-**soop**-ee-al] n (pl -s) animal that carries its young in a pouch
marsupialians n ▷ marsupial
marsupials n ▷ marsupial
mart n (pl -s) market
marts n ▷ mart
marten n (pl -s) weasel-like animal
martens n ▷ marten
martial adj of war, warlike
martian [**marsh**-an] adj of Mars ► n (pl -s) supposed inhabitant of Mars
martians n ▷ martian
martin n (pl -s) bird with a slightly forked tail
martins n ▷ martin
martinet n (pl -s) person who maintains strict discipline
martinets n ▷ martinet
martini n (pl -s) cocktail of vermouth and gin
martinis n ▷ martini
martyr n (pl -s) person who dies or suffers for his or her beliefs ► v (-s, -ing, -ed) make a martyr of ► **martyrdom** n (pl -s)
martyrdom n ▷ martyr
martyrdoms n ▷ martyr
martyred v ▷ martyr
martyring v ▷ martyr
martyrs n, v ▷ martyr
marvel v (-s, -velling, -velled) be filled with wonder ► n wonderful thing

marvelled v ▷ marvel
marvelling v ▷ marvel
marvellous adj amazing
marvels v ▷ marvel
marzipan n (pl -s) paste of ground almonds, sugar, and egg whites
marzipans n ▷ marzipan
mascara n (pl -s) cosmetic for darkening the eyelashes
mascaras n ▷ mascara
mascot n (pl -s) person, animal, or thing supposed to bring good luck
mascots n ▷ mascot
masculine adj relating to males > **masculinity** n (pl -ties)
masculinities n ▷ masculine
masculinity n ▷ masculine
mash n (pl -es) (Informal) mashed potatoes ► v (-es, -ing, -ed) crush into a soft mass
mashed v ▷ mash
mashes n, v ▷ mash
mashing v ▷ mash
mask n (pl -s) covering for the face, as a disguise or protection ► v (-s, -ing, -ed) cover with a mask
masked v ▷ mask
masking v ▷ mask
masks n, v ▷ mask
masochism [**mass**-oh-kiz-zum] n (pl -s) condition in which (sexual) pleasure is obtained from feeling pain or from being humiliated > **masochist** n (pl -s) > **masochistic** adj
masochist n ▷ masochism
masochistic n ▷ masochism
masochists n ▷ masochism
mason n (pl -s) person who works with stone
masonic adj of Freemasonry
masonry n (pl -ries) stonework
masonries n (pl -ries) stonework
masons n ▷ mason
masque [mask] n (pl -s) (HIST) 16th–17th-century form of dramatic entertainment
masques n ▷ masque
masquerade [mask-er-**aid**] n (pl -s) deceptive show or pretence ► v (-des, -ding, -ded) pretend to be someone or something else
masqueraded v ▷ masquerade
masquerades n, v ▷ masquerade
masquerading v ▷ masquerade
mass n (pl -es) coherent body of matter ► adj large-scale ► v (-es, -ing, -ed) form into a mass
massacre [**mass**-a-ker] n (pl -s) indiscriminate killing of large numbers of people ► v (-res, -ring, -red) kill in large numbers

massacred v ▷ massacre

massacres n, v ▷ massacre

massacring v ▷ massacre

massage [mass-ahzh] n (pl -s) rubbing and kneading of parts of the body to reduce pain or stiffness ▶ v (-ges, -ging, -ged) give a massage to

massaged v ▷ massage

massages n, v ▷ massage

massaging v ▷ massage

massed v ▷ mass

masses n, v ▷ mass

masseur, fem masseuse n (pl -s) person who gives massages

masseurs n ▷ masseur

masseuse n ▷ masseuses

massing v ▷ mass

massive adj large and heavy

massif [mass-seef] n (pl -s) connected group of mountains

massifs n ▷ massif

mast¹ n (pl -s) tall pole for supporting something, esp. a ship's sails

mast² n (pl -s) fruit of the beech, oak, etc., used as pig fodder

masts n ▷ mast¹,²

mastectomies n ▷ mastectomy

mastectomy [mass-tek-tom-ee] n (pl -mies) surgical removal of a breast

master n (pl -s) person in control, such as an employer or an owner of slaves or animals ▶ adj overall or controlling ▶ v (-s, -ing, -ed) acquire knowledge of or skill in

mastered v ▷ master

masterful adj domineering

masteries n ▷ mastery

mastering v ▷ master

masterly adj showing great skill

mastermind v plan and direct (a complex task) n person who plans and directs a complex task

masterpiece n outstanding work of art

masters n, v ▷ master

mastery n (pl -ries) expertise

mastic n (pl -s) gum obtained from certain trees

mastics n ▷ mastic

masticate v (-tes, -ting, -ted) chew > mastication n (pl -s)

masticated v ▷ masticate

masticates v ▷ masticate

masticating v ▷ masticate

mastication n ▷ masticate

mastications n ▷ masticate

mastiff n (pl -s) large dog

mastiffs n ▷ mastiff

mastitis n (pl -tises) inflammation of a breast or udder

mastitises n ▷ mastitis

mastodon n (pl -s) extinct elephant-like mammal

mastodons n ▷ mastodon

mastoid n (pl -s) projection of the bone behind the ear

mastoids n ▷ mastoid

masturbate v (-tes, -ting, -ted) fondle the genitals (of) > masturbation n (pl -s)

masturbated v ▷ masturbate

masturbates v ▷ masturbate

masturbating v ▷ masturbate

masturbation n ▷ masturbate

masturbations n ▷ masturbate

mat n (pl -s) piece of fabric used as a floor covering or to protect a surface ▶ v (-s, -tting, -tted) tangle or become tangled into a dense mass

matador n (pl -s) man who kills the bull in bullfights

matadors n ▷ matador

match¹ n (pl -es) contest in a game or sport ▶ v (-es, -ing, -ed) be exactly like, equal to, or in harmony with

match² n small stick with a tip which ignites when scraped on a rough surface > matchbox n (pl -es)

matchbox n ▷ match²

matchboxes n ▷ match²

matched v ▷ match¹

matches v ▷ match¹ ▶ n ▷ match¹,²

matching v ▷ match¹

matchless adj unequalled

matchmaker n (pl -s) person who schemes to bring about a marriage > matchmaking n (pl -s) adj

matchmakers n ▷ matchmaker

matchmaking n ▷ matchmaker

matchmakings n ▷ matchmaker

matchstick n (pl -s) wooden part of a match ▶ adj (of drawn figures) thin and straight

matchsticks n ▷ matchstick

matchwood n (pl -s) small splinters

matchwoods n ▷ matchwood

mate¹ n (pl -s) (Informal) friend ▶ v (-tes, -ting, -ted) pair (animals) or (of animals) be paired for reproduction

mate² n (pl -s) checkmate ▶ v (-tes, -ting, -ted) (CHESS) checkmate

mated v ▷ mate¹,²

mates n, v ▷ mate¹,²

mating v ▷ mate¹,²

material n (pl -s) substance of which a thing is made ▶ adj of matter or substance > **materialist** adj, n ▷ **materialistic** adj
materialism n (pl -s) excessive interest in or desire for money and possessions
materialisms n ▷ materialism
materialist adj, n (pl -s) ▷ material
materialistic adj ▷ material
materialists n ▷ material
materialize v (-zes, -zing, -zed) actually happen > **materialization** n (pl -s)
materialization n ▷ materialize
materializations n ▷ materialize
materialized v ▷ materialize
materializes v ▷ materialize
materializing v ▷ materialize
materially adv considerably
materials n ▷ material
maternal adj of a mother ▶ adj of or for pregnant women
maternities n ▷ maternity
maternity n (pl -ties) motherhood
matey adj (-tier, -tiest) (BRIT) (Informal) friendly or intimate
mathematics n science of number, quantity, shape, and space > **mathematical** adj > **mathematically** adv > **mathematician** n (pl -s)
mathematical adj ▷ mathematics
mathematically adv ▷ mathematics
mathematician n ▷ mathematics
mathematicians n ▷ mathematics
maths n (Informal) mathematics
matier adj ▷ matey
matiest adj ▷ matey
matilda n (pl -s) (AUST HIST) swagman's bundle of belongings
matildas n ▷ matilda
matinée [mat-in-nay] n (pl -s) afternoon performance in a theatre or cinema
matinées n ▷ matinée
matins pl n early morning service in various Christian Churches
matriarch [mate-ree-ark] n (pl -s) female head of a tribe or family > **matriarchal** adj
matriarchal n ▷ matriarch
matriarchies n ▷ matriarchy
matriarchs n ▷ matriarch
matriarchy n (pl -chies) society governed by a female, in which descent is traced through the female line
matrices n ▷ matrix
matricide n (pl -s) crime of killing one's mother
matricides n ▷ matricide
matriculate v (-tes, -ting, -ted) enrol or

be enrolled in a college or university > **matriculation** n (pl -s)
matriculated v ▷ matriculate
matriculates v ▷ matriculate
matriculating v ▷ matriculate
matriculation n ▷ matriculate
matriculations n ▷ matriculate
matrimonial adj ▷ matrimony
matrimonies n ▷ matrimony
matrimony n (pl -nies) marriage > **matrimonial** adj
matrix [may-trix] n (pl -trices) substance or situation in which something originates, takes form, or is enclosed
matron n (pl -s) staid or dignified married woman > **matronly** adj
matrons n ▷ matron
mats n, v ▷ mat
matt adj dull, not shiny
matted v ▷ mat
matter n (pl -s) substance of which something is made ▶ v (-s, -ing, -ed) be of importance
mattered v ▷ matter
mattering v ▷ matter
matters n, v ▷ matter
matting v ▷ mat
mattock n (pl -s) large pick with one of its blade ends flattened for loosening soil
mattocks n ▷ mattock
mattress n (pl -es) large stuffed flat case, often with springs, used on or as a bed
mattresses n ▷ mattress
mature adj fully developed or grown-up ▶ v (-res, -ring, -red) make or become mature > **maturation** n (pl -s)
maturation n ▷ mature
maturations n ▷ mature
matured v ▷ mature
matures v ▷ mature
maturing v ▷ mature
maturities n ▷ maturity
maturity n (pl -ties) state of being mature
maudlin adj foolishly or tearfully sentimental
maul v (-s, -ing, -ed) handle roughly
mauled v ▷ maul
mauling v ▷ maul
mauls v ▷ maul
maunder v (-s, -ing, -ed) talk or act aimlessly or idly
maundered v ▷ maunder
maundering v ▷ maunder
maunders v ▷ maunder
mausoleum [maw-so-lee-um] n (pl -s) stately tomb
mausoleums n ▷ mausoleum

mauve adj (**-r, -est**) pale purple
mauver adj ▷ mauve
mauvest adj ▷ mauve
maverick n (pl -s) ▷ adj independent and unorthodox (person)
mavericks n ▷ maverick
maw n (pl -s) animal's mouth, throat, or stomach
maws n ▷ maw
mawkish adj foolishly sentimental

max n (**maxes**). Max is a short form of **maximum**. This is a useful word, particularly if you find yourself with an X toward the end of the game, with limited opportunity to play it. Max scores 12 points.

maxim n (pl -s) general truth or principle
maxima n ▷ maximum
maximal adj ▷ maxim
maxims n ▷ maxim
maximum adj, n (pl -s, -ma) greatest possible (amount or number) > **maximal** adj
maximize v (-zes, -zing, -zed) increase to a maximum
maximized v ▷ maximize
maximizes v ▷ maximize
maximizing v ▷ maximize
maximums n ▷ maximum
may[1] v (past tense **might**) used as an auxiliary to express possibility, permission, opportunity, etc.
may[2] n (pl -s) ▷ hawthorn
mays n ▷ may[2]
maybe adv perhaps, possibly
mayday n (pl -s) international radio distress signal
maydays n ▷ mayday
mayflies n ▷ mayfly
mayfly n (pl -lies) short-lived aquatic insect
mayhem n (pl -s) violent destruction or confusion
mayhems n ▷ mayhem
mayonnaise n (pl -s) creamy sauce of egg yolks, oil, and vinegar
mayonnaises n ▷ mayonnaise
mayor n (pl -s) head of a municipality
mayoralties n ▷ mayoralty
mayoralty n (pl -ies) (term of) office of a mayor
mayoress n (pl -es) mayor's wife
mayoresses n ▷ mayoress
mayors n ▷ mayor
maypole n (pl -s) pole set up for dancing round on the first day of May to celebrate spring
maypoles n ▷ maypole
maze n (pl -s) complex network of paths or

lines designed to puzzle
mazes n ▷ maze
mazurka n (pl -s) lively Polish dance
mazurkas n ▷ mazurka
me pron ▷ I
mead n (pl -s) alcoholic drink made from honey
meads n ▷ mead
meadow n (pl -s) piece of grassland
meadows n ▷ meadow
meadowsweet n (pl -s) plant with dense heads of small fragrant flowers
meadowsweets n ▷ meadowsweet
meagre adj scanty or insufficient
meal[1] n (pl -s) occasion when food is served and eaten
meal[2] n (pl -s) grain ground to powder > **mealy** **-lier, -liest**) ▷ adj
mealie n (pl -s) (S AFR) maize
mealier adj ▷ meal[2]
mealies n ▷ mealie
mealiest adj ▷ meal[2]
meals n ▷ meal[1,2]
mealy adj ▷ meal[2]
mealymouthed adj not outspoken enough
mean[1] v (-s, -ing, meant) intend to convey or express > **meaningful** adj > **meaningless** adj
mean[2] adj (-er, -est) miserly, ungenerous, or petty > **meanly** adv > **meanness** n (pl -es)
mean[3] n (pl -s) middle point between two extremes ▶ pl method by which something is done ▶ adj intermediate in size or quantity
meaner adj ▷ mean[2]
meanest adj ▷ mean[2]
meaning n (pl -s) sense, significance
meaningful adj ▷ mean[1]
meaningless adj ▷ mean[1]
meanings n ▷ meaning
meanly adv ▷ mean[2]
meanness n ▷ mean[2]
meannesses n ▷ mean[2]
means v ▷ mean[1] ▶ n ▷ mean[3]
meander [mee-and-er] v (-s, -ing, -ed) follow a winding course ▶ n (pl -s) winding course
meandered v ▷ meander
meandering v ▷ meander
meanders v, n ▷ meander
meantime n (pl -s) intervening period ▶ adv meanwhile
meantimes n ▷ meantime
meanwhile adv during the intervening period
measles n infectious disease producing red spots
measly adj (Informal) meagre
measure n (pl -s) size or quantity ▶ v (-res, -ring, -red) determine the size or quantity of

> **measurable** adj
measurable adj ▷ measure
measured adj slow and steady ▶ v ▷ measure
measurement n (pl -s) measuring
measures n, v ▷ measure
measuring v ▷ measure
meat n (pl -s) animal flesh as food
meatier adj ▷ meaty
meatiest adj ▷ meaty
meats n ▷ meat
meaty adj (-tier, -tiest) (tasting) of or like meat
mechanic n (pl -s) person skilled in repairing or operating machinery
mechanical adj of or done by machines
> **mechanically** adv
mechanically adv ▷ mechanical
mechanics n scientific study of motion and force ▷ mechanic
mechanism n (pl -s) way a machine works
mechanisms n ▷ mechanism
mechanization n ▷ mechanize
mechanizations n ▷ mechanism
mechanize v (-zes, -zing, -zed) equip with machinery > **mechanization** n (pl -s)
mechanized v ▷ mechanize
mechanizes v ▷ mechanize
mechanizing v ▷ mechanize
medal n (pl -s) piece of metal with an inscription etc., given as a reward or memento
medallion n (pl -s) disc-shaped ornament worn on a chain round the neck
medallions n ▷ medallion
medallist n (pl -s) winner of a medal
medallists n ▷ medallist
medals n ▷ medal
meddle v (-les, -ling, -led) interfere annoyingly
> **meddler** n (pl -s) > **meddlesome** adj
meddled v ▷ meddle
meddler n ▷ meddle
meddlers n ▷ meddle
meddles v ▷ meddle
meddlesome adj ▷ meddle
meddling v ▷ meddle
media n (pl -iae) ▷ medium the mass media collectively
mediae n ▷ media
mediaeval adj ▷ medieval
medial adj of or in the middle
median adj, n (pl -s) middle (point or line)
medians n ▷ median
mediate v (-tes, -ting, -ted) intervene in a dispute to bring about agreement
> **mediation** n (pl -s) > **mediator** n (pl -s)
mediated v ▷ mediate

mediates v ▷ mediate
mediating v ▷ mediate
mediation n ▷ mediate
mediations n ▷ mediate
mediator n ▷ mediate
mediators n ▷ mediate
medic n (pl -s) (Informal) doctor or medical student
medics n ▷ medic
medical adj of the science of medicine
▶ n (pl -s) (Informal) medical examination
> **medically** adv
medically adv ▷ medical
medicals n ▷ medical
medicate v (-tes, -ting, -ted) treat with a medicinal substance
medicated v ▷ medicate
medicates v ▷ medicate
medicating v ▷ medicate
medication n (pl -s) (treatment with) a medicinal substance
medications n ▷ medication
medicine n (pl -s) substance used to treat disease
medicinal [med-**diss**-in-al] adj having therapeutic properties
medicines n ▷ medicine
medieval [med-ee-**eve**-al] adj of the Middle Ages
mediocre [mee-dee-**oak**-er] adj average in quality > **mediocrity** [mee-dee-**ok**-rit-ee] ▶ n (pl -ties)
mediocrities n ▷ mediocre
mediocrity n ▷ mediocre
meditate v (-tes, -ting, -ted) reflect deeply, esp. on spiritual matters > **meditation** n (pl -s) > **meditative** adj > **meditatively** adv
> **meditator** n (pl -s)
meditated v ▷ meditate
meditates v ▷ meditate
meditating v ▷ meditate
meditation n ▷ meditate
meditations n ▷ meditate
meditative adj ▷ meditate
meditatively adv ▷ meditate
meditator n ▷ meditate
meditators n ▷ meditate
medium adj midway between extremes, average ▶ n (pl -dia, -diums) middle state, degree, or condition
mediums n ▷ medium
medlar n (pl -s) apple-like fruit of a small tree, eaten when it begins to decay
medlars n ▷ medlar
medley n (pl -s) miscellaneous mixture

medleys n ▷ medley
medulla [mid-**dull**-la] n (pl -las, -lae) marrow, pith, or inner tissue
medullae n ▷ medulla
medullas n ▷ medulla
meek adj (-er, -est) submissive or humble > **meekly** adv > **meekness** n (pl -es)
meeker adj ▷ meek
meekest adj ▷ meek
meekly adv ▷ meek
meekness n ▷ meek
meeknesses n ▷ meek
meerkat n (pl -s) S African mongoose
meerkats n ▷ meerkat
meerschaum [**meer**-shum] n (pl -s) white substance like clay
meerschaums n ▷ meerschaum
meet[1] v (-s, meeting, met) come together (with) ▶ n (pl -s) meeting, esp. a sports meeting
meet[2] adj (-er, -est) (Obs) fit or suitable
meeter adj ▷ meet[2]
meetest adj ▷ meet[2]
meeting n (pl -s) coming together ▶ v ▷ meet[1]
meets v, n ▷ meek[1]
megabyte n (pl -s) (COMPUTERS) 2^{20} or 1 048 576 bytes
megabytes n ▷ megabyte
megahertz n one million hertz
megalith n (pl -s) great stone, esp. as part of a prehistoric monument ▶ **megalithic** adj
megalithic adj ▷ megalith
megaliths n ▷ megalith
megalomania n (pl -s) craving for or mental delusions of power > **megalomaniac** adj, n (pl -s)
megalomaniac n ▷ megalomania
megalomaniacs n ▷ megalomania
megalomanias n ▷ megalomania
megaphone n (pl -s) cone-shaped instrument used to amplify the voice
megaphones n ▷ megaphone
megapode n (pl -s) bird of Australia, New Guinea, and adjacent islands
megapodes n ▷ megapode
megaton n (pl -s) explosive power equal to that of one million tons of TNT
megatons n ▷ megaton
melaleuca [mel-a-**loo**-ka] n (pl -s) Australian shrub or tree with a white trunk and black branches
melaleucas n ▷ melaleuca
melancholia [mel-an-**kole**-lee-a] n (pl -s) state of depression
melancholias n ▷ melancholia

melancholic adj ▷ melancholy
melancholies n ▷ melancholy
melancholy [**mel**-an-kol-lee] n (pl -ies) sadness or gloom ▶ adj sad or gloomy > **melancholic** adj, n (pl -s)
melange [may-**lahnzh**] n (pl -s) mixture
melanges n ▷ melange
melanin n (pl -s) dark pigment found in the hair, skin, and eyes of humans and animals
melanins n ▷ melanin
mêlée [**mel**-lay] n (pl -s) noisy confused fight or crowd
mêlées n ▷ mêlée
mellifluous [mel-**lif**-flew-uss] adj (of sound) smooth and sweet
mellow adj soft, not harsh ▶ v (-s, -ing, -ed) make or become mellow
mellowed v ▷ mellow
mellowing v ▷ mellow
mellows v ▷ mellow
melodic [mel-**lod**-ik] adj of melody
melodious [mel-**lode**-ee-uss] adj pleasing to the ear
melodrama n (pl -s) play full of extravagant action and emotion > **melodramatic** adj
melodramas n ▷ melodrama
melodramatic adj ▷ melodrama
melody n (pl -dies) series of musical notes which make a tune
melon n (pl -s) large round juicy fruit with a hard rind
melons n ▷ melon
melt v (-s, -ing, -ed) (cause to) become liquid by heat
meltdown n (pl -s) (in a nuclear reactor) melting of the fuel rods, with the possible release of radiation
meltdowns n ▷ meltdown
melted v ▷ melt
melting v ▷ melt
melts v ▷ melt
member n (pl -s) individual making up a body or society > **membership** n (pl -s)
members n ▷ member
membership n ▷ member
memberships n ▷ member
membrane n (pl -s) thin flexible tissue in a plant or animal body > **membranous** adj
membranes n ▷ membrane
membranous adj ▷ membrane
memento n (pl -tos, -toes) thing serving to remind, souvenir
mementoes n ▷ memento
mementos n ▷ memento
memo n (pl -s) ▷ memorandum

memos n ▷ memo

memoir [**mem**-wahr] n (pl -s) biography or historical account based on personal knowledge ► pl collection of these

memoirs n ▷ memoir

memorable adj worth remembering, noteworthy > **memorably** adv

memorably adv ▷ memorable

memoranda n ▷ memorandum

memorandum n (pl -dums, -da) written record or communication within a business

memorandums n ▷ memorandum

memorial n (pl -s) something serving to commemorate a person or thing ► adj serving as a memorial

memorials n ▷ memorandum

memorize v (-zes, -zing, -zed) commit to memory

memorized v ▷ memorize

memorizes v ▷ memorize

memorizing v ▷ memorize

memory n (pl -ries) ability to remember

men n ▷ man

menace n (pl -s) threat ► v (-ces, -cing, -ced) threaten, endanger > **menacing** adj

menaced v ▷ menace

menaces n, v ▷ menace

menacing v, adj ▷ menace

ménage [may-**nahzh**] n (pl -s) household

ménages n ▷ ménage

menagerie [min-**naj**-er-ee] n (pl -s) collection of wild animals for exhibition

menageries n ▷ menagerie

mend v (-s, -ing, -ed) repair or patch ► n (pl -s) mended area

mendacious adj ▷ mendacity

mendacities n ▷ mendacity

mendacity n (pl -ties) (tendency to) untruthfulness > **mendacious** adj

mended v ▷ mend

mendicant adj begging ► n (pl -s) beggar

mendicants n ▷ mendicant

mending v ▷ mend

mends v, n ▷ mend

menhir [**men**-hear] n (pl -s) single upright prehistoric stone

menhirs n ▷ menhir

menial [**mean**-nee-al] adj involving boring work of low status ► n (pl -s) person with a menial job

menials n ▷ menial

meningitis [men-in-**jite**-iss] n (pl -es) inflammation of the membranes of the brain

meningitises n ▷ meningitis

meniscus n (pl -ci) curved surface of a liquid

menisci n ▷ meniscus

menopausal adj ▷ menopause

menopause n (pl -s) time when a woman's menstrual cycle ceases > **menopausal** adj

menopauses n ▷ menopause

menservants n ▷ manservant

menstruation n (pl -s) approximately monthly discharge of blood and cellular debris from the womb of a nonpregnant woman > **menstruate** v (-tes, -ting, -ted) > **menstrual** adj

menstrual adj ▷ menstruation

menstruated v ▷ menstruation

menstruates v ▷ menstruation

menstruating v ▷ menstruation

menstruations n ▷ menstruation

mensuration n (pl -s) measuring, esp. in geometry

mensurations n ▷ mensuration

mental adj of, in, or done by the mind > **mentally** adv

mentalities n ▷ mentality

mentality n (pl -ties) way of thinking

mentally adv ▷ mental

menthol n (pl -s) organic compound found in peppermint, used medicinally

menthols n ▷ menthol

mention v (-s, -ing, -ed) refer to briefly ► n (pl -s) brief reference to a person or thing

mentioned v ▷ mention

mentioning v ▷ mention

mentions v, n ▷ mention

mentor n (pl -s) adviser or guide

mentors n ▷ mentor

menu n (pl -s) list of dishes to be served, or from which to order

menus n ▷ menu

mercantile adj of trade or traders

mercenaries n ▷ mercenary

mercenary adj influenced by greed ► n (pl -ries) hired soldier

merchandises n ▷ merchandise

merchandise n (pl -s) commodities

merchant n (pl -s) person engaged in trade, wholesale trader

merchantman n (pl -men) trading ship

merchantmen n ▷ merchantman

merchants n ▷ merchant

merciful adj compassionate

merciless adj ▷ mercy

mercurial adj lively, changeable

mercuries n ▷ mercury

mercury n (pl -s) (CHEM) silvery liquid metal

mercy n (pl -cies) compassionate treatment of an offender or enemy who is in one's power

> **merciless** adj

mere¹ adj (-r, -st) nothing more than > **merely** adv

mere² n (pl -s) (BRIT) (Obs) lake
merely adv ▷ mere¹
merer adj ▷ mere¹
meres n ▷ mere²
merest adj ▷ mere¹

meretricious adj superficially or garishly attractive but of no real value

merganser [mer-**gan**-ser] n (pl -s) large crested diving duck
mergansers n ▷ merganser

merge v (-ges, -ging, -ged) combine or blend
merged v ▷ merge

merger n (pl -s) combination of business firms into one
mergers n ▷ merger
merges v ▷ merge
merging v ▷ merge
mergings n ▷ merge

meridian n (pl -s) imaginary circle of the earth passing through both poles
meridians n ▷ meridian

meringue [mer-**rang**] n (pl -s) baked mixture of egg whites and sugar
meringues n ▷ meringue

merino n (pl -s) breed of sheep with soft wool
merinos n ▷ merino

merit n (pl -s) excellence or worth ▶ pl admirable qualities ▶ v (-s, -ing, -ed) deserve
merited v ▷ merit
meriting v ▷ merit
meritocracies n ▷ meritocracy

meritocracy [mer-it-**tok**-rass-ee] n (pl -s) rule by people of superior talent or intellect
meritorious adj deserving praise
merits n, v ▷ merit

merlin n (pl -s) small falcon
merlins n ▷ merlin

mermaid n (pl -s) imaginary sea creature with the upper part of a woman and the lower part of a fish
mermaids n ▷ mermaid
merrier adj ▷ merry
merriest adj ▷ merry
merrily adv ▷ merry
merriment n ▷ merry
merriments n ▷ merry

merry adj (-rier, -rriest) cheerful or jolly > **merrily** adv > **merriment** n (pl -s)

merrymaking n (pl -s) noisy, cheerful celebrations or fun
merrymakings n ▷ merrymaking
mesdames n ▷ madame

mesdemoiselles n ▷ mademoiselle

mesh n (pl -es) network or net ▶ v (-es, -ing, -ed) (of gear teeth) engage
meshed v ▷ mesh
meshes n, v ▷ mesh
meshing v ▷ mesh

mesmerize v (-zes, -zing, -zed) hold spellbound
mesmerized v ▷ mesmerize
mesmerizes v ▷ mesmerize
mesmerizing v ▷ mesmerize

meson [**mee**-zon] n (pl -s) elementary atomic particle
mesons n ▷ meson

mess n (pl -es) untidy or dirty confusion ▶ v (-es, -ing, -ed) muddle or dirty
message n (pl -s) communication sent
messages n ▷ message

messaging n (pl -s) sending and receiving of textual communications by mobile phone
messagings n ▷ message
messed v ▷ mess
messeigneurs n ▷ monseigneur

messenger n (pl -s) bearer of a message
messengers n ▷ messenger
messes n, v ▷ mess

messiah n (pl -s) promised deliverer > **messianic** adj
messiahs n ▷ messiah
messianic adj ▷ messiah
messier adj ▷ messy
messiest adj ▷ messy
messieurs n ▷ monsieur
messily adv ▷ messy
messing v ▷ mess

messy adj (-ssier, -ssiest) dirty, confused, or untidy > **messily** adv
met v ▷ meet¹
metabolic adj ▷ metabolism

metabolism [met-**tab**-oh-liz-zum] n (pl -s) chemical processes of a living body > **metabolic** adj
metabolisms n ▷ metabolism

metabolize v (-zes, -zing, -zed) produce or be produced by metabolism
metabolized v ▷ metabolize
metabolizes v ▷ metabolize
metabolizing v ▷ metabolize

metal n (pl -s) chemical element, such as iron or copper, that is malleable and capable of conducting heat and electricity > **metallic** adj
metallic adj ▷ metal
metallurgical adj ▷ metallurgy
metallurgist n ▷ metallurgy
metallurgists n ▷ metallurgy

metallurgy n (pl -gies) scientific study of the structure, properties, extraction, and refining of metals > **metallurgical** adj
> **metallurgist** n (pl -s)
metals n ▷ metal
metamorphic adj (of rocks) changed in texture or structure by heat and pressure
metamorphose v (-ses, -sing, -sed) transform
metamorphosed v ▷ metamorphose
metamorphoses n, v ▷ metamorphosis
metamorphosing v ▷ metamorphose
metamorphosis [met-a-**more**-foss-is] n (pl -ses) [-foss-eez] change of form or character
metaphor n (pl -s) figure of speech in which a term is applied to something it does not literally denote in order to imply a resemblance > **metaphorical** adj
> **metaphorically** adv
metaphorically adv ▷ metaphor
metaphors n ▷ metaphor
metaphysical adj ▷ metaphysics
metaphysics n branch of philosophy concerned with being and knowing
> **metaphysical** adj
mete v (-tes, -ting, -ted) (usu. with **out**) deal out as punishment
meted v ▷ mete
meteor n (pl -s) small fast-moving heavenly body, visible as a streak of incandescence if it enters the earth's atmosphere
meteoric [meet-ee-**or**-rik] adj of a meteor
meteorite n (pl -s) meteor that has fallen to earth
meteorites n ▷ meteorite
meteorological adj ▷ meteorology
meteorologies n ▷ meteorology
meteorologist n ▷ meteorology
meteorologists n ▷ meteorology
meteorology n (pl -gies) study of the earth's atmosphere, esp. for weather forecasting
> **meteorological** adj > **meteorologist** n (pl -s)
meteors n ▷ meteor
meter n (pl -s) instrument for measuring and recording something, such as the consumption of gas or electricity ▶ v (-s, -ing, -ed) measure by meter
meters n, v ▷ meter
metes v ▷ mete
meting v ▷ mete
methane n (pl -s) colourless inflammable gas
methanes n ▷ methane
methanol n (pl -s) colourless poisonous liquid used as a solvent and fuel (also **methyl alcohol**)
methanols n ▷ methanol

methinks v (past tense methought) (Obs) it seems to me
method n (pl -s) way or manner
methodical adj orderly > **methodically** adv
methodically adv ▷ methodical
methodism n ▷ methodist
methodisms n ▷ methodist
methodist n (pl -s) member of any of the Protestant churches originated by John Wesley and his followers ▶ adj of methodists or their Church > **methodism** n (pl -s)
methodists n ▷ methodist
methodologies n ▷ methodology
methodology n (pl -gies) particular method or procedure
methods n ▷ method
meths n (Informal) methylated spirits
methyl n (pl -s) (compound containing) a saturated hydrocarbon group of atoms
methyls n ▷ methyl
meticulous adj very careful about details
> **meticulously** adv
meticulously adv ▷ meticulous
métier [met-ee-ay] n (pl -s) profession or trade
métiers n ▷ métier
metonymies n ▷ metonymy
metonymy [mit-**on**-im-ee] n (pl -mies) figure of speech in which one thing is replaced by another associated with it, such as 'the Crown' for 'the queen'
metre n (pl -s) basic unit of length equal to about 1.094 yards (100 centimetres)
metres n ▷ metre
metric adj of the decimal system of weights and measures based on the metre
metrical adj of measurement
metrication n (pl -s) conversion to the metric system
metrications n ▷ metrication
metronome n (pl -s) instrument which marks musical time by means of a ticking pendulum
metronomes n ▷ metronome
metropolis [mit-**trop**-oh-liss] n (pl -es) chief city of a country or region
metropolises n ▷ metropolis
metropolitan adj of a metropolis
metrosexual adj, n (pl -s) (of) a heterosexual man who is preoccupied with his appearance
metrosexuals n ▷ metrosexual
mettle n (pl -s) courage or spirit
mettles n ▷ mettle
mew n (pl -s) cry of a cat ▶ v (-s, -ing, -ed) utter this cry
mewed v ▷ mew
mewing v ▷ mew

mews *n, v* ▷ mew

> **mezquit (mezquit).** A mezquit is a small spiny tree or shrub. With its combination of Q and Z, mezquit is a very high-scoring word. As it contains seven letters, mezquit can earn you a bonus of 50 points if you manage to use all the letters on your rack to form it. Mezquit scores 28 points.

mezzanine [mez-zan-een] *n* (*pl* -s) intermediate storey, esp. between the ground and first floor
mezzanines *n* ▷ mezzanine
mezzotint [met-so-tint] *n* (*pl* -s) method of engraving by scraping the roughened surface of a metal plate
mezzotints *n* ▷ mezzotint

> **mi** *n* (**mis**). Mi is the third degree of a major scale in music. This isn't a high-scoring word, but can be very helpful when you want to form words in more than one direction. Mi scores 4 points.

miaow [mee-ow] *n* (*pl* -s) ▶ *v* (-s, -ing, -wed) ▷ mew
miaowed *v* ▷ miaow
miaowing *v* ▷ miaow
miaows *v, n* ▷ miaow
miasma [mee-azz-ma] *n* (*pl* -mata) unwholesome or foreboding atmosphere
miasmata *n* ▷ miasma
mica [my-ka] *n* (*pl* -s) glasslike mineral used as an electrical insulator
micas *n* ▷ mica
mice *n* ▷ mouse
microbe *n* (*pl* -s) minute organism, esp. one causing disease > **microbial** *adj*
microbes *n* ▷ microbe
microbial *adj* ▷ microbe
microchip *n* (*pl* -s) small wafer of silicon containing electronic circuits
microchips *n* ▷ microchip
microcomputer *n* (*pl* -s) computer with a central processing unit contained in one or more silicon chips
microcomputers *n* ▷ microcomputer
microcosm *n* (*pl* -s) miniature representation of something
microcosms *n* ▷ microcosm
microfiche [my-kroh-feesh] *n* (*pl* -s) microfilm in sheet form
microfiches *n* ▷ microfiche
microfilm *n* (*pl* -s) miniaturized recording of books or documents on a roll of film
microfilms *n* ▷ microfilm
microlight *n* (*pl* -s) very small light private

aircraft with large wings
microlights *n* ▷ microlight
micrometer [my-krom-it-er] *n* (*pl* -s) instrument for measuring very small distances or angles
micrometers *n* ▷ micrometer
micron [my-kron] *n* (*pl* -s) one millionth of a metre
microns *n* ▷ micron
microorganism *n* (*pl* -ms) organism of microscopic size
microorganisms *n* ▷ microorganism
microphone *n* (*pl* -s) instrument for amplifying or transmitting sounds
microphones *n* ▷ microphone
microprocessor *n* (*pl* -s) integrated circuit acting as the central processing unit in a small computer
microprocessors *n* ▷ microprocessor
microscope *n* (*pl* -s) instrument with lens(es) which produces a magnified image of a very small object > **microscopic** *adj* too small to be seen except with a microscope > **microscopically** *adv*
microscopes *n* ▷ microscope
microscopic *adj* ▷ microscope
microscopically *adv* ▷ microscope
microscopies *n* ▷ microscopy
microscopy *n* (*pl* -pies) use of a microscope
microsurgeries *n* ▷ microsurgery
microsurgery *n* (*pl* -ries) intricate surgery using a special microscope and miniature precision instruments
microwave *n* (*pl* -s) electromagnetic wave with a wavelength of a few centimetres, used in radar and cooking ▶ *v* (-ves, -ving, -ved) cook in a microwave oven
microwaved *v* ▷ microwave
microwaves *n, v* ▷ microwave
microwaving *v* ▷ microwave
mid *adj* intermediate, middle
midday *n* (*pl* -s) noon
middays *n* ▷ midday
midden *n* (*pl* -s) (BRIT & AUST) dunghill or rubbish heap
middens *n* ▷ midden
middle *adj* equidistant from two extremes ▶ *n* (*pl* -s) middle point or part
middleman *n* (*pl* -men) trader who buys from the producer and sells to the consumer
middlemen *n* ▷ middleman
middles *n* ▷ middle
middleweight *n* (*pl* -s) boxer weighing up to 16olb (professional) or 75kg (amateur)
middleweights *n* ▷ middleweight

middling adj mediocre
midge n (pl -s) small mosquito-like insect
  midges n ▷ midge
midget n (pl -s) very small person or thing
  midgets n ▷ midget
midland n (pl -s) (BRIT, AUST & US) middle part
  of a country
  midlands n ▷ midland
midnight n (pl -s) twelve o'clock at night
  midnights n ▷ midnight
midriff n (pl -s) middle part of the body
  midriffs n ▷ midriff
midshipman n (pl -men) naval officer of the
  lowest commissioned rank
  midshipmen n ▷ midshipman
midsummer n (pl -s) middle of summer
  midsummers n ▷ midsummer
midway adj, adv halfway
midwife n (pl -wives) trained person who
  assists at childbirth > **midwifery** n (pl -ries)
  midwiferies n ▷ midwife
  midwifery n ▷ midwife
  midwives n ▷ midwife
midwinter n (pl -s) middle or depth of winter
  midwinters n ▷ midwinter
mien [mean] n (pl -s) (Lit) person's bearing,
  demeanour, or appearance
  miens n ▷ mien
miffed adj (Informal) offended or upset
might¹ ▷ may
might² n (pl -s) power or strength
  mightier adj ▷ mighty
  mightiest adj ▷ mighty
  mightily adv ▷ mighty
mighty adj (-tier, -tiest) powerful ▶ adv (US &
  AUST) (Informal) very > **mightily** adv
migraine [mee-grain] n (pl -s) severe headache,
  often with nausea and visual disturbances
  migraines n ▷ migraine
migrant n (pl -s) person or animal that moves
  from one place to another ▶ adj moving from
  one place to another
  migrants n ▷ migrant
migrate v (-tes, -ting, -ted) move from one
  place to settle in another > **migration** n (pl -s)
  migrated v ▷ migrate
  migrates v ▷ migrate
  migrating v ▷ migrate
  migration n ▷ migrate
  migrations n ▷ migrate
migratory adj (of an animal) migrating every
  year
mike n (pl -s) (Informal) microphone
  mikes n ▷ mike
milch adj (CHIEFLY BRIT) (of a cow) giving milk

mild adj (-er, -est) not strongly flavoured
  > **mildly** adv **mildness** n (pl -es)
  milder adj ▷ mild
  mildest adj ▷ mild
mildew n (pl -s) destructive fungus on plants
  or things exposed to damp > **mildewed** adj
  mildewed adj ▷ mildew
  mildews n ▷ mildew
  mildly adv ▷ mild
  mildness n ▷ mild
  mildnesses n ▷ mild
mile n (pl -s) unit of length equal to 1760 yards
  or 1.609 kilometres
mileage n (pl -s) distance travelled in miles
  mileages n ▷ mileage
mileometer n (pl -s) (BRIT) device that records
  the number of miles a vehicle has travelled
  mileometers n ▷ mileometer
  miles n ▷ mile
milestone n (pl -s) significant event
  milestones n ▷ milestone
milieu [meal-yer] n (pl milieux, milieus) [meal-
  yerz] environment or surroundings
  milieus n ▷ milieu
  milieux n ▷ milieu
  militancies n ▷ militant
  militancy n ▷ militant
militant adj aggressive or vigorous in support
  of a cause > **militancy** n (pl -cies)
  militants n ▷ militant
  militaries n ▷ military
militarism n (pl -s) belief in the use of military
  force and methods
  militarisms n ▷ militarism
  militarist n ▷ military
  militarists n ▷ military
  militarized adj ▷ military
military adj of or for soldiers, armies, or war
  ▶ n (pl -ries) armed services > **militarist** n (pl
  -s) > **militarized** adj
militate v (-tes, -ting, -ted) (usu. with **against**
  or **for**) have a strong influence or effect
  militated v ▷ militate
  militates v ▷ militate
  militating v ▷ militate
militia [mill-ish-a] n (pl -s) military force of
  trained citizens for use in emergency only
  militias n ▷ militia
milk n (pl -s) white fluid produced by female
  mammals to feed their young ▶ v (-s, -ing, -ed)
  draw milk from > **milky** adj (-kier, -kiest)
  milked v ▷ milk
  milkier adj ▷ milk
  milkiest adj ▷ milk
  milking v ▷ milk

milkmaid n (pl -s) (esp. in former times) woman who milks cows
milkmaids n ▷ milkmaid
milkman n (pl -men) (BRIT, AUST & NZ) man who delivers milk to people's houses
milkmen n ▷ milkman
milks n, v ▷ milk
milkshake n (pl -s) frothy flavoured cold milk drink
milkshakes n ▷ milkshake
milksop n (pl -s) feeble man
milksops n ▷ milk
milky adj ▷ milk
mill n (pl -s) factory ▶ v (-s, -ing, -ed) grind, press, or process in or as if in a mill
milled v ▷ mill
millennium n (pl -nnia, -nniums) period of a thousand years
millennia n ▷ mill
millenniums n ▷ mill
miller n (pl -s) person who works in a mill
millers n ▷ miller
millet n (pl -s) type of cereal grass
millets n ▷ millet
millibar n (pl -s) unit of atmospheric pressure
millibars n ▷ millibar
millimetre n (pl -s) thousandth part of a metre
millimetres n ▷ millimetre
milliner n (pl -s) maker or seller of women's hats > **millinery** n (pl -ries)
millineries n ▷ milliner
milliners n ▷ milliner
millinery n ▷ milliner
milling v ▷ mill
million n (pl -s) one thousand thousands
> **millionth** adj, n (pl -s)
millionaire n (pl -s) person who owns at least a million pounds, dollars, etc.
millionaires n ▷ millionaire
millions n ▷ million
millionths n ▷ million
millipede n (pl -s) small animal with a jointed body and many pairs of legs
millipedes n ▷ millipede
mills n, v ▷ mill
millstone n (pl -s) flat circular stone for grinding corn
millstones n ▷ millstone
millwheel n (pl -s) waterwheel that drives a mill
millwheels n ▷ millwheel
milometer n (pl -s) (BRIT) ▷ mileometer
milometers n ▷ milometer
milt n (pl -s) sperm of fish
milts n ▷ milt

mime n (pl -s) acting without the use of words ▶ v (-mes, -ming, -med) act in mime
mimed v ▷ mime
mimes n, v ▷ mime
miming v ▷ mime
mimic v (-ics, -icking, -icked) imitate (a person or manner), esp. for satirical effect ▶ n (pl -s) person or animal that is good at mimicking
> **mimicry** n (pl -ries)
mimicked v ▷ mimic
mimicking v ▷ mimic
mimicry n ▷ mimic
mimics n, v ▷ mimic
mina n ▷ myna
minas n ▷ myna
minaret n (pl -s) tall slender tower of a mosque
minarets n ▷ minaret
mince v (-ces, -cing, -ced) cut or grind into very small pieces ▶ n (pl -s) minced meat
minced v ▷ mince
mincemeat n (pl -s) sweet mixture of dried fruit and spices
mincemeats n ▷ mincemeat
mincer n (pl -s) machine for mincing meat
mincers n ▷ mince
minces v, n ▷ mince
mincing adj affected in manner ▶ v ▷ mince
mind n (pl -s) thinking faculties ▶ v (-s, -ing, -ed) take offence at
minded adj having an inclination as specified ▶ v ▷ mind
minder n (pl -s) (Informal) aide or bodyguard
minders n ▷ minder
mindful adj heedful
minding v ▷ mind
mindless adj stupid
minds n, v ▷ mind
mine[1] pron belonging to me
mine[2] n (pl -s) deep hole for digging out coal, ores, etc. ▶ v (-nes, -ning, -ned) dig for minerals
mined v ▷ mine
minefield n (pl -s) area of land or water containing mines
minefields n ▷ minefield
miner n (pl -s) person who works in a mine
mineral n (pl -s) naturally occurring inorganic substance, such as metal ▶ adj of, containing, or like minerals
mineralogies n ▷ mineralogy
mineralogy [min-er-al-a-jee] n (pl -gies) study of minerals
minerals n ▷ mineral
miners n ▷ miner
mines n, v ▷ mine

minestrone [min-ness-**strone**-ee] n (pl -s) soup containing vegetables and pasta
minestrones n ▷ minestrone
minesweeper n (pl -s) ship for clearing away mines
minesweepers n ▷ minesweeper
mining v ▷ mine
minger n (pl -s) (BRIT) (Informal) unattractive person
mingers n ▷ minger
mingier adj ▷ mingy
mingiest adj ▷ mingy
minging adj (BRIT) (Informal) unattractive or unpleasant
mingle v (-les, -ling, -led) mix or blend
mingled v ▷ mingle
mingles v ▷ mingle
mingling v ▷ mingle
mingy adj (-gier, -giest) (Informal) miserly
mini n (pl -s) ▶ adj (-ier, -iest) (something) small or miniature
minier adj ▷ mini
miniest adj ▷ mini
minis n ▷ mini
miniature n (pl -s) small portrait, model, or copy ▶ adj small-scale > **miniaturist** n (pl -s)
miniatures n ▷ miniature
miniaturist n ▷ miniature
miniaturists n ▷ miniature
miniaturize v (-zes, -zing, -zed) make to a very small scale
miniaturized v ▷ miniaturize
miniaturizes v ▷ miniaturize
miniaturizing v ▷ miniaturize
minibar n (pl -s) selection of drinks and confectionery provided in a hotel room
minibus n (pl -es) small bus
minibuses n ▷ minibus
minicab n (pl -s) (BRIT) ordinary car used as a taxi
minicabs n ▷ minicab
minicomputer n (pl -s) computer smaller than a mainframe but more powerful than a microcomputer
minicomputers n ▷ minicomputer
minidisc n (pl -s) small recordable compact disc
minidiscs n ▷ minidisc
minim n (pl -s) (MUSIC) note half the length of a semibreve
minima n ▷ minimum
minimal adj minimum
minimize v (-zes, -zing, -zed) reduce to a minimum
minimized v ▷ minimize

minimizes v ▷ minimize
minimizing v ▷ minimize
minims n ▷ minim
minimum adj, n (pl -mums, -ma) least possible (amount or number)
minimums n ▷ minimum
minion n (pl -s) servile assistant
minions n ▷ minion
miniseries n (pl -ries) TV programme shown in several parts, often on consecutive days
miniseries n ▷ miniseries
minister n (pl -s) head of a government department ▶ v (-s, -ing, -ed) (foll. by **to**) attend to the needs of > **ministerial** adj
ministered v ▷ minister
ministerial adj ▷ minister
ministering v ▷ minister
ministers n, v ▷ minister
ministration n (pl -s) giving of help
ministrations n ▷ ministration
ministries n ▷ ministry
ministry n (pl -tries) profession or duties of a clergyman
mink n stoatlike animal
minnow n (pl -s) small freshwater fish
minnows n ▷ minnow
minor adj lesser ▶ n (pl -s) person regarded legally as a child
minorities n ▷ minority
minority n (pl -ties) lesser number
minors n ▷ minor
minster n (pl -s) (BRIT) cathedral or large church
minsters n ▷ minster
minstrel n (pl -s) medieval singer or musician
minstrels n ▷ minstrel
mint¹ n (pl -s) plant with aromatic leaves used for seasoning and flavouring
mint² n place where money is coined ▶ v (-s, -ing, -ed) make (coins)
minted v ▷ mint²
minting v ▷ mint²
mints n ▷ mint¹,² ▶ v ▷²
minuet [min-new-**wet**] n (pl -s) stately dance
minuets n ▷ minuet
minus prep, adj indicating subtraction ▶ adj less than zero ▶ n (pl -es) sign (-) denoting subtraction or a number less than zero
minuses n ▷ minus
minuscule [min-niss-skyool] adj very small
minute¹ [min-it] n (pl -s) 60th part of an hour or degree ▶ pl record of the proceedings of a meeting ▶ v (-tes, -ting, -ted) record in the minutes
minute² [my-**newt**] adj (-r, -st) very small
> **minutely** adv

minuted v ▷ minute¹
minutely adv ▷ minute²
minuter adj ▷ minute²
minutes n, v ▷ minute¹
minutest adj ▷ minute²
minutiae [my-**new**-shee-eye] pl n trifling or precise details
minuting v ▷ minute¹
minx n (pl -es) bold or flirtatious girl
minxes n ▷ minx
miracle n (pl -s) wonderful supernatural event
> **miraculous** adj > **miraculously** adv
miracles n ▷ miracle
miraculous adj ▷ miracle
miraculously adv ▷ miracle
mirage [mir-**rahzh**] n (pl -s) optical illusion, esp. one caused by hot air
mirages n ▷ mirage
mire n (pl -s) swampy ground
mires n ▷ mire
mirror n (pl -s) coated glass surface for reflecting images ▶ v (-s, -ing, -ed) reflect in or as if in a mirror
mirrored v ▷ mirror
mirroring v ▷ mirror
mirrors n, v ▷ mirror
mirth n (pl -s) laughter, merriment, or gaiety
> **mirthful** adj > **mirthless** adj
mirthful adv ▷ mirth
mirthless adj ▷ mirth
mirths n ▷ mirth
misadventure n (pl -s) unlucky chance
misadventures n ▷ misadventure
misanthrope [miz-zan-thrope] n (pl -s) person who dislikes people in general
> **misanthropic** [miz-zan-**throp**-ik] ▶ adj
> **misanthropy** [miz-**zan**-throp-ee] ▶ n (pl -pies)
misanthropes n ▷ misanthrope
misanthropies n ▷ misanthrope
misanthropic adj ▷ misanthrope
misanthropy n ▷ misanthrope
misapprehend v (-s, -ing, -ed) misunderstand ▶ **misapprehension** n (pl -s)
misapprehended v ▷ misapprehend
misapprehending v ▷ misapprehend
misapprehends v ▷ misapprehend
misapprehension n ▷ misapprehend
misapprehensions n ▷ misapprehend
misappropriate v (-tes, -ting, -ted) take and use (money) dishonestly ▶ **misappropriation** n (pl -s)
misappropriated v ▷ misappropriate
misappropriates v ▷ misappropriate
misappropriating v ▷ misappropriate
misappropriation n ▷ misappropriate

misappropriations n ▷ misappropriate
miscarriage n (pl -s) spontaneous premature expulsion of a fetus from the womb
miscarriages n ▷ miscarriage
miscarried v ▷ miscarry
miscarries v ▷ miscarry
miscarry v (-ries, -rying, -ried) have a miscarriage
miscarrying v ▷ miscarry
miscast v (-s, -ing, -cast) cast (a role or actor) in (a play or film) inappropriately
miscasting v ▷ miscast
miscasts v ▷ miscast
miscegenation [miss-ij-in-**nay**-shun] n (pl -s) interbreeding of races
miscegenations n ▷ miscegenation
miscellaneous [miss-sell-**lane**-ee-uss] adj mixed or assorted
miscellanies n ▷ miscellany
miscellany [miss-**sell**-a-nee] n (pl -nies) mixed assortment
mischance n (pl -es) unlucky event
mischances n ▷ mischance
mischief n (pl -s) annoying but not malicious behaviour
mischiefs n ▷ mischief
mischievous adj full of mischief
> **mischievously** adv
mischievously adv ▷ mischievous
miscible [**miss**-sib-bl] adj able to be mixed
misconception n (pl -s) wrong idea or belief
misconceptions n ▷ misconception
misconduct n (pl -s) immoral or unethical behaviour
misconducts n ▷ misconduct
miscreant [**miss**-kree-ant] n (pl -s) wrongdoer
miscreants n ▷ miscreant
misdeed n (pl -s) wrongful act
misdeeds n ▷ misdeed
misdemeanour n (pl -s) minor wrongdoing
misdemeanours n ▷ misdemeanour
miser n (pl -s) person who hoards money and hates spending it ▶ **miserly** adj
miserable adj very unhappy, wretched
miseries adj ▷ misery
miserly adj ▷ miser
misers n ▷ miser
misery n (pl -ries) great unhappiness
misfire v (-res, -ring, -red) (of a firearm or engine) fail to fire correctly
misfired v ▷ misfire
misfires v ▷ misfire
misfiring v ▷ misfire
misfit n (pl -s) person not suited to his or her social environment

misfits n ▷ misfit
misfortune n (pl -s) (piece of) bad luck
misfortunes n ▷ misfortune
misgiving n (pl -s) feeling of fear or doubt
misgivings n ▷ misgiving
misguided adj mistaken or unwise
mishandle v (-les, -ling, -led) handle badly or inefficiently
mishandled v ▷ mishandle
mishandles v ▷ mishandle
mishandling v ▷ mishandle
mishap n (pl -s) minor accident
mishaps n ▷ mishap
misinform v (-s, -ing, -ed) give incorrect information to ▷ **misinformation** n (pl -s)
misinformation n ▷ misinform
misinformations n ▷ misinform
misinformed v ▷ misinform
misinforming v ▷ misinform
misinforms v ▷ misinform
misjudge v (-ges, -ging, -ged) judge wrongly or unfairly ▷ **misjudgment, misjudgement** n (pl -s)
misjudged v ▷ misjudge
misjudgement n ▷ misjudge
misjudges v ▷ misjudge
misjudging v ▷ misjudge
misjudgment n ▷ misjudge
mislaid v ▷ mislay
mislay v (-s, -ing, -laid) lose (something) temporarily
mislaying v ▷ mislay
mislays v ▷ mislay
mislead v (-s, -ing, -led) give false or confusing information to ▷ **misleading** adj
misleading v, adj ▷ mislead
misleads v ▷ mislead
misled v ▷ mislead
mismanage v (-ges, -ging, -ged) organize or run (something) badly ▷ **mismanagement** n (pl -s)
mismanaged v ▷ mismanage
mismanagement n ▷ mismanage
mismanagements n ▷ mismanage
mismanages v ▷ mismanage
mismanaging v ▷ mismanage
misnomer [miss-no-mer] n (pl -s) incorrect or unsuitable name
misnomers n ▷ misnomer
misogyny [miss-oj-in-ee] n (pl -nies) hatred of women ▷ **misogynist** n (pl -s)
misogynies n ▷ misogyny
misogynist n ▷ misogyny
misogynists n ▷ misogyny
misplace v (-ces, -cing, -ced) mislay

misplaced v ▷ misplace
misplaces v ▷ misplace
misplacing v ▷ misplace
misprint n (pl -s) printing error
misprints n ▷ misprint
misrepresent v (-s, -ing, -ed) represent wrongly or inaccurately
misrepresented v ▷ misrepresent
misrepresenting v ▷ misrepresent
misrepresents v ▷ misrepresent
miss v (-es, -ing, -ed) fail to notice, hear, hit, reach, find, or catch ▶ n (pl -es) fact or instance of missing
missed v ▷ miss
misses v, n ▷ miss
missing adj lost or absent ▶ v ▷ miss
missal n (pl -s) book containing the prayers and rites of the Mass
missals n ▷ missal
misshapen adj badly shaped, deformed
missile n (pl -s) object or weapon thrown, shot, or launched at a target
missiles n ▷ missile
mission n (pl -s) specific task or duty
missionaries n ▷ mission
missionary n (pl -ries) person sent abroad to do religious and social work
missions n ▷ mission
missive n (pl -s) letter
missives n ▷ missive
misspent adj wasted or misused
mist n (pl -s) thin fog
mists n ▷ mist
mistake n (pl -s) error or blunder ▶ v (-takes, -taking, -took, -taken) misunderstand
mistaken v ▷ mistake
mistakes n, v ▷ mistake
mistaking v ▷ mistake
mister n (pl -s) an informal form of address for a man
misters n ▷ mister
mistier adj ▷ misty
mistiest adj ▷ misty
mistletoe n (pl -s) evergreen plant with white berries growing as a parasite on trees
mistletoes n ▷ mistletoe
mistook v ▷ mistake
mistral n (pl -s) strong dry northerly wind of S France
mistrals n ▷ mistral
mistress n (pl -es) woman who has a continuing sexual relationship with a married man
mistresses n ▷ mistress
mistrial n (pl -s) (LAW) trial made void because

of some error

mistrials n ▷ mistrial

mistrust v (-s, -ing, -ed) have doubts or suspicions about ▶ n (pl -s) lack of trust
> **mistrustful** adj

mistrusted v ▷ mistrust

mistrustful adj ▷ mistrust

mistrusting v ▷ mistrust

mistrusts v, n ▷ mistrust

misty adj full of mist

misunderstand v (-stands, -standing, -stood) fail to understand properly
> **misunderstanding** n (pl -s)

misunderstanding v, n ▷ misunderstand

misunderstandings n ▷ misunderstand

misunderstands v ▷ misunderstand

misunderstood v ▷ misunderstand

misuse n (pl -s) incorrect, improper, or careless use ▶ v (-es, -sing, -sed) use wrongly

misused v ▷ misuse

misuses n, v ▷ misuse

misusing v ▷ misuse

mite n (pl -s) very small spider-like animal

mites n ▷ mite

mitigate v (-tes, -ting, -ted) make less severe
> **mitigation** n (pl -s)

mitigated v ▷ mitigate

mitigating v ▷ mitigate

mitigates v ▷ mitigate

mitigation n ▷ mitigate

mitigations n ▷ mitigate

mitre [my-ter] n (pl -s) bishop's pointed headdress ▶ v (-res, -ring, -red) join with a mitre joint

mitred v ▷ mitre

mitres n, v ▷ mitre

mitring v ▷ mitre

mitt n (pl -s) baseball catcher's glove

mitts n ▷ mitt

mitten n (pl -s) glove with one section for the thumb and one for the four fingers together

mittens n ▷ mitten

mix v (-es, -ing, -ed) combine or blend into one mass ▶ n (pl -es) mixture > **mixed** adj > **mixup** n (pl -s) > **mixer** n (pl -s)

mixed v, adj ▷ mix

mixer n ▷ mix

mixers n ▷ mix

mixes v, n ▷ mix

mixing v ▷ mix

mixture n (pl -s) something mixed

mixtures n ▷ mixture

mixup n ▷ mix

mixups n ▷ mix

▓ **miz** n (**mizzes**). Miz is an informal short

form of **misery**. This is a useful word, giving a high score for three letters. Remember that you'll need a blank tile for the second Z if you want to form the plural. Miz scores 14 points.

mizzenmast n (pl -s) (on a vessel with three or more masts) third mast from the bow

mizzenmasts n ▷ mizzenmast

▓ **mm** interj. Mm is a sound that people make to express satisfaction. This two-letter word with no vowels can be very handy when forming several words at once. Mm scores 6 points.

mnemonic [nim-**on**-ik] n (pl -s) ▶ adj (something, such as a rhyme) intended to help the memory

mnemonics n ▷ mnemonic

▓ **mo** n (**mos**). Mo is an informal short form of **moment**. This word can come in handy when you are trying to play words in more than one direction at once. Mo scores 4 points.

moa n (pl -s) large extinct flightless New Zealand bird

moas n ▷ moa

moan n (pl -s) low cry of pain ▶ v (-s, -ing, -ed) make or utter with a moan

moaned v ▷ moan

moaning v ▷ moan

moans n, v ▷ moan

moat n (pl -s) deep wide ditch, esp. round a castle

moats n ▷ moat

mob n (pl -s) disorderly crowd ▶ v (-s, -bbing, -bbed) surround in a mob to acclaim or attack

mobbed v ▷ mob

mobbing v ▷ mob

mobs n, v ▷ mob

mobile adj able to move ▶ n (pl -s) hanging structure designed to move in air currents
> **mobility** n (pl -ties)

mobiles n ▷ mobile

mobilities n ▷ mobile

mobility n ▷ mobile

mobilization n ▷ mobilize

mobilizations n ▷ mobilize

mobilize v (-zes, -zing, -zed) (of the armed services) prepare for active service
> **mobilization** n (pl -s)

mobilized v ▷ mobilize

mobilizes v ▷ mobilize

mobilizing v ▷ mobilize

moccasin n (pl -s) soft leather shoe

moccasins n ▷ moccasin

mocha [**mock**-a] n (pl -s) kind of strong dark

coffee

mochas n ▷ mocha

mock v (-s, -ing, -ed) make fun of ▶ adj sham or imitation

mocked v ▷ mock

mockeries n ▷ mockery

mockery n (pl -ries) derision

mocking v ▷ mock

mockingbird n (pl -s) N American bird which imitates other birds' songs

mockingbirds n ▷ mockingbird

mocks pl n (Informal) (in England and Wales) practice exams taken before public exams ▶ ▷ mock

mock-up n (pl -s) full-scale model for test or study

mock-ups n ▷ mock-up

mode n (pl -s) method or manner

modes n ▷ mode

model n (pl -s) (miniature) representation ▶ v (-s, -elling, -elled) make a model of

modelled v ▷ model

modelling n ▷ model

models n ▷ model

modem [mode-em] n (pl -s) device for connecting two computers by a telephone line

modems n ▷ modem

moderate adj not extreme ▶ n (pl -s) person of moderate views ▶ v (-tes, -ting, -ted) make or become less violent or extreme ▶ **moderately** adv ▷ **moderation** (pl -s) n

moderated v ▷ moderate

moderately adv ▷ moderate

moderates n, v ▷ moderate

moderating v ▷ moderate

moderation n ▷ moderate

moderations n ▷ moderate

moderator n (pl -s) (Presbyterian Church) minister appointed to preside over a Church court, general assembly, etc.

moderators n ▷ moderate

modern adj (-er, -est) of present or recent times > **modernity** n (pl -ties)

moderner adj ▷ modern

modernest adj ▷ modern

modernism n (pl -s) (support of) modern tendencies, thoughts, or styles > **modernist** adj, n (pl -s)

modernism n ▷ modern

modernisms n ▷ modern

modernist n ▷ modern

modernists n ▷ modern

modernities n ▷ modern

modernity n ▷ modern

modernization n ▷ modernize

modernizations n ▷ modernize

modernize v (-izes, -izing, -ized) bring up to date > **modernization** n (pl -s)

modest adj (-er, -est) not vain or boastful > **modestly** adv > **modesty** n (pl -s)

modester adj ▷ modest

modestest adj ▷ modest

modesties n ▷ modest

modestly adv ▷ modest

modesty n ▷ modest

modicum n (pl -s) small quantity

modicums n ▷ modicum

modify v (-fies, -fying, -fied) change slightly > **modification** n (pl -s)

modified v ▷ modify

modifier n (pl -s) word that qualifies the sense of another

modifiers n ▷ modifier

modish [mode-ish] adj in fashion

modulate v (-tes, -ting, -ted) vary in tone > **modulation** n (pl -s) > **modulator** n (pl -s)

modulated v ▷ modulate

modulates v ▷ modulate

modulating v ▷ modulate

modulation n ▷ modulate

modulations n ▷ modulate

module n (pl -s) self-contained unit, section, or component with a specific function

modules n ▷ module

mogul [moh-gl] n (pl -s) important or powerful person

moguls n ▷ mogul

mohair n (pl -s) fine hair of the Angora goat

mohairs n ▷ mohair

mohican n (pl -s) punk hairstyle with shaved sides and a stiff central strip of hair, often brightly coloured

mohicans n ▷ mohican

moieties n ▷ moieties

moiety [moy-it-ee] n (pl -ties) half

moist adj (-er, -est) slightly wet

moisten v (-s, -ing, -ed) make or become moist

moistened v ▷ moisten

moistening v ▷ moisten

moistens v ▷ moisten

moister adj ▷ moist

moistest adj ▷ moist

moisture n (pl -s) liquid diffused as vapour or condensed in drops

moistures n ▷ moisture

moisturize v (-zes, -zing, -zed) add moisture to (the skin etc.)

moisturized v ▷ moisten

moisturizes v ▷ moisten

moisturizing v ▷ moisten

molar n (pl -s) large back tooth used for grinding

molars n ▷ molar

molasses n dark syrup, a by-product of sugar refining

mole[1] n (pl -s) small dark raised spot on the skin

mole[2] n (pl -s) small burrowing mammal

mole[3] n (pl -s) unit of amount of substance

mole[4] n (pl -s) breakwater

molecule [mol-lik-kyool] n (pl -s) simplest freely existing chemical unit, composed of two or more atoms > **molecular** [mol-**lek**-yew-lar] ▶ adj

molecular adj ▷ molecule

molecules n ▷ molecule

moles n ▷ mole[1,2,3,4]

molest v (-s, -ing, -ed) interfere with sexually > **molester** n (pl -s) > **molestation** n (pl -s)

molested v ▷ molest

molester n ▷ molest

molesters n ▷ molest

molesting v ▷ molest

molests v ▷ molest

moll n (pl -s) (Slang) gangster's female accomplice

mollified v ▷ mollify

mollifies v ▷ mollify

mollify v (-fies, -fying, -fied) pacify or soothe

mollifying v ▷ mollify

molls n ▷ moll

mollusc n (pl -s) soft-bodied, usu. hard-shelled, animal, such as a snail or oyster

molluscs n ▷ mollusc

mollycoddle v (-les, -ling, -led) pamper

mollycoddled v ▷ mollycoddle

mollycoddles v ▷ mollycoddle

mollycoddling v ▷ mollycoddle

molten adj liquefied or melted

molybdenum [mol-**lib**-din-um] n (pl -s) (CHEM) hard silvery-white metallic element

molybdenums n ▷ molybdenum

moment n (pl -s) short space of time

momenta n ▷ momentum

momentarily adv ▷ momentary

momentary adj lasting only a moment > **momentarily** adv

momentous [moh-**men**-tuss] adj of great significance

moments n ▷ moment

momentum n (pl -ta) impetus of a moving body

monarch n (pl -s) sovereign ruler of a state > **monarchical** adj

monarchical adj ▷ monarch

monarchies n ▷ monarchy

monarchist n (pl -s) supporter of monarchy

monarchists n ▷ monarchist

monarchs n ▷ monarch

monarchy n (pl -chies) government by or a state ruled by a sovereign

monasteries n ▷ monastery

monastery n (pl -ries) residence of a community of monks > **monasticism** n (pl -s)

monastic adj of monks, nuns, or monasteries

monasticism n ▷ monastery

monasticisms n ▷ monastery

monetarism n (pl -s) theory that inflation is caused by an increase in the money supply > **monetarist** n (pl -s) adj

monetarisms n ▷ monetarism

monetarist n, adj ▷ monetarism

monetarists n ▷ monetarism

monetary adj of money or currency

money n (pl -s) medium of exchange, coins or banknotes > **moneyed, monied** adj rich

moneyed adj ▷ money

moneys n ▷ money

mongoose n (pl -s) stoatlike mammal of Asia and Africa that kills snakes

mongooses n ▷ money

mongrel n (pl -s) animal, esp. a dog, of mixed breed ▶ adj of mixed breed or origin

mongrels n ▷ mongrel

monied adj ▷ money

monitor n (pl -s) person or device that checks, controls, warns, or keeps a record of something ▶ v (-s, -ing, -ed) watch and check on

monitored v ▷ monitor

monitoring v ▷ monitor

monitors n, v ▷ monitor

monk n (pl -s) member of an all-male religious community bound by vows > **monkish** adj

monkey n (pl -s) long-tailed primate ▶ v (-s, -ing, -ed) (usu. foll. by about or around) meddle or fool

monkeyed v ▷ monkey

monkeying v ▷ monkey

monkeys n, v ▷ monkey

monkish adj ▷ monk

monks n ▷ monk

monochrome adj (PHOTOG) black-and-white

monocle n (pl -s) eyeglass for one eye only

monocles n ▷ monocle

monogamies n ▷ monogamy

monogamy n (pl -mies) custom of being married to one person at a time

monogram n (pl -s) design of combined

letters, esp. a person's initials
monograms n ▷ monogram

monograph n (pl -s) book or paper on a single subject
monographs n ▷ monograph

monolith n (pl -s) large upright block of stone > **monolithic** adj
monolithic n ▷ monolith
monoliths n ▷ monolith

monologue n (pl -s) long speech by one person
monologues n ▷ monologue

monomania n (pl -s) obsession with one thing > **monomaniac** n, adj
monomaniac adj ▷ monomania
monomanias n ▷ monomania

monoplane n (pl -s) aeroplane with one pair of wings
monoplanes n ▷ monoplane
monopolies n ▷ monopoly

monopolize v (-zes, -zing, -zed) have or take exclusive possession of
monopolized v ▷ monopoly
monopolizes v ▷ monopoly
monopolizing v ▷ monopoly

monopoly n (pl -lies) exclusive possession of or right to do something

monorail n (pl -s) single-rail railway
monorails n ▷ monorail

monotheism n (pl -s) belief in only one God > **monotheistic** adj
monotheisms n ▷ monorail
monotheistic adj ▷ monotheism

monotone n (pl -s) unvaried pitch in speech or sound > **monotony** n (pl -s)
monotones n ▷ monotone
monotonies n ▷ monotony

monotonous adj tedious due to lack of variety > **monotonously** adv
monotonously adv ▷ monotonous

monseigneur [mon-sen-**nyur**] n (pl messeigneurs) [may-sen-**nyur**] title of French prelates

monsieur [muss-**syur**] n (pl messieurs) [may-**syur**] French title of address equivalent to sir or Mr

monsignor n (pl -s) (RC CHURCH) title attached to certain offices
monsignors n ▷ monsignor

monsoon n (pl -s) seasonal wind of SE Asia
monsoons n ▷ monsoon

monster n (pl -s) imaginary, usu. frightening, beast ▶ adj huge
monsters n ▷ monster

monstrance n (pl -ces) (RC CHURCH) container in which the consecrated Host is exposed for adoration
monstrances n ▷ monstrance
monstrocities n ▷ monstrosity

monstrosity n (pl -ties) large ugly thing
monstrous adj unnatural or ugly > **monstrously** adv
monstrously adv ▷ monstrous

montage [mon-**tahzh**] n (pl -s) (making of) a picture composed from pieces of others
montages n ▷ montage

month n (pl -s) one of the twelve divisions of the calendar year
monthlies n ▷ month

monthly adj happening or payable once a month ▶ adv once a month ▶ n (pl -lies) monthly magazine
months n ▷ month

monument n (pl -s) something, esp. a building or statue, that commemorates something
monumental adj large, impressive, or lasting > **monumentally** adv
monumentally adv ▷ monumental
monuments n ▷ monument

moo n (pl -s) long deep cry of a cow ▶ v (-s, -ing, -ed) make this noise
mooed v ▷ moo
mooing v ▷ moo
moos n, v ▷ moo

mooch v (-es, -ing, -ed) (Slang) loiter about aimlessly
mooched v ▷ mooch
mooches v ▷ mooch
mooching v ▷ mooch

mood[1] n (pl -s) temporary (gloomy) state of mind

mood[2] n (GRAMMAR) form of a verb indicating whether it expresses a fact, wish, supposition, or command
moodier adj ▷ moody
moodiest adj ▷ moody
moodily adv ▷ moody
moods n ▷ mood[1,2]

moody adj (-dier, -iest) sullen or gloomy > **moodily** adv

moon n (pl -s) natural satellite of the earth ▶ v (-s, -ing, -ed) (foll. by **about** or **around**) be idle in a listless or dreamy way
mooned v ▷ moon
mooning v ▷ moon

moonlight n (pl -s) light from the moon ▶ v (-s, -ing, -ed) (Informal) work at a secondary job, esp. illegally
moonlighted v ▷ moonlight
moonlighting v ▷ moonlight
moonlights n, v ▷ moonlight

moons *n*, *v* ▷ moon
moonshine *n* (*pl* **-s**) (US & CANADIAN) illicitly distilled whisky
  moonshines *n* ▷ moonshine
moonstone *n* (*pl* **-s**) translucent semiprecious stone
  moonstones *n* ▷ moonstone
moonstruck *adj* slightly mad or odd
moor[1] *n* (*pl* **-s**) (BRIT) tract of open uncultivated ground covered with grass and heather
moor[2] *v* (**-s**, **-ing**, **-ed**) secure (a ship) with ropes etc. ▷ **mooring** *n* (*pl* **-s**)
  moored *v* ▷ moor[2]
moorhen *n* (*pl* **-s**) small black water bird
  moorhens *n* ▷ moorhen
  mooring *v*, *n* ▷ moor[2]
  moors *n* ▷ moor[1] ▶ *v* ▷ moor[2]
moose *n* large N American deer
moot *adj* (**-er**, **-est**) debatable ▶ *v* (**-s**, **-ing**, **-ed**) bring up for discussion
  mooted *v* ▷ moot
  mooter *adj* ▷ moot
  mootest *adj* ▷ moot
  mooting *v* ▷ moot
  moots *v* ▷ moot
mop *n* (*pl* **-s**) long stick with twists of cotton or a sponge on the end, used for cleaning ▶ *v* (**-s**, **-pping**, **-pped**) clean or soak up with or as if with a mop
mope *v* (**-pes**, **-ping**, **-ped**) be gloomy and apathetic
moped *n* (*pl* **-s**) light motorized cycle ▶ *v* ▷ mope
  mopeds *v* ▷ mope
  mopes *v* ▷ mope
  moping *v* ▷ mope
mopoke *n* (*pl* **-s**) small spotted owl of Australia and New Zealand
  mopokes *n* ▷ mopoke
  mopped *v* ▷ mop
  mopping *v* ▷ mop
  mops *n*, *v* ▷ mop
moraine *n* (*pl* **-s**) accumulated mass of debris deposited by a glacier
  moraines *n* ▷ moraine
moral *adj* concerned with right and wrong conduct ▶ *n* (*pl* **-s**) lesson to be obtained from a story or event ▷ **morally** *adv*
morale [mor-**rahl**] *n* (*pl* **-s**) degree of confidence or hope of a person or group
  morales *n* ▷ morale
moralist *n* (*pl* **-s**) person with a strong sense of right and wrong
  moralists *n* ▷ moralist
  moralities *n* ▷ morality

morality *n* (*pl* **-ties**) good moral conduct
moralize *v* (**-zes**, **-zing**, **-zed**) make moral pronouncements
  moralized *v* ▷ moralize
  moralizes *v* ▷ moralize
  moralizing *v* ▷ moralize
  morally *adv* ▷ moral
  morals *n* ▷ moral
morass *n* (*pl* **-es**) marsh
  morasses *n* ▷ morass
  moratoria *n* ▷ moratorium
moratorium *n* (*pl* **-ria**, **-riums**) legally authorized ban or delay
  moratoriums *n* ▷ moratorium
moray *n* (*pl* **-s**) large voracious eel
  morays *n* ▷ moray
morbid *adj* unduly interested in death or unpleasant events
mordant *adj* sarcastic or scathing ▶ *n* (*pl* **-s**) substance used to fix dyes
  mordants *n* ▷ mordant
more *adj* greater in amount or degree ▷ much, many ▶ *adv* to a greater extent ▶ *pron* greater or additional amount or number
moreover *adv* in addition to what has already been said
mores [**more**-rayz] *pl n* customs and conventions embodying the fundamental values of a community
morgue *n* (*pl* **-s**) mortuary
  morgues *n* ▷ morgue
moribund *adj* without force or vitality
morn *n* (*pl* **morns**) (*Poetic*) morning
  morns *n* ▷ morn
morning *n* (*pl* **-s**) part of the day before noon
  mornings *n* ▷ morning
morocco *n* (*pl* **-s**) goatskin leather
  moroccos *n* ▷ morocco
moron *n* (*pl* **-s**) (*Informal*) foolish or stupid person ▷ **moronic** *adj*
  moronic *adj* ▷ moron
  morons *n* ▷ moron
morose [mor-**rohss**] *adj* (**-r**, **-st**) sullen or moody
  moroser *adj* ▷ morose
  morosest *adj* ▷ morose
  morphia *n* ▷ morphine
  morphines *n* ▷ morphine
morphine, morphia *n* (*pl* **-s**) drug extracted from opium, used as an anaesthetic and sedative
  morphological *adj* ▷ morphology
  morphologies *n* ▷ morphology
morphology *n* (*pl* **-gies**) science of forms and structures of organisms or words ▷ **morphological** *adj*

morrow *n* (*pl* -s) (*Poetic*) next day
  morrows *n* ▷ morrow
morse *n* (*pl* -s) clasp or fastening
morsel *n* (*pl* -s) small piece, esp. of food
  morsels *n* ▷ morsel
  morses *n* ▷ morse
mortal *adj* subject to death ▶ *n* (*pl* -s) human
  being > **mortally** *adv*
  mortalities *n* ▷ mortal
mortality *n* (*pl* -ties) state of being mortal
  mortally *adj* ▷ mortal
  mortals *n* ▷ mortal
mortar *n* (*pl* -s) small cannon with a short
  range
mortarboard *n* (*pl* -s) black square academic
  cap
  mortarboards *n* ▷ mortarboard
  mortars *n* ▷ mortar
mortgage *n* (*pl* -s) conditional pledging of
  property, esp. a house, as security for the
  repayment of a loan ▶ *v* (-ges, -ging, -ged)
  pledge (property) as security thus
  mortgaged *v* ▷ mortgage
mortgagee *n* (*pl* -s) creditor in a mortgage
  mortgagees *n* ▷ mortgagee
  mortgages *n, v* ▷ mortgage
  mortgaging *v* ▷ mortgage
mortgagor *n* (*pl* -s) debtor in a mortgage
  mortgagors *n* ▷ mortgagor
mortice, mortise [**more**-tiss] *n* (*pl* -s) hole in
  a piece of wood or stone shaped to receive a
  matching projection on another piece
  mortices *n* ▷ mortice
mortification *n* ▷ mortify
  mortifications *n* ▷ mortify
  mortified *v* ▷ mortify
  mortifies *v* ▷ mortify
mortify *v* (-fies, -fying, -fied) humiliate
  > **mortification** *n* (*pl* -s)
  mortifying *v* ▷ mortify
  mortise *n* ▷ mortice
  mortises *n* ▷ mortice
  mortuaries *n* ▷ mortuary
mortuary *n* (*pl* -aries) building where corpses
  are kept before burial or cremation
mosaic [mow-**zay**-ik] *n* (*pl* -s) design or
  decoration using small pieces of coloured
  stone or glass
  mosaics *n* ▷ mosaic
mosque *n* (*pl* -s) Muslim temple
  mosques *n* ▷ mosque
mosquito *n* (*pl* -toes, -tos) blood-sucking
  flying insect
  mosquitoes *n* ▷ mosquito
  mosquitos *n* ▷ mosquito

moss *n* (*pl* -es) small flowerless plant growing
  in masses on moist surfaces > **mossy** *adj*
  (-sier, -siest)
  mosses *n* ▷ moss
  mossier *adj* ▷ moss
  mossiest *adj* ▷ moss
  mossy *adj* (-sier, -siest) ▷ moss
most *n* greatest number or degree ▶ *adj*
  greatest in number or degree ▷ much, many
  ▶ *adv* in the greatest degree
mostly *adv* for the most part, generally
motel *n* (*pl* -s) roadside hotel for motorists
  motels *n* ▷ motel
motet *n* (*pl* -s) short sacred choral song
  motets *n* ▷ motet
moth *n* (*pl* -s) nocturnal insect like a butterfly
mothball *n* (*pl* -s) small ball of camphor or
  naphthalene used to repel moths from stored
  clothes ▶ *v* (-ed, -ing, -ed) store (something
  operational) for future use
  mothballed *v* ▷ moth
  mothballing *v* ▷ moth
  mothballs *n, v* ▷ moth
  moths *n* ▷ moth
mother *n* (*pl* -s) female parent ▶ *adj* native
  or inborn ▶ *v* (-s, -ing, -ed) look after as a
  mother > **motherhood** *n* (*pl* -s) > **motherly** *adj*
  > **motherless** *adj*
  mothered *v* ▷ mother
  motherhood *n* ▷ mother
  motherhoods *n* ▷ mother
  mothering *v* ▷ mother
  motherless *adj* ▷ mother
  motherly *adj* ▷ mother
  mothers *n, v* ▷ mother
  mothers-in-law *n* ▷ mother-in-law
motif [moh-**teef**] *n* (*pl* -s) (recurring) theme
  or design
  motifs *n* ▷ motif
motion *n* (*pl* -s) process, action, or way of
  moving ▶ *v* (-s, -ing, -ed) direct (someone)
  by gesture
  motioned *v* ▷ motion
  motioning *v* ▷ motion
motionless *adj* not moving
  motions *n, v* ▷ motion
motivate *v* (-tes, -ting, -ted) give incentive to
  > **motivation** *n* (*pl* -s)
  motivated *v* ▷ motivate
  motivates *v* ▷ motivate
  motivating *v* ▷ motivate
  motivation *n* ▷ motivate
  motivations *n* ▷ motivate
motive *n* (*pl* -s) reason for a course of action
  ▶ *adj* causing motion

motives *n* ▷ motive

motley *adj* miscellaneous

motocross *n* (*pl* -es) motorcycle race over a rough course

motocrosses *n* ▷ motocross

motor *n* (*pl* -s) engine, esp. of a vehicle ▶ *v* (-s, -ing, -ed) travel by car > **motorized** *adj* equipped with a motor or motor transport
> **motorbike** *n* (*pl* -s) > **motorboat** *n* (*pl* -s)
> **motorcar** *n* (*pl* -s) > **motorcycle** *n* (*pl* -s)
> **motorcyclist** *n* (*pl* -s)

motorbike *n* ▷ motor

motorbikes *n* ▷ motor

motorboat *n* ▷ motor

motorboats *n* ▷ motor

motorcar *n* ▷ motor

motorcars *n* ▷ motor

motorcycle *n* ▷ motor

motorcycles *n* ▷ motor

motorcyclist *n* ▷ motor

motorcyclists *n* ▷ motor

motored *v* ▷ motor

motoring *v* ▷ motor

motorist *n* (*pl* -s) driver of a car

motorists *n* ▷ motorist

motorized *adj* ▷ motor

motors *n*, *v* ▷ motor

motorway *n* (*pl* -s) main road for fast-moving traffic

motorways *n* ▷ motorway

mottled *adj* marked with blotches

motto *n* (*pl* -ttoes, -ttos) saying expressing an ideal or rule of conduct

mottoes *n* ▷ motto

mottos *n* ▷ motto

mould¹ *n* (*pl* -s) hollow container in which metal etc. is cast ▶ *v* (-s, -ing, -ed) shape

mould² *n* (*pl* -s) fungal growth caused by dampness

mould³ *n* (*pl* -s) loose soil

moulded *v* ▷ mould¹

moulder *v* (-s, -ing, -ed) decay into dust

mouldered *v* ▷ moulder

mouldering *v* ▷ moulder

moulders *v* ▷ moulder

mouldier *adj* ▷ mouldy

mouldiest *adj* ▷ mouldy

moulding *n* (*pl* -s) moulded ornamental edging ▶ *v* ▷ mould¹

moulds *n* ▷ mould¹,²,³ ▶ *v* ▷ mould¹

mouldy *adj* (-dier, -diest) stale or musty; dull or boring

moult *v* (-s, -ing, -ed) shed feathers, hair, or skin to make way for new growth ▶ *n* (*pl* -s) process of moulting

moulted *v* ▷ moult

moulting *v* ▷ moult

moults *v*, *n* ▷ moult

mound *n* (*pl* -s) heap, esp. of earth or stones

mounds *n* ▷ mound

mount *v* (-s, -ing, -ed) climb or ascend ▶ *n* (*pl* -s) backing or support on which something is fixed

mountain *n* (*pl* -s) hill of great size
> **mountainous** *adj* full of mountains
n (*pl* -s) person who climbs mountains
> **mountaineering** *n* (*pl* -s)

mountaineering *n* ▷ mountaineer

mountaineerings *n* ▷ mountaineer

mountaineers *n* ▷ mountaineer

mountains *n* ▷ mountain

mountebank *n* (*pl* -s) charlatan or fake

mountebanks *n* ▷ mountebank

mounted *v* ▷ mount

mounting *v* ▷ mount

mounts *v*, *n* ▷ mount

mourn *v* (-s, -ing, -ed) feel or express sorrow for (a dead person or lost thing)

mourned *v* ▷ mourn

mourner *n* (*pl* mourners) person attending a funeral

mourners *n* ▷ mourner

mournful *adj* (-ler, -lest) sad or dismal
> **mournfully** *adv*

mournfuller *adj* ▷ mournful

mournfullest *adj* ▷ mournful

mournfully *adv* ▷ mournful

mourning *n* (*pl* -s) grieving ▶ *v* ▷ mourn

mournings *n* ▷ mourning

mourns *v* ▷ mourn

mouse *n* (*pl* mice) small long-tailed rodent

mouser *n* (*pl* -s) cat used to catch mice

mousers *n* ▷ mouser

mousse *n* (*pl* -s) dish of flavoured cream whipped and set

mousses *n* ▷ mousse

moustache *n* (*pl* -s) hair on the upper lip

moustaches *n* ▷ moustache

mousy *adj* like a mouse, esp. in hair colour

mouth *n* (*pl* -s) opening in the head for eating and issuing sounds ▶ *v* (-s, -ing, -ed) form (words) with the lips without speaking

mouthed *v* ▷ mouth

mouthful *n* (*pl* -s) amount of food or drink put into the mouth at any one time when eating or drinking

mouthfuls *n* ▷ mouthful

mouthing *v* ▷ mouth

mouthpiece *n* (*pl* -s) part of a telephone into which a person speaks mouthpieces n ▷ mouthpiece

mouths n, v ▷ mouth

move v (-ves, -ving, -ved) change in place or position ▸ n (pl -s) moving > movable, moveable adj

movement n (pl -s) action or process of moving

movements n ▷ movement

moved v ▷ move

moves v, n ▷ move

movie n (pl -s) (Informal) cinema film

movies n ▷ movie

moving v ▷ move

mow v (-s, -ing, -ed or mown) cut (grass or crops)

mowed v ▷ mow

mower n (pl -s) machine for cutting grass

mowers n ▷ mower

mowing v ▷ mow

mown v ▷ mow

mows v ▷ mow

> **moz** n (**mozes**). Moz is an old Australian slang word for a jinx or hex. This is an unusual word that is worth remembering as it can be very useful if you have a Z but little chance to play it on a crowded board. Moz scores 14 points.

mozzarella [mot-sa-**rel**-la] n (pl -s) moist white cheese originally made in Italy from buffalo milk

mozzarellas n ▷ mozzarella

> **mu** n (**mus**). Mu is the 12th letter in the Greek alphabet. This is a useful word to remember: it won't score you many points on its own, but it can be very helpful on a crowded board when you need to form words in different directions. Mu scores 4 points.

much adj (more, most) large amount or degree of ▸ n large amount or degree ▸ adv (more, most) to a great degree

mucilage [**mew**-sill-ij] n (pl -s) gum or glue

mucilages n ▷ mucilage

muck n (pl -s) dirt, filth > mucky adj

mucks n ▷ mucks

mucky adj ▷ mucks

mucus [**mew**-kuss] n (pl -s) slimy secretion of the mucous membranes

mucuses n ▷ mucus

mud n (pl -s) wet soft earth > muddy adj

muddier adj ▷ mud

muddiest adj ▷ mud

muddy adj (-dier, -ddiest) ▷ mud

mudguard n (pl -s) cover over a wheel to prevent mud or water being thrown up by it

mudguards n ▷ mudguard

muds n ▷ mud

muddle v (-les, -ling, -led) (often foll. by **up**) confuse ▸ n (pl -s) state of confusion

muddled v ▷ muddle

muddles v, n ▷ muddle

muddling v ▷ muddle

muesli [**mewz**-lee] n (pl -s) mixture of grain, nuts, and dried fruit, eaten with milk

mueslis n ▷ muesli

muezzin [moo-**ezz**-in] n (pl -s) official who summons Muslims to prayer

muezzins n ▷ muezzin

muff[1] n (pl -s) tube-shaped covering to keep the hands warm

muff[2] v (-s, -ing, -ed) bungle (an action)

muffed v ▷ muff

muffin n (pl -s) light round flat yeast cake

muffing v ▷ muff

muffins n ▷ muffin

muffs n ▷ muff[1] ▸ v ▷ muff[2]

muffle v (-les, -ling, -led) wrap up for warmth or to deaden sound

muffled v ▷ muffle

muffler n (pl -s) (BRIT) scarf

mufflers n ▷ muffle

muffles v ▷ muffle

muffling v ▷ muffle

mufti n (pl -s) civilian clothes worn by a person who usually wears a uniform

muftis n ▷ mufti

mug[1] n (pl -s) large drinking cup

mug[2] n (pl -s) (Slang) face ▸ v (-s, -gging, -gged) (Informal) attack in order to rob > mugger n (pl -s)

mug[3] v (-s, -gging, -gged) (foll. by **up**) (Informal) study hard

mugged v ▷ mug[2,3]

mugger v ▷ mug[2]

muggers v ▷ mug[2]

muggier adj ▷ muggy

muggiest adj ▷ muggy

mugging v ▷ mug[2,3]

muggins n (Informal) stupid or gullible person

muggy adj (-ggier, -ggiest) (of weather) damp and stifling

mugs n ▷ mug[1,2]

mulatto [mew-**lat**-toe] n (pl -tos, -toes) child of one Black and one White parent

mulattoes adj ▷ mulatto

mulattos adj ▷ mulatto

mulberries n ▷ mulberry

mulberry n (pl -rries) tree whose leaves are used to feed silkworms

mulch n (pl -es) mixture of wet straw, leaves, etc., used to protect the roots of plants ▶ v (-es, -ing, -ed) cover (land) with mulch
  mulched v ▷ mulch
  mulches n, v ▷ mulch
  mulching v ▷ mulch
mule[1] n (pl -s) offspring of a horse and a donkey > **mulish** adj obstinate
mule[2] n backless shoe or slipper
  mules n ▷ mule[1,2]
mulga n (pl -s) Australian acacia shrub growing in desert regions
  mulgas n ▷ mulga
  mulish adj ▷ mule[1]
mull v (-s, -ing, -ed) think (over) or ponder > **mulled** adj (of wine or ale) flavoured with sugar and spices and served hot
mullah n (pl -s) Muslim scholar, teacher, or religious leader
  mullahs n ▷ mullah
  mulled v, adj ▷ mull
mullet[1] n (pl -s) edible sea fish
mullet[2] n (pl -s) haircut in which the hair is short at the top and sides and long at the back
  mullets n ▷ mullet[1,2]
  mulling v ▷ mull
  mulls v ▷ mull
  mulligatawnies n ▷ mulligatawny
mulligatawny n (pl -nies) soup made with curry powder
mullion n (pl -s) vertical dividing bar in a window > **mullioned** adj
  mullioned adj ▷ mullion
  mullions n ▷ mullion
mulloway n (pl -s) large Australian sea fish, valued for sport and food
  mulloways n ▷ mulloway
multifarious [mult-ee-**fare**-ee-uss] adj having many various parts
multiple adj having many parts ▶ n (pl -s) quantity which contains another an exact number of times
  multiples n ▷ multiple
multiplex n (pl -es) purpose-built complex containing several cinemas and usu. restaurants and bars ▶ adj having many elements, complex
  multiplexes n ▷ multiplex
  multiplicities n ▷ multiplicity
multiplicity n (pl -ties) large number or great variety
multiply v (-lies, -lying, -lied) (cause to) increase in number, quantity, or degree > **multiplication** n (pl -s)

multiplicand n (pl -s) (MATHS) number to be multiplied
  multiplicands n ▷ multiplicand
  multiplication n ▷ multiply
  multiplications n ▷ multiply
  multiplied v ▷ multiply
  multiplies v ▷ multiply
  multiplying v ▷ multiply
multipurpose adj having many uses
multitude n (pl -s) great number
  multitudes n ▷ multitude
multitudinous adj very numerous
mum n (pl -s) (Informal) mother
  mums n ▷ mum
mumble v (-les, -ling, -led) speak indistinctly, mutter
  mumbled v ▷ mumble
  mumbles v ▷ mumble
  mumbling v ▷ mumble
mummer n (pl -s) actor in a traditional English folk play or mime
  mummers n ▷ mummer
  mummies n ▷ mummer
mummified adj (of a body) preserved as a mummy
mummy[1] n (pl -mmies) body embalmed and wrapped for burial in ancient Egypt
mummy[2] n (pl -mmies) ▷ mother
mumps n infectious disease with swelling in the glands of the neck
munch v (-es, -ing, -ed) chew noisily and steadily
  munched v ▷ munch
  munches v ▷ munch
  munching v ▷ munch
mundane adj everyday
municipal adj relating to a city or town
  municipalities n ▷ municipality
municipality n (pl -ties) city or town with local self-government
munificence n ▷ munificent
  munificences n ▷ munificent
munificent [mew-**niff**-fiss-sent] adj very generous > **munificence** n (pl -s)
muniments pl n title deeds or similar documents
munitions pl n military stores
munted adj (NZ) (Slang) destroyed or ruined
mural n (pl -s) painting on a wall
  murals n ▷ mural
murder n (pl -s) unlawful intentional killing of a human being ▶ v (-s, -ing, -ed) kill in this way > **murderer, murderess** n (pl -s) > **murderous** adj
  murdered v ▷ murder

murderer n ▷ murder
murderers n ▷ murder
murderess n ▷ murder
murderesses n ▷ murder
murdering v ▷ murder
murderous adj ▷ murder
murders v, n ▷ murder
murk n (pl -s) thick darkness
  murkier adj ▷ murky
  murkiest adj ▷ murky
  murks n ▷ murk
murky adj (-kier, -kiest) dark or gloomy
murmur v (-s, -ing, -ed) speak or say in a quiet
  indistinct way ▶ n (pl -s) continuous low
  indistinct sound
  murmured v ▷ murmur
  murmuring v ▷ murmur
  murmurs v, n ▷ murmur
muscle n (pl -s) tissue in the body which
  produces movement by contracting
  muscles n ▷ muscle
muscular adj with well-developed muscles
muse v (-ses, -sing, -sed) ponder quietly
  mused v ▷ muse
  musing v ▷ muse
  muses v ▷ muse
museum n (pl -s) building where natural,
  artistic, historical, or scientific objects are
  exhibited and preserved
  museums n ▷ museum
mush n (pl -es) soft pulpy mass > **mushy** adj
  (-shier, -shiest)
  mushes n ▷ mush
  mushier adj ▷ mush
  mushiest adj ▷ mush
mushroom n (pl -s) edible fungus with a stem
  and cap ▶ v (-s, -ing, -ed) grow rapidly
  mushroomed v ▷ mushroom
  mushrooming v ▷ mushroom
  mushrooms n, v ▷ mushroom
mushy (-shier, -shiest) adj ▷ mush
music n (pl -s) art form using a melodious
  and harmonious combination of notes ▶ n
  (pl -s) play or film with songs and dancing
  > **musician** n (pl -s)
musical adj of or like music > **musically** adv
  musically adv ▷ musical
  musician n ▷ music
  musicians n ▷ music
  musicologies n ▷ musicology
  musicologist n ▷ musicology
  musicologists n ▷ musicology
musicology n (pl -gies) scientific study of
  music > **musicologist** n (pl -s)
  musics n ▷ music

musk n (pl -s) scent obtained from a gland
  of the musk deer or produced synthetically
  > **musky** adj (-kier, -kiest)
musket n (pl -s) (HIST) long-barrelled gun
  > **musketeer** n (pl -s)
  musketeer n ▷ musket
  musketeers n ▷ musket
  musketries n ▷ musketry
musketry n (pl -ries) (use of) muskets
  muskets n ▷ musket
  muskier adj ▷ musk
  muskiest adj ▷ musk
muskrat n (pl -s) N American beaver-like
  rodent
  muskrats n ▷ muskrat
  musks n ▷ musk
  musky adj (-kier, -kiest) ▷ musk
muslin n (pl -s) fine cotton fabric
  muslins n ▷ muslin
mussel n (pl -s) edible shellfish with a dark
  hinged shell
  mussels n ▷ mussel
must[1] used as an auxiliary to express
  obligation, certainty, or resolution ▶ n (pl -s)
  essential or necessary thing
must[2] n (pl -s) newly pressed grape juice
  musts n ▷ must[1,2]
mustang n (pl -s) wild horse of SW USA
  mustangs n ▷ mustang
mustard n (pl -s) paste made from the
  powdered seeds of a plant, used as a
  condiment
  mustards n ▷ mustard
muster v (-s, -ing, -ed) assemble ▶ n (pl -s)
  assembly of military personnel
  mustered v ▷ muster
  mustering v ▷ muster
  musters v, n ▷ muster
  mustier adj ▷ musty
  mustiest adj ▷ musty
  mustiness n ▷ musty
  mustinesses n ▷ musty
musty adj (mustier, mustiest) smelling
  mouldy and stale > **mustiness** n (pl -es)
  mutabilities n ▷ mutable
  mutability n ▷ mutable
mutable [mew-tab-bl] adj liable to change
  > **mutability** n (pl -ties)
mutant n (pl -s) mutated animal, plant, etc.
  mutants n ▷ mutant
mutate v (-tes, -ting, -ted) (cause to) undergo
  mutation
  mutated v ▷ mutate
  mutates v ▷ mutate
  mutating v ▷ mutate

mutation n (pl -s) (genetic) change
  mutations n ▷ mutation
mute adj (-r, -st) silent ▶ n (pl -s) person who is unable to speak > **mutely** adv
muted adj (of sound or colour) softened
  mutely adv ▷ mute
  muter adj ▷ mute
  mutes n ▷ mute
  mutest adj ▷ mute
muti [moo-ti] n (pl -s) (S AFR) (Informal) medicine, esp. herbal medicine
  mutis n ▷ muti
mutilate [mew-till-ate] v (-tes, -ting, -ted) deprive of a limb or other part > **mutilation** n (pl -s)
  mutilated v ▷ mutilate
  mutilates v ▷ mutilate
  mutilating v ▷ mutilate
  mutilation n ▷ mutilate
  mutilations n ▷ mutilate
  mutineer n ▷ mutiny
  mutineers n ▷ mutiny
  mutinied v ▷ mutiny
  mutinies n ▷ mutiny
  mutinous n ▷ mutiny
mutiny [mew-tin-ee] n (pl -nies) rebellion against authority, esp. by soldiers or sailors ▶ v (-nies, -nying, -nied) commit mutiny > **mutineer** n (pl -s) > **mutinous** adj
  mutinying v ▷ mutiny
mutt n (pl -s) (Slang) mongrel dog
  mutts n ▷ mutt
mutter v (-s, -ing, -ed) utter or speak indistinctly ▶ n (pl -s) muttered sound or grumble
  muttered v ▷ mutter
  muttering v ▷ mutter
  mutters v, n ▷ mutter
mutton n (pl -s) flesh of sheep, used as food
  muttons n ▷ mutton
mutual [mew-chew-al] adj felt or expressed by each of two people about the other > **mutually** adv
  mutually adv ▷ mutual

> **mux** v (muxes, muxing, muxed). Mux is an old American word meaning to make a mess of something. This word is very useful not only because it contains an X, but because its verb forms can enable you to clear your rack of unpromising letters. Mux scores 12 points.

> **muzjik** n (muzjiks). A muzjik is a Russian peasant. This is a great high-scoring word, combining Z, J and K. If

> you can play the plural using all of your tiles, you'll get a bonus of 50 points. Muzjik scores 28 points.

muzzle n (pl -s) animal's mouth and nose ▶ v (-les, -ling, -led) prevent from being heard or noticed
  muzzled v ▷ muzzle
  muzzles n, v ▷ muzzle
  muzzling v ▷ muzzle
muzzy adj (-zzier, -zziest) confused or muddled
my adj belonging to me
myall n (pl -s) Australian acacia with hard scented wood
  myalls n ▷ myall
mycology n (pl -gies) study of fungi
  mycologies n ▷ mycology
myna, mynah, mina n (pl -s) Asian bird which can mimic human speech
  mynah n ▷ myna
  mynahs n ▷ myna
  mynas n ▷ myna
myopia [my-oh-pee-a] n (pl -s) short-sightedness > **myopic** [my-op-ik] ▶ adj
  myopias n ▷ myopia
  myopic adj ▷ myopia
myriad [mir-ee-ad] adj innumerable ▶ n (pl -s) large indefinite number
  myriads n ▷ myriad
myrrh [mur] n (pl -s) aromatic gum used in perfume, incense, and medicine
  myrrhs n ▷ myrrh
myrtle [mur-tl] n (pl -s) flowering evergreen shrub
  myrtles n ▷ myrtle
  myself pron ▷ I
  mysteries n ▷ mystery
  mysterious adj ▷ mystery
  mysteriously adv ▷ mystery
mystery n (pl -ries) strange or inexplicable event or phenomenon > **mysterious** adj > **mysteriously** adv
mystic n (pl -s) person who seeks spiritual knowledge ▶ adj mystical > **mysticism** n (pl -s)
mystical adj having a spiritual or religious significance beyond human understanding
  mysticism n ▷ mystic
  mysticisms n ▷ mystic
  mystics n ▷ mystic
  mystification v ▷ mystify
  mystifications v ▷ mystify
  mystified v ▷ mystify
  mystifies v ▷ mystify
mystify v (-fies, -fying, -fied) bewilder or puzzle > **mystification** n (pl -s)
  mystifying v ▷ mystify

mystique [miss-**steek**] *n* (*pl* -s) aura of mystery
or power
  mystiques *n* ▷ mystique
myth *n* (*pl* -s) tale with supernatural
characters, usu. of how the world and
mankind began > **mythical, mythic** *adj*
  mythic *adj* ▷ myth
  mythical *adj* ▷ myth

  mythological *adj* ▷ mythology
  mythologies *n* ▷ mythology
mythology *n* (*pl* -gies) myths collectively
  > **mythological** *adj*
  myths *n* ▷ myth
  myxomatoses *n* ▷ myxomatosis
myxomatosis [mix-a-mat-**oh**-siss] *n* (*pl* -ses)
contagious fatal viral disease of rabbits

Nn

Along with R and T, N is one of the most common consonants in Scrabble. As you'll often have it on your rack, it's well worth learning what N can do in different situations. N is useful when you need short words, as it begins two-letter words with every vowel except I, and with Y as well. There are plenty of three-letter words starting with N, but there aren't many high-scoring ones. Remember words like **nab** (5 points), **nag** (4), **nap** (5), **nay** (6), **new** (6), **nib** (5), **nob** (5), **nod** (4) and **now** (6).

na *interj*. Na is a Scots word for **no** or **not**. This word can be very convenient when you need short words to form words in different directions. Na scores 2 points.

naan *n (pl -s)* nan bread
  naans *n* ▷ naan
naartjie [nahr-chee] *n (pl -s)* (S AFR) tangerine
  naartjies *n* ▷ naartjie
nab *v (-s, -bbing, -bbed)* (*Informal*) arrest (someone)
  nabbed *v* ▷ nab
  nabbing *v* ▷ nab
  nabs *v* ▷ nab
nadir *n (pl -s)* point in the sky opposite the zenith
  nadiral *adj* ▷ nadir
  nadirs *n* ▷ nadir
  naevi *n* ▷ naevus
naevus [nee-vuss] *n (pl -vi)* birthmark or mole
naff *adj (-er, -est)* (BRIT) (*Slang*) lacking quality or taste
  naffer *adj* ▷ naff
  naffest *adj* ▷ naff
nag¹ *v (-s, -gging, -gged)* scold or find fault constantly ▶ *n (pl -s)* person who nags
  > **nagging** *adj, n (pl -s)*
nag² *n (pl -s)* (*Informal*) old horse
  nagged *v* ▷ nag¹
  nagging *v, adj n* ▷ nag¹
  naggings *n* ▷ nag¹
  nags *v* ▷ nag¹ ▷ *n* ▷ nag¹, ²
naiad [nye-ad] *n (pl -s)* (GREEK MYTH) nymph living in a lake or river
  naiads *n* ▷ naiad
nail *n (pl -s)* pointed piece of metal with a head, hit with a hammer to join two objects together ▶ *v (-s, -ing, -ed)* attach (something) with nails

  nailed *v* ▷ nail
  nailing *v* ▷ nail
  nails *n, v* ▷ nail
naive [nye-eev] *adj (-r, -st)* innocent and gullible > **naively** *adv* > **naivety** [nye-**eev**-tee] *n (pl -ties)*, **naïveté** *(pl -s)*
  naively *adv* ▷ naive
  naiver *adj* ▷ naive
  naivest *adj* ▷ naive
  naïveté *n* ▷ naive
  naïvetés *n* ▷ naive
  naiveties *n* ▷ naive
  naivety *n* ▷ naive
naked *adj (-er, -est)* without clothes > **nakedness** *n (pl -es)*
  nakeder *adj* ▷ naked
  nakedest *adj* ▷ naked
  nakedness *n* ▷ naked
  nakednesses *n* ▷ naked
name *n (pl -s)* word by which a person or thing is known ▶ *v (-mes, -ming, -med)* give a name to
  named *v* ▷ name
nameless *adj* without a name
namely *adv* that is to say
  names *n, v* ▷ name
namesake *n (pl -s)* person with the same name as another
  namesakes *n* ▷ namely
  naming *v* ▷ name
  nannies *n* ▷ nanny
nanny *n (pl -nnies)* woman whose job is looking after young children
nap¹ *n (pl -s)* short sleep ▶ *v (-s, -pping, -pped)* have a short sleep
nap² *n (pl -s)* raised fibres of velvet or similar cloth

nap³ n (pl -s) card game similar to whist
napalm n (pl -s) highly inflammable jellied petrol, used in bombs
napalms n ▷ napalm
nape n (pl -s) back of the neck
napes n ▷ nape
naphtha n (pl -s) liquid mixture distilled from coal tar or petroleum, used as a solvent and in petrol
naphthalene n (pl -s) white crystalline product distilled from coal tar or petroleum, used in disinfectants, mothballs, and explosives
naphthalenes n ▷ naphthalene
naphthas n ▷ naphtha
napkin n (pl -s) piece of cloth or paper for wiping the mouth or protecting the clothes while eating
napkins n ▷ napkin
napped v ▷ nap¹
nappies n ▷ nappy
napping v ▷ nap¹
nappy n (pl -ppies) piece of absorbent material fastened round a baby's lower torso to absorb urine and faeces
naps n ▷ nap ▶ v ▷ nap¹
narcissism n (pl -s) exceptional interest in or admiration for oneself > **narcissistic** adj
narcissisms n ▷ narcissism
narcissistic adj ▷ narcissism
narcissi n ▷ narcissus
narcissus n (pl -cissi) yellow, orange, or white flower related to the daffodil
narcoses n ▷ narcosis
narcosis n (pl -s) effect of a narcotic
narcotic n (pl -s) ▶ adj (of) a drug, such as morphine or opium, which produces numbness and drowsiness, used medicinally but addictive
narcotics n ▷ narcotic
nark (Slang) v (-s, -ing, -ed) annoy ▶ n (pl -s) informer or spy
narked v ▷ nark
narkier adj ▷ narky
narkiest adj ▷ narky
narking v ▷ nark
narks v, n ▷ nark
narky adj (Slang) (-kier, -kiest) irritable or complaining
narrate v (-tes, -ting, -ted) tell (a story) > **narration** n (pl -s) > **narrator** n (pl -s)
narrated v ▷ narrate
narrates v ▷ narrate
narrating v ▷ narrate
narration n ▷ narrate

narrations n ▷ narrate
narrative n (pl -s) account, story
narratives n ▷ narrative
narrator n ▷ narrate
narrators n ▷ narrate
narrow adj (-er, -est) small in breadth in comparison to length ▶ v (-s, -ing, -ed) make or become narrow > **narrowly** adv > **narrowness** n (pl -es)
narrowed v ▷ narrow
narrower adj ▷ narrow
narrowest adj ▷ narrow
narrowing v ▷ narrow
narrowly adv ▷ narrow
narrowness n ▷ narrow
narrownesses n ▷ narrow
narrows v ▷ narrow ▶ pl n narrow part of a strait, river, or current
narwhal n (pl -s) arctic whale with a long spiral tusk
narwhals n ▷ narwhal
nasal adj of the nose > **nasally** adv
nasally adv ▷ nasal
nascent adj starting to grow or develop
nastier adj ▷ nasty
nastiest adj ▷ nasty
nastily adv ▷ nasty
nastiness n ▷ nasty
nastinesses n ▷ nasty
nasturtium n (pl -s) plant with yellow, red, or orange trumpet-shaped flowers
nasturtiums n ▷ nasturtium
nasty adj (-tier, -tiest) unpleasant > **nastily** adv > **nastiness** n (pl -es)
natal adj of or relating to birth
nation n (pl nations) people of one or more cultures or races organized as a single state
nations n ▷ nation
national adj characteristic of a particular nation ▶ n (pl -s) citizen of a nation > **nationally** adv
nationalism n (pl -s) policy of national independence > **nationalist** n (pl -s) adj
nationalisms n ▷ nationalism
nationalist n ▷ nationalism
nationalists n ▷ nationalism
nationalities n ▷ nationality
nationality n (pl -ties) fact of being a citizen of a particular nation
nationalization n ▷ nationalize
nationalizations n ▷ nationalize
nationalize v (-izes, -izing, -ized) put (an industry or a company) under state control > **nationalization** n (pl -s)
nationalized v ▷ nationalize

nationalizes v ▷ nationalize
nationalizing v ▷ nationalize
nationally adv ▷ national
nationals n ▷ national
native adj relating to a place where a person was born ▶ n (pl -s) person born in a specified place
natives n ▷ native
nativities n ▷ nativity
nativity n (pl -ties) birth or origin
natter (Informal) v (-s, -ing, -ed) talk idly or chatter ▶ n (pl -s) long idle chat
nattered v ▷ natter
nattering v ▷ natter
natters v, n ▷ natter
nattier adj ▷ natty
nattiest adj ▷ natty
natty adj (-tier, -tiest) (Informal) smart and spruce
natural adj normal or to be expected ▶ n (pl -s) person with an inborn talent or skill
naturalism n (pl -s) movement in art and literature advocating detailed realism > **naturalistic** adj
naturalisms n ▷ naturalism
naturalist n (pl -s) student of natural history
naturalistic n ▷ naturalism
naturalists n ▷ naturalist
naturalization n ▷ naturalize
naturalizations n ▷ naturalize
naturalize v (-izes, -izing, -ized) give citizenship to (a person born in another country) > **naturalization** n (pl -s)
naturalized v ▷ naturalize
naturalizes v ▷ naturalize
naturalizing v ▷ naturalize
naturally adv of course
naturals n ▷ natural
nature n (pl -s) whole system of the existence, forces, and events of the physical world that are not controlled by human beings
natures n ▷ nature
naturism n (pl -s) nudism > **naturist** n (pl -s)
naturisms n ▷ naturism
naturist n ▷ naturism
naturists n ▷ naturism
naught n (pl -s) (Lit) nothing
naughtier adj ▷ naughty
naughtiest adj ▷ naughty
naughtily adv ▷ naughty
naughtiness n ▷ naughty
naughtinesses n ▷ naughty
naughts n ▷ naught
naughty adj (-tier, -tiest) disobedient or mischievous > **naughtily** adv > **naughtiness**

n (pl -es)
nausea [naw-zee-a] n (pl -s) feeling of being about to vomit
nauseas n ▷ nausea
nauseate v (-tes, -ting, -ted) make (someone) feel sick
nauseated v ▷ nauseate
nauseates v ▷ nauseate
nauseating v ▷ nauseate
nauseous adj as if about to vomit
nautical adj of the sea or ships
nautili n ▷ nautilus
nautilus n (pl -luses, -li) shellfish with many tentacles
nautiluses n ▷ nautilus
naval adj ▷ navy
nave n (pl -s) long central part of a church
navel n (pl -s) hollow in the middle of the abdomen where the umbilical cord was attached
navels n ▷ navel
naves n ▷ nave
navies n ▷ navy
navigable adj wide, deep, or safe enough to be sailed through
navigate v (-tes, -ting, -ted) direct or plot the path or position of a ship, aircraft, or car > **navigation** n (pl -s) > **navigator** n (pl -s)
navigated v ▷ navigate
navigates v ▷ navigate
navigating v ▷ navigate
navigation n ▷ navigate
navigations n ▷ navigate
navigator n ▷ navigate
navigators n ▷ navigate
navvies n ▷ navvy
navvy n (pl -vvies) (BRIT) labourer employed on a road or a building site
navy n (pl -vies) branch of a country's armed services comprising warships with their crews and organization
nay interj (Obs) no

> **ne** adv. Ne is an old word meaning **not.** This handy little word can be very helpful when you are trying to form several words at once. Ne scores 2 points.

neanderthal [nee-ann-der-tahl] adj of a type of primitive man that lived in Europe before 12 000 BC
near prep, adv adj (-er, -est) indicating a place or time not far away ▶ adj almost being the thing specified ▶ v (-s, -ing, -ed) draw close (to) > **nearness** n (pl -es)
nearby adj not far away

neared v ▷ near
nearer adj ▷ near
nearest adj ▷ near
nearing v ▷ near
nearly adv almost
nearness n ▷ near
nearnesses n ▷ near
nears v ▷ near
nearside n (pl -s) side of a vehicle that is nearer the kerb
nearsides n ▷ nearside
neat adj (-er, -est) tidy and clean > **neatly** adv > **neatness** n (pl -es)
neater adj ▷ neat
neatest adj ▷ neat
neatly adv ▷ neat
neatness n ▷ neat
neatnesses n ▷ neat
nebula n (pl -lae) (ASTRONOMY) hazy cloud of particles and gases > **nebulous** adj vague and unclear
nebulae n ▷ nebula
nebulous adj ▷ nebula
necessarily adv ▷ necessary
necessary adj needed to obtain the desired result > **necessarily** adv
necessitate v (-tes, -ting, -ted) compel or require
necessitated v ▷ necessitate
necessitates v ▷ necessitate
necessitating v ▷ necessitate
necessities n ▷ necessity
necessity n (pl -ties) circumstances that inevitably require a certain result
neck n (pl -s) part of the body joining the head to the shoulders ▶ v (-s, -ing, -ed) (Slang) kiss and cuddle
necked v ▷ neck
neckerchief n (pl -s) piece of cloth worn tied round the neck
neckerchiefs n ▷ neckerchief
necking v ▷ neck
necklace n (pl -s) decorative piece of jewellery worn around the neck
necklaces n ▷ necklace
necks n, v ▷ neck
necromancies n ▷ necromancy
necromancy n (pl -cies) communication with the dead
necropolis [neck-**rop**-pol-liss] n (pl -ses) cemetery
necropolises n ▷ necropolis
nectar n (pl -s) sweet liquid collected from flowers by bees
nectars n ▷ nectar

nectarine n (pl -s) smooth-skinned peach
nectarines n ▷ nectarine
née [nay] prep indicating the maiden name of a married woman
need v (-s, -ing, -ed) require or be in want of ▶ n (pl -s) condition of lacking something
needed v ▷ need
needful adj necessary or required
needier adj ▷ needy
neediest adj ▷ needy
needing v ▷ need
needle n (pl -s) thin pointed piece of metal with an eye through which thread is passed for sewing ▶ v (-les, -ling, -led) (Informal) goad or provoke
needled v ▷ needle
needles n, v ▷ needle
needless adj unnecessary
needlework n (pl -s) sewing and embroidery
needleworks n ▷ needlework
needling v ▷ needle
needs v, n ▷ need ▶ adv (preceded or foll. by must) necessarily
needy adj (-dier, -diest) poor, in need of financial support
nefarious [nif-**fair**-ee-uss] adj wicked
negate v (-tes, -ting, -ted) invalidate > **negation** n (pl -s)
negated v ▷ negate
negates v ▷ negate
negating v ▷ negate
negation n ▷ negate
negations n ▷ negate
negative adj expressing a denial or refusal ▶ n (pl -s) negative word or statement
negatives n ▷ negative
neglect v (-s, -ing, -ed) take no care of ▶ n (pl -s) neglecting or being neglected > **neglectful** adj
neglected v ▷ neglect
neglectful adj ▷ neglect
neglecting v ▷ neglect
neglects v, n ▷ neglect
negligee [neg-lee-zhay] n (pl -s) woman's lightweight usu. lace-trimmed dressing gown
negligees n ▷ negligee
negligence n (pl -s) neglect or carelessness > **negligent** adj > **negligently** adv
negligences n ▷ negligence
negligent adj ▷ negligence
negligently adv ▷ negligence
negligible adj so small or unimportant as to be not worth considering
negotiable adj ▷ negotiate

negotiate v (-tes, -ting, -ted) discuss in order to reach (an agreement) ▸ **negotiation** n (pl -s) ▸ **negotiator** n (pl -s) ▸ **negotiable** adj
negotiated v ▷ negotiate
negotiates v ▷ negotiate
negotiating v ▷ negotiate
negotiation n ▷ negotiate
negotiations n ▷ negotiate
negotiator n ▷ negotiate
negotiators n ▷ negotiate
neigh n (pl -s) loud high-pitched sound made by a horse ▸ v (-s, -ing, -ed) make this sound
neighed v ▷ neigh
neighing v ▷ neigh
neighs n, v ▷ neigh
neighbour n (pl -s) person who lives or is situated near another
neighbourhood n (pl -s) district
neighbourhoods n ▷ neighbourhood
neighbouring adj situated nearby
neighbourly adj kind, friendly, and helpful
neighbours n ▷ neighbour
neither adj, pron not one nor the other ▸ conj not
nemeses n ▷ nemesis
nemesis [nem-miss-iss] n (pl -ses) retribution or vengeance
neo- combining form new, recent, or a modern form of
neolith n (pl -s) stone implement from the Neolithic age
neoliths n ▷ neolith
neologism [nee-ol-a-jiz-zum] n (pl -s) newly-coined word or an established word used in a new sense
neologisms n ▷ neologism
neon n (pl -s) (CHEM) colourless odourless gaseous element used in illuminated signs and lights
neons n ▷ neon
neophyte n (pl -s) beginner or novice
neophytes n ▷ neophyte
nephew n (pl -s) son of one's sister or brother
nephews n ▷ nephew
nephritis [nif-frite-tiss] n (pl -tises) inflammation of a kidney
nephritises n ▷ nephritis
nepotism [nep-a-tiz-zum] n (pl -s) favouritism in business shown to relatives and friends
nepotisms n ▷ nepotism
nerd n (pl -s) (Slang) boring person obsessed with a particular subject
nerds n ▷ nerd
nerve n (pl -s) cordlike bundle of fibres that conducts impulses between the brain and other parts of the body
nerveless adj numb, without feeling
nerves n ▷ nerve ▸ pl n anxiety or tension
nervier adj ▷ nervy
nerviest adj ▷ nervy
nervous adj apprehensive or worried ▸ **nervously** adv ▸ **nervousness** n (pl -es)
nervously adv ▷ nervous
nervousness n ▷ nervous
nervousnesses n ▷ nervous
nervy adj (-vier, -viest) excitable or nervous
nest n (pl -s) place or structure in which birds or certain animals lay eggs or give birth to young ▸ v (-s, -ing, -ed) make or inhabit a nest
nested v ▷ nest
nesting v ▷ nest
nests v, n ▷ nest
nestle v (-les, -ling, -led) snuggle
nestled v ▷ nestle
nestles v ▷ nestle
nestling n (pl -s) bird too young to leave the nest ▸ v ▷ nestle
nestlings n ▷ nestling
net[1] n (pl -s) fabric of meshes of string, thread, or wire with many openings ▸ v (-s, -tting, -tted) catch (a fish or animal) in a net
net[2], **nett** adj left after all deductions ▸ v (-s, -tting, -tted) yield or earn as a clear profit
netball n (pl -s) team game in which a ball has to be thrown through a net hanging from a ring at the top of a pole
netballs n ▷ netball
nether adj lower
nets v ▷ net[1, 2]
nets n ▷ net[1]
nett adj ▷ net[2]
netted v ▷ net[1, 2]
netting v ▷ net[1, 2] ▸ n (pl -s) material made of net
nettings n ▷ netting
nettle n (pl -s) plant with stinging hairs on the leaves
nettled adj irritated or annoyed
nettles n ▷ nettle
network n (pl -s) system of intersecting lines, roads, etc.
networks n ▷ network
neural adj of a nerve or the nervous system
neuralgia n (pl -s) severe pain along a nerve
neuralgias n ▷ neuralgia
neuritis [nyoor-rite-tiss] n (pl -tises) inflammation of a nerve or nerves
neuritises n ▷ neuritis
neurologies n ▷ neurology
neurologist n ▷ neurology

neurologists n ▷ neurology

neurology n (pl -gies) scientific study of the nervous system > **neurologist** n (pl -s)

neuroses n ▷ neurosis

neurosis n (pl -ses) mental disorder producing hysteria, anxiety, depression, or obsessive behaviour

neurotic adj emotionally unstable ▶ n (pl -s) neurotic person

neurotics n ▷ neurotic

neuter adj belonging to a particular class of grammatical inflections in some languages ▶ v (-s, -ing, -ed) castrate (an animal)

neutered v ▷ neuter

neutering v ▷ neuter

neuters v ▷ neuter

neutral adj taking neither side in a war or dispute ▶ n (pl -s) neutral person or nation > **neutrality** n (pl -ties)

neutralities n ▷ neutral

neutrality n ▷ neutral

neutralize v (-izes, -izing, -ized) make ineffective or neutral

neutralized v ▷ neutralize

neutralizes v ▷ neutralize

neutralizing v ▷ neutralize

neutrals n ▷ neutral

neutrino [new-tree-no] n (pl -nos) elementary particle with no mass or electrical charge

neutrinos n ▷ neutrino

neutron n (pl -s) electrically neutral elementary particle of about the same mass as a proton

neutrons n ▷ neutron

never adv at no time

nevertheless adv in spite of that

new adj (-er, -est) not existing before (foll. by to) ▶ adv recently

newbie (Informal) n (pl -s) person new to a job, club, etc

newbies n ▷ newbie

newborn adj recently or just born

newcomer n (pl -s) recent arrival or participant

newcomers n ▷ newcomer

newel n (pl -s) post at the top or bottom of a flight of stairs that supports the handrail

newels n ▷ newel

newer adj ▷ new

newest adj ▷ new

newfangled adj objectionably or unnecessarily modern

newlyweds pl n recently married couple

newness n (pl -es) novelty

newnesses n ▷ newness

news n important or interesting new happenings

newsagent n (pl -s) (BRIT) shopkeeper who sells newspapers and magazines

newsagents n ▷ newsagent

newscaster n ▷ newsreader

newscasters n ▷ newsreader

newsflash n (pl -es) brief important news item, which interrupts a radio or television programme

newsflashes n ▷ newsflash

newsier adj ▷ newsy

newsiest adj ▷ newsy

newsletter n (pl -s) bulletin issued periodically to members of a group

newsletters n ▷ newsletter

newspaper n (pl -s) weekly or daily publication containing news

newspapers n ▷ newspaper

newsprint n (pl -s) inexpensive paper used for newspapers

newsprints n ▷ newsprint

newsreader, newscaster n (pl -s) person who reads the news on the television or radio

newsreaders n ▷ newsreader

newsreel n (pl -s) short film giving news

newsreels n ▷ newsreel

newsroom n (pl -s) room where news is received and prepared for publication or broadcasting

newsrooms n ▷ newsroom

newsworthy adj sufficiently interesting to be reported as news

newsy adj (-sier, -siest) full of news

newt n (pl -s) small amphibious creature with a long slender body and tail

newton n (pl -s) unit of force

newtons n ▷ newton

newts n ▷ newt

next adj, adv immediately following

nexus n (pl nexus) connection or link

nib n (pl -s) writing point of a pen

nibble v (-les, -ling, -led) take little bites (of) ▶ n (pl -les) little bite

nibbled v ▷ nibble

nibbles v, n ▷ nibble

nibbling v ▷ nibble

nibs n (pl ▷ nib

nibses n ▷ nibs

nice adj (-r, -st) pleasant > **nicely** adv > **niceness** n (pl -es)

nicely adv ▷ nice

niceness n ▷ nice

nicenesses n ▷ nice

nicer adj ▷ nice

nicest adj ▷ nice
niceties n ▷ nicety
nicety n (pl -ties) subtle point
niche [neesh] n (pl -s) hollow area in a wall
niches n ▷ niche
nick v (-s, -ing, -ed) make a small cut in ▶ n (pl -s) small cut
nicked v ▷ nick
nickel n (pl -s) (CHEM) silvery-white metal often used in alloys
nickelodeon n (pl -s) (US) early type of jukebox
nickelodeons n ▷ nickelodeon
nickels n ▷ nickel
nicking v ▷ nick
nickname n (pl -s) familiar name given to a person or place ▶ v (-mes, -ming, -med) call by a nickname
nicknamed v ▷ nickname
nicknames n, v ▷ nickname
nicknaming v ▷ nickname
nicks v, n ▷ nick
nicotine n (pl -s) poisonous substance found in tobacco
nicotines n ▷ nicotine
niece n (pl -s) daughter of one's sister or brother
nieces n ▷ niece
niftier adj ▷ nifty
niftiest adj ▷ nifty
nifty adj (-tier, -tiest) (Informal) neat or smart
niggard n ▷ niggardly
niggardly adj stingy > **niggard** n (pl -s) stingy person
niggards n ▷ niggardly
niggle v (-les, -ling, -led) worry slightly ▶ n (pl -s) small worry or doubt
niggled v ▷ niggle
niggles v, n ▷ niggle
niggling v ▷ niggle
nigh adv, prep (Lit) near
night n (pl -s) time of darkness between sunset and sunrise
nightcap n (pl -s) drink taken just before bedtime
nightcaps n ▷ nightcap
nightclub n (pl -s) establishment for dancing, music, etc., open late at night
nightclubs n ▷ nightclub
nightdress n (pl -es) woman's loose dress worn in bed
nightdresses n ▷ nightdress
nightfall n (pl -s) approach of darkness
nightfalls n ▷ nightfall
nightie n (pl -s) (Informal) nightdress
nighties n ▷ nightie

nightingale n (pl -s) small bird with a musical song usu. heard at night
nightingales n ▷ nightingale
nightjar n (pl -s) nocturnal bird with a harsh cry
nightjars n ▷ nightjar
nightlife n (pl -s) entertainment and social activities available at night in a town or city
nightlifes n ▷ nightlife
nightly adj, adv (happening) each night
nightmare n (pl -s) very bad dream
nightmares n ▷ nightmare
nights n ▷ night
nightshade n (pl -s) plant with bell-shaped flowers which are often poisonous
nightshades n ▷ nightshade
nightshirt n (pl -s) long loose shirt worn in bed
nightshirts n ▷ nightshirt
nihilism [nye-ill-liz-zum] n (pl -s) rejection of all established authority and institutions > **nihilist** n (pl -s) > **nihilistic** adj
nihilisms n ▷ nihilism
nihilist n ▷ nihilism
nihilistic adj ▷ nihilism
nihilists n ▷ nihilism
nil n (pl -s) nothing, zero
nils n ▷ nil
nimbi n ▷ nimbus
nimble adj (-r, -st) agile and quick > **nimbly** adv
nimbler adj ▷ nimble
nimblest adj ▷ nimble
nimbly adv ▷ nimble
nimbus n (pl -bi, -buses) dark grey rain cloud
nimbuses n ▷ nimbus
nincompoop n (pl -s) (Informal) stupid person
nincompoops n ▷ nincompoop
nine adj, n (pl -s) one more than eight
ninepins n game of skittles
nines n ▷ nine
nineteen adj, n (pl -s) ten and nine > **nineteenth** adj, n (pl -s)
nineteens n ▷ nineteen
nineteenth adj, n ▷ nineteen
nineteenths n ▷ nineteen
nineties n ▷ ninety
ninetieth adj, n ▷ ninety
ninetieths n ▷ ninety
ninety adj, n (pl -ties) ten times nine > **ninetieth** adj, n
ninth adj, n (pl -s) (of) number nine in a series
ninths n ▷ ninth
niobium n (pl -s) (CHEM) white superconductive metallic element
niobiums n ▷ niobium
nip¹ v (-s, -pping, -pped) (Informal) hurry ▶ n (pl

-s) pinch or light bite

nip² n (pl **nips**) small alcoholic drink
 nipped v ▷ nip¹

nipper n (pl -s) (BRIT, AUST & NZ) (Informal) small child
 nippers n ▷ nipper
 nippier adj ▷ nippy
 nippiest adj ▷ nippy
 nipping v ▷ nip¹

nipple n (pl -s) projection in the centre of a breast
 nipples n ▷ nipple

nippy adj (Informal) (-pier, -piest) frosty or chilly
 nips v ▷ nip¹ ▶ n ▷ nip¹, ²

nirvana [near-**vah**-na] n (pl -s) (BUDDHISM) (HINDUISM) absolute spiritual enlightenment and bliss
 nirvanas n ▷ nirvana

nit n (pl -s) egg or larva of a louse (Informal)
 ▷ nitwit

nitrate n (pl -s) compound of nitric acid, used as a fertilizer
 nitrates n ▷ nitrate

nitric, nitrous, nitrogenous adj of or containing nitrogen

nitrogen [**nite**-roj-jen] n (pl -s) (CHEM) colourless odourless gas that forms four fifths of the air
 nitrogenous n ▷ nitric
 nitrogens n ▷ nitrogen

nitroglycerin n ▷ nitroglycerine

nitroglycerine, nitroglycerin n (pl -s) explosive liquid
 nitroglycerines n ▷ nitroglycerine
 nitroglycerins n ▷ nitroglycerine

nitrous adj ▷ nitric

nits n ▷ nit

nitwit n (pl -s) (Informal) stupid person
 nitwits n ▷ nitwit

> **nix** n (**nixes**). A nix is a water sprite in Germanic mythology. This is a handy little word, combining X with two of the most common tiles in the game. If you have an X on your rack, look out for opportunities on the board to play this as there's most likely an N or I available. Nix scores 10 points.

no interj expresses denial, disagreement, or refusal ▶ adj not any, not a ▶ adv not at all ▶ n (pl **noes, nos**) answer or vote of 'no'

nob n (pl -s) (CHIEFLY BRIT) (Slang) person of wealth or social distinction
 nobs n ▷ nob

nobble v (-les, -ling, -led) (BRIT) (Slang) attract the attention of (someone) in order to talk to him or her

nobbled v ▷ nobble
 nobbles v ▷ nobble
 nobbling v ▷ nobble

nobelium n (pl -s) (CHEM) artificially-produced radioactive element
 nobeliums n ▷ nobelium

nobilities n ▷ nobility

nobility n (pl -ties) quality of being noble
 > **nobleman, noblewoman** n (pl -men)

noble adj (-r, -st) showing or having high moral qualities ▶ n (pl -s) member of the nobility
 > **nobly** adv

nobleman n ▷ nobility
 noblemen n ▷ nobility
 nobler adj ▷ noble
 nobles n ▷ noble
 noblest adj ▷ noble
 noblewoman n ▷ nobility
 noblewomen n ▷ nobility
 nobly adv ▷ noble
 nobodies n ▷ nobody

nobody pron no person ▶ n (pl -dies) person of no importance

nocturnal adj of the night

nocturne n (pl -s) short dreamy piece of music
 nocturnes n ▷ nocturne

nod v (-s, -dding, -dded) lower and raise (one's head) briefly in agreement or greeting ▶ n (pl -s) act of nodding
 nodded v ▷ nod
 nodding v ▷ nod

noddle n (pl s) (CHIEFLY BRIT) (Informal) the head
 noddles n ▷ noddle

node n (pl -s) point on a plant stem from which leaves grow
 nodes n ▷ node
 nods v, n ▷ nod

nodule n (pl -s) small knot or lump
 nodules n ▷ nodule

noel n (pl -s) Christmas carol
 noels n ▷ noel
 noes n ▷ no

noggin n (pl -s) (Informal) head
 noggins n ▷ noggin

noise n (pl -s) sound, usu. a loud or disturbing one > **noiseless** adj
 noiseless adj ▷ noise
 noises n ▷ noise
 noisier adj ▷ noisy
 noisiest adj ▷ noisy
 noisily adv ▷ noisy

noisy adj (-sier, -siest) making a lot of noise
 > **noisily** adv

noisome adj (of smells) offensive

nomad n (pl -s) member of a tribe with no fixed

dwelling place, wanderer ▷ **nomadic** adj
nomadic adj ▷ nomad
nomads n ▷ nomad
nomenclature n (pl -s) system of names used in a particular subject
nomenclatures n ▷ nomenclature
nominal adj in name only > **nominally** adv
nominally adv ▷ nominal
nominate v (-tes, -ting, -ted) suggest as a candidate > **nomination** n (pl -s)
nominated v ▷ nominate
nominates v ▷ nominate
nominating v ▷ nominate
nomination n ▷ nominate
nominations n ▷ nominate
nominative n (pl -s) form of a noun indicating the subject of a verb
nominatives n ▷ nominative
nominee n (pl -s) candidate
nominees n ▷ nominee
non- prefix indicating: negation
nonagenarian n (pl -s) person aged between ninety and ninety-nine
nonagenarians n ▷ nonagenarian
nonaggression n (pl -s) policy of not attacking other countries
nonaggressions n ▷ nonaggression
nonagon n (pl -s) geometric figure with nine sides
nonagons n ▷ nonagon
nonalcoholic adj containing no alcohol
nonaligned adj (of a country) not part of a major alliance or power bloc
nonce n (pl -s) for the present
nonces n ▷ nonce
nonchalance n ▷ nonchalant
nonchalances n ▷ nonchalant
nonchalant adj casually unconcerned or indifferent > **nonchalantly** adv
> **nonchalance** n (pl -s)
nonchalantly adv ▷ nonchalant
noncombatant n (pl -s) member of the armed forces whose duties do not include fighting
noncombatants n ▷ noncombatant
noncommittal adj not committing oneself to any particular opinion
nonconductor n (pl -s) substance that is a poor conductor of heat, electricity, or sound
nonconductors n ▷ nonconductor
nonconformist n (pl -s) person who does not conform to generally accepted patterns of behaviour or thought (N-) ▶ adj (of behaviour or ideas) not conforming to accepted patterns > **nonconformity** n (pl -ties)
nonconformists n ▷ nonconformist

nonconformities n ▷ nonconformist
nonconformity n ▷ nonconformist
noncontributory adj (BRIT) denoting a pension scheme for employees, the premiums of which are paid entirely by the employer
nondescript adj lacking outstanding features
none pron not any
nonentities n ▷ nonentity
nonentity [non-**enn**-tit-tee] n (pl -ties) insignificant person or thing
nonetheless adv despite that, however
nonevent n (pl -s) disappointing or insignificant occurrence
nonevents n ▷ nonevent
nonflammable adj not easily set on fire
nonintervention n (pl refusal to intervene in the affairs of others
nonpareil [non-par-**rail**] n (pl -s) person or thing that is unsurpassed
nonpareils n ▷ nonpareil
nonpayment n (pl -s) failure to pay money owed
nonpayments n ▷ nonpayment
nonplussed adj perplexed
nonsense n (pl -s) something that has or makes no sense > **nonsensical** adj
nonsenses n ▷ nonsense
nonsensical adj ▷ nonsense
nonstandard adj denoting language that is not regarded as correct by educated native speakers
nonstarter n (pl -s) person or idea that has little chance of success
nonstarters n ▷ nonstarter
nonstick adj coated with a substance that food will not stick to when cooked
nonstop adj, adv without a stop
nontoxic adj not poisonous
noodles pl n long thin strips of pasta
nook n (pl -s) sheltered place
nooks n ▷ nook
noon n (pl -s) twelve o'clock midday
noonday adj happening at noon
noons n ▷ noon
noose n (pl -s) loop in the end of a rope, tied with a slipknot
nooses n ▷ noose
nor conj and not
norm n (pl -s) standard that is regarded as normal
normal adj usual, regular, or typical
> **normally** adv > **normality** n (pl -ties)
> **normalize** v (-izes, -izing, -ized)
normalities n ▷ normal

normality n ▷ normal
normalized v ▷ normal
normalizes v ▷ normal
normalizing v ▷ normal
normally adv ▷ normal
norms n ▷ norm
north n (pl -s) direction towards the North Pole, opposite south ▶ adj to or in the north ▶ adv in, to, or towards the north > northerly adj > northern adj > northward adj, adv > northwards adv
northerly adj ▷ north
northern adj ▷ north
northerner n (pl -s) person from the north of a country or area
northerners n ▷ northerner
norths n ▷ north
northward adj, adv ▷ north
northwards adv ▷ north
nos n ▷ no
nose n (pl -s) organ of smell, used also in breathing ▶ v (-ses, -sing, -sed) move forward slowly and carefully
nosed v ▷ nose
nosegay n (pl -s) small bunch of flowers
nosegays n ▷ nosegay
noses n, v ▷ nose
nosey, nosy adj (Informal) (-sier, -siest) prying or inquisitive > nosiness n (pl -es)
nosier adj ▷ nosey
nosiest adj ▷ nosey
nosiness n ▷ nosey
nosinesses n ▷ nosey
nosing v ▷ nosey
nosh n (pl -es) (BRIT, AUST & NZ) (Slang) food ▶ v (-shes, -shing, -shed) eat
noshed v ▷ nosh
noshes n, v ▷ nosh
noshing v ▷ nosh
nostalgia n (pl -s) sentimental longing for the past > nostalgic adj
nostalgias n ▷ nostalgia
nostalgic adj ▷ nostalgia
nostril n (pl -s) one of the two openings at the end of the nose
nostrils n ▷ nostril
nostrum n (pl -s) quack medicine
nostrums n ▷ nostrum
nosy adj (-sier, -siest) ▷ nosey
not adv expressing negation, refusal, or denial
notable adj worthy of being noted, remarkable ▶ n (pl -s) person of distinction > notably adv
notabilities n ▷ notability
notability n (pl -ties)

notables n ▷ notable
notably adv ▷ notable
notaries n ▷ notary
notary n (pl -ries) person authorized to witness the signing of legal documents
notation n (pl -s) representation of numbers or quantities in a system by a series of symbols
notations n ▷ notation
notch n (pl -es) V-shaped cut ▶ v (-ches, -ching, -ched) make a notch in (foll. by up)
notched v ▷ notch
notches n, v ▷ notch
notching v ▷ notch
note n (pl -s) short letter ▶ v (-tes, -ting, -ted) notice, pay attention to
notebook n (pl -s) book for writing in
notebooks n ▷ notebook
noted v ▷ note ▶ adj well-known
notes n, v ▷ note
noteworthy adj worth noting, remarkable
nothing pron not anything ▶ adv not at all
nothingness n (pl -es) nonexistence
nothingnesses n ▷ nothingness
notice n (pl -s) observation or attention ▶ v (-ces, -cing, -ced) become aware of
noticeable adj easily seen or detected, appreciable
noticed v ▷ notice
notices n, v ▷ notice
noticing v ▷ notice
notifiable adj having to be reported to the authorities
notification n ▷ notify
notifications n ▷ notify
notified v ▷ notify
notifies v ▷ notify
notify v (-fies, -fying, -fied) inform > notification n (pl -s)
notifying v ▷ notify
noting v ▷ note
notion n (pl -s) idea or opinion
notional adj speculative, imaginary, or unreal
notions n ▷ notion
notorieties n ▷ notorious
notoriety n ▷ notorious
notorious adj well known for something bad > notoriously adv > notoriety n (pl -ties)
notoriously adv ▷ notorious
notwithstanding prep in spite of
nougat n (pl -s) chewy sweet containing nuts and fruit
nougats n ▷ nougat
nought n (pl -s) figure o
noughties pl n (Informal) decade from 2000 to 2009

noughts n ▷ nought
noun n (pl -s) word that refers to a person, place, or thing
nouns n ▷ noun
nourish v (-shes, -shing, -shed) feed
  > **nourishment** n (pl -s)
nourished v ▷ nourish
nourishes v ▷ nourish
nourishing adj providing the food necessary for life and growth ▶ v ▷ nourish
nourishment n ▷ nourish
nourishments n ▷ nourish
nova n (pl -vae, -vas) star that suddenly becomes brighter and then gradually decreases to its original brightness
novae n ▷ nova
novas n ▷ nova
novel[1] n (pl -s) long fictitious story in book form
novel[2] adj fresh, new, or original > **novelist** n (pl -s) writer of novels
novelists n ▷ novelist
novella n (pl -s, -llae) short novel
novellae n ▷ novella
novellas n ▷ novella
novels n ▷ novel[1]
novelties n ▷ novelty
novelty n (pl -ties) newness
novena [no-vee-na] n (pl -s) (RC CHURCH) set of prayers or services on nine consecutive days
novenas n ▷ novena
novice n (pl -s) beginner
novices n ▷ novice
now adv at or for the present time ▶ conj seeing that, since
nowadays adv in these times
nowhere adv not anywhere

nox n (**noxes**). In chemistry, nox is short for nitrogen oxide. This can come in useful in the later stages of the game when there isn't much space left, or when you have an X but can't form a longer word with it. Nox scores 10 points.

noxious adj poisonous or harmful
nozzle n (pl -s) projecting spout through which fluid is discharged
nozzles n ▷ nozzle

nth adv. In mathematics, nth represents an unspecified ordinal number. Nth is a good word to remember for awkward situations on the board, as it's one of very few three-letter words that doesn't contain a vowel. Nth scores 6 points.

nu n nus. Nu is the 13th letter in the Greek alphabet. This word can be really useful when you want to form short words in the process of playing a longer one. Nu scores 2 points.

nuance [new-ahnss] n (pl -s) subtle difference in colour, meaning, or tone
nuances n ▷ nuance
nub n (pl -s) point or gist (of a story etc.)
nubs n ▷ nub
nubile [new-bile] adj (of a young woman) sexually attractive
nuclear adj of nuclear weapons or energy
nuclei n ▷ nucleus
nucleus n (pl -clei) centre, esp. of an atom or cell
nude adj (-r, -st) naked ▶ n (pl -s) naked figure in painting, sculpture, or photography > **nudity** n (pl -ties)
nuder adj ▷ nude
nudes n ▷ nude
nudest adj ▷ nude
nudge v (-dges, -dging, -dged) push gently, esp. with the elbow ▶ n (pl -s) gentle push or touch
nudged v ▷ nudge
nudges v, n ▷ nudge
nudging v ▷ nudge
nudism n (pl -s) practice of not wearing clothes > **nudist** n (pl -s)
nudisms n ▷ nudism
nudist n ▷ nudism
nudists n ▷ nudism
nudities n ▷ nude
nudity n ▷ nude
nugatory [new-gat-tree] adj of little value
nugget n (pl -s) small lump of gold in its natural state ▶ v (-s, -tting, -tted) (NZ & S AFR) polish footwear
nuggeted v ▷ nugget
nuggeting v ▷ nugget
nuggets n, v ▷ nugget
nuggetted v ▷ nugget
nuggetting v ▷ nugget
nuisance n (pl -s) something or someone that causes annoyance or bother
nuisances n ▷ nuisance
nuke (Slang) v (-kes, -king, -ked) attack with nuclear weapons ▶ n (pl -s) nuclear weapon
nuked v ▷ nuke
nukes v, n ▷ nuke
nuking v ▷ nuke
null adj not legally valid > **nullity** n (pl -s)
nullified v ▷ nullify
nullifies v ▷ nullify

nullify v (-fies, -fying, -fied) make ineffective
  nullifying v ▷ nullify
  nullities n ▷ null
  nullity n ▷ null
numb adj (-er, -est) without feeling, as through cold, shock, or fear ▶ v (-s, -ing, -ed) make numb > **numbly** adv > **numbness** n (pl -es)
numbat n (pl -s) small Australian marsupial with a long snout and tongue
  numbats n ▷ numbat
  numbed v ▷ numb
  number¹ adj ▷ numb
number² n (pl -s) sum or quantity ▶ v (-s, -ing, -ed) count
  numbered v ▷ number
  numbering v ▷ number
numberless adj too many to be counted
numberplate n (pl -s) plate on a car showing the registration number
  numberplates n ▷ numberplate
  numbers n, v ▷ number
  numbest adj ▷ numb
  numbing v ▷ numb
  numbly adv ▷ numb
  numbness n ▷ numb
  numbnesses n ▷ numb
  numbs v ▷ numb
numbskull n (pl -s) stupid person
  numbskulls n ▷ numbskull
  numeracies n ▷ numerate
  numeracy n ▷ numerate
numeral n (pl -s) word or symbol used to express a sum or quantity
  numerals n ▷ numeral
numerate adj able to do basic arithmetic > **numeracy** n (pl -cies)
numeration n (pl -s) act or process of numbering or counting
  numerations n ▷ numeration
numerator n (pl -s) (MATHS) number above the line in a fraction
  numerators n ▷ numerator
numerical adj measured or expressed in numbers > **numerically** adv
  numerically adv ▷ numerical
numerous adj existing or happening in large numbers
numismatist n (pl -s) coin collector
  numismatists n ▷ numismatist
numskull n (pl -s) ▷ numbskull
  numskulls n ▷ numskull
nun n (pl -s) female member of a religious order
nuncio n (pl -s) (RC CHURCH) pope's ambassador
  nuncios n ▷ nuncio

  nunneries n ▷ nunnery
nunnery n (pl -ries) convent
  nuns n ▷ nun
nuptial adj relating to marriage
nuptials pl n wedding
nurse n (pl -s) person employed to look after sick people, usu. in a hospital ▶ v (-ses, -sing, -sed) look after (a sick person)
  nursed v ▷ nurse
  nurseries n ▷ nursery
nursery n (pl -ries) room where children sleep or play
nurseryman n (pl -men) person who raises plants for sale
  nurserymen n ▷ nurseryman
  nurses n, v ▷ nurse
  nursing v ▷ nurse
nurture n (pl -s) act or process of promoting the development of a child or young plant ▶ v (-res, -ring, -red) promote or encourage the development of
  nurtured v ▷ nurture
  nurtures n, v ▷ nurture
  nurturing v ▷ nurture
nut n (pl -s) fruit consisting of a hard shell and a kernel
nutcracker n (pl -s) device for cracking the shells of nuts
  nutcrackers n ▷ nutcracker
nuthatch n (pl -es) small songbird
  nuthatches n ▷ nuthatch
nutmeg n (pl -s) spice made from the seed of a tropical tree
  nutmeg n ▷ nutmeg
nutria n (pl -s) fur of the coypu
  nutrias n ▷ nutria
nutrient n (pl -s) substance that provides nourishment
  nutrients n ▷ nutrient
nutriment n (pl -s) food or nourishment required by all living things to grow and stay healthy
  nutriments n ▷ nutriment
nutrition n (pl -s) process of taking in and absorbing nutrients > **nutritional** adj
  nutritional adj ▷ nutrition
  nutritions n ▷ nutrition
nutritious, nutritive adj nourishing
  nutritive adj ▷ nutritious
  nuts n ▷ nut
nutter n (pl -s) (BRIT) (Slang) insane person
  nutters n ▷ nutter
  nuttier adj ▷ nutty
  nuttiest adj ▷ nutty
nutty adj (-ttier, -ttiest) containing or

resembling nuts

nuzzle v (-**les**, -**ling**, -**led**) push or rub gently with the nose or snout
    nuzzled v ▷ nuzzle
    nuzzles v ▷ nuzzle
    nuzzling v ▷ nuzzle

> **ny** adj, adv. Ny is an old spelling of **nigh.** This word can be useful when you're forming one word adjacent to another, and so need to form two-letter words where the two words meet. Ny is also unusual in that it doesn't contain a vowel. Ny scores 5 points.

nylon n (pl -**s**) synthetic material used for clothing etc.
    nylons n ▷ nylon ▶ pl n stockings made of nylon

nymph n (pl -**s**) mythical spirit of nature, represented as a beautiful young woman
    nymphs n ▷ nymph

nymphet n (pl -**s**) sexually precocious young girl
    nymphets n ▷ nymphet

Oo

With eight Os in the bag, you're likely to have at least one on your rack during a game. There are plenty of good two-letter words starting with O. It's worth knowing that O will form a two-letter word in front of every other vowel except A, as well as in front of Y. O also combines well with X, with **ox** (9 points) as the obvious starting point, and several words that refer to **oxygen** (17). Don't forget the short everyday words that begin with O. While **on** and **or** (2 each) won't earn you many points, they can be very helpful when you are trying to score in more than one direction at a time. **Of** and **oh** (5 each) can also prove very useful.

oaf n (pl -s) stupid or clumsy person ▷ **oafish** adj
  oafish adj ▷ oaf
  oafs n ▷ oaf
oak n (pl -s) deciduous forest tree ▷ **oaken** adj
  oaken adj ▷ oak
  oaks n ▷ oak
oakum n (pl -s) fibre obtained by unravelling old rope
  oakums n ▷ oakum
oar n (pl -s) pole with a broad blade, used for rowing a boat
  oars n ▷ oar
oasis n (pl -ses) fertile area in a desert
  oases n ▷ oasis
oast n (pl -s) (CHIEFLY BRIT) oven for drying hops
  oasts n ▷ oast
oat n (pl -s) hard cereal grown as food ▶ pl grain of this cereal
oath n (pl -s) solemn promise, esp. to be truthful in court
  oaths n ▷ oath
oatmeal adj pale brownish-cream
  oats n ▷ oat
obbligato [ob-lig-**gah**-toe] n (pl -os) (MUSIC) essential part or accompaniment
  obbligatos n ▷ obbligato
  obduracies n ▷ obdurate
  obduracy n ▷ obdurate
obdurate adj hardhearted or stubborn ▷ **obduracy** n (pl -cies)
obedience n ▷ obedient
  obediences n ▷ obedient
obedient adj obeying or willing to obey ▷ **obedience** n (pl -s) ▷ **obediently** adv
  obediently adv ▷ obedient
obeisance [oh-**bay**-sanss] n (pl -s) attitude of respect
  obeisances n ▷ obeisance
obelisk [**ob**-bill-isk] n (pl -s) four-sided stone column tapering to a pyramid at the top
  obelisks n ▷ obelisk
obese [oh-**beess**] adj (-r, -st) very fat ▷ **obesity** n (pl -ties)
  obeser adj ▷ obese
  obesest adj ▷ obese
  obesities n ▷ obese
  obesity n ▷ obese
obey v (-s, -ing, -ed) carry out instructions or orders
  obeyed v ▷ obey
  obeying v ▷ obey
  obeys v ▷ obey
obfuscate v (-tes, -ting, -ted) make (something) confusing
  obfuscated v ▷ obfuscate
  obfuscates v ▷ obfuscate
  obfuscating v ▷ obfuscate
  obituaries n ▷ obituary
  obituarist n ▷ obituary
  obituarists n ▷ obituary
obituary n (pl -ies) announcement of someone's death, esp. in a newspaper ▷ **obituarist** n (pl -s)
object[1] n (pl -s) physical thing
object[2] v (-s, -ing, -ed) express disapproval ▷ **objection** n (pl -s) ▷ **objector** n (pl -s)
  objected v ▷ object[2]
  objecting v ▷ object[2]
  objection n ▷ object[2]
objectionable adj unpleasant
  objections n ▷ object[2]
objective n (pl -s) aim or purpose ▶ adj not

biased > **objectively** adv > **objectivity** n (pl -ties)

objectively adv ▷ objective

objectives n ▷ objective

objectivities n ▷ objective

objectivity n ▷ objective

objector n ▷ object²

objectors n ▷ object²

objects n, v ▷ object¹, ²

oblation n (pl -s) religious offering

oblations n ▷ oblation

obligated adj obliged to do something

obligation n (pl -s) duty

obligations n ▷ obligation

obligatory adj required by a rule or law

oblige v (-ges, -ging, -ged) compel (someone) morally or by law to do something

obliged v ▷ oblige

obliges v ▷ oblige

obliging adj ready to help other people ▶ v ▷ oblige > **obligingly** adv

obligingly adv ▷ oblige

oblique [oh-**bleak**] adj (-r, -st) slanting ▶ n (pl -s) the symbol (/) > **obliquely** adv

obliquely adv ▷ oblique

obliquer adj ▷ oblique

obliques n ▷ oblique

obliquest adj ▷ oblique

obliterate v (-tes, -ting, -ted) wipe out, destroy > **obliteration** n (pl -s)

obliterated v ▷ obliterate

obliterates v ▷ obliterate

obliterating v ▷ obliterate

obliteration n ▷ obliterate

obliterations n ▷ obliterate

oblivion n (pl -s) state of being forgotten

oblivions n ▷ oblivion

oblivious adj unaware

oblong adj having two long sides, two short sides, and four right angles ▶ n (pl -s) oblong figure

oblongs n ▷ oblong

obloquies n ▷ obloquy

obloquy [ob-**lock**-wee] n (pl -quies) verbal abuse

obnoxious adj offensive

oboe n (pl -s) double-reeded woodwind instrument > **oboist** n (pl -s)

oboes n ▷ oboe

oboist n ▷ oboe

oboists n ▷ oboe

obscene adj (-r, -st) portraying sex offensively > **obscenity** n (pl -ies)

obscener adj ▷ obscene

obscenest adj ▷ obscene

obscenities n ▷ obscene

obscenity n ▷ obscene

obscure adj (-r, -st) not well known ▶ v (-res, -ring, -red) make (something) obscure > **obscurity** n (pl -ties)

obscured v ▷ obscure

obscurer adj ▷ obscure

obscures v ▷ obscure

obscurest adj ▷ obscure

obscuring v ▷ obscure

obscurities n ▷ obscure

obscurity n ▷ obscure

obsequies [ob-**sick**-weez] pl n funeral rites

obsequious [ob-**seek**-wee-uss] adj overattentive in order to gain favour > **obsequiousness** n

obsequiousness n ▷ obsequious

observe v (-ves, -ving, -ved) see or notice > **observable** adj

observable adj ▷ observe

observance n (pl -s) observing of a custom

observances n ▷ observance

observant adj quick to notice things

observation n (pl -s) action or habit of observing

observations n ▷ observation

observatories n ▷ observatory

observatory n (pl -ries) building equipped for studying the weather and the stars

observed v ▷ observe

observer n (pl -s) person who observes, esp. one who watches someone or something carefully

observers n ▷ observer

observes v ▷ observe

observing v ▷ observe

obsess v (-es, -ing, -ed) preoccupy (someone) compulsively > **obsessed** adj > **obsessive** adj > **obsession** n (pl -s)

obsessed v, adj ▷ obsess

obsesses v ▷ obsess

obsessing v ▷ obsess

obsession n ▷ obsess

obsessions n ▷ obsess

obsessive adj ▷ obsess

obsidian n (pl -s) dark glassy volcanic rock

obsidians n ▷ obsidian

obsolescence n ▷ obsolescent

obsolescences n ▷ obsolescent

obsolescent adj becoming obsolete > **obsolescence** n (pl -s)

obsolete adj no longer in use

obstacle n (pl -s) something that makes progress difficult

obstacles n ▷ obstacle

obstetric adj ▷ obstetrics

obstetrician n ▷ obstetrics
obstetricians n ▷ obstetrics
obstetrics n branch of medicine concerned with pregnancy and childbirth > **obstetric** adj > **obstetrician** n (pl -s)
obstinacy n ▷ obstinate
obstinacies n ▷ obstinate
obstinate adj stubborn > **obstinately** adv > **obstinacy** n (pl -cies)
obstinately adv ▷ obstinate
obstreperous adj unruly, noisy
obstruct v (-s, -ing, -ed) block with an obstacle > **obstruction** n (pl -s) > **obstructive** adj
obstructed v ▷ obstruct
obstructing v ▷ obstruct
obstruction n ▷ obstruct
obstructions n ▷ obstruct
obstructive adj ▷ obstruct
obstructs v ▷ obstruct
obtain v (-s, -ing, -ed) acquire intentionally > **obtainable** adj
obtainable adj ▷ obtain
obtained v ▷ obtain
obtaining v ▷ obtain
obtains v ▷ obtain
obtrude v (-des, -ding, -ded) push oneself or one's ideas on others
obtruded v ▷ obtrude
obtrudes v ▷ obtrude
obtruding v ▷ obtrude
obtuse adj (-r, -st) mentally slow > **obtuseness** n (pl -es)
obtuseness n ▷ obtuse
obtusenesses n ▷ obtuse
obtuser adj ▷ obtuse
obtusest adj ▷ obtuse
obtrusive adj unpleasantly noticeable > **obtrusively** adv
obtrusively adv ▷ obstrusive
obverse n (pl -s) opposite way of looking at an idea
obverses n ▷ obverse
obviate v (-tes, -ting, -ted) make unnecessary
obviated v ▷ obviate
obviates v ▷ obviate
obviating v ▷ obviate
obvious adj easy to see or understand, evident > **obviously** adv
obviously adv ▷ obvious
ocarina n (pl -s) small oval wind instrument
ocarinas n ▷ ocarina
occasion n (pl -s) time at which a particular thing happens ▶ v (-s, -ing, -ed) cause
occasional adj happening sometimes > **occasionally** adv

occasionally adv ▷ occasional
occasioned v ▷ occasion
occasioning v ▷ occasion
occasions n, v ▷ occasion
occident n (pl occidents) (Lit) west > **occidental** adj
occidental adj ▷ occident
occidents n ▷ occident
occiput [ox-sip-put] n (pl -s) back of the head
occiputs n ▷ occiput
occlude v (-des, -ding, -ded) obstruct > **occlusion** n (pl -s)
occluded v ▷ occlude
occludes v ▷ occlude
occluding v ▷ occlude
occlusion n ▷ occlude
occlusions n ▷ occlude
occult adj relating to the supernatural
occupancies n ▷ occupancy
occupancy n (pl -cies) (length of) a person's stay in a specified place
occupant n (pl -s) person occupying a specified place
occupants n ▷ occupant
occupation n (pl -s) profession > **occupational** adj
occupational adj ▷ occupation
occupations n ▷ occupation
occupied v ▷ occupy
occupier n ▷ occupy
occupiers n ▷ occupy
occupies v ▷ occupy
occupy v (-pies, -pying, -pied) live or work in (a building) > **occupier** n (pl -s)
occur v (-s, -rring, -rred) happen
occurrence n (pl -s) something that occurs
occurrences n ▷ occurrence
occurred v ▷ occur
occurring v ▷ occur
occurs v ▷ occur
ocean n (pl -s) vast area of sea between continents > **oceanic** adj
oceanic adj ▷ ocean
oceanographies n ▷ oceanography
oceanography n (pl -phies) scientific study of the oceans
oceans n ▷ ocean
ocelot [oss-ill-lot] n (pl -s) American wild cat with a spotted coat
ocelots n ▷ ocelot
oche [ok-kee] n (pl -s) (DARTS) mark on the floor behind which a player must stand
oches n ▷ oche
ochre [oak-er] adj, n (pl -s) brownish-yellow (earth)

ochres n ▷ ochre

octagon n (pl -s) geometric figure with eight sides > **octagonal** adj

octagonal adj ▷ octagon

octagons n ▷ octagon

octahedra n ▷ octahedron

octahedron [ok-ta-**heed**-ron] n (pl -drons, -dra) three-dimensional geometric figure with eight faces

octahedrons n ▷ octahedra

octane n (pl -s) hydrocarbon found in petrol

octanes n ▷ octane

octave n (pl -s) (MUSIC) (interval between the first and) eighth note of a scale

octaves n ▷ octave

octet n (pl -s) group of eight performers

octets n ▷ octet

octogenarian n (pl -s) person aged between eighty and eighty-nine

octogenarians n ▷ octogenarian

octopus n (pl -es) sea creature with a soft body and eight tentacles

octopuses n ▷ octopus

ocular adj relating to the eyes or sight

odd (-er, -est) adj unusual

odder adj ▷ odd

oddest adj ▷ odd

oddities n ▷ oddity

oddity n (pl -ties) odd person or thing

oddments pl n things left over

oddness n (pl -es) quality of being odd

oddnesses n ▷ oddness

odds pl n (ratio showing) the probability of something happening

ode n (pl -s) lyric poem, usu. addressed to a particular subject

odes n ▷ ode

odious adj offensive

odium [oh-dee-um] n (pl -s) widespread dislike

odiums n ▷ odium

odorous adj ▷ odour

odour n (pl -s) particular smell > **odorous** adj > **odourless** adj

odourless adj ▷ odour

odours n ▷ odour

odyssey [odd-iss-ee] n (pl -s) long eventful journey

odysseys n ▷ odyssey

> **oe** n (oes). Oe is a Scots word for a grandchild. This is a good word to remember, as it combines two of the most common letters in the game without using any consonants. Oe scores 2 points.

oedema [id-**deem**-a] n (pl -mata) (MED) abnormal swelling

oedemata n ▷ oedema

oesophagi n ▷ oesophagus

oesophagus [ee-**soff**-a-guss] n (pl -gi) passage between the mouth and stomach

oestrogen [ee-stra-jen] n (pl -s) female hormone that controls the reproductive cycle

oestrogens n ▷ oestrogen

of prep belonging to

off prep away from ▶ adv away ▶ adj not operating ▶ n (pl -s) (CRICKET) side of the field to which the batsman's feet point

offal n (pl -s) edible organs of an animal, such as liver or kidneys

offals n ▷ offal

offcut n (pl -s) piece remaining after the required parts have been cut out

offcuts n ▷ offcut

offend v (-s, -ing, -ed) hurt the feelings of, insult

offence n (pl -s) (cause of) hurt feelings or annoyance

offences n ▷ offence

offended v ▷ offend

offender n (pl -s) person who commits a crime

offenders n ▷ offender

offending v ▷ offend

offends v ▷ offend

offensive adj disagreeable ▶ n (pl -s) position or action of attack

offensives n ▷ offensive

offer v (-s, -ing, -ed) present (something) for acceptance or rejection ▶ n (pl -s) instance of offering something

offering n (pl -s) thing offered

offered v ▷ offer

offering v ▷ offer

offerings n ▷ offering

offers v, n ▷ offer

offertories n ▷ offertory

offertory n (-ries) (CHRISTIANITY) offering of the bread and wine for Communion

offhand adj casual, curt ▶ adv without preparation

office n (pl -s) room or building where people work at desks

officer n (pl -s) person in authority in the armed services

officers n ▷ officer

offices n ▷ office

official adj of a position of authority ▶ n (pl -s) person who holds a position of authority > **officially** adv

officialdom n (pl -s) officials collectively

officialdoms n ▷ officialdom

officially adv ▷ official
officials n ▷ official
officiate v (-tes, -ting, -ted) act in an official role
officiated v ▷ officiate
officiates v ▷ officiate
officiating v ▷ officiate
officious adj interfering unnecessarily
offing n (pl -s) area of the sea visible from the shore
offings n ▷ offing
offs n ▷ off
offset v (-sets, -setting, -set) cancel out, compensate for
offsets v ▷ offset
offsetting v ▷ offset
offshoot n (pl -s) something developed from something else
offshoots n ▷ offshoot
offside adj, adv (SPORT) (positioned) illegally ahead of the ball
offspring n (pl -s) child
offsprings n ▷ offspring
oft adv (Poetic) often
often adv frequently, much of the time
ogle v (-les, -ling, -led) stare at (someone) lustfully
ogled v ▷ ogle
ogles v ▷ ogle
ogling v ▷ ogle
ogre n (pl -s) giant that eats human flesh
ogres n ▷ ogre
oh interj exclamation of surprise, pain, etc.
ohm n (pl -s) unit of electrical resistance
ohms n ▷ ohm

> **oi** interj. Oi is something people shout to attract attention. This is a good word to remember, as it combines two of the most common letters in the game without using any consonants. Oi scores 2 points.

oil n (pl -s) viscous liquid, insoluble in water and usu. flammable ▷ petroleum ▶ pl oil-based paints used in art ▶ v (-s, -ing, -ed) lubricate (a machine) with oil > **oily** adj (-lier, -liest)
oiled v ▷ oil
oilfield n (-s) area containing oil reserves
oilfields n ▷ oilfield
oilier adj ▷ oil
oiliest adj ▷ oil
oiling v ▷ oil
oils n, v ▷ oil
oilskin n (pl -s) (garment made from) waterproof material

oilskins n ▷ oilskin
oily adj ▷ oil
ointment n (pl -s) greasy substance used for healing skin or as a cosmetic
ointments n ▷ ointment
okapi [ok-kah-pee] n (pl -s) African animal related to the giraffe but with a shorter neck
okapis n ▷ okapi
okra n (pl -s) tropical plant with edible green pods
okras n ▷ okra
okay (Informal) interj expression of approval ▶ v (-s, -ing, -ed) approve (something) ▶ n (pl -s) approval
okayed v ▷ okay
okaying v ▷ okay
okays v, n ▷ okay
old adj (-er, -est) having lived or existed for a long time
olden adj old
older adj ▷ old
oldest adj ▷ old
oldie n (pl -s) (Informal) old but popular song or film
oldies n ▷ oldie
oleaginous [ol-lee-aj-in-uss] adj oily, producing oil
oleander [ol-lee-ann-der] n (pl -s) Mediterranean flowering evergreen shrub
oleanders n ▷ oleander
olfactory adj relating to the sense of smell
oligarchic adj ▷ oiligarchy
oligarchical adj ▷ oligarchy
oligarchies n ▷ oligarchy
oligarchy [ol-lee-gark-ee] n (pl -ies) government by a small group of people > **oligarchic, oligarchical** adj
olive n (pl -s) small green or black fruit used as food or pressed for its oil ▶ adj greyish-green
olives n ▷ olive
ombudsman n (pl -men) official who investigates complaints against government organizations
ombudsmen n ▷ ombudsman
omelette n (pl -s) dish of eggs beaten and fried
omelettes n ▷ omelette
omen n (pl (pl -s) happening or object thought to foretell success or misfortune
omens n ▷ omen
ominous adj worrying, seeming to foretell misfortune
omit v (-s, -tting, -tted) leave out > **omission** n (pl -s)
omission n ▷ omit
omissions n ▷ omit

omits v ▷ omit
omitted v ▷ omit
omitting v ▷ omit
omnibus n (pl -es) several books or TV or radio programmes made into one
omnibuses n ▷ omnibus
omnipotence n ▷ omnipotent
omnipotences n ▷ omnipotent
omnipotent adj having unlimited power > **omnipotence** n (pl -s)
omnipresence n ▷ omnipresent
omnipresences n ▷ omnipresent
omnipresent adj present everywhere > **omnipresence** n (pl -s)
omniscience n ▷ omniscient
omnisciences n ▷ omniscient
omniscient [om-niss-ee-ent] adj knowing everything > **omniscience** n (pl -s)
omnivore n (pl -s) omnivorous animal
omnivores n ▷ omnivore
omnivorous [om-niv-vor-uss] adj eating food obtained from both animals and plants
on prep indicating position above, attachment, closeness, etc. ▶ adv in operation ▶ adj operating ▶ n (pl -s) (CRICKET) side of the field on which the batsman stands
once adv on one occasion ▶ conj as soon as
oncogene [on-koh-jean] n (pl -s) gene that can cause cancer when abnormally activated
oncogenes n ▷ oncogene
oncoming adj approaching from the front
one adj single, lone ▶ n (pl -s) number or figure 1 ▶ pron any person
oneness n (pl -es) unity
onenesses n ▷ oneness
onerous [own-er-uss] adj (of a task) difficult to carry out
ones n ▷ one
oneself pron ▷ one
ongoing adj in progress, continuing
onion n (pl -s) strongly flavoured edible bulb
onions n ▷ onion
online adj (of a computer) directly controlled by a central processor
onlooker n (pl -s) person who watches without taking part
onlookers n ▷ onlooker
only adj alone of its kind ▶ adv exclusively ▶ conj but
onomatopoeia [on-a-mat-a-pee-a] n (pl -s) use of a word which imitates the sound it represents, such as hiss > **onomatopoeic** adj
onomatopoeias n ▷ onomatopoeia
onomatopoeic adj ▷ onomatopoeia
onset n (pl -s) beginning

onsets n ▷ onset
onslaught n (pl -s) violent attack
onslaughts n ▷ onslaught
onto prep to a position on
ontological adj ▷ ontology
ontologies n ▷ ontology
ontology n (pl -gies) branch of philosophy concerned with existence > **ontological** adj
onus [own-uss] n (pl -es) responsibility or burden
onuses n ▷ onus
onward adj directed or moving forward ▶ adv (also **onwards**) ahead, forward
onwards see ▷ onward
onyx n (pl -es) type of quartz with coloured layers
onyxes n ▷ onyx

oo n (oos). Oo is a Scots word for **wool**. This is a good word to remember, as it combines two of the most common letters in the game without using any consonants. Oo scores two points.

oodles pl n (Informal) great quantities
ooze[1] v (-zes, -zing, -zed) flow slowly ▶ n (pl -s) sluggish flow > **oozy** adj (-zier, -ziest)
ooze[2] n (-s) soft mud at the bottom of a lake or river
oozed v ▷ ooze
oozes v, n ▷ ooze[1, 2]
oozier adj ▷ ooze[1]
ooziest adj ▷ ooze[1]
oozing v ▷ ooze
oozy adj ▷ ooze[1]
opacities n ▷ opaque
opacity n ▷ opaque
opal n (pl -s) iridescent precious stone
opalescent adj iridescent like an opal
opals n ▷ opal
opaque adj (-r, -st) not able to be seen through, not transparent > **opacity** n (-ties)
opaquer adj ▷ opaque
opaquest adj ▷ opaque
open adj (-er, -est) not closed ▶ v (-s, -ing, -ed) (cause to) become open ▶ n (pl -s) (SPORT) competition which all may enter
opened v ▷ open
opener n instrument for opening containers
openest adj ▷ open
opening n (pl -s) opportunity ▶ adj first ▶ v ▷ open
openings n ▷ opening
openly adv without concealment
opens v, n ▷ open
opera[1] n (pl -s) drama in which the text is sung to an orchestral accompaniment > **operatic**

adj

opera² *n* ▷ opus

operas *n* ▷ opera

operate *v* (-tes, -ting, -ted) (cause to) work > **operator** *n* (*pl* -s)

operated *v* ▷ operate

operates *v* ▷ operate

operatic *adj* ▷ opera¹

operating *v* ▷ operate

operation *n* (*pl* -s) method or procedure of working

operational *adj* in working order

operations *n* ▷ operation

operative *adj* working ▶ *n* (*pl* -s) worker with a special skill

operatives *n* ▷ operative

operator *n* ▷ operate

operators *n* ▷ operate

operetta *n* (*pl* -s) light-hearted comic opera

operettas *n* ▷ operetta

ophthalmic *adj* relating to the eye

ophthalmologies *n* ▷ ophthalmology

ophthalmologist *n* ▷ ophthalmology

ophthalmologists *n* ▷ ophthalmology

ophthalmology *n* (*pl* -gies) study of the eye and its diseases > **ophthalmologist** *n* (*pl* -s)

opiate *n* (*pl* -s) narcotic drug containing opium

opiates *n* ▷ opiate

opine *v* (-nes, -ning, -ned) (*Old-fashioned*) express an opinion

opined *v* ▷ opine

opines *v* ▷ opine

opining *v* ▷ opine

opinion *n* (*pl* -s) personal belief or judgment

opinionated *adj* having strong opinions

opinions *n* ▷ opinion

opium *n* (*pl* -s) addictive narcotic drug made from poppy seeds

opiums *n* ▷ opium

opossum *n* (*pl* -s) small marsupial of America or Australasia

opossums *n* ▷ opossum

opponent *n* (*pl* -s) person one is working against in a contest, battle, or argument

opponents *n* ▷ opponent

opportune *adj* happening at a suitable time

opportunism *n* ▷ opportunist

opportunisms , ▷ opportunist

opportunist *n* (*pl* -s) ▶ *adj* (person) doing whatever is advantageous without regard for principles > **opportunism** *n* (*pl* -s)

opportunists *n* ▷ opportunist

opportunities *n* ▷ opportunity

opportunity *n* (*pl* -ties) favourable time or condition

oppose *v* (-ses, -sing, -sed) work against

opposed *v* ▷ oppose

opposes *v* ▷ oppose

opposing *v* ▷ oppose

opposition *n* (*pl* -s) obstruction or hostility

oppositions *n* ▷ opposition

opposite *adj* situated on the other side ▶ *n* (*pl* -s) person or thing that is opposite ▶ *prep* facing ▶ *adv* on the other side

opposites *n* ▷ opposite

oppress *v* (-es, -ing, -ed) control by cruelty or force > **oppression** *n* (*pl* -s) > **oppressor** *n* (*pl* -s)

oppressed *v* ▷ oppress

oppresses *v* ▷ oppress

oppressing *v* ▷ oppress

oppression *n* ▷ oppress

oppressions *n* ▷ oppress

oppressive *adj* tyrannical > **oppressively** *adv*

oppressively *adv* ▷ oppressive

oppressor *n* ▷ oppress

oppressors *n* ▷ oppress

opprobrium [op-probe-ree-um] *n* (*pl* -s) state of being criticized severely for wrong one has done

opprobriums *n* ▷ opprobrium

opt *v* (-s, -ing, -ed) show a preference, choose

opted *v* ▷ opt

opting *v* ▷ opt

opts *v* ▷ opt

optic *adj* relating to the eyes or sight > **optical** *adj*

optical *adj* ▷ optic

optics *n* science of sight and light

optician *n* (*pl* -s) (*also* **ophthalmic optician**) person qualified to prescribe glasses (*also* **dispensing optician**)

opticians *n* ▷ optician

optimism *n* (*pl* -s) tendency to take the most hopeful view > **optimist** *n* (*pl* -s) > **optimistic** *adj* > **optimistically** *adv*

optimisms *n* ▷ optimism

optimist *n* ▷ optimism

optimistic *adj* ▷ optimism

optimistically *adv* ▷ optimism

optimists *n* ▷ optimism

optima *n* ▷ optimum

optimal *adj* ▷ optimum

optimize *v* (-zes, -zing, -zed) make the most of

optimized *v* ▷ optimize

optimizes *v* ▷ optimize

optimizing *v* ▷ optimize

optimum *n* (*pl* -ma, -mums) best possible conditions ▶ *adj* most favourable > **optimal** *adj*

optimums *n* ▷ optimum
option *n* (*pl* -s) choice
optional *adj* possible but not compulsory
options *n* ▷ option
optometries *n* ▷ optometry
optometrist *n* (*pl* -s) person qualified to prescribe glasses > **optometry** *n* (-ries)
optometrists *n* ▷ optometrist
optometry *n* ▷ optometrist
opulence *n* ▷ opulent
opulences *n* ▷ opulent
opulent [op-pew-lent] *adj* having or indicating wealth > **opulence** *n* (-s)
opus *n* (*pl* opuses, opera) artistic creation, esp. a musical work
opuses *n* ▷ opus
or *conj* used to join alternatives
oracle *n* (*pl* -s) shrine of an ancient god > **oracular** *adj*
oracles *n* ▷ oracle
oracular *adj* ▷ oracle
oral *adj* spoken ▶ *n* (*pl* -s) spoken examination > **orally** *adv*
orally *adv* ▷ oral
orals *n* ▷ oral
orange *n* (*pl* -s) reddish-yellow citrus fruit ▶ *adj* reddish-yellow
orangeade *n* (BRIT) orange-flavoured, usu. fizzy drink
orangeades *n* ▷ orangeade
orangeries *n* ▷ orangery
orangery *n* (*pl* -ries) greenhouse for growing orange trees
oranges *n* ▷ orange
oration *n* (*pl* -s) formal speech
orations *n* ▷ oration
orator [or-rat-tor] *n* (*pl* -s) skilful public speaker
oratorical *adj* ▷ oratory
oratories *n* ▷ oratory[1, 2]
oratorio [or-rat-tor-ee-oh] *n* (*pl* -s) musical composition for choir and orchestra, usu. with a religious theme
oratorios *n* ▷ oratorio
orators *n* ▷ orator
oratory[1] [or-rat-tree] *n* (*pl* -ries) art of making speeches > **oratorical** *adj*
oratory[2] *n* (*pl* -ries) small private chapel
orb *n* (*pl* -s) ceremonial decorated sphere with a cross on top, carried by a monarch
orbs *n* ▷ orb
orbit *n* (*pl* -s) curved path of a planet, satellite, or spacecraft around another body ▶ *v* (-s, -ing, -ed) move in an orbit around > **orbital** *adj*
orbital *adj* ▷ orbit
orbited *v* ▷ orbit

orbiting *v* ▷ orbit
orbits *n*, *v* ▷ orbit
orchard *n* (*pl* -s) area where fruit trees are grown
orchards *n* ▷ orchard
orchestra *n* (*pl* -s) large group of musicians, esp. playing a variety of instruments (also **orchestra pit**) > **orchestral** *adj*
orchestral *adj* ▷ orchestra
orchestras *n* ▷ orchestra
orchestrate *v* (-tes, -ting, -ted) arrange (music) for orchestra > **orchestration** *n* (*pl* -s)
orchestrated *v* ▷ orchestrate
orchestrates *v* ▷ orchestrate
orchestrating *v* ▷ orchestrate
orchestration *n* ▷ orchestrate
orchestrations *n* ▷ orchestrate
orchid *n* (*pl* -s) plant with flowers that have unusual lip-shaped petals
orchids *n* ▷ orchid
ordain *v* (-s, -ing, -ed) make (someone) a member of the clergy
ordained *v* ▷ ordain
ordaining *v* ▷ ordain
ordains *v* ▷ ordain
ordeal *n* (*pl* -s) painful or difficult experience
ordeals *n* ▷ ordeal
order *n* (*pl* -s) instruction to be carried out ▶ *v* (-s, -ing, -ed) give an instruction to
orderlies *n* ▷ orderly
orderliness *n* ▷ orderly
orderlinesses *n* ▷ orderly
orderly *adj* well-organized ▶ *n* (*pl* -lies) male hospital attendant > **orderliness** *n* (*pl* -es)
ordered *v* ▷ order
ordering *v* ▷ order
orders *n*, *v* ▷ order
ordinance *n* (*pl* -s) official rule or order
ordinances *n* ▷ ordinance
ordinarily *adv* ▷ ordinary
ordinary *adj* usual or normal > **ordinarily** *adv*
ordination *n* (*pl* -s) act of making someone a member of the clergy
ordinations *n* ▷ ordination
ordnance *n* (*pl* -s) weapons and military supplies
ordnances *n* ▷ ordnance
ordure *n* (*pl* -s) excrement
ordures *n* ▷ ordure
ore *n* (*pl* -s) (rock containing) a mineral which yields metal
ores *n* ▷ ore
oregano [or-rig-gah-no] *n* (*pl* -nos) sweet-smelling herb used in cooking
oreganos *n* ▷ oregano

organ n (pl -s) part of an animal or plant that has a particular function, such as the heart or lungs

organdie n (pl -s) fine cotton fabric

organdies n ▷ organdie

organic adj of or produced from animals or plants (CHEM) > **organically** adv

organically adv ▷ organic

organism n (-s) any living animal or plant

organisms n ▷ organism

organist n (pl -s) organ player

organists n ▷ organist

organization n (pl -s) group of people working together > **organizational** adj

organizational adj ▷ organization

organizations n ▷ organization

organize v (-zes, -zing, -zed) make arrangements for > **organizer** n (pl -s)

organized v ▷ organize

organizer n ▷ organize

organizers n ▷ organize

organizes v ▷ organize

organizing v ▷ organize

organs n ▷ organ

orgasm n (pl -s) most intense point of sexual pleasure > **orgasmic** adj

orgasmic adj ▷ orgasm

orgasms n ▷ orgasm

orgiastic adj ▷ orgy

orgies n ▷ orgy

orgy n (pl -gies) party involving promiscuous sexual activity > **orgiastic** adj

orient¹, orientate v (-s, -ing, -ed) position (oneself) according to one's surroundings > **orientation** n (pl -s)

orient² n (pl -s) (Lit) east > **oriental** adj

oriental adj ▷ orient²

orientate v ▷ orient

orientated v ▷ orient

orientates v ▷ orient

orientating v ▷ orient

orientation n ▷ orient

orientations n ▷ orient

oriented v ▷ orient

orienteering n (pl -s) sport in which competitors hike over a course using a compass and map

orienteerings n ▷ orienteering

orienting v ▷ orient

orients v ▷ orient

Orients n ▷ Orient

Orientalist n (pl -s) specialist in the languages and history of the Far East

Orientalists n ▷ Orientalist

orifice [or-rif-fiss] n (pl -s) opening or hole

orifices n ▷ orifice

origami [or-rig-gah-mee] n (pl -mis) Japanese decorative art of paper folding

origamis n ▷ origami

origin n (pl -s) point from which something develops

original adj first or earliest ▶ n (pl -s) first version, from which others are copied > **originality** n (pl -ies) > **originally** adv

originalities n ▷ original

originality n ▷ original

originally adv ▷ original

originals n ▷ original

originate v (-tes, -ting, -ted) come or bring into existence > **origination** n (pl -s) > **originator** n (pl -s)

originated v ▷ originate

originates v ▷ originate

originating v ▷ originate

origination n ▷ originate

originations n ▷ originate

originator n ▷ originate

originator n ▷ originate

origins n ▷ origin

oriole n (pl -s) tropical or American songbird

orioles n ▷ oriole

ormolu n (pl -lus) gold-coloured alloy used for decoration

ormolus n ▷ ormolu

ornament n (pl -s) decorative object ▶ v (-s, -ing, -ed) decorate > **ornamental** adj > **ornamentation** n (pl -s)

ornamental adj ▷ ornament

ornamentation n ▷ ornament

ornamentations n ▷ ornament

ornamented v ▷ ornament

ornamenting v ▷ ornament

ornaments n, v ▷ ornament

ornate adj highly decorated, elaborate

ornithological adj ▷ ornithology

ornithologies n ▷ ornithology

ornithologist n ▷ ornithology

ornithologists n ▷ ornithology

ornithology n (pl -gies) study of birds > **ornithological** adj > **ornithologist** n (pl -s)

orphan n (pl -s) child whose parents are dead

orphanage n (pl -s) children's home for orphans

orphanages n ▷ orphanage

orphaned adj having no living parents

orphans n ▷ orphan

orreries n ▷ orrery

orrery n (pl -ries) mechanical model of the solar system

orris n (pl -es) kind of iris (also **orris root**)

orrises n ▷ orris

orthodontics n (pl branch of dentistry concerned with correcting irregular teeth > **orthodontist** n (pl -s)
orthodontist n ▷ orthodontics
orthodontists n ▷ orhtodontics

orthodox adj conforming to established views > **orthodoxy** n (pl -ies)
orthodoxies n ▷ orthodox
orthodoxy n ▷ orthodox

orthography n (pl -phies) correct spelling
orthographies n ▷ orthography
orthopaedic adj ▷ orthopaedics

orthopaedics n (pl branch of medicine concerned with disorders of the bones or joints > **orthopaedic** adj

oryx n (pl -es) large African antelope
oryxes n ▷ oryx

os n (ossa). Os is a technical word for **bone.** This word won't score many points on its own, but will allow you to connect a word beginning with O to one ending in S (e.g. most plurals). Os scores 2 points.

oscillate [oss-ill-late] v (-tes, -ting, -ted) swing back and forth > **oscillation** n (pl -s) > **oscillator** n (pl -s)
oscillated v ▷ oscillate
oscillates v ▷ oscillate
oscillating v ▷ oscillate
oscillation n ▷ oscillate
oscillation n ▷ oscillate
oscillations n ▷ oscillate
oscillator n ▷ oscillate
oscillators n ▷ oscillate

oscilloscope [oss-sill-oh-scope] n (pl -s) instrument that shows the shape of a wave on a cathode-ray tube
oscilloscopes n ▷ oscilloscope

osier [oh-zee-er] n (pl -s) willow tree
osiers n ▷ osier

osmium n (pl -s) (CHEM) heaviest known metallic element
osmiums n ▷ osmium

osmosis n (pl -ses) movement of a liquid through a membrane from a lower to a higher concentration > **osmotic** adj
osmoses n ▷ osmosis
osmotic adj ▷ osmosis

osprey n (pl -s) large fish-eating bird of prey
ospreys n ▷ osprey
ossification n ▷ ossify
ossifications n ▷ ossify
ossified v ▷ ossify
ossifies v ▷ ossify

ossify v (-fies, -fying, -fied) (cause to) become bone, harden > **ossification** n (pl -s)
ossifying v ▷ ossify

ostensible adj apparent, seeming > **ostensibly** adv
ostensibly adv ▷ ostensible

ostentation n (pl -s) pretentious display > **ostentatious** adj > **ostentatiously** adv
ostentations n ▷ ostentation
ostentatious adj ▷ ostentation
ostentatiously adv ▷ ostentation

osteopath n ▷ osteopathy
osteopathies n ▷ osteopathy
osteopaths n ▷ osteopathy

osteopathy n (pl -thies) medical treatment involving manipulation of the joints > **osteopath** n (pl -s)

osteoporosis n (pl -ses) brittleness of the bones, caused by lack of calcium
osteoporoses n ▷ osteoporosis

ostracism n ▷ ostracize
ostracisms n ▷ ostracize

ostracize v (-zes, -zing, -zed) exclude (a person) from a group > **ostracism** n (pl -s)
ostracized v ▷ ostracize
ostracizes v ▷ ostracize
ostracizing v ▷ ostracize

ostrich n (pl -es) large African bird that runs fast but cannot fly
ostriches n ▷ ostrich

other adj remaining in a group of which one or some have been specified ▶ n (pl -s) other have or thing
others n ▷ other

otherwise conj or else, if not ▶ adv differently, in another way

otherworldly adj concerned with spiritual rather than practical matters

otiose [oh-tee-oze] adj not useful

otter n (pl -s) small brown freshwater mammal that eats fish
otters n ▷ otter

ottoman n (pl -mans) storage chest with a padded lid for use as a seat
ottomans n ▷ ottoman

ou n (ous). Ou is a South African slang word for a man. This word doesn't score many points, but is very useful when you are trying to form words in more than one direction. Ou scores 2 points.

oubliette [oo-blee-ett] n (pl -s) dungeon entered only by a trapdoor
oubliettes n ▷ oubliette

ouch interj exclamation of sudden pain

ought *v* used to express: obligation
ounce *n* (*pl* -s) unit of weight equal to one sixteenth of a pound (28.4 grams)
  ounces *n* ▷ ounce
our *adj* belonging to us
ours *pron* thing(s) belonging to us
  ourselves *pron* ▷ we, us
  ousel *n* (*pl* -s) ▷ dipper
  ousels *n* ▷ ousel
oust *v* (-s, -ing, -ed) force (someone) out, expel
  ousted *v* ▷ oust
  ousting *v* ▷ oust
  ousts *v* ▷ oust
out *adv, adj* denoting movement or distance away from, a state of being used up or extinguished, public availability, etc. ▶ *v* (-s, -ing, -ed) (*Informal*) name (a public figure) as being homosexual
outback *n* (*pl* -s) remote bush country of Australia
  outbacks *n* ▷ outback
outbid *v* (-bids, -bidding, -bid, -bidden) offer a higher price than
  outbid *v* ▷ outbid
  outbidden *v* ▷ outbid
  outbidding *v* ▷ outbid
  outbids *v* ▷ outbid
outbreak *n* (*pl* -s) sudden occurrence (of something unpleasant)
  outbreaks *n* ▷ outbreak
outburst *n* (*pl* -s) sudden expression of emotion
  outbursts *n* ▷ outburst
outcast *n* (*pl* -s) person rejected by a particular group
  outcasts *n* ▷ outcast
outclass *v* (-es, -ing, -ed) surpass in quality
  outclassed *v* ▷ outclass
  outclasses *v* ▷ outclass
  outclassing *v* ▷ outclass
outcome *n* (*pl* -s) result
  outcomes *n* ▷ outcome
  outcries *n* ▷ outcry
outcrop *n* (*pl* -s) part of a rock formation that sticks out of the earth
  outcrops *n* ▷ outcrop
outcry *n* (*pl* -ries) vehement or widespread protest
outdo *v* (-does, -doing, -did, -done) surpass in performance
  outdid *v* ▷ outdo
  outdoes *v* ▷ outdo
  outdoing *v* ▷ outdo
  outdone *v* ▷ outdo
  outdoor *adj* ▷ outdoors

outdoors *adv* in(to) the open air ▶ *n* (*pl* the open air > **outdoor** *adj*
  outed *v* ▷ out
outer *adj* on the outside
outermost *adj* furthest out
outface *v* (-ces, -cing, -ced) subdue or disconcert (someone) by staring
  outfaced *v* ▷ outface
  outfaces *v* ▷ outface
  outfacing *v* ▷ outface
outfield *n* (*pl* -s) (CRICKET) area far from the pitch
  outfields *n* ▷ outfield
outfit *n* (*pl* -s) matching set of clothes
  outfits *n* ▷ outfit
outfitter *n* (*pl* -s) supplier of men's clothes
  outfitters *n* ▷ outfitter
outflank *v* (-s, -ing, -ed) get round the side of (an enemy army)
  outflanked *v* ▷ outflank
  outflanking *v* ▷ outflank
  outflanks *v* ▷ outflank
outgoing *adj* leaving
outgoings *pl n* expenses
outgrow *v* (-grows, -growing, -grew, -grown) become too large or too old for
  outgrew *v* ▷ outgrow
  outgrowing *v* ▷ outgrow
  outgrown *v* ▷ outgrow
  outgrows *v* ▷ outgrow
outgrowth *n* natural development
  outgrowths *n* ▷ outgrowth
outhouse *n* (*pl* -s) building near a main building
  outhouses *n* ▷ outhouse
outing *n* (*pl* -s) leisure trip ▶ *v* ▷ out
  outings *n* ▷ outing

> **outjinx** *v* (outjinxes, outjinxing, outjinxed). Outjinx means to outmanoeuvre. If someone else plays **jinx**, you can outjinx them by adding O, U and T! If you can form the whole word using all of your letters, you'll get a 50-point bonus. Outjinx scores 21 points.

outlandish *adj* extremely unconventional
outlaw *n* (*pl* -s) (HIST) criminal deprived of legal protection, bandit ▶ *v* (-s, -ing, -ed) make illegal (HIST)
  outlawed *v* ▷ outlaw
  outlawing *v* ▷ outlaw
  outlaws *n, v* ▷ outlaw
outlay *n* (*pl* -s) expenditure
  outlays *n* ▷ outlay
outlet *n* (*pl* -s) means of expressing emotion
  outlets *n* ▷ outlet

outline n (pl -s) short general explanation ▸ v (-nes, -ning, -ned) summarize
  outlined v ▷ outline
  outlines n, v ▷ outline
  outlining v ▷ outline

outlook n (pl -s) attitude
  outlooks n ▷ outlook

outlying adj distant from the main area

outmanoeuvre v (-res, -ring, -red) get an advantage over
  outmanoeuvred v ▷ outmanoeuvre
  outmanoeuvres v ▷ outmanoeuvre
  outmanoeuvring v ▷ outmanoeuvre

outmoded adj no longer fashionable or accepted

outnumber v (-s, -ing, -ed) exceed in number
  outnumbered v ▷ outnumber
  outnumbering v ▷ outnumber
  outnumbers v ▷ outnumber

outpatient n (pl -s) patient who does not stay in hospital overnight
  outpatients n ▷ outpatient

outpost n (pl -s) outlying settlement
  outposts n ▷ outpost

outpouring n (pl -s) passionate outburst
  outpourings n ▷ outpouring

output n (pl -s) amount produced ▸ v (-puts, -putting, -putted) (COMPUTERS) produce (data) at the end of a process
  outputted v ▷ output
  outputting v ▷ output
  outputs n, v ▷ output

outrage n (pl -s) great moral indignation ▸ v (-s, -ing, -ed) offend morally
  outraged v ▷ outrage

outrageous adj shocking > **outrageously** adv
  outrageously adv ▷ outrageous
  outrages n, v ▷ outrage
  outraging v ▷ outrage

outré [oo-tray] adj shockingly eccentric

outrider n (pl -s) motorcyclist acting as an escort
  outriders n ▷ outrider

outrigger n (pl -s) stabilizing frame projecting from a boat
  outriggers n ▷ outrigger

outright adj, adv absolute(ly)

outrun v (-runs, -running, -ran, -run) run faster than
  outran v ▷ outrun
  outrun v ▷ outrun
  outrunning v ▷ outrun
  outruns v ▷ outrun
  outs v ▷ out

outset n (pl -s) beginning

outsets n ▷ outset

outshine v (-shines, -shining, -shone) surpass (someone) in excellence
  outshines v ▷ outshine
  outshining v ▷ outshine
  outshone v ▷ outshine

outside prep, adj adv indicating movement to or position on the exterior ▸ adj unlikely ▸ n (pl -s) external area or surface

outsider n (pl -s) person outside a specific group
  outsiders n ▷ outsider
  outsides n ▷ outside

outsize, outsized adj larger than normal
  outsized adj ▷ outsize

outskirts pl n outer areas, esp. of a town

outsmart v (-s, -ing, -ed) (Informal) outwit
  outsmarted v ▷ outsmart
  outsmarting v ▷ outsmart
  outsmarts v ▷ outsmart

outspan v (-s, -nning, -nned) (S AFR) relax
  outspanned v ▷ outspan
  outspanning v ▷ outspan
  outspans v ▷ outspan

outspoken adj tending to say what one thinks

outstanding adj excellent

outstrip v (-s, -pping, -pped) surpass
  outstripped v ▷ outstrip
  outstripping v ▷ outstrip
  outstrips v ▷ outstrip

outtake n (pl -s) unreleased take from a recording session, film, or TV programme
  outtakes n ▷ outtake

outward adj apparent ▸ adv (also **outwards**) away from somewhere > **outwardly** adv
  outwardly adv ▷ outward

outweigh v (-s, -ing, -ed) be more important, significant, or influential than
  outweighed v ▷ outweigh
  outweighing v ▷ outweigh
  outweighs v ▷ outweigh

outwit v (-s, -tting, -tted) get the better of (someone) by cunning
  outwits v ▷ outwit
  outwitted v ▷ outwit
  outwitting v ▷ outwit

ouzel [ooze-el] n (pl -s) ▷ dipper
  ouzels n ▷ ouzel

ova n ▷ ovum

oval adj egg-shaped ▸ n (pl -s) anything that is oval in shape
  ovals n ▷ oval

ovarian adj ▷ ovary

ovaries n ▷ ovary

ovary n (pl -ries) female egg-producing organ

> **ovarian** *adj*

ovation *n* (*pl* -s) enthusiastic round of applause

ovations *n* ▷ ovation

oven *n* (*pl* -s) heated compartment or container for cooking or for drying or firing ceramics

ovens *n* ▷ oven

over *prep*, *adv* indicating position on the top of, movement to the other side of, amount greater than, etc. ▶ *adj* finished ▶ *n* (*pl* -s) (CRICKET) series of six balls bowled from one end

overall *adj*, *adv* in total ▶ *n* (*pl* -s) coat-shaped protective garment ▶ *pl* protective garment consisting of trousers with a jacket or bib and braces attached

overalls *n* ▷ overall

overarm *adj*, *adv* (thrown) with the arm above the shoulder

overawe *v* (-wes, -wing, -wed) affect (someone) with an overpowering sense of awe

overawed *v* ▷ overawe
overawes *v* ▷ overawe
overawing *v* ▷ overawe

overbalance *v* (-ces, -cing, -ced) lose balance
overbalanced *v* ▷ overbalance
overbalances *v* ▷ overbalance
overbalancing *v* ▷ overbalance

overbearing *adj* unpleasantly forceful

overblown *adj* excessive

overboard *adv* from a boat into the water

overcame *v* ▷ overcome

overcast *adj* (of the sky) covered by clouds

overcoat *n* (*pl* -s) heavy coat

overcoats *n* ▷ overcoat

overcome *v* (-comes, -coming, -came, -come) gain control over after an effort

overcomes *v* ▷ overcome
overcoming *v* ▷ overcome

overcrowded *adj* containing more people or things than is desirable

overdid *v* ▷ overdo

overdo *v* (-does, -doing, -did, -done) do to excess

overdoes *v* ▷ overdo
overdoing *v* ▷ overdo
overdone *v* ▷ overdo

overdose *n* (*pl* -s) excessive dose of a drug ▶ *v* (-ses, -sing, -sed) take an overdose

overdosed *n* ▷ overdose
overdoses *n*, *v* ▷ overdose
overdosing *v* ▷ overdose

overdraft *n* (*pl* -s) overdrawing

overdrafts *n* ▷ overdraft

overdraw *v* (-draws, -drawing, -drew, -drawn) withdraw more money than is in (one's bank account)

overdrawing *v* ▷ overdraw
overdrawn *v* ▷ overdraw
overdraws *v* ▷ overdraw
overdrew *v* ▷ overdraw

overdrawn *adj* having overdrawn one's account

overdrive *n* (*pl* -s) very high gear in a motor vehicle

overdrives *n* ▷ overdrive

overdue *adj* still due after the time allowed

overgrown *adj* thickly covered with plants and weeds

overhaul *v* (-s, -ing, -ed) examine and repair ▶ *n* (*pl* -s) examination and repair

overhauled *v* ▷ overhaul
overhauling *v* ▷ overhaul
overhauls *v*, *n* ▷ overhaul

overhead *adv*, *adj* above one's head

overheads *pl n* general cost of maintaining a business

overhear *v* (-hears, -hearing, -heard) hear (a speaker or remark) unintentionally or without the speaker's knowledge

overheard *v* ▷ overhear
overhearing *v* ▷ overhear
overhears *v* ▷ overhear

overjoyed *adj* extremely pleased

overkill *n* (*pl* -s) treatment that is greater than required

overkills *n* ▷ overkill

overland *adj*, *adv* by land

overlap *v* (-s, -pping, -pped) share part of the same space or period of time (as) ▶ *n* (*pl* -s) area overlapping

overlapped *v* ▷ overlap
overlapping *v* ▷ overlap
overlaps *v*, *n* ▷ overlap

overleaf *adv* on the back of the current page

overlook *v* (-s, -ing, -ed) fail to notice
overlooked *v* ▷ overlook
overlooking *v* ▷ overlook
overlooks *v* ▷ overlook

overly *adv* excessively

overnight *adj*, *adv* (taking place) during one night

overpower *v* (-s, -ing, -ed) subdue or overcome (someone)

overpowered *v* ▷ overpower
overpowering *v* ▷ overpower
overpowers *v* ▷ overpower

overran *v* ▷ overrun

overreach v (-es, -ing, -ed) fail by trying to be too clever
  overreached v ▷ overreach
  overreaches v ▷ overreach
  overreaching v ▷ overreach
override v (-rides, -riding, -rode, -ridden) overrule
  overridden v ▷ override
  overrides v ▷ override
  overriding v ▷ override
  overrode v ▷ override
overrule v (-les, -ling, -led) reverse the decision of (a person with less power)
  overruled v ▷ overrule
  overrules v ▷ overrule
  overruling v ▷ overrule
overrun v (-runs, -running, -ran, -run) spread over (a place) rapidly
  overrunning v ▷ overrun
  overruns v ▷ overrun
  overs n ▷ over
  oversaw v ▷ oversee
overseas adv, adj to, of, or from a distant country
oversee v (-sees, -seeing, -saw, -seen) watch over from a position of authority > **overseer** n (-s)
  overseeing v ▷ oversee
  overseen v ▷ oversee
  overseer n ▷ oversee
  overseers n ▷ oversee
  oversees v ▷ oversee
overshadow v (-s, -ing, -ed) reduce the significance of (a person or thing) by comparison
  overshadowed v ▷ overshadow
  overshadowing v ▷ overshadow
  overshadows v ▷ overshadow
oversight n (pl -s) mistake caused by not noticing something
  oversights n ▷ oversight
overspill n (pl -s) (BRIT) rehousing of people from crowded cities in smaller towns
  overspills n ▷ overspill
overstay v (-s, -ing, -ed) stay longer than one's host or hostess would like
  overstayed v ▷ overstay
overstayer n (-s) (NZ) person who remains in New Zealand after their permit has expired
  overstayers n ▷ overstyer
  overstaying v ▷ overstay
  overstays v ▷ overstay
overt adj open, not hidden > **overtly** adv
  overtly adv ▷ overt
overtake v (-takes, -taking, -took, -taken) move past (a vehicle or person) travelling in the same direction
  overtaken v ▷ overtake
  overtakes v ▷ overtake
  overtaking v ▷ overtake
  overtook v ▷ overtake
  overthrew v ▷ overthrow
overthrow v (-throws, -throwing, -threw, -thrown) defeat and replace ▶ n (pl -s) downfall, destruction
  overthrowing v ▷ overthrow
  overthrown v ▷ overthrow
  overthrows v, n ▷ overthrow
overtime n, adv (pl -s) (paid work done) in addition to one's normal working hours
  overtimes n ▷ overtime
overtone n (pl -s) additional meaning
  overtones n ▷ overtone
overture n (pl -s) (MUSIC) orchestral introduction ▶ pl opening moves in a new relationship
  overtures n ▷ overture
overturn v (-s, -ing, -ed) turn upside down
  overturned v ▷ overturn
  overturning v ▷ overturn
  overturns v ▷ overturn
overweight adj weighing more than is healthy
overwhelm v (-s, -ing, -ed) overpower, esp. emotionally > **overwhelming** adj > **overwhelmingly** adv
  overwhelmed v ▷ overwhelm
  overwhelming v, adj ▷ overwhelm
  overwhelmingly adv ▷ overwhelm
  overwhelms v ▷ overwhelm
overwrought adj nervous and agitated
ovoid [oh-void] adj egg-shaped
ovulate [ov-yew-late] v (-tes, -ting, -ted) produce or release an egg cell from an ovary > **ovulation** n (-s)
  ovulated v ▷ ovulate
  ovulates v ▷ ovulate
  ovulating v ▷ ovulate
  ovulation n ▷ ovulate
  ovulations n ▷ ovulate
ovum [oh-vum] n (pl ova) unfertilized egg cell
owe v (owes, owing, owed) be obliged to pay (a sum of money) to (a person)
  owed v ▷ owe
  owes v ▷ owe
  owing v ▷ owe
owl n (pl -s) night bird of prey > **owlish** adj
  owlish adj ▷ owl
  owls n ▷ owl
own adj used to emphasize possession

▶ v (-s, -ing, -ed) possess ▶ **owner** n (pl -s)
▶ **ownership** n (pl -s)
owned v ▷ own
owner n ▷ own
owners n ▷ own
ownership n ▷ own
ownerships n ▷ own
owning v ▷ own
owns v ▷ own
ox n (pl oxen) castrated bull
oxen n ▷ ox
oxide n (pl -s) compound of oxygen and one other element
oxides n ▷ oxide
oxidize v (-zes, -zing, -zed) combine chemically with oxygen, as in burning or rusting
oxidized v ▷ oxidize
oxidizes v ▷ oxidize
oxidizing v ▷ oxidize
oxygen n (pl -s) (CHEM) gaseous element

essential to life and combustion
oxygenate v (-tes, -ting, -ted) add oxygen to
oxygenated v ▷ oxygenate
oxygenates v ▷ oxygenate
oxygenating v ▷ oxygenate
oxygens n ▷ oxygen
oxymora n ▷ oxymoron
oxymoron [ox-see-**more**-on] n (pl -mora, -morons) figure of speech that combines two apparently contradictory ideas
oxymorons n ▷ oxymoron
oyez interj (HIST) shouted three times by a public crier, listen
oyster n (pl -s) edible shellfish
oystercatcher n (pl -s) wading bird with black-and-white feathers
oystercatchers n ▷ oystercatcher
oysters n ▷ oyster
ozone n (pl -s) strong-smelling form of oxygen
ozones n ▷ ozone

Pp

P forms a two-letter word in front of every vowel except U, which makes it very useful for joining a new word to one already on the board. It also forms several three-letter words with X: **pax, pix, pox** (12 points each) and **pyx** (15). You should also remember one of the strangest words in Scrabble – **pH** (7), which is valid because it doesn't start with a capital letter. When you have the letter P on your rack, look for an H on the board, as they may allow you to play a word beginning or ending in PH, adding to your options.

pa n (pl -s) (NZ) (formerly) a fortified Maori settlement

pace n (pl -s) single step in walking ▶ v (-ces, -cing, -ced) walk up and down, esp. in anxiety
paced v ▷ pace

pacemaker n (pl -s) electronic device surgically implanted in a person with heart disease to regulate the heartbeat
pacemakers n ▷ pacemaker
paces n, v ▷ pace

pachyderm [pak-ee-durm] n (pl -s) thick-skinned animal such as an elephant
pachyderms n ▷ pachyderm
pacification n ▷ pacify
pacifications n ▷ pacify
pacified v ▷ pacify
pacifies v ▷ pacify
pacifism n ▷ pacifist
pacifisms n ▷ pacifist

pacifist n (pl -s) person who refuses on principle to take part in war > **pacifism** n (pl -s)
pacifists n ▷ pacifist

pacify v (-fies, -fying, -fied) soothe, calm > **pacification** n (pl -s)
pacifying v ▷ pacify
pacing v ▷ pace

pack v (-s, -ing, -ed) put (clothes etc.) together in a suitcase or bag ▶ n (pl -s) bag carried on a person's or animal's back
packed v ▷ pack
packing v ▷ pack
packs v, n ▷ pack

package n (pl -s) small parcel ▶ v (-ges, -ging, -ged) put into a package > **packaging** n (pl -s)
packaged v ▷ package

packages n, v ▷ package
packaging v, n ▷ package
packagings n ▷ package

packet n (pl -s) small container (and contents)
packets n ▷ packet

packhorse n (pl -s) horse used for carrying goods
packhorses n ▷ packhorse

pact n (pl -s) formal agreement
pacts n ▷ pact

pad n (pl -s) piece of soft material used for protection, support, absorption of liquid, etc. ▶ v (padding, padded) protect or fill with soft material
padded v ▷ pad
paddies n ▷ paddy

padding n (pl -s) soft material used to pad something ▶ v ▷ pad
paddings n ▷ padding

paddle¹ n (pl -s) short oar with a broad blade at one or each end ▶ v (-les, -ling, -led) move (a canoe etc.) with a paddle

paddle² v (-les, -ling, -led) walk barefoot in shallow water
paddled v ▷ paddle¹, ²
paddles n, v ▷ paddle¹, ²
paddling v ▷ paddle¹, ²

paddock n (pl -s) small field or enclosure for horses
paddocks n ▷ paddock

paddy n (pl -ies) (BRIT) (Informal) fit of temper
paddymelons n ▷ pademelon

pademelon, paddymelon [pad-ee-mel-an] n (pl -s) small Australian wallaby
pademelons n ▷ pademelon

padlock n (pl -s) detachable lock with a hinged

hoop fastened over a ring on the object to be secured
padlocks n ▷ padlock
padre [pah-dray] n (pl -s) chaplain to the armed forces
padres n ▷ padre
pads v, n ▷ pad
paean [pee-an] n (pl -s) song of triumph or thanksgiving
paeans n ▷ paean
paediatrics n branch of medicine concerned with diseases of children > **paediatrician** n
paella [pie-ell-a] n (pl -s) Spanish dish of rice, chicken, shellfish, and vegetables
paellas n ▷ paella
pagan n (pl -s) ▶ adj (person) not belonging to one of the world's main religions
pagans n ▷ pagan
page¹ n (pl -s) (one side of) a sheet of paper forming a book etc.
page² n (also **pageboy**) small boy who attends a bride at her wedding ▶ v (-ges, -ging, -ged) summon (someone) by bleeper or loudspeaker, in order to pass on a message
pageant n (pl -s) parade or display of people in costume, usu. illustrating a scene from history > **pageantry** n (pl -ries)
pageantries n ▷ pageant
pageantry n ▷ pageant
pageants n ▷ pageant
paged v ▷ page²
pages n, v ▷ page¹, ²
pagination n (pl -s) numbering of the pages of a book etc.
paginations n ▷ pagination
paging v ▷ page²
pagoda n (pl -s) pyramid-shaped Asian temple or tower
pagodas n ▷ pagoda
paid v ▷ pay
pail n (pl -s) (contents of) a bucket
pails n ▷ pail
pain n (pl -s) physical or mental suffering ▶ pl trouble, effort > **painful** adj > **painfully** adv > **painless** adj > **painlessly** adv
painful adj ▷ pain
painfully adv ▷ pain
painkiller n (pl -s) drug that relieves pain
painkillers n ▷ painkiller
painless adj ▷ pain
painlessly adv ▷ pain
pains n ▷ pain
painstaking adj extremely thorough and careful
paint n (pl -s) coloured substance, spread on a

surface with a brush or roller ▶ v (-s, -ing, -ed) colour or coat with paint ▶ **painter** n (pl -s)
> **painting** n (pl -s)
painted v ▷ paint
painter¹ n ▷ paint
painter² n (pl -s) rope at the front of a boat, for tying it up
painters n ▷ paint painter²
painting v, n ▷ paint
paintings n ▷ paint
paints n, v ▷ paint
pair n (pl -s) set of two things matched for use together ▶ v (-s, -ing, -ed) group or be grouped in twos
paired v ▷ pair
pairing v ▷ pair
pairs n, v ▷ pair
pakeha [pah-kee-ha] n (pl -s) (NZ) New Zealander who is not of Maori descent
pakehas n ▷ pakeha
pal n (pl -s) (Informal) (Old-fashioned in NZ) friend
pals n ▷ pal
palace n (pl -s) residence of a king, bishop, etc.
palaces n ▷ palace
palaeographies n ▷ palaeography
palaeography [pal-ee-og-ra-fee] n (pl -ies) study of ancient manuscripts
palaeolithic [pal-ee-oh-lith-ik] adj of the Old Stone Age
palaeontologies n ▷ palaeontology
palaeontology [pal-ee-on-tol-a-jee] n (pl -ies) study of past geological periods and fossils
palagi [pa-lang-gee] n (pl -s) (NZ) Samoan name for a pakeha
palagis n ▷ palagi
palatable adj pleasant to taste
palate n (pl -s) roof of the mouth
palates n ▷ palate
palatial adj like a palace, magnificent
palaver [pal-lah-ver] n (pl -s) time-wasting fuss
palavers n ▷ palaver
pale¹ adj (-er, -est) light, whitish ▶ v (-les, -ling, -led) become pale
pale² n (pl -s) wooden or metal post used in fences
paled v ▷ pale
paler adj ▷ pale¹
pales v ▷ pale¹, ²
palest adj ▷ pale¹
paling v ▷ pale
palette n (pl -s) artist's flat board for mixing colours on
palettes n ▷ palette
palindrome n (pl -s) word or phrase that reads the same backwards as forwards

palindromes n ▷ palindrome
paling n (pl -s) wooden or metal post used in fences
palings n ▷ paling
palisade n (pl -s) fence made of wooden posts driven into the ground
palisades n ▷ palisade
pall¹ n (pl -s) cloth spread over a coffin
pall² v (-s, -ing, -ed) become boring
pallbearer n (pl -s) person who helps to carry the coffin at a funeral
pallbearers n ▷ pallbearer
palled v ▷ pall²
palling v ▷ pall²
palls n ▷ pall¹ ▶ v ▷ pall²
palladium n (pl -s) (CHEM) silvery-white element of the platinum metal group
palladiums n ▷ palladium
pallet¹ n (pl -s) portable platform for storing and moving goods
pallet² n straw-filled mattress or bed
pallets n ▷ pallet¹, ²
palliate v (-tes, -ting, -ted) lessen the severity of (something) without curing it
palliated v ▷ palliate
palliates v ▷ palliate
palliating v ▷ palliate
palliative adj giving temporary or partial relief ▶ n (pl -s) something, for example a drug, that palliates
palliatives n ▷ palliative
pallid adj (-er, -est) pale, esp. because ill or weak > **pallor** n (pl -s)
pallider adj ▷ pallid
pallidest adj ▷ pallid
pallier adj ▷ pally
palliest adj ▷ pally
pallor n ▷ pallid
pallors n ▷ pallid
pally adj (-llier, -lliest) (Informal) on friendly terms
palm¹ n (pl -s) inner surface of the hand
palm² n (pl -s) tropical tree with long pointed leaves growing out of the top of a straight trunk
palmist n ▷ palmistry
palmistries n ▷ palmistry
palmistry n (pl -ries) fortune-telling from lines on the palm of the hand > **palmist** n (pl -s)
palmists n ▷ palmistry
palms n ▷ palm¹, ²
palmtop adj (of a computer) small enough to be held in the hand ▶ n (pl -s) computer small enough to be held in the hand
palmtops n ▷ palmtop

palomino n (pl -s) gold-coloured horse with a white mane and tail
palominos n ▷ palomino
palpable adj obvious > **palpably** adv
palpably adv ▷ palpable
palpate v (-tes, -ting, -ted) (MED) examine (an area of the body) by touching
palpated v ▷ palpate
palpates v ▷ palpate
palpating v ▷ palpate
palpitate v (-tes, -ting, -ted) (of the heart) beat rapidly > **palpitation** n (pl -s)
palpitated v ▷ palpitate
palpitates v ▷ palpitate
palpitating v ▷ palpitate
palpitation n ▷ palpitate
palpitations v ▷ palpitate
palsied adj affected with palsy
palsies n ▷ palsy
palsy [pawl-zee] n (pl -sies) paralysis
paltrier adj ▷ paltry
paltriest adj ▷ paltry
paltry adj (-rier, -riest) insignificant
pampas pl n vast grassy plains in S America
pamper v (-s, -ing, -ed) treat (someone) with great indulgence, spoil
pampered v ▷ pamper
pampering v ▷ pamper
pampers v ▷ pamper
pamphlet n (pl -s) thin paper-covered booklet
pamphleteer n (pl -s) writer of pamphlets
pamphleteers n ▷ pamphleteer
pamphlets n ▷ pamphlet
pan¹ n (pl -s) wide long-handled metal container used in cooking ▶ v (-s, -nning, -nned) sift gravel from (a river) in a pan to search for gold (Informal)
pan² v (-s, -nning, -nned) (of a film camera) be moved slowly so as to cover a whole scene or follow a moving object
panacea [pan-a-see-a] n (pl -s) remedy for all diseases or problems
panaceas n ▷ panacea
panache [pan-ash] n (pl -s) confident elegant style
panaches n ▷ panache
panatella n (pl -s) long slender cigar
panatellas n ▷ panatella
pancake n (pl -s) thin flat circle of fried batter
pancakes n ▷ pancake
panchromatic adj (PHOTOG) sensitive to light of all colours
pancreas [pang-kree-ass] n (pl -es) large gland behind the stomach that produces insulin and helps digestion > **pancreatic** adj

pancreases n ▷ pancreas

pancreatic adj ▷ pancreas

panda n (pl -s) large black-and-white bearlike mammal from China

pandas n ▷ panda

pandemic adj (of a disease) occurring over a wide area

pandemonium n (pl -s) wild confusion, uproar

pandemoniums n ▷ pandemonium

pander¹ v (-s, -ing, -ed) (foll. by **to**) indulge (a person his or her desires)

pander² n (pl -s) (Old-fashioned) person who procures a sexual partner for someone

pandered v ▷ pander

pandering v ▷ pander

panders v, n ▷ pander¹, ²

pane n (pl -s) sheet of glass in a window or door

panes n ▷ pane

panegyric [pan-ee-**jire**-ik] n (pl -s) formal speech or piece of writing in praise of someone or something

panegyrics n ▷ panegyric

panel n (pl -s) flat distinct section of a larger surface, for example in a door ▶ v (-s, -lling, -lled) cover or decorate with panels

panelled v ▷ panel

panelling n (pl -s) panels collectively, esp. on a wall ▶ v ▷ panel

panellings n ▷ panelling

panellist n (pl -s) member of a panel

panellists n ▷ panellist

panels n ▷ panel

pang n (pl -s) sudden sharp feeling of pain or sadness

pangs n ▷ pang

pangolin n (pl -s) animal of tropical countries with a scaly body and a long snout for eating ants and termites (also **scaly anteater**)

pangolins n ▷ pangolin

panic n (pl -s) sudden overwhelming fear, often affecting a whole group of people ▶ v (-s, -cking, -cked) feel or cause to feel panic ▷ **panicky** adj (-ier, -iest)

panicked v ▷ panic

panickier adj ▷ panic

panickiest adj ▷ panic

panicking v ▷ panic

panicky adj ▷ panic

panics n, v ▷ panic

panic-stricken adj ▷ panic

pannier n (pl -s) bag fixed on the back of a cycle

panniers n ▷ pannier

panoplies n ▷ panoply

panoply n (pl -ies) magnificent array

panorama n (pl -s) wide unbroken view of a scene ▷ **panoramic** adj

panoramas n ▷ panorama

panoramic adj ▷ panorama

pansies n ▷ pansy

pansy n (pl -sies) small garden flower with velvety purple, yellow, or white petals

pant v (-s, -ing, -ed) breathe quickly and noisily during or after exertion

pantaloons pl n baggy trousers gathered at the ankles

pantechnicon n (pl -s) large van for furniture removals

pantechnicons n ▷ pantechnicon

panted v ▷ pant

pantheism n (pl -s) belief that God is present in everything ▷ **pantheist** n (pl -s) ▷ **pantheistic** adj

pantheisms n ▷ pantheism

pantheist n ▷ pantheism

pantheistic adj ▷ pantheism

pantheists n ▷ pantheism

pantheon n (pl -s) (in ancient Greece and Rome) temple built to honour all the gods

pantheons n ▷ pantheon

panther n (pl -s) leopard, esp. a black one

panthers n ▷ panther

panties pl n women's underpants

pantile n (pl -s) roofing tile with an S-shaped cross section

pantiles n ▷ pantile

panting v ▷ pant

pantomime n (pl -s) play based on a fairy tale, performed at Christmas time

pantomimes n ▷ pantomime

pantries n ▷ pantry

pantry n (pl -ries) small room or cupboard for storing food

pants v ▷ pant

pants pl n undergarment for the lower part of the body

pap n (pl -s) soft food for babies or invalids

papacies n ▷ papacy

paps n ▷ pap

papacy [**pay**-pa-see] n (pl -cies) position or term of office of a pope

papal adj of the pope

paparazzi n ▷ paparazzo

paparazzo [pap-a-**rat**-so] n (pl -razzi) photographer specializing in candid photographs of famous people

papaya [pa-**pie**-ya] n (pl -s) large sweet West Indian fruit

papayas n ▷ papaya

paper n (pl -s) material made in sheets from wood pulp or other fibres ▶ pl personal documents ▶ v (-s, -ing, -ed) cover (walls) with wallpaper

paperback n (pl -s) book with covers made of flexible card

paperbacks n ▷ paperback

papering v ▷ paper

papered v ▷ paper

papers n, v ▷ paper

paperweight n (pl -s) heavy decorative object placed on top of loose papers

paperweights n ▷ paperweight

paperwork n (pl -s) clerical work, such as writing reports and letters

paperworks n ▷ paperwork

papoose n (pl -s) Native American child

papooses n ▷ papoose

paprika n (pl -s) mild powdered seasoning made from red peppers

paprikas n ▷ paprika

papyri n ▷ papyrus

papyrus [pap-**ire**-uss] n (pl -ri, -ruses) tall water plant

papyruses n ▷ papyrus

par n (pl -s) usual or average condition

parable n (pl -s) story that illustrates a religious teaching

parables n ▷ parable

parabola [par-**ab**-bol-a] n (pl -s) regular curve resembling the course of an object thrown forward and up ▷ **parabolic** adj

parabolas n ▷ parabola

parabolic adj ▷ parabola

paracetamol n (pl -s) mild pain-relieving drug

paracetamols n ▷ paracetamol

parachute n (pl -s) large fabric canopy that slows the descent of a person or object from an aircraft ▶ v (-tes, -ting, -ted) land or drop by parachute ▷ **parachutist** n (pl -s)

parachuted n, v ▷ parachute

parachutes v ▷ parachute

parachuting v ▷ parachute

parachutist n ▷ parachute

parachutists n ▷ parachute

parade n (pl -s) procession or march ▶ v (-des, -ding, -ded) display or flaunt

paraded v ▷ parade

parades n, v ▷ parade

parading v ▷ parade

paradigm [**par**-a-dime] n (pl -s) example or model

paradigms n ▷ paradigm

paradise n (pl -s) heaven

paradises n ▷ paradise

paradox n (pl -xes) statement that seems self-contradictory but may be true ▷ **paradoxical**

adj ▷ **paradoxically** adv

paradoxes n ▷ paradox

paradoxical adj ▷ paradox

paradoxically adv ▷ paradox

paraffin n (pl -s) (BRIT & S AFR) liquid mixture distilled from petroleum and used as a fuel or solvent

paraffins n ▷ paraffin

paragliding n (pl -s) cross-country gliding wearing a parachute shaped like wings

paraglidings n ▷ paragliding

paragon n (pl -s) model of perfection

paragons n ▷ paragon

paragraph n (pl -s) section of a piece of writing starting on a new line

paragraphs n ▷ paragraph

parakeet n (pl -s) small long-tailed parrot

parakeets n ▷ parakeet

parallax n (pl -es) apparent change in an object's position due to a change in the observer's position

parallaxes n ▷ parallax

parallel adj separated by an equal distance at every point ▶ n (pl -s) line separated from another by an equal distance at every point ▶ v (-s, -ing, -ed) correspond to

paralleled n ▷ parallel

paralleling v ▷ parallel

parallels n, v ▷ parallel

parallelogram n (pl -s) four-sided geometric figure with opposite sides parallel

parallelograms n ▷ parallelogram

paralyse v (-ses, -sing, -sed) affect with paralysis

paralysed v ▷ paralyse

paralyses v ▷ paralyse ▶ n ▷ paralysis

paralysing ▷ paralyse

paralysis n (pl -ses) inability to move or feel, because of damage to the nervous system

paralytic n (pl -s) ▶ adj (person) affected with paralysis

paralytics n ▷ paralytic

paramedic n (pl -s) person working in support of the medical profession ▷ **paramedical** adj

paramedical adj ▷ paramedic

paramedics n ▷ paramedic

parameter [par-**am**-it-er] n (pl -s) limiting factor, boundary

parameters n ▷ parameter

paramilitary adj organized on military lines

paramount adj of the greatest importance

paramour n (pl -s) (Old-fashioned) lover, esp. of a person married to someone else

paramours n ▷ paramour

paranoia n (pl -s) mental illness causing

delusions of grandeur or persecution
(*Informal*) > **paranoid, paranoiac** *adj*, *n* (*pl* -s)
  paranoiac *adj*, *n* ▷ paranoia
  paranoiacs *n* ▷ paranoia
  paranoias *n* ▷ paranoia
  paranoid *adj*, *n* ▷ paranoia
  paranoids *n* ▷ paranoia
paranormal *adj* beyond scientific explanation
parapet *n* (*pl* -s) low wall or railing along the
  edge of a balcony or roof
  parapets *n* ▷ parapet
paraphernalia *n* (*pl* -s) personal belongings or
  bits of equipment
  paraphernalias *n* ▷ paraphernalia
paraphrase *v* (-ses, -sing, -sed) put (a
  statement or text) into other words
  paraphrased *v* ▷ paraphrase
  paraphrases *n* ▷ paraphrase
  paraphrasing *v* ▷ paraphrase
paraplegia [par-a-**pleej**-ya] *n* (*pl* -s) paralysis
  of the lower half of the body > **paraplegic**
  adj, *n* (*pl* -s)
  paraplegias *n* ▷ paraplegia
  paraplegic *adj*, *n* ▷ paraplegia
  paraplegics *n* ▷ paraplegia
  parapsychologies *n* ▷ parapsychology
parapsychology *n* (*pl* -gies) study of mental
  phenomena such as telepathy
parasite *n* (*pl* -s) animal or plant living in or on
  another > **parasitic** *adj*
  parasites *n* ▷ parasite
  parasitic *adj* ▷ parasite
parasol *n* (*pl* -s) umbrella-like sunshade
  parasols *n* ▷ parasol
paratrooper *n* (*pl* -s) soldier trained to be
  dropped by parachute into a battle area
  > **paratroops** *pl n*
  paratroopers *n* ▷ paratrooper
  paratroops *n* ▷ paratrooper
parboil *v* (-s, -ing, -ed) boil until partly cooked
  parboiled *v* ▷ parboil
  parboiling *v* ▷ parboil
  parboils *v* ▷ parboil
parcel *n* (*pl* -s) something wrapped up,
  package ▶ *v* (-s, -lling, -lled) (*often foll. by* **up**)
  wrap up
  parcelled *v* ▷ parcel
  parcelling *v* ▷ parcel
  parcels *n*, *v* ▷ parcel
parch *v* (-es, -ing, -ed) make very hot and dry
  parched *v* ▷ parch
  parches *v* ▷ parch
  parching *v* ▷ parch
parchment *n* (*pl* -s) thick smooth writing
  material made from animal skin

  parchments *n* ▷ parchment
pardon *v* (-s, -ing, -ed) forgive, excuse ▶ *n* (*pl* -s)
  forgiveness > **pardonable** *adj*
  pardonable *adj* ▷ pardon
  pardoned *v* ▷ pardon
  pardoning *v* ▷ pardon
  pardons *v* ▷ pardon
pare *v* (-res, -ring, -red) cut off the skin or top
  layer of (*often foll. by* **down**)
  pared *v* ▷ pare
  pares *v* ▷ pare
  paring *v* ▷ pare ▶ *n* (*pl* -s) piece pared off
  parings *n* ▷ pareing
parent *n* (*pl* -s) father or mother > **parental** *adj*
  > **parenthood** *n*
parentage *n* (*pl* -s) ancestry or family
  parentages *n* ▷ parentage
  parental *adj* ▷ parent
  parenthood *n* ▷ parent
  parenthoods *n* ▷ parent
parenting *n* (*pl* -s) activity of bringing up
  children
  parentings *n* ▷ parenting
  parents *n* ▷ parent
parenthesis [par-**en**-thiss-iss] *n* (*pl* -ses) word or
  sentence inserted into a passage, marked off
  by brackets or dashes ▶ *pl* round brackets, ( )
  > **parenthetical** *adj*
  parentheses *n* ▷ parenthesis
  parenthetical *adj* ▷ parenthesis
pariah [par-**rye**-a] *n* (*pl* -s) social outcast
  pariahs *n* ▷ pariah
parietal [par-**rye**-it-al] *adj* of the walls of a body
  cavity such as the skull
parish *n* (*pl* -es) area that has its own church
  and a priest or pastor
  parishes *n* ▷ parish
parishioner *n* (*pl* -s) inhabitant of a parish
  parishioners *n* ▷ parishioner
  parities *n* ▷ parity
parity *n* (*pl* -ties) equality or equivalence
park *n* (*pl* -s) area of open land for recreational
  use by the public ▶ *v* (-s, -ing, -ed) stop and
  leave (a vehicle) temporarily
  parked *v* ▷ park
  parking *v* ▷ park
  parks *n*, *v* ▷ park
parka *n* (*pl* -s) large waterproof jacket with
  a hood
  parkas *n* ▷ parka
  parkier *adj* ▷ parky
  parkiest *adj* ▷ parky
parky *adj* (-kier, -kiest) (BRIT) (*Informal*) (of the
  weather) chilly
parlance *n* (*pl* -s) particular way of speaking,

idiom

parlances n ▷ parlance

parley n (pl -s) meeting between leaders or representatives of opposing forces to discuss terms ▶ v (-s, -ing, -ed) have a parley

parleyed v ▷ parley

parleying v ▷ parley

parleys n, v ▷ parley

parliament n (pl -s) law-making assembly of a country > **parliamentary** adj

parliamentary adj ▷ parliament

parliaments n ▷ parliament

parlour n (pl -s) (Old-fashioned) living room for receiving visitors

parlours n ▷ parlour

parlous adj (Old-fashioned) dire

parochial adj narrow in outlook
> **parochialism** n (pl -s)

parochialism n ▷ parochial

parochialisms n ▷ parochial

parodied v ▷ parody

parodies n, v ▷ parody

parody n (pl -dies) exaggerated and amusing imitation of someone else's style ▶ v (-ies, -ying, -ied) make a parody of

parodying v ▷ parody

parole n (pl -s) early freeing of a prisoner on condition that he or she behaves well ▶ v (-les, -ling, -led) put on parole

paroled v ▷ parole

paroles n, v ▷ parole

paroling v ▷ parole

paroxysm n (pl -s) uncontrollable outburst of rage, delight, etc.

paroxysms n ▷ paroxysm

parquet [par-kay] n (pl -s) floor covering made of wooden blocks arranged in a geometric pattern > **parquetry** n (pl -ies)

parquetries n ▷ parquet

parquetry n ▷ parquet

parquets n ▷ parquet

parricide n (pl -s) crime of killing either of one's parents

parricides n ▷ parricide

parried v ▷ parry

parries v ▷ parry

parrot n (pl -s) tropical bird with a short hooked beak and an ability to imitate human speech ▶ v (-s, -ing, -ed) repeat (someone else's words) without thinking

parroted v ▷ parrot

parroting v ▷ parrot

parrots n, v ▷ parrot

parry v (-rries, -rrying, -rried) ward off (an attack)

parrying v ▷ parry

pars n ▷ par

parse [parz] v (-ses, -sing, -sed) analyse (a sentence) in terms of grammar

parsed v ▷ parse

parses v ▷ parse

parsing v ▷ parse

parsimonies n ▷ parsimony

parsimonious adj ▷ parsimony

parsimony n (pl -nies) extreme caution in spending money > **parsimonious** adj

parsley n (pl -s) herb used for seasoning and decorating food

parsleys n ▷ parsley

parsnip n (pl -s) long tapering cream-coloured root vegetable

parsnips n ▷ parsnip

parson n (pl -s) Anglican parish priest

parsons n ▷ parson

parsonage n (pl -s) parson's house

parsonages n ▷ parsonage

part n (pl -s) one of the pieces that make up a whole ▶ v (-s, -ing, -ed) divide or separate

partake v (-takes, -taking, -took, -taken) (foll. by of) take (food or drink)

partaken v ▷ partake

partakes v ▷ partake

partaking v ▷ partake

partial adj not complete > **partiality** n (pl -ties)
> **partially** adv

partialities n ▷ partial

partiality n ▷ partial

partially adv ▷ partial

parted v ▷ part

participate v (-tes, -ting, -ted) become actively involved > **participant** n (pl -s)
> **participation** n (pl -s)

participant n ▷ participate

participants n ▷ participate

participated v ▷ participate

participates v ▷ participate

participating v ▷ participate

participation n ▷ participate

participations n ▷ participations

participle n (pl -s) form of a verb used in compound tenses or as an adjective

participles n ▷ participle

particle n (pl -s) extremely small piece or amount

particles n ▷ particle

particular adj relating to one person or thing, not general ▶ n (pl -s) item of information, detail > **particularly** adv

particularize v (-zes, -zing, -zed) give details about

particularized v ▷ particularize
particularizes v ▷ particularize
particularizing v ▷ particularize
particularly adv ▷ particular
particulars n ▷ particular
parties n ▷ party
parting n (pl -s) occasion when one person leaves another ▶ v ▷ part
partings n ▷ parting
partisan n (pl -s) strong supporter of a party or group ▶ adj prejudiced or one-sided
partisans n ▷ partisan
partition n (pl -s) screen or thin wall that divides a room ▶ v (-s, -ing, -ed) divide with a partition
partitioned v ▷ partition
partitioning v ▷ partition
partitions n, v ▷ partition
partly adv not completely
partner n (pl -s) either member of a couple in a relationship or activity ▶ v (-s, -ing, -ed) be the partner of
partnered v ▷ partner
partnering v ▷ partner
partners n, v ▷ partner
partnership n (pl -s) joint business venture between two or more people
partnerships n ▷ partnership
partook v ▷ partake
partridge n (pl -s) game bird of the grouse family
partridges n ▷ partridge
parts n, v ▷ part
parturition n (pl -s) act of giving birth
party n (pl -ties) social gathering for pleasure
parvenu [par-ven-new] n (pl -s) person newly risen to a position of power or wealth
parvenus n ▷ parvenu
pas n ▷ pa
pascal n (pl -s) unit of pressure
pascals n ▷ pascal
paspalum [pass-**pale**-um] n (pl -s) (AUST & NZ) type of grass with wide leaves
paspalums n ▷ paspalum
pass v (-es, -ing, -ed) go by, past, or through (SPORT) ▶ n (pl -es) successful result in a test or examination
passable adj (just) acceptable
passage n (pl -s) channel or opening providing a way through
passages n ▷ passage
passageway n (pl -s) passage or corridor
passageways n ▷ passageway
passbook n (pl -s) book issued by a bank or building society for keeping a record of

deposits and withdrawals
passbooks n ▷ passbook
passé [pas-say] adj out-of-date
passed v ▷ pass
passenger n (pl -s) person travelling in a vehicle driven by someone else
passengers n ▷ passenger
passes v, n ▷ pass
passim adv (LATIN) everywhere, throughout
passing adj brief or transitory ▶ v ▷ pass
passion n (pl -s) intense sexual love
> **passionate** adj
passionate adj ▷ passion
passionflower n (pl -s) tropical American plant
passionflowers n ▷ passionflower
passions n ▷ passion
passive adj not playing an active part
> **passivity** n (pl -ties)
passivities n ▷ passive
passivity n ▷ passive
passport n (pl -s) official document of nationality granting permission to travel abroad
passports n ▷ passport
password n (pl -s) secret word or phrase that ensures admission
passwords n ▷ password
past adj of the time before the present ▶ n (pl -s) period of time before the present ▶ adv by, along ▶ prep beyond
pasta n (pl -s) type of food, such as spaghetti, that is made in different shapes from flour and water
pastas n ▷ pasta
paste n (pl -s) moist soft mixture, such as toothpaste ▶ v (-tes, -ting, -ted) fasten with paste
pasteboard n (pl -s) stiff thick paper
pasteboards n ▷ pasteboard
pasted v ▷ paste
pastel n (pl -s) coloured chalk crayon for drawing ▶ adj pale and delicate in colour
pastels n ▷ pastel
pastes n, v ▷ paste
pasteurize v (-zes, -zing, -zed) sterilize by heating > **pasteurization** n (pl -s)
pasteurization n ▷ pasteurize
pasteurizations n ▷ pasteurize
pasteurized v ▷ pasteurize
pasteurizes v ▷ pasteurize
pasteurizing v ▷ pasteurize
pastiche [pass-teesh] n (pl -s) work of art that mixes styles or copies the style of another artist
pastiches n ▷ pastiche

pastier adj ▷ pasty¹
pasties n ▷ pasty²
pastiest adj ▷ pasty¹
pastille n (pl -s) small fruit-flavoured and sometimes medicated sweet
pastilles n ▷ pastille
pastime n (pl -s) activity that makes time pass pleasantly
pastimes n ▷ pastime
pasting n (pl -s) (Informal) heavy defeat ▶ v ▷ paste
pastings n ▷ pasting
pastor n (pl -s) member of the clergy in charge of a congregation
pastoral adj of or depicting country life
pastors n ▷ pastor
pastrami n (pl -s) highly seasoned smoked beef
pastramis n ▷ pastrami
pastries n ▷ pastry
pastry n (pl -ries) baking dough made of flour, fat, and water
pasts n ▷ past
pasture n (pl -s) grassy land for farm animals to graze on
pastures n ▷ pasture
pasty¹ [pay-stee] adj (-tier, -tiest) (of a complexion) pale and unhealthy
pasty² [pass-tee] n (pl -ties) round of pastry folded over a savoury filling
pat¹ v (-s, -tting, -tted) tap lightly ▶ n (pl -s) gentle tap or stroke
pat² adj quick, ready, or glib
patch n (pl -es) piece of material sewn on a garment ▶ v (-es, -ing, -ed) mend with a patch
patched v ▷ patch
patches n, v ▷ patch
patchier adj ▷ patchy
patchiest adj ▷ patchy
patching v ▷ patch
patchwork n (pl -s) needlework made of pieces of different materials sewn together
patchworks n ▷ patchwork
patchy adj (-hier, -hiest) of uneven quality or intensity
pate n (pl -s) (Old-fashioned) head
pates n ▷ pate
pâté [pat-ay] n (pl -s) spread of finely minced liver etc.
pâtés n ▷ pâté
patella n (pl -ae) kneecap
patellae n ▷ patella
patent n (pl -es) document giving the exclusive right to make or sell an invention ▶ adj open to public inspection ▶ v (-s, -ing, -ed) obtain

a patent for
patented v ▷ patent
patenting v ▷ patent
patently adv obviously
patents n, v ▷ patent
paternal adj fatherly
paternities n ▷ paternity
paternity n (pl -ties) fact or state of being a father
paternalism n (pl -s) authority exercised in a way that limits individual responsibility > **paternalistic** adj
paternalisms n ▷ paternalism
paternalistic adj ▷ paternalism
path n (pl -s) surfaced walk or track
pathname n (pl -s) (COMPUTERS) file name listing the sequence of directories leading to a particular file or directory
pathnames n ▷ pathname
paths n ▷ path
pathetic adj causing feelings of pity or sadness > **pathetically** adv
pathetically adv ▷ pathetic
pathogen n (pl -s) thing that causes disease > **pathogenic** adj
pathogenic adj ▷ pathogen
pathogens n ▷ pathogen
pathologies n ▷ pathology
pathology n (pl -gies) scientific study of diseases > **pathologist** n (pl -s)
pathological adj of pathology
pathological n ▷ pathology
pathologists n ▷ pathology
pathos n (pl -es) power of arousing pity or sadness
pathoses n ▷ pathos
patience n (pl -s) quality of being patient
patiences n ▷ patience
patient adj enduring difficulties or delays calmly ▶ n (pl -s) person receiving medical treatment
patients n ▷ patient
patina n (pl -s) fine layer on a surface
patinas n ▷ patina
patio n (pl -s) paved area adjoining a house
patios n ▷ patio
patois [pat-wah] n (pl patois) [pat-wahz] regional dialect, esp. of French
patriarch n (pl -s) male head of a family or tribe > **patriarchal** adj
patriarchal adj ▷ patriarch
patriarchies n ▷ patriarchy
patriarchs n ▷ patriarch
patriarchy n (pl -hies) society in which men have most of the power

patrician n (pl -s) member of the nobility ▶ adj of noble birth
patricians n ▷ patrician
patricide n (pl -s) crime of killing one's father
patricides n ▷ patricide
patrimonies n ▷ patrimony
patrimony n (pl -nies) property inherited from ancestors
patriot n (pl -s) person who loves his or her country and supports its interests > **patriotic** adj > **patriotism** n (pl -s)
patriotic adj ▷ patriot
patriotism n ▷ patriot
patriotisms n ▷ patriot
patriots n ▷ patriot
patrol n (pl -s) regular circuit by a guard ▶ v (-s, -lling, -lled) go round on guard, or reconnoitring
patrolled v ▷ patrol
patrolling v ▷ patrol
patrols n, v ▷ patrol
patron n (pl -s) person who gives financial support to charities, artists, etc.
patronage n (pl -s) support given by a patron
patronages n ▷ patronage
patronize v (-zes, -zing, -zed) treat in a condescending way
patronized v ▷ patronize
patronizes v ▷ patronize
patronizing v ▷ patronize
patrons n ▷ patron
patronymic n (pl -s) name derived from one's father or a male ancestor
patronymics n ▷ patronymic
pats v, n ▷ pat¹
patted v, n ▷ pat¹
patter¹ v (-s, -ing, -ed) make repeated soft tapping sounds ▶ n (pl -s) quick succession of taps
patter² n (pl -s) glib rapid speech
pattered v ▷ patter¹
pattering v ▷ patter¹
patters v, n ▷ patter¹, ²
pattern n (pl -s) arrangement of repeated parts or decorative designs
patterned adj decorated with a pattern
patterns n ▷ pattern
patties n ▷ patty
patting v ▷ pat¹
patty n (pl -tties) small flattened cake of minced food
paucities n ▷ paucity
paucity n (pl -ties) scarcity
paunch n (pl -es) protruding belly
paunches n ▷ paunch

pauper n (pl -s) very poor person
paupers n ▷ pauper
pause v (-ses, -sing, -sed) stop for a time ▶ n (pl -s) stop or rest in speech or action
paused v ▷ pause
pauses v, n ▷ pause
pausing v ▷ pause
pave v (-ves, -ving, -ved) form (a surface) with stone or brick
paved v ▷ pave
pavement n (pl -s) paved path for pedestrians
pavements n ▷ pavement
paves v ▷ pave
paving v ▷ pave
pavilion n (pl -s) building on a playing field etc.
pavilions n ▷ pavilion
paw n (pl -s) animal's foot with claws and pads ▶ v (-s, -ing, -ed) scrape with the paw or hoof
pawed v ▷ paw
pawing v ▷ paw
paws n, v ▷ paw
pawn¹ v (-s, -ing, -ed) deposit (an article) as security for money borrowed
pawn² n (pl -s) chessman of the lowest value
pawnbroker n (pl -s) lender of money on goods deposited
pawnbrokers n ▷ pawnbroker
pawned v ▷ pawn¹
pawning v ▷ pawn¹
pawns v, n ▷ pawn¹, ²
pay v (-s, -ing, paid) give money etc. in return for goods or services ▶ n (pl -s) wages or salary
payable adj due to be paid
payee n (pl -s) person to whom money is paid or due
payees n ▷ payee
paying v ▷ pay
payload n (pl -s) passengers or cargo of an aircraft
payloads n ▷ payload
payment n (pl -s) act of paying
payments n ▷ payment
payola n (pl -s) (CHIEFLY US) (Informal) bribe to get special treatment, esp. to promote a commercial product
pays v, n ▷ pay
payolas n ▷ payola

> **pax** n (paxes). A pax is a period of peace, especially when there is one dominant nation. If you have a P and an X on your rack, there is likely to be an A available on the board. Pax gives a decent score for a three-letter word, so watch out for chances to play it on a bonus square. Pax scores 12 points.

pe *n* (**pes**). Pe is the 17th letter in the Hebrew alphabet. This is a very handy word because it allows you to connect words beginning with P to those ending in E, or vice versa and E is the most common tile in the game. Pe scores 4 points.

pea *n* (*pl* -s) climbing plant with seeds growing in pods
  peas *n* ▷ pea

peace *n* (*pl* -s) calm, quietness > **peaceful** *adj* > **peacefully** *adv*

peaceable *adj* inclined towards peace > **peaceably** *adv*
  peaceably *adv* ▷ peaceable
  peaceful *adj* ▷ peace
  peacefully *adv* ▷ peace
  peaces *n* ▷ peace

peach *n* (*pl* -es) soft juicy fruit with a stone and a downy skin ▶ *adj* pinkish-orange
  peaches *n* ▷ peach

peacock *n* (*pl* -s) large male bird with a brilliantly coloured fanlike tail > **peahen** *n* *fem* (*pl* -s)
  peacocks *n* ▷ peacock
  peahen *n* ▷ peacock
  peahens *n* ▷ peacock

peak *n* (*pl* -s) pointed top, esp. of a mountain ▶ *v* (-s, -ing, -ed) form or reach a peak ▶ *adj* of or at the point of greatest demand > **peaked** *adj*
  peaked *adj*, *v* ▷ peak
  peakier *adj* ▷ peaky
  peakiest *adj* ▷ peaky
  peaking *v* ▷ peak
  peaks *n*, *v* ▷ peak

peaky *adj* (-kier, -kiest) pale and sickly

peal *n* (*pl* -s) long loud echoing sound, esp. of bells or thunder ▶ *v* (-s, -ing, -ed) sound with a peal or peals
  pealed *v* ▷ peal
  pealing *v* ▷ peal
  peals *n*, *v* ▷ peal

peanut *n* (*pl* -s) pea-shaped nut that ripens underground ▶ *pl* (*Informal*) trifling amount of money
  peanuts *n* ▷ peanut

pear *n* (*pl* -s) sweet juicy fruit with a narrow top and rounded base
  pears *n* ▷ pear

pearl *n* (*pl* -s) hard round shiny object found inside some oyster shells and used as a jewel > **pearly** *adj* (-lier, -liest)
  pearlier *adj* ▷ pearl
  pearliest *adj* ▷ peral

pearls *n* ▷ pearl
pearly *adj* ▷ pearl

peasant *n* (*pl* -s) person working on the land, esp. in poorer countries or in the past
  peasantries *n* ▷ peasantry

peasantry *n* (*pl* -ries) peasants collectively
  peasants *n* ▷ peasant

peat *n* (*pl* -s) decayed vegetable material found in bogs, used as fertilizer or fuel
  peats *n* ▷ peat

pebble *n* (*pl* -s) small roundish stone > **pebbly** *adj* (-lier, -liest)
  pebbles *n* ▷ pebble
  pebblier *adj* ▷ pebble
  pebbliest *adj* ▷ pebble
  pebbly *adj* ▷ pebble

pecan [pee-kan] *n* (*pl* -s) edible nut of a N American tree
  pecans *n* ▷ pecan

peccadillo *n* (*pl* -lloes, -llos) trivial misdeed
  peccadilloes *n* ▷ peccadillo
  peccadillos *n* ▷ peccadillo

peck *v* (-s, -ing, -ed) strike or pick up with the beak ▶ *n* (*pl* -s) pecking movement
  pecked *v* ▷ peck
  pecking *v* ▷ peck

peckish *adj* (*Informal*) slightly hungry
  pecks *v*, *n* ▷ peck

pecs *pl* *n* (*Informal*) pectoral muscles

pectin *n* (*pl* -s) substance in fruit that makes jam set
  pectins *n* ▷ pectin

pectoral *adj* of the chest or thorax ▶ *n* (*pl* -s) pectoral muscle or fin
  pectorals *n* ▷ pectoral

peculiar *adj* strange
  peculiarities *n* ▷ peculiarity

peculiarity *n* (*pl* -ties) oddity, eccentricity

pecuniary *adj* relating to, or consisting of, money

pedagogue *n* (*pl* -s) schoolteacher, esp. a pedantic one
  pedagogues *n* ▷ pedagogue

pedal *n* (*pl* -s) foot-operated lever used to control a vehicle or machine, or to modify the tone of a musical instrument ▶ *v* (-s, -lling, -lled) propel (a bicycle) by using its pedals
  pedalled *v* ▷ pedal
  pedalling *v* ▷ pedal
  pedals *n* ▷ pedal

pedant *n* (*pl* -s) person who is excessively concerned with details and rules, esp. in academic work > **pedantic** *adj* > **pedantry** *n* (*pl* -ries)
  pedantic *adj* ▷ pedant

pedantries n ▷ pedant
pedantry n ▷ pedant
pedants n ▷ pedant
peddle v (-les, -ling, -led) sell (goods) from door to door
  peddled v ▷ peddle
  peddles v ▷ peddle
  peddling v ▷ peddle
peddler n (pl -s) person who sells illegal drugs
  peddlers n ▷ peddler
pedestal n (pl -s) base supporting a column, statue, etc.
  pedestals n ▷ pedestal
pedestrian n (pl -s) person who walks ▶ adj dull, uninspiring
  pedestrians n ▷ pedestrian
pedicure n (pl -s) medical or cosmetic treatment of the feet
  pedicures n ▷ pedicure
pedigree n (pl -s) register of ancestors, esp. of a purebred animal
  pedigrees n ▷ pedigree
pediment n (pl -s) triangular part over a door etc.
  pediments n ▷ pediment
pedlar n (pl -s) person who sells goods from door to door
  pedlars n ▷ pedlar
pee (Informal) v (-s, -ing, peed) urinate ▶ n (-s) act of urinating
  peed v ▷ pee
  peeing v ▷ pee
  pees v, n ▷ pee
peek v, n (pl -s) peep or glance
  peeks n ▷ peek
peel v (-s, -ing, -ed) remove the skin or rind of (a vegetable or fruit) ▶ n (-s) rind or skin
  > **peelings** pl n
  peeled v ▷ peel
  peeling v ▷ peel
  peelings n ▷ peel
  peels v, n ▷ peel
peep[1] v (-s, -ing, -ed) look slyly or quickly ▶ n (pl -s) peeping look
peep[2] v (-s, -ing, -ed) make a small shrill noise ▶ n (-s) small shrill noise
  peeped v ▷ peep[1, 2]
  peeping v ▷ peep[1, 2]
  peeps v, n ▷ peep[1, 2]
peer[1] n (pl -s), fem **peeress** (pl -es) (in Britain) member of the nobility
peer[2] v (-s, -ing, -ed) look closely and intently
peerage n (BRIT) whole body of peers
  peerages n ▷ peerage
  peered v ▷ peer[2]

peeress n ▷ peer
peeresses n ▷ peer
peering v ▷ peer[2]
peerless adj unequalled, unsurpassed
peers n, v ▷ peer[1, 2]
peers v ▷ peer
peering v ▷ peer
peered v ▷ peer
peeved adj (Informal) annoyed
peevish adj fretful or irritable > **peevishly** adv
  peevishly adv ▷ peevish
peewee n (pl -s) black-and-white Australian bird
  peewees n ▷ peewee
peewit n (pl -s) ▷ lapwing
  peewits n ▷ peewit
peg n (pl -s) pin or clip for joining, fastening, marking, etc. ▶ v (-s, -gging, -gged) fasten with pegs
  pegged v ▷ peg
  pegging v ▷ peg
  pegs n, v ▷ peg
peignoir [pay-nwahr] n (pl -s) woman's light dressing gown
  peignoirs n ▷ peignoir
pejorative [pij-jor-a-tiv] adj (of words etc.) with an insulting or critical meaning
pelargonium n (pl -s) plant with red, white, purple, or pink flowers
  pelargoniums n ▷ pelargonium
pelican n (pl -s) large water bird with a pouch beneath its bill for storing fish
  pelicans n ▷ pelican
pellagra n (pl -s) disease caused by lack of vitamin B
  pellagras n ▷ pellagra
pellet n (pl -s) small ball of something
  pellets n ▷ pellet
pellucid adj very clear
pelmet n (pl -s) ornamental drapery or board, concealing a curtain rail
  pelmets n ▷ pelmet
pelt[1] v (-s, -ing, -ed) throw missiles at
pelt[2] n (pl -s) skin of a fur-bearing animal
  pelted v ▷ pelt[1]
  pelting v ▷ pelt[1]
  pelts v, n ▷ pelt[1, 2]
pelvic adj ▷ pelvis
pelvis n (pl -es) framework of bones at the base of the spine, to which the hips are attached
  > **pelvic** adj
  pelvises n ▷ pelvis
pen[1] n (pl -s) instrument for writing in ink ▶ v (-s, -nning, -nned) write or compose
pen[2] n small enclosure for domestic animals

▶ v (-s, -nning, -nned) put or keep in a pen

pen³ n (pl -s) female swan

penal [pee-nal] adj of or used in punishment

penalize (-zes, -zing, -zed) v impose a penalty on

  penalized v ▷ penalize

  penalizes v ▷ penalize

  penalizing v ▷ penalize

  penalties n ▷ penalty

penalty n (pl -ties) punishment for a crime or offence

penance n (pl -s) voluntary self-punishment to make amends for wrongdoing

  penances n ▷ penance

pence n (BRIT) ▷ penny

penchant [pon-shon] n (pl -s) inclination or liking

  penchants n ▷ penchant

pencil n (pl -s) thin cylindrical instrument containing graphite, for writing or drawing ▶ v (-s, -lling, -lled) draw, write, or mark with a pencil

  pencilled v ▷ pencil

  pencilling v ▷ pencil

  pencils n, v ▷ pencil

pendant n (pl -s) ornament worn on a chain round the neck

  pendants n ▷ pendant

pendent adj hanging

pending prep while waiting for ▶ adj not yet decided or settled

pendulous adj hanging, swinging

pendulum n (pl -s) suspended weight swinging to and fro, esp. as a regulator for a clock

  pendulums n ▷ pendulum

penetrate v (-tes, -ting, -ted) find or force a way into or through > **penetration** n (pl -s)

penetrable adj capable of being penetrated

  penetrated v ▷ penetrate

  penetrates v ▷ penetrate

penetrating adj (of a sound) loud and unpleasant ▶ v ▷ penetrate

  penetration n ▷ penetrate

  penetrations n ▷ penetrate

penguin n (pl -s) flightless black-and-white sea bird of the southern hemisphere

  penguins n ▷ penguin

penicillin n (pl -s) antibiotic drug effective against a wide range of diseases and infections

  penicillins n ▷ penicillin

peninsula n (pl -s) strip of land nearly surrounded by water > **peninsular** adj

  penisular adj ▷ penisula

  peninsulas n ▷ peninsula

penis n (pl -es) organ of copulation and urination in male mammals

  penises n ▷ penis

  penitence n ▷ penitent

  penitences n ▷ penitent

penitent adj feeling sorry for having done wrong ▶ n (pl -s) someone who is penitent

  > **penitence** n (pl -s)

  penitentiaries n ▷ penitentiary

penitentiary n (pl -ries) (US) prison ▶ adj (also **penitential**) relating to penance

  penitents n ▷ penitent

penknife n (pl -knives) small knife with blade(s) that fold into the handle

  penknives n ▷ penknife

pennant n (pl -s) long narrow flag

  pennants n ▷ pennant

  penned v ▷ pen¹, ²

  pennies n ▷ penny

penniless adj very poor

  penning v ▷ pen¹, ²

penny n (pl pence, pennies) British bronze coin worth one hundredth of a pound

  pens n ▷ pen¹, ², ³

pension¹ n (pl -s) regular payment to people above a certain age, retired employees, widows, etc. > **pensionable** adj

pension² [pon-syon] n (pl -s) boarding house in Europe

  pensionable adj ▷ pension

pensioner n (pl -s) person receiving a pension

  pensioners n ▷ pension

  pensions n ▷ pension¹, ²

pensive adj deeply thoughtful, often with a tinge of sadness

pentagon n (pl -s) geometric figure with five sides > **pentagonal** adj

  pentagonal adj ▷ pentagon

  pentagons n ▷ pentagon

pentameter [pen-tam-it-er] n (pl -s) line of poetry with five metrical feet

  pentameters n ▷ pentameter

penthouse n (pl -s) flat built on the roof or top floor of a building

  penthouses n ▷ penthouse

penultimate adj second last

penumbra n (pl -brae, -bras) (in an eclipse) the partially shadowed region which surrounds the full shadow

  penumbrae n ▷ penumbra

  penumbras n ▷ penumbra

  penuries n ▷ penury

  penurious adj ▷ penury

penury n (pl -ries) extreme poverty

> **penurious** adj

peonies n ▷ peony

peony n (pl -nies) garden plant with showy red, pink, or white flowers

people pl n persons generally ▶ n (pl -s) race or nation ▶ v (-les, -ling, -led) provide with inhabitants

peopled v ▷ people

peoples n, v ▷ people

peopling v ▷ people

pep n (pl -s) (*Informal*) high spirits, energy, or enthusiasm

pepper n (pl -s) sharp hot condiment made from the fruit of an East Indian climbing plant ▶ v (-s, -ing, -ed) season with pepper

peppercorn n dried berry of the pepper plant

peppercorns n ▷ peppercorn

peppered v ▷ pepper

pepperier adj ▷ peppery

pepperiest adj ▷ peppery

peppering v ▷ pepper

peppermint n (pl -s) plant that yields an oil with a strong sharp flavour

peppermints n ▷ peppermint

peppers n, v ▷ pepper

peppery adj (-rier, -riest) tasting of pepper

peps n ▷ pep

peptic adj relating to digestion or the digestive juices

per prep for each

perambulate v (-tes, -ting, -ted) (*Old-fashioned*) walk through or about (a place) > **perambulation** n (pl -s)

perambulated v ▷ perambulate

perambulates v ▷ perambulate

perambulating v ▷ perambulate

perambulation n ▷ perambulate

perambulations n ▷ perambulate

perambulator n (pl -s) pram

perambulators n ▷ perambulator

perceive v (-ves, -ving, -ved) become aware of (something) through the senses

perceived v ▷ perceive

perceives v ▷ perceive

perceiving v ▷ perceive

perceptible adj discernible, recognizable

perception n (pl -s) act of perceiving > **perceptive** adj

perceptions n ▷ perception

perceptive adj ▷ perception

perch¹ n (pl -es) resting place for a bird ▶ v (-es, -ing, -ed) alight, rest, or place on or as if on a perch

perch² n (pl -es) any of various edible fishes

perchance adv (*Old-fashioned*) perhaps

perches n, v ▷ perch¹, ²

perching v ▷ perch¹, ²

perched v ▷ perch¹, ²

percipient adj quick to notice things, observant

percolate v (-tes, -ting, -ted) pass or filter through small holes > **percolation** n

percolated v ▷ percolate

percolates v ▷ percolate

percolating v ▷ percolate

percolation n ▷ percolate

percolations n ▷ percolate

percolator n (pl -s) coffeepot in which boiling water is forced through a tube and filters down through coffee

percolators n ▷ percolator

percussion n (pl -s) striking of one thing against another

percussions n ▷ percussion

perdition n (pl -s) (CHRISTIANITY) spiritual ruin

perditions n ▷ perdition

peregrination n (pl -s) (*Obs*) travels, roaming

peregrinations n ▷ peregrination

peremptory adj authoritative, imperious

perennial adj lasting through many years ▶ n (pl -s) plant lasting more than two years > **perennially** adv

perennially adv ▷ perennial

perennials n ▷ perennial

perfect adj (-er, -est) having all the essential elements ▶ n (GRAMMAR) perfect tense ▶ v (-s, -ing, -ed) improve > **perfectly** adv

perfected n ▷ perfect

perfecter adj ▷ perfect

perfectest adj ▷ perfect

perfecting v ▷ perfect

perfection n (pl -s) state of being perfect

perfectionist n (pl -s) person who demands the highest standards of excellence > **perfectionism** n (pl -s)

perfectionism n ▷ perfectionist

perfectionisms n ▷ perfectionist

perfectionists n ▷ perfectionist

perfections n ▷ perfection

perfectly adv ▷ perfect

perfects n, v ▷ perfect

perfidious adj (*Lit*) treacherous, disloyal > **perfidy** n (pl -ies)

perfidies n ▷ perfidious

perfidy n ▷ perfidious

perforate v (-es, -ing, -ed) make holes in > **perforation** n (pl -s)

perforated v ▷ perforate

perforates v ▷ perforate

perforating v ▷ perforate

perforation n ▷ perforate
perforations n ▷ perforate
perforce adv of necessity
perform v (-s, -ing, -ed) carry out (an action)
> **performance** n (pl -s) > **performer** n (pl -s)
performance n ▷ perform
performances n ▷ perform
performed v ▷ perform
performer n ▷ perform
performers n ▷ perform
performing v ▷ perform
performs v ▷ perform
perfume n (pl -s) liquid cosmetic worn for
its pleasant smell ▶ v (-es, -ing, -ed) give a
pleasant smell to
perfumed v ▷ perfume
perfumeries n ▷ perfumery
perfumery n (pl -ries) perfumes in general
perfumes n, v ▷ perfume
perfuming v ▷ perfume
perfunctorily adv ▷ perfunctory
perfunctory adj done only as a matter of
routine, superficial > **perfunctorily** adv
pergola n (pl -s) arch or framework of trellis
supporting climbing plants
pergolas n ▷ pergola
perhaps adv possibly, maybe
pericardia n ▷ pericardum
pericardium n (pl -dia) membrane enclosing
the heart
perihelia n ▷ perihelion
perihelion n (pl -lia) point in the orbit of a
planet or comet that is nearest to the sun
peril n (pl -s) great danger > **perilous** adj
> **perilously** adv
perilous adj ▷ peril
perilously adv ▷ peril
perils n ▷ peril
perimeter [per-**rim**-it-er] n (pl -s) (length of) the
outer edge of an area
perimeters n ▷ perimeter
perinatal adj of or in the weeks shortly before
or after birth
period n (pl -s) particular portion of time (US)
▶ adj (of furniture, dress, a play, etc.) dating
from or in the style of an earlier time
periodic adj recurring at intervals
periodical n (pl -s) magazine issued at regular
intervals ▶ adj periodic
periodicals n ▷ periodical
periods n ▷ period
peripatetic [per-rip-a-**tet**-ik] adj travelling
about from place to place
peripheral [per-**if**-er-al] adj unimportant, not
central

peripheries n ▷ periphery
periphery [per-**if**-er-ee] n (pl -ries) boundary
or edge
periscope n (pl -s) instrument used, esp. in
submarines, to give a view of objects on a
different level
periscopes n ▷ periscope
perish v (-es, -ing, -ed) be destroyed or die
perishable adj liable to rot quickly
perished v ▷ perish
perishes v ▷ perish
perishing adj (Informal) very cold ▶ v ▷ perish
peritonea n ▷ peritoneum
peritoneum [per-rit-toe-**nee**-um] n (pl -nea,
-neums) membrane lining the internal
surface of the abdomen
peritoneums n ▷ peritoneum
peritonitis [per-rit-tone-**ite**-iss] n (pl -tises)
inflammation of the peritoneum
peritonitises n ▷ peritonitis
periwinkle[1] n (pl -s) small edible shellfish,
the winkle
periwinkle[2] n (pl -s) plant with trailing stems
and blue flowers
periwinkles n ▷ periwinkle[1, 2]
perjuries n ▷ perjury
perjury n (pl -ies) act or crime of lying while
under oath in a court
perk n (pl -s) (Informal) incidental benefit
gained from a job, such as a company car
perkier adj ▷ perk
perkiest adj ▷ perk
perks n ▷ perk
perky adj (-kier, -kiest) lively or cheerful
perlemoen n (pl -s) (S AFR) edible sea creature
with a shell lined with mother of pearl
perlemoens n ▷ perlemoen
perm n (pl -s) long-lasting curly hairstyle
produced by treating the hair with chemicals
▶ v (-s, -ing, -ed) give (hair) a perm
permafrost n (pl -s) permanently frozen
ground
permafrosts n ▷ permafrost
permanence n ▷ permanent
permanences n ▷ permanent
permanent adj lasting forever > **permanence**
n (pl -s) > **permanently** adv
permanently adv ▷ permanent
permeate v (-tes, -ting, -ted) pervade or pass
through the whole of (something)
permeable adj able to be permeated, esp.
by liquid
permeated v ▷ permeate
permeates v ▷ permeate
permeating v ▷ permeate

permed v ▷ perm
perming v ▷ perm
permissible adj ▷ permit
permission n (pl -s) authorization to do something
permissions n ▷ permission
permissive adj (excessively) tolerant, esp. in sexual matters
permit v (-s, -tting, -tted) give permission, allow ▶ n (pl -s) document giving permission to do something > **permissible** adj
permits v, n ▷ permit
permitted v ▷ permit
permitting v ▷ permit
perms n, v ▷ perm
permutation n (pl -s) any of the ways a number of things can be arranged or combined
permutations n ▷ permutation
pernicious adj wicked
pernickety adj (Informal) (excessively) fussy about details
peroration n (pl -s) concluding part of a speech, usu. summing up the main points
perorations n ▷ peroration
peroxide n (pl -s) hydrogen peroxide used as a hair bleach
peroxides n ▷ peroxide
perpendicular adj at right angles to a line or surface ▶ n (pl -s) line or plane at right angles to another
perpendiculars n ▷ perpendicular
perpetrate v (-tes, -ting, -ted) commit or be responsible for (a wrongdoing) > **perpetration** n (pl -s) > **perpetrator** n (pl -s)
perpetrated v ▷ perpetrate
perpetrates v ▷ perpetrate
perpetrating v ▷ perpetrate
perpetration n ▷ perpetrate
perpetrations n ▷ perpetrate
perpetrator n ▷ perpetrate
perpetrators n ▷ perpetrate
perpetual adj lasting forever > **perpetually** adv
perpetually adv ▷ perpetual
perpetuate v (-tes, -ting, -ted) cause to continue or be remembered > **perpetuation** n (pl -s)
perpetuated v ▷ perpetuate
perpetuates v ▷ perpetuate
perpetuating v ▷ perpetuate
perpetuation n ▷
perpetuations n ▷
perplex v (-es, -ing, -ed) puzzle, bewilder > **perplexity** n (pl -ties)
perplexed v ▷ perplex

perplexes v ▷ perplex
perplexing v ▷ perplex
perplexities n ▷ perplex
perplexity n ▷ perplex
perquisite n (pl -s) (Formal) ▷ perk
perquisites n ▷ perquisite
perries n ▷ perry
perry n (pl -rries) alcoholic drink made from fermented pears
persecute v (-tes, -ting, -ted) treat cruelly because of race, religion, etc. > **persecution** n (pl -s) > **persecutor** n (pl -s)
persecuted v ▷ persecute
persecutes v ▷ persecute
persecuting v ▷ persecute
persecution n ▷ persecute
persecutions n ▷ persecute
persecutor n ▷ persecute
persecutors n ▷ persecute
persevere v (-res, -ring, -red) keep making an effort despite difficulties > **perseverance** n (pl -s)
perseverance n ▷ persevere
perseverances n ▷ persevere
persevered v ▷ persevere
perseveres v ▷ persevere
persevering v ▷ persevere
persimmon n (pl -s) sweet red tropical fruit
persimmons n ▷ persimmon
persist v (-s, -ing, -ed) continue to be or happen, last > **persistent** adj > **persistently** adv > **persistence** n (pl -s)
persisted v ▷ persist
persistence adj ▷ persist
persistences adj ▷ persist
persistent adj ▷ persist
persistently v ▷ persist
persisting v ▷ persist
persists v ▷ persist
person n (pl -s) human being
persons n ▷ person
persona [per-soh-na] n (pl -nae) [-nee] someone's personality as presented to others
personable adj pleasant in appearance and personality
personae n ▷ persona
personage n (pl -s) important person
personages n ▷ personage
personal adj individual or private
personalities n ▷ personality
personality n (pl -ties) person's distinctive characteristics
personally adv directly, not by delegation to others
personification n ▷ personify

personifications n ▷ personify

personified v ▷ personify

personifies v ▷ personify

personify v (-fies, -fying, -fied) give human characteristics to ▷ **personification** n (pl -s)

personifying v ▷ personify

personnel n (pl -s) people employed in an organization

personnels n ▷ personnel

perspective n (pl -s) view of the relative importance of situations or facts

perspectives n ▷ perspective

perspicacious adj having quick mental insight ▷ **perspicacity** n (pl -ties)

perspicacities n ▷ perspicacious

perspicacity n ▷ perspicacious

perspiration n ▷ perspire

perspirations n ▷ perspire

perspire v (-res, -ring, -red) sweat ▷ **perspiration** n (pl -s)

perspired v ▷ perspire

perspires v ▷ perspire

perspiring v ▷ perspire

persuade v (-des, -ding, -ded) make (someone) do something by argument, charm, etc. ▷ **persuasive** adj

persuasion n (pl -s) act of persuading

persuasions n ▷ persuasion

persuasive adj ▷ persuade

persuaded v ▷ persuade

persuades v ▷ persuade

persuading v ▷ persuade

pert adj (-er, -est) saucy and cheeky

pertain v (-s, -ing, -ed) belong or be relevant (to)

pertained v ▷ pertain

pertaining v ▷ pertain

pertains v ▷ pertain

perter adj ▷ pert

pertest adj ▷ pert

pertinacious adj (Formal) very persistent and determined ▷ **pertinacity** n (pl -ties)

pertinacities n ▷ pertinacious

pertinacity n ▷ pertinacious

pertinence n ▷ pertinent

pertinences n ▷ pertinent

pertinent adj relevant ▷ **pertinence** n (pl -s)

perturb v (-s, -ing, -ed) disturb greatly ▷ **perturbation** n (pl -s)

perturbation n ▷ perturb

perturbation n ▷ perturb

perturbed v ▷ perturb

perturbing v ▷ perturb

perturbs v ▷ perturb

perusal n ▷ peruse

perusals n ▷ peruse

peruse v (-ses, -sing, -sed) read in a careful or leisurely manner ▷ **perusal** n (pl -s)

perused v ▷ peruse

peruses v ▷ peruse

perusing v ▷ peruse

pervade v (-des, -ding, -ded) spread right through (something) ▷ **pervasive** adj

pervaded v ▷ pervade

pervades v ▷ pervade

pervading v ▷ pervade

pervasive adj ▷ pervade

perverse adj (-r, -st) deliberately doing something different from what is thought normal or proper ▷ **perversely** adv ▷ **perversity** n (pl -ties)

perversely n ▷ perverse

perverser adj ▷ perverse

perversest adj ▷ perverse

perversion n (pl -s) sexual act or desire considered abnormal

perversions n ▷ perversion

perversities n ▷ perverse

perversity n ▷ perverse

pervert v (-s, -ing, -ed) use or alter for a wrong purpose ▶ n (pl -s) person who practises sexual perversion

perverted v ▷ pervert

perverting v ▷ pervert

perverts v, n ▷ pervert

pervious adj able to be penetrated, permeable

peseta [pa-**say**-ta] n (pl -s) former monetary unit of Spain

pesetas n ▷ peseta

pessaries n ▷ pessary

pessary n (pl -ries) appliance worn in the vagina, either to prevent conception or to support the womb

pessimism n (pl -s) tendency to expect the worst in all things ▷ **pessimist** n (pl -s) ▷ **pessimistic** adj ▷ **pessimistically** adv

pessimisms n ▷ pessimism

pessimist n ▷ pessimism

pessimistic adj ▷ pessimism

pessimistically adv ▷ pessimism

pessimists n ▷ pessimism

pest n (pl -s) annoying person

pesticide n (pl -s) chemical for killing insect pests

pesticides n ▷ pesticide

pester v (-s, -ing, -ed) annoy or nag continually

pestered v ▷ pester

pestering v ▷ pester

pesters v ▷ pester

pestilence n (pl -s) deadly epidemic disease

pestilences n ▷ pestilence

pestilent adj annoying, troublesome
> **pestilential** adj

pestilential adj ▷ pestilent

pestle n (pl -s) club-shaped implement for grinding things to powder in a mortar

pestles n ▷ pestle

pests n ▷ pest

pet n (pl -s) animal kept for pleasure and companionship ▶ adj particularly cherished ▶ v (-s, -tting, -tted) treat as a pet

petal n (pl -s) one of the brightly coloured outer parts of a flower > **petalled** adj

petalled adj ▷ petal

petals n ▷ petal

petard n (pl -s) being the victim of one's own schemes

petards n ▷ petard

petite adj (of a woman) small and dainty

petition n (pl -s) formal request, esp. one signed by many people and presented to parliament ▶ v (-s, -ing, -ed) present a petition to > **petitioner** n (pl -s)

petitioned v ▷ petition

petitioner n ▷ petition

petitioners n ▷ petition

petitioning v ▷ petition

petitions n, v ▷ petition

petrel n (pl -s) sea bird with a hooked bill and tubular nostrils

petrels n ▷ petrel

petrification n ▷ petrify

petrifications n ▷ petrify

petrified v ▷ petrify

petrifies v ▷ petrify

petrify v (-fies, -fying, -fied) frighten severely > **petrification** n (pl -s)

petrochemical n (pl -s) substance, such as acetone, obtained from petroleum

petrochemicals n ▷ petrochemical

petrol n (pl -s) flammable liquid obtained from petroleum, used as fuel in internal-combustion engines

petroleum n (pl -s) thick dark oil found underground

petroleums n ▷ petroleums

petrols n ▷ petrol

pets n, v ▷ pet

petted v ▷ pet

petticoat n (pl -s) woman's skirt-shaped undergarment

petticoats n ▷ petticoat

pettier adj ▷ petty

pettiest adj ▷ petty

pettifogging adj excessively concerned with unimportant detail

pettiness n ▷ petty

pettinesses n ▷ petty

petting v ▷ pet

petty adj (-ttier, -ttiest) unimportant, trivial > **pettiness** n (pl -es)

petulance n ▷ petulant

petulances n ▷ petulant

petulant adj childishly irritable or peevish > **petulance** n (pl -s) > **petulantly** adv

petulantly adv ▷ petulant

petunia n (pl -s) garden plant with funnel-shaped flowers

petunias n ▷ petunia

pew n (pl -s) fixed benchlike seat in a church

pews n ▷ pew

pewter n (pl -s) greyish metal made of tin and lead

pewters n ▷ pewter

phalanger n (pl -s) long-tailed Australian tree-dwelling marsupial

phalangers n ▷ phalanger

phalanx n (pl -es) closely grouped mass of people

phalanxes n ▷ phalanx

phalli n ▷ phallus

phallic adj ▷ phallus

phallus n (pl -lluses, -lli) penis, esp. as a symbol of reproductive power in primitive rites > **phallic** adj

phalluses n ▷ phallus

phantasm n (pl -s) unreal vision, illusion > **phantasmal** adj

phantasmal adj ▷ phantasm

phantasms n ▷ phantasm

phantasmagoria n (pl -s) shifting medley of dreamlike figures

phantasmagorias n ▷ phantasmagoria

phantom n (pl -s) ghost

phantoms n ▷ phantom

pharmaceutical adj of pharmacy

pharmacies n ▷ pharmacy

pharmacist n (pl -s) person qualified to prepare and sell drugs and medicines

pharmacists n ▷ pharmacist

pharmacological adj ▷ pharmacology

pharmacologies n ▷ pharmacology

pharmacologist n ▷ pharmacology

pharmacologists n ▷ pharmacology

pharmacology n (pl -gies) study of drugs > **pharmacological** adj > **pharmacologist** n (pl -s)

pharmacopoeia [far-ma-koh-**pee**-a] n (pl -s) book with a list of and directions for the use of drugs

pharmacopoeias n ▷ pharmacopoeia
pharmacy n (pl -cies) preparation and dispensing of drugs and medicines
pharynges n ▷ pharynx
pharyngitis [far-rin-**jite**-iss] n (pl -tes) inflammation of the pharynx
pharyngitises n ▷ pharynx
pharynx [far-rinks] n (pl -nges, -nxes) cavity forming the back part of the mouth
pharynxes ▷ pharynx
phase n (pl -s) any distinct or characteristic stage in a development or chain of events
▶ v (-ses, -sing, -sed) arrange or carry out in stages or to coincide with something else
phased v ▷ phase
phases n, v ▷ phase
phasing v ▷ phase
pheasant n (pl -s) game bird with bright plumage
pheasants n ▷ pheasant
phenobarbitone n (pl -s) drug inducing sleep or relaxation
phenobarbitones n ▷ phenobarbitone
phenol n (pl -s) chemical used in disinfectants and antiseptics
phenols n ▷ phenol
phenomena n ▷ phenomenon
phenomenal adj extraordinary, outstanding
> **phenomenally** adv
phenomenally adv ▷ phenomenal
phenomenon n (pl -mena) anything appearing or observed
phial n (pl -s) small bottle for medicine etc.
phials n ▷ phial
philadelphus n (pl -es) shrub with sweet-scented flowers
philadelphuses n ▷ philadelphus
philanderer n (pl -s) man who flirts or has many casual love affairs > **philandering** adj, n (pl -s)
philanderers n ▷ philanderer
philandering n ▷ philanderer
philanderings n ▷ philanderer
philanthropic adj ▷ philanthropy
philanthropies n ▷ philanthropy
philanthropist n ▷ philanthropy
philanthropists n ▷ philanthropy
philanthropy n (pl -pies) practice of helping people less well-off than oneself
> **philanthropic** adj > **philanthropist** n (pl -s)
philatelies n ▷ philately
philatelist n ▷ philately
philatelists n ▷ philately
philately [fill-**lat**-a-lee] n (pl -lies) stamp collecting > **philatelist** n (pl -s)

philharmonic adj (in names of orchestras etc.) music-loving
philistine adj, n (pl -s) boorishly uncultivated (person) > **philistinism** n (pl -s)
philistines n ▷ philistine
philistinism n ▷ philistine
philistinisms n ▷ philistine
philological adj ▷ philology
philologies n ▷ philology
philologist n ▷ philology
philologists n ▷ philology
philology n (pl -gies) science of the structure and development of languages > **philological** adj > **philologist** n (pl -s)
philosopher n (pl -s) person who studies philosophy
philosophers n ▷ philosopher
philosophize v (-zes, -zing, -zed) discuss in a philosophical manner
philosophized v ▷ philosophize
philosophizes v ▷ philosophize
philosophizing v ▷ philosophize
philosophic adj ▷ philosophy
philosophical adj ▷ philosophy
philosophically adv ▷ philosophy
philosophies n ▷ philosophy
philosophy n (pl -phies) study of the meaning of life, knowledge, thought, etc. > **philosophical, philosophic** adj of philosophy > **philosophically** adv
philtre n (pl -s) magic drink supposed to arouse love in the person who drinks it
philtres n ▷ philtre
phlebitis [fleb-**bite**-iss] n (pl -es) inflammation of a vein
phlebitises n ▷ phlebitis
phlegm [flem] n (pl -s) thick yellowish substance formed in the nose and throat during a cold
phlegmatic [fleg-**mat**-ik] adj not easily excited, unemotional > **phlegmatically** adv
phlematically adv ▷ phlegmatic
phlegms n ▷ phlegm
phlox n (pl phlox, -xes) flowering garden plant
phloxes n ▷ phlox
phobia n (pl -s) intense and unreasoning fear or dislike
phobias n ▷ phobia
phoenix n (pl -es) legendary bird said to set fire to itself and rise anew from its ashes
phoenixes n ▷ phoenix
phone n, v (-nes, -ning, -ned) (Informal) telephone
phonecard n (pl -s) card used to operate certain public telephones

phonecards n ▷ phonecard
phoned v ▷ phone
phones v ▷ phone
phonetic adj of speech sounds > **phonetically** adv
phonetically adv ▷ phonetic
phonetics n science of speech sounds
phoney, phony (Informal) adj (-nier, -niest) not genuine ▶ n (pl -neys, -nies) phoney person or thing
phoneys n ▷ phoney
phonier adj ▷ phoney
phonies n ▷ phoney
phoniest adj ▷ phoney
phoning v ▷ phone
phonograph n (pl -s) (US) (old-fashioned) record player
phonographs n ▷ phonograph
phony adj ▷ phoney
phosphorescence n (pl -s) faint glow in the dark > **phosphorescent** adj
phosphorescences n ▷ phosphorescence
phosphorescent adj ▷ phosphorescence
phosphate n (pl -s) compound of phosphorus
phosphates n ▷ phosphate
phosphorus n (pl -es) (CHEM) toxic flammable nonmetallic element which appears luminous in the dark
phosphoruses n ▷ phosphorus
photo n (pl -s) ▷ photograph
photocopied v ▷ photocopy
photocopier n ▷ photocopy
photocopiers n ▷ photocopy
photocopies n, v ▷ photocopy
photocopy n (pl -pies) photographic reproduction ▶ v (-pies, -pying, -pied) make a photocopy of > **photocopier** n (pl -s)
photocopying v ▷ photocopy
photoelectric adj using or worked by electricity produced by the action of light
photogenic adj always looking attractive in photographs
photograph n (pl -s) picture made by the chemical action of light on sensitive film ▶ v (-s, -ing, -ed) take a photograph of > **photographic** adj
photographed v ▷ photograph
photographer n (pl -s) person who takes photographs, esp. professionally
photographers n ▷ photographer
photographic adj ▷ photograph
photographing v ▷ photograph
photographs n, v ▷ photograph
photographies n ▷ photography
photography n (pl -s) art of taking photographs
photos n ▷ photo
photostat n (pl -s) copy made by photocopying machine
photostats n ▷ photostat
photosyntheses n ▷ photosynthesis
photosynthesis n (pl -ses) process by which a green plant uses sunlight to build up carbohydrate reserves
phrase n (pl -s) group of words forming a unit of meaning, esp. within a sentence ▶ v (-ses, -sing, -sed) express in words
phrased v ▷ phrase
phrases n, v ▷ phrase
phrasing v ▷ phrase
phraseologies n ▷ phraseology
phraseology n (pl -gies) way in which words are used
physical adj of the body, as contrasted with the mind or spirit > **physically** adv
physically adv ▷ physical
physician n (pl -s) doctor of medicine
physicians n ▷ physician
physics n science of the properties of matter and energy
physicist n (pl -s) person skilled in or studying physics
physicists n ▷ physicist
physiognomies n ▷ physiognomy
physiognomy [fiz-ee-on-om-ee] n (pl -mies) face
physiological adj ▷ physiology
physiologies n ▷ physiology
physiologist n ▷ physiology
physiologists n ▷ physiology
physiology n (pl -gies) science of the normal function of living things > **physiological** adj > **physiologist** n (pl -s)
physiotherapies n ▷ physiotherapy
physiotherapist n ▷ physiotherapy
physiotherapists n ▷ physiotherapy
physiotherapy n (pl -pies) treatment of disease or injury by physical means such as massage, rather than by drugs > **physiotherapist** n (pl -s)
physique n (pl -s) person's bodily build and muscular development
physiques n ▷ physique
pi n (pl -s) (MATHS) ratio of the circumference of a circle to its diameter
pis n ▷ pi
pianissimo adv (MUSIC) very quietly
piano[1] n (pl -os) musical instrument with strings which are struck by hammers worked by a keyboard (also **pianoforte**) (pl -s) > **pianist**

n (*pl* -s)
pianist *n* ▷ piano¹
pianists *n* ▷ piano¹
piano² *adv* (MUSIC) quietly
pianoforte *n* ▷ piano¹
pianofortes *n* ▷ piano¹
pianos *n* ▷ piano¹
piazza *n* (*pl* -s) square or marketplace, esp. in Italy
piazzas *n* ▷ piazza
pic *n* (*pl* -s, pix) (*Informal*) photograph or illustration
picador *n* (*pl* -s) mounted bullfighter with a lance
picadors *n* ▷ picador
picaresque *adj* denoting a type of fiction in which the hero, a rogue, has a series of adventures
piccalilli *n* (*pl* -s) pickle of vegetables in mustard sauce
piccalillis *n* ▷ piccalilli
piccolo *n* (*pl* -os) small flute
piccolos *n* ▷ piccolo
pick¹ *v* (-s, -ing, -ed) choose ▶ *n* (*pl* -s) choice
pick² *n* (*pl* -s) tool with a curved iron crossbar and wooden shaft, for breaking up hard ground or rocks
pickaxe *n* (*pl* -s) large pick
pickaxes *n* ▷ pickaxe
picked *v* ▷ pick¹
picket *n* (*pl* -s) person or group standing outside a workplace to deter would-be workers during a strike ▶ *v* (-s, -ing, -ed) form a picket outside (a workplace)
picketed *v* ▷ picket
picketing *v* ▷ picket
pickets *n*, *v* ▷ picket
picking *v* ▷ pick¹
pickings *pl n* money easily acquired
pickle *n* (*pl* -s) food preserved in vinegar or salt water ▶ *v* (-les, -ling, -led) preserve in vinegar or salt water
pickled *adj* (of food) preserved ▶ *n* ▷ pickle
pickles *n*, *v* ▷ pickle
pickling *v* ▷ pickle
pickpocket *n* (*pl* -s) thief who steals from someone's pocket
pickpockets *n* ▷ pickpocket
picks *n*, *v* ▷ pick¹, ²
picnic *n* (*pl* -s) (*Informal*) meal out of doors ▶ *v* (-s, -cking, -cked) have a picnic
picnicked *v* ▷ picnic
picnicking *v* ▷ picnic
picnics *n*, *v* ▷ picnic

pics *n* ▷ pic
pictorial *adj* of or in painting or pictures
picture *n* (*pl* -s) drawing or painting ▶ *pl* cinema ▶ *v* (-res, -ring, -red) visualize, imagine
pictured *v* ▷ picture
pictures *n*, *v* ▷ picture
picturesque *adj* (of a place or view) pleasant to look at
picturing *v* ▷ picture
piddle *v* (-les, -ling, -led) (*Informal*) urinate
piddled *v* ▷ piddle
piddles *v* ▷ piddle
piddling *v* ▷ piddle
pidgin *n* (*pl* -s) language, not a mother tongue, made up of elements of two or more other languages
pidgins *n* ▷ pidgin
pie *n* (*pl* -s) dish of meat, fruit, etc. baked in pastry
pies *n* ▷ pie
piebald *adj*, *n* (*pl* -s) (horse) with irregular black-and-white markings
piebalds *n* ▷ piebald
piece *n* (*pl* -s) separate bit or part
pieces *n* ▷ piece
piecemeal *adv* bit by bit
piecework *n* (*pl* -s) work paid for according to the quantity produced
pieceworks *n* ▷ piecework
pied *adj* having markings of two or more colours
pier *n* (*pl* -s) platform on stilts sticking out into the sea
piers *n* ▷ pier
pierce *v* (-ces, -cing, -ced) make a hole in or through with a sharp instrument
pierced *v* ▷ pierce
pierces *v* ▷ pierce
piercing *adj* (of a sound) shrill and high-pitched ▶ *v* ▷ pierce
pierrot [pier-roe] *n* (*pl* -s) pantomime clown with a whitened face
pierrots *n* ▷ pierrot
pieties *n* ▷ piety
piety *n* (*pl* -ties) deep devotion to God and religion
piffle *n* (*pl* -s) (*Informal*) nonsense
piffles *n* ▷ piffle
pig *n* (*pl* -s) animal kept and killed for pork, ham, and bacon
pigeon¹ *n* (*pl* -s) bird with a heavy body and short legs, sometimes trained to carry messages
pigeon² *n* (*Informal*) concern or responsibility

pigeonhole n (-s) compartment for papers in a desk etc. ▶ v (-les, -ling, -led) classify
pigeonholed v ▷ pigeonhole
pigeonholing v ▷ pigeonhole
pigeonholes n, v ▷ pigeonhole
pigeons n ▷ pigeon¹,²
piggeries n ▷ piggery
piggery n (pl -ries) place for keeping and breeding pigs
piggier adj ▷ piggy
piggiest adj ▷ piggy
piggish, piggy (-ggier, -ggiest) adj (Informal) dirty
piggy adj ▷ piggish
piggyback n (pl -s) ride on someone's shoulders ▶ adv carried on someone's shoulders
piggybacks n ▷ piggyback
pigment n (pl -s) colouring matter, paint or dye ▷ **pigmentation** n (pl -s)
pigmentation n ▷ pigment
pigmentations n ▷ pigment
pigments n ▷ pigment
pigmies n ▷ pigmy
pigmy n (pl -mies) ▷ pygmy
pigs n ▷ pig
pigtail n (pl -s) plait of hair hanging from the back or either side of the head
pigtails n ▷ pigtail
pike¹ n (pl -s) large predatory freshwater fish
pike² n (pl -s) (HIST) long-handled spear
pikes n ▷ pike¹,²
pikelet n (pl -s) (AUST & NZ) small thick pancake
pikelets n ▷ pikelet
piker n (pl -s) (AUST & NZ) (Slang) shirker
pikers n ▷ piker
pilaster n (pl -s) square column, usu. set in a wall
pilasters n ▷ pilaster
pilau, pilaf, pilaff n (pl -s) Middle Eastern dish of meat, fish, or poultry boiled with rice, spices, etc.
pilaffs n ▷ pilaff
pilafs n ▷ pilaf
pilchard n (pl -s) small edible sea fish of the herring family
pilchards n ▷ pilchard
pile¹ n (pl -s) number of things lying on top of each other ▶ v (-les, -ling, -led) collect into a pile
pile² n (pl -s) (HIST) beam driven into the ground, esp. as a foundation for building
pile³ n (pl -s) fibres of a carpet or a fabric, esp. velvet, that stand up from the weave
piled v ▷ pile¹

piling v ▷ pile¹
piles pl n swollen veins in the rectum, haemorrhoids ▶ v, n ▷ pile¹,²,³
pilfer v (-s, -ing, -ed) steal in small quantities
pilfered v ▷ pilfer
pilfering v ▷ pilfer
pilfers v ▷ pilfer
pilgrim n (pl -s) person who journeys to a holy place ▷ **pilgrimage** n (pl -s)
pilgrimage n ▷ pilgrim
pilgrimages n ▷ pilgrim
pilgrims n ▷ pilgrim
pill n (pl -s) small ball of medicine swallowed whole
pills n ▷ pill
pillage v (-ges, -ging, -ged) steal property by violence in war ▶ n (pl -s) violent seizure of goods, esp. in war
pillaged v ▷ pillage
pillages v, n ▷ pillage
pillaging v ▷ pillage
pillar n (pl -s) upright post, usu. supporting a roof
pillars n ▷ pillar
pillion n (pl -s) seat for a passenger behind the rider of a motorcycle
pillions n ▷ pillion
pilloried v ▷ pillory
pillories n, v ▷ pillory
pillory n (pl -ries) (HIST) frame with holes for the head and hands in which an offender was locked and exposed to public abuse ▶ v (-ies, -ying, -ied) ridicule publicly
pillow n (pl -s) stuffed cloth bag for supporting the head in bed ▶ v (-s, -ing, -ed) rest as if on a pillow
pillowcase, pillowslip n (pl -s) removable cover for a pillow
pillowcases n ▷ pillowcase
pillowed v ▷ pillow
pillowing v ▷ pillow
pillows n, v ▷ pillow
pillowslip n ▷ pillowcase
pillowslips n ▷ pillowcase
pilot n (pl -s) person qualified to fly an aircraft or spacecraft ▶ adj experimental and preliminary ▶ v (-s, -ing, -ed) act as the pilot of
piloted v ▷ pilot
piloting v ▷ pilot
pilots n, v ▷ pilot
pimento n (pl -tos) mild-tasting red pepper
pimentos n ▷ pimento
pimp n (pl -s) man who gets customers for a prostitute in return for a share of his or her earnings ▶ v (-s, -ing, -ed) act as a pimp

pimped v ▷ pimp
pimpernel n (pl -s) wild plant with small star-shaped flowers
pimpernels n ▷ pimpernel
pimping v ▷ pimp
pimple n (pl -s) small pus-filled spot on the skin > **pimply** adj (-lier, -liest)
pimples n ▷ pimple
pimplier v ▷ pimple
pimpliest v ▷ pimple
pimply v ▷ pimple
pimps n, v ▷ pimp
pin n (pl -s) short thin piece of stiff wire with a point and head, for fastening things ▶ v (-s, -ning, -ned) fasten with a pin
pinafore n (pl -s) apron
pinafores n ▷ pinafore
pinball n (pl -s) electrically operated table game in which a small ball is shot through various hazards
pinballs n ▷ pinball
pincers pl n tool consisting of two hinged arms, for gripping
pinch v (-es, -ing, -ed) squeeze between finger and thumb ▶ n (pl -es) act of pinching
pinchbeck n (pl -s) alloy of zinc and copper, used as imitation gold
pinchbecks n ▷ pinchbeck
pinched v ▷ pinch
pinches v, n ▷ pinch
pinching v ▷ pinch
pinned v ▷ pin
pinning v ▷ pin
pins n, v ▷ pin
pine¹ n (pl -s) evergreen coniferous tree
pine² v (-nes, -ning, -ned) (foll. by for) feel great longing (for)
pineapple n (pl -s) large tropical fruit with juicy yellow flesh and a hard skin
pineapples n ▷ pineapple
pined v ▷ pine²
pines n, v ▷ pine¹, ²
ping v (-s, -ing, -ed) ▶ n (pl -s) (make) a short high-pitched sound
pinged v ▷ ping
pinging v ▷ ping
pings v, n ▷ ping
pining v ▷ pine²
pinion¹ n (pl -s) bird's wing ▶ v (-s, -ing, -ed) immobilize (someone) by tying or holding his or her arms
pinion² n (pl -s) small cogwheel
pinioned v ▷ pinion
pinioning v ▷ pinion
pinions n, v ▷ pinion¹, ²

pink n (pl -s) pale reddish colour ▶ adj (-er, -est) of the colour pink ▶ v (-s, -ing, -ed) (of an engine) make a metallic noise because not working properly, knock
pinked v ▷ pink
pinker adj ▷ pink
pinkest adj ▷ pink
pinking v ▷ pink
pinks n, v ▷ pink
pinnacle n (pl -s) highest point of fame or success
pinnacles n ▷ pinnacle
pinotage [pin-no-tajj] n (pl -s) blended red wine of S Africa
pinotages n ▷ pinotage
pinpoint v (-s, -ing, -ed) locate or identify exactly
pinpointed v ▷ pinpoint
pinpointing v ▷ pinpoint
pinpoints v ▷ pinpoint
pinstripe n (pl -s) very narrow stripe in fabric
pinstripes n ▷ pinstripe
pint n (pl -s) liquid measure, 1/8 gallon (.568 litre)
pints n ▷ pint
pioneer n (pl -s) explorer or early settler of a new country ▶ v (-s, -ing, -ed) be the pioneer or leader of
pioneered v ▷ pioneer
pioneering v ▷ pioneer
pioneers n, v ▷ pioneer
pious adj deeply religious, devout
pip¹ n (pl -s) small seed in a fruit
pip² n high-pitched sound used as a time signal on radio (Informal)
pips n ▷ pip¹, ²
pipe n (pl -s) tube for conveying liquid or gas ▶ pl bagpipes ▶ v (-pes, -ping, -ped) play on a pipe
piped v ▷ pipe
piper n (pl -s) player on a pipe or bagpipes
pipers n ▷ piper
piping n (pl -s) system of pipes ▶ v ▷ pipe
pipings n ▷ piping
pipeline n (pl -s) long pipe for transporting oil, water, etc.
pipelines n ▷ pipeline
pipes n, v ▷ pipe
pipette n (pl -s) slender glass tube used to transfer or measure fluids
pipettes n ▷ pipette
pipi n (pl -s) (AUST) mollusc often used as bait
pipit n (pl -s) small brownish songbird
pipits n ▷ pipit
pippin n (pl -s) type of eating apple

pippins n ▷ pippin
pips n ▷ pip[1, 2]
piquancies n ▷ piquant
piquancy n ▷ piquant
piquant [pee-kant] adj having a pleasant spicy taste > **piquancy** n (pl -cies)
pique [peek] n (pl -s) feeling of hurt pride, baffled curiosity, or resentment ▶ v (-ques, -quing, -qued) hurt the pride of
piqué [pee-kay] n (pl -s) stiff ribbed cotton fabric
piqued v ▷ pique
piques n, v ▷ pique
piqués n ▷ piqué
piquing v ▷ pique
piquet [pik-ket] n (pl -s) card game for two
piquets n ▷ piquet
piracies n ▷ pirate
piracy n ▷ pirate
piranha n (pl -s) small fierce freshwater fish of tropical America
piranhas n ▷ piranha
pirate n (pl -s) sea robber ▶ v (-tes, -ting, -ted) sell or reproduce (artistic work etc.) illegally > **piracy** n (pl -cies) > **piratical** adj
pirated v ▷ pirate
pirates n, v ▷ pirate
piratical adj ▷ pirate
pirating v ▷ pirate
pirouette v, n (pl -s) (make) a spinning turn balanced on the toes of one foot
pirouettes n ▷ pirouette
pistachio n (pl -s) edible nut of a Mediterranean tree
pistachios n ▷ pistachio
piste [peest] n (pl -s) ski slope
pistes n ▷ piste
pistil n (pl -s) seed-bearing part of a flower
pistils n ▷ pistil
pistol n (pl -s) short-barrelled handgun
pistols n ▷ pistol
piston n (pl -s) cylindrical part in an engine that slides to and fro in a cylinder
pistons n ▷ piston
pit n (pl -s) deep hole in the ground ▷ orchestra
pit ▶ v (-s, -tting, -tted) mark with small dents or scars
pitch[1] v (-es, -ing, -ed) throw, hurl ▶ n (pl -es) area marked out for playing sport
pitch[2] n dark sticky substance obtained from tar
pitched v ▷ pitch[1]
pitches v, n ▷ pitch[1]
pitching v ▷ pitch[1]
pitchblende n (pl -s) mineral composed largely of uranium oxide, yielding radium
pitchblendes n ▷ pitchblende
pitcher n (pl -s) large jug with a narrow neck
pitchers n ▷ pitcher
pitchfork n (pl -s) large long-handled fork for lifting hay ▶ v (-s, -ing, -ed) thrust abruptly or violently
pitchforked v ▷ pitchfork
pitchforking v ▷ pitchfork
pitchforks n, v ▷ pitchfork
piteous, pitiable adj arousing pity
pitfall n (pl -s) hidden difficulty or danger
pitfalls n ▷ pitfall
pith n (pl -s) soft white lining of the rind of oranges etc.
pithier adj ▷ pithy
pithiest adj ▷ pithy
piths n ▷ pith
pithy adj (-thier, -thiest) short and full of meaning
pitiable adj ▷ piteous
pitied v ▷ pity
pities n, v ▷ pity
pitiful adj arousing pity > **pitifully** adv
pitifully adv ▷ pitiful
pitiless adj feeling no pity or mercy > **pitilessly** adv
pitilessly adv ▷ pitiless
piton [peet-on] n (pl -s) metal spike used in climbing to secure a rope
pitons n ▷ piton
pits n, v ▷ pit
pittance n (pl -s) very small amount of money
pittances n ▷ pittance
pitted v ▷ pit
pitting v ▷ pit
pituitaries n ▷ pituitary
pituitary n (pl -ies) gland at the base of the brain, that helps to control growth
pity n (pl -ties) sympathy or sorrow for others' suffering ▶ v (-ies, -ying, -ied) feel pity for
pitying v ▷ pity
pivot n (pl -s) central shaft on which something turns ▶ v (-s, -ing, -ed) provide with or turn on a pivot
pivotal adj of crucial importance
pivoted v ▷ pivot
pivoting v ▷ pivot
pivots n, v ▷ pivot
pix n (Informal) ▷ pic
pixie n (pl -s) (in folklore) fairy
pixies n ▷ pixie
pizza n (pl -s) flat disc of dough covered with a wide variety of savoury toppings and baked
pizzas n ▷ pizza

pizzazz n (pl -es) (Informal) attractive combination of energy and style
pizzazzes n ▷ pizzazz

pizzicato [pit-see-**kah**-toe] adj (MUSIC) played by plucking the string of a violin etc. with the finger

placard n (pl -s) notice that is carried or displayed in public
placards n ▷ placard

placate v (-tes, -ting, -ted) make (someone) stop feeling angry or upset **placatory** adj
placated v ▷ placate
placates v ▷ placate
placating v ▷ placate
placatory adj ▷ placate

place n (pl -s) particular part of an area or space ▷ v (-ces, -cing, -ced) put in a particular place
placed v ▷ place
places n, v ▷ place

placebo [plas-**see**-bo] n (pl -bos, -boes) sugar pill etc. given to an unsuspecting patient instead of an active drug
placeboes n ▷ placebo
placebos n ▷ placebo

placenta [plass-**ent**-a] n (pl -tas, -tae) organ formed in the womb during pregnancy, providing nutrients for the fetus ▷ **placental** adj
placentae n ▷ placenta
placental adj ▷ placenta
placentas n ▷ placenta

placid adj (-er, -est) not easily excited or upset, calm ▷ **placidity** n (pl -ties)
placider adj ▷ placid
placidest adj ▷ placid
placidities n ▷ placid
placidity n ▷ placid
placing v ▷ place

plagiarize [play-**jer**-ize] v (-zes, -zing, -zed) steal ideas, passages, etc. from (someone else's work) and present them as one's own ▷ **plagiarism** n (pl -s)
plagiarism n ▷ plagiarize
plagiarisms n ▷ plagiarize
plagiarized v ▷ plagiarize
plagiarizes v ▷ plagiarize
plagiarizing v ▷ plagiarize

plague n (pl -s) fast-spreading fatal disease ▷ v (-gues, -guing, -gued) trouble or annoy continually
plagued v ▷ plague
plagues n, v ▷ plague
plaguing v ▷ plague

plaice n (pl plaice) edible European flatfish

plaid n (pl -s) long piece of tartan cloth worn as part of Highland dress
plaids n ▷ plaid

plain (-er, -est) adj easy to see or understand ▷ n (pl -s) large stretch of level country ▷ **plainly** adv ▷ **plainness** n (pl -es)
plainer adj ▷ plain
plainest adj ▷ plain
plainly adj ▷ plain
plainness n ▷ plain
plainnesses n ▷ plain
plains n ▷ plain

plainsong n (pl -s) unaccompanied singing, esp. in a medieval church
plainsongs n ▷ plainsong

plaintiff n (pl -s) person who sues in a court of law
plaintiffs n ▷ plaintiff

plaintive adj sad, mournful ▷ **plaintively** adv
plaintively adv ▷ plaintive

plait [platt] n (pl -s) intertwined length of hair ▷ v (-s, -ing, -ed) intertwine separate strands in a pattern
plaited v ▷ plait
plaiting v ▷ plait
plaits n, v ▷ plait

plan n (pl -s) way thought out to do or achieve something ▷ v (-s, -nning, -nned) arrange beforehand ▷ **planner** n (pl -s)

plane¹ n (pl -s) aeroplane ▷ adj perfectly flat or level ▷ v (-nes, -ning, -ned) glide or skim
plane² n (pl -s) tool for smoothing wood ▷ v (-nes, -ning, -ned) smooth (wood) with a plane
plane³ n (pl -s) tree with broad leaves
planed v ▷ plane¹, ², ³
planes n, v ▷ plane¹, ², ³

planet n (pl -s) large body in space that revolves round the sun or another star ▷ **planetary** adj
planetaria n ▷ planetarium

planetarium n (pl -iums, -ia) building where the movements of the stars, planets, etc. are shown by projecting lights on the inside of a dome
planetariums n ▷ planetarium
planetary adj ▷ planet
planets n ▷ planet

plangent adj (of sounds) mournful and resounding
planing v ▷ plane¹, ²

plank n (pl -s) long flat piece of sawn timber
planks n ▷ plank

plankton n (pl -s) minute animals and plants floating in the surface water of a sea or lake

planktons *n* ▷ plankton
planned *v* ▷ plan
planner *n* ▷ plan
planners *n* ▷ plan
planning *v* ▷ plan
plans *n, v* ▷ plan
plant *n (pl -s)* living organism that grows in the ground and has no power to move ▸ *v (-s, -ing, -ed)* put in the ground to grow
plantain¹ *n (pl -s)* low-growing wild plant with broad leaves
plantain² *n (-s)* tropical fruit like a green banana
plantains *n* ▷ plantain¹, ²
plantation *n (pl -s)* estate for the cultivation of tea, tobacco, etc.
plantations *n* ▷ plantation
planted *v* ▷ plant
planter *n (pl -s)* owner of a plantation
planters *n* ▷ planter
planting *v* ▷ plant
plants *n, v* ▷ plant
plaque *n (pl -s)* inscribed commemorative stone or metal plate
plaques *n* ▷ plaque
plasma *n (pl -s)* clear liquid part of blood
plasmas *n* ▷ plasma
plaster *n (pl -s)* mixture of lime, sand, etc. for coating walls ▸ *v (-s, -ing, -ed)* cover with plaster
plastered *adj (Slang)* drunk ▸ *v* ▷ plaster
plastering *v* ▷ plaster
plasters *n, v* ▷ plaster
plastic *n (pl -s)* synthetic material that can be moulded when soft but sets in a hard long-lasting shape ▸ *adj* made of plastic
plasticities *n* ▷ plasticity
plasticity *n (pl -ties)* ability to be moulded
plastics *n* ▷ plastic
plate *n (pl -s)* shallow dish for holding food ▸ *v (-s, -ting, -ted)* cover with a thin coating of gold, silver, or other metal ▷ **plateful** *n (pl -s)*
plateau *n (pl -teaus, -teaux)* area of level high land
plateaus *n* ▷ plateau
plateaux *n* ▷ plateau
plated *v* ▷ plate
plateful *n* ▷ plate
platefuls *n* ▷ plate
platen *n (pl -s)* roller of a typewriter, against which the paper is held
platens *n* ▷ platen
plates *n, v* ▷ plate
platform *n (pl -s)* raised floor
platforms *n* ▷ platform

plating *v* ▷ plate
platinum *n (pl -s)* (CHEM) valuable silvery-white metal
platinums *n* ▷ platinum
platitude *n (pl -s)* remark that is true but not interesting or original ▷ **platitudinous** *adj*
platitudes *n* ▷ platitude
platitudinous *adj* ▷ platitude
platonic *adj* (of a relationship) friendly or affectionate but not sexual
platoon *n (pl -s)* smaller unit within a company of soldiers
platoons *n* ▷ platoon
platteland *n (pl -s)* (S AFR) rural district
plattelands *n* ▷ plattelands
platter *n (pl -s)* large dish
platters *n* ▷ platter
platypus *n (pl -es)* Australian egg-laying amphibious mammal, with dense fur, webbed feet, and a ducklike bill (*also* **duck-billed platypus**)
platypuses *n* ▷ platypus
plaudits *pl n* expressions of approval
plausible *adj* apparently true or reasonable ▷ **plausibly** *adv* ▷ **plausibility** *n (pl -ties)*
plausibilities *n* ▷ plausible
plausibility *n* ▷ plausible
plausibly *adj* ▷ plausible
play *v (-s, -ing, -ed)* occupy oneself in (a game or recreation) ▸ *n (pl -s)* story performed on stage or broadcast
playboy *n (pl -s)* rich man who lives only for pleasure
playboys *n* ▷ playboy
playcentre *n (pl -s)* (NZ & S AFR) centre for preschool children run by parents
playcentres *n* ▷ playcentre
played *v* ▷ play
player *n (pl -s)* person who plays a game or sport
players *n* ▷ player
playful *adj* lively
playgroup *n (pl -s)* regular meeting of very young children for supervised play
playgroups *n* ▷ playgroup
playhouse *n* theatre
playhouses *n* ▷ playhouse
playing *v* ▷ play
plays *v, n* ▷ play
playschool *n (pl -s)* nursery group for young children
playschools *n* ▷ playschool
plaything *n* toy
playthings *n* ▷ plaything
playwright *n* author of plays

playwrights n ▷ playwright

plaza n (pl -s) open space or square

plazas n ▷ plaza

plea n (pl -s) serious or urgent request, entreaty

pleas n ▷ plea

plead v (-s, -ing, -ed) ask urgently or with deep feeling (LAW)

pleaded v ▷ plead

pleading v ▷ plead

pleads v ▷ plead

pleasant adj (-er, -est) pleasing, enjoyable > **pleasantly** adv

pleasanter adj ▷ pleasant

pleasantest adj ▷ pleasant

pleasantly adv ▷ pleasant

pleasantries n ▷ pleasantry

pleasantry n (pl -ries) polite or joking remark

please v (-ses, -sing, -sed) give pleasure or satisfaction to ▶ adv polite word of request > **pleased** adj > **pleasing** adj

pleased v, adj ▷ please

pleasing v, adj ▷ please

pleases v ▷ please

pleasurable adj giving pleasure > **pleasurably** adv

pleasurably adv ▷ pleasurable

pleasure n (pl -s) feeling of happiness and satisfaction

pleasures n ▷ pleasure

pleat n (pl -s) fold made by doubling material back on itself ▶ v (-s, -ing, -ed) arrange (material) in pleats

pleated v ▷ pleat

pleating v ▷ pleat

pleats n, v ▷ pleat

plebeian [pleb-ee-an] adj of the lower social classes ▶ n (pl -s) (also **pleb**) member of the lower social classes

plebeians n ▷ plebeian

plebiscite [pleb-iss-ite] n (pl -s) decision by direct voting of the people of a country

plebiscites n ▷ plebiscite

plectra n ▷ plectrum

plectrum n (pl -rums, -ra) small implement for plucking the strings of a guitar etc.

plectrums n ▷ plectrum

pledge n (pl -s) solemn promise ▶ v (-ges, -ging, -ged) promise solemnly

pledged v ▷ pledge

pledges n, v ▷ pledge

pledging v ▷ pledge

plenary adj (of a meeting) attended by all members

plenipotentiary adj having full powers

▶ n diplomat or representative having full powers

plenitude n (pl -s) completeness, abundance

plenitudes n ▷ plenitude

plenteous adj plentiful

plenties n ▷ plenty

plenty n (pl -ties) large amount or number

plentiful adj existing in large amounts or numbers > **plentifully** adv

plentifully adv ▷ plentiful

pleonasm n (pl -s) use of more words than necessary

pleonasms n ▷ pleonasm

plethora n (pl -s) excess

plethoras n ▷ plethora

pleurisies n ▷ pleurisy

pleurisy n (pl -sies) inflammation of the membrane covering the lungs

pliabilities n ▷ pliable

pliability n ▷ pliable

pliable adj easily bent > **pliability** n (pl -ties)

pliancies n ▷ pliant

pliancy n ▷ pliant

pliant adj pliable > **pliancy** n (pl -cies)

plied v ▷ ply

plies v, n ▷ ply

pliers pl n tool with hinged arms and jaws for gripping

plight[1] n (pl -s) difficult or dangerous situation

plight[2] v (-s, -ing, -ed) pledge

plighted v ▷ plight[2]

plighting v ▷ plight[2]

plights n, v ▷ plight[1, 2]

plimsolls pl n (BRIT) rubber-soled canvas shoes

plinth n (pl -s) slab forming the base of a statue, column, etc.

plinths n ▷ plinth

plod v (-s, -dding, -dded) walk with slow heavy steps > **plodder** n (pl -s)

plodded v ▷ plod

plodder n ▷ plod

plodders n ▷ plod

plodding v ▷ plod

plods v ▷ plod

plonk[1] v (-s, -ing, -ed) put (something) down heavily and carelessly

plonk[2] n (pl -s) (Informal) cheap inferior wine

plonked v ▷ plonk[1]

plonking v ▷ plonk[1]

plonks v, n ▷ plonk[1, 2]

plop n (pl -s) sound of an object falling into water without a splash ▶ v (-s, -pping, -pped) make this sound

plopped v ▷ plop

plopping v ▷ plop

plops n, v ▷ plop

plot[1] n (pl -s) secret plan to do something illegal or wrong ▶ v (-s, -tting, -tted) plan secretly, conspire

plot[2] n (-s) small piece of land

plotted v ▷ plot[1]

plotting v ▷ plot[1]

plots n, v ▷ plot[1, 2]

plough n (pl -s) agricultural tool for turning over soil ▶ v (-s, -ing, -ed) turn over (earth) with a plough > **ploughman** n (pl -men)

ploughed v ▷ plough

ploughing v ▷ plough

ploughman n ▷ plough

ploughmen n ▷ plough

ploughs n, v ▷ plough

ploughshare n (pl -s) blade of a plough

ploughshares n ▷ ploughshare

plover n (pl -s) shore bird with a straight bill and long pointed wings

plovers n ▷ plover

ploy n (pl -s) manoeuvre designed to gain an advantage

ploys n ▷ ploy

pluck v (-s, -ing, -ed) pull or pick off ▶ n (pl -s) courage

plucked v ▷ pluck

pluckier adj ▷ plucky

pluckiest adj ▷ plucky

pluckily adj ▷ plucky

plucking v ▷ pluck

plucks v, n ▷ pluck

plucky adj (-kier, -kiest) brave > **pluckily** adv

plug n (pl -s) thing fitting into and filling a hole ▶ v (-s, -gging, -gged) block or seal (a hole or gap) with a plug

plugged v ▷ plug

plugging v ▷ plug

plugs n, v ▷ plug

plum n (pl -s) oval usu. dark red fruit with a stone in the middle ▶ adj dark purplish-red

plumage n (pl -s) bird's feathers

plumages n ▷ plumage

plumb v (-s, -ing, -ed) understand (something obscure) ▶ adv exactly

plumbed v ▷ plumb

plumber n (pl -s) person who fits and repairs pipes and fixtures for water and drainage systems

plumbers n ▷ plumber

plumbing n pipes and fixtures used in water and drainage systems ▶ v ▷ plumb

plumbs v ▷ plumb

plume n (pl -s) feather, esp. one worn as an ornament

plumes n ▷ plume

plummet v (-s, -ing, -ed) plunge downward

plummeted v ▷ plummet

plummeting v ▷ plummet

plummets v ▷ plummet

plump[1] adj (-er, -est) moderately or attractively fat > **plumpness** n (pl -es)

plump[2] v (-s, -ing, -ed) sit or fall heavily and suddenly

plumper adj ▷ plump[1]

plumpest adj ▷ plump[1]

plumped v ▷ plump[2]

plumping v ▷ plump[2]

plumpness n ▷ plump

plumpnesses n ▷ plump

plumps v ▷ plump[2]

plums n ▷ plum

plunder v (-s, -ing, -ed) take by force, esp. in time of war ▶ n (pl -s) things plundered, spoils

plundered v ▷ plunder

plundering v ▷ plunder

plunders v, n ▷ plunder

plunge v (-ges, -ging, -ged) put or throw forcibly or suddenly (into) ▶ n (pl -s) plunging, dive

plunged v ▷ plunge

plunger n (pl -s) rubber suction cup used to clear blocked pipes

plungers n ▷ plunge

plunges v, n ▷ plunge

plunging v ▷ plunge

pluperfect adj, n (pl -s) (GRAMMAR) (tense) expressing an action completed before a past time, e.g. had gone in his wife had gone already

pluperfects n ▷ pluperfect

plural adj of or consisting of more than one ▶ n (pl -s) word indicating more than one

plurals n ▷ plural

pluralism n (pl -s) existence and toleration of a variety of peoples, opinions, etc. in a society > **pluralist** n (pl -s) > **pluralistic** adj

pluralisms n ▷ pluralism

pluralist n ▷ pluralism

pluralists n ▷ pluralism

pluralistic adj ▷ pluralism

plus prep, adj indicating addition ▶ adj more than zero ▶ n (pl -es) sign (+) denoting addition

pluses n ▷ plus

plush n (pl -es) fabric with long velvety pile ▶ adj (-er, -est) (also **plushy**) (-ier, -iest) luxurious

plusher adj ▷ plush

plushest adj ▷ plush

plushes n ▷ plush

plushier adj ▷ plush

plushiest adj ▷ plush

plutocrat n (pl -s) person who is powerful because of being very rich > **plutocratic** adj

plutocratic adj ▷ plutocrat

plutocrats n ▷ plutocrat

plutonium n (pl -s) (CHEM) radioactive metallic element used esp. in nuclear reactors and weapons

plutoniums n ▷ plutonium

ply[1] v (-ies, -ying, -ied) work at (a job or trade)

ply[2] n (pl -ies) thickness of wool, fabric, etc.

plying v ▷ ply[1]

plywood n (pl -s) board made of thin layers of wood glued together

plywoods n ▷ plywood

pneumatic adj worked by or inflated with wind or air

pneumonia n (pl -s) inflammation of the lungs

pneumonias n ▷ pneumonia

> **po** n (pos). A po is an informal word for a chamber pot. This is a good word to have ready in case you see an opportunity to play a good word beginning with P next to a word ending in O, or vice versa. Po scores 4 points.

poach[1] v (-es, -ing, -ed) catch (animals) illegally on someone else's land

poach[2] v (-es, -ing, -ed) simmer (food) gently in liquid

poached v ▷ poach

poacher n (pl -s) person who catches animals illegally on someone else's land

poachers n ▷ poacher

poaches v ▷ poach

poaching v ▷ poach

pocket n (pl -s) small bag sewn into clothing for carrying things ▶ v (-s, -ing, -ed) put into one's pocket ▶ adj small

pocketed v ▷ pocket

pocketing v ▷ pocket

pockets n, v ▷ pocket

pockmarked adj (of the skin) marked with hollow scars where diseased spots have been

pod n (pl -s) long narrow seed case of peas, beans, etc.

podgier adj ▷ podgy

podgiest adj ▷ podgy

pods n ▷ pod

podgy adj (-gier, -giest) short and fat

podia n ▷ podium

podium n (pl -diums, -dia) small raised platform for a conductor or speaker

podiums n ▷ podium

poem n (pl -s) imaginative piece of writing in rhythmic lines

poems n ▷ poem

poep n (pl -s) (S AFR) (Slang) emission of gas from the anus

poeps n ▷ poep

poesies n ▷ poesy

poesy n (pl -sies) (Obs) poetry

poet n (pl -s) writer of poems

poetic, poetical adj of or like poetry > **poetically** adv

poetical adj ▷ poetic

poetically adv ▷ poetic

poetries n ▷ poetry

poetry n (pl -ries) poems

poets n ▷ poet

pogrom n (pl -s) organized persecution and massacre

pogroms n ▷ pogrom

poignancies n ▷ poignant

poignancy n ▷ poignant

poignant adj sharply painful to the feelings > **poignancy** n (pl -cies)

poinsettia n (pl -s) Central American shrub widely grown for its clusters of scarlet leaves, which resemble petals

poinsettias n ▷ poinsettia

point n (pl -s) main idea in a discussion, argument, etc. ▶ v (-s, -ing, -ed) show the direction or position of something or draw attention to it by extending a finger or other pointed object towards it

pointed adj having a sharp end ▶ v ▷ point > **pointedly** adv

pointedly adv ▷ pointed

pointer n (pl -s) helpful hint

pointers n ▷ pointer

pointing v ▷ point

pointless adj meaningless, irrelevant

points n, v ▷ point

poise n (pl -s) calm dignified manner

poised adj absolutely ready

poises n ▷ poise

poison n (pl -s) substance that kills or injures when swallowed or absorbed ▶ v (-s, -ing, -ed) give poison to > **poisoner** n (pl -s) > **poisonous** adj

poisoned v ▷ poison

poisoner n ▷ poison

poisoners n ▷ poison

poisoning v ▷ poison

poisonous adj ▷ poison

poisons n, v ▷ poison

poke v (-kes, -king, -ked) jab or prod with one's finger, a stick, etc. ▶ n (pl -s) poking poked v ▷ poke

poker¹ n (pl -s) metal rod for stirring a fire

poker² n (pl -s) card game in which players bet on the hands dealt

pokers n ▷ poker¹,²

pokier adj ▷ poky

pokiest adj ▷ poky

poking v ▷ poke

pokes v, n ▷ poke

poky adj (-kier, -kiest) small and cramped

polar adj of or near either of the earth's poles

polarize v (-zes, -zing, -zed) form or cause to form into groups with directly opposite views > polarization n (pl -s)

polarization n ▷ polarize

polarizations n ▷ polarize

polarized v ▷ polarize

polarizes v ▷ polarize

polarizing v ▷ polarize

polder n (pl -s) land reclaimed from the sea, esp. in the Netherlands

polders n ▷ polder

pole¹ n (pl -s) long rounded piece of wood etc.

pole² n (pl -s) point furthest north or south on the earth's axis of rotation

poleaxe v (-xes, -xing, -xed) hit or stun with a heavy blow

poleaxed v ▷ poleaxe

poleaxes v ▷ poleaxe

poleaxing v ▷ poleaxe

polecat n (pl -s) small animal of the weasel family

polecats n ▷ polecat

polemic [pol-em-ik] n (pl -s) fierce attack on or defence of a particular opinion, belief, etc. > polemical adj

polemical adj ▷ polemic

polemics n ▷ polemic

poles n ▷ pole¹,²

police n organized force in a state which keeps law and order ▶ v (-ces, -cing, -ced) control or watch over with police or a similar body

policed v ▷ police

policeman, policewoman n (pl -men, -women) member of a police force

policemen n ▷ policeman

polices v ▷ police

policewomen n ▷ policeman

policies n ▷ policy¹,²

policing v ▷ police

policy¹ n (pl -cies) plan of action adopted by a person, group, or state

policy² n (pl -cies) document containing an insurance contract

polio n (pl -s) disease affecting the spinal cord, which often causes paralysis (also poliomyelitis)

polios n ▷ polio

polish v (-es, -ing, -ed) make smooth and shiny by rubbing ▶ n (pl -es) substance used for polishing

polished adj accomplished ▶ v ▷ polish

polishing v ▷ polish

polishes v, n ▷ polish

polite adj showing consideration for others in one's manners, speech, etc. > politely adv > politeness n (pl -es)

politely adv ▷ polite

politeness n ▷ polite

politenesses n ▷ politeness

politic adj wise and likely to prove advantageous

political adj of the state, government, or public administration > politically adv

politically adv ▷ political

politician n (pl -s) person actively engaged in politics, esp. a member of parliament

politicians n ▷ politician

politics n winning and using of power to govern society

polka n (pl -s) lively 19th-century dance

polkas n ▷ polka

poll n (pl -s) (also opinion poll) questioning of a random sample of people to find out general opinion ▶ v (-s, -ing, -ed) receive (votes)

pollarded adj (of a tree) growing very bushy because its top branches have been cut short

polled v ▷ poll

pollen n (pl -s) fine dust produced by flowers to fertilize other flowers

pollens n ▷

pollinate v (-tes, -ting, -ted) fertilize with pollen

pollinated v ▷ pollinate

pollinates v ▷ pollinate

pollinating v ▷ pollinate

polling v ▷ poll

polls n, v ▷ poll

pollster n (pl -s) person who conducts opinion polls

pollsters n ▷ pollster

pollute v (-tes, -ting, -ted) contaminate with something poisonous or harmful > pollution n (pl -s)

pollutant n (pl -s) something that pollutes

pollutants n ▷ pollutant

polluted v ▷ pollute

pollutes v ▷ pollute

polluting v ▷ pollute

pollution n ▷ pollute

pollutions n ▷ pollute

polo n (pl -s) game like hockey played by teams of players on horseback

polonaise n (pl -s) old stately dance

polonaises n ▷ polonaise

polonium n (pl -s) (CHEM) radioactive element that occurs in trace amounts in uranium ores

poloniums n ▷ polonium

polos n ▷ polo

poltergeist n (pl -s) spirit believed to move furniture and throw objects around

poltergeists n ▷ poltergeist

poltroon n (pl -s) (Obs) utter coward

poltroons n ▷ poltroon

polyandries n ▷ polyandry

polyandry n (pl -ries) practice of having more than one husband at the same time

polyanthus n (pl -es) garden primrose

polyanthuses n ▷ polyanthus

polychromatic adj many-coloured

polyester n (pl -s) synthetic material used to make plastics and textile fibres

polyesters n ▷ polyester

polygamies n ▷ polygamy

polygamist n ▷ polygamy

polygamists n ▷ polygamy

polygamous adj ▷ polygamy

polygamy [pol-ig-a-mee] n (pl -mies) practice of having more than one husband or wife at the same time > **polygamous** adj > **polygamist** n (pl -s)

polyglot adj, n (pl -s) (person) able to speak or write several languages

polyglots n ▷ polyglot

polygon n (pl -s) geometrical figure with three or more angles and sides > **polygonal** adj

polygonal adj ▷ polygon

polygons n ▷ polygon

polyhedra n ▷ polyhedron

polyhedron n (pl -rons, -ra) solid figure with four or more sides

polyhedrons n ▷ polyhedron

polymer n (pl -s) chemical compound with large molecules made of simple molecules of the same kind

polymerize v (-zes, -zing, -zed) form into polymers > **polymerization** n (pl -s)

polymerization n ▷ polymerize

polymerizations n ▷ polymerize

polymerized v ▷ polymerize

polymerizes v ▷ polymerize

polymerizing v ▷ polymerize

polymers n ▷ polymer

polyp n (pl -s) small simple sea creature with a hollow cylindrical body

polyps n ▷ polyp

polyphonic adj (MUSIC) consisting of several melodies played simultaneously

polystyrene n (pl -s) synthetic material used esp. as white rigid foam for packing and insulation

polystyrenes n ▷ polystyrene

polytechnic n (pl -s) (in New Zealand and formerly in Britain) college offering courses in many subjects at and below degree level

polytechnics n ▷ polytechnic

polytheism n (pl -s) belief in many gods > **polytheistic** adj

polytheisms n ▷ polytheism

polytheistic n ▷ polytheism

polythene n (pl -s) light plastic used for bags etc.

polythenes n ▷ polythene

polyunsaturated adj of a group of fats that do not form cholesterol in the blood

polyurethane n (pl -s) synthetic material used esp. in paints

polyurethanes n ▷ polyurethane

pom n (pl -s) (AUST & NZ) (Slang) person from England (also **pommy**) (pl -mmies)

pomander n (pl -s) (container for) a mixture of sweet-smelling petals, etc.

pomanders n ▷ pomander

pomegranate n (pl -s) round tropical fruit with a thick rind containing many seeds in a red pulp

pomegranates n ▷ pomegranate

pommel n (pl -s) raised part on the front of a saddle

pommels n ▷ pommel

pommies n ▷ pom

pommy n ▷ pom

poms n ▷ pom

pomp n (pl -s) stately display or ceremony

pomps n ▷ pomp

pompom n (pl -s) decorative ball of tufted wool, silk, etc.

pompoms n ▷ pompom

pomposities n ▷ pompous

pomposity n ▷ pompous

pompous adj foolishly serious and grand, self-important > **pompously** adv > **pomposity** n (pl -ties)

pompously adv ▷ pompous

poncho n (pl -os) loose circular cloak with a hole for the head

ponchos n ▷ poncho

pond n (pl -s) small area of still water

ponds n ▷ pond

ponder v (-s, -ing, -ed) think thoroughly or

deeply (about)

pondered v ▷ ponder

pondering v ▷ ponder

ponderous adj serious and dull > **ponderously** adv

ponderously adv ▷ ponderous

ponders v ▷ ponder

pong v, n (pl -s) (Informal) (give off) a strong unpleasant smell

pongs n ▷ pong

ponies n ▷ pony

pontiff n (pl -s) the Pope

pontiffs n ▷ pontiff

pontificate v (-tes, -ting, -ted) state one's opinions as if they were the only possible correct ones ▶ n (pl -s) period of office of a Pope

pontificated v ▷ pontificate

pontificates v, n ▷ pontificate

pontificating v ▷ pontificate

pontoon[1] n (pl -s) floating platform supporting a temporary bridge

pontoon[2] n (pl -s) gambling card game

pontoons n ▷ pontoon[1, 2]

pony n (pl -nies) small horse

ponytail n (pl -s) long hair tied in one bunch at the back of the head

ponytails n ▷ ponytail

poodle n (pl -s) dog with curly hair often clipped fancifully

poodles n ▷ poodle

pool[1] n (pl -s) small body of still water

pool[2] n (pl -s) shared fund or group of workers or resources ▶ pl (BRIT) ▷ football pools ▶ v (-s, -ing, -ed) put in a common fund

pooled v ▷ pool[2]

pooling v ▷ pool[2]

pools n, v ▷ pool[1, 2]

poop n (pl -s) raised part at the back of a sailing ship

poops n ▷ poop

poor adj having little money and few possessions

poorlier adj ▷ poorly

poorliest adj ▷ poorly

poorly adv in a poor manner ▶ adj (-lier, -liest) not in good health

pop[1] v (-s, -pping, -pped) make or cause to make a small explosive sound (Informal) ▶ n small explosive sound (BRIT)

pop[2] n (pl -s) music of general appeal, esp. to young people

pop[3] n (pl -s) (Informal) father

popcorn n (pl -s) grains of maize heated until they puff up and burst

popcorns n ▷ popcorn

pope n (pl -s) head of the Roman Catholic Church

popes n ▷ pope

poplar n (pl -s) tall slender tree

poplars n ▷ poplar

poplin n (pl -s) ribbed cotton material

poplins n ▷ poplin

poppadom n (pl -s) thin round crisp Indian bread

poppadoms n ▷ poppadom

popped v ▷ pop[1]

poppies n ▷ poppy

popping v ▷ pop[1]

poppy n (pl -ppies) plant with a large red flower

pops n ▷ pop

populace n (pl -s) the ordinary people

populaces n ▷ populace

popular adj widely liked and admired > **popularly** adv > **popularity** n (pl -ties)

popularize v (-zes, -zing, -zed) make popular

popularized v ▷ popularize

popularizes v ▷ popularize

popularizing v ▷ popularize

popularities n ▷ popular

popularity n ▷ popular

popularly adv ▷ popular

populate v (-tes, -ting, -ted) live in, inhabit

populated v ▷ populate

populates v ▷ populate

populating v ▷ populate

population n (pl -s) all the people who live in a particular place

populations n ▷ population

populous adj densely populated

porbeagle n (pl -s) kind of shark

porbeagles n ▷ porbeagle

porcelain n (pl -s) fine china

porcelains n ▷ porcelain

porch n (pl -es) covered approach to the entrance of a building

porches n ▷ porch

porcine adj of or like a pig

porcupine n (pl -s) animal covered with long pointed quills

porcupines n ▷ porcupine

pore n (pl -s) tiny opening in the skin or in the surface of a plant

pores n ▷ pore

pork n (pl -s) pig meat

porker n (pl -s) pig raised for food

porkers n ▷ porker

porks n ▷ pork

porn, porno adj, n (pl -s) (Informal) ▷ pornography, pornographic

pornographies n ▷ pornography
pornography n (pl -hies) writing, films, or pictures designed to be sexually exciting > **pornographic** adj
pornographer n (pl -s) producer of pornography
pornographers n ▷ pornographer
pornographic n ▷ pornography
pornos n ▷ porn
porns n ▷ porn
porosities n ▷ porous
porosity n ▷ porous
porous adj allowing liquid to pass through gradually > **porosity** n (pl -ties)
porphyries n ▷ porphyry
porphyry [por-fir-ee] n (pl -ries) reddish rock with large crystals in it
porpoise n (pl -s) fishlike sea mammal
porpoises n ▷ porpoise
porridge n (pl -s) breakfast food made of oatmeal cooked in water or milk
porridges n ▷ porridge
port[1] n (pl -s) (town with) a harbour
port[2] n (pl -s) left side of a ship or aircraft when facing the front of it
port[3] n (pl -s) strong sweet wine, usu. red
port[4] n (pl -s) opening in the side of a ship
portabilities n ▷ portable
portability n ▷ portable
portable adj easily carried > **portability** n (pl -ties)
portal n (pl -s) large imposing doorway or gate
portals n ▷ portal
portcullis n (pl -es) grating suspended above a castle gateway, that can be lowered to block the entrance
portcullises n ▷ portcullis
portend v (-s, -ing, -ed) be a sign of
portended v ▷ portend
portending v ▷ portend
portends v ▷ portend
portent n (pl -s) sign of a future event
portentous adj of great or ominous significance
portents n ▷ portent
porter[1] n (pl -s) man who carries luggage
porter[2] n (pl -s) doorman or gatekeeper of a building
porters n ▷ porter[1, 2]
portfolio n (pl -s) (flat case for carrying) examples of an artist's work
portfolios n ▷ portfolio
porthole n (pl -s) small round window in a ship or aircraft
portholes n ▷ porthole

portico n (pl -coes, -cos) porch or covered walkway with columns supporting the roof
porticoes n ▷ portico
porticos n ▷ portico
portion n (pl -s) part or share
portions n ▷ portion
portlier adj ▷ portly
portliest adj ▷ portly
portly adj (-lier, -liest) rather fat
portmanteau n (pl -eaus, -eaux) (Old-fashioned) large suitcase that opens into two compartments ▶ adj combining aspects of different things
portmanteaus n ▷ portmanteau
portmanteaux n ▷ portmanteau
portrait n (pl -s) picture of a person
portraits n ▷ portrait
portray v (-s, -ing, -ed) describe or represent by artistic means, as in writing or film > **portrayal** n (pl -s)
portrayal n ▷ portray
portrayals n ▷ portray
portrayed v ▷ portray
portraying v ▷ portray
portrays v ▷ portray
ports n ▷ port[1, 2, 3, 4]
pose v (-ses, -sing, -sed) place in or take up a particular position to be photographed or drawn ▶ n (pl -s) position while posing
posed v ▷ pose
poser n (pl -s) puzzling question
posers n ▷ poser
poses v, n ▷ pose
poseur n (pl -s) person who behaves in an affected way to impress others
poseurs n ▷ poseur
posies n ▷ posy
posing v ▷ pose
posh adj (Informal) smart, luxurious
posit [pozz-it] v (-s, -ing, -ed) lay down as a basis for argument
posited v ▷ posit
positing v ▷ posit
position n (pl -s) place ▶ v (-s, -ing, -ed) place
positioned v ▷ position
positioning v ▷ position
positions n, v ▷ position
posits v ▷ posit
positive adj feeling no doubts, certain (MATHS) > **positively** adv
positively adv ▷ positive
positron n (pl -s) (PHYSICS) particle with same mass as electron but positive charge
positrons n ▷ positron
posse [poss-ee] n (pl -s) (US) group of men

organized to maintain law and order

posses n ▷ posse

possess v (-es, -ing, -ed) have as one's property > **possessor** n (pl -s)

possessed v ▷ possess

possesses v ▷ possess

possessing v ▷ possess

possession n (pl -s) state of possessing, ownership ▶ pl things a person possesses

possessions n ▷ possession

possessive adj wanting all the attention or love of another person > **possessiveness** n

possessiveness n ▷ possessive

possessor n ▷ possess

possessors n ▷ possess

possibilities n ▷ possibility

possibility n ▷ possibility

possible adj able to exist, happen, or be done ▶ n (pl -s) person or thing that might be suitable or chosen > **possibility** n (pl -ties)

possibles n ▷ possible

possibly adv perhaps, not necessarily

possum n (pl -s) ▷ opossum (AUST & NZ) ▷ phalanger

possums n ▷ possum

post[1] n (pl -s) official system of delivering letters and parcels ▶ v (-s, -ing, -ed) send by post > **postal** adj

post[2] n (pl -s) length of wood, concrete, etc. fixed upright to support or mark something ▶ v (-s, -ing, -ed) put up (a notice) in a public place

post[3] n (pl -s) job ▶ v (-s, -ing, -ed) send (a person) to a new place to work

postage n charge for sending a letter or parcel by post

postages n ▷ postage

postal adj ▷ post[1]

postbag n (pl -s) postman's bag

postbags n ▷ postbag

postcard n (pl -s) card for sending a message by post without an envelope

postcards n ▷ postcard

postcode n system of letters and numbers used to aid the sorting of mail

postcodes n ▷ postcode

postdate v (-tes, -ting, -ted) write a date on (a cheque) that is later than the actual date

postdated v ▷ postdate

postdates v ▷ postdate

postdating v ▷ postdate

posted v ▷ post[1, 2, 3]

poster n (pl -s) large picture or notice stuck on a wall

posterior n (pl -s) buttocks ▶ adj behind, at

the back of

posteriors n ▷ posterior

posterities n ▷ posterity

posterity n (pl -ties) future generations, descendants

postern n (pl -s) small back door or gate

posterns n ▷ postern

posters n ▷ poster

postgraduate n (pl -s) person with a degree who is studying for a more advanced qualification

postgraduates n ▷ postgraduate

posthaste adv with great speed

posthumous [poss-tume-uss] adj occurring after one's death > **posthumously** adv

posthumously adv ▷ posthumous

postie n (pl -s) (SCOT, AUST & NZ) (Informal) postman

posties n ▷ postie

postilion, postillion n (pl -s) (HIST) person riding one of a pair of horses drawing a carriage

postilions n ▷ postilion

postillion n ▷ postilion

postillions n ▷ postilion

posting v ▷ post[1, 2, 3]

postman, postwoman n (pl -men, -women) person who collects and delivers post

postmark n (pl -s) official mark stamped on letters showing place and date of posting

postmarks n ▷ postmark

postmen n ▷ postman

postmaster, postmistress n (pl -s, -es) (in some countries) official in charge of a post office

postmasters n ▷ postmaster

postmistress n ▷ postmaster

postmistresses n ▷ postmaster

postmortem ▶ n (pl -s) medical examination of a body to establish the cause of death

postmortems n ▷ postmortem

postnatal adj occurring after childbirth

postpone v (-nes, -ning, -ned) put off to a later time > **postponement** n (pl -s)

postponed v ▷ postpone

postponement n ▷ postpone

postponements n ▷ postpone

postpones v ▷ postpone

postponing v ▷ postpone

posts n, v ▷ post[1, 2, 3]

postscript n (pl -s) passage added at the end of a letter

postscripts n ▷ postscript

postulant n (pl -s) candidate for admission to a religious order

postulants n ▷ postulant

postulate v (-tes, -ting, -ted) assume to be true as the basis of an argument or theory

postulated v ▷ postulate

postulates v ▷ postulate

postulating v ▷ postulate

posture n (pl -s) position or way in which someone stands, walks, etc. ▶ v (-res, -ring, -red) behave in an exaggerated way to get attention

postured v ▷ posture

postures n, v ▷ posture

posturing v ▷ posture

postwomen [pote-a-bl] ▷ postman

posy n (pl -sies) small bunch of flowers

pot¹ n (pl -s) round deep container ▶ pl (Informal) large amount ▶ v (-s, -tting, -tted) plant in a pot

pot² n (Slang) cannabis

potted adj grown in a pot ▶ v ▷ pot¹

potting v ▷ pot¹

pots n ▷ pot¹

potable [pote-a-bl] adj drinkable

potash n (pl -es) white powdery substance obtained from ashes and used as fertilizer

potashes n ▷ potash

potassium n (pl -s) (CHEM) silvery metallic element

potassiums n ▷ potassium

potato ▶ n (pl -oes) roundish starchy vegetable that grows underground

potatoes n ▷ potato

poteen n (pl -s) (in Ireland) illegally made alcoholic drink

poteens n ▷ poteen

potencies n ▷ potent

potency n ▷ potent

potent adj having great power or influence > **potency** n (pl -cies)

potentate n (pl -s) ruler or monarch

potentates n ▷ potentate

potential adj possible but not yet actual ▶ n (pl -s) ability or talent not yet fully used > **potentially** adv > **potentiality** n (pl -ties)

potentialities n ▷ potential

potentiality n ▷ potential

potentially adv ▷ potential

potentials n ▷ potential

pothole n (pl -s) hole in the surface of a road

potholer n ▷ potholing

potholers n ▷ potholing

potholes n ▷ pothole

potholing n (pl -s) sport of exploring underground caves > **potholer** n (pl -s)

potholings n ▷ potholing

potion n (pl -s) dose of medicine or poison

potions n ▷ potion

potoroo n (pl -s) Australian leaping rodent

potoroos n ▷ potoroo

potpourri [po-poor-ee] n (pl -s) fragrant mixture of dried flower petals

potpourris n ▷ potpourri

pottage n (pl -s) (Old-fashioned) thick soup or stew

pottages n ▷ pottage

potter¹ n (pl -s) person who makes pottery

potter² v (-s, -ing, -ed) be busy in a pleasant but aimless way

pottered v ▷ potter²

potteries n ▷ pottery

pottering v ▷ potter²

potters n, v ▷ potter¹, ²

pottery n (pl -ies) articles made from baked clay

pottier adj ▷ potty

potties n ▷ potty²

pottiest adj ▷ potty

potty¹ adj (-ttier, -ttiest) (Informal) crazy or silly

potty² n (pl -tries) bowl used by a small child as a toilet

pouch n (pl -es) small bag

pouches n ▷ pouch

pouf, pouffe [poof] n (pl -s) large solid cushion used as a seat

pouffe n ▷ pouf

pouffes n ▷ pouf

poufs n ▷ pouf

poulterer n (pl -s) (BRIT) person who sells poultry

poulterers n ▷ poulterer

poultice [pole-tiss] n (pl -s) moist dressing, often heated, applied to inflamed skin

poultices n ▷ poultice

poultries n ▷ poultry

poultry n (pl -ies) domestic fowls

pounce v (-ces, -cing, -ced) spring upon suddenly to attack or capture ▶ n (pl -s)

pouncing

pounced v ▷ pounce

pouncing v ▷ pounce

pounces v, n ▷ pounce

pound¹ n (pl -s) monetary unit of Britain and some other countries

pound² v (-s, -ing, -ed) hit heavily and repeatedly

pound³ n (pl -s) enclosure for stray animals or officially removed vehicles

pounded v ▷ pound²

pounding v ▷ pound²

pounds n, v ▷ pound¹, ³

pour v (-s, -ing, -ed) flow or cause to flow out in a stream
poured v ▷ pour
pouring v ▷ pour
pours v ▷ pour
pout v (-s, -ing, -ed) thrust out one's lips, look sulky ▶ n (pl -s) pouting look
pouted v ▷ pout
pouting v ▷ pout
pouts v, n ▷ pout
poverties n ▷ poverty
poverty n (pl -ties) state of being without enough food or money
powder n (pl -s) substance in the form of tiny loose particles ▶ v (-s, -ing, -ed) apply powder to > **powdery** adj (-rier, -riest)
powdered adj, v ▷ powder
powderier adj ▷ powder
powderiest adj ▷ powder
powdering v ▷ powder
powders n, v ▷ powder
power n (pl -s) ability to do or act > **powerful** adj > **powerless** adj
powered adj having or operated by mechanical or electrical power
powerful adj ▷ power
powerless adj ▷ power
powers n ▷ power
powwow n (pl -s) (Informal) talk or conference
powwows n ▷ powwow
pox n (pl -es) disease in which skin pustules form
poxes n ▷ pox

> **poz** adj. Poz is an old-fashioned short form of **positive**. This is a good word for a crowded board towards the end of the game, especially if you can form another word in the process, or form it on a bonus square. Poz scores 24 points.

practicabilities n ▷ practicable
practicability n ▷ practicable
practicable adj capable of being done successfully > **practicability** n (pl -ties)
practical adj involving experience or actual use rather than theory ▶ n (pl -s) examination in which something has to be done or made > **practically** adv
practically adv ▷ practical
practicals n ▷ practical
practice n (pl -s) something done regularly or habitually
practices n ▷ practice
practise v (-ses, -sing, -sed) do repeatedly so as to gain skill

practised v ▷ practise
practises v ▷ practise
practising v ▷ practise
practitioner n (pl -s) person who practises a profession
practitioners n ▷ practitioner
pragmatic adj concerned with practical consequences rather than theory
> **pragmatism** n (pl -s) > **pragmatist** n (pl -s)
pragmatism n ▷ pragmatic
pragmatisms n ▷ pragmatic
pragmatist n ▷ pragmatic
pragmatists n ▷ pragmatic
prairie n (pl -s) large treeless area of grassland, esp. in N America and Canada
prairies n ▷ prairie
praise v (-ses, -sing, -sed) express approval or admiration of (someone or something)
▶ n (pl -s) something said or written to show approval or admiration > **praiseworthy** adj
praised v ▷ praise
praises v, n ▷ praise
praiseworthy adj ▷ praise
praising v ▷ praise
praline [prah-leen] n (pl -s) sweet made of nuts and caramelized sugar
pralines n ▷ praline
pram n (pl -s) four-wheeled carriage for a baby, pushed by hand
prams n ▷ pram
prance v (-ces, -cing, -ced) walk with exaggerated bouncing steps
pranced v ▷ prance
prances v ▷ prance
prancing v ▷ prance
prang v, n (pl -s) (Slang) (have) a crash in a car or aircraft
prangs n ▷ prang
prank n (pl -s) mischievous trick
pranks n ▷ prank
prat n (pl -s) (BRIT, AUST & NZ) (Informal) stupid person
prats n ▷ prat
prattle v (-les, -ling, -led) chatter in a childish or foolish way ▶ n (pl -s) childish or foolish talk
prattled v ▷ prattle
prattles v, n ▷ prattle
prattling v ▷ prattle
prawn n (pl -s) edible shellfish like a large shrimp
prawns n ▷ prawn
praxis n (pl praxises) practice as opposed to theory
praxises n ▷ praxis
pray v (-s, -ing, -ed) say prayers

prayed v ▷ pray

prayer n (pl -s) thanks or appeal addressed to one's God

prayers n ▷ prayer

praying v ▷ pray

prays v ▷ pray

preach v (-es, -ing, -ed) give a talk on a religious theme as part of a church service

preached v ▷ preach

preaches v ▷ preach

preaching v ▷ preach

preacher n (pl -s) person who preaches, esp. in church

preachers n ▷ preacher

preamble n (pl -s) introductory part to something said or written

preambles n ▷ preamble

prearranged adj arranged beforehand

prebendaries n ▷ prebendary

prebendary n (pl -ries) clergyman who is a member of the chapter of a cathedral

precarious adj insecure, unsafe, likely to fall or collapse > **precariously** adv

precariously adv ▷ precarious

precaution n (pl -s) action taken in advance to prevent something bad happening > **precautionary** adj

precautionary adj ▷ precaution

precautions n ▷ precaution

precede v (-des, -ding, -ded) go or be before

preceded v ▷ precede

precedence [press-ee-denss] n (pl -s) formal order of rank or position

precedences n ▷ precedence

precedent n (pl -s) previous case or occurrence regarded as an example to be followed

precedents n ▷ precedent

precedes v ▷ precede

preceding v ▷ precede

precentor n (pl -s) person who leads the singing in a church

precentors n ▷ precentor

precept n (pl -s) rule of behaviour > **preceptive** adj

preceptive adj ▷ precept

precepts n ▷ precept

precinct n (pl -s) (BRIT, AUST & S AFR) area in a town closed to traffic ▶ pl surrounding region

precincts n ▷ precinct

precious adj of great value and importance

precipice n (pl -s) very steep face of cliff or rockface

precipices n ▷ precipice

precipitate v (-tes, -ting, -ted) cause to happen suddenly ▶ adj done rashly or hastily

▶ n (pl -s) (CHEM) substance precipitated from a solution > **precipitately** adv > **precipitation** n (pl -s) precipitating

precipitated v, n ▷ precipitate

precipitately adv ▷ precipitate

precipitates v, n ▷ precipitate

precipitating v ▷ precipitate

precipitation n ▷ precipitate

precipitations n ▷ precipitate

precipitous adj sheer

précis [pray-see] n (pl précis) short written summary of a longer piece ▶ v (-ses, -sing, -sed) make a précis of

precise adj (-r, -st) exact, accurate in every detail > **precisely** adv > **precision** n (pl -s)

précised v ▷ précis

précises v ▷ précis

precisely adv ▷ precise

preciser adj ▷ precise

precisest adj ▷ precise

précising v ▷ précis

precision n ▷ precise

precisions n ▷ precise

preclude v (-des, -ding, -ded) make impossible to happen

precluded v ▷ preclude

precludes v ▷ preclude

precluding v ▷ preclude

precocious adj having developed or matured early or too soon > **precocity** n (pl -ties)

precocities n ▷ precocious

precocity n ▷ precocious

precognition n (pl -s) alleged ability to foretell the future

precognitions n ▷ precognition

preconceived adj (of an idea) formed without real experience or reliable information > **preconception** n (pl -s)

preconception n ▷ preconceived

preconceptions n ▷ preconcieve

precondition n (pl -s) something that must happen or exist before something else can

preconditions n ▷ precondition

precursor n (pl -s) something that precedes and is a signal of something else, forerunner

precursors n ▷ precursor

predate v (-tes, -ting, -ted) occur at an earlier date than

predated v ▷ predate

predates v ▷ predate

predating v ▷ predate

predator n (pl -s) predatory animal

predators n ▷ predators

predatory [pred-a-tree] adj habitually hunting and killing other animals for food

predecease v (-ses, -sing, -sed) die before (someone else)
  predeceased v ▷ predecease
  predeceases v ▷ predecease
  predeceasing v ▷ predecease
predecessor n (pl -s) person who precedes another in an office or position
  predecessors n ▷ predecessor
predestination n (pl -s) (THEOLOGY) belief that future events have already been decided by God or fate > **predestined** adj
  predestinations n ▷ predestine
  predestined adj ▷ predestination
predetermined adj decided in advance
predicament n (pl -s) embarrassing or difficult situation
  predicaments n ▷ predicament
predicate n (pl -tes) (GRAMMAR) part of a sentence in which something is said about the subject, e.g. went home in I went home ▶ v (-tes, -ting, -ted) declare or assert
  predicated v ▷ predicate
  predicates n, v ▷ predicate
  predicating v ▷ predicate
predict v (-s, -ing, -ed) tell about in advance, prophesy > **predictable** adj > **prediction** n (pl -s)
  predictable adj ▷ predict
  predicted v ▷ predict
  predicting v ▷ predict
  prediction n ▷ predict
  predictions n ▷ predict
predictive adj relating to or able to make predictions
  predicts v ▷ predict
predilection n (pl -s) (Formal) preference or liking
  predilections n ▷ predilection
predispose v (-ses, -sing, -sed) influence (someone) in favour of something > **predisposition** n (pl -s)
  predisposed v ▷ predispose
  predisposes v ▷ predispose
  predisposing v ▷ predispose
  predisposition n ▷ predispose
  predispositions n ▷ predispose
predominate v (-tes, -ting, -ted) be the main or controlling element > **predominance** n (pl -s) > **predominant** adj > **predominantly** adv
  predominance n ▷ predominances
  predominances n ▷ predominate
  predominant n ▷ predominate
  predominantly adv ▷ predominate
  predominated v ▷ predominate
  predominates v ▷ predominate
  predominating v ▷ predominate
preen v (-s, -ing, -ed) (of a bird) clean or trim (feathers) with the beak
  preened v ▷ preen
  preening v ▷ preen
  preens v ▷ preen
prefab n (pl -s) prefabricated house
prefabricated adj (of a building) manufactured in shaped sections for rapid assembly on site
  prefabs n ▷ prefab
preface [pref-iss] n (pl -s) introduction to a book ▶ v (-ces, -cing, -ced) serve as an introduction to (a book, speech, etc.) > **prefatory** adj
  prefaced v ▷ preface
  prefaces n, v ▷ preface
  prefacing v ▷ preface
  prefatory adj ▷ preface
prefect n (pl -s) senior pupil in a school, with limited power over others
  prefects n ▷ prefect
prefecture n (pl -s) office or area of authority of a prefect
  prefectures n ▷ prefecture
prefer v (-s, -rring, -rred) like better > **preference** n (pl -s)
preferable adj more desirable > **preferably** adv
  preferably adv ▷ preferable
  preference n ▷ prefer
  preferences n ▷ prefer
preferential adj showing preference
preferment n (pl -s) promotion or advancement
  preferments n ▷ preferment
  preferred v ▷ prefer
  preferring v ▷ prefer
  prefers v ▷ prefer
prefigure v (-res, -ring, -red) represent or suggest in advance
  prefigured v ▷ prefigure
  prefigures v ▷ prefigure
  prefiguring v ▷ prefigure
prefix n (pl -es) letter or group of letters put at the beginning of a word to make a new word, such as un- in unhappy ▶ v (-es, -ing, -ed) put as an introduction or prefix (to)
  prefixed v ▷ prefix
  prefixes n, v ▷ prefix
  prefixing v ▷ prefix
  pregnacies n ▷ pregnant
  pregnancy n ▷ pregnant
pregnant adj carrying a fetus in the womb > **pregnancy** n (pl -cies)
prehensile adj capable of grasping

prehistoric adj of the period before written history begins > **prehistory** n (pl -ries)

prehistories n ▷ prehistoric

prehistory n ▷ prehistoric

prejudice n (pl -s) unreasonable or unfair dislike or preference ▶ (-ces, -cing, -ced) cause (someone) to have a prejudice > **prejudicial** adj disadvantageous, harmful

prejudiced v ▷ prejudice

prejudicial adj ▷ prejudice

prejudicing v ▷ prejudice

prejudices n, v ▷ prejudice

prelate [prel-it] n (pl -s) bishop or other churchman of high rank

prelates n ▷ prelate

preliminaries n ▷ preliminary

preliminary adj happening before and in preparation, introductory ▶ n (pl -ries) preliminary remark, contest, etc.

prelude n (pl -s) introductory movement in music

preludes n ▷ prelude

premarital adj occurring before marriage

premature adj happening or done before the normal or expected time > **prematurely** adv

prematurely adv ▷ premature

premeditated adj planned in advance > **premeditation** n (pl -s)

premeditation n ▷ premeditated

premeditations n ▷ premeditated

premenstrual adj occurring or experienced before a menstrual period

premier n (pl -s) prime minister ▶ adj chief, leading > **premiership** n (pl -s)

première n (pl -s) first performance of a play, film, etc.

premières n ▷ première

premiers n ▷ premier

premiership n ▷ premier

premierships n ▷ premier

premise, premiss n (pl -s, -es) statement assumed to be true and used as the basis of reasoning

premises n ▷ premise

premises pl n house or other building and its land

premisses n ▷ premise

premium n (pl -s) additional sum of money, as on a wage or charge

premiums n ▷ premium

premonition n (pl -s) feeling that something unpleasant is going to happen; foreboding > **premonitory** adj

premonitions n ▷ premonition

premonitory adj ▷ premonition

prenatal adj before birth, during pregnancy

preoccupied v ▷ preoccupy

preoccupies v ▷ preoccupy

preoccupy v (-pied, -pying, -pied) fill the thoughts or attention of (someone) to the exclusion of other things > **preoccupation** n (pl -s)

preoccupation n ▷ preoccupy

preoccupations n ▷ preoccupy

preoccupying v ▷ preoccupy

preordained adj decreed or determined in advance

prep. preparatory

prepacked adj sold already wrapped

prepaid adj paid for in advance

prepare v (-res, -ring, -red) make or get ready

preparation n (pl -s) preparing

preparations n ▷ preparation

preparatory [prip-par-a-tree] adj preparing for

prepared adj willing ▶ v ▷ prepare

prepares v ▷ prepare

preparing v ▷ prepare

preponderance n (pl -s) greater force, amount, or influence > **preponderant** adj

preponderances adj ▷ preponderance

preponderant adj ▷ preponderance

preposition n (pl -s) word used before a noun or pronoun to show its relationship with other words, such as by in go by bus > **prepositional** adj

prepositional n ▷ preposition

prepositions n ▷ preposition

prepossessing adj making a favourable impression, attractive

preposterous adj utterly absurd

prepuce [pree-pyewss] n (pl -s) retractable fold of skin covering the tip of the penis, foreskin

prepuces n ▷ prepuce

prerecorded adj recorded in advance to be played or broadcast later

prerequisite adj, n (pl -s) (something) required before something else is possible

prerequisites n ▷ prerequisite

prerogative n (pl -s) special power or privilege

prerogatives n ▷ prerogative

presage [press-ij] v (-ges, -ging, -ged) be a sign or warning of

presaged v ▷ presage

presages v ▷ presage

presaging v ▷ presage

presbyteries n ▷ presbytery

presbytery n (pl -ies) (PRESBYTERIAN CHURCH) local church court

prescience [press-ee-enss] n (pl -s) knowledge of events before they happen > **prescient** adj

presciences n ▷ prescience
prescient adj ▷ prescience
prescribe v (-bes, -bing, -bed) recommend the use of (a medicine)
prescribed v ▷ prescribe
prescribes v ▷ prescribe
prescribing v ▷ prescribe
prescription n written instructions from a doctor for the making up and use of a medicine
prescriptions n ▷ prescription
prescriptive adj laying down rules
presence n (pl -s) fact of being in a specified place
presences n ▷ presence
present¹ adj being in a specified place ▶ n (pl -s) present time or tense
present² n something given to bring pleasure to another person ▶ v (-s, -ing, -ed) introduce formally or publicly > **presentation** n (pl -s)
presentable adj attractive, neat, fit for people to see
presented n ▷ present²
presenter n (pl -s) person introducing a TV or radio show
presenters n ▷ presenter
presentiment [priz-**zen**-tim-ent] n (pl -s) sense of something unpleasant about to happen
presentiments n ▷ presentiment
presenting v ▷ present²
presently adv soon (US & SCOT)
presents n, v ▷ present¹, ²
preserve v (-ves, -ving, -ved) keep from being damaged, changed, or ended ▶ n (pl -s) area of interest restricted to a particular person or group > **preservation** n (pl -s)
preservation n ▷ preserve
preservations n ▷ preserve
preservative n (pl -s) chemical that prevents decay
preservatives n ▷ preservative
preserved v ▷ preserve
preserves v, n ▷ preserve
preserving v ▷ preserve
preshrunk adj (of fabric or a garment) having been shrunk during manufacture so that further shrinkage will not occur when washed
preside v (-des, -ding, -ded) be in charge, esp. of a meeting
presided v ▷ preside
presidencies n ▷ president
presidency n ▷ president
president n (pl -s) head of state in many countries > **presidential** adj > **presidency** n

(pl -cies)
presidential n ▷ president
presidents n ▷ president
presides v ▷ preside
presiding v ▷ preside
press v (-es, -ing, -ed) apply force or weight to ▶ n (pl -es) printing machine
pressed v ▷ press
presses v, n ▷ press
pressing adj urgent ▶ v ▷ press
presses n ▷ press
pressure n (pl -s) force produced by pressing
pressures n ▷ pressure
prestidigitation n (pl -s) skilful quickness with the hands, conjuring
prestidigitations n ▷ prestidigitation
prestige n (pl -s) high status or respect resulting from success or achievements
> **prestigious** adj
prestiges n ▷ prestige
prestigious adj ▷ prestige
presumed v ▷ presume
presto adv (MUSIC) very quickly
prestressed adj (of concrete) containing stretched steel wires to strengthen it
presume v (-mes, -ing, -med) suppose to be the case
presumably adv one supposes (that)
presumed v ▷ presume
presumes v ▷ presume
presuming v ▷ presume
presumption (pl -s) n bold insolent behaviour
presumption n ▷ presumption
presumptive adj assumed to be true or valid until the contrary is proved
presumptuous adj doing things one has no right to do
presuppose v (-ses, -sing, -sed) need as a previous condition in order to be true
> **presupposition** n (pl -s)
presupposed v ▷ presuppose
presupposes v ▷ presuppose
presupposing v ▷ presuppose
presupposition n ▷ presuppose
presuppositions v ▷ presuppose
pretence n (pl -s) behaviour intended to deceive, pretending
pretences n ▷ pretence
pretend v (-s, -ing, -ed) claim or give the appearance of (something untrue) to deceive or in play
pretended v ▷ pretend
pretender n (pl -s) person who makes a false or disputed claim to a position of power
pretenders n ▷ pretender

pretending v ▷ pretend
pretends v ▷ pretend
pretension n ▷ pretentious
pretensions n ▷ pretentious
pretentious adj making (unjustified) claims to special merit or importance > **pretension** n (pl -s)
preternatural adj beyond what is natural, supernatural
pretext n (pl -s) false reason given to hide the real one
pretexts n ▷ pretext
prettier adj ▷ pretty
prettiest adj ▷ pretty
prettily adv ▷ pretty
prettiness n ▷ pretty
prettinesses n ▷ pretty
pretty adj (-tier, -ttiest) pleasing to look at ▶ adv fairly, moderately > **prettily** adv > **prettiness** n (pl -es)
pretzel n (pl -s) brittle salted biscuit
pretzels n ▷ pretzel
prevail v (-s, -ing, -ed) gain mastery
prevailed v ▷ prevail
prevailing adj widespread ▶ v ▷ prevail
prevails v ▷ prevail
prevalence n ▷ prevalent
prevalences n ▷ prevalent
prevalent adj widespread, common > **prevalence** n (pl -s)
prevaricate v (-tes, -ting, -ted) avoid giving a direct or truthful answer > **prevarication** n (pl -s)
prevaricated v ▷ prevaricate
prevaricates v ▷ prevaricate
prevaricating v ▷ prevaricate
prevarication n ▷ prevaricate
prevarications n ▷ prevaricate
prevent v (-s, -ing, -ed) keep from happening or doing > **preventable** adj > **prevention** n (pl -s) > **preventive** adj, n (pl -s)
preventable adj ▷ prevent
prevented v ▷ prevent
preventing v ▷ prevent
prevention n ▷ prevent
preventions n ▷ prevent
preventive adj, n ▷ prevent
preventives n ▷ prevent
prevents v ▷ prevent
preview n (pl -s) advance showing of a film or exhibition before it is shown to the public
previews n ▷ preview
previous adj coming or happening before > **previously** adv
previously adv ▷ previous

prey n (pl -s) animal hunted and killed for food by another animal
preys n ▷ prey
price n (pl -s) amount of money for which a thing is bought or sold ▶ v (-ces, -cing, -ced) fix or ask the price of
priced v ▷ price
priceless adj very valuable
prices n, v ▷ price
pricier adj ▷ pricey
priciest adj ▷ pricey
pricing v ▷ price
pricey adj (-cier, -ciest) (Informal) expensive
prick v (-s, -ing, -ed) pierce lightly with a sharp point ▶ n (pl -s) sudden sharp pain caused by pricking
pricked v ▷ prick
pricking v ▷ prick
prickle n (pl -s) thorn or spike on a plant ▶ v (-les, -ling, -led) have a tingling or pricking sensation > **prickly** adj (-lier, -liest)
prickled v ▷ prickle
prickles n, v ▷ prickle
pricklier adj ▷ prickle
prickliest adj ▷ prickle
prickling v ▷ prickle
prickly adj ▷ prickle
pricks v, n ▷ prick
pride n (pl -s) feeling of pleasure and satisfaction when one has done well
prides n ▷ pride
pried v ▷ pry
pries v ▷ pry
priest n (pl -s) (in the Christian church) a person who can administer the sacraments and preach > **priestess** n fem (pl -es) > **priesthood** n (pl -s) > **priestly** adj (-lier, -liest)
priestess n ▷ priest
priestesses n ▷ priest
priesthood n ▷ priest
priesthoods n ▷ priest
priestlier adj ▷ priest
priestliest adj ▷ priest
priestly adj ▷ priest
priests n ▷ priest
prig n (pl -s) self-righteous person who acts as if superior to others > **priggish** adj > **priggishness** n (pl -s)
priggish adj ▷ prig
priggishness n ▷ prig
priggishnesses n ▷ prig
prigs n ▷ prig
prim adj (-mmer, -mmest) formal, proper, and rather prudish > **primly** adv
primacies n ▷ primacy

primacy *n* (*pl* -ies) state of being first in rank, grade, etc.
  primaeval *adj* ▷ primeval
primal *adj* of basic causes or origins
  primarily *adv* ▷ primary
primary *adj* chief, most important > **primarily** *adv*
primate[1] *n* (*pl* -s) member of an order of mammals including monkeys and humans
primate[2] *n* (*pl* -s) archbishop
  primates *n* ▷ primate[1, 2]
prime *adj* main, most important ▶ *n* (*pl* -s) time when someone is at his or her best or most vigorous ▶ *v* (-mes, -ming, -med) give (someone) information in advance to prepare them for something
  primed *v* ▷ prime
primer *n* (*pl* -s) special paint applied to bare wood etc. before the main paint
  primers *n* ▷ primer
  primes *n*, *v* ▷ prime
  priming *v* ▷ prime
primeval [prime-**ee**-val] *adj* of the earliest age of the world
primitive *adj* of an early simple stage of development
  primly *adv* ▷ prim
  primmer *adj* ▷ prim
  primmest *adj* ▷ prim
primogeniture *n* (*pl* -s) system under which the eldest son inherits all his parents' property
  primogenitures *n* ▷ primogeniture
primordial *adj* existing at or from the beginning
primrose *n* (*pl* -s) pale yellow spring flower
  primroses *n* ▷ primrose
primula *n* (*pl* -s) type of primrose with brightly coloured flowers
  primulas *n* ▷ primula
prince *n* (*pl* -s) male member of a royal family, esp. the son of the king or queen
  princelier *adj* ▷ princely
  princeliest *adj* ▷ princely
princely *adj* (-lier, -liest) of or like a prince
princess *n* (*pl* -es) female member of a royal family, esp. the daughter of the king or queen
  princes *n* ▷ prince
  princesses *n* ▷ princess
principal *adj* main, most important ▶ *n* (*pl* -s) head of a school or college > **principally** *adv*
  principalities *n* ▷ principality
principality *n* (*pl* -ties) territory ruled by a prince
  principally *adv* ▷ principal

  principals *n* ▷ principal
principle *n* (*pl* -s) moral rule guiding behaviour
  principles *n* ▷ principle
print *v* (-s, -ing, -ed) reproduce (a newspaper, book, etc.) in large quantities by mechanical or electronic means ▶ *n* (*pl* -s) printed words etc. > **printing** *n* (*pl* -s)
  printed *v* ▷ print
printer *n* (*pl* -s) person or company engaged in printing
  printers *n* ▷ printer
  printing *n*, *v* ▷ print
  printings *n* ▷ print
  prints *v* ▷ print
  printing *v* ▷ print
  printed *v* ▷ print
  prints *n* ▷ print
prior[1] *adj* earlier
prior[2] *n* (*pl* -s) head monk in a priory
prioress *n* (*pl* -es) deputy head nun in a convent
  prioresses *n* ▷ prioress
  priories *n* ▷ priory
  priors *n* ▷ prior[2]
priory *n* (*pl* -ries) place where certain orders of monks or nuns live
  priors *n* ▷ prior
  priorities *n* ▷ priority
priority *n* (*pl* -ties) most important thing that must be dealt with first
prise *v* (-ses, -sing, -sed) force open by levering
  prised *v* ▷ prise
  prises *v* ▷ prise
  prising *v* ▷ prise
prism *n* (*pl* -s) transparent block usu. with triangular ends and rectangular sides, used to disperse light into a spectrum or refract it in optical instruments
prismatic *adj* of or shaped like a prism
  prisms *n* ▷ prism
prison *n* (*pl* -s) building where criminals and accused people are held
  prisons *n* ▷ prison
prisoner *n* (*pl* -s) person held captive
  prisoners *n* ▷ prisoner
  prissier *adj* ▷ prissy
  prissiest *adj* ▷ prissy
  prissily *adv* ▷ prissy
prissy *adj* (-ssier, -ssiest) prim, correct, and easily shocked > **prissily** *adv*
pristine *adj* clean, new, and unused
  privacies *n* ▷ private
  privacy *n* ▷ private
private *adj* for the use of one person or group only ▶ *n* (*pl* -s) soldier of the lowest rank

> **privately** adv > **privacy** n (pl **-cies**)
privately adv ▷ private
privates n ▷ private
privateer n (pl **-s**) (HIST) privately owned armed vessel authorized by the government to take part in a war
privateers n ▷ privateer
privation n (pl **-s**) loss or lack of the necessities of life
privations n ▷ privation
privatization n ▷ privatize
privatizations n ▷ privatize
privatize v (**-zes**, **-zing**, **-zed**) sell (a publicly owned company) to individuals or a private company > **privatization** n (pl **-s**)
privatized v ▷ privatize
privatizes v ▷ privatize
privatizing v ▷ privatize
privet n (pl **-s**) bushy evergreen shrub used for hedges
privets n ▷ privet
privier adj ▷ privy
privies n ▷ privy
priviest adj ▷ privy
privilege n (pl **-s**) advantage or favour that only some people have
privileged adj enjoying a special right or immunity
privileges n ▷ privilege
privy adj (**-vier**, **-viest**) sharing knowledge of something secret ▶ n (pl **-ies**) (Obs) toilet, esp. an outside one
prize¹ n (pl **-s**) reward given for success in a competition etc. ▶ adj winning or likely to win a prize
prize² v (**-zes**, **-zing**, **-zed**) value highly
prize³ v ▷ prise
prized v ▷ prize
prizefighter n (pl **-s**) boxer who fights for money
prizefighters n ▷ prizefighter
prizes n, v ▷ prize¹, ²
prizing v ▷ prize²
pro¹ adv, prep in favour of
pro² n (pl **-s**) (Informal) professional
probabilities n ▷ probable
probability n ▷ probable
probable adj likely to happen or be true > **probability** n (pl **-ies**)
probably adv in all likelihood
probate n (pl **-s**) process of proving the validity of a will
probates n ▷ probate
probation n (pl **-s**) system of dealing with law-breakers, esp. juvenile ones, by placing them

under supervision
probationer n (pl **-s**) person on probation
probationers n ▷ probationer
probations n ▷ probation
probe v (**-bes**, **-bing**, **-bed**) search into or examine closely ▶ n (pl **-s**) surgical instrument used to examine a wound, cavity, etc.
probed v ▷ probe
probes v, n ▷ probe
probing v ▷ probe
probiotic adj, n (pl **-s**) (of) a bacterium that protects the body from harmful bacteria
probiotics n ▷ probiotic
probities n ▷ probity
probity n (pl **-ties**) honesty, integrity
problem n (pl **-s**) something difficult to deal with or solve > **problematic, problematical** adj
problematic adj ▷ problem
problematical adj ▷ problem
problems n ▷ problem
proboscis [pro-**boss**-iss] n (pl **-scises**) long trunk or snout
proboscises n ▷ proboscis
procedural adj ▷ procedure
procedure n (pl **-s**) way of doing something, esp. the correct or usual one > **procedural** adj
procedures n ▷ procedure
proceed v (**-s**, **-ing**, **-ed**) start or continue doing
proceeded v ▷ proceed
proceeds pl n money obtained from an event or activity ▶ v ▷ proceed
proceeding v ▷ proceed
proceedings pl n organized or related series of events
process n (pl **-es**) series of actions or changes ▶ v (**-es**, **-ing**, **-ed**) handle or prepare by a special method of manufacture > **processor** n (pl **-s**)
processed adj (of food) treated to prevent it decaying ▶ v ▷ process
processes n, v ▷ process
processing v ▷ process
procession n (pl **-s**) line of people or vehicles moving forward together in order
processions n ▷ procession
processor n ▷ process
processors n ▷ process
proclaim v (**-s**, **-ing**, **-ed**) declare publicly > **proclamation** n (pl **-s**)
proclaimed v ▷ proclaim
proclaiming v ▷ proclaim
proclaims v ▷ proclaim
proclamation n ▷ proclaim
proclamations n ▷ proclaim

proclivities *n* ▷ proclivity
proclivity *n* (*pl* -ties) inclination, tendency
procrastinate *v* (-tes, -ting, -ted) put off taking action, delay > **procrastination** *n* (*pl* -s)
  procrastinated *v* ▷ procrastinate
  procrastinates *v* ▷ procrastinate
  procrastinating *v* ▷ procrastinate
  procrastination *n* ▷ procrastinate
  procrastinations *n* ▷ procrastinate
procreate *v* (-tes, -ting, -ted) (*Formal*) produce offspring > **procreation** *n* (*pl* -s)
  procreated *v* ▷ procreate
  procreates *v* ▷ procreate
  procreating *v* ▷ procreate
  procreation *n* ▷ procreate
  procreations *n* ▷ procreate
procure *v* (-res, -ring, -red) get, provide > **procurement** *n* (*pl* -s)
  procured *v* ▷ procure
  procurement *n* ▷ procure
  procurements *n* ▷ procure
procurer, procuress *n* (*pl* -s, -es) person who obtains people to act as prostitutes
  procurers *n* ▷ procurer
  procures *v* ▷ procure
  procuress *n* ▷ procurer
  procuresses *n* ▷ procurer
  procuring *v* ▷ procure
prod *v* (-s, -dding, -dded) poke with something pointed ▶ *n* (*pl* -s) prodding
  prodded *v* ▷ prod
  prodding *v* ▷ prod
prodigal *adj* recklessly extravagant, wasteful > **prodigality** *n* (*pl* -s)
  prodigalities *n* ▷ prodigal
  prodigality *n* ▷ prodigal
  prodigies *n* ▷ prodigy
prodigious *adj* very large, immense > **prodigiously** *adv*
  prodigiously *adv* ▷ prodigious
prodigy *n* (*pl* -gies) person with some marvellous talent
prods *v*, *n* ▷ prod
produce *v* (-ces, -cing, -ced) bring into existence ▶ *n* (*pl* -s) food grown for sale
  produced *v* ▷ produce
producer *n* (*pl* -s) person with control over the making of a film, record, etc.
  producers *n* ▷ producer
  produces *v*, *n* ▷ produce
  producing *v* ▷ produce
product *n* (*pl* -s) something produced
production *n* (*pl* -s) producing
  productions *n* ▷ production
productive *adj* producing large quantities

  > **productivity** *n* (*pl* -ies)
  productivities *n* ▷ productive
  productivity *n* ▷ productive
  products *n* ▷ product
profane *adj* showing disrespect for religion or holy things ▶ *v* (-nes, -ning, -ned) treat (something sacred) irreverently, desecrate
profanation *n* (*pl* -s) act of profaning
  profanations *n* ▷ profanation
  profaned *v* ▷ profane
  profanes *v* ▷ profane
  profaning *v* ▷ profane
  profanities *n* ▷ profanity
profanity *n* (*pl* -ties) profane talk or behaviour, blasphemy
profess *v* (-es, -ing, -ed) state or claim (something as true), sometimes falsely > **professed** *adj* supposed
professed *v*, *adj* ▷ profess
  professes *v* ▷ profess
  professing *v* ▷ profess
profession *n* (*pl* -s) type of work, such as being a doctor, that needs special training
professional *adj* working in a profession ▶ *n* person who works in a profession > **professionally** *adv* > **professionalism** *n* (*pl* -s)
  professionally *adv* ▷ professional
  professionalism *n* ▷ professional
  professionalisms *n* ▷ professional
  professions *n* ▷ profession
professor *n* (*pl* -s) teacher of the highest rank in a university > **professorial** *adj* > **professorship** *n* (*pl* -s)
  professorial *adj* ▷ professor
  professors *n* ▷ professor
  professorship *n* ▷ professor
  professorships *n* ▷ professor
proffer *v* (-s, -ing, -ed) offer
  proffered *v* ▷ proffer
  proffering *v* ▷ proffer
  proffers *v* ▷ proffer
  proficiencies *n* ▷ proficient
  proficiency *n* ▷ proficient
proficient *adj* skilled, expert > **proficiency** *n* (*pl* -cies)
profile *n* (*pl* -s) outline, esp. of the face, as seen from the side
  profiles *n* ▷ profile
profit *n* (*pl* -s) money gained ▶ *v* (-s, -ing, -ed) gain or benefit
profitable *adj* making profit > **profitably** *adv* > **profitability** *n* (*pl* -ties)
  profitabilities *n* ▷ profitable
  profitability *n* ▷ profitable

profitably adv ▷ profitable
profited v ▷ profit
profiteer n (pl -s) person who makes excessive profits at the expense of the public > **profiteering** n (pl -s)
profiteering n ▷ profiteer
profiteerings n ▷ profiteer
profiteers n ▷ profiteer
profiting v ▷ profit
profits n, v ▷ profit
profligacies n ▷ profligate
profligacy n ▷ profligate
profligate adj recklessly extravagant ▶ n (pl -s) profligate person > **profligacy** n (pl -cies)
profligates n ▷ profligate
profound adj (-er, -est) showing or needing great knowledge > **profundity** n (pl -ties)
profounder adj ▷ profound
profoundest adj ▷ profound
profundities n ▷ profound
profundity n ▷ profound
profuse adj plentiful > **profusion** n (pl -s)
profusion n ▷ profuse
profusions n ▷ profuse
progenies n ▷ progeny
progeny [proj-in-ee] n (pl -nies) children
progenitor [pro-jen-it-er] n (pl -s) ancestor
progenitors n ▷ progenitor
progesterone n (pl -s) hormone which prepares the womb for pregnancy and prevents further ovulation
progesterones n ▷ progesterone
prognoses n ▷ prognosis
prognosis n (pl -noses) doctor's forecast about the progress of an illness
prognostication n (pl -s) forecast or prediction
prognostications n ▷ prognostication
program n (pl -s) sequence of coded instructions for a computer ▶ v (-s, -mming, --mmed) arrange (data) so that it can be processed by a computer > **programmer** n (pl -s) > **programmable** adj
programmable adj ▷ program
programmed v ▷ program
programmer n ▷ program
programmers n ▷ program
programming v ▷ program
programs n, v ▷ program
programme n (pl -s) planned series of events
programmes n ▷ programme
progress n (pl -es) improvement, development ▶ v (-es, -ing, -ed) become more advanced or skilful > **progression** n (pl -s)
progressed v ▷ progress

progresses v ▷ progress
progressing v ▷ progress
progression n ▷ progress
progressions n ▷ progress
progressive adj favouring political or social reform > **progressively** adv
progressively adv ▷ progressive
prohibit v (-s, -ing, -ed) forbid or prevent from happening
prohibited v ▷ prohibit
prohibiting v ▷ prohibit
prohibition n (pl -s) act of forbidding
prohibitions n ▷ prohibition
prohibitive adj (of prices) too high to be affordable > **prohibitively** adv
prohibitively adv ▷ prohibitive
prohibits v ▷ prohibit
project n (pl projects) planned scheme to do or examine something over a period ▶ v (-s, -ing, -ed) make a forecast based on known data > **projection** n (pl -s)
projected v ▷ project
projectile n (pl -s) object thrown as a weapon or fired from a gun
projectiles n ▷ projectile
projecting v ▷ project
projection n ▷ project
projectionist n (pl -s) person who operates a projector
projectionists n ▷ projectionist
projections n ▷ project
projector n (pl -s) apparatus for projecting photographic images, films, or slides on a screen
projectors n ▷ projector
projects n, v ▷ project
prolapse n (pl -s) slipping down of an internal organ of the body from its normal position
prolapses n ▷ prolapse
prole adj, n (pl -s) (CHIEFLY BRIT) (Slang) proletarian
proles n ▷ prole
proletariat [pro-lit-air-ee-at] n (pl -s) working class > **proletarian** adj, n (pl -s)
proletarian n ▷ proletariat
proletarians n ▷ proletariat
proletariats n ▷ proletariat
proliferate v (-tes, -ting, -ted) grow or reproduce rapidly > **proliferation** n (pl -s)
proliferated v ▷ proliferate
proliferates v ▷ proliferate
proliferating v ▷ proliferate
proliferation n ▷ proliferate
proliferations n ▷ proliferate
prolific adj very productive > **prolifically** adv

prolifically *adv* ▷ prolific

prolix *adj* (of speech or a piece of writing) overlong and boring

prologue *n* (*pl* -s) introduction to a play or book

prologues *n* ▷ prologue

prolong *v* (-s, -ing, -ed) make (something) last longer > **prolongation** *n* (*pl* -s)

prolongation *n* ▷ prolong

prolongations *n* ▷ prolong

prolonged *v* ▷ prolong

prolonging *v* ▷ prolong

prolongs *v* ▷ prolong

prom *n* (*pl* -s) ▷ promenade

promenade *n* (*pl* -s) (CHIEFLY BRIT) paved walkway along the seafront at a holiday resort ▶ *v* (-des, -ding, -ded) ▶ *n* (Old-fashioned) (take) a leisurely walk

promenaded *v* ▷ promenade

promenades *n, v* ▷ promenade

promenading *v* ▷ promenade

prominence *n* ▷ prominent

prominences *n* ▷ prominent

prominent *adj* very noticeable > **prominently** *adv* > **prominence** *n* (*pl* -s)

prominently *adv* ▷ prominent

promiscuities *n* ▷ promiscuous

promiscuity *n* ▷ promiscuous

promiscuous *adj* having many casual sexual relationships > **promiscuity** *n* (*pl* -ties)

promise *v* (-es, -sing, -sed) say that one will definitely do or not do something ▶ *n* (*pl* -s) undertaking to do or not to do something

promised *v* ▷ promise

promises *v* ▷ promise

promising *adj* likely to succeed or turn out well ▶ *v* ▷ promise

promo *n* (*pl* -os) (Informal) short film to promote a product

promontories *n* ▷ promontory

promontory *n* (*pl* -ries) point of high land jutting out into the sea

promos *n* ▷ promo

promote *v* (-tes, -ting, -ted) help to make (something) happen or increase > **promotion** *n* (*pl* -s) > **promotional** *adj*

promoted *v* ▷ promote

promoter *n* (*pl* -s) person who organizes or finances an event etc.

promoters *n* ▷ promoter

promotes *v* ▷ promote

promoting *v* ▷ promote

promotion *n* ▷ promote

promotional *adj* ▷ promote

promotions *n* ▷ promote

prompt *v* (-s, -ing, -ed) cause (an action) ▶ *adj* done without delay ▶ *adv* exactly > **promptness** *n* (*pl* -es)

prompted *v* ▷ prompt

prompter, prompt *n* (*pl* -s) person offstage who prompts actors

prompter *n* ▷ prompter

prompting *v* ▷ prompt

promptly *adv* immediately, without delay

promptness *n* ▷ prompt

promptnesses *n* ▷ prompt

prompts *v, n* ▷ prompt

proms *n* ▷ prom

promulgate *v* (-tes, -ting, -ted) put (a law etc.) into effect by announcing it officially > **promulgation** *n* (*pl* -s)

promulgated *v* ▷ promulgate

promulgates *v* ▷ promulgate

promulgating *v* ▷ promulgate

promulgation *n* ▷ promulgate

promulgations *n* ▷ promulgate

prone *adj* (-r, -st) (foll. by to) likely to do or be affected by (something)

proner *adj* ▷ prone

pronest *adj* ▷ prone

prong *n* (*pl* -s) one spike of a fork or similar instrument > **pronged** *adj*

pronged *adj* ▷ prong

prongs *n* ▷ prong

pronoun *n* (*pl* -s) word, such as *she* or *it*, used to replace a noun

pronouns *n* ▷ pronoun

pronounce *v* (-ces, -cing, -ced) form the sounds of (words or letters), esp. clearly or in a particular way > **pronounceable** *adj*

pronouncable *adj* ▷ pronounce

pronounced *adj* very noticeable ▶ *v* ▷ pronounce

pronounces *v* ▷ pronounce

pronouncement *n* (*pl* -s) formal announcement

pronouncements *n* ▷ pronouncement

pronouncing *v* ▷ pronounce

pronunciation *n* (*pl* -s) way in which a word or language is pronounced

pronunciations *n* ▷ pronunciation

pronto *adv* (Informal) at once

proof *n* (*pl* -s) evidence that shows that something is true or has happened ▶ *adj* able to withstand

proofread *v* (-s, -ing, -read) read and correct (printer's proofs) > **proofreader** *n* (*pl* -s)

proofreader *n* ▷ proofread

proofreaders *n* ▷ proofread

proofreading *v* ▷ proofread

proofreads v ▷ proofread
proofs n ▷ proof
prop[1] v (-s, -pping, -pped) support (something) so that it stays upright or in place ▶ n (pl -s) pole, beam, etc. used as a support
prop[2] n (pl -s) movable object used on the set of a film or play
prop[3] n (pl -s) (Informal) propeller
propaganda n (organized promotion of) information to assist or damage the cause of a government or movement ▷ **propagandist** n (pl -s)
propagandas n ▷ propaganda
propagandist n ▷ propaganda
propagandists n ▷ propaganda
propagate v (-tes, -ting, -ted) spread (information and ideas) ▷ **propagation** n (pl -s)
propagated v ▷ propagate
propagates v ▷ propagate
propagating v ▷ propagate
propagation n ▷ propagate
propagations n ▷ propagate
propane n (pl -s) flammable gas found in petroleum and used as a fuel
propanes n ▷ propane
propel v (-s, -lling, -lled) cause to move forward
propellant n (pl -s) something that provides or causes propulsion
propellants n ▷ propellant
propelled v ▷ propel
propeller n (pl -s) revolving shaft with blades for driving a ship or aircraft
propellers n ▷ propeller
propelling v ▷ propel
propels v ▷ propel
propped v ▷ prop[1]
propping v ▷ prop[1]
props v, n ▷ prop[1, 2, 3]
propulsion n (pl -s) method by which something is propelled
propulsions n ▷ propulsion
propensities n ▷ propensity
propensity n (pl -ies) natural tendency
proper adj (-er, -est) real or genuine ▷ **properly** adv
properer adj ▷ proper
properest adj ▷ proper
properly adv ▷ proper
properties n ▷ property
property n (pl -ties) something owned
prophecies n ▷ prophecy
prophecy n (pl -cies) prediction
prophesied v ▷ prophesy
prophesies v ▷ prophesy

prophesy v (-sies, -sying, -sied) foretell
prophesying v ▷ prophesy
prophet n (pl -s) person supposedly chosen by God to spread His word ▷ **prophetic** adj ▷ **prophetically** adv
prophetic adj ▷ prophet
prophetically adv ▷ prophet
prophets n ▷ prophet
prophylactic n (pl -s) ▶ adj (drug) used to prevent disease
prophylactics n ▷ prophylactic
propitiate v (-tes, -ting, -ted) appease, win the favour of ▷ **propitiation** n
propitiated v ▷ propitiate
propitiates v ▷ propitiate
propitiating v ▷ propitiate
propitiation n ▷ propitiate
propitiations n ▷ propitiate
propitious adj favourable or auspicious
proponent n (pl -s) person who argues in favour of something
proponents n ▷ proponent
proportion n (pl -s) relative size or extent ▶ pl dimensions or size ▶ v (-s, -ing, -ed) adjust in relative amount or size
proportional, proportionate adj being in proportion ▷ **proportionally, proportionately** adv
proportionally adv ▷ proportional
proportionate adj ▷ proportional
proportionately adv ▷ proportional
proportioned v ▷ proportion
proportioning v ▷ proportion
proportions n, v ▷ proportion
propose v (-ses, -sing, -sed) put forward for consideration ▷ **proposal** n (pl -s)
proposal n ▷ propose
proposals n ▷ propose
proposed v ▷ propose
proposes v ▷ propose
proposing v ▷ propose
proposition n (pl -s) offer ▶ v (-s, -ing, -ed) (Informal) ask (someone) to have sexual intercourse
propositioned v ▷ proposition
propositioning v ▷ proposition
propositions n, v ▷ proposition
propound v (-s, -ing, -ed) put forward for consideration
propounded v ▷ propound
propounding v ▷ propound
propounds v ▷ propound
proprietor n (pl -s) owner of a business establishment ▷ **proprietress** n fem (pl -es)
proprietary adj made and distributed under

a trade name
proprieties n ▷ propriety
proprietors n ▷ proprietor
proprietress n ▷ proprietor
proprietresses n ▷ proprietor
propriety n (pl -ties) correct conduct
propulsion n ▷ propel
prorogue v (-gues, -guing, -gued) suspend (parliament) without dissolving it
> **prorogation** n (pl -s)
prorogation n ▷ prorogue
prorogations n ▷ prorogue
prorogued v ▷ prorogue
prorogues v ▷ prorogue
proroguing v ▷ prorogue
pros n ▷ pro
prosaic [pro-zay-ik] adj lacking imagination, dull > **prosaically** adv
prosaically adv ▷ prosaic
proscenia n ▷ proscenium
proscenium n (pl -nia, -niums) arch in a theatre separating the stage from the auditorium
prosceniums n ▷ proscenium
proscribe v (-bes, -bing, -bed) prohibit, outlaw
> **proscription** n (pl -s) > **proscriptive** adj
proscribed v ▷ proscribe
proscribes v ▷ proscribe
proscribing v ▷ proscribe
proscription n ▷ proscribe
proscriptions n ▷ proscribe
proscriptive adj ▷ proscribe
prose n (pl -s) ordinary speech or writing in contrast to poetry
proses n ▷ prose
prosecute v (-tes, -ting, -ted) bring a criminal charge against > **prosecution** n (pl -s)
> **prosecutor** n (pl -s)
prosecuted v ▷ prosecute
prosecutes v ▷ prosecute
prosecuting v ▷ prosecute
prosecution n ▷ prosecute
prosecutions n ▷ prosecute
prosecutor n ▷ prosecute
prosecutors n ▷ prosecute
proselyte [pross-ill-ite] n (pl -s) recent convert
proselytes n ▷ proselyte
proselytize [pross-ill-it-ize] v (-zes, -zing, -zed) attempt to convert
proselytized v ▷ proselytize
proselytizes v ▷ proselytize
proselytizing v ▷ proselytize
prospect n (pl -s) something anticipated (Old-fashioned) ▶ pl probability of future success ▶ v (-s, -ing, -ed) explore, esp. for gold

> **prospector** n (pl -s)
prospected v ▷ prospect
prospecting v ▷ prospect
prospective adj future
prospector n ▷ prospect
prospectors n ▷ prospect
prospects n, v ▷ prospect
prospectus n (pl -es) booklet giving details of a university, company, etc.
prospectuses n ▷ prospectus
prosper v (-s, -ing, -ed) be successful
> **prosperous** adj
prospered v ▷ prosper
prospering v ▷ prosper
prosperities n ▷ prosperity
prosperity n success and wealth
prosperous adj ▷ prosper
prospers v ▷ prosper
prostate n (pl -s) gland in male mammals that surrounds the neck of the bladder
prostates n ▷ prostate
prostheses n ▷ prosthesis
prosthesis [pross-**theess**-iss] n (pl -ses) [-seez] artificial body part, such as a limb or breast
> **prosthetic** adj
prosthetic adj ▷ prosthesis
prostitute n (pl -s) person who offers sexual intercourse in return for payment
▶ v (-tes, -ting, -ted) make a prostitute of
> **prostitution** n (pl -s)
prostituted v ▷ prostitute
prostitutes n, v ▷ prostitute
prostituting v ▷ prostitute
prostitution n ▷ prostitute
prostitutions n ▷ prostitute
prostrate adj lying face downwards ▶ v (-tes, -ting, -ted) lie face downwards > **prostration** n (pl -s)
prostrated v ▷ prostrate
prostrates v ▷ prostrate
prostrating v ▷ prostrate
prostration n ▷ prostrate
prostrations n ▷ prostrate
protagonist n (pl -s) supporter of a cause
protagonists n ▷ protagonist
protea [pro-tee-a] n (pl -s) African shrub with showy flowers
protean [pro-tee-an] adj constantly changing
proteas n ▷ protea
protect v (-s, -ing, -ed) defend from trouble, harm, or loss > **protection** n (pl -s)
protected v ▷ protect
protecting v ▷ protect
protection n ▷ protect
protectionism n policy of protecting

industries by taxing competing imports
> **protectionist** n (pl **-s**) adj

protectionisms n ▷ protectionism

protectionist n ▷ protectionism

protectionists n ▷ protectionism

protections n ▷ protect

protective adj giving protection

protector n (pl **-s**) person or thing that protects

protectorate n (pl **-s**) territory largely controlled by a stronger state

protectorates n ▷ protectorate

protectors n ▷ protector

protects v ▷ protect

protégé, fem **protégée** [pro-ti-zhay] n (pl **-s**) person who is protected and helped by another

protégés n ▷ protégé

protein n (pl **-s**) any of a group of complex organic compounds that are essential for life

proteins n ▷ protein

protest n (pl **-s**) declaration or demonstration of objection ▸ v (**-s**, **-ing**, **-ed**) object, disagree

protestant n (pl **-s**) one who protests

protestants n ▷ protestant

protestation n (pl **-s**) strong declaration

protestations n ▷ protestation

protested v ▷ protest

protesting v ▷ protest

protests n, v ▷ protest

protocol n (pl **-s**) rules of behaviour for formal occasions

protocols n ▷ protocol

proton n (pl **-s**) positively charged particle in the nucleus of an atom

protons n ▷ proton

protoplasm n (pl **-s**) substance forming the living contents of a cell

protoplasms n ▷ protoplasm

prototype n (pl **-s**) original or model to be copied or developed

prototypes n ▷ prototype

protozoa n ▷ protozoan

protozoan [pro-toe-**zoe**-an] n (pl **-zoa**) microscopic one-celled creature

protracted adj lengthened or extended

protractor n (pl **-s**) instrument for measuring angles

protractors n ▷ protractor

protrude v (**-des**, **-ding**, **-ded**) stick out, project
> **protrusion** n (pl **-s**)

protruded v ▷ protrude

protrudes v ▷ protrude

protruding v ▷ protrude

protrusion n ▷ protrude

protrusions n ▷ protrude

protuberance n ▷ protuberant

protuberances n ▷ protuberant

protuberant adj swelling out, bulging
> **protuberance** n (pl **-s**)

proud adj (**-er**, **-est**) feeling pleasure and satisfaction > **proudly** adv

prouder adj ▷ proud

proudest adj ▷ proud

proudly adv ▷ proud

prove v (**-ves**, **-ving**, **-ved** or **-ven**) establish the validity of

proved v ▷ prove

proven adj known from experience to work
▸ v ▷ prove

provenance [**prov**-in-anss] n (pl **-s**) place of origin

provenances n ▷ provenance

provender n (pl **-s**) (Old-fashioned) fodder

provenders n ▷ provender

proverb n (pl **-s**) short saying that expresses a truth or gives a warning > **proverbial** adj

proverbial adj ▷ proverb

proverbs n ▷ proverb

proves v ▷ prove

provide v (**-des**, **-ding**, **-ded**) make available
> **provider** n (pl **-s**)

provided v ▷ provide

providence n (pl **-s**) God or nature seen as a protective force that arranges people's lives

providences n ▷ providence

provident adj thrifty

providential adj lucky

provider n ▷ provide

providers n ▷ provide

provides v ▷ provide

providing v ▷ provide

province n (pl **-s**) area governed as a unit of a country or empire ▸ pl parts of a country outside the capital

provincial adj of a province or the provinces
▸ n (pl **-s**) unsophisticated person

provincialism n (pl **-s**) narrow-mindedness and lack of sophistication

provincialisms n ▷ provincialism

provincials n ▷ provincial

provinces n ▷ province

proving v ▷ prove

provision n (pl **-s**) act of supplying something
▸ pl food ▸ v (**-s**, **-ing**, **-ed**) supply with food

provisional adj temporary or conditional
> **provisionally** adv

provisionally adv ▷ provisional

provisioned v ▷ provision

provisioning v ▷ provision

provisions n, v ▷ provision
proviso [pro-**vize**-oh] n (pl -**sos, -soes**) condition, stipulation
provisoes n ▷ proviso
provisos n ▷ proviso
provocation n ▷ provoke
provocations n ▷ provoke
provocative adj ▷ provoke
provoke v (-**kes, -king, -ked**) deliberately anger > **provocation** n (pl -**s**) > **provocative** adj
provoked v ▷ provoke
provokes v ▷ provoke
provoking v ▷ provoke
provost n (pl -**s**) head of certain university colleges in Britain
provosts n ▷ provost
prow n (pl -**s**) bow of a vessel
prows n ▷ prow
prowess n (pl -**es**) superior skill or ability
prowesses n ▷ prowess
prowl v (-**s, -ing, -ed**) move stealthily around a place as if in search of prey or plunder ▶ n (pl -**s**) prowling
prowled v ▷ prowl
prowler n (pl -**s**) person who moves stealthily around a place as if in search of prey or plunder
prowlers n ▷ prowler
prowling v ▷ prowl
prowls v, n ▷ prowl
proxies n ▷ proxy
proximate n ▷ proximity
proximities n ▷ proximity
proximity n (pl -**ties**) nearness in space or time > **proximate** adj
proxy n (pl -**xies**) person authorized to act on behalf of someone else
prude n (pl -**s**) person who is excessively modest, prim, or proper > **prudish** adj > **prudery** n (pl -**ries**)
prudence n ▷ prudent
prudences n ▷ prudent
prudent adj cautious, discreet, and sensible > **prudence** n (pl -**s**)
prudential adj (Old-fashioned) prudent
prudes n ▷ prude
pruderies n ▷ prude
prudery n ▷ prude
prudish adj ▷ prude
prune¹ n (pl -**s**) dried plum
prune² v (-**nes, -ning, -ned**) cut off dead parts or excessive branches from (a tree or plant)
pruned v ▷ prune
prunes n, v ▷ prune¹,²
pruning v ▷ prune

prurience n ▷ prurient
pruriences n ▷ prurient
prurient adj excessively interested in sexual matters > **prurience** n (pl -**s**)
pry v (**prys, prying, pried**) make an impertinent or uninvited inquiry into a private matter
prying v ▷ pry
psalm n (pl -**s**) sacred song
psalmist n (pl -**s**) writer of psalms
psalmists n ▷ psalmist
psalms n ▷ psalm
psalter n (pl -**s**) book containing (a version of) psalms from the Bible
psalteries n ▷ psalter
psaltery n (pl -**ries**) ancient instrument played by plucking strings
psalters n ▷ psalter
psephologies n ▷ psephology
psephology [sef-**fol**-a-jee] n (pl -**gies**) statistical study of elections
pseud n (pl -**s**) (Informal) pretentious person
pseuds n ▷ pseud
pseudonym n (pl -**s**) fictitious name adopted esp. by an author > **pseudonymous** adj
pseudonymous adj ▷ pseudonym
pseudonyms n ▷ pseudonym

> **psi** n (**psis**). Psi is the 23rd letter of the Greek alphabet. This word can be useful if you have a difficult rack, especially if you can form another word at the same time. Psi scores 5 points.

psittacosis n (pl -**ses**) disease of parrots that can be transmitted to humans
psittacoses n ▷ psittacosis

> **pst** interj. Pst is a sound people make when they want to draw someone's attention to something without making too much noise. This is a useful word to remember because it doesn't use any vowels, and so can be useful if you have no vowels on your rack. Pst scores 5 points.

psyche [**sye**-kee] n (pl -**s**) human mind or soul
psychedelic adj denoting a drug that causes hallucinations
psyche n ▷ psyche
psychiatric adj ▷ psychiatry
psychiatries n ▷ psychiatry
psychiatrist n ▷ psychiatry
psychiatrists n ▷ psychiatry
psychiatry n (pl -**ries**) branch of medicine concerned with mental disorders > **psychiatric** adj > **psychiatrist** n

psychic *adj (also* **psychical**) having mental powers which cannot be explained by natural laws ▶ *n (pl -s)* person with psychic powers **psychics** *n* ▷ psychic

psycho *n (pl -s)* (*Informal*) psychopath

psychoanalyse *v* ▷ psychoanalysis

psychoanalysed *v* ▷ psychoanalysis

psychoanalyses *n, v* ▷ psychoanalysis

psychoanalysing *v* ▷ psychoanalysis

psychoanalysis *n (pl -ses)* method of treating mental and emotional disorders by discussion and analysis of one's thoughts and feelings > **psychoanalyse** *v (-ses, -sing, -sed)* > **psychoanalyst** *n (pl -s)*

psychoanalyst *n* ▷ psychoanalysis

psychoanalysts *n* ▷ psychoanalysis

psychological *adj* of or affecting the mind > **psychologically** *adv*

psychologically *adv* ▷ psychological

psychologies *n* ▷ psychology

psychologist *n* ▷ psychology

psychologists *n* ▷ psychology

psychology *n (pl -gies)* study of human and animal behaviour > **psychologist** *n (pl -s)*

psychopath *n (pl -s)* person afflicted with a personality disorder causing him or her to commit antisocial or violent acts > **psychopathic** *adj*

psychopathic *adj* ▷ psychopath

psychopaths *n* ▷ psychopath

psychos *n* ▷ psycho

psychoses *n* ▷ psychosis

psychosis *n (pl -ses)* severe mental disorder in which the sufferer's contact with reality becomes distorted > **psychotic** *adj*

psychosomatic *adj* (of a physical disorder) thought to have psychological causes

psychotherapeutic *adj* ▷ psychotherapy

psychotherapies *n* ▷ psychotherapy

psychotherapist *n* ▷ psychotherapy

psychotherapists *n* ▷ psychotherapy

psychotherapy *n (pl -pies)* treatment of nervous disorders by psychological methods > **psychotherapeutic** *adj* > **psychotherapist** *n* **psychotic** *adj* ▷ psychosis

ptarmigan [tar-mig-an] *n (pl -s)* bird of the grouse family which turns white in winter **ptarmigans** *n* ▷ ptarmigan

pterodactyl [terr-roe-**dak**-til] *n (pl -s)* extinct flying reptile with batlike wings **pterodactyls** *n* ▷ pterodactyl

ptomaine [toe-**main**] *n (pl -s)* any of a group of poisonous alkaloids found in decaying matter **ptomaines** *n* ▷ ptomaine

pub *n (pl -s)* building with a bar licensed to sell alcoholic drinks

pubertal *adj* ▷ puberty

puberties *n* ▷ puberty

puberty *n (pl -ties)* beginning of sexual maturity > **pubertal** *adj*

pubic *adj* of the lower abdomen

public *adj* of or concerning the people as a whole ▶ *n (pl -s)* the community, people in general > **publicly** *adv*

publican *n (pl -s)* (BRIT, AUST & NZ) person who owns or runs a pub

publicans *n* ▷ publican

publication *n* ▷ publish

publications *n* ▷ publish

publicist *n (pl -s)* person, esp. a press agent or journalist, who publicizes something

publicists *n* ▷ publicist

publicities *n* ▷ publicity

publicity *n (pl -ties)* process or information used to arouse public attention

publicize *v (-zes, -zing, -zed)* bring to public attention

publicized *v* ▷ publicize

publicizes *v* ▷ publicize

publicizing *v* ▷ publicize

publicly *adv* ▷ public

publics *n* ▷ public

publish *v (-es, -ing, -ed)* produce and issue (printed matter) for sale > **publication** *n (pl -s)* > **publisher** *n (pl -s)*

published *v* ▷ publish

publisher *n* ▷ publish

publishers *n* ▷ publish

publishes *v* ▷ publish

publishing *v* ▷ publish

pubs *n* ▷ pub

puce *adj (pucer, pucest)* purplish-brown

pucer *adj* ▷ puce

pucest *adj* ▷ puce

puck¹ *n (pl -s)* small rubber disc used in ice hockey

puck² *n (pl -s)* mischievous or evil spirit > **puckish** *adj*

pucker *v (-s, -ing, -ed)* gather into wrinkles ▶ *n (pl -s)* wrinkle or crease

puckered *v* ▷ pucker

puckering *v* ▷ pucker

puckers *v, n* ▷ pucker

puckish *adj* ▷ puck²

pucks *n* ▷ puck¹, ²

pudding *n (pl -s)* dessert, esp. a cooked one served hot

puddings *n* ▷ pudding

puddle *n (pl -s)* small pool of water, esp. of rain

puddles n ▷ puddle

puerile adj silly and childish

puerperal [pew-er-per-al] adj concerning the period following childbirth

puff n (pl -s) (sound of) a short blast of breath, wind, etc. ▶ v (-s, -ing, -ed) blow or breathe in short quick draughts > **puffy** adj (-ffier, -ffiest)

puffball n (pl -s) ball-shaped fungus

puffballs n ▷ puffball

puffed v ▷ puff

puffier adj ▷ puff

puffiest adj ▷ puff

puffin n (pl -s) black-and-white sea bird with a brightly-coloured beak

puffins n ▷ puffin

puffing v ▷ puff

puffs n, v ▷ puff

puffy adj ▷ puff

pug n (pl -s) small snub-nosed dog

pugs n ▷ pug

pugilist [pew-jil-ist] n (pl -s) boxer > **pugilism** n (pl -s) > **pugilistic** adj

pugilism n ▷ pugilist

pugilisms n ▷ pugilist

pugilistic adj ▷ pugilist

pugilists n ▷ pugilist

pugnacious adj ready and eager to fight > **pugnacity** n (pl -ties)

pugnacities n ▷ pugnacious

pugnacity n ▷ pugnacious

puissance [pwee-sonce] n (pl -s) showjumping competition that tests a horse's ability to jump large obstacles

puissances n ▷ puissance

puke (Slang) v (-kes, -king, -ked) vomit ▶ n (pl -s) act of vomiting

puked v ▷ puke

pukes v, n ▷ puke

puking v ▷ puke

pulchritude n (pl -s) (Lit) beauty

pulchritudes n ▷ pulchritude

pull v (-s, -ing, -ed) exert force on (an object) to move it towards the source of the force ▶ n (pl -s) act of pulling

pulled v ▷ pull

pullet n (pl -s) young hen

pullets n ▷ pullet

pulley n (pl -s) wheel with a grooved rim in which a belt, chain, or piece of rope runs in order to lift weights by a downward pull

pulleys n ▷ pulley

pulling v ▷ pull

pullover n (pl -s) sweater that is pulled on over the head

pullovers n ▷ pullover

pulls v, n ▷ pull

pulmonary adj of the lungs

pulp n (pl -s) soft wet substance made from crushed or beaten matter ▶ v (-s, -ing, -ed) reduce to pulp

pulped v ▷ pulp

pulping v ▷ pulp

pulpit n (pl -s) raised platform for a preacher

pulpits n ▷ pulpit

pulps n, v ▷ pulp

pulsar n (pl -s) small dense star which emits regular bursts of radio waves

pulsars n ▷ pulsar

pulsate v ▷ pulse[1]

pulsated v ▷ pulse[1]

pulsates v ▷ pulse[1]

pulsating v ▷ pulse[1]

pulsation n ▷ pulse[1]

pulsations n ▷ pulse[1]

pulse[1] n (pl -s) regular beating of blood through the arteries at each heartbeat > **pulsate** v (-s, -ing, -ed) throb, quiver > **pulsation** n (pl -s)

pulse[2] n (-s) edible seed of a pod-bearing plant such as a bean or pea

pulses n ▷ pulse[1, 2]

pulverize v (-zes, -zing, -zed) reduce to fine pieces

pulverized v ▷ pulverize

pulverizes v ▷ pulverize

pulverizing v ▷ pulverize

puma n (pl -s) large American wild cat with a greyish-brown coat

pumas n ▷ puma

pumice [pumm-iss] n (pl -s) light porous stone used for scouring

pumices n ▷ pumice

pummel v (-s, -lling, -lled) strike repeatedly with or as if with the fists

pummelled v ▷ pummel

pummelling v ▷ pummel

pummels v ▷ pummel

pump[1] n (pl -s) machine used to force a liquid or gas to move in a particular direction ▶ v (-s, -ing, -ed) raise or drive with a pump

pump[2] n (pl -s) light flat-soled shoe

pumped v ▷ pump

pumping v ▷ pump

pumpkin n (pl -s) large round fruit with an orange rind, soft flesh, and many seeds

pumpkins n ▷ pumpkin

pumps n, v ▷ pump[1, 2]

pun n (pl -s) use of words to exploit double meanings for humorous effect ▶ v (-s, -nning, -nned) make puns

punch¹ v (-es, -ing, -ed) strike at with a clenched fist ▶ n (pl -es) blow with a clenched fist (*Informal*)

punch² n (pl -es) tool or machine for shaping, piercing, or engraving ▶ v (-es, -ing, -ed) pierce, cut, stamp, shape, or drive with a punch

punch³ n (pl -es) drink made from a mixture of wine, spirits, fruit, sugar, and spices
punched v ▷ punch¹, ²
punches v, n ▷ punch
punchier adj ▷ punchy
punchiest adj ▷ punchy
punching v ▷ punch¹, ²
punchy adj (-chier, -chiest) forceful
punctilious adj paying great attention to correctness in etiquette
punctual adj arriving or taking place at the correct time > **punctuality** n (pl -ties)
> **punctually** adv
punctualities n ▷ punctual
punctuality n ▷ punctual
punctually adv ▷ punctual
punctuate v (-tes, -ting, -ted) put punctuation marks in
punctuated v ▷ punctuate
punctuates v ▷ punctuate
punctuating v ▷ punctuate
punctuation n (pl -s) (use of) marks such as commas, colons, etc. in writing, to assist in making the sense clear
punctuations n ▷ punctuation
puncture n (pl -s) small hole made by a sharp object, esp. in a tyre ▶ v (-res, -ring, -red) pierce a hole in
punctured v ▷ puncture
punctures n, v ▷ puncture
puncturing v ▷ puncture
pundit n (pl -s) expert who speaks publicly on a subject
pundits n ▷ pundit
pungencies n ▷ pungent
pungency n ▷ pungent
pungent adj having a strong sharp bitter flavour > **pungency** n (pl -cies)
punier adj ▷ puny
puniest adj ▷ puny
punish v (-es, -ing, -ed) cause (someone) to suffer or undergo a penalty for some wrongdoing > **punishment** n (pl -s)
punished v ▷ punish
punishes v ▷ punish
punishing adj harsh or difficult ▶ v ▷ punish
punishment n ▷ punish
punishments n ▷ punish

punitive [pew-nit-tiv] adj relating to punishment
punk n (pl -s) anti-Establishment youth movement and style of rock music of the late 1970s
punks n ▷ punk
punned v ▷ pun
punnet n (pl -s) small basket for fruit
punnets n ▷ punnet
punning v ▷ pun
puns n, v ▷ pun
punt¹ n (pl -s) open flat-bottomed boat propelled by a pole ▶ v (-s, -ing, -ed) travel in a punt
punt² (SPORT) n (pl -s) kick of a ball before it touches the ground when dropped from the hands ▶ v (-s, -ing, -ed) kick (a ball) in this way
punt³ n (pl -s) former monetary unit of the Irish Republic
punted v ▷ punt
punter n (pl -s) person who bets
punters n ▷ punter
punting v ▷ punt
punts n, v ▷ punt¹, ², ³
puny adj (-nier, -niest) small and feeble
pup n (pl -s) young of certain animals, such as dogs and seals
pupa n (pl -pae, -pas) insect at the stage of development between a larva and an adult
pupae n ▷ pupa
pupas n ▷ pupa
pupil¹ n (pl -s) person who is taught by a teacher
pupil² n (pl -s) round dark opening in the centre of the eye
pupils n ▷ pupil¹, ²
puppet n (pl -s) small doll or figure moved by strings or by the operator's hand > **puppeteer** n (pl -s)
puppeteer n ▷ puppet
puppeteers n ▷ puppet
puppets n ▷ puppet
puppies n ▷ puppy
puppy n (pl -ppies) young dog
pups n ▷ pup
purchase v (-ses, -sing, -sed) obtain by payment ▶ n (pl -s) thing that is bought
> **purchaser** n (pl -s)
purchased v ▷ purchase
purchaser n ▷ purchase
purchasers n ▷ purchase
purchases v, n ▷ purchase
purchasing v ▷ purchase
purdah n (pl -s) Muslim and Hindu custom of keeping women in seclusion, with clothing

that conceals them completely when they go out
purdahs n ▷ purdah

pure adj (-r, -st) unmixed, untainted > **purely** adv > **purity** n (pl -ies)
purely adv ▷ pure

purée [pure-ray] n (pl -s) pulp of cooked food ▶ v (-s, -réeing, -réed) make into a purée
puréed v ▷ purée
puréeing v ▷ purée
purées n, v ▷ purée

purer adj ▷ pure
purest adj ▷ pure
purgatorial adj ▷ purgatory
purgatories n ▷ purgatory
purgatory n (pl -ries) place or state of temporary suffering > **purgatorial** adj

purge v (-ges, -ging, -ged) rid (a thing or place) of (unwanted things or people) ▶ n (pl -s) purging
purgative n, adj (medicine) designed to cause defecation
purgatives n ▷ purgative
purged v ▷ purge
purges v, n ▷ purge
purging v ▷ purge
purification n ▷ purify
purifications n ▷ purify
purified v ▷ purify
purifies v ▷ purify

purify v (-fies, -fying, -fied) make or become pure > **purification** n (pl -s)
purifying v ▷ purify

purist n (pl -s) person concerned with strict obedience to the traditions of a subject
purists n ▷ purist

puritan n (pl -s) person with strict moral and religious principles > **puritanical** adj > **puritanism** n (pl -s)
puritanical adj ▷ puritan
puritanism n ▷ puritan
puritanisms n ▷ puritan
puritans n ▷ puritan
purities n ▷ pure
purity n ▷ pure

purl n (pl -s) stitch made by knitting a plain stitch backwards ▶ v (-s, -ing, -ed) knit in purl
purled v ▷ purl

purlieus [per-lyooz] pl n (Lit) outskirts
purling v ▷ purl

purloin v (-s, -ing, -ed) steal
purloined v ▷ purloin
purloining v ▷ purloin
purloins v ▷ purloin
purls n, v ▷ purl

purple adj, n (pl -s) (of) a colour between red and blue
purples n ▷ purple

purport v (-s, -ing, -ed) claim (to be or do something) ▶ n (pl -s) apparent meaning, significance
purported v ▷ purport
purporting v ▷ purport
purports v, n ▷ purport

purpose n (pl -s) reason for which something is done or exists
purposely adv intentionally
purposes n ▷ purpose

purr v (-s, -ing, -ed) (of cats) make low vibrant sound, usu. when pleased ▶ n (pl -s) this sound
purred v ▷ purr
purring v ▷ purr
purrs v, n ▷ purr

purse n (pl -s) small bag for money (US & NZ) ▶ v (-ses, -sing, -sed) draw (one's lips) together into a small round shape
pursed v ▷ purse

purser n (pl -s) ship's officer who keeps the accounts
pursers n ▷ purser
purses n, v ▷ purse
pursing v ▷ purse

pursue v (-sues, -suing, -sued) chase > **pursuer** n (pl -s)
pursued v ▷ pursue
pursuer n ▷ pursue
pursuers n ▷ pursue
pursues v ▷ pursue
pursuing v ▷ pursue

pursuit n (pl -s) pursuing
pursuits n ▷ pursuit

purulent [pure-yoo-lent] adj of or containing pus

purvey v (-s, -ing, -ed) supply (provisions) > **purveyor** n (pl -s)
purveyed v ▷ purvey
purveying v ▷ purvey
purveyor n ▷ purvey
purveyors n ▷ purvey
purveys v ▷ purvey

purview n (pl -s) scope or range of activity or outlook
purviews n ▷ purview

pus n (pl -es) yellowish matter produced by infected tissue
puses n ▷ pus

push v (-es, -ing, -ed) move or try to move by steady force (Informal) ▶ n (pl -es) act of pushing

pushed v ▷ push
pusher n (pl -s) person who sells illegal drugs
  pushers n ▷ pusher
pushes v, n ▷ push
  pushier adj ▷ pushy
  pushiest adj ▷ pushy
  pushing v ▷ push
pushy adj (-shier, -shiest) too assertive or ambitious
pushchair n (pl -s) (BRIT) folding chair on wheels for a baby
  pushchairs n ▷ pushchair
pusillanimous adj timid and cowardly
  > **pusillanimity** n (pl -ies)
  pusillanimities n ▷ pusillanimous
  pusillanimity n ▷ pusillanimous
puss, pussy n (pl -es, -ies) (Informal) cat
  pusses n ▷ puss
  pussies n ▷ puss
pussyfoot v (-s, -ing, -ed) (Informal) behave too cautiously
  pussyfooted v ▷ pussyfoot
  pussyfooting v ▷ pussyfoot
  pussyfoots v ▷ pussyfoot
pustule n (pl -s) pimple containing pus
  pustules n ▷ pustule
put v (puts, putting, put) cause to be (in a position, state, or place) ▶ n (pl -s) throw in putting the shot
putative adj reputed, supposed
  putrefied v ▷ putrify
  putrefies v ▷ putrify
putrefy v (-fies, -fying, -fied) rot and produce an offensive smell > **putrefaction** n (pl -s)
  putrefaction n ▷ putrefy
  putrefactions n ▷ putrefy
  putrefying v ▷ putrefy
putrescent adj rotting
putrid adj rotten and foul-smelling
  puts v, n ▷ put
putsch n (pl -es) sudden violent attempt to remove a government from power
  putsches n ▷ putsch
putt (GOLF) n (pl -s) stroke on the putting green to roll the ball into or near the hole ▶ v (-s, -ing, -ed) strike (the ball) in this way
  putted n, v ▷ putt
putter n (pl -s) golf club for putting
  putters n ▷ putter

putties n ▷ putty
putting v ▷ put putt
putts v, n ▷ putt
putty n (pl -ies) adhesive used to fix glass into frames and fill cracks in woodwork
puzzle v (-les, -ling, -led) perplex and confuse or be perplexed or confused ▶ n (pl -s) problem that cannot be easily solved > **puzzlement** n (pl -s) > **puzzling** adj
  puzzled v ▷ puzzle
  puzzlement n ▷ puzzle
  puzzlements n ▷ puzzle
  puzzles v, n ▷ puzzle
puzzling v, adj ▷ puzzle
  pygmies n ▷ pygmy
pygmy n (pl -ies) something that is a very small example of its type ▶ adj (p-) very small
pyjamas pl n loose-fitting trousers and top worn in bed
pylon n (pl -s) steel tower-like structure supporting electrical cables
  pylons n ▷ pylon
pyramid n (pl -s) solid figure with a flat base and triangular sides sloping upwards to a point > **pyramidal** adj
  pyramidal adj ▷ pyramid
  pyramids n ▷ pyramid
pyre n (pl -s) pile of wood for burning a corpse on
  pyres n ▷ pyre
pyromania n (pl -s) uncontrollable urge to set things on fire > **pyromaniac** n (pl -s)
  pyromanias n ▷ pyromania
  pyromaniac n ▷ pyromania
  pyromaniacs n ▷ pyromania
pyrotechnics n art of making fireworks > **pyrotechnic** adj
  pyrotechnic adj ▷ pyrotechnics
python n (pl -s) large nonpoisonous snake that crushes its prey
  pythons n ▷ python

> **pyx** n (**pyxes**). A **pyx** is a container used for testing the weight of coins. This word can also be spelt **pix**. It's a great word to know as it earns a good score and doesn't use any vowels very helpful if you have a difficult rack. Pyx scores 15 points.

Qq

With a value of 10 points, Q is one of the best tiles to have on your rack. It can, however, be a difficult letter to use, especially if you don't have a U to play it with. It's therefore a good idea to remember the short words beginning with Q that don't need a U. This is easy, as there's only one two-letter word starting with Q: **qi** (11 points). There are three three-letter words, only one of which needs a U: **qua** (12). The other two are **qat** and **qis** (12 each). If you do have a U, remember **quiz** (22), which is a very useful word. If you have a blank tile for the second Z, you may be able to form its plural or verb inflections: **quizzes** (24), **quizzed** (25) and **quizzing** (26). This is especially worth remembering in case someone else plays quiz. Don't forget **quartz** (24) either.

qat n (**qats**). Qat is a shrub that grows in Africa and Arabia. This is a great word as it combines Q with two of the most common letters in the game, and thus is very handy if there isn't a U on your rack or the board. Qat scores 12 points.

qi n (**qis**). In Chinese medicine, qi is vital energy believed to circulate in the body. This is an exceptionally useful word, as it's the only two-letter word containing Q, and doesn't contain a U. The plural is one of only three three-letter words that begin with Q. As I is one of the more common tiles on the board, it's highly likely that you will be able to play qi if you have a Q. Qi scores 11 points.

qua prep. Qua means in the capacity of. This is the only three-letter word beginning with Q that needs a U, and is useful when you have a U, or there is a U on the board, but don't have any promising tiles to go with it. Qua scores 12 points.

quack¹ v (**-s, -ing, -ed**) (of a duck) utter a harsh guttural sound ▶ n (pl -s) sound made by a duck

quack² n (pl -s) unqualified person who claims medical knowledge
    quacked v ▷ quack¹
    quacking v ▷ quack¹
    quacks v ▷ quack¹ ▶ n ▷ quack¹, ²

quad n (pl -s) ▷ quadrangle ▶ adj ▷ quadraphonic

quadrangle n (pl -s) (also **quad**) rectangular courtyard with buildings on all four sides > **quadrangular** adj
    quadrangles n ▷ quadrangle
    quadrangular adj ▷ quadrangle

quadrant n (pl -s) quarter of a circle
    quadrants n ▷ quadrant

quadraphonic adj (also **quad**) using four independent channels to reproduce or record sound

quadratic (MATHS) n (pl -s) equation in which the variable is raised to the power of two, but nowhere raised to a higher power ▶ adj of the second power
    quadratics n ▷ quadratic

quadrennial adj occurring every four years

quadrilateral adj having four sides ▶ n (pl -s) polygon with four sides
    quadrilaterals n ▷ quadrilateral

quadrille n (pl -s) square dance for four couples
    quadrilles n ▷ quadrille

quadriplegia n (pl -s) paralysis of all four limbs
    quadriplegias n ▷ quadriplegia

quadruped [kwod-roo-ped] n (pl -s) any animal with four legs
    quadrupeds n ▷ quadruped

quadruple v (**-les, -ling, -led**) multiply by four ▶ adj four times as much or as many
    quadrupled v ▷ quadruple
    quadruples v ▷ quadruple

quadruplet n (pl -s) one of four offspring born

at one birth
quadruplets *n* ▷ quadruplet
quadrupling *v* ▷ quadruple
quads *n* ▷ quad
quaff [kwoff] *v* (-s, -ing, -ed) drink heartily or in one draught
quaffed *v* ▷ quaff
quaffing *v* ▷ quaff
quaffs *v* ▷ quaff
quagmire [kwog-mire] *n* (*pl* -s) soft wet area of land
quagmires *n* ▷ quagmire
quail[1] *n* (*pl* -s) small game bird of the partridge family
quail[2] *v* (-s, -ing, -ed) shrink back with fear
quailed *v* ▷ quail
quailing *v* ▷ quail
quails *n* ▷ quail[1] ▸ *v* ▷ quail[2]
quaint *adj* (-er, -est) attractively unusual, esp. in an old-fashioned style ▷ **quaintly** *adv*
quainter *adj* ▷ quaint
quaintest *adj* ▷ quaint
quaintly *adv* ▷ quaint
quake *v* (-kes, -king, -ked) shake or tremble with or as if with fear ▸ *n* (*pl* -s) (*Informal*) earthquake
quaked *v*, *n* ▷ quake
quakes *v* ▷ quake
quaking *v* ▷ quake
qualification *n* (*pl* -s) official record of achievement in a course or examination
qualifications *n* ▷ qualification
qualified *v*, *adj* ▷ qualify
qualifies *v* ▷ qualify
qualify *v* (-fies, -fying, -fied) provide or be provided with the abilities necessary for a task, office, or duty ▷ **qualified** *adj*
qualifying *v* ▷ qualify
qualitative *adj* of or relating to quality
qualities *n* ▷ quality
quality *n* (*pl* -ties) degree or standard of excellence ▸ *adj* excellent or superior
qualm [kwahm] *n* (*pl* -s) pang of conscience
qualms *n* ▷ qualm
quandaries *n* ▷ quandary
quandary *n* (*pl* -ries) difficult situation or dilemma
quandong [kwon-dong] *n* (*pl* -s) small Australian tree with edible fruit and nuts used in preserves
quandongs *n* ▷ quandong
quango *n* (*pl* -s) (CHIEFLY BRIT) quasi-autonomous nongovernmental organization: any partly independent official body set up by a government

quangos *n* ▷ quango
quanta *n* ▷ quantum
quantifiable *adj* ▷ quantify
quantification *n* ▷ quantify
quantifications *n* ▷ quantify
quantified *v* ▷ quantify
quantifies *v* ▷ quantify
quantify *v* (-fies, -fying, -fied) discover or express the quantity of ▷ **quantifiable** *adj* ▷ **quantification** *n* (*pl* -s)
quantifying *v* ▷ quantify
quantitative *adj* of or relating to quantity
quantities *n* ▷ quantity
quantity *n* (*pl* -ties) specified or definite amount or number
quantum *n* (*pl* -ta) desired or required amount, esp. a very small one
quarantine *n* (*pl* -s) period of isolation of people or animals to prevent the spread of disease ▸ *v* (-nes, -ning, -ned) isolate in or as if in quarantine
quarantined *v* ▷ quarantine
quarantines *n*, *v* ▷ quarantine
quarantining *v* ▷ quarantine
quark *n* (*pl* -s) (PHYSICS) subatomic particle thought to be the fundamental unit of matter
quarks *n* ▷ quark
quarrel *n* (*pl* -s) angry disagreement ▸ *v* (-s, -lling, -lled) have a disagreement or dispute ▷ **quarrelsome** *adj*
quarrelled *v* ▷ quarrel
quarrelling *v* ▷ quarrel
quarrels *n*, *v* ▷ quarrel
quarrelsome *adj* ▷ quarrel
quarried *v* ▷ quarry[1]
quarries *n* ▷ quarry[1, 2] ▸ *v* ▷ quarry[1]
quarry[1] *n* (*pl* -rries) place where stone is dug from the surface of the earth ▸ *v* (-rries, -rrying, -rried) extract (stone) from a quarry
quarry[2] *n* (*pl* -rries) person or animal that is being hunted
quart *n* (*pl* -s) unit of liquid measure equal to two pints (1.136 litres)
quarter *n* (*pl* -s) one of four equal parts of something ▸ *v* (-s, -ing, -ed) divide into four equal parts
quarterdeck *n* (*pl* -s) (NAUT) rear part of the upper deck of a ship
quarterdecks *n* ▷ quarterdeck
quartered *v* ▷ quarter
quarterfinal *n* (*pl* -s) round before the semifinal in a competition
quarterfinals *n* ▷ quarterfinal
quartering *v* ▷ quarter

quarterlies n ▷ quarterly

quarterly adj occurring, due, or issued at intervals of three months ▶ n (pl -lies) magazine issued every three months ▶ adv once every three months

quartermaster n (pl -s) military officer responsible for accommodation, food, and equipment

quartermasters n ▷ quartermaster

quarters n, v ▷ quarter

quartet n (pl -s) group of four performers

quartets n ▷ quartet

quarto n (pl -s) book size in which the sheets are folded into four leaves

quarto n ▷ quarto

quarts n ▷ quart

quartz n (pl -es) hard glossy mineral

quartzes n ▷ quartz

quasar [kway-zar] n (pl -s) extremely distant starlike object that emits powerful radio waves

quasars n ▷ quasar

quash v (-shes, -shing, -shed) annul or make void

quashed v ▷ quash

quashes v ▷ quash

quashing v ▷ quash

quatrain n (pl -s) stanza or poem of four lines

quatrains n ▷ quatrain

quaver v (-s, -ing, -ed) (of a voice) quiver or tremble ▶ n (pl -s) (MUSIC) note half the length of a crotchet

quavered v ▷ quaver

quavering v ▷ quaver

quavers v, n ▷ quaver

quay [kee] n (pl -s) wharf built parallel to the shore

quays n ▷ quay

queasier adj ▷ queasy

queasiest adj ▷ queasy

queasiness n ▷ queasy

queasinesses n ▷ queasy

queasy adj (-sier, -siest) having the feeling that one is about to vomit ▷ **queasiness** n (pl -es)

queen n (pl -s) female sovereign who is the official ruler or head of state ▷ **queenly** adj

queenly adj ▷ queen

queens n ▷ queen

queer adj (-er, -est) not normal or usual

queerer adj ▷ queer

queerest adj ▷ queer

quell v (-s, -ing, -ed) suppress

quelled v ▷ quell

quelling v ▷ quell

quells v ▷ quell

quench v (-es, -ing, -ed) satisfy (one's thirst)

quenched v ▷ quench

quenches v ▷ quench

quenching v ▷ quench

queried v ▷ query

queries n, v ▷ query

quern n (pl -s) stone hand mill for grinding corn

querns n ▷ quern

querulous [kwer-yoo-luss] adj complaining or whining ▷ **querulously** adv

querulously adv ▷ querulous

query n (pl -ries) question, esp. one raising doubt ▶ v (-ries, -rying, -ried) express uncertainty, doubt, or an objection concerning (something)

querying v ▷ query

quest n (pl -s) long and difficult search ▶ v (-s, -ing, -ed) (foll. by for or after) go in search of

quested v ▷ quest

questing v ▷ quest

question n (pl -s) form of words addressed to a person in order to obtain an answer ▶ v (-s, -ing, -ed) put a question or questions to (a person)

questionable adj of disputable value or authority ▷ **questionably** adv

questionably adv ▷ questionable

questioned v ▷ question

questioning v ▷ question

questionnaire n (pl -s) set of questions on a form, used to collect information from people

questionnaires n ▷ questionnaire

questions n, v ▷ question

quests n, v ▷ quest

> **quetzal** or **quezal** n (**quetzals, quezales, quezals**). The quetzal is a crested bird of Central and South America. This is a great word if you can get the tiles to play quetzal or quezals, so it's well worth remembering both spellings and the three plural forms. If you can use all your letters to play quetzal or quezals, you'll earn a bonus of 50 points. Quetzal scores 25 points.

queue n (pl -s) line of people or vehicles waiting for something ▶ v (**queues, queuing** or **queueing, queued**) (often foll. by up) form or remain in a line while waiting

queued v ▷ queue

queueing v ▷ queue

queues n, v ▷ queue

queuing v ▷ queue

quibble v (-les, -ling, -led) make trivial

objections ▶ *n* (*pl* -s) trivial objection

quibbled *v* ▷ quibble

quibbles *v*, *n* ▷ quibble

quibbling *v* ▷ quibble

quiche [keesh] *n* (*pl* -s) savoury flan with an egg custard filling to which vegetables etc. are added

quiches *n* ▷ quiche

quick *adj* (-er, -est) speedy, fast ▶ *n* (*pl* -s) area of sensitive flesh under a nail ▶ *adv* (*Informal*) in a rapid manner > **quickly** *adv*

quicken *v* (-s, -ing, -ed) make or become faster

quickened *v* ▷ quicken

quickening *v* ▷ quicken

quickens *v* ▷ quicken

quicker *adj* ▷ quick

quickest *adj* ▷ quick

quicklime *n* (*pl* -s) white solid used in the manufacture of glass and steel

quicklimes *n* ▷ quicklime

quickly *adv* ▷ quick

quicks *n* ▷ quick

quicksand *n* (*pl* -s) deep mass of loose wet sand that sucks anything on top of it into it

quicksands *n* ▷ quicksand

quicksilver *n* (*pl* -s) mercury

quicksilvers *n* ▷ quicksilver

quickstep *n* (*pl* -s) fast modern ballroom dance

quicksteps *n* ▷ quickstep

quid *n* (*pl* quid, -s) (BRIT) (*Slang*) pound (sterling)

quids *n* ▷ quid

quiescence *n* ▷ quiescent

quiescences *n* ▷ quiescent

quiescent [kwee-ess-ent] *adj* quiet, inactive, or dormant > **quiescence** *n* (*pl* -s)

quiet *adj* (-er, -est) with little noise ▶ *n* (*pl* -s) quietness ▶ *v* (-s, -ing, -ed) make or become quiet > **quietly** *adv* > **quietness** *n* (*pl* -es)

quieted *v* ▷ quiet

quieten *v* (-s, -ing, -ed) (*often foll. by* down) make or become quiet

quieter *adj* ▷ quiet

quietest *adj* ▷ quiet

quieting *v* ▷ quiet

quietism *n* (*pl* -s) passivity and calmness of mind towards external events

quietisms *n* ▷ quietism

quietly *adv* ▷ quiet

quietness *n* ▷ quiet

quietnesses *n* ▷ quiet

quiets *v*, *n* ▷ quiet

quietude *n* (-s) quietness, peace, or tranquillity

quietudes *n* ▷ quietude

quiff *n* (*pl* -s) tuft of hair brushed up above the forehead

quiffs *n* ▷ quiff

quill *n* (*pl* -s) pen made from the feather of a bird's wing or tail

quills *n* ▷ quill

quilt *n* (*pl* -s) padded covering for a bed

quilted *adj* consisting of two layers of fabric with a layer of soft material between them

quilts *n* ▷ quilt

quince *n* (*pl* -s) acid-tasting pear-shaped fruit

quinces *n* ▷ quince

quinine *n* (*pl* -s) bitter drug used as a tonic and formerly to treat malaria

quinines *n* ▷ quinine

quinquennial *adj* occurring every five years

quins *n* ▷ quin

quinsies *n* ▷ quinsy

quinsy *n* (*pl* -sies) inflammation of the throat or tonsils

quintessence *n* (*pl* -s) most perfect representation of a quality or state > **quintessential** *adj*

quintessences *n* ▷ quintessence

quintessential *adj* ▷ quintessence

quintet *n* (*pl* -s) group of five performers

quintets *n* ▷ quintet

quintuplet *n* (*pl* -s) one of five offspring born at one birth

quintuplets *n* ▷ quintuplet

> **quinze** *n* (**quinzes**). Quinze is a card game. This is a high-scoring word, and if you can use all of your tiles to form the plural, you'll get a 50-points bonus. Quinze scores 24 points.

quip *n* (*pl* -s) witty saying ▶ *v* (-s, -pping, -pped) make a quip

quipped *v* ▷ quip

quipping *v* ▷ quip

quips *n*, *v* ▷ quip

quire *n* (*pl* -s) set of 24 or 25 sheets of paper

quires *n* ▷ quire

quirk *n* (*pl* -s) peculiarity of character > **quirky** *adj* (-kier, -kiest)

quirks *n* ▷ quirk

quirky *adj* ▷ quirk

quisling *n* (*pl* -s) traitor who aids an occupying enemy force

quislings *n* ▷ quisling

quit *v* (quits, quitting, quit) stop (doing something)

quite *adv* somewhat ▶ *interj* expression of agreement

quits *adj* (*Informal*) on an equal footing ▶ *v* ▷ quit

quitter *n* (*pl* -s) person who lacks perseverance

quitters n ▷ quitter
quitting v ▷ quit
quiver[1] v (-s, -ing, -ed) shake with a tremulous movement ▸ n (pl -s) shaking or trembling
quiver[2] n (pl -s) case for arrows
quivered v ▷ quiver[1]
quivering v ▷ quiver[1]
quivers v ▷ quiver[1] ▸ n ▷ quiver[1, 2]

> **quixote** n (**quixotes**). A quixote is an impractically idealistic person. This is a high-scoring word; if you have all the letters to play it, and can place them on the board, you'll score a 50-point bonus for using all of your tiles. Quixote scores 23 points.

quixotic [kwik-**sot**-ik] adj romantic and unrealistic > **quixotically** adv
quixotically adv ▷ quixotic
quiz n (pl -**zzes**) entertainment in which the knowledge of the players is tested by a series of questions ▸ v (-**zzes**, -**zzing**, -**zzed**) investigate by close questioning
quizzed v ▷ quiz
quizzes n, v ▷ quiz
quizzical adj questioning and mocking > **quizzically** adv
quizzically adv ▷ quizzical
quizzing v ▷ quiz
quod n (pl -s) (BRIT) (Slang) jail
quods n ▷ quod
quoit n (pl -s) large ring used in the game of

quoits ▸ pl game in which quoits are tossed at a stake in the ground in attempts to encircle it
quoits n ▷ quoit
quokka n (pl -s) small Australian wallaby
quokkas n ▷ quokka
quorum n (pl -s) minimum number of people required to be present at a meeting before any transactions can take place
quorums n ▷ quorum
quota n (pl -s) share that is due from, due to, or allocated to a group or person
quotable adj ▷ quote
quotas n ▷ quota
quotation n (pl -s) written or spoken passage repeated exactly in a later work, speech, or conversation
quotations n ▷ quotation
quote v (-**tes**, -**ting**, -**ted**) repeat (words) exactly from (an earlier work, speech, or conversation) ▸ n (pl -s) (Informal) quotation > **quotable** adj
quoted v ▷ quote
quotes v, n ▷ quote
quoth v (Obs) said
quotidian adj daily
quotient n (pl -s) result of the division of one number or quantity by another
quotients n ▷ quotient
quoting v ▷ quote

Rr

R is one of the most common consonants in Scrabble, along with N and T. Despite this, however, there is only one two-letter word beginning with R: **re** (2 points). This is worth remembering, as you won't need to waste time trying to think of others. There are some good three-letter words with R, however, some of which are quite unusual: **raj, rax, rex** (10 each), **rez** and **riz** (12 each). Also, don't forget common words like **raw, ray** and **row** (6 each).

rabbi [rab-bye] *n* (*pl* -s) Jewish spiritual leader > **rabbinical** *adj*
  rabbinical *adj* ▷ rabbi
  rabbis *n* ▷ rabbi
rabbit *n* (*pl* -s) small burrowing mammal with long ears
  rabbits *n* ▷ rabbit
rabble *n* (*pl* -s) disorderly crowd of noisy people
  rabbles *n* ▷ rabble
rabid *adj* (-er, -est) fanatical > **rabidly** *adv*
  rabider *adj* ▷ rabid
  rabidest *adj* ▷ rabid
  rabidly *adv* ▷ rabid
rabies [ray-beez] *n* usu. fatal viral disease transmitted by dogs and certain other animals
raccoon *n* (*pl* -s) small N American mammal with a long striped tail
  raccoons *n* ▷ raccoon
race[1] *n* (*pl* -s) contest of speed ▶ *pl* meeting for horse racing ▶ *v* (-ces, -cing, -ced) compete with in a race > **racer** *n* (*pl* -s) > **racecourse** *n* (*pl* -s) > **racehorse** *n* (*pl* -s) > **racetrack** *n* (*pl* -s)
race[2] *n* (*pl* -s) group of people of common ancestry with distinguishing physical features, such as skin colour > **racial** *adj*
raced *n, v* ▷ race[1]
  racecourse *n* ▷ race[1]
  racecourses *n* ▷ race[1]
  raced *n, v* ▷ race[1]
racehorse *n* ▷ race[1]
  racehorses *n* ▷ race[1]
raceme [rass-eem] *n* (*pl* -s) cluster of flowers along a central stem, as in the foxglove
  racemes *n* ▷ raceme
racer *n* ▷ race[1]
  racers *n* ▷ race[1]
races *n* ▷ race[1, 2] ▶ *v* ▷ race[1]

racetrack *n* ▷ race[1]
  racetracks *n* ▷ race[1]
racial *adj* ▷ race[2]
racialism *n* ▷ racism
  racialisms *adj, n* ▷ racism
racialist *n* ▷ racism
  racialists *n* ▷ racism
racier *adj* ▷ racy
raciest *adj* ▷ racy
racing *v* ▷ race
racism, racialism *n* (*pl* -s) hostile attitude or behaviour to members of other races, based on a belief in the innate superiority of one's own race > **racist, racialist** *adj, n* (*pl* -s)
  racisms *n* ▷ racism
racist *n* ▷ racism
  racists *n* ▷ racism
rack *n* (*pl* -s) framework for holding particular articles, such as coats or luggage (HIST) ▶ *v* (-s, -ing, -ed) cause great suffering to
  racked *v* ▷ rack
racket[1] *n* (*pl* -s) noisy disturbance
racket[2], **racquet** *n* (-s) bat with strings stretched in an oval frame, used in tennis etc.
racketeer *n* (*pl* -s) person making illegal profits
  racketeers *n* ▷ racketeer
rackets *n* ball game played in a paved walled court ▶ *n* ▷ racket[1, 2]
  racking *v* ▷ rack
  racks *n, v* ▷ rack
raconteur [rak-on-tur] *n* (*pl* -s) skilled storyteller
  raconteurs *n* ▷ raconteur
  racquet *n* ▷ racket[2]
  racquets *n* ▷ racket[2]
racy *adj* (-cier, -ciest) slightly shocking
radar *n* (*pl* -s) device for tracking distant objects by bouncing high-frequency radio

pulses off them

radars n ▷ radar

radial adj spreading out from a common central point

radiance n ▷ radiant

radiances n ▷ radiant

radiant adj looking happy ▷ **radiance** n (-s)

radiate v (-tes, -ting, -ted) spread out from a centre

radiated v ▷ radiate

radiates v ▷ radiate

radiating v ▷ radiate

radiation n (pl -s) transmission of energy from one body to another

radiations n ▷ radiation

radiator n (-s) (BRIT) arrangement of pipes containing hot water or steam to heat a room

radiators n ▷ radiator

radical adj fundamental ▶ n (pl -s) person advocating fundamental (political) change ▷ **radically** adv ▷ **radicalism** n (-s)

radicalism n ▷ radical

radicalisms n ▷ radical

radically adv ▷ radical

radicals n ▷ radical

radicle n (pl -s) small or developing root

radicles n ▷ radicle

radii n ▷ radius

radio n (pl -s) use of electromagnetic waves for broadcasting, communication, etc. ▶ v (-s, -ing, -ed) transmit (a message) by radio

radioactive adj emitting radiation as a result of nuclear decay ▷ **radioactivity** n (pl -ies)

radioactivities n ▷ radioactive

radioactivity n ▷ radioactive

radioed v ▷ radio

radiographer n ▷ radiography

radiographers n ▷ radiography

radiographies n ▷ radiography

radiography [ray-dee-og-ra-fee] n (pl -phies) production of an image on a film or plate by radiation ▷ **radiographer** n (pl -s)

radioing v ▷ radio

radiologies n ▷ radiology

radiologist n ▷ radiology

radiologists n ▷ radiology

radiology [ray-dee-ol-a-jee] n (pl -gies) science of using x-rays in medicine ▷ **radiologist** n (pl -s)

radios n, v ▷ radio

radiotherapies n ▷ radiotherapy

radiotherapist n ▷ radiotherapy

radiotherapists n ▷ radiotherapy

radiotherapy n (pl -pies) treatment of disease,

esp. cancer, by radiation ▷ **radiotherapist** n (pl -s)

radish n (pl -es) small hot-flavoured root vegetable eaten raw in salads

radishes n ▷ radish

radium n (pl -s) (CHEM) radioactive metallic element

radiums n ▷ radium

radius n (pl radii, radiuses) (length of) a straight line from the centre to the circumference of a circle

radiuses n ▷ radius

radon [ray-don] n (pl -s) (CHEM) radioactive gaseous element

radons n ▷ radon

raffia n (pl -s) prepared palm fibre for weaving mats etc.

raffias n ▷ raffia

raffish adj slightly disreputable

raffle n (pl -s) lottery with goods as prizes ▶ v (-les, -ling, -led) offer as a prize in a raffle

raffled v ▷ raffle

raffles n, v ▷ raffle

raffling v ▷ raffle

raft n (pl -s) floating platform of logs, etc.

rafter n (pl -s) one of the main beams of a roof

rafters n ▷ rafter

raftings n ▷ raft

rafts n ▷ raft

rag¹ n (pl -s) fragment of cloth ▶ pl tattered clothing

rag² (BRIT) v (-s, -gging, -gged) tease ▶ adj, n (pl -s) (of) events organized by students to raise money for charities

rage n (pl -s) violent anger or passion ▶ v (-ges, -ging, -ged) speak or act with fury

raged v ▷ rage

rages n, v ▷ rage

ragamuffin n (pl -s) ragged dirty child

ragamuffins n ▷ ragamuffin

ragged [rag-gid] adj dressed in shabby or torn clothes ▶ v ▷ rag²

ragging v ▷ rag²

raging v ▷ rage

raglan adj (of a sleeve) joined to a garment by diagonal seams from the neck to the underarm

ragout [rag-goo] n (pl -s) richly seasoned stew of meat and vegetables

ragouts n ▷ ragout

rags n, v ▷ rag¹,²

ragtime n (pl -s) style of jazz piano music

ragtimes n ▷ ragtime

raid n (pl -s) sudden surprise attack or search ▶ v (-s, -ing, -ed) make a raid on ▷ **raider** n

(*pl* -s)
raided *v* ▷ raid
raider *n* ▷ raid
raiders *n* ▷ raid
raiding *v* ▷ raid
raidings *n* ▷ raid
raids *n, v* ▷ raid
rail[1] *n* (*pl* -s) horizontal bar, esp. as part of a fence or track
rail[2] *v* (-s, -ing, -ed) (foll. by **at** or **against**) complain bitterly or loudly
rail[3] *n* (*pl* -s) small marsh bird
railed *v* ▷ rail[2]
railing *n* (*pl* -s) fence made of rails supported by posts ▶ *v* ▷ rail[2]
railings *n* ▷ railing
railleries *n* ▷ raillery
raillery *n* (*pl* -ies) teasing or joking
rails *n* ▷ rail[1, 2, 3] *v* ▷ rail[2]
railway *n* (*pl* -s) track of iron rails on which trains run
railways *n* ▷ railway
raiment *n* (*pl* -s) (Obs) clothing
raiments *n* ▷ raiment
rain *n* (*pl* -s) water falling in drops from the clouds ▶ *v* (-s, -ing, -ed) fall or pour down as rain > **rainy** *adj* (-nier, -niest)
rainbow *n* (*pl* -s) arch of colours in the sky
rainbows *n* ▷ rainbow
raincoat *n* (*pl* -s) water-resistant overcoat
raincoats *n* ▷ raincoat
rained *v* ▷ rain
rainier *adj* ▷ rainy
rainiest *adj* ▷ rainy
rainfall *n* (*pl* -s) amount of rain
rainfalls *n* ▷ rainfall
rainforest *n* (*pl* -s) dense forest in tropical and temperate areas
rainforests *n* ▷ rainforest
raining *v* ▷ rain
rains *n, v* ▷ rain
rainy *adj* ▷ rain
raise *v* (-ses, -sing, -sed) lift up
raised *v* ▷ raise
raises *v* ▷ raise
raisin *n* (*pl* -s) dried grape
raising *v* ▷ raise
raisins *n* ▷ raisin

> **raj** *n* (rajes). Raj is an Indian word for government. This can be very useful when there isn't much space. If you can't play raj, remember it's just **jar** backwards, you might be able to fit that in. Raj scores 10 points.

raja, rajah *n* (*pl* -s) (HIST) Indian prince or ruler

rajah *n* ▷ raja
rajahs *n* ▷ raja
rajas *n* ▷ raja
rake[1] *n* (*pl* -s) tool with a long handle and a crosspiece with teeth, used for smoothing earth or gathering leaves, hay, etc. ▶ *v* (-kes, -king, -ked) gather or smooth with a rake
rake[2] *n* (*pl* -s) dissolute or immoral man
raked *v* ▷ rake[1]
rakes *n, v* ▷ rake[1, 2] ▶ *v* ▷ rake[1]
raking *v* ▷ rake[1]
rakish *adj* dashing or jaunty
rallied *v* ▷ rally
rallies *n, v* ▷ rally
rally *n* (*pl* -ies) large gathering of people for a meeting ▶ *v* (-ies, -ying, -ied) bring or come together after dispersal or for a common cause
rallying *v* ▷ rally
ram *n* (*pl* -s) male sheep ▶ *v* (-s, -mming, -mmed) strike against with force
ramble *v* (-les, -ling, -led) walk without a definite route ▶ *n* (*pl* -s) walk, esp. in the country
rambled *v* ▷ ramble
rambler *n* (*pl* -s) person who rambles
ramblers *n* ▷ rambler
rambles *v, n* ▷ ramble
rambling *v* ▷ ramble
ramekin [ram-ik-in] *n* (*pl* -s) small ovenproof dish for a single serving of food
ramekins *n* ▷ ramekin
ramifications *pl n* consequences resulting from an action
rammed *v* ▷ ram
ramming *v* ▷ ram
ramp *n* (*pl* -s) slope joining two level surfaces
rampage *v* (-ges, -ging, -ged) dash about violently
rampaged *v* ▷ rampage
rampages *v* ▷ rampage
rampaging *v* ▷ rampage
rampant *adj* growing or spreading uncontrollably
rampart *n* (*pl* -s) mound or wall for defence
ramparts *n* ▷ rampart
ramps *n* ▷ ramp
rams *n, v* ▷ ram
ramshackle *adj* tumbledown, rickety, or makeshift
ran *v* ▷ run
ranch *n* (*pl* -es) large cattle farm in the American West > **rancher** *n* (*pl* -s)
rancher *n* ▷ ranch
ranchers *n* ▷ ranch

ranches n ▷ ranch

rancid adj (of bacon, etc.) stale and having an offensive smell > rancidity n (pl -ies)

rancidities n ▷ rancidity

rancidity n ▷ rancid

rancorous adj ▷ rancour

rancorousnesses n ▷ rancour

rancour n (pl -s) deep bitter hate > rancorous adj

rancours n ▷ rancour

rand n (pl -s) monetary unit of S Africa

randier adj ▷ randy

randiest adj ▷ randy

random adj made or done by chance or without plan

rands n ▷ rand

randy adj (-ier, -iest) (Informal) sexually aroused

rang v ▷ ring[1]

range n (pl -s) limits of effectiveness or variation ▶ v (-ges, -ging, -ged) vary between one point and another

ranged v ▷ range

ranger n (pl -s) official in charge of a nature reserve etc.

rangers n ▷ ranger

rangefinder n (pl -s) instrument for finding how far away an object is

rangefinders n ▷ rangefinder

ranges n, v ▷ range

rangier adj ▷ rangy

rangiest adj ▷ rangy

ranging v ▷ range

rangy [rain-jee] adj (-ier, -iest) having long slender limbs

rank[1] n (pl -s) relative place or position ▶ v (-s, -ing, -ed) have a specific rank or position

rank[2] adj complete or absolute

ranked v ▷ rank

ranking v ▷ rank

rankle v (-les, -ling, -led) continue to cause resentment or bitterness

rankled v ▷ rankle

rankles v ▷ rankle

rankling v ▷ rankle

ranks n, v ▷ rank[1]

ransack v (-s, -ing, -ed) search thoroughly

ransacked v ▷ ransack

ransacking v ▷ ransack

ransacks v ▷ ransack

ransom n (pl -s) money demanded in return for the release of someone who has been kidnapped

ransoms n ▷ ransom

rant v (-s, -ing, -ed) talk in a loud and excited way > ranter n (pl -s)

ranted v ▷ rant

ranter n ▷ rant

ranters n ▷ rant

ranting v ▷ rant

rants v ▷ rant

rap v (-s, -pping, -pped) hit with a sharp quick blow ▶ n (pl -s) quick sharp blow > rapper n (pl -s)

rapacious adj greedy or grasping > rapacity n (pl -ies)

rapacities n ▷ rapacious

rapacity n ▷ rapacious

rape[1] v (-pes, -ping, -ped) force to submit to sexual intercourse ▶ n (pl -s) act of raping > rapist n (pl -s)

rape[2] n (pl -s) plant with oil-yielding seeds, also used as fodder

raped v ▷ rape[1]

rapes v ▷ rape[1] ▶ n ▷ rape[1,2]

rapid adj (-er, -est) quick, swift > rapidly adv > rapidity n (pl -ies)

rapider adj ▷ rapid

rapidest adj ▷ rapid

rapidities n ▷ rapid

rapidity n ▷ rapid

rapidly adv ▷ rapid

rapids pl n part of a river with a fast turbulent current

rapier [ray-pyer] n (pl -s) fine-bladed sword

rapiers n ▷ rapier

raping v ▷ rape[1]

rapist n ▷ rape[1]

rapists n ▷ rape[1]

rapped v ▷ rap

rapper n ▷ rap

rappers n ▷ rap

rapping v ▷ rap

rapport [rap-pore] n (pl -s) harmony or agreement

rapports n ▷ rapport

rapprochement [rap-prosh-mong] n (pl -s) re-establishment of friendly relations, esp. between nations

rapprochements n ▷ rapprochement

raps v, n ▷ rap

rapt adj engrossed or spellbound

rapture n (pl -s) ecstasy > rapturous adj

raptures n ▷ rapture

rapturous adj ▷ rapture

rare[1] adj (-r, -st) uncommon > rarity n (pl -ies)

rare[2] adj (-r, -st) (of meat) lightly cooked

rarebit n (pl -s) dish of melted cheese on toast

rarebits n ▷ rarebit

rarefied [rare-if-ide] adj highly specialized, exalted

rarely *adv* seldom
rarer *adj* ▷ rare¹,²
rarest *adj* ▷ rare¹,²
raring *adj* enthusiastic, willing, or ready to
rarities *n* ▷ rare¹
rarity *n* ▷ rare¹
rascal *n* (*pl* -s) rogue > **rascally** *adj* (-ier, -iest)
rascalliest *adj* ▷ rascal
rascally *adj* ▷ rascal
rascals *n* ▷ rascal
rash¹ *adj* (-er, -est) hasty, reckless, or incautious > **rashly** *adv*
rash² *n* (*pl* -es) eruption of spots or patches on the skin
rasher *n* (*pl* -s) thin slice of bacon ▶ *adj* ▷ rash¹
rashers *n* ▷ rasher
rashes *n* ▷ rash²
rashest *adj* ▷ rash¹
rashly *adv* ▷ rash¹
rasp *n* (*pl* -s) harsh grating noise ▶ *v* (-s, -ing, -ed) speak in a grating voice
raspberries *n* ▷ raspberry
raspberry *n* (*pl* -ies) red juicy edible berry (*Informal*)
rasped *v* ▷ rasp
rasping *v* ▷ rasp
rasps *n*, *v* ▷ rasp
rat *n* (*pl* -s) small rodent (*Informal*) ▶ *v* (-s, -tting, -tted) (*Informal*) inform (on)
ratafia [rat-a-**fee**-a] *n* (*pl* -s) fruit liqueur
ratafias *n* ▷ ratafia
ratatouille [rat-a-**twee**] *n* (*pl* -s) vegetable casserole of tomatoes, aubergines, etc.
ratatouilles *n* ▷ ratatouille
ratchet *n* (*pl* -s) set of teeth on a bar or wheel allowing motion in one direction only
ratchets *n* ▷ ratchet
rate *n* (*pl* -s) degree of speed or progress ▶ *pl* local tax on business ▶ *v* (-tes, -ting, -ted) consider or value > **ratepayer** *n* (*pl* -s)
rateable *adj* able to be rated
rated *v* ▷ rate
ratepayer *n* ▷ rate
ratepayers *n* ▷ rate
rates *n*, *v* ▷ rate
rather *adv* to some extent
ratification *n* ▷ ratify
ratifications *n* ▷ ratify
ratified *v* ▷ ratify
ratifies *v* ▷ ratify
ratify *v* (-ies, -ying, -ied) give formal approval to > **ratification** *n* (*pl* -s)
ratifying *v* ▷ ratify
rating *n* (*pl* -s) valuation or assessment ▶ *pl* size of the audience for a TV programme ▶ *v*

▷ rate
ratings *n* ▷ rating
ratio *n* (*pl* -s) relationship between two numbers or amounts expressed as a proportion
ration *n* (*pl* -s) fixed allowance of food etc. ▶ *v* (-s, -ing, -ed) limit to a certain amount per person
rational *adj* reasonable, sensible > **rationally** *adv* > **rationality** *n* (*pl* -ies)
rationale [rash-a-**nahl**] *n* (*pl* -s) reason for an action or decision
rationales *n* ▷ rationale
rationalism *n* (*pl* -s) philosophy that regards reason as the only basis for beliefs or actions > **rationalist** *n* (*pl* -s)
rationalisms *n* ▷ rationalism
rationalist *n* ▷ rationalism
rationalists *n* ▷ rationalism
rationalities *n* ▷ rational
rationality *n* ▷ rational
rationalize *v* (-zes, -zing, -zed) justify by plausible reasoning > **rationalization** *n* (*pl* -s)
rationalization *n* ▷ rationalize
rationalizations *n* ▷ rationalize
rationalized *v* ▷ rationalize
rationalizes *v* ▷ rationalize
rationalizing *v* ▷ rationalize
rationally *adv* ▷ rational
rationed *v* ▷ ration
rationing *v* ▷ ration
rations *n*, *v* ▷ ration
ratios *n* ▷ ratio
rats *n* ▷ rat
rattan *n* (*pl* -s) climbing palm with jointed stems used for canes
rattans *n* ▷ rattan
ratted *v* ▷ rat
rattier *adj* ▷ ratty
rattiest *adj* ▷ ratty
rattinesses *n* ▷ ratty
ratting *v* ▷ rat
rattle *v* (-les, -ling, -led) give out a succession of short sharp sounds ▶ *n* (*pl* -s) short sharp sound
rattled *v* ▷ rattle
rattlesnake *n* (*pl* -s) poisonous snake with loose horny segments on the tail that make a rattling sound
rattlesnakes *n* ▷ rattlesnake
rattles *v*, *n* ▷ rattle
rattling *v* ▷ rattle
ratty *adj* (-ier, -iest) (BRIT & NZ) (*Informal*) bad-tempered, irritable
raucous *adj* hoarse or harsh

raunchier adj ▷ raunchy
raunchiest adj ▷ raunchy
raunchy adj (-chier, -chiest) (Slang) earthy, sexy
ravage v (-ges, -ging, -ged) cause extensive damage to
ravaged v ▷ ravage
ravages pl n damaging effects ▶ v ▷ ravage
ravaging v ▷ ravage
rave v (-ves, -ving, -ved) talk wildly or with enthusiasm ▶ n (pl -s) (Slang) large-scale party with electronic dance music
raved v ▷ rave
ravel v (-s, -lling, -lled) tangle or become entangled
ravelled v ▷ ravel
ravelling v ▷ ravel
ravels v ▷ ravel
raven n (pl -s) black bird like a large crow ▶ adj (of hair) shiny black
ravens n ▷ raven
ravenous adj very hungry
raves v, n ▷ rave
ravine [rav-veen] n (pl -s) narrow steep-sided valley worn by a stream
ravines n ▷ ravine
raving adj delirious ▶ v ▷ rave
ravioli pl n small squares of pasta with a savoury filling
ravish v (-es, -ing, -ed) enrapture
ravished v ▷ ravish
ravishes v ▷ ravish
ravishing adj, v ▷ ravish
raw adj (-er, -est) uncooked
rawer adj ▷ raw
rawest adj ▷ raw
rawhide n (pl -s) untanned hide
rawhides n ▷ rawhide

> **rax** v (**raxes, raxing, raxed**). Rax is a Scots word that means to stretch or extend. This is a good word to have ready when you have an X on your rack, as there is probably an A or R on the board already. The verb forms can also help you to get a better score. Rax scores 10 points.

ray[1] n (pl -s) single line or narrow beam of light
ray[2] n (pl -s) large sea fish with a flat body and a whiplike tail
rays n ▷ ray[1, 2]
rayon n (pl -s) (fabric made of) a synthetic fibre
rayons n ▷ rayon
raze v (-zes, -zing, -zed) destroy (buildings or a town) completely
razed v ▷ raze
razes v ▷ raze
razing v ▷ raze
razor n (pl -s) sharp instrument for shaving
razorbill n (pl -s) sea bird of the North Atlantic with a stout sideways flattened bill
razorbills n ▷ razorbill
razors n ▷ razor

> **re** n (res). Re is a musical note. This is the only two-letter word beginning with R, and so is a good one to remember. Re is very useful as it allows you to connect a word beginning with R to one ending in E, or vice versa. Re scores 2 points.

reach v (-es, -ing, -ed) arrive at ▶ n (pl -es) distance that one can reach; stretch of a river
> **reachable** adj
reachable adj ▷ reach
reached v ▷ reach
reaches v, n ▷ reach
reaching v ▷ reach
react v (-s, -ing, -ed) act in response (to) (foll. by **against**)
reactance n (pl -s) (ELECTRICITY) resistance to the flow of an alternating current caused by the inductance or capacitance of the circuit
reactances n ▷ reactance
reacted v ▷ react
reacting v ▷ react
reaction n (pl -s) physical or emotional response to a stimulus
reactionaries n ▷ reactionary
reactionary n, adj (pl -ies) (person) opposed to change, esp. in politics
reactionary n ▷ reaction
reactionisms n ▷ reactionary
reactions n ▷ reaction
reactive adj chemically active
reactor n (pl -s) apparatus in which a nuclear reaction is maintained and controlled to produce nuclear energy
reactors n ▷ reactor
reacts v ▷ react
read v (-s, -ing, read) look at and understand or take in (written or printed matter) ▶ n matter suitable for reading ▶ **reading** n (pl -s)
readable adj enjoyable to read
reader n (pl -s) person who reads
readers n ▷ reader
readership n (pl -s) readers of a publication collectively
readerships n ▷ readership
readier adj ▷ ready
readiest adj ▷ ready
readily adv ▷ ready
readiness n ▷ ready

readinesses n ▷ ready
reading n, v ▷ read
readings n ▷ read
readjust v (-s, -ing, -ed) adapt to a new situation > **readjustment** n (pl -s)
readjusted v ▷ readjust
readjusting v ▷ readjust
readjustment n ▷ readjust
readjustments n ▷ readjust
readjusts v ▷ readjust
reads v ▷ read
ready adj (-dier, -diest) prepared for use or action > **readily** adv > **readiness** n (pl -es)
reagent [ree-**age**-ent] n (pl -s) chemical substance that reacts with another, used to detect the presence of the other
reagents n ▷ reagent
real adj (-er, -est) existing in fact
realism n ▷ realistic
realisms n ▷ realistic
realist n ▷ realistic
realistically adv ▷ realistic
realists n ▷ realistic
realistic adj seeing and accepting things as they really are, practical > **realistically** adv > **realism** n (pl -s) > **realist** n (pl -s)
realities n ▷ reality
reality n (pl -ies) state of things as they are
realize v (-zes, -zing, -zed) become aware or grasp the significance of > **realization** n (pl -s)
realization n ▷ realize
realizations n ▷ realize
realized v ▷ realize
realizes v ▷ realize
realizing v ▷ realize
really adv very ▶ interj exclamation of dismay, doubt, or surprise
realm n (pl -s) kingdom
realms n ▷ realm
ream n (pl -s) twenty quires of paper, generally 500 sheets ▶ pl (Informal) large quantity (of written matter)
reams n ▷ ream
reap v (-s, -ing, -ed) cut and gather (a harvest) > **reaper** n (pl -s)
reaped v ▷ reap
reaper n ▷ reap
reapers n ▷ reap
reaping v ▷ reap
reappear v (-s, -ing, -ed) appear again > **reappearance** n (pl -s)
reappearance n ▷ reappear
reappearances n ▷ reappear
reappeared v ▷ reappear
reappearing v ▷ reappear

reappears v ▷ reappear
reaps v ▷ reap
rear¹ n (pl -s) back part ▶ **rearmost** adj
rear² v (-s, -ing, -ed) care for and educate (children)
reared v ▷ rear
rearguard n (pl -s) troops protecting the rear of an army
rearguards n ▷ rearguard
rearing v ▷ rear
rearmost adj ▷ rear¹
rearrange v (-ges, -ging, -ged) organize differently, alter > **rearrangement** n (pl -s)
rearranged v ▷ rearrange
rearrangement n ▷ rearrange
rearrangements n ▷ rearrange
rearranges v ▷ rearrange
rearranging v ▷ rearrange
rears n ▷ rear¹ ▶ v ▷ rear²
reason n (pl -s) cause or motive ▶ v (-s, -ing, -ed) think logically in forming conclusions
reasonable adj sensible > **reasonably** adv
reasoned v ▷ reason
reasoning v ▷ reason
reasons n, v ▷ reason
reassess v (-es, -ing, -ed) reconsider the value or importance of
reassessed v ▷ reassess
reassesses v ▷ reassess
reassessing v ▷ reassess
reassure v (-res, -ring, -red) restore confidence to > **reassurance** n (pl -s)
reassurance n ▷ reassure
reassurances n ▷ reassure
reassured v ▷ reassure
reassures v ▷ reassure
reassuring v ▷ reassure
rebate n (pl -s) discount or refund
rebates n ▷ rebate
rebel v (-s, -lling, -lled) revolt against the ruling power ▶ n (pl -s) person who rebels > **rebellious** adj
rebelled v ▷ rebel
rebelling v ▷ rebel
rebellion n (pl -s) organized open resistance to authority
rebellions n ▷ rebellion
rebellious adj ▷ rebel
rebels v, n ▷ rebel
rebore, reboring n (pl -s) boring of a cylinder to restore its true shape
rebores n ▷ rebore
reboring n ▷ rebore
reborings n ▷ rebore
rebound v (-s, -ing, -ed) spring back

rebounded v ▷ rebound

rebounding v ▷ rebound

rebounds v ▷ rebound

rebuff v (-s, -ing, -ed) reject or snub ▶ n (pl -s) blunt refusal, snub

rebuffed v ▷ rebuff

rebuffing v ▷ rebuff

rebuffs v, n ▷ rebuff

rebuke v (-kes, -king, -ked) scold sternly ▶ n (pl -s) stern scolding

rebuked v ▷ rebuke

rebukes v, n ▷ rebuke

rebuking v ▷ rebuke

rebus n (pl -es) puzzle consisting of pictures and symbols representing words or syllables

rebuses n ▷ rebus

rebut v (-s, -ting, -tted) prove that (a claim) is untrue ▶ **rebuttal** n (pl -s)

rebuts v ▷ rebut

rebuttal n ▷ rebut

rebuttals n ▷ rebut

rebutted v ▷ rebut

rebutting v ▷ rebut

recalcitrant adj wilfully disobedient > **recalcitrance** n (pl -s)

recalcitrance n ▷ recalcitrant

recalcitrances n ▷ recalcitrant

recall v (-s, -ing, -ed) recollect or remember ▶ n (pl (l -s) ability to remember

recalled v ▷ recall

recalling v ▷ recall

recalls v, n ▷ recall

recant v (-s, -ing, -ed) withdraw (a statement or belief) publicly > **recantation** n (pl -s)

recantation n ▷ recant

recantations n ▷ recant

recanted v ▷ recant

recanting v ▷ recant

recants v ▷ recant

recap (Informal) v (-s, -pping, -pped) recapitulate ▶ n (pl -s) recapitulation

recapitulate v (-tes, -ting, -ted) state again briefly, repeat > **recapitulation** n (pl -s)

recapitulated v ▷ recapitulate

recapitulates v ▷ recapitulate

recapitulating v ▷ recapitulate

recapitulation n ▷ recapitulate

recapitulations n ▷ recapitulate

recapped v ▷ recap

recapping v ▷ recap

recaps v, n ▷ recap

recapture v (-res, -ring, -red) experience again

recaptured v ▷ recapture

recaptures v ▷ recapture

recapturing v ▷ recapture

recce (CHIEFLY BRIT) (Slang) v (-s, -ceing, -ced or -ceed) reconnoitre ▶ n (pl -s) reconnaissance

recced v ▷ recce

recceed v ▷ recce

recceing v ▷ recce

recces v, n ▷ recce

recede v (-des, -ding, -ded) move to a more distant place

receded v ▷ recede

recedes v ▷ recede

receding v ▷ recede

receipt n (pl -s) written acknowledgment of money or goods received

receipts n ▷ receipt

receive v (-ves, -ving, -ved) take, accept, or get

received adj generally accepted ▶ v ▷ receive

receiver n (pl -s) part of telephone that is held to the ear

receivers n ▷ receiver

receivership n (pl -s) state of being administered by a receiver

receiverships n ▷ receivership

receives v ▷ receive

receiving v ▷ receive

recent adj (-er, -est) having happened lately > **recently** adv

recenter adj ▷ recent

recentest adj ▷ recent

recently adv ▷ recent

receptacle n (pl -s) object used to contain something

receptacles n ▷ receptacle

reception n (pl -s) area for receiving guests, clients, etc.

receptionist n (pl -s) person who receives guests, clients, etc.

receptionists n ▷ receptionist

receptions n ▷ reception

receptive adj willing to accept new ideas, suggestions, etc. > **receptivity** n (pl -ies)

receptivities n ▷ receptive

receptivity n ▷ receptive

recess n (pl -es) niche or alcove

recessed adj hidden or placed in a recess

recesses n ▷ recess

recession n (pl -s) period of economic difficulty when little is being bought or sold

recessions n ▷ recession

recessive adj receding

recherché [rish-air-shay] adj refined or elegant

recidivism n (pl -s) habitual relapse into crime > **recidivist** n (pl -s)

recidivisms n ▷ recidivism

recidivist n ▷ recidivism

recidivists n ▷ recidivism

recipe n (pl -s) directions for cooking a dish
  recipes n ▷ recipe
recipient n (pl -s) person who receives
  something
  recipients n ▷ recipient
reciprocal [ris-**sip**-pro-kl] adj mutual
  > **reciprocally** adv
  reciprocally adv ▷ reciprocal
reciprocate v (-tes, -ting, -ted) give or feel in
  return > **reciprocation** n (pl -s) > **reciprocity**
  n (pl -s)
  reciprocated v ▷ reciprocate
  reciprocates v ▷ reciprocate
  reciprocating v ▷ reciprocate
  reciprocation n ▷ reciprocate
  reciprocations n ▷ reciprocate
  reciprocities n ▷ reciprocate
  reciprocity n ▷ reciprocate
recital n (pl -s) musical performance by a
  soloist or soloists
  recitals n ▷ recital
recitation n (pl -s) recital, usu. from memory,
  of poetry or prose
  recitations n ▷ recitation
recitative [ress-it-a-**teev**] n (pl -s) speechlike
  style of singing, used esp. for narrative
  passages in opera
  recitatives n ▷ recitative
recite v (-tes, -ting, -ted) repeat (a poem etc.)
  aloud to an audience
  recited v ▷ recite
  recites v ▷ recite
  reciting v ▷ recite
reckless adj heedless of danger > **recklessly**
  adv > **recklessness** n (pl -s)
  recklessly adv ▷ reckless
  recklessness n ▷ reckless
  recklessnesses n ▷ reckless
reckon v (-s, -ing, -ed) consider or think
  > **reckoning** n (pl -s)
  reckoned v ▷ reckon
  reckoning v, n ▷ reckon
  reckonings n ▷ reckon
  reckons v ▷ reckon
reclaim v (-s, -ing, -ed) regain possession of
  > **reclamation** n (pl -s)
  reclaimed v ▷ reclaim
  reclaiming v ▷ reclaim
  reclaims v ▷ reclaim
  reclamation n ▷ reclaim
  reclamations n ▷ reclaim
recline v (-nes, -ning, -ned) rest in a leaning
  position > **reclining** adj
  reclined v ▷ recline
  reclines v ▷ recline

  reclining v, adj ▷ recline
recluse n (pl -s) person who avoids other
  people > **reclusive** adj
  recluses n ▷ recluse
  reclusive adj ▷ recluse
recognition n ▷ recognize
  recognitions n ▷ recognize
  recognizable adj ▷ recognize
recognizance [rik-og-**nizz**-anss] n (pl -s)
  undertaking before a court to observe some
  condition
  recognizances n ▷ recognizance
recognize v (-zes, -zing, -zed) identify
  as (a person or thing) already known
  > **recognition** n (pl -s) > **recognizable** adj
  recognized v ▷ recognize
  recognizes v ▷ recognize
  recognizing v ▷ recognize
recoil v (-s, -ing, -ed) jerk or spring back ▶ n (pl
  -s) backward jerk
  recoiled v ▷ recoil
  recoiling v ▷ recoil
  recoils v, n ▷ recoil
recollect v (-s, -ing, -ed) call back to mind,
  remember > **recollection** n (pl -s)
  recollected v ▷ recollect
  recollecting v ▷ recollect
  recollection n ▷ recollect
  recollections n ▷ recollect
  recollects v ▷ recollect
recommend v (-s, -ing, -ed) advise or counsel
  > **recommendation** n (pl -s)
  recommendation n ▷ recommend
  recommendations n ▷ recommend
  recommended v ▷ recommend
  recommending v ▷ recommend
  recommends v ▷ recommend
recompense v (-ses, -sing, -sed) pay or reward
  ▶ n (pl -s) compensation
  recompensed v ▷ recompense
  recompenses v, n ▷ recompense
  recompensing v ▷ recompense
reconcile v (-les, -ling, -led) harmonize
  (conflicting beliefs etc.) > **reconciliation**
  n (pl -s)
  reconciled v ▷ reconcile
  reconciles v ▷ reconcile
  reconciliation n ▷ reconcile
  reconciliations n ▷ reconcile
  reconciling v ▷ reconcile
recondite adj difficult to understand
recondition v (-s, -ing, -ed) restore to good
  condition or working order
  reconditioned v ▷ recondition
  reconditioning v ▷ recondition

reconditions v ▷ recondition
reconnaissance [rik-**kon**-iss-anss] n (pl -s) survey for military or engineering purposes
reconnaissances n ▷ reconnaissance
reconnoitre [rek-a-**noy**-ter] v (-res, -ring, -red) make a reconnaissance of
reconnoitred v ▷ reconnoitre
reconnoitres v ▷ reconnoitre
reconnoitring v ▷ reconnoitre
reconsider v (-s, -ing, -ed) think about again, consider changing
reconsidered v ▷ reconsider
reconsidering v ▷ reconsider
reconsiders v ▷ reconsider
reconstitute v (-tes, -ting, -ted) reorganize > **reconstitution** n (pl -s)
reconstituted v ▷ reconstitute
reconstitutes v ▷ reconstitute
reconstituting v ▷ reconstitute
reconstitution n ▷ reconstitute
reconstitutions n ▷ reconstitute
reconstruct v (-s, -ing, -ed) rebuild > **reconstruction** n (pl -s)
reconstructed v ▷ reconstruct
reconstructing v ▷ reconstruct
reconstruction n ▷ reconstruct
reconstructions n ▷ reconstruct
reconstructs v ▷ reconstruct
record n (pl -s) [**rek**-ord] document or other thing that preserves information ▶ v (-s, -ing, -ed) [rik-**kord**] put in writing > **recording** n (pl -s)
recorded v ▷ record
recorder n (pl -s) person or machine that records, esp. a video, cassette, or tape recorder
recorders n ▷ recorder
recording v ▷ record
records n, v ▷ record
recount v (-s, -ing, -ed) tell in detail
recounted v ▷ recount
recounting v ▷ recount
recounts v ▷ recount
recoup [rik-**koop**] v (-s, -ing, -ed) regain or make good (a loss)
recouped v ▷ recoup
recouping v ▷ recoup
recoups v ▷ recoup
recourse n (pl -s) source of help
recourses n ▷ recourse
recover v (-s, -ing, -ed) become healthy again > **recovery** n (pl -ies) > **recoverable** adj
recoverable adj ▷ recover
recovered v ▷ recover
recoveries n ▷ recover

recovering v ▷ recover
recovers v ▷ recover
recovery v ▷ recover
recreation n (pl -s) agreeable or refreshing occupation, relaxation, or amusement > **recreational** adj
recreational adj ▷ recreation
recreations n ▷ recreation
recrimination n (pl -s) mutual blame > **recriminatory** adj
recriminations n ▷ recrimination
recriminatory adj ▷ recrimination
recruit v (-s, -ing, -ed) enlist (new soldiers, members, etc.) ▶ n (pl -s) newly enlisted soldier > **recruitment** n (pl -s)
recruited v ▷ recruit
recruiting v ▷ recruit
recruitment n ▷ recruit
recruitments n ▷ recruit
recruits v, n ▷ recruit
recta n ▷ rectum
rectangle n (pl -s) oblong four-sided figure with four right angles > **rectangular** adj
rectangles n ▷ rectangle
rectangular adj ▷ rectangle
rectification n ▷ rectify
rectifications n ▷ rectify
rectified v ▷ rectify
rectifier n ▷ rectify
rectifiers n ▷ rectify
rectifies v ▷ rectify
rectify v (-ies, -ying, -ied) put right, correct (CHEM) (ELECTRICITY) > **rectification** n (pl -s)
rectifying v ▷ rectify
rectilinear adj in a straight line
rectitude n (pl -s) moral correctness
rectitudes n ▷ rectitude
recto n (pl -os) right-hand page of a book
rector n (pl -s) clergyman in charge of a parish
rectories n ▷ rectory
rectors n ▷ rector
rectory n (pl -s) rector's house
rectos n ▷ recto
rectum n (pl -tums, -ta) final section of the large intestine
rectums n ▷ rectum
recumbent adj lying down
recuperate v (-tes, -ting, -ted) recover from illness > **recuperation** n (pl -s) > **recuperative** adj
recuperated v ▷ recuperate
recuperates v ▷ recuperate
recuperating v ▷ recuperate
recuperation n ▷ recuperate
recuperations n ▷ recuperate

recuperative *adj* ▷ recuperate
recur *v* (-s, -rring, -rred) happen again
> **recurrence** *n* (*pl* -s) repetition > **recurrent**
adj
recurred *v* ▷ recur
recurrence *n* ▷ recur
recurrences *n* ▷ recur
recurrent *adj* ▷ recur
recurring *v* ▷ recur
recurs *v* ▷ recur
recycle *v* (-les, -ling, -led) reprocess (used
materials) for further use > **recyclable** *adj*
recyclable *adj* ▷ recycle
recycled *v* ▷ recycle
recycles *v* ▷ recycle
recycling *v* ▷ recycle
red *adj* (-dder, -ddest) of a colour varying from
crimson to orange and seen in blood, fire, etc.
▶ *n* (*pl* -s) red colour > **reddish** *adj* > **redness**
n (*pl* -es)
redbrick *adj* (of a university in Britain)
founded in the late 19th or early 20th century
redcoat *n* (*pl* -s) (HIST) British soldier
redcoats *n* ▷ redcoat
redcurrant *n* (*pl* -s) small round edible red
berry
redcurrants *n* ▷ redcurrant
redden *v* (-s, -ing, -ed) make or become red
reddened *v* ▷ redden
reddening *v* ▷ redden
reddens *v* ▷ redden
redder *adj* ▷ red
reddest *adj* ▷ red
reddish *adj* ▷ red
redeem *v* (-s, -ing, -ed) make up for
> **redeemable** *adj* > **redemption** *n* (*pl* -s)
> **redemptive** *adj*
redeemable *adj* ▷ reddem
redeemed *v* ▷ redeem
redeeming *v* ▷ redeem
redeems *v* ▷ redeem
redemption *adj* ▷ reddem
redemptions *adj* ▷ reddem
redemptive *adj* ▷ reddem
redeploy *v* (-s, -ing, -ed) assign to a new
position or task > **redeployment** *n* (*pl* -s)
redeployed *v* ▷ redeploy
redeploying *v* ▷ redeploy
redeployment *n* ▷ redeploy
redeployment *n* ▷ redeploy
redeploys *v* ▷ redeploy
redevelop *v* (-s, -ing, -ed) rebuild or renovate
(an area or building) > **redevelopment** *n* (*pl* -s)
redeveloped *v* ▷ redevelop
redeveloping *v* ▷ redevelop

redevelopment *n* ▷ redevelop
redevelopments *n* ▷ redevelop
redevelops *v* ▷ redevelop
redness *n* ▷ red
redolent *adj* reminiscent (of)
redouble *v* (-les, -ling, -led) increase, multiply,
or intensify
redoubled *v* ▷ redouble
redoubles *v* ▷ redouble
redoubling *v* ▷ redouble
redoubt *n* (*pl* -s) small fort defending a hilltop
or pass
redoubtable *adj* formidable
redoubts *n* ▷ redoubt
redound *v* (-s, -ing, -ed) cause advantage or
disadvantage (to)
redounded *v* ▷ redound
redounding *v* ▷ redound
redounds *v* ▷ redound
redox *n* (*pl* -es) chemical reaction in which
one substance is reduced and the other is
oxidized
redoxes *n* ▷ redox
redress *v* (-es, -ing, -ed) make amends for ▶ *n*
(*pl* -es) compensation or amends
redressed *v* ▷ redress
redresses *v*, *n* ▷ redress
redressing *v* ▷ redress
reds *n* ▷ red
reduce *v* (-ces, -cing, -ced) bring down, lower
> **reducible** *adj* > **reduction** *n* (*pl* -s)
reduced *v* ▷ reduce
reduces *v* ▷ reduce
reducible *adj* ▷ reduce
reducing *v* ▷ reduce
reduction *n* ▷ reduce
reductions *n* ▷ reduce
redundancies *n* ▷ redundant
redundancy *n* ▷ redundant
redundant *adj* (of a worker) no longer needed
> **redundancy** *n* (*pl* -s)
reed *n* (*pl* -s) tall grass that grows in swamps
and shallow water
reedier *adj* ▷ reedy
reediest *n* ▷ reedy
reeds *n* ▷ reed
reedy (-dier, -diest) *adj* harsh and thin in tone
reef¹ *n* (*pl* -s) ridge of rock or coral near the
surface of the sea
reef² *n* (*pl* -s) part of a sail which can be rolled
up to reduce its area ▶ *v* (-s, -ing, -ed) take
in a reef of
reefed *v* ▷ reef²
reefer *n* (*pl* -s) short thick jacket worn esp.
by sailors

reefers n ▷ reefer
reefing v ▷ reef²
reefs n ▷ reef¹, ² ▶ v ▷ reef²
reek v (-s, -ing, -ed) smell strongly ▶ n (pl -s) strong unpleasant smell
reeked v ▷ reek
reeking v ▷ reek
reeks v, n ▷ reek
reel n (pl -s) cylindrical object on which film, tape, thread, or wire is wound
reel² v (-s, -ing, -ed) stagger, sway, or whirl
reel³ n (pl -s) lively Scottish dance
reeled v ▷ reel²
reeling v ▷ reel²
reels n ▷ reel¹, ³ ▶ v ▷ reel²
ref n (pl -s) (Informal) referee in sport
refectories n ▷ refectory
refectory n (pl -ies) room for meals in a college etc.
refer v (-s, -rring, -rred) (foll. by **to**) allude (to) > **referral** n (pl -s)
referee n (pl -s) umpire in sports, esp. soccer or boxing ▶ v (-s, -ing, -eed) act as referee of
refereed v ▷ referee
refereeing v ▷ referee
referees n, v ▷ referee
reference n (pl -s) act of referring
references n ▷ reference
referenda n ▷ referendum
referendum n (pl -dums, -da) direct vote of the electorate on an important question
referendums n ▷ referendum
referral n ▷ refer
referrals n ▷ refer
referred v ▷ refer
referring v ▷ refer
refers v ▷ refer
refill v (-s, -ing, -ed) fill again ▶ n (pl -s) second or subsequent filling
refilled v ▷ refill
refilling v ▷ refill
refills v, n ▷ refill
refine v (-nes, -ning, -ned) purify
refined adj cultured or polite ▶ v ▷ refine
refinement n (pl -s) improvement or elaboration
refinements n ▷ refinement
refineries n ▷ refinery
refinery n (pl -ies) place where sugar, oil, etc. is refined
refines v ▷ refine
refining v ▷ refine
reflate v ▷ reflation
reflated v ▷ reflation
reflates v ▷ reflation

reflating v ▷ reflation
reflation n (pl -s) increase in the supply of money and credit designed to encourage economic activity > **reflate** v (-tes, -ting, -ted) > **reflationary** adj
reflationary adj ▷ reflation
reflations n ▷ reflation
reflect v (-s, -ing, -ed) throw back, esp. rays of light, heat, etc.
reflected v ▷ reflect
reflecting v ▷ reflect
reflection n (pl -s) act of reflecting
reflections n ▷ reflect
reflective adj quiet, contemplative
reflector n (pl -s) polished surface for reflecting light etc.
reflectors n ▷ reflector
reflects v ▷ reflect
reflex n (pl -es) involuntary response to a stimulus or situation ▶ adj (of a muscular action) involuntary
reflexes n ▷ reflex
reflexive adj (GRAMMAR) denoting a verb whose subject is the same as its object
reflexologies n ▷ reflexology
reflexology n (pl -ies) foot massage as a therapy in alternative medicine
reform n (pl -s) improvement ▶ v (-s, -ing, -ed) improve > **reformer** n (pl -s)
reformation n (pl -s) act or instance of something being reformed
reformations n ▷ reformation
reformatories n ▷ reformatory
reformatory n (pl -ies) (formerly) institution for reforming young offenders
reformed v ▷ reform
reformer n ▷ reform
reformers n ▷ reform
reforming v ▷ reform
reforms n, v ▷ reform
refract v (-s, -ing, -ed) change the course of (light etc.) passing from one medium to another > **refraction** n (pl -s) > **refractive** adj > **refractor** n (pl -s)
refracted v ▷ refract
refracting v ▷ refract
refraction n ▷ refract
refractions n ▷ refract
refractive adj ▷ refract
refractor n ▷ refract
refractors n ▷ refract
refractory adj unmanageable or rebellious
refracts v ▷ refract
refrain¹ v (-s, -ing, -ed) keep oneself from doing
refrain² n (pl -s) frequently repeated part of

a song

refrained v ▷ refrain[1]

refraining v ▷ refrain[1]

refrains n ▷ refrain[1, 2] ▶ v ▷ refrain[2]

refresh v (-es, -ing, -ed) revive or reinvigorate, as through food, drink, or rest > **refresher** n (pl -s)

refreshed v ▷ refresh

refresher n ▷ refresh

refreshers n ▷ refresh

refreshes v ▷ refresh

refreshing adj having a reviving effect ▶ v ▷ refresh

refreshment n (pl -s) something that refreshes, esp. food or drink

refreshments n ▷ refreshment

refrigerate v (-tes, -ting, -ted) cool or freeze in order to preserve > **refrigeration** n (pl -s)

refrigerated v ▷ refrigerate

refrigerates v ▷ refrigerate

refrigerating v ▷ refrigerate

refrigeration n ▷ refrigerate

refrigerations n ▷ refrigerate

refrigerator n (pl -s) ▷ fridge

refrigerators n ▷ refrigerator

refs n ▷ ref

refuge n (pl -s) (source of) shelter or protection

refugee n (pl -s) person who seeks refuge, esp. in a foreign country

refugees n ▷ refugee

refuges n ▷ refuge

refulgent adj shining, radiant

refund v (-s, -ing, -ed) pay back ▶ n (pl -s) return of money

refunded v ▷ refund

refunding v ▷ refund

refunds v, n ▷ refund

refurbish v (-es, -ing, -ed) renovate and brighten up

refurbished v ▷ refurbish

refurbishes v ▷ refurbish

refurbishing v ▷ refurbish

refusal n (pl -s) denial of anything demanded or offered

refusals n ▷ refusal

refuse[1] v (-ses, -sing, -sed) decline, deny, or reject

refuse[2] n (pl -s) rubbish or useless matter

refused v ▷ refuse[1]

refuses v ▷ refuse[1] ▶ n ▷ refuse[2]

refusing v ▷ refuse[1]

refute v (-tes, -ting, -ted) disprove > **refutation** n (pl -s)

refutation n ▷ refute

refutations n ▷ refute

refuted v ▷ refute

refutes v ▷ refute

refuting v ▷ refute

regain v (-s, -ing, -ed) get back or recover

regained v ▷ regain

regaining v ▷ regain

regains v ▷ regain

regal adj of or like a king or queen > **regally** adv

regalia pl n ceremonial emblems of royalty or high office

regale v (-les, -ling, -led) entertain (someone) with stories etc.

regaled v ▷ regale

regales v ▷ regale

regaling v ▷ regale

regally adv ▷ regal

regard v (-s, -ing, -ed) consider ▶ n (pl -s) respect or esteem ▶ pl expression of goodwill

regarded v ▷ regard

regarding in respect of, concerning v ▷ regard

regardless adj heedless ▶ adv in spite of everything

regards v, n ▷ regard

regatta n (pl -s) meeting for yacht or boat races

regattas n ▷ regatta

regenerate v (-tes, -ting, -ted) (cause to) undergo spiritual, moral, or physical renewal > **regeneration** n (pl -s) > **regenerative** adj

regenerated v ▷ regenerate

regenerates v ▷ regenerate

regenerating v ▷ regenerate

regeneration n ▷ regenerate

regenerations n ▷ regenerate

regenerative adj ▷ regenerate

regencies n ▷ regency

regency n (pl -ies) status or period of office of a regent

regent n (pl -s) ruler of a kingdom during the absence, childhood, or illness of its monarch ▶ adj ruling as a regent

regents n ▷ regent

reggae n (pl -s) style of Jamaican popular music with a strong beat

reggaes n ▷ reggae

regicide n (pl -s) killing of a king

regicides n ▷ regicide

regime [ray-**zheem**] n (pl -s) system of government

regimen n (pl -s) prescribed system of diet etc.

regimens n ▷ regimen

regiment n (pl -s) organized body of troops as a unit of the army > **regimental** adj > **regimentation** n (pl -s)

regimental adj ▷ regiment

regimentation n ▷ regiment

regimentations n ▷ regiment
regimented adj very strictly controlled
regiments n ▷ regiment
regimes n ▷ regime
region n (pl -s) administrative division of a country > **regional** adj
regional adj ▷ region
regions n ▷ region
register n (pl -s) (book containing) an official list or record of things ▶ v (-s, -ing, -ed) enter in a register or set down in writing > **registration** n (pl -s)
registered v ▷ register
registering v ▷ register
registers n, v ▷ register
registrar n (pl -s) keeper of official records
registrars n ▷ registrar
registration n ▷ register
registrations n ▷ registers
regress v (-es, -ing, -ed) revert to a former worse condition
regressed v ▷ regress
regresses v ▷ regress
regressing v ▷ regress
regression n (pl -s) act of regressing (PSYCHOL) > **regressive** adj
regressions n ▷ regression
regressive adj ▷ regression
regret v (-s, -tting, -tted) feel sorry about ▶ n (pl -s) feeling of repentance, guilt, or sorrow > **regretful** adj > **regrettable** adj
regretful adj ▷ regret
regrets v ▷ regret
regrettable adj ▷ regret
regretted v ▷ regret
regretting v ▷ regret
regular adj normal, customary, or usual ▶ n (pl -s) regular soldier > **regularity** n (pl -s) > **regularize** v (-zes, -zing, -zed) > **regularly** adv
regularities n ▷ regular
regularity n ▷ regular
regularize v ▷ regular
regularized v ▷ regular
regularizes v ▷ regular
regularizing v ▷ regular
regularly adv ▷ regular
regulars n ▷ regular
regulate v (-tes, -ting, -ted) control, esp. by rules
regulated v ▷ regulate
regulates v ▷ regulate
regulating v ▷ regulate
regulation n (pl -s) rule
regulations n ▷ regulation

regulator n (pl -s) device that automatically controls pressure, temperature, etc.
regulators n ▷ regulator
regurgitate v (-tes, -ting, -ted) vomit > **regurgitation** n (pl -s)
regurgitated v ▷ regurgitate
regurgitates v ▷ regurgitate
regurgitating v ▷ regurgitate
regurgitation n ▷ regurgitate
regurgitations n ▷ regurgitate
rehabilitate v (-tes, -ting, -ted) help (a person) to readjust to society after illness, imprisonment, etc. > **rehabilitation** n (pl -s)
rehabilitated v ▷ rehabilitate
rehabilitates v ▷ rehabilitate
rehabilitating v ▷ rehabilitate
rehabilitation n ▷ rehabilitate
rehabilitations n ▷ rehabilitate
rehash v (-es, -ing, -ed) rework or reuse ▶ n (pl -es) old ideas presented in a new form
rehashed v ▷ rehash
rehashes v, n ▷ rehash
rehashing v ▷ rehash
rehearse v (-es, -sing, -sed) practise (a play, concert, etc.) > **rehearsal** n (pl -s)
rehearsal n ▷ rehearse
rehearsals n ▷ rehearse
rehearsed v ▷ rehearse
rehearses v ▷ rehearse
rehearsing v ▷ rehearse
rehouse v (-ses, -sing, -sed) provide with a new (and better) home
rehoused v ▷ rehouse
rehouses v ▷ rehouse
rehousing v ▷ rehouse
reign n (pl -s) period of a sovereign's rule ▶ v (-s, -ing, -ed) rule (a country)
reigned v ▷ reign
reigning v ▷ reign
reigns n, v ▷ reign
reimburse v (-ses, -sing, -sed) refund, pay back > **reimbursement** n (pl -s)
reimbursed v ▷ reimburse
reimbursement n ▷ reimburse
reimbursements n ▷ reimburse
reimburses v ▷ reimburse
reimbursing v ▷ reimburse
rein v (-s, -ing, -ed) check or manage with reins
reincarnation n (pl -s) rebirth of a soul in successive bodies > **reincarnate** v (-tes, -ting, -ted)
reincarnate v ▷ reincarnation
reincarnated v ▷ reincarnation
reincarnates v ▷ reincarnation
reincarnating v ▷ reincarnation

reincarnations n ▷ reincarnation
reindeer n (pl -deer, -deers) deer of arctic regions with large branched antlers
reindeers n ▷ reindeer
reined v ▷ rein
reining v ▷ rein
reinforce v (-ces, -cing, -ced) strengthen with new support, material, or force > **reinforcement** n (pl -s)
reinforced v ▷ reinforce
reinforcement n ▷ reinforce
reinforcements n ▷ reinforce
reinforces v ▷ reinforce
reinforcing v ▷ reinforce
reins pl n narrow straps attached to a bit to guide a horse ▶ v ▷ rein
reinstate v (-tes, -ting, -ted) restore to a former position > **reinstatement** n (pl -s)
reinstated v ▷ reinstate
reinstatement n ▷ reinstate
reinstatements n ▷ reinstate
reinstates v ▷ reinstate
reinstating v ▷ reinstate
reiterate v (-tes, -ting, -ted) repeat again and again > **reiteration** n (pl -s)
reiterated v ▷ reiterate
reiterates v ▷ reiterate
reiterating v ▷ reiterate
reiteration n ▷ reiterate
reiterations n ▷ reiterate
reject v (-s, -ing, -ed) refuse to accept or believe ▶ n (pl -s) person or thing rejected as not up to standard > **rejection** n (pl -s)
rejected v ▷ reject
rejecting v ▷ reject
rejection n ▷ reject
rejections n ▷ reject
rejects v, n ▷ reject
rejig v (-s, -gging, -gged) re-equip (a factory or plant)
rejigged v ▷ rejig
rejigging v ▷ rejig
rejigs v ▷ rejig
rejoice v (-ces, -cing, -ced) feel or express great happiness
rejoiced v ▷ rejoice
rejoices v ▷ rejoice
rejoicing v ▷ rejoice
rejoin[1] v (-s, -ing, -ed) join again
rejoin[2] v (-s, -ing, -ed) reply
rejoinder (pl -s) n answer, retort
rejoinders n ▷ rejoinder
rejoined v ▷ rejoin[1, 2]
rejoining v ▷ rejoin[1, 2]
rejoins v ▷ rejoin[1, 2]

rejuvenate v (-tes, -ting, -ted) restore youth or vitality to > **rejuvenation** n (pl -s)
rejuvenated v ▷ rejuvenate
rejuvenates v ▷ rejuvenate
rejuvenating v ▷ rejuvenate
rejuvenation n ▷ rejuvenate
rejuvenations v ▷ rejuvenate
relapse v (-ses, -sing, -sed) fall back into bad habits, illness, etc. ▶ n (pl -s) return of bad habits, illness, etc.
relapsed v ▷ relapse
relapses v, n ▷ relapse
relapsing v ▷ relapse
relate v (-tes, -ting, -ted) establish a relation between > **related** adj
related adj, v ▷ relate
relates v ▷ relate
relating v ▷ relate
relation n (pl -s) connection between things ▶ pl social or political dealings
relations n ▷ relation
relationship n (pl -s) dealings and feelings between people or countries
relationships n ▷ relationship
relative adj dependent on relation to something else, not absolute ▶ n (pl -s) person connected by blood or marriage > **relatively** adv
relatively adv ▷ relative
relatives n ▷ relative
relativities n ▷ relativity
relativity n (pl -ies) subject of two theories of Albert Einstein, dealing with relationships of space, time, and motion, and acceleration and gravity
relax v (-es, -ing, -ed) make or become looser, less tense, or less rigid > **relaxing** adj > **relaxation** n (pl -s)
relaxation n ▷ relax
relaxations n ▷ relax
relaxed v ▷ relax
relaxes v ▷ relax
relaxing v, adj ▷ relax
relay n (pl -s) fresh set of people or animals relieving others ▶ v (-s, -ing, -ed) pass on (a message)
relayed v ▷ relay
relaying v ▷ relay
relays n, v ▷ relay
release v (-ses, -sing, -sed) set free ▶ n (pl -s) setting free
released v ▷ release
releases v, n ▷ release
releasing v ▷ release
relegate v (-tes, -ting, -ted) put in a less

important position > **relegation** n (pl -s)
relegated v ▷ relegate
relegates v ▷ relegate
relegating v ▷ relegate
relegation n ▷ relegate
relegations n ▷ relegate
relent v (-s, -ing, -ed) give up a harsh intention, become less severe
relented v ▷ relent
relenting v ▷ relent
relentless adj unremitting
relents v ▷ relent
relevance n ▷ relevant
relevances n ▷ relevant
relevant adj to do with the matter in hand
> **relevance** n (pl -s)
reliabilities n ▷ reliable
reliability n ▷ reliable
reliable adj able to be trusted, dependable
> **reliably** adv > **reliability** n (pl -ies)
reliably adv ▷ reliable
reliance n (pl -s) dependence, confidence, or trust > **reliant** adj
reliances n ▷ reliance
reliant adj ▷ reliance
relic n (pl -s) something that has survived from the past ▶ pl remains or traces
relics n ▷ relic
relict n (pl -s) (Obs) widow
relicts n ▷ relict
relied v ▷ rely
relief n (pl -s) gladness at the end or removal of pain, distress, etc.
reliefs n ▷ relief
relies v ▷ rely
relieve v (-ves, -ving, -ved) bring relief to
relieved v ▷ relieve
relieves v ▷ relieve
relieving v ▷ relieve
religion n (pl -s) system of belief in and worship of a supernatural power or god
religious adj of religion > **religiously** adv
religiously adv ▷ religious
religions n ▷ religion
relinquish v (-es, -ing, -ed) give up or abandon
relinquished v ▷ relinquish
relinquishes v ▷ relinquish
relinquishing v ▷ relinquish
reliquaries n ▷ reliquary
reliquary n (pl -ies) case or shrine for holy relics
relish v (-es, -ing, -ed) enjoy, like very much ▶ n (pl -es) liking or enjoyment
relished v ▷ relish
relishes v, n ▷ relish
relishing v ▷ relish

relocate v (-tes, -ting, -ted) move to a new place to live or work > **relocation** n (pl -s)
relocated v ▷ relocate
relocates v ▷ relocate
relocating v ▷ relocate
relocation n ▷ relocate
relocations n ▷ relocate
reluctance n ▷ reluctant
reluctances n ▷ reluctant
reluctant adj unwilling or disinclined
> **reluctantly** adv > **reluctance** n (pl -s)
reluctantly adv ▷ reluctant
rely v (-ies, -ying, -ied) depend (on)
relying v ▷ rely
remain v (-s, -ing, -ed) continue
remainder n (pl -s) part which is left ▶ v (-s, -ing, -ed) offer (copies of a poorly selling book) at reduced prices
remaindered v ▷ remainders
remaindering v ▷ remainders
remainders n, v ▷ remainders
remained v ▷ remain
remaining v ▷ remain
remains pl n relics, esp. of ancient buildings
▶ v ▷ remain
remand v (-s, -ing, -ed) send back into custody or put on bail before trial
remanded v ▷ remand
remanding v ▷ remand
remands v ▷ remand
remark v (-s, -ing, -ed) make a casual comment (on) ▶ n (pl -s) observation or comment
remarkable adj worthy of note or attention
> **remarkably** adv
remarkably adv ▷ remarkable
remarked v ▷ remark
remarking v ▷ remark
remarks v, n ▷ remark
remedial adj intended to correct a specific disability, handicap, etc.
remedied v ▷ remedy
remedies n, v ▷ remedy
remedy n (pl -ies) means of curing pain or disease ▶ v (-ies, -ying, -ied) put right
remedying v ▷ remedy
remember v (-s, -ing, -ed) retain in or recall to one's memory
remembered v ▷ remember
remembering v ▷ remember
remembers v ▷ remember
remembrance n (pl -s) memory
remembrances n ▷ remembrance
remind v (-s, -ing, -ed) cause to remember
reminded v ▷ remind
reminder n (pl -s) something that recalls the

past
reminders n ▷ reminder
reminding v ▷ remind
reminds v ▷ remind
reminisce v (-ces, -cing, -ced) talk or write of past times, experiences, etc.
reminisced v ▷ reminisce
reminiscence n (pl -s) remembering ▶ pl memoirs
reminiscences n ▷ reminiscence
reminiscent adj reminding or suggestive (of)
reminisces v ▷ reminisce
reminiscing v ▷ reminisce
remiss adj negligent or careless
remission n (pl -s) reduction in the length of a prison term
remissions n ▷ remission
remit v (-s, -tting, -tted) send (money) for goods, services, etc., esp. by post ▶ n (pl -s) [ree-mitt] area of competence or authority
remits v, n ▷ remit
remittance n (pl -s) money sent as payment
remittances n ▷ remittance
remitted v ▷ remit
remitting v ▷ remit
remnant n (pl -s) small piece, esp. of fabric, left over
remnants n ▷ remnant
remonstrance n ▷ remonstrate
remonstrances n ▷ remonstrate
remonstrate v (-tes, -ting, -ted) argue in protest > **remonstrance** n (pl -s)
remonstrated v ▷ remonstrate
remonstrates v ▷ remonstrate
remonstrating v ▷ remonstrate
remorse n (pl -s) feeling of sorrow and regret for something one did > **remorseful** adj
remorseful adj ▷ remorse
remorseless adj pitiless > **remorselessly** adv
remorselessly adv ▷ remorseless
remorses n ▷ remorse
remote adj (-er, -est) far away, distant > **remotely** adv
remoter adj ▷ remote
remotest adj ▷ remote
remotely adv ▷ remote
remould v (-s, -ing, -ed) (BRIT) renovate (a worn tyre) ▶ n (pl -s) (BRIT) renovated tyre
remoulded v ▷ remould
remoulding v ▷ remould
remoulds v ▷ remould
remove v (-ves, -ving, -ved) take away or off ▶ n (pl -s) degree of difference > **removable** adj
removable adj ▷ remove
removal n (pl -s) removing, esp. changing

residence
removals n ▷ removal
removed v ▷ remove
removes v, n ▷ remove
removing v ▷ remove
remunerate v (-tes, -ting, -ted) reward or pay > **remunerative** adj
remunerated v ▷ remunerate
remunerates v ▷ remunerate
remunerating v ▷ remunerate
remuneration n (pl -s) reward or payment
remunerations n ▷ remuneration
remunerative adj ▷ remuneration
renaissance n (pl -s) revival or rebirth
renaissances n ▷ renaissance
renal [ree-nal] adj of the kidneys
renascent adj becoming active or vigorous again
rend v (-s, -ing, rent) tear or wrench apart
render v (-s, -ing, -ed) cause to become
rendered v ▷ render
rendering v ▷ render
renders v ▷ render
rendezvous [ron-day-voo] n (pl -vous) appointment ▶ v (-vous, -vousing, -voused) meet as arranged
rendezvoused v ▷ rendezvous
rendezvousing v ▷ rendezvous
rending v ▷ rend
rendition n (pl -s) performance
renditions n ▷ rendition
rends v ▷ rend
renegade n (pl -s) person who deserts a cause
renegades n ▷ renegade
renege [rin-nayg] v (-ges, -ging, -ged) go back (on a promise etc.)
reneged v ▷ renege
reneges v ▷ renege
reneging v ▷ renege
renew v (-s, -ing, -ed) begin again > **renewable** adj > **renewal** n (pl -s)
renewable adj ▷ renew
renewal n ▷ renew
renewals n ▷ renew
renewed v ▷ renew
renewing v ▷ renew
renews v ▷ renew
rennet n (pl -s) substance for curdling milk to make cheese
rennets n ▷ rennet
renounce v (-ces, -cing, -ced) give up (a belief, habit, etc.) voluntarily > **renunciation** n (pl -s)
renounced v ▷ renounce
renounces v ▷ renounce
renouncing v ▷ renounce

renovate v (-tes, -ting, -ted) restore to good condition > **renovation** n (pl -s)
renovated v ▷ renovate
renovates v ▷ renovate
renovating v ▷ renovate
renovation n ▷ renovate
renovations n ▷ renovate
renown n (pl -s) widespread good reputation
renowned adj famous
renowns n ▷ renown
rent¹ v (-s, -ing, -ed) give or have use of in return for regular payments ▶ n (pl -s) regular payment for use of land, a building, etc.
rent² n (pl -s) tear or fissure ▶ v ▷ rend
rental n (pl -s) sum payable as rent
rentals n ▷ rental
rented v ▷ rent¹
renting v ▷ rent¹
rentings n ▷ rent¹
rents v ▷ rent¹ ▶ n ▷ rent²
renunciation n ▷ renounce
renunciations n ▷ renounce
reorganize v (-zes, -zing, -zed) organize in a new and more efficient way > **reorganization** n (pl -s)
reorganization n ▷ reorganize
reorganizations n ▷ reorganize
reorganized v ▷ reorganize
reorganizes v ▷ reorganize
reorganizing v ▷ reorganize
rep¹ n (pl -s) repertory company
rep² n (pl -s) ▷ representative
repair¹ v (-s, -ing, -ed) restore to good condition, mend ▶ n (pl -s) act of repairing
repair² v (-s, -ing, -ed) go (to)
repaired v ▷ repair¹, ²
repairing v ▷ repair¹, ²
repairs v ▷ repair¹, ² ▶ n ▷ repair¹
reparation n (pl -s) something done or given as compensation
reparations n ▷ reparation
repartee n (pl -s) interchange of witty retorts
repartees n ▷ repartee
repast n (pl -s) meal
repasts n ▷ repast
repatriate v (-tes, -ting, -ted) send (someone) back to his or her own country > **repatriation** n (pl -s)
repatriated v ▷ repatriate
repatriates v ▷ repatriate
repatriating v ▷ repatriate
repatriation n ▷ repatriate
repatriations n ▷ repatriate
repay v (-s, -ing, -paid) pay back, refund > **repayable** adj > **repayment** n (pl -s)

repayable adj ▷ repay
repaying v ▷ repay
repayment n ▷ repay
repayments n ▷ repay
repays v ▷ repay
repeal v (-s, -ing, -ed) cancel (a law) officially ▶ n (pl -s) act of repealing
repealed v ▷ repeal
repealing v ▷ repeal
repeals v, n ▷ repeal
repeat v (-s, -ing, -ed) say or do again ▶ n (pl -s) act or instance of repeating > **repeatedly** adv
repeated v ▷ repeat
repeatedly adv ▷ repeat
repeater n (pl -s) firearm that may be discharged many times without reloading
repeaters n ▷ repeater
repeating v ▷ repeat
repeats v, n ▷ repeat
repel v (-s, -lling, -lled) be disgusting to
repelled v ▷ repel
repellent adj distasteful ▶ n (pl -s) something that repels, esp. a chemical to repel insects
repellents n ▷ repellent
repelling v ▷ repel
repels v ▷ repel
repent v (-s, -ing, -ed) feel regret for (a deed or omission) > **repentance** n (pl -s) > **repentant** adj
repentance n ▷ repent
repentances n ▷ repent
repentant adj ▷ repent
repented v ▷ repent
repenting v ▷ repent
repents v ▷ repent
repercussions pl n indirect effects, often unpleasant
repertoire n (pl -s) stock of plays, songs, etc. that a player or company can give
repertoires n ▷ repertoire
repertories n ▷ repertory
repertory n (pl -ies) repertoire
repetition n (pl -s) act of repeating
repetitions n ▷ repetition
repetitious adj ▷ repetitive
repetitive, repetitious adj full of repetition
rephrase v (-ses, -sing, -sed) express in different words
rephrased v ▷ rephrase
rephrases v ▷ rephrase
rephrasing v ▷ rephrase
repine v (-nes, -ning, -ned) fret or complain
repined v ▷ repine
repines v ▷ repine
repining v ▷ repine

replace v (-ces, -cing, -ced) substitute for
> **replacement** n (pl -s)
  replaced v ▷ replace
  replacement n ▷ replace
  replacements n ▷ replace
  replaces v ▷ replace
  replacing v ▷ replace
replay n (pl -s) immediate reshowing on TV
of an incident in sport, esp. in slow motion
▶ v (-s, -ing, -ed) play (a match, recording,
etc.) again
  replayed v ▷ replay
  replaying v ▷ replay
  replays n, v ▷ replay
replenish v (-es, -ing, -ed) fill up again,
resupply > **replenishment** n (pl -s)
  replenished v ▷ replenish
  replenishes v ▷ replenish
  replenishing v ▷ replenish
  replenishment n ▷ replenish
  replenishments n ▷ replenish
replete adj filled or gorged
replica n (pl -s) exact copy
  replicas n ▷ replica
replicate v (-s, -ing, -ed) make or be a copy of
  replicated v ▷ replicate
  replicates v ▷ replicate
  replicating v ▷ replicate
  replied v ▷ reply
  replies v, n ▷ reply
reply v (-ies, -ying, -ied) answer or respond ▶ n
(pl -ies) answer or response
  replying v ▷ reply
report v (-s, -ing, -ed) give an account of ▶ n (pl
-s) account or statement
  reported v ▷ report
reportedly adv according to rumour
reporter n (pl -s) person who gathers news for
a newspaper, TV, etc.
  reporters n ▷ reporter
  reporting v ▷ report
  reports v, n ▷ report
repose n (pl -s) peace ▶ v (-ses, -sing, -sed) lie
or lay at rest
  reposed v ▷ repose
  reposes n, v ▷ repose
  reposing v ▷ repose
  repositories n ▷ repository
repository n (pl -ies) place where valuables are
deposited for safekeeping, store
repossess v (-es, -ing, -ed) (of a lender) take
back property from a customer who is behind
with payments > **repossession** n (pl -s)
  repossessed v ▷ repossess
  repossesses v ▷ repossess

  repossessing v ▷ repossess
  repossession n ▷ repossess
  repossessions n ▷ repossess
reprehensible adj open to criticism,
unworthy
represent v (-s, -ing, -ed) act as a delegate or
substitute for > **representation** n (pl -s)
  representation n ▷ represent
  representations n ▷ represent
representative n (pl -s) person chosen to
stand for a group ▶ adj typical
  representatives n ▷ representative
  represented v ▷ represent
  representing v ▷ represent
  represents v ▷ represent
repress v (-es, -ing, -ed) keep (feelings) in
check > **repression** n (pl -s) > **repressive** adj
  repressed v ▷ repress
  represses v ▷ repress
  repressing v ▷ repress
  repression n ▷ repress
  repressions n ▷ repress
  repressive adj ▷ repress
reprieve v (-ves, -ving, -ved) postpone the
execution of (a condemned person) ▶ n (pl
-s) (document granting) postponement or
cancellation of a punishment
  reprieved v ▷ reprieve
  reprieves n, v ▷ reprieve
  reprieving v ▷ reprieve
reprimand v (-s, -ing, -ed) blame (someone)
officially for a fault ▶ n (pl -s) official blame
  reprimanded v ▷ reprimand
  reprimanding v ▷ reprimand
  reprimands v, n ▷ reprimand
reprint v (-s, -ing, -ed) print further copies of (a
book) ▶ n (pl -s) reprinted copy
  reprinted v ▷ reprint
  reprinting v ▷ reprint
  reprints v, n ▷ reprint
reprisal n (pl -s) retaliation
  reprisals n ▷ reprisal
reproach n, v (-s, -ing, -ed) blame, rebuke
> **reproachful** adj > **reproachfully** adv
  reproached v ▷ reproach
  reproaches v ▷ reproach
  reproachful adj ▷ reproach
  reproachfully adv ▷ reproach
  reproaching v ▷ reproach
reprobate adj, n (pl -s) depraved or
disreputable (person)
  reprobates n ▷ reprobate
reproduce v (-ces, -cing, -ced) produce a copy
of > **reproducible** adj
  reproduced v ▷ reproduce

reproduces v ▷ reproduce
reproducible adj ▷ reproduce
reproducing v ▷ reproduce
reproduction n (pl -s) process of reproducing > **reproductive** adj
reproductions n ▷ reproduction
reproductive adj ▷ reproduction
reproof n (pl -s) severe blaming of someone for a fault
reproofs n ▷ reproof
reprove v (-ves, -ving, -ved) speak severely to (someone) about a fault
reproved v ▷ reprove
reproves v ▷ reprove
reproving v ▷ reprove
reps n ▷ rep¹,²
reptile n (pl -s) cold-blooded egg-laying vertebrate with horny scales or plates, such as a snake or tortoise > **reptilian** adj
reptiles n ▷ reptile
reptilian adj ▷ reptile
republic n (pl -s) form of government in which the people or their elected representatives possess the supreme power
republican n (pl -s) supporter or advocate of a republic > **republicanism** n (pl -s)
republicans n ▷ republican
republicanism n ▷ republican
republicanisms n ▷ republican
republics n ▷ republic
repudiate [rip-**pew**-dee-ate] v (-tes, -ting, -ted) reject the authority or validity of > **repudiation** n (pl -s)
repudiated v ▷ repudiate
repudiates v ▷ repudiate
repudiating v ▷ repudiate
repudiation n ▷ repudiate
repudiations n ▷ repudiate
repugnance n ▷ repugnant
repugnances n ▷ repugnant
repugnant adj offensive or distasteful > **repugnance** n (pl -s)
repulse v (-ses, -sing, -sed) be disgusting to ▶ n (pl -s) driving back
repulsed v ▷ repulse
repulsing v ▷ repulse
repulses v, n ▷ repulse
repulsion n (pl -s) distaste or aversion
repulsions n ▷ repulsion
repulsive adj loathsome, disgusting
reputable adj of good reputation, respectable
reputation n (pl -s) estimation in which a person is held
reputations n ▷ reputation
repute n (pl -s) reputation

reputed adj supposed > **reputedly** adv
reputedly adv ▷ reputed
reputes n ▷ repute
request v (-s, -ing, -ed) ask ▶ n (pl -s) asking
requested v ▷ request
requesting v ▷ request
requests v, n ▷ request
requiem [**rek**-wee-em] n (pl -s) Mass for the dead
requiems n ▷ requiem
require v (-res, -ring, -red) want or need
required v ▷ require
requirement n (pl -s) essential condition
requirements v ▷ requirement
requires v ▷ require
requiring v ▷ require
requisite [**rek**-wizz-it] adj necessary, essential ▶ n (pl -s) essential thing
requisites n ▷ requisite
requisition v (-s, -ing, -ed) demand (supplies) ▶ n (pl -s) formal demand, such as for materials or supplies
requisitioned v ▷ requisition
requisitioning v ▷ requisition
requisitions v, n ▷ requisition
requite v (-tes, -ting, -ted) return to someone (the same treatment or feeling as received)
requited v ▷ requite
requites v ▷ requite
requiting v ▷ requite
reredos [**rear**-doss] n (pl -es) ornamental screen behind an altar
reredoses n ▷ reredos
resat v ▷ resit
rescind v (-s, -ing, -ed) annul or repeal
rescinded v ▷ rescind
rescinding v ▷ rescind
rescinds v ▷ rescind
rescue v (-cues, -cuing, -cued) deliver from danger or trouble, save ▶ n (pl -s) rescuing > **rescuer** n (pl -s)
rescued v ▷ rescue
rescuer n ▷ rescue
rescuers n ▷ rescue
rescues v, n ▷ rescue
rescuing v ▷ rescue
research n (pl -es) systematic investigation to discover facts or collect information ▶ v (-es, -ing, -ed) carry out investigations > **researcher** n (pl -s)
researched v ▷ research
researcher n ▷ research
researchers n ▷ research
researches n, v ▷ research
researching v ▷ research

resemblance *n* ▷ resemble
resemblances *n* ▷ resemble
resemble *v* (-s, -ling, -led) be or look like
> **resemblance** *n* (*pl* -s)
resembled *v* ▷ resemble
resembles *v* ▷ resemble
resembling *v* ▷ resemble
resent *v* (-s, -ing, -ed) feel bitter about
> **resentful** *adj* > **resentment** *n* (*pl* -s)
resented *v* ▷ resent
resentful *adj* ▷ resent
resenting *v* ▷ resent
resentment *n* ▷ resent
resentments *n* ▷ resent
resents *v* ▷ resent
reservation *n* (*pl* -s) doubt
reservations *n* ▷ reservation
reserve *v* (-ves, -ving, -ved) set aside, keep for
future use ▶ *n* (*pl* -s) something, esp. money
or troops, kept for emergencies (SPORT)
reserved *adj* not showing one's feelings,
lacking friendliness ▶ *v* ▷ reserve
reserves *v*, *n* ▷ reserve
reserving *v* ▷ reserve
reservist *n* (*pl* -s) member of a military reserve
reservists *n* ▷ reservist
reservoir *n* (*pl* -s) natural or artificial lake
storing water for community supplies
reservoirs *n* ▷ reservoir
reshuffle *n* (*pl* -s) reorganization ▶ *v* (-s, -ing,
-ed) reorganize
reshuffled *n* ▷ reshuffle
reshuffles *n*, *v* ▷ reshuffle
reshuffling *v* ▷ reshuffle
reside *v* (-des, -ding, -ded) dwell permanently
resided *v* ▷ reside
residence *n* (*pl* -s) home or house
residences *n* ▷ residence
resident *n* (*pl* -s) person who lives in a place
▶ *adj* living in a place
residential *adj* (of part of a town) consisting
mainly of houses
residents *n* ▷ resident
resides *v* ▷ reside
residing *v* ▷ reside
residue *n* (*pl* -s) what is left, remainder
> **residual** *adj*
residual *adj* ▷ residue
residues *n* ▷ residue
resign *v* (-s, -ing, -ed) give up office, a job, etc.
resignation *n* (*pl* -s) resigning
resignations *n* ▷ resignation
resigned *adj* content to endure ▶ *v* ▷ resign
resigning *v* ▷ resign
resigns *v* ▷ resign

resilience *n* ▷ resilient
resiliences *n* ▷ resilient
resilient *adj* (of a person) recovering quickly
from a shock etc. > **resilience** *n* (*pl* -s)
resin [rezz-in] *n* (*pl* -s) sticky substance from
plants, esp. pines > **resinous** *adj*
resinous *adj* ▷ resin
resins *n* ▷ resin
resist *v* (-s, -ing, -ed) withstand or oppose
> **resistant** *adj* > **resistible** *adj*
resistance *n* (*pl* -s) act of resisting
resistances *n* ▷ resistance
resistant *adj* ▷ resist
resisted *v* ▷ resist
resistible *adj* ▷ resist
resisting *v* ▷ resist
resistor *n* (*pl* -s) component of an electrical
circuit producing resistance
resistors *n* ▷ resistor
resists *v* ▷ resist
resit *v* (-s, -tting, -sat) take (an exam) again ▶ *n*
(*pl* -s) exam that has to be taken again
resitting *v* ▷ resit
resits *v*, *n* ▷ resit
resolute *adj* firm in purpose > **resolutely** *adv*
resolutely *adv* ▷ resolute
resolution *n* (*pl* -s) firmness of conduct or
character
resolutions *n* ▷ resolution
resolve *v* (-ves, -ving, -ved) decide with an
effort of will
resolved *adj* determined ▶ *v* ▷ resolve
resolves *v* ▷ resolve
resolving *v* ▷ resolve
resonance *n* (*pl* -s) echoing, esp. with a deep
sound > **resonant** *adj* > **resonate** *v* (-tes,
-ting, -ted)
resonances *n* ▷ resonance
resonant *adj* ▷ resonance
resonate *v* ▷ resonance
resonated *v* ▷ resonance
resonates *v* ▷ resonance
resonating *v* ▷ resonance
resort *v* (-s, -ing, -ed) have recourse (to) for
help etc. ▶ *n* (*pl* -s) place for holidays
resorted *v* ▷ resort
resorting *v* ▷ resort
resorts *v*, *n* ▷ resort
resound [riz-zownd] *v* (-s, -ing, -ed) echo or ring
with sound
resounded *v* ▷ resound
resounding *adj* echoing ▶ *v* ▷ resound
resounds *v* ▷ resound
resource *n* (*pl* -s) thing resorted to for
support ▶ *pl* sources of economic wealth

> resourceful adj > resourcefulness n
resourceful adj ▷ resource
resourcefulness n ▷ resource
resources n ▷ resource
respect n (pl -s) consideration ▸ v (-s, -ing, -ed) treat with esteem > respecter n (pl -s)
> respectful adj
respectable adj worthy of respect
> respectably adv > respectability n (pl -ies)
respectabilities n ▷ respectable
respectability n ▷ respectable
respectably adv ▷ respectable
respected v ▷ respect
respecter n ▷ respect
respecters n ▷ respect
respectful adj ▷ respect
respecting prep concerning ▸ v ▷ respect
respective adj relating separately to each of those in question > respectively adv
respectively adv ▷ respective
respects n, v ▷ respect
respiration [ress-per-ray-shun] n (pl -s) breathing > respiratory adj
respirations n ▷ respiration
respirator n apparatus worn over the mouth and breathed through as protection against dust, poison gas, etc., or to provide artificial respiration
respirators n ▷ respirator
respiratory adj ▷ respiration
respire v (-res, -ring, -red) breathe
respired v ▷ respire
respires v ▷ respire
respiring v ▷ respire
respite n (pl -s) pause, interval of rest
respites n ▷ respite
resplendence n ▷ resplendent
resplendences n ▷ resplendent
resplendent adj brilliant or splendid
> resplendence n (pl -s)
respond v (-s, -ing, -ed) answer
responded v ▷ respond
respondent n (pl -s) (LAW) defendant
respondents n ▷ respondent
responding v ▷ respond
responds v ▷ respond
response n (pl -s) answer
responses n ▷ response
responsibilities n ▷ responsibility
responsibility n (pl -ies) state of being responsible
responsible adj having control and authority
> responsibly adv
responsibly adv ▷ responsible
responsive adj readily reacting to some

influence > responsiveness n
responsiveness n ▷ responsive
rest¹ n (pl -s) freedom from exertion etc. ▸ v (-s, -ing, -ed) take a rest > restful adj > restless adj
rest² n what is left ▸ v (-s, -ing, -ed) remain, continue to be
restaurant n (pl -s) commercial establishment serving meals
restaurants n ▷ restaurant
restaurateur [rest-er-a-tur] n (pl -s) person who owns or runs a restaurant
restaurateurs n ▷ restaurateur
rested v ▷ rest¹, ²
restful (-ler, -lest) adj ▷ rest¹
restfuller adj ▷ restful
restfullest adj ▷ restful
resting v ▷ rest¹, ²
restitution n (pl -s) giving back
restitutions n ▷ restitution
restive adj restless or impatient
restless adj ▷ rest¹
restore v (-res, -ring, -red) return (a building, painting, etc.) to its original condition
> restoration n (pl -s) > restorer n (pl -s)
restoration n ▷ restore
restorations n ▷ restore
restorative adj restoring ▸ n (pl -s) food or medicine to strengthen etc.
restoratives n ▷ restorative
restored v ▷ restore
restorer n ▷ restore
restorers n ▷ restore
restores v ▷ restore
restoring v ▷ restore
restrain v (-s, -ing, -ed) hold (someone) back from action
restrained adj not displaying emotion ▸ v ▷ restrain
restraining v ▷ restrain
restrains v ▷ restrain
restraint n (pl -s) control, esp. self-control
restraints n ▷ restraint
restrict v (-s, -ing, -ed) confine to certain limits > restriction n (pl -s) > restrictive adj
restricted v ▷ restrict
restricting v ▷ restrict
restriction n ▷ restrict
restrictions n ▷ restrict
restrictive adj ▷ restrict
restricts v ▷ restrict
restructure v (-res, -ring, -red) organize in a different way
restructured v ▷ restructure
restructures v ▷ restructure
restructuring v ▷ restructure

rests n, v ▷ rest¹, ²
result n (pl -s) outcome or consequence ▷ v (-s, -ing, -ed) (foll. by **from**) be the outcome or consequence (of) > **resultant** adj
  resultant adj ▷ result
  resulted v ▷ result
  resulting v ▷ result
  results n, v ▷ result
resume v (-mes, -ming, -med) begin again
  > **resumption** n (pl -s)
résumé [rezz-yew-may] n (pl -s) summary
  resumed v ▷ resume
  resumes v ▷ resume
  résumés n ▷ résumé
  resuming v ▷ resume
  resumption n ▷ resume
  resumptions n ▷ resume
resurgence n (pl -s) rising again to vigour
  > **resurgent** adj
  resurgences n ▷ resurgence
  resurgent adj ▷ resurgence
resurrect v (-s, -ing, -ed) restore to life
  resurrected v ▷ resurrect
  resurrecting v ▷ resurrect
resurrection n (pl -s) rising again (esp. from the dead)
  resurrections n ▷ resurrection
  resurrects v ▷ resurrect
resuscitate [ris-**suss**-it-tate] v (-tes, -ting, -ted) restore to consciousness > **resuscitation** n (pl -s)
  resuscitated v ▷ resuscitate
  resuscitates v ▷ resuscitate
  resuscitating v ▷ resuscitate
  resuscitation n ▷ resuscitate
  resuscitations n ▷ resuscitate
retail n (pl -s) selling of goods individually or in small amounts to the public ▷ adv by retail ▷ v (-s, -ing, -ed) sell or be sold retail
  retailed v ▷ retail
retailer n (pl -s) person or company that sells goods to the public
  retailers n ▷ retailer
  retailing v ▷ retail
  retails n, v ▷ retail
retain v (-s, -ing, -ed) keep in one's possession
  retained v ▷ retain
retainer n (pl -s) fee to retain someone's services
  retainers n ▷ retainer
  retaining v ▷ retain
  retains v ▷ retain
retaliate v (-tes, -ting, -ted) repay an injury or wrong in kind > **retaliation** n (pl -s)
  > **retaliatory** adj

retaliated v ▷ retaliate
retaliates v ▷ retaliate
retaliating v ▷ retaliate
retaliation n ▷ retaliate
retaliations n ▷ retaliate
retaliatory adj ▷ retaliate
retard v (-s, -ing, -ed) delay or slow (progress or development) > **retardation** n (pl -s)
  retardation n ▷ retard
  retardations n ▷ retard
retarded adj underdeveloped, esp. mentally
  ▷ v ▷ retard
  retarding v ▷ retard
  retards v ▷ retard
retch v (-es, -ing, -ed) try to vomit
  retched v ▷ retch
  retches v ▷ retch
  retching v ▷ retch
rethink v (-s, -ing, -thought) consider again, esp. with a view to changing one's tactics
  rethinks v ▷ rethink
  rethinking v ▷ rethink
  rethought v ▷ rethink
  reticence n ▷ reticent
  reticences n ▷ reticent
reticent adj uncommunicative, reserved
  > **reticence** n (pl -s)
retina n (pl -nas, -nae) light-sensitive membrane at the back of the eye
  retinae n ▷ retina
  retinas n ▷ retina
retinue n (pl -s) band of attendants
  retinues n ▷ retinue
retire v (-res, -ring, -red) (cause to) give up office or work, esp. through age > **retirement** n (pl -s)
retired adj having retired from work etc. ▷ v
  ▷ retire
  retirement n ▷ retire
  retirements n ▷ retire
  retires v ▷ retire
retiring adj shy ▷ v ▷ retire
retort¹ v (-s, -ing, -ed) reply quickly, wittily, or angrily ▷ n (pl -s) quick, witty, or angry reply
retort² n (pl -s) glass container with a bent neck used for distilling
  retorted v ▷ retort¹
  retorting v ▷ retort¹
  retorts v ▷ retort¹▷ n ▷ retort¹, ²
retouch v (-es, -ing, -ed) restore or improve by new touches, esp. of paint
  retouched v ▷ retouch
  retouches v ▷ retouch
  retouching v ▷ retouch
retrace v (-ces, -cing, -ced) go back over (a

route etc.) again

retraced v ▷ retrace

retraces v ▷ retrace

retracing v ▷ retrace

retract v (-s, -ing, -ed) withdraw (a statement etc.) > **retraction** n (pl -s)

retractable, retractile adj able to be retracted

retracted v ▷ retract

retractile adj ▷ retractable

retracting v ▷ retract

retracts v ▷ retract

retraction n ▷ retract

retractions n ▷ retract

retread v (-s, -ing, -ed) ▶ n (pl -s) ▷ remould

retreaded v ▷ retread

retreading v ▷ retread

retreads v, n ▷ retread

retreat v (-s, -ing, -ed) move back from a position, withdraw ▶ n (pl -s) act of or military signal for retiring or withdrawal

retreated v ▷ retreat

retreating v ▷ retreat

retreats v, n ▷ retreat

retrench v (-es, -ing, -ed) reduce expenditure, cut back > **retrenchment** n (pl -s)

retrenched v ▷ retrench

retrenches v ▷ retrench

retrenching v ▷ retrench

retrenchment n ▷ retrench

retrenchments n ▷ retrench

retrial n (pl -s) second trial of a case or defendant in a court of law

retrials n ▷ retrial

retribution n (pl -s) punishment or vengeance for evil deeds > **retributive** adj

retributions n ▷ retribution

retributive adj ▷ retribution

retrieve v (-ves, -ving, -ved) fetch back again > **retrievable** adj > **retrieval** n (pl -s)

retrievable adj ▷ retrieve

retrieval n ▷ retrieve

retrievals n ▷ retrieve

retrieved v ▷ retrieve

retriever n (pl -s) dog trained to retrieve shot game

retrievers n ▷ retrieve

retrieves v ▷ retrieve

retrieving v ▷ retrieve

retroactive adj effective from a date in the past

retrograde adj tending towards an earlier worse condition

retrogressive adj going back to an earlier worse condition > **retrogression** n (pl -s)

retrogression n ▷ retrogressive

retrogressions n ▷ retrogressive

retrorocket n (pl -s) small rocket engine used to slow a spacecraft

retrorockets n ▷ retrorocket

retrospective adj looking back in time ▶ n (pl -s) exhibition of an artist's life's work

retrospectives n ▷ retrospective

retroussé [rit-troo-say] adj (of a nose) turned upwards

retsina n (pl -s) Greek wine flavoured with resin

retsinas n ▷ retsina

return v (-s, -ing, -ed) go or come back ▶ n (pl -s) returning > **returnable** adj

returnable adj ▷ return

returned v ▷ return

returning v ▷ return

returns v, n ▷ return

reunion n (pl -s) meeting of people who have been apart

reunions n ▷ reunion

reunite v (-tes, -ting, -ted) bring or come together again after a separation

reunited v ▷ reunite

reunites v ▷ reunite

reuniting v ▷ reunite

reuse v (-ses, -sing, -sed) use again > **reusable** adj

reusable adj ▷ reuse

reused v ▷ reuse

reuses v ▷ reuse

reusing v ▷ reuse

rev (Informal) n (pl -s) revolution (of an engine) ▶ v (-s, -vving, -vved) (foll. by up) increase the speed of revolution of (an engine)

revalue v (-ues, -uing, -ued) adjust the exchange value of (a currency) upwards > **revaluation** n (pl -s)

revaluation n ▷ revalue

revaluations n ▷ revalue

revalued v ▷ revalue

revalues v ▷ revalue

revaluing v ▷ revalue

revamp v (-s, -ing, -ed) renovate or restore

revamped v ▷ revamp

revamping v ▷ revamp

revamps v ▷ revamp

reveal v (-s, -ing, -ed) make known > **revelation** n (pl -s)

revealed v ▷ reveal

revealing v ▷ reveal

reveals v ▷ reveal

reveille [riv-val-ee] n (pl -s) morning bugle call to waken soldiers

reveilles n ▷ reveille

revel v (-s, -lling, -lled) take pleasure (in)
> **reveller** n (pl -s)
revelation n ▷ revel
revelations n ▷ revel
revelled v ▷ revel
reveller n ▷ revel
revellers n ▷ revel
revelling v ▷ revel
revelries n ▷ revelry
revelry n (pl -s) festivity
revels pl n merrymaking ▶ v ▷ revel
revenge n (pl -s) retaliation for wrong done
 ▶ v (-ges, -ging, -ged) make retaliation for
> **revengeful** adj
revenged v ▷ revenge
revengeful adj ▷ revenge
revenges n, v ▷ revenge
revenging v ▷ revenge
revenue n (pl -s) income, esp. of a state
revenues n ▷ revenue
reverberate v (-tes, -ting, -ted) echo or
resound > **reverberation** n (pl -s)
reverberated v ▷ reverberate
reverberates v ▷ reverberate
reverberating v ▷ reverberate
reverberation n ▷ reverberate
reverberations n ▷ reverberate
revere v (-s, -ing, -ed) be in awe of and respect
greatly
revered v ▷ revere
reverence n (pl -s) awe mingled with respect
and esteem
reverences n ▷ reverence
reverent adj showing reverence > **reverently**
adv
reverential adj marked by reverence
reverently adv ▷ reverent
reveres v ▷ revere
revering v ▷ revere
reverie n (pl -s) absent-minded daydream
reveries n ▷ reverie
revers [riv-**veer**] n (pl -s) turned back part of a
garment, such as the lapel
reverse v (-ses, -sing, -sed) turn upside down
or the other way round ▶ n (pl -s) opposite
 ▶ adj opposite or contrary > **reversal** n (pl -s)
> **reversible** adj
reversal n ▷ reverse
reversals n ▷ reverse
reversed v ▷ reverse
reverses v, n ▷ reverse
reversible adj ▷ reverse
reversing v ▷ reverse
reversion n ▷ revert
reversions n ▷ revert

revert v (-s, -ing, -ed) return to a former state
> **reversion** n (pl -s)
reverted v ▷ revert
reverting v ▷ revert
reverts v ▷ revert
review n (pl -s) critical assessment of a book,
concert, etc. ▶ v (-s, -ing, -ed) hold or write
a review of
reviewed v ▷ review
reviewer n (pl -s) writer of reviews
reviewers n ▷ reviewer
reviewing v ▷ review
reviews n, v ▷ review
revile v (-les, -ling, -led) be abusively scornful
of
reviled v ▷ revile
reviles v ▷ revile
reviling v ▷ revile
revise v (-ses, -sing, -sed) change or alter
> **revision** n (pl -s)
revised v ▷ revise
revises v ▷ revise
revising v ▷ revise
revision n ▷ revive
revisions n ▷ revive
revival n (pl -s) reviving or renewal
> **revivalism** n (pl -s) > **revivalist** n (pl -s)
revivalism n ▷ revival
revivalisms n ▷ revival
revivalists n ▷ revival
revivalist n ▷ revival
revivals n ▷ revival
revive v (-ves, -ving, -ved) bring or come back
to life, vigour, use, etc.
revived v ▷ revive
revives v ▷ revive
reviving v ▷ revive
revocation n ▷ revoke
revocations n ▷ revoke
revoke v (-kes, -king, -ked) cancel (a will,
agreement, etc.) > **revocation** n (pl -s)
revoked v ▷ revoke
revokes v ▷ revoke
revoking v ▷ revoke
revolt n (pl -s) uprising against authority ▶ v
(-s, -ing, -ed) rise in rebellion
revolted v ▷ revolt
revolting adj disgusting, horrible ▶ v ▷ revolt
revolts n, v ▷ revolt
revolution n (pl -s) overthrow of a government
by the governed
revolutionaries n ▷ revolutionary
revolutionary adj advocating or engaged in
revolution ▶ n (pl -ies) person advocating or
engaged in revolution

revolutionize v (-zes, -zing, -zed) change considerably
revolutionized v ▷ revolutionize
revolutionizes v ▷ revolutionize
revolutionizing v ▷ revolutionize
revolutions n ▷ revolution
revolve v (-ves, -ving, -ved) turn round, rotate
revolved v ▷ revolve
revolver n (pl -s) repeating pistol
revolvers n ▷ revolver
revolves v ▷ revolve
revolving v ▷ revolve
revs n, v ▷ rev
revue n (pl -s) theatrical entertainment with topical sketches and songs
revues n ▷ revue
revulsion n (pl -s) strong disgust
revulsions n ▷ revulsion
revved v ▷ rev
revving v ▷ rev
reward n (pl -s) something given in return for a service ▶ v (-s, -ing, -ed) pay or give something to (someone) for a service, information, etc.
rewarded v ▷ reward
rewarding v ▷ reward
rewards n, v ▷ reward
rewind v (-s, -ing, -wound) run (a tape or film) back to an earlier point in order to replay
rewinding v ▷ rewind
rewinds v ▷ rewind
rewire v (-res, -ring, -red) provide (a house, engine, etc.) with new wiring
rewired v ▷ rewire
rewires v ▷ rewire
rewiring v ▷ rewire
rewound v ▷ rewire
rewrite v (-tes, -ting, -wrote, -written) write again in a different way ▶ n (pl -s) something rewritten
rewrites v, n ▷ rewrite
rewriting v ▷ rewrite
rewritten v ▷ rewrite
rewrote v ▷ rewrite

> **rex** n (**rexes**). Rex is a Latin word for king. This is a very useful word, as it combines X with two of the most common letters on the board, making it one to look for when you get an X. Rex scores 10 points.

> **rez** n (**rezes**). Rez is a short informal word for reservation. Combining Z with two of the most common tiles on the board, this is one of the first words to think about when you draw a Z and

> don't have the letters for a longer word. Rez scores 12 points.

rhapsodic adj ▷ rhapsody
rhapsodies n ▷ rhapsody
rhapsodize v (-zes, -zing, -zed) speak or write with extravagant enthusiasm
rhapsodized v ▷ rhapsodize
rhapsodizes v ▷ rhapsodize
rhapsodizing v ▷ rhapsodize
rhapsody n (pl -ies) freely structured emotional piece of music > **rhapsodic** adj
rhea [ree-a] n (pl -s) S American three-toed ostrich
rheas n ▷ rhea
rhenium n (pl -s) (CHEM) silvery-white metallic element with a high melting point
rheniums n ▷ rhenium
rheostat n (pl -s) instrument for varying the resistance of an electrical circuit
rheostats n ▷ rheostat
rhesus [ree-suss] n (pl -es) small long-tailed monkey of S Asia
rhesuses n ▷ rhesus
rhetoric n (pl -s) art of effective speaking or writing
rhetorical adj (of a question) not requiring an answer > **rhetorically** adv
rhetorically adv ▷ rhetorical
rhetorics n ▷ rhetoric
rheumatic n, adj (pl -s) (person) affected by rheumatism
rheumatics n ▷ rheumatic
rheumatism n (pl -s) painful inflammation of joints or muscles
rheumatisms n ▷ rheumatism
rheumatoid adj of or like rheumatism
rhinestone n (pl -s) imitation diamond
rhinestones n ▷ rhinestone
rhino n (pl -s) rhinoceros
rhinoceros n (pl -oses, -os) large thick-skinned animal with one or two horns on its nose
rhinoceroses n ▷ rhinoceros
rhinos n ▷ rhino
rhizome n (pl -s) thick underground stem producing new plants
rhizomes n ▷ rhizome

> **rho** n (**rhos**). Rho is the 17th letter of the Greek alphabet. It's useful to remember words that start with RH, as there are quite a few that can come in useful. If you or someone else plays rho, remember that it could be expanded to **rhodium, rhombus** or **rhomboid**. Rho scores 6 points.

rhodium n (pl -s) (CHEM) hard metallic element

rhodiums *n* ▷ rhodium
rhododendron *n* (*pl* -s) evergreen flowering shrub
rhododendrons *n* ▷ rhododendron
rhombi *n* ▷ rhombus
rhomboid *n* (*pl* -s) parallelogram with adjacent sides of unequal length
rhomboids *n* ▷ rhomboid
rhombus *n* (*pl* -buses, -bi) parallelogram with sides of equal length but no right angles, diamond-shaped figure
rhombuses *n* ▷ rhombus
rhubarb *n* (*pl* -s) garden plant of which the fleshy stalks are cooked as fruit
rhubarbs *n* ▷ rhubarb

> **rhy** *n* (**rhys**). Rhy is an alternative spelling of rye. This is a useful word as it doesn't contain a vowel, and so can be helpful when you have a poor combination of tiles on your rack. Rhy scores 9 points.

rhyme *n* (*pl* -s) sameness of the final sounds at the ends of lines of verse, or in words ▶ *v* (-mes, -ming, -med) make a rhyme
rhymed *v* ▷ rhyme
rhymes *n*, *v* ▷ rhyme
rhyming *v* ▷ rhyme
rhythm *n* (*pl* -s) any regular movement or beat > **rhythmic, rhythmical** *adj* > **rhythmically** *adv*
rhythmic *adj* ▷ rhythm
rhythmical *adj* ▷ rhythm
rhythmically *adv* ▷ rhythm
rhythms *n* ▷ rhythm
rib¹ *n* (*pl* -s) one of the curved bones forming the framework of the upper part of the body ▶ *v* (-s, -bbing, -bbed) provide or mark with ribs > **ribbed** *adj* > **ribbing** *n* (*pl* -s)
rib² *v* (-s, -bbing, -bbed) (*Informal*) tease or ridicule > **ribbing** *n* (*pl* -s)
ribald *adj* humorously or mockingly rude or obscene > **ribaldry** *n* (*pl* -s)
ribaldries *n* ▷ ribald
ribaldry *n* ▷ ribald
ribbed *v*, *adj* ▷ rib¹
ribbing *v*, *n* ▷ rib¹, ²
ribbings *n* ▷ rib¹, ²
ribbon *n* (*pl* -s) narrow band of fabric used for trimming, tying, etc.
ribbons *n* ▷ ribbon
ribcage *n* (*pl* -s) bony structure of ribs enclosing the lungs
ribcages *n* ▷ ribcage
riboflavin [rye-boe-**flay**-vin] *n* (*pl* -s) form of vitamin B

riboflavins *n* ▷ riboflavin
ribs *n*, *v* ▷ rib¹, ²
rice *n* (*pl* -s) cereal plant grown on wet ground in warm countries
rices *n* ▷ rice
rich *adj* (-er, -est) owning a lot of money or property, wealthy > **richness** *n* (*pl* -es)
richer *adj* ▷ rich
riches *pl n* wealth
richest *adj* ▷ rich
richly *adv* elaborately
richness *n* ▷ rich
richnesses *n* ▷ rich
rick¹ *n* (*pl* -s) stack of hay etc.
rick² *v*, *n* (-s, -ing, -ed) sprain or wrench
ricked *v* ▷ rick²
ricketier *adj* ▷ rickety
ricketiest *adj* ▷ rickety
rickets *n* disease of children marked by softening of the bones, bow legs, etc., caused by vitamin D deficiency
rickety *adj* (-tier, -tiest) shaky or unstable
ricking *v* ▷ rick¹
ricks *n* ▷ rick¹ ▶ *v* ▷ rick²
rickshaw *n* (*pl* -s) light two-wheeled man-drawn Asian vehicle
rickshaws *n* ▷ rickshaw
ricochet [**rik**-osh-ay] *v* (-s, -ing, -ed) (of a bullet) rebound from a solid surface ▶ *n* (*pl* -s) such a rebound
ricocheted *v* ▷ ricochet
ricocheting *v* ▷ ricochet
ricochets *v*, *n* ▷ ricochet
rid *v* (-s, -dding, rid) clear or relieve (of)
ridden *v* ▷ ride ▶ *adj* afflicted or affected by the thing specified
ridding *v* ▷ rid
riddle¹ *n* (*pl* -s) question made puzzling to test one's ingenuity
riddle² *v* (-les, -ling, -led) pierce with many holes ▶ *n* (*pl* -s) coarse sieve for gravel etc.
riddled *v* ▷ riddle²
riddles *n* ▷ riddle¹, ² ▶ *v* ▷ riddle²
riddling *v* ▷ riddle²
ride *v* (-des, -ding, rode, ridden) sit on and control or propel (a horse, bicycle, etc.) ▶ *n* (*pl* -s) journey on a horse etc., or in a vehicle
rider *n* (*pl* -s) person who rides
riders *n* ▷ rider
rides *v*, *n* ▷ ride
ridge *n* (*pl* -s) long narrow hill > **ridged** *adj*
ridged *adj* ▷ ridge
ridges *n* ▷ ridge
ridicule *n* (*pl* -s) treatment of a person or thing as ridiculous ▶ *v* (-les, -ling, -led) laugh at,

make fun of
ridiculed v ▷ ridicule
ridicules n, v ▷ ridicule
ridiculing v ▷ ridicule
ridiculous adj deserving to be laughed at, absurd
riding¹ v ▷ ride
riding² n (pl -s) (in Canada) parliamentary constituency
ridings n ▷ riding
rids v ▷ rid
riesling n (pl -s) type of white wine
rieslings n ▷ riesling
rife adj (-r, -st) widespread or common
rifer adj ▷ rife
rifest adj ▷ rife
riff n (pl -s) (JAZZ, ROCK) short repeated melodic figure
riffle v (-les, -ling, -led) flick through (pages etc.) quickly
riffled v ▷ riffle
riffles v ▷ riffle
riffling v ▷ riffle
riffraff n (pl -s) rabble, disreputable people
riffraffs n ▷ riffraff
riffs n ▷ riff
rifle¹ n (pl -s) firearm with a long barrel
rifle² v (-les, -ling, -led) search and rob
rifled v ▷ rifle²
rifles n ▷ rifle¹ ▶ v ▷ rifle²
rifling v ▷ rifle²
rift n (pl -s) break in friendly relations
rifts n ▷ rift
rig v (-s, -gging, -gged) arrange in a dishonest way ▶ n (pl -s) apparatus for drilling for oil and gas
rigged v ▷ rig
rigging n ship's spars and ropes ▶ v ▷ rig
right adj (-er, -est) just ▶ adv properly ▶ n (pl -s) claim, title, etc. ▶ v (-s, -ing, -ed) bring or come back to a normal or correct state > **rightly** adv > **rightful** adj > **rightfully** adv
righted v ▷ right
righteous [rye-chuss] adj upright, godly, or virtuous > **righteousness** n (pl -s)
righteousness n ▷ righteous
righteousnesses n ▷ righteous
righter adj ▷ right
rightest adj ▷ right
rightful adj ▷ right
rightfully adv ▷ right
righting v ▷ right
rightist n (pl -s) ▶ adj (person) on the political right

rightists n ▷ rightist
rightly adv ▷ right
rights n, v ▷ right
rigid adj (-er, -est) inflexible or strict > **rigidly** adv > **rigidity** n (pl -s)
rigider adj ▷ rigid
rigidest adj ▷ rigid
rigidities n ▷ rigid
rigidity n ▷ rigid
rigidly n ▷ rigid
rigmarole n (pl -s) long complicated procedure
rigmaroles n ▷ rigmarole
rigorous adj harsh, severe, or stern
rigour n (pl -s) harshness, severity, or strictness
rigours n ▷ rigour
rigs v, n ▷ rig
rile v (-les, -ling, -led) anger or annoy
riled v ▷ rile
riles v ▷ rile
riling v ▷ rile
rill n (pl -s) small stream
rills n ▷ rill
rim n (pl -s) edge or border > **rimmed** adj
rime n (pl -s) (Lit) hoarfrost
rimes n ▷ rime
rimmed adj ▷ rim
rims n ▷ rim
rimu n (pl -s) (NZ) New Zealand tree whose wood is used for building and furniture
rimus n ▷ rimu
rind n (pl -s) tough outer coating of fruits, cheese, or bacon
rinds n ▷ rind
ring¹ v (-s, -ing, rang, rung) give out a clear resonant sound, as a bell ▶ n (pl -s) ringing
ring² n (pl -s) circle of gold etc., esp. for a finger ▶ v (-s, -ing, -ed) put a ring round
ringed v ▷ ring²
ringer n (pl -s) (BRIT, AUST & NZ) (Slang) person or thing apparently identical to another
ringers n ▷ ringer
ringing v ▷ ring¹, ²
ringleader n (pl -s) instigator of a mutiny, riot, etc.
ringleaders n ▷ ringleader
ringlet n (pl -s) curly lock of hair
ringlets n ▷ ringlet
rings n, v ▷ ring¹, ²
ringside n (pl -s) row of seats nearest a boxing or circus ring
ringsides n ▷ ringside
ringtail n (pl -s) (AUST) possum with a curling tail used to grip branches while climbing
ringtails n ▷ ringtail

ringtone n (pl -s) tune played by a mobile phone when it receives a call
  ringtones n ▷ ringtone
ringworm n (pl -s) fungal skin disease in circular patches
  ringworms n ▷ ringworm
rink n (pl -s) sheet of ice for skating or curling
  rinks n ▷ rink
rinse v (-ses, -sing, -sed) remove soap from (washed clothes, hair, etc.) by applying clean water ▶ n (pl -s) rinsing
  rinsed v ▷ rinse
  rinses v, n ▷ rinse
  rinsing v ▷ rinse
riot n (pl -s) disorderly unruly disturbance ▶ v (-s, -ing, -ed) take part in a riot
  rioted v ▷ riot
  rioting v ▷ riot
riotous adj unrestrained
  riots n, v ▷ riot
rip v (-s, -pping, -pped) tear violently (Informal) ▶ n (pl -s) split or tear
riparian [rip-**pair**-ee-an] adj of or on the banks of a river
ripcord n (pl -s) cord pulled to open a parachute
  ripcords n ▷ ripcord
ripe adj (-er, -est) ready to be reaped, eaten, etc.
ripen v (-s, -ing, -ed) grow ripe
  ripened v ▷ ripen
  ripening v ▷ ripen
  ripens v ▷ ripen
  riper adj ▷ ripe
  ripest adj ▷ ripe
riposte [rip-**posst**] n (pl -s) verbal retort ▶ v (-tes, -ting, -ted) make a riposte
  riposted v ▷ riposte
  ripostes n, v ▷ riposte
  riposting v ▷ riposte
  ripped v ▷ rip
  ripping v ▷ rip
ripple n (pl -s) slight wave or ruffling of a surface ▶ v (-les, -ling, -led) flow or form into little waves (on)
  rippled v ▷ ripple
  ripples n, v ▷ ripple
  rippling v ▷ ripple
  rips v, n ▷ rip
rise v (-ses, -sing, rose, risen) get up from a lying, sitting, or kneeling position ▶ n (pl -s) rising
  risen v ▷ rise
riser n (pl -s) person who rises, esp. from bed
  risers n ▷ riser
  rises v, n ▷ rise

rising n (pl -s) revolt ▶ adj increasing in rank or maturity ▶ v ▷ rise
  risings n ▷ rising
risible [**riz**-zib-bl] adj causing laughter, ridiculous
risk n (pl -s) chance of disaster or loss ▶ v (-s, -ing, -ed) act in spite of the possibility of (injury or loss)
  risked v ▷ risk
  riskier adj ▷ risky
  riskiest adj ▷ risky
  risking v ▷ risk
  risks n, v ▷ risk
risky adj (-kier, -kiest) full of risk, dangerous
risotto n (pl -s) dish of rice cooked in stock with vegetables, meat, etc.
  risottos n ▷ risotto
risqué [**risk**-ay] adj bordering on indecency
rissole n (pl -s) cake of minced meat, coated with breadcrumbs and fried
  rissoles n ▷ rissole
rite n (pl -s) formal practice or custom, esp. religious
  rites n ▷ rite
ritual n (pl -s) prescribed order of rites ▶ adj concerning rites > **ritually** adv
ritualistic adj like a ritual
  ritually adv ▷ ritual
  rituals n ▷ ritual
  ritzier adj ▷ ritzy
  ritziest adj ▷ ritzy
ritzy adj (-zier, -ziest) (Slang) luxurious or elegant
rival n (pl -s) person or thing that competes with or equals another for favour, success, etc. ▶ adj in the position of a rival ▶ v (-s, -lling, -lled) (try to) equal
  rivalled v ▷ rival
  rivalling v ▷ rival
  rivalries n ▷ rivalry
rivalry n (pl -s) keen competition
  rivals v, n ▷ rival
riven adj split apart
river n (pl -s) large natural stream of water
  rivers n ▷ river
rivet [**riv**-vit] n (pl -s) bolt for fastening metal plates, the end being put through holes and then beaten flat ▶ v (-s, -ing, -ed) fasten with rivets
  riveted v ▷ rivet
riveting adj very interesting and exciting ▶ v ▷ rivet
  rivets n, v ▷ rivet
rivulet n (pl -s) small stream
  rivulets n ▷ rivulet

riz v. Riz is the past tense of rise in some US dialects. This unusual word can be very useful if you get a Z in the later stages of the game, as you will probably be able to find either I or R on the board already. Riz scores 12 points.

roach n (pl -es) Eurasian freshwater fish
roaches n ▷ roach
road n (pl -s) way prepared for passengers, vehicles, etc.
roadblock n (pl -s) barricade across a road to stop traffic for inspection etc.
roadblocks n ▷ roadblock
roadhouse n (pl -s) (BRIT, AUST & S AFR) pub or restaurant on a country road
roadhouses n ▷ roadhouse
roadie n (pl -s) (BRIT, AUST & NZ) (Informal) person who transports and sets up equipment for a band
roadies n ▷ roadie
roads n ▷ road
roadside n (pl -s) ▶ adj by the road
roadsides n ▷ roadside
roadway n (pl -s) the part of a road used by vehicles
roadways n ▷ roadway
roadworks pl n repairs to a road, esp. blocking part of the road
roadworthy adj (of a vehicle) mechanically sound
roam v (-s, -ing, -ed) wander about
roamed v ▷ roam
roaming v ▷ roam
roams v ▷ roam
roan adj (of a horse) having a brown or black coat sprinkled with white hairs ▶ n (pl -s) roan horse
roans n ▷ roan
roar v (-s, -ing, -ed) make or utter a loud deep hoarse sound like that of a lion ▶ n (pl -s) such a sound
roared v ▷ roar
roaring v ▷ roar
roars v, n ▷ roar
roast v (-s, -ing, -ed) cook by dry heat, as in an oven ▶ n (pl -s) roasted joint of meat ▶ adj roasted
roasted v ▷ roast
roasting (Informal) adj extremely hot ▶ n (pl -s) severe criticism or scolding ▶ v ▷ roast
roastings n ▷ roasting
roasts v, n ▷ roast
rob v (-s, -bbing, -bbed) steal from > **robber** n (pl -s) > **robbery** n (pl -ies)
robbed v ▷ rob

robber n ▷ rob
robberies n ▷ rob
robbers n ▷ rob
robbery n ▷ rob
robbing v ▷ rob
robe n (pl -s) long loose outer garment ▶ v (-bes, -bing, -bed) put a robe on
robed v ▷ robe
robes v, n ▷ robe
robin n (pl -s) small brown bird with a red breast
robing v ▷ robe
robins n ▷ robin
robot n (pl -s) automated machine, esp. one performing functions in a human manner > **robotic** adj
robotic adj ▷ robot
robotics n science of designing and using robots
robots n ▷ robot
robs v ▷ rob
robust adj (-er, -est) very strong and healthy > **robustly** adv > **robustness** n (pl -s)
robuster adj ▷ robust
robustest adj ▷ robust
robustly adv ▷ robust
robustness n ▷ robust
robustnesses n ▷ robust
roc n (pl -s) monstrous bird of Arabian mythology
rock¹ n (pl -s) hard mineral substance that makes up part of the earth's crust, stone
rock² v (-s, -ing, -ed) (cause to) sway to and fro ▶ n style of pop music with a heavy beat
rocked v ▷ rock²
rocker n (pl -s) rocking chair
rockeries n ▷ rockery
rockers n ▷ rocker
rockery n (pl -ies) mound of stones in a garden for rock plants
rocket n (pl -s) self-propelling device powered by the burning of explosive contents (used as a firework, weapon, etc.) ▶ v (-s, -ing, -ed) move fast, esp. upwards, like a rocket
rocketed v ▷ rocket
rocketing v ▷ rocket
rockets n, v ▷ rocket
rockier adj ▷ rocky¹, rocky²
rockiest adj ▷ rocky¹, rocky²
rocking v ▷ rock²
rocks n ▷ rock¹ ▶ v ▷ rock²
rocky¹ adj (-ier, -iest) having many rocks
rocky² adj (-ier, -iest) shaky or unstable
rococo [rok-koe-koe] adj (of furniture, architecture, etc.) having much elaborate

decoration in an early 18th-century style
rocs n ▷ roc
rod n (pl -s) slender straight bar, stick
rode v ▷ ride
rodent n (pl -s) animal with teeth specialized
for gnawing, such as a rat, mouse, or squirrel
rodents n ▷ rodent
rodeo n (pl -s) display of skill by cowboys, such
as bareback riding
rodeos n ▷ rodeo
rods n ▷ rod
roe¹ n (pl -s) mass of eggs in a fish, sometimes
eaten as food
roe² n (pl -s) small species of deer
roentgen [ront-gan] n (pl -s) unit measuring a
radiation dose
roentgens n ▷ roentgen
roes n ▷ roe¹, ²
rogue n (pl -s) dishonest or unprincipled
person ▶ adj (of a wild beast) having a savage
temper and living apart from the herd
▷ **roguish** adj
rogues n ▷ rogue
roguish adj ▷ rogee
roister v (-s, -ing, -ed) make merry noisily or
boisterously
roistered v ▷ roister
roistering v ▷ roister
roisters v ▷ roister

> **rok** n (roks). Rok is an alternative
> spelling of **roc**. This uncommon word
> can be helpful if you have a K without
> the tiles needed for a longer word. Rok
> scores 7 points.

role n (pl -s) task or function
roles n ▷ role
roll v (-s, -ing, -ed) move by turning over and
over ▶ n (pl -s) act of rolling over or from side
to side
rolled v ▷ roll
roller n (pl -s) rotating cylinder used for
smoothing or supporting a thing to be
moved, spreading paint, etc.
rollers n ▷ roller
rollicking adj boisterously carefree
rolling v ▷ roll
rolls v, n ▷ roll
roman n roman type or print
romance n (pl -s) love affair
romances n ▷ romance
romantic adj of or dealing with love ▶ n (pl -s)
romantic person or artist ▷ **romantically** adv
▷ **romanticism** n (pl -s)
romantically adv ▷ romantic
romanticism n ▷ romantic

romanticisms n ▷ romantic
romanticize v (-zes, -zing, -zed) describe or
regard in an idealized and unrealistic way
romanticized v ▷ romanticize
romanticizes v ▷ romanticize
romanticizing v ▷ romanticize
romantics n ▷ romantic
romp v (-s, -ing, -ed) play wildly and joyfully ▶ n
(pl -s) boisterous activity
romped v ▷ romp
rompers pl n child's overalls
romping v ▷ romp
romps v, n ▷ romp
rondo n (pl -s) piece of music with a leading
theme continually returned to
rondos n ▷ rondo
roo n (pl -s) (AUST) (Informal) kangaroo
rood n (pl -s) (CHRISTIANITY) the Cross
roods n ▷ rood
roof n (pl -s) outside upper covering of a
building, car, etc. ▶ v put a roof on
roofs n ▷ roofs
rooibos [roy-boss] n (pl -es) (S AFR) tea prepared
from the dried leaves of an African plant
rooiboses n ▷ rooibos
rook¹ n (pl -s) Eurasian bird of the crow family
rook² n (pl -s) chess piece shaped like a castle
rookeries n ▷ rookery
rookery n (pl -ies) colony of rooks, penguins,
or seals
rookie n (pl -s) (Informal) new recruit
rookies n ▷ rookie
rooks n ▷ rook
room n (pl -s) enclosed area in a building ▶ pl
lodgings
roomier adj ▷ roomy
roomiest adj ▷ roomy
rooms n ▷ room
roomy adj (-ier, -iest) spacious
roos n ▷ roo
roost n (pl -s) perch for fowls ▶ v (-s, -ing, -ed)
perch
roosted v ▷ roost
rooster n (pl -s) domestic cock
roosters n ▷ rooster
roosting v ▷ roost
roosts v, n ▷ roost
root¹ n (pl -s) part of a plant that grows down
into the earth obtaining nourishment ▶ pl
person's sense of belonging ▶ v (-s, -ing, -ed)
establish a root and start to grow
root² v (-s, -ing, -ed) dig or burrow
rooted v ▷ root¹, ²
rooting v ▷ root¹, ²
rootless adj having no sense of belonging

roots n ▷ root¹ ▶ v ▷ root¹, ²
rope n (pl -s) thick cord
ropes n ▷ rope
ropey, ropy adj (-pier, -piest) (BRIT) (Informal) inferior or inadequate
ropier adj ▷ ropy
ropiest adj ▷ ropy
ropy adj ▷ ropy
rorqual n (pl -s) toothless whale with a dorsal fin
rorquals n ▷ rorqual
rort (AUST) (Informal) n (pl -s) dishonest scheme ▶ v (-s, -ing, -ed) take unfair advantage of something
rorted v ▷ rort
rorting v ▷ rort
rorts n, v ▷ rort
rosaries n ▷ rosary
rosary n (pl -ies) series of prayers
rose¹ n (pl -s) shrub or climbing plant with prickly stems and fragrant flowers ▶ adj pink
rose² v ▷ rise
roseate [roe-zee-ate] adj rose-coloured
rosehip n (pl -s) berry-like fruit of a rose plant
rosehips n ▷ rosehip
rosella n (pl -s) type of Australian parrot
rosellas n ▷ rosella
rosemaries n ▷ rosemary
rosemary n (pl -ies) fragrant flowering shrub
roses n ▷ rose¹
rosette n (pl -s) rose-shaped ornament, esp. a circular bunch of ribbons
rosettes n ▷ rosette
rosewood n (pl -s) fragrant wood used to make furniture
rosewoods n ▷ rosewood
rosier adj ▷ rosy
rosiest adj ▷ rosy
rosin [rozz-in] n (pl -s) resin used for treating the bows of violins etc.
rosins n ▷ rosin
roster n (pl -s) list of people and their turns of duty
rosters n ▷ roster
rostra n ▷ rostrum
rostrum n (pl -trums, -tra) platform or stage
rostrums n ▷ rostrum
rosy adj (-sier, -siest) pink-coloured
rot v (-s, -tting, -tted) decompose or decay ▶ n (pl -s) decay (Informal)
rota n (pl -s) list of people who take it in turn to do a particular task
rotas n ▷ rota
rotary adj revolving
rotate v (-tes, -ting, -ted) (cause to) move

round a centre or on a pivot > **rotation** n (pl -s)
rotated v ▷ rotate
rotates v ▷ rotate
rotating v ▷ rotate
rotation n ▷ rotate
rotations n ▷ rotate
rote n (pl -s) mechanical repetition
rotes n ▷ rote
rotisserie n (pl -s) rotating spit for cooking meat
rotisseries n ▷ rotisserie
rotor n (pl -s) revolving portion of a dynamo, motor, or turbine
rotors n ▷ rotor
rots v, n ▷ rot
rotted v ▷ rot
rotten adj (-er, -est) decaying (Informal)
rottener adj ▷ rotten
rottenest adj ▷ rotten
rotter n (pl -s) (CHIEFLY BRIT) (Slang) despicable person
rotters n ▷ rotter
rotting v ▷ rot
rotund [roe-tund] adj round and plump > **rotundity** n (pl -ies)
rotunda n (pl -s) circular building or room, esp. with a dome
rotundas n ▷ rotunda
rotundities n ▷ rotund
rotundity n ▷ rotund
rouble [roo-bl] n (pl -s) monetary unit of Russia, Belarus, and Tajikistan
roubles n ▷ rouble
roué [roo-ay] n (pl -s) man given to immoral living
roués n ▷ roué
rouge n (pl -s) red cosmetic used to colour the cheeks
rouges n ▷ rouge
rough adj (-er, -est) uneven or irregular ▶ v (-s, -ing, -ed) make rough ▶ n (pl -s) rough state or area > **roughen** v (-s, -ing, -ed) > **roughly** adv > **roughness** n (pl -s)
roughage n (pl -s) indigestible constituents of food which aid digestion
roughages n ▷ roughage
roughcast n (pl -s) mixture of plaster and small stones for outside walls ▶ v (-s, -ing, -cast) coat with this
roughcasting v ▷ roughcast
roughcasts n, v ▷ roughcast
roughed v ▷ rough
roughen v ▷ rough
roughened v ▷ rough
roughening v ▷ rough

roughens v ▷ rough
rougher adj ▷ rough
roughest adj ▷ rough
roughhouse n (pl -s) (CHIEFLY US) (Slang) fight
roughhouses n ▷ roughhouse
roughing v ▷ rough
roughly adv ▷ rough
roughness n ▷ rough
roughnesses n ▷ rough
roughs v, n ▷ rough
roughshod adv with total disregard
roulette n (pl -s) gambling game played with a revolving wheel and a ball
roulettes n ▷ roulette
round adj (-er, -est) spherical, cylindrical, circular, or curved ▶ adv, prep indicating an encircling movement, presence on all sides, etc. ▶ v (-s, -ing, -ed) move round ▶ n (pl -s) customary course, as of a milkman
roundabout n (pl -s) road junction at which traffic passes round a central island ▶ adj not straightforward
roundabouts n ▷ roundabout
rounded v ▷ round
roundel n (pl -s) small disc
roundelay n (pl -s) simple song with a refrain
roundelays n ▷ roundelay
roundels n ▷ roundel
rounder adj ▷ round
roundest adj ▷ round
rounders n bat-and-ball team game
rounding v ▷ round
roundly adv thoroughly
rounds v, n ▷ round
rouse[1] [rhymes with **cows**] v (-ses, -sing, -sed) wake up
rouse[2] [rhymes with **mouse**] v (-ses, -sing, -sed) (foll. by **on**) (AUST) scold or rebuke
rouseabout n (pl -s) (AUST & NZ) labourer in a shearing shed
rouseabouts n ▷ rouseabout
roused v ▷ rouse[1, 2]
rouses v ▷ rouse[1, 2]
rousing v ▷ rouse[1, 2]
roustabout n (pl -s) labourer on an oil rig
roustabouts n ▷ roustabout
rout n (pl -s) overwhelming defeat ▶ v (-s, -ing, -ed) defeat and put to flight
route n (pl -s) roads taken to reach a destination
routed v ▷ rout
routes n ▷ route
routine n (pl -s) usual or regular method of procedure ▶ adj ordinary or regular
routines n ▷ routine

routing v ▷ rout
routs n, v ▷ rout
roux [roo] n (pl roux) fat and flour cooked together as a basis for sauces
rove v (-ves, -ving, -ved) wander
roved v ▷ rove
rover n (pl -s) wanderer, traveller
rovers n ▷ rover
roves v ▷ rove
roving v ▷ rove
row[1] [rhymes with **go**] n (pl -s) straight line of people or things
row[2] [rhymes with **go**] v (-s, -ing, -ed) propel (a boat) by oars ▶ n (-s) spell of rowing
row[3] [rhymes with **now**] (Informal) n (-s) dispute ▶ v (-s, -ing, -ed) quarrel noisily
rowan n (pl -s) tree producing bright red berries, mountain ash
rowans n ▷ rowan
rowdier adj ▷ rowdy
rowdiest adj ▷ rowdy
rowdies n ▷ rowdy
rowdy adj (-dier, -diest) disorderly, noisy, and rough ▶ n (pl -ies) person like this
rowed v ▷ row[2, 3]
rowel [rhymes with **towel**] n (pl -s) small spiked wheel on a spur
rowels n ▷ rowel
rowing v ▷ row[2, 3]
rowlock [rol-luk] n (pl -s) device on a boat that holds an oar in place
rowlocks n ▷ rowlock
rows n ▷ row[1, 2, 3] ▶ v ▷ row[2, 3]
royal adj (-er, -lest) of, befitting, or supported by a king or queen ▶ n (pl -s) (Informal) member of a royal family > **royally** adv
royalist n (pl -s) supporter of monarchy
royalists n ▷ royalist
royaller adj ▷ royal
royallest adj ▷ royal
royally adv ▷ royal
royals n ▷ royal
royalties n ▷ royalty
royalty n (pl -ies) royal people
rub v (-s, -bbing, -bbed) apply pressure and friction to (something) with a circular or backwards-and-forwards movement ▶ n (-s) act of rubbing
rubato adv, n (pl -s) (MUSIC) (with) expressive flexibility of tempo
rubatos n ▷ rubato
rubbed v ▷ rub
rubber[1] n (pl -s) strong waterproof elastic material, orig. made from the dried sap of a tropical tree, now usu. synthetic ▶ adj made

of or producing rubber > **rubbery** adj (-rier, -riest)

rubber² n (pl -s) match consisting of three games of bridge, whist, etc.
rubberier adj ⊳ rubber¹
rubberiest adj ⊳ rubber¹
rubberneck v (-s, -ing, -ed) stare with unthinking curiosity
rubbernecked v ⊳ rubberneck
rubbernecking v ⊳ rubberneck
rubbernecks v ⊳ rubberneck
rubbers n ⊳ rubber¹, ²
rubbery adj ⊳ rubber¹
rubbing v ⊳ rub
rubbish n (pl -es) waste matter > **rubbishy** adj
rubbishes n ⊳ rubbish
rubbishy adj ⊳ rubbish
rubble n (pl -s) fragments of broken stone, brick, etc.
rubbles n ⊳ rubble
rubella n (pl -s) ⊳ German measles
rubellas n ⊳ rubella
rubicund adj ruddy
rubidium n (pl -s) (CHEM) soft highly reactive radioactive element
rubidiums n ⊳ rubidium
rubies n ⊳ ruby
rubric n (pl -s) heading or explanation inserted in a text
rubrics n ⊳ rubric
rubs v, n ⊳ rub
ruby n (pl -ies) red precious gemstone ▸ adj deep red
ruck¹ n (pl -s) rough crowd of common people
ruck² n, v (-s, -ing, -ed) wrinkle or crease
rucked v ⊳ ruck²
rucking v ⊳ ruck²
rucks n ⊳ ruck¹, ² ▸ v ⊳ ruck²
rucksack n (pl -s) (BRIT, AUST & S AFR) large pack carried on the back
rucksacks n ⊳ rucksack
ructions pl n (Informal) noisy uproar
rudder n (pl -s) vertical hinged piece at the stern of a boat or at the rear of an aircraft, for steering
rudders n ⊳ rudder
ruddier adj ⊳ ruddy
ruddiest adj ⊳ ruddy
ruddy adj (-dier, -diest) of a fresh healthy red colour
rude adj (-r, -st) impolite or insulting > **rudely** adv > **rudeness** n (pl -s)
rudely adv ⊳ rude
rudeness n ⊳ rude
rudenesses n ⊳ rude

ruder adj ⊳ rude
rudest adj ⊳ rude
rudimentary adj basic, elementary
rudiments pl n simplest and most basic stages of a subject
rue¹ v (rues, ruing, rued) feel regret for
rue² n (pl -s) plant with evergreen bitter leaves
rueful adj regretful or sorry > **ruefully** adv
ruefully adv ⊳ rueful
rued v ⊳ rue¹
rues v ⊳ rue¹ ▸ n ⊳ rue²
ruff n (pl -s) starched and frilled collar
ruffian n (pl -s) violent lawless person
ruffians n ⊳ ruffian
ruffle v (-les, -ling, -led) disturb the calm of ▸ n (pl -s) frill or pleat
ruffled v ⊳ ruffle
ruffles v, n ⊳ ruffle
ruffling v ⊳ ruffle
ruffs n ⊳ ruff
rug n (pl -s) small carpet
rugbies n ⊳ rugby
rugby n (pl -ies) form of football played with an oval ball which may be handled by the players
rugged [rug-gid] adj rocky or steep
rugger n (pl -s) (CHIEFLY BRIT) (Informal) rugby
ruggers n ⊳ rugger
rugs n ⊳ rug
ruin v (-s, -ing, -ed) destroy or spoil completely ▸ n (pl -s) destruction or decay
ruination n (pl -s) act of ruining
ruinations n ⊳ ruination
ruined v ⊳ ruin
ruing v ⊳ rue¹
ruining v ⊳ ruin
ruinous adj causing ruin > **ruinously** adv
ruinously adv ⊳ ruinous
ruins v, n ⊳ ruin
rule n (pl -s) statement of what is allowed, for example in a game or procedure ▸ v (-les, -ling, -led) govern
ruled v ⊳ rule
ruler n (pl -s) person who governs
rulers n ⊳ ruler
rules n, v ⊳ rule
ruling n (pl -s) formal decision ▸ v ⊳ rule
rulings n ⊳ ruling
rum n (pl -s) alcoholic drink distilled from sugar cane
rumba n (pl -s) lively ballroom dance of Cuban origin
rumbas n ⊳ rumba
rumble v (-les, -ling, -led) make a low continuous noise (BRIT) (Informal) ▸ n (pl -s) deep resonant sound

rumbled v ▷ rumble
rumbles v, n ▷ rumble
rumbling v ▷ rumble
rumbustious adj boisterous or unruly
ruminate v (-tes, -ting, -ted) chew the cud
ruminant adj, n (pl -s) cud-chewing (animal, such as a cow, sheep, or deer)
ruminants n ▷ ruminant
ruminated v ▷ ruminate
ruminates v ▷ ruminate
ruminating v ▷ ruminate
rumination n (pl -ies) quiet meditation and reflection > **ruminative** adj
ruminations n ▷ rumination
ruminative adj ▷ rumination
rummage v (-ges, -ging, -ged) search untidily and at length ▶ n (pl -s) untidy search through a collection of things
rummaged v ▷ rummage
rummages v, n ▷ rummage
rummaging v ▷ rummage
rummies n ▷ rummy
rummy n (pl -ies) card game in which players try to collect sets or sequences
rumour n (pl -s) unproved statement
rumoured adj suggested by rumour
rumours n ▷ rumour
rump n (pl -s) buttocks
rumple v (-les, -ling, -led) make untidy, crumpled, or dishevelled
rumpled v ▷ rumple
rumples v ▷ rumple
rumpling v ▷ rumple
rumps n ▷ rump
rumpus n (pl -es) noisy commotion
rumpuses n ▷ rumpus
rums n ▷ rum
run v (runs, running, ran, run) move with a more rapid gait than walking ▶ n (pl -s) act or spell of running
rune n (pl -s) any character of the earliest Germanic alphabet > **runic** adj
runes n ▷ rune
rung¹ n (pl -s) crossbar on a ladder
rung² v ▷ ring¹
rungs n ▷ rung¹
runic adj ▷ rune
runnel n (pl -s) small brook
runnels n ▷ runnel
runner n (pl -s) competitor in a race
runners n ▷ runner
runnier adj ▷ runny
runniest adj ▷ runny
running adj continuous ▶ n (pl -s) act of moving or flowing quickly ▶ v ▷ run

runnings n ▷ running
runny adj (-nier, -niest) tending to flow
runs v, n ▷ run
runt n (pl -s) smallest animal in a litter
runts n ▷ runt
runway n (pl -s) hard level roadway where aircraft take off and land
runways n ▷ runway
rupee n (pl -s) monetary unit of India and Pakistan
rupees n ▷ rupee
rupture n (pl -s) breaking, breach ▶ v (-res, -ring, -red) break, burst, or sever
ruptured v ▷ rupture
ruptures n, v ▷ rupture
rupturing v ▷ rupture
rural adj in or of the countryside
ruse [rooz] n (pl -s) stratagem or trick
ruses n ▷ ruse
rush¹ v (-es, -ing, -ed) move or do very quickly ▶ n (pl -es) sudden quick or violent movement ▶ pl first unedited prints of a scene for a film ▶ adj done with speed, hasty
rush² n (pl -es) marsh plant with a slender pithy stem
rushed v ▷ rush¹
rushes v, n ▷ rush¹, ²
rushier adj ▷ rushy
rushiest adj ▷ rushy
rushing v ▷ rush¹
rushy adj (-shier, -shiest) full of rushes
rusk n (pl -s) hard brown crisp biscuit, used esp. for feeding babies
rusks n ▷ rusk
russet adj reddish-brown ▶ n (pl -s) apple with rough reddish-brown skin
russets n ▷ russet
rust n (pl -s) reddish-brown coating formed on iron etc. that has been exposed to moisture ▶ adj reddish-brown ▶ v (-s, -ing, -ed) become coated with rust
rusted v ▷ rust
rustic adj of or resembling country people ▶ n (pl -s) person from the country
rustics n ▷ rustic
rustier adj ▷ rusty
rustiest adj ▷ rusty
rusting v ▷ rust
rustle¹ v, n (pl -s) (make) a low whispering sound
rustle² v (-les, -ling, -led) (US) steal (cattle)
rustled v ▷ rustle
rustler n (pl -s) (US) cattle thief
rustlers n ▷ rustler
rustles n, v ▷ rustle

rustling *v* ▷ rustle
rusts *n*, *v* ▷ rust
rusty *adj* (-tier, -tiest) coated with rust
rut¹ *n* (*pl* -s) furrow made by wheels
rut² *n* recurrent period of sexual excitability in male deer ▶ *v* (-s, -tting, -tted) be in a period of sexual excitability
ruthenium *n* (*pl* -s) (CHEM) rare hard brittle white element
rutheniums *n* ▷ ruthenium
ruthless *adj* pitiless, merciless > **ruthlessly** *adv*

> **ruthlessness** *n* (*pl* -es)
ruthlessly *adv* ▷ ruthless
ruthlessness *n* ▷ ruthless
ruthlessnesses *n* ▷ ruthless
ruts *n* ▷ rut¹, ² ▶ *v* ▷ rut²
rutted *v* ▷ rut²
rutting *v* ▷ rut²
rye *n* (*pl* -s) kind of grain used for fodder and bread
ryes *n* ▷ rye

Ss

S begins only four two-letter words, **sh** (5 points), **si**, **so** and **st** (2 each). These are easy to remember, and it's worth noting that two of them, **sh** and **st**, don't use any vowels. Interestingly, there are quite a few three-letter words beginning with S that don't contain vowels, some of which give good scores. These are **shh** (9), **shy** (9), **sky** (10), **sly** (6), **sny** (6), **spy** (8), **sty** (6), **swy** (9) and **syn** (6). S also forms a number of three-letter words with X. These are easy to remember as they use every vowel except U: **sax**, **sex**, **six** and **sox** (10 each). Apart from the two- and three-letter words, don't forget **squeeze** (25), which uses the two highest-scoring tiles in the game.

sabbath n (pl -s) day of worship and rest: Saturday for Jews, Sunday for Christians
   sabbaths n ▷ sabbath

sabbatical adj, n (pl -s) (denoting) leave for study
   sabbaticals n ▷ sabbatical

sable n (pl -s) dark fur from a small weasel-like Arctic animal ▶ adj black
   sables n ▷ sable

sabot [sab-oh] n (pl -s) wooden shoe traditionally worn by peasants in France

sabotage n (pl -s) intentional damage done to machinery, systems, etc. ▶ v (-ges, -ging, -ged) damage intentionally
   sabotaged v ▷ sabotage
   sabotages n, v ▷ sabotage
   sabotaging v ▷ sabotage

saboteur n (pl -s) person who commits sabotage
   saboteurs n ▷ saboteur
   sabots n ▷ sabot

sabre n (pl -s) curved cavalry sword
   sabres n ▷ sabre

sac n (pl -s) pouchlike structure in an animal or plant

saccharin n (pl -s) artificial sweetener > **saccharine** adj excessively sweet
   saccharine adj ▷ saccharin
   saccharins n ▷ saccharin

sacerdotal adj of priests

sachet n (pl -s) small envelope or bag containing a single portion
   sachets n ▷ sachet

sack[1] n (pl -s) large bag made of coarse material ▶ v (-s, -ing, -ed) (Informal) dismiss

sack[2] n (pl -s) plundering of a captured town ▶ v (-s, -ing, -ed) plunder (a captured town)

sackcloth n (pl -s) coarse fabric used for sacks, formerly worn as a penance
   sackcloths n ▷ sackcloth
   sacked v ▷ sack[1, 2]
   sacking v ▷ sack[1, 2]
   sacks v, n ▷ sack[1, 2]
   sacra n ▷ sacrum

sacrament n (pl -s) ceremony of the Christian Church, esp. Communion > **sacramental** adj
   sacramental adj ▷ sacrament
   sacraments n ▷ sacrament

sacred adj holy

sacrifice n (pl -s) giving something up ▶ v (-es, -ing, -ced) offer as a sacrifice > **sacrificial** adj
   sacrificed v ▷ sacrifice
   sacrifices n, v ▷ sacrifice
   sacrificial adj ▷ sacrifice
   sacrificing v ▷ sacrifice

sacrilege n (pl -s) misuse or desecration of something sacred > **sacrilegious** adj
   sacrileges n ▷ sacrilege
   sacrilegious adj ▷ sacrilege

sacristan n (pl -s) person in charge of the contents of a church
   sacristans n ▷ sacristan
   sacristies n ▷ sacristy

sacristy n (pl -ties) room in a church where sacred objects are kept

sacrosanct adj regarded as sacred, inviolable

sacrum [say-krum] n (pl -cra) wedge-shaped bone at the base of the spine
   sacs n ▷ sac

sad adj (-dder, -ddest) sorrowful, unhappy

> **sadly** *adv* > **sadness** *n* (*pl* -es)
sadden *v* (-s, -ing, -ed) make sad
  saddened *v* > sadden
  saddening *v* > sadden
  saddens *v* > sadden
  sadder *adj* > sad
  saddest *adj* > sad
saddle *n* (*pl* -les) rider's seat on a horse or
bicycle ▶ *v* (-les, -ling, -led) put a saddle on
(a horse)
  saddled *v* > saddle
saddler *n* (*pl* -s) maker or seller of saddles
  saddlers *n* > saddler
  saddles *n*, *v* > saddle
  saddling *v* > saddle
saddo *n* (*pl* -s, -es) (BRIT) (*Informal*) socially
inadequate or pathetic person
  saddoes *n* > saddo
  saddos *n* > saddo
sadism [**say**-dizz-um] *n* (*pl* -s) gaining of
(sexual) pleasure from inflicting pain > **sadist**
n (*pl* -s) > **sadistic** *adj* > **sadistically** *adv*
  sadisms *n* > sadism
  sadist *n* > sadism
  sadistic *adj* > sadism
  sadistically *adv* > sadism
  sadists *n* > sadism
  sadly *adv* > sad
  sadness *n* > sad
  sadnesses *n* > sad
sadomasochism *n* (*pl* -s) combination of
sadism and masochism > **sadomasochist**
n (*pl* -s)
  sadomasochisms *n* > sadomasochism
  sadomasochist *n* > sadomasochism
  sadomasochists *n* > sadomasochism
safari *n* (*pl* -s) expedition to hunt or observe
wild animals, esp. in Africa
  safaris *n* > safari
safe *adj* (-r, -st) secure, protected ▶ *n* (*pl* -s)
strong lockable container > **safely** *adv*
safeguard *v* (-s, -ing, -ed) protect ▶ *n* (*pl* -s)
protection
  safeguarded *v* > safeguard
  safeguarding *v* > safeguard
  safeguards *v*, *n* > safeguard
safekeeping *n* (*pl* -s) protection
  safekeepings *n* > safekeeping
  safely *adv* > safe
  safer *adj* > safe
  safes *n* > safe
  safest *adj* > safe
  safeties *n* > safety
safety *n* (*pl* -ties) state of being safe
saffron *n* (*pl* -s) orange-coloured flavouring

obtained from a crocus ▶ *adj* orange
  saffrons *n* > saffron
sag *v* (sags, sagging, sagged) sink in the
middle ▶ *n* (*pl* -s) droop
saga [**sah**-ga] *n* (*pl* -s) legend of Norse heroes
sagacious *adj* wise > **sagacity** *n* (*pl* -ties)
  sagacities *n* > sagacious
  sagacity *n* > sagacious
  sagas *n* > saga
sage[1] *n* (*pl* -s) very wise man ▶ *adj* (-r, -st) (*Lit*)
wise > **sagely** *adv*
sage[2] *n* (*pl* -s) aromatic herb with grey-green
leaves
  sagely *adv* > sage[1]
  sager *adj* > sage[1]
  sages *n* > sage[1, 2]
  sagest *adj* > sage[1]
  sagged *v* > sag
  sagging *v* > sag
sago *n* (*pl* -s) starchy cereal from the powdered
pith of the sago palm tree
  sagos *n* > sago
  sags *v*, *n* > sag
  said *v* > say
sail *n* (*pl* -s) sheet of fabric stretched to catch
the wind for propelling a sailing boat ▶ *v* (-s,
-ing, -ed) travel by water
sailboard *n* (*pl* -s) board with a mast and single
sail, used for windsurfing
  sailboards *n* > sailboard
  sailed *v* > sail
  sailing *v* > sail
sailor *n* (*pl* -s) member of a ship's crew
  sailors *n* > sailor
  sails *n*, *v* > sail
saint *n* (*pl* -s) (CHRISTIANITY) person venerated
after death as specially holy > **saintly** *adj*
  > **saintliness** *n* (*pl* -es)
  saintliness *n* > saint
  saintlinesses *n* > saint
  saintly *adj* > saint
  saints *n* > saint
sake[1] *n* (*pl* -s) benefit
sake[2], **saki** [**sah**-kee] *n* (*pl* -s) Japanese alcoholic
drink made from fermented rice
  sakes *n* > sake[1, 2]
  saki *n* > sake[2]
  sakis *n* > sake[2]
salaam [sal-**ahm**] *n* (*pl* -s) low bow of greeting
among Muslims
  salaams *n* > salaam
salacious *adj* excessively concerned with sex
salad *n* (*pl* -s) dish of raw vegetables, eaten as a
meal or part of a meal
  salads *n* > salad

salamander n (pl -s) amphibian which looks like a lizard
  salamanders n ▷ salamander
salami n (pl -s) highly spiced sausage
  salamis n ▷ salami
  salaried adj ▷ salary
  salaries n ▷ salary
salary n (pl -ries) fixed regular payment, usu. monthly, to an employee > **salaried** adj
sale n (pl -s) exchange of goods for money > **saleable** adj fit or likely to be sold
  saleable adj ▷ sale
  sales n ▷ sale
salesman, saleswoman (pl -men, -women) > **salesperson** (pl -people) n person who sells goods
salesmanship n (pl -s) skill in selling
  salesmanships n ▷ salesmanship
  salesmen n ▷ salesman
  salespeople n ▷ salesman
  salesperson n ▷ salesman
  saleswoman n ▷ salesman
  saleswomen n ▷ salesman
salient [say-lee-ent] adj prominent, noticeable
  ▶ n (pl -s) (MIL) projecting part of a front line
  salients n ▷ salient
saline [say-line] adj containing salt > **salinity** n (pl -ties)
  salinities n ▷ saline
  salinity n ▷ saline
saliva n (pl -s) liquid that forms in the mouth, spittle > **salivary** adj
  salivary adj ▷ saliva
  salivas n ▷ saliva
salivate v (-tes, -ting, -ted) produce saliva
  salivated v ▷ salivate
  salivates v ▷ salivate
  salivating v ▷ salivate
sallee n (pl -s) (AUST) SE Australian eucalyptus with a pale grey bark
  sallees n ▷ sallee
  sallied v ▷ sally
  sallies n, v ▷ sally
sallow adj (-er, -est) of an unhealthy pale or yellowish colour
  sallower adj ▷ sallow
  sallowest adj ▷ sallow
sally n (pl -lies) witty remark ▶ v (-lies, -lying, -lied) (foll. by forth) rush out
  sallying v ▷ sally
salmon n (pl -lies) large fish with orange-pink flesh valued as food ▶ adj orange-pink
salmonella n (pl -lae) bacterium causing food poisoning
  salmonellae n ▷ salmonella

  salmons n ▷ salmon
salon n (pl -s) commercial premises of a hairdresser, beautician, etc.
  salons n ▷ salon
saloon n (pl -s) two-door or four-door car with body closed off from rear luggage area
  saloons n ▷ saloon
salt n (pl -s) white crystalline substance used to season food ▶ v (-s, -ing, -ed) season or preserve with salt > **salty** adj (-tier, -tiest)
saltbush n (pl -es) shrub that grows in alkaline desert regions
  saltbushes n ▷ saltbush
  salted v ▷ salt
  saltier adj ▷ salt
  saltiest adj ▷ salt
  salting v ▷ salt
saltire n (pl -s) (HERALDRY) diagonal cross on a shield
  saltires n ▷ saltire
saltpetre n (pl -s) compound used in gunpowder and as a preservative
  saltpetres n ▷ saltpetre
  salts n, v ▷ salt
  salty adj ▷ salt
salubrious adj favourable to health
saluki n (pl -s) tall hound with a silky coat
  salukis n ▷ saluki
salutary adj producing a beneficial result
salutation n (pl -s) greeting by words or actions
  salutations n ▷ salutation
salute n (pl -s) motion of the arm as a formal military sign of respect ▶ v (-tes, -ting, -ted) greet with a salute
  saluted v ▷ salute
  salutes n, v ▷ salute
  saluting v ▷ salute
salvage n (pl -s) saving of a ship or other property from destruction ▶ v (-ges, -ging, -ged) save from destruction or waste
  salvaged v ▷ salvage
  salvages n, v ▷ salvage
  salvaging v ▷ salvage
salvation n (pl -s) fact or state of being saved from harm or the consequences of sin
  salvations n ▷ salvation
salve n (pl -s) healing or soothing ointment ▶ v (-ves, -ving, -ved) soothe or appease
  salved v ▷ salve
salver n (pl -s) (silver) tray on which something is presented
  salvers n ▷ salver
  salves n, v ▷ salve
salvia n (pl -s) plant with blue or red flowers

salvias n ▷ salvia
salving v ▷ salve
salvo n (pl -s, -es) simultaneous discharge of guns etc.
salvoes n ▷ salvo
salvos n ▷ salvo
samaritan n (pl -s) person who helps people in distress
samaritans n ▷ samaritan
samba n (pl -s) lively Brazilian dance
sambas n ▷ samba
same adj identical, not different, unchanged ▷ **sameness** n (pl -es)
sameness n ▷ same
samenesses n ▷ same
samovar n (pl -s) Russian tea urn
samovars n ▷ samovar
sampan n (pl -s) small boat with oars used in China
sampans n ▷ sampan
samphire n (pl -s) plant found on rocks by the seashore
samphires n ▷ samphire
sample n (pl -s) part taken as representative of a whole ▶ v (-les, -ling, -led) take and test a sample of ▷ **sampling** n (pl -s)
sampled v ▷ sample
sampler n (pl -s) piece of embroidery showing the embroiderer's skill
samplers n ▷ sampler
samples v, n ▷ sample
sampling v, n ▷ sample
samplings n ▷ sample
samurai n (pl -rai) member of an ancient Japanese warrior caste
sanatoria n ▷ sanatorium
sanatorium n (pl -riums, -ria) institution for invalids or convalescents
sanatoriums n ▷ sanatorium
sancta n ▷ sanctum
sanctified v ▷ sanctify
sanctifies v ▷ sanctify
sanctify v (-fies, -fying, -fied) make holy
sanctifying v ▷ sanctify
sanctimonious adj pretending to be religious and virtuous
sanction n (pl -s) permission, authorization ▶ v (-s, -ing, -ed) allow, authorize
sanctioned v ▷ sanction
sanctioning v ▷ sanction
sanctions n, v ▷ sanction
sanctities n ▷ sanctity
sanctity n (pl -ties) sacredness, inviolability
sanctuaries n ▷ sanctuary
sanctuary n (pl -ries) holy place

sanctum n (pl -tums, -ta) sacred place
sanctums n ▷ sanctum
sand n (pl -s) substance consisting of small grains of rock, esp. on a beach or in a desert ▶ v (-s, -ing, -ed) smooth with sandpaper
sandal n (pl -s) light shoe consisting of a sole attached by straps
sandals n ▷ sandal
sandalwood n (pl -s) sweet-scented wood
sandalwoods n ▷ sandalwood
sandbag n (pl -s) bag filled with sand, used as protection against gunfire or flood water
sandbags n ▷ sandbag
sandblast v (-s, -ing, -ed) ▶ n (pl -s) (clean with) a jet of sand blown from a nozzle under pressure
sandblasted v ▷ sandblast
sandblasting v ▷ sandblast
sandblasts v, n ▷ sandblast
sanded v ▷ sand
sander n (pl -s) power tool for smoothing surfaces
sanders n ▷ sander
sandier adj ▷ sandy
sandiest adj ▷ sandy
sanding v ▷ sand
sandpaper n (pl -s) paper coated with sand for smoothing a surface
sandpapers n ▷ sandpaper
sandpiper n (pl -s) shore bird with a long bill and slender legs
sandpipers n ▷ sandpiper
sands n, v ▷ sand ▶ pl n stretches of sand forming a beach or desert
sandstone n (pl -s) rock composed of sand
sandstones n ▷ sandstone
sandstorm n (pl -s) desert wind that whips up clouds of sand
sandstorms n ▷ sandstorm
sandwich n (pl -es) two slices of bread with a layer of food between ▶ v (-es, -ing, -ed) insert between two other things
sandwiched v ▷ sandwich
sandwiches n, v ▷ sandwich
sandwiching v ▷ sandwich
sandy adj (-dier, -diest) covered with sand
sane adj (-r, -st) of sound mind ▷ **sanity** n (pl -ties)
saner adj ▷ sane
sanest adj ▷ sane
sang v ▷ sing
sangoma n (pl -s) (S AFR) witch doctor or herbalist
sangomas n ▷ sangoma
sanguinary adj accompanied by bloodshed

sanguine *adj* cheerful, optimistic
sanitary *adj* promoting health by getting rid of dirt and germs
sanitation *n* (*pl* -s) sanitary measures, esp. drainage or sewerage
  sanitations *n* ▷ sanitation
  sanities *n* ▷ sane
  sanity *n* ▷ sane
  sank *v* ▷ sink
sap[1] *n* (*pl* -s) moisture that circulates in plants
sap[2] *v* (saps, sapping, sapped) undermine
sapient [say-pee-ent] *adj* (*Lit*) wise, shrewd
sapling *n* (*pl* -s) young tree
  saplings *n* ▷ sapling
  sapped *v* ▷ sap[2]
sapper *n* (*pl* -s) soldier in an engineering unit
  sappers *n* ▷ sapper
sapphire *n* (*pl* -s) blue precious stone ▶ *adj* deep blue
  sapphires *n* ▷ sapphire
  sapping *v* ▷ sap[2]
  saps *n* ▷ sap[1] ▶ *v* ▷ sap[2]
  saraband *n* ▷ sarabande
sarabande, saraband *n* (*pl* -s) slow stately Spanish dance
  sarabandes *n* ▷ sarabande
  sarabands *n* ▷ sarabande
sarcasm *n* (*pl* -s) (use of) bitter or wounding ironic language > **sarcastic** *adj* > **sarcastically** *adv*
  sarcasms *n* ▷ sarcasm
  sarcastic *adj* ▷ sarcasm
  sarcastically *adv* ▷ sarcasm
  sarcophagi *n* ▷ sarcophagus
sarcophagus *n* (*pl* -gi, -guses) stone coffin
  sarcophaguses *n* ▷ sarcophagus
sardine *n* (*pl* -s) small fish of the herring family, usu. preserved tightly packed in tins
  sardines *n* ▷ sardine
sardonic *adj* mocking or scornful > **sardonically** *adv*
  sardonically *adv* ▷ sardonic
  saree *n* ▷ sari
  sarees *n* ▷ sari
  sargasso *n* ▷ sargassum
  sargassos *n* ▷ sargassum
sargassum, sargasso *n* (*pl* -s) type of floating seaweed
  sargassums *n* ▷ sargassum
sari, saree *n* (*pl* -s) long piece of cloth draped around the body and over one shoulder, worn by Hindu women
  saris *n* ▷ sari
sarmie *n* (*pl* -s) (S AFR) (*Slang*) sandwich
  sarmies *n* ▷ sarmie

sarong *n* (*pl* -s) long piece of cloth tucked around the waist or under the armpits, worn esp. in Malaysia
  sarongs *n* ▷ sarong
sarsaparilla *n* (*pl* -s) soft drink, orig. made from the root of a tropical American plant
  sarsaparillas *n* ▷ sarsaparilla
sartorial *adj* of men's clothes or tailoring
sash[1] *n* (*pl* -es) decorative strip of cloth worn round the waist or over one shoulder
sash[2] *n* (*pl* -es) wooden frame containing the panes of a window
  sashes *n* ▷ sash[1,2]
sassafras *n* (*pl* -rases) American tree with aromatic bark used medicinally
  sassafrases *n* ▷ sassafras
  sat *v* ▷ sit
satanic *adj* of Satan
satanism *n* (*pl* -s) worship of Satan
  satanisms *n* ▷ satanism
satay, saté [sat-ay] *n* (*pl* -s) Indonesian and Malaysian dish consisting of pieces of chicken, pork, etc., grilled on skewers and served with peanut sauce
  satays *n* ▷ satay
satchel *n* (*pl* -s) bag, usu. with a shoulder strap, for carrying books
  satchels *n* ▷ satchel
sate *v* (-tes, -ting, -ted) satisfy (a desire or appetite) fully
  sated *v* ▷ sate
satellite *n* (*pl* -s) man-made device orbiting in space ▶ *adj* of or used in the transmission of television signals from a satellite to the home
  satellites *n* ▷ satellite
  sates *v* ▷ sate
satiate [say-she-ate] *v* (-tes, -ting, -ted) provide with more than enough, so as to disgust
  satiated *v* ▷ satiate
  satiates *v* ▷ satiate
  satiating *v* ▷ satiate
  satieties *n* ▷ satiety
satiety [sat-tie-a-tee] *n* (*pl* -ties) feeling of having had too much
satin *n* (*pl* -s) silky fabric with a glossy surface on one side
  sating *v* ▷ sate
  satins *n* ▷ satin
satinwood *n* (*pl* -s) tropical tree yielding hard wood
  satinwoods *n* ▷ satinwood
satiny *adj* of or like satin
satire *n* (*pl* -s) use of ridicule to expose vice or folly > **satirical** *adj* > **satirist** *n* (*pl* -s)

satires n ▷ satire
satirical adj ▷ satire
satirist n ▷ satire
satirists n ▷ satire
satirize v (-zes, -zing, -zed) ridicule by means of satire
satirized v ▷ satirize
satirizes v ▷ satirize
satirizing v ▷ satirize
satisfaction n ▷ satisfy
satisfactions n ▷ satisfy
satisfactory adj ▷ satisfy
satisfied v ▷ satisfy
satisfies v ▷ satisfy
satisfy v (-fies, -fying, -fied) please, content > **satisfaction** n (pl -s) > **satisfactory** adj
satisfying v ▷ satisfy
satnav n (pl -s) (MOTORING) (Informal) satellite navigation
satnavs n ▷ satnav
satsuma n (pl -s) kind of small orange
satsumas n ▷ satsuma
saturate v (-tes, -ting, -ted) soak thoroughly > **saturation** n (pl -s)
saturated v ▷ saturate
saturates v ▷ saturate
saturating v ▷ saturate
saturation n ▷ saturate
saturations n ▷ saturate
saturnalia n (pl -s) wild party or orgy
saturnalias n ▷ saturnalia
saturnine adj gloomy in temperament or appearance
satyr n (pl -s) woodland god, part man, part goat
satyrs n ▷ satyr
sauce n (pl -s) liquid added to food to enhance flavour
saucepan n (pl -s) cooking pot with a long handle
saucepans n ▷ saucepan
saucer n (pl -s) small round dish put under a cup
saucers n ▷ saucer
sauces n ▷ sauce
saucier adj ▷ saucy
sauciest adj ▷ saucy
saucily adv ▷ saucy
saucy adj (-cier, -ciest) impudent > **saucily** adv
sauerkraut n (pl -s) shredded cabbage fermented in brine
sauerkrauts n ▷ sauerkraut
sauna n (pl -s) Finnish-style steam bath
saunas n ▷ sauna
saunter v (-s, -ing, -ed) walk in a leisurely manner, stroll ▶ n (pl -s) leisurely walk
sauntered v ▷ saunter
sauntering v ▷ saunter
saunters v, n ▷ saunter
sausage n (pl -s) minced meat in an edible tube-shaped skin
sausages n ▷ sausage
sauté [so-tay] v (-tés, -téing or -téeing, -téed) fry quickly in a little fat
sautéed v ▷ sauté
sautéeing v ▷ sauté
sautéing v ▷ sauté
sautés v ▷ sauté
savage adj (-r, -st) wild, untamed ▶ n (pl -s) uncivilized person ▶ v (-ges, -ging, -ged) attack ferociously > **savagely** adv > **savagery** n (pl -ries)
savaged v ▷ savage
savagely adv ▷ savage
savager adj ▷ savage
savageries n ▷ savage
savagery n ▷ savage
savages n, v ▷ savage
savagest adj ▷ savage
savaging v ▷ savage
savanna n ▷ savannah
savannah, savanna n (pl -s) extensive open grassy plain in Africa
savannahs n ▷ savannah
savannas n ▷ savanna
savant n (pl -s) learned person
savants n ▷ savant
save v (-ves, -ving, -ved) rescue or preserve from harm, protect ▶ n (pl -s) (SPORT) act of preventing a goal > **saver** n (pl -s)
saved v ▷ save
saveloy n (pl -s) (BRIT, AUST & NZ) spicy smoked sausage
saveloys n ▷ saveloy
saver n ▷ save
savers n ▷ save
saves v, n ▷ save
saving v ▷ save ▶ n (pl -s) economy
savings n pl money put by for future use
saviour n (pl -s) person who rescues another
saviours n ▷ saviour
savories n ▷ savory
savory n (pl -ries) aromatic herb used in cooking
savour v (-s, -ing, -ed) enjoy, relish (foll. by of) ▶ n (pl -s) characteristic taste or odour
savoured v ▷ savour
savourier adj ▷ savoury
savouries n ▷ savoury
savouriest adj ▷ savoury

savouring v ▷ savour
savours v, n ▷ savour
savoury adj (-rier, -riest) salty or spicy ▶ n (pl -ries) savoury dish served before or after a meal
savoy n (pl -s) variety of cabbage
savoys n ▷ savoy
savvied v ▷ savvy
savvies v, n ▷ savvy
savvy (Slang) v (-vies, -vying, -vied) understand ▶ n (-vies) understanding, intelligence
savvying v ▷ savvy
saw[1] n (pl -s) cutting tool with a toothed metal blade ▶ v (-s, -ing, -ed, -ed or **sawn**) cut with a saw
saw[2] ▷ see[1]
saw[3] n (pl -s) wise saying, proverb
sawdust n (pl -s) fine wood fragments made in sawing
sawdusts n ▷ sawdust
sawed v ▷ saw[1]
sawfish n (pl -es) fish with a long toothed snout
sawfishes n ▷ sawfish
sawing v ▷ saw[1]
sawmill n (pl -s) mill where timber is sawn into planks
sawmills n ▷ sawmill
sawn v ▷ saw[1]
saws n ▷ saw[1, 3] ▶ v ▷ saw[1]
sawyer n (pl -s) person who saws timber for a living
sawyers n ▷ sawyer
sax n (pl -es) (Informal) ▷ saxophone
saxes n ▷ sax
saxifrage n (pl -s) alpine rock plant with small flowers
saxifrages n ▷ saxifrage
saxophone n (pl -s) brass wind instrument with keys and a curved body > **saxophonist** n (pl -s)
saxophones n ▷ saxophone
saxophonist n ▷ saxophone
saxophonists n ▷ saxophonist
say v (-s, -ing, said) speak or utter ▶ n (pl -s) right or chance to speak
saying n (pl -s) maxim, proverb ▶ v ▷ say
sayings n ▷ saying
says v, n ▷ say

> **saz** n (**sazes**). A saz is a Turkish musical instrument. This is a very useful word, and one to remember for when you get a Z in the later stages of the game, with little space left on the board. Saz scores 12 points.

scab n (pl -s) crust formed over a wound
scabbard n (pl -s) sheath for a sword or dagger
scabbards n ▷ scabbard
scabbier adj ▷ scabby
scabbiest adj ▷ scabby
scabby adj (-bbier, -bbiest) covered with scabs
scabies [skay-beez] n itchy skin disease
scabrous [skay-bruss] adj rough and scaly
scabs n ▷ scab
scaffold n (pl -s) temporary platform for workmen
scaffolding n (pl -s) (materials for building) scaffolds
scaffoldings n ▷ scaffolding
scaffolds n ▷ scaffold
scalar n (pl -s) ▶ adj (variable quantity) having magnitude but no direction
scalars n ▷ scalar
scald v (-s, -ing, -ed) burn with hot liquid or steam ▶ n (pl -s) injury by scalding
scalded v ▷ scald
scalding v ▷ scald
scalds v, n ▷ scald
scale[1] n (pl -s) one of the thin overlapping plates covering fishes and reptiles ▶ v (-les, -ling, -led) remove scales from > **scaly** adj (-lier, -liest)
scale[2] n (pl -s) (often pl) weighing instrument
scale[3] n (pl -s) graduated table or sequence of marks at regular intervals, used as a reference in making measurements ▶ v (-les, -ling, -led) climb
scaled v ▷ scale[1, 3]
scalene adj (of a triangle) with three unequal sides
scales n ▷ scale[1, 2, 3] ▶ v ▷ scale[1, 3]
scalier adj ▷ scale[1]
scaliest adj ▷ scale[1]
scaling v ▷ scale[1, 3]
scallop n (pl -s) edible shellfish with two fan-shaped shells
scalloped adj decorated with small curves along the edge
scallops n ▷ scallop
scallywag n (pl -s) (Informal) scamp, rascal
scallywags n ▷ scallywag
scalp n (pl -s) skin and hair on top of the head ▶ v (-s, -ing, -ed) cut off the scalp of
scalped v ▷ scalp
scalpel n (pl -s) small surgical knife
scalpels n ▷ scalpel
scalping v ▷ scalp
scalps n, v ▷ scalp
scaly adj ▷ scale[1]
scam n (pl -s) (Informal) dishonest scheme

scamp n (pl -s) mischievous child
scamper v (-s, -ing, -ed) run about hurriedly or in play ▶ n (pl -s) scampering
  scampered v ▷ scamper
  scampering v ▷ scamper
  scampers v, n ▷ scamper
scampi pl n large prawns
  scamps n ▷ scamp
  scams n ▷ scam
scan v (-s, -nning, -nned) scrutinize carefully ▶ n (pl -s) scanning
scandal n (pl -s) disgraceful action or event
  > **scandalous** adj
scandalize v (-zes, -zing, -zed) shock by scandal
  scandalized v ▷ scandalize
  scandalizes v ▷ scandalize
  scandalizing v ▷ scandalize
  scandalous adj ▷ scandal
  scandals n ▷ scandal
scandium n (pl -s) (CHEM) rare silvery-white metallic element
  scandiums n ▷ scandium
  scanned v ▷ scan
scanner n (pl -s) electronic device used for scanning
  scanners n ▷ scanner
  scanning v ▷ scan
  scans v, n ▷ scan
scansion n (pl -s) metrical scanning of verse
  scansions n ▷ scansion
scant adj (-er, -est) barely sufficient, meagre
  scanter adj ▷ scant
  scantest adj ▷ scant
  scantier adj ▷ scanty
  scantiest adj ▷ scanty
  scantily adv ▷ scanty
scanty adj (-tier, -tiest) barely sufficient or not sufficient > **scantily** adv
scapegoat n (pl -s) person made to bear the blame for others
  scapegoats n ▷ scapegoat
scapula n (pl -lae, -las) shoulder blade
  > **scapular** adj
  scapulae n ▷ scapula
  scapular adj ▷ scapula
  scapulas n ▷ scapula
scar n (pl -s) mark left by a healed wound ▶ v (-s, -rring, -rred) mark or become marked with a scar
scarab n (pl -s) sacred beetle of ancient Egypt
  scarabs n ▷ scarab
scarce adj (-r, -st) insufficient to meet demand
  > **scarcity** n (pl -ties)
  scarcely adv hardly at all

scarcer adj ▷ scarce
scarcest adj ▷ scarce
scarcities n ▷ scarcity
scarcity n ▷ scarce
scare v (-res, -ring, -red) frighten or be frightened ▶ n (pl -s) fright, sudden panic
scarecrow n (pl -s) figure dressed in old clothes, set up to scare birds away from crops
  scarecrows n ▷ scarecrow
  scared v ▷ scare
scaremonger n (pl -s) person who spreads alarming rumours
  scaremongers n ▷ scaremonger
  scares v, n ▷ scare
scarf¹ n (pl scarves, -s) piece of material worn round the neck, head, or shoulders
scarf² n (pl -s) joint between two pieces of timber made by notching the ends and fastening them together ▶ v (-s, -ing, -ed) join in this way
  scarfed v ▷ scarf²
  scarfing v ▷ scarf²
  scarfs n ▷ scarf¹, ² ▶ v ▷ scarf²
  scarier adj ▷ scary
  scariest adj ▷ scary
  scarification n ▷ scarify
  scarifications n ▷ scarify
  scarified v ▷ scarify
  scarifies v ▷ scarify
scarify v (-fies, -fying, -fied) scratch or cut slightly all over > **scarification** n (pl -s)
  scarifying v ▷ scarify
  scaring v ▷ scare
scarlatina n (pl -s) scarlet fever
  scarlatinas n ▷ scarlatina
scarlet adj, n (pl -s) brilliant red
  scarlets n ▷ scarlet
scarp n (pl -s) steep slope
scarper v (-s, -ing, -ed) (BRIT) (Slang) run away
  scarpered v ▷ scarper
  scarpering v ▷ scarper
  scarpers v ▷ scarper
  scarps n ▷ scarp
  scarred v ▷ scar
  scarring v ▷ scar
  scars n, v ▷ scar
  scarves n ▷ scarf¹
scary adj (-rier, -riest) (Informal) frightening
scat¹ v (-s, -tting, -tted) (Informal) go away
scat² n (pl -s) jazz singing using improvised vocal sounds instead of words
scathing adj harshly critical
scatological adj preoccupied with obscenity, esp. with references to excrement
  > **scatology** n (pl -gies)

scatologies n ▷ scatology
scatology n ▷ scatological
scats n ▷ scat² ▶ v ▷ scat¹
scatted v ▷ scat¹
scatter v (-s, -ing, -ed) throw about in various directions
scatterbrain n (pl -s) empty-headed person
scatterbrains n ▷ scatterbrain
scattered v ▷ scatter
scattering v ▷ scatter
scatters v ▷ scatter
scattier adj ▷ scatty
scattiest adj ▷ scatty
scatting v ▷ scat¹
scatty adj (-tier, -tiest) (Informal) empty-headed
scavenge v (-ges, -ging, -ged) search for (anything usable) among discarded material
scavenged v ▷ scavenge
scavenger n (pl -s) person who scavenges
scavengers n ▷ scavenger
scavenges v ▷ scavenge
scavenging v ▷ scavenge
scenario n (pl -rios) summary of the plot of a play or film
scenarios n ▷ scenario
scene n (pl -s) place of action of a real or imaginary event
sceneries n ▷ scenery
scenery n (pl -ries) natural features of a landscape
scenes n ▷ scene
scenic adj picturesque
scent n (pl -s) pleasant smell ▶ v (-s, -ing, -ed) detect by smell
scented v ▷ scent
scenting v ▷ scent
scents n, v ▷ scent
sceptic [skep-tik] n (pl -s) person who habitually doubts generally accepted beliefs
> **sceptical** adj > **sceptically** adv > **scepticism** n (pl -s)
sceptical adj ▷ sceptic
sceptically adv ▷ sceptic
scepticism n ▷ sceptic
scepticisms n ▷ sceptic
sceptics n ▷ sceptic
sceptre n (pl -s) ornamental rod symbolizing royal power
sceptres n ▷ sceptre
schedule n (pl -s) plan of procedure for a project ▶ v (-les, -ling, -led) plan to occur at a certain time
scheduled v ▷ schedule
schedules n, v ▷ schedule

scheduling v ▷ schedule
schema n (pl -mata) overall plan or diagram
schematic adj presented as a plan or diagram
scheme n (pl -s) systematic plan ▶ v (-mes, -ming, -med) plan in an underhand manner
> **scheming** adj, n (pl -s)
schemed v ▷ scheme
schemes n, v ▷ scheme
scheming v, adj n ▷ scheme
schemings n ▷ scheme
scherzi n ▷ scherzo
scherzo [skairt-so] n (pl -zos, -zi) brisk lively piece of music
scherzos n ▷ scherzo
schism [skizz-um] n (pl -s) (group resulting from) division in an organization
> **schismatic** adj, n (pl -s)
schismatic adj, n ▷ schism
schismatics n ▷ schism
schisms n ▷ schism
schist [shist] n (pl -s) crystalline rock which splits into layers
schists n ▷ schist
schizoid adj abnormally introverted ▶ n (pl -s) schizoid person
schizoids n ▷ schizoid
schizophrenia n (pl -s) mental disorder involving deterioration of or confusion about the personality > **schizophrenic** adj, n (pl -s)
schizophrenias n ▷ schizophrenia
schizophrenic adj, n ▷ schizophrenia
schizophrenics n ▷ schizophrenia
schmaltz n (pl -es) excessive sentimentality
> **schmaltzy** adj (-zier, -ziest)
schmaltzes n ▷ schmaltz
schmaltzier adj ▷ schmaltz
schmaltziest adj ▷ schmaltz
schmaltzy adj ▷ schmaltz
schnapps n (pl -es) strong alcoholic spirit
schnappses n ▷ schnapps
schnitzel n (pl -s) thin slice of meat, esp. veal
schnitzels n ▷ schnitzel
scholar n (pl -s) learned person
scholarly adj learned
scholars n ▷ scholar
scholarship n (pl -s) learning
scholarships n ▷ scholarship
scholastic adj of schools or scholars
school¹ n (pl -s) place where children are taught or instruction is given in a subject ▶ v (-s, -ing, -ed) educate or train
school² n (pl -s) shoal of fish, whales, etc.
schooled v ▷ school¹
schoolie n (pl -s) (AUST) schoolteacher or high-school student

schoolies n ▷ schoolie
schooling v ▷ school[1]
schools n ▷ school[1, 2] ▶ v ▷ school[1]
schooner n (pl -s) sailing ship rigged fore-and-aft
schooners n ▷ schooner
sciatic adj of the hip
sciatica n (pl -s) severe pain in the large nerve in the back of the leg
sciaticas n ▷ sciatica
science n (pl -s) systematic study and knowledge of natural or physical phenomena
sciences n ▷ science
scientific adj of science > **scientifically** adv
scientifically adv ▷ scientific
scientist n (pl -s) person who studies or practises a science
scientists n ▷ scientist
scimitar n (pl -s) curved oriental sword
scimitars n ▷ scimitar
scintillate v (-tes, -ting, -ted) give off sparks
scintillated v ▷ scintillate
scintillates v ▷ scintillate
scintillating adj very lively and amusing ▶ v ▷ scintillate
scion [sy-on] n (pl -s) descendant or heir
scions n ▷ scion
scissors pl n cutting instrument with two crossed pivoted blades
scleroses n ▷ sclerosis
sclerosis n (pl -ses) abnormal hardening of body tissues
scoff[1] v (-s, -ing, -ed) express derision
scoff[2] v (-s, -ing, -ed) (Informal) eat rapidly
scoffed v ▷ scoff[1, 2]
scoffing v ▷ scoff[1, 2]
scoffs v ▷ scoff[1, 2]
scold v (-s, -ing, -ed) find fault with, reprimand ▶ n (pl -s) person who scolds > **scolding** n (pl -s)
scolded v ▷ scold
scolding v, n ▷ scold
scoldings n ▷ scold
scolds v, n ▷ scold
sconce n (pl -s) bracket on a wall for holding candles or lights
sconces n ▷ sconce
scone n (pl -s) small plain cake baked in an oven or on a griddle
scones n ▷ scone
scoop n (pl -s) shovel-like tool for ladling or hollowing out ▶ v (-s, -ing, -ed) take up or hollow out with or as if with a scoop
scooped v ▷ scoop
scooping v ▷ scoop
scoops n, v ▷ scoop

scoot v (-s, -ing, -ed) (Slang) leave or move quickly
scooted v ▷ scoot
scooter n (pl -s) child's vehicle propelled by pushing on the ground with one foot
scooters n ▷ scooter
scooting v ▷ scoot
scoots v ▷ scoot
scope n (pl -s) opportunity for using abilities
scopes n ▷ scope
scorch v (-es, -ing, -ed) burn on the surface ▶ n (pl -es) slight burn
scorched v ▷ scorch
scorcher n (pl -s) (Informal) very hot day
scorchers n ▷ scorcher
scorches v, ▷ scorch
scorching v ▷ scorch
score n (pl -s) points gained in a game or competition ▶ v (-res, -ring, -red) gain (points) in a game
scored v ▷ score
scores n, v ▷ score ▶ pl n lots
scoring v ▷ score
scorn n (pl -s) open contempt ▶ v (-s, -ing, -ed) despise > **scornful** adj > **scornfully** adv
scorned v ▷ scorn
scornful adj ▷ scorn
scornfully adv ▷ scorn
scorning v ▷ scorn
scorns n, v ▷ scorn
scorpion n (pl -s) small lobster-shaped animal with a sting at the end of a jointed tail
scorpions n ▷ scorpion
scotch v (-es, -ing, -ed) put an end to
scotched v ▷ scotch
scotches v ▷ scotch
scotching v ▷ scotch
scoundrel n (pl -s) (Old-fashioned) cheat or deceiver
scoundrels n ▷ scoundrel
scour[1] v (-s, -ing, -ed) clean or polish by rubbing with something rough
scour[2] v (-s, -ing, -ed) search thoroughly and energetically
scoured v ▷ scour[1, 2]
scourer n (pl -s) small rough nylon pad used for cleaning pots and pans
scourers n ▷ scourer
scourge n (pl -s) person or thing causing severe suffering ▶ v (-ges, -ging, -ged) cause severe suffering to
scourged v ▷ scourge
scourges n, v ▷ scourge
scourging v ▷ scourge
scouring v ▷ scour[1, 2]

scours v ▷ scour[1, 2]

scout n (pl -s) person sent out to reconnoitre ▶ v (-s, -ing, -ed) act as a scout
  scouted v ▷ scout
  scouting v ▷ scout
  scouts n, v ▷ scout

scowl v (-s, -ing, -ed) ▶ n (pl -s) (have) an angry or sullen expression
  scowled v ▷ scowl
  scowling v ▷ scowl
  scowls v, n ▷ scowl

scrabble v (-les, -ling, -led) scrape at with the hands, feet, or claws
  scrabbled v ▷ scrabble
  scrabbles v ▷ scrabble
  scrabbling v ▷ scrabble

scrag n (pl -s) thin end of a neck of mutton
  scraggier adj ▷ scraggy
  scraggiest adj ▷ scraggy

scraggy adj (-ggier, -ggiest) thin, bony
  scrags n ▷ scrag

scram v (-s, -mming, -mmed) (Informal) go away quickly

scramble v (-les, -ling, -led) climb or crawl hastily or awkwardly ▶ n (pl -les) scrambling
  scrambled v ▷ scramble

scrambler n (pl -s) electronic device that makes transmitted speech unintelligible
  scramblers n ▷ scrambler
  scrambles v, n ▷ scramble
  scrambling v ▷ scramble
  scrammed v ▷ scram
  scramming v ▷ scram
  scrams v ▷ scram

scrap[1] n (pl -s) small piece ▶ v (-s, -pping, -pped) discard as useless

scrap[2] n (pl -s) ▶ v (-s, -pping, -pped) (Informal) fight or quarrel

scrapbook n (pl -s) book with blank pages in which newspaper cuttings or pictures are stuck
  scrapbooks n ▷ scrapbook

scrape v (-pes, -ping, -ped) rub with something rough or sharp ▶ n (pl -s) act or sound of scraping > **scraper** n (pl -s)
  scraped v ▷ scrape
  scraper n ▷ scrape
  scrapers n ▷ scrape
  scrapes v, n ▷ scrape
  scraping v ▷ scrape
  scrapped v ▷ scrap[1, 2]
  scrappier adj ▷ scrappy
  scrappiest adj ▷ scrappy
  scrapping v ▷ scrap[1, 2]

scrappy adj (-pier, -ppiest) fragmentary, disjointed
  scraps v ▷ scrap[1, 2] ▶ n ▷ scrap[1, 2] ▶ pl n leftover food

scratch v (-es, -ing, -ed) mark or cut with claws, nails, or anything rough or sharp ▶ n (pl -es) wound, mark, or sound made by scratching ▶ adj put together at short notice > **scratchy** adj (-chier, -chiest)

scratchcard n (pl -s) ticket that reveals whether or not the holder has won a prize when the surface is removed by scratching
  scratchcards n ▷ scratchcard
  scratched v ▷ scratch
  scratches v, n ▷ scratch
  scratchier adj ▷ scratch
  scratchiest adj ▷ scratch
  scratching v ▷ scratch
  scratchy adj ▷ scratch

scrawl v (-s, -ing, -ed) write carelessly or hastily ▶ n (pl -s) scribbled writing
  scrawled v ▷ scrawl
  scrawling v ▷ scrawl
  scrawls v, n ▷ scrawl
  scrawnier adj ▷ scrawny
  scrawniest adj ▷ scrawny

scrawny adj (-nier, -niest) thin and bony

scream v (-s, -ing, -ed) utter a piercing cry, esp. of fear or pain ▶ n (pl -s) shrill piercing cry
  screamed v ▷ scream
  screaming v ▷ scream
  screams v, n ▷ scream

scree n (pl -s) slope of loose shifting stones

screech v (-es, -ing, -ed) ▶ n (pl -es) (utter) a shrill cry
  screeched v ▷ screech
  screeches v, n ▷ screech
  screeching v ▷ screech

screed n (pl -s) long tedious piece of writing
  screeds n ▷ screed

screen n (pl -s) surface of a television set, VDU, etc., on which an image is formed ▶ v (-s, -ing, -ed) shelter or conceal with or as if with a screen
  screened v ▷ screen
  screening v ▷ screen
  screens n, v ▷ screen
  screes n ▷ scree

screw n (pl -s) metal pin with a spiral ridge along its length, twisted into materials to fasten them together ▶ v (-s, -ing, -ed) turn (a screw)

screwdriver n (pl -s) tool for turning screws
  screwdrivers n ▷ screwdriver
  screwed v ▷ screw
  screwier adj ▷ screwy

screwiest adj ▷ screwy
screwing v ▷ screw
screws n, v ▷ screw
screwy adj (-wier, -wiest) (Informal) crazy or eccentric
scribble v (-les, -ling, -led) write hastily or illegibly ▶ n (pl -s) something scribbled
scribbled v ▷ scribble
scribbles v, n ▷ scribble
scribbling v ▷ scribble
scribe n (pl -s) person who copied manuscripts before the invention of printing
scribes n ▷ scribe
scrimmage n (pl -s) rough or disorderly struggle
scrimmages n ▷ scrimmage
scrimp v (-s, -ing, -ed) be very economical
scrimped v ▷ scrimp
scrimping v ▷ scrimp
scrimps v ▷ scrimp
scrip n (pl -s) certificate representing a claim to stocks or shares
scrips n ▷ scrip
script n (pl -s) text of a film, play, or TV programme
scripts n ▷ script
scriptural adj ▷ scripture
scripture n (pl -s) sacred writings of a religion > **scriptural** adj
scriptures n ▷ scripture
scrofula n (pl -s) tuberculosis of the lymphatic glands > **scrofulous** adj
scrofulas n ▷ scrofula
scrofulous adj ▷ scrofula
scroggin n (pl -s) (NZ) mixture of nuts and dried fruits
scroggins n ▷ scroggin
scroll n (pl -s) roll of parchment or paper ▶ v (-s, -ing, -ed) move (text) up or down on a VDU screen
scrolled v ▷ scroll
scrolling v ▷ scroll
scrolls n, v ▷ scroll
scrota n ▷ scrotum
scrotum n (pl -ta, -tums) pouch of skin containing the testicles
scrotums n ▷ scrotum
scrounge v (-ges, -ging, -ged) (Informal) get by cadging or begging > **scrounger** n (pl -s)
scrounged v ▷ scrounge
scrounger n ▷ scrounge
scroungers n ▷ scrounge
scrounges v ▷ scrounge
scrounging v ▷ scrounge
scrub¹ v (-s, -bbing, -bbed) clean by rubbing,

often with a hard brush and water ▶ n (pl -s) scrubbing
scrub² n (pl -s) stunted trees
scrubbed v ▷ scrub¹
scrubbier adj ▷ scrubby
scrubbiest adj ▷ scrubby
scrubbing v ▷ scrub¹
scrubby adj (-bbier, -bbiest) covered with scrub
scrubs v ▷ scrub¹ ▶ n ▷ scrub¹, ²
scruff¹ n (pl -s) nape (of the neck)
scruff² n (pl -s) (Informal) untidy person
scruffier adj ▷ scruffy
scruffiest adj ▷ scruffy
scruffs n ▷ scruff¹, ²
scruffy adj (-ffier, -ffiest) unkempt or shabby
scrum, scrummage n (pl -s) (RUGBY) restarting of play in which opposing packs of forwards push against each other to gain possession of the ball
scrummage n ▷ scrum
scrummages n ▷ scrum
scrumptious adj (Informal) delicious
scrums n ▷ scrum
scrunch v (-es, -ing, -ed) crumple or crunch or be crumpled or crunched ▶ n (pl -es) act or sound of scrunching
scrunched v ▷ scrunch
scrunches v, n ▷ scrunch
scrunching v ▷ scrunch
scruple n (pl -s) doubt produced by one's conscience or morals ▶ v (-les, -ling, -led) have doubts on moral grounds
scrupled v ▷ scruple
scruples n, v ▷ scruple
scrupling v ▷ scruple
scrupulous adj very conscientious > **scrupulously** adv
scrupulously adv ▷ scrupulous
scrutinies n ▷ scrutiny
scrutinize v (-zes, -zing, -zed) examine closely
scrutinized v ▷ scrutinize
scrutinizes v ▷ scrutinize
scrutinizing v ▷ scrutinize
scrutiny n (pl -nies) close examination
scud v (-s, -dding, -dded) move along swiftly
scudded v ▷ scud
scudding v ▷ scud
scuds v ▷ scud
scuff v (-s, -ing, -ed) drag (the feet) while walking ▶ n (pl -s) mark caused by scuffing
scuffed v ▷ scuff
scuffing v ▷ scuff
scuffle v (-les, -ling, -led) fight in a disorderly manner ▶ n (pl -s) disorderly struggle

scuffled v ▷ scuffle
scuffles v, n ▷ scuffle
scuffling v ▷ scuffle
scuffs v, n ▷ scuff
scull n (pl -s) small oar ▶ v (-s, -ing, -ed) row (a boat) using sculls
sculled v ▷ scull
sculleries n ▷ scullery
scullery n (pl -ries) small room where washing-up and other kitchen work is done
sculling v ▷ scull
sculls n, v ▷ scull
sculptor n ▷ sculpture
sculptors n ▷ sculpture
sculptress n ▷ sculpture
sculptresses n ▷ sculpture
sculptural adj ▷ sculpture
sculpture n (pl -s) art of making figures or designs in wood, stone, etc. ▶ v (-res, -ring, -red) (also **sculpt**) represent in sculpture > **sculptor, sculptress** (pl -s, -es) > **sculptural** adj
sculptured v ▷ sculpture
sculptures n, v ▷ sculpture
sculpturing v ▷ sculpture
scum n (pl -s) impure or waste matter on the surface of a liquid > **scummy** adj (-mmier, -mmiest)
scummier adj ▷ scum
scummiest adj ▷ scum
scummy adj ▷ scum
scums n ▷ scum
scungier adj ▷ scungy
scungiest adj ▷ scungy
scungy adj (-ier, -iest) (AUST & NZ) (Informal) sordid or dirty
scupper v (-s, -ing, -ed) (Informal) defeat or ruin
scuppered v ▷ scupper
scuppering v ▷ scupper
scuppers v ▷ scupper
scurf n (pl -s) flaky skin on the scalp
scurfs n ▷ scurf
scurried v ▷ scurry
scurries v, n ▷ scurry
scurrilous adj untrue and defamatory
scurry v (-ries, -rying, -ried) move hastily ▶ n (pl -ries) act or sound of scurrying
scurrying v ▷ scurry
scurvies n ▷ scurvy
scurvy n (pl -vies) disease caused by lack of vitamin C
scut n (pl -s) short tail of the hare, rabbit, or deer
scuts n ▷ scut
scuttle¹ n (pl -s) fireside container for coal

scuttle² v (-les, -ling, -led) run with short quick steps ▶ n (pl -s) hurried run
scuttle³ v (-les, -ling, -ed) make a hole in (a ship) to sink it
scuttled v ▷ scuttle²,³
scuttles n (pl -s 1, 2) ▶ v ▷ scuttle²,³
scuttling v ▷ scuttle²,³
scythe n (pl -s) long-handled tool with a curved blade for cutting grass ▶ v (-thes, -thing, -thed) cut with a scythe
scythed v ▷ scythe
scythes n, v ▷ scythe
scything v ▷ scythe
sea n (pl -s) mass of salt water covering three quarters of the earth's surface
seaboard n (pl -s) coast
seaboards n ▷ seaboard
seafaring adj working or travelling by sea
seafood n (pl -s) edible saltwater fish or shellfish
seafoods n ▷ seafood
seagull n (pl -s) gull
seagulls n ▷ seagull
seal¹ n (pl -s) piece of wax, lead, etc. with a special design impressed upon it, attached to a letter or document as a mark of authentication ▶ v (-s, -ing, -ed) close with or as if with a seal
seal² n (pl -s) amphibious mammal with flippers as limbs > **sealskin** n (pl -s)
sealant n (pl -s) any substance used for sealing
sealants n ▷ sealant
sealed v ▷ seal¹
sealing v ▷ seal¹
seals n ▷ seal¹,² ▶ v ▷ seal¹
sealskin n ▷ seal²
sealskins n ▷ seal²
seam n (pl -s) line where two edges are joined, as by stitching ▶ v (-s, -ing, -ed) mark with furrows or wrinkles > **seamless** adj
seaman n (pl -men) sailor
seamed v ▷ seam
seamen n ▷ seaman
seamier adj ▷ seamy
seamiest adj ▷ seamy
seaming v ▷ seam
seamless adj ▷ seam
seams n, v ▷ seam
seamstress n (pl -es) woman who sews, esp. professionally
seamstresses n ▷ seamstress
seamy adj (-mier, -miest) sordid
seance [say-anss] n (pl -s) meeting at which spiritualists attempt to communicate with the dead

seances n ▷ seance

seaplane n (pl -s) aircraft designed to take off from and land on water

seaplanes n ▷ seaplane

sear v (-s, -ing, -ed) scorch, burn the surface of

search v (-es, -ing, -ed) examine closely in order to find something ▶ n (pl -es) searching

searched v ▷ search

searches v, n ▷ search

searching adj keen or thorough ▶ v ▷ search

searchlight n (pl -s) powerful light with a beam that can be shone in any direction

searchlights n ▷ searchlight

seared v ▷ sear

searing adj (of pain) very sharp ▶ v ▷ sear

sears v ▷ sear

seas n ▷ sea

seasick adj suffering from nausea caused by the motion of a ship > **seasickness** n (pl -es)

seasickness n ▷ seasick

seasicknesses n ▷ seasick

seaside n (pl -s) area, esp. a holiday resort, on the coast

seasides n ▷ seaside

season n (pl -s) one of four divisions of the year, each of which has characteristic weather conditions ▶ v (-s, -ing, -ed) flavour with salt, herbs, etc.

seasonable adj appropriate for the season

seasonal adj depending on or varying with the seasons

seasoned adj experienced ▶ v ▷ season

seasoning v ▷ season ▶ n (pl -s) salt, herbs, etc. added to food to enhance flavour

seasonings n ▷ seasoning

seasons n, v ▷ season

seat n (pl -s) thing designed or used for sitting on ▶ v (-s, -ing, -ed) cause to sit

seated v ▷ seat

seating v ▷ seat

seats n, v ▷ seat

seaweed n (pl -s) plant growing in the sea

seaweeds n ▷ seaweed

seaworthy adj (of a ship) in fit condition for a sea voyage

sebaceous adj of, like, or secreting fat or oil

secateurs pl n small pruning shears

secede v (-des, -ding, -ded) withdraw formally from a political alliance or federation > **secession** n (pl -s)

seceded v ▷ secede

secedes v ▷ secede

seceding v ▷ secede

secession n ▷ secede

secessions n ▷ secede

seclude v (-des, -ding, -ded) keep (a person) from contact with others

secluded adj private, sheltered ▶ v ▷ seclude > **seclusion** n (pl -s)

secludes v ▷ seclude

secluding v ▷ seclude

seclusion n ▷ secluded

seclusions n ▷ secluded

second[1] adj coming directly after the first ▶ n (pl -s) person or thing coming second ▶ v (-s, -ing, -ed) express formal support for (a motion proposed in a meeting) > **secondly** adv

second[2] n (pl -s) sixtieth part of a minute of an angle or time

second[3] [si-kond] v (-s, -ing, -ed) transfer (a person) temporarily to another job > **secondment** n (pl -s)

secondary adj of less importance

seconded v ▷ second[1, 3]

secondhand adj bought after use by another

seconding v ▷ second[1, 3]

secondly adv ▷ second[1]

secondment n ▷ second[3]

secondments n ▷ second[3]

seconds v ▷ second[1, 3] ▶ n ▷ second[1, 2] ▶ pl n inferior goods

secrecies n ▷ secret

secrecy n ▷ secret

secret adj kept from the knowledge of others ▶ n (pl -s) something kept secret > **secretly** adv > **secrecy** n (pl -cies)

secretarial adj ▷ secretary

secretariat n (pl -s) administrative office or staff of a legislative body

secretariats n ▷ secretariat

secretaries n ▷ secretary

secretary n (pl -ries) person who deals with correspondence and general clerical work > **secretarial** adj

secrete[1] v (-tes, -ting, -ted) (of an organ, gland, etc.) produce and release (a substance) > **secretion** n (pl -s) > **secretory** [sek-reet-or-ee] adj

secrete[2] v (-tes, -ting, -ted) hide or conceal

secreted v ▷ secrete[1, 2]

secretes v ▷ secrete[1, 2]

secreting v ▷ secrete[1, 2]

secretion n ▷ secrete[1]

secretions n ▷ secrete[1]

secretive adj inclined to keep things secret > **secretiveness** n (pl -es)

secretiveness n ▷ secretive

secretivenesses n ▷ secretive

secretly adv ▷ secret

secretory adj ▷secrete¹
secrets n ▷secret
sect n (pl -s) subdivision of a religious or political group, esp. one with extreme beliefs
sectarian adj of a sect
section n (pl -s) part cut off ▶ v (-s, -ing, -ed) cut or divide into sections > **sectional** adj
  sectional adj ▷section
  sectioned v ▷section
  sectioning v ▷section
  sections n, v ▷section
sector n (pl -s) part or subdivision
  sectors n ▷sector
  sects n ▷sect
secular adj worldly, as opposed to sacred
secure adj (-r, -st) free from danger ▶ v (-res, -ring, -red) obtain > **securely** adv
  secured v ▷secure
  securely adv ▷secure
  securer adj ▷secure
  secures v ▷secure
  securest adj ▷secure
  securing v ▷secure
  securities n ▷security
security n (pl -ties) precautions against theft, espionage, or other danger
sedan n (pl -s) (US, AUST & NZ) two-door or four-door car with the body closed off from the rear luggage area
  sedans n ▷sedan
sedate¹ adj (-r, -st) calm and dignified > **sedately** adv
sedate² v (-tes, -ting, -ted) give a sedative drug to > **sedation** n (pl -s)
  sedated v ▷sedate²
  sedately adv ▷sedate¹
  sedater adj ▷sedate¹
  sedates v ▷sedate²
  sedatest adj ▷sedate¹
  sedating v ▷sedate²
  sedation n ▷sedate²
  sedations n ▷sedate²
sedative adj having a soothing or calming effect ▶ n (pl -s) sedative drug
  sedatives n ▷sedative
sedentary adj done sitting down, involving little exercise
sedge n (pl -s) coarse grasslike plant growing on wet ground
  sedges n ▷sedge
sediment n (pl -s) matter which settles to the bottom of a liquid > **sedimentary** adj
  sedimentary adj ▷sediment
  sediments n ▷sediment
sedition n (pl -s) speech or action encouraging

rebellion against the government > **seditious** adj
  seditions n ▷sedition
  seditious adj ▷sedition
seduce v (-ces, -cing, -ced) persuade into sexual intercourse > **seducer, seductress** n (pl -s, -es) > **seduction** n (pl -s) > **seductive** adj
  seduced v ▷seduce
  seducer n ▷seduce
  seducers n ▷seduce
  seduces v ▷seduce
  seducing v ▷seduce
  seduction n ▷seduce
  seductions n ▷seduce
  seductive adj ▷seduce
  seductress n ▷seduce
  seductresses n ▷seduce
sedulous adj diligent or persevering > **sedulously** adv
  sedulously adv ▷sedulous
see¹ v (-s, -ing, saw, seen) perceive with the eyes or mind
see² n (pl -s) diocese of a bishop
seed n (pl -s) mature fertilized grain of a plant ▶ v (-s, -ing, -ed) sow with seed
  seeded v ▷seed
  seedier adj ▷seedy
  seediest adj ▷seedy
  seeding v ▷seed
seedling n (pl -s) young plant raised from a seed
  seedlings n ▷seedling
  seeds n, v ▷seed
seedy adj (-dier, -diest) shabby
seeing conj in view of the fact that ▶ v ▷see¹
seek v (-s, -ing, sought) try to find or obtain
  seeking v ▷seek
  seeks v ▷seek
seem v (-s, -ing, -ed) appear to be
  seemed v ▷seem
seeming adj apparent but not real > **seemingly** adv, v ▷seem
  seemingly adv ▷seeming
  seemlier adj ▷seemly
  seemliest adj ▷seemly
seemly adj (-lier, -liest) proper or fitting
  seems v ▷seem
  seen v ▷see¹
seep v (-s, -ing, -ed) trickle through slowly, ooze > **seepage** n (pl -s)
  seepage n ▷seep
  seepages n ▷seep
  seeped v ▷seep
  seeping v ▷seep
  seeps v ▷seep

seer n (pl -s) prophet
  seers n ▷ seer
seersucker n (pl -s) light cotton fabric with a slightly crinkled surface
  seersuckers n ▷ seersucker
sees n ▷ see² ▶ v ▷ see¹
seesaw n (pl -s) plank balanced in the middle so that two people seated on either end ride up and down alternately ▶ v (-s, -ing, -ed) move up and down
  seesawed v ▷ seesaw
  seesawing v ▷ seesaw
  seesaws n, v ▷ seesaw
seethe v (-thes, -thing, -thed) be very agitated
  seethed v ▷ seethe
  seethes v ▷ seethe
  seething v ▷ seethe
segment n (pl -s) one of several sections into which something may be divided ▶ v (-s, -ing, -ed) divide into segments > **segmentation** n (pl -s)
  segmentation n ▷ segment
  segmentations n ▷ segment
  segmented v ▷ segment
  segmenting v ▷ segment
  segments n, v ▷ segment
segregate v (-tes, -ting, -ted) set apart > **segregation** n (pl -s)
  segregated v ▷ segregate
  segregates v ▷ segregate
  segregating v ▷ segregate
  segregation n ▷ segregate
  segregations n ▷ segregate
seine [sane] n (pl -s) large fishing net that hangs vertically from floats
  seines n ▷ seine
seismic adj relating to earthquakes
seismograph, seismometer n (pl -s) instrument that records the strength of earthquakes
  seismographs n ▷ seismograph
  seismological adj ▷ seismology
  seismologies n ▷ seismology
  seismologist n ▷ seismology
  seismologists n ▷ seismology
seismology n (pl -gies) study of earthquakes > **seismological** adj > **seismologist** n (pl -s)
  seismometer n ▷ seismograph
  seismometers n ▷ seismograph
seize v (-zes, -zing, -zed) take hold of forcibly or quickly (usu. foll. by **up**)
  seized v ▷ seize
  seizes v ▷ seize
  seizing v ▷ seize
seizure n (pl -s) sudden violent attack of an

illness
  seizures n ▷ seizure
seldom adv not often, rarely
select v (-s, -ing, -ed) pick out or choose ▶ adj chosen in preference to others > **selector** n (pl -s)
  selected v ▷ select
  selecting v ▷ select
selection n (pl -s) selecting
  selections n ▷ selection
selective adj chosen or choosing carefully > **selectively** adv > **selectivity** n (pl -ties)
  selectively adv ▷ selective
  selectivities n ▷ selective
  selectivity n ▷ selective
  selector n ▷ select
  selectors n ▷ select
  selects v ▷ select
selenium n (pl -s) (CHEM) nonmetallic element with photoelectric properties
  seleniums n ▷ selenium
self n (pl selves) distinct individuality or identity of a person or thing
selfish adj caring too much about oneself and not enough about others > **selfishly** adv > **selfishness** n (pl -es)
  selfishly adv ▷ selfish
  selfishness n ▷ selfish
  selfishnesses n ▷ selfish
selfless adj unselfish
selfsame adj the very same
sell v (-s, -ing, sold) exchange (something) for money (foll. by **for**) ▶ n (pl -s) manner of selling > **seller** n (pl -s)
  seller n ▷ sell
  sellers n ▷ sell
  selling v ▷ sell
sellotape n (pl -s) ® type of adhesive tape ▶ v (-pes, -ping, -ped) stick with sellotape
  sellotaped v ▷ sellotape
  sellotapes n, v ▷ sellotape
  sellotaping v ▷ sellotape
sellout n (pl -s) performance of a show etc. for which all the tickets are sold
  sellouts n ▷ sellout
  sells v, n ▷ sell
selvage, selvedge n (pl -s) edge of cloth, woven so as to prevent unravelling
  selvages n ▷ selvage
  selvedge n ▷ selvage
  selvedges n ▷ selvage
  selves n ▷ self
semantic adj relating to the meaning of words
semantics n study of linguistic meaning
semaphore n (pl -s) system of signalling by

holding two flags in different positions to represent letters of the alphabet

semaphores n ▷ semaphore

semblance n (pl -s) outward or superficial appearance

semblances n ▷ semblance

semen n (pl -s) sperm-carrying fluid produced by male animals

semens n ▷ semen

semester n (pl -s) either of two divisions of the academic year

semesters n ▷ semester

semi n (pl -s) (BRIT & S AFR) (Informal) semidetached house

semibreve n (pl -s) musical note four beats long

semibreves n ▷ semibreve

semicolon n (pl -s) the punctuation mark (;)

semicolons n ▷ semicolon

semiconductor n (pl -s) substance with an electrical conductivity that increases with temperature

semiconductors n ▷ semiconductor

semidetached adj (of a house) joined to another on one side

semifinal n (pl -s) match or round before the final > **semifinalist** n (pl -s)

semifinalist n ▷ semifinal

semifinalists n ▷ semifinal

semifinals n ▷ semifinal

seminal adj original and influential

seminar n (pl -s) meeting of a group of students for discussion

seminaries n ▷ seminary

seminars n ▷ seminar

seminary n (pl -ries) college for priests

semiprecious adj (of gemstones) having less value than precious stones

semiquaver n (pl -s) musical note half the length of a quaver

semiquavers n ▷ semiquaver

semis n ▷ semi

semitone n (pl -s) smallest interval between two notes in Western music

semitones n ▷ semitone

semitrailer n (pl -s) (AUST) large truck in two separate sections joined by a pivoted bar

semitrailers n ▷ semitrailer

semolina n (pl -s) hard grains of wheat left after the milling of flour, used to make puddings and pasta

semolinas n ▷ semolina

senate n (pl -s) upper house of some parliaments; governing body of some universities

senates n ▷ senate

senator n (pl -s) member of a senate > **senatorial** adj

senatorial adj ▷ senator

senators n ▷ senator

send v (-s, -ing, sent) cause (a person or thing) to go to or be taken or transmitted to a place

sending v ▷ send

sendoff n (pl -s) demonstration of good wishes at a person's departure

sendoffs n ▷ sendoff

sends v ▷ send

sendup n (pl -s) (Informal) imitation

sendups n ▷ sendup

senile adj mentally or physically weak because of old age > **senility** n (pl -ties)

senilities n ▷ senile

senility n ▷ senile

senior adj superior in rank or standing ▶ n (pl -s) senior person > **seniority** n (pl -ties)

seniorities n ▷ senior

seniority n ▷ senior

seniors n ▷ senior

senna n (pl -s) tropical plant

sennas n ▷ senna

señor [sen-**nyor**] n (pl -ores) Spanish term of address equivalent to sir or Mr

señora [sen-**nyor**-a] n (pl -s) Spanish term of address equivalent to madam or Mrs

señoras n ▷ señora

señorita [sen-nyor-**ee**-ta] n (pl -s) Spanish term of address equivalent to madam or Miss

señoritas n ▷ señorita

señors n ▷ señor

sensation n (pl -s) ability to feel things physically

sensational adj causing intense shock, anger, or excitement

sensationalism n (pl -s) deliberate use of sensational language or subject matter > **sensationalist** adj, n (pl -s)

sensationalisms n ▷ sensationalism

sensationalist adj, n ▷ sensationalism

sensationalists n ▷ sensationalism

sensations n ▷ sensation

sense n (pl -s) any of the faculties of perception or feeling (sight, hearing, touch, taste, or smell ▶ v (-ses, -sing, -sed) perceive > **senseless** adj

sensed v ▷ sense

senseless adj ▷ sense

senses n, v ▷ sense

sensibilities n ▷ sensibility

sensibility n (pl -ties) ability to experience deep feelings

sensible *adj* (**-r, -st**) having or showing good sense > **sensibly** *adv*
  sensibler *adj* ▷ sensible
  sensiblest *adj* ▷ sensible
  sensibly *adv* ▷ sensible
  sensing *v* ▷ sense
sensitive *adj* easily hurt or offended
  > **sensitively** *adv* > **sensitivity** *n* (*pl* -s)
  sensitively *adv* ▷ sensitive
  sensitivities *n* ▷ sensitive
  sensitivity *n* ▷ sensitive
sensitize *v* (**-zes, -zing, -zed**) make sensitive
  sensitized *v* ▷ sensitize
  sensitizes *v* ▷ sensitize
  sensitizing *v* ▷ sensitize
sensor *n* (*pl* -s) device that detects or measures the presence of something, such as radiation
  sensors *n* ▷ sensor
sensory *adj* of the senses or sensation
sensual *adj* giving pleasure to the body and senses rather than the mind > **sensually** *adv*
  > **sensuality** *n* (*pl* -ties) > **sensualist** *n* (*pl* -s)
  sensualist *n* ▷ sensual
  sensualists *n* ▷ sensual
  sensualities *n* ▷ sensual
  sensuality *n* ▷ sensual
  sensually *adj* ▷ sensual
sensuous *adj* pleasing to the senses
  > **sensuously** *adv*
  sensuously *adv* ▷ sensuous
sent *v* ▷ send
sentence *n* (*pl* -s) sequence of words capable of standing alone as a statement, question, or command ▸ *v* (**-ces, -cing, -ced**) pass sentence on (a convicted person)
  sentenced *v* ▷ sentence
  sentences *n, v* ▷ sentence
  sentencing *n, v* ▷ sentence
sententious *adj* trying to sound wise
  sentience *n* ▷ sentient
  sentiences *n* ▷ sentient
sentient [sen-tee-ent] *adj* capable of feeling
  > **sentience** *n* (*pl* -s)
sentiment *n* (*pl* -s) thought, opinion, or attitude
sentimental *adj* excessively romantic or nostalgic > **sentimentalism** *n* (*pl* -s)
  > **sentimentality** *n* (*pl* -ties)
  sentimentalism *n* ▷ sentimental
  sentimentalisms *n* ▷ sentimental
  sentimentalities *n* ▷ sentimentality
  sentimentality *n* ▷ sentimental
sentimentalize *v* (**-zes, -zing, -zed**) make sentimental
  sentimentalized *v* ▷ sentimentalize

  sentimentalizes *v* ▷ sentimentalize
  sentiments *n* ▷ sentiment
sentinel *n* (*pl* -s) sentry
  sentinels *n* ▷ sentinel
  sentries *n* ▷ sentry
sentry *n* (*pl* -tries) soldier on watch
sepal *n* (*pl* -s) leaflike division of the calyx of a flower
  sepals *n* ▷ sepal
  separable *adj* ▷ separate
separate *v* (**-tes, -ting, -ted**) act as a barrier between ▸ *adj* not the same, different
  > **separable** *adj* > **separately** *adv*
  separated *v* ▷ separate
  separately *adv* ▷ separate
  separates *v* ▷ separate
  separating *v* ▷ separate
separation *n* (*pl* -s) separating or being separated
  separations *n* ▷ separation
  separatism *n* ▷ separatist
  separatisms *n* ▷ separatist
separatist *n* (*pl* -s) person who advocates the separation of a group from an organization or country > **separatism** *n* (*pl* -s)
  separatists *n* ▷ separatist
sepia *adj, n* (*pl* -s) reddish-brown (pigment)
  sepias *n* ▷ sepia
  sepses *n* ▷ sepsis
sepsis *n* (*pl* -ses) poisoning caused by pus-forming bacteria
septet *n* (*pl* -s) group of seven performers
  septets *n* ▷ septet
septic *adj* (of a wound) infected
septicaemia [sep-tis-**see**-mee-a] *n* (*pl* -s) infection of the blood
  septicaemias *n* ▷ septicaemia
septuagenarian *n* (*pl* -s) person aged between seventy and seventy-nine
  septuagenarians *n* ▷ septuagenarian
sepulchral [sip-**pulk**-ral] *adj* gloomy
sepulchre [**sep**-pull-ker] *n* (*pl* -s) tomb or burial vault
  sepulchres *n* ▷ sepulchre
sequel *n* (*pl* -s) novel, play, or film that continues the story of an earlier one
  sequels *n* ▷ sequel
sequence *n* (*pl* -s) arrangement of two or more things in successive order > **sequential** *adj*
  sequences *n* ▷ sequence
  sequential *adj* ▷ sequence
sequester *v* (**-s, -ing, -ed**) seclude
  sequestered *v* ▷ sequester
  sequestering *v* ▷ sequester
  sequesters *v* ▷ sequester

sequestrate v (-tes, -ting, -ted) confiscate (property) until its owner's debts are paid or a court order is complied with > **sequestration** n (pl -s)

sequestrated v ▷ sequestrate
sequestrates v ▷ sequestrate
sequestrating v ▷ sequestrate
sequestration n ▷ sequestrate
sequestrations n ▷ sequestrate

sequin n (pl -s) small ornamental metal disc on a garment > **sequined** adj
sequined adj ▷ sequin
sequins n ▷ sequin

sequoia n (pl -s) giant Californian coniferous tree
sequoias n ▷ sequoia

seraglio [sir-ah-lee-oh] n (pl -s) harem of a Muslim palace
seraglios n ▷ seraglio

seraph n (pl -s, -aphim) member of the highest order of angels > **seraphic** adj
seraphic adj ▷ seraph
seraphim n ▷ seraph
seraphs n ▷ seraph

serenade n (pl -s) music played or sung to a woman by a lover ▶ v (-des, -ding, -ded) sing or play a serenade to (someone)
serenaded v ▷ serenade
serenades n, v ▷ serenade
serenading v ▷ serenade
serendipities n ▷ serendipity

serendipity n (pl -ties) gift of making fortunate discoveries by accident

serene adj (-r, -st) calm, peaceful > **serenely** adv > **serenity** n (pl -ties)
serenely adv ▷ serene
serener adj ▷ serene
serenest adj ▷ serene
serenities n ▷ serene
serenity n ▷ serene

serf n (pl -s) medieval farm labourer who could not leave the land he worked on > **serfdom** n (pl -s)
serfdom n ▷ serf
serfdoms n ▷ serf
serfs n ▷ serf

serge n (pl -s) strong woollen fabric

sergeant n (pl -s) noncommissioned officer in the army
sergeants n ▷ sergeant
serges n ▷ serge

serial n (pl -s) story or play produced in successive instalments ▶ adj of or forming a series

serialize v (-zes, -zing, -zed) publish or present as a serial
serialized v ▷ serialize
serializes v ▷ serialize
serializing v ▷ serialize
serials n ▷ serial

series n (pl series) group or succession of related things, usu. arranged in order

serious adj giving cause for concern > **seriously** adv > **seriousness** n (pl -es)
seriously adv ▷ serious
seriousness n ▷ serious
seriousnesses n ▷ serious

sermon n (pl -s) speech on a religious or moral subject by a clergyman in a church service

sermonize v (-zes, -zing, -zed) make a long moralizing speech
sermonized v ▷ sermonize
sermonizes v ▷ sermonize
sermonizing v ▷ sermonize
sermons n ▷ sermon

serpent n (pl -s) (Lit) snake

serpentine adj twisting like a snake
serpents n ▷ serpent

serrated adj having a notched or sawlike edge

serried adj in close formation

serum [seer-um] n (pl -s) watery fluid left after blood has clotted
serums n ▷ serum

servant n (pl -s) person employed to do household work for another
servants n ▷ servant

serve v (-s, -ing, -ed) work for (a person, community, or cause) ▶ n (pl -s) (TENNIS ETC.) act of serving the ball
served v ▷ serve

server n (pl -s) player who serves in racket games
servers n ▷ server
serves n, v ▷ serve

service n (pl -s) system that provides something needed by the public ▶ v (-ces, -cing, -ced) overhaul (a machine or vehicle)

serviceable adj useful or helpful
serviced v ▷ service

serviceman, servicewoman n (pl -men, -women) member of the armed forces
servicemen n ▷ serviceman
services n, v ▷ service ▶ pl n armed forces
servicewoman n ▷ serviceman
servicewomen n ▷ serviceman
servicing v ▷ service

serviette n (pl -s) table napkin
serviettes n ▷ serviette

servile adj too eager to obey people, fawning > **servility** n (pl -s)

servilities n ▷servile

servility n ▷servile

serving v ▷serve

servitude n (pl -s) bondage or slavery

servitudes n ▷servitude

sesame [sess-am-ee] n (pl -s) plant cultivated for its seeds and oil, which are used in cooking

sesames n ▷sesame

session n (pl -s) period spent in an activity

sessions n ▷session

set[1] v (-s, -tting, set) put in a specified position or state ▶ n (pl -s) scenery used in a play or film ▶ adj fixed or established beforehand

set[2] n (pl -s) number of things or people grouped or belonging together

setback n (pl -s) anything that delays progress

setbacks n ▷setback

sets v ▷set[1] ▶ n ▷set[2]

sett, set n (p -s) badger's burrow

settee n (pl -s) couch

settees n ▷settee

setter n (pl -s) long-haired gun dog

setters n ▷setter

setting n (pl -s) background or surroundings ▶ v ▷set

settings n ▷setting

settle[1] v (-les, -ling, -led) arrange or put in order

settle[2] n (pl -s) long wooden bench with high back and arms

settled v ▷settle[1]

settlement n (pl -s) act of settling

settlements n ▷settlement

settler n (pl -s) colonist

settlers n ▷settler

settles v ▷settle[1] ▶ n ▷settle[2]

settling v ▷settle[1]

setts n ▷sett

setup n (pl -s) way in which anything is organized or arranged

setups n ▷setup

seven adj, n (pl -s) one more than six

sevens n ▷seven

seventeen adj, n (pl -s) ten and seven > **seventeenth** adj, n (pl -s)

seventeens n ▷seventeen

seventeenth n ▷seventeen

seventeenths n ▷seventeen

seventh adj, n (pl -s) (of) number seven in a series

sevenths n ▷seventh

seventies n ▷seventy

seventieth n ▷seventy

seventieths n ▷seventy

seventy adj, n (pl -ties) ten times seven > **seventieth** adj, n (pl -s)

sever v (-s, -ing, -ed) cut through or off > **severance** n (pl -s)

several adj some, a few

severally adv separately

severance n ▷sever

severances n ▷sever

severe adj (-r, -st) strict or harsh > **severely** adv > **severity** n (pl -ties)

severed v ▷sever

severely adv ▷severe

severer adj ▷severe

severest adj ▷severe

severing v ▷sever

severities n ▷severe

severity n ▷severe

severs v ▷sever

sew v (-s, -ing, -ed, sewn or -ed) join with thread repeatedly passed through with a needle

sewage n (pl -s) waste matter or excrement carried away in sewers

sewages n ▷sewage

sewed v ▷sew

sewer n (pl -s) drain to remove waste water and sewage > **sewerage** n (pl -s) system of sewers

sewerage n ▷sewer

sewerages n ▷sewer

sewers n ▷sewer

sewing v ▷sew

sewn v ▷sew

sews v ▷sew

sex n (pl -es) state of being male or female ▶ v (-es, -ing, -ed) find out the sex of > **sexual** adj > **sexually** adv > **sexuality** n (pl -ties)

sexagenarian n (pl -s) person aged between sixty and sixty-nine

sexagenarians n ▷sexagenarian

sexed v ▷sex

sexes n, v ▷sex

sexier adj ▷sexy

sexiest adj ▷sexy

sexing v ▷sex

sexism n (pl -s) discrimination on the basis of a person's sex > **sexist** adj, n (pl -s)

sexisms n ▷sexism

sexist n ▷sexism

sexists n ▷sexism

sextant n (pl -s) navigator's instrument for measuring angles, as between the sun and horizon, to calculate one's position

sextants n ▷sextant

sextet n (pl -s) group of six performers

sextets n ▷ sextet
sexton n (pl -s) official in charge of a church and churchyard
  sextons n ▷ sexton
sexual adj ▷ sex
sexualities n ▷ sex
sexuality n ▷ sex
sexually adv ▷ sex
sexy adj (-xier, -xiest) sexually exciting or attractive

> **sez** v. Sez is an short informal form of **says**. This word can be very useful when there isn't much space on the board, as it gives a good score. Sez scores 12 points.
> **sh** interj. Sh is a sound people make to request silence or quiet. This is one of two two-letter words beginning with S that do not contain a vowel. It's useful when you want to connect a word beginning with H to one ending in S or vice versa. Sh scores 5 points.

shabbier adj ▷ shabby
shabbiest adj ▷ shabby
shabbily adv ▷ shabby
shabbiness n ▷ shabby
shabbinesses n ▷ shabby
shabby adj (-bier, -biest) worn or dilapidated in appearance > **shabbily** adv > **shabbiness** n (pl -es)
shack n (pl -s) rough hut
shackle n (pl -s) one of a pair of metal rings joined by a chain, for securing a person's wrists or ankles ▶ v (-les, -ling, -led) fasten with shackles
  shackled v ▷ shackle
  shackles n, v ▷ shackle
  shackling v ▷ shackle
  shacks n ▷ shack
shad n (pl -s) herring-like fish
shade n (pl -s) relative darkness ▶ v (-des, -ding, -ded) screen from light > **shady** adj (-dier, -diest) situated in or giving shade
  shaded v ▷ shade
  shades n, v ▷ shade ▶ pl n (Slang) sunglasses
  shadier adj ▷ shade
  shadiest adj ▷ shade
  shading v ▷ shade
shadow n (pl -s) dark shape cast on a surface when something stands between a light and the surface ▶ v (-s, -ing, -ed) cast a shadow over > **shadowy** adj (-wier, -wiest)
shadowboxing n (pl -s) boxing against an imaginary opponent for practice
  shadowboxings n ▷ shadowboxing

shadowed v ▷ shadow
shadowier adj ▷ shadow
shadowiest adj ▷ shadow
shadowing v ▷ shadow
shadows n, v ▷ shadow
shadowy adj ▷ shadow
shads n ▷ shad
shady adj ▷ shade
shaft n (pl -s) long narrow straight handle of a tool or weapon
  shafts n ▷ shaft
shag[1] n (pl -s) coarse shredded tobacco ▶ adj (of a carpet) having a long pile
shag[2] n (pl -s) kind of cormorant
  shaggier adj ▷ shaggy
  shaggiest adj ▷ shaggy
shaggy adj (-ggier, -ggiest) covered with rough hair or wool
shagreen n (pl -s) sharkskin
  shagreens n ▷ shagreen
  shags n ▷ shag[1, 2]
shah n (pl -s) formerly, ruler of Iran
  shahs n ▷ shah
shake v (-kes, -king, shook, -en) move quickly up and down or back and forth ▶ n (pl -s) shaking (Informal)
  shaken v ▷ shake
  shakes v, n ▷ shake
  shakier adj ▷ shaky
  shakiest adj ▷ shaky
  shakily adv ▷ shaky
  shaking v ▷ shake
shaky adj (-kier, -kiest) unsteady > **shakily** adv
shale n (pl -s) flaky sedimentary rock
  shales n ▷ shale
shall v (past tense should) used as an auxiliary to make the future tense or to indicate intention, obligation, or inevitability
shallot n (pl -s) kind of small onion
  shallots n ▷ shallot
shallow adj (-er, -est) not deep > **shallowness** n (pl -es)
  shallower adj ▷ shallow
  shallowest adj ▷ shallow
  shallowness n ▷ shallow
  shallownesses n ▷ shallow
shallows pl n area of shallow water
sham n (pl -s) thing or person that is not genuine ▶ adj not genuine ▶ v (-s, -mming, -mmed) fake, feign
shamble v (-les, -ling, -led) walk in a shuffling awkward way
  shambled v ▷ shamble
shambles n (pl disorderly event or place ▶ v ▷ shamble

shambling v ▷ shamble

shame n (pl -s) painful emotion caused by awareness of having done something dishonourable or foolish ▶ v (-mes, -ming, -med) cause to feel shame ▶ interj (S AFR) (Informal) exclamation of sympathy or endearment

shamed v ▷ shame

shamefaced adj looking ashamed

shameful adj causing or deserving shame > **shamefully** adv

shamefully adv ▷ shameful

shameless adj with no sense of shame

shames n, v ▷ shame

shaming v ▷ shame

shammed v ▷ sham

shammies n ▷ shammy

shamming v ▷ sham

shammy n (pl -mies) (Informal) piece of chamois leather

shampoo n (pl -s) liquid soap for washing hair, carpets, or upholstery ▶ v (-s, -ing, -ed) wash with shampoo

shampooed v ▷ shampoo

shampooing v ▷ shampoo

shampoos n, v ▷ shampoo

shamrock n (pl -s) clover leaf, esp. as the Irish emblem

shamrocks n ▷ shamrock

shams n, v ▷ sham

shandies n ▷ shandy

shandy n (pl -dies) drink made of beer and lemonade

shanghai v (-hais, -haiing, -haied) force or trick (someone) into doing something ▶ n (pl -s) (AUST & NZ) catapult

shanghaied v ▷ shanghai

shanghaiing v ▷ shanghai

shanghais v, n ▷ shanghai

shank n (pl -s) lower leg

shanks n ▷ shank

shanties n ▷ shanty¹, ²

shantung n (pl -s) soft Chinese silk with a knobbly surface

shantungs n ▷ shantung

shanty¹ n (pl -ties) shack or crude dwelling

shanty² n (pl -ties) sailor's traditional song

shantytown n (pl -s) slum consisting of shanties

shantytowns n ▷ shantytown

shape n (pl -s) outward form of an object ▶ v (-pes, -ping, -ped) form or mould > **shapeless** adj

shaped v ▷ shape

shapeless adj ▷ shape

shapelier adj ▷ shapely

shapeliest adj ▷ shapely

shapely adj (-lier, -liest) having an attractive shape

shapes n, v ▷ shape

shaping v ▷ shape

shard n (pl -s) broken piece of pottery or glass

shards n ▷ shard

share¹ n (pl -s) part of something that belongs to or is contributed by a person ▶ v (-res, -ring, -red) give or take a share of (something) > **shareholder** n (pl -s)

share² n (pl -s) blade of a plough

shared v ▷ share¹

shareholder n ▷ share¹

shareholders n ▷ share¹

sharemilker n (pl -s) (NZ) person who works on a dairy farm belonging to someone else

sharemilkers n ▷ sharemilker

shares v ▷ share¹ ▶ n ▷ share¹, ²

sharing v ▷ share¹

shark n (pl -s) large usu. predatory sea fish

sharks n ▷ shark

sharkskin n (pl -s) stiff glossy fabric

sharkskins n ▷ sharkskin

sharp adj having a keen cutting edge or fine point ▶ adv promptly ▶ n (pl -s) (MUSIC) symbol raising a note one semitone above natural pitch > **sharply** adv > **sharpness** n (pl -es)

sharpen v (-s, -ing, -ed) make or become sharp or sharper > **sharpener** n (pl -s)

sharpened v ▷ sharpen

sharpener n ▷ sharpen

sharpeners n ▷ sharpen

sharpening v ▷ sharpen

sharpens v ▷ sharpen

sharply adv ▷ sharp

sharpness n ▷ sharp

sharpnesses n ▷ sharp

sharps n ▷ sharp

sharpshooter n (pl -s) marksman

sharpshooters n ▷ sharpshooter

shatter v (-s, -ing, -ed) break into pieces

shattered adj (Informal) completely exhausted ▶ v ▷ shatter

shattering v ▷ shatter

shatters v ▷ shatter

shave v (-ves, -ving, -ved, -ved or **shaven**) remove (hair) from (the face, head, or body) with a razor or shaver ▶ n (pl -s) shaving

shaved v ▷ shave

shaven v ▷ shave

shaver n (pl -s) electric razor

shavers n ▷ shaver

shaves v, n ▷ shave

shaving v ▷ shave

shavings pl n parings

shawl n (pl -s) piece of cloth worn over a woman's head or shoulders or wrapped around a baby

shawls n ▷ shawl

she pron refers to: female person or animal previously mentioned

sheaf n (pl sheaves) bundle of papers

shear v (-s, -ing, -ed, -ed or shorn) clip hair or wool from ▷ **shearer** n (pl -s)

sheared v ▷ shear

shearer n ▷ shear

shearers n ▷ shear

shearing v ▷ shear

shears pl n large scissors or a cutting tool shaped like these ▶ v ▷ shear

shearwater n (pl -s) medium-sized sea bird

shearwaters n ▷ shearwater

sheath n (pl -s) close-fitting cover, esp. for a knife or sword

sheathe v (-thes, -thing, -thed) put into a sheath

sheathed v ▷ sheathe

sheathes v ▷ sheathe

sheathing v ▷ sheathe

sheaths n ▷ sheath

sheaves n ▷ sheaf

shebeen n (pl -s) (SCOT, IRISH & S AFR) place where alcohol is sold illegally

shebeens n ▷ shebeen

shed¹ n (pl -s) building used for storage or shelter or as a workshop

shed² v (-s, -dding, shed) pour forth (tears)

shedding v ▷ shed²

sheds n ▷ shed¹ ▶ v ▷ shed²

sheen n (pl -s) glistening brightness on the surface of something

sheens n ▷ sheen

sheep n (pl sheep) ruminant animal bred for wool and meat

sheepdog n (pl -s) dog used for herding sheep

sheepdogs n ▷ sheepdog

sheepish adj embarrassed because of feeling foolish ▷ **sheepishly** adv

sheepishly adv ▷ sheepish

sheepskin n (pl -s) skin of a sheep with the fleece still on, used for clothing or rugs

sheepskins n ▷ sheepskin

sheer¹ adj (-er, -est) absolute, complete

sheer² v (-s, -ing, -ed) change course suddenly

sheered v ▷ sheer²

sheerer adj ▷ sheer¹

sheerest adj ▷ sheer¹

sheering v ▷ sheer²

sheers v ▷ sheer²

sheet¹ n (pl -s) large piece of cloth used as an inner bed cover

sheet² n (pl -s) rope for controlling the position of a sail

sheets n ▷ sheet¹, ²

sheikdom n ▷ sheikh

sheikdoms n ▷ sheikh

sheikh, sheik [shake] n (pl -s) Arab chief ▷ **sheikhdom, sheikdom** n (pl -s)

sheikhdoms n ▷ sheikhdom

sheikhs n ▷ sheikh

sheiks n ▷ sheikh

sheila n (pl -s) (AUST & NZ) (Slang) girl or woman

sheilas n ▷ sheila

shekel n (pl -s) monetary unit of Israel

shekels n ▷ shekel ▶ pl n (Informal) money

shelf n (pl -ves) board fixed horizontally for holding things

shell n (pl -s) hard outer covering of an egg, nut, or certain animals ▶ v (-s, -lling, -lled) take the shell from

shellac n (pl -s) resin used in varnishes ▶ v (-cs, -cking, -cked) coat with shellac

shellacked v ▷ shellac

shellacking v ▷ shellac

shellacs n, v ▷ shellac

shelled v ▷ shell

shellfish n (pl -s) sea-living animal, esp. one that can be eaten, with a shell

shellfishes n ▷ shellfish

shelling v ▷ shell

shells n, v ▷ shell

shelter n (pl -s) structure providing protection from danger or the weather ▶ v (-s, -ing, -ed) give shelter to

sheltered v ▷ shelter

sheltering v ▷ shelter

shelters n, v ▷ shelter

shelve¹ v (-ves, -ving, -ved) put aside or postpone

shelve² v (-ves, -ving, -ved) slope

shelved v ▷ shelve¹, ²

shelves v ▷ shelve¹, ² ▶ n ▷ shelf

shelving n (pl -s) (material for) shelves ▶ v ▷ shelve¹, ²

shenanigans pl n (Informal) mischief or nonsense

shepherd n (pl -s) person who tends sheep ▶ v (-s, -ing, -ed) guide or watch over (people) ▷ **shepherdess** n fem (pl -s)

shepherded v ▷ shepherd

shepherdess n ▷ shepherd

shepherdesses n ▷ shepherd

shepherding v ▷ shepherd

shepherds *n, v* ▷ shepherd
sherbet *n (pl -s)* (BRIT, AUST & NZ) fruit-flavoured fizzy powder
  sherbets *n* ▷ sherbet
sheriff *n (pl -s)* (in the US) chief law enforcement officer of a county
  sheriffs *n* ▷ sheriff
  sherries *n* ▷ sherry
sherry *n (pl -ries)* pale or dark brown fortified wine

> **shh** *interj.* Shh is a sound people make to request silence or quiet. As it doesn't contain a vowel, shh can help you to clear an unpromising rack. Shh scores 9 points.

shibboleth *n (pl -s)* slogan or principle, usu. considered outworn, characteristic of a particular group
  shibboleths *n* ▷ shibboleth
  shied *v* ▷ shy[1,2]
shield *n (pl -s)* piece of armour carried on the arm to protect the body from blows or missiles ▶ *v (-s, -ing, -ed)* protect
  shielded *v* ▷ shield
  shielding *v* ▷ shield
  shields *n, v* ▷ shield
  shies *v* ▷ shy[1,2] ▶ *n* ▷ shy[2]
shift *v (-s, -ing, -ed)* move ▶ *n (pl -s)* shifting
  shifted *v* ▷ shift
  shiftier *adj* ▷ shifty
  shiftiest *adj* ▷ shifty
  shiftiness *n* ▷ shifty
  shiftinesses *n* ▷ shifty
  shifting *v* ▷ shift
shiftless *adj* lacking in ambition or initiative
  shifts *v, n* ▷ shift
shifty *adj (-tier, -tiest)* evasive or untrustworthy > **shiftiness** *n (pl -es)*
shillelagh [shil-**lay**-lee] *n (pl -s)* (in Ireland) a cudgel
  shillelaghs *n* ▷ shillelagh
shilling *n (pl -s)* former British coin, replaced by the 5p piece
  shillings *n* ▷ shilling
  shillyshallied *v* ▷ shillyshally
  shillyshallies *v* ▷ shillyshally
shillyshally *v (-lies, -lying, -lied)* (Informal) be indecisive
  shillyshallying *v* ▷ shillyshally
shimmer *v (-s, -ing, -ed)* ▶ *n (pl -s)* (shine with) a faint unsteady light
  shimmered *v* ▷ shimmer
  shimmering *v* ▷ shimmer
  shimmers *v, n* ▷ shimmer
shin *n (pl -s)* front of the lower leg ▶ *v (-s,*

-nning, -nned) climb by using the hands or arms and legs
shinbone *n (pl -s)* tibia
  shinbones *n* ▷ shinbone
shindig *n (pl -s)* (Informal) noisy party
  shindigs *n* ▷ shindig
shine *v (-s, -ing, shone)* give out or reflect light ▶ *n (pl -s)* brightness or lustre > **shiny** *adj (-nier, -niest)*
shiner *n (pl -s)* (Informal) black eye
  shiners *n* ▷ shiner
  shines *v, n* ▷ shine
shingle[1] *n (pl -s)* wooden roof tile ▶ *v (-les, -ling, -led)* cover (a roof) with shingles
shingle[2] *n (pl -s)* coarse gravel found on beaches
  shingled *v* ▷ shingle[1]
shingles *n* disease causing a rash of small blisters along a nerve ▷ shingle[1,2] ▶ *v* ▷ shingle[1]
  shingling *v* ▷ shingle[1]
  shinier *adj* ▷ shine
  shiniest *adj* ▷ shine
  shining *v* ▷ shine
  shinned *v* ▷ shin
  shinning *v* ▷ shin
  shins *n, v* ▷ shin
  shinties *n* ▷ shinty
shinty *n (pl -ties)* game like hockey
  shiny *adj* ▷ shine
ship *n (pl -s)* large seagoing vessel ▶ *v (-s, -pping, -pped)* send or transport by carrier, esp. a ship
shipment *n (pl -s)* act of shipping cargo
  shipments *n* ▷ shipment
  shipped *v* ▷ ship
shipping *n (pl -s)* freight transport business ▶ *v* ▷ ship
  shippings *n* ▷ shipping
  ships *n, v* ▷ ship
shipshape *adj* orderly or neat
shipwreck *n (pl -s)* destruction of a ship through storm or collision ▶ *v (-s, -ing, -ed)* cause to undergo shipwreck
  shipwrecked *v* ▷ shipwreck
  shipwrecking *v* ▷ shipwreck
  shipwrecks *n, v* ▷ shipwreck
shipyard *n (pl -s)* place where ships are built
  shipyards *n* ▷ shipyard
shire *n (pl -s)* (BRIT) county
  shires *n* ▷ shire
shirk *v (-s, -ing, -ed)* avoid (duty or work) > **shirker** *n (pl -s)*
  shirked *v* ▷ shirk
  shirker *n* ▷ shirk

shirkers n ▷ shirk
shirking v ▷ shirk
shirks v ▷ shirk
shirt n (pl -s) garment for the upper part of the body
shirtier adj ▷ shirty
shirtiest adj ▷ shirty
shirts n ▷ shirt
shirty adj (-tier, -tiest) (CHIEFLY BRIT) (Slang) bad-tempered or annoyed
shiver[1] v (-s, -ing, -ed) tremble, as from cold or fear ▶ n (pl -s) shivering
shiver[2] v (-s, -ing, -ed) splinter into pieces
shivered v ▷ shiver[1, 2]
shivering v ▷ shiver[1, 2]
shivers v ▷ shiver[1, 2] ▶ n ▷ shiver[1]
shoal[1] n (pl -s) large number of fish swimming together
shoal[2] n (pl -s) stretch of shallow water
shoals n ▷ shoal[1, 2]
shock[1] v (-s, -ing, -ed) horrify, disgust, or astonish ▶ n (pl -s) sudden violent emotional disturbance ▷ **shocker** n (pl -s)
shock[2] n (pl -s) bushy mass (of hair)
shocked v ▷ shock[1]
shocker n ▷ shock[1]
shockers n ▷ shock[1]
shocking adj causing horror, disgust, or astonishment ▶ v ▷ shock[1]
shocks v ▷ shock[1] ▶ n ▷ shock[1, 2]
shod v ▷ shoe
shoddier adj ▷ shoddy
shoddiest adj ▷ shoddy
shoddy adj (-dier, -diest) made or done badly
shoe n (pl -s) outer covering for the foot, ending below the ankle ▶ v (shoes, shoeing, shod) fit with a shoe or shoes
shoehorn n (pl -s) smooth curved implement inserted at the heel of a shoe to ease the foot into it
shoehorns n ▷ shoehorn
shoeing v ▷ shoe
shoes n, v ▷ shoe
shoestring n (pl -s) (foll. by **on a**) using a very small amount of money
shoestrings n ▷ shoestring
shone v ▷ shine
shonkier adj ▷ shonky
shonkiest adj ▷ shonky
shonky adj (-kier, -kiest) (AUST & NZ) (Informal) unreliable or unsound
shoo interj go away! ▶ v (-s, -ing, -ed) drive away as by saying 'shoo'
shooed v ▷ shoo
shooing v ▷ shoo

shook v ▷ shake
shoos v ▷ shoo
shoot v (-s, -ing, shot) hit, wound, or kill with a missile fired from a weapon ▶ n (pl -s) new branch or sprout of a plant
shooting v ▷ shoot
shoots v, n ▷ shoot
shop n (pl -s) place for sale of goods and services ▶ v (-s, -pping, -pped) visit a shop or shops to buy goods
shoplifter n (pl -s) person who steals from a shop
shoplifters n ▷ shoplifter
shopped v ▷ shop
shopping v ▷ shop
shops n, v ▷ shop
shopsoiled adj soiled or faded from being displayed in a shop
shore[1] n (pl -s) edge of a sea or lake
shore[2] v (-res, -ring, -red) (foll. by **up**) prop or support
shored v ▷ shore[2]
shores n ▷ shore[1] ▶ v ▷ shore[2]
shoring v ▷ shore[2]
shorn v ▷ shear
short adj (-er, -est) not long ▶ adv abruptly ▶ n (pl -s) drink of spirits
shortage n (pl -s) deficiency
shortages n ▷ shortage
shortbread, shortcake n (pl -s) crumbly biscuit made with butter
shortbreads n ▷ shortbread
shortcake n ▷ shortbread
shortcakes n ▷ shortbread
shortchange v (-ges, -ging, -ed) give (someone) less than the correct amount of change
shortchanged v ▷ shortchange
shortchanges v ▷ shortchange
shortchanging v ▷ shortchange
shortcoming n (pl -s) failing or defect
shortcomings n ▷ shortcoming
shorten v (-s, -ing, -ed) make or become shorter
shortened v ▷ shorten
shortening v ▷ shorten
shortens v ▷ shorten
shorter adj ▷ short
shortest adj ▷ short
shortfall n (pl -s) deficit
shortfalls n ▷ shortfall
shorthand n (pl -s) system of rapid writing using symbols to represent words
shorthanded adj not having enough workers
shorthands n ▷ shorthand

shortlist v (-s, -ing, -ed) put on a short list
  shortlisted v ▷ shortlist
  shortlisting v ▷ shortlist
  shortlists v ▷ shortlist
shortly adv soon
shorts n ▷ short ▶ pl n short trousers
shortsighted adj unable to see distant things clearly
shot n (pl -s) shooting ▶ v ▷ shoot
shotgun n (pl -s) gun for firing a charge of shot at short range
  shotguns n ▷ shotgun
  shots n ▷ shot
  should v ▷ shall
shoulder n (pl -s) part of the body to which an arm, foreleg, or wing is attached ▶ v (-s, -ing, -ed) bear (a burden or responsibility)
  shouldered v ▷ shoulder
  shouldering v ▷ shoulder
  shoulders v ▷ shoulder
shout n (pl -s) loud cry (Informal) ▶ v (-s, -ing, -ed) cry out loudly
  shouted v ▷ shout
  shouting v ▷ shout
  shouts n, v ▷ shout
shove v (-ves, -ving, -ved) push roughly ▶ n (pl -s) rough push
  shoved v ▷ shove
shovel n (pl -s) tool for lifting or moving loose material ▶ v (-s, -lling, -lled) lift or move as with a shovel
  shovelled v ▷ shovel
  shovelling v ▷ shovel
  shovels n, v ▷ shovel
  shoves n ▷ shove
  shoving v ▷ shove
show v (-s, -ing, -ed, shown or showed) make, be, or become noticeable or visible ▶ n (pl -s) public exhibition
showcase n (pl -s) situation in which something is displayed to best advantage
  showcases n ▷ showcase
showdown n (pl -s) confrontation that settles a dispute
  showdowns n ▷ showdown
  showed v ▷ show
shower n (pl -s) kind of bath in which a person stands while being sprayed with water ▶ v (-s, -ing, -ed) wash in a shower > **showery** adj (-rier, -riest)
  showered v ▷ shower
  showerier adj ▷ shower
  showeriest adj ▷ shower
  showering v ▷ shower
  showers n, v ▷ shower

showery adj ▷ shower
showier adj ▷ showy
showiest adj ▷ showy
showily adv ▷ showy
showing v ▷ show
showjumping n (pl -s) competitive sport of riding horses to demonstrate skill in jumping
  showjumpings n ▷ showjumping
showman n (pl -men) man skilled at presenting anything spectacularly
  > **showmanship** n (pl -s)
  showmanship n ▷ showman
  showmanships n ▷ showman
  showmen n ▷ showman
  shown v ▷ show
showoff n (pl -s) (Informal) person who shows off
  showoffs n ▷ showoff
showpiece n (pl -s) excellent specimen shown for display or as an example
  showpieces n ▷ showpiece
showroom n (pl -s) room in which goods for sale are on display
  showrooms n ▷ showroom
  shows v, n ▷ show
showy adj (-wier, -wiest) gaudy > **showily** adv
shrank v ▷ shrink
shrapnel n (pl -s) artillery shell filled with pellets which scatter on explosion
  shrapnels n ▷ shrapnel
shred n (pl -s) long narrow strip torn from something ▶ v (-s, -dding, -dded or shred) tear to shreds
  shredded v ▷ shred
  shredding v ▷ shred
  shreds n, v ▷ shred
shrew n (pl -s) small mouselike animal
  > **shrewish** adj
shrewd adj (-er, -est) clever and perceptive
  > **shrewdly** adv > **shrewdness** n (pl -es)
  shrewder adj ▷ shrewd
  shrewdest adj ▷ shrewd
  shrewdly adv ▷ shrewd
  shrewdness n ▷ shrewd
  shrewdnesses n ▷ shrewd
  shrewish adj ▷ shrew
  shrews n ▷ shrew
shriek n (pl -s) shrill cry ▶ v (-s, -ing, -ed) utter (with) a shriek
  shrieked v ▷ shriek
  shrieking v ▷ shriek
  shrieks n, v ▷ shriek
shrike n (pl -s) songbird with a heavy hooked bill
  shrikes n ▷ shrike

shrill adj (-er, -est) (of a sound) sharp and high-pitched ▷ **shrillness** n (pl -es) ▷ **shrilly** adv
  shriller adj ▷ shrill
  shrillest adj ▷ shrill
  shrillness n ▷ shrill
  shrillnesses n ▷ shrill
  shrilly adv ▷ shrill
shrimp n (pl -s) small edible shellfish (Informal)
shrimping n (pl -s) fishing for shrimps
  shrimpings n ▷ shrimping
  shrimps n ▷ shrimp
shrine n (pl -s) place of worship associated with a sacred person or object
  shrines n ▷ shrine
shrink v (-s, -ing, shrank or shrunk, shrunk or shrunken) become or make smaller ▶ n (pl -s) (Slang) psychiatrist
shrinkage n (pl -s) decrease in size, value, or weight
  shrinkages n ▷ shrinkage
  shrinking v ▷ shrink
  shrinks v, n ▷ shrink
shrivel v (-s, -lling, -lled) shrink and wither
  shrivelled v ▷ shrivel
  shrivelling v ▷ shrivel
  shrivels v ▷ shrivel
shroud n (pl -s) piece of cloth used to wrap a dead body ▶ v (-s, -ing, -ed) conceal
  shrouded v ▷ shroud
  shrouding v ▷ shroud
  shrouds n, v ▷ shroud
shrub n (pl -s) woody plant smaller than a tree
  shrubberies n ▷ shrubbery
shrubbery n (pl -ries) area planted with shrubs
  shrubs n ▷ shrub
shrug v (-s, -gging, -gged) raise and then drop (the shoulders) as a sign of indifference, ignorance, or doubt ▶ n (pl -s) shrugging
  shrugged v ▷ shrug
  shrugging v ▷ shrug
  shrugs v, n ▷ shrug
  shrunk v ▷ shrink
  shrunken v ▷ shrink
shudder v (-s, -ing, -ed) shake or tremble violently, esp. with horror ▶ n (pl -s) shaking or trembling
  shuddered v ▷ shudder
  shuddering v ▷ shudder
  shudders v, n ▷ shudder
shuffle v (-les, -ling, -led) walk without lifting the feet ▶ n (pl -s) shuffling
  shuffled v ▷ shuffle
  shuffles v, n ▷ shuffle
  shuffling v ▷ shuffle
shun v (-s, -nning, -nned) avoid

  shunned v ▷ shun
  shunning v ▷ shun
  shuns v ▷ shun
shunt v (-s, -ing, -ed) move (objects or people) to a different position
  shunted v ▷ shunt
  shunting v ▷ shunt
  shunts v ▷ shunt
shush interj be quiet!
shut v (-s, -tting, shut) bring together or fold, close
shutdown n (pl -s) closing
  shutdowns n ▷ shutdown
  shuts v ▷ shut
shutter n (pl -s) hinged doorlike cover for closing off a window
  shutters n ▷ shutter
  shutting v ▷ shut
shuttle n (pl -s) vehicle going to and fro over a short distance ▶ v (-les, -ling, -led) travel by or as if by shuttle
shuttlecock n (pl -s) small light cone with feathers stuck in one end, struck to and fro in badminton
  shuttlecocks n ▷ shuttlecock
  shuttled v ▷ shuttle
  shuttles n, v ▷ shuttle
  shuttling v ▷ shuttle
shy¹ adj (-er, -est) not at ease in company (foll. by of) ▶ v (shies, shying, shied) start back in fear (foll. by away from) ▷ **shyly** adv ▷ **shyness** n (pl -es)
shy² v (shies, shying, shied) throw ▶ n (pl shies) throw
  shyer adj ▷ shy¹
  shyest adj ▷ shy¹
  shying v ▷ shy¹, ²
  shyly adv ▷ shy¹
  shyness n ▷ shy¹
  shynesses n ▷ shy¹

> **si** n (**sis**). Si means the same as **te**, a musical note This is an unusual word which can be helpful when you want to form words in more than one direction Si scores 2 points

sibilant adj hissing ▶ n (pl -s) consonant pronounced with a hissing sound
  sibilants n ▷ sibilant
sibling n (pl -s) brother or sister
  siblings n ▷ sibling
sibyl n (pl -s) (in ancient Greece and Rome) prophetess
  sibyls n ▷ sibyl
sic (LATIN) thus: used to indicate that an odd spelling or reading is in fact accurate

sick adj (-er, -est) vomiting or likely to vomit ▷ **sickness** n (pl -es)

sicken v (-s, -zing, -ed) make nauseated or disgusted

sickened v ▷ sicken

sickening v ▷ sicken

sickens v ▷ sicken

sicker adj ▷ sick

sickest adj ▷ sick

sickle n (pl -s) tool with a curved blade for cutting grass or grain

sickles n ▷ sickle

sicklier adj ▷ sickly

sickliest adj ▷ sickly

sickly adj (-lier, -liest) unhealthy, weak

sickness n ▷ sick

sicknesses n ▷ sick

side n (pl -s) line or surface that borders anything ▶ adj at or on the side

sideboard n (pl -s) piece of furniture for holding plates, cutlery, etc. in a dining room

sideboards n ▷ sideboard ▶ pl n ▷ sideburns

sideburns, sideboards pl n man's side whiskers

sidekick n (pl -s) (Informal) close friend or associate

sidekicks n ▷ sidekick

sidelight n (pl -s) either of two small lights on the front of a vehicle

sidelights n ▷ sidelight

sideline n (pl -s) subsidiary interest or source of income

sidelines n ▷ sideline

sidelong adj sideways ▶ adv obliquely

sidereal [side-**eer**-ee-al] adj of or determined with reference to the stars

sides n ▷ side

sidesaddle n (pl -s) saddle designed to allow a woman rider to sit with both legs on the same side of the horse

sidesaddles n ▷ sidesaddle

sidestep v (-s, -pping, -pped) dodge (an issue)

sidestepped v ▷ sidestep

sidestepping v ▷ sidestep

sidesteps v ▷ sidestep

sidetrack v (-s, -ing, -ed) divert from the main topic

sidetracked v ▷ sidetrack

sidetracking v ▷ sidetrack

sidetracks v ▷ sidetrack

sidewalk n (pl -s) (us) paved path for pedestrians, at the side of a road

sidewalks n ▷ sidewalk

sideways adv to or from the side

siding n (pl -s) short stretch of railway track on which trains or wagons are shunted from the main line

sidings n ▷ siding

sidle v (-les, -ling, -led) walk in a furtive manner

sidled v ▷ sidle

sidles v ▷ sidle

sidling v ▷ sidle

siege n (pl -s) surrounding and blockading of a place

sieges n ▷ siege

sienna n (pl -s) reddish- or yellowish-brown pigment made from natural earth

siennas n ▷ sienna

sierra n (pl -s) range of mountains in Spain or America with jagged peaks

sierras n ▷ sierra

siesta n (pl -s) afternoon nap, taken in hot countries

siestas n ▷ siesta

sieve [siv] n (pl -s) utensil with mesh through which a substance is sifted or strained ▶ v (-ves, -ving, -ved) sift or strain through a sieve

sieved v ▷ sieve

sieves n, v ▷ sieve

sieving v ▷ sieve

sift v (-s, -ing, -ed) remove the coarser particles from a substance with a sieve

sifted v ▷ sift

sifting v ▷ sift

sifts v ▷ sift

sigh n (pl -s) long audible breath expressing sadness, tiredness, relief, or longing ▶ v (-s, -ing, -ed) utter a sigh

sighed v ▷ sigh

sighing v ▷ sigh

sighs n, v ▷ sigh

sight n (pl -s) ability to see ▶ v (-s, -ing, -ed) catch sight of

sighted v ▷ sight

sighting v ▷ sight

sightless adj blind

sights n, v ▷ sight

sightseeing n (pl -s) visiting places of interest ▷ **sightseer** n (pl -s)

sightseeings n ▷ sightseeing

sightseer n ▷ sightseeing

sightseers n ▷ sightseeing

sign n (pl -s) indication of something not immediately or outwardly observable ▶ v (-s, -ing, -ed) write (one's name) on (a document or letter) to show its authenticity or one's agreement

signal n (pl -s) sign or gesture to convey information ▶ adj (Formal) very important

▶ v (-s, -lling, -lled) convey (information) by signal > **signally** adv

signalled v ▷ signal

signalling v ▷ signal

signally adv ▷ signal

signalman n (pl -men) railwayman in charge of signals and points

signalmen n ▷ signalman

signals n, v ▷ signal

signatories n ▷ signatory

signatory n (pl -ries) one of the parties who sign a document

signature n (pl -s) person's name written by himself or herself in signing something

signatures n ▷ signature

signed v ▷ sign

signet n (pl -s) small seal used to authenticate documents

signets n ▷ signet

significance n ▷ significant

significances n ▷ significant

significant adj important > **significantly** adv > **significance** n (pl -s)

significantly adv ▷ significant

signification n ▷ signify

significations n ▷ signify

signified v ▷ signify

signifies v ▷ signify

signify v (-fies, -fying, -fied) indicate or suggest > **signification** n (pl -s)

signifying v ▷ signify

signing n (pl -s) system of communication by gestures, as used by deaf people ▶ v ▷ sign

signings n ▷ signing

signor [see-**nyor**] n (pl -s) Italian term of address equivalent to *sir* or *Mr*

signora [see-**nyor**-a] n (pl -s) Italian term of address equivalent to *madam* or *Mrs*

signoras n ▷ signora

signorina [see-nyor-**ee**-na] n (pl -s) Italian term of address equivalent to *madam* or *Miss*

signorinas n ▷ signorina

signors n ▷ signor

signpost n (pl -s) post bearing a sign that shows the way

signposts n ▷ signpost

signs n, v ▷ sign

silage [**sile**-ij] n (pl -s) fodder crop harvested while green and partially fermented in a silo or plastic bags

silages n ▷ silage

silence n (pl -s) absence of noise or speech ▶ v (-ces, -cing, -ced) make silent > **silent** adj > **silently** adv

silenced v ▷ silence

silencer n (pl -s) device to reduce the noise of an engine exhaust or gun

silencers n ▷ silencer

silences n, v ▷ silence

silencing v ▷ silence

silent adj ▷ silencet

silently adv ▷ silence

silhouette n (pl -s) outline of a dark shape seen against a light background ▶ v (-s, -ing, -ed) show in silhouette

silhouetted v ▷ silhouette

silhouettes n, v ▷ silhouette

silhouetting v ▷ silhouette

silica n (pl -s) hard glossy mineral found as quartz and in sandstone

silicas n ▷ silica

silicon n (pl -s) (CHEM) brittle nonmetallic element widely used in chemistry and industry

silicone n (pl -s) tough synthetic substance made from silicon and used in lubricants, paints, and resins

silicones n ▷ silicone

silicons n ▷ silicon

silicoses n ▷ silicosis

silicosis n (pl -ses) lung disease caused by inhaling silica dust

silk n (pl -s) fibre made by the larva of a certain moth

silken adj ▷ silky

silkier adj ▷ silky

silkiest adj ▷ silky

silks n ▷ silk

silky (-ier, -iest), **silken** adj of or like silk

sill n (pl -s) ledge at the bottom of a window or door

sillier adj ▷ silly

silliest adj ▷ silly

silliness n ▷ silly

sillinesses n ▷ silly

sills n ▷ sill

silly adj (-lier, -liest) foolish > **silliness** n (pl -es)

silo n (pl -los) pit or airtight tower for storing silage or grains

silos n ▷ silo

silt n (pl -s) mud deposited by moving water ▶ v (-s, -ing, -ed) (foll. by **up**) fill or be choked with silt

silted v ▷ silt

silting v ▷ silt

silts n, v ▷ silt

silvan adj ▷ sylvan

silver n (pl -s) white precious metal ▶ adj made of or of the colour of silver

silverbeet n (pl -s) (AUST & NZ) leafy green

vegetable with white stalks
silverbeets n ▷ silverbeet
silverfish n (pl -es) small wingless silver-coloured insect
silverfishes n ▷ silverfish
silvers n ▷ silver
silverside n (pl -s) cut of beef from below the rump and above the leg
silversides n ▷ silverside
sim n (pl -s) computer game that simulates an activity such as flying or playing a sport
simian adj, n (pl -s) (of or like) a monkey or ape
simians n ▷ simian
similar adj alike but not identical > **similarity** n (pl -s) > **similarly** adv
similarities n ▷ similar
similarity n ▷ similar
similarly adv ▷ similar
simile [sim-ill-ee] n (pl -s) figure of speech comparing one thing to another, using 'as' or 'like'
similes n ▷ simile
similitude n (pl -s) similarity, likeness
similitudes n ▷ similitude
simmer v (-s, -ing, -ed) cook gently at just below boiling point
simmered v ▷ simmer
simmering v ▷ simmer
simmers v ▷ simmer
simper v (-s, -ing, -ed) smile in a silly or affected way ▶ n (pl -s) simpering smile
simpered v ▷ simper
simpering v ▷ simper
simpers v, n ▷ simper
simple adj (-r, -st) easy to understand or do > **simply** adv > **simplicity** n (pl -ties)
simpler adj ▷ simple
simplest adj ▷ simple
simpleton n (pl -s) foolish or half-witted person
simpletons n ▷ simpleton
simplicities n ▷ simple
simplicity n ▷ simple
simplification n ▷ simplify
simplifications n ▷ simplify
simplified v ▷ simplify
simplifies v ▷ simplify
simplify v (-fies, -fying, -fied) make less complicated > **simplification** n (pl -s)
simplifying v ▷ simplify
simplistic adj too simple or naive
simply adv ▷ simpl
sims n ▷ sim
simulate v (-tes, -ting, -ted) make a pretence of > **simulation** n (pl -s) > **simulator** n (pl -s)

simulated v ▷ simulate
simulates v ▷ simulate
simulating v ▷ simulate
simulation n ▷ simulate
simulations n ▷ simulate
simulator n ▷ simulate
simulators n ▷ simulate
simultaneous adj occurring at the same time > **simultaneously** adv
simultaneously adv ▷ simultaneous
sin¹ n (pl -s) breaking of a religious or moral law ▶ v (-s, -nning, -nned) commit a sin > **sinner** n (pl -s)
sin² (MATHS) sine
since prep during the period of time after ▶ conj from the time when ▶ adv from that time
sincere adj (-r, -st) without pretence or deceit > **sincerely** adv > **sincerity** n (pl -ties)
sincerely adv ▷ sincere
sincerer adj ▷ sincere
sincerest adj ▷ sincere
sincerities n ▷ sincere
sincerity n ▷ sincere
sine n (pl -s) (in trigonometry) ratio of the length of the opposite side to that of the hypotenuse in a right-angled triangle
sinecure [sin-ee-cure] n (pl -s) paid job with minimal duties
sinecures n ▷ sinecure
sines n ▷ sine
sinew n (pl -s) tough fibrous tissue joining muscle to bone > **sinewy** adj (-wier, -wiest)
sinewier adj ▷ sinew
sinewiest adj ▷ sinew
sinews n ▷ sinew
sinewy adj ▷ sinew
sinful adj guilty of sin > **sinfully** adv
sinfully adv ▷ sinful
sing v (-s, -ing, sang, sung) make musical sounds with the voice
singe v (-ges, -geing, -ged) burn the surface of ▶ n (pl -s) superficial burn
singed v ▷ singe
singeing v ▷ singe
singer n (pl -s) person who sings, esp. professionally
singers n ▷ singer
singes v, n ▷ singe
singing v ▷ sing
single adj one only ▶ n (pl -s) single thing ▶ v (-les, -ling, -led) (foll. by out) pick out from others > **singly** adv
singled v ▷ single
singles n, v ▷ single ▶ pl n game between two players

singlet n (pl -s) sleeveless vest
  singlets n ▷ singlet
  singling v ▷ single
  singly adv ▷ single
  sings v ▷ sing
singsong n (pl -s) informal singing session
  ▶ adj (of the voice) repeatedly rising and
  falling in pitch
  singsongs n ▷ singsong
singular adj (of a word or form) denoting one
  person or thing ▶ n (pl -s) singular form of a
  word ▷ **singularity** n (pl -ties) ▷ **singularly** adv
  singularities n ▷ singular
  singularity n ▷ singular
  singularly adv ▷ singular
  singulars n ▷ singular
sinister adj threatening or suggesting evil
  or harm
sink v (-s, -ing, sank, sunk or sunken) submerge
  (in liquid) ▶ n (pl -s) fixed basin with a water
  supply and drainage pipe
sinker n (pl -s) weight for a fishing line
  sinkers n ▷ sinker
  sinking v ▷ sink
  sinks v, n ▷ sink
  sinned v ▷ sin¹
  sinner n ▷ sin¹
  sinners n ▷ sin¹
  sinning v ▷ sin¹
  sins n, v ▷ sin¹
sinuous adj curving ▷ **sinuously** adv
  sinuously adv ▷ sinuous
sinus [sine-uss] n (pl -nuses) hollow space in
  a bone, esp. an air passage opening into
  the nose
  sinuses n ▷ sinus
sip v (-s, -pping, -pped) drink in small
  mouthfuls ▶ n (pl -s) amount sipped
siphon n (pl -s) bent tube which uses air
  pressure to draw liquid from a container ▶ v
  (-s, -ing, -ed) draw off thus
  siphoned v ▷ siphon
  siphoning v ▷ siphon
  siphons n, v ▷ siphon
  sipped v ▷ sip
  sipping v ▷ sip
  sips v, n ▷ sip
sir n (pl -s) polite term of address for a man
sire n (pl -s) male parent of a horse or other
  domestic animal ▶ v (-res, -ring, -red) father
  sired v ▷ sire
siren n (pl -s) device making a loud wailing
  noise as a warning
  sirens n ▷ siren
  sires n, v ▷ sire

  siring v ▷ sire
sirloin n (pl -s) prime cut of loin of beef
  sirloins n ▷ sirloin
sirocco n (pl -s) hot wind blowing from N Africa
  into S Europe
  siroccos n ▷ sirocco
  sirs n ▷ sir
sis interj (S AFR) (Informal) exclamation of disgust
sisal [size-al] n (pl -s) (fibre of) plant used in
  making ropes
  sisals n ▷ sisal
siskin n (pl -s) yellow-and-black finch
  siskins n ▷ siskin
  sissier adj ▷ sissy
  sissies n ▷ sissy
  sissiest adj ▷ sissy
sissy adj (-ssier, -ssiest) ▶ n (pl -ssies) weak or
  cowardly (person)
sister n (pl -s) girl or woman with the same
  parents as another person ▶ adj closely
  related, similar ▷ **sisterly** adj
sisterhood n (pl -s) state of being a sister
  sisterhoods n ▷ sisterhood
  sisterly adj ▷ sister
  sisters n ▷ sister
sit v (-s, -tting, sat) rest one's body upright on
  the buttocks
sitar n (pl -s) Indian stringed musical
  instrument
  sitars n ▷ sitar
sitcom n (pl -s) (Informal) situation comedy
  sitcoms n ▷ sitcom
site n (pl -s) place where something is, was, or
  is intended to be located ▷ website ▶ v (-tes,
  -ting, -ted) provide with a site
  sited v ▷ site
  sites n, v ▷ site
  siting v ▷ site
  sits v ▷ sit
  sitting v ▷ sit
situate v (-tes, -ting, -ted) place
  situated v ▷ situate
  situates v ▷ situate
  situating v ▷ situate
situation n (pl -s) state of affairs
  situations n ▷ situation
six adj, n (pl -es) one more than five
  sixes n ▷ six
sixteen adj, n (pl -s) six and ten ▷ **sixteenth**
  adj, n (pl -s)
  sixteens n ▷ sixteen
  sixteenth n ▷ sixteen
  sixteenths n ▷ sixteen
sixth adj, n (pl -s) (of) number six in a series
  sixths n ▷ sixth

sixties n ▷ sixty
sixtieth n ▷ sixty
sixtieths n ▷ sixty
sixty adj, n (pl -s) six times ten > **sixtieth** adj, n (pl -s)
sizable adj ▷ sizeable
size¹ n (pl -s) dimensions, bigness ▶ v (-zes, -zing, -zed) arrange according to size
size² n (pl -s) gluey substance used as a protective coating
sizeable, sizable adj quite large
sized v ▷ size¹
sizes n ▷ size¹,² ▶ v ▷ size¹
sizing v ▷ size¹
sizzle v (-les, -ling, -led) make a hissing sound like frying fat
sizzled v ▷ sizzle
sizzles v ▷ sizzle
sizzling v ▷ sizzle
skankier adj ▷ skanky
skankiest adj ▷ skanky
skanky adj (-kier, -kiest) (Slang) dirty or unattractive
skate¹ n (pl -s) boot with a steel blade or sets of wheels attached to the sole for gliding over ice or a hard surface ▶ v (-tes, -ting, -ted) glide on or as if on skates
skate² n (pl -s) large marine flatfish
skateboard n (pl -s) board mounted on small wheels for riding on while standing up > **skateboarding** n (pl -s)
skateboarding n ▷ skateboard
skateboardings n ▷ skateboard
skateboards n ▷ skateboard
skated v ▷ skate¹
skates n ▷ skate¹,² ▶ v ▷ skate¹
skating v ▷ skate¹
skedaddle v (-les, -ling, -led) (Informal) run off
skedaddled v ▷ skedaddle
skedaddles v ▷ skedaddle
skedaddling v ▷ skedaddle
skein n (pl -s) yarn wound in a loose coil
skeins n ▷ skein
skeletal adj ▷ skeleton
skeleton n (pl -s) framework of bones inside a person's or animal's body ▶ adj reduced to a minimum > **skeletal** adj
skeletons n ▷ skeleton
sketch n (pl -es) rough drawing ▶ v (-es, -ing, -ed) make a sketch (of)
sketched v ▷ sketch
sketches n, v ▷ sketch
sketchier adj ▷ sketchy
sketchiest adj ▷ sketchy
sketching v ▷ sketch

sketchy adj (-chier, -chiest) incomplete or inadequate
skew v (-s, -ing, -ed) make slanting or crooked ▶ adj slanting or crooked
skewed v ▷ skew
skewer n (pl -s) pin to hold meat together during cooking ▶ v (-s, -ing, -ed) fasten with a skewer
skewered v ▷ skewer
skewering v ▷ skewer
skewers n, v ▷ skewer
skewing v ▷ skew
skews v ▷ skew
skewwhiff adj (BRIT) (Informal) slanting or crooked
ski n (pl -s) one of a pair of long runners fastened to boots for gliding over snow or water ▶ v (skis, skiing, skied) travel on skis > **skier** n (pl -s)
skid v (-s, -dding, -dded) (of a moving vehicle) slide sideways uncontrollably ▶ n (pl -s) skidding
skidded v ▷ skid
skidding v ▷ skid
skids v, n ▷ skid
skied v ▷ ski
skier n ▷ ski
skiers n ▷ ski
skies n ▷ sky
skiff n (pl -s) small boat
skiffs n ▷ skiff
skiing v ▷ ski
skilful adj having or showing skill > **skilfully** adv
skilfully adv ▷ skilful
skill n (pl -s) special ability or expertise > **skilled** adj
skilled adj ▷ skill
skillet n (pl -s) small frying pan or shallow cooking pot
skillets n ▷ skillet
skills n ▷ skill
skim v (-s, -mming, -mmed) remove floating matter from the surface of (a liquid)
skimmed v ▷ skim
skimming v ▷ skim
skimp v (-s, -ing, -ed) not invest enough time, money, material, etc.
skimped v ▷ skimp
skimpier adj ▷ skimpy
skimpiest adj ▷ skimpy
skimping v ▷ skimp
skimps v ▷ skimp
skimpy adj (-pier, -piest) scanty or insufficient
skims v ▷ skim

skin n (pl -s) outer covering of the body ▶ v (-s, -nning, -nned) remove the skin of > **skinless** adj

skinflint n (pl -s) miser

skinflints n ▷ skinflint

skinhead n (pl -s) youth with very short hair

skinheads n ▷ skinhead

skinless adj ▷ skin

skinned v ▷ skin

skinnier adj ▷ skinny

skinniest adj ▷ skinny

skinning v ▷ skin

skinny adj (-nnier, -nniest) thin

skins n, v ▷ skin

skint adj (BRIT) (Slang) having no money

skip[1] v (-s, -pping, -pped) leap lightly from one foot to the other ▶ n (pl -s) skipping

skip[2] n (pl -s) large open container for builders' rubbish

skipped v ▷ skip[1]

skipper n (pl -s) ▶ v (-s, -ing, -ed) captain

skippered v ▷ skipper

skippering v ▷ skipper

skippers n, v ▷ skipper

skipping v ▷ skip[1]

skips v ▷ skip[1] ▶ n ▷ skip[1, 2]

skirl n (pl -s) sound of bagpipes

skirls n ▷ skirl

skirmish n (pl -es) brief or minor fight or argument ▶ v (-es, -ing, -ed) take part in a skirmish

skirmished v ▷ skirmish

skirmishes n, v ▷ skirmish

skirmishing v ▷ skirmish

skirt n (pl -s) woman's garment hanging from the waist ▶ v (-s, -ing, -ed) border

skirted v ▷ skirt

skirting v ▷ skirt

skirts n, v ▷ skirt

skis n, v ▷ ski

skit n (pl -s) brief satirical sketch

skite v (-tes, -ting, -ted) ▶ n (pl -s) (AUST & NZ) boast

skited v ▷ skite

skites v, n ▷ skite

skiting v ▷ skite

skits n ▷ skit

skittish adj playful or lively

skittle n (pl -s) bottle-shaped object used as a target in some games

skittles n ▷ skittle ▶ pl n game in which players try to knock over skittles by rolling a ball at them

skive v (-ves, -ving, -ved) (BRIT) (Informal) evade work or responsibility

skived v ▷ skive

skives v ▷ skive

skiving v ▷ skive

skivvies n ▷ skivvy

skivvy n (pl -vies) (BRIT) female servant who does menial work

skua n (pl -s) large predatory gull

skuas n ▷ skua

skulduggeries n ▷ skulduggery

skulduggery n (pl -ries) (Informal) trickery

skulk v (-s, -ing, -ed) move stealthily

skulked v ▷ skulk

skulking v ▷ skulk

skulks v ▷ skulk

skull n (pl -s) bony framework of the head

skullcap n (pl -s) close-fitting brimless cap

skullcaps n ▷ skullcap

skulls n ▷ skull

skunk n (pl -s) small black-and-white N American mammal which emits a foul-smelling fluid when attacked

skunks n ▷ skunk

sky n (pl skies) upper atmosphere as seen from the earth

skydiving n (pl -s) sport of jumping from an aircraft and performing manoeuvres before opening one's parachute

skydivings n ▷ skydiving

skylark n (pl -s) lark that sings while soaring at a great height

skylarks n ▷ skylark

skylight n (pl -s) window in a roof or ceiling

skylights n ▷ skylight

skyscraper n (pl -s) very tall building

skyscrapers n ▷ skyscraper

slab n (pl -s) broad flat piece

slabs n ▷ slab

slack adj (-er, -est) not tight ▶ n (pl -s) slack part ▶ v (-s, -ing, -ed) neglect one's work or duty > **slacker** n (pl -s) > **slackness** n (pl -es)

slacked v ▷ slack

slacken v (-s, -ing, -ed) make or become slack

slackened v ▷ slacken

slackening v ▷ slacken

slackens v ▷ slacken

slacker n, adj ▷ slack

slackers n ▷ slack

slackest adj ▷ slack

slacking v ▷ slack

slackness n ▷ slack

slacknesses n ▷ slack

slacks n, v ▷ slack ▶ pl n informal trousers

slag n (pl -s) waste left after metal is smelted ▶ v (-s, -gging, -gged) (foll. by **off**) (BRIT, AUST & NZ) (Slang) criticize

slagged v ▷ slag
slagging v ▷ slag
slags n ▷ slag
slain v ▷ slay
slake v (-kes, -king, -ked) satisfy (thirst or desire)
slaked v ▷ slake
slakes v ▷ slake
slaking v ▷ slake
slalom n (pl -s) skiing or canoeing race over a winding course
slaloms n ▷ slalom
slam v (-s, -mming, -mmed) shut, put down, or hit violently and noisily ▶ n (pl -s) act or sound of slamming
slammed v ▷ slam
slamming v ▷ slam
slams v, n ▷ slam
slander n (pl -s) false and malicious statement about a person ▶ v (-s, -ing, -ed) utter slander about > **slanderous** adj
slandered v ▷ slander
slandering v ▷ slander
slanderous adj ▷ slander
slanders n, v ▷ slander
slang n (pl -s) very informal language > **slangy** adj (-gier, -giest)
slangier adj ▷ slang
slangiest adj ▷ slang
slangs n ▷ slang
slangy adj ▷ slang
slant v (-s, -ing, -ed) lean at an angle, slope ▶ n (pl -s) slope > **slanting** adj
slanted v ▷ slant
slanting v, adj ▷ slant
slants v, n ▷ slant
slap n (pl -s) blow with the open hand or a flat object ▶ v (-s, -pping, -pped) strike with the open hand or a flat object
slapdash adj careless and hasty
slaphappy adj (Informal) cheerfully careless
slapped v ▷ slap
slapping v ▷ slap
slaps n, v ▷ slap
slapstick n (pl -s) boisterous knockabout comedy
slapsticks n ▷ slapstick
slash v (-es, -ing, -ed) cut with a sweeping stroke ▶ n (pl -es) sweeping stroke
slashed v ▷ slash
slashes v, n ▷ slash
slashing v ▷ slash
slat n (pl -s) narrow strip of wood or metal
slate¹ n (pl -s) rock which splits easily into thin layers

slate² v (-tes, -ting, -ted) (Informal) criticize harshly
slated v ▷ slate²
slates n ▷ slate¹ ▶ v ▷ slate²
slating v ▷ slate²
slats n ▷ slat
slattern n (pl -s) (Old-fashioned) slovenly woman > **slatternly** adj
slatternly adv ▷ slattern
slatterns n ▷ slattern
slaughter v (-s, -ing, -ed) kill (animals) for food ▶ n (pl -s) slaughtering
slaughtered v ▷ slaughter
slaughterhouse n (pl -s) place where animals are killed for food
slaughterhouses n ▷ slaughterhouse
slaughtering v ▷ slaughter
slaughters v, n ▷ slaughter
slave n (pl -s) person owned by another for whom he or she has to work ▶ v (-ves, -ing, -ved) work like a slave
slaved v ▷ slave
slaver n (pl -s) person or ship engaged in the slave trade ▶ v [slav-ver] (-s, -ing, -ed) dribble saliva from the mouth
slavered v ▷ slaver
slaveries n ▷ slavery
slavering v ▷ slaver
slavers n, v ▷ slaver
slavery n (pl -ries) state or condition of being a slave
slaves v, n ▷ slave
slaving v ▷ slave
slavish adj of or like a slave
slay v (-s, -ing, slew, slain) kill
slaying v ▷ slay
slays v ▷ slay
sleazes n ▷ sleaze
sleazier adj ▷ sleazy
sleaziest adj ▷ sleazy
sleazy adj (-zier, -ziest) run-down or sordid > **sleaze** n (pl -s)
sled n (pl -s) ▶ v (-s, -dding, -dded) ▷
sledded v ▷ sled
sledding v ▷ sled
sledge¹ n (pl -s) carriage on runners for sliding on snow ▶ v (-dges, -dging, -dged) travel by sledge
sledge², **sledgehammer** n (pl -s) heavy hammer with a long handle
sledged v ▷ sledge¹
sledgehammer n ▷ sledge
sledgehammers n ▷ sledge
sledges n ▷ sledge¹,² ▶ v ▷ sledge¹
sledging v ▷ sledge¹

sleds *n, v* ▷ sled
sleek *adj* (-er, -est) glossy, smooth, and shiny
  sleeker *adj* ▷ sleek
  sleekest *adj* ▷ sleek
sleep *n* (*pl* -s) state of rest characterized by
  unconsciousness ▶ *v* (-s, -ing, slept) be in
  or as if in a state of sleep > **sleepy** *adj* (-pier,
  -piest) > **sleepily** *adv* > **sleepiness** *n* (*pl* -es)
  > **sleepless** *adj*
sleeper *n* (*pl* -s) railway car fitted for sleeping
  in
  sleepers *n* ▷ sleeper
  sleepier *adj* ▷ sleep
  sleepiest *adj* ▷ sleep
  sleepily *adv* ▷ sleep
  sleepiness *n* ▷ sleep
  sleepinesses *n* ▷ sleep
  sleeping *v* ▷ sleep
  sleepless *adj* ▷ sleep
sleepout *n* (*pl* -s) (NZ) small building for
  sleeping in
  sleepouts *n* ▷ sleepout
sleepover *n* (*pl* -s) occasion when a person
  stays overnight at a friend's house
  sleepovers *n* ▷ sleepover
  sleeps *n, v* ▷ sleep
  sleepy *adj* ▷ sleep
sleet *n* (*pl* -s) rain and snow or hail falling
  together
  sleets *n* ▷ sleet
sleeve *n* (*pl* -s) part of a garment which covers
  the arm > **sleeveless** *adj*
  sleeveless *adj* ▷ sleeve
  sleeves *n* ▷ sleeve
sleigh *n* (*pl* -s) ▶ *v* (-s, -ing, -ed) sledge
  sleighed *v* ▷ sleigh
  sleighing *v* ▷ sleigh
  sleighs *n, v* ▷ sleigh
slender *adj* (-er, -est) slim
  slenderer *adj* ▷ slender
  slenderest *adj* ▷ slender
  slept *v* ▷ sleep
sleuth [slooth] *n* (*pl* -s) detective
  sleuths *n* ▷ sleuth
slew¹ *v* ▷ slay
slew² *v* (-s, -ing, -ed) twist or swing round
  slewed *v* ▷ slew²
  slewing *v* ▷ slew²
  slews *v* ▷ slew²
slice *n* (*pl* -s) thin flat piece cut from something
  ▶ *v* (-ces, -cing, -ced) cut into slices
  sliced *v* ▷ slice
  slices *n, v* ▷ slice
  slicing *v* ▷ slice
slick *adj* (-er, -est) persuasive and glib ▶ *n* (*pl* -s)

patch of oil on water ▶ *v* (-s, -ing, -ed) make
  smooth or sleek
  slicked *v* ▷ slick
  slicker *adj* ▷ slick
  slickest *adj* ▷ slick
  slicking *v* ▷ slick
  slicks *n, v* ▷ slick
  slid *v* ▷ slide
slide *v* (-des, -ding, slid) slip smoothly along (a
  surface) ▶ *n* (*pl* -s) sliding
  slides *v, n* ▷ slide
  sliding *v* ▷ slide
  slier *adj* ▷ sly
  sliest *adj* ▷ sly
slight *adj* (-er, -est) small in quantity or extent
  ▶ *v* (-s, -ing, -ed) ▶ *n* (*pl* -s) snub > **slightly** *adv*
  slighted *v* ▷ slight
  slighter *adj* ▷ slight
  slightest *adj* ▷ slight
  slighting *v* ▷ slight
  slightly *adv* ▷ slight
  slights *v, n* ▷ slight
slim *adj* (-mmer, -mmest) not heavy or stout,
  thin ▶ *v* (-s, -mming, -mmed) make or become
  slim by diet and exercise > **slimmer** *n* (*pl* -s)
slime *n* (*pl* -s) unpleasant thick slippery
  substance
  slimes *n* ▷ slime
  slimier *adj* ▷ slimy
  slimiest *adj* ▷ slimy
  slimmed *v* ▷ slim
  slimmer *adj, n* ▷ slim
  slimmers *n* ▷ slim
  slimmest *adj* ▷ slim
  slimming *v* ▷ slim
  slims *v* ▷ slim
slimy *adj* (-mier, -miest) of, like, or covered
  with slime
sling¹ *n* (*pl* -s) bandage hung from the neck to
  support an injured hand or arm ▶ *v* (-s, -ing,
  slung) throw
sling² *n* (*pl* -s) sweetened drink with a spirit
  base
  slinging *v* ▷ sling¹
  slings *n* ▷ sling¹, ² ▶ *v* ▷ sling¹
slink *v* (-s, -ing, slunk) move furtively or guiltily
  slinkier *adj* ▷ slinky
  slinkiest *adj* ▷ slinky
  slinking *v* ▷ slink
  slinks *v* ▷ slink
slinky *adj* (-kier, -kiest) (of clothes) figure-
  hugging
slip¹ *v* (-s, -pping, -pped) lose balance by sliding
  ▶ *n* (*pl* -s) slipping
slip² *n* (*pl* -s) small piece (of paper)

slip³ n (pl -s) clay mixed with water used for decorating pottery

slipknot n (pl -s) knot tied so that it will slip along the rope round which it is made
  slipknots n ▷ slipknot
  slipped v ▷ slip¹

slipper n (pl -s) light shoe for indoor wear
  slipperier adj ▷ slippery
  slipperiest adj ▷ slippery
  slippers n ▷ slipper

slippery adj (-rier, -riest) so smooth or wet as to cause slipping or be difficult to hold
  slippier adj ▷ slippy
  slippiest adj ▷ slippy
  slipping v ▷ slip¹

slippy adj (-ppier, -ppiest) (Informal) slippery
  slips n ▷ slip¹, ², ³ ▷ v ▷ slip¹

slipshod adj (of an action) careless

slipstream n (pl -s) stream of air forced backwards by a fast-moving object
  slipstreams n ▷ slipstream

slipway n (pl -s) launching slope on which ships are built or repaired
  slipways n ▷ slipway

slit n (pl -s) long narrow cut or opening ▷ v (-s, -tting, slit) make a long straight cut in

slither v (-s, -ing, -ed) slide unsteadily
  slithered v ▷ slither
  slithering v ▷ slither
  slithers v ▷ slither
  slits n, v ▷ slit
  slitting v ▷ slit

sliver [sliv-ver] n (pl -s) small thin piece
  slivers n ▷ sliver

slob n (pl -s) (Informal) lazy and untidy person
  > **slobbish** adj

slobber v (-s, -ing, -ed) dribble or drool
  > **slobbery** adj
  slobbered v ▷ slobber
  slobbering v ▷ slobber
  slobbers v ▷ slobber
  slobbery adj ▷ slobber
  slobbish adj ▷ slob
  slobs n ▷ slob

sloe n (pl -s) sour blue-black fruit
  sloes n ▷ sloe

slog v (-s, -gging, -gged) work hard and steadily ▷ n (pl -s) long and exhausting work or walk

slogan n (pl -s) catchword or phrase used in politics or advertising
  slogans n ▷ slogan
  slogged v ▷ slog
  slogging v ▷ slog
  slogs v, n ▷ slog

sloop n (pl -s) small single-masted ship
  sloops n ▷ sloop

slop v (-s, -pping, -pped) splash or spill ▷ n (pl -s) spilt liquid

slope v (-pes, -ping, -ped) slant ▷ n (pl -s) sloping surface
  sloped v ▷ slope

slopes v, n ▷ slope ▷ pl n hills
  sloping v ▷ slope
  slopped v ▷ slop
  sloppier adj ▷ sloppy
  sloppiest adj ▷ sloppy
  slopping v ▷ slop

sloppy adj (-ppier, -ppiest) careless or untidy

slops v, n ▷ slop ▷ pl n liquid refuse and waste food used to feed animals

slosh v (-es, -ing, -ed) splash carelessly ▷ n (pl -es) splashing sound

sloshed adj (Slang) drunk ▷ v ▷ slosh
  sloshes v, n ▷ slosh
  sloshing v ▷ slosh

slot n (pl -s) narrow opening for inserting something ▷ v (-s, -tting, -tted) make a slot or slots in

sloth [rhymes with **both**] n (pl -s) slow-moving animal of tropical America

slothful adj lazy or idle
  sloths n ▷ sloth
  slots n, v ▷ slot
  slotted v ▷ slot
  slotting v ▷ slot

slouch v (-es, -ing, -ed) sit, stand, or move with a drooping posture ▷ n (pl -es) drooping posture
  slouched v ▷ slouch
  slouches v, n ▷ slouch
  slouching v ▷ slouch

slough¹ [rhymes with **now**] n (pl -s) bog

slough² [**sluff**] v (-s, -ing, -ed) (of a snake) shed (its skin) or (of a skin) be shed
  sloughed v ▷ slough²
  sloughing v ▷ slough²
  sloughs n ▷ slough¹ ▷ v ▷ slough²

sloven n (pl -s) habitually dirty or untidy person
  slovenlier adj ▷ slovenly
  slovenliest adj ▷ slovenly

slovenly adj (-lier, -liest) dirty or untidy
  slovens n ▷ sloven

slow adj (-er, -est) taking a longer time than is usual or expected ▷ v (-s, -ing, -ed) reduce the speed (of) > **slowly** adv > **slowness** n (pl -es)

slowcoach n (pl -es) (Informal) person who moves or works slowly
  slowcoaches n ▷ slowcoach

slowed v ▷ slow
slower adj ▷ slow
slowest adj ▷ slow
slowing v ▷ slow
slowly adv ▷ slow
slowness n ▷ slow
slownesses n ▷ slow
slows v ▷ slow
slowworm n (pl -s) small legless lizard
slowworms n ▷ slowworm
sludge n (pl -s) thick mud
sludges n ▷ sludge
slug[1] n (pl -s) land snail with no shell
slug[2] n (pl -s) bullet (Informal)
slug[3] v (-s, -gging, -gged) hit hard ▶ n (pl -s) heavy blow
sluggard n (pl -s) lazy person
sluggards n ▷ sluggard
slugged v ▷ slug[3]
slugging v ▷ slug[3]
sluggish adj slow-moving, lacking energy > **sluggishly** adv > **sluggishness** n (pl -es)
sluggishly adv ▷ sluggish
sluggishness n ▷ sluggish
sluggishnesses n ▷ sluggish
slugs n ▷ slug[1, 2, 3] ▶ v ▷ slug[3]
sluice n (pl -s) channel carrying off water ▶ v (-ces, -cing, -ced) pour a stream of water over or through
sluiced v ▷ sluice
sluices n, v ▷ sluice
sluicing v ▷ sluice
slum n (pl -s) squalid overcrowded house or area ▶ v (-s, -mming, -mmed) temporarily and deliberately experience poorer places or conditions than usual
slumber v (-s, -ing, -ed) ▶ n (pl -s) (Lit) sleep
slumbered v ▷ slumber
slumbering v ▷ slumber
slumbers v, n ▷ slumber
slummed v ▷ slum
slumming v ▷ slum
slump v (-s, -ing, -ed) (of prices or demand) decline suddenly ▶ n (pl -s) sudden decline in prices or demand
slumped v ▷ slump
slumping v ▷ slump
slumps v, n ▷ slump
slums n, v ▷ slum
slung v ▷ sling[1]
slunk v ▷ slink
slur v (-s, -rring, -rred) pronounce or utter (words) indistinctly ▶ n (pl -s) slurring of words
slurp (Informal) v (-s, -ing, -ed) eat or drink

noisily ▶ n (pl -s) slurping sound
slurped v ▷ slurp
slurping v ▷ slurp
slurps v, n ▷ slurp
slurred v ▷ slur
slurries n ▷ slurry
slurring v ▷ slur
slurry n (pl -ries) muddy liquid mixture
slurs v, n ▷ slur
slush n (pl -es) watery muddy substance > **slushy** adj (-shier, -shiest)
slushes n ▷ slush
slushier adj ▷ slush
slushiest adj ▷ slush
slushy adj ▷ slush
sly adj (slyer, slyest or slier, sliest) crafty > **slyly** adv > **slyness** n (pl -es)
slyer adj ▷ sly
slyest adj ▷ sly
slyly adv ▷ sly
slyness n ▷ sly
slynesses n ▷ sly
smack[1] v (-s, -ing, -ed) slap sharply ▶ n (pl -s) sharp slap ▶ adv (Informal) squarely or directly
smack[2] n (pl -s) slight flavour or trace ▶ v (-s, -ing, -ed) have a slight flavour or trace (of)
smack[3] n (pl -s) small single-masted fishing boat
smacked v ▷ smack[1, 2]
smacker n (pl -s) (Slang) loud kiss
smackers n ▷ smacker
smacking v ▷ smack[1, 2]
smacks n ▷ smack[1, 2, 3] ▶ v ▷ smack[1, 2]
small adj (-er, -est) not large in size, number, or amount ▶ n (pl -s) narrow part of the lower back > **smallness** n (pl -es)
smaller adj ▷ small
smallest adj ▷ small
smallholding n (pl -s) small area of farming land
smallholdings n ▷ smallholding
smallness n ▷ small
smallnesses n ▷ small
smallpox n (pl -es) contagious disease with blisters that leave scars
smallpoxes n ▷ smallpox
smalls n ▷ small ▶ pl n (Informal) underwear
smarmier adj ▷ smarmy
smarmiest adj ▷ smarmy
smarmy adj (-mier, -miest) (Informal) unpleasantly suave or flattering
smart adj (-er, -est) well-kept and neat ▶ v (-s, -ing, -ed) feel or cause stinging pain ▶ n (pl -s) stinging pain > **smartly** adv > **smartness** n (pl -es)

smarted v ▷ smart
smarten v (-s, -ing, -ed) make or become smart
smartened v ▷ smarten
smartening v ▷ smarten
smartens v ▷ smarten
smarter adj ▷ smart
smartest adj ▷ smart
smarting v ▷ smart
smartly adv ▷ smart
smartness n ▷ smart
smartnesses n ▷ smart
smarts v, n ▷ smart
smash v (-es, -ing, -ed) break violently and noisily ▶ n (pl -es) act or sound of smashing
smashed v ▷ smash
smasher n (pl -s) (Informal) attractive person or thing
smashers n ▷ smasher
smashes v, n ▷ smash
smashing adj (Informal) excellent ▶ v ▷ smash
smattering n (pl -s) slight knowledge
smatterings n ▷ smattering
smear v (-s, -ing, -ed) spread with a greasy or sticky substance ▶ n (pl -s) dirty mark or smudge
smeared v ▷ smear
smearing v ▷ smear
smears v, n ▷ smear
smell v (-s, -ing, smelt or -ed) perceive (a scent or odour) by means of the nose ▶ n (pl -s) ability to perceive odours by the nose
smelled v ▷ smell
smellier adj ▷ smelly
smelliest adj ▷ smelly
smelling v ▷ smell
smells v, n ▷ smell
smelly adj (-llier, -lliest) having a nasty smell
smelt¹ v (-s, -ing, -ed) extract (a metal) from (an ore) by heating
smelt² n (pl smelt) small fish of the salmon family
smelt³ v ▷ smell
smelted v ▷ smelt¹
smelter n (pl -s) industrial plant where smelting is carried out
smelters n ▷ smelter
smelting v ▷ smelt¹
smelts v ▷ smelt¹
smile n (pl -s) turning up of the corners of the mouth to show pleasure, amusement, or friendliness ▶ v (-les, -ing, -led) give a smile
smiled v ▷ smile
smiles n, v ▷ smile
smiley n (pl -s) symbol depicting a smile or

other facial expression, used in e-mail
smileys n ▷ smiley
smiling v ▷ smile
smirch v (-es, -ing, -ed) ▶ n (pl -es) stain
smirched v ▷ smirch
smirches v, n ▷ smirch
smirching v ▷ smirch
smirk n (pl -s) smug smile ▶ v (-s, -ing, -ed) give a smirk
smirked v ▷ smirk
smirking v ▷ smirk
smirks n, v ▷ smirk
smite v (-tes, -ting, smote, smitten) (Old-fashioned) strike hard
smites v ▷ smite
smith n (pl -s) worker in metal
smithereens pl n shattered fragments
smithies n ▷ smithy
smiths n ▷ smith
smithy n (pl -thies) blacksmith's workshop
smiting v ▷ smite
smitten v ▷ smite
smock n (pl -s) loose overall ▶ v (-s, -ing, -ed) gather (material) by sewing in a honeycomb pattern > **smocking** n (pl -s)
smocked v ▷ smock
smocking v, n ▷ smock
smockings n ▷ smock
smocks n, v ▷ smock
smog n (pl -s) mixture of smoke and fog
smogs n ▷ smog
smoke n (pl -s) cloudy mass that rises from something burning ▶ v (-kes, -king, -ked) give off smoke > **smokeless** adj > **smoker** n (pl -s) > **smoky** adj (-kier, -kiest)
smoked v ▷ smoke
smokeless adj ▷ smoke
smoker n ▷ smok
smokers n ▷ smok
smokes n, v ▷ smoke
smokier adj ▷ smoke
smokiest adj ▷ smoke
smoking v ▷ smoke
smoky adj ▷ smoke
smooch (Informal) v (-es, -ing, -ed) kiss and cuddle ▶ n (pl -es) smooching
smooched v ▷ smooch
smooches v, n ▷ smooch
smooching v ▷ smooch
smooth adj (-er, -est) even in surface, texture, or consistency ▶ v (-s, -ing, -ed) make smooth > **smoothly** adv
smoothed v ▷ smooth
smoother adj ▷ smooth
smoothest adj ▷ smooth

smoothie n (pl -thies) (*Informal*) charming but possibly insincere man
smoothies n ▷ smoothie
smoothing v ▷ smooth
smoothly adv ▷ smooth
smooths v ▷ smooth
smorgasbord n (pl -s) buffet meal of assorted dishes
smorgasbords n ▷ smorgasbord
smote v ▷ smite
smother v (-s, -ing, -ed) suffocate or stifle
smothered v ▷ smother
smothering v ▷ smother
smothers v ▷ smother
smoulder v (-s, -ing, -ed) burn slowly with smoke but no flame
smouldered v ▷ smoulder
smouldering v ▷ smoulder
smoulders v ▷ smoulder
smudge v (-ges, -ging, -ged) make or become smeared or soiled ▶ n (pl -s) dirty mark > **smudgy** adj (-gier, -giest)
smudged v ▷ smudge
smudges v, n ▷ smudge
smudgier adj ▷ smudge
smudgiest adj ▷ smudge
smudging v ▷ smudge
smudgy adj ▷ smudge
smug adj (-gger, -ggest) self-satisfied > **smugly** adv > **smugness** n (pl -es)
smugger adj ▷ smug
smuggest adj ▷ smug
smuggle v (-les, -ling, -led) import or export (goods) secretly and illegally > **smuggler** n (pl -s)
smuggled v ▷ smuggle
smuggler n ▷ smuggle
smugglers n ▷ smuggle
smuggles v ▷ smuggle
smuggling v ▷ smuggle
smugly adv ▷ smug
smugness n ▷ smug
smugnesses n ▷ smug
smut n (pl -s) obscene jokes, pictures, etc. > **smutty** adj (-ttier, -ttiest)
smuts n ▷ smut
smuttier adj ▷ smut
smuttiest adj ▷ smut
smutty adj ▷ smut
snack n (pl -s) light quick meal
snacks n ▷ snack
snaffle n (pl -s) jointed bit for a horse ▶ v (-les, -ling, -led) (BRIT, AUST & NZ) (*Slang*) steal
snaffled v ▷ snaffle
snaffles n, v ▷ snaffle

snaffling v ▷ snaffle
snag n (pl -s) difficulty or disadvantage ▶ v (-s, -gging, -gged) catch or tear on a point
snagged v ▷ snag
snagging v ▷ snag
snags n, v ▷ snag
snail n (pl -s) slow-moving mollusc with a spiral shell
snails n ▷ snail
snake n (pl -s) long thin scaly limbless reptile ▶ v (-kes, -king, -ked) move in a winding course like a snake
snaked v ▷ snake
snakes n, v ▷ snake
snakier adj ▷ snaky
snakiest adj ▷ snaky
snaking v ▷ snake
snaky adj (-kier, -kiest) twisted or winding
snap v (-s, -pping, -pped) break suddenly ▶ n (pl -s) act or sound of snapping ▶ adj made on the spur of the moment
snapdragon n (pl -s) plant with flowers that can open and shut like a mouth
snapdragons n ▷ snapdragon
snapped v ▷ snap
snapper n (pl -s) food fish of Australia and New Zealand with a pinkish body covered with blue spots
snappers n ▷ snapper
snappier adj ▷ snappy
snappiest adj ▷ snappy
snapping v ▷ snap
snappish adj ▷ snappy
snappy adj (-ppier, -ppiest) (*also* **snappish**) irritable
snaps v, n ▷ snap
snapshot n (pl -s) informal photograph
snapshots n ▷ snapshot
snare n (pl -s) trap with a noose ▶ v (-res, -ring, -red) catch in or as if in a snare
snared v ▷ snare
snares n, v ▷ snare
snaring v ▷ snare
snarl¹ v (-s, -ing, -ed) (of an animal) growl with bared teeth ▶ n (pl -s) act or sound of snarling
snarl² n (pl -s) tangled mess ▶ v (-s, -ing, -ed) make tangled
snarled v ▷ snarl¹, ²
snarling v ▷ snarl¹, ²
snarls n, v ▷ snarl¹, ²
snatch v (-es, -ing, -ed) seize or try to seize suddenly ▶ n (pl -es) snatching
snatched v ▷ snatch
snatches v, n ▷ snatch
snatching v ▷ snatch

snazzier adj ▷ snazzy

snazziest adj ▷ snazzy

snazzy adj (-zzier, -zziest) (Informal) stylish and flashy

sneak v (-s, -ing, -ed) move furtively ▶ n (pl -s) cowardly or underhand person > **sneaky** adj (-kier, -kiest)

sneaked v ▷ sneak

sneakers pl n canvas shoes with rubber soles

sneakier adj ▷ sneak

sneakiest adj ▷ sneak

sneaking adj slight but persistent ▶ v ▷ sneak

sneaks v, n ▷ sneak

sneaky adj ▷ sneak

sneer n (pl -s) contemptuous expression or remark ▶ v (-s, -ing, -ed) show contempt by a sneer

sneered v ▷ sneer

sneering v ▷ sneer

sneers n, v ▷ sneer

sneeze v (-zes, -zing, -zed) expel air from the nose suddenly, involuntarily, and noisily ▶ n (pl -s) act or sound of sneezing

sneezed v ▷ sneeze

sneezes v, n ▷ sneeze

sneezing v ▷ sneeze

snicker n (pl -s) ▶ v (-s, -ing, -ed) ▷ snigger

snickered v ▷ snicker

snickering v ▷ snicker

snickers n, v ▷ snicker

snide adj (-r, -st) critical in an unfair and nasty way

snider adj ▷ snide

snidest adj ▷ snide

sniff v (-s, -ing, -ed) inhale through the nose in short audible breaths ▶ n (pl -s) act or sound of sniffing

sniffed v ▷ sniff

sniffing v ▷ sniff

sniffle v (-les, -ling, -led) sniff repeatedly, as when suffering from a cold ▶ n (pl -s) slight cold

sniffled v ▷ sniffle

sniffles v, n ▷ sniffle

sniffling v ▷ sniffle

sniffs v, n ▷ sniff

snifter n (pl -s) (Informal) small quantity of alcoholic drink

snifters n ▷ snifter

snigger n (pl -s) sly disrespectful laugh, esp. one partly stifled ▶ v (-s, -ing, -ed) utter a snigger

sniggered v ▷ snigger

sniggering v ▷ snigger

sniggers n, v ▷ snigger

snip v (-s, -pping, -pped) cut in small quick strokes with scissors or shears ▶ n (pl -s) (Informal) bargain

snipe n (pl -s) wading bird with a long straight bill ▶ v (-pes, -ping, -ped) (foll. by **at**) shoot at (a person) from cover

sniped v ▷ snipe

sniper n (pl -s) person who shoots at someone from cover

snipers n ▷ sniper

snipes n, v ▷ snipe

sniping v ▷ snipe

snipped v ▷ snip

snippet n (pl -s) small piece

snippets n ▷ snippet

snipping v ▷ snip

snips v, n ▷ snip

snitch (Informal) v (-es, -ing, -ed) act as an informer ▶ n (pl -es) informer

snitched v ▷ snitch

snitches v, n ▷ snitch

snitching v ▷ snitch

snivel v (-s, -lling, -lled) cry in a whining way

snivelled v ▷ snivel

snivelling v ▷ snivel

snivels v ▷ snivel

snob n (pl -s) person who judges others by social rank > **snobbery** n (pl -ries) > **snobbish** adj

snobberies n ▷ snob

snobbery n ▷ snob

snobbish adj ▷ snob

snobs n ▷ snob

snoek n (pl -s) (S AFR) edible marine fish

snoeks n ▷ snoek

snood n (pl -s) pouch, often of net, loosely holding a woman's hair at the back

snoods n ▷ snood

snook n (pl -s) gesture of contempt

snooker n (pl -s) game played on a billiard table ▶ v (-s, -ing, -ed) leave (a snooker opponent) in a position such that another ball blocks the target ball

snookered v ▷ snooker

snookering v ▷ snooker

snookers n, v ▷ snooker

snooks n ▷ snook

snoop (Informal) v (-s, -ing, -ed) pry ▶ n (pl -s) snooping > **snooper** n (pl -s)

snooped v ▷ snoop

snooper n ▷ snoop

snoopers n ▷ snoop

snooping v ▷ snoop

snoops v, n ▷ snoop

snootier adj ▷ snooty

snootiest adj ▷ snooty

snooty adj (-tier, -tiest) (*Informal*) haughty

snooze (*Informal*) v (-zes, -zing, -zed) take a brief light sleep ▶ n (pl -s) brief light sleep

  snoozed v ▷ snooze

  snoozes v, n ▷ snooze

  snoozing v ▷ snooze

snore v (-res, -ring, -red) make snorting sounds while sleeping ▶ n (pl -s) sound of snoring

  snored v ▷ snore

  snores v, n ▷ snore

  snoring v ▷ snore

snorkel n (pl -s) tube allowing a swimmer to breathe while face down on the surface of the water ▶ v (-s, -lling, -lled) swim using a snorkel

  snorkelled v ▷ snorkel

  snorkelling v ▷ snorkel

  snorkels n, v ▷ snorkel

snort v (-s, -ing, -ed) exhale noisily through the nostrils ▶ n (pl -s) act or sound of snorting

  snorted v ▷ snort

  snorting v ▷ snort

  snorts v, n ▷ snort

snot n (pl -s) (*Slang*) mucus from the nose

  snots n ▷ snot

snout n (pl -s) animal's projecting nose and jaws

  snouts n ▷ snout

snow n (pl -s) frozen vapour falling from the sky in flakes ▶ v (-s, -ing, -ed) fall as or like snow > **snowy** adj (-wier, -wiest)

snowball n (pl -s) snow pressed into a ball for throwing ▶ v (-s, -ing, -ed) increase rapidly

  snowballed v ▷ snowball

  snowballing v ▷ snowball

  snowballs n, v ▷ snowball

snowboard n (pl -s) board on which a person stands to slide across the snow > **snowboarding** n (pl -s)

  snowboarding n ▷ snowboard

  snowboardings n ▷ snowboard

  snowboards n ▷ snowboard

snowdrift n (pl -s) bank of deep snow

  snowdrifts n ▷ snowdrift

snowdrop n (pl -s) small white bell-shaped spring flower

  snowdrops n ▷ snowdrop

  snowed v ▷ snow

snowflake n (pl -s) single crystal of snow

  snowflakes n ▷ snowflake

  snowier adj ▷ snow

  snowiest adj ▷ snow

  snowing v ▷ snow

snowman n (pl -men) figure shaped out of snow

  snowmen n ▷ snowman

snowplough n (pl -s) vehicle for clearing away snow

  snowploughs n ▷ snowplough

  snows n, v ▷ snow

snowshoes pl n racket-shaped shoes for travelling on snow

  snowy adj ▷ snow

snub v (-s, -bbing, -bbed) insult deliberately ▶ n (pl -s) deliberate insult ▶ adj (of a nose) short and blunt

  snubbed v ▷ snub

  snubbing v ▷ snub

  snubs v, n ▷ snub

snuff n (pl -s) powdered tobacco for sniffing up the nostrils

snuff² v (-s, -ing, -ed) extinguish (a candle)

  snuffed v ▷ snuff²

  snuffing v ▷ snuff²

snuffle v (-les, -ling, -led) breathe noisily or with difficulty

  snuffled v ▷ snuffle

  snuffles v ▷ snuffle

  snuffling v ▷ snuffle

  snuffs n ▷ snuff¹ ▶ v ▷ snuff²

snug adj (-gger, -ggest) warm and comfortable ▶ n (pl -s) (in Britain and Ireland) small room in a pub > **snugly** adv

  snugger adj ▷ snug

  snuggest adj ▷ snug

snuggle v (-les, -ling, -led) nestle into a person or thing for warmth or from affection

  snuggled v ▷ snuggle

  snuggles v ▷ snuggle

  snuggling v ▷ snuggle

  snugly adv ▷ snug

  snugs n ▷ snug

> **sny** n (**snys**). Sny is a Canadian word for a side channel of a river. This word doesn't contain a vowel, so it can help you to clear an awkward rack. Sny scores 6 points.

so adv to such an extent ▶ conj in order that ▶ interj exclamation of surprise, triumph, or realization

soak v (-s, -ing, -ed) make wet ▶ n (pl -s) soaking > **soaking** n (pl -s) adj

  soaked v ▷ soak

soaking v, n, adj ▷ soak

  soakings n ▷ soak

  soaks v, n ▷ soak

soap n (pl -s) compound of alkali and fat, used with water as a cleaning agent ▶ v (-s, -ing,

-ed) apply soap to ▶ **soapy** adj (-pier, -piest)
soaped v ▷ soap
soapier adj ▷ soap
soapiest adj ▷ soap
soaping v ▷ soap
soaps n, v ▷ soap
soapy adj ▷ soap
soar v (-s, -ing, -ed) rise or fly upwards
soared v ▷ soar
soaring v ▷ soar
soars v ▷ soar
sob v (-s, -bbing, -bbed) weep with convulsive
gasps ▶ n (pl -s) act or sound of sobbing
sobbed v ▷ sob
sobbing v ▷ sob
sober adj (-er, -est) not drunk ▶ v (-s, -ing, -ed)
make or become sober > **soberly** adv
sobered v ▷ sober
soberer adj ▷ sober
soberest adj ▷ sober
sobering v ▷ sober
soberly adv ▷ sober
sobers v ▷ sober
sobrieties n ▷ sobriety
sobriety n (pl -ties) state of being sober
sobriquet [so-brik-ay] n (pl -s) nickname
sobriquets n ▷ sobriquet
sobs v, n ▷ sob
soccer n (pl -s) football played by two teams of
eleven kicking a spherical ball
soccers n ▷ soccer
sociabilities n ▷ sociable
sociability n ▷ sociable
sociable adj friendly or companionable
> **sociability** n (pl -ties) > **sociably** adv
sociably adv ▷ sociable
social adj living in a community ▶ n (pl -s)
informal gathering > **socially** adv
socialism n (pl -s) political system which
advocates public ownership of industries,
resources, and transport
socialisms n ▷ socialism
socialist n (pl -s) ▶ adj
socialists n ▷ socialist
socialite n (pl -s) member of fashionable
society
socialites n ▷ socialite
socialize v (-zes, -zing, -zed) meet others
socially
socialized v ▷ socialize
socializes v ▷ socialize
socializing v ▷ socialize
socially adv ▷ social
socials n ▷ social
societies n ▷ society

society n (pl -ties) human beings considered
as a group
sociological adj ▷ sociology
sociologies n ▷ sociology
sociologist n ▷ sociology
sociologists n ▷ sociology
sociology n (pl -gies) study of human societies
> **sociological** adj > **sociologist** n (pl -s)
sock[1] n (pl -s) knitted covering for the foot
sock[2] (Slang) v (-s, -ing, -ed) hit hard ▶ n (pl -s)
hard blow
socked v ▷ sock[2]
socket n (pl -s) hole or recess into which
something fits
sockets n ▷ socket
socking v ▷ sock[2]
socks v ▷ sock[2] ▶ n ▷ sock[1, 2]
sod n (pl -s) (piece of) turf
soda n (pl -s) compound of sodium
sodas n ▷ soda
sodden adj soaked
sodium n (pl -s) (CHEM) silvery-white metallic
element
sodiums n ▷ sodium
sods n ▷ sod
sofa n (pl -s) couch
sofas n ▷ sofa
soft adj (-er, -s) easy to shape or cut > **softly** adv
soften v (-s, -ing, -ed) make or become soft
or softer
softened v ▷ soften
softening v ▷ soften
softens v ▷ soften
softer adj ▷ soft
softest adj ▷ soft
softly adv ▷ soft
software n (pl -s) computer programs
softwares n ▷ software
softwood n (pl -s) wood of a coniferous tree
softwoods n ▷ softwood
soggier adj ▷ soggy
soggiest adj ▷ soggy
sogginess n ▷ soggy
sogginesses n ▷ soggy
soggy adj (-ggier, -ggiest) soaked > **sogginess**
n (pl -es)
soigné, fem **soignée** [swah-nyay] adj well-
groomed, elegant
soil[1] n (pl -s) top layer of earth
soil[2] v (-s, -ing, -ed) make or become dirty
soiled v ▷ soil
soiling v ▷ soil
soils n ▷ soil[1] ▶ v ▷ soil[2]
soiree [swah-ray] n (pl -s) evening party or
gathering

soirees n ▷ soiree
sojourn [soj-urn] n (pl -s) temporary stay ▶ v (-s, -ing, -ed) stay temporarily
  sojourned v ▷ sojourn
  sojourning v ▷ sojourn
  sojourns n, v ▷ sojourn
solace [sol-iss] n, v (-ces, -cing, -ced) comfort in distress
  solaced v ▷ solace
  solaces v ▷ solace
  solacing v ▷ solace
solar adj of the sun
  solaria n ▷ solarium
solarium n (pl -riums, -ria) place with beds and ultraviolet lights used for acquiring an artificial suntan
  solariums n ▷ solarium
sold v ▷ sell
solder n (pl -s) soft alloy used to join two metal surfaces ▶ v (-s, -ing, -ed) join with solder
  soldered v ▷ solder
  soldering v ▷ solder
  solders n, v ▷ solder
soldier n (pl -s) member of an army ▶ v (-s, -ing, -ed) serve in an army > **soldierly** adj
  soldiered v ▷ soldier
  soldiering v ▷ soldier
  soldierly adj ▷ soldier
  soldiers n, v ▷ soldier
sole[1] adj one and only
sole[2] n (pl -s) underside of the foot ▶ v (-les, -ling, -led) provide (a shoe) with a sole
sole[3] n (pl -s) small edible flatfish
solecism [sol-iss-izz-um] n (pl -s) minor grammatical mistake
  solecisms n ▷ solecism
  soled v ▷ sole[2]
solely adv only, completely
solemn adj (-er, -est) serious, deeply sincere > **solemnly** adv > **solemnity** n (pl -ties)
  solemner adj ▷ solemn
  solemnest adj ▷ solemn
  solemnities n ▷ solemn
  solemnity n ▷ solemn
  solemnly adv ▷ solemn
solenoid [sole-in-oid] n (pl -s) coil of wire magnetized by passing a current through it
  solenoids n ▷ solenoid
  soles n ▷ sole[2,3] ▶ v ▷ sole[2]
solicit v (-s, -ing, -ed) request > **solicitation** n (pl -s)
  solicitation n ▷ solicit
  solicitations n ▷ solicit
  solicited v ▷ solicit
  soliciting v ▷ solicit

solicitor n (pl -s) (BRIT, AUST & NZ) lawyer who advises clients and prepares documents and cases
  solicitors n ▷ solicitor
solicitous adj anxious about someone's welfare > **solicitude** n (pl -s)
  solicits v ▷ solicit
  solicitude n ▷ solicitous
  solicitudes n ▷ solicitous
solid adj (-er, -est) (of a substance) keeping its shape ▶ n (pl -s) three-dimensional shape > **solidity** n (pl -ties) > **solidly** adv
  solidarities n ▷ solidarity
solidarity n (pl -ties) agreement in aims or interests, total unity
  solider adj ▷ solid
  solidest adj ▷ solid
  solidified v ▷ solidify
  solidifies v ▷ solidify
solidify v (-fies, -fying, -fied) make or become solid or firm
  solidifying v ▷ solidify
  solidities n ▷ solid
  solidity n ▷ solid
  solidly adv ▷ solid
  solids n ▷ solid
  soliloquies n ▷ soliloquy
soliloquy n (pl -quies) speech made by a person while alone, esp. in a play
  soling v ▷ sole[2]
solipsism n (pl -s) doctrine that the self is the only thing known to exist > **solipsist** n (pl -s)
  solipsisms n ▷ solipsism
  solipsist n ▷ solipsism
  solipsists n ▷ solipsism
solitaire n (pl -s) game for one person played with pegs set in a board
  solitaires n ▷ solitaire
solitary adj alone, single
solitude n (pl -s) state of being alone
  solitudes n ▷ solitude
solo n (pl -s) music for one performer ▶ adj done alone ▶ adv by oneself, alone > **soloist** n (pl -s)
  soloist n ▷ solo
  soloists n ▷ solo
  solos n ▷ solo
solstice n (pl -s) either the shortest (in winter) or longest (in summer) day of the year
  solstices n ▷ solstice
  solubilities n ▷ soluble
  solubility n ▷ soluble
soluble adj able to be dissolved > **solubility** n (pl -ties)
solution n (pl -s) answer to a problem
  solutions n ▷ solution

solvable *adj* ▷ solve
solve *v* (-ves, -ving, -ved) find the answer to (a problem) > **solvable** *adj*
solved *v* ▷ solve
solvencies *n* ▷ solvent
solvency *n* ▷ solvent
solvent *adj* having enough money to pay one's debts ▶ *n* (*pl* -s) liquid capable of dissolving other substances > **solvency** *n* (*pl* -cies)
solvents *n* ▷ solvent
solves *v* ▷ solve
solving *v* ▷ solve
sombre *adj* (-r, -st) dark, gloomy
sombrer *adj* ▷ sombre
sombrero *n* (*pl* -s) wide-brimmed Mexican hat
sombreros *n* ▷ sombrero
sombrest *adj* ▷ sombre
some *adj* unknown or unspecified (*Informal*) ▶ *pron* certain unknown or unspecified people or things
somebodies *n* ▷ somebody
somebody *pron* some person ▶ *n* (*pl* -dies) important person
somehow *adv* in some unspecified way
someone *pron* somebody
somersault *n* (*pl* -s) leap or roll in which the trunk and legs are turned over the head ▶ *v* (-s, -ing, -ed) perform a somersault
somersaulted *v* ▷ somersault
somersaulting *v* ▷ somersault
somersaults *n*, *v* ▷ somersault
something *pron* unknown or unspecified thing or amount
sometime *adv* at some unspecified time ▶ *adj* former
sometimes *adv* from time to time, now and then
somewhat *adv* to some extent, rather
somewhere *adv* in, to, or at some unspecified or unknown place
somnambulism *n* ▷ somnambulist
somnambulisms *n* ▷ somnambulist
somnambulist *n* (*pl* -s) person who walks in his or her sleep > **somnambulism** *n* (*pl* -s)
somnambulists *n* ▷ somnambulist
somnolent *adj* drowsy
son *n* (*pl* -s) male offspring
sonar *n* (*pl* -s) device for detecting underwater objects by the reflection of sound waves
sonars *n* ▷ sonar
sonata *n* (*pl* -s) piece of music in several movements for one instrument with or without piano
sonatas *n* ▷ sonata
song *n* (*pl* -s) music for the voice

songbird *n* (*pl* -s) any bird with a musical call
songbirds *n* ▷ songbird
songs *n* ▷ song
songster, songstress *n* (*pl* -s, -es) singer
songsters *n* ▷ songster
songstress *n* ▷ songster
songstresses *n* ▷ songster
sonic *adj* of or producing sound
sonnet *n* (*pl* -s) fourteen-line poem with a fixed rhyme scheme
sonnets *n* ▷ sonnet
sonorities *n* ▷ sonorous
sonority *n* ▷ sonorous
sonorous *adj* (of sound) deep or resonant > **sonorously** *adv* > **sonority** *n* (*pl* -ties)
sonorously *adv* ▷ sonorous
sons *n* ▷ son
soon *adv* in a short time
sooner *adv* rather
soot *n* (*pl* -s) black powder formed by the incomplete burning of an organic substance > **sooty** *adj* (-tier, -tiest)
soothe *v* (-thes, -thing, -thed) make calm
soothed *v* ▷ soothe
soothes *v* ▷ soothe
soothing *v* ▷ soothe
soothsayer *n* (*pl* -s) seer or prophet
soothsayers *n* ▷ soothsayer
sootier *adj* ▷ soot
sootiest *adj* ▷ soot
soots *n* ▷ soot
sooty *adj* ▷ soot
sop *n* (*pl* -s) concession to pacify someone ▶ *v* (-s, -pping, -pped) mop up or absorb (liquid)
sophism *n* ▷ sophistry
sophisms *n* ▷ sophistry
sophist *n* (*pl* -s) person who uses clever but invalid arguments
sophisticate *v* (-tes, -ting, -ted) make less natural or innocent ▶ *n* (*pl* -s) sophisticated person
sophisticated *adj* having or appealing to refined or cultured tastes and habits ▶ *v* ▷ sophisticate > **sophistication** *n* (*pl* -s)
sophisticates *v*, *n* ▷ sophisticate
sophisticating *v* ▷ sophisticate
sophistication *n* ▷ sophisticated
sophistications *n* ▷ sophisticated
sophistries *n* ▷ sophistry
sophistry, sophism *n* (*pl* -ries, -s) clever but invalid argument
sophists *n* ▷ sophist
sophomore *n* (*pl* -s) (*US*) student in second year at college
sophomores *n* ▷ sophomore

soporific adj causing sleep ▶ n (pl -s) drug that causes sleep
  soporifics n ▷ soporific
sopped v ▷ sop
soppier adj ▷ soppy
soppiest adj ▷ soppy
sopping adj completely soaked ▶ v ▷ sop
soppy adj (soppier, soppiest) (Informal) oversentimental
soprano n (pl -s) (singer with) the highest female or boy's voice
  sopranos n ▷ soprano
sops n, v ▷ sop
sorbet n (pl -s) flavoured water ice
  sorbets n ▷ sorbet
sorcerer n (pl -s) magician > **sorceress** n fem (pl -s)
  sorcerers n ▷ sorcerer
  sorceress n ▷ sorcerer
  sorceresses n ▷ sorcerer
  sorceries n ▷ sorcery
sorcery n (pl -ries) witchcraft or magic
sordid adj dirty, squalid > **sordidly** adv > **sordidness** n (pl -es)
  sordider adj ▷ sordid
  sordidest adj ▷ sordid
  sordidly adv ▷ sordid
  sordidness n ▷ sordid
  sordidnesses n ▷ sordid
sore adj (-r, -st) painful ▶ n (pl -s) painful area on the body ▶ adv (Obs) greatly > **soreness** n (pl -es)
sorely adv greatly
  soreness n ▷ sore
  sorenesses n ▷ sore
  sorer adj ▷ sore
  sores n ▷ sore
  sorest adj ▷ sore
sorghum n (pl -s) kind of grass cultivated for grain
  sorghums n ▷ sorghum
sorrel n (pl -s) bitter-tasting plant
  sorrels n ▷ sorrel
  sorrier adj ▷ sorry
  sorriest adj ▷ sorry
sorrow n (pl -s) grief or sadness ▶ v (-s, -ing, -ed) grieve > **sorrowful** adj > **sorrowfully** adv
  sorrowed v ▷ sorrow
  sorrowful adj ▷ sorrow
  sorrowfully adv ▷ sorrow
  sorrowing v ▷ sorrow
  sorrows n, v ▷ sorrow
sorry adj (-rier, -riest) feeling pity or regret
sort n (pl -s) group all sharing certain qualities or characteristics ▶ v (-s, -ing, -ed) arrange according to kind
  sorted v ▷ sort
sortie n (pl -s) relatively short return trip
  sorties n ▷ sortie
  sorting v ▷ sort
  sorts n, v ▷ sort
sot n (pl -s) habitual drunkard
  sots n ▷ sot
soubriquet [so-brik-ay] n (pl -s) ▷ sobriquet
  soubriquets n ▷ soubriquet
soufflé [soo-flay] n (pl -s) light fluffy dish made with beaten egg whites and other ingredients
  soufflés n ▷ soufflé
sough [rhymes with **now**] v (-s, -ing, -ed) (of the wind) make a sighing sound
  soughed v ▷ sough
  soughing v ▷ sough
  soughs v ▷ sough
  sought [sawt] v ▷ seek
souk [sook] n (pl -s) marketplace in Muslim countries, often open-air
  souks n ▷ souk
soul n (pl -s) spiritual and immortal part of a human being
soulful adj full of emotion
soulless adj lacking human qualities, mechanical
  souls n ▷ soul
sound[1] n (pl -s) something heard, noise ▶ v (-s, -ing, -ed) make or cause to make a sound
sound[2] adj (-er, -est) in good condition > **soundly** adv
sound[3] v (-s, -ing, -ed) find the depth of (water etc.)
sound[4] n (pl -s) channel or strait
  sounded v ▷ sound[1, 3]
  sounder adj ▷ sound[2]
  soundest adj ▷ sound[2]
  sounding v ▷ sound[1, 3]
soundings pl n measurements of depth taken by sounding
  soundly adv ▷ sound[2]
soundproof adj not penetrable by sound ▶ v (-s, -ing, -ed) make soundproof
  soundproofed v ▷ soundproof
  soundproofing v ▷ soundproof
  soundproofs v ▷ soundproof
  sounds n ▷ sound[1, 4] ▶ v ▷ sound[1, 3]
soundtrack n (pl -s) recorded sound accompaniment to a film
  soundtracks n ▷ soundtrack
soup n (pl -s) liquid food made from meat, vegetables, etc. > **soupy** adj (-pier, -piest)
soupçon [soop-sonn] n (pl -s) small amount

soupçons n ▷ soupçon
soupier adj ▷ soup
soupiest adj ▷ soup
soups n ▷ soup
soupy adj ▷ soup
sour adj (-er, -est) sharp-tasting ▶ v (-s, -ing, -ed) make or become sour > **sourly** adv
> **sourness** n (pl -s)
source n (pl -s) origin or starting point
sources n ▷ source
soured v ▷ sour
sourer adj ▷ sour
sourest adj ▷ sour
souring v ▷ sour
sourly adv ▷ sour
sourness n ▷ sour
sournesses n ▷ sour
sours v ▷ sour
souse v (-ses, -sing, -sed) plunge (something) into liquid
soused v ▷ souse
souses v ▷ souse
sousing v ▷ souse
soutane [soo-tan] n (pl -s) Roman Catholic priest's cassock
soutanes n ▷ soutane
south n (pl -s) direction towards the South Pole, opposite north ▶ adj to or in the south ▶ adv in, to, or towards the south > **southerly** adj > **southern** adj > **southward** adj, adv
> **southwards** adv
southerly adj ▷ south
southern adj ▷ south
southerner n (pl -s) person from the south of a country or area
southerners n ▷ southerner
southpaw n (pl -s) (Informal) left-handed person, esp. a boxer
southpaws n ▷ southpaw
souths n ▷ south
southward adj, adv ▷ south
southwards adv ▷ south
souvenir n (pl -s) keepsake, memento
souvenirs n ▷ souvenir
sou'wester n (pl -s) seaman's waterproof hat covering the head and back of the neck
sou'westers n ▷ sou'wester
sovereign n (pl -s) king or queen ▶ adj (of a state) independent > **sovereignty** n (pl -ties)
sovereigns n ▷ sovereign
sovereignties n ▷ sovereign
sovereignty n ▷ sovereign
soviet n (pl -s) formerly, elected council at various levels of government in the USSR
▶ adj

soviets n ▷ soviet
sow[1] [rhymes with **know**] v (-s, -ing, -ed, sown or -ed) scatter or plant (seed) in or on (the ground)
sow[2] [rhymes with **cow**] n (pl -s) female adult pig
sowed v ▷ sow[1]
sowing v ▷ sow[1]
sown v ▷ sow[1]
sows n ▷ sow[2] ▶ v ▷ sow[1]

> **sox** pl n. Sox is an informal word for **socks**. This is a good word to remember for when you find an X on your rack without the space or tiles to play a longer word. Sox scores 10 points.

soya n (pl -s) plant whose edible bean is used for food and as a source of oil
soyas n ▷ soya
sozzled adj (BRIT, AUST & NZ) (Slang) drunk
spa n (pl -s) resort with a mineral-water spring
space n (pl -s) unlimited expanse in which all objects exist and move ▶ v (-ces, -cing, -ced) place at intervals
spacecraft, spaceship n (pl -s) vehicle for travel beyond the earth's atmosphere
spacecrafts n ▷ spacecraft
spaced v ▷ space
spaces n, v ▷ space
spaceship n ▷ spacecraft
spaceships n ▷ spacecraft
spacesuit n (pl -s) sealed pressurized suit worn by an astronaut
spacesuits n ▷ spacesuit
spacing v ▷ space
spacious adj having a large capacity or area
spade[1] n (pl -s) tool for digging
spade[2] n (pl -s) playing card of the suit marked with black leaf-shaped symbols
spades n ▷ spade[1, 2]
spadework n (pl -s) hard preparatory work
spadeworks n ▷ spadework
spaghetti n (pl -s) pasta in the form of long strings
spaghettis n ▷ spaghetti
span n (pl -s) space between two points ▶ v (-s, -nning, -nned) stretch or extend across
spangle n (pl -les) small shiny metallic ornament ▶ v (-les, -ling, -led) decorate with spangles
spangled v ▷ spangle
spangles n, v ▷ spangle
spangling v ▷ spangle
spaniel n (pl -s) dog with long ears and silky hair
spaniels n ▷ spaniel

spank v (-s, -ing, -ed) slap with the open hand, on the buttocks or legs ▶ n (pl -s) such a slap
> **spanking** n (pl -s)
spanked v ▷ spank

spanking adj (Informal) outstandingly fine or smart ▶ v ▷ spank ▶ n ▷ spank
spankings n ▷ spank
spanks v, n ▷ spank
spanned v ▷ span

spanner n (pl -s) tool for gripping and turning a nut or bolt
spanners n ▷ spanner
spanning v ▷ span
spans n, v ▷ span

spar[1] n (pl -s) pole used as a ship's mast, boom, or yard
spar[2] v (-s, -rring, -rred) box or fight using light blows for practice

spare adj extra ▶ n (pl -s) duplicate kept in case of damage or loss ▶ v (-res, -ring, -red) refrain from punishing or harming
spared v ▷ spare
spares n, v ▷ spare
sparing adj economical ▶ v ▷ spare

spark n (pl -s) fiery particle thrown out from a fire or caused by friction ▶ v (-s, -ing, -ed) give off sparks
sparked v ▷ spark

sparkie n (pl -s) (NZ) (Informal) electrician
sparkies n ▷ sparkie
sparking v ▷ spark

sparkle v (-les, -ling, -led) glitter with many points of light ▶ n (pl -s) sparkling points of light
sparkled v ▷ sparkle

sparkler n (pl -s) hand-held firework that emits sparks
sparklers n ▷ sparkler
sparkles v, n ▷ sparkle

sparkling adj (of wine or mineral water) slightly fizzy ▶ v ▷ sparkle
sparks v, n ▷ spark
sparred v ▷ spar[2]
sparring v ▷ spar[2]

sparrow n (pl -s) small brownish bird
sparrowhawk n (pl -s) small hawk
sparrowhawks n ▷ sparrowhawk
sparrows n ▷ sparrow
spars n ▷ spar[1] ▶ v ▷ spar[2]

sparse adj (-r, -st) thinly scattered > **sparsely** adv > **sparseness** n (pl -es)
sparsely adv ▷ sparse
sparseness n ▷ sparse
sparsenesses n ▷ sparse
sparser adj ▷ sparse

sparsest adj ▷ sparse
spartan adj strict and austere
spas n ▷ spa

spasm n (pl -s) involuntary muscular contraction

spasmodic adj occurring in spasms
> **spasmodically** adv
spasmodically adv ▷ spasmodic
spasms n ▷ spasm

spastic n (pl -s) person with cerebral palsy ▶ adj suffering from cerebral palsy
spastics n ▷ spastic
spat[1] n (pl -s) slight quarrel
spat[2] v ▷ spit[1]

spate n (pl -s) large number of things happening within a period of time
spates n ▷ spate
spatial adj of or in space

spats pl n coverings formerly worn over the ankle and instep ▶ n ▷ spat[1]

spatter v (-s, -ing, -ed) scatter or be scattered in drops over (something) ▶ n (pl -s) spattering sound
spattered v ▷ spatter
spattering v ▷ spatter
spatters n, v ▷ spatter

spatula n (pl -s) utensil with a broad flat blade for spreading or stirring
spatulas n ▷ spatula

spawn n (pl -s) jelly-like mass of eggs of fish, frogs, or molluscs ▶ v (-s, -ing, -ed) (of fish, frogs, or molluscs) lay eggs
spawned v ▷ spawn
spawning v ▷ spawn
spawns n, v ▷ spawn

spay v (-s, -ing, -ed) remove the ovaries from (a female animal)
spayed v ▷ spay
spaying v ▷ spay
spays v ▷ spay

speak v (-s, -ing, spoke, spoken) say words, talk
speaker n (pl -s) person who speaks, esp. at a formal occasion
speakers n ▷ speaker
speaking v ▷ speak
speaks v ▷ speak

spear[1] n (pl -s) weapon consisting of a long shaft with a sharp point ▶ v (-s, -ing, -ed) pierce with or as if with a spear
spear[2] n (pl -s) slender shoot
speared v ▷ spear[1]

spearhead v (-es, -ing, -ed) lead (an attack or campaign) ▶ n (pl -s) leading force in an attack or campaign
spearheaded v ▷ spearhead

spearheading v ▷ spearhead
spearheads v, n ▷ spearhead
spearing v ▷ spear[1]
spearmint n (pl -s) type of mint
spearmints n ▷ spearmint
spears n ▷ spear[1, 2] ▶ v ▷ spear[1]
spec n (pl -s) (Informal) speculation
special adj distinguished from others of its kind ▶ **specially** adv
specialist n (pl -s) expert in a particular activity or subject
specialists n ▷ specialist
specialities n ▷ speciality
speciality n (pl -ties) special interest or skill
specialization n ▷ specialize
specializations n ▷ specialize
specialize v (-zes, -zing, -zed) be a specialist ▶ **specialization** n (pl -s)
specialized v ▷ specialize
specializes v ▷ specialize
specializing v ▷ specialize
specially adv ▷ special
specie n coins as distinct from paper money
species n (pl species) group of plants or animals that are related closely enough to interbreed naturally
specific adj particular, definite ▶ n (pl -s) drug used to treat a particular disease ▶ **specifically** adv
specifically adv ▷ specific
specification n (pl -s) detailed description of something to be made or done
specifications n ▷ specification
specifics n ▷ specific ▶ pl n particular details
specified v ▷ specify
specifies v ▷ specify
specify v (-fies, -fying, -fied) refer to or state specifically
specifying v ▷ specify
specimen n (pl -s) individual or part typifying a whole
specimens n ▷ specimen
specious [spee-shuss] adj apparently true, but actually false
speck n (pl -s) small spot or particle
speckle n (pl -s) small spot ▶ v (-les, -ling, -led) mark with speckles
speckled v ▷ speckle
speckles n, v ▷ speckle
speckling v ▷ speckle
specks n ▷ speck
specs pl n (Informal) ▷ spectacles ▶ n ▷ spec
spectacle n (pl -s) strange, interesting, or ridiculous sight
spectacles n ▷ spectacle ▶ pl n pair of glasses

for correcting faulty vision
spectacles n ▷ spectacle
spectacular adj impressive ▶ n (pl -s) spectacular public show > **spectacularly** adv
spectacularly adv ▷ spectacular
spectaculars n ▷ spectacular
spectate v (-tes, -ting, -ted) watch
spectated v ▷ spectate
spectates v ▷ spectate
spectating v ▷ spectate
spectator n (pl -s) person viewing anything, onlooker
spectators n ▷ spectator
spectra n ▷ spectrum
spectral adj ▷ spectre
spectre n (pl -s) ghost > **spectral** adj
spectres n ▷ spectre
spectroscope n (pl -s) instrument for producing or examining spectra
spectroscopes n ▷ spectroscope
spectrum n (pl -tra) range of different colours, radio waves, etc. in order of their wavelengths
speculate v (-tes, -ting, -ted) guess, conjecture > **speculation** n (pl -s) > **speculative** adj > **speculator** n (pl -s)
speculated v ▷ speculate
speculates v ▷ speculate
speculating v ▷ speculate
speculation n ▷ speculate
speculations n ▷ speculate
speculative adj ▷ speculate
speculator n ▷ speculate
speculators n ▷ speculate
sped v ▷ speed
speech n (pl -es) act, power, or manner of speaking
speeches n ▷ speech
speechless adj unable to speak because of great emotion
speed n (pl -s) swiftness ▶ v (-s, -ing, sped or -ed) go quickly
speedboat n (pl -s) light fast motorboat
speedboats n ▷ speedboat
speeded v ▷ speed
speedier adj ▷ speedy
speediest adj ▷ speedy
speedily adv ▷ speedy
speeding v ▷ speed
speedometer n (pl -s) instrument to show the speed of a vehicle
speedometers n ▷ speedometer
speeds n, v ▷ speed
speedway n (pl -s) track for motorcycle racing
speedways n ▷ speedway

speedwell n (pl -s) plant with small blue flowers
speedwells n ▷ speedwell
speedy adj (-dier, -diest) prompt ▷ **speedily** adv
speleologies n ▷ speleology
speleology n (pl -gies) study and exploration of caves
spell[1] v (-s, -ing, spelt or -ed) give in correct order the letters that form (a word)
spell[2] n (pl -s) formula of words supposed to have magic power
spell[3] n (pl -s) period of time of weather or activity
spellbound adj entranced
spellchecker n (pl -s) (COMPUTING) program that highlights wrongly spelled words in a word-processed document
spellcheckers n ▷ spellchecker
spelled v ▷ spell[1]
spelling n (pl -s) way a word is spelt ▶ v ▷ spell[1]
spellings n ▷ spelling
spells v ▷ spell[1] ▶ n ▷ spell[2, 3]
spelt v ▷ spell[1]
spend v (-s, -ing, spent) pay out (money)
spending v ▷ spend
spends v ▷ spend
spendthrift n (pl -s) person who spends money wastefully
spendthrifts n ▷ spendthrift
spent v ▷ spend
sperm n (pl -s or **sperm**) male reproductive cell
spermaceti [sper-ma-**set**-ee] n (pl -s) waxy solid obtained from the sperm whale
spermacetis n ▷ spermaceti
spermatozoa n ▷ spermatozoon
spermatozoon [sper-ma-toe-**zoe**-on] n (pl -zoa) sperm
spermicide n (pl -s) substance that kills sperm
spermicides n ▷ spermicide
sperms n ▷ sperm
spew v (-s, -ing, -ed) vomit
spewed v ▷ spew
spewing v ▷ spew
spews v ▷ spew
sphagnum n (pl -s) moss found in bogs
sphagnums n ▷ sphagnum
sphere n (pl -s) perfectly round solid object ▷ **spherical** adj
spheres n ▷ sphere
spherical adj ▷ sphere
sphincter n (pl -s) ring of muscle which controls the opening and closing of a hollow organ
sphincters n ▷ sphincter
sphinx n (pl -es) enigmatic person

sphinxes n ▷ sphinx
spice n (pl -s) aromatic substance used as flavouring ▶ v (-ces, -cing, -ced) flavour with spices
spiced v ▷ spice
spices n, v ▷ spice
spicier adj ▷ spicy
spiciest adj ▷ spicy
spicing v ▷ spice
spicy adj (-cier, -ciest) flavoured with spices
spider n (pl -s) small eight-legged creature which spins a web to catch insects for food ▷ **spidery** adj
spiders n ▷ spider
spidery adj ▷ spider
spied v ▷ spy
spiel n (pl -s) speech made to persuade someone to do something
spiels n ▷ spiel
spies v, n ▷ spy
spigot n (pl -s) stopper for, or tap fitted to, a cask
spigots n ▷ spigot
spike n (pl -s) sharp point ▶ v (-kes, -king, -ked) put spikes on ▷ **spiky** adj (-kier, -kiest)
spiked v ▷ spike
spikes n, v ▷ spike ▶ pl n sports shoes with spikes for greater grip
spikier adj ▷ spike
spikiest adj ▷ spike
spiking v ▷ spike
spiky adj ▷ spike
spill[1] v (-s, -ing, spilt or spilled) pour from or as if from a container ▶ n (pl -s) fall ▷ **spillage** n (pl -s)
spill[2] n (pl -s) thin strip of wood or paper for lighting pipes or fires
spillage n ▷ spill[1]
spillages n ▷ spill[1]
spilled v ▷ spill[1]
spilling v ▷ spill[1]
spills n ▷ spill[1, 2] ▶ v ▷ spill[1]
spilt v ▷ spill[1]
spin v (-s, -nning, spun) revolve or cause to revolve rapidly ▶ n (pl -s) revolving motion ▷ **spinner** n (pl -s)
spinach n (pl -es) dark green leafy vegetable
spinaches n ▷ spinach
spinal adj of the spine
spindle n (pl -s) rotating rod that acts as an axle
spindles n ▷ spindle
spindlier adj ▷ spindly
spindliest adj ▷ spindly
spindly adj (-lier, -liest) long, slender, and frail

spine n (pl -s) backbone
spineless adj lacking courage
  spines n ▷ spine
spinet n (pl -s) small harpsichord
  spinets n ▷ spinet
  spinier adj ▷ spiny
  spiniest adj ▷ spiny
spinifex n (pl -es) coarse spiny Australian grass
  spinifexes n ▷ spinifex
spinnaker n (pl -s) large sail on a racing yacht
  spinnakers n ▷ spinnaker
  spinner n ▷ spin
  spinners n ▷ spin
spinney n (pl -s) (CHIEFLY BRIT) small wood
  spinneys n ▷ spinney
  spinning v ▷ spin
  spins v, n ▷ spin
spinster n (pl -s) unmarried woman
  spinsters n ▷ spinster
spiny adj (-nier, -niest) covered with spines
spiral n (pl -s) continuous curve formed by
  a point winding about a central axis at an
  ever-increasing distance from it ▶ v (-s, -lling,
  -lled) move in a spiral ▶ adj having the form
  of a spiral
  spiralled v ▷ spiral
  spiralling v ▷ spiral
  spirals n, v ▷ spiral
spire n (pl -s) pointed part of a steeple
  spires n ▷ spire
spirit[1] n (pl -s) nonphysical aspect of a person
  concerned with profound thoughts ▶ v (-s,
  -ing, -ed) carry away mysteriously
spirit[2] n (pl -s) liquid obtained by distillation
spirited adj lively ▶ v ▷ spirit[1]
  spiriting v ▷ spirit[1]
spirits n ▷ spirit[1, 2] ▶ pl n emotional state ▶ v
  ▷ spirit[1]
spiritual adj relating to the spirit ▶ n (pl -s)
  type of religious folk song originating among
  Black slaves in America > **spiritually** adv
  > **spirituality** n (pl -ties)
spiritualism n (pl -s) belief that the spirits of
  the dead can communicate with the living
  > **spiritualist** n (pl -s)
  spiritualisms n ▷ spiritualism
  spiritualist n ▷ spiritualism
  spiritualists n ▷ spiritualism
  spiritualities n ▷ spiritual
  spirituality n ▷ spiritual
  spiritually adv ▷ spiritual
  spirituals n ▷ spiritual
spit[1] v (-s, -tting, spat) eject (saliva or food)
  from the mouth ▶ n (pl -s) saliva
spit[2] n (pl -s) sharp rod on which meat is

skewered for roasting
spite n (pl -s) deliberate nastiness ▶ v (-tes,
  -ting, -ted) annoy or hurt from spite > **spiteful**
  adj > **spitefully** adv
  spited v ▷ spite
  spiteful adj ▷ spite
  spitefully adv ▷ spite
  spites n, v ▷ spite
spitfire n (pl -s) person with a fiery temper
  spitfires n ▷ spitfire
  spiting v ▷ spite
  spits n ▷ spit[1, 2] ▶ v ▷ spit[1]
  spitting v ▷ spit[1]
spittle n (pl -s) fluid produced in the mouth,
  saliva
  spittles n ▷ spittle
spittoon n (pl -s) bowl to spit into
  spittoons n ▷ spittoon
spiv n (pl -s) (BRIT, AUST & NZ) (Slang) smartly
  dressed man who makes a living by shady
  dealings
  spivs n ▷ spiv
splash v (-es, -ing, -ed) scatter liquid on
  (something) ▶ n (pl -es) splashing sound
  splashed v ▷ splash
  splashes v, n ▷ splash
  splashing v, n ▷ splash
splatter v (-s, -ing, -ed) ▶ n (pl -s) splash
  splattered v ▷ splatter
  splattering v ▷ splatter
  splatters v, n ▷ splatter
splay v (-s, -ing, -ed) spread out, with ends
  spreading in different directions
  splayed v ▷ splay
  splaying v ▷ splay
  splays v ▷ splay
spleen n (pl -s) abdominal organ which filters
  bacteria from the blood
  spleens n ▷ spleen
splendid adj (-er, -est) excellent > **splendidly**
  adv > **splendour** n (pl -s)
  splendider adj ▷ splendid
  splendidest adj ▷ splendid
  splendidly adv ▷ splendid
  splendour n ▷ splendid
  splendours n ▷ splendid
splenetic adj spiteful or irritable
splice v (-ces, -cing, -ced) join by interweaving
  or overlapping ends
  spliced v ▷ splice
  splices v ▷ splice
  splicing v ▷ splice
splint n (pl -s) rigid support for a broken bone
splinter n (pl -s) thin sharp piece broken off,
  esp. from wood ▶ v (-s, -ing, -ed) break into

fragments

splintered v ▷ splinter

splintering v ▷ splinter

splinters n, v ▷ splinter

splints n ▷ splint

split v (-s, -tting, split) break into separate pieces ▶ n (pl -s) crack or division caused by splitting

splits v ▷ split ▶ n ▷ split ▶ pl n act of sitting with the legs outstretched in opposite directions

splitting v ▷ split

splodge n (pl -s) ▶ v (-ges, -ging, -ged) ▷ splotch

splodged v ▷ splodge

splodges n, v ▷ splodge

splodging v ▷ splodge

splotch n (pl -s) ▶ v (-ches, -ching, -ched) splash, daub

splotched v ▷ splotch

splotches n, v ▷ splotch

splotching v ▷ splotch

splurge v (-ges, -ging, -ged) spend money extravagantly ▶ n (pl -s) bout of extravagance

splurged v ▷ splurge

splurges v, n ▷ splurge

splurging v ▷ splurge

splutter v (-s, -ing, -ed) utter with spitting or choking sounds ▶ n (pl -s) spluttering

spluttered v ▷ splutter

spluttering v ▷ splutter

splutters v, n ▷ splutter

spoil v (-s, -ing, -spoilt or -ed) damage

spoiled v ▷ spoil

spoiling v ▷ spoil

spoils pl n booty ▶ v ▷ spoil

spoilsport n (pl -s) person who spoils the enjoyment of others

spoilsports n ▷ spoilsport

spoilt v ▷ spoil

spoke¹ v ▷ speak

spoke² n (pl -s) bar joining the hub of a wheel to the rim

spoken v ▷ speak

spokes n ▷ spoke²

spokesman, spokeswoman, spokesperson n (pl -men, -women, -persons, -people) person chosen to speak on behalf of a group

spokesmen n ▷ spokesman

spokespeople n ▷ spokesman

spokesperson n ▷ spokesman

spokespersons n ▷ spokesman

spokeswoman n ▷ spokesman

spokeswomen n ▷ spokesman

spoliation n (pl -s) plundering

spoliations n ▷ spoliation

sponge n (pl -s) sea animal with a porous absorbent skeleton ▶ v (-ges, -ging, -ged) wipe with a sponge > **spongy** adj (-gier, -giest)

sponged v ▷ sponge

sponger n (pl -s) (Slang) person who sponges on others

spongers n ▷ sponge

sponges n, v ▷ sponge

spongier adj ▷ sponge

spongiest adj ▷ sponge

sponging v ▷ sponge

spongy adj ▷ sponge

sponsor n (pl -s) person who promotes something ▶ v (-s, -ing, -ed) act as a sponsor for > **sponsorship** n (pl -s)

sponsored v ▷ sponsor

sponsoring v ▷ sponsor

sponsors n, v ▷ sponsor

sponsorship n ▷ sponsor

sponsorships n ▷ sponsor

spontaneities n ▷ spontaneous

spontaneity n ▷ spontaneous

spontaneous adj not planned or arranged > **spontaneously** adv > **spontaneity** n (pl -ties)

spontaneously adv ▷ spontaneous

spoof n (pl -s) mildly satirical parody

spoofs n ▷ spoof

spook n (pl -s) (Informal) ghost > **spooky** adj (-kier, -kiest)

spookier adj ▷ spook

spookiest adj ▷ spook

spooks n ▷ spook

spooky adj ▷ spook

spool n (pl -s) cylinder round which something can be wound

spools n ▷ spool

spoon n (pl -s) shallow bowl attached to a handle for eating, stirring, or serving food ▶ v (-s, -ing, -ed) lift with a spoon > **spoonful** n (pl -s)

spoonbill n (pl -s) wading bird of warm regions with a long flat bill

spoonbills n ▷ spoonbill

spooned v ▷ spoon

spoonerism n (pl -s) accidental changing over of the initial sounds of a pair of words, such as half-warmed fish for half-formed wish

spoonerisms n ▷ spoonerism

spoonful n ▷ spoon

spoonfuls n ▷ spoon

spooning v ▷ spoon

spoons n, v ▷ spoon

spoor n (pl -s) trail of an animal

spoors n ▷ spoor

sporadic *adj* intermittent, scattered
> **sporadically** *adv*
sporadically *adv* ▷ sporadic
spore *n* (*pl* -s) minute reproductive body of some plants
spores *n* ▷ spore
sporran *n* (*pl* -s) pouch worn in front of a kilt
sporrans *n* ▷ sporran
sport *n* (*pl* -s) activity for pleasure, competition, or exercise *v* (-s, -ing, -ed) wear proudly > **sporty** *adj* (-tier, -tiest)
sported *v* ▷ sport
sportier *adj* ▷ sport
sportiest *adj* ▷ sport
sporting *adj* of sport ▶ *v* ▷ sport
sportive *adj* playful
sports *n*, *v* ▷ sport
sportsman, sportswoman *n* (*pl* -men, -women) person who plays sports
> **sportsmanlike** *adj* > **sportsmanship** *n* (*pl* -s)
sportsmanlike *adj* ▷ sportsman
sportsmanship *n* ▷ sportsman
sportsmanships *n* ▷ sportsman
sportsmen *n* ▷ sportsman
sportswoman *n* ▷ sportsman
sportswomen *n* ▷ sportsman
sporty *adj* ▷ sport
spot *n* (*pl* -s) small mark on a surface (*Informal*)
▶ *v* (-s, -tting, -tted) notice
spotless *adj* absolutely clean > **spotlessly** *adv*
spotlessly *adv* ▷ spotless
spotlight *n* (*pl* -s) powerful light illuminating a small area
spotlights *n* ▷ spotlight
spots *n*, *v* ▷ spot
spotted *v* ▷ spot
spottier *adj* ▷ spotty
spottiest *adj* ▷ spotty
spotting *v* ▷ spot
spotty *adj* (-tier, -ttiest) with spots
spouse *n* (*pl* -s) husband or wife
spouses *n* ▷ spouse
spout *v* (-s, -ing, -ed) pour out in a stream or jet (*Slang*) ▶ *n* (*pl* -s) projecting tube or lip for pouring liquids
spouted *v* ▷ spout
spouting *v* ▷ spout
spouts *v*, *n* ▷ spout
sprain *v* (-s, -ing, -ed) injure (a joint) by a sudden twist ▶ *n* (*pl* -s) such an injury
sprained *v* ▷ sprain
spraining *v* ▷ sprain
sprains *v*, *n* ▷ sprain
sprang *v* ▷ spring
sprat *n* (*pl* -s) small sea fish

sprats *n* ▷ sprat
sprawl *v* (-s, -ing, -ed) lie or sit with the limbs spread out ▶ *n* (*pl* -s) part of a city that has spread untidily over a large area
sprawled *v* ▷ sprawl
sprawling *v* ▷ sprawl
sprawls *v*, *n* ▷ sprawl
spray¹ *n* (*pl* -s) (device for producing) fine drops of liquid ▶ *v* (-s, -ing, -ed) scatter in fine drops
spray² *n* (*pl* -s) branch with buds, leaves, etc.
sprayed *v* ▷ spray¹
spraying *v* ▷ spray¹
sprayings *n* ▷ spray¹
sprays *v* ▷ spray¹, ²
spread *v* (-s, -ing, spread) open out or be displayed to the fullest extent ▶ *n* (*pl* -s) spreading (*Informal*)
spreading *v* ▷ spread
spreads *v*, *n* ▷ spread
spreadsheet *n* (*pl* -s) computer program for manipulating figures
spreadsheets *n* ▷ spreadsheet
spree *n* (*pl* -s) session of overindulgence, usu. in drinking or spending money
sprees *n* ▷ spree
sprier *adj* ▷ spry
spriest *adj* ▷ spry
sprig *n* (*pl* -s) twig or shoot
sprightlier *adj* ▷ sprightly
sprightliest *adj* ▷ sprightly
sprightliness *n* ▷ sprightly
sprightlinesses *n* ▷ sprightly
sprightly *adj* (-lier, -liest) lively and brisk
> **sprightliness** *n* (*pl* -es)
sprigs *n* ▷ sprig
spring *v* (-s, -ing, sprang *or* sprung) move suddenly upwards or forwards in a single motion, jump ▶ *n* (*pl* -s) season between winter and summer
springboard *n* (*pl* -s) flexible board used to gain height or momentum in diving or gymnastics
springboards *n* ▷ springboard
springbok *n* (*pl* -s) S African antelope
springboks *n* ▷ springbok
springer *n* (*pl* -s) small spaniel
springers *n* ▷ springer
springier *adj* ▷ springy
springiest *adj* ▷ springy
springing *v* ▷ spring
springs *v*, *n* ▷ springs
springy *adj* (-gier, -giest) elastic
sprinkle *v* (-les, -ling, -led) scatter (liquid or powder) in tiny drops or particles over (something) > **sprinkler** *n* (*pl* -s)

sprinkled v ▷ sprinkle

sprinkler n ▷ sprinkle

sprinklers n ▷ sprinkle

sprinkles v ▷ sprinkle

sprinkling v ▷ sprinkle ▶ n (pl -s) small quantity or number

sprinklings n ▷ sprinkling

sprint n (pl -s) short race run at top speed ▶ v (-s, -ing, -ed) run a short distance at top speed > **sprinter** n (pl -s)

sprinted v ▷ sprint

sprinter n ▷ sprint

sprinters n ▷ sprint

sprinting v ▷ sprint

sprints n, v ▷ sprint

sprite n (pl -s) elf

sprites n ▷ sprite

sprocket n (pl -s) wheel with teeth on the rim, that drives or is driven by a chain

sprockets n ▷ sprocket

sprout v (-s, -ing, -ed) put forth shoots ▶ n (pl -s) shoot

sprouted v ▷ sprout

sprouting v ▷ sprout

sprouts v, n ▷ sprout

spruce[1] n (pl -s) kind of fir

spruce[2] adj (-r, -st) neat and smart

sprucer adj ▷ spruce[2]

spruces n ▷ spruce[1]

sprucest adj ▷ spruce[2]

sprung v ▷ spring

spry adj (-yer, -yest or **sprier**) (spriest) active or nimble

spryer adj ▷ spry

spryest adj ▷ spry

spud n (pl -s) (Informal) potato

spuds n ▷ spud

spume n (pl -s) ▶ v (-mes, -ming, -med) froth

spumed v ▷ spume

spumes v, n ▷ spume

spuming v ▷ spume

spun v ▷ spin

spunk n (pl -s) (Informal) courage, spirit > **spunky** adj (-kier, -kiest)

spunkier adj ▷ spunk

spunkiest adj ▷ spunk

spunks n ▷ spunk

spunky adj ▷ spunk

spur n (pl -s) stimulus or incentive ▶ v (-s, -rring, -rred) urge on, incite (someone)

spurge n (pl -s) plant with milky sap

spurges n ▷ spurge

spurious adj not genuine

spurn v (-s, -ing, -ed) reject with scorn

spurned v ▷ spurn

spurning v ▷ spurn

spurns v ▷ spurn

spurred v ▷ spur

spurring v ▷ spur

spurs n, v ▷ spur

spurt v (-s, -ing, -ed) gush or cause to gush out in a jet ▶ n (pl -s) short sudden burst of activity or speed

spurted v ▷ spurt

spurting v ▷ spurt

spurts v, n ▷ spurt

sputa n ▷ sputum

sputnik n (pl -s) early Soviet artificial satellite

sputniks n ▷ sputnik

sputter v (-es, -ing, -ed) ▶ n (pl -s) splutter

sputtered v ▷ sputter

sputtering v ▷ sputter

sputters v, n ▷ sputter

sputum n (pl -ta) spittle, usu. mixed with mucus

spy n (pl spies) person employed to obtain secret information ▶ v (spies, spying, spied) act as a spy

spying v ▷ spy

squabble v (-les, -ling, -led) ▶ n (pl -s) (engage in) a petty or noisy quarrel

squabbled v ▷ squabble

squabbles v, n ▷ squabble

squabbling v ▷ squabble

squad n (pl -s) small group of people working or training together

squadron n (pl -s) division of an air force, fleet, or cavalry regiment

squadrons n ▷ squadron

squads n ▷ squad

squalid adj (-er, -est) dirty and unpleasant

squalider adj ▷ squalid

squalidest adj ▷ squalid

squall[1] n (pl -s) sudden strong wind

squall[2] v (-s, -ing, -ed) cry noisily, yell ▶ n (pl -s) harsh cry

squalled v ▷ squall[2]

squalling v ▷ squall[2]

squalls v ▷ squall[2] ▶ n ▷ squall[1, 2]

squalor n (pl -s) disgusting dirt and filth

squalors n ▷ squalor

squander v (-s, -ing, -ed) waste (money or resources)

squandered v ▷ squander

squandering v ▷ squander

squanders v ▷ squander

square n (pl -s) geometric figure with four equal sides and four right angles ▶ adj square in shape ▶ v (-res, -ring, -red) multiply (a number) by itself ▶ adv squarely, directly

squared v ▷ square

squarely adv in a direct way

squares n, v ▷ square

squaring v ▷ square

squash[1] v (-es, -ing, -ed) crush flat ▶ n (pl -es) sweet fruit drink diluted with water > **squashy** adj (-shier, -shiest)

squash[2] n (pl -es) marrow-like vegetable

squashed v ▷ squash[1]

squashes n ▷ squash[1, 2] ▶ v ▷ squash[1]

squashier adj ▷ squash[1]

squashiest adj ▷ squash[1]

squashing v ▷ squash[1]

squashy adj ▷ squash[1]

squat v (-s, -tting, -tted) crouch with the knees bent and the weight on the feet ▶ n (pl -s) place where squatters live ▶ adj (-tter, -ttest) short and broad

squats v, n ▷ squat

squatted v ▷ squat

squatter n (pl -s) illegal occupier of unused premises ▶ adj ▷ squat

squatters n ▷ squatter

squattest n ▷ squat

squatting v ▷ squat

squaw n (pl -s) (Offens) Native American woman

squawk n (pl -s) loud harsh cry ▶ v (-s, -ing, -ed) utter a squawk

squawked v ▷ squawk

squawking v ▷ squawk

squawks v ▷ squawk

squaws n ▷ squaw

squeak n (pl -s) short shrill cry or sound ▶ v (-s, -ing, -ed) make or utter a squeak > **squeaky** adj (-kier, -kiest)

squeaked v ▷ squeak

squeakier adj ▷ squeak

squeakiest adj ▷ squeak

squeaking v ▷ squeak

squeaks n, v ▷ squeak

squeaky adj ▷ squeak

squeal n (pl -s) long shrill cry or sound ▶ v (-s, -ing, -ed) make or utter a squeal (Slang)

squealed v ▷ squeal

squealing v ▷ squeal

squeals n, v ▷ squeal

squeamish adj easily sickened or shocked

squeegee n (pl -s) tool with a rubber blade for clearing water from a surface

squeegees n ▷ squeegee

squeeze v (-zes, -zing, -zed) grip or press firmly ▶ n (pl -s) squeezing

squeezed v ▷ squeeze

squeezes v, n ▷ squeeze

squeezing v ▷ squeeze

squelch v (-es, -ing, -ed) make a wet sucking sound, as by walking through mud ▶ n (pl -es) squelching sound

squelched v ▷ squelch

squelches n ▷ squelch

squelching v ▷ squelch

squib n (pl -s) small firework that hisses before exploding

squibs n ▷ squib

squid n (pl -s) sea creature with a long soft body and ten tentacles

squids n ▷ squid

squiggle n (pl -s) wavy line > **squiggly** adj (-lier, -liest)

squiggles n ▷ squiggle

squigglier adj ▷ squiggle

squiggliest adj ▷ squiggle

squiggly adj ▷ squiggle

squint v (-s, -ing, -ed) have eyes which face in different directions ▶ n (pl -s) squinting condition of the eye ▶ adj crooked (-er, -est)

squinted v ▷ squint

squinter adj ▷ squint

squintest adj ▷ squint

squinting v ▷ squint

squints v, n ▷ squint

squire n (pl -s) country gentleman, usu. the main landowner in a community

squires n ▷ squire

squirm v (-s, -ing, -ed) wriggle, writhe ▶ n (pl -s) wriggling movement

squirmed v ▷ squirm

squirming v ▷ squirm

squirms v, n ▷ squirm

squirrel n (pl -s) small bushy-tailed tree-living animal

squirrels n ▷ squirrel

squirt v (-s, -ing, -ed) force (a liquid) or (of a liquid) be forced out of a narrow opening ▶ n (pl -s) jet of liquid

squirted v ▷ squirt

squirting v ▷ squirt

squirts n, v ▷ squirt

squish v (-es, -ing, -ed) ▶ n (pl -es) (make) a soft squelching sound > **squishy** adj (-shier, -shiest)

squished v ▷ squish

squishes n, v ▷ squish

squishier adj ▷ squish

squishiest adj ▷ squish

squishing v ▷ squish

squishy adj ▷ squish

> **squiz** n (**squizzes**). Squiz is an informal word for a look or glance. This is a

useful word to remember, both for when you have the most of the tiles to form it and when someone else plays **quiz** which you can then add an S to for a good score. Squiz scores 23 points.

st *interj.* St is a sound people make to request silence or quiet. This is one of two two-letter words beginning with S that do not contain a vowel. It's useful when you want to connect a word beginning with H to one ending in T or vice versa. St scores 2 points.

stab v (-s, -bbing, -bbed) pierce with something pointed ▶ n (pl -s) stabbing

stabbed v ▷ stab

stabbing v ▷ stab

stabilities n ▷ stable²

stability n ▷ stable²

stabilization n ▷ stabilize

stabilizations n ▷ stabilize

stabilize v (-zes, -zing, -zed) make or become stable > **stabilization** n (pl -s)

stabilized v ▷ stabilize

stabilizer n (pl -s) device for stabilizing a child's bicycle, an aircraft, or a ship

stabilizers n ▷ stabilizer

stabilizes v ▷ stabilize

stabilizing v ▷ stabilize

stable¹ n (pl -s) building in which horses are kept ▶ v (-les, -ling, -led) put or keep (a horse) in a stable

stable² adj (-r, -st) firmly fixed or established > **stability** n (pl -ties)

stabled v ▷ stable¹

stabler adj ▷ stable²

stables n, v ▷ stable¹

stablest adj ▷ stable²

stabling v ▷ stable¹

stabs v, n ▷ stab

staccato [stak-ah-toe] adv (MUSIC) with the notes sharply separated ▶ adj consisting of short abrupt sounds

stack n (pl -s) ordered pile ▶ v (-s, -ing, -ed) pile in a stack

stacked v ▷ stack

stacking v ▷ stack

stacks n, v ▷ stack

stadia n ▷ stadium

stadium n (pl -diums, -dia) sports arena with tiered seats for spectators

stadiums n ▷ stadium

staff¹ n (pl -s) people employed in an organization ▶ v (-s, -ing, -ed) supply with personnel

staff² n (pl staves) set of five horizontal lines

on which music is written

staffed v ▷ staff¹

staffing v ▷ staff¹

staffs n, v ▷ staff¹

stag n (pl -s) adult male deer

stage n (pl -s) step or period of development ▶ v (-ges, -ging, -ged) put (a play) on stage

stagecoach n (pl -es) large horse-drawn vehicle formerly used to carry passengers and mail

stagecoaches n ▷ stagecoach

staged v ▷ stage

stages n, v ▷ stage

stagey adj (-gier, -giest) overtheatrical

stagger v (-s, -ing, -ed) walk unsteadily ▶ n (pl -s) staggering

staggered v ▷ stagger

staggering v ▷ stagger

staggers v, n ▷ stagger

stagier adj ▷ stagey

stagiest adj ▷ stagey

staging v ▷ stage

stagnant adj (of water or air) stale from not moving

stagnate v (-tes, -ting, -ted) be stagnant > **stagnation** n (pl -s)

stagnated v ▷ stagnate

stagnates v ▷ stagnate

stagnating v ▷ stagnate

stagnation n ▷ stagnate

stagnations n ▷ stagnate

stags n ▷ stag

staid adj (-er, -est) sedate, serious, and rather dull

staider adj ▷ staid

staidest adj ▷ staid

stain v (-s, -ing, -ed) discolour, mark ▶ n (pl -s) discoloration or mark > **stainless** adj

stained v ▷ stain

staining v ▷ stain

stainless adj ▷ stain

stains v, n ▷ stain

staircase, stairway n (pl -s) flight of stairs with a handrail or banisters

staircases n ▷ staircase

stairs pl n flight of steps between floors, usu. indoors

stairway n ▷ staircase

stairways n ▷ staircase

stake¹ n (pl -s) pointed stick or post driven into the ground as a support or marker ▶ v (-kes, -king, -ked) support or mark out with stakes

stake² n (pl -s) money wagered ▶ v (-kes, -king, -ked) wager, risk

staked v ▷ stake¹, ²

stakeholder n (pl -s) person who has a concern or interest in something, esp. a business
   stakeholders n ▷ stakeholder
   stakes v ▷ stake¹,² ▶ n ▷ stake¹,²
   staking v ▷ stake¹,²

stalactite n (pl -s) lime deposit hanging from the roof of a cave
   stalactites n ▷ stalactite

stalagmite n (pl -s) lime deposit sticking up from the floor of a cave
   stalagmites n ▷ stalagmite

stale adj (-r, -st) not fresh > **staleness** n (pl -es)

stalemate n (pl -s) (CHESS) position in which any of a player's moves would put his king in check, resulting in a draw
   stalemates n ▷ stalemate
   staleness n ▷ stale
   stalenesses n ▷ stale
   staler adj ▷ stale
   stalest adj ▷ stale

stalk¹ n (pl -s) plant's stem

stalk² v (-s, -ing, -ed) follow or approach stealthily
   stalked v ▷ stalk²

stalker n (pl -s) person who follows or stealthily approaches a person or an animal
   stalkers n ▷ stalker
   stalking v ▷ stalk²

stalking-horse n (pl -s) pretext
   stalking-horses n ▷ stalking-horse
   stalks n ▷ stalk¹ ▶ v ▷ stalk²

stall¹ n (pl -s) small stand for the display and sale of goods ▶ v (-s, -ing, -ed) stop (a motor vehicle or engine) or (of a motor vehicle or engine) stop accidentally

stall² v (-s, -ing, -ed) employ delaying tactics
   stalled v ▷ stall¹,²
   stalling v ▷ stall¹,²

stallion n (pl -s) uncastrated male horse
   stallions n ▷ stallion
   stalls n ▷ stall¹ ▶ v ▷ stall¹,² ▶ pl n ground-floor seats in a theatre or cinema

stalwart [stawl-wart] adj strong and sturdy ▶ n (pl -s) stalwart person
   stalwarts n ▷ stalwart

stamen n (pl -s) pollen-producing part of a flower
   stamens n ▷ stamen

stamina n (pl -s) enduring energy and strength
   staminas n ▷ stamina

stammer v (-s, -ing, ed) speak or say with involuntary pauses or repetition of syllables ▶ n (pl -s) tendency to stammer
   stammered v ▷ stammer
   stammering v ▷ stammer

stammers v, n ▷ stammer

stamp n (pl -s) piece of gummed paper stuck to an envelope or parcel to show that the postage has been paid ▶ v (-s, -ing, -ed) bring (one's foot) down forcefully
   stamped v ▷ stamp

stampede n (pl -s) sudden rush of frightened animals or of a crowd ▶ v (-des, -ding, -ded) (cause to) take part in a stampede
   stampeded v ▷ stampede
   stampedes n, v ▷ stampede
   stampeding v ▷ stampede
   stamping v ▷ stamp
   stamps n, v ▷ stamp

stance n (pl -s) attitude
   stances n ▷ stance

stanch [stahnch] v (-es, -ing, -ed) ▷ staunch²
   stanched v ▷ stanch
   stanches v ▷ stanch
   stanching v ▷ stanch

stanchion n (pl -s) upright bar used as a support
   stanchions n ▷ stanchion

stand v (-s, -ing, stood) be in, rise to, or place in an upright position ▶ n (pl -s) stall for the sale of goods

standard n (pl -s) level of quality ▶ adj usual, regular, or average
   standardization n ▷ standardize

standardize v (-zes, -zing, -zed) cause to conform to a standard > **standardization** n (pl -s)
   standardized v ▷ standardize
   standardizes v ▷ standardize
   standardizing v ▷ standardize
   standards n ▷ standard

standing adj permanent, lasting ▶ n (pl -s) reputation or status ▶ v ▷ stand
   standings n ▷ standing

standoffish adj reserved or haughty

standpipe n (pl -s) tap attached to a water main to provide a public water supply
   standpipes n ▷ standpipe

standpoint n (pl -s) point of view
   standpoints n ▷ standpoint
   stands v, n ▷ stand

standstill n (pl -s) complete halt
   standstills n ▷ standstill
   stank v ▷ stink

stanza n (pl -s) verse of a poem
   stanzas n ▷ stanza

staple¹ n (pl -s) U-shaped piece of metal used to fasten papers or secure things ▶ v (-les, -ling, -led) fasten with staples

staple² adj of prime importance, principal ▶ n

(pl -s) main constituent of anything
stapled v ▷ staple¹

stapler n (pl -s) small device for fastening papers together
staplers n ▷ stapler
staples n ▷ staple¹, ² ▶ v ▷ staple¹
stapling v ▷ staple¹

star n (pl -s) hot gaseous mass in space, visible in the night sky as a point of light ▶ v (-s, -rring, -rred) feature or be featured in a main role ▶ adj leading, famous

starboard n (pl -s) right-hand side of a ship, when facing forward ▶ adj of or on this side
starboards n ▷ starboard

starch n (pl -es) carbohydrate forming the main food element in bread, potatoes, etc., and used mixed with water for stiffening fabric ▶ v (-es, -ing, -ed) stiffen (fabric) with starch
starched v ▷ starch
starches n, v ▷ starch
starchier adj ▷ starchy
starchiest adj ▷ starchy
starching v ▷ starch

starchy adj (-chier, -chiest) containing starch

stardom n (pl -s) status of a star in the entertainment or sports world
stardoms n ▷ stardom

stare v (-res, -ring, -red) look or gaze fixedly (at) ▶ n (pl -s) fixed gaze
stared v ▷ stare
stares v, n ▷ stare

starfish n (pl -es) star-shaped sea creature
starfishes n ▷ starfish
staring v ▷ stare

stark adj (-er, -est) harsh, unpleasant, and plain ▶ adv completely
starker adj ▷ stark
starkest adj ▷ stark

starling n (pl -s) songbird with glossy black speckled feathers
starlings n ▷ starling
starred v ▷ star
starrier adj ▷ starry
starriest adj ▷ starry
starring v ▷ star

starry adj (-rrier, -rriest) full of or like stars

stars n, v ▷ star ▶ pl n astrological forecast, horoscope

start v (-s, -ing, -ed) take the first step, begin ▶ n (pl -s) first part of something
started v ▷ start

starter n (pl -s) first course of a meal
starters n ▷ starter
starting v ▷ start

startle v (-les, -ling, -led) slightly surprise or frighten
startled v ▷ startle
startles v ▷ startle
startling v ▷ startle
starts v, n ▷ start

starvation n ▷ starve
starvations n ▷ starve

starve v (-ves, -ving, -ved) die or suffer or cause to die or suffer from hunger > **starvation** n (pl -s)
starved v ▷ starve
starves v ▷ starve
starving v ▷ starve

stash (Informal) v (-es, -ing, -ed) store in a secret place ▶ n (pl -es) secret store
stashed v ▷ stash
stashes v, n ▷ stash
stashing v ▷ stash

state n (pl -s) condition of a person or thing ▶ adj of or concerning the State ▶ v (-tes, -ting, -ted) express in words
stated v ▷ state

statehouse n (pl -s) (nz) publicly-owned house rented to a low-income tenant
statehouses n ▷ statehouse
statelier adj ▷ stately
stateliest adj ▷ stately

stately adj (-lier, -liest) dignified or grand

statement n (pl -s) something stated
statements n ▷ statement

stateroom n (pl -s) private cabin on a ship
staterooms n ▷ stateroom
states n, v ▷ state

statesman, stateswoman n (pl -men, -women) experienced and respected political leader > **statesmanship** n (pl -s)
statesmanship n ▷ statesman
statesmanships n ▷ statesman
statesmen n ▷ statesman
stateswoman n ▷ statesman
stateswomen n ▷ statesman

static adj stationary or inactive ▶ n (pl -s) crackling sound or speckled picture caused by interference in radio or television reception
statics n ▷ static
stating v ▷ state

station n (pl -s) place where trains stop for passengers ▶ v (-s, -ing, -ed) assign (someone) to a particular place

stationary adj not moving
stationed v ▷ station

stationer n (pl -s) dealer in stationery
stationeries n ▷ stationery

stationers n ▷ stationer
stationery n (pl -ries) writing materials such as paper and pens
stationing v ▷ station
stations n, v ▷ station
statistic n (pl -s) numerical fact collected and classified systematically > **statistical** adj > **statistically** adv
statistical adj ▷ statistic
statistically adv ▷ statistic
statistician n (pl -s) person who compiles and studies statistics
statisticians n ▷ statistician
statistics n ▷ statistic
statuaries n ▷ statuary
statuary n (pl -ries) statues collectively
statue n (pl -s) large sculpture of a human or animal figure
statues n ▷ statue
statuesque adj (of a woman) tall and well-proportioned
statuette n (pl -s) small statue
statuettes n ▷ statuette
stature n (pl -s) person's height
statures n ▷ stature
status n (pl -ses) social position
statuses n ▷ status
statute n (pl -s) written law > **statutory** adj required or authorized by law
statutes n ▷ statute
statutory adj ▷ statute
staunch¹ adj (-er, -est) loyal, firm
staunch², **stanch** v (-ches, -ching, -ched) stop (a flow of blood)
staunched v ▷ staunch²
stauncher adj ▷ staunch¹
staunches v ▷ staunch²
staunchest adj ▷ staunch¹
staunching v ▷ staunch²
stave n (pl -s) one of the strips of wood forming a barrel
staves n ▷ staff²
stay¹ v (-s, -ing, -ed) remain in a place or condition ▶ n (pl -s) period of staying in a place
stay² n (pl -s) prop or buttress
stay³ n (pl -s) rope or wire supporting a ship's mast
stayed v ▷ stay¹
staying v ▷ stay¹
stays n ▷ stay¹, ², ³ ▶ v ▷ stay¹ ▶ pl n corset
stead n (pl -s) in someone's place
steadfast adj firm, determined > **steadfastly** adv
steadfastly adv ▷ steadfast

steadied v ▷ steady
steadier adj ▷ steady
steadiest adj ▷ steady
steadily adv ▷ steady
steadiness n ▷ steady
steadinesses n ▷ steady
steads n ▷ stead
steady adj (-dier, -diest) not shaky or wavering ▶ v (-dies, -dying, -died) make steady ▶ adv in a steady manner > **steadily** adv > **steadiness** n (pl -es)
steadying v ▷ steady
steak n (pl -s) thick slice of meat, esp. beef
steaks n ▷ steak
steal v (-s, -ing, stole, stolen) take unlawfully or without permission
stealing v ▷ steal
steals v ▷ steal
stealth n (pl -s) secret or underhand behaviour ▶ adj (of technology) able to render an aircraft almost invisible to radar > **stealthy** adj (-thier, -thiest) > **stealthily** adv
stealthier adj ▷ stealth
stealthiest adj ▷ stealth
stealthily adv ▷ stealth
stealths n ▷ stealth
stealthy adj ▷ stealth
steam n (pl -s) vapour into which water changes when boiled ▶ v (-s, -ing, -ed) give off steam
steamed v ▷ steam
steamer n (pl -s) steam-propelled ship
steamers n ▷ steamer
steaming v ▷ steam
steamroller n (pl -s) steam-powered vehicle with heavy rollers, used to level road surfaces ▶ v (-s, -ing, -ed) use overpowering force to make (someone) do what one wants
steamrollered v ▷ steamroller
steamrollering v ▷ steamroller
steamrollers n, v ▷ steamroller
steams n, v ▷ steam
steed n (pl -s) (Lit) horse
steeds n ▷ steed
steel n (pl -s) hard malleable alloy of iron and carbon ▶ v (-s, -ing, -ed) prepare (oneself) for something unpleasant > **steely** adj (-lier, -liest)
steeled v ▷ steel
steelier adj ▷ steel
steeliest adj ▷ steel
steeling v ▷ steel
steels n, v ▷ steel
steely adj ▷ steel
steep¹ adj (-er, -est) sloping sharply > **steeply**

adv ▷ **steepness** *n* (*pl* -es)
steep² *v* (-s, -ing, -ed) soak or be soaked in liquid
steeped *v* ▷ steep²
steeper *adj* ▷ steep¹
steepest *adj* ▷ steep¹
steeping *v* ▷ steep²
steeple *n* (*pl* -s) church tower with a spire
steeplechase *n* (*pl* -s) horse race with obstacles to jump
steeplechases *n* ▷ steeplechase
steeplejack *n* (*pl* -s) person who repairs steeples and chimneys
steeplejacks *n* ▷ steeplejack
steeples *n* ▷ steeple
steeply *n* ▷ steep¹
steepness *n* ▷ steep¹
steepnesses *n* ▷ steep¹
steeps *v* ▷ steep²
steer¹ *v* (-s, -ing, -ed) direct the course of (a vehicle or ship)
steer² *n* (*pl* -s) castrated male ox
steerage *n* (*pl* -s) cheapest accommodation on a passenger ship
steerages *n* ▷ steerage
steered *v* ▷ steer¹
steering *v* ▷ steer¹
steers *v* ▷ steer¹ ▶ *n* ▷ steer²
stein [stine] *n* (*pl* -s) earthenware beer mug
steins *n* ▷ stein
stellar *adj* of stars
stem¹ *n* (*pl* -s) long thin central part of a plant ▶ *v* (-s, -mming, -mmed) originate from
stem² *v* (-s, -mming, -mmed) stop (the flow of something)
stemmed *v* ▷ stem¹, ²
stemming *v* ▷ stem¹, ²
stems *v* ▷ stem¹, ² ▶ *n* ▷ stem¹
stench *n* (*pl* -es) foul smell
stenches *n* ▷ stench
stencil *n* (*pl* -s) thin sheet with cut-out pattern through which ink or paint passes to form the pattern on the surface below ▶ *v* (-s, -lling, -lled) make (a pattern) with a stencil
stencilled *v* ▷ stencil
stencilling *v* ▷ stencil
stencils *n*, *v* ▷ stencil
stenographer *n* (*pl* -s) shorthand typist
stenographers *n* ▷ stenographer
stent *n* (*pl* -s) surgical implant used to keep an artery open
stentorian *adj* (of a voice) very loud
stents *n* ▷ stent
step *v* (-s, -pping, -pped) move and set down the foot, as when walking ▶ *n* (*pl* -s) stepping

stepladder *n* (*pl* -s) folding portable ladder with supporting frame
stepladders *n* ▷ stepladder
stepped *v* ▷ step
steppes *pl* *n* wide grassy treeless plains in Russia and Ukraine
stepping *v* ▷ step
steps *pl* *n* stepladder ▶ *n*, *v* ▷ step
stereo *adj* ▷ stereophonic ▶ *n* (*pl* -s) stereophonic record player
stereophonic *adj* using two separate loudspeakers to give the effect of naturally distributed sound
stereos *n* ▷ stereo
stereotype *n* (*pl* -s) standardized idea of a type of person or thing ▶ *v* (-pes, -ping, -ped) form a stereotype of
stereotyped *v* ▷ stereotype
stereotypes *n*, *v* ▷ stereotype
stereotyping *v* ▷ stereotype
sterile *adj* free from germs > **sterility** *n* (*pl* -ties)
sterilities *n* ▷ sterile
sterility *n* ▷ sterile
sterilization *n* ▷ sterilize
sterilizations *n* ▷ sterilize
sterilize *v* (-zes, -zing, -zed) make sterile > **sterilization** *n* (*pl* -s)
sterilized *v* ▷ sterilize
sterilizes *v* ▷ sterilize
sterilizing *v* ▷ sterilize
sterling *n* (*pl* -s) British money system ▶ *adj* genuine and reliable
sterlings *n* ▷ sterling
stern¹ *adj* (-er, -est) severe, strict > **sternly** *adv* > **sternness** *n* (*pl* -es)
stern² *n* (*pl* -s) rear part of a ship
sterna *n* ▷ sternum
sterner *adj* ▷ stern¹
sternest *adj* ▷ stern¹
sternly *adv* ▷ stern¹
sternness *n* ▷ stern¹
sternnesses *n* ▷ stern¹
sterns *n* ▷ stern²
sternum *n* (*pl* -na, -nums) ▷ breastbone
sternums *n* ▷ sternum
steroid *n* (*pl* -s) organic compound containing a carbon ring system, such as many hormones
steroids *n* ▷ steroid
stethoscope *n* (*pl* -s) medical instrument for listening to sounds made inside the body
stethoscopes *n* ▷ stethoscope
stevedore *n* (*pl* -s) person who loads and unloads ships
stevedores *n* ▷ stevedore

stew *n* (*pl* -s) food cooked slowly in a closed pot ▶ *v* (-s, -ing, -ed) cook slowly in a closed pot
steward *n* (*pl* -s) person who looks after passengers on a ship or aircraft > **stewardess** *n fem* (*pl* -es)
 stewardess *n* ▷ steward
 stewardesses *n* ▷ steward
 stewards *n* ▷ steward
 stewed *v* ▷ stew
 stewing *v* ▷ stew
 stews *n, v* ▷ stew
stick[1] *n* (*pl* -s) long thin piece of wood
stick[2] *v* (-s, -ing, stuck) push (a pointed object) into (something)
sticker *n* (*pl* -s) adhesive label or sign
 stickers *n* ▷ sticker
 stickier *adj* ▷ sticky
 stickiest *adj* ▷ sticky
 sticking *v* ▷ stick[2]
stickleback *n* (*pl* -s) small fish with sharp spines on its back
 sticklebacks *n* ▷ stickleback
stickler *n* (*pl* -s) person who insists on something
 sticklers *n* ▷ stickler
 sticks *n* ▷ stick[1] ▶ *v* ▷ stick[2]
stickup *n* (*pl* -s) (*Slang*) robbery at gunpoint
 stickups *n* ▷ stickup
sticky *adj* (-ckier, -ckiest) covered with an adhesive substance
 sties *n* ▷ sty
stiff *adj* (-er, -est) not easily bent or moved ▶ *n* (*pl* -s) (*Slang*) corpse > **stiffly** *adv* > **stiffness** *n* (*pl* -es)
stiffen *v* (-s, -ing, -ed) make or become stiff
 stiffened *v* ▷ stiffen
 stiffening *v* ▷ stiffen
 stiffens *v* ▷ stiffen
 stiffer *adj* ▷ stiff
 stiffest *adj* ▷ stiff
 stiffly *adv* ▷ stiff
 stiffness *n* ▷ stiff
 stiffnesses *n* ▷ stiff
 stiffs *n* ▷ stiff
stifle *v* (-les, -ling, -led) suppress
 stifled *v* ▷ stifle
 stifles *v* ▷ stifle
 stifling *v* ▷ stifle
stigma *n* (*pl* -mas, -mata) mark of social disgrace
 stigmas *n* ▷ stigma
stigmata *pl n* marks resembling the wounds of the crucified Christ ▶ *n* ▷ stigma
stigmatize *v* (-zes, -zing, -zed) mark as being shameful

 stigmatized *v* ▷ stigmatize
 stigmatizes *v* ▷ stigmatize
 stigmatizing *v* ▷ stigmatize
stile *n* (*pl* -s) set of steps allowing people to climb a fence
 stiles *n* ▷ stile
stiletto *n* (*pl* -s) high narrow heel on a woman's shoe
 stilettos *n* ▷ stiletto
still[1] *adv* now or in the future as before ▶ *adj* (-er, -est) motionless ▶ *n* (*pl* -s) photograph from a film scene ▶ *v* (-s, -ing, -ed) make still > **stillness** *n* (*pl* -es)
still[2] *n* (*pl* -s) apparatus for distilling alcoholic drinks
stillborn *adj* born dead
 stilled *v* ▷ still[1]
 stiller *adj* ▷ still[1]
 stillest *adj* ▷ still[1]
 stilling *v* ▷ still[1]
 stillness *n* ▷ still[1]
 stillnesses *n* ▷ still[1]
 stills *n* ▷ still[1, 2] ▶ *v* ▷ still[1]
stilted *adj* stiff and formal in manner
stilts *pl n* pair of poles with footrests for walking raised from the ground
stimulant *n* (*pl* -s) something, such as a drug, that acts as a stimulus
 stimulants *n* ▷ stimulant
stimulate *v* (-tes, -ting, -ted) act as a stimulus (on) > **stimulation** *n* (*pl* -s)
 stimulated *v* ▷ stimulate
 stimulates *v* ▷ stimulate
 stimulating *v* ▷ stimulate
 stimulation *n* ▷ stimulate
 stimulations *n* ▷ stimulate
 stimuli *n* ▷ stimulus
stimulus *n* (*pl* -li) something that rouses a person or thing to activity
sting *v* (-s, -ing, stung) (of certain animals or plants) wound by injecting with poison ▶ *n* (*pl* -s) wound or pain caused by or as if by stinging
 stingier *adj* ▷ stingy
 stingiest *adj* ▷ stingy
 stinginess *n* ▷ stingy
 stinginesses *n* ▷ stingy
 stinging *v* ▷ sting
 stings *v, n* ▷ sting
stingy *adj* (-gier, -giest) mean or miserly > **stinginess** *n* (*pl* -es)
stink *n* (*pl* -s) strong unpleasant smell ▶ *v* (-s, -ing, stank or stunk) (stunk) give off a strong unpleasant smell
 stinking *v* ▷ stink

stinks n, v ▷ stink

stint v (-s, -ing, -ed) (foll. by **on**) be miserly with (something) ▶ n (pl -s) allotted amount of work

stinted v ▷ stint

stinting v ▷ stint

stints v, n ▷ stint

stipend [sty-pend] n (pl -s) regular allowance or salary, esp. that paid to a clergyman
> **stipendiary** adj receiving a stipend

stipendiary adj ▷ stipend

stipends n ▷ stipend

stipple v (-les, -ling, -led) paint, draw, or engrave using dots

stippled v ▷ stipple

stipples v ▷ stipple

stippling v ▷ stipple

stipulate v (-tes, -ting, -ted) specify as a condition of an agreement > **stipulation** n (pl -s)

stipulated v ▷ stipulate

stipulates v ▷ stipulate

stipulating v ▷ stipulate

stipulation n ▷ stipulate

stipulations n ▷ stipulate

stir v (-s, -rring, -rred) mix up (a liquid) by moving a spoon etc. around in it ▶ n (pl -s) a stirring

stirred v ▷ stir

stirring v ▷ stir

stirrup n (pl -s) metal loop attached to a saddle for supporting a rider's foot

stirrups n ▷ stirrup

stirs v, n ▷ stir

stitch n (pl -es) link made by drawing thread through material with a needle ▶ v (-es, -ing, -ed) sew

stitched v ▷ stitch

stitches n, v ▷ stitch

stitching v ▷ stitch

stoat n (pl -s) small mammal of the weasel family, with brown fur that turns white in winter

stoats n ▷ stoat

stock n (pl -s) total amount of goods available for sale in a shop ▶ adj kept in stock, standard ▶ v (-s, -ing, -ed) keep for sale or future use

stockade n (pl -s) enclosure or barrier made of stakes

stockades n ▷ stockade

stockbroker n (pl -s) person who buys and sells stocks and shares for customers

stockbrokers n ▷ stockbroker

stocked v ▷ stock

stockier adj ▷ stocky

stockiest adj ▷ stocky

stocking n (pl -s) close-fitting covering for the foot and leg ▶ v ▷ stock

stockings n ▷ stocking

stockist n (pl -s) dealer who stocks a particular product

stockists n ▷ stockist

stockpile v (-les, -ling, -led) store a large quantity of (something) for future use ▶ n (pl -s) accumulated store

stockpiled v ▷ stockpile

stockpiles v, n ▷ stockpile

stockpiling v ▷ stockpile

stocks n pl (HIST) instrument of punishment consisting of a wooden frame with holes into which the hands and feet of the victim were locked ▶ n, v ▷ stock

stocktaking n (pl -s) counting and valuing of the goods in a shop

stocktakings n ▷ stocktaking

stocky adj (-ckier, -ckiest) (of a person) broad and sturdy

stodge n (pl -s) (BRIT, AUST & NZ) heavy starchy food

stodges n ▷ stodge

stodgier adj ▷ stodgy

stodgiest adj ▷ stodgy

stodgy adj (-gier, -giest) (of food) heavy and starchy

stoep [stoop] n (pl -s) (S AFR) verandah

stoeps n ▷ stoep

stoic [stow-ik] n (pl -s) person who suffers hardship without showing his or her feelings ▶ adj (also **stoical**) suffering hardship without showing one's feelings > **stoically** adv > **stoicism** [stow-iss-izz-um] n (pl -s)

stoical adj ▷ stoic

stoically adv ▷ stoic

stoicism n ▷ stoic

stoicisms n ▷ stoic

stoics n ▷ stoic

stoke v (-kes, -king, -ked) feed and tend (a fire or furnace) > **stoker** n (pl -s)

stoked v ▷ stoke

stoker n ▷ stoke

stokers n ▷ stoke

stokes v ▷ stoke

stoking v ▷ stoke

stole¹ v ▷ steal

stole² n (pl -s) long scarf or shawl

stolen v ▷ steal

stoles n ▷ stole²

stolid adj (-er, -est) showing little emotion or interest > **stolidly** adv

stolider adj ▷ stolid

stolidest adj ▷ stolid
stolidly adv ▷ stolid
stomach n (pl -s) organ in the body which digests food ▶ v (-s, -ing, -ed) put up with
stomached v ▷ stomach
stomaching v ▷ stomach
stomachs n, v ▷ stomach
stomp v (-s, -ing, -ed) (Informal) tread heavily
stomped v ▷ stomp
stomping v ▷ stomp
stomps v ▷ stomp
stone n (pl -s) material of which rocks are made ▶ v (-nes, -ning, -ned) throw stones at
stoned adj (Slang) under the influence of alcohol or drugs ▶ v ▷ stone
stones n, v ▷ stone
stonewall v (-s, -ing, -ed) obstruct or hinder discussion
stonewalled v ▷ stonewall
stonewalling v ▷ stonewall
stonewalls v ▷ stonewall
stoneware n (pl -s) hard kind of pottery fired at a very high temperature
stonewares n ▷ stoneware
stonier adj ▷ stony
stoniest adj ▷ stony
stonily adv ▷ stony
stoning v ▷ stone
stony adj (-nier, -niest) of or like stone
> **stonily** adv
stood v ▷ stand
stooge n (pl -es) actor who feeds lines to a comedian or acts as the butt of his jokes
stooges n ▷ stooge
stool n (pl -s) chair without arms or back
stools n ▷ stool
stoop v (-s, -ing, -ed) bend (the body) forward and downward ▶ n (pl -s) stooping posture
stooped v ▷ stoop
stooping v ▷ stoop
stoops v, n ▷ stoop
stop v (-s, -pping, -pped) cease or cause to cease from doing (something) ▶ n (pl -s) stopping or being stopped > **stoppage** n (pl -s)
stopcock n (pl -s) valve to control or stop the flow of fluid in a pipe
stopcocks n ▷ stopcock
stopgap n (pl -s) temporary substitute
stopgaps n ▷ stopgap
stopover n (pl -s) short break in a journey
stopovers n ▷ stopover
stoppage n ▷ stop
stoppages n ▷ stop
stopped v ▷ stop
stopper n (pl -s) plug for closing a bottle etc.

stoppers n ▷ stopper
stopping v ▷ stop
stops v, n ▷ stop
stopwatch n (pl -es) watch which can be stopped instantly for exact timing of a sporting event
stopwatches n ▷ stopwatch
storage n (pl -s) storing
storages n ▷ storage
store v (-res, -ring, -red) collect and keep (things) for future use ▶ n (pl -s) shop
stored v ▷ store
stores v, n ▷ store ▶ n pl stock of provisions
storey n (pl -s) floor or level of a building
storeys n ▷ storey
stories n ▷ story
storing v ▷ store
stork n (pl -s) large wading bird
storks n ▷ stork
storm n (pl -s) violent weather with wind, rain, or snow ▶ v (-s, -ing, -ed) attack or capture (a place) suddenly
stormed v ▷ storm
stormier adj ▷ stormy
stormiest adj ▷ stormy
storming v ▷ storm
storms n, v ▷ storm
stormy adj (-mier, -miest) characterized by storms
story n (pl -ries) description of a series of events told or written for entertainment
stoup [stoop] n (pl -s) small basin for holy water
stoups n ▷ stoup
stout adj (-er, -est) fat ▶ n (pl -s) strong dark beer > **stoutly** adv
stouter adj ▷ stout
stoutest adj ▷ stout
stoutly adv ▷ stout
stouts n ▷ stout
stove n (pl -s) apparatus for cooking or heating
stoves n ▷ stove
stow v (-s, -ing, -ed) pack or store
stowaway n (pl -s) person who hides on a ship or aircraft in order to travel free
stowaways n ▷ stowaway
stowed v ▷ stow
stowing v ▷ stow
stows v ▷ stow
straddle v (-les, -ling, -led) have one leg or part on each side of (something)
straddled v ▷ straddle
straddles v ▷ straddle
straddling v ▷ straddle
strafe v (-fes, -fing, -fed) attack (an enemy) with machine guns from the air

strafed v ▷ strafe
strafes v ▷ strafe
strafing v ▷ strafe
straggle v (-les, -ling, -led) go or spread in a rambling or irregular way ▶ **straggler** n (pl -s) > **straggly** adj (-lier, -liest)
straggled v ▷ straggle
straggler n ▷ straggle
stragglers n ▷ straggle
straggles v ▷ straggle
stragglier adj ▷ straggle
straggliest adj ▷ straggle
straggling v ▷ straggle
straggly adj ▷ straggle
straight adj (-er, -est) not curved or crooked ▶ adv in a straight line ▶ n (pl -s) straight part, esp. of a racetrack > **straighten** v (-s, -ing, -ed)
straightaway adv immediately
straighten v ▷ straight
straightened v ▷ straight
straightening v ▷ straight
straightens v ▷ straighn
straighter adj ▷ straight
straightest adj ▷ straight
straightforward adj honest, frank
straightlaced adj ▷ straitlaced
straights n ▷ straight
strain¹ v (-s, -ing, -ed) cause (something) to be used or tested beyond its limits ▶ n (pl -s) tension or tiredness
strain² n (pl -s) breed or race
strained adj not natural, forced ▶ v ▷ strain¹
strainer n (pl -s) sieve
strainers n ▷ strainer
straining v ▷ strain¹
strains n ▷ strain¹, ² ▶ v ▷ strain¹
strait n (pl -s) position of acute difficulty
straitened adj not having much money
straitjacket n (pl -s) strong jacket with long sleeves used to bind the arms of a violent person
straitjackets n ▷ straitjacket
straitlaced, straightlaced adj prudish or puritanical
straits n ▷ strait ▶ n pl narrow channel connecting two areas of sea
strand¹ v (-s, -ing, -ed) run aground ▶ n (pl -s) (Poetic) shore
strand² n (pl -s) single thread of string, wire, etc.
stranded v ▷ strand¹
stranding v ▷ strand¹
strands n ▷ strand¹, ² ▶ v ▷ strand¹
strange adj (-r, -st) odd or unusual > **strangely** adv > **strangeness** n (pl -es)

strangely adv ▷ strange
strangeness n ▷ strange
strangenesses n ▷ strange
stranger n (pl -s) person who is not known or is new to a place or experience ▶ adj ▷ strange
strangers n ▷ stranger
strangest adj ▷ strange
strangle v (-les, -ling, -led) kill by squeezing the throat > **strangler** n (pl -s)
strangled v ▷ strangle
stranglehold n (pl -s) strangling grip in wrestling
strangleholds n ▷ stranglehold
strangler n ▷ strangle
stranglers n ▷ strangle
strangles v ▷ strangle
strangling v ▷ strangle
strangulation n (pl -s) strangling
strangulations n ▷ strangulation
strap n (pl -s) strip of flexible material for lifting, fastening, or holding in place ▶ v (-s, -pping, -pped) fasten with a strap or straps
strapped n ▷ strap
strapping adj tall and sturdy ▶ v ▷ strap
straps n, v ▷ strap
strata n ▷ stratum
stratagem n (pl -s) clever plan, trick
stratagems n ▷ stratagem
strategic [strat-ee-jik] adj advantageous > **strategically** adv
strategically adv ▷ strategic
strategies n ▷ strategy
strategist n ▷ strategy
strategists n ▷ strategy
strategy n (pl -gies) overall plan > **strategist** n (pl -s)
strathspey n (pl -s) Scottish dance with gliding steps
strathspeys n ▷ strathspey
stratification n ▷ stratified
stratifications n ▷ stratified
stratified adj divided into strata > **stratification** n (pl -s)
stratosphere n (pl -s) atmospheric layer between about 15 and 50 kilometres above the earth
stratospheres n ▷ stratosphere
stratum [strah-tum] n (pl -ta) layer, esp. of rock
straw n (pl -s) dried stalks of grain
strawberries n ▷ strawberry
strawberry n (pl -ries) sweet fleshy red fruit with small seeds on the outside
straws n ▷ straw
stray v (-s, -ing, -ed) wander ▶ adj having strayed ▶ n (pl -s) stray animal

strayed v ▷ stray

straying v ▷ stray

strays v, n ▷ stray

streak n (pl -s) long band of contrasting colour or substance ▶ v (-s, -ing, -ed) mark with streaks > **streaker** n (pl -s) > **streaky** adj (-kier, -kiest)

streaked v ▷ streak

streaker n ▷ streak

streakers n ▷ streak

streakier adj ▷ streak

streakiest adj ▷ streak

streaking v ▷ streak

streaks n, v ▷ streak

streaky adj ▷ streak

stream n (pl -s) small river ▶ v (-s, -ing, -ed) flow steadily

streamed v ▷ stream

streamer n (pl -s) strip of coloured paper that unrolls when tossed

streamers n ▷ streamer

streaming v ▷ stream

streamline v (-nes, -ning, -ned) make more efficient by simplifying

streamlined v ▷ streamline

streamlines v ▷ streamline

streamlining v ▷ streamline

streams n, v ▷ stream

street n (pl -s) public road, usu. lined with buildings

streetcar n (us) tram

streetcars n ▷ streetcar

streets n ▷ street

streetwise adj knowing how to survive in big cities

strength n (pl -s) quality of being strong > **strengthen** v (-s, -ing, -ed)

strengthen v ▷ strength

strengthened v ▷ strength

strengthening v ▷ strength

strengthens v ▷ strength

strengths n ▷ strength

strenuous adj requiring great energy or effort > **strenuously** adv

strenuously adv ▷ strenuous

streptococci n ▷ streptococcus

streptococcus [strep-toe-kok-uss] n (pl -cocci) bacterium occurring in chains, many species of which cause disease

stress n (pl -es) tension or strain ▶ v (-es, -ing, -ed) emphasize

stressed v ▷ stress

stresses n, v ▷ stress

stressing v ▷ stress

stretch v (-es, -ing, -ed) extend or be extended

▶ n (pl -es) stretching > **stretchy** adj (-chier, -chiest)

stretched v ▷ stretch

stretcher n (pl -s) frame covered with canvas, on which an injured person is carried

stretchers n ▷ stretcher

stretches v, n ▷ stretch

stretchier adj ▷ stretch

stretchiest adj ▷ stretch

stretching v ▷ stretch

stretchy adj ▷ stretch

strew v (-s, -ing, -ed or strewn) scatter (things) over a surface

strewed v ▷ strew

strewing v ▷ strew

strewn v ▷ strew

strews v ▷ strew

striated adj having a pattern of scratches or grooves

stricken adj seriously affected by disease, grief, pain, etc.

strict adj (-er, -est) stern or severe > **strictly** adv > **strictness** n (pl -es)

stricter adj ▷ strict

strictest adj ▷ strict

strictly adv ▷ strict

strictness n ▷ strict

strictnesses n ▷ strict

stricture n (pl -s) severe criticism

strictures n ▷ stricture

stridden v ▷ stride

stride v (-des, -ding, strode, stridden) walk with long steps ▶ n (pl -s) long step

stridencies n ▷ strident

stridency n ▷ strident

strident adj loud and harsh > **stridently** adv > **stridency** n (pl -cies)

stridently adv ▷ strident

strides v, n ▷ stride ▶ n pl progress

striding v ▷ stride

strife n (pl -s) conflict, quarrelling

strifes n ▷ strife

strike v (-kes, -king, struck) cease work as a protest ▶ n (pl -s) stoppage of work as a protest

striker n (pl -s) striking worker

strikers n ▷ striker

strikes v, n ▷ strike

striking adj impressive ▶ v ▷ strike

string n (pl -s) thin cord used for tying ▶ v (-s, -ing, strung) provide with a string or strings

stringed adj (of a musical instrument) having strings that are plucked or played with a bow

stringencies n ▷ stringent

stringency n ▷ stringent

stringent [strin-jent] *adj* strictly controlled or enforced ▷ **stringently** *adv* ▷ **stringency** *n* (*pl* -cies)

stringently *adv* ▷ stringent

stringier *adj* ▷ stringy

stringiest *adj* ▷ stringy

stringing *v* ▷ string

strings *n, v* ▷ string ▶ *n pl* restrictions or conditions

stringy *adj* (-gier, -giest) like string

stringybark *n* (*pl* -s) Australian eucalyptus with a fibrous bark

stringybarks *n* ▷ stringybark

strip¹ *v* (-s, -pping, -pped) take (the covering or clothes) off

strip² *n* (*pl* -s) long narrow piece

stripe *n* (*pl* -s) long narrow band of contrasting colour or substance ▷ **striped, stripy, stripey** *adj* (-pier, -piest)

striped *adj* ▷ stripe

stripes *n* ▷ stripe

stripey *adj* ▷ stripe

stripier *adj* ▷ stripe

stripiest *adj* ▷ stripe

stripling *n* (*pl* -s) youth

striplings *n* ▷ stripling

stripped *v* ▷ strip¹

stripper *n* (*pl* -s) person who performs a striptease

strippers *n* ▷ stripper

stripping *v* ▷ strip¹

strips *v* ▷ strip¹ ▶ *n* ▷ strip²

striptease *n* (*pl* -s) entertainment in which a performer undresses to music

stripteases *n* ▷ striptease

stripy *adj* ▷ stripe

strive *v* (-ves, -ving, strove, striven) make a great effort

striven *v* ▷ strive

strives *v* ▷ strive

striving *v* ▷ strive

strobe *n* (*pl* -s) ▷ stroboscope

strobes *n* ▷ strobe

stroboscope *n* (*pl* -s) instrument producing a very bright flashing light

stroboscopes *n* ▷ stroboscope

strode *v* ▷ stride

stroke *v* (-kes, -king, -ked) touch or caress lightly with the hand ▶ *n* (*pl* -s) light touch or caress with the hand

stroked *v* ▷ stroke

strokes *v, n* ▷ stroke

stroking *v* ▷ stroke

stroll *v* (-s, -ing, -ed) walk in a leisurely manner ▶ *n* (*pl* -s) leisurely walk

strolled *v* ▷ stroll

strolling *v* ▷ stroll

strolls *v, n* ▷ stroll

strong *adj* (-er, -est) having physical power ▷ **strongly** *adv*

stronger *adj* ▷ strong

strongest *adj* ▷ strong

stronghold *n* (*pl* -s) area of predominance of a particular belief

strongholds *n* ▷ stronghold

strongly *adv* ▷ strong

strongnesses *n* ▷ strong

strongroom *n* (*pl* -s) room designed for the safekeeping of valuables

strongrooms *n* ▷ strongroom

strontium *n* (*pl* -s) (CHEM) silvery-white metallic element

strontiums *n* ▷ strontium

strop *n* (*pl* -s) leather strap for sharpening razors

stroppier *adj* ▷ stroppy

stroppiest *adj* ▷ stroppy

stroppy *adj* (-pier, -piest) (*Slang*) angry or awkward

strops *n* ▷ strop

strove *v* ▷ strive

struck *v* ▷ strike

structural *adj* ▷ structure

structuralism *n* (*pl* -s) approach to literature, etc., which sees changes in the subject as caused and organized by a hidden set of universal rules ▷ **structuralist** *n* (*pl* -s) *adj*

structuralisms *n* ▷ structuralism

structuralist *n, adj* ▷ structuralism

structuralists *n* ▷ structuralism

structure *n* (*pl* -s) complex construction ▶ *v* (-res, -ring, -red) give a structure to ▷ **structural** *adj*

structured *v* ▷ structure

structures *n, v* ▷ structure

structuring *v* ▷ structure

strudel *n* (*pl* -s) thin sheet of filled dough rolled up and baked, usu. with an apple filling

strudels *n* ▷ strudel

struggle *v* (-les, -ling, -led) work, strive, or make one's way with difficulty ▶ *n* (*pl* -s) striving

struggled *v* ▷ struggle

struggles *v, n* ▷ struggle

struggling *v* ▷ struggle

strum *v* (-s, -mming, -mmed) play (a guitar or banjo) by sweeping the thumb or a plectrum across the strings

strummed *v* ▷ strum

strumming *v* ▷ strum

strumpet n (pl -s) (Old-fashioned) prostitute
  strumpets n ▷ strumpet
  strums v ▷ strum
  strung v ▷ string
strut v (-s, -tting, -tted) walk pompously, swagger ▶ n (pl -s) bar supporting a structure
  struts v, n ▷ strut
  strutted v ▷ strut
  strutting v ▷ strut
strychnine [strik-neen] n (pl -s) very poisonous drug used in small quantities as a stimulant
  strychnines n ▷ strychnine
stub n (pl -s) short piece left after use ▶ v (-s, -bbing, -bbed) strike (the toe) painfully against an object
  stubbed v ▷ stub
  stubbier adj ▷ stubby
  stubbiest adj ▷ stubby
  stubbing v ▷ stub
stubble n (pl -s) short stalks of grain left in a field after reaping > **stubbly** adj (-lier, -liest)
  stubbles n ▷ stubble
  stubblier adj ▷ stubble
  stubbliest adj ▷ stubble
  stubbly adj ▷ stubble
stubborn adj (-er, -est) refusing to agree or give in > **stubbornly** adv > **stubbornness** n (pl -es)
  stubborner adj ▷ stubborn
  stubbornest adj ▷ stubborn
  stubbornly adv ▷ stubborn
  stubbornness n ▷ stubborn
  stubbornnesses n ▷ stubborn
stubby adj (-bbier, -bbiest) short and broad
  stubs n, v ▷ stub
stucco n (pl -oes) plaster used for coating or decorating walls
  stuccoes n ▷ stucco
  stuck v ▷ stick[2]
stud[1] n (pl -s) small piece of metal attached to a surface for decoration ▶ v (-s, -dding, -dded) set with studs
  studded v ▷ stud[1]
  studding v ▷ stud[1]
stud[2] n (pl -s) male animal, esp. a stallion, kept for breeding
  student n (pl -s) person who studies a subject, esp. at university
  students n ▷ student
studied adj carefully practised or planned ▶ v ▷ study
  studies v, n ▷ study
studio n (pl -s) workroom of an artist or photographer
  studios n ▷ studio

studious adj fond of study > **studiously** adv
  studiously adv ▷ studious
  studs n ▷ stud[1, 2] ▶ v ▷ stud[1]
study v (-dies, -dying, -died) be engaged in learning (a subject) ▶ n (pl -dies) act or process of studying
  studying v ▷ study
stuff n (pl -s) substance or material ▶ v (-s, -ing, -ed) pack, cram, or fill completely
  stuffed v ▷ stuff
  stuffier adj ▷ stuffy
  stuffiest adj ▷ stuffy
stuffing n (pl -s) seasoned mixture with which food is stuffed ▶ v ▷ stuff
  stuffings n ▷ stuffing
  stuffs n, v ▷ stuff
stuffy adj (-ffier, -ffiest) lacking fresh air
stultifying adj very boring and repetitive
stumble v (-les, -ling, -led) trip and nearly fall ▶ n (pl -s) stumbling
  stumbled v ▷ stumble
  stumbles n ▷ stumble
  stumbling v ▷ stumble
stump n (pl -s) base of a tree left when the main trunk has been cut away ▶ v (-s, -ing, -ed) baffle
  stumped v ▷ stump
  stumpier adj ▷ stumpy
  stumpiest adj ▷ stumpy
  stumping v ▷ stump
  stumps n, v ▷ stump
stumpy adj (-pier, -piest) short and thick
stun v (-s, -nning, -nned) shock or overwhelm
  stung v ▷ sting
  stunk v ▷ stink
  stunned v ▷ stun
stunning adj very attractive or impressive ▶ v ▷ stun
  stuns v ▷ stun
stunt[1] v (-ts, -ing, -ed) prevent or impede the growth of > **stunted** adj
stunt[2] n (pl -s) acrobatic or dangerous action
  stunted v, adj ▷ stunt[1]
  stunting v ▷ stunt[1]
  stunts v ▷ stunt[1] ▶ n ▷ stunt[2]
  stupefaction n ▷ stupefy
  stupefactions n ▷ stupefy
  stupefied v ▷ stupefy
  stupefies v ▷ stupefy
stupefy v (-fies, -fying, -fied) make insensitive or lethargic > **stupefaction** n (pl -s)
  stupefying v ▷ stupefy
stupendous adj very large or impressive > **stupendously** adv
  stupendously adv ▷ stupendous

stupid *adj* (-er, -est) lacking intelligence
> **stupidity** *n* (*pl* -ties) > **stupidly** *adv*
stupider *adj* ▷ stupid
stupidest *adj* ▷ stupid
stupidities *n* ▷ stupid
stupidity *n* ▷ stupid
stupidly *adv* ▷ stupid
stupor *n* (*pl* -s) dazed or unconscious state
stupors *n* ▷ stupor
sturdier *adj* ▷ sturdy
sturdiest *adj* ▷ sturdy
sturdily *adv* ▷ sturdy
sturdy *adj* (-dier, -diest) healthy and robust
> **sturdily** *adv*
sturgeon *n* (*pl* -s) fish from which caviar is
obtained
sturgeons *n* ▷ sturgeon
stutter *v* (-s, -ing, -ed) speak with repetition
of initial consonants ▶ *n* (*pl* -s) tendency to
stutter
stuttered *v* ▷ stutter
stuttering *v* ▷ stutter
stutters *v*, *n* ▷ stutter
sty *n* (*pl* sties) pen for pigs
stye *n* (*pl* styes) inflammation at the base of
an eyelash
styes *n* ▷ stye
style *n* (*pl* -s) shape or design ▶ *v* (-les, -ling,
-led) shape or design
styled *v* ▷ style
styles *n*, *v* ▷ style
styli *n* ▷ stylus
styling *v* ▷ style
stylish *adj* smart, elegant, and fashionable
> **stylishly** *adv*
stylishly *adv* ▷ stylish
stylist *n* (*pl* -s) hairdresser
stylistic *adj* of literary or artistic style
stylists *n* ▷ stylist
stylize *v* (-zes, -zing, -zed) cause to conform to
an established stylistic form
stylized *v* ▷ stylize
stylizes *v* ▷ stylize
stylizing *v* ▷ stylize
stylus *n* (*pl* -li, -luses) needle-like device on a
record player that rests in the groove of the
record and picks up the sound signals
styluses *n* ▷ stylus
stymie *v* (-mies, -mieing, -mied) hinder or
thwart
stymied *v* ▷ stymie
stymieing *v* ▷ stymie
stymies *v* ▷ stymie
styptic *n* (*pl* -s) ▶ *adj* (drug) used to stop
bleeding

styptics *n* ▷ styptic
suave [swahv] *adj* smooth and sophisticated in
manner > **suavely** *adv*
suavely *adv* ▷ suave
sub *n* (*pl* -s) subeditor ▶ *v* (-s, -bbing, -bbed) act
as a substitute
subaltern *n* (*pl* -s) British army officer below
the rank of captain
subalterns *n* ▷ subaltern
subatomic *adj* of or being one of the particles
which make up an atom
subbed *v* ▷ sub
subbing *v* ▷ sub
subcommittee *n* (*pl* -s) small committee
formed from some members of a larger
committee
subcommittees *n* ▷ subcommittee
subconscious *adj* happening or existing
without one's awareness ▶ *n* (*pl* -es)
(PSYCHOANALYSIS) that part of the mind of which
one is not aware but which can influence
one's behaviour > **subconsciously** *adv*
subconsciouses *n* ▷ subconscious
subconsciously *adv* ▷ subconscious
subcontinent *n* (*pl* -s) large land mass that is a
distinct part of a continent
subcontinents *n* ▷ subcontinent
subcontract *n* (*pl* -s) secondary contract by
which the main contractor for a job puts
work out to others ▶ *v* (-s, -ing, -ed) put out
(work) on a subcontract > **subcontractor**
n (*pl* -s)
subcontracted *v* ▷ subcontract
subcontracting *v* ▷ subcontract
subcontractor *n* ▷ subcontract
subcontractors *n* ▷ subcontract
subcontracts *n*, *v* ▷ subcontract
subcutaneous [sub-cute-**ayn**-ee-uss] *adj* under
the skin
subdivide *v* (-des, -ding, -ded) divide (a part of
something) into smaller parts > **subdivision**
n (*pl* -s)
subdivided *v* ▷ subdivide
subdivides *v* ▷ subdivide
subdividing *v* ▷ subdivide
subdivision *n* ▷ subdivide
subdivisions *n* ▷ subdivide
subdue *v* (-dues, -duing, -dued) overcome
subdued *v* ▷ subdue
subdues *v* ▷ subdue
subduing *v* ▷ subdue
subeditor *n* (*pl* -s) person who checks and
edits text for a newspaper or magazine
subeditors *n* ▷ subeditor
subject *n* (*pl* -s) person or thing being dealt

with or studied ▶ *adj* being under the rule of a monarch or government ▶ *v* (-s, -ing, -ed) (*foll. by* **to**) cause to undergo > **subjection** *n* (*pl* -s)

subjected *v* ▷ subject

subjecting *v* ▷ subject

subjection *n* ▷ subject

subjections *n* ▷ subject

subjective *adj* based on personal feelings or prejudices > **subjectively** *adv*

subjectively *adv* ▷ subjective

subjects *n, v* ▷ subject

subjugate *v* (-tes, -ting, -ted) bring (a group of people) under one's control > **subjugation** *n* (*pl* -s)

subjugated *v* ▷ subjugate

subjugates *v* ▷ subjugate

subjugating *v* ▷ subjugate

subjugation *n* ▷ subjugate

subjugations *n* ▷ subjugate

subjunctive (GRAMMAR) *n* (*pl* -s) mood of verbs used when the content of the clause is doubted, supposed, or wished ▶ *adj* in or of that mood

subjunctives *n* ▷ subjunctive

sublet *v* (-s, -letting, -let) rent out (property rented from someone else)

sublets *v* ▷ sublet

subletting *v* ▷ sublet

sublimate *v* (-tes, -ting, -ted) (PSYCHOL) direct the energy of (a strong desire, esp. a sexual one) into socially acceptable activities > **sublimation** *n* (*pl* -s)

sublimated *v* ▷ sublimate

sublimates *v* ▷ sublimate

sublimating *v* ▷ sublimate

sublimation *n* ▷ sublimate

sublimations *n* ▷ sublimate

sublime *adj* (-r, -st) of high moral, intellectual, or spiritual value ▶ *v* (-mes, -ming, -med) (CHEM) change from a solid to a vapour without first melting > **sublimely** *adv*

sublimed *v* ▷ sublime

sublimely *adv* ▷ sublime

sublimer *adj* ▷ sublime

sublimes *v* ▷ sublime

sublimest *adj* ▷ sublime

subliminal *adj* relating to mental processes of which the individual is not aware

subliming *v* ▷ sublime

submarine *n* (*pl* -s) vessel which can operate below the surface of the sea ▶ *adj* below the surface of the sea

submarines *n* ▷ submarine

submerge *v* (-ges, -ging, -ged) put or go below the surface of water or other liquid

> **submersion** *n* (*pl* -s)

submerged *v* ▷ submerge

submerges *v* ▷ submerge

submerging *v* ▷ submerge

submersion *n* ▷ submerge

submersions *n* ▷ submerge

submission *n* (*pl* -s) submitting

submissions *n* ▷ submission

submissive *adj* meek and obedient

submit *v* (-s, -tting, -tted) surrender

submits *v* ▷ submit

submitted *v* ▷ submit

submitting *v* ▷ submit

subordinate *adj* of lesser rank or importance ▶ *n* (*pl* -s) subordinate person or thing ▶ *v* (-tes, -ting, -ted) make or treat as subordinate > **subordination** *n* (*pl* -s)

subordinated *v* ▷ subordinate

subordinates *n, v* ▷ subordinate

subordinating *v* ▷ subordinate

subordination *n* ▷ subordinate

subordinations *n* ▷ subordinate

suborn *v* (-s, -ing, -ed) (*Formal*) bribe or incite (a person) to commit a wrongful act

suborned *v* ▷ suborn

suborning *v* ▷ suborn

suborns *v* ▷ suborn

subpoena [sub-**pee**-na] *n* (*pl* -s) writ requiring a person to appear before a law court ▶ *v* (-nas, -naing, -naed) summon (someone) with a subpoena

subpoenaed *v* ▷ subpoena

subpoenaing *v* ▷ subpoena

subpoenas *n, v* ▷ subpoena

subs *n, v* ▷ sub

subscribe *v* (-bes, -bing, -bed) pay (a subscription) > **subscriber** *n* (*pl* -s)

subscribed *v* ▷ subscribe

subscriber *n* ▷ subscribe

subscribers *n* ▷ subscribe

subscribes *v* ▷ subscribe

subscribing *v* ▷ subscribe

subscription *n* (*pl* -s) payment for issues of a publication over a period

subscriptions *n* ▷ subscription

subsection *n* (*pl* -s) division of a section

subsections *n* ▷ subsection

subsequent *adj* occurring after, succeeding > **subsequently** *adv*

subsequently *adv* ▷ subsequent

subservience *n* ▷ subservient

subserviences *n* ▷ subservient

subservient *adj* submissive, servile > **subservience** *n* (*pl* -s)

subside *v* (-des, -ding, -ded) become less

intense

subsided v ▷ subside

subsidence n (pl -s) act or process of subsiding

subsidences n ▷ subsidence

subsides v ▷ subside

subsidiaries n ▷ subsidiary

subsidiary adj of lesser importance ▶ n (pl -ries) subsidiary person or thing

subsidies n ▷ subsidy

subsiding v ▷ subside

subsidize v (-izes, -izing, -ized) help financially

subsidized v ▷ subsidize

subsidizes v ▷ subsidize

subsidizing v ▷ subsidize

subsidy n (pl -dies) financial aid

subsist v (-s, -ing, -ed) manage to live
> **subsistence** n (pl -s)

subsisted v ▷ subsist

subsistence n ▷ subsist

subsistences n ▷ subsist

subsisting v ▷ subsist

subsists v ▷ subsist

subsonic adj moving at a speed less than that of sound

substance n (pl -s) physical composition of something

substances n ▷ substance

substantial adj of considerable size or value
> **substantially** adv

substantially adv ▷ substantial

substantiate v (-tes, -ting, -ted) support (a story) with evidence > **substantiation** n (pl -s)

substantiated v ▷ substantiate

substantiates v ▷ substantiate

substantiating v ▷ substantiate

substantiation n ▷ substantiate

substantiations n ▷ substantiate

substantive n (pl -s) noun ▶ adj of or being the essential element of a thing

substantives n ▷ substantive

substitute v (-tes, -ting, -ted) take the place of or put in place of another ▶ n (pl -s) person or thing taking the place of (another)
> **substitution** n (pl -s)

substituted v ▷ substitute

substitutes v, n ▷ substitute

substituting v ▷ substitute

substitution n ▷ substitute

substitutions n ▷ substitute

subsume v (-mes, -ming, -med) include (an idea, case, etc.) under a larger classification or group

subsumed v ▷ subsume

subsumes v ▷ subsume

subsuming v ▷ subsume

subterfuge n (pl -s) trick used to achieve an objective

subterfuges n ▷ subterfuge

subterranean adj underground

subtitle n (pl -s) secondary title of a book ▶ v (-les, -ling, -led) provide with a subtitle or subtitles

subtitled v ▷ subtitle

subtitles v, n ▷ subtitle ▶ pl n printed translation at the bottom of the picture in a film with foreign dialogue

subtitling v ▷ subtitle

subtle adj (-r, -st) not immediately obvious
> **subtly** adv > **subtlety** n (pl -ties)

subtler adj ▷ subtle

subtlest adj ▷ subtle

subtleties n ▷ subtle

subtlety n ▷ subtle

subtly adv ▷ subtle

subtract v (-s, -ing, -ed) take (one number or quantity) from another > **subtraction** n (pl -s)

subtracted v ▷ subtract

subtracting v ▷ subtract

subtraction n ▷ subtract

subtractions n ▷ subtract

subtracts v ▷ subtract

subtropical adj of the regions bordering on the tropics

suburb n (pl -s) residential area on the outskirts of a city

suburban adj of or inhabiting a suburb

suburbia n (pl -s) suburbs and their inhabitants

suburbias n ▷ suburbia

suburbs n ▷ suburb

subvention n (pl -s) (Formal) subsidy

subventions n ▷ subvention

subversion n ▷ subvert

subversions n ▷ subvert

subversive adj, n ▷ subvert

subversives n ▷ subvert

subvert v (-s, -ing, -ed) overthrow the authority of > **subversion** n (pl -s)
> **subversive** adj, n (pl -s)

subverted v ▷ subvert

subverting v ▷ subvert

subverts v ▷ subvert

subway n (pl -s) passage under a road or railway

subways n ▷ subway

succeed v (-s, -ing, -ed) accomplish an aim

succeeded v ▷ succeed

succeeding v ▷ succeed

succeeds v ▷ succeed

success n (pl -es) achievement of something

attempted

successes n ▷ success

successful adj having success > **successfully** adv

successfully adv ▷ successful

succession n (pl -s) series of people or things following one another in order

successions n ▷ succession

successive adj consecutive > **successively** adv

successively adv ▷ successive

successor n (pl -s) person who succeeds someone in a position

successors n ▷ successor

succinct adj (-er, -est) brief and clear > **succinctly** adv

succincter adj ▷ succinct

succinctest adj ▷ succinct

succinctly adv ▷ succinct

succour v (-s, -ing, -ed) ▶ n (pl -s) help in distress

succoured v ▷ succour

succouring v ▷ succour

succours v, n ▷ succour

succulence n ▷ succulent

succulences n ▷ succulent

succulent adj juicy and delicious ▶ n (pl -s) succulent plant > **succulence** n (pl -s)

succulent n ▷ succulent

succulents n ▷ succulent

succumb v (-s, -ing, -ed) (foll. by **to**) give way (to something overpowering)

succumbed v ▷ succumb

succumbing v ▷ succumb

succumbs v ▷ succumb

such adj of the kind specified ▶ pron such things

suchlike pron such or similar things

suck v (-s, -ing, -ed) draw (liquid or air) into the mouth ▶ n (pl -s) sucking

sucked v ▷ suck

sucker n (pl -s) (Slang) person who is easily deceived or swindled

suckers n ▷ sucker

sucking v ▷ suck

suckle v (-les, -ling, -led) feed at the breast

suckled v ▷ suckle

suckles v ▷ suckle

suckling n (pl -s) unweaned baby or young animal ▶ v ▷ suckle

sucklings n ▷ suckling

sucks v, n ▷ suck

sucrose [soo-kroze] n (pl -s) chemical name for sugar

sucroses n ▷ sucrose

suction n (pl -s) sucking

suctions n ▷ suction

sudden adj done or occurring quickly and unexpectedly > **suddenly** adv > **suddenness** n (pl -es)

suddenly adv ▷ sudden

suddenness n ▷ suddenness

suddennesses n ▷ suddenness

sudorific [syoo-dor-**if**-ik] n (pl -s) ▶ adj (drug) causing sweating

sudorifics n ▷ sudorific

suds pl n froth of soap and water, lather

sue v (-ues, -uing, -ued) start legal proceedings against

sued v ▷ sue

suede n (pl -s) leather with a velvety finish on one side

suedes n ▷ suede

sues v ▷ sue

suet n (pl -s) hard fat obtained from sheep and cattle, used in cooking

suets n ▷ suet

suffer v (-s, -ing, -ed) undergo or be subjected to > **sufferer** n (pl -s) > **suffering** n (pl -s) > **sufferance** n (pl -s)

sufferance n ▷ suffer

sufferances n ▷ suffer

suffered v ▷ suffer

sufferer n ▷ suffer

sufferers n ▷ suffer

suffering n, v ▷ suffer

sufferings n ▷ suffer

suffers v ▷ suffer

suffice [suf-**fice**] v (-ces, -cing, -ced) be enough for a purpose

sufficed v ▷ suffice

suffices v ▷ suffice

sufficiencies n ▷ sufficiency

sufficiency n (pl -cies) adequate amount

sufficient adj enough, adequate > **sufficiently** adv

sufficiently adv ▷ sufficient

sufficing v ▷ suffice

suffix n (pl -es) letter or letters added to the end of a word to form another word, such as -s and -ness in dogs and softness

suffixes n ▷ suffix

suffocate v (-tes, -ting, -ted) kill or be killed by deprivation of oxygen > **suffocation** n (pl -s)

suffocated v ▷ suffocate

suffocates v ▷ suffocate

suffocating v ▷ suffocate

suffocation n ▷ suffocate

suffocations n ▷ suffocate

suffragan n (pl -s) bishop appointed to assist an archbishop

suffragans n ▷ suffragan
suffrage n (pl -s) right to vote in public elections
suffrages n ▷ suffrage
suffragette n (pl -s) (in Britain in the early 20th century) a woman who campaigned militantly for the right to vote
suffragettes n ▷ suffragette
suffuse v (-ses, -sing, -sed) spread through or over (something) > **suffusion** n (pl -s)
suffused v ▷ suffuse
suffuses v ▷ suffuse
suffusing v ▷ suffuse
suffusion n ▷ suffuse
suffusions n ▷ suffuse
sugar n (pl -s) sweet crystalline carbohydrate found in many plants and used to sweeten food and drinks ▶ v (-s, -ing, -ed) sweeten or cover with sugar > **sugary** adj (-rier, -riest)
sugared v ▷ sugar
sugarier adj ▷ sugar
sugariest adj ▷ sugar
sugaring v ▷ sugar
sugars n, v ▷ sugar
sugary adj ▷ sugar
suggest v (-s, -ing, -ed) put forward (an idea) for consideration
suggested v ▷ suggest
suggestible adj easily influenced
suggesting v ▷ suggest
suggestion n (pl -s) thing suggested
suggestions n ▷ suggestion
suggestive adj suggesting something indecent > **suggestively** adv
suggestively adv ▷ suggestive
suggests v ▷ suggest
suicidal adj liable to commit suicide > **suicidally** adv
suicidally adv ▷ suicide
suicide n (pl -s) killing oneself intentionally
suicides n ▷ suicide
suing v ▷ sue
suit n (pl -s) set of clothes designed to be worn together ▶ v (-s, -ing, -ed) be appropriate for
suitabilities n ▷ suitable
suitability n ▷ suitable
suitable adj appropriate or proper > **suitably** adv > **suitability** n (pl -ties)
suitably adv ▷ suitable
suitcase n (pl -s) portable travelling case for clothing
suitcases n ▷ suitcase
suite n (pl -s) set of connected rooms in a hotel
suited v ▷ suit
suites n ▷ suite

suiting v ▷ suit
suitor n (pl -s) (Old-fashioned) man who is courting a woman
suitors n ▷ suitor
suits n, v ▷ suit
sulk v (-s, -ing, -ed) be silent and sullen because of resentment or bad temper ▶ n (pl -s) resentful or sullen mood > **sulky** adj (-kier, -kiest) > **sulkily** adv
sulked v ▷ sulk
sulkier adj ▷ sulk
sulkiest adj ▷ sulk
sulkily adv ▷ sulk
sulking v ▷ sulk
sulks v, n ▷ sulk
sulky adj ▷ sulk
sullen adj (-er, -est) unwilling to talk or be sociable > **sullenly** adv > **sullenness** n (pl -es)
sullener adj ▷ sullen
sullenest adj ▷ sullen
sullenly adv ▷ sullen
sullenness n ▷ sullen
sullennesses n ▷ sullen
sullied v ▷ sully
sullies v ▷ sully
sully v (-lies, -lying, -lied) ruin (someone's reputation)
sullying v ▷ sully
sulphate n (pl -s) salt or ester of sulphuric acid
sulphates n ▷ sulphate
sulphide n (pl -s) compound of sulphur with another element
sulphides n ▷ sulphide
sulphite n (pl -s) salt or ester of sulphurous acid
sulphites n ▷ sulphite
sulphonamide [sulf-on-a-mide] n (pl -s) any of a class of drugs that prevent the growth of bacteria
sulphonamides n ▷ sulphonamide
sulphur n (pl -s) (CHEM) pale yellow nonmetallic element
sulphuric, sulphurous adj of or containing sulphur
sulphurous adj ▷ sulphuric
sulphurs n ▷ sulphur
sultan n (pl -s) sovereign of a Muslim country
sultana n (pl -s) kind of raisin
sultanas n ▷ sultana
sultanate n (pl -s) territory of a sultan
sultanates n ▷ sultanate
sultans n ▷ sultan
sultrier n ▷ sultry
sultriest n ▷ sultry
sultry adj (-trier, -triest) (of weather or

climate) hot and humid

sum n (pl -s) result of addition, total
  summaries n ▷ summary
  summarily adv ▷ summary
summarize v (-izes, -izing, -ized) make or be a summary of (something)
  summarized v ▷ summarize
  summarizes v ▷ summarize
  summarizing v ▷ summarize
summary n (pl -ries) brief account giving the main points of something ▶ adj done quickly, without formalities > **summarily** adv
summation n (pl -s) summary
  summations n ▷ summation
summer n (pl -s) warmest season of the year, between spring and autumn > **summery** adj (-rier, -riest)
summerhouse n (pl -s) small building in a garden
  summerhouses n ▷ summerhouse
  summerier adj ▷ summer
  summeriest adj ▷ summer
  summers n ▷ summer
summertime n (pl -s) period or season of summer
  summertimes n ▷ summertime
  summery adj ▷ summer
summit n (pl -s) top of a mountain or hill
  summits n ▷ summit
summon v (-s, -ing, -ed) order (someone) to come
  summoned v ▷ summon
  summoning v ▷ summon
summons n (pl -es) command summoning someone ▶ v (-es, -ing, -ed) order (someone) to appear in court ▶ v ▷ summon
  summonsed n ▷ summons
  summonses v, n ▷ summons
  summonsing v ▷ summons
sumo n (pl -s) Japanese style of wrestling
  sumos n ▷ sumo
sump n (pl -s) container in an internal-combustion engine into which oil can drain
  sumps n ▷ sump
sumptuous adj lavish, magnificent > **sumptuously** adv
  sumptuously adv ▷ sumptuous
  sums n ▷ sum
sun n (pl -s) star around which the earth and other planets revolve ▶ v (-s, sunning, sunned) expose (oneself) to the sun's rays > **sunless** adj
sunbathe v (-thes, -thing, -thed) lie in the sunshine in order to get a suntan
  sunbathed v ▷ sunbathe

sunbathes v ▷ sunbathe
  sunbathing v ▷ sunbathe
sunbeam n (pl -s) ray of sun
  sunbeams n ▷ sunbeam
sunburn n (pl -s) painful reddening of the skin caused by overexposure to the sun > **sunburnt, sunburned** adj
  sunburned adj ▷ sunburn
  sunburns n ▷ sunburn
  sunburnt adj ▷ sunburn
sundae n (pl -s) ice cream topped with fruit etc.
  sundaes n ▷ sundae
sundial n (pl -s) device showing the time by means of a pointer that casts a shadow on a marked dial
  sundials n ▷ sundial
sundown n (pl -s) sunset
  sundowns n ▷ sundown
sundries pl n several things of various sorts
sundry adj several, various
sunflower n (pl -s) tall plant with large golden flowers
  sunflowers n ▷ sunflower
  sung v ▷ sing
  sunk v ▷ sink
  sunken v ▷ sink
  sunless adj ▷ sun
  sunned v ▷ sun
  sunnier adj ▷ sunny
  sunniest adj ▷ sunny
  sunning v ▷ sun
sunny adj (-nnier, -nniest) full of or exposed to sunlight
sunrise n (pl -s) daily appearance of the sun above the horizon
  sunrises n ▷ sunrise
  suns n, v ▷ sun
sunset n (pl -s) daily disappearance of the sun below the horizon
  sunsets n ▷ sunset
sunshine n (pl -s) light and warmth from the sun
  sunshines n ▷ sunshine
sunspot n (pl -s) dark patch appearing temporarily on the sun's surface
  sunspots n ▷ sunspot
sunstroke n (pl -s) illness caused by prolonged exposure to intensely hot sunlight
  sunstrokes n ▷ sunstroke
suntan n (pl -s) browning of the skin caused by exposure to the sun
  suntans n ▷ suntan
sup v (-s, -pping, -pped) take (liquid) by sips ▶ n (pl -s) sip

super *adj* (*Informal*) excellent

superannuated *adj* discharged with a pension, owing to old age or illness

superannuation *n* (*pl* -s) regular payment by an employee into a pension fund

  superannuations *n* ▷ superannuation

superb *adj* excellent, impressive, or splendid > **superbly** *adv*

  superbly *adv* ▷ superb

superbug *n* (*pl* -s) (*Informal*) bacterium resistant to antibiotics

  superbugs *n* ▷ superbug

supercharged *adj* (of an engine) having a supercharger

supercharger *n* (*pl* -s) device that increases the power of an internal-combustion engine by forcing extra air into it

  superchargers *n* ▷ supercharger

supercilious *adj* showing arrogant pride or scorn

superconductor *n* (*pl* -s) substance which has almost no electrical resistance at very low temperatures

  superconductors *n* ▷ superconductor

superficial *adj* not careful or thorough > **superficially** *adv* > **superficiality** *n* (*pl* -ties)

  superficialities *n* ▷ superficial

  superficiality *n* ▷ superficial

  superficially *adv* ▷ superficial

  superfluities *n* ▷ superfluous

  superfluity *n* ▷ superfluous

superfluous [soo-per-flew-uss] *adj* more than is needed > **superfluity** *n* (*pl* -ties)

superhuman *adj* beyond normal human ability or experience

superimpose *v* (-ses, -sing, -sed) place (something) on or over something else

  superimposed *v* ▷ superimpose

  superimposes *v* ▷ superimpose

  superimposing *v* ▷ superimpose

superintend *v* (-s, -ing, -ed) supervise (a person or activity)

  superintended *v* ▷ superintend

superintendent *n* (*pl* -s) senior police officer

  superintendents *n* ▷ superintendent

  superintending *v* ▷ superintend

  superintends *v* ▷ superintend

superior *adj* greater in quality, quantity, or merit ▶ *n* (*pl* -s) person of greater rank or status > **superiority** *n* (*pl* -ties)

  superiorities *n* ▷ superior

  superiority *n* ▷ superior

  superiors *n* ▷ superior

superlative [soo-per-lat-iv] *adj* of outstanding quality ▶ *n* (*pl* -s) (GRAMMAR) word expressing this

  superlatives *n* ▷ superlative

superman *n* (*pl* -men) man with great physical or mental powers

supermarket *n* (*pl* -s) large self-service store selling food and household goods

  supermarkets *n* ▷ supermarket

  supermen *n* ▷ superman

supermodel *n* (*pl* -s) famous and highly-paid fashion model

  supermodels *n* ▷ supermodel

supernatural *adj* of or relating to things beyond the laws of nature

supernova *n* (*pl* -vae, -vas) star that explodes and briefly becomes exceptionally bright

  supernovae *n* ▷ supernova

  supernovas *n* ▷ supernova

  supernumeraries *n* ▷ supernumerary

supernumerary *adj* exceeding the required or regular number ▶ *n* (*pl* -ries) supernumerary person or thing

superpower *n* (*pl* -s) extremely powerful nation

  superpowers *n* ▷ superpower

superscript *n* (*pl* -s) ▶ *adj* (character) printed above the line

  superscripts *n* ▷ superscript

supersede *v* (-des, -ding, -ded) replace, supplant

  superseded *v* ▷ supersede

  supersedes *v* ▷ supersede

  superseding *v* ▷ supersede

supersonic *adj* of or travelling at a speed greater than the speed of sound

superstition *n* (*pl* -s) belief in omens, ghosts, etc. > **superstitious** *adj*

  superstitions *n* ▷ superstition

  superstitious *adj* ▷ superstition

superstore *n* (*pl* -s) large supermarket

  superstores *n* ▷ superstore

superstructure *n* (*pl* -s) structure erected on something else

  superstructures *n* ▷ superstructure

supervene *v* (-nes, -ning, -ned) occur as an unexpected development

  supervened *v* ▷ supervene

  supervenes *v* ▷ supervene

  supervening *v* ▷ supervene

supervise *v* (-ses, -sing, -sed) watch over to direct or check > **supervision** *n* (*pl* -s) > **supervisor** *n* (*pl* -s) > **supervisory** *adj*

  supervised *v* ▷ supervise

  supervises *v* ▷ supervise

  supervising *v* ▷ supervise

  supervision *n* ▷ supervise

supervisions n ▷ supervise
supervisor n ▷ supervise
supervisors n ▷ supervise
supervisory adj ▷ supervise
supine adj lying flat on one's back
supped v ▷ sup
supper n (pl -s) light evening meal
suppers n ▷ supper
supping v ▷ sup
supplant v (-s, -ing, -ed) take the place of, oust
supplanted v ▷ supplant
supplanting v ▷ supplant
supplants v ▷ supplant
supple adj (-r, -st) (of a person) moving and
   bending easily and gracefully > **suppleness**
   n (pl -es)
supplement n (pl -s) thing added to complete
   something or make up for a lack ▶ v (-s,
   -ing, -ed) provide or be a supplement to
   (something) > **supplementary** adj
supplementary adj ▷ supplement
supplemented v ▷ supplement
supplementing v ▷ supplement
supplements n, v ▷ supplement
suppleness n ▷ supple
supplenesses n ▷ supple
suppler adj ▷ supple
supplest adj ▷ supple
supplicant n (pl -s) person who makes a
   humble request
supplicants n ▷ supplicant
supplication n (pl -s) humble request
supplications n ▷ supplication
supplied v ▷ supply
supplier n ▷ supply
suppliers n ▷ supply
supplies pl n food or equipment ▶ v ▷ supply
supply v (-lies, -lying, -lied) provide with
   something required ▶ n (pl -lies) supplying
   > **supplier** n (pl -s)
supplying v ▷ supply
support v (-s, -ing, -ed) bear the weight of ▶ n
   (pl -s) supporting > **supportive** adj
supported v ▷ support
supporter n (pl -s) person who supports a
   team, principle, etc.
supporters n ▷ supporter
supporting v ▷ support
supportive adj ▷ support
supports v, n ▷ support
suppose v (-ses, -sing, -sed) presume to be true
supposed adj presumed to be true without
   proof, doubtful ▶ v ▷ suppose > **supposedly**
   adv
supposedly adv ▷ supposed

supposes v ▷ suppose
supposing v ▷ suppose
supposition n (pl -s) supposing
suppositions n ▷ supposition
suppositories n ▷ suppository
suppository n (pl -ries) solid medication
   inserted into the rectum or vagina and left
   to melt
suppress v (-es, -ing, -ed) put an end to
   > **suppression** n (pl -s)
suppressed v ▷ suppress
suppresses v ▷ suppress
suppressing v ▷ suppress
suppression n ▷ suppress
suppressions n ▷ suppress
suppurate v (-tes, -ting, -ted) (of a wound etc.)
   produce pus
suppurated v ▷ suppurate
suppurates v ▷ suppurate
suppurating v ▷ suppurate
supremacies n ▷ supremacy
supremacy n (pl -cies) supreme power
supreme adj highest in authority, rank, or
   degree
supremely adv extremely
supremo n (pl -s) (Informal) person in overall
   authority
supremos n ▷ supremo
sups n, v ▷ sup

> **suq** n (**suqs**). A suq is an open-air
> marketplace in Arabic-speaking
> countries. This unusual word can be
> very useful. Usually, when you have a
> Q and a U, you will be looking to play
> words with QU in them. But look out
> for opportunities to play suq instead.
> Suq scores 12 points.

surcharge n (pl -s) additional charge
surcharges n ▷ surcharge
surd n (pl -s) (MATHS) number that cannot be
   expressed in whole numbers
surds n ▷ surd
sure adj (-r, -st) free from uncertainty or doubt
   ▶ adv, interj (Informal) certainly
surefooted adj unlikely to slip or stumble
surely adv it must be true that
surer adj ▷ sure
surest adj ▷ sure
sureties n ▷ surety
surety n (pl -ties) person who takes
   responsibility, or thing given as a guarantee,
   for the fulfilment of another's obligation
surf n (pl -s) foam caused by waves breaking on
   the shore ▶ v (-s, -ing, -ed) take part in surfing
   > **surfer** n (pl -s)

surface n (pl -s) outside or top of an object ▶ v
(-ces, -cing, -ced) rise to the surface
  surfaced v ▷ surface
  surfaces n, v ▷ surface
  surfacing v ▷ surface
surfboard n (pl -s) long smooth board used
in surfing
  surfboards n ▷ surfboard
  surfed v ▷ surf
surfeit n (pl -s) excessive amount
  surfeits n ▷ surfeit
  surfer n ▷ surf
  surfers n ▷ surf
surfing n (pl -s) sport of riding towards the
shore on a surfboard on the crest of a wave
▶ v ▷ surf
  surfings n ▷ surfing
  surfs n, v ▷ surf
surge n (pl -s) sudden powerful increase ▶ v
(-ges, -ging, -ged) increase suddenly
  surged v ▷ surge
surgeon n (pl -s) doctor who specializes in
surgery
  surgeons n ▷ surgeon
  surgeries n ▷ surgery
surgery n (pl -ries) treatment in which the
patient's body is cut open in order to treat the
affected part > **surgical** adj > **surgically** adv
  surges n, v ▷ surge
  surgical adj ▷ surgery
  surgically adv ▷ surgery
  surging v ▷ surge
  surlier adj ▷ surly
  surliest adj ▷ surly
  surliness n ▷ surly
  surlinesses n ▷ surly
surly adj (-lier, -liest) ill-tempered and rude
> **surliness** n (pl -es)
surmise v (-ises, -ising, -ised) ▶ n (pl -s) guess,
conjecture
  surmised v ▷ surmise
  surmises n, v ▷ surmise
  surmising v ▷ surmise
surmount v (-s, -ing, -ed) overcome (a
problem) > **surmountable** adj
  surmountable adj ▷ surmount
  surmounted v ▷ surmount
  surmounting v ▷ surmount
  surmounts v ▷ surmount
surname n (pl -s) family name
  surnames n ▷ surname
surpass v (-es, -ing, -ed) be greater than or
superior to
  surpassed v ▷ surpass
  surpasses v ▷ surpass

  surpassing v ▷ surpass
surplice n (pl -s) loose white robe worn by
clergymen and choristers
  surplices n ▷ surplice
surplus n (pl -es) amount left over in excess of
what is required
  surpluses n ▷ surplus
surprise n (pl -ses) unexpected event ▶ v
(-ses, -sing, -sed) cause to feel amazement
or wonder
  surprised v ▷ surprise
  surprises n, v ▷ surprise
  surprising v ▷ surprise
surreal adj bizarre ▶ **surrealist** n (pl -s) adj
> **surrealistic** adj
surrealism n (pl -s) movement in art and
literature involving the combination of
incongruous images, as in a dream
  surrealisms n ▷ surrealism
  surrealist n, adj ▷ surreal
  surrealistic adj ▷ surreal
  surrealists n ▷ surreal
surrender v (-s, -ing, -ed) give oneself up ▶ n (pl
-s) surrendering
  surrendered v ▷ surrender
  surrendering v ▷ surrender
  surrenders v, n ▷ surrender
surreptitious adj done secretly or stealthily
> **surreptitiously** adv
  surreptitiously adv ▷ surreptitious
surrogate n (pl -s) substitute
  surrogates n ▷ surrogate
surround v (-s, -ing, -ed) be, come, or place all
around (a person or thing) ▶ n (pl -s) border
or edging
  surrounded v ▷ surround
  surrounding v ▷ surround
surroundings pl n area or environment
around a person, place, or thing
  surrounds v, n ▷ surround
surveillance n (pl -s) close observation
  surveillances n ▷ surveillance
survey v (-s, -ing, -ed) view or consider in a
general way ▶ n (pl -s) surveying > **surveyor**
n (pl -s)
  surveyed v ▷ survey
  surveying v ▷ survey
  surveyor n ▷ survey
  surveyors n ▷ survey
  surveys v, n ▷ survey
survival n (pl -s) condition of having survived
  survivals n ▷ survival
survive v (-ves, -ing, -ved) continue to live or
exist after (a difficult experience) > **survivor**
n (pl -s)

survived v ▷ survive
survives v ▷ survive
surviving v ▷ survive
survivor n ▷ survive
survivors n ▷ survive
susceptibilities n ▷ susceptible
susceptibility n ▷ susceptible
susceptible adj liable to be influenced or affected by > **susceptibility** n (pl -ties)
sushi [soo-shee] n (pl -s) Japanese dish of small cakes of cold rice with a topping of raw fish
sushis n ▷ sushi
suspect v (-s, -ing, -ed) believe (someone) to be guilty without having any proof ▶ adj not to be trusted ▶ n (pl -s) person who is suspected
suspected v ▷ suspect
suspecting v ▷ suspect
suspects v, n ▷ suspect
suspend v (-s, -ing, -ed) hang from a high place
suspended v ▷ suspend
suspenders pl n straps for holding up stockings
suspending v ▷ suspend
suspends v ▷ suspend
suspense n (pl -s) state of uncertainty while awaiting news, an event, etc.
suspenses n ▷ suspense
suspension n (pl -s) suspending or being suspended
suspensions n ▷ suspension
suspicion n (pl -s) feeling of not trusting a person or thing
suspicions n ▷ suspicion
suspicious adj feeling or causing suspicion > **suspiciously** adv
suspiciously adv ▷ suspicious
sustain v (-s, -ing, -ed) maintain or prolong
sustained v ▷ sustain
sustaining v ▷ sustain
sustains v ▷ sustain
sustenance n (pl -s) food
sustenances n ▷ sustenance
suture [soo-cher] n (pl -s) stitch joining the edges of a wound
sutures n ▷ suture
suzerain n (pl -s) state or sovereign with limited authority over another self-governing state > **suzerainty** n (pl -ties)
suzerains n ▷ suzerain
suzerainties n ▷ suzerain
suzerainty n ▷ suzerain
svelte adj (-r, -st) attractively or gracefully slim
svelter adj ▷ svelte
sveltest adj ▷ svelte
swab n (pl -s) small piece of cotton wool used

to apply medication, clean a wound, etc.
▶ v (-s, -bbing, -bbed) clean (a wound) with a swab
swabbed v ▷ swab
swabbing v ▷ swab
swabs n, v ▷ swab
swaddle v (-les, -ling, -led) wrap (a baby) in swaddling clothes
swaddled v ▷ swaddle
swaddles v ▷ swaddle
swaddling v ▷ swaddle
swag n (pl -s) (Slang) stolen property
swagger v (-s, -ing, -ed) walk or behave arrogantly ▶ n (pl -s) arrogant walk or manner
swaggered v ▷ swagger
swaggering v ▷ swagger
swaggers v, n ▷ swagger
swagman n (pl -men) (AUST HIST) tramp who carries his belongings in a bundle on his back
swagmen n ▷ swagman
swags n ▷ swag
swain n (pl -s) (Poetic) suitor
swains n ▷ swain
swallow¹ v (-s, -ing, -ed) cause to pass down one's throat ▶ n (pl -s) swallowing
swallow² n (pl -s) small migratory bird with long pointed wings and a forked tail
swallowed v ▷ swallow¹
swallowing v ▷ swallow¹
swallows v ▷ swallow¹ ▶ n ▷ swallow¹, ²
swam v ▷ swim
swamp n (pl -s) watery area of land, bog ▶ v (-s, -ing, -ed) cause (a boat) to fill with water and sink > **swampy** adj (-pier, -piest)
swamped v ▷ swamp
swampier adj ▷ swamp
swampiest adj ▷ swamp
swamping v ▷ swamp
swamps n, v ▷ swamp
swampy adj ▷ swamp
swan n (pl -s) large usu. white water bird with a long graceful neck ▶ v (-s, -nning, -nned) (Informal) wander about idly
swank (Slang) v (-s, -ing, -ed) show off or boast ▶ n (pl -s) showing off or boasting
swanked v ▷ swank
swankier adj ▷ swanky
swankiest adj ▷ swanky
swanking v ▷ swank
swanks v, n ▷ swank
swanky adj (-kier, -kiest) (Slang) expensive and showy, stylish
swanned n ▷ swan
swanning n ▷ swan
swans n, v ▷ swan

swap v (-s, -pping, -pped) exchange (something) for something else ▶ n (pl -s) exchange
swapped v ▷ swap
swapping v ▷ swap
swaps v, n ▷ swap
sward n (pl -s) stretch of short grass
swards n ▷ sward
swarm[1] n (pl -s) large group of bees or other insects ▶ v (-s, -ing, -ed) move in a swarm
swarm[2] v (-s, -ing, -ed) (foll. by **up**) climb (a ladder or rope) by gripping with the hands and feet
swarmed v ▷ swarm[1, 2]
swarming v ▷ swarm[1, 2]
swarms v ▷ swarm[1, 2] ▶ n ▷ swarm[1]
swarthier adj ▷ swarthy
swarthiest adj ▷ swarthy
swarthy adj (-thier, -thiest) dark-complexioned
swashbuckler n ▷ swashbuckling
swashbucklers n ▷ swashbuckling
swashbuckling adj having the exciting behaviour of pirates, esp. those depicted in films > **swashbuckler** n (pl -s)
swastika n (pl -s) symbol in the shape of a cross with the arms bent at right angles, used as the emblem of Nazi Germany
swastikas n ▷ swastika
swat v (-s, -tting, -tted) hit sharply ▶ n (pl -s) sharp blow
swatch n (pl -es) sample of cloth
swatches n ▷ swatch
swath [swawth] n (pl -s) ▷ swathe
swathe v (-thes, -thing, -thed) wrap in bandages or layers of cloth ▶ n (pl -s) long strip of cloth wrapped around something (also **swath**)
swathed v ▷ swathe
swathes v, n ▷ swathe
swathing v ▷ swathe
swaths n ▷ swath
swats v, n ▷ swat
swatted v ▷ swat
swatting v ▷ swat
sway v (-s, -ing, -ed) swing to and fro or from side to side ▶ n (pl -s) power or influence
swayed v ▷ sway
swaying v ▷ sway
sways v, n ▷ sway
swear v (-s, -ing, swore, sworn) use obscene or blasphemous language
swearing v ▷ swear
swears v ▷ swear
swearword n (pl -s) word considered obscene or blasphemous
swearwords n ▷ swearword
sweat n (pl -s) salty liquid given off through the pores of the skin ▶ v (-s, -ing, -ed) have sweat coming through the pores > **sweaty** adj (-tier, -tiest)
sweatband n (pl -s) strip of cloth tied around the forehead or wrist to absorb sweat
sweatbands n ▷ sweatband
sweated v ▷ sweat
sweater n (pl -s) (woollen) garment for the upper part of the body
sweaters n ▷ sweater
sweatier adj ▷ sweat
sweatiest adj ▷ sweat
sweating v ▷ sweat
sweats n, v ▷ sweat
sweatshirt n (pl -s) long-sleeved cotton jersey
sweatshirts n ▷ sweatshirt
sweatshop n (pl -s) place where employees work long hours in poor conditions for low pay
sweatshops n ▷ sweatshop
sweaty adj ▷ sweat
swede n (pl -des) kind of turnip
swedes n ▷ swede
sweep v (-s, -ing, swept) remove dirt from (a floor) with a broom ▶ n (pl -s) sweeping
sweeping adj wide-ranging ▶ v ▷ sweep
sweeps v, n ▷ sweep
sweepstake n (pl -s) lottery in which the stakes of the participants make up the prize
sweepstakes n ▷ sweepstake
sweet adj (-er, -est) tasting of or like sugar ▶ n (pl -s) shaped piece of food consisting mainly of sugar > **sweetly** adv > **sweetness** n (pl -es) > **sweeten** v (-s, -ing, -ed)
sweetbread n (pl -s) animal's pancreas used as food
sweetbreads n ▷ sweetbread
sweetened v ▷ sweet
sweetener n (pl -s) sweetening agent that does not contain sugar
sweeteners n ▷ sweetener
sweetening v ▷ sweet
sweetens v ▷ sweet
sweetheart n (pl -s) lover
sweethearts n ▷ sweetheart
sweetly adv ▷ sweet
sweetmeat n (pl -s) (Old-fashioned) sweet delicacy such as a small cake
sweetmeats n ▷ sweetmeat
sweetness n ▷ sweet
sweetnesses n ▷ sweet
sweets n ▷ sweet

swell v (-lls, -lling, -lled, swollen or swelled) expand or increase ▸ n (pl -s) swelling or being swollen ▸ adj (-er, -est) (US) (Slang) excellent or fine
  swelled v ▷ swell
  sweller adj ▷ swell
  swellest adj ▷ swell
swelling n (pl -s) enlargement of part of the body, caused by injury or infection ▸ v ▷ swell
  swells v, n ▷ swell
swelter v (-s, -ing, -ed) feel uncomfortably hot
  sweltered v ▷ swelter
sweltering adj uncomfortably hot ▸ v ▷ swelter
  swelters v ▷ swelter
  swept v ▷ sweep
swerve v (-ves, -ving, -ved) turn aside from a course sharply or suddenly ▸ n (pl -s) swerving
  swerved v ▷ swerve
  swerves v, n ▷ swerve
  swerving v ▷ swerve
swift adj (-er, -est) moving or able to move quickly ▸ n (pl -s) fast-flying bird with pointed wings > **swiftly** adv > **swiftness** n (pl -es)
  swifter adj ▷ swift
  swiftest adj ▷ swift
  swiftly adv ▷ swift
  swiftness n ▷ swift
  swiftnesses n ▷ swift
  swifts n ▷ swift
swig n (pl -s) large mouthful of drink ▸ v (-s, -gging, -gged) drink in large mouthfuls
  swigged v ▷ swig
  swigging v ▷ swig
  swigs n, v ▷ swig
swill v (-s, -ing, -ed) drink greedily ▸ n (pl -s) sloppy mixture containing waste food, fed to pigs
  swilled v ▷ swill
  swilling v ▷ swill
  swills v, n ▷ swill
swim v (-s, -mming, swam, swum) move along in water by movements of the limbs ▸ n (pl -s) act or period of swimming > **swimmer** n (pl -s)
  swimmer n ▷ swim
  swimmers n ▷ swim
  swimming v ▷ swim
swimmingly adv successfully and effortlessly
  swims v, n ▷ swim
swindle v (-les, -ling, -led) cheat (someone) out of money ▸ n (pl -s) instance of swindling > **swindler** n (pl -s)
  swindled v ▷ swindle
  swindler n ▷ swindle
  swindlers n ▷ swindle

swindles v, n ▷ swindle
swindling v ▷ swindle
swine n (pl -s) contemptible person
  swines n ▷ swine
swing v (-s, -ing, swung) move to and fro, sway ▸ n (pl -s) swinging
swingeing [swin-jing] adj punishing, severe
  swinging v ▷ swing
  swings v, n ▷ swing
swipe v (-ipes, -iping, -iped) strike (at) with a sweeping blow ▸ n (pl -s) hard blow
  swiped v ▷ swipe
  swipes v, n ▷ swipe
  swiping v ▷ swipe
swirl v (-s, -ing, -ed) turn with a whirling motion ▸ n (pl -s) whirling motion
  swirled v ▷ swirl
  swirling v ▷ swirl
  swirls v, n ▷ swirl
swish v (-es, -ing, -ed) move with a whistling or hissing sound ▸ n (pl -es) whistling or hissing sound ▸ adj (-er, -est) (Informal) fashionable, smart
  swished v ▷ swish
  swisher adj ▷ swish
  swishes v, n ▷ swish
  swishest adj ▷ swish
  swishing v ▷ swish
switch n (pl -es) device for opening and closing an electric circuit ▸ v (-ches, -ching, -ched) change abruptly
switchback n (pl -s) road or railway with many sharp hills or bends
  switchbacks n ▷ switchback
switchboard n (pl -s) installation in a telephone exchange or office where telephone calls are connected
  switchboards n ▷ switchboard
  switched v ▷ switch
  switches n, v ▷ switch
  switching v ▷ switch
swivel v (-s, -elling, -elled) turn on a central point ▸ n (pl -s) coupling device that allows an attached object to turn freely
  swivelled v ▷ swivel
  swivelling v ▷ swivel
  swivels v, n ▷ swivel
  swollen v ▷ swell
swoon v (-s, -ing, -ed) ▸ n (pl -s) faint
  swooned v ▷ swoon
  swooning v ▷ swoon
  swoons v, n ▷ swoon
swoop v (-s, -ing, -ed) sweep down or pounce on suddenly ▸ n (pl -s) swooping
  swooped v ▷ swoop

swooping v ▷ swoop
swoops v, n ▷ swoop
swop v (-s, -pping, -pped) ▶ n (pl -s) ▷ swap
swopped v ▷ swop
swopping v ▷ swop
swops v, n ▷ swop
sword n (pl -s) weapon with a long sharp blade
swordfish n (pl -es) large fish with a very long upper jaw
swordfishes n ▷ swordfish
swords n ▷ sword
swordsman n (pl -men) person skilled in the use of a sword
swordsmen n ▷ swordsman
swore v ▷ swear
sworn v ▷ swear ▶ adj bound by or as if by an oath
swot (Informal) v (-s, -tting, -tted) study hard ▶ n (pl -s) person who studies hard
swots v, n ▷ swot
swotted v ▷ swot
swotting v ▷ swot
swum v ▷ swim
swung v ▷ swing

> **swy** n (**swys**) Swy is an Australian gambling game. This is a very unusual word which doesn't contain a vowel, so it can be useful in helping you to clear a difficult rack. Swy scores 9 points.

sybarite [sib-bar-ite] n (pl -s) lover of luxury > **sybaritic** adj
sybarites n ▷ sybarite
sybaritic adj ▷ sybarite
sycamore n (pl -s) tree with five-pointed leaves and two-winged fruits
sycamores n ▷ sycamore
sycophancies n ▷ sycophant
sycophancy n ▷ sycophant
sycophant n (pl -s) person who uses flattery to win favour from people with power or influence > **sycophantic** adj > **sycophancy** n (pl -cies)
sycophantic adj ▷ sycophant
sycophants n ▷ sycophant
syllabi n ▷ syllabus
syllabic adj ▷ syllable
syllable n (pl -s) part of a word pronounced as a unit > **syllabic** adj
syllables n ▷ syllable
syllabub n (pl -s) dessert of beaten cream, sugar, and wine
syllabubs n ▷ syllabub
syllabus n (pl -buses, -bi) list of subjects for a course of study

syllabuses n ▷ syllabus
syllogism n (pl -s) form of logical reasoning consisting of two premises and a conclusion
syllogisms n ▷ syllogism
sylph n (pl -s) slender graceful girl or woman > **sylphlike** adj
sylphlike adj ▷ sylph
sylphs n ▷ sylph
sylvan adj (Lit) relating to woods and trees
symbioses n ▷ symbiosis
symbiosis n (pl -oses) close association of two species living together to their mutual benefit > **symbiotic** adj
symbiotic adj ▷ symbiosis
symbol n (pl -s) sign or thing that stands for something else > **symbolic** adj > **symbolically** adv
symbolic adj ▷ symbol
symbolically adv ▷ symbol
symbolism n (pl -s) representation of something by symbols > **symbolist** n (pl -s) adj
symbolisms n ▷ symbolism
symbolist n ▷ symbolism
symbolists n ▷ symbolism
symbolize v (-izes, -izing, -ized) be a symbol of
symbolized v ▷ symbolize
symbolizes v ▷ symbolize
symbolizing v ▷ symbolize
symbols n ▷ symbol
symmetrical adj ▷ symmetry
symmetrically adv ▷ symmetry
symmetries n ▷ symmetry
symmetry n (pl -tries) state of having two halves that are mirror images of each other > **symmetrical** adj > **symmetrically** adv
sympathetic adj feeling or showing sympathy > **sympathetically** adv
sympathetically adv ▷ sympathetic
sympathies n ▷ sympathy
sympathize v (-zes, -izing, -ized) feel or express sympathy > **sympathizer** n (pl -s)
sympathized v ▷ sympathize
sympathizer n ▷ sympathize
sympathizers n ▷ sympathize
sympathizes v ▷ sympathize
sympathizing v ▷ sympathize
sympathy n (pl -thies) compassion for someone's pain or distress
symphonic adj ▷ symphony
symphonies n ▷ symphony
symphony n (pl -nies) composition for orchestra, with several movements > **symphonic** adj
symposia n ▷ symposium
symposium n (pl -iums, -sia) conference for

discussion of a particular topic

symposiums n ▷ symposium

symptom n (pl -s) sign indicating the presence of an illness > **symptomatic** adj

symptomatic adj ▷ symptom

symptoms n ▷ symptom

> **syn** adv. (**Syn**) is a Scots word for **since**. This is a good word to remember for when you have a shortage of vowels. Syn scores 6 points.

synagogue n (pl -s) Jewish place of worship and religious instruction

synagogues n ▷ synagogue

sync, synch (Informal) n (pl -s) synchronization ▶ v (-s, -ing, -ed) synchronize

synced v ▷ sync

synched v ▷ sync

synching v ▷ sync

synchromesh adj (of a gearbox) having a device that synchronizes the speeds of gears before they engage

synchronization n ▷ synchronize

synchronizations n ▷ synchronize

synchronize v (-izes, -izing, -ized) (of two or more people) perform (an action) at the same time > **synchronization** n (pl -s)

synchronized v ▷ synchronize

synchronizes v ▷ synchronize

synchronizing v ▷ synchronize

synchronous adj happening or existing at the same time

synchs n, v ▷ sync

syncing v ▷ sync

syncopate v (-tes, -ting, -ted) (MUSIC) stress the weak beats in (a rhythm) instead of the strong ones > **syncopation** n (pl -s)

syncopated v ▷ syncopate

syncopates v ▷ syncopate

syncopating v ▷ syncopate

syncopation n ▷ syncopate

syncopations n ▷ syncopate

syncope [sing-kop-ee] n (pl -s) (MED) a faint

syncopes n ▷ syncope

syncs n, v ▷ sync

syndicate n (pl -s) group of people or firms undertaking a joint business project ▶ v (-tes, -ting, -ted) publish (material) in several newspapers > **syndication** n (pl -s)

syndicated v ▷ syndicate

syndicates n, v ▷ syndicate

syndicating v ▷ syndicate

syndication n ▷ syndicate

syndications n ▷ syndicate

syndrome n (pl -s) combination of symptoms indicating a particular disease

syndromes n ▷ syndrome

synergies n ▷ synergy

synergy n (pl -gies) potential ability for people or groups to be more successful working together than on their own

synod n (pl -s) church council

synods n ▷ synod

synonym n (pl -s) word with the same meaning as another > **synonymous** adj

synonymous adj ▷ synonym

synonyms n ▷ synonym

synopses n ▷ synopsis

synopsis n (pl -ses) summary or outline

syntactic adj ▷ syntax

syntax n (pl -es) (GRAMMAR) way in which words are arranged to form phrases and sentences > **syntactic** adj

syntaxes n ▷ syntax

syntheses n ▷ synthesis

synthesis n (pl -ses) combination of objects or ideas into a whole

synthesize v (-izes, -izing, -ized) produce by synthesis

synthesized v ▷ synthesize

synthesizer n (pl -s) electronic musical instrument producing a range of sounds

synthesizers n ▷ synthesizer

synthesizes v ▷ synthesize

synthesizing v ▷ synthesize

synthetic adj (of a substance) made artificially > **synthetically** adv

synthetically adv ▷ synthetic

syphilis n (pl -es) serious sexually transmitted disease > **syphilitic** adj

syphilises n ▷ syphilis

syphilitic adj ▷ syphilis

syphon n (pl -s) ▶ v (-s, -ing, -ed) ▷ siphon

syphoned v ▷ syphon

syphoning v ▷ syphon

syphons n, v ▷ syphon

syringe n (pl -s) device for withdrawing or injecting fluids, consisting of a hollow cylinder, a piston, and a hollow needle ▶ v (-ges, -ging, -ged) wash out or inject with a syringe

syringed v ▷ syringe

syringes n, v ▷ syringe

syringing v ▷ syringe

syrup n (pl -s) solution of sugar in water > **syrupy** adj (-pier, -piest)

syrupier adj ▷ syrup

syrupiest adj ▷ syrup

syrups n ▷ syrup

syrupy adj ▷ syrup

system n (pl -s) method or set of methods

> **systematic** adj > **systematically** adv
systematic adj ▷ system
systematically adv ▷ system
systematization n ▷ systematize
systematizations n ▷ systematize
systematize v (-izes, -izing, -ized) organize using a system
systematization n (pl -s) systemizing
  systematized v ▷ systematize

systematizes v ▷ systematize
systematizing v ▷ systematize
systemic adj affecting the entire animal or body
systems n ▷ system
systole [siss-tol-ee] n (pl -s) regular contraction of the heart as it pumps blood > **systolic** adj
systoles n ▷ systole
systolic adj ▷ systole

Tt

T is one of the most common consonants in Scrabble. There are only four two-letter words that begin with T, but they are easy to remember as there is one for every vowel except U. Like S, T begins a number of three-letter words that don't use vowels, which are well worth remembering. These are: **thy** (6 points), **try** (6), **tsk** (7), **twp** (8) and **tyg** (7). There are also some useful three-letter words using X: **tax**, **tix** and **tux** (10 each). If you have an X during a game, remember words like **text** (11), **texts** (12), **textile** (14), **textual** (14) and **texture** (14). The last three of these have seven letters, and so will earn you 50-point bonuses if you use all your tiles to form them.

ta *interj* (*Informal*) thank you
tab *n* (*pl* -s) small flap or projecting label
tabard *n* (*pl* -s) short sleeveless tunic decorated with a coat of arms, worn in medieval times
  tabards *n* ▷ tabard
  tabbies *n* ▷ tabby
tabby *n* (*pl* -bbies) ▶ *adj* (cat) with dark stripes on a lighter background
tabernacle *n* (*pl* -s) portable shrine of the Israelites
  tabernacles *n* ▷ tabernacle
tabla *n* (*pl* -bla, -blas) one of a pair of Indian drums played with the hands
  tablas *n* ▷ tabla
table *n* (*pl* -s) piece of furniture with a flat top supported by legs ▶ *v* (-les, -ling, -led) submit (a motion) for discussion by a meeting
  tabled *v* ▷ table
tableland *n* (*pl* -s) high plateau
  tablelands *n* ▷ tableland
tablespoon *n* (*pl* -s) large spoon for serving food
  tablespoons *n* ▷ tablespoon
tableau [tab-loh] *n* (*pl* -leaux) silent motionless group arranged to represent some scene
  tableaux *n* ▷ tableau
  tabled *v* ▷ table
  tables *n*, *v* ▷ table
tablet *n* (*pl* -s) pill of compressed medicinal substance
  tablets *n* ▷ tablet
  tabling *v* ▷ table
tabloid *n* (*pl* -s) small-sized newspaper with many photographs and a concise, usu. sensational style

  tabloids *n* ▷ tabloid
taboo *n* (*pl* -s) prohibition resulting from religious or social conventions ▶ *adj* forbidden by a taboo
  taboos *n* ▷ taboo
  tabs *n* ▷ tab
tabular *adj* arranged in a table
tabulate *v* (-tes, -ting, -ted) arrange (information) in a table ▶ **tabulation** *n* (*pl* -s)
  tabulated *v* ▷ tabulate
  tabulates *v* ▷ tabulate
  tabulating *v* ▷ tabulate
  tabulation *n* ▷ tabulate
  tabulations *n* ▷ tabulate
tachograph *n* (*pl* -s) device for recording the speed and distance travelled by a motor vehicle
  tachographs *n* ▷ tachograph
tachometer *n* (*pl* -s) device for measuring speed, esp. that of a revolving shaft
  tachometers *n* ▷ tachometer
tacit [tass-it] *adj* implied but not spoken ▷ **tacitly** *adv*
  tacitly *adv* ▷ tacit
taciturn [tass-it-turn] *adj* habitually uncommunicative ▷ **taciturnity** *n* (*pl* -ties)
  taciturnities *n* ▷ taciturnity
  taciturnity *n* ▷ taciturn
tack¹ *n* (*pl* -s) short nail with a large head ▶ *v* (-s, -ing, -ed) fasten with tacks
tack² *n* (*pl* -s) course of a ship sailing obliquely into the wind ▶ *v* (-s, -ing, -ed) sail into the wind on a zigzag course
tack³ *n* (*pl* -s) riding harness for horses
  tacked *v* ▷ tack¹, ²
  tackier *adj* ▷ tacky¹, ²

tackies, takkies pl n (sing **tacky**) (S AFR) (*Informal*) tennis shoes or plimsolls
tackiest adj ▷ tacky[1, 2]
tacking v ▷ tack[1, 2]
tackle v (-les, -ling, -led) deal with (a task) (SPORT) ▶ n (pl -les) (SPORT) act of tackling an opposing player
tackled v ▷ tackle
tackles v, n ▷ tackle
tackling v ▷ tackle ▶
tacks n ▷ tack[1, 2, 3] ▶ v ▷ tack[1, 2]
tacky[1] adj (-ckier, -ckiest) slightly sticky
tacky[2] adj (-ckier, -ckiest) (*Informal*) vulgar and tasteless
tacky[3] n ▷ tackies
taco [tah-koh] n (pl -s) (MEXICAN COOKERY) tortilla fried until crisp, served with a filling
tacos n ▷ taco
tact n (pl -s) skill in avoiding giving offence
> **tactful** adj > **tactfully** adv > **tactless** adj
> **tactlessly** adv
tactful adj ▷ tact
tactfully adv ▷ tact
tactic n (pl -s) method or plan to achieve an end > **tactical** adj > **tactician** n (pl -s)
tactical adj ▷ tactic
tactician n ▷ tactic
tacticians n ▷ tactic
tactics pl n art of directing military forces in battle ▶ n ▷ tactic
tactile adj of or having the sense of touch
tactless adj ▷ tact
tactlessly adv ▷ tact
tacts n ▷ tact
tadpole n (pl -s) limbless tailed larva of a frog or toad
tadpoles n ▷ tadpole
taffeta n (pl -s) shiny silk or rayon fabric
taffetas n ▷ taffeta
tag[1] n (pl -s) label bearing information ▶ v (-s, -gging, -gged) attach a tag to
tag[2] n (pl -s) children's game where the person being chased becomes the chaser upon being touched ▶ v (-s, -gging, -gged) touch and catch in this game
tagged v ▷ tag[1, 2]
tagging v ▷ tag[1, 2]
tagliatelle n pasta in long narrow strips
tags n, v ▷ tag[1, 2]
tail n (pl -s) rear part of an animal's body, usu. forming a flexible appendage ▶ adj at the rear ▶ v (-s, -ing, -ed) (*Informal*) follow (someone) secretly > **tailless** adj
tailback n (pl -s) (BRIT) queue of traffic stretching back from an obstruction

tailbacks n ▷ tailback
tailboard n (pl -s) removable or hinged rear board on a truck etc.
tailboards n ▷ tailboard
tailed v ▷ tail
tailing v ▷ tail
tailless adj ▷ tail
tailor n (pl -s) person who makes men's clothes ▶ v (-s, -ing, -ed) adapt to suit a purpose
tailored v ▷ tailor
tailoring v ▷ tailor
tailors n, v ▷ tailor
tailplane n (pl -s) small stabilizing wing at the rear of an aircraft
tailplanes n ▷ tailplane
tails adv with the side of a coin uppermost that does not have a portrait or a head on it ▶ pl n (*Informal*) tail coat ▶ n, v ▷ tail
tailspin n (pl -s) uncontrolled spinning dive of an aircraft
tailspins n ▷ tailspin
tailwind n (pl -s) wind coming from the rear
tailwinds n ▷ tailwind
taint v (-s, -ing, -ed) spoil with a small amount of decay, contamination, or other bad quality ▶ n (pl -s) something that taints
tainted v ▷ taint
tainting v ▷ taint
taints v, n ▷ taint
taipan n (pl -s) large poisonous Australian snake
taipans n ▷ taipan

> **taj** n (**tajes**). A taj is a tall conical cap worn by some Muslims. This unusual word can be helpful if you are struggling to use J because there aren't any good opportunities for longer words on the board. Taj scores 10 points.

take v (**takes, taking, took, taken**) remove from a place ▶ n (pl -s) one of a series of recordings from which the best will be used
takeaway n (pl -s) shop or restaurant selling meals for eating elsewhere
takeaways n ▷ takeaway
taken v ▷ take
takeoff n (pl -s) (of an aircraft) act of leaving the ground
takeoffs n ▷ takeoff
takeover n (pl -s) act of taking control of a company by buying a large number of its shares
takeovers n ▷ takeover
takes v, n ▷ take
taking adj charming ▶ v ▷ take

takings pl n money received by a shop
takkies pl n ▷ takkies
talc n (pl -s) talcum powder
talcs n ▷ talc
tale n (pl -s) story
talent n (pl -s) natural ability > **talented** adj
talented adj ▷ talent
talents n ▷ talent
tales n ▷ tale
talisman n (pl -s) object believed to have magic power > **talismanic** adj
talismanic adj ▷ talisman
talismans n ▷ talisman
talk v (-s, -ing, -ed) express ideas or feelings by means of speech ▶ n (pl -s) speech or lecture
talkative adj fond of talking
talkback n (pl -s) (NZ) broadcast in which telephone comments or questions from the public are transmitted live
talkbacks n ▷ talkback
talked v ▷ talk
talker n (pl -s) person who talks
talkers n ▷ talker
talking v ▷ talk
talks v, n ▷ talk
tall (-er, -est) adj higher than average
tallboy n (pl -s) high chest of drawers
tallboys n ▷ tallboy
taller adj ▷ tall
tallest adj ▷ tall
tallied v ▷ tally
tallies v, n ▷ tally
tallow n (pl -s) hard animal fat used to make candles
tallows n ▷ tallow
tally v (-llies, -llying, -llied) (of two things) correspond ▶ n (pl -lies) record of a debt or score
tallying v ▷ tally
talon n (pl -s) bird's hooked claw
talons n ▷ talon
tamarind n (pl -s) tropical tree
tamarinds n ▷ tamarind
tamarisk n (pl -s) evergreen shrub with slender branches and feathery flower clusters
tamarisks n ▷ tamarisk
tambourine n (pl -s) percussion instrument like a small drum with jingling metal discs attached
tambourines n ▷ tambourine
tame adj (-r, -est) (of animals) brought under human control ▶ v (-mes, -ming, -med) make tame > **tamely** adv
tamed v ▷ tame
tamely adv ▷ tame

tamer n (pl -s) person who tames wild animals ▶ adj ▷ tame
tamers n ▷ tamer
tames v ▷ tame
tamest adj ▷ tame
taming v ▷ tame
tamp v (-s, -ing, -ed) pack down by repeated taps
tamped v ▷ tamp
tamper v (-s, -ing, -ed) (foll. by with) interfere
tampered v ▷ tamper
tampering v ▷ tamper
tampers v ▷ tamper
tamping v ▷ tamp
tampon n (pl -s) absorbent plug of cotton wool inserted into the vagina during menstruation
tampons n ▷ tampon
tamps v ▷ tamp
tan n (pl -s) brown coloration of the skin from exposure to sunlight ▶ v (-s, -nning, -nned) (of skin) go brown from exposure to sunlight ▶ adj (-ner, -nest) yellowish-brown
tandem n (pl -s) bicycle for two riders, one behind the other
tandems n ▷ tandem
tandoori adj (of food) cooked in an Indian clay oven
tang n (pl -s) strong taste or smell > **tangy** adj (-gier, -giest)
tangent n (pl -s) line that touches a curve without intersecting it
tangential adj of superficial relevance only > **tangentially** adv
tangentially adv ▷ tangential
tangents n ▷ tangent
tangerine n (pl -s) small orange-like fruit of an Asian citrus tree
tangerines n ▷ tangerine
tangible adj able to be touched > **tangibly** adv
tangibly adv ▷ tangible
tangier adj ▷ tang
tangiest adj ▷ tang
tangle n (pl -les) confused mass or situation ▶ v (-les, -ling, -led) twist together in a tangle
tangled v ▷ tangle
tangles n, v ▷ tangle
tangling v ▷ tangle
tango n (pl -gos) S American dance ▶ v (-goes, -going, -goed) dance a tango
tangoed v ▷ tango
tangoes v ▷ tango
tangoing v ▷ tango
tangos v ▷ tango
tangs n ▷ tang

tangy adj ▷ tang
taniwha [tun-ee-fah] n (pl -s) (NZ) mythical Maori monster that lives in water
  taniwhas n ▷ taniwha
tank n (pl -s) container for liquids or gases
tankard n (pl -s) large beer-mug, often with a hinged lid
  tankards n ▷ tankard
tanker n (pl -s) ship or truck for carrying liquid in bulk
  tankers n ▷ tanker
  tanks n ▷ tank
  tanned v ▷ tan
  tanner adj ▷ tan
  tanneries n ▷ tannery
tannery n (pl -ries) place where hides are tanned
  tannest adj ▷ tan
tannin n (pl -s) vegetable substance used in tanning
  tanning v ▷ tan
  tannins n ▷ tannin
  tans n, v ▷ tan
  tansies n ▷ tansy
tansy n (pl -sies) yellow-flowered plant
tantalize v (-zes, -zing, -zed) torment by showing but withholding something desired > **tantalizingly** adv
  tantalized v ▷ tantalize
  tantalizes v ▷ tantalize
  tantalizing v, adj ▷ tantalize
  tantalizingly adv ▷ tantalize
tantalum n (pl -s) (CHEM) hard greyish-white metallic element
  tantalums n ▷ tantalum
tantamount adj equivalent in effect to
tantrum n (pl -s) childish outburst of temper
  tantrums n ▷ tantrum
tap¹ v (taps, tapping, -pped) knock lightly and usu. repeatedly ▶ n (pl -s) light knock
tap² n (pl -s) valve to control the flow of liquid from a pipe or cask ▶ v (taps, tapping, tapped) listen in on (a telephone call) secretly by making an illegal connection
tape n (pl -s) narrow long strip of material ▶ v (tapes, taping, taped) record on magnetic tape
  taped v ▷ tape
taper v (-s, -ing, -ed) become narrower towards one end ▶ n (pl -s) long thin candle
  tapered v ▷ taper
  tapering v ▷ taper
  tapers v, n ▷ taper
  tapes n, v ▷ tape
  tapestries n ▷ tapestry

tapestry n (pl -tries) fabric decorated with coloured woven designs
tapeworm n (pl -s) long flat parasitic worm living in the intestines of vertebrates
  tapeworms n ▷ tapeworm
tapioca n (pl -s) beadlike starch made from cassava root, used in puddings
  tapiocas n ▷ tapioca
  taping v ▷ tape
tapir [tape-er] n (pl -s) piglike mammal of tropical America and SE Asia, with a long snout
  tapirs n ▷ tapir
  tapped v ▷ tap¹, ²
tappet n (pl -s) short steel rod in an engine, transferring motion from one part to another
  tappets n ▷ tappet
  tapping v ▷ tap¹, ²
taproot n (pl -s) main root of a plant, growing straight down
  taproots n ▷ taproot
  taps n, v ▷ tap¹, ²
tar n (pl -rs) thick black liquid distilled from coal etc. ▶ v (-s, -rring, -rred) coat with tar
taramasalata n (pl -s) creamy pink pâté made from fish roe
  taramasalatas n ▷ taramasalata
tarantella n (pl -s) lively Italian dance
  tarantellas n ▷ tarantella
tarantula n (pl -s) large hairy spider with a poisonous bite
  tarantulas n ▷ tarantula
  tardier adj ▷ tardy
  tardiest adj ▷ tardy
  tardily adv ▷ tardy
  tardiness n ▷ tardy
  tardinesses n ▷ tardy
tardy adj (-dier, -diest) slow or late > **tardily** adv > **tardiness** n (pl -es)
tare n (pl -s) type of vetch plant
  tares n ▷ tare
target n (pl -s) object or person a missile is aimed at ▶ v (-gets, -geting, -geted) aim or direct
  targeted v ▷ target
  targeting v ▷ target
  targets n, v ▷ target
tariff n (pl -s) tax levied on imports
  tariffs n ▷ tariff
tarn n (pl -s) small mountain lake
tarnish v (-shes, -shing, -shed) make or become stained or less bright ▶ n (pl -es) discoloration or blemish
  tarnished v ▷ tarnish
  tarnishes v, n ▷ tarnish

tarnishing v ▷ tarnish

tarns n ▷ tarn

tarot [tarr-oh] n (pl -s) special pack of cards used mainly in fortune-telling

tarots n ▷ tarot

tarpaulin n (pl -s) (sheet of) heavy waterproof fabric

tarpaulins n ▷ tarpaulin

tarragon n (pl -s) aromatic herb

tarragons n ▷ tarragon

tarred v ▷ tar

tarried v ▷ tarry

tarries v ▷ tarry

tarring v ▷ tar

tarry v (tarries, tarrying, tarried) (Old-fashioned) linger or delay

tarrying v ▷ tarry

tars n, v ▷ tar

tarsi n ▷ tarsus

tarsus n (pl -si) bones of the heel and ankle collectively

tart¹ n (pl -s) pie or flan with a sweet filling

tart² adj (-er, -est) sharp or bitter > **tartly** adv > **tartness** n (pl -es)

tart³ n (pl -s) (Informal) sexually provocative or promiscuous woman

tartan n (pl -s) design of straight lines crossing at right angles, esp. one associated with a Scottish clan

tartans n ▷ tartan

tartar¹ n (pl -s) hard deposit on the teeth

tartar² n (pl -s) fearsome or formidable person

tartars n ▷ tartar¹, ²

tarter adj ▷ tart²

tartest adj ▷ tart²

tartly adv ▷ tart²

tartness n ▷ tart²

tartnesses n ▷ tart²

tartrazine [tar-traz-zeen] n (pl -s) artificial yellow dye used in food etc.

tartrazines n ▷ tartrazine

tarts n ▷ tart¹, ³

task n (pl -s) (difficult or unpleasant) piece of work to be done

taskmaster n (pl -s) person who enforces hard work

taskmasters n ▷ taskmaster

tasks n ▷ task

tassel n (pl -s) decorative fringed knot of threads

tassels n ▷ tassel

taste n (pl -s) sense by which the flavour of a substance is distinguished in the mouth ▶ v (-tes, -ting, -ted) distinguish the taste of (a substance)

tasted v ▷ taste

tasteful adj having or showing good taste > **tastefully** adv

tastefully adv ▷ tasteful

tasteless adj bland or insipid > **tastelessly** adv

tastelessly adv ▷ tasteless

tastes n, v ▷ taste

tastier adj ▷ tasty

tastiest adj ▷ tasty

tasting v ▷ taste

tasty adj (-tier, -tiest) pleasantly flavoured

tat n (pl -s) (BRIT) tatty or tasteless article(s)

tats n ▷ tat

tattered adj ragged or torn

tattier n ▷ tatty

tattiest n ▷ tatty

tattle v (-les, -ling, -led), n (pl -les) (BRIT, AUST & NZ) gossip or chatter

tattled v ▷ tattle

tattles n ▷ tattle

tattling v ▷ tattle

tattoo¹ n (pl -s) pattern made on the body by pricking the skin and staining it with indelible inks ▶ v (-toos, -tooing, -tooed) make such a pattern on the skin > **tattooist** n (pl -s)

tattoo² n (pl -s) military display or pageant

tattooed n ▷ tattoo¹

tattooing n ▷ tattoo¹

tattooist n ▷ tattoo¹

tattooists n ▷ tattoo¹

tattoos n ▷ tattoo¹, ² ▶ v ▷ tattoo¹

tatty adj (-tier, -tiest) shabby or worn out

taught v ▷ teach

taunt v (-s, -ing, -ed) tease with jeers ▶ n (pl -s) jeering remark

taunted v ▷ taunt

taunting v ▷ taunt

taunts v, n ▷ taunt

taupe adj brownish-grey

taut adj (-er, -est) drawn tight

tauten v (-s, -ing, -ed) make or become taut

tautened v ▷ tauten

tautening v ▷ tauten

tautens v ▷ tauten

tauter adj ▷ taut

tautest adj ▷ taut

tautological adj ▷ tautology

tautologies n ▷ tautology

tautology n (pl -gies) use of words which merely repeat something already stated > **tautological** adj

tavern n (pl -s) (Old-fashioned) pub

taverns n ▷ tavern

tawdrier adj ▷ tawdry

tawdriest adj ▷ tawdry
tawdry adj (-drier, -driest) cheap, showy, and of poor quality
tawnier adj ▷ tawny
tawniest adj ▷ tawny
tawny adj (-nier, -niest) yellowish-brown
tax n (pl -es) compulsory payment levied by a government on income, property, etc. to raise revenue ▶ v (-es, -ing, -ed) levy a tax on ▷ **taxable** adj ▷ **taxpayer** n (pl -s)
taxable adj ▷ tax
taxation n (pl -s) levying of taxes
taxations n ▷ taxation
taxed v ▷ tax
taxes n, v ▷ tax
taxi n (pl -s) car with a driver that may be hired to take people to any specified destination ▶ v (taxis, taxiing, taxied) (of an aircraft) run along the ground before taking off or after landing
taxidermies n ▷ taxidermy
taxidermist n ▷ taxidermy
taxidermists n ▷ taxidermy
taxidermy n (pl -mies) art of stuffing and mounting animal skins to give them a lifelike appearance ▷ **taxidermist** n (pl -s)
taxied v ▷ taxi
taxiing v ▷ taxi
taxing v ▷ taxi
taxis n, v ▷ taxi
taxonomic adj ▷ taxonomy
taxonomies n ▷ taxonomy
taxonomist n ▷ taxonomy
taxonomists n ▷ taxonomy
taxonomy n (pl -mies) classification of plants and animals into groups ▷ **taxonomic** adj ▷ **taxonomist** n (pl -s)
taxpayer n ▷ tax
taxpayers n ▷ tax

te n (tes). Te is the seventh note of a musical scale. Although it won't earn you many points on its own, te is extremely useful as it allows you to connect a word beginning with T to one ending in E, or vice versa, which is very helpful as T and E are two of the most common tiles in the game. Te scores 2 points.

tea n (pl -s) drink made from infusing the dried leaves of an Asian bush in boiling water
teapot n (pl -s) container with a lid, spout, and handle for making and serving tea
teapots n ▷ teapot
teaspoon n (pl -s) small spoon for stirring tea
teaspoons n ▷ teaspoon

teach v (-es, -ing, taught) tell or show (someone) how to do something ▷ **teaching** n (pl -s)
teacher n (pl -s) person who teaches, esp. in a school
teachers n ▷ teacher
teaches v ▷ teach
teaching v, n ▷ teach
teachings n ▷ teach
teak n (pl -s) very hard wood of an E Indian tree
teaks n ▷ teak
teal n (pl -s) kind of small duck
teals n ▷ teal
team n (pl -s) group of people forming one side in a game
teams n ▷ team
teamster n (pl -s) (US) commercial vehicle driver
teamsters n ▷ teamster
teamwork n (pl -s) cooperative work by a team
teamworks n ▷ teamwork
tear¹, teardrop n (pl -s) drop of fluid appearing in and falling from the eye
tear² v (-s, -ing, tore, torn) rip a hole in ▶ n (pl -s) hole or split
tearaway n (pl -s) wild or unruly person
tearaways n ▷ tearaway
teardrop n ▷ tear¹
teardrops n ▷ tear¹
tearful adj weeping or about to weep
tearing v ▷ tear²
tears n ▷ tear¹,² ▶ v ▷ tear²
teas n ▷ tea
tease v (-ses, -sing, -sed) make fun of (someone) in a provoking or playful way ▶ n (pl -s) person who teases ▷ **teasing** adj, n (pl -s)
teased v ▷ tease
teasel, teazel, teazle n (pl -s) plant with prickly leaves and flowers
teasels n ▷ teasel
teases v, n ▷ tease
teasing v, adj n ▷ tease
teasings n ▷ tease
teat n (pl -s) nipple of a breast or udder
teats n ▷ teat
teazel n ▷ teasel
teazels n ▷ teasel
teazle n ▷ teasel
teazles n ▷ teasel
tech n (pl -s) (Informal) technical college
techie (Informal) n (pl -s) person who is skilled in the use of technology ▶ adj relating to or skilled in the use of technology
techies n ▷ techie
technetium [tek-**neesh**-ee-um] n (pl -s) (CHEM)

artificially produced silvery-grey metallic element
technetiums n ▷ technetium
technical adj of or specializing in industrial, practical, or mechanical arts and applied sciences > **technically** adv
technicalities n ▷ technicality
technicality n (pl -s) petty point based on a strict application of rules
technically adv ▷ technical
technician n (pl -s) person skilled in a particular technical field
technicians n ▷ technician
technicolor adj garishly coloured
technique n (pl -s) method or skill used for a particular task
techniques n ▷ technique
techno n (pl -s) type of electronic dance music with a very fast beat
technocracies n ▷ technocracy
technocracy n (pl -cies) government by technical experts > **technocrat** n (pl -s)
technocrat n ▷ technocracy
technocrats n ▷ technocracy
technological adj ▷ technology
technologies n ▷ technology
technologist n ▷ technology
technologists n ▷ technology
technology n (pl -gies) application of practical or mechanical sciences to industry or commerce > **technological** adj > **technologist** n (pl -s)
technos n ▷ techno
techs n ▷ tech
tectonics n study of the earth's crust and the forces affecting it
teddies n ▷ teddy
teddy n (pl -dies) teddy bear
tedious adj causing fatigue or boredom > **tediously** adv
tediously adv ▷ tedious
tedium n (pl -s) monotony
tediums n ▷ tedium
tee n (pl -s) small peg from which a golf ball can be played at the start of each hole
teem[1] v (-s, -ing, -ed) be full of
teem[2] v (-s, -ing, -ed) rain heavily
teemed v ▷ teem[1, 2]
teeming v ▷ teem[1, 2]
teems v ▷ teem[1, 2]
teenage adj ▷ teenager
teenager n (pl -s) person aged between 13 and 19 > **teenage** adj
teenagers n ▷ teenager
teens pl n period of being a teenager

teepee n (pl -s) ▷ tepee
teepees n ▷ teepee
tees n ▷ tee
teeter v (-s, -ing, -ed) wobble or move unsteadily
teetered v ▷ teeter
teetering v ▷ teeter
teeters v ▷ teeter
teeth n ▷ tooth
teethe v (-thes, -thing, -thed) (of a baby) grow his or her first teeth
teethed v ▷ teethe
teethes v ▷ teethe
teething v ▷ teethe
teetotal adj drinking no alcohol > **teetotaller** n (pl -s)
teetotaller n ▷ teetotal
teetotallers n ▷ teetotal
telecommunications n communications using telephone, radio, television, etc.
telegram n (pl -s) formerly, a message sent by telegraph
telegrams n ▷ telegram
telegraph n (pl -s) formerly, a system for sending messages over a distance along a cable ▶ v (-s, -ing, -ed) communicate by telegraph > **telegraphic** adj > **telegraphist** n (pl -s)
telegraphed v ▷ telegraph
telegraphic adj ▷ telegraph
telegraphies n ▷ telegraphy
telegraphing v ▷ telegraph
telegraphist n ▷ telegraph
telegraphists n ▷ telegraph
telegraphs n, v ▷ telegraph
telegraphy n (pl -phies) science or use of a telegraph
telekinesis n (pl -eses) movement of objects by thought or willpower
telekineses n ▷ telekinesis
telemetries n ▷ telemetry
telemetry n (pl -tries) use of electronic devices to record or measure a distant event and transmit the data to a receiver
teleological adj ▷ teleology
teleologies n ▷ teleology
teleology n (pl -gies) belief that all things have a predetermined purpose > **teleological** adj
telepathic adj ▷ telepathy
telepathically adv ▷ telepathy
telepathies n ▷ telepathy
telepathy n (pl -thies) direct communication between minds > **telepathic** adj > **telepathically** adv
telephone n (pl -s) device for transmitting

sound over a distance ▶ v (-nes, -ning, -ned) call or talk to (a person) by telephone > **telephony** n (pl -nies) > **telephonic** adj
telephoned v ▷ telephone
telephones n, v ▷ telephone
telephonic adj ▷ telephone
telephonies n ▷ telephone
telephoning v ▷ telephone
telephonist n (pl -s) person operating a telephone switchboard
telephonists n ▷ telephonist
telephony n ▷ telephone
teleprinter n (pl -s) (BRIT) apparatus like a typewriter for sending and receiving typed messages by wire
teleprinters n ▷ teleprinter
telesales n selling of a product or service by telephone
telescope n (pl -s) optical instrument for magnifying distant objects ▶ v (-pes, -ping, -ped) shorten > **telescopic** adj
telescoped v ▷ telescope
telescopes n, v ▷ telescope
telescopic adj ▷ telescope
telescoping v ▷ telescope
televise v (-ses, -sing, -sed) broadcast on television
televised v ▷ televise
televises v ▷ televise
televising v ▷ televise
television n (pl -s) system of producing a moving image and accompanying sound on a distant screen > **televisual** adj
televisions n ▷ television
televisual adj ▷ television
telex n (pl -es) international communication service using teleprinters ▶ v (-es, -ing, -ed) transmit by telex
telexed v ▷ telex
telexes n, v ▷ telex
telexing v ▷ telex
tell v (-s, -lling, told) make known in words
teller n (pl -s) narrator
tellers n ▷ teller
tellies n ▷ telly
telling adj having a marked effect ▶ v ▷ tell
tells v ▷ tell
telltale n (pl -s) person who reveals secrets ▶ adj revealing
telltales n ▷ telltale
tellurium n (pl -s) (CHEM) brittle silvery-white nonmetallic element
telluriums n ▷ tellurium
telly n (pl -lies) (Informal) television
temerities n ▷ temerity

temerity [tim-merr-it-tee] n (pl -ties) boldness or audacity
temp (BRIT) (Informal) n (pl -s) temporary employee, esp. a secretary ▶ v (-s, -ing, -ed) work as a temp
temped v ▷ temp
temper n (pl -s) outburst of anger ▶ v (-s, -ing, -ed) make less extreme
tempera n (pl -s) painting medium for powdered pigments
temperas n ▷ tempera
temperament n (pl -s) person's character or disposition
temperamental adj having changeable moods > **temperamentally** adv
temperamentally adv ▷ temperamental
temperaments n ▷ temperament
temperance n (pl -s) moderation
temperances n ▷ temperance
temperate adj (of climate) not extreme
temperature n (pl -s) degree of heat or cold
temperatures n ▷ temperature
tempered v ▷ temper
tempering v ▷ temper
tempers n, v ▷ temper
tempest n (pl -s) violent storm
tempests n ▷ tempest
tempestuous adj violent or stormy
tempi n ▷ tempo
temping v ▷ temp
template n (pl -s) pattern used to cut out shapes accurately
templates n ▷ template
temple¹ n (pl -s) building for worship
temple² n (pl -s) region on either side of the forehead
temples n ▷ temple¹, ²
tempo n (pl -pi, -pos) rate or pace
temporal adj of time
temporarily adv ▷ temporary
temporary adj lasting only for a short time > **temporarily** adv
temporize v (-zes, -zing, -zed) gain time by negotiation or evasiveness
temporized v ▷ temporize
temporizes v ▷ temporize
temporizing v ▷ temporize
tempos n ▷ tempo
temps n, v ▷ temp
tempt v (-s, -ing, -ed) entice (a person) to do something wrong > **tempter, temptress** n (pl -s, -es)
temptation n (pl -s) tempting
temptations n ▷ temptation
tempted v ▷ tempt

tempter n ▷ tempt
tempters n ▷ tempt
tempting adj attractive or inviting ▶ v ▷ tempt
temptress n ▷ tempt
temptresses n ▷ tempt
tempts v ▷ tempt
ten adj, n (pl -s) one more than nine
tenable adj able to be upheld or maintained
tenacious adj holding fast > **tenaciously** adv
> **tenacity** n (pl -ties)
tenaciously adv ▷ tenacious
tenacities n ▷ tenacious
tenacity n ▷ tenacious
tenancies n ▷ tenant
tenancy n ▷ tenant
tenant n (pl -s) person who rents land or a building > **tenancy** n (pl -cies)
tenants n ▷ tenant
tench n (pl -es) freshwater game fish of the carp family
tenches n ▷ tench
tend[1] v (-s, -ing, -ed) be inclined
tend[2] v (-s, -ing, -ed) take care of
tended v ▷ tend[1, 2]
tendencies n ▷ tendency
tendency n (pl -cies) inclination to act in a certain way > **tendentious** adj biased, not impartial
tendentious adj ▷ tendency
tender[1] adj (-er, -est) not tough > **tenderly** adv
> **tenderness** n (pl -es)
tender[2] v (-s, -ing, -ed) offer ▶ n (pl -s) such an offer
tender[3] n (pl -s) small boat that brings supplies to a larger ship in a port
tendered v ▷ tender[2]
tenderer adj ▷ tender[1]
tenderest adj ▷ tender[1]
tendering v ▷ tender[2]
tenderize v (-zes, -zing, -zed) soften (meat) by pounding or treatment with a special substance
tenderized v ▷ tenderize
tenderizes v ▷ tenderize
tenderizing v ▷ tenderize
tenderly adv ▷ tender[1]
tenderness n ▷ tender[1]
tendernesses n ▷ tender[1]
tenders n ▷ tender[2, 3] ▷ v ▷ tender[2]
tending v ▷ tend[1, 2]
tendon n (pl -s) strong tissue attaching a muscle to a bone
tendons n ▷ tendon
tendril n (pl -s) slender stem by which a climbing plant clings

tendrils n ▷ tendril
tends v ▷ tend[1, 2]
tenement n (pl -s) (esp. in Scotland or the US) building divided into several flats
tenements n ▷ tenement
tenet [ten-nit] n (pl -s) doctrine or belief
tenets n ▷ tenet
tenner n (pl -s) (BRIT) (Informal) ten-pound note
tenners n ▷ tenner
tennis n (pl -es) game in which players use rackets to hit a ball back and forth over a net
tennises n ▷ tennis
tenon n (pl -s) projecting end on a piece of wood fitting into a slot in another
tenons n ▷ tenon
tenor n (pl -s) (singer with) the second highest male voice ▶ adj (of a voice or instrument) between alto and baritone
tenors n ▷ tenor
tens n ▷ ten
tense[1] adj (-r, -st) emotionally strained ▶ v (-ses, -sing, -sed) make or become tense
tense[2] n (pl -s) (GRAMMAR) form of a verb showing the time of action
tensed v ▷ tense[1]
tenser adj ▷ tense[1]
tenses n ▷ tense[2] ▶ v ▷ tense[1]
tensest adj ▷ tense[1]
tensile adj of tension
tensing v ▷ tense[1]
tension n (pl -s) hostility or suspense
tensions n ▷ tension
tent n (pl -s) portable canvas shelter
tentacle n (pl -s) flexible organ of many invertebrates, used for grasping, feeding, etc.
tentacles n ▷ tentacle
tentative adj provisional or experimental
> **tentatively** adv
tentatively adv ▷ tentative
tenterhooks pl n tension
tenth adj, n (pl -s) (of) number ten in a series
tenths n ▷ tenth
tents n ▷ tent
tenuous adj slight or flimsy > **tenuously** adv
tenuously adv ▷ tenuous
tenure n (pl -s) (period of) the holding of an office or position
tenures n ▷ tenure
tepee, teepee [tee-pee] n (pl -s) cone-shaped tent, formerly used by Native Americans
tepees n ▷ tepee
tepid adj (-er, -est) slightly warm
tepider adj ▷ tepid
tepidest adj ▷ tepid
tequila n (pl -s) Mexican alcoholic drink

tequilas n ▷ tequila
tercentenaries n ▷ tercentenary
tercentenary adj, n (pl -ries) (of) a three hundredth anniversary
term n (pl -s) word or expression ▶ v (-s, -ing, -ed) name or designate
termed v ▷ term
terminal adj (of an illness) ending in death ▶ n (pl -s) place where people or vehicles begin or end a journey > **terminally** adv
terminally adv ▷ terminal
terminals n ▷ terminal
terminate v (-tes, -ting, -ted) bring or come to an end > **termination** n (pl -s)
terminated v ▷ terminate
terminates v ▷ terminate
terminating v ▷ terminate
termination n ▷ terminate
terminations n ▷ terminate
terming v ▷ term
termini n ▷ terminus
terminologies n ▷ terminology
terminology n (pl -gies) technical terms relating to a subject
terminus n (pl -ni, -nuses) railway or bus station at the end of a line
terminuses n ▷ terminus
termite n (pl -s) white antlike insect that destroys timber
termites n ▷ termite
terms n, v ▷ term ▶ pl n conditions
tern n (pl -s) gull-like sea bird with a forked tail and pointed wings
ternary adj consisting of three parts
terns n ▷ tern
terrace n (pl -s) row of houses built as one block ▶ v (-ces, -cing, -ced) form into or provide with a terrace
terraced v ▷ terrace
terraces n, v ▷ terrace ▶ pl n (also **terracing**) tiered area in a stadium where spectators stand
terracing v ▷ terrace
terracotta adj, n (pl -s) (made of) brownish-red unglazed pottery ▶ adj brownish-red
terracottas n ▷ terracotta
terrain n (pl -s) area of ground, esp. with reference to its physical character
terrains n ▷ terrain
terrapin n (pl -s) small turtle-like reptile
terrapins n ▷ terrapin
terraria n ▷ terrarium
terrarium n (pl -raria, -rariums) enclosed container for small plants or animals
terrariums n ▷ terrarium

terrazzo n (pl -s) floor of marble chips set in mortar and polished
terrazzos n ▷ terrazzo
terrestrial adj of the earth
terrible adj very serious > **terribly** adv
terribly adv ▷ terrible
terrier n (pl -s) any of various breeds of small active dog
terriers n ▷ terrier
terries n ▷ terry
terrific adj great or intense
terrified v, adj ▷ terrify
terrifies v ▷ terrify
terrify v (-fies, -fying, -fied) fill with fear > **terrified** adj > **terrifying** adj
terrifying v, adj ▷ terrify
terrine [terr-**reen**] n (pl -s) earthenware dish with a lid
terrines n ▷ terrine
territorial adj ▷ territory
territories n ▷ territory
territory n (pl -ries) district > **territorial** adj
terror n (pl -s) great fear
terrorism n (pl -s) use of violence and intimidation to achieve political ends > **terrorist** n (pl -s) adj
terrorisms n ▷ terrorism
terrorist n, adj ▷ terrorism
terrorists n ▷ terrorism
terrorize v (-zes, -zing, -zed) force or oppress by fear or violence
terrorized v ▷ terrorize
terrorizes v ▷ terrorize
terrorizing v ▷ terrorize
terrors n ▷ terror
terry n (pl -ries) fabric with small loops covering both sides, used esp. for making towels
terse adj (-r, -st) neat and concise > **tersely** adv
tersely adv ▷ terse
terser adj ▷ terse
tersest adj ▷ terse
tertiary [tur-**shar**-ee] adj third in degree, order, etc.
tessellated adj paved or inlaid with a mosaic of small tiles
test v (-s, -ing, -ed) try out to ascertain the worth, capability, or endurance of ▶ n (pl -s) critical examination > **testing** n
testament n (pl -s) proof or tribute
testaments n ▷ testament
testator [test-**tay**-tor], fem **testatrix** [test-**tay**-triks] n (pl -s, -xes) maker of a will
testators n ▷ testator
testatrix n ▷ testator

testatrixes n ▷ testator
tested v ▷ test
testes n ▷ testis
testicle n (pl -s) either of the two male
reproductive glands
testicles n ▷ testicle
testier adj ▷ testy
testiest adj ▷ testy
testified v ▷ testify
testifies v ▷ testify
testify v (-fies, -fying, -fied) give evidence
under oath
testifying v ▷ testify
testily adv ▷ testy
testimonial n (pl -s) recommendation of the
worth of a person or thing
testimonials n ▷ testimonial
testimonies n ▷ testimony
testimony n (pl -nies) declaration of truth
or fact
testiness n ▷ testy
testinesses n ▷ testy
testing v, n ▷ test
testis n (pl -tes) testicle
testosterone n (pl -s) male sex hormone
secreted by the testes
testosterones n ▷ testosterone
tests v, n ▷ test
testy adj (-tier, -tiest) irritable or touchy
>**testily** adv > **testiness** n (pl -es)
tetanus n (pl -es) acute infectious disease
producing muscular spasms and convulsions
tetanuses n ▷ tetanus
tether n (pl -s) rope or chain for tying an
animal to a spot ▶ v (-s, -ing, -ed) tie up with
rope
tethered v ▷ tether
tethering v ▷ tether
tethers n, v ▷ tether
tetrahedra n ▷ tetrahedron
tetrahedron [tet-ra-**heed**-ron] n (pl -drons, -dra)
solid figure with four faces
tetrahedrons n ▷ tetrahedron
tetralogies n ▷ tetralogy
tetralogy n (pl -gies) series of four related
works
text n (pl -s) main body of a book as distinct
from illustrations etc. ▶ v (-s, -ing, -ed) send a
text message to (someone) >**textual** adj
textbook n (pl -s) standard book on a
particular subject ▶ adj perfect
textbooks n ▷ textbook
texted v ▷ text
textile n (pl -s) fabric or cloth, esp. woven
textiles n ▷ textile

texting v ▷ text
texts n, v ▷ text
textual adj ▷ text
textural adj ▷ texture
texture n (pl -s) structure, feel, or consistency
>**textured** adj >**textural** adj
textured adj ▷ texture
textures n ▷ texture
thalidomide [thal-**lid**-oh-mide] n (pl -s) drug
formerly used as a sedative, but found to
cause abnormalities in developing fetuses
thalidomides n ▷ thalidomide
thallium n (pl -s) (CHEM) highly toxic metallic
element
thalliums n ▷ thallium
than conj, prep used to introduce the second
element of a comparison
thane n (pl -s) (HIST) Anglo-Saxon or medieval
Scottish nobleman
thanes n ▷ thane
thank v (-s, -ing, -ed) express gratitude to
thanked v ▷ thank
thankful adj grateful
thanking v ▷ thank
thankless adj unrewarding or unappreciated
thanks pl n words of gratitude ▶ interj polite
expression of gratitude ▶ v ▷ thank
that adj, pron used to refer to something
already mentioned or familiar, or further
away ▶ conj used to introduce a clause ▶ pron
used to introduce a relative clause
thatch n (pl -es) roofing material of reeds or
straw ▶ v (-ches, -ching, -ched) roof (a house)
with reeds or straw
thatched v ▷ thatch
thatches n, v ▷ thatch
thatching v ▷ thatch
thaw v (-s, -ing, -ed) make or become unfrozen
▶ n (pl -s) thawing
thawed v ▷ thaw
thawing v ▷ thaw
thaws v, n ▷ thaw
the adj the definite article, used before a noun
theatre n (pl -s) place where plays etc. are
performed
theatres n ▷ theatre
theatrical adj of the theatre >**theatrically** adv
>**theatricality** n (pl -ties)
theatricalities n ▷ theatrical
theatricality n ▷ theatrical
theatrically adv ▷ theatrical
theatricals pl n (amateur) dramatic
performances
thee pron (Obs) you
theft n (pl -s) act or an instance of stealing

thefts n ▷ theft
their adj of or associated with them
theirs pron (thing or person) belonging to them
theism [thee-iz-zum] n (pl -s) belief in a God or gods > **theist** n (pl -s) adj > **theistic** adj
theisms n ▷ theism
theist n, adj ▷ theism
theistic adj ▷ theism
theists n ▷ theism
them pron refers to people or things other than the speaker or those addressed
thematic adj ▷ theme
theme n (pl -s) main idea or subject being discussed > **thematic** adj
themes n ▷ theme
themselves pron ▷ they, them
then adv at that time
thence adv from that place or time
theocracies n ▷ theocracy
theocracy n (pl -cies) government by a god or priests > **theocratic** adj
theocratic adj ▷ theocracy
theodolite [thee-odd-oh-lite] n (pl -s) surveying instrument for measuring angles
theodolites n ▷ theodolite
theologian n ▷ theology
theologians n ▷ theology
theological adj ▷ theology
theologically adv ▷ theology
theologies n ▷ theology
theology n (pl -gies) study of religions and religious beliefs > **theologian** n (pl -s) > **theological** adj > **theologically** adv
theorem n (pl -s) proposition that can be proved by reasoning
theorems n ▷ theorem
theoretical adj based on theory rather than practice or fact > **theoretically** adv
theoretically adv ▷ theoretical
theories n ▷ theory
theorist n ▷ theory
theorists n ▷ theory
theorize v (-zes, -zing, -zed) form theories, speculate
theorized v ▷ theorize
theorizes v ▷ theorize
theorizing v ▷ theorize
theory n (pl -ries) set of ideas to explain something > **theorist** n (pl -s)
theosophical adj ▷ theosophy
theosophies n ▷ theosophy
theosophy n (pl -phies) religious or philosophical system claiming to be based on intuitive insight into the divine nature

> **theosophical** adj
therapeutic [ther-rap-pew-tik] adj curing
therapeutics n art of curing
therapies n ▷ therapy
therapist n ▷ therapy
therapists n ▷ therapy
therapy n (pl -pies) curing treatment > **therapist** n (pl -s)
there adv in or to that place
thereby adv by that means
therefore adv consequently, that being so
thereupon adv immediately after that
therm n (pl -s) unit of measurement of heat
thermal adj of heat ▶ n (pl -s) rising current of warm air
thermals n ▷ thermal
thermodynamics n scientific study of the relationship between heat and other forms of energy
thermometer n (pl -s) instrument for measuring temperature
thermometers n ▷ thermometer
thermonuclear adj involving nuclear fusion
thermoplastic adj (of a plastic) softening when heated and resetting on cooling
thermosetting adj (of a plastic) remaining hard when heated
thermostat n (pl -s) device for automatically regulating temperature > **thermostatic** adj
thermostatic adj ▷ thermostat
thermostats n ▷ thermostat
therms n ▷ therm
thesaurus [thiss-sore-uss] n (pl -ruses) book containing lists of synonyms and related words
thesauruses n ▷ thesaurus
these adj, pron ▷ this
theses n ▷ thesis
thesis n (pl theses) written work submitted for a degree
thespian n (pl -s) actor or actress ▶ adj of the theatre
thespians n ▷ thespian
they pron refers to: people or things other than the speaker or people addressed
thiamine n (pl -s) vitamin found in the outer coat of rice and other grains
thiamines n ▷ thiamine
thick adj (-er, -est) of great or specified extent from one side to the other > **thickly** adv
thicken v (-s, -ing, -ed) make or become thick or thicker
thickened v ▷ thicken
thickening v ▷ thicken
thickens v ▷ thicken

thicker adj ▷ thick
thickest adj ▷ thick
thicket n (pl -s) dense growth of small trees
thickets n ▷ thicket
thickly adv ▷ thick
thickness n (pl -es) state of being thick
thicknesses n ▷ thickness
thickset adj stocky in build
thief n (pl thieves) person who steals
thieve v (-ves, -ving, -ved) steal > **thieving** adj
thieved v ▷ thieve
thieves v ▷ thieve ▶ n ▷ thief
thieving v, adj ▷ thieve
thigh n (pl -s) upper part of the human leg
thighs n ▷ thigh
thimble n (pl -s) cap protecting the end of the finger when sewing
thimbles n ▷ thimble
thin adj (-nner, -nnest) not thick ▶ v (-s, -nning, -nned) make or become thin > **thinly** adv
> **thinness** n (pl -es)
thine pron, adj (Obs) (something) of or associated with you (thou)
thing n (pl -s) material object
things n ▷ thing ▶ pl n possessions, clothes, etc.
think v (-s, -ing, thought) consider, judge, or believe > **thinker** n (pl -s) > **thinking** adj, n (pl -s)
thinker n ▷ think
thinkers n ▷ think
thinking v, adj, n ▷ think
thinkings n ▷ think
thinks v ▷ think
thinly adv ▷ thin
thinned v ▷ thin
thinner adj ▷ thin
thinness n ▷ thin
thinnesses n ▷ thin
thinnest adj ▷ thin
thinning v ▷ thin
thins v ▷ thin
third adj of number three in a series ▶ n (pl -s) one of three equal parts
thirds n ▷ third
thirst n (pl -s) desire to drink ▶ v (-s, -ing, -ed) feel thirst > **thirsty** adj (-tier, -tiest) > **thirstily** adv
thirsted v ▷ thirst
thirstier adj ▷ thirst
thirstiest adj ▷ thirst
thirstily adv ▷ thirst
thirsting v ▷ thirst
thirsts n, v ▷ thirst
thirsty adj (-tier, -tiest) ▷ thirst

thirteen adj, n (pl -s) three plus ten
> **thirteenth** adj, n (pl -s)
thirteens n ▷ thirteen
thirteenth n ▷ thirteen
thirteenths n ▷ thirteen
thirties n ▷ thirty
thirtieth n ▷ thirty
thirtieths n ▷ thirty
thirty adj, n (pl -ties) three times ten
> **thirtieth** adj, n (pl -s)
this adj, pron used to refer to a thing or person nearby, just mentioned, or about to be mentioned ▶ adj used to refer to the present time
thistle n (pl -s) prickly plant with dense flower heads
thistles n ▷ thistle
thither adv (Obs) to or towards that place
thong n (pl -s) thin strip of leather etc.
thongs n ▷ thong
thoraces n ▷ thorax
thoracic adj ▷ thorax
thorax n (pl -xes, -races) part of the body between the neck and the abdomen
> **thoracic** adj
thoraxes n ▷ thorax
thorn n (pl -s) prickle on a plant > **thorny** adj (-ier, -iest)
thornier adj ▷ thorn
thorniest adj ▷ thorn
thorns n ▷ thorn
thorny adj ▷ thorn
thorough adj complete > **thoroughly** adv
> **thoroughness** n (pl -es)
thoroughbred n (pl -s) ▶ adj (animal) of pure breed
thoroughbreds n ▷ thoroughbred
thoroughfare n (pl -s) way through from one place to another
thoroughfares n ▷ thoroughfare
thoroughly adv ▷ thorough
thoroughness n ▷ thorough
thoroughnesses n ▷ thorough
those adj, pron ▷ that
thou pron (Obs) you
though conj despite the fact that ▶ adv nevertheless
thought v ▷ think ▶ n (pl -s) thinking
> **thoughtful** adj considerate
thoughtful adj ▷ thought
thoughtless adj inconsiderate
thoughts n ▷ thought
thousand adj, n (pl -s) ten hundred
thousands n ▷ thousand
thousandth adj, n (pl -s) (of) number one

thousand in a series
thousandths n ▷ thousandth
thrall n (pl -s) state of being in the power of another person
thralls n ▷ thrall
thrash v (-es, -ing, -ed) beat, esp. with a stick or whip
thrashed v ▷ thrash
thrashes v ▷ thrash
thrashing n (pl -s) severe beating ▶ v ▷ thrash
thread n (pl -s) fine strand or yarn ▶ v (-s, -ing, -ed) pass thread through
threadbare adj (of fabric) with the nap worn off
threaded v ▷ thread
threading v ▷ thread
threads n, v ▷ thread
threat n (pl -s) declaration of intent to harm
threaten v (-s, -ing, -ed) make or be a threat to
threatened v ▷ threaten
threatening v ▷ threaten
threatens v ▷ threaten
threats n ▷ threat
three adj, n (pl -s) one more than two
threes n ▷ three
threesome n (pl -s) group of three
threesomes n ▷ threesome
threnodies n ▷ threnody
threnody n (pl -dies) lament for the dead
thresh v (-es, -ing, -ed) beat (wheat etc.) to separate the grain from the husks and straw
threshed v ▷ thresh
threshes v ▷ thresh
threshing v ▷ thresh
threshold n (pl -s) bar forming the bottom of a doorway
thresholds n ▷ threshold
threw v ▷ throw
thrice adv (Lit) three times
thrift n (pl -s) wisdom and caution with money > **thrifty** adj
thrifts n ▷ thrift
thrifty adj ▷ thrift
thrill n (pl -s) sudden feeling of excitement ▶ v (-s, -ing, -ed) (cause to) feel a thrill ▶ **thrilling** adj
thrilled v ▷ thrill
thriller n (pl -s) book, film, etc. with an atmosphere of mystery or suspense
thrillers n ▷ thriller
thrilling v, adj ▷ thrill
thrills n, v ▷ thrill
thrive v (-ves, -ving, -ved or **throve**, thrived or **thriven**) flourish or prosper
thrived v ▷ thrive

thriven v ▷ thrive
thrives v ▷ thrive
thriving v ▷ thrive
throat n (pl -s) passage from the mouth and nose to the stomach and lungs
throatier adj ▷ throaty
throatiest adj ▷ throaty
throats n ▷ throat
throaty adj (-tier, -tiest) (of the voice) hoarse
throb v (-s, -bbing, -bbed) pulsate repeatedly ▶ n (pl -s) throbbing
throbbed v ▷ throb
throbbing v ▷ throb
throbs v, n ▷ throb
throes pl n violent pangs or pains
thrombosis n (pl -oses) forming of a clot in a blood vessel or the heart
thromboses n ▷ thrombosis
throne n (pl -s) ceremonial seat of a monarch or bishop
thrones n ▷ throne
throng n (pl -s) ▶ v (-s, -ing, -ed) crowd
thronged v ▷ throng
thronging v ▷ throng
throngs n, v ▷ throng
throstle n (pl -s) song thrush
throstles n ▷ throstle
throttle n (pl -s) device controlling the amount of fuel entering an engine ▶ v (-les, -ling, -led) strangle
throttled v ▷ throttle
throttles n, v ▷ throttle
throttling v ▷ throttle
through prep from end to end or side to side of ▶ adj finished
throughout prep, adv in every part (of)
throughput n (pl -s) amount of material processed
throughputs n ▷ throughput
throve v ▷ thrive
throw v (-s, -ing, threw, thrown) hurl through the air ▶ n (pl -s) throwing
throwaway adj done or said casually
throwback n (pl -s) person or thing that reverts to an earlier type
throwbacks n ▷ throwback
throwing v ▷ throw
thrown v ▷ throw
throws v, n ▷ throw
thrush[1] n (pl -es) brown songbird
thrush[2] n (pl -es) fungal disease of the mouth or vagina
thrushes n ▷ thrush[1, 2]
thrust v (-s, -ing, thrust) push forcefully ▶ n (pl -s) forceful stab

thrusting v ▷ thrust

thrusts v, n ▷ thrust

thud n (pl -s) dull heavy sound ▶ v (-s, -dding, -dded) make such a sound

thudded v ▷ thud

thudding v ▷ thud

thuds n, v ▷ thud

thug n (pl -s) violent man, esp. a criminal > **thuggery** n (pl -ries) > **thuggish** adj

thuggeries n ▷ thug

thuggery n ▷ thug

thuggish adj ▷ thug

thugs n ▷ thug

thumb n (pl -s) short thick finger set apart from the others ▶ v (-s, -ing, -ed) touch or handle with the thumb

thumbed v ▷ thumb

thumbing v ▷ thumb

thumbs n, v ▷ thumb

thump n (pl -s) (sound of) a dull heavy blow ▶ v (-s, -ing, -ed) strike heavily

thumped v ▷ thump

thumping v ▷ thump

thumps n, v ▷ thump

thunder n (pl -s) loud noise accompanying lightning ▶ v (-s, -ing, -ed) rumble with thunder > **thunderous** adj > **thundery** (-rier, -riest) adj

thunderbolt n (pl -s) lightning flash

thunderbolts n ▷ thunderbolt

thunderclap n (pl -s) peal of thunder

thunderclaps n ▷ thunderclap

thundered v ▷ thunder

thunderier adj ▷ thunder

thunderiest adj ▷ thunder

thundering v ▷ thunder

thunderous adj ▷ thunder

thunders v, n ▷ thunder

thunderstruck adj amazed

thundery adj ▷ thunder

thus adv therefore

thwack v (-s, -ing, -ed) ▶ n (pl -s) whack

thwacked v ▷ thwack

thwacking v ▷ thwack

thwacks v, n ▷ thwack

thwart v (-s, -ing, -ed) foil or frustrate ▶ n (pl -s) seat across a boat

thwarted v ▷ thwart

thwarting v ▷ thwart

thwarts v, n ▷ thwart

thy adj (Obs) of or associated with you (thou)

thylacine n (pl -s) extinct doglike Tasmanian marsupial

thylacines n ▷ thylacine

thyme [time] n (pl -s) aromatic herb

thymes n ▷ thyme

thymi n ▷ thymus

thymus n (pl -muses, -mi) small gland at the base of the neck

thymuses n ▷ thymus

thyroid adj, n (pl -s) (of) a gland in the neck controlling body growth

thyroids n ▷ thyroid

thyself pron (Obs) ▷ thou

> **ti** n (tis). Ti means the same as **te**. This is a useful word when you want to form words in more than one direction. Ti scores 2 points.

tiara n (pl -s) semicircular jewelled headdress

tiaras n ▷ tiara

tibia n (pl -biae, -bias) inner bone of the lower leg > **tibial** adj

tibiae n ▷ tibia

tibial adj ▷ tibia

tibias n ▷ tibia

tic n (pl -s) spasmodic muscular twitch

tick[1] n (pl -s) mark (✓) used to check off or indicate the correctness of something ▶ v (-s, -ing, -ed) mark with a tick

tick[2] n (pl -s) tiny bloodsucking parasitic animal

tick[3] n (pl -s) (Informal) credit or account

ticked v ▷ tick[1]

ticket n (pl -s) card or paper entitling the holder to admission, travel, etc. (CHIEFLY US & NZ) ▶ v (-s, -ing, -ed) attach or issue a ticket to

ticketed v ▷ ticket

ticketing v ▷ ticket

tickets n, v ▷ ticket

ticking n (pl -s) strong material for mattress covers ▶ v ▷ tick[1]

tickings n ▷ ticking

tickle v (-les, -ling, -led) touch or stroke (a person) to produce laughter ▶ n (pl -s) tickling

tickled v ▷ tickle

tickles v, n ▷ tickle

tickling v ▷ tickle

ticklish adj sensitive to tickling

ticks v ▷ tick[1] ▶ n ▷ tick[1, 2, 3]

ticktack n (pl -s) (BRIT) bookmakers' sign language

ticktacks n ▷ ticktack

tics n ▷ tic

tidal adj ▷ tide

tiddler n (pl -s) (Informal) very small fish

tiddlers n ▷ tiddler

tiddlier adj ▷ tiddly[1, 2]

tiddliest adj ▷ tiddly[1, 2]

tiddly[1] adj (-dlier, -dliest) tiny

tiddly[2] adj (-dlier, -dliest) (Informal) slightly

drunk

tiddlywink n small plastic disc

tiddlywinks n game in which players try to flip small plastic discs into a cup

tide n (pl -s) rise and fall of the sea caused by the gravitational pull of the sun and moon > **tidal** adj

  tides n ▷ tide

  tidied v ▷ tidy

  tidier adj ▷ tidy

  tidies v ▷ tidy

  tidiest adj ▷ tidy

  tidily adv ▷ tidy

  tidiness n ▷ tidy

  tidinesses n ▷ tidy

tidings pl n news

tidy adj (-dier, -diest) neat and orderly ▶ v (-dies, -dying, -died) put in order > **tidily** adv > **tidiness** n (pl -es)

  tidying v ▷ tidy

tie v (ties, tying, tied) fasten or be fastened with string, rope, etc. ▶ n (pl -s) long narrow piece of material worn knotted round the neck

  tied v ▷ tie ▶ adj (BRIT) (of a cottage etc.) rented to the tenant only as long as he or she is employed by the owner

tier n (pl -s) one of a set of rows placed one above and behind the other

  tiers n ▷ tier

  ties v, n ▷ tie

tiff n (pl -s) petty quarrel

  tiffs n ▷ tiff

tiger n (pl -s) large yellow-and-black striped Asian cat

  tigers n ▷ tiger

tight adj (-er, -est) stretched or drawn taut > **tightly** adv

tighten v (-s, -ing, -ed) make or become tight or tighter

  tightened v ▷ tighten

  tightening v ▷ tighten

  tightens v ▷ tighten

  tighter adj ▷ tight

  tightest adj ▷ tight

  tightly adv ▷ tight

tightrope n (pl -s) rope stretched taut on which acrobats perform

  tightropes n ▷ tightrope

tights pl n one-piece clinging garment covering the body from the waist to the feet

tigress n (pl -s) female tiger

  tigresses n ▷ tigress

tiki n (pl -s) (NZ) small carving of a grotesque person worn as a pendant

  tikis n ▷ tiki

tikka adj (INDIAN COOKERY) marinated in spices and dry-roasted

tilde n (pl -s) mark (~) used in Spanish to indicate that the letter 'n' is to be pronounced in a particular way

  tildes n ▷ tilde

tile n (pl -s) flat piece of ceramic, plastic, etc. used to cover a roof, floor, or wall ▶ v (-les, -ling, -led) cover with tiles > **tiled** adj

  tiled v, adj ▷ tile

  tiles n, v ▷ tile

tiling n (pl -s) tiles collectively ▶ v ▷ tile

  tilings n ▷ tiling

till¹ conj, prep until

till² v (-s, -ing, -ed) cultivate (land) > **tillage** n (pl -s)

till³ n (pl -s) drawer for money, usu. in a cash register

  tillage n ▷ till²

  tillages n ▷ till²

  tilled v ▷ till²

tiller n (pl -s) lever to move a rudder of a boat

  tillers n ▷ tiller

  tilling v ▷ till²

  tills v ▷ till² ▶ n ▷ till³

tilt v (-s, -ing, -ed) slant at an angle ▶ n (pl -s) slope

  tilted v ▷ tilt

  tilting v ▷ tilt

  tilts v, n ▷ tilt

timber n (pl -s) wood as a building material > **timbered** adj

  timbered adj ▷ timber

  timbers n ▷ timber

timbre [tam-bra] n (pl -s) distinctive quality of sound of a voice or instrument

  timbres n ▷ timbre

time n (pl -s) past, present, and future as a continuous whole ▶ v (-mes, -ming, -med) note the time taken by

  timed v ▷ time

timeless adj unaffected by time

  timelier adj ▷ timely

  timeliest adj ▷ timely

timely adj (-lier, -liest) at the appropriate time

timepiece n (pl -s) watch or clock

  timepieces n ▷ timepiece

  times n, v ▷ time

timeserver n (pl -s) person who changes his or her views to gain support or favour

  timeservers n ▷ timeserver

timetable n (pl -s) plan showing the times when something takes place, the departure and arrival times of trains or buses, etc.

timetables n ▷ timetable

timid adj (-er, -est) easily frightened > timidly adv ▷ timidity n (pl -dies)

timider adj ▷ timid

timidest adj ▷ timid

timidities n ▷ timid

timidity n ▷ timid

timidly adv ▷ timid

timing v ▷ time

timorous adj timid

timpani [tim-pan-ee] pl n set of kettledrums > timpanist n (pl -s)

timpanist n ▷ timpani

timpanists n ▷ timpani

tin n (pl -s) soft metallic element

tincture n (pl -s) medicinal extract in a solution of alcohol

tinctures n ▷ tincture

tinder n (pl -s) dry easily-burning material used to start a fire > tinderbox n (pl -es)

tinderbox n ▷ tinder

tinderboxes n ▷ tinder

tinders n ▷ tinder

tine n (pl -s) prong of a fork or antler

tines n ▷ tine

ting n (pl -s) high metallic sound, as of a small bell

tinge n (pl -s) slight tint ▶ v (-ges, -geing, -ged) give a slight tint or trace to

tinged v ▷ tinge

tinges n, v ▷ tinge

tinging v ▷ tinge

tingle v (-les, -ling, -led) ▶ n (pl -s) (feel) a prickling or stinging sensation

tingled v ▷ tingle

tingles v, n ▷ tingle

tingling v ▷ tingle

tings n ▷ ting

tinier adj ▷ tiny

tiniest adj ▷ tiny

tinker n (pl -s) travelling mender of pots and pans ▶ v (-s, -ing, -ed) fiddle with (an engine etc.) in an attempt to repair it

tinkered v ▷ tinker

tinkering v ▷ tinker

tinkers n, v ▷ tinker

tinkle v (-les, -ling, -led) ring with a high tinny sound like a small bell ▶ n (pl -s) this sound or action

tinkled v ▷ tinkle

tinkles v, n ▷ tinkle

tinkling v ▷ tinkle

tinned adj (of food) preserved by being sealed in a tin

tinnier adj ▷ tinny

tinniest adj ▷ tinny

tinny adj (-nnier, -nniest) (of sound) thin and metallic

tinpot adj (Informal) worthless or unimportant

tins n ▷ tin

tinsel n (pl -s) decorative metallic strips or threads

tinsels n ▷ tinsel

tint n (pl -s) (pale) shade of a colour ▶ v (-s, -ing, -ed) give a tint to

tinted v ▷ tint

tinting v ▷ tint

tints n, v ▷ tint

tiny adj (-ier, -iest) very small

tip¹ n (pl -s) narrow or pointed end of anything ▶ v (-s, -pping, -pped) put a tip on

tip² n (pl -s) money given in return for service ▶ v (-s, -pping, -pped) give a tip to

tip³ v (-s, -pping, -pped) tilt or overturn ▶ n (pl -s) rubbish dump

tipped v ▷ tip¹,²,³

tipping v ▷ tip¹,²,³

tipple v (-les, -ling, -led) drink alcohol habitually, esp. in small quantities ▶ n (pl -s) alcoholic drink > tippler n (pl -s)

tippled v ▷ tipple

tippler n ▷ tipple

tipplers n ▷ tipple

tipples v, n ▷ tipple

tippling v ▷ tipple

tips n, v ▷ tip¹,²,³

tipsier adj ▷ tipsy

tipsiest adj ▷ tipsy

tipster n (pl -s) person who sells tips about races

tipsters n ▷ tipster

tipsy adj (-sier, -siest) slightly drunk

tiptoe v (-toes, -toeing, -toed) walk quietly with the heels off the ground

tiptoed v ▷ tiptoe

tiptoeing v ▷ tiptoe

tiptoes v ▷ tiptoe

tiptop adj of the highest quality or condition

tirade n (pl -s) long angry speech

tirades n ▷ tirade

tire v (-res, -ring, -red) reduce the energy of, as by exertion > tiring adj

tired adj (-er, -est) exhausted ▶ v ▷ tire

tireder adj ▷ tired

tiredest adj ▷ tired

tireless adj energetic and determined

tires v ▷ tire

tiresome adj boring and irritating

tiring v, adj ▷ tire

tissue n (pl -s) substance of an animal body

or plant

tissues n ▷ tissue

tit¹ n (pl -s) any of various small songbirds

tit² n (pl -s) (Slang) female breast

titanic adj huge or very important

titanium n (pl -s) (CHEM) strong light metallic element used to make alloys

titaniums n ▷ titanium

titbit n (pl -s) tasty piece of food

titbits n ▷ titbit

tithe n (pl -s) esp. formerly, one tenth of one's income or produce paid to the church as a tax

tithes n ▷ tithe

titian [tish-an] adj (of hair) reddish-gold

titillate v (-tes, -ting, -ted) excite or stimulate pleasurably > **titillating** adj > **titillation** n (pl -s)

titillated v ▷ titillate

titillates v ▷ titillate

titillating v, adj ▷ titillate

titillation n ▷ titillate

titillations n ▷ titillate

titivate v (-tes, -ting, -ted) smarten up

titivated v ▷ titivate

titivates v ▷ titivate

titivating v ▷ titivate

title n (pl -s) name of a book, film, etc.

titled adj aristocratic

titles n ▷ title

tits n ▷ tit¹, ²

titter v (-s, -ing, -ed) laugh in a suppressed way ▶ n (pl -s) suppressed laugh

tittered v ▷ titter

tittering v ▷ titter

titters v, n ▷ titter

titular adj in name only

tizzies n ▷ tizzy

tizzy n (pl -zies) (Informal) confused or agitated state

tix pl n. Tix is an informal word for **tickets**. This is a good word if you are struggling to use an X towards the end of a game.

to prep indicating movement towards, equality or comparison, etc. ▶ adv to a closed position

toad n (pl -s) animal like a large frog

toadied v ▷ toady

toadies n, v ▷ toady

toads n ▷ toad

toadstool n (pl -s) poisonous fungus like a mushroom

toadstools n ▷ toadstool

toady n (pl -dies) ingratiating person ▶ v (-dies, -dying, -died) be ingratiating

toadying v ▷ toady

toast¹ n (pl -s) sliced bread browned by heat ▶ v (-s, -ing, -ed) brown (bread) by heat

toast² n (pl -s) tribute or proposal of health or success marked by people raising glasses and drinking together ▶ v (-s, -ing, -ed) drink a toast to

toasted v, n ▷ toast¹, ²

toaster n (pl -s) electrical device for toasting bread

toasters n ▷ toaster

toasting n, v ▷ toast¹, ²

toasts n, v ▷ toast¹, ²

tobacco n (pl -os, -oes) plant with large leaves dried for smoking

tobaccoes n ▷ tobacco

tobacconist n (pl -s) person or shop selling tobacco, cigarettes, etc.

tobacconists n ▷ tobacconist

tobaccos n ▷ tobacco

toboggan n (pl -s) narrow sledge for sliding over snow ▶ v (-s, -ing, -ed) ride a toboggan

tobogganed v ▷ toboggan

tobogganing v ▷ toboggan

toboggans n, v ▷ toboggan

toccata [tok-kah-ta] n (pl -s) rapid piece of music for a keyboard instrument

toccatas n ▷ toccata

today n (pl -s) this day ▶ adv on this day

todays n ▷ today

toddies n ▷ toddy

toddle v (-les, -ling, -led) walk with short unsteady steps

toddled v ▷ toddle

toddler n (pl -s) child beginning to walk

toddlers n ▷ toddler

toddles v ▷ toddle

toddling v ▷ toddle

toddy n (pl -dies) sweetened drink of spirits and hot water

toe n (pl -s) digit of the foot ▶ v (toes, toeing, toed) touch or kick with the toe

toed v ▷ toe

toeing v ▷ toe

toes n, v ▷ toe

toff n (pl -s) (BRIT) (Slang) well-dressed or upper-class person

toffee n (pl -s) chewy sweet made of boiled sugar

toffees n ▷ toffee

toffs n ▷ toff

tofu n (pl -s) soft food made from soya-bean curd

tofus n ▷ tofu

tog n (pl -s) unit for measuring the insulating

power of duvets

toga [toe-ga] n (pl -s) garment worn by citizens of ancient Rome

togas n ▷ toga

together adv in company ▶ adj (Informal) organized

toggle n (pl -s) small bar-shaped button inserted through a loop for fastening

toggles n ▷ toggle

togs n ▷ tog

toil n (pl -s) hard work ▶ v (-s, -ing, -ed) work hard

toiled v ▷ toil

toilet n (pl -s) (room with) a bowl connected to a drain for receiving and disposing of urine and faeces

toiletries n ▷ toiletry

toiletry n (pl -ries) object or cosmetic used to clean or groom oneself

toilets n ▷ toilet

toiling v ▷ toil

toils n, v ▷ toil

token n (pl -s) sign or symbol ▶ adj nominal or slight

tokenism n (pl -s) policy of making only a token effort, esp. to comply with a law

tokenisms n ▷ tokenism

tokens n ▷ token

told v ▷ tell

tolerable adj bearable > **tolerably** adv

tolerably adv ▷ tolerable

tolerance n (pl -s) acceptance of other people's rights to their own opinions or actions > **tolerant** adj > **tolerantly** adv > **toleration** n (pl -s)

tolerances n ▷ tolerance

tolerant adj ▷ tolerance

tolerantly adv ▷ tolerance

tolerate v (-tes, -ting, -ted) allow to exist or happen

tolerated v ▷ tolerate

tolerates v ▷ tolerate

tolerating v ▷ tolerate

toleration n ▷ tolerance

tolerations n ▷ tolerance

toll v (-s, -ing, -ed) ring (a bell) slowly and regularly, esp. to announce a death ▶ n (pl -s) tolling

toll² n (pl -s) charge for the use of a bridge or road

tolled v ▷ toll¹

tolling v ▷ toll¹

tolls n ▷ toll¹, ² v ▷ toll¹

tom n (pl -s) male cat

tomahawk n (pl -s) fighting axe of the Native Americans

tomahawks n ▷ tomahawk

tomato n (pl -es) red fruit used in salads and as a vegetable

tomatoes n ▷ tomato

tomb n (pl -s) grave

tombola n (pl -s) lottery with tickets drawn from a revolving drum

tombolas n ▷ tombola

tomboy n (pl -s) girl who acts or dresses like a boy

tomboys n ▷ tomboy

tombs n ▷ tomb

tombstone n (pl -s) gravestone

tombstones n ▷ tombstone

tome n (pl -s) large heavy book

tomes n ▷ tome

tomfooleries n ▷ tomfoolery

tomfoolery n (pl -ries) foolish behaviour

tomorrow adv, n (pl -s) (on) the day after today

tomorrows n ▷ tomorrow

toms n ▷ tom

ton n (pl -s) unit of weight equal to 2240 pounds or 1016 kilograms or, in the US, 2000 pounds or 907 kilograms

tonal adj (MUSIC) written in a key > **tonality** n (pl -ties)

tonalities n ▷ tonal

tonality n ▷ tonal

tone n (pl -s) sound with reference to its pitch, volume, etc. ▶ v (-nes, -ning, -ned) harmonize (with) > **toneless** adj

toned v ▷ tone

toneless adj ▷ tone

tones n, v ▷ tone

tongs pl n large pincers for grasping and lifting

tongue n (pl -s) muscular organ in the mouth, used in speaking and tasting

tongues n ▷ tongue

tonic n (pl -s) medicine to improve body tone ▶ adj invigorating

tonics n ▷ tonic

tonight adv, n (pl -s) (in or during) the night or evening of this day

tonights n ▷ tonight

toning v ▷ tone

tonnage n (pl -s) weight capacity of a ship

tonnages n ▷ tonnage

tonne [tunn] n (pl -s) unit of weight equal to 1000 kilograms

tonnes n ▷ tonne

tons n ▷ ton

tonsil n (pl -s) small gland in the throat

tonsillectomies n ▷ tonsillectomy

tonsillectomy n (pl -mies) surgical removal

of the tonsils

tonsillitis n (pl -tises) inflammation of the tonsils

tonsillitises n ▷ tonsillitis

tonsils n ▷ tonsil

tonsure n (pl -s) shaving of all or the top of the head as a religious or monastic practice > **tonsured** adj

tonsured adj ▷ tonsure

tonsures n ▷ tonsure

too adv also, as well

took v ▷ take

tool n (pl -s) implement used by hand

tools n ▷ tool

toot n (pl -s) short hooting sound ▶ v (-s, -ing, -ed) (cause to) make such a sound

tooted v ▷ toot

tooth n (pl teeth) bonelike projection in the jaws of most vertebrates for biting and chewing > **toothless** adj

toothless adj ▷ tooth

toothpaste n (pl -s) paste used to clean the teeth

toothpastes n ▷ toothpaste

toothpick n (pl -s) small stick for removing scraps of food from between the teeth

toothpicks n ▷ toothpick

tooting v ▷ toot

toots n, v ▷ toot

top¹ n (pl -s) highest point or part ▶ adj at or of the top ▶ v (-s, -pping, -pped) form a top on

top² n (pl -s) toy which spins on a pointed base

topaz [toe-pazz] n (pl -es) semiprecious stone in various colours

topazes n ▷ topaz

topee, topi [toe-pee] n (pl -s) lightweight hat worn in tropical countries

topees n ▷ topee

topi n ▷ topee

topiaries n ▷ topiary

topiary [tope-yar-ee] n (pl -ries) art of trimming trees and bushes into decorative shapes

topic n (pl -s) subject of a conversation, book, etc.

topical adj relating to current events > **topicality** n (pl -ties)

topicalities n ▷ topical

topicality n ▷ topical

topics n ▷ topic

topis n ▷ topee

topless adj (of a costume or woman) with no covering for the breasts

topmost adj highest or best

topographer n ▷ topography

topographers n ▷ topography

topographical adj ▷ topography

topographies n ▷ topography

topography n (pl -phies) (science of describing) the surface features of a place > **topographer** n (pl -s) > **topographical** adj

topological adj ▷ topology

topologies n ▷ topology

topology n (pl -gies) geometry of the properties of a shape which are unaffected by continuous distortion > **topological** adj

topped n ▷ top¹

topping n (pl -s) sauce or garnish for food ▶ v ▷ top¹

toppings n ▷ topping

topple v (-les, -ling, -led) (cause to) fall over

toppled v ▷ topple

topples v ▷ topple

toppling v ▷ topple

top-notch adj excellent, first-class

tops n ▷ top¹, ² ▶ v ▷ top¹

topsoil n (pl -s) surface layer of soil

topsoils n ▷ topsoil

toque [toke] n (pl -s) small round hat

toques n ▷ toque

tor n (pl -s) high rocky hill

torch n (pl -es) small portable battery-powered lamp ▶ v (-es, -ing, -ed) (Informal) deliberately set (a building) on fire

torched v ▷ torch

torches n, v ▷ torch

torching v ▷ torch

tore v ▷ tear²

toreador [torr-ee-a-dor] n (pl -s) bullfighter

toreadors n ▷ toreador

torment v (-s, -ing, -ed) cause (someone) great suffering ▶ n (pl -s) great suffering > **tormentor** n (pl -s)

tormented v ▷ torment

tormenting v ▷ torment

tormentor n ▷ torment

tormentors n ▷ torment

torments v, n ▷ torment

torn v ▷ tear²

tornado n (pl -s, -es) violent whirlwind

tornadoes n ▷ tornado

tornados n ▷ tornado

torpedo n (pl -es) self-propelled underwater missile ▶ v (-es, -ing, -ed) attack or destroy with or as if with torpedoes

torpedoed v ▷ torpedo

torpedoes n, v ▷ torpedo

torpedoing v ▷ torpedo

torpid adj sluggish and inactive

torpor n (pl -s) torpid state

torpors n ▷ torpor

torque [tork] n (pl -s) force causing rotation
  torques n ▷ torque
torrent n (pl -s) rushing stream
torrential adj (of rain) very heavy
  torrents n ▷ torrent
torrid adj (-er, -est) very hot and dry
  torrider adj ▷ torrid
  torridest adj ▷ torrid
  tors n ▷ tor
torsion n (pl -s) twisting of a part by equal
  forces being applied at both ends but in
  opposite directions
  torsions n ▷ torsion
torso n (pl -s) trunk of the human body
  torsos n ▷ torso
tort n (pl -s) (LAW) civil wrong or injury for
  which damages may be claimed
tortilla n (pl -s) thin Mexican pancake
  tortillas n ▷ tortilla
tortoise n (pl -s) slow-moving land reptile with
  a dome-shaped shell
  tortoises n ▷ tortoise
tortoiseshell n (pl -s) mottled brown shell of
  a turtle, used for making ornaments ▶ adj
  having brown, orange, and black markings
  tortoiseshells n ▷ tortoiseshell
  torts n ▷ tort
tortuous adj winding or twisting
torture v (-res, -ring, -red) cause (someone)
  severe pain or mental anguish ▶ n (pl -s)
  severe physical or mental pain > **torturer**
  n (pl -s)
  tortured v ▷ torture
  torturer n ▷ torture
  torturers n ▷ torture
  tortures v, n ▷ torture
  torturing v ▷ torture
toss v (-es, -ing, -ed) throw lightly ▶ n (pl -es)
  tossing
  tossed v ▷ toss
  tosses v, n ▷ toss
  tossing v ▷ toss
tot¹ n (pl -s) small child
tot² v (-s, -tting, -tted) add (numbers) together
total n (pl -s) whole, esp. a sum of parts ▶ adj
  complete ▶ v (-s, -lling, -lled) amount to
  > **totally** adv > **totality** n (pl -ties)
totalitarian adj of a dictatorial one-party
  government > **totalitarianism** n (pl -s)
  totalitarianism n ▷ totalitarian
  totalitarianisms n ▷ totalitarian
  totalities n ▷ total
  totality n ▷ total
  totalled v ▷ total
  totalling v ▷ total

totally adv ▷ total
  totals n, v ▷ total
tote¹ v (-tes, -ting, -ted) carry (a gun etc.)
tote² n (pl -s) > totalizator
  toted v ▷ tote¹
totem n (pl -s) tribal badge or emblem
  totems n ▷ totem
  totes v ▷ tote¹ ▶ n ▷ tote²
  toting v ▷ tote¹
  tots n ▷ tot¹ ▶ v ▷ tot²
  totted v ▷ tot²
totter v (-s, -ing, -ed) move unsteadily
  tottered v ▷ totter
  tottering v ▷ totter
  totters v ▷ totter
  totting v ▷ tot²
toucan n (pl -s) tropical American bird with
  a large bill
  toucans n ▷ toucan
touch v (-es, -ing, -ed) come into contact
  with ▶ n (pl -es) sense by which an object's
  qualities are perceived when they come into
  contact with part of the body ▶ adj of a non-
  contact version of particular sport
touché [too-shay] interj acknowledgment of
  the striking home of a remark or witty reply
touched adj emotionally moved ▶ v ▷ touch
  touches v, n ▷ touch
  touchier adj ▷ touchy
  touchiest adj ▷ touchy
touching adj emotionally moving ▶ v ▷ touch
touchline n (pl -s) side line of the pitch in some
  games
  touchlines n ▷ touchline
touchstone n (pl -s) standard by which a
  judgment is made
  touchstones n ▷ touchstone
touchy adj (-chier, -chiest) easily offended
tough adj (-er, -est) strong or resilient ▶ n (pl -s)
  (Informal) rough violent person > **toughness**
  n (pl -es)
toughen v (-s, -ing, -ed) make or become
  tough or tougher
  toughened v ▷ toughen
  toughening v ▷ toughen
  toughens v ▷ toughen
  tougher adj ▷ tough
  toughest adj ▷ tough
  toughness n ▷ tough
  toughnesses n ▷ tough
  toughs n ▷ tough
toupee [too-pay] n (pl -s) small wig
  toupees n ▷ toupee
tour n (pl -s) journey visiting places of interest
  along the way ▶ v (-s, -ing, -ed) make a tour

(of)

toured v ▷ tour

touring v ▷ tour

tourism n (pl -s) tourist travel as an industry
 tourisms n ▷ tourism

tourist n (pl -s) person travelling for pleasure
 tourists n ▷ tourist

touristy adj (Informal) (often derogatory) full of tourists or tourist attractions

tournament n (pl -s) sporting competition with several stages to decide the overall winner
 tournaments n ▷ tournament

tourniquet [tour-nick-kay] n (pl -s) something twisted round a limb to stop bleeding
 tourniquets n ▷ tourniquet

tours n, v ▷ tour

tousled adj ruffled and untidy

tout [rhymes with **shout**] v (-s, -ing, -ed) seek business in a persistent manner ▶ n (pl -s) person who sells tickets for a popular event at inflated prices
 touted v ▷ tout
 touting v ▷ tout
 touts v, n ▷ tout

tow[1] v (-s, -ing, -ed) drag, esp. by means of a rope ▶ n (pl -s) towing

tow[2] n (pl -s) fibre of hemp or flax

toward n ▷ towards

towards, toward prep in the direction of

towbar n (pl -s) metal bar on a car for towing vehicles
 towbars n ▷ towbar

towed v ▷ tow[1]

towel n (pl -s) cloth for drying things

towelling n (pl -s) material used for making towels
 towellings n ▷ towelling
 towels n ▷ towel

tower n (pl -s) tall structure, often forming part of a larger building
 towers n ▷ tower

towing v ▷ tow[1]

town n (pl -s) group of buildings larger than a village
 towns n ▷ town

township n (pl -s) small town
 townships n ▷ township

towpath n (pl -s) path beside a canal or river, originally for horses towing boats
 towpaths n ▷ towpath
 tows n ▷ tow[1, 2] ▶ v ▷ tow[1]

toxaemia [tox-**seem**-ya] n (pl -s) blood poisoning
 toxaemias n ▷ toxaemia

toxic adj poisonous > **toxicity** n (pl -ties)
 toxicities n ▷ toxic
 toxicity n ▷ toxic
 toxicologies n ▷ toxicology

toxicology n (pl -gies) study of poisons

toxin n (pl -s) poison of bacterial origin
 toxins n ▷ toxin

toy n (pl -s) something designed to be played with ▶ adj (of a dog) of a variety much smaller than is normal for that breed ▶ v (-s, -ing, -ed) play
 toyed v ▷ toy
 toying v ▷ toy
 toys n, v ▷ toy

trace v (-ces, -cing, -ced) track down and find ▶ n (pl -s) track left by something > **traceable** adj
 traceable adj ▷ trace
 traced v ▷ trace

tracer n (pl -s) projectile which leaves a visible trail
 traceries n ▷ tracery
 tracers n ▷ tracer

tracery n (pl -ries) pattern of interlacing lines

traces v, n ▷ trace ▶ pl n strap by which a horse pulls a vehicle

trachea [track-**kee**-a] n (pl -cheae) windpipe
 tracheae n ▷ trachea
 tracheotomies n ▷ tracheotomy

tracheotomy [track-ee-ot-a-mee] n (pl -mies) surgical incision into the trachea

tracing n (pl -s) traced copy ▶ v ▷ trace

track n (pl -s) rough road or path ▶ v (-s, -ing, -ed) follow the trail or path of
 tracked v ▷ track
 tracking v ▷ track
 tracks n, v ▷ track

tracksuit n (pl -s) warm loose-fitting suit worn by athletes etc., esp. during training
 tracksuits n ▷ tracksuit

tract[1] n (pl -s) wide area

tract[2] n (pl -s) pamphlet, esp. a religious one

tractable adj easy to manage or control

traction n (pl -s) pulling, esp. by engine power
 tractions n ▷ traction

tractor n (pl -s) motor vehicle with large rear wheels for pulling farm machinery
 tractors n ▷ tractor
 tracts n ▷ tract[1, 2]

trade n (pl -s) buying, selling, or exchange of goods ▶ v (-des, -ding, -ded) buy and sell > **trader** n (pl -s) > **trading** n (pl -s)
 traded v ▷ trade

trademark n (pl -s) (legally registered) name or symbol used by a firm to distinguish its

goods
trademarks n ▷ trademark
trader n ▷ trade
traders n ▷ trade
trades n, v ▷ trade
tradesman n (pl -men) skilled worker
tradesmen n ▷ tradesman
trading v, n ▷ trade
tradings n ▷ trad
tradition n (pl -s) body of beliefs, customs, etc. handed down from generation to generation > traditional adj > traditionally adv
traditional adj ▷ tradition
traditionally adv ▷ tradition
traditions n ▷ tradition
traduce v (-ces, -cing, -ced) slander
traduced v ▷ traduce
traduces v ▷ traduce
traducing v ▷ traduce
traffic n (pl -s) vehicles coming and going on a road ▶ v (-s, -cking, -cked) trade, usu. illicitly > trafficker n (pl -s)
trafficked v ▷ traffic
trafficker n ▷ traffic
traffickers n ▷ traffic
trafficking v ▷ traffic
traffics n, v ▷ traffic
tragedian [traj-jee-dee-an], tragedienne [traj-jee-dee-enn] n (pl -s) person who acts in or writes tragedies
tragedians n ▷ tragedian
tragedies n ▷ tragedy
tragedy n (pl -dies) shocking or sad event
tragic adj of or like a tragedy > tragically adv
tragically adv ▷ tragic
tragicomedies n ▷ tragicomedy
tragicomedy n (pl -s) play with both tragic and comic elements
trail n (pl -s) path, track, or road ▶ v (-s, -ing, -ed) drag along the ground
trailed v ▷ trail
trailer n (pl -s) vehicle designed to be towed by another vehicle
trailers n ▷ trailer
trailing v ▷ trail
trails n, v ▷ trail
train v (-s, -ing, -ed) instruct in a skill ▶ n (pl -s) line of railway coaches or wagons drawn by an engine
trained v ▷ train
trainee n (pl -s) person being trained
trainees n ▷ trainee
trainer n (pl -s) person who trains an athlete or sportsman
trainers n ▷ trainer

training v ▷ train
trains v, n ▷ train
traipse v (-pses, -psing, -psed) (Informal) walk wearily
traipsed v ▷ traipse
traipses v ▷ traipse
traipsing v ▷ traipse
trait n (pl -s) characteristic feature
traitor n (pl -s) person guilty of treason or treachery > traitorous adj
traitorous adj ▷ traitor
traitors n ▷ traitor
traits n ▷ trait
trajectories n ▷ trajectory
trajectory n (pl -ries) line of flight, esp. of a projectile
tram n (pl -s) public transport vehicle powered by an overhead wire and running on rails laid in the road
tramlines pl n track for trams
tramp v (-s, -ing, -ed) travel on foot, hike ▶ n (pl -s) homeless person who travels on foot
tramped v ▷ tramp
tramping v ▷ tramp
trample v (-les, -ling, -led) tread on and crush
trampled v ▷ trample
tramples v ▷ trample
trampling v ▷ trample
trampoline n (pl -s) tough canvas sheet attached to a frame by springs, used by acrobats etc. ▶ v (-nes, -ning, -ned) bounce on a trampoline
trampolined v ▷ trampoline
trampolines n, v ▷ trampoline
trampolining v ▷ trampoline
tramps n ▷ tramp
trams n ▷ tram
trance n (pl -s) unconscious or dazed state
trances n ▷ trance
tranche n (pl -s) portion of something large, esp. a sum of money
tranches n ▷ tranche
tranquil adj (-ler, -lest) calm and quiet > tranquilly adv > tranquillity n (pl -ties)
tranquiller adj ▷ tough
tranquillest adj ▷ tough
tranquillities n ▷ tranquil
tranquillity n ▷ tranquil
tranquillize v (-zes, -zing, -zed) make calm
tranquillized v ▷ tranquillize
tranquillizer n (pl -s) drug which reduces anxiety or tension
tranquillizers n ▷ tranquillizer
tranquillizes v ▷ tranquillize
tranquillizing v ▷ tranquillize

tranquilly adv ▷ tranquil

transact v (-s, -ing, -ed) conduct or negotiate (a business deal)

    transacted v ▷ transact

    transacting v ▷ transact

transaction n (pl -s) business deal transacted

    transactions n ▷ transaction

    transacts v ▷ transact

transatlantic adj on, from, or to the other side of the Atlantic

transceiver n (pl -s) transmitter and receiver of radio or electronic signals

    transceivers n ▷ transceiver

transcend v (-s, -ing, -ed) rise above > **transcendence** n (pl -s) > **transcendent** adj

    transcended v ▷ transcend

    transcendence n ▷ transcend

    transcendences n ▷ transcend

    transcendent adj ▷ transcend

transcendental adj based on intuition rather than experience

    transcending v ▷ transcend

    transcends v ▷ transcend

transcribe v (-bes, -bing, -bed) write down (something said)

    transcribed v ▷ transcribe

    transcribes v ▷ transcribe

    transcribing v ▷ transcribe

transcript n (pl -s) copy

    transcripts n ▷ transcript

transducer n (pl -s) device that converts one form of energy to another

    transducers n ▷ transducer

transept n (pl -s) either of the two shorter wings of a cross-shaped church

    transepts n ▷ transept

    transexual n ▷ transsexual

    transexuals n ▷ transsexual

transfer v (-fers, -ferring, -ferred) move or send from one person or place to another ▶ n (pl -s) transferring > **transferable** adj

    transferable adj ▷ transfer

transference n (pl -s) transferring

    transferences n ▷ transference

    transferred v ▷ transfer

    transferring v ▷ transfer

    transfers v, n ▷ transfer

    transfiguration n ▷ transfigure

    transfigurations n ▷ transfigure

transfigure v (-res, -ring, -red) change in appearance > **transfiguration** n (pl -s)

    transfigured v ▷ transfigure

    transfigures v ▷ transfigure

    transfiguring v ▷ transfigure

transfix v (-es, -ing, -ed) astound or stun

    transfixed v ▷ transfix

    transfixes v ▷ transfix

    transfixing v ▷ transfix

transform v (-s, -ing, -ed) change the shape or character of > **transformation** n (pl -s)

    transformation n ▷ transform

    transformations n ▷ transform

    transformed v ▷ transform

transformer n (pl -s) device for changing the voltage of an alternating current

    transformers n ▷ transformer

    transforming v ▷ transform

    transforms v ▷ transform

transfuse v (-ses, -sing, -sed) give a transfusion to

    transfused v ▷ transfuse

    transfuses v ▷ transfuse

    transfusing v ▷ transfuse

transfusion n (pl -s) injection of blood into the blood vessels of a patient

    transfusions n ▷ transfusion

transgress v (-es, -ing, -ed) break (a moral law) > **transgression** n (pl -s) > **transgressor** n (pl -s)

    transgressed v ▷ transgress

    transgresses v ▷ transgress

    transgressing v ▷ transgress

    transgression n ▷ transgress

    transgressions n ▷ transgress

    transgressor n ▷ transgress

    transgressors n ▷ transgress

    transience n ▷ transient

    transiences n ▷ transient

transient adj lasting only for a short time > **transience** n (pl -s)

transistor n (pl -s) semiconducting device used to amplify electric currents

    transistors n ▷ transistor

transit n (pl -s) movement from one place to another

transition n (pl -s) change from one state to another > **transitional** adj

    transitional adj ▷ transition

    transitions n ▷ transition

transitive adj (GRAMMAR) (of a verb) requiring a direct object

transitory adj not lasting long

    transits n ▷ transit

translate v (-tes, -ting, -ted) turn from one language into another > **translation** n (pl -s) > **translator** n (pl -s)

    translated v ▷ translate

    translates v ▷ translate

    translating v ▷ translate

    translation n ▷ translat

translations n ▷ translat
translator n ▷ translate
translators n ▷ translate
transliterate v (-tes, -ting, -ted) convert to the letters of a different alphabet > **transliteration** n (pl -s)
transliterated v ▷ transliterate
transliterates v ▷ transliterate
transliterating v ▷ transliterate
transliteration n ▷ transliterate
translucence n ▷ translucence
translucences n ▷ translucent
translucencies n ▷ translucent
translucency n ▷ translucent
translucent adj letting light pass through, but not transparent > **translucency, translucence** n (pl -cies, -ces)
transmigrate v (-tes, -ting, -ted) (of a soul) pass into another body > **transmigration** n (pl -s)
transmigrated v ▷ transmigrate
transmigrates v ▷ transmigrate
transmigrating v ▷ transmigrate
transmigration n ▷ transmigrate
transmigrations n ▷ transmigrate
transmission n (pl -s) transmitting
transmissions n ▷ transmission
transmit v (-mits, -mitting, -mitted) pass (something) from one person or place to another > **transmittable** adj > **transmitter** n (pl -s)
transmits v ▷ transmit
transmittable adj ▷ transmit
transmitted v ▷ transmit
transmitter n ▷ transmit
transmitters n ▷ transmit
transmitting v ▷ transmit
transmogrified v ▷ transmogrify
transmogrifies v ▷ transmogrify
transmogrify v (-fies, -fying, -fied) (Informal) change completely
transmogrifying v ▷ transmogrify
transmutation n ▷ transmute
transmutations n ▷ transmute
transmute v (-tes, -ting, -ted) change the form or nature of > **transmutation** n (pl -s)
transmuted v ▷ transmute
transmutes v ▷ transmute
transmuting v ▷ transmute
transom n (pl -s) horizontal bar across a window
transoms n ▷ transom
transparencies n ▷ transparency
transparency n (pl -cies) transparent quality
transparent adj able to be seen through, clear

> **transparently** adv
transparently adv ▷ transparent
transpiration n ▷ transpire
transpirations n ▷ transpire
transpire v (-res, -ring, -red) become known > **transpiration** n (pl -s)
transpired v ▷ transpire
transpires v ▷ transpire
transpiring v ▷ transpire
transplant v (-s, -ing, -ed) transfer (an organ or tissue) surgically from one part or body to another ▶ n (pl -s) surgical transplanting > **transplantation** n (pl -s)
transplantation n ▷ transplant
transplantations n ▷ transplant
transplanted v ▷ transplant
transplanting v ▷ transplant
transplants v, n ▷ transplant
transport v (-s, -ing, -ed) convey from one place to another ▶ n (pl -s) business or system of transporting > **transportation** n (pl -s)
transportation n ▷ transport
transportations n ▷ transport
transported v ▷ transport
transporter n (pl -s) large goods vehicle
transporters n ▷ transporter
transporting v ▷ transport
transports v, n ▷ transport
transpose v (-ses, -sing, -sed) interchange two things > **transposition** n (pl -s)
transposed v ▷ transpose
transposes v ▷ transpose
transposing v ▷ transpose
transposition n ▷ transpose
transpositions n ▷ transpose
transsexual, transexual n (pl -s) person of one sex who believes his or her true identity is of the opposite sex
transsexuals n ▷ transsexual
transuranic [tranz-yoor-ran-ik] adj (of an element) having an atomic number greater than that of uranium
transverse adj crossing from side to side
transvestite n (pl -s) person who seeks sexual pleasure by wearing the clothes of the opposite sex > **transvestism** n (pl -s)
transvestism n ▷ transvestite
transvestisms n ▷ transvestite
transvestites n ▷ transvestite
trap n (pl -s) device for catching animals ▶ v (-s, -pping, -pped) catch
trapdoor n (pl -s) door in floor or roof
trapdoors n ▷ trapdoor
trapeze n (pl -s) horizontal bar suspended from two ropes, used by circus acrobats

trapezes n ▷ trapeze
trapezia n ▷ trapezium
trapezium n (pl -ziums, -zia) quadrilateral with two parallel sides of unequal length
trapeziums n ▷ trapezium
trapezoid [trap-piz-zoid] n (pl -s) quadrilateral with no sides parallel
trapezoids n ▷ trapezoid
trapped n ▷ trap
trapper. n (pl -s) person who traps animals for their fur
trappers n ▷ trapper
trapping n ▷ trap
trappings pl n accessories that symbolize an office or position
traps n, v ▷ trap
trash n (pl -es) anything worthless > **trashy** adj (-shier, -shiest)
trashes n ▷ trash
trashier adj ▷ trash
trashiest adj ▷ trash
trashy adj ▷ trash
trauma [traw-ma] n (pl -mata, -s) emotional shock > **traumatic** adj > **traumatize** v (-zes, -zing, -zed)
traumas n ▷ trauma
traumata n ▷ trauma
traumatic adj ▷ trauma
traumatized v ▷ trauma
traumatizes v ▷ trauma
traumatizing v ▷ trauma
travail n (pl -s) (Lit) labour or toil
travails n ▷ travail
travel v (-s, -lling, -lled) go from one place to another, through an area, or for a specified distance ▶ n (pl -s) travelling, esp. as a tourist > **traveller** n (pl -s)
travelled v ▷ travel
traveller n ▷ travel
travellers n ▷ travel
travelling v ▷ travel
travelogue n (pl -s) film or talk about someone's travels
travelogues n ▷ travelogue
travels v, n ▷ travel ▶ pl n (account of) travelling
traverse v (-ses, -sing, -sed) move over or back and forth over
traversed v ▷ traverse
traverses v ▷ traverse
traversing v ▷ traverse
travesties n ▷ travesty
travesty n (pl -ties) grotesque imitation or mockery
trawl n (pl -s) net dragged at deep levels behind a fishing boat ▶ v (-s, -ing, -ed) fish with such a net
trawled v ▷ trawl
trawler n (pl -s) trawling boat
trawlers n ▷ trawler
trawling v ▷ trawl
trawls n, v ▷ trawl
tray n (pl -s) flat board, usu. with a rim, for carrying things
trays n ▷ tray
treacheries n ▷ treachery
treacherous adj disloyal > **treacherously** adv
treacherously adv ▷ treacherous
treachery n (pl -ries) wilful betrayal
treacle n (pl -s) thick dark syrup produced when sugar is refined > **treacly** adj (-lier, -liest)
treacles n ▷ treacle
treaclier adj ▷ treacle
treacliest adj ▷ treacle
treacly adj ▷ treacle
tread v (-s, -ing, trod, trodden or trod) set one's foot on ▶ n (pl -s) way of walking or dancing
treading v ▷ tread
treadle [tred-dl] n (pl -s) lever worked by the foot to turn a wheel
treadles n ▷ treadle
treadmill n (pl -s) (HIST) cylinder turned by treading on steps projecting from it
treadmills n ▷ treadmill
treads v, n ▷ tread
treason n (pl -s) betrayal of one's sovereign or country > **treasonable** adj
treasonable adj ▷ treason
treasons n ▷ treason
treasure n (pl -s) collection of wealth, esp. gold or jewels ▶ v (-res, -ring, -red) prize or cherish
treasured v ▷ treasure
treasurer n (pl -s) official in charge of funds
treasurers n ▷ treasurer
treasures n, v ▷ treasure
treasuries n ▷ treasury
treasuring v ▷ treasure
treasury n (pl -ries) storage place for treasure
treat v (-s, -ing, -ed) deal with or regard in a certain manner ▶ n (pl -s) pleasure, entertainment, etc. given or paid for by someone else
treated v ▷ treat
treaties n ▷ treaty
treating v ▷ treat
treatise [treat-izz] n (pl -s) formal piece of writing on a particular subject
treatises n ▷ treatise
treatment n (pl -s) medical care

treatments n ▷ treatment
treats v, n ▷ treat
treaty n (pl -ties) signed contract between states
treble adj triple (MUSIC) ▶ n (pl -s) (singer with or part for) a soprano voice ▶ v (-les, -ling, -led) increase three times > **trebly** adv
 trebled v ▷ treble
 trebles n, v ▷ treble
 trebling v ▷ treble
 trebly adv ▷ treble
tree n (pl -s) large perennial plant with a woody trunk > **treeless** adj
 treeless adj ▷ tree
 trees n ▷ tree
trefoil [tref-foil] n (pl -s) plant, such as clover, with a three-lobed leaf
 trefoils n ▷ trefoil
trek n (pl -s) long difficult journey, esp. on foot ▶ v (-s, -kking, -kked) make such a journey
 trekked v ▷ trek
 trekking v ▷ trek
 treks n, v ▷ trek
trellis n (pl -ises) framework of horizontal and vertical strips of wood
 trellises n ▷ trellis
tremble v (-les, -ling, -led) shake or quiver ▶ n (pl -les) trembling > **trembling** adj
 trembled v ▷ tremble
 trembles v, n ▷ tremble
 trembling v, adj ▷ tremble
tremendous adj huge > **tremendously** adv
 tremendously adv ▷ tremendous
tremolo n (pl -s) (MUSIC) quivering effect in singing or playing
 tremolos n ▷ tremolo
tremor n (pl -s) involuntary shaking
 tremors n ▷ tremor
tremulous adj trembling, as from fear or excitement
trench n (pl -es) long narrow ditch, esp. one used as a shelter in war
trenchant adj incisive
trencher n (pl -s) (HIST) wooden plate for serving food
trencherman n (pl -men) hearty eater
 trenchermen n ▷ trencherman
 trenchers n ▷ trencher
 trenches n ▷ trench
trend n (pl -s) general tendency or direction
 trendier adj ▷ trendy
 trendies n ▷ trendy
 trendiest adj ▷ trendy
 trendiness n ▷ trendy
 trendinesses n ▷ trendy

trends n ▷ trend
trendy adj (-dier, -diest) ▶ n (pl -dies) (Informal) consciously fashionable (person) > **trendiness** n (pl -es)
trepidation n (pl -s) fear or anxiety
 trepidations n ▷ trepidation
trespass v (-es, -ing, -ed) go onto another's property without permission ▶ n (pl -es) trespassing > **trespasser** n (pl -s)
 trespassed v ▷ trespass
 trespasser n ▷ trespass
 trespassers n ▷ trespass
 trespasses v, n ▷ trespass
 trespassing v ▷ trespass
tresses pl n long flowing hair
trestle n (pl -s) board fixed on pairs of spreading legs, used as a support
 trestles n ▷ trestle
 trevallies n ▷ trevally
trevally n (pl -lies) (AUST & NZ) any of various food and game fishes
trews pl n close-fitting tartan trousers
triad n (pl -s) group of three
 triads n ▷ triad
trial n (pl -s) investigation of a case before a judge
 trials n ▷ trial ▶ pl n sporting competition for individuals
triangle n (pl -s) geometric figure with three sides > **triangular** adj
 triangles n ▷ triangle
 triangular adj ▷ triangle
 tribal adj ▷ tribe
tribalism n (pl -s) loyalty to a tribe
 tribalisms n ▷ tribalism
tribe n (pl -s) group of clans or families believed to have a common ancestor > **tribal** adj
 tribes n ▷ tribe
tribulation n (pl -s) great distress
 tribulations n ▷ tribulation
tribunal n (pl -s) board appointed to inquire into a specific matter
 tribunals n ▷ tribunal
tribune n (pl -s) people's representative, esp. in ancient Rome
 tribunes n ▷ tribune
 tributaries n ▷ tributary
tributary n (pl -ries) stream or river flowing into a larger one ▶ adj (of a stream or river) flowing into a larger one
tribute n (pl -s) sign of respect or admiration
 tributes n ▷ tribute
trice n (pl -s) moment
triceps n (pl -pses) muscle at the back of the upper arm

tricepses n ▷ triceps

trices n ▷ trice

trichologies n ▷ trichology

trichologist n ▷ trichology

trichologists n ▷ trichology

trichology [trick-ol-a-jee] n (pl -gies) study and treatment of hair and its diseases
> **trichologist** n (pl -s)

trick n (pl -s) deceitful or cunning action or plan ▸ v (-s, -ing, -ed) cheat or deceive
> **trickery** n (pl -ries) > **trickster** n (pl -s)

tricked v ▷ trick

trickeries n ▷ trick

trickery n ▷ trick

trickier adj ▷ tricky

trickiest adj ▷ tricky

tricking v ▷ trick

trickle v (-les, -ling, -led) (cause to) flow in a thin stream or drops ▸ n (pl -s) gradual flow

trickled v ▷ trickle

trickles v, n ▷ trickle

trickling v ▷ trickle

tricks n, v ▷ trick

trickster n ▷ trick

tricksters n ▷ trick

tricky adj (-kier, -kiest) difficult, needing careful handling

tricolour [trick-kol-lor] n (pl -s) three-coloured striped flag

tricolours n ▷ tricolour

tricycle n (pl -s) three-wheeled cycle

tricycles n ▷ tricycle

trident n (pl -s) three-pronged spear

tridents n ▷ trident

tried v ▷ try

triennial adj happening every three years

tries v, n ▷ try

trifle n (pl -s) insignificant thing or amount

trifles n ▷ trifle

trifling adj insignificant

trigger n (pl -s) small lever releasing a catch on a gun or machine ▸ v (-s, -ing, -ed) set (an action or process) in motion

triggered v ▷ trigger

triggering v ▷ trigger

triggers n, v ▷ trigger

trigonometries n ▷ trigonometry

trigonometry n (pl -ries) branch of mathematics dealing with relations of the sides and angles of triangles

trike n (pl -s) (Informal) tricycle

trikes n ▷ trike

trilateral adj having three sides

trilbies n ▷ trilby

trilby n (pl -bies) man's soft felt hat

trill n (pl -s) (MUSIC) rapid alternation between two notes ▸ v (-s, -ing, -ed) play or sing a trill

trilled v ▷ trill

trilling v ▷ trill

trillion n (pl -s) one million million, 10^{12}

trillions n ▷ trillion

trills n, v ▷ trill

trilobite [trile-oh-bite] n (pl -s) small prehistoric sea animal

trilobites n ▷ trilobite

trilogies n ▷ trilogy

trilogy n (pl -gies) series of three related books, plays, etc.

trim adj (-mmer, -mmest) neat and smart ▸ v (-s, -mming, -mmed) cut or prune into good shape ▸ n (pl -s) decoration

trimaran [trime-a-ran] n (pl -s) three-hulled boat

trimarans n ▷ trimaran

trimmed v ▷ trim

trimmer adj ▷ trim

trimmest adj ▷ trim

trimming n (pl -s) decoration ▸ v ▷ trim

trimmings n ▷ trimming ▸ pl n usual accompaniments

trims v, n ▷ trim

trinities n ▷ trinity

trinitrotoluene n (pl -s) TNT

trinitrotoluenes n ▷ trinitrotoluene

trinity n (pl -ties) group of three

trinket n (pl -s) small or worthless ornament or piece of jewellery

trinkets n ▷ trinket

trio n (pl -s) group of three

trios n ▷ trio

trip n (pl -s) journey to a place and back, esp. for pleasure ▸ v (-s, -pping, -pped) (cause to) stumble

tripe n (pl -s) stomach of a cow used as food

tripes n ▷ tripe

triple adj having three parts ▸ v (-les, -ling, -led) increase three times

tripled v ▷ triple

triples v ▷ triple

triplet n (pl -s) one of three babies born at one birth

triplets n ▷ triplet

triplicate adj triple

tripling v ▷ triple

tripod [tripe-pod] n (pl -s) three-legged stand, stool, etc.

tripods n ▷ tripod

tripos [tripe-poss] n (pl -poses) final examinations for an honours degree at Cambridge University

triposes n ▷ tripos

tripped v ▷ trip
tripper n (pl -s) tourist
trippers n ▷ tripper
tripping v ▷ trip
trips n, v ▷ trip
triptych [trip-tick] n (pl -s) painting or carving on three hinged panels, often forming an altarpiece
triptychs n ▷ triptych
trite adj (of a remark or idea) commonplace and unoriginal
tritium n (pl -s) radioactive isotope of hydrogen
tritiums n ▷ tritium
triumph n (pl -s) (happiness caused by) victory or success ▶ v (-s, -ing, -ed) be victorious or successful
triumphal adj celebrating a triumph
triumphant adj feeling or showing triumph
triumphed v ▷ triumph
triumphing v ▷ triumph
triumphs n, v ▷ triumph
triumvirate [try-umm-vir-rit] n (pl -s) group of three people in joint control
triumvirates n ▷ triumvirate
trivet [triv-vit] n (pl -s) metal stand for a pot or kettle
trivets n ▷ trivet
trivia pl n trivial things or details
trivial adj of little importance > **trivially** adv
> **triviality** n (pl -ties)
trivialities n ▷ trivial
triviality n ▷ trivial
trivialize v (-zes, -zing, -zed) make (something) seem less important or complex than it is
trivialized v ▷ trivialize
trivializes v ▷ trivialize
trivializing v ▷ trivialize
trivially adv ▷ trivial
trod v ▷ tread
trodden v ▷ tread
troglodyte n (pl -s) cave dweller
troglodytes n ▷ troglodyte
troika n (pl -s) Russian vehicle drawn by three horses abreast
troikas n ▷ troika
troll n (pl -s) giant or dwarf in Scandinavian folklore
trolley n (pl -s) small wheeled table for food and drink
trolleys n ▷ trolley
trollop n (pl -s) (Old-fashioned) promiscuous or slovenly woman
trollops n ▷ trollop

trolls n ▷ troll
trombone n (pl -s) brass musical instrument with a sliding tube > **trombonist** n (pl -s)
trombones n ▷ trombone
trombonist n ▷ trombone
trombonists n ▷ trombone
troop n (pl -s) large group ▶ v (-s, -ing, -ed) move in a crowd
trooped v ▷ troop
trooper n (pl -s) cavalry soldier
troopers n ▷ trooper
trooping v ▷ troop
troops n, v ▷ troop ▶ pl n soldiers
trope n (pl -s) figure of speech
tropes n ▷ trope
trophies n ▷ trophy
trophy n (pl -phies) cup, shield, etc. given as a prize
tropic n (pl -s) either of two lines of latitude at 23½°N (**tropic of Cancer**) or 23½°S (**tropic of Capricorn**) ▶ pl n part of the earth's surface between these lines
tropical adj of or in the tropics
tropics n ▷ tropic
trot v (-s, -tting, -tted) (of a horse) move at a medium pace, lifting the feet in diagonal pairs ▶ n (pl -s) trotting
troth [rhymes with **growth**] n (pl -s) (Obs) pledge of devotion, esp. a betrothal
troths n ▷ troth
trots v, n ▷ trot
trotted v ▷ trot
trotter n (pl -s) pig's foot
trotters n ▷ trotter
trotting v ▷ trot
troubadour [troo-bad-oor] n (pl -s) medieval travelling poet and singer
troubadours n ▷ troubadour
trouble n (pl -s) (cause of) distress or anxiety ▶ v (-les, -ling, -led) (cause to) worry
> **troubled** adj > **troublesome** adj
troubled v, adj ▷ trouble
troubles n, v ▷ trouble
troubleshooter n (pl -s) person employed to locate and deal with faults or problems
troubleshooters n ▷ troubleshooter
troublesome adj ▷ trouble
troubling v ▷ trouble
trough [troff] n (pl -s) long open container, esp. for animals' food or water
troughs n ▷ trough
trounce v (-ces, -cing, -ced) defeat utterly
trounced v ▷ trounce
trounces v ▷ trounce
trouncing v ▷ trounce

troupe [troop] *n* (*pl* -s) company of performers
> **trouper** *n* (*pl* -s)
  trouper *n* ▷ troupe
  troupers *n* ▷ troupe
  troupes *n* ▷ troupe
trouser *adj* of trousers
trousers *pl n* two-legged outer garment with legs reaching usu. to the ankles
trousseau [troo-so] *n* (*pl* -seaux, -seaus) bride's collection of clothing etc. for her marriage
  trousseaus *n* ▷ trousseau
  trousseaux *n* ▷ trousseau
trout *n* (*pl* trout, trouts) game fish related to the salmon
  trouts *n* ▷ trout
trowel *n* (*pl* -s) hand tool with a wide blade for spreading mortar, lifting plants, etc.
  trowels *n* ▷ trowel
  truancies *n* ▷ truant
  truancy *n* ▷ truant
truant *n* (*pl* -s) pupil who stays away from school without permission > **truancy** *n* (*pl* -cies)
  truants *n* ▷ truant
truce *n* (*pl* -s) temporary agreement to stop fighting
  truces *n* ▷ truce
truck[1] *n* (*pl* -s) railway goods wagon
truck[2] *n* (*pl* -s) commercial goods
trucker *n* (*pl* -s) truck driver
  truckers *n* ▷ trucker
  trucks *n* ▷ truck[1, 2]
  truculence *n* ▷ truculent
  truculences *n* ▷ truculent
truculent [truck-yew-lent] *adj* aggressively defiant > **truculence** *n* (*pl* -s)
trudge *v* (-dges, -dging, -dged) walk heavily or wearily ▶ *n* (*pl* -s) long tiring walk
  trudged *v* ▷ trudge
  trudges *v, n* ▷ trudge
  trudging *v* ▷ trudge
true *adj* (truer, truest) in accordance with facts > **truly** *adv*
  truer *adj* ▷ true
  truest *adj* ▷ true
truffle *n* (*pl* -s) edible underground fungus
  truffles *n* ▷ truffle
trug *n* (*pl* -s) (BRIT) long shallow basket used by gardeners
  trugs *n* ▷ trug
truism *n* (*pl* -s) self-evident truth
  truisms *n* ▷ truism
  truly *adv* ▷ true
trump[1] *n* (*pl* -s) ▶ *adj* (card) of the suit outranking the others ▶ *v* (-s, -ing, -ed) play a trump card on (another card)

trump[2] *n* (*pl* -s) (*Lit*) (sound of) a trumpet
  trumped *v* ▷ trump[1]
trumpet *n* (*pl* -s) valved brass instrument with a flared tube ▶ *v* (-s, -ing, -ed) proclaim loudly
> **trumpeter** *n* (*pl* -s)
  trumpeted *v* ▷ trumpet
  trumpeter *n* ▷ trumpet
  trumpeters *n* ▷ trumpet
  trumpeting *v* ▷ trumpet
  trumpets *n, v* ▷ trumpet
  trumping *v* ▷ trump[1]
  trumps *n* ▷ trump[1, 2] ▶ *pl n* suit outranking the others ▶ *v* ▷ trump[1]
truncate *v* (-tes, -ting, -ted) cut short
  truncated *v* ▷ truncate
  truncates *v* ▷ truncate
  truncating *v* ▷ truncate
truncheon *n* (*pl* -s) club carried by a policeman
  truncheons *n* ▷ truncheon
trundle *v* (-les, -ling, -led) move heavily on wheels
  trundled *v* ▷ trundle
  trundles *v* ▷ trundle
  trundling *v* ▷ trundle
trunk *n* (*pl* -s) main stem of a tree
  trunks *n* ▷ trunk ▶ *pl n* man's swimming shorts
truss *v* (-es, -ing, -ed) tie or bind up ▶ *n* (*pl* -es) device for holding a hernia in place
  trussed *v* ▷ truss
  trusses *v, n* ▷ truss
  trussing *v* ▷ truss
trust *v* (-s, -ing, -ed) believe in and rely on ▶ *n* (*pl* -s) confidence in the truth, reliability, etc. of a person or thing
  trusted *v* ▷ trust
trustee *n* (*pl* -s) person holding property on another's behalf
  trustees *n* ▷ trustee
trustful, trusting *adj* inclined to trust others
  trustier *adj* ▷ trusty
  trustiest *adj* ▷ trusty
  trusting *v* ▷ trust ▶ *adj* ▷ trustful
  trusts *n, v* ▷ trust
trustworthy *adj* reliable or honest
trusty *adj* (-tier, -tiest) faithful or reliable
truth *n* (*pl* -s) state of being true
truthful *adj* honest > **truthfully** *adv*
  truthfully *adv* ▷ truthful
  truths *n* ▷ truth
try *v* (tries, trying, tried) make an effort or attempt ▶ *n* (*pl* tries) attempt or effort
trying *adj* (*Informal*) difficult or annoying ▶ *v* ▷ try
tryst *n* (*pl* -s) arrangement to meet
  trysts *n* ▷ tryst

tsar, czar [zahr] n (pl -s) (HIST) Russian emperor
tsars n ▷ tsar

tsk interj. Tsk is a sound people make to show disapproval. This is a useful word because it enables you to play K without using vowels, which is handy if your rack is low on vowel tiles. Tsk scores 7 points.

tsunami n (pl -mis, -mi) tidal wave, usu. caused by an earthquake under the sea
tsunamis n ▷ tsunami

tuatara n (pl -s) large lizard-like New Zealand reptile
tuataras n ▷ tuatara

tub n (pl -s) open, usu. round container

tuba [tube-a] n (pl -s) valved low-pitched brass instrument
tubas n ▷ tuba
tubbier adj ▷ tubby
tubbiest adj ▷ tubby

tubby adj (tubbier, tubbiest) (of a person) short and fat

tube n (pl -s) hollow cylinder

tuber [tube-er] n (pl -s) fleshy underground root of a plant such as a potato > **tuberous** adj

tubercle [tube-er-kl] n (pl -s) small rounded swelling
tubercles n ▷ tubercle
tubercular adj ▷ tuberculosis

tuberculin n (pl -s) extract from a bacillus used to test for tuberculosis
tuberculins n ▷ tuberculin

tuberculosis [tube-berk-yew-lohss-iss] n (pl -ses) infectious disease causing tubercles, esp. in the lungs > **tubercular** adj
tuberculoses n ▷ tuberculosis
tuberous adj ▷ tuber
tubers n ▷ tuber
tubes n ▷ tube

tubing n (pl -s) length of tube
tubings n ▷ tubing
tubs n ▷ tub

tubular [tube-yew-lar] adj of or shaped like a tube

tuck v (-s, -ing, -ed) push or fold into a small space ▶ n (pl -s) stitched fold
tucked v ▷ tuck

tucker n (pl -s) (AUST & NZ) (Informal) food
tuckers n ▷ tucker
tucking v ▷ tuck
tucks v, n ▷ tuck

tufa [tew-fa] n (pl -s) porous rock formed as a deposit from springs
tufas n ▷ tufa

tuffet n (pl -s) small mound or seat

tuffets n ▷ tuffet

tuft n (pl -s) bunch of feathers, grass, hair, etc. held or growing together at the base
tufts n ▷ tuft

tug v (-s, -gging, -gged) pull hard ▶ n (pl -s) hard pull
tugged v ▷ tug
tugging v ▷ tug
tugs v, n ▷ tug

tuition n (pl -s) instruction, esp. received individually or in a small group
tuitions n ▷ tuition

tulip n (pl -s) plant with bright cup-shaped flowers
tulips n ▷ tulip

tulle [tewl] n (pl -s) fine net fabric of silk etc.
tulles n ▷ tulle

tumble v (-les, -ling, -led) (cause to) fall, esp. awkwardly or violently ▶ n (pl -s) fall
tumbled v ▷ tumble

tumbledown adj dilapidated

tumbler n (pl -s) stemless drinking glass
tumblers n ▷ tumbler
tumbles v, n ▷ tumble
tumbling v ▷ tumble
tumbrel n ▷ tumbril
tumbrels n ▷ tumbril

tumbril, tumbrel n (pl -s) farm cart used during the French Revolution to take prisoners to the guillotine
tumbrils n ▷ tumbril

tumescent [tew-mess-ent] adj swollen or becoming swollen
tummies n ▷ tummy

tummy n (pl -mies) (Informal) stomach

tumour [tew-mer] n (pl -s) abnormal growth in or on the body
tumours n ▷ tumour
tumuli n ▷ tumulus

tumult n (pl -s) uproar or commotion > **tumultuous** [tew-mull-tew-uss] ▶ adj
tumults n ▷ tumult
tumultuous adj ▷ tumult

tumulus n (pl -li) burial mound

tun n (pl -s) large beer cask

tuna n (pl -s) large marine food fish
tunas n ▷ tuna

tundra n (pl -s) vast treeless Arctic region with permanently frozen subsoil
tundras n ▷ tundra

tune n (pl -s) (pleasing) sequence of musical notes ▶ v (-nes, -ning, -ned) adjust (a musical instrument) so that it is in tune > **tuneful** adj > **tunefully** adv > **tuneless** adj > **tuner** n (pl -s)
tuned v ▷ tune

tuneful *adj* ▷ tune
tunefully *adv* ▷ tune
tuneless *adj* ▷ tune
tuner *n* ▷ tune
tuners *n* ▷ tune
tunes *n, v* ▷ tune
tungsten *n* (*pl* -s) (CHEM) greyish-white metal
tungstens *n* ▷ tungsten
tunic *n* (*pl* -s) close-fitting jacket forming part of some uniforms
tunics *n* ▷ tunic
tuning *v* ▷ tune
tunnel *n* (*pl* -s) underground passage ▶ *v* (-s, -lling, -lled) make a tunnel (through)
tunnelled *v* ▷ tunnel
tunnelling *v* ▷ tunnel
tunnels *n, v* ▷ tunnel
tunnies *n* ▷ tunny
tunny *n* (*pl* -nies, -ny) tuna
tuns *n* ▷ tun
tup *n* (*pl* -s) male sheep
tups *n* ▷ tup
turban *n* (*pl* -s) Muslim, Hindu, or Sikh man's head covering, made by winding cloth round the head
turbans *n* ▷ turban
turbid *adj* muddy, not clear
turbine *n* (*pl* -s) machine or generator driven by gas, water, etc. turning blades
turbines *n* ▷ turbine
turbot *n* (*pl* -s) large European edible flatfish
turbots *n* ▷ turbot
turbulence *n* (*pl* -s) confusion, movement, or agitation ▶ **turbulent** *adj*
turbulences *n* ▷ turbulence
turbulent *adj* ▷ turbulence
tureen *n* (*pl* -s) serving dish for soup
tureens *n* ▷ tureen
turf *n* (*pl* -s, turves) short thick even grass ▶ *v* (-s, -ing, -ed) cover with turf
turfed *v* ▷ turf
turfing *v* ▷ turf
turfs *n, v* ▷ turf
turgid [tur-jid] *adj* (-er, -est) (of language) pompous
turgider *adj* ▷ turgid
turgidest *adj* ▷ turgid
turkey *n* (*pl* -s) large bird bred for food
turkeys *n* ▷ turkey
turmeric *n* (*pl* -s) yellow spice obtained from the root of an Asian plant
turmerics *n* ▷ turmeric
turmoil *n* (*pl* -s) agitation or confusion
turmoils *n* ▷ turmoil
turn *v* (-s, -ing, -ed) change the position or

direction (of) ▶ *n* (*pl* -s) turning ▶ **turner** *n* (*pl* -s)
turncoat *n* (*pl* -s) person who deserts one party or cause to join another
turncoats *n* ▷ turncoat
turned *v* ▷ turn
turner *n* ▷ turn
turners *n* ▷ turn
turning *n* (*pl* -s) road or path leading off a main route ▶ *v* ▷ turn
turnings *n* ▷ turning
turnip *n* (*pl* -s) root vegetable with orange or white flesh
turnips *n* ▷ turnip
turnout *n* (*pl* -s) number of people appearing at a gathering
turnouts *n* ▷ turnout
turnover *n* (*pl* -s) total sales made by a business over a certain period
turnovers *n* ▷ turnover
turnpike *n* (*pl* -s) (BRIT) road where a toll is collected at barriers
turnpikes *n* ▷ turnpike
turns *v, n* ▷ turn
turnstile *n* (*pl* -s) revolving gate for admitting one person at a time
turnstiles *n* ▷ turnstile
turntable *n* (*pl* -s) revolving platform
turntables *n* ▷ turntable
turnup *n* (*pl* -s) turned-up fold at the bottom of a trouser leg
turnups *n* ▷ turnup
turpentine *n* (*pl* -s) (oil made from) the resin of certain trees
turpentines *n* ▷ turpentine
turpitude *n* (*pl* -s) wickedness
turpitudes *n* ▷ turpitude
turps *n* turpentine oil
turquoise *adj* blue-green ▶ *n* (*pl* -s) blue-green precious stone
turquoises *n* ▷ turquoise
turret *n* (*pl* -s) small tower
turrets *n* ▷ turret
turtle *n* (*pl* -s) sea tortoise
turtledove *n* (*pl* -s) small wild dove
turtledoves *n* ▷ turtledove
turtleneck *n* (*pl* -s) (sweater with) a round high close-fitting neck
turtlenecks *n* ▷ turtleneck
turtles *n* ▷ turtle
turves *n* ▷ turf
tusk *n* (*pl* -s) long pointed tooth of an elephant, walrus, etc.
tusks *n* ▷ tusk
tussle *n* (*pl* -s) ▶ *v* (-les, -ling, -led) fight or

scuffle

tussled v ▷ tussle

tussles n, v ▷ tussle

tussling v ▷ tussle

tussock n (pl -s) tuft of grass

tussocks n ▷ tussock

tutelage [tew-till-lij] n (pl -s) instruction or guidance, esp. by a tutor > **tutelary** [tew-till-lar-ee] ▶ adj

tutelages n ▷ tutelage

tutelary adj ▷ tutelage

tutor n (pl -s) person teaching individuals or small groups ▶ v (-s, -ing, -ed) act as a tutor to

tutored v ▷ tutor

tutorial n (pl -s) period of instruction with a tutor

tutorials n ▷ tutorial

tutoring v ▷ tutor

tutors n, v ▷ tutor

tutu n (pl -s) short stiff skirt worn by ballerinas

tutus n ▷ tutu

> **tux** n (**tuxes**). Tux is a short form of **tuxedo.** This is a very useful word, as U and T are common tiles, so look for opportunities to play it when you get an X. Tux scores 10 points.

tuxedo n (pl -s) (US & AUST) dinner jacket

tuxedos n ▷ tuxedo

twaddle n (pl -s) silly or pretentious talk or writing

twaddles n ▷ twaddle

twain n (pl -s) (Obs) two

twains n ▷ twain

twang n (pl -s) sharp ringing sound ▶ v (-s, -ing, -ed) (cause to) make a twang

twanged v ▷ twang

twanging v ▷ twang

twangs n, v ▷ twang

tweak v (-s, -ing, -ed) pinch or twist sharply ▶ n (pl -s) tweaking

tweaked v ▷ tweak

tweaking v ▷ tweak

tweaks v, n ▷ tweak

twee adj (Informal) (-r, -st) too sentimental, sweet, or pretty

tweed n (pl -s) thick woollen cloth > **tweedy** adj (-dier, -diest)

tweedier adj ▷ tweed

tweediest adj ▷ tweed

tweeds n ▷ tweed ▶ pl n suit of tweed

tweedy adj ▷ tweed

tweer adj ▷ twee

tweest adj ▷ twee

tweet n (pl -s) ▶ v (-s, -ing, -ed) chirp

tweeted v ▷ tweet

tweeter n (pl -s) loudspeaker reproducing high-frequency sounds

tweeters n ▷ tweeter

tweeting v ▷ tweet

tweets n, v ▷ tweet

tweezers pl n small pincer-like tool

twelfth adj, n (pl -s) (of) number twelve in a series

twelfths n ▷ twelfth

twelve adj, n (pl -s) two more than ten

twelves n ▷ twelve

twenties n ▷ twenty

twentieth adj, n ▷ twenty

twentieths n ▷ twenty

twenty adj, n (pl -ties) two times ten > **twentieth** adj, n (pl -s)

twerp n (pl -s) (Informal) silly person

twerps n ▷ twerp

twice adv two times

twiddle v (-les, -ling, -led) fiddle or twirl in an idle way

twiddled v ▷ twiddle

twiddles v ▷ twiddle

twiddling v ▷ twiddle

twig¹ n (pl -s) small branch or shoot

twig² v (-s, -gging, -gged) (Informal) realize or understand

twigged v ▷ twig¹

twigging v ▷ twig¹

twigs n ▷ twig¹ ▶ v ▷ twig²

twilight n (pl -s) soft dim light just after sunset

twilights n ▷ twilight

twill n (pl -s) fabric woven to produce parallel ridges

twills n ▷ twill

twin n (pl -s) one of a pair, esp. of two children born at one birth ▶ v (-s, -nning, -nned) pair or be paired

twine n (pl -es) string or cord ▶ v (-nes, -ning, -ned) twist or coil round

twined v ▷ twine

twines n, v ▷ twine

twining v ▷ twine

twinge n (pl -s) sudden sharp pain or emotional pang

twinges n ▷ twinge

twinkle v (-les, -ling, -led) shine brightly but intermittently ▶ n (pl -les) flickering brightness

twinkled v ▷ twinkle

twinkles v, n ▷ twinkle

twinkling v ▷ twinkle

twinned v ▷ twin

twinning v ▷ twin

twins n, v ▷ twin

twirl v (-s, -ing, -ed) turn or spin around quickly
  twirled v ▷ twirl
  twirling v ▷ twirl
  twirls v ▷ twirl
twist v (-s, -ing, -ed) turn out of the natural position ▶ n (pl -s) twisting
twisted adj (of a person) cruel or perverted ▶ v ▷ twist
twister n (pl -s) (BRIT) (Informal) swindler
  twisters n ▷ twister
  twisting v ▷ twist
  twists v, n ▷ twist
twit[1] v (-s, -tting, -tted) poke fun at (someone)
twit[2] n (pl -s) (Informal) foolish person
twitch v (-es, -ing, -ed) move spasmodically ▶ n (pl -es) nervous muscular spasm
  twitched v ▷ twitch
  twitches v, n ▷ twitch
  twitching v ▷ twitch
  twits n ▷ twit[2] ▶ v ▷ twit[1]
  twitted v ▷ twit[1]
twitter v (-s, -ing, -ed) (of birds) utter chirping sounds ▶ n (pl -s) act or sound of twittering
  twittered v ▷ twitter
  twittering v ▷ twitter
  twitters v, n ▷ twitter
  twitting v ▷ twit[1]
two adj, n (pl -s) one more than one
  twos n ▷ two

> **twp** adj. This is a Welsh word that means stupid or daft. This is a useful word because it contains no vowels, and can thus help when you have an awkward rack. Twp scores 8 points.

tycoon n (pl -s) powerful wealthy businessman
  tycoons n ▷ tycoon

> **tyg** n (**tygs**). A tyg is a cup with more than one handle. This word is useful because it uses no vowels, and can thus help when you are short of them. Tyg scores 7 points.

tying v ▷ tie
tyke n (pl -s) (BRIT, AUST & NZ) (Informal) small cheeky child
  tykes n ▷ tyke
type n (pl -s) class or category ▶ v (-pes, -ping, -ped) print with a typewriter or word processor
typecast v (-s, -ing, -ed) continually cast (an actor or actress) in similar roles
  typecasted v ▷ typecast
  typecasting v ▷ typecast
  typecasts v ▷ typecast
  typed v ▷ type

types n, v ▷ type
typewriter n (pl -s) machine which prints a character when the appropriate key is pressed
  typewriters n ▷ typewriter
  typing v ▷ type
typist n (pl -s) person who types with a typewriter or word processor
  typists n ▷ typist
typhoon n (pl -s) violent tropical storm
  typhoons n ▷ typhoon
typhus n (pl -uses) infectious feverish disease
  typhuses n ▷ typhus
typical adj true to type, characteristic
  > **typically** adv
  typically adv ▷ typical
  typified v ▷ typify
  typifies v ▷ typify
typify v (-fies, -fying, -fied) be typical of
  typifying v ▷ typify
  typographer n ▷ typography
  typographers n ▷ typography
  typographical adj ▷ typography
  typographies n ▷ typography
typography n (pl -phies) art or style of printing
  > **typographical** adj > **typographer** n (pl -s)
tyrannical adj like a tyrant, oppressive
  tyrannies n ▷ tyranny
tyrannize v (-zes, -zing, -zed) exert power (over) oppressively or cruelly > **tyrannous** adj
  tyrannized v ▷ tyrannize
  tyrannizes v ▷ tyrannize
  tyrannizing v ▷ tyrannize
tyrannosaurus [tirr-ran-oh-**sore**-uss] n (pl -es) large two-footed flesh-eating dinosaur
  tyrannosauruses n ▷ tyrannosaurus
  tyrannous n ▷ tyrannize
tyranny n (pl -nies) tyrannical rule
tyrant n (pl -s) oppressive or cruel ruler
  tyrants n ▷ tyrant
tyre n (pl -s) rubber ring, usu. inflated, over the rim of a vehicle's wheel to grip the road
  tyres n ▷ tyre
tyro n (pl -ros) novice or beginner
  tyros n ▷ tyro

> **tzaddiq** n (**tzaddiqim, tzaddiqs**). A tzaddiq is a Hasidic Jewish leader. This is a fantastic word if you can get the necessary tiles. If someone has played add, you might be able to form it around that; if you can form the whole word using all your tiles you'll earn a 50-point bonus. Tzaddiq scores 27 points.

U u

U can be a difficult tile to use effectively. Although there are quite a few two-letter words beginning with U, most of them are quite unusual, and so difficult to remember. Only **up** (4 points) and **us** (2) are immediately obvious, so it's well worth learning words like **ug** (3), **uh** (5), **um** (4), and **un**, **ur** and **ut** (2 each). Three-letter words beginning with U can also be difficult to remember. If you are trying to use a Q, X or Z, bear in mind that there aren't any valid three-letter words with these letters that start with U. Knowing this can save you valuable time. It's also helpful to remember that there aren't any particularly high-scoring two- or three-letter words starting with U.

ubiquities n ▷ ubiquitous
ubiquitous [yew-bik-wit-uss] *adj* being or seeming to be everywhere at once > **ubiquity** n (*pl* -ties)
 ubiquity n ▷ ubiquitous
udder n (*pl* -s) large baglike milk-producing gland of cows, sheep, or goats
 udders n ▷ udder

> **ug** v (**ugs, ugging, ugged**). Ug is an old word meaning to loathe. The different verb forms of this word can be useful, and remember that if someone plays ug or its inflections, you can put B, L, M or T in front of it to form another valid word. Ug scores 3 points.

ugh *interj*. Ugh is a sound that people make when they dislike something or are disgusted by it. Together with uke, this is the highest-scoring three-letter word starting with U. Ugh scores 7 points.

uglier *adj* ▷ ugly
ugliest *adj* ▷ ugly
ugliness n ▷ ugly
 uglinesses n ▷ ugly
ugly *adj* (-lier, -liest) of unpleasant appearance > **ugliness** n (*pl* -es)

> **uh** *interj*. Uh is a sound that people make when they are unsure about something. This useful little word can help when you are trying to form words in more than one direction. Uh scores 5 points.

> **uke** n (**ukes**). Uke is a short form of ukulele. Together with ugh, this is the highest-scoring three-letter word

starting with U. Uke scores 7 points.
ukelele n ▷ ukulele
 ukeleles n ▷ ukulele
ukulele, ukelele [yew-kal-**lay**-lee] n (*pl* -s) small guitar with four strings
 ukuleles n ▷ ukulele
ulcer n (*pl* -s) open sore on the surface of the skin or mucous membrane. > **ulceration** n (*pl* -s)
ulcerated *adj* made or becoming ulcerous
 ulceration n ▷ ulcer
 ulcerations n ▷ ulcer
ulcerous *adj* of, like, or characterized by ulcers
 ulcers n ▷ ulcer
ulna n (*pl* -nae, -nas) inner and longer of the two bones of the human forearm
 ulnae n ▷ ulna
 ulnas n ▷ ulna
ulterior *adj* (of an aim, reason, etc.) concealed or hidden
ultimate *adj* final in a series or process > **ultimately** *adv*
 ultimately *adv* ▷ ultimate
ultimatum [ult-im-**may**-tum] n (*pl* -s) final warning stating that action will be taken unless certain conditions are met
 ultimatums n ▷ ultimatum
ultramarine *adj* vivid blue
ultrasonic *adj* of or producing sound waves with a higher frequency than the human ear can hear
ultraviolet *adj*, n (*pl* -s) (of) light beyond the limit of visibility at the violet end of the spectrum
 ultraviolets n ▷ ultraviolet
ululate [**yewl**-yew-late] v (-tes, -ting, -ted) howl

or wail ▷ **ululation** n (pl -s)
ululated v ▷ ululate
ululates v ▷ ululate
ululating v ▷ ululate
ululation n ▷ ululate
ululations n ▷ ululate

um interj. Um is a sound people make when hesitating in speech. If someone plays this word, remember that lots of words end in UM (dictum, podium and rostrum, for example) and look out for chances to play them. Um scores 4 points.

umber adj dark brown to reddish-brown
umbilical adj of the navel
umbrella n (pl -s) portable device used for protection against rain, consisting of a folding frame covered in material attached to a central rod
umbrellas n ▷ umbrella
umpire n (pl -s) official who rules on the playing of a game ▶ v (-res, -ring, -red) act as umpire in (a game)
umpired v ▷ umpire
umpires n, v ▷ umpire
umpiring v ▷ umpire
umpteen adj (Informal) very many ▷ **umpteenth** n (pl -s) adj
umpteenth n, adj ▷ umpteen
umpteenths n ▷ umpteen

un pron. Un is a dialect word for one. If someone plays this, remember that you can form lots of words by placing letters after UN. Un scores 2 points.

unable adj lacking the necessary power, ability, or authority to (do something)
unaccountable adj unable to be explained ▷ **unaccountably** adv
unaccountably adv ▷ unaccountable
unadulterated adj with nothing added, pure
unanimities n ▷ unanimous
unanimity n ▷ unanimous
unanimous [yew-nan-im-uss] adj in complete agreement ▷ **unanimity** n (pl -ties)
unarmed adj without weapons
unassuming adj modest or unpretentious
unaware adj not aware or conscious
unawares adv by surprise
unbalanced adj biased or one-sided
unbearable adj not able to be endured ▷ **unbearably** adv
unbearably adv ▷ unbearable
unbeknown adv without the knowledge of (a person)
unbend v (-s, -ing, unbent) (Informal) become

less strict or more informal in one's attitudes or behaviour ▷ **unbending** adj
unbending v, adj ▷ unbend
unbends v ▷ unbend
unbent v ▷ unbend
unbidden adj not ordered or asked
unborn adj not yet born
unbosom v (-s, -ing, -ed) relieve (oneself) of (secrets or feelings) by telling someone
unbosomed v ▷ unbosom
unbosoming v ▷ unbosom
unbosoms v ▷ unbosom
unbridled adj (of feelings or behaviour) not controlled in any way
unburden v (-s, -ing, -ed) relieve (one's mind or oneself) of a worry by confiding in someone
unburdened v ▷ unburden
unburdening v ▷ unburden
unburdens v ▷ unburden
uncannier adj ▷ uncanny
uncanniest adj ▷ uncanny
uncannily adv ▷ uncanny
uncanny adj (-nnier, -nniest) weird or mysterious ▷ **uncannily** adv
unceremonious adj relaxed and informal ▷ **unceremoniously** adv
unceremoniously adv ▷ unceremonious
uncertain adj not able to be accurately known or predicted ▷ **uncertainty** n (pl -ties)
uncertainties n ▷ uncertain
uncertainty n ▷ uncertain
uncle n (pl -s) brother of one's father or mother
unclean adj lacking moral, spiritual, or physical cleanliness
uncles n ▷ uncle
uncomfortable adj not physically relaxed
uncommon adj (-er, -est) not happening or encountered often ▷ **uncommonly** adv
uncommoner adj ▷ uncommon
uncommonest adj ▷ uncommon
uncommonly adv ▷ uncommon
uncompromising adj not prepared to compromise
unconcerned adj lacking in concern or involvement ▷ **unconcernedly** adv
unconcernedly adv ▷ unconcerned
unconditional adj without conditions or limitations
unconscionable adj having no principles, unscrupulous
unconscious adj lacking normal awareness through the senses ▶ n (pl -es) part of the mind containing instincts and ideas that exist without one's awareness ▷ **unconsciously** adv ▷ **unconsciousness** n

(*pl* -es)
unconsciouses *n* ▷ unconscious
unconsciously *adv* ▷ unconscious
unconsciousness *n* ▷ unconscious
unconsciousnesses *n* ▷ unconscious
uncooperative *adj* not willing to help other people with what they are doing
uncouth *adj* (-er, -est) lacking in good manners, refinement, or grace
uncouther *adj* ▷ uncouth
uncouthest *adj* ▷ uncouth
uncover *v* (-s, -ing, -ed) reveal or disclose
uncovered *v* ▷ uncover
uncovering *v* ▷ uncover
uncovers *v* ▷ uncover
unction *n* (*pl* -s) act of anointing with oil in sacramental ceremonies
unctions *n* ▷ unction
unctuous *adj* pretending to be kind and concerned
undecided *adj* not having made up one's mind
undeniable *adj* unquestionably true
> **undeniably** *adv*
undeniably *adv* ▷ undeniable
under *prep*, *adv* indicating movement to or position beneath the underside or base ▶ *prep* less than
underage *adj* below the required or standard age
underarm *adj* (SPORT) denoting a style of throwing, bowling, or serving in which the hand is swung below shoulder level ▶ *adv* (SPORT) in an underarm style
undercarriage *n* (*pl* -s) landing gear of an aircraft
undercarriages *n* ▷ undercarriage
underclass *n* (*pl* -es) class consisting of the most disadvantaged people, such as the long-term unemployed
underclasses *n* ▷ underclass
undercoat *n* (*pl* -s) coat of paint applied before the final coat
undercoats *n* ▷ undercoat
undercover *adj* done or acting in secret
undercurrent *n* (*pl* -s) current that is not apparent at the surface
undercurrents *n* ▷ undercurrent
undercut *v* (-cuts, -cutting, -cut) charge less than (a competitor) to obtain trade
undercuts *v* ▷ undercut
undercutting *v* ▷ undercut
underdog *n* (*pl* -s) person or team in a weak or underprivileged position
underdogs *n* ▷ underdog
underdone *adj* not cooked enough

underestimate *v* (-tes, -ting, -ted) make too low an estimate of
underestimated *v* ▷ underestimate
underestimates *v* ▷ underestimate
underestimating *v* ▷ underestimate
underfoot *adv* under the feet
undergarment *n* (*pl* -s) any piece of underwear
undergarments *n* ▷ undergarment
undergo *v* (-goes, -going, -went, -gone) experience, endure, or sustain
undergoes *v* ▷ undergo
undergoing *v* ▷ undergo
undergone *v* ▷ undergo
undergraduate *n* (*pl* -s) person studying in a university for a first degree
undergraduates *n* ▷ undergraduate
underground *adj* occurring, situated, used, or going below ground level ▶ *n* (*pl* -s) electric passenger railway operated in underground tunnels
undergrounds *n* ▷ underground
undergrowth *n* (*pl* -s) small trees and bushes growing beneath taller trees in a wood or forest
undergrowths *n* ▷ undergrowth
underhand *adj* sly, deceitful, and secretive
underlain *v* ▷ underlie
underlay *v* ▷ underlie
underlie *v* (-lies, -lying, -lay, underlain) lie or be placed under > **underlying** *adj* fundamental or basic
underlies *v* ▷ underlie
underline *v* (-s, -ning, -d) draw a line under
underlined *v* ▷ underline
underlines *v* ▷ underline
underling *n* (*pl* -s) subordinate
underlings *n* ▷ underling
underlining *v* ▷ underline
underlying *v*, *adj* ▷ underlie
undermine *v* (-nes, -ning, -ned) weaken gradually
undermined *v* ▷ undermine
undermines *v* ▷ undermine
undermining *v* ▷ undermine
underneath *prep*, *adv* under or beneath ▶ *adj*, *n* (*pl* -s) lower (part or surface)
underneaths *n* ▷ underneath
underpants *pl n* man's undergarment for the lower part of the body
underpass *n* (*pl* -es) section of a road that passes under another road or a railway line
underpasses *n* ▷ underpass
underpin *v* (-pins, -pinning, -pinned) give strength or support to

underpinned v ▷ underpin
underpinning v ▷ underpin
underpins v ▷ underpin
underprivileged adj lacking the rights and advantages of other members of society
underrate v (-tes, -ting, -ted) not realize the full potential of > **underrated** adj
underrated v, adj ▷ underrate
underrates v ▷ underrate
underrating v ▷ underrate
underseal n (pl -s) (CHIEFLY BRIT) coating of tar etc. applied to the underside of a motor vehicle to prevent corrosion
underseals n ▷ underseal
underside n (pl -s) bottom or lower surface
undersides n ▷ underside
understand v (-s, -ing, -stood) know and comprehend the nature or meaning of > **understandable** adj > **understandably** adv
understandable adj ▷ understand
understandably adj ▷ understand
understanding n (pl -s) ability to learn, judge, or make decisions ▶ adj kind and sympathetic ▶ v ▷ understand
understandings n ▷ understanding
understands v ▷ understand
understate v (-tes, -ting, -ted) describe or represent (something) in restrained terms > **understatement** n (pl -s)
understated v ▷ understate
understatement n ▷ understate
understatements n ▷ understate
understates v ▷ understate
understating v ▷ understate
understood v ▷ understand
understudied v ▷ understudy
understudies n, v ▷ understudy
understudy n (pl -dies) actor who studies a part in order to be able to replace the usual actor if necessary ▶ v (-dies, -dying, -died) act as an understudy for
understudying v ▷ understudy
undertake v (-takes, -taking, -took, -taken) agree or commit oneself to (something) or to do (something)
undertaken v ▷ undertake
undertaker n (pl -s) person whose job is to prepare corpses for burial or cremation and organize funerals
undertakers n ▷ undertaker
undertakes v ▷ undertake
undertaking n (pl -s) task or enterprise ▶ v ▷ undertake
undertakings n ▷ undertaking
undertone n (pl -s) quiet tone of voice

undertones n ▷ undertone
undertook v ▷ undertake
undertow n (pl -s) strong undercurrent flowing in a different direction from the surface current
undertows n ▷ undertow
underwear n (pl -s) clothing worn under the outer garments and next to the skin
underwears n ▷ underwear
underwent v ▷ undergo
underworld n (pl -s) criminals and their associates
underworlds n ▷ underworld
underwrite v (-writes, -writing, -wrote, -written) accept financial responsibility for (a commercial project)
underwriter n (pl -s) person who underwrites (esp. an insurance policy)
underwriters n ▷ underwriter
underwrites v ▷ underwrite
underwriting v ▷ underwrite
underwritten v ▷ underwrite
underwrote v ▷ underwrite
undesirable adj not desirable or pleasant, objectionable ▶ n (pl -s) objectionable person
undesirables n ▷ undesirable
undid v ▷ undo
undo v (-does, -doing, -did, -done) open, unwrap > **undone** adj
undoes v ▷ undo
undoing n (pl -s) cause of someone's downfall ▶ v ▷ undo
undoings n ▷ undoing
undone v, adj ▷ undo
undoubted adj certain or indisputable > **undoubtedly** adv
undoubtedly adv ▷ undoubted
undue adj greater than is reasonable, excessive > **unduly** adv
undulate v (-tes, -ting, -ted) move in waves > **undulation** n (pl -s)
undulated v ▷ undulate
undulates v ▷ undulate
undulating v ▷ undulate
undulation n ▷ undulate
undulations n ▷ undulate
unduly adv ▷ undue
undying adj never ending, eternal
unearth v (-s, -ing, -ed) reveal or discover by searching
unearthed v ▷ unearth
unearthing v ▷ unearth
unearthly adj ghostly or eerie
unearths v ▷ unearth
unease n (pl -s) feeling of anxiety

uneases n ▷ unease
uneasier adj ▷ uneasy
uneasiest adj ▷ uneasy
uneasily adv ▷ uneasy
uneasiness n ▷ uneasy
uneasinesses n ▷ uneasy
uneasy adj (-sier, -siest) (of a person) anxious or apprehensive > **uneasily** adv > **uneasiness** n (pl -es)
unemployed adj out of work
 > **unemployment** n (pl -s)
unemployment n ▷ unemployed
unemployments n ▷ unemployed
unequivocal adj completely clear in meaning
 > **unequivocally** adv
unequivocally adv ▷ unequivocal
unerring adj never mistaken, consistently accurate
unexceptionable adj beyond criticism or objection
unfailing adj continuous or reliable
 > **unfailingly** adv
unfailingly adv ▷ unfailing
unfair adj (-er, -est) not right, fair, or just
 > **unfairly** adv > **unfairness** n (pl -es)
unfairer adj ▷ unfair
unfairest adj ▷ unfair
unfairly adv ▷ unfair
unfairness n ▷ unfair
unfairnesses n ▷ unfair
unfaithful adj having sex with someone other than one's regular partner > **unfaithfulness** n (pl -es)
unfaithfulness n ▷ unfaithful
unfaithfulnesses n ▷ unfaithful
unfeeling adj without sympathy
unfit adj unqualified or unsuitable
unflappabilities n ▷ unflappable
unflappability n ▷ unflappable
unflappable adj (Informal) not easily upset
 > **unflappability** n (pl -ties)
unfold v (-s, -ing, -ed) open or spread out from a folded state
unfolded v ▷ unfold
unfolding v ▷ unfold
unfolds v ▷ unfold
unforgettable adj impossible to forget, memorable
unfortunate adj unlucky, unsuccessful, or unhappy > **unfortunately** adv
unfortunately adv ▷ unfortunate
unfrock v (-s, -ing, -ed) deprive (a priest in holy orders) of his or her priesthood
unfrocked v ▷ unfrock
unfrocking v ▷ unfrock

unfrocks v ▷ unfrock
ungainlier adj ▷ ungainly
ungainliest adj ▷ ungainly
ungainly adj (-lier, -liest) lacking grace when moving
ungodlier adj ▷ ungodly
ungodliest adj ▷ ungodly
ungodly adj (-lier, -liest) (Informal) unreasonable or outrageous
ungrateful adj not grateful or thankful
unguarded adj not protected
unguent [ung-gwent] n (pl -s) (Lit) ointment
unguents n ▷ unguent
unhand v (-s, -ing, -ed) (Old-fashioned or lit) release from one's grasp
unhanded v ▷ unhand
unhanding v ▷ unhand
unhands v ▷ unhand
unhappier adj ▷ unhappy
unhappiest adj ▷ unhappy
unhappily adv ▷ unhappy
unhappiness n ▷ unhappy
unhappinesses n ▷ unhappy
unhappy adj (-ppier, -ppiest) sad or depressed
 > **unhappily** adv > **unhappiness** n (pl -es)
unhealthier adj ▷ unhealthy
unhealthiest adj ▷ unhealthy
unhealthy adj (-thier, -thiest) likely to cause poor health
unhinge v (-ges, -ging, -ged) derange or unbalance (a person or his or her mind)
unhinged v ▷ unhinge
unhinges v ▷ unhinge
unhinging v ▷ unhinge
unicorn n (pl -s) imaginary horselike creature with one horn growing from its forehead
unicorns n ▷ unicorn
unification n ▷ unify
unifications n ▷ unify
unified v ▷ unify
unifies v ▷ unify
uniform n (pl -s) special identifying set of clothes for the members of an organization, such as soldiers ▶ adj regular and even throughout, unvarying > **uniformly** adv
 > **uniformity** n (pl -ties)
uniformities n ▷ uniform
uniformity n ▷ uniform
uniformly adv ▷ uniform
uniforms n ▷ uniform
unify v (-fies, -fying, -fied) make or become one > **unification** n (pl -s)
unifying v ▷ unify
unilateral adj made or done by only one person or group > **unilaterally** adv

unilaterally adv ▷ unilateral

unimpeachable adj completely honest and reliable

uninterested adj having or showing no interest in someone or something

union n (pl -s) uniting or being united

unionist n (pl -s) member or supporter of a trade union
    unionists n ▷ unionist
    unionization n ▷ unionize
    unionizations n ▷ unionize

unionize v (-zes, -zing, -zed) organize (workers) into a trade union > **unionization** n (pl -s)
    unionized v ▷ unionize
    unionizes v ▷ unionize
    unionizing v ▷ unionize
    unions n ▷ union

unique [yoo-**neek**] adj being the only one of a particular type > **uniquely** adv
    uniquely adv ▷ unique

unisex adj designed for use by both sexes

unison n (pl -s) complete agreement
    unisons n ▷ unison

unit n (pl -s) single undivided entity or whole

unitary adj consisting of a single undivided whole

unite v (-tes, -ting, -ted) make or become an integrated whole
    united v ▷ unite
    unites n ▷ unite
    unities n ▷ unity
    uniting v ▷ unite
    units n ▷ unit

unity n (pl -ties) state of being one

universal adj of or typical of the whole of mankind or of nature > **universally** adv > **universality** n (pl -ties)
    universalities n ▷ universal
    universality n ▷ universal
    universally adv ▷ universal

universe n (pl -s) whole of all existing matter, energy, and space
    universes n ▷ universe
    universities n ▷ university

university n (pl -ties) institution of higher education with the authority to award degrees

unkempt adj (of the hair) not combed

unknown adj not known ▶ n (pl -s) unknown person, quantity, or thing
    unknowns n ▷ unknown

unleaded adj (of petrol) containing less tetraethyl lead, in order to reduce environmental pollution

unless conj except under the circumstances that

unlike adj dissimilar or different ▶ prep not like or typical of

unlikely adj improbable

unload v (-s, -ing, -ed) remove (cargo) from (a ship, truck, or plane)
    unloaded v ▷ unload
    unloading v ▷ unload
    unloads v ▷ unload

unmask v (-s, -ing, -ed) remove the mask or disguise from
    unmasked v ▷ unmask
    unmasking v ▷ unmask
    unmasks v ▷ unmask

unmentionable adj unsuitable as a topic of conversation

unmistakable, unmistakeable adj not ambiguous, clear > **unmistakably, unmistakeably** adv
    unmistakably adv ▷ unmistakable
    unmistakeable adj ▷ unmistakable
    unmistakeably adv ▷ unmistakable

unmitigated adj not reduced or lessened in severity etc.

unmoved adj not affected by emotion, indifferent

unnatural adj strange and frightening because not usual

unnerve v (-ves, -ving, -ved) cause to lose courage, confidence, or self-control
    unnerved v ▷ unnerve
    unnerves v ▷ unnerve
    unnerving v ▷ unnerve

unnumbered adj countless

unorthodox adj (of ideas, methods, etc.) unconventional and not generally accepted

unpack v (-s, -ing, -ed) remove the contents of (a suitcase, trunk, etc.)
    unpacked v ▷ unpack
    unpacking v ▷ unpack
    unpacks v ▷ unpack

unparalleled adj not equalled, supreme

unpick v (-s, -ing, -ed) undo (the stitches) of (a piece of sewing)
    unpicked v ▷ unpick
    unpicking v ▷ unpick
    unpicks v ▷ unpick

unpleasant adj not pleasant or agreeable > **unpleasantly** adv > **unpleasantness** n (pl -s)
    unpleasantly adv ▷ unpleasant
    unpleasantness n ▷ unpleasant
    unpleasantnesses n ▷ unpleasant

unprintable adj unsuitable for printing for reasons of obscenity or libel

unprofessional *adj* contrary to the accepted code of a profession ▷ **unprofessionally** *adv*
unprofessionally *adv* ▷ unprofessional
unqualified *adj* lacking the necessary qualifications
unravel *v* (-vels, -velling, -velled) reduce (something knitted or woven) to separate strands
unravelled *v* ▷ unravel
unravelling *v* ▷ unravel
unravels *v* ▷ unravel
unremitting *adj* never slackening or stopping
unrequited *adj* not returned
unrest *n* (pl -s) rebellious state of discontent
unrests *n* ▷ unrest
unrivalled *adj* having no equal
unroll *v* (-s, -ing, -ed) open out or unwind (something rolled or coiled) or (of something rolled or coiled) become opened out or unwound
unrolled *v* ▷ unroll
unrolling *v* ▷ unroll
unrolls *v* ▷ unroll
unrulier *adj* ▷ unruly
unruliest *adj* ▷ unruly
unruly *adj* (-lier, -liest) difficult to control or organize
unsavoury *adj* distasteful or objectionable
unscathed *adj* not harmed or injured
unscrupulous *adj* prepared to act dishonestly, unprincipled
unseat *v* (-s, -ing, -ed) throw or displace from a seat or saddle
unseated *v* ▷ unseat
unseating *v* ▷ unseat
unseats *v* ▷ unseat
unsettled *adj* lacking order or stability
unsightlier *adj* ▷ unsightly
unsightliest *adj* ▷ unsightly
unsightly *adj* (-lier, -liest) unpleasant to look at
unsociable *adj* ▷ unsocial
unsocial *adj* (also **unsociable**) avoiding the company of other people
unsound *adj* unhealthy or unstable
unstable *adj* (-r, -st) lacking stability or firmness
unstabler *adj* ▷ unstable
unstablest *adj* ▷ unstable
unsuitable *adj* not right or appropriate for a particular purpose ▷ **unsuitably** *adv*
unsuitably *adv* ▷ unsuitable
unsuited *adj* not appropriate for a particular task or situation
unswerving *adj* firm, constant, not changing

unthinkable *adj* out of the question, inconceivable
untidier *adj* ▷ untidy
untidiest *adj* ▷ untidy
untidily *adv* ▷ untidy
untidiness *n* ▷ untidy
untidinesses *n* ▷ untidy
untidy *adj* (-dier, -diest) messy and disordered ▷ **untidily** *adv* > **untidiness** *n* (pl -es)
untie *v* (-ties, -tying, -tied) open or free (something that is tied)
untied *v* ▷ untie
unties *v* ▷ untie
until *conj* up to the time that ▶ *prep* in or throughout the period before
untimelier *adj* ▷ untimely
untimeliest *adj* ▷ untimely
untimely *adj* (-lier, -liest) occurring before the expected or normal time
unto *prep* (Old-fashioned) to
untold *adj* incapable of description
untouchable *adj* above reproach or suspicion ▶ *n* (pl -s) member of the lowest Hindu caste in India
untouchables *n* ▷ untouchable
untoward *adj* causing misfortune or annoyance
untrue *adj* (-r, -st) incorrect or false
untruer *adj* ▷ untrue
untruest *adj* ▷ untrue
untruth *n* (pl -s) statement that is not true, lie
untruths *n* ▷ untruth
untying *v* ▷ untie
unusual *adj* uncommon or extraordinary ▷ **unusually** *adv*
unusually *adv* ▷ unusual
unutterable *adj* incapable of being expressed in words ▷ **unutterably** *adv*
unutterably *adv* ▷ unutterable
unvarnished *adj* not elaborated upon
unwieldier *adj* ▷ unwieldy
unwieldiest *adj* ▷ unwieldy
unwieldy *adj* (-dier, -diest) too heavy, large, or awkward to be easily handled
unwind *v* (-s, -ing, unwound) relax after a busy or tense time
unwinding *v* ▷ unwind
unwinds *v* ▷ unwind
unwitting *adj* not intentional ▷ **unwittingly** *adv*
unwittingly *adv* ▷ unwitting
unwonted *adj* out of the ordinary
unworthier *adj* ▷ unworthy
unworthiest *adj* ▷ unworthy
unworthy *adj* (-thier, -thiest) not deserving

or worthy

unwound v ▷ unwind

unwrap v (-s, -pping, -pped) remove the wrapping from (something)

unwrapped v ▷ unwrap

unwrapping v ▷ unwrap

unwraps v ▷ unwrap

unwritten adj not printed or in writing

up prep, adv indicating movement to or position at a higher place ▶ adv indicating readiness, intensity or completeness, etc. ▶ adj of a high or higher position ▶ v (-s, -pping, -pped) increase or raise ▶ adv (also **upwards**) from a lower to a higher place, level, or condition

upbeat adj (Informal) cheerful and optimistic ▶ n (pl -s) (MUSIC) unaccented beat

upbeats n ▷ upbeat

upbraid v (-s, -ing, -ded) scold or reproach

upbraided v ▷ upbraid

upbraiding v ▷ upbraid

upbraids v ▷ upbraid

upbringing n (pl -s) education of a person during the formative years

upbringings n ▷ upbringing

update v (-tes, -ting, -ted) bring up to date

updated v ▷ update

updates v ▷ update

updating v ▷ update

upend v (-s, -ing, -ed) turn or set (something) on its end

upended v ▷ upend

upending v ▷ upend

upends v ▷ upend

upfront adj open and frank ▶ adv, adj (of money) paid out at the beginning of a business arrangement

upgrade v (-des, -ding, -ded) promote (a person or job) to a higher rank

upgraded v ▷ upgrade

upgrades v ▷ upgrade

upgrading v ▷ upgrade

upheaval n (pl -s) strong, sudden, or violent disturbance

upheavals n ▷ upheaval

upheld v ▷ uphold

uphill adj sloping or leading upwards ▶ adv up a slope ▶ n (pl -s) (S AFR) difficulty

uphills n ▷ uphill

uphold v (-s, -ing, upheld) maintain or defend against opposition ▶ **upholder** n (pl -s)

upholder n ▷ uphold

upholders n ▷ uphold

upholding v ▷ uphold

upholds v ▷ uphold

upholster v (-s, -ing, -ed) fit (a chair or sofa) with padding, springs, and covering ▶ **upholsterer** n (pl -s)

upholstered v ▷ upholster

upholsterer n ▷ upholster

upholsterers n ▷ upholster

upholsteries n ▷ upholstery

upholstering v ▷ upholster

upholsters v ▷ upholster

upholstery n (pl -ries) soft covering on a chair or sofa

upkeep n (pl -s) act, process, or cost of keeping something in good repair

upkeeps n ▷ upkeep

upland adj of or in an area of high or relatively high ground ▶ **uplands** pl n area of high or relatively high ground

uplands pl n ▷ upland

uplift v (-s, -ing, -ed) raise or lift up ▶ n (pl -s) act or process of improving moral, social, or cultural conditions ▶ **uplifting** adj

uplifted v ▷ uplift

uplifting v, adj ▷ uplift

uplifts v, n ▷ uplift

upload v (-s, -ing, -ed) transfer (data or a program) from one's own computer into the memory of another computer

uploaded v ▷ upload

uploading v ▷ upload

uploads v ▷ upload

upon prep on

upped v ▷ up

upper adj higher or highest in physical position, wealth, rank, or status ▶ n (pl -s) part of a shoe above the sole

uppermost adj highest in position, power, or importance ▶ adv in or into the highest place or position

uppers n ▷ upper

upping v ▷ up

uppish, uppity adj (BRIT) (Informal) snobbish, arrogant, or presumptuous

uppity adj ▷ uppish

upright adj vertical or erect ▶ adv vertically or in an erect position ▶ n (pl -s) vertical support, such as a post ▶ **uprightness** n (pl -s)

uprightness n ▷ upright

uprightnesses n ▷ upright

uprights n ▷ upright

uprising n (pl -s) rebellion or revolt

uprisings n ▷ uprising

uproar n (pl -s) disturbance characterized by loud noise and confusion

uproarious adj very funny ▶ **uproariously** adv

uproariously adv ▷ uproarious

uproars n ▷ uproar
uproot v (-s, -ing, -ed) pull up by or as if by the roots
uprooted v ▷ uproot
uprooting v ▷ uproot
uproots v ▷ uproot
ups v ▷ up
upset adj emotionally or physically disturbed or distressed ▶ v (-s, -tting, upset) tip over ▶ n (pl -s) unexpected defeat or reversal > **upsetting** adj
upsets v, n ▷ upset
upsetting v, adj ▷ upset
upshot n (pl -s) final result or conclusion
upshots n ▷ upshot
upstage adj at the back half of the stage ▶ v (-ges, -ging, -ged) (Informal) draw attention to oneself from (someone else)
upstaged v ▷ upstage
upstages v ▷ upstage
upstaging v ▷ upstage
upstairs adv to or on an upper floor of a building ▶ n upper floor
upstanding adj of good character
upstart n (pl -s) person who has risen suddenly to a position of power and behaves arrogantly
upstarts n ▷ upstart
upstream adv, adj in or towards the higher part of a stream
upsurge n (pl -s) rapid rise or swell
upsurges n ▷ upsurge
uptake n (pl -s) (Informal) quick or slow to understand or learn
uptakes n ▷ uptake
uptight adj (Informal) nervously tense, irritable, or angry
upturn n (pl -s) upward trend or improvement > **upturned** adj facing upwards
upturned adj ▷ upturn
upturns n ▷ upturn
upward adj directed or moving towards a higher place or level
upwards adv ▷ up

> **ur** interj. Ur is a sound people make when hesitating in speech. If someone plays this, you may be able to use it to form words that begin with UR. Ur is also handy for connecting words beginning with U to those ending in R. Ur scores 2 points.

uranium n (pl -s) (CHEM) radioactive silvery-white metallic element, used chiefly as a source of nuclear energy
uraniums n ▷ uranium

urban adj of or living in a city or town
urbane adj (-r, -st) characterized by courtesy, elegance, and sophistication > **urbanity** n (pl -ties)
urbaner adj ▷ urbane
urbanest adj ▷ urbane
urbanities n ▷ urbane
urbanity n ▷ urbane
urbanization n ▷ urbanize
urbanizations n ▷ urbanize
urbanize v (-zes, -zing, -zed) make (a rural area) more industrialized and urban > **urbanization** n (pl -s)
urbanized v ▷ urbanize
urbanizes v ▷ urbanize
urbanizing v ▷ urbanize
urchin n (pl -s) mischievous child
urchins n ▷ urchin
urethra [yew-reeth-ra] n (pl -rae) canal that carries urine from the bladder out of the body
urethrae n ▷ urethra
urge n (pl -s) strong impulse, inner drive, or yearning ▶ v (-urges, -urging, -urged) plead with or press (a person to do something)
urged v ▷ urge
urgencies n ▷ urgent
urgency n ▷ urgent
urgent adj requiring speedy action or attention > **urgency** n (pl -cies) > **urgently** adv
urgently adv ▷ urgent
urges n, v ▷ urge
urging v ▷ urge
urinal n (pl -s) sanitary fitting used by men for urination
urinals n ▷ urine
urinary adj ▷ urine
urinate v (-tes, -ting, -ted) discharge urine > **urination** n (pl -s)
urinated v ▷ urinate
urinates v ▷ urinate
urinating v ▷ urinate
urination n ▷ urinate
urinations n ▷ urinate
urine n (pl -s) pale yellow fluid excreted by the kidneys to the bladder and passed as waste from the body > **urinary** adj
urines n ▷ urine
urn n (pl -s) vase used as a container for the ashes of the dead
urns n ▷ urn
ursine adj of or like a bear
us pron ▷ we
usable adj able to be used
usage n (pl -s) regular or constant use
usages n ▷ usage

use v (-ses, -sing, -sed) put into service or action ▶ n (pl -s) using or being used **> user** n (pl -s) **> useful** adj **> usefully** adv **> usefulness** n (pl -es) **> useless** adj **> uselessly** adv **> uselessness** n (pl -es)

used adj second-hand ▶ v **> use**
  useful adj ▷ use
  usefully adv ▷ use
  usefulness n ▷ use
  usefulnesses n ▷ use
  useless adj ▷ use
  uselessly adv ▷ use
  uselessness n ▷ use
  uselessnesses n ▷ use
  user n ▷ use
username n (pl -s) (COMPUTERS) name entered into a computer for identification purposes
  usernames n ▷ username
  users n ▷ use
  uses v, n ▷ use
usher n (pl -s) official who shows people to their seats, as in a church ▶ v (-s, -ing, -ed) conduct or escort
  ushered v ▷ usher
usherette n (pl -s) female assistant in a cinema who shows people to their seats
  usherettes n ▷ usherette
  ushering v ▷ usher
  ushers n, v ▷ usher
  using v ▷ use
usual adj of the most normal, frequent, or regular type
usually adv most often, in most cases
  usurer n ▷ usury
  usurers n ▷ usury
  usuries n ▷ usury
usurp [yewz-zurp] v (-s, -ing, -ed) seize (a position or power) without authority **> usurpation** n (pl -s) **> usurper** n (pl -s)
  usurpation n ▷ usurp
  usurpations n ▷ usurp
  usurped v ▷ usurp
  usurper n ▷ usurp
  usurpers n ▷ usurp
  usurping v ▷ usurp
  usurps v ▷ usurp
usury n (pl -ries) practice of lending money at an extremely high rate of interest **> usurer** [yewz-yoor-er] ▶ n (pl -s)

> **ut** n (uts). Ut is a musical note. This unusual word is useful for connecting words beginning with U to those ending with T. Ut scores 2 points.

ute [yoot] n (pl -s) (AUST & NZ) (Informal) utility truck
utensil n (pl -s) tool or container for practical use
  utensils n ▷ utensil
  uteri n ▷ uterus
  uterine adj ▷ uterus
uterus [yew-ter-russ] n (pl uteri) womb **> uterine** adj
  utes n ▷ ute
utilitarian adj useful rather than beautiful
utilitarianism n (pl -s) (ETHICS) doctrine that the right action is the one that brings about the greatest good for the greatest number of people
  utilitarianisms n ▷ utilitarianism
  utilities n ▷ utility
utility n (pl -ties) usefulness ▶ adj designed for use rather than beauty
  utilization n ▷ utilize
  utilizations n ▷ utilize
utilize v (-zes, -zing, -zed) make practical use of **> utilization** n (pl -s)
  utilized v ▷ utilize
  utilizes v ▷ utilize
  utilizing v ▷ utilize
utmost, uttermost adj, n (pl -s) (of) the greatest possible degree or amount
  utmosts n ▷ utmost
utopia [yew-tope-ee-a] n (pl -s) any real or imaginary society, place, or state considered to be perfect or ideal **> utopian** adj
  utopian adj ▷ utopia
  utopias n ▷ utopia
utter[1] v (-s, -ing, -ed) express (something) in sounds or words
utter[2] adj total or absolute **> utterly** adv
utterance n (pl -s) something uttered
  utterances n ▷ utterance
  uttered v ▷ utter[1]
  uttering v ▷ utter[1]
  utterly adv ▷ utter[2]
  uttermost adj, n (pl -s) ▷ utmost
  uttermosts n ▷ uttermost
  utters v ▷ utter[1]
uvula [yew-view-la] n (pl -s) small fleshy part of the soft palate that hangs in the back of the throat **> uvular** adj
  uvular adj ▷ uvula
  uvulas n ▷ uvula
uxorious [ux-or-ee-uss] adj excessively fond of or dependent on one's wife

Vv

If you have a V on your rack, the first thing to remember is that there are no valid two-letter words beginning with V. In fact, there are no two-letter words that end in V either, so you can't form any two-letter words using V. Remembering this will stop you wasting time trying to think of some. While V is useless for two-letter words, it does start some good three-letter words. **Vex** and **vox** (13 points each) are the best of these, while **vaw, vow** and **vly** (9 each) are also useful.

vac n (**vacs**). Vac is a short form of vacuum cleaner. This word can prove useful when you have a V but not much space to play it in. Remember that if you have the letters for vac, you might be able to form **cave** using an E that is already on the board. Vac scores 8 points.

vacancies n ▷ vacancy
vacancy n (pl -**cies**) unfilled job
vacant adj (of a toilet, room, etc.) unoccupied
> **vacantly** adv
    vacantly adv ▷ vacant
vacate v (-**tes, -ting, -ted**) cause (something) to be empty by leaving
    vacated v ▷ vacate
    vacates v ▷ vacate
    vacating v ▷ vacate
vacation n time when universities and law courts are closed
    vacations n ▷ vacation
vaccinate v (-**tes, -ting, -ted**) inject with a vaccine > **vaccination** n (pl -**s**)
    vaccinated v ▷ vaccinate
    vaccinates v ▷ vaccinate
    vaccinating v ▷ vaccinate
    vaccination n ▷ vaccinate
    vaccinations n ▷ vaccinate
vaccine n (pl -**s**) substance designed to cause a mild form of a disease to make a person immune to the disease itself
    vaccines n ▷ vaccine
vacillate [vass-ill-late] v (-**tes, -ting, -ted**) keep changing one's mind or opinions
> **vacillation** n (pl -**s**)
    vacillated v ▷ vacillate
    vacillates v ▷ vacillate
    vacillating v ▷ vacillate

    vacillation n ▷ vacillate
    vacillations n ▷ vacillate
vacua n ▷ vacuum
vacuous adj not expressing intelligent thought > **vacuity** n (pl -**ties**)
vacuum n (pl -**cuums, -cua**) empty space from which all or most air or gas has been removed
▶ v (-**s, -ing, -ed**) clean with a vacuum cleaner
    vacuumed v ▷ vacuum
    vacuuming v ▷ vacuum
    vacuums n ▷ vacuum
vagabond n (pl -**s**) person with no fixed home, esp. a beggar
    vagabonds n ▷ vagabond
    vagaries n ▷ vagary
vagary [vaig-a-ree] n (pl -**ries**) unpredictable change
vagina [vaj-jine-a] n (pl -**s**) (in female mammals) passage from the womb to the external genitals > **vaginal** adj
    vaginal adj ▷ vagina
    vaginas n ▷ vagina
    vagrancies n ▷ vagrancy
    vagrancy n ▷ vagrant
vagrant [vaig-rant] n (pl -**s**) person with no settled home ▶ adj wandering > **vagrancy** n (pl -**cies**)
    vagrants n ▷ vagrant
vague adj (-**guer, -guest**) not clearly explained
> **vaguely** adv
    vaguely adv ▷ vague
    vaguer adj ▷ vague
    vaguest adj ▷ vague
vain adj (-**er, -est**) excessively proud, esp. of one's appearance
    vainer adj ▷ vain
    vainest adj ▷ vain
vainglorious adj (Lit) boastful

valance [**val**-lenss] n (pl -s) piece of drapery round the edge of a bed
    valances n ▷ valance
vale n (pl -s) (Lit) valley
valediction n (pl -s) farewell speech
    valedictions n ▷ valediction
valedictory [val-lid-**dik**-tree] adj (of a speech, performance, etc.) intended as a farewell
valence [**vale**-ence] n (pl -s) molecular bonding between atoms
    valences n ▷ valence
    valencies n ▷ valency
valency n (pl -cies) power of an atom to make molecular bonds
valentine n (pl -s) (person to whom one sends) a romantic card on Saint Valentine's Day, 14th February
    valentines n ▷ valentine
valerian n (pl -s) herb used as a sedative
    valerians n ▷ valerian
    vales n ▷ vale
valet n (pl -s) man's personal male servant
    valets n ▷ valet
valetudinarian [val-lit-yew-din-**air**-ee-an] n (pl -s) person with a long-term illness
    valetudinarians n ▷ valetudinarian
valiant adj brave or courageous
valid adj (-er, -est) soundly reasoned > **validity** n (pl -ies)
validate v (-tes, -ting, -ted) make valid > **validation** n (pl -s)
    validated v ▷ validate
    validates v ▷ validate
    validating v ▷ validate
    validation n ▷ validate
    validations n ▷ validate
    valider adj ▷ valid
    validest adj ▷ valid
    validities n ▷ valid
    validity n ▷ valid
valise [val-**leez**] n (pl -s) (Old-fashioned) small suitcase
    valises n ▷ valise
valley n (pl -s) low area between hills, often with a river running through it
    valleys n ▷ valley
valour n (pl -s) (Lit) bravery
    valours n ▷ valour
valuable adj having great worth
valuables pl n valuable personal property
valuation n (pl -s) assessment of worth
    valuations n ▷ valuation
value n (pl -s) importance, usefulness ▶ pl moral principles ▶ v (-ues, -uing, -ued) assess the worth or desirability of > **valueless** adj

    > **valuer** n (pl -s)
    valued v ▷ value
    valueless adj ▷ value
    valuer n ▷ value
    valuers n ▷ value
    values n, v ▷ value
    valuing v ▷ value
valve n (pl -s) device to control the movement of fluid through a pipe > **valvular** adj
    valves n ▷ valve
    valvular adj ▷ valve
vamp[1] n (pl -s) (Informal) sexually attractive woman who seduces men
vamp[2] v (-s, -ing, -ed) make (a story, piece of music, etc.) seem new by inventing additional parts
    vamped v ▷ vamp[2]
    vamping v ▷ vamp[2]
vampire n (pl -s) (in folklore) corpse that rises at night to drink the blood of the living
    vampires n ▷ vampire
    vamps n, v ▷ vamp[1, 2]
van[1] n (pl -s) motor vehicle for transporting goods
van[2] n (pl -s) ▷ vanguard
vanadium n (pl -s) (CHEM) metallic element, used in steel
    vanadiums n ▷ vanadium
vandal n (pl -s) person who deliberately damages property > **vandalism** n (pl -s) > **vandalize** v (-zes, -zing, -zed)
    vandalism n ▷ vandal
    vandalisms n ▷ vandal
    vandalize n ▷ vandal
    vandalized n ▷ vandal
    vandalizes n ▷ vandal
    vandalizing v ▷ vandal
    vandals n ▷ vandal
vane n (pl -s) flat blade on a rotary device such as a weathercock or propeller
    vanes n ▷ vane
vanguard n (pl -s) unit of soldiers leading an army
    vanguards n ▷ vanguard
vanilla n (pl -s) seed pod of a tropical climbing orchid, used for flavouring
    vanillas n ▷ vanilla
vanish v (-es, -ing, -ed) disappear suddenly or mysteriously
    vanished v ▷ vanish
    vanishes v ▷ vanish
    vanishing v ▷ vanish
    vanities n ▷ vanity
vanity n (pl -ies) (display of) excessive pride
vanquish v (-es, -ing, -ed) (Lit) defeat

vanquished v ▷ vanquish
vanquishes v ▷ vanquish
vanquishing v ▷ vanquish
vans n ▷ van[1, 2]

vantage n (pl -s) position that gives one an overall view
vantages n ▷ vantage

vapid adj (-er, -est) lacking character, dull
vapider adj ▷ vapid
vapidest adj ▷ vapid
vaporize v ▷ vapour
vaporized v ▷ vapour
vaporizer n ▷ vapour
vaporizers n ▷ vapour
vaporizes v ▷ vapour
vaporizing v ▷ vapour
vaporous adj ▷ vapour

vapour n (pl -s) moisture suspended in air as steam or mist > **vaporize** v (-zes, -zing, -zed) > **vaporizer** n (pl -s) > **vaporous** adj
vapours n ▷ vapour
variabilities n ▷ variable
variability n ▷ variable

variable adj not always the same, changeable ▶ n (pl -s) (MATHS) expression with a range of values > **variability** n (pl -ties)
variables n ▷ variable

variant adj differing from a standard or type ▶ n (pl -s) something that differs from a standard or type
variants n ▷ variant

variation n (pl -s) something presented in a slightly different form
variations n ▷ variation
varied v, adj ▷ vary

variegated adj having patches or streaks of different colours > **variegation** n (pl -s)
variegation n ▷ variegate
variegations n ▷ variegate
varies adj ▷ vary
varieties n ▷ variety

variety n (pl -ies) state of being diverse or various

various adj of several kinds > **variously** adv
variously adv ▷ various

varnish n (pl -es) solution of oil and resin, put on a surface to make it hard and glossy ▶ v (-es, -ing, -ed) apply varnish to
varnished v ▷ varnish
varnishes n, v ▷ varnish
varnishing v ▷ varnish

vary v (-ries, -rying, -ried) change > **varied** adj
varying v ▷ vary

vascular adj (BIOL) relating to vessels

vase n (pl -s) ornamental jar, esp. for flowers
vasectomies n ▷ vasectomy

vasectomy n (pl -mies) surgical removal of part of the vas deferens, as a contraceptive method
vases n ▷ vase

vassal n (pl -s) (HIST) man given land by a lord in return for military service > **vassalage** n (pl -s)
vassalage n ▷ vassal
vassalages n ▷ vassal
vassals n ▷ vassal

vast adj (-er, -est) extremely large > **vastly** adv > **vastness** n (pl -es)
vaster adj ▷ vast
vastest adj ▷ vast
vastly adv ▷ vast
vastness n ▷ vast
vastnesses n ▷ vast

vat n (pl -s) large container for liquids
vats n ▷ vat

vaudeville n (pl -s) variety entertainment of songs and comic turns
vaudevilles n ▷ vaudeville

vault[1] n (pl -s) secure room for storing valuables

vault[2] v (-s, -ing, -ed) jump over (something) by resting one's hand(s) on it. ▶ n such a jump
vaulted adj having an arched roof ▶ v ▷ vault[2]
vaulting v ▷ vault[2]
vaults n, v ▷ vault[1, 2]

vaunt v (-s, -ing, -ed) describe or display (success or possessions) boastfully > **vaunted** adj
vaunted adj, v ▷ vaunt
vaunting v ▷ vaunt
vaunts v ▷ vaunt

> **vaw** n (vaws). Vaw is a letter of the Hebrew alphabet. This is a very unusual word that can be useful when you are short of options. If you have the tiles for vaw, look out for opportunities to play **wave** or **wavy** using an E or Y that is already on the board. Vaw scores 9 points.

veal n (pl -s) calf meat
veals n ▷ veal

vector n (pl -s) (MATHS) quantity that has size and direction, such as force
vectors n ▷ vector

veer v (-s, -ing, -ed) change direction suddenly
veered v ▷ veer
veering v ▷ veer
veers v ▷ veer

> **veg** n (veges). Veg is a short form of **vegetable**. If someone plays this, look

out for opportunities to form **vegan** or **vegetate** from it. Veg scores 7 points.

vegan [vee-gan] n (pl-s) person who eats no meat, fish, eggs, or dairy products ▶ adj suitable for a vegan > **veganism** n (pl-s)
veganism n ▷ vegan
veganisms n ▷ vegan
vegans n ▷ vegan
vegetable n (pl-s) edible plant ▶ adj of or like plants or vegetables
vegetables n ▷ vegetable
vegetarian n (pl-s) person who eats no meat or fish ▶ adj suitable for a vegetarian > **vegetarianism** n (pl-s)
vegetarianism n ▷ vegetarian
vegetarianisms n ▷ vegetarian
vegetarians n ▷ vegetarian
vegetate v (-tes, -ting, -ted) live a dull boring life with no mental stimulation
vegetated v ▷ vegetate
vegetates v ▷ vegetate
vegetating v ▷ vegetate
vegetation n (pl-s) plant life of a given place
vegetations n ▷ vegetation
vehemence n ▷ vehement
vehemences n ▷ vehement
vehement adj expressing strong feelings > **vehemence** n > **vehemently** adv
vehemently adv ▷ vehement
vehicle n (pl-s) machine, esp. with an engine and wheels, for carrying people or objects > **vehicular** adj
vehicles n ▷ vehicle
vehicular adj ▷ vehicle
veil n (pl-s) piece of thin cloth covering the head or face ▶ v (-s, -ing, -ed) cover with or as if with a veil
veiled adj disguised ▶ v ▷ veil
veiling v ▷ veil
veils n, v ▷ veil
vein n (pl-s) tube that takes blood to the heart > **veined** adj
veined adj ▷ vein
veins n ▷ vein
veld, veldt n (pl-s) high grassland in southern Africa
velds n ▷ veld
veldskoen, velskoen n (pl-s) (S AFR) leather ankle boot
veldskoens n ▷ veldskoen
veldts n ▷ veld
vellum n (pl-s) fine calfskin parchment
vellums n ▷ vellum
velocities n ▷ velocity
velocity n (pl-ties) speed of movement in a

given direction
velour, velours [vel-loor] n (pl-s) fabric similar to velvet
velours n ▷ velour
velskoen n ▷ veldskoen
velskoens n ▷ veldskoen
velvet n (pl-s) fabric with a thick soft pile
velveteen n (pl-s) cotton velvet
velveteens n ▷ velveteen
velvetier adj ▷ velvety
velvetiest adj ▷ velvety
velvets n ▷ velvet
velvety adj (-tier, -tiest) soft and smooth
venal adj easily bribed
vend v (-s, -ing, -ed) sell > **vendor** n (pl-s)
vended v ▷ vend
vendetta n (pl-s) prolonged quarrel between families, esp. one involving revenge killings
vendettas n ▷ vendetta
vending v ▷ vend
vendor n ▷ vend
vendors n ▷ vend
vends v ▷ vend
veneer n (pl-s) thin layer of wood etc. covering a cheaper material
veneers n ▷ veneer
venerable adj worthy of deep respect
venerate v (-tes, -ting, -ted) hold (a person) in deep respect > **veneration** n (pl-s)
venerated v ▷ venerate
venerates v ▷ venerate
venerating v ▷ venerate
veneration n ▷ venerate
venerations n ▷ venerate
vengeance n (pl-s) revenge
vengeances n ▷ vengeance
vengeful adj wanting revenge
venial [veen-ee-al] adj (of a sin or fault) easily forgiven
venison n (pl-s) deer meat
venisons n ▷ venison
venom n (pl-s) malice or spite > **venomous** adj
venomous adj ▷ venom
venoms n ▷ venom
venous adj (ANAT) of veins
vent[1] n (pl-s) outlet releasing fumes or fluid ▶ v (-s, -ing, -ed) express (an emotion) freely
vent[2] n (pl-s) vertical slit in a jacket
vented v ▷ vent[1]
ventilate v (-tes, -ting, -ted) let fresh air into > **ventilation** n (pl-s) > **ventilator** n (pl-s)
ventilated v ▷ ventilate
ventilates v ▷ ventilate
ventilating v ▷ ventilate
ventilation n ▷ ventilate

ventilations n ▷ ventilate
ventilator n ▷ ventilate
ventilators n ▷ ventilate
venting v ▷ vent¹
ventral adj relating to the front of the body
ventricle n (pl -s) (ANAT) one of the four cavities of the heart or brain
ventricles n ▷ ventricle
ventriloquism n ▷ ventriloquist
ventriloquisms n ▷ ventriloquist
ventriloquist n (pl -s) entertainer who can speak without moving his or her lips, so that a voice seems to come from elsewhere > **ventriloquism** n (pl -s)
ventriloquists n ▷ ventriloquist
vents n, v ▷ vent¹, ²
venture n (pl -s) risky undertaking, esp. in business ▶ v (-res, -ring, -red) do something risky
ventured v ▷ venture
ventures n, v ▷ venture
venturesome adj daring
venturing v ▷ venture
venue n (pl -s) place where an organized gathering is held
venues n ▷ venue
veracious adj ▷ veracity
veracities n ▷ veracity
veracity n (pl -ties) habitual truthfulness > **veracious** adj
veranda n ▷ verandah
verandah, veranda n (pl -s) open porch attached to a house
verandahs n ▷ verandah
verandas n ▷ verandah
verb n (pl -s) word that expresses the idea of action, happening, or being
verbal adj spoken > **verbally** adv
verbalize v (-s, -ing, -ed) express (something) in words
verbalized v ▷ verbalize
verbalizes n ▷ verbalize
verbalizing v ▷ verbalize
verbally adv ▷ verbal
verbatim [verb-**bait**-im] adv, adj word for word
verbena n (pl -s) plant with sweet-smelling flowers
verbenas n ▷ verbena
verbiage n (pl -s) excessive use of words
verbiages n ▷ verbiage
verbose [verb-**bohss**] adj (-r, -st) speaking at tedious length > **verbosity** n (pl -ties)
verboser adj ▷ verbose
verbosest adj ▷ verbose
verbosities n ▷ verbose

verbosity n ▷ verbose
verbs n ▷ verb
verdant adj (Lit) covered in green vegetation
verdict n (pl -s) decision of a jury
verdicts n ▷ verdict
verdigris [**ver**-dig-riss] n (pl -es) green film on copper, brass, or bronze
verdigrises n ▷ verdigris
verdure n (pl -s) (Lit) flourishing green vegetation
verdures n ▷ verdure
verge n (pl -s) grass border along a road
verger n (pl -s) (C OF E) church caretaker
vergers n ▷ verger
verges n ▷ verge
verifiable adj ▷ verify
verification n ▷ verify
verifications n ▷ verify
verified v ▷ verify
verifies v ▷ verify
verify v (-fies, -fying, -fied) check the truth or accuracy of > **verifiable** adj > **verification** n (pl -s)
verifying v ▷ verify
verily adv (Obs) in truth
verisimilitude n (pl -s) appearance of being real or true
verisimilitudes n ▷ verisimilitude
veritable adj rightly called, without exaggeration > **veritably** adv
veritably adv ▷ veritable
verities n ▷ verity
verity n (pl -ies) true statement or principle
vermicelli [ver-me-**chell**-ee] n (pl -s) fine strands of pasta
vermicellis n ▷ vermicelli
vermiform adj shaped like a worm
vermilion adj orange-red
vermin pl n (pl -s) animals, esp. insects and rodents, that spread disease or cause damage > **verminous** adj
verminous adj ▷ vermin
vermins n ▷ vermin
vermouth [ver-**muth**] n (pl -s) wine flavoured with herbs
vermouths n ▷ vermouth
vernacular [ver-**nak**-yew-lar] n (pl -s) most widely spoken language of a particular people or place
vernaculars n ▷ vernacular
vernal adj occurring in spring
vernier [**ver**-nee-er] n (pl -s) movable scale on a graduated measuring instrument for taking readings in fractions
verniers n ▷ vernier

veronica n (pl -s) plant with small blue, pink, or white flowers
   veronicas n ▷ veronica
verruca [ver-**roo**-ka] n (pl -s) wart, usu. on the foot
   verrucas n ▷ verruca
versatile adj having many skills or uses
   > **versatility** n (pl -ties)
   versatilities n ▷ versatile
   versatility n ▷ versatile
verse n (pl -s) group of lines forming part of a song or poem
   verses n ▷ verse
versification n (pl -s) writing in verse
   versifications n ▷ versification
version n (pl -s) form of something, such as a piece of writing, with some differences from other forms
   versions n ▷ version
verso n (pl -s) left-hand page of a book
   versos n ▷ verso
versus prep in opposition to or in contrast with
vertebra n (pl -rae) one of the bones that form the spine ▶ **vertebral** adj
   vertebrae n ▷ vertabra
   vertebral adj ▷ vertebra
vertebrate n, adj (pl -s) (animal) having a spine
   vertebrates n ▷ vertebrate
vertex n (pl -texes, -tices) (MATHS) point on a geometric figure where the sides form an angle
   vertexes n ▷ vertex
vertical adj straight up and down ▶ n (pl -s) vertical direction
   verticals n ▷ vertical
   vertices n ▷ vertex
   vertiginous adj ▷ vertigo
vertigo n (pl -s) dizziness, usu. when looking down from a high place > **vertiginous** adj
   vertigoes n ▷ vertigo
vervain n (pl -s) plant with spikes of blue, purple, or white flowers
   vervains n ▷ vervain
verve n (pl -s) enthusiasm or liveliness
   verves n ▷ verve
very adv more than usually, extremely ▶ adj absolute, exact
vesicle n (pl -s) (BIOL) sac or small cavity, esp. one containing fluid
   vesicles n ▷ vesicle
vespers pl n (RC CHURCH) (service of) evening prayer
vessel n (pl -s) ship
   vessels n ▷ vessel

vest n (pl -s) undergarment worn on the top half of the body ▶ v (-s, -ing, -ed) (foll. by **in** or **with**) give (authority) to (someone)
   vested v ▷ vest
vestibule n (pl -s) small entrance hall
   vestibules n ▷ vestibule
vestige [**vest**-ij] n (pl -s) small amount or trace
   > **vestigial** adj
   vestiges n ▷ vestige
   vestigial adj ▷ vestige
   vesting v ▷ vest
vestments pl n priest's robes
   vestries n ▷ vestry
vestry n (pl -ies) room in a church used as an office by the priest or minister
   vests n, v ▷ vest
vet[1] n (pl -s) ▷ veterinary surgeon ▶ v (-s, -tting, -tted) check the suitability of
vet[2] n (pl -s) (US, AUST & NZ) military veteran
vetch n (pl -es) climbing plant with a beanlike fruit used as fodder
   vetches n ▷ vetch
veteran n (pl -s) person with long experience in a particular activity, esp. military service ▶ adj long-serving
   veterans n ▷ veteran
veterinary adj concerning animal health
veto n (pl -es) official power to cancel a proposal ▶ v (-es, -ing, -ed) enforce a veto against
   vetoed v ▷ veto
   vetoes n, v ▷ veto
   vetoing v ▷ veto
   vets n, v ▷ vet[1,2]
   vetted v ▷ vet[1]
   vetting v ▷ vet[1]
vex v (-es, -ing, -ed) frustrate, annoy
vexation n (pl -s) something annoying
   > **vexatious** adj
   vexations n ▷ vexation
   vexatious adj ▷ vexation
   vexed v ▷ vex
   vexes v ▷ vex
   vexing v ▷ vex
via prep by way of
   viabilities n ▷ viable
   viability n ▷ viable
viable adj able to be put into practice
   > **viability** n (pl -ties)
viaduct n (pl -s) bridge over a valley
   viaducts n ▷ viaduct
vial n (pl -s) ▷ phial
   vials n ▷ vial
viands pl n (Obs) food
vibes pl n (Informal) emotional reactions

between people

vibrant [**vibe**-rant] *adj* vigorous in appearance, energetic

vibraphone *n* (*pl* -s) musical instrument with metal bars that resonate electronically when hit

  vibraphones *n* ▷ vibraphone

vibrate *v* (-tes, -ting, -ted) move back and forth rapidly > **vibration** *n* (*pl* -s)

  vibrated *v* ▷ vibrate
  vibrates *v* ▷ vibrate
  vibrating *v* ▷ vibrate
  vibration *n* ▷ vibrate
  vibrations *n* ▷ vibrate

vibrato *n* (*pl* -s) (MUSIC) rapid fluctuation in the pitch of a note

vibrator *n* (*pl* -s) device that produces vibratory motion, used for massage or as a sex aid > **vibratory** *adj*

  vibrators *n* ▷ vibrator
  vibratos *n* ▷ vibrato

vicar *n* (*pl* -s) (C of E) member of the clergy in charge of a parish

vicarage *n* (*pl* -s) vicar's house

  vicarages *n* ▷ vicarage

vicarious [vick-**air**-ee-uss] *adj* felt indirectly by imagining what another person experiences > **vicariously** *adv*

  vicariously *adv* ▷ vicarious
  vicars *n* ▷ vicar

vice¹ *n* (*pl* -s) immoral or evil habit or action

vice² *n* (*pl* -s) tool with a pair of jaws for holding an object while working on it

vice³ *adj* serving in place of

  viceregal *adj* ▷ viceroy

viceroy *n* (*pl* -s) governor of a colony who represents the monarch > **viceregal** *adj*

  viceroys *n* ▷ viceroy
  vices *n* ▷ vice¹,²
  vicinities *n* ▷ vicinity

vicinity [viss-**in**-it-ee] *n* (*pl* -ties) surrounding area

vicious *adj* cruel and violent > **viciously** *adv*

  viciously *adv* ▷ vicious

vicissitudes [viss-**iss**-it-yewds] *pl n* changes in fortune

victim *n* (*pl* -s) person or thing harmed or killed

  victimization *n* ▷ victimize
  victimizations *n* ▷ victimize

victimize *v* (-zes, -zing, -zed) punish unfairly > **victimization** *n* (*pl* -s)

  victimized *v* ▷ victimize
  victimizes *v* ▷ victimize
  victimizing *v* ▷ victimize
  victims *n* ▷ victim

victor *n* (*pl* -s) person who has defeated an opponent, esp. in war or in sport

  victories *n* ▷ victory
  victorious *adj* ▷ victory
  victors *n* ▷ victor

victory *n* (*pl* -ries) winning of a battle or contest > **victorious** *adj*

victuals [**vit**-tals] *pl n* (*Old-fashioned*) food and drink

vicuña [vik-**koo**-nya] *n* (*pl* -s) S American animal like the llama

  vicuñas *n* ▷ vicuña

video *n* (*pl* -s) ▷ video cassette (recorder) ▶ *v* (-s, -ing, -ed) record (a TV programme or event) on video ▶ *adj* relating to or used in producing television images

  videoed *v* ▷ video
  videoing *v* ▷ video
  videos *n, v* ▷ video

videotext *n* (*pl* -s) means of representing on a TV screen information that is held in a computer

  videotexts *n* ▷ videotext

vie *v* (vies, vying, vied) compete (with someone)

  vied *v* ▷ vie
  vies *v* ▷ vie

view *n* (*pl* -s) opinion or belief ▶ *v* (-s, -ing, -ed) think of (something) in a particular way

viewdata *n* (*pl* -as) ® videotext service linking users to a computer by telephone

  viewdatas *n* ▷ viewdata
  viewed *v* ▷ view

viewer *n* person who watches television

  viewers *n* ▷ viewer

viewfinder *n* (*pl* -s) window on a camera showing what will appear in a photograph

  viewfinders *n* ▷ viewfinder
  viewing *v* ▷ view
  views *n, v* ▷ view

vigil [**vij**-ill] *n* (*pl* -s) night-time period of staying awake to look after a sick person, pray, etc.

  vigilance *n* ▷ vigilant
  vigilances *n* ▷ vigilant

vigilant *adj* watchful in case of danger > **vigilance** *n* (*pl* -s)

vigilante [vij-ill-**ant**-ee] *n* (*pl* -s) person, esp. as one of a group, who takes it upon himself or herself to enforce the law

  vigilantes *n* ▷ vigilante
  vigils *n* ▷ vigil

vignette [vin-**yet**] *n* (*pl* -s) concise description of the typical features of something

  vignettes *n* ▷ vignette

vigorous adj ▷ vigour
vigorously adv ▷ vigour
vigour n (pl -s) physical or mental energy
> **vigorous** adj > **vigorously** adv
vigours n ▷ vigour
viking n (pl -s) (HIST) seafaring raider and settler from Scandinavia
vikings n ▷ viking
vile (-r, -st) adj very wicked > **vilely** adv
> **vileness** n (pl -s)
vilely adv ▷ vile
vileness n ▷ vile
vilenesses n ▷ vile
viler adj ▷ vile
vilest adj ▷ vile
vilification n ▷ vilify
vilifications n ▷ vilify
vilified v ▷ vilify
vilifies v ▷ vilify
vilify v (-fies, -fying, -fied) attack the character of > **vilification** n (pl -s)
vilifying v ▷ vilify
villa n (pl -s) large house with gardens
village n (pl -s) small group of houses in a country area > **villager** n (pl -s)
villager n ▷ village
villagers n ▷ village
villages n ▷ village
villain n (pl -s) wicked person > **villainous** adj
> **villainy** n (pl -nies)
villainies n ▷ villian
villainous adj ▷ villain
villains n ▷ villian
villas n ▷ villa
villein [vill-an] n (pl -s) (HIST) peasant bound in service to his lord
villeins n ▷ villein
villiany n ▷ villian

> **vim** n (**vims**). Vim means vigour or energy. This word can be helpful when you're stuck with unpromising letters, and gives a reasonable score for a three-letter word. Vim scores 8 points.

vinaigrette n (pl -s) salad dressing of oil and vinegar
vinaigrettes n ▷ vinaigrette
vindicate v (-tes, -ting, -ted) clear (someone) of guilt > **vindication** n (pl -s)
vindicated v ▷ vindicate
vindicates v ▷ vindicate
vindicating v ▷ vindicate
vindication n ▷ vindicate
vindications n ▷ vindicate
vindictive adj maliciously seeking revenge
> **vindictiveness** n (pl -es) > **vindictively** adv

vindictively adv ▷ vindictive
vindictiveness n ▷ vindictive
vindictivenesses n ▷ vindictive
vine n (pl -s) climbing plant, esp. one producing grapes
vinegar n (pl -s) acid liquid made from wine, beer, or cider > **vinegary** adj
vinegars n ▷ vinegar
vinegary adj ▷ vinegar
vines n ▷ vine
vineyard [vinn-yard] n (pl -s) plantation of grape vines, esp. for making wine
vineyards n ▷ vineyard
vino [vee-noh] n (pl -s) (Informal) wine
vinos n ▷ vino
vintage n (pl -s) wine from a particular harvest of grapes ▶ adj best and most typical
vintages n ▷ vintage
vintner n (pl -s) dealer in wine
vintners n ▷ vintner
vinyl [vine-ill] n (pl -s) type of plastic, used in mock leather and records
vinyls n ▷ vinyl
viol [vie-oll] n (pl -s) early stringed instrument preceding the violin
viola[1] [vee-oh-la] n (pl -s) stringed instrument lower in pitch than a violin
viola[2] [vie-ol-la] n (pl -s) variety of pansy
violas n ▷ viola[1, 2]
violate v (-tes, -ting, -ted) break (a law or agreement) > **violation** n > **violator** n
violated v ▷ violate
violates v ▷ violate
violating v ▷ violate
violation n ▷ violate
violations n ▷ violate
violator n ▷ violate
violators n ▷ violate
violence n (pl -s) use of physical force, usu. intended to cause injury or destruction
> **violent** adj > **violently** adv
violences n ▷ violence
violent adj ▷ violence
violently adv ▷ violent
violet n (pl -s) plant with bluish-purple flowers ▶ adj bluish-purple
violets n ▷ violet
violin n (pl -s) small four-stringed musical instrument played with a bow. > **violinist** n (pl -s)
violinist n ▷ violin
violinists n ▷ violin
violins n ▷ violin
viols n ▷ viol
viper n (pl -s) poisonous snake

vipers *n* ▷ viper

virago [vir-**rah**-go] *n* (*pl* -**goes**, -**gos**) aggressive woman

viragoes *n* ▷ virago

viragos *n* ▷ virago

viral *adj* of or caused by a virus

virgin *n* (*pl* -**s**) person, esp. a woman, who has not had sexual intercourse ▶ *adj* not having had sexual intercourse > **virginity** *n* (*pl* -**ties**)

virginal *adj* like a virgin ▶ *n* early keyboard instrument like a small harpsichord

virginities *n* ▷ virgin

virginity *n* ▷ virgin

virgins *n* ▷ virgin

virile *adj* having the traditional male characteristics of physical strength and a high sex drive > **virility** *n* (*pl* -**ties**)

virilities *n* ▷ virile

virility *n* ▷ virile

virologies *n* ▷ virology

virologies *n* ▷ virology

virology *n* (*pl* -**gies**) study of viruses

virtual *adj* having the effect but not the form of > **virtually** *adv* practically, almost

virtually *adv* ▷ virtual

virtue *n* (*pl* -**s**) moral goodness

virtues *n* ▷ virtue

virtuosi *n* ▷ virtuoso

virtuosities *n* ▷ virtuoso

virtuosity *n* ▷ virtuoso

virtuoso *n* (*pl* -**sos**, -**si**) person with impressive esp. musical skill > **virtuosity** *n* (*pl* -**ies**)

virtuosos *n* ▷ virtuoso

virtuous *adj* morally good > **virtuously** *adv*

virtuously *adv* ▷ virtuous

virulent [**vir**-yew-lent] *adj* very infectious

virus *n* (*pl* -**es**) microorganism that causes disease in humans, animals, and plants

viruses *n* ▷ virus

visa *n* (*pl* -**s**) permission to enter a country, granted by its government and shown by a stamp on one's passport

visage [**viz**-zij] *n* (*pl* -**s**) (*Lit*) face

visages *n* ▷ visage

visas *n* ▷ visa

viscera [**viss**-er-a] *pl n* large abdominal organs

visceral [**viss**-er-al] *adj* instinctive

viscid [**viss**-id] *adj* sticky

viscose *n* (*pl* -**s**) synthetic fabric made from cellulose

viscoses *n* ▷ viscose

viscosities *n* ▷ viscous

viscosity *n* ▷ viscous

viscount [**vie**-count] *n* (*pl* -**s**) British nobleman ranking between an earl and a baron

viscountess [**vie**-count-iss] *n* (*pl* -**es**) woman holding the rank of viscount in her own right

viscountesses *n* ▷ viscountess

viscounts *n* ▷ viscount

viscous *adj* thick and sticky > **viscosity** *n* (*pl* -**ties**)

visibilities *n* ▷ visibility

visibility *n* (*pl* -**ties**) range or clarity of vision

visible *adj* able to be seen > **visibly** *adv*

visibly *adv* ▷ visible

vision *n* (*pl* -**s**) ability to see

visionaries *n* ▷ visionary

visionary *adj* showing foresight ▶ *n* (*pl* -**ries**) visionary person

visions *n* ▷ vision

visit *v* (-**s**, -**ing**, -**ed**) go or come to see ▶ *n* instance of visiting > **visitor** *n* (*pl* -**s**)

visitation *n* (*pl* -**s**) formal visit or inspection

visitations *n* ▷ visitation

visited *v* ▷ visit

visiting *v* ▷ visit

visitor *n* ▷ visit

visitors *n* ▷ visit

visits *v* ▷ visit

visor [**vize**-or] *n* (*pl* -**s**) transparent part of a helmet that pulls down over the face

visors *n* ▷ visor

vista *n* (*pl* -**s**) (beautiful) extensive view

vistas *n* ▷ vista

visual *adj* done by or used in seeing

visualization *n* ▷ visualize

visualizations *n* ▷ visualize

visualize *v* (-**zes**, -**zing**, -**zed**) form a mental image of > **visualization** *n* (*pl* -**s**)

visualized *v* ▷ visualize

visualizes *v* ▷ visualize

visualizing *v* ▷ visualize

vital *adj* essential or highly important > **vitally** *adv*

vitalities *n* ▷ vitality

vitality *n* (*pl* -**ties**) physical or mental energy

vitally *adv* ▷ vital

vitals *pl n* bodily organs necessary to maintain life

vitamin *n* (*pl* -**s**) one of a group of substances that are essential in the diet for specific body processes

vitamins *n* ▷ vitamin

vitiate [**vish**-ee-ate] *v* (-**tes**, -**ting**, -**ted**) spoil the effectiveness of

vitiated *v* ▷ vitiate

vitiates *v* ▷ vitiate

vitiating *v* ▷ vitiate

viticulture *n* (*pl* -**s**) cultivation of grapevines

viticultures *n* ▷ viticulture

vitreous *adj* like or made from glass
vitriol *n* (*pl* -s) language expressing bitterness and hatred > **vitriolic** *adj*
vitriolic *adj* ▷ vitriol
vitriols *n* ▷ vitriol
vituperation *n* ▷ vituperative
vituperations *n* ▷ vituperative
vituperative [vite-tyew-pra-tiv] *adj* bitterly abusive > **vituperation** *n* (*pl* -s)
viva[1] *interj* long live (a person or thing)
viva[2] *n* (*pl* -s) (BRIT) examination in the form of an interview
vivace [viv-vah-chee] *adv* (MUSIC) in a lively manner
vivacious *adj* full of energy and enthusiasm > **vivacity** *n* (*pl* -ties)
vivacities *n* ▷ vivacious
vivacity *n* ▷ vivacious
vivas *n* ▷ viva[2]
vivid *adj* (-er, -est) very bright > **vividly** *adv* > **vividness** *n* (*pl* -es)
vivider *adj* ▷ vivid
vividest *adj* ▷ vivid
vividly *adv* ▷ vivid
vividness *n* ▷ vivid
vividnesses *n* ▷ vivid
vivisection *n* (*pl* -s) performing surgical experiments on living animals > **vivisectionist** *n* (*pl* -s)
vivisectionist *n* ▷ vivisection
vivisectionists *n* ▷ vivisection
vivisections *n* ▷ vivisection
vixen *n* (*pl* -s) female fox
vixens *n* ▷ vixen
vizier [viz-zeer] *n* (*pl* -s) high official in certain Muslim countries
viziers *n* ▷ vizier
vizor *n* (*pl* -s) ▷ visor
vizors *n* ▷ vizor

> **vly** *n* (**vlys**). Vly is a South African word meaning an area of low marshy ground. This is a good word to remember because it doesn't contain any vowels, making it useful when you are short of vowel tiles. Vly scores 9 points.

vocabularies *n* ▷ vocabulary
vocabulary *n* (*pl* -ries) all the words that a person knows
vocal *adj* relating to the voice
vocalist *n* (*pl* -s) singer
vocalists *n* ▷ vocalist
vocalization *n* ▷ vocalize
vocalizations *n* ▷ vocalize
vocalize *v* (-zes, -zing, -zed) express with or

use the voice > **vocalization** *n* (*pl* -s)
vocalizes *v* ▷ vocalize
vocalizes *v* ▷ vocalize
vocalizing *v* ▷ vocalize
vocally *adv* ▷ vocal
vocals *pl n* singing part of a piece of pop music > **vocally** *adv*
vocation *n* (*pl* -s) profession or trade
vocational *adj* directed towards a particular profession or trade
vocations *n* ▷ vocation
vociferous *adj* shouting, noisy
vodka *n* (*pl* -s) (Russian) spirit distilled from potatoes or grain
vodkas *n* ▷ vodka
vogue *n* (*pl* -s) popular style
vogues *n* ▷ vogue
voice *n* (*pl* -s) (quality of) sound made when speaking or singing ▶ *v* (-ces, -cing, -ced) express verbally > **voiceless** *adj*
voiced *v* ▷ voice
voiceless *adj* ▷ voice
voices *n*, *v* ▷ voice
voicing *v* ▷ voice
void *adj* not legally binding ▶ *n* (*pl* -s) empty space ▶ *v* (-s, -ing, -ed) make invalid
voided *v* ▷ void
voiding *v* ▷ void
voids *n*, *v* ▷ void
voile [voyl] *n* (*pl* -s) light semitransparent fabric
voiles *n* ▷ voile
volatile *adj* liable to sudden change, esp. in behaviour > **volatility** *n* (*pl* -ties)
volatilities *n* ▷ volatile
volatility *n* ▷ volatile
volcanic *adj* ▷ volcano
volcano *n* (*pl* -noes, -nos) mountain with a vent through which lava is ejected > **volcanic** *adj*
volcanoes *n* ▷ volcano
volcanos *n* ▷ volcano
vole *n* (*pl* -s) small rodent
voles *n* ▷ vole
volition *n* (*pl* -s) ability to decide things for oneself
volitions *n* ▷ volition
volley *n* (*pl* -s) simultaneous discharge of ammunition ▶ *v* (-s, -ing, -ed) discharge (ammunition) in a volley
volleyball *n* (*pl* -s) team game where a ball is hit with the hands over a high net
volleyballs *n* ▷ volleyball
volleyed *v* ▷ volley
volleying *v* ▷ volley

volleys n, v ▷ volley
volt n (pl -s) unit of electric potential
voltage n (pl -s) electric potential difference expressed in volts
voltages n ▷ voltage
voltmeter n instrument for measuring voltage
voltmeters n ▷ voltmeter
volts n ▷ volt
volubilities n ▷ voluble
volubility n ▷ voluble
voluble adj talking easily and at length > **volubility** n (pl -ties) > **volubly** adv
volubly adv ▷ voluble
volume n (pl -s) size of the space occupied by something
volumes n ▷ volume
volumetric adj relating to measurement by volume
voluminous adj (of clothes) large and roomy
voluntaries n ▷ voluntary
voluntarily adv ▷ voluntary
voluntary adj done by choice ▶ n (pl -ries) organ solo in a church service > **voluntarily** adv
volunteer n (pl -s) person who offers voluntarily to do something ▶ v (-s, -ing, -ed) offer one's services
volunteered v ▷ volunteer
volunteering v ▷ volunteer
volunteers n, v ▷ volunteer
voluptuaries n ▷ voluptuary
voluptuary n (pl -ries) person devoted to sensual pleasures
voluptuous adj (of a woman) sexually alluring through fullness of figure
volute n (pl -s) spiral or twisting turn, form, or object
volutes n ▷ volute
vomit v (-s, -ing, -ed) eject (the contents of the stomach) through the mouth ▶ n (pl -s) matter vomited
vomited v ▷ vomit
vomiting v ▷ vomit
vomits v, n ▷ vomit
voodoo n (pl -s) religion involving ancestor worship and witchcraft, practised by Black people in the West Indies, esp. in Haiti.
voodoos n ▷ voodoo
voracious adj craving great quantities of food > **voraciously** adv > **voracity** n (pl -ties)
voraciously adv ▷ voracious
voracities n ▷ voracious
voracity n ▷ voracious
vortex n (pl -texes, -tices) whirlpool

vortexes n ▷ vortex
vortices n ▷ vortex
vote n (pl -s) choice made by a participant in a shared decision, esp. in electing a candidate ▶ v (-tes, -ting, -ted) make a choice by a vote
> **voter** n (pl -s)
voted v ▷ vote
voter n ▷ vote
voters n ▷ vote
votes n, v ▷ vote
voting v ▷ vote
votive adj done or given to fulfil a vow
vouch v (-es, -ing, -ed) give one's personal assurance about
vouched v ▷ vouch
voucher n (pl -s) ticket used instead of money to buy specified goods
vouchers n ▷ voucher
vouches v ▷ vouch
vouching v ▷ vouch
vouchsafe v (-fes, -fing, -fed) (Old-fashioned) give, entrust
vouchsafed v ▷ vouchsafe
vouchsafes v ▷ vouchsafe
vouchsafing v ▷ vouchsafe
vow n (pl -s) solemn and binding promise ▶ pl formal promises made when marrying or entering a religious order ▶ v (-s, -ing, -ed) promise solemnly
vowed v ▷ vow
vowel n (pl -s) speech sound made without obstructing the flow of breath
vowels n ▷ vowel
vowing v ▷ vow
vows n, v ▷ vow

> **vox** n (**voces**). Vox means a voice or sound. Along with **vex**, this is the highest-scoring three-letter word beginning with V. Vox scores 13 points.

voyage n (pl -s) long journey by sea or in space ▶ v (-ges, -ging, -ged) make a voyage
> **voyager** n (pl -s)
voyaged v ▷ voyage
voyager n ▷ voyager
voyagers n ▷ voyager
voyages n, v ▷ voyage
voyaging v ▷ voyage
voyeur n (pl -s) person who obtains pleasure from watching people undressing or having sex > **voyeurism** n (pl -s)
voyeurism n ▷ voyeur
voyeurisms n ▷ voyeur
voyeurs n ▷ voyeur

> **vug** n (**vugs**). A vug is a small cavity in a rock. This is a very unusual word

that can be useful when you have an uninspiring combination of letters. Vug scores 7 points.

vulcanize v (-zes, -zing, -zed) strengthen (rubber) by treating it with sulphur
vulcanized v ▷ vulcanize
vulcanizes v ▷ vulcanize
vulcanizing v ▷ vulcanize
vulgar adj (-er, -est) showing lack of good taste, decency, or refinement > **vulgarly** adv > **vulgarity** n (pl -ies)
vulgarer adj ▷ vulgar
vulgarest adj ▷ vulgar
vulgarian n (pl -s) vulgar (rich) person
vulgarians n ▷ vulgarian

vulgarities n ▷ vulgar
vulgarities n ▷ vulgar
vulgarly adv ▷ vulgar
vulnerabilities n ▷ vulnerable
vulnerability n ▷ vulnerable
vulnerable adj liable to be physically or emotionally hurt > **vulnerability** n (pl -s)
vulpine adj of or like a fox
vulture n (pl -s) large bird that feeds on the flesh of dead animals
vultures n ▷ vulture
vulva n (pl -vae) woman's external genitals
vulvae n ▷ vulva
vying v ▷ vie

Ww

W is a useful tile to have on your rack as it earns 4 points on its own and produces a number of high-scoring short words. There are, however, only two two-letter words begin with W: **we** and **wo** (5 points each). If you know this, though, you won't waste time looking for others. There are lots of everyday three-letter words that earn good scores: **wax** (13) with its two old-fashioned variants **wex** and **wox** (also 13 each) and **way**, **who**, **why**, **wow** and **wry** (9 each). Don't forget **wok** (10) either, which can be as useful on the Scrabble board as in the kitchen!

wackier *adj* ▷ wacky
wackiest *adj* ▷ wacky
wackiness *n* ▷ wacky
wackinesses *n* ▷ wacky
wacky *adj* (-ckier, -ckiest) (*Informal*) eccentric or funny > **wackiness** *n* (*pl* -es)
wad *n* (*pl* -s) small mass of soft material
waddies *n* ▷ waddy
wadding *n* (*pl* -s) soft material used for padding or stuffing
waddings *n* ▷ wadding
waddle *v* (-les, -ling, -led) walk with short swaying steps ▶ *n* (*pl* -s) swaying walk
waddled *v*, *n* ▷ waddle
waddles *v* ▷ waddle
waddling *v* ▷ waddle
waddy *n* (*pl* -ies) heavy wooden club used by Australian Aborigines
wade *v* (-des, -ding, -ded) walk with difficulty through water or mud
waded *v* ▷ wade
wader *n* (*pl* -s) long-legged water bird ▶ *pl* angler's long waterproof boots
waders *n* ▷ wader
wades *v* ▷ wade
wadi [wod-dee] *n* (*pl* -s) (in N Africa and Arabia) river which is dry except in the wet season
wading *v* ▷ wade
wadis *n* ▷ wadi
wads *n* ▷ wad
wafer *n* (*pl* -s) thin crisp biscuit
wafers *n* ▷ wafer
waffle¹ (*Informal*) *v* (-les, -ling, -led) speak or write in a vague wordy way ▶ *n* (*pl* -s) vague wordy talk or writing
waffle² *n* (*pl* -s) square crisp pancake with a gridlike pattern

waffled *v* ▷ waffle¹
waffles *v*, *n* ▷ waffle¹,²
waffling *v* ▷ waffle¹
waft *v* (-s, -ing, -ed) drift or carry gently through the air ▶ *n* (*pl* -s) something wafted
wafted *v* ▷ waft
wafting *v* ▷ waft
wafts *v*, *n* ▷ waft
wag *v* (-s, -gging, -gged) move rapidly from side to side ▶ *n* (*pl* -s) wagging movement
wage *n* (*pl* -s) (*often pl*) payment for work done, esp. when paid weekly ▶ *v* (-ges, -ging, -ged) engage in (an activity)
waged *v* ▷ wage
wager *n*, *v* (-s, -ing, -ed) bet on the outcome of something
wagered *v* ▷ wager
wagering *v* ▷ wager
wagers *n*, *v* ▷ wager
wages *n*, *v* ▷ wage
wagged *v* ▷ wag
wagging *v* ▷ wag
waggle *v* (-les, -ling, -led) move with a rapid shaking or wobbling motion
waggled *v* ▷ waggle
waggles *v* ▷ waggle
waggling *v* ▷ waggle
waggon *n* ▷ wagon
waggons *n* ▷ wagon
waging *v* ▷ wag
wagon, waggon *n* (*pl* -s) four-wheeled vehicle for heavy loads
wagons *n* ▷ wagon
wags *v* ▷ wag
wagtail *n* (*pl* -s) small long-tailed bird
wagtail *n* ▷ wagtails
wahoo *n* (*pl* -s) food and game fish of tropical

seas

wahoos n ▷ wahoo

waif n (pl -s) young person who is, or seems, homeless or neglected

waifs n ▷ waif

wail v (-s, -ing, -ed) cry out in pain or misery ▶ n (pl -s) mournful cry

wailed v ▷ wail

wailing v ▷ wail

wails v, n ▷ wail

wain n (pl -s) (Poetic) farm wagon

wains n ▷ wain

wainscot, wainscoting n (pl -s) wooden lining of the lower part of the walls of a room

wainscoting n ▷ wainscot

wainscotings n ▷ wainscot

wainscots n ▷ wainscot

waist n (pl -s) part of the body between the ribs and hips

waistband n (pl -s) band of material sewn on to the waist of a garment to strengthen it

waistbands n ▷ waistband

waistcoat n (pl -s) sleeveless garment which buttons up the front, usu. worn over a shirt and under a jacket

waistcoats n ▷ waistcoat

waistline n (pl -s) (size of) the waist of a person or garment

waistlines n ▷ waistline

waists n ▷ waist

wait v (-s, -ing, -ed) remain inactive in expectation (of something) ▶ n (pl -s) act or period of waiting

waited v ▷ wait

waiter n (pl -s) man who serves in a restaurant etc. > **waitress** n fem (pl -es)

waiters n ▷ waiter

waiting v ▷ wait

waitress n ▷ waiter

waitresses n ▷ waiter

waits v, n ▷ wait

waive v (-ves, -ving, -ved) refrain from enforcing (a law, right, etc.)

waived v ▷ waive

waiver n (pl -s) act or instance of voluntarily giving up a claim, right, etc.

waivers n ▷ waiver

waives v ▷ waive

waiving v ▷ waive

waka n (pl -s) (NZ) Maori canoe

wakas n ▷ waka

wake[1] v (-kes, -king, woke, woken) rouse from sleep or inactivity ▶ n (pl -s) vigil beside a corpse the night before the funeral > **wakeful** adj

wake[2] n (pl -s) track left by a moving ship

wakeful adj ▷ wake[1]

waken v (-s, -ing, -ed) wake

wakened v ▷ waken

wakening v ▷ waken

wakens v ▷ waken

wakes n ▷ wake[1, 2]

waking v ▷ wake[1]

walk v (-s, -ing, -ed) move on foot with at least one foot always on the ground ▶ n (pl -s) act or instance of walking > **walker** n (pl -s)

walkabout n (pl -s) informal walk among the public by royalty etc.

walkabouts n ▷ walkabout

walked v ▷ walk

walker n ▷ walk

walkers n ▷ walk

walking v ▷ walk

walkout n (pl -s) strike

walkouts n ▷ walkout

walkover n (pl -s) easy victory

walkovers n ▷ walkover

walks v, n ▷ walk

wall n (pl -s) structure of brick, stone, etc. used to enclose, divide, or support ▶ v (-s, -ing, -ed) enclose or seal with a wall or walls

wallabies n ▷ wallaby

wallaby n (pl -bies) marsupial like a small kangaroo

wallaroo n (pl -s) large stocky Australian kangaroo of rocky regions

wallaroos n ▷ wallaroo

walled v ▷ wall

wallet n (pl -s) small folding case for paper money, documents, etc.

wallets n ▷ wallet

walleye n (pl -s) fish with large staring eyes (also dory)

walleyes n ▷ walleye

wallflower n (pl -s) fragrant garden plant

wallflowers n ▷ wallflower

wallies n ▷ wally

walling v ▷ wall

wallop (Informal) v (-s, -ing, -ed) hit hard ▶ n (pl -s) hard blow

walloped v ▷ wallop

walloping (Informal) n thrashing ▶ adj large or great ▶ v ▷ wallop

wallops v, n ▷ wallop

wallow v (-s, -ing, -ed) revel in an emotion ▶ n (pl -s) act or instance of wallowing

wallowed v ▷ wallow

wallowing v ▷ wallow

wallows v, n ▷ wallow

wallpaper n (pl -s) decorative paper to cover

interior walls

wallpapers n ▷ wallpaper

walls n, v ▷ wall

wally n (pl -ies) (BRIT) (Slang) stupid person

walnut n (pl -s) edible nut with a wrinkled shell

walnuts n ▷ walnut

walrus n (pl -ruses, -rus) large sea mammal with long tusks

walruses n ▷ walrus

waltz n (pl -es) ballroom dance ▶ v (-zes, -zing, -zed) dance a waltz

waltzed v ▷ waltz

waltzes n, v ▷ waltz

waltzing v ▷ waltz

wampum [wom-pum] n (pl -s) shells woven together, formerly used by Native Americans for money and ornament

wampums n ▷ wampum

wan [rhymes with swan] adj (-nner, -nnest) pale and sickly looking

wand n (pl -s) thin rod, esp. one used in performing magic tricks

wander v (-s, -ing, -ed) move about without a definite destination or aim ▶ n (pl -s) act or instance of wandering > **wanderer** n (pl -s)

wandered v ▷ wander

wanderer n ▷ wander

wanderers n ▷ wander

wandering v ▷ wander

wanderlust n (pl -s) great desire to travel

wanderlusts n ▷ wanderlust

wanders v, n ▷ wander

wands n ▷ wand

wane v (-nes, -ning, -ned) decrease gradually in size or strength

waned v ▷ wane

wanes v ▷ wane

wangle v (-les, -ling, -led) (Informal) get by devious methods

wangled v ▷ wangle

wangles v ▷ wangle

wangling v ▷ wangle

waning v ▷ wane

wanner adj ▷ wan

wannest adj ▷ wan

want v (-s, -ing, -ed) need or long for ▶ n (pl -s) act or instance of wanting

wanted adj sought by the police ▶ v ▷ want

wanting adj lacking ▶ v ▷ want

wanton adj (-er, -est) without motive, provocation, or justification

wantoner adj ▷ wanton

wantonest adj ▷ wanton

wants v, n ▷ want

war n (pl -s) fighting between nations ▶ adj of, like, or caused by war ▶ v (-s, -rring, -rred) conduct a war > **warring** adj

waratah n (pl -s) Australian shrub with crimson flowers

waratahs n ▷ waratah

warble v (-les, -ling, -led) sing in a trilling voice

warbled v ▷ warble

warbler n (pl -s) any of various small songbirds

warblers n ▷ warbler

warbles v ▷ warble

warbling v ▷ warble

ward n (pl -s) room in a hospital for patients needing a similar kind of care

warden n (pl -s) person in charge of a building and its occupants

wardens n ▷ warden

warder n (pl -s) prison officer > **wardress** n fem (pl -es)

warders n ▷ warder

wardress n ▷ warder

wardresses n ▷ warder

wardrobe n (pl -s) cupboard for hanging clothes in

wardrobes n ▷ wardrobe

wardroom n (pl -s) officers' quarters on a warship

wardrooms n ▷ wardroom

wards n ▷ ward

ware n (pl -s) articles of a specified type or material ▶ pl goods for sale

warehouse n (pl -s) building for storing goods prior to sale or distribution

warehouses n ▷ warehouse

wares n ▷ ware

warfare n (pl -s) fighting or hostilities

warfares n ▷ warfare

warhead n (pl -s) explosive front part of a missile

warheads n ▷ warhead

warier adj ▷ wary

wariest n ▷ wary

warily adv ▷ wary

wariness n ▷ wary

warinesses n ▷ wary

warlike adj of or relating to war

warlock n (pl -s) man who practises black magic

warlocks n ▷ warlock

warm adj (-er, -est) moderately hot ▶ v (-s, -ing, -ed) make or become warm > **warmly** adv

warmed v ▷ warm

warmer adj ▷ warm

warmest adj ▷ warm

warming v ▷ warm

warmly adv ▷ warm

warmonger n (pl -s) person who encourages war
  warmongers n ▷ warmonger
  warms v ▷ warm
warmth n (pl -s) mild heat
  warmths n ▷ warmth
warn v (-s, -ing, -ed) make aware of possible danger or harm
  warned v ▷ warn
warning n (pl -s) something that warns ▶ v ▷ warn
  warnings n ▷ warning
  warns v ▷ warn
warp v (-s, -ing, -ed) twist out of shape ▶ n (pl -s) state of being warped
  warped v ▷ warp
  warping v ▷ warp
  warps v, n ▷ warp
warrant n (pl -s) (document giving) official authorization ▶ v (-s, -ing, -ed) make necessary
  warranted v ▷ warrant
  warranties n ▷ warranty
  warranting v ▷ warrant
  warrants n, v ▷ warrant
warranty n (pl -ties) (document giving) a guarantee
  warred v ▷ war
warren n (pl -s) series of burrows in which rabbits live
  warrens n ▷ warren
warrigal (AUST) n (pl -s) dingo ▶ adj wild
  warrigals n ▷ warrigal
  warring v ▷ war
warrior n (pl -s) person who fights in a war
  warriors n ▷ warrior
  wars n, v ▷ war
warship n (pl -s) ship designed and equipped for naval combat
  warships n ▷ warship
wart n (pl -s) small hard growth on the skin
  warts n ▷ wart
wary [ware-ree] adj (-rier, -riest) watchful or cautious > **warily** adv > **wariness** n (pl -es)
  was v ▷ be
wash v (-es, -ing, -ed) clean (oneself, clothes, etc.) with water and usu. soap (Informal) ▶ n (pl -es) act or process of washing > **washable** adj
  washable adj ▷ wash
  washed v ▷ wash
washer n (pl -s) ring put under a nut or bolt or in a tap as a seal
  washers n ▷ washer
  washes v, n ▷ wash
washing n (pl -s) clothes to be washed ▶ v

▷ wash
  washings n ▷ washing
washout n (pl -s) (Informal) complete failure
  washouts n ▷ washouts
wasp n (pl -s) stinging insect with a slender black-and-yellow striped body
waspish adj bad-tempered
  wasps n ▷ wasp
wastage n (pl -s) loss by wear or waste
  wastages n ▷ wastage
waste v (-tes, -ting, -ted) use pointlessly or thoughtlessly ▶ n (pl -s) act of wasting or state of being wasted ▶ pl desert ▶ adj rejected as worthless or surplus to requirements
  wasted v ▷ waste
wasteful adj extravagant > **wastefully** adv
  wastefully adv ▷ waste
waster, wastrel n (pl -s) layabout
  wasters n ▷ waster
  wastes v, n ▷ waste
  wasting v ▷ waste
  wastrel n ▷ waster
  wastrels n ▷ waster
watch v (-es, -ing, -ed) look at closely ▶ n (pl -es) portable timepiece for the wrist or pocket > **watchable** adj > **watcher** n (pl -s)
  watchable adj ▷ watch
watchdog n (pl -s) dog kept to guard property
  watchdogs n ▷ watchdog
  watched v ▷ watch
  watcher n ▷ watch
  watchers n ▷ watch
  watches v, n ▷ watch
watchful adj vigilant or alert > **watchfully** adv
  watchfully adv ▷ watchful
  watching v ▷ watch
watchman n (pl -men) man employed to guard a building or property
  watchmen n ▷ watchman
watchword n (pl -s) word or phrase that sums up the attitude of a particular group
  watchwords n ▷ watchword
water n (pl -s) clear colourless tasteless liquid that falls as rain and forms rivers etc. ▶ v (-s, -ing, -ed) put water on or into > **watery** adj (-rier, -riest)
watercolour n (pl -s) paint thinned with water
  watercolours n ▷ watercolour
watercourse n (pl -s) bed of a stream or river
  watercourses n ▷ watercourse
watercress n (pl -es) edible plant growing in clear ponds and streams
  watercresses n ▷ watercress
  watered v ▷ water
waterfall n (pl -s) place where the waters of a

river drop vertically
waterfalls n ▷ waterfall
waterfront n (pl -s) part of a town alongside a body of water
waterfronts n ▷ waterfront
waterier adj ▷ watery
wateriest adj ▷ watery
watering v ▷ water
watermark n (pl -s) faint translucent design in a sheet of paper
watermarks n ▷ watermark
watermelon n (pl -s) melon with green skin and red flesh
watermelons n ▷ watermelon
waterproof adj not letting water through ▶ n (pl -s) waterproof garment ▶ v (-s, -ing, -ed) make waterproof
waterproofed v ▷ waterproof
waterproofing v ▷ waterproof
waterproofs n, v ▷ waterproof
waters n, v ▷ water
watershed n (pl -s) important period or factor serving as a dividing line
watersheds n ▷ watershed
watersider n (pl -s) (NZ) person employed to load and unload ships
watersiders n ▷ watersider
waterskiing n (pl -s) sport of riding over water on skis towed by a speedboat
waterskiings n ▷ waterskiing
watertight adj not letting water through
watery adj ▷ water
watt [wott] n (pl -s) unit of power
wattage n (pl -s) electrical power expressed in watts
wattages n ▷ wattage
wattle [wott-tl] n (pl -s) branches woven over sticks to make a fence making fences
wattles n ▷ wattle
watts n ▷ watt
wave v (-ves, -ving, -ved) move the hand to and fro as a greeting or signal ▶ n (pl -s) moving ridge on water ▷ **wavy** adj (-vier, -viest)
waved v ▷ wave
wavelength n (pl -s) distance between the same points of two successive waves
wavelengths n ▷ wavelength
waver v (-s, -ing, -ed) hesitate or be irresolute ▷ **waverer** n (pl -s)
wavered v ▷ waver
waverer n ▷ waver
waverers n ▷ waver
wavering v ▷ waver
wavers v ▷ waver
waves v, n ▷ wave

wavier adj ▷ wave
waviest adj ▷ wave
waving v ▷ wave
wavy adj ▷ wave
wax[1] n (pl -es) solid shiny fatty or oily substance used for sealing, making candles, etc. ▶ v (-es, -ing, -ed) coat or polish with wax ▷ **waxy** adj (-xier, -xiest)
wax[2] v (-es, -ing, -ed) increase in size or strength
waxed v ▷ wax[1, 2]
waxen adj made of or like wax
waxes n, v ▷ wax[1, 2]
waxier adj ▷ wax
waxiest adj ▷ wax
waxing v ▷ wax[1, 2]
waxwork n (pl -s) lifelike wax model of a (famous) person ▶ pl place exhibiting these
waxworks n ▷ waxwork
waxy adj ▷ wax[1]
way n (pl -s) manner or method
wayfarer n (Lit) traveller
wayfarers n ▷ wayfarer
waylaid v ▷ waylay
waylay v (-lays, -laying, -laid) lie in wait for and accost or attack
waylaying v ▷ waylay
waylays v ▷ waylay
ways n ▷ way
wayside adj, n (pl -s) (situated by) the side of a road
waysides n ▷ wayside
wayward adj erratic, selfish, or stubborn ▷ **waywardness** n (pl -es)
waywardness n ▷ waywardness
waywardnesses n ▷ waywardness
we pron (used as the subject of a verb) the speaker or writer and one or more others
weak adj (-er, -est) lacking strength
weaken v (-s, -ing, -ed) make or become weak
weakened v ▷ weaken
weakening v ▷ weaken
weakens v ▷ weaken
weaker adj ▷ weak
weakest adj ▷ weak
weakling n feeble person or animal
weaklings n ▷ weakling
weakly adv feebly
weakness n (-es) being weak
weaknesses n ▷ weakness
weal n (pl -s) raised mark left on the skin by a blow
weals n ▷ weal
wealth n (pl -s) state of being rich ▷ **wealthy** adj (-thier, -thiest)

wealthier adj ▷ wealth
wealthiest adj ▷ wealth
wealthy adj ▷ wealth
wean v (-s, -ing, -ed) accustom (a baby or young mammal) to food other than mother's milk
weaned v ▷ wean
weaning v ▷ wean
weans v ▷ wean
weapon n (pl -s) object used in fighting
weaponries n ▷ weapon
weaponry n (pl -ries) weapons collectively
weapons n ▷ weapon
wear v (-s, -ing, wore, worn) have on the body as clothing or ornament ▶ n (pl -s) clothes suitable for a particular time or purpose
> **wearer** n (pl -s)
wearer n ▷ wear
wearers n ▷ wear
wearied v ▷ weary
wearier adj ▷ weary
wearies v ▷ weary
weariest adj ▷ weary
wearily adv ▷ weary
weariness n ▷ weary
wearinesses n ▷ weary
wearing v ▷ wear
wearisome adj tedious
wears n, v ▷ wear
weary adj (-rier, -riest) tired or exhausted ▶ v (-ries, -rying, -ried) make or become weary
> **wearily** adv ▷ **weariness** n (pl -es)
wearying v ▷ weary
weasel n (pl -s) small carnivorous mammal with a long body and short legs
weasels n ▷ weasel
weather n (pl -s) day-to-day atmospheric conditions of a place ▶ v (-s, -ing, -ed) (cause to) be affected by the weather
weathercock, weathervane n device that revolves to show the direction of the wind
weathercocks n ▷ weathercock
weathered v ▷ weather
weathering v ▷ weather
weathers v, n ▷ weather
weathervanes n ▷ weathervane
weave v (-s, -ving, wove or weaved, woven or weaved) make (fabric) by interlacing (yarn) on a loom > **weaver** n (pl -s)
weaved v ▷ weave
weaver n ▷ weave
weavers n ▷ weave
weaves v ▷ weave
web n (pl -s) net spun by a spider > **webbed** adj
webbed adj ▷ web

webbing n (pl -s) strong fabric woven in strips
webbings n ▷ web
webcam n (pl -s) camera that transmits images over the Internet
webcams n ▷ webcam
webcast n (pl -s) broadcast of an event over the Internet
webcasts n ▷ webcast
weblog n (pl -s) person's online journal (also **blog**)
weblogs n ▷ weblog
webs n ▷ web
website n (pl -s) group of connected pages on the World Wide Web
websites n ▷ website
wed v (-s, -dding, -dded or wed) marry
wedded v ▷ wed
wedding n (pl -s) act or ceremony of marriage ▶ v ▷ wed
weddings n ▷ wedding
wedge n (pl wedges) piece of material thick at one end and thin at the other ▶ v (-ges, -ging, -ged) fasten or split with a wedge
wedged v ▷ wedge
wedges v, n ▷ wedge
wedging v ▷ wedge
wedlock n (pl -s) marriage
wedlocks n ▷ wedlock
wee adj (-r, -st) (BRIT, AUST & NZ) (Informal) small or short
weed n (pl -s) plant growing where undesired (Informal) ▶ v (-s, -ing, -ed) clear of weeds
weeded v ▷ weed
weedier adj ▷ weedy
weediest adj ▷ weddy
weeding v ▷ weed
weeds n, v ▷ weed ▶ pl n (Obs) widow's mourning clothes
weedy adj (-dier, -diest) (Informal) (of a person) thin and weak
week n (pl -s) period of seven days, esp. one beginning on a Sunday
weekday n (pl -s) any day of the week except Saturday or Sunday
weekdays n ▷ weekday
weekend n (pl -s) Saturday and Sunday
weekends n ▷ weekend
weeklies n ▷ weekly
weekly adj, adv happening, done, etc. once a week ▶ n (pl -lies) newspaper or magazine published once a week
weeks n ▷ week
weep v (-s, -ing, wept) shed tears
weepier adj ▷ weepy
weepiest adj ▷ weepy

weeping v ▷ weep

weeps v ▷ weep

weepy adj (-pier, -piest) liable to cry

weer adj ▷ wee

weest adj ▷ wee

weevil n (pl -s) small beetle which eats grain etc.

weevils n ▷ weevil

weft n (pl -s) cross threads in weaving

wefts n ▷ weft

weigh v (-s, -ing, -ed) have a specified weight

weighbridge n (pl -s) machine for weighing vehicles by means of a metal plate set into the road

weighbridges n ▷ weighbridge

weighed v ▷ weigh

weighing v ▷ weigh

weighs v ▷ weigh

weight n (pl -s) heaviness of an object ▶ v (-s, -ing, -ed) add weight to ▷ **weightless** adj ▷ **weightlessness** n

weighted v ▷ weight

weightier adj ▷ weighty

weightiest adj ▷ weighty

weightily adv ▷ weighty

weighting v ▷ weight ▶ n (pl -s) (BRIT) extra allowance paid in special circumstances

weightings n ▷ weighting

weightless adj ▷ weight

weightlessness n ▷ weight

weights n, v ▷ weight

weighty adj (-tier, -tiest) important or serious ▷ **weightily** adv

weir n (pl -s) river dam

weird (-er, -est) adj strange or bizarre

weirder adj ▷ weird

weirdest adj ▷ weird

weirdo n (pl -s) (Informal) peculiar person

weirdos n ▷ weirdo

weirs n ▷ weir

welch v (-es, -ing, -ed) ▷ welsh

welched v ▷ welch

welches v ▷ welch

welching v ▷ welch

welcome v (-mes, -ming, -med) greet with pleasure ▶ n (pl -s) kindly greeting ▶ adj received gladly

welcomed v ▷ welcome

welcomes v, n ▷ welcome

welcoming v ▷ welcome

weld v (-s, -ing, -ed) join (pieces of metal or plastic) by softening with heat ▶ n (pl -s) welded joint ▷ **welder** n (pl -s)

welded v ▷ weld

welder n ▷ weld

welders n ▷ weld

welding v ▷ weld

welds v, n ▷ weld

welfare n (pl -s) wellbeing

welfares n ▷ welfare

well¹ adv (better, best) satisfactorily ▶ adj in good health ▶ interj exclamation of surprise, interrogation, etc.

well² n (pl -s) hole sunk into the earth to reach water, oil, or gas ▶ v (-s, -ing, -ed) flow upwards or outwards

wellbeing n (pl -s) state of being well, happy, or prosperous

wellbeings n ▷ wellbeing

welled v ▷ well²

wellies pl n (BRIT & AUST) (Informal) wellingtons

welling v ▷ well²

wellingtons pl n (BRIT & AUST) high waterproof rubber boots

wells n, v ▷ well²

welsh v (-es, -ing, -ed) fail to pay a debt or fulfil an obligation

welshed v ▷ welsh

welshes v ▷ welsh

welshing v ▷ welsh

welt n (pl -s) raised mark on the skin produced by a blow

welter n (pl -s) jumbled mass

welters n ▷ welter

welterweight n (pl -s) boxer weighing up to 147lb (professional) or 67kg (amateur)

welterweights n ▷ welterweight

welts n ▷ welt

wen n (pl -s) cyst on the scalp

wench n (pl -es) (facetious) young woman

wenches n ▷ wench

wend v (-s, -ing, -ed) go or travel

wended v ▷ wend

wending v ▷ wend

wends v ▷ wend

wens n ▷ wen

went v ▷ go

wept v ▷ weep

were v form of the past tense of **be** used after we, you, they, or a plural noun ▷ be

werewolf n (pl -wolves) (in folklore) person who can turn into a wolf

werewolves n ▷ werewolf

west n (pl -s) (direction towards) the part of the horizon where the sun sets ▶ adj to or in the west ▶ adv in, to, or towards the west ▷ **westerly** adj ▷ **westward** adj, adv ▷ **westwards** adv

westerly adj ▷ west

western adj of or in the west ▶ n (pl -s) film or

story about cowboys in the western US

westernize v (-zes, -zing, -zed) adapt to the customs and culture of the West
westernized v ▷ westernize
westernizes v ▷ westernize
westernizing v ▷ westernize
westerns n ▷ western
wests n ▷ west
westward adj ▷ west
westwards adv ▷ west

wet adj (-tter, -ttest) covered or soaked with water or another liquid (BRIT) (Informal) ▶ n moisture or rain (BRIT) (Informal) ▶ v (-s, -tting, wet or wetted) make wet
wetland n (pl -s) area of marshy land
wetlands n ▷ wetland
wetted v ▷ wet
wetter adj ▷ wet
wettest adj ▷ wet
wetting v ▷ wet

wex n (wexes). Wex is an old word for **wax**. This gives a very good score for a three-letter word, and is a good one to look for when you have an X. Wex scores 13 points.

whack v (-s, -ing, -ed) strike with a resounding blow ▶ n (pl -s) such a blow
whacked adj exhausted ▶ v ▷ whack
whacking adj (Informal) huge ▶ v ▷ whack
whacks v, n ▷ whack
whale n large fish-shaped sea mammal
whaler n ship or person involved in whaling
whalers n ▷ whaler
whales n ▷ whale
whaling n (pl -s) hunting of whales for food and oil
whalings n ▷ whaling
wharf n (pl wharves, wharfs) platform at a harbour for loading and unloading ships
wharfie n (pl -s) (AUST) person employed to load and unload ships
wharfies n ▷ wharfie
wharfs n ▷ wharf
wharves n ▷ wharf
what pron which thing ▶ interj exclamation of anger, surprise, etc. ▶ adv in which way, how much
whatnot n (pl -s) (Informal) similar unspecified things
whatnots n ▷ whatnot
whatsoever adj at all
wheat n (pl -s) grain used in making flour, bread, and pasta > **wheaten** adj
wheatear n (pl -s) small songbird
wheatears n ▷ wheatear

wheaten adj ▷ wheat
wheats n ▷ wheat
wheedle v (-les, -ling, -led) coax or cajole
wheedled v ▷ wheedle
wheedles v ▷ wheedle
wheedling v ▷ wheedle
wheel n (pl -s) disc that revolves on an axle ▶ v (-s, -ing, -ed) push or pull (something with wheels)
wheelbarrow n (pl -s) shallow box for carrying loads, with a wheel at the front and two handles
wheelbarrows n ▷ wheelbarrow
wheelbase n (pl -s) distance between a vehicle's front and back axles
wheelbases n ▷ wheelbase
wheelchair n (pl -s) chair mounted on wheels for use by people who cannot walk
wheelchairs n ▷ wheelchair
wheeled v ▷ wheel
wheeling v ▷ wheel
wheels n, v ▷ wheel
wheeze v (-zes, -zing, -zed) breathe with a hoarse whistling noise ▶ n (pl -s) wheezing sound (Informal) > **wheezy** adj (-zier, -ziest)
wheezed v ▷ wheeze
wheezes v, n ▷ wheeze
wheezier adj ▷ wheeze
wheeziest adj ▷ wheeze
wheezing v ▷ wheeze
wheezy adj ▷ wheeze
whelk n (pl -s) edible snail-like shellfish
whelks n ▷ whelk
whelp n (pl -s) pup or cub ▶ v (-s, -ing, -ed) (of an animal) give birth
whelped v ▷ whelp
whelping v ▷ whelp
whelps n, v ▷ whelp
when adv at what time? ▶ conj at the time that ▶ pron at which time
whence adv, conj (Obs) from what place or source
whenever adv, conj at whatever time
where adv in, at, or to what place? ▶ pron in, at, or to which place ▶ conj in the place at which
whereabouts n present position ▶ adv at what place
whereas conj but on the other hand
whereby pron by which
wherefore (Obs) adv why ▶ conj consequently
whereupon conj at which point
wherever conj, adv at whatever place
wherewithal n (pl -s) necessary funds, resources, etc.
wherewithals n ▷ wherewithals

whet v (-s, -tting, -tted) sharpen (a tool)

whether conj used to introduce an indirect question or a clause expressing doubt or choice

whets v ▷ whet

whetstone n (pl -s) stone for sharpening tools

whetstones n ▷ whetstone

whetted v ▷ whet

whetting v ▷ whet

whey [way] n (pl -s) watery liquid that separates from the curd when milk is clotted

wheys n ▷ whey

which adj, pron used to request or refer to a choice from different possibilities ▶ pron used to refer to a thing already mentioned

whichever adj, pron any out of several

whiff n (pl -s) puff of air or odour

whiffs n ▷ whiff

whig n (pl -s) member of a British political party of the 18th–19th centuries that sought limited reform

whigs n ▷ whig

while conj at the same time that ▶ n (pl -s) period of time

whiles n ▷ while

whilst conj while

whim n (pl -s) sudden fancy

whimper v (-s, -ing, -ed) cry in a soft whining way ▶ n (pl -s) soft plaintive whine

whimpered v ▷ whimper

whimpering v ▷ whimper

whimpers v, n ▷ whimper

whims n ▷ whim

whimsical adj unusual, playful, and fanciful

whimsies n ▷ whimsy

whimsy n (pl -ies) capricious idea

whin n (pl -s) (BRIT) gorse

whine n (pl -s) high-pitched plaintive cry ▶ v (-nes, -ning, -ned) make such a sound > **whining** n, adj (pl -s)

whined v ▷ whine

whines n, v ▷ whine

whinge (BRIT, AUST & NZ) (Informal) v (-ges, -geing, -ged) complain ▶ n (pl -s) complaint

whinged v ▷ whinge

whingeing v ▷ whinge

whinges v, n ▷ whinge

whining v, n adj ▷ whine

whinings n ▷ whine

whinnied v ▷ whinny

whinnies v, n ▷ whinny

whinny v (-nnies, -nnying, -nnied) neigh softly ▶ n (pl -nnies) soft neigh

whinnying v ▷ whinny

whins n ▷ whin

whip n (pl -s) cord attached to a handle, used for beating animals or people ▶ v (-s, -pping, -pped) strike with a whip, strap, or cane

whipped v ▷ whip

whippet n (pl -s) racing dog like a small greyhound

whippets n ▷ whippet

whipping v ▷ whip

whips v, n ▷ whip

whir v ▷ whirr

whirl v (-s, -ing, -ed) spin or revolve ▶ n (pl -s) whirling movement

whirled v ▷ whirl

whirling v ▷ whirl

whirlpool n (pl -s) strong circular current of water

whirlpools n ▷ whirlpool

whirls v, n ▷ whirl

whirlwind n (pl -s) column of air whirling violently upwards in a spiral ▶ adj much quicker than normal

whirlwinds n ▷ whirlwind

whirr, whir n (pl -s) prolonged soft buzz ▶ v (-s, -rring, -rred) (cause to) make a whirr

whirred v ▷ whirr

whirring v ▷ whirr

whirrs n, v ▷ whirr

whirs v ▷ whirr

whisk v (-s, -ing, -ed) move or remove quickly ▶ n (pl -s) egg-beating utensil

whisked v ▷ whisk

whisker n (pl -s) any of the long stiff hairs on the face of a cat or other mammal ▶ pl hair growing on a man's face

whiskers n ▷ whisker

whiskey n (pl -s) Irish or American whisky

whiskeys n ▷ whiskey

whiskies n ▷ whisky

whisking v, v ▷ whisk

whisks n ▷ whisk

whisky n (pl -ies) spirit distilled from fermented cereals

whisper v (-s, -ing, -ed) speak softly, without vibration of the vocal cords ▶ n (pl -s) soft voice (Informal)

whispered v ▷ whisper

whispering v ▷ whisper

whispers v, n ▷ whisper

whist n (pl -s) card game in which one pair of players tries to win more tricks than another pair

whistle v (-les, -ling, -led) produce a shrill sound, esp. by forcing the breath through pursed lips ▶ n (pl -s) whistling sound > **whistling** n, adj (pl -s)

whistled v ▷ whistle
whistles v, n ▷ whistle
whistling v, n ▷ whistle
whistlings n ▷ whistle
whists n ▷ whist
whit n (pl -s) not the slightest amount
white adj (-r, -st) of the colour of snow ▶ n (pl -s) colour of snow **> whiteness** n (pl -es) **> whitish** adj
whitebait n (pl -s) small edible fish
whitebaits n ▷ whitebait
whiten v (-s, -ing, -ed) make or become white or whiter
whitened v ▷ whiten
whiteness n ▷ white
whitenesses n ▷ white
whitening v ▷ whiten
whitens v ▷ whiten
whiter adj ▷ white
whites n ▷ white
whitest adj ▷ white
whitewash n (pl -es) substance for whitening walls ▶ v (-es, -ing, -ed) cover with whitewash
whitewashed v ▷ whitewash
whitewashes n, v ▷ whitewash
whitewashing v ▷ whitewash
whither adv (Obs) to what place
whiting n (pl -s) edible sea fish
whitings n ▷ whiting
whitish adj ▷ white
whittle v (-les, -ling, -led) cut or carve (wood) with a knife
whittled v ▷ whittle
whittles v ▷ whittle
whittling v ▷ whittle
whiz v ▷ whizz
whizz, whiz v (-es, -ing, -ed) make a loud buzzing sound (Informal) ▶ n (pl -es) loud buzzing sound (Informal)
whizzed v ▷ whizz
whizzes v, n ▷ whizz
whizzing v ▷ whizz
who pron which person
whodunnit, whodunit [hoo-**dun**-nit] n (pl -s) (Informal) detective story, play, or film
whodunnits n ▷ whodunnit
whoever pron any person who
whole adj containing all the elements or parts ▶ n (pl -s) complete thing or system **> wholly** adv
wholefood n (pl -s) food that has been processed as little as possible
wholefoods n ▷ wholefood
wholehearted adj sincere or enthusiastic
wholemeal adj (of flour) made from the whole

wheat grain
wholes n ▷ whole
wholesale adj, adv dealing by selling goods in large quantities to retailers **> wholesaler** n (pl -s)
wholesaler n ▷ wholesale
wholesalers n ▷ wholesale
wholesome adj physically or morally beneficial
wholly adv ▷ whole
whom pron ▷ who
whoop v, n (pl -s) shout or cry to express excitement
whoopee interj (Informal) cry of joy
whoops n ▷ whoop
whopper n (pl -s) (Informal) anything unusually large **> whopping** adj
whoppers n ▷ whopper
whopping adj ▷ whopper
whore [hore] n (pl -s) prostitute
whores n ▷ whore
whorl n (pl -s) ring of leaves or petals
whorls n ▷ whorl
whose pron of whom or of which
why adv for what reason ▶ pron because of which
wick n (pl -s) cord through a lamp or candle which carries fuel to the flame
wicked (-er, -est) adj morally bad **> wickedly** adv **> wickedness** n (pl -s)
wickedly adv ▷ wicked
wickedness n ▷ wicked
wickednesses n ▷ wicked
wicker adj made of woven cane **> wickerwork** n (pl -s)
wickerwork n ▷ wicker
wickerworks n ▷ wicker
wicket n (pl -s) set of three cricket stumps and two bails
wickets n ▷ wicket
wicks n ▷ wick
wide adj (-r, -st) large from side to side ▶ adv to the full extent **> widely** adv
widely adv ▷ wide
widen v (-s, -ing, -ed) make or become wider
widened v ▷ widen
widening v ▷ widen
widens v ▷ widen
wider adj ▷ wide
widespread adj affecting a wide area or a large number of people
widest adj ▷ wide
widgeon n (pl -s) ▷ wigeon
widgeons n ▷ widgeon
widow n (pl -s) woman whose husband is dead

and who has not remarried ▸ **widowed** adj
▸**widowhood** n (pl -s)
   widowed adj ▷widow
widower n (pl -s) man whose wife is dead and
who has not remarried
   widowers n ▷widower
   widowhood n ▷widow
   widowhoods n ▷widow
   widows n ▷widow
width n (pl -s) distance from side to side
   widths n ▷width
wield v (-s, -ing, -ed) hold and use (a weapon)
   wielded v ▷wield
   wielding v ▷wield
   wields v ▷wield
wife n (pl wives) woman to whom a man is
married
wig n (pl -s) artificial head of hair
wigeon n (pl -s) duck found in marshland
   wigeons n ▷wigeon
wiggle v (-les, -ling, -led) move jerkily from
side to side ▸ n (pl -les) wiggling movement
   wiggled v ▷wiggle
   wiggles v, n ▷wiggle
   wiggling v ▷wiggle
   wigs n ▷wig
wigwam n (pl -s) Native American's tent
   wigwams n ▷wigwam
wild adj (-er, -est) (of animals) not tamed or
domesticated ▷ **wildly** adv ▷ **wildness** n (pl
-es)
wildcat n (pl -s) European wild animal like a
large domestic cat
   wildcats n ▷wildcat
wildebeest n (pl -s) gnu
   wildebeests n ▷wildebeest
   wilder adj ▷wild
wilderness n (pl -es) uninhabited uncultivated
region
   wildernesses n ▷wilderness
   wildest adj ▷wild
wildlife n (pl -s) wild animals and plants
collectively
   wildlifes n ▷wildlife
   wildly adv ▷wild
   wildness n ▷wild
   wildnesses n ▷wild
wilds pl n desolate or uninhabited place
wiles pl n tricks or ploys
wilful adj headstrong or obstinate ▷ **wilfully**
adv
   wilfully adv ▷wilful
   wilier adj ▷wily
   wiliest adj ▷wily
will¹ v (past would) used as an auxiliary to form

the future tense or to indicate intention,
ability, or expectation
will² n (pl -s) strong determination ▸ v (-s,
-ing, -ed) use one's will in an attempt to do
(something)
   willed v ▷will²
willing adj ready or inclined (to do something)
▸ v ▷will² ▸ **willingly** adv ▸ **willingness** n
(pl -es)
   willingly adv ▷willing
   willingness n ▷willing
   willingnesses n ▷willing
willow n (pl -s) tree with thin flexible branches
   willowier adj ▷willowy
   willowiest adj ▷willowy
   willows n ▷willow
willowy adj (-wier, -wiest) slender and graceful
willpower n (pl -s) ability to control oneself
and one's actions
   willpowers n ▷willpower
   wills n, v ▷will²
wilt v (-s, -ing, -ed) (cause to) become limp or
lose strength
   wilted v ▷wilt
   wilting v ▷wilt
   wilts v ▷wilt
wily adj (-lier, -liest) crafty or sly
wimp n (pl -s) (Informal) feeble ineffectual
person
wimple n (pl -s) garment framing the face,
worn by medieval women and now by nuns
   wimples n ▷wimple
   wimps n ▷wimp
win v (-s, -nning, won) come first in (a
competition, fight, etc.) ▸ n (pl -s) victory, esp.
in a game ▸ **winner** n (pl -s)
wince v (-ces, -cing, -ced) draw back, as if in
pain ▸ n (pl -s) wincing
   winced v ▷wince
   winces v, n ▷wince
winch n (pl -es) machine for lifting or hauling
using a cable or chain wound round a drum
▸ v (-es, -ing, -ed) lift or haul using a winch
   winched v ▷winch
   winches n, v ▷winch
   winching v ▷winch
   wincing v ▷wince
wind¹ n (pl -s) current of air ▸ v (-s, -ing, -ed)
render short of breath ▷ **windy** adj (-dier,
-diest)
wind² v (-s, -ing, wound) coil or wrap around
   winded v ▷wind¹
windfall n (pl -s) unexpected good luck
   windfalls n ▷windfall
   windier adj ▷wind¹

windiest adj ▷ wind¹
winding v ▷ wind¹, ²
windlass n (pl -es) winch worked by a crank
windlasses n ▷ windlass
windmill n (pl -s) machine for grinding or pumping driven by sails turned by the wind
windmills n ▷ windmill
window n (pl -s) opening in a wall to let in light or air
windows n ▷ window
windpipe n (pl -s) tube linking the throat and the lungs
windpipes n ▷ windpipe
winds n, v ▷ wind¹, ²
windscreen n (pl -s) front window of a motor vehicle
windscreens n ▷ windscreen
windsock n (pl -s) cloth cone on a mast at an airfield to indicate wind direction
windsocks n ▷ windsock
windsurfing n (pl -s) sport of riding on water using a surfboard propelled and steered by a sail
windsurfings n ▷ windsurfing
windward adj, n (pl -s) (of or in) the direction from which the wind is blowing
windwards n ▷ windward
windy adj ▷ wind¹
wine n (pl -s) alcoholic drink made from fermented grapes
wines n ▷ wine
wing n (pl -s) one of the limbs or organs of a bird, insect, or bat that are used for flying ▶ pl sides of a stage ▶ v (-s, -ing, -ed) fly ▶ **winged** adj
winged v, adj ▷ wing
winger n (pl -s) (SPORT) player positioned on the side of the pitch
wingers n ▷ winger
winging v ▷ wing
wings n, v ▷ wing
wink v (-s, -ing, -ed) close and open (an eye) quickly as a signal ▶ n (pl -s) winking
winked v ▷ wink
winking v ▷ wink
winkle n (pl -s) shellfish with a spiral shell
winkles n ▷ winkle
winks v, n ▷ wink
winner n ▷ win
winners n ▷ win
winning adj gaining victory ▶ v ▷ win
winnings pl n sum won, esp. in gambling
winnow v (-s, -ing, -ed) (pl -s) separate (chaff) from (grain)
winnowed v ▷ winnow

winnowing v ▷ winnow
winnows v, n ▷ winnow
winsome adj (-r, -st) charming or winning
winsomer adj ▷ winsome
winsomest adj ▷ winsome
winter n (pl -s) coldest season ▶ v (-s, -ing, -ed) spend the winter
wintered v ▷ winter
wintering v ▷ winter
winters n, v ▷ winter
wintrier adj ▷ wintry
wintriest adj ▷ wintry
wintry adj (-rier, -riest) of or like winter
wipe v (-pes, -ping, -ped) clean or dry by rubbing ▶ n (pl -s) wiping
wiped v ▷ wipe
wipes v, n ▷ wipe
wiping v ▷ wipe
wire n (pl -s) thin flexible strand of metal (Obs) ▶ v (-res, -ring, -red) equip with wires
wired v ▷ wire
wirehaired adj (of a dog) having a stiff wiry coat
wireless n (pl -es) (Old-fashioned) ▷ radio ▶ adj (of a computer network) connected by radio rather than by cables or fibre optics
wirelesses n ▷ wireless
wires n, v ▷ wire
wirier adj ▷ wiry
wiriest adj ▷ wiry
wiring n (pl -s) system of wires ▶ v ▷ wire
wirings n ▷ wiring
wiry adj (-rier, -riest) lean and tough
wisdom n (pl -s) good sense and judgment
wisdoms n ▷ wisdom
wise¹ adj (-r, -st) having wisdom > **wisely** adv
wise² n (pl -s) (Obs) manner
wiseacre n (pl -s) person who wishes to seem wise
wiseacres n ▷ wiseacre
wisecrack (Informal) n (pl -s) clever, sometimes unkind, remark ▶ v (-s, -ing, -ed) make a wisecrack
wisecracked v ▷ wisecrack
wisecracking v ▷ wisecrack
wisecracks n, v ▷ wisecrack
wisely adv ▷ wise¹
wiser adj ▷ wise¹
wises n ▷ wise²
wisest adj ▷ wise¹
wish v (-es, -ing, -ed) want or desire ▶ n (pl -es) expression of a desire
wishbone n (pl -s) V-shaped bone above the breastbone of a fowl
wishbones n ▷ wishbone

wished v ▷ wish

wishes v, n ▷ wish

wishful adj too optimistic

wishing v ▷ wish

wisp n (pl -s) light delicate streak > **wispy** adj (-pier, -piest)

wispier adj ▷ wisp

wispiest adj ▷ wisp

wisps n ▷ wisp

wispy adj ▷ wisp

wisteria n (pl -s) climbing shrub with blue or purple flowers

wisterias n ▷ wisteria

wistful adj sadly longing > **wistfully** adv

wistfully adv ▷ wistful

wit n (pl -s) ability to use words or ideas in a clever and amusing way

witch n (pl -es) person, usu. female, who practises (black) magic

witchcraft n (pl -s) use of magic

witchcrafts n ▷ witchcraft

witches n ▷ witch

with prep indicating presence alongside, possession, means of performance, characteristic manner, etc.

withdraw v (-drawing, -drew, -drawn) take or move out or away ▶ withdrawal n (pl -s)

withdrawal n ▷ withdraw

withdrawals n ▷ withdraw

withdrawn adj unsociable ▶ v ▷ withdraw

withdraws v ▷ withdraw

withdrew v ▷ withdraw

wither v (-s, -ing, -ed) wilt or dry up

withered v ▷ wither

withering adj (of a look or remark) scornful ▶ v ▷ wither

withers v ▷ wither ▶ pl n ridge between a horse's shoulder blades

withheld v ▷ withhold

withhold v (-s, -ing, -held) refrain from giving

withholding v ▷ withhold

withholds v ▷ withhold

within prep, adv in or inside

without prep not accompanied by, using, or having

withstand v (-s, -ing, -stood) oppose or resist successfully

withstanding v ▷ withstand

withstands v ▷ withstand

withstood v ▷ withstand

witless adj foolish

witness n (pl -es) person who has seen something happen ▶ v (-es, -ing, -ed) see at first hand

witnessed v ▷ witness

witnesses n, v ▷ witness

witnessing v ▷ witness

wits n ▷ wit

witter v (-s, -ing, -ed) (CHIEFLY BRIT) chatter pointlessly or at unnecessary length

wittered v ▷ witter

wittering v ▷ witter

witters v ▷ witter

witticism n (pl -s) witty remark

witticisms n ▷ witticism

wittier adj ▷ witty

wittiest adj ▷ witty

wittily adv ▷ witty

wittingly adv intentionally

witty adj (-tier, -tiest) clever and amusing > **wittily** adv

wives n ▷ wife

wiz n (wizzes). Wiz is a short form of **wizard.** This is the highest-scoring three-letter word beginning with W, and can be especially useful when there isn't much room to manoeuvre. Wiz scores 15 points.

wizard n (pl -s) magician > **wizardry** n (pl -ies)

wizardries n ▷ wizard

wizardry n ▷ wizard

wizards n ▷ wizard

wizened [wiz-zend] adj shrivelled or wrinkled

wo n (wos). Wo is an old-fashioned spelling of **woe.** This unusual word is handy for joining words ending in W to those beginning in O. Wo scores 5 points.

woad n (pl -s) blue dye obtained from a plant, used by the ancient Britons as a body dye

woads n ▷ woad

wobbegong n (pl -s) Australian shark with brown-and-white skin

wobbegongs n ▷ wobbegong

wobble v (-les, -ling, -led) move unsteadily ▶ n (pl -s) wobbling movement or sound > **wobbly** adj (-lier, -liest)

wobbled v ▷ wobble

wobbles v, n ▷ wobble

wobblier adj ▷ wobble

wobbliest adj ▷ wobble

wobbling v ▷ wobble

wobbly adj ▷ wobble

wodge n (pl -s) (Informal) thick lump or chunk

wodges n ▷ wodge

woe n (pl -s) grief

woebegone adj looking miserable

woeful adj extremely sad > **woefully** adv

woefully adv ▷ woeful

woes n ▷ woe

wok n (pl -s) bowl-shaped Chinese cooking pan, used for stir-frying
woke v ▷ wake¹
woken v ▷ wake¹
woks n ▷ wok
wold n (pl -s) high open country
wolds n ▷ wold
wolf n (pl wolves) wild predatory canine mammal ▶ v eat ravenously
wolverine n (pl -s) carnivorous mammal of Arctic regions
wolverines n ▷ wolverine
wolves n ▷ wolf
woman n (pl women) adult human female > **womanhood** n (pl -s)
womanhood n ▷ woman
womanhoods n ▷ woman
womanish adj effeminate
womanizer n ▷ womanizing
womanizers n ▷ womanizing
womanizing n (pl -s) practice of indulging in casual affairs with women > **womanizer** n (pl -s)
womanizings n ▷ womanizing
womanly adj having qualities traditionally associated with a woman
womb n (pl -s) hollow organ in female mammals where babies are conceived and develop
wombat n (pl -s) small heavily-built burrowing Australian marsupial
wombats n ▷ wombat
wombs n ▷ womb
women n ▷ woman
won v ▷ win
wonder v (-s, -ing, -ed) be curious about ▶ n (pl -s) wonderful thing ▶ adj spectacularly successful > **wonderment** n (pl -s)
wondered v ▷ wonder
wonderful adj very fine > **wonderfully** adv
wonderfully adv ▷ wonderful
wondering v ▷ wonder
wonderment n ▷ wonder
wonderments n ▷ wonder
wonders v, n ▷ wonder
wondrous adj (Old-fashioned) wonderful
wonkier adj ▷ wonky
wonkiest adj ▷ wonky
wonky adj (-kier, -kiest) (BRIT, AUST & NZ) (Informal) shaky or unsteady
wont [rhymes with **don't**] adj accustomed ▶ n (pl -s) custom
wonts n ▷ wont
woo v (-s, -ing, -ed) try to persuade (Old-fashioned)

wood n (pl -s) substance trees are made of, used in carpentry and as fuel > **woody** adj (-dier, -diest)
woodbine n (pl -s) honeysuckle
woodbines n ▷ woodbine
woodcock n (pl -s) game bird
woodcocks n ▷ woodcock
woodcut n (pl -s) (print made from) an engraved block of wood
woodcuts n ▷ woodcut
wooded adj covered with trees
wooden adj made of wood
woodier adj ▷ wood
woodiest adj ▷ wood
woodland n (pl -s) forest
woodlands n ▷ woodland
woodlice n ▷ woodlouse
woodlouse n (pl -lice) small insect-like creature with many legs
woodpecker n (pl -s) bird which searches tree trunks for insects
woodpeckers n ▷ woodpecker
woods n ▷ wood
woodwind adj, n (pl -s) (of) a type of wind instrument made of wood
woodwinds n ▷ woodwind
woodworm n insect larva that bores into wood
woodworms n ▷ woodworm
woody adj ▷ wood
wooed v ▷ woo
woof¹ n (pl -s) cross threads in weaving
woof² n (pl -s) barking noise made by a dog
woofer n (pl -s) loudspeaker reproducing low-frequency sounds
woofers n ▷ woofer
woofs n ▷ woof¹, ²
wooing v ▷ woo
wool n (pl -s) soft hair of sheep, goats, etc. > **woollen** adj
woollen adj ▷ wool
woollier adj ▷ woolly
woolliest adj ▷ woolly
woolly adj (-llier, -lliest) of or like wool ▶ n knitted woollen garment
wools n ▷ wool
woomera n (pl -s) notched stick used by Australian Aborigines to aid the propulsion of a spear
woomeras n ▷ woomera
woos v ▷ woo
woozier adj ▷ woozy
wooziest adj ▷ woozy
woozy adj (-zier, -ziest) (Informal) weak, dizzy, and confused

word n (pl -s) smallest single meaningful unit of speech or writing ▶ v (-s, -ing, -ed) express in words
worded v ▷ word
wordier adj ▷ wordy
wordiest adj ▷ wordy
wording n (pl -s) choice and arrangement of words ▶ v ▷ word
wordings n ▷ wording
words n, v ▷ word
wordy adj (-dier, -diest) using too many words
wore v ▷ wear
work n (pl -s) physical or mental effort directed to making or doing something ▶ pl factory (Informal) ▶ adj of or for work ▶ v (-s, -ing, -ed) (cause to) do work > **workable** adj > **worker** n (pl -s)
workable adj ▷ work
workaholic n (pl -s) person obsessed with work
workaholics n ▷ workaholic
worked v ▷ work
worker n ▷ work
workers n ▷ work
workhorse n (pl -s) person or thing that does a lot of dull or routine work
workhorses n ▷ workhorse
workhouse n (pl -s) (in England, formerly) institution where the poor were given food and lodgings in return for work
workhouses n ▷ workhouse
working v ▷ work
workman n (pl -men) manual worker
workmanship n (pl -s) skill with which an object is made
workmanships n ▷ workmanship
workmen n ▷ workman
works n, v ▷ work
workshop n (pl -s) room or building for a manufacturing process
workshops n ▷ w
worktop n (pl -s) surface in a kitchen, used for food preparation
worktops n ▷ worktop
world n (pl -s) the planet earth ▶ adj of the whole world
worldlier adj ▷ worldly
worldliest adj ▷ worldly
worldly adj (-ier, -iest) not spiritual
worlds n ▷ world
worm n (pl -s) small limbless invertebrate animal ▶ pl illness caused by parasitic worms in the intestines ▶ v (-s, -ing, -ed) rid of worms > **wormy** adj (-mier, -miest)
wormed v ▷ worm

wormier adj ▷ worm
wormiest adj ▷ worm
worming v ▷ worm
worms n, v ▷ worm
wormwood n (pl -s) bitter plant
wormwoods n ▷ wormwood
wormy adj ▷ worm
worn v ▷ wear
worried v, adj ▷ worry
worries v, n ▷ worry
worry v (-ies, -ying, -ied) (cause to) be anxious or uneasy ▶ n (pl -ies) (cause of) anxiety or concern > **worried** adj > **worrying** adj, n
worrying v, adj ▷ worry
worse adj, adv ▷ bad, badly
worsen v (-s, -ing, -ed) make or grow worse
worsened v ▷ worsen
worsening v ▷ worsen
worsens v ▷ worsen
worship v (-s, -pping, -pped) show religious devotion to ▶ n (pl -s) act or instance of worshipping > **worshipper** n (pl -s)
worshipful adj worshipping
worshipped v ▷ worship
worshipper n ▷ worship
worshippers n ▷ worship
worshipping v ▷ worship
worships v, n ▷ worship
worst adj, adv ▷ bad, badly ▶ n worst thing
worsted [wooss-tid] n (pl -s) type of woollen yarn or fabric
worsteds n ▷ worsted
worth prep having a value of ▶ n (pl -s) value or price > **worthless** adj
worthier adj ▷ worthy
worthiest adj ▷ worthy
worthily adv ▷ worthy
worthiness n ▷ worthy
worthinesses n ▷ worthy
worthless adj ▷ worth
worths n ▷ worth
worthwhile adj worth the time or effort involved
worthy adj (-thier, -thiest) deserving admiration or respect ▶ n (Informal) notable person > **worthily** adv > **worthiness** n (pl -es)
would v ▷ will¹
wound¹ n (pl -s) injury caused by violence ▶ v (-s, -ing, -ed) inflict a wound on
wound² v ▷ wind²
wounded v ▷ wound¹
wounding v ▷ wound¹
wounds n, v ▷ wound¹
wove v ▷ weave
woven v ▷ weave

wow *interj* exclamation of astonishment ▶ *n* (*pl* -s) (*Informal*) astonishing person or thing
  wows *n* ▷ wow
wowser *n* (*pl* -s) (AUST & NZ) (*Slang*) puritanical person
  wowsers *n* ▷ wowser

wox *n* (**woxes**). Wox is an old past tense of the verb **wax**. This gives a very good score for a three-letter word, and is a good one to look for when you have an X. Wox scores 13 points.

wrack *n* (*pl* -s) seaweed
  wracks *n* ▷ wrack
wraith *n* (*pl* -s) ghost
  wraiths *n* ▷ wraith
wrangle *v* (-les, -ling, -led) argue noisily ▶ *n* (*pl* -s) noisy argument
  wrangled *v* ▷ wrangle
  wrangles *v, n* ▷ wrangle
  wrangling *v* ▷ wrangle
wrap *v* (-s, -pping, -pped) fold (something) round (a person or thing) so as to cover ▶ *n* (*pl* -s) garment wrapped round the shoulders
  wrapped *v* ▷ wrap
wrapper *n* (*pl* -s) cover for a product
  wrappers *n* ▷ wrapper
wrapping *n* (*pl* -s) material used to wrap ▶ *v* ▷ wrap
  wrappings *n* ▷ wrapping
  wraps *v, n* ▷ wrap
wrasse *n* (*pl* -s) colourful sea fish
  wrasses *n* ▷ wrasse
wrath [roth] *n* (*pl* -s) intense anger > **wrathful** *adj*
  wrathful *adj* ▷ wrath
  wraths *n* ▷ wrath
wreak *v* (-s, -ing, -ed) cause (chaos)
  wreaked *v* ▷ wreak
  wreaking *v* ▷ wreak
  wreaks *v* ▷ wreak
wreath *n* (*pl* -s) twisted ring or band of flowers or leaves used as a memorial or tribute
  wreathed *adj* surrounded or encircled
  wreaths *n* ▷ wreath
wreck *v* (-s, -ing, -ed) destroy ▶ *n* (*pl* -s) remains of something that has been destroyed or badly damaged, esp. a ship > **wrecker** *n* (*pl* -s)
wreckage *n* (*pl* -s) wrecked remains
  wreckages *n* ▷ wreckage
  wrecked *v* ▷ wreck
  wrecker *n* ▷ wreck
  wreckers *n* ▷ wreck
  wrecking *v* ▷ wreck
  wrecks *v, n* ▷ wreck
wren *n* (*pl* -s) small brown songbird

wrench *v* (-es, -ing, -ed) twist or pull violently ▶ *n* (*pl* -es) violent twist or pull
  wrenched *v* ▷ wrench
  wrenches *v, n* ▷ wrench
  wrenching *v* ▷ wrench
  wrens *n* ▷ wren
wrest *v* (-s, -ing, -ed) twist violently
  wrested *v* ▷ wrest
  wresting *v* ▷ wrest
wrestle *v* (-les, -ling, -led) fight, esp. as a sport, by grappling with and trying to throw down an opponent > **wrestler** *n* (*pl* -s) > **wrestling** *n* (*pl* -s)
  wrestled *v* ▷ wrestle
  wrestler *n* ▷ wrestle
  wrestlers *n* ▷ wrestle
  wrestles *v* ▷ wrestle
  wrestling *v, n* ▷ wrestle
  wrestlings *n* ▷ wrestle
  wrests *v* ▷ wrest
wretch *n* (*pl* -es) despicable person
wretched [retch-id] *adj* (-er, -est) miserable or unhappy > **wretchedly** *adv* > **wretchedness** *n* (*pl* -es)
  wretcheder *adj* ▷ wretched
  wretchedest *adj* ▷ wretched
  wretchedly *adv* ▷ wretched
  wretchedness *n* ▷ wretched
  wretchednesses *n* ▷ wretched
  wretches *n* ▷ wretch
  wrier *adj* ▷ wry
  wriest *adj* ▷ wry
wriggle *v* (-les, -ling, -led) move with a twisting action ▶ *n* (*pl* -s) wriggling movement
  wriggled *v* ▷ wriggle
  wriggles *v, n* ▷ wriggle
  wriggling *v* ▷ wriggle
wright *n* (*pl* -s) maker
  wrights *n* ▷ wright
wring *v* (-s, -ing, wrung) twist, esp. to squeeze liquid out of
  wringing *v* ▷ wring
  wrings *v* ▷ wring
wrinkle *n* (*pl* -s) slight crease, esp. one in the skin due to age ▶ *v* (-les, -ling, -led) make or become slightly creased > **wrinkly** *adj* (-lier, -liest)
  wrinkled *v* ▷ wrinkle
  wrinkles *n, v* ▷ wrinkle
  wrinklier *adj* ▷ wrinkle
  wrinkliest *adj* ▷ wrinkle
  wrinkling *v* ▷ wrinkle
  wrinkly *adj* ▷ wrinkle
wrist *n* (*pl* -s) joint between the hand and

the arm
wrists n ▷ wrist
wristwatch n (pl -es) watch worn on the wrist
  wristwatches n ▷ wristwatch
writ n (pl -s) written legal command
write v (-tes, -ting, wrote, written) mark paper
  etc. with symbols or words > **writing** n (pl -s)
writer n (pl -s) author
  writers n ▷ writer
writhe v (-thes, -thing, -thed) twist or squirm
  in or as if in pain
  writhed v ▷ writhe
  writhes v ▷ writhe
  writhing v ▷ writhe
  writing v, n ▷ write
  writings n ▷ write
  writs n ▷ writ
  written v ▷ write
wrong adj incorrect or mistaken ▶ adv in a
  wrong manner ▶ n (pl -s) something immoral
  or unjust ▶ v (-s, -ing, -ed) treat unjustly
  > **wrongly** adv > **wrongful** adj > **wrongfully**
  adv
  wrongdoer n ▷ wrongdoing
  wrongdoers n ▷ wrongdoing

wrongdoing n (pl -s) immoral or illegal
  behaviour > **wrongdoer** n (pl -s)
  wrongdoings n ▷ wrongdoing
  wronged v ▷ wrong
  wrongful adj ▷ wrong
  wrongfully adv ▷ wrong
  wronging v ▷ wrong
  wrongly adv ▷ wrong
  wrongs n, v ▷ wrong
  wrote v ▷ write
wrought [rawt] v (Lit) ▷ work ▶ adj (of metals)
  shaped by hammering or beating
  wrung v ▷ wring
wry adj (wrier, wriest or wryer) (wryest) drily
  humorous > **wryly** adv
  wryer adj ▷ wry
  wryest adj ▷ wry
  wryly adv ▷ wry

> **wye** n (**wyes**). Wye is the letter Y. If you
> have W and Y on your rack, look for an
> E on the board that will allow you to
> play this especially if you can land on
> a bonus square as a result. Wye scores
> 9 points.

X x

Worth 8 points on its own, X is one of the best tiles in the game. It doesn't, however, start many two- and three-letter words. There are only two valid two-letter words, **xi** and **xu** (9 points each), beginning with X, and only one three-letter word, **xis.** Therefore, if you have an X on your rack and need to play short words, you're probably better off thinking of words that end in X or have X in them rather than those that start with X.

xebec *n* (**xebecs**). A xebec is an Algerian ship. This is a good high-scoring word. If you have an X, you'll probably only need one E as well as B and C to play it, as there is likely to be an available E on the board already. Xebec scores 16 points.

xenon *n* (*pl* -s) (CHEM) colourless odourless gas found in very small quantities in the air
xenons *n* ▷ xenon

xenophobia [zen-oh-**fobe**-ee-a] *n* (*pl* -s) fear or hatred of people from other countries
xenophobias *n* ▷ xenophobia

xi *n* (**xis**). Xi is the 14th letter of the Greek alphabet. The plural of this word is the only three-letter word that starts with X. Xi scores 9 points.

xoanon *n* (**xoanons**) A xoanon is a primitive carving of a god. If you have all the tiles for the plural, and are able to place them all on the board, you'll earn a 50-point bonus. Xoanon scores 13 points.

xu *n* (**xu**). The xu is a unit of currency in Vietnam. The plural form of this word is the same as its singular, so be sure to challenge anyone who adds an S to it! Xu scores 9 points.

xylem [**zy**-lem] *n* (*pl* -s) plant tissue that conducts water and minerals from the roots to all other parts
xylems *n* ▷ xylem

xylophone [zile-oh-fone] *n* (*pl* -s) musical instrument made of a row of wooden bars played with hammers
xylophones *n* ▷ xylophone

Yy

Y is a useful tile to have on your rack. It's worth 4 points on its own, and so often gives you good scores. There are only four two-letter words beginning with Y, but these are easy to remember as there's one for every vowel except I: **ya, ye, yo** and **yu** (5 points each). There are quite a few useful three-letter words: **yew** (9) and **yob** (8) and remember that yob was originally **boy** backwards: if you can't fit in yob, you may be able to use boy instead. And while his half-brother the **zo** (or **dzo** or **dso** or **zho**) gets all the attention, don't forget that the **yak** (10) earns quite a decent score!

ya *interj* (S AFR) yes
  yabbies *n* ▷ yabby
yabby *n* (*pl* -bbies) (AUST) small freshwater crayfish
yacht [yott] *n* (*pl* -s) large boat with sails or an engine, used for racing or pleasure cruising ▷ **yachting** *n* (*pl* -s) ▷ **yachtsman** *n* (*pl* -men) ▷ **yachtswoman** *n* (*pl* -women)
  yachting *n* ▷ yacht
  yachtings *n* ▷ yacht
  yachts *n* ▷ yacht
  yachtsman *n* ▷ yacht
  yachtsmen *n* ▷ yacht
  yachtswoman *n* ▷ yacht
  yachtswomen *n* ▷ yacht
yak[1] *n* (*pl* -s) Tibetan ox with long shaggy hair
yak[2] *v* (yaks, yakking, yakked) (*Slang*) talk continuously about unimportant matters
yakka *n* (*pl* -s) (AUST & NZ) (*Informal*) work
  yakkas *n* ▷ yakka
  yakked *v* ▷ yak[2]
  yakking *v* ▷ yak[2]
  yaks *n* ▷ yak[1] ▶ *v* ▷ yak[2]
yam *n* (*pl* -s) tropical root vegetable
  yams *n* ▷ yam
yank *v* (-s, -ing, -ed) pull or jerk suddenly ▶ *n* (*pl* -s) sudden pull or jerk
  yanked *v* ▷ yank
  yanking *v* ▷ yank
  yanks *v, n* ▷ yank
yap *v* (-s, -pping, -pped) bark with a high-pitched sound (*Informal*) ▶ *n* (*pl* -s) high-pitched bark
  yapped *v* ▷ yap
  yapping *v* ▷ yap

  yaps *v* ▷ yap
yard[1] *n* (*pl* -s) unit of length equal to 36 inches or about 91.4 centimetres > **yardstick** *n* (*pl* -s) standard against which to judge other people or things
yard[2] *n* (*pl* -s) enclosed area, usu. next to a building and often used for a particular purpose
  yards *n* ▷ yard[1, 2]
  yardstick *n* ▷ yard[1]
  yardsticks *n* ▷ yard[1]
yarmulke [yar-mull-ka] *n* (*pl* -s) skullcap worn by Jewish men
  yarmulkes *n* ▷ yarmulke
yarn *n* (*pl* -s) thread used for knitting or making cloth
  yarns *n* ▷ yarn
yashmak *n* (*pl* -s) veil worn by a Muslim woman to cover her face in public
  yashmaks *n* ▷ yashmak
yaw *v* (-s, -ing, -ed) (of an aircraft or ship) turn to one side or from side to side while moving
  yawed *v* ▷ yaw
  yawing *v* ▷ yaw
yawl *n* (*pl* -s) two-masted sailing boat
  yawls *n* ▷ yawl
yawn *v* (-s, -ing, -ed) open the mouth wide and take in air deeply, often when sleepy or bored ▶ *n* (*pl* -s) act of yawning > **yawning** *adj*
  yawned *v* ▷ yawn
  yawning ▷ yawn
  yawns *v, n* ▷ yawn
  yaws *v* ▷ yaw
ye [yee] *pron* (*Obs*) you
year *n* (*pl* -s) time taken for the earth to make

one revolution around the sun, about 365 days

yearling n (pl -s) animal between one and two years old

yearlings n ▷ yearling

yearly adj, adv (happening) every year or once a year

yearn v (-s, -ing, -ed) want (something) very much > **yearning** n (pl -s) adj

yearned v ▷ yearn

yearning v, n ▷ yearn

yearnings n ▷ yearn

yearns v ▷ yearn

years n ▷ year

yeast n (pl -s) fungus used to make bread rise and to ferment alcoholic drinks > **yeasty** adj

yeasts n ▷ yeast

yebo interj (S AFR) (Informal) yes

yell v (-s, -ing, -ed) shout or scream in a loud or piercing way ▶ n (pl -s) loud cry of pain, anger, or fear

yelled v ▷ yell

yelling v ▷ yell

yellow n (pl -s) the colour of gold, a lemon, etc. ▶ adj (-er, -est) of this colour ▶ v (-s, -ing, -ed) make or become yellow

yellowed v ▷ yellow

yellower adj ▷ yellow

yellowest adj ▷ yellow

yellowhammer n (pl -s) European songbird with a yellow head and body

yellowhammers n ▷ yellowhammer

yellowing v ▷ yellow

yellows n, v ▷ yellow

yells v, n ▷ yell

yelp v (-s, -ing, -ed) ▶ n (pl -s) (give) a short sudden cry

yelped v ▷ yelp

yelping v ▷ yelp

yelps v, n ▷ yelp

yen[1] n (pl yen) monetary unit of Japan

yen[2] n (pl yen) (Informal) longing or desire

yeoman [yo-man] n (pl -men) (HIST) farmer owning and farming his own land

yeomen n ▷ yeoman

yes interj expresses consent, agreement, or approval

yesterday adv, n (pl -s) (on) the day before today

yesterdays n ▷ yesterday

yet conj nevertheless, still ▶ adv up until then or now

yeti n (pl yetis) large apelike creature said to live in the Himalayas

yetis n ▷ yeti

yew n (pl -s) evergreen tree with needle-like leaves and red berries

yews n ▷ yew

> **yex** v (**yexes, yexing, yexed**). Yex is a Scots word that means to hiccup or cough. This word gives you a good score, and the verb forms offer the chance to expand it if someone else plays it, or if you get the chance later on. Yex scores 13 points.

yield v (-s, -ing, -ed) produce or bear ▶ n (pl -s)

yielded v ▷ yield

yielding adj submissive ▶ v ▷ yield

yields v, n ▷ yield

> **yo** interj. Yo is an informal greeting. This is useful for connecting words ending in Y with ones beginning in O. Yo scores 5 points.

yob n (pl -s) (Slang) bad-mannered aggressive youth

yobbo n (pl -bboes or -bbos) yob

yobboes n ▷ yobbo

yobbos n ▷ yobbo

yobs n ▷ yob

yodel v (-s, -lling, -lled) sing with abrupt changes between a normal and a falsetto voice

yodelled v ▷ yodel

yodelling v ▷ yodel

yodels v ▷ yodel

yoga n (pl -s) Hindu method of exercise and discipline aiming at spiritual, mental, and physical wellbeing

yogas n ▷ yoga

yoghurt n ▷ yogurt

yoghurts n ▷ yogurt

yogi n (pl -s) person who practises yoga

yogis n ▷ yogi

yogurt, yoghurt n (pl -s) slightly sour custard-like food made from milk that has had bacteria added to it, often sweetened and flavoured with fruit

yogurts n ▷ yogurt

> **yok** n (**yoks**). A yok is a noisy laugh. This unusual word is useful if there isn't much space on the board, as there's likely to be an O available to form it around. Yok scores 10 points.

yoke n (pl -s) wooden bar put across the necks of two animals to hold them together (Lit) ▶ v (-kes, -king, -ked) put a yoke on

yoked v ▷ yoke

yokel n (pl yokels) (Offens) person who lives in the country and is usu. simple and old-fashioned

yokels *n* ▷ yokel
yokes *n, v* ▷ yoke
yoking *v* ▷ yoke
yolk *n (pl -s)* yellow part of an egg that provides food for the developing embryo
yolks *n* ▷ yolk
yonder *adj, adv* (situated) over there
yonks *pl n (Informal)* very long time
yore *n (pl -s)* (Lit) a long time ago
yores *n* ▷ yore
you *pron* refers to: the person or people addressed
young *adj* in an early stage of life or growth
▶ *pl n* young people in general
youngster *n (pl -s)* young person
youngsters *n* ▷ youngster
your *adj* of, belonging to, or associated with you > **yourself** *pron*
yours *pron* something belonging to you
yourself *pron* ▷ your
youth *n (pl -s)* time of being young > **youthful** *adj* > **youthfulness** *n (pl -es)*
youthful *adj* ▷ youth
youthfulness *adj* ▷ youth
youthfulnesses *adj* ▷ youth
youths *n* ▷ youth
yowl *v, n (pl -s)* (produce) a loud mournful cry

yowls *n* ▷ yowl
yttrium [it-ree-um] *n (pl -s)* (CHEM) silvery metallic element used in various alloys
yttriums *n* ▷ yttrium

> **yu** *n* (**yus**). Yu is a Chinese word that means precious jade. This word is good for connecting words ending in Y with ones beginning in U. Yu scores 5 points.

yucca *n (pl -s)* tropical plant with spikes of white leaves
yuccas *n* ▷ yucca
yuckier *adj* ▷ yucky
yuckiest *adj* ▷ yucky
yucky *adj* (**-ckier, -ckiest**) (Slang) disgusting, nasty

> **yuk** *interj*. Yuk is a noise people make to express disgust or dislike. This funny little word is worth remembering as it give a good score and uses an unpromising combination of letters. Yuk scores 10 points.

yuppie *n (pl -s)* young highly-paid professional person, esp. one who has a materialistic way of life ▶ *adj* typical of or reflecting the values of yuppies
yuppies *n* ▷ yuppie

Zz

Scoring the same as Q but easier to use, Z is the most valuable tile in Scrabble. There is only one two-letter word beginning with Z, **zo** (11 points), but remembering this will save you wasting time looking for others. There some very good three-letter words starting with Z, however. These include another variant of **zo**, **zho** (15), as well as **zax** and **zex** (19 each), **zap** (14), **zip** (14) and **zoo** (12).

zanier adj ▷ zany

zaniest ▷ zany

> **zanja** n (**zanjas**). A zanja is an irrigation canal. This unusual word is very useful because of its combination of J and Z. As there are many As in the game, if you are lucky enough to get J and Z together, you may well be able to play this somewhere. Zanja scores 21 points.
>
> **zanjero** n (**zanjeros**). A zanjero is a supervisor of irrigation canals. If you can use all your tiles to play zanjero, you'll earn a 50-point bonus. Zanjero scores 23 points.

zany [zane-ee] adj (-nier, -niest) comical in an endearing way

zap v (-s, -ping, -pped) (*Slang*) kill (by shooting)

zapped v ▷ zap

zapping v ▷ zap

zaps v ▷ zap

> **zax** n (**zaxes**). A zax a small axe for cutting slates. This is great word combining X and Z. If you get a Z late in the game, check if X has already been played, and whether there is an opportunity to form zax or **zex**. Zax scores 19 points.

zeal n (pl -s) great enthusiasm or eagerness

zealot [zel-lot] n (pl -s) fanatic or extreme enthusiast

zealots n ▷ zealot

zealous [zel-luss] adj extremely eager or enthusiastic > **zealously** adv

zealously adv ▷ zealous

zeals n ▷ zeal

zebra n (pl -s) black-and-white striped African animal of the horse family

zebras n ▷ zebra

zebu [zee-boo] n (pl -s) Asian ox with a humped back and long horns

zebus n ▷ zebu

> **zed** n (**zeds**). Zed is the letter Z. This is a handy word when you have a Z but no space or letters for a longer word. Zed scores 13 points.
>
> **zee** n (**zees**). Zee is the American pronunciation of the letter Z. This word can be very useful because E is the most common tile in Scrabble, so keep it in mind if you draw a Z. Zee scores 12 points.

zenith n (pl -s) highest point of success or power

zeniths n ▷ zenith

zephyr [zef-fer] n (pl -s) soft gentle breeze

zephyrs n ▷ zephyr

zeppelin n (pl -s) (HIST) large cylindrical airship

zeppelins n ▷ zeppelin

zero n (pl -ros, -roes) (symbol representing) the number 0 ▶ adj having no measurable quantity or size

zeroes n ▷ zero

zeros n ▷ zero

zest n (pl -s) enjoyment or excitement

zests n ▷ zest

> **zeuxite** n (**zeuxites**). Zeuxite is a mineral. This unusual word is great if you have the letters for it. If you can use all of your tiles to play zeuxite, you'll get a 50-point bonus. Zeuxite scores 23 points.
>
> **zex** n (**zexes**). Zex means the same as **zax.** If you get a Z late in the game, check if X has already been played, and whether there is an opportunity to form zax. Zex scores 19 points.

zho n (**zhos**) Zho is one of several spelling for a Tibetan animal bred from yaks and cattle. The other forms are **dso**, **dzo** and **zo**, and it's worth remembering all of them. Zho scores 15 points.

zigzag n (pl -s) line or course having sharp turns in alternating directions ▶ v (-zags, -zagging, -zagged) move in a zigzag ▶ adj formed in or proceeding in a zigzag
zigzagged v ▷ zigzag
zigzagging v ▷ zigzag
zigzags n, v ▷ zigzag

zinc n (pl -s) (CHEM) bluish-white metallic element used in alloys and to coat metal
zincs n ▷ zinc

zing n (pl -s) (Informal) quality in something that makes it lively or interesting
zings n ▷ zing

zip n (pl -s) fastener with two rows of teeth that are closed or opened by a small clip pulled between them ▶ v (-s, -pping, -pped) fasten with a zip
zipped v ▷ zip
zipping v ▷ zip
zips n, v ▷ zip

zircon n (pl -s) mineral used as a gemstone and in industry

zirconium n (pl -s) (CHEM) greyish-white metallic element that is resistant to corrosion
zirconiums n ▷ zirconium
zircons n ▷ zircon

zit n (**zits**). A zit is a pimple. This nasty little word can be very useful during a game, especially when there's not much space left on the board. Zit scores 12 points.

zither n (pl -s) musical instrument consisting of strings stretched over a flat box and plucked to produce musical notes
zithers n ▷ zither

zo n (**zos**). Zo is one of several spelling for a Tibetan animal bred from yaks and cattle. The other forms are **dso**, **dzo** and **zho**, and it's worth remembering all of them. If someone plays zo and you have a D, remember that you can form dzo from it. Zo is the

only two-letter word beginning with Z, and scores 11 points.

zodiac n (pl -s) imaginary belt in the sky within which the sun, moon, and planets appear to move, divided into twelve equal areas, called signs of the zodiac, each named after a constellation
zodiacs n ▷ zodiac
zombi n ▷ zombie

zombie, zombi n (pl -s) person who appears to be lifeless, apathetic, or totally lacking in independent judgment
zombies n ▷ zombie
zombis n ▷ zombie
zonal adj ▷ zone

zone n (pl -s) area with particular features or properties ▶ v (-nes, -ning, -ned) divide into zones > **zonal** adj
zoned v ▷ zone
zones n, v ▷ zone
zoning v ▷ zone

zoo n (pl -s) place where live animals are kept for show
zoological adj ▷ zoology
zoologies n ▷ zoology
zoologist n ▷ zoology
zoologists n ▷ zoology

zoology n (pl -gies) study of animals > **zoologist** n (pl -s) > **zoological** adj

zoom v (-s, -ing, -ed) move or rise very rapidly
zoomed v ▷ zoom
zooming v ▷ zoom
zooms v ▷ zoom
zoos n ▷ zoo

zootaxy n (**zootaxies**). Zootaxy is the scientific classification of animals. If you're lucky enough to have the letters for this word, you can earn a 50-point bonus by using all of your tiles to form it. Zootaxy scores 26 points.

zucchini [zoo-**keen**-ee] n (pl -ni, -nis) (US & AUST) courgette
zucchinis n ▷ zucchini

zulu n (pl -s) member of a tall Black people of southern Africa
zulus n ▷ zulu

zygote n (pl -s) fertilized egg cell
zygotes n ▷ zygote